ADOLESCENCE

ADOLESCENCE

9TH EDITION

JOHN W. SANTROCK

UNIVERSITY OF TEXAS AT DALLAS

Boston   Burr Ridge, IL   Dubuque, IA   Madison, WI   New York   San Francisco   St. Louis
Bangkok   Bogotá   Caracas   Kuala Lumpur   Lisbon   London   Madrid   Mexico City
Milan   Montreal   New Delhi   Santiago   Seoul   Singapore   Sydney   Taipei   Toronto

McGraw-Hill Higher Education

*A Division of The **McGraw-Hill** Companies*

ADOLESCENCE, NINTH EDITION

Published by McGraw-Hill, a business unit of The McGraw-Hill Companies, Inc., 1221 Avenue of the Americas, New York, NY 10020. Copyright © 2003, 2001, 1998 by The McGraw-Hill Companies, Inc. All rights reserved. No part of this publication may be reproduced or distributed in any form or by any means, or stored in a database or retrieval system, without the prior written consent of The McGraw-Hill Companies, Inc., including, but not limited to, in any network or other electronic storage or transmission, or broadcast for distance learning.

Some ancillaries, including electronic and print components, may not be available to customers outside the United States.

This book is printed on acid-free paper.

International   1 2 3 4 5 6 7 8 9 0 QPD/QPD 0 9 8 7 6 5 4 3 2
Domestic   2 3 4 5 6 7 8 9 0 QPD/QPD 0 9 8 7 6 5 4 3 2

ISBN 0–07–249199–X
ISBN 0–07–121297–3 (ISE)

Vice president and editor-in-chief: *Thalia Dorwick*
Publisher: *Stephen D. Rutter*
Senior sponsoring editor: *Rebecca H. Hope*
Senior marketing manager: *Chris Hall*
Project manager: *Richard H. Hecker*
Production supervisor: *Enboge Chong*
Coordinator of freelance design: *Michelle D. Whitaker*
Cover/interior designer: *Diane Beasley*
Cover image: *David Young-Wolff/Getty Images, Inc.*
Lead photo research coordinator: *Carrie K. Burger*
Photo research: *LouAnn K. Wilson*
Senior supplement producer: *David A. Welsh*
Media technology producer: *Ginger Warner*
Compositor: *GAC–Indianapolis*
Typeface: *10.5/12 Minion*
Printer: *Quebecor World Dubuque, IA*

The credits section for this book begins on page C-1 and is considered an extension of the copyright page.

Library of Congress Cataloging-in-Publication Data

Santrock, John W.
    Adolescence / John W. Santrock. — 9th ed.
      p.   cm.
    Includes bibliographical references and indexes.
    ISBN 0–07–249199–X (alk. paper) — ISBN 0–07–121297–3 (ISE : alk. paper)
    1. Adolescence. 2. Adolescent psychology. I. Title.

HQ796 .S26   2003
305.235—dc21   2002022713
                                                                         CIP

INTERNATIONAL EDITION ISBN 0–07–121297–3
Copyright © 2003. Exclusive rights by The McGraw-Hill Companies, Inc., for manufacture and export. This book cannot be re-exported from the country to which it is sold by McGraw-Hill. The International Edition is not available in North America.

www.mhhe.com

TO TRACY AND JENNIFER,
WHO, AS THEY HAVE MATURED,
HAVE HELPED ME APPRECIATE
THE MARVELS OF
ADOLESCENT DEVELOPMENT

ABOUT THE AUTHOR

JOHN W. SANTROCK received his Ph.D. from the University of Minnesota in 1973. He taught at the University of Charleston and the University of Georgia before joining the psychology department at the University of Texas at Dallas. He has been a member of the editorial boards of *Developmental Psychology* and *Child Development.* His research on father custody is widely cited and used in expert witness testimony to promote flexibility and alternative considerations in custody disputes. John has also authored these exceptional McGraw-Hill texts: *Child Development,* Ninth Edition, *Life-Span Development,* Eighth Edition, *Children,* 7th Edition, *Psychology,* Seventh Edition, and *Educational Psychology,* First Edition.

John Santrock has been teaching an undergraduate course on adolescent development every year since 1981 and continues to teach this course and a range of other undergraduate courses at the University of Texas at Dallas.

BRIEF CONTENTS

CONTENTS

Preface   xvi

SECTION 2

BIOLOGICAL AND COGNITIVE DEVELOPMENT   73

CHAPTER 3
PUBERTY, HEALTH, AND BIOLOGICAL FOUNDATIONS   75

SECTION 3
THE CONTEXTS OF ADOLESCENT DEVELOPMENT   145

CHAPTER 6
PEERS   185

CHAPTER 7
SCHOOLS   219

CHAPTER 8
CULTURE   255

SECTION 4

SOCIAL, EMOTIONAL, AND PERSONALITY DEVELOPMENT   289

CHAPTER 12
MORAL DEVELOPMENT, VALUES,
AND RELIGION   379

SECTION 5

ADOLESCENT PROBLEMS   437

PREFACE

More undergraduate students in the world continue to learn about the field of adolescent development from this text than from any other. The ninth edition appears some 21 years after the first edition, signaling its status in development as an emerging adult. As with human development, there have been major changes and transitions across these nine editions. Through these many changes, though, is a basic core of topics and content that serves as the foundation for adolescent development.

I believe there are three main aspects to creating a textbook for undergraduates that maximizes learning about the field of adolescent development: (1) research, (2) applications, and (3) pedagogy/student-friendliness.

> ■ *"This is an exceptional text."*
> —Sam Givhan
> *Mississippi State University*

Research

Above all else, the field of adolescent development is based on a solid foundation of research. We are fortunate that an increasing number of researchers are studying adolescent development and this is leading to a better understanding of how adolescents develop.

Contemporary Research

As an indication of the breadth of updating in the ninth edition of this book, it includes more than 450 twenty-first-century citations. You will find substantial research updating in each of the 14 chapters of *Adolescence*, ninth edition.

> ■ *"The research is great in John Santrock's text."*
> —Jennifer Fager
> *Central Michigan University*
>
> ■ *"John Santrock's coverage of research is an important strength. The references are up-to-date and material is presented that often is not covered in other adolescence texts."*
> —Tara Kuther
> *Western Connecticut State University*
>
> ■ *"The research in John Santrock's text is current, relevant, and accurate."*
> —Belinda Blevins-Knabe
> *University of Arkansas–Little Rock*

Expanded Research Emphases

As with any new edition, some areas were updated and expanded more than others. In the ninth edition of *Adolescence*, these areas were given increased attention:

■ Health and Well-Being of Adolescents

The health and well-being of adolescents continues to be a major concern and research in areas related to this topic has expanded considerably in recent years. Here are some of the areas where there was substantial research updating related to the health and well-being of adolescents:

- Adolescent health, chapter 3
- Adjustment in stepfamilies, chapter 5
- Bullying, chapter 6
- Youth organizations, chapter 6
- TV viewing and adolescent obesity, chapter 8
- Adolescent sexuality, chapter 11
- Achievement and career development, chapter 13
- Problems and disorders, chapter 14

■ Biological Foundations

Chapter 3, "Puberty, Health, and Biological Foundations," was extensively revised and updated based on feedback from instructors and expert consultants. The sequence of topics within the chapter is now puberty, the brain, then health, and finally biological foundations. The discussion of puberty has been expanded with a great deal of new material included. Also the section on adolescent health now includes major new sections on the brain and sleep, areas that are emerging as major topics in adolescent development. At the request of reviewers, the discussion of some aspects of evolution and heredity were reduced.

■ Transitions in Development

Currently, there is increased interest in two transitions in adolescent development: the transition from childhood to adolescence and the transition from adolescence to adulthood. Consequently, we expanded the coverage of these transitions, especially the transition from adolescence to adulthood, to augment the emphasis on transitions already present in the text. For example, in chapter 1, a new section is devoted to transitions in adolescent development, with an introduction to the transition from childhood to adolescence and the transition from adolescence to adulthood. In addition to the new section in chapter 1, here are some of the other locations where new material on adolescent transitions appears:

The pubertal transition from childhood through early adolescence, chapter 3

Changes in the brain from childhood through early adolescence and from adolescence to adulthood, chapter 3

Changes in sleep patterns from childhood through early adolescence, chapter 3

Changes in cognitive development from adolescence through early adulthood, chapter 4

The emergence of dating and romantic involvement in young adolescents, chapter 6

The transition from high school to college, chapter 7

Changing sex roles in U.S. college students, chapter 10

Sex education in the transition from childhood to early adolescence, chapter 11

Developing values in early adolescence and the college years, chapter 12

The role of parents in the transition from childhood to adolescence in achievement and career development, chapter 13

Achievement, careers, and the college transition, chapter 13

Link between alcohol abuse in adolescence and reduced brain activity in adulthood, chapter 14

Binge-drinking trajectories from early adolescence through emerging adulthood, chapter 14

Link between cigarette smoking in adolescence and anxiety disorders in emerging adulthood, chapter 14

Sexual activity, pubertal transition, and dieting, chapter 14

Adult developmental outcomes of anorexia nervosa in adolescence, chapter 14

Bulimia nervosa in emerging adulthood, chapter 14

■ Culture and Ethnicity

Beginning with the first edition of *Adolescence,* culture and ethnicity have been important themes in this book. *Adolescence,* ninth edition, has an entire chapter (chapter 8) devoted to culture and ethnicity and other discussions of these topics are embedded in every chapter. In the ninth edition of *Adolescence,* we removed the Explorations in Adolescence boxes, many of which focused on culture and ethnicity, and integrated coverage of culture and ethnicity in a more seamless fashion in the text. In addition, there was a significant updating and expansion of material on culture and ethnicity. Here are some of the locations where the updated and expanded discussions of ethnicity and culture can be found:

Cross-cultural comparisons of exercise in adolescence, chapter 3

Parent-adolescent communication in dyadic and triadic interactions in African American families

Parent-adolescent conflict in African American families, chapter 5

Parent-adolescent conflict and autonomy in American and Japanese families, chapter 5

The emergence of dating and romantic relationships in Latina adolescents, chapter 6

Ethnicity and Schools, chapter 7

African American identity as a buffer to perceived discrimination in adolescents, chapter 8

Cross-cultural comparisons of the initiation of sexual activity in adolescence, chapter 11

Cross-cultural comparisons of adolescent pregnancy, chapter 11

U.S. adolescent pregnancy rates in ethnic groups, chapter 11

Cross-cultural comparisons of AIDS in adolescents, chapter 11

Values of adolescents in seven different countries, chapter 12

Positive value of work in low-income, urban adolescents, chapter 13

Cross-cultural comparison of adolescent obesity in China, Russia, and the United States, chapter 14

■ *"This is the best chapter on culture I've ever read."*
—Dan Houlihan
Minnesota State University

■ *"A strength of the text is the detail of each chapter's inclusion of culturally different societies."*
—Celina Echols
Southeastern Louisiana State University

Expert Consultants

No single author can be an expert in all areas of a complex, growing field like adolescent development. The ninth edition of *Adolescence* is the third edition in which the world's leading experts in particular domains of adolescent development have served as consultants and guided me in providing students with the most accurate and contemporary research. They thoroughly examined one or two chapters in their area of expertise in considerable detail. The consultants for the ninth edition of *Adolescence* truly are among the world's leading experts in the field of adolescent development. Photographs and biographies of the consultants are presented on page xxvii.

Applications

A second major theme of *Adolescence,* ninth edition, is the application of information to the real lives of adolescents with the goal of improving their opportunities to successfully negotiate the path from childhood to adulthood. As in past editions, these applications have been integrated within each chapter, and they also appear periodically in material on social policy and adolescent development.

■ *"John Santrock's text is one of the best at providing applied material and examples."*
—Laura Duvall
Heartland Community College

A new aspect of applications in this edition is the emphasis on careers in adolescent development.

■ Careers in Adolescent Development

Instructors and students told us that they would like to see more information about the range of careers in adolescent development. To meet this need, we did two things:

1. Created a *Careers in Adolescent Development Appendix,* which follows chapter 1, in which students can read about the nature of careers in these areas: education/research; clinical/counseling/medical; families/relationships.

2. Developed inserts, called *Careers in Adolescent Development,* that profile a number of actual people in a wide variety of careers in adolescent development. The career profiles provide information about the person's education, the nature of their work, and a photograph of the individual at work. These appear throughout the book, often multiple times in individual chapters. Examples of career profiles include Pam Reid, Educational and Developmental Psychologist (chapter 2, page 67); Martha Chan, Marriage and Family Therapist (chapter 5, page 160); Jimmy Furlow, Secondary School Teacher (chapter 7, page 240); and Armando Ronquillo, High School Counselor/College Advisor (chapter 13, page 427).

> ■ *"The Careers in Adolescent Development material is very interesting, creative, and motivating."*
> —Anne R. Gayles-Felton
> *Florida A&M University*

Pedagogy/Student-Friendliness

Students should not only be challenged to study hard and think more deeply and productively about adolescent development, they also should be provided with a pedagogical framework to help them learn more effectively. *Adolescence,* ninth edition, has the most extensive, systematic pedagogical system in texts on adolescent development.

> ■ *"I can't say enough about how well I enjoy using this book. I am equally pleased with student responses."*
> —Celina Echols
> *Southwestern Louisiana State University*

Already widely acclaimed for its student friendliness, an important new learning system involving Learning Goals was developed for this new, ninth edition of the book.

■ The Learning Goals System

My recent experience in writing texts in the areas of college success and educational psychology led me to develop a new **Learning Goals system.** We know that an important aspect of learning is to set learning goals and systematically review material related to those goals as reading and studying proceed.

Thus, we created a new Learning Goals system that is integrated throughout each chapter. At the beginning of each chapter, students read four to seven Learning Goals for the chapter. Then, after they have read a portion of a chapter, they review material related to the Learning Goals tied to that portion of the chapter. Finally, at the end of the chapter, in a section called **Reach Your Learning Goals,** students are encouraged to engage in a final summary review of content related to the Learning Goals stated at the beginning of the chapter.

A full overview of all of the many learning elements involved in *Adolescence,* ninth edition, is presented in a **Visual Student Preface,** which appears on page xxix.

Content Changes in Individual Chapters

As mentioned earlier, substantial changes and updating of content occurred in every chapter of the book. Here are some of the main content changes in each chapter:

CHAPTER 1 INTRODUCTION

- New section on "Old Centuries and New Centuries," focusing on the new trend in positive psychology applied to adolescent development (Seligman & Csikszentmihalyi, 2000)
- New section on "Generational Perceptions and Memories"
- New Careers Profile on Peter Benson, Director of the Search Institute
- New conceptualization by Reed Larson (2000) of the importance of developing the initiative of adolescents
- New section on developmental transitions, including childhood to adolescence, and adolescence to adulthood (Barber & others, 2001; Raynor & others, 2001)
- New Careers Profile on Louis Vargas, Child Clinical Psychologist

> ■ *"The discussion of social policy and adolescent development is a very interesting, creative, and motivating topic. . . . It is a strength of the chapter."*
> —Anne R. Gayles-Felton
> *Florida A&M University*

APPENDIX CAREERS IN ADOLESCENT DEVELOPMENT

- New Appendix, which follows chapter 1, that profiles a number of careers in adolescent development

CHAPTER 2 THE SCIENCE OF ADOLESCENT DEVELOPMENT

- New section on evaluating the psychoanalytic theories
- Revision and updating of the information-processing approach
- New section on evaluating the cognitive theories
- New section on evaluating the behavioral and cognitive theories
- New section on evaluating ecological, contextual theory

- New section, "Who Will the Participants Be?"
- New discussion of techniques for measuring brain activity (Thompson & others, 2001)
- Revised and updated discussion of ethics in research (Jones, 2000)

■ *"The new discussion of the information-processing approach is excellent. It makes the material more understandable and practical."*
—Anne R. Gayles-Felton
Florida A&M University

■ *"Research design is covered well. The section on "Being a Wise Consumer of Research" is very valuable to students."*
—Tara Kuther
Western Connecticut State University

 ## CHAPTER 3 PUBERTY, HEALTH, AND BIOLOGICAL FOUNDATIONS

- Extensive reorganization of chapter with chapter now following this sequence: puberty, the brain, then adolescent health, and finally heredity and environment
- Much expanded, updated discussion of hormones, including figure 3.1, showing how the feedback system of sex hormones works
- New section on the growth hormone (Susman, Dorn, & Schiefelbein, in press)
- New section on adrenarache and gonadarche (Archibald, Graber, & Brooks-Gunn, in press)
- New section on weight, body fat, and leptin (Mantzoros, 2000)
- More detailed information about changes in body weight during puberty
- New section, "Secular Trends in Puberty" (de Muinich Keizer, 2001; Kaplowitz & others, 2001)
- New section under Psychological Dimensions of Puberty on links between hormones and behavior (Archibald, Graber, & Brooks-Gunn, in press)
- New Careers profile on Anne Petersen, Researcher and Administrator
- New section on the brain, including the nature and change in neurons and structural changes in the brain, including new figure 3.9, Synaptic Density in the Human Brain from Infancy to Adulthood (Dahl, 2001; De Bellis & others, 2001; Thompson & Fox, 2001; Thompson & others, 2001)
- Much expanded and updated coverage of exercise, including recent U.S. studies (American Sports Data, 2001) and cross-cultural comparisons (World Health Organization, 2000)
- New section on sports in adolescence, including recent research on participation (Cornock, Bowker, & Gadbois, 2001; Pate & others, 2000)
- New section on sleep practices in adolescence, including sleep deprivation and possible links to problems in school (Carskadon, Acebo, & Seifer, 2001; Fukuda & Ishira, 2001)
- New Careers profile on Marilyn Billingsly, Adolescent Medicine Specialist

- New section on molecular genetics and the Human Genome Project (Magee, Gordon, & Whelan, 2001)

■ *"The primary strength of this chapter is that it provides the most extraordinarily comprehensive presentation of all biologically related issues as they relate to adolescence that I have ever seen in a chapter in an undergraduate text.*
—Mark S. Chapell
Rowan University

■ *"John Santrock's chapter on puberty, health, and biological foundations is current in its orientation, comprehensive, and innovative."*
—Elizabeth J. Susman
Pennsylvania State University

 ## CHAPTER 4 COGNITIVE DEVELOPMENT

- Expanded, updated comments about the neo-Piagetian view of Robbie Case (2000)
- New section, "Is There a Fifth, Postformal stage?" (Labouvie-Vief & Diehl, 1999; Perry, 1999)
- Expanded, updated discussion of improved automaticity, capacity, and familiarity in content of information processing during adolescence
- New section on working memory emphasizing Baddeley's (2000) view and a recent developmental study that highlights improvements in working memory during adolescence (Swanson, 1999). Includes new figure 4.6, Developmental Changes in Working Memory
- New Careers profile on Laura Bickford, Secondary School Teacher

■ *"I give John Santrock's chapter on cognitive development an A. It is an excellent overview of the complicated issues about adolescent cognitive development. It is easy to read while still being challenging. The new edition has retained the strengths of the earlier treatment but brought it to currency both in terms of the thinking in the field and in the literature.*
—Daniel Keating
University of Toronto

■ *"I am a tough grader on textbooks and I like this book. John Santrock has a knack for writing in a clear, succinct, and engaging style.*
—James Byrnes
University of Maryland

■ *"This is a chapter that students often find difficult and John Santrock's chapter especially impresses me. The examples and content are well written, comprehensive, and engaging.*
—Tara Kuther
Western Connecticut State University

 ## CHAPTER 5 FAMILIES

- New research on communication in dyadic and triadic parent/adolescent interactions in African American families (Smetana, Abernethy, & Harris, 2000)

- Recent research on parental monitoring and adolescent competence (Jacobson & Crockett, 2000)
- New research on parent-adolescent conflict in African American families (Smetana & Gaines, 2000).
- New Careers profile on Martha Chan, Marriage and Family Therapist
- New research on gender differences in autonomy granting during adolescence (Bumpus, Crouder, & McHale, 2001)
- New cross-cultural research on Japanese and American differences in autonomy and parent-adolescent conflict (Rothbaum & others, 2000)
- New research on older siblings as sources of social support for younger siblings (Tucker, McHale, & Crouder, 2001)
- New research on male sibling pairs and female sibling pairs (Cole & Kerns, 2001)
- Extensively revised and updated section on stepfamilies, including recent research (Bray, Berger, & Boethel, 1999; Dunn & others) and discussion of types of stepfamilies and adjustment

- *"John Santrock's chapter on families continues his fine tradition of clarity, engagement, and a sense of the real lives of youth and families that will help students make sense of the lives of youth and put knowledge to work on their behalf."*
  —Catherine Cooper
  University of California at Santa Cruz

- *"This chapter has good all-around coverage of the topic of families. Contradictory research findings are pointed out, which tends to engage students and encourage discussion."*
  —Alice Alexander
  Old Dominion University

CHAPTER 6   PEERS

- New commentary about adolescents having a larger number of acquaintances in their peer networks than children do (Connolly & others, 2000)
- Extensively revised and updated coverage of bullying, including a recent national survey (Nansel & others, 2001) and other research (Haynie & others, 2001)
- Reorganization and updating of discussion of crowds and cliques, including better differentiation of these concepts
- Discussion of Larson's (2000) ideas on how structured voluntary organizations are well-suited to help adolescents develop initiative
- New longitudinal study of adolescents' romantic relationships (Buhrmester, 2001)
- New research on the emergence of Latina adolescents' dating and romantic involvement (Raffaelli & Ontai, in press)
- Recent research on young adolescent girls' dating and depression (Joyner & Udry, 2000)
- Recent research on the role of peers in the emergence of romantic involvement in adolescence (Connolly, Furman, & Konarksi, 2000)

- *"John Santrock's chapter on peers provides excellent coverage of the central issues in adolescent peer relationships, as revealed in current research trends. An important feature of the chapter is the excellent manner in which theoretical perspectives are presented and research findings are integrated into these ideas."*
  —Jennifer Connolly
  York University

CHAPTER 7   SCHOOLS

- New research on school teams and a lower sense of social isolation, as well as activities participation and higher self-esteem (Stone & others, 2001)
- Updated research on college freshmen's experience of stress and depression (Sax & others, 2001)
- Updated figures on high school dropouts (National Center for Education Statistics, 2000)
- New Careers profile on Donna Smith, School Psychologist
- New Careers profile on Jimmy Furlow, Secondary School Teacher
- New research on African American adolescents, Latino adolescents, and education (Cooper & others, 2001; Ginorio & Huston, 2001)
- New research on evaluation of the Comer School Development Program (Cook, Hunt, & Murphy, 2001)
- New Careers profile on James Comer, Psychiatrist
- Recent research on a combination of drug and behavioral therapy in the treatment of ADHD (Evans & others, 2001)
- New Careers profile on Sterling Jones, Supervisor of Gifted and Talented Education

- *"Issues and concepts are clear and well explained in the chapter on schools. A broad range of topics is discussed in appropriate depth."*
  —Alice Alexander
  Old Dominion University

- *"John Santrock's chapter on schools is excellent and the balance is terrific."*
  —Jennifer Fager
  Western Michigan University

CHAPTER 8   CULTURE

- Integration of material on El Puente, designed to improve the lives of adolescents in low-income areas
- New Careers profile on Carola Suárez-Orozco, Lecturer, Researcher, and Co-Director of Immigration Projects
- Recent research on African American adolescents' connection to their ethnic group as a buffer to threats of discrimination (Wong, Eccles, & Sameroff, 2001)
- Recent research on the link between TV watching and obesity in adolescent girls (Anderson & others, 2001)

- Recent research on the link between watching educational TV programs in early childhood and success in school during early adolescence (Anderson & others, 2001)

> *"The chapter on culture has well-organized broad coverage including some international comparisons."*
> —Alice Alexander
> *Old Dominion University*

CHAPTER 9   THE SELF AND IDENTITY

- Recent research on link between possible selves to health behaviors in early adolescence (Aloise-Young, Hennigan, & Leong, 2001)
- Integration of material on multiple selves and culture into text
- New conceptualization of identity styles in terms of how individuals process self-relevant information (Berzonsky, 2000)
- New discussion of Janet Helms' stages of ethnic identity development
- New Careers profile on Nicole Langlais, College Counselor

> *"John Santrock's coverage of the self and identity is extensive, current, and complete. The issues are presented in a readable and engaging fashion—in such a way that one actually wants to read the material, something that is rare in a textbook. Please don't delete anything."*
> —James Marcia
> *Simon Fraser University*

> *"Key strengths of this chapter are the rich portrayal of the self, identity, and intimacy with clear and compelling links across these areas."*
> —Catherine Cooper
> *University of California at Santa Cruz*

CHAPTER 10   GENDER

- Integration of culture and gender material into text
- New discussion of college students' changing attitudes about gender roles, including new figure 10.3
- New Careers profile on Carol Gilligan, Professor and Chair of Gender Studies Program

CHAPTER 11   SEXUALITY

- New cross-cultural comparison of adolescent sexuality in Japan and the United States (Rothbaum & others, 2000)
- New cross-cultural comparisons of the timing of teenage sexual initiation (Singh & others, 2000)
- New discussion of the link between suicide and sexual orientation in adolescence
- New research on ethnic variations in adolescent pregnancy (Child Trends, 2001)

- New cross-cultural comparisons on adolescent pregnancy (Centers for Disease Control & Prevention, 2001)
- New Careers profile on Lynn Blankenship, Family and Consumer Science Educator
- New research on the increase in abstinence-only instruction in sex education (Darroch, Landry, & Singh, 2000)
- New cross-cultural comparisons of AIDS in adolescence, especially the epidemic of AIDS in sub-Saharan adolescent girls (World Health Organization, 2000)
- Recent research on sexual abuse in dating relationships during adolescence (Silverman & others, 2001)
- Recent research evaluation of a program, "Safer Choices" (Basen-Enquist & others, 2001)

> *"I like the fact that John Santrock's chapter includes a section on sex as a normal aspect of adolescence and that it separates problem outcomes from normal outcomes. The material is quite up-to-date and contains references to the major research in the field."*
> —Shirley Feldman
> *Stanford University*

> *"John Santrock's chapter on adolescent sexuality is well written, well organized, and very up to date in its references. Many important topics are covered in a balanced and thoughtful way."*
> —Ronald Craig
> *Cincinnati State Technological and Community College*

CHAPTER 12   MORAL DEVELOPMENT, VALUES, AND RELIGION

- Extensively revised and updated section, "Reasoning in Different Social Cognitive Domains" (Nucci, 2001), including recent research (Killen, McGlotlin, & Lee-Kim, in press)
- New commentary about Gilligan's view of moral education
- Recent updating of college students' values (Sax & others, 2001)
- New research on values in seven different countries (Bowes & Flanagan, 2000)
- New Careers profile on Constance Flanagan, Professor of Youth Civic Development

> *"John Santrock's chapter is an excellent overview of theories and applications in the area of moral development and religion in adolescence . . . the chapter is informative, engaging, thought-provoking, and current."*
> —Lawrence Walker
> *University of British Columbia*

> *"The chapter on moral development, my specialty area, is simply outstanding. It is the best textbook chapter on the topic I have ever read."*
> —Elizabeth Vozzda
> *St. Joseph College*

CHAPTER 13   ACHIEVEMENT, CAREERS, AND WORK

- New Careers profile on Jaime Escalante, Secondary School Math Teacher
- New research on the development of attitudes and acquisition of skills necessary to achieve career goals and expectations (Csikszentmihalyi & Schneider, 2000)
- New research on comparing adolescent ambition in the 1990s and the 1980s/1970s (Scheider & Stevenson, 1999)
- New Careers profile on Grace Leaf, College/Career Counselor
- New conceptualization and research on how parents can potentially influence adolescents' occupations through their communication about occupations and values, as well as their behavior (Jodl & others, 2001)
- New Careers profile on Armando Ronquillo, High School Counselor/College Advisor
- New research on the positive role of work in low-income, urban adolescents (Leventhal, Graber, & Brooks-Gunn, 2001)

> ■ *"I've found this chapter to be weak in many adolescence texts but John Santrock handles it well. I give the chapter 5 points on a 5-point scale."*
> —Dan Houlihan
> *Minnesota State University*

CHAPTER 14   ADOLESCENT PROBLEMS

- Substantially revised introduction to adolescent problems and deletion of emphasis on abnormal behavior
- Movement of discussion of resilience from the end of the chapter to first section of chapter
- Very recent research by Johnston and others (2001) on trends in U.S. adolescent drug use
- New research on heavy, regular drinking in adolescence and brain impairment, including new figure 14.3 (DeBellis & others, 2000; Tapert & others, 2000)
- New research on peer pressure and adolescent alcohol use (Borden & others, 2001)
- New research on three types of adolescent drinkers, including association of drinking and adolescent crowds (Barber, Eccles, & Stone, 2001)
- New research on binge drinking in college students (Wechsler & others, 2000)
- New research on binge-drinking trajectories from early adolescence through emerging adulthood (Chassin, Pitts, & Prost, 2001)
- New research on cigarette smoking in adolescence and emotional problems (Goodman & Capitman, 2000; Johnson & others, 2000)
- New discussion of the increase in use of Ecstasy and its social context of raves
- New Careers profile on Cheryl Perry, Epidemiologist, School of Public Health

- Recent research on the importance of parental involvement and limit setting in lower drug use by adolescents (National Center for Addiction and Substance Abuse, 2001)
- Recent research on the importance of early intervention in drug abuse (Shin, 2001)
- New research on heavy drug use by peers and initial drug use by adolescents (Simons, Walker-Barnes, & Mason, 2001)
- New discussion of the Pittsburgh Youth Study (Loeber & others, 1998)
- New research on siblings and delinquency (Slomkowski & others, 2001)
- New research on peers and delinquency (Henry, Tolan, & Gorman-Smith, 2001)
- Recent research on students who carry a gun to school (National Center for Health Statistics, 2000)
- Updated coverage of youth violence (Garbarino, 2001)
- New Careers profile on Rodney Hammond, Health Psychologist
- Updated, recent statistics on adolescent suicide (National Center for Health Statistics, 2000; National Vital Statistics Report, 2001)
- New discussion of "copycat" suicides
- New research on dating, puberty, and dieting in girls (Field & others, 2001)
- Recent national survey of the increase in adolescent obesity (National Center for Health Statistics, 2000), including new figure 14.9
- Recent research on adolescents with overweight parents (Dowda & others, 2001)
- Expanded, updated discussion of anorexia nervosa and bulimia nervosa
- New research on connections between anorexia nervosa in adolescence and outcomes in adulthood (Herpertz & others, 2001; Lowe & others, 2001)
- Expanded, updated coverage of the nature of coping in adolescence (Compas & others, 2001)

> ■ *"I was pleased with the coverage and communication style in John Santrock's chapter on adolescent problems."*
> —Gerald Patterson
> *Oregon Social Learning Center*
>
> ■ *"I like the breadth of coverage and the updated and more detailed description of research evidence to support the points made."*
> —Susan Shonk
> *State University of New York at Brockport*

Ancillaries

The supplements listed here may accompany Santrock, *Adolescence*, ninth edition. Please contact your McGraw-Hill representative for details concerning policies, prices, and availability as some restrictions may apply.

For the Instructor

Instructor's Manual

Rita M. Curl
Minot State University

The *Instructor's Manual* includes updated lecture material and suggested lecture topics, key terms, classroom discussions and in-class activities, student research projects, and essay questions. New to the ninth edition, and a proven tool to help instructors plan for the course, the Total Teaching Reference Package fully integrates the many McGraw-Hill resources to help enhance the material and organize the course. Instructors will find that all of the course resources available have been correlated to the main concepts and goals for each chapter. The *Instructor's Manual's* other features include teaching tips, a guide for using the Internet in teaching, and comprehensive transparency, video, and film resources. The *Instructor's Manual* is organized by chapter, and integrates the new Learning Goals found in the text.

Printed Test Bank

Jane P. Sheldon
University of Michigan–Dearborn

This comprehensive Test Bank includes a wide range of approximately 1,400 multiple-choice and up to 140 short essay and critical thinking questions. Every question includes the answer, the type of question, its level of difficulty, as well as the page number where the corresponding material can be found. The Test Bank questions relate to the newly implemented Learning Goals for each chapter.

Dual-Platform Computerized Test Bank on CD-ROM

The Computerized Test Bank on CD-ROM, which includes questions identical to those found in the printed Test Bank, is compatible for both Macintosh and Windows platforms. The CD-ROM provides an editing feature that enables instructors to integrate their own questions, scramble items, and modify questions. The CD-ROM also offers an instructor the option of implanting the following features unique to this program: Online Testing Program, Internet Testing, and Grade Management.

PowerPoint Slide Presentations

The PowerPoint slides follow the chapter organization of *Adolescence,* and include related text images for a more effective lecture presentation.

Instructor's Resource CD-ROM

This CD-ROM offers instructors the opportunity to customize McGraw-Hill materials to prepare for and create their lecture presentations. Among the resources included on the CD-ROM are the *Instructor's Manual,* Test Bank, PowerPoint slides, and the Image Database for *Adolescence.*

McGraw-Hill Developmental Psychology Image Database

This set of 200 full-color images was developed using the best selection of McGraw-Hill Higher Education's human development art and tables, and is available on the Instructor's Resource CD-ROM as well as on the text's Online Learning Center at www.mhhe.com/santrocka9.

Adolescence Overhead Transparencies

This set of 174 full-color images was developed using the best selection of all of McGraw-Hill Higher Education's adolescent development illustrations and tables, and is available in a print overhead transparency set.

Online Learning Center

This extensive website, designed specifically to accompany Santrock, *Adolescence,* ninth edition, offers an array of resources for both instructor and student. Hotlinks can be found for the text's topical web links that appear in the margins as well as for the *Taking It to the Net* exercises that appear at the end of each chapter. These resources and more can be found by logging on to the text's OLC at http://www.mhhe.com/santrocka9.

McGraw-Hill's Developmental Supersite

This comprehensive web page provides a superstructure that organizes and houses all of our developmental text websites. The Developmental Tree serves as a portal through which instructors and students can access each text-specific online learning center as well as many universally useful teaching and study tools. Visit us at http://www.mhhe.com/developmental.

TThe Critical Thinker

Richard Mayer and Fiona Goodchild of the University of California, Santa Barbara, use excerpts from introductory psychology textbooks to show how to think critically about psychology.

Annual Editions—Adolescent Psychology

Published by Dushkin/McGraw-Hill, this is a collection of articles on topics related to the latest research and thinking in adolescent development. These editions are updated annually and contain helpful features including a topic guide, an annotated table of contents, unit overviews, and a topical index. An instructor's guide containing testing materials is also available. Visit http://www.dushkin.com.

For the Student

Student Study Guide

Daniel Houlihan, University of Minnesota–Mankato

This comprehensive Study Guide includes chapter outlines, chapter maps, key terms and concepts, key people, multiple-choice questions, and several useful exercises to enhance what is covered in the text. Designed to help students make the most of their time when reviewing for an exam, this guide also integrates the new Learning Goals system found in the main text.

Student CD-ROM

This user-friendly CD-ROM gives students an opportunity to test their comprehension of the course material. This book-specific CD contains Making the Grade test questions and concept maps for each chapter, as well as key terms and key people for each section. Several interactive activities are available for each section to enhance the material and help the student to better understand it. In addition, the CD contains a Guide to Electronic Research, Learning Styles Assessment, an Internet Primer, and additional Psychology Resources.

Online Learning Center

This extensive website, designed specifically to accompany this edition of *Adolescence,* offers a wide variety of resources for both instructors and students. The student side of the website includes chapter outlines, overviews, and summaries for each of the text's chapters, as well as the Learning Goals of the text. There are a variety of self-quizzes to help students test their knowledge of the book's content, including multiple-choice, fill-in-the-blank, true/false, and matching quizzes. Also available on this site are a selection of scenarios for the student to determine "what would you do" in certain circumstances in the field of adolescent developmental psychology. Also helpful to the student are a set of interactive flash cards and crossword puzzles and the text glossary.

McGraw-Hill's Developmental Supersite

This useful web page provides a superstructure that organizes and houses all of our developmental text websites. The Developmental Tree serves as a portal through which instructors and students can access each text-specific online learning center as well as many universally useful teaching and study tools. Visit us at http://www.mhhe.com/developmental.

Acknowledgments

A project of this magnitude requires the efforts of many people. I owe a special gratitude to Rebecca Hope, Senior Sponsoring Editor, for providing outstanding guidance and support. I also thank Glenn Turner and his Burrston House staff for their developmental and marketing work on the book. I also very much

benefited from the excellent production supervision of the book by Rick Hecker. Thanks also go to Jane Sheldon, University of Michigan–Dearborn and Rita M. Curl, Minot State University, for creating effective, significantly improved ancillaries. Additional thanks to Jane Sheldon for her proofreading efforts.

I also owe special thanks to the reviewers of *Adolescence,* ninth edition. Many of the improvements in the book are the outgrowth of their comments about what they want in an adolescent development text for their course. In this regard, I sincerely appreciate the time and effort in reviewing provided by the following instructors:

Peer Reviewers

Alice Alexander
Old Dominion University

Belinda Blevins-Knabe
University of Arkansas

Mark S. Chapell
Rowan University

Ronald K. Craig
Cincinnati State College

Mark W. Durm
Athens State University

Laura Duvall
Heartland Community College

Celina Echols
Southern Louisiana State
    University

Jennifer Fager
Western Michigan University

Mary Fraser
San Jose State University

Anne R. Gayles-Felton
Florida A&M University

Sam Givhan
Mississippi State University

Dan Houlihan
Minnesota State University

Tara Kuther
Western Connecticut State
    University

Philip Langer
University of Colorado

Heidi Legg Burross
University of Arizona

Jessica Miller
Mesa State College

Kim Shifren
Towson University

Susan Shonk
State University of New York

Elizabeth Vozzola
Saint Joseph's College

Shelli Wynants
California State University

Expert Consultants

James Byrnes
University of Maryland

Carol Dweck
Columbia University

Beth Manke
University of Houston

James Marcia
Simon Fraser University

Ruby Takanishi
Foundation for Child
    Development

Lawrence Walker
University of British Columbia

The following expert consultants also gave valuable feedback on previous editions of the book:

Joseph Allen
University of Virginia

Carole Beale
University of Massachusetts

Nancy Busch-Rossnagel
Fordham University

P. Lindsay Chase-Lansdale
University of Chicago

Joy Dryfoos
Hastings-on-Hudson,
New York

Glen Elder
University of North Carolina

Wyndol Furman
University of Denver

Harold Grotevant
University of Minnesota

Daniel Keating
University of Toronto

Daniel Lapsley
Brandon University

Nancy Leffert
Search Institute, Minneapolis

James Marcia
Simon Fraser University

Daniel Offer
University of Michigan

James Rest
University of Minnesota

Elizabeth Susman
Pennsylvania State University

Allan Wigfield
University of Maryland

In addition, I thank the following peer reviewers for their evaluations of previous editions:

Previous Edition Peer Reviewers

Frank Ascione
Utah State University

Luciane A. Berg
Southern Utah University

David K. Bernhardt
Carleton University

Fredda Blanchard-Fields
Louisiana State University

Robert Bornstein
Miami University

Geraldine Brookins
University of Minnesota

Deborah Brown
Friends University

Christy Buchanan
Wake Forest University

Duane Buhrmester
University of Texas at Dallas

William Bukowski
Concordia University

James Byrnes
University of Maryland

Cheryl A. Camenzuli
Hofstra University

Elaine Cassel
Marymount University

Stephanie M. Clancy
Southern Illinois University
at Carbondale

Rita M. Curl
Minot State University

Peggy A. DeCooke
Northern Illinois University

R. Daniel DiSalvi
Kean College

James A. Doyle
Roane State Community
College

Richard M. Ehlenz
Lakewood Community
College

Gene Elliott
Glassboro State University

Robert Enright
University of
Wisconsin–Madison

Douglas Fife
Plymouth State College

Urminda Firlan
Michigan State University

Martin E. Ford
Stanford University

Gregory T. Fouts
University of Calgary

Charles Fry
University of Virginia

Nancy Galambos
University of Victoria

Margaret J. Gill
Kutztown University

William Gnagey
Illinois State University

Sandra Graham
UCLA

B. Jo Hailey
University of Southern
Mississippi

Dick E. Hammond
Southwest Texas State
University

Frances Harnick
University of New Mexico,
Indian Children's Program,
and Lovelace-Bataan
Pediatric Clinic

Algea Harrison
Oakland University

Susan Harter
University of Denver

June V. Irving
Ball State University

Beverly Jennings
University of Colorado–Denver

Joline Jones
Worcester State College

Alfred L. Karlson
University of
Massachusetts–Amherst

Lynn F. Katz
University of Pittsburgh

Roger Kobak
University of Delaware

Emmett C. Lampkin
Scott Community College

Royal Louis Lange
Ellsworth Community College

Bonnie Leadbeater
University of Victoria

Neal E. Lipsitz
Boston College

Nancey G. Lobb
Alvin Community College

Daniel Lynch
University of
Wisconsin–Oshkosh

Beth Manke
University of Houston

Joseph G. Marrone
Siena College

Ann McCabe
University of Windsor

Susan McCammon
East Carolina University

Sherri McCarthy-Tucker
Northern Arizona University

E. L. McGarry
California State
University–Fullerton

John J. Mirich
Metropolitan State College

John J. Mitchell
University of Alberta

Suzanne F. Morrow
Old Dominion University

Lloyd D. Noppe
University of Wisconsin–
Green Bay

Michelle Paludi
Michelle Paludi & Associates

Joycelyn G. Parish
Kansas State University

Peggy G. Perkins
University of Nevada, Las Vegas

James D. Reid
Washington University

Anne Robertson
University of
Wisconsin–Milwaukee

Tonie E. Santmire
University of Nebraska

Douglas Sawin
University of Texas

Jane Sheldon
University of
Michigan–Dearborn

Dale Shunk
Purdue University

Vern Tyler
Western Washington
University

Rhoda Unger
Montclair State College

Barry Wagner
Catholic University of America

Lawrence Walker
University of British Columbia

Rob Weisskirch
California State University,
Fullerton

Wanda Willard
State University of New York,
Oswego

Carolyn L. Williams
University of Minnesota

A final note of thanks goes to my family. My wife, Mary Jo Santrock, has lived through nine editions of *Adolescence*. I sincerely appreciate the support and encouragement she has given to my writing. My two daughters—Tracy and Jennifer—have provided me with firsthand experience of watching adolescents develop. Through the years, they have helped me render a treatment of adolescent development that captures its complexity, its subtlety, and its humanity.

EXPERT CONSULTANTS

Catherine R. Cooper is Professor of Psychology and Education at the University of California, Santa Cruz, where she was founding director of the doctoral program in developmental psychology. Cooper's work focuses on cultural perspectives on childhood and adolescence, by tracing how youth forge identities that coordinate the values of their cultural and family traditions with those of their schools, peers, communities, and work. With colleagues, students, and community partners, she has developed a theoretical model of Bridging Multiple Worlds across a range of cultural communities. Cooper is a member of the John D. and Catherine T. MacArthur Foundation Research Network on Successful Pathways through Middle Childhood and director of the Program on Families, Schools, Peers, and Communities of the Center for Research on Education, Diversity, and Excellence (CREDE) of the U.S. Office of Education, Research, and Improvement (OERI). Professor Cooper is one of the world's leading experts on many aspects of adolescent development, especially in the areas of family processes and identity.

Shirley Feldman has taught at Stanford University since 1971. She served as Director of the Stanford Center for the Study of Families, Children, and Youth for 4 years (1991–1995) and is currently serving as Associate Director of the Human Biology Program and as Director for the Curriculum on Children and Society. Her research concerns socialization of children and adolescents. In recent years her interests have focused specifically on adolescent development and she co-edited the influential volume "At the Threshold: The Developing Adolescence" (Harvard University Press, 1990). She has conducted longitudinal studies which span two important transitions—from childhood into early adolescence, and from mid adolescence into adulthood—in which she focuses particularly on family influences on both normal and pathological development (including school success, peer relations, depression, delinquency, romantic intimacy, sexuality, promiscuity). Her most recent research focuses on adolescent sexuality and intimacy. She teaches in the Human Biology Program and in the Division of Child Psychiatry. Professor Feldman is one of the world's leading experts on adolescent sexuality.

Daniel P. Keating is the Atkinson Professor of Human Development and Applied Psychology at the Ontario Institute for Studies in Education, University of Toronto. He is also a Fellow of the Canadian Institute for Advanced Research (CIAR), and Director of the CIAR Program in Human Development. Dr. Keating has written extensively on human development and education, particularly on intellectual and social development across the lifespan, on the developmental sources of human diversity, and on the prospects for human development in a learning society. He has written, edited, or co-edited seven books (including *Developmental Health and the Wealth of Nations;* a three-volume series on *Applied Developmental Psychology;* and *Intellectual Talent: Research and Development*), and has contributed numerous papers to scientific journals and scholarly collections.

He is frequently invited to address research, professional, and community groups in Canada, the United States, and Europe to discuss his work on how our social environments shape the way we develop, and how social institutions need to change in order to promote human development in the face of emerging social and economic challenges. He is also investigating the impact and the potential uses of advanced information technology for human development (www.webforum2001.net). Professor Keating is one of the world's leading experts on adolescent cognition.

Elizabeth J. Susman is the Jean Phillips Shibley Professor of Biobehavioral Health in the Department of Biobehavioral Health, at Penn State. Dr. Susman is a registered nurse, received a Ph.D. in human development and completed postdoctoral training in developmental psychology and pediatric oncology. After completing her postdoctoral training, Dr. Susman was a senior fellow at the National Institute of Mental Health (NIMH) intramural program working collaboratively in Developmental Endocrinology in the National Institute of Child Health and Human Development (NICHD). Since coming to Penn State in 1986, she holds appointments in the Department of Biobehavioral Health, School of Nursing, and the Department of Human Development and Family Studies. Dr. Susman also has been a visiting professor at the Harvard School of Public Health; Stockholm University; Halsohogskolan, College of Health and Care, Jonkoping, Sweden; and Louis Pasteur University, Strasbourg, France.

Dr. Susman's research focuses on reproductive transitions, specifically, puberty and pregnancy, and the endocrinology of stress. The research examines interactions between hypothalamic releasing hormones and gonadal and adrenal hormones and antisocial behavior, depression, and anxiety. Dr. Susman and her colleagues at NIH were the first to show the relationship between changes in gonadal and adrenal hormones at puberty and aggressive behavior. She and colleagues also were the first to show the effect of cortisol reactivity in early pregnancy and depression in the postpartum period and the links between corticotropin releasing hormone and antisocial behavior in adolescent girls. Her ongoing research continues to focus on hormone changes at puberty and changes in antisocial behavior and emotions.

Gerald R. Patterson has been a research scientist at the Oregon Social Learning Center since 1977. He received his B.S. and M.A. from the University of Oregon–Eugene, and his Ph.D. in psychology from the University of Minnesota–Twin Cities. His major research interests include behavior modification, marital conflict, social learning theory, observation techniques, social interaction, antisocial behavior, delinquency, and therapy process. Dr. Patterson has won a number of awards, most recently an honorary Doctor's degree in psychology from the University of Bergen, Norway, an Outstanding Achievement Award from the University of Minnesota, and the G. Stanley Hall Award for Distinguished Contribution to Developmental Psychology from the American Psychological Association. He has won grants for his research from the National Institute of Mental Health and the National Institute of Drug Abuse. He is currently co-editing "Antisocial Behavior in Children and Adolescents: A Developmental Analysis and Model for Intervention," which will summarize 30 years of research.

Dr. Jennifer Connolly is an Associate Professor in the Department of Psychology at York University in Toronto. Dr. Connolly completed her graduate training in clinical-developmental psychology at Concordia University in Montreal, Canada. Her research and publications focus on peer and romantic relationships in adolescence. Her current research projects examine romance and sexuality in early adolescence; how intimacy and autonomy mature in adolescents' peer and romantic relationships; peer and media influences on dating aggression; sexual harassment and bullying in high school. Dr. Connolly is on the Editorial Board of the *Journal of Adolescent Research*. She is currently the Director (Acting) of the LaMarsh Centre for Research on Violence and Conflict Resolution at York University. Professor Connolly is one of the world's leading experts on romantic relationships and peer group processes.

VISUAL STUDENT PREFACE

■ BEGINNING OF CHAPTER

NEW!
Chapter Map

This provides students with a visual overview of the entire chapter.

Quotations

These appear at the beginning of the chapter and occasionally in the margins to stimulate further thought about a topic.

Images of Adolescence

Each chapter opens with a high-interest story that is linked to the chapter's content.

NEW!
Learning Goals

At the beginning of each chapter, you will read four to seven learning goals for the chapter.

■ WITHIN CHAPTER

Web Icons

Web icons appear a number of times in each chapter, signaling students to go to the McGraw-Hill website for Santrock's *Adolescence*, 9th edition, where they will find connecting links that provide additional information. The labels under the Internet icons match the links at the Santrock website, making for easy access to the relevant websites.

Through the Eyes of Psychologists

This feature, appearing several times throughout each chapter, includes a photograph and quotation from leading psychologists to stimulate further thinking about the content.

Mini Chapter Maps

These mini-maps appear three to five times per chapter and provide students with a more detailed, visual look at the organization of the chapter.

Cross-Linkage

This system, unique to this text in the field of adolescent development refers students to the primary discussion of key concepts. A specific page reference appears in the text with a backward-pointing arrow each time a key topic occurs in a chapter subsequent to its initial coverage.

Through the Eyes of Adolescents

This feature, appearing one or more times in each chapter, provides a glimpse of the real worlds of adolescents in their own words.

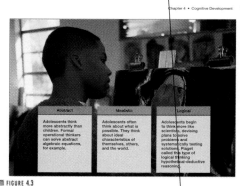

Thinking Critically

These critical thinking boxes appear periodically in each chapter to challenge students to stretch their minds.

Critical Thinking Captions

Most photos have a caption that ends with a critical thinking or knowledge question.

NEW! For Your Review

Several times in each chapter, we review what has been discussed so far in that chapter by displaying the information in For Your Review sections. This learning device helps students get a handle on material several times a chapter, so they don't have to wait until the end of a chapter and have too much information to digest. The For Your Review sections are tied to the Learning Goals stated at the beginning of the chapter.

Key Terms Definitions

Key terms appear in boldface type with their definitions immediately following in italic type and they also appear nearby in the margin. This provides the student with a clear understanding of important concepts.

NEW! Careers in Adolescent Development

This feature, appearing in each chapter, explores a variety of careers in the field of adolescent development.

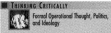

■ END OF CHAPTER

NEW!
Reach Your Learning Goals

The chapter endmatter includes Reach Your Learning Goals (new), chapter map, key terms, and key people. Reach Your Learning Goals is connected to the For Your Review sections within the chapter and the Learning Goals stated at the beginning of the chapter.

Resources for Improving the Lives of Adolescents

Students are provided information about both academic and practical resources in this feature. The resources include books, phone numbers, agencies, research journals, and organizations.

Taking It to the Net

This presents students with questions to explore on the Internet that are related to the chapter. By going to the Santrock website under *Taking It to the Net*, students will be able to connect to other websites, where they can find information that will help them think more deeply about the questions posed.

NEW!
OLC Preview

This directs you to the Online Learning Center for this book, where you will find many learning activities to improve your knowledge and understanding of the chapter.

ADOLESCENCE

THE NATURE OF ADOLESCENT DEVELOPMENT

□

In no order of things is adolescence the simple time of life.
—Jean Erskine Stewart
American Writer, 20th Century

Adolescence is a transitional period in the human life span, linking childhood and adulthood. Understanding the meaning of adolescence is important because adolescents are the future of any society. This first section contains two chapters: chapter 1, "Introduction," and chapter 2, "The Science of Adolescent Development."

CHAPTER
1

CHAPTER MAP

HISTORICAL PERSPECTIVE

Early History

A Positive View of Adolescence

The Twentieth Century

Stereotyping Adolescents

TODAY'S ADOLESCENTS

The Current Status of Adolescents

Social Policy and Adolescents' Development

THE NATURE OF DEVELOPMENT

Processes and Periods

Developmental Issues

Developmental Transitions

UNDERSTANDING ADOLESCENCE: WHAT MATTERS?

Biological Processes Matter

Critical Thinking Matters

Cognitive Processes Matter

Science Matters

Contexts Matter

Problems and Disorders Matter

Social and Personality Development Matters

■ THE YOUTHS OF JEFFREY DAHMER AND ALICE WALKER

Jeffrey Dahmer had a troubled childhood and adolescence. His parents constantly bickered before they divorced. His mother had emotional problems and doted on his younger brother. He felt that his father neglected him, and he had been sexually abused by another boy when he was 8 years old. But the vast majority of people who suffered through a painful childhood and adolescence never go on to commit the grisly crimes that Dahmer committed in the 1970s to 1990s. Dahmer murdered his first victim in 1978 with a barbell and went on to kill 16 other individuals.

A decade before Dahmer's first murder, Alice Walker, who would later win a Pulitzer Prize for her book *The Color Purple,* spent her days battling racism in Mississippi. Walker knew the brutal effects of poverty, born the eighth child of Georgia sharecroppers. Despite the counts against her, she went on to become an award-winning novelist. Walker writes about people who, as she puts it, "make it, who come out of nothing. People who triumph."

What leads one adolescent, so full of promise, to commit brutal acts of violence and another to turn poverty and trauma into a rich literary harvest? How can we attempt to explain how one adolescent can pick up the pieces of a life shattered by tragedy, such as a loved one's death, whereas another one seems to come unhinged by life's minor hassles? Why is it that some adolescents are whirlwinds—successful in school, involved in a network of friends, and full of energy—while others hang out on the sidelines, mere spectators of life? If you have ever wondered what makes adolescents tick, you have asked yourself the central question we explore in this book.

A few years ago, it occurred to me that, when I was a teenager, in the early Depression years, there were no teenagers! Teenagers have sneaked up on us in our own lifetime, and yet it seems they always have been with us. . . . The teenager had not yet been invented, though, and there did not yet exist a special class of beings, bounded in a certain way—not quite children and certainly not adults.

—P. Musgrove
American Writer, 20th Century

Jeffrey Dahmer's senior portrait in high school.

Alice Walker

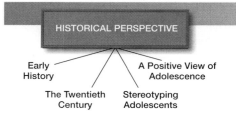

HISTORICAL PERSPECTIVE

Early History — A Positive View of Adolescence

The Twentieth Century — Stereotyping Adolescents

Children are the legacy we leave for the time we will not live to see.

—Aristotle
Greek Philosopher, 4th Century B.C.

HISTORICAL PERSPECTIVE

What have the portraits of adolescence been like at different points in history? When did the scientific study of adolescence begin?

Early History

In early Greece, both Plato and Aristotle commented about the nature of youth. According to Plato (fourth century B.C.), reasoning is not a characteristic of children, but rather makes its first appearance in adolescence. Plato thought that children should spend time in sports and music and adolescents should study science and mathematics.

Aristotle (fourth century B.C.) argued that the most important aspect of adolescence is the ability to choose and that this self-determination becomes a hallmark of maturity. Aristotle's emphasis on the development of self-determination is not unlike some contemporary views that see independence, identity, and career choice as the key themes of adolescence. Aristotle also recognized adolescents' egocentrism, once commenting that adolescents think they know everything and are quite sure about it.

In the Middle Ages, children and adolescents were viewed as miniature adults. They also were treated with harsh discipline in this historical period. In the eighteenth century, French philosopher Jean-Jacques Rousseau offered a more enlightened view of adolescence, restoring the belief that being a child or an adolescent is not the same as being an adult. Like Plato, Rousseau thought that reasoning develops in adolescence. He said that curiosity especially should be encouraged in the education of 12- to 15-year-olds. Rousseau believed that from 15 to 20 years of age, individuals mature emotionally and that their selfishness becomes replaced by an interest in others. Thus, Rousseau helped to restore the belief that development has distinct phases. But Rousseau's ideas were speculative. It wasn't until the beginning of the twentieth century that the scientific exploration of adolescence began.

The Twentieth Century

The end of the nineteenth century and the early part of the twentieth century was an important period in the invention of the concept we now call adolescence. Subsequent changes that adolescents experienced later in the twentieth century also influenced their lives in substantial ways.

The Turn of the Century   Between 1890 and 1920, a number of psychologists, urban reformers, educators, youth workers, and counselors began to mold the concept of adolescence. At this time, young people, especially boys, no longer were viewed as decadent problem causers, but instead were seen as increasingly passive and vulnerable—qualities previously associated only with the adolescent female. When G. Stanley Hall's book on adolescence was published in 1904, as discussed in the next section, it played a major role in restructuring thinking about adolescents. Hall said that although many adolescents appear to be passive, they are experiencing considerable turmoil within.

Educators, counselors, and psychologists began to develop norms of behavior for adolescents. Hall's storm-and-stress concept substantially influenced these norms. As a result, adults attempted to impose conformity and passivity on adolescents in the 1900 to 1920 period. Examples of this conformity included the encouragement of school spirit, loyalty, and hero worship on athletic teams.

G. Stanley Hall   Historians label G. Stanley Hall (1844–1924) the father of the scientific study of adolescence. Hall's ideas were first published in the two-volume set *Adolescence* in 1904.

Hall was strongly influenced by Charles Darwin, the famous evolutionary theorist. Hall applied the scientific and biological dimensions of Darwin's view to the study of adolescent development. Hall believed that all development is controlled by genetically determined physiological factors and that environment plays a minimal role in development, especially during infancy and childhood. He did acknowledge, however, that environment accounts for more change in development in adolescence than in earlier periods. Thus, at least with regard to adolescence, Hall believed—as we do today—that heredity interacts with environmental influences to determine the individual's development.

According to Hall, adolescence is the period from 12 to 23 years of age and is filled with storm and stress. The **storm-and-stress view** *is Hall's concept that adolescence is a turbulent time charged with conflict and mood swings.* Hall borrowed the label *storm and stress* from the *Sturm und Drang* descriptions of German writers, such as Goethe and Schiller, who wrote novels full of idealism, commitment to goals, passion, feeling, and revolution. Hall sensed that there was a parallel between the themes of the German authors and the psychological development of adolescents. In Hall's view, adolescents' thoughts, feelings, and actions oscillate between conceit and humility, good and temptation, happiness and sadness. The adolescent might be nasty to a peer one moment and kind the next moment. At one moment, the adolescent might want to be alone, but seconds later might seek companionship.

Hall was a giant in the field of adolescence. It was he who began the theorizing, the systematizing, and the questioning that went beyond mere speculating and philosophizing. Indeed, we owe the beginnings of the scientific study of adolescent development to Hall.

Margaret Mead's Sociocultural View of Adolescence   Anthropologist Margaret Mead (1928) studied adolescents on the South Sea island of Samoa. She concluded that the basic nature of adolescence is not biological, as Hall envisioned, but rather sociocultural. She argued that when cultures provide a smooth, gradual transition from childhood to adulthood, which is the way adolescence is handled in Samoa, little storm and stress is associated with the period. Mead's observations of Samoan adolescents revealed that their lives were relatively free of turmoil. Mead concluded that cultures that allow adolescents to observe sexual relations, see babies born, regard death as natural, do important work, engage in sex play, and know clearly what their adult roles will be promote a relatively stress-free adolescence. However, in cultures like the United States, in which children are considered very different from adults and where adolescence is not characterized by the aforementioned experiences, adolescence is more likely to be stressful.

storm-and-stress view
G. Stanley Hall's concept that adolescence is a turbulent time charged with conflict and mood swings.

Anthropologist Margaret Mead (*left*) with a Samoan adolescent girl. Mead found that adolescence in Samoa was relatively stress-free, although recently her findings have been criticized. *How does Mead's view of adolescence contrast with Hall's view?*

inventionist view

The view that adolescence is a sociohistorical creation. Especially important in this view are the sociohistorical circumstances at the beginning of the twentieth century, a time when legislation was enacted that ensured the dependency of youth and made their move into the economic sphere more manageable.

More than half a century after Mead's Samoan findings, her work was criticized as biased and error-prone (Freeman, 1983). The current criticism also states that Samoan adolescence is more stressful than Mead observed and that delinquency appears among Samoan adolescents just as it does among Western adolescents. In the current controversy over Mead's findings, some researchers have defended Mead's work (Holmes, 1987).

The Inventionist View   Although adolescence has a biological base, as G. Stanley Hall believed, it also has a sociocultural base, as Margaret Mead believed. Indeed, sociohistorical conditions contributed to the emergence of the concept of adolescence. In the quote that opens this chapter, P. Musgrove comments about the teenager sneaking up on us in our own lifetime. At a point not too long ago in history, the teenager had not yet been invented. The **inventionist view** *states that adolescence is a sociohistorical creation. Especially important in the inventionist view of adolescence are the sociohistorical circumstances at the beginning of the twentieth century, a time when legislation was enacted that ensured the dependency of youth and made their move into the economic sphere more manageable.* We discussed many of these sociohistorical circumstances in our overview of the historical background of adolescence. They included the decline in apprenticeship; increased mechanization during the Industrial Revolution, which also involved upgraded skill requirements of labor and specialized divisions of labor; the separation of work and home; the writings of G. Stanley Hall; urbanization; the appearance of youth groups, such as the YMCA and the Boy Scouts; and age-segregated schools.

Schools, work, and economics are important dimensions of the inventionist view of adolescence (Elder, 1975; Fasick, 1994; Lapsley, Enright, & Serlin, 1985). Some scholars on adolescence argue that the concept of adolescence was invented mainly as a by-product of the motivation to create a system of compulsory public education. In this view, the function of secondary schools is to transmit intellectual skills to youth. However, other scholars on adolescence argue that the primary purpose of secondary schools is to deploy youth within the economic sphere and to serve as an important cog in the culture's authority structure (Lapsley, Enright, & Serlin, 1985). In this view, the American society "inflicted" the status of adolescence on its youth through child-saving legislation. By developing laws for youth, the adult power structure placed youth in a submissive position that restricted their options, encouraged their dependency, and made their move into the world of work more manageable.

Historians now call the period between 1890 and 1920 the "age of adolescence" because they believe it was during this time frame that the concept of adolescence was invented. In this period, a great deal of compulsory legislation aimed at youth was enacted. In virtually every state, laws were passed that excluded youth from most employment and required them to attend secondary school. Much of this legislation included extensive enforcement provisions.

Two clear changes resulted from this legislation: decreased youth employment and increased school attendance by youth. From 1910 to 1930, the number of 10- to 15-year-olds who were gainfully employed dropped about 75 percent. In addition, between 1900 and 1930 the number of high school graduates substantially increased. Approximately 600 percent more individuals graduated from high school in this 30-year time frame.

An analysis of the content of the oldest continuing journal in developmental psychology (*Journal of Genetic Psychology*—earlier called *Pedagogical Seminary*) provided further evidence of history's role in the perception of adolescents (Enright & others,

1987). Four historical periods—the depressions of the 1890s and 1930s, and the two world wars—were evaluated. During the depression periods, scholars wrote about the psychological immaturity of youth and their educational needs. In contrast, during the world wars, scholars did not describe youth as immature, but rather underscored their importance as draftees and factory workers.

Further Changes in the Twentieth Century   In the three decades from 1920 to 1950, adolescents gained a more prominent status in society as they went through a number of complex changes. The lives of adolescents took a turn for the better in the 1920s but moved through difficult times in the 1930s and 1940s. In the 1920s, the Roaring Twenties atmosphere rubbed off on adolescents. Passivity and conformity to adult leadership were replaced by increased autonomy and conformity to peer values. Adults began to model the styles of youth, rather than vice versa. If a new dance came into vogue, the adolescent girl did it first and her mother learned it from her. Prohibition was the law of the time, but many adolescents drank heavily. More permissive attitudes toward the opposite sex developed, and kissing parties were standard fare. Short skirts even led to a campaign by the YWCA against such "abnormal" behavior.

Just when adolescence was getting to be fun, the Great Depression arrived in the 1930s, followed by World War II in the 1940s. Serious economic and political concerns replaced the hedonistic adolescent values of the 1920s. Radical protest groups that were critical of the government increased in number during the 1930s, and World War II exposed adolescents to another serious life-threatening event. Military service provided travel and exposure to other youth from different parts of the United States. This experience promoted a broader perspective on life and a greater sense of independence.

By 1950, the developmental period we refer to as adolescence had come of age—not only did it possess physical and social identity, but legal attention was paid to it as well. Every state had developed special laws for youth between the ages of 16 and 18 or 20. Adolescents in the 1950s have been described as the silent generation. Life was much better for adolescents in the 1950s than it had been in the 1930s and 1940s. The government was paying for many individuals' college educations through the GI Bill, and television was beginning to invade most homes. Getting a college degree, the key to a good job, was on the minds of many adolescents during the 1950s—so were getting married, having a family, and settling down to the life of luxury displayed in television commercials.

While the pursuit of higher education persisted among adolescents in the 1960s, it became painfully apparent that many African American adolescents not only were being denied a college education, but were receiving an inferior secondary education as well. Ethnic conflicts in the form of riots and sit-ins were pervasive, with college-age adolescents among the most vocal participants.

The political protest of adolescents reached a peak in the late 1960s and early 1970s, when millions of adolescents violently reacted to what they saw as immoral American participation in the Vietnam War. As parents watched the 1968 Democratic Convention, they saw not only political speeches in support of candidates but their adolescents fighting with the police, yelling obscenities at adults, and staging sit-ins.

Parents became more concerned in the 1960s about teenage drug use and abuse than in past eras. Sexual permissiveness in the form of premarital sex, cohabitation, and endorsement of previously prohibited sexual conduct also increased.

By the mid 1970s, much of the radical protest of adolescents had abated and was replaced by increased concern for an achievement-oriented, upwardly mobile career to be attained through hard work in high school, college, or a vocational training school. Material interests began to dominate adolescent motives again, while ideological challenges to social institutions seemed to become less central.

Protest in the 1970s also involved the women's movement. The descriptions of adolescents in America in earlier years pertained more to males than to females. The family and career objectives of adolescent females today would barely be recognized by the adolescent females of the 1890s and early 1900s.

(*a*) The Roaring Twenties was a time when adolescents began to behave more permissively. Adults began to model the styles of youth. Adolescent drinking increased dramatically. (*b*) In the 1940s, many youth served in World War II. Military service exposed many youth to life-threatening circumstances and allowed them to see firsthand the way people in other countries live. (*c*) In the 1950s, many youth developed a stronger orientation toward education. Television was piped into many homes for the first time. One of the fads of the 1950s, shown here, was seeing how many people could squeeze into a phone booth. (*d*) In the late 1960s, many youth protested U.S. participation in the Vietnam War. Parents became more concerned about adolescent drug use as well. (*e*) Since the 1970s, much of the radical protest of youth quieted down. Today's adolescents are achievement-oriented, more likely to be working at a job, experiencing adult roles earlier, showing more interest in equality of the sexes, and heavily influenced by the media.

For many years, barriers prevented many females and ethnic minority individuals from entering the field of adolescent development. Females and ethnic minority individuals who obtained doctoral degrees were very dedicated and overcame considerable bias. One pioneering female was Leta Hollingworth, who conducted important research on adolescent development, mental retardation, and gifted children (see

FIGURE 1.1
Leta Hollingworth

Women have often been overlooked in the history of psychology. In the field of adolescence, one such overlooked individual is Leta Hollingworth. She was the first individual to use the term *gifted* to describe youth who scored exceptionally high on intelligence tests (Hollingworth, 1916). She also played an important role in criticizing theories of her time that promoted the idea that males were superior to females (Hollingworth, 1914). For example, she conducted a research study refuting the myth that phases of the menstrual cycle are associated with a decline in performance in females.

figure 1.1). Pioneering African American psychologists included Kenneth and Mamie Clark, who conducted research on the self-esteem of African American children (Clark & Clark, 1939). And in 1932, George Sanchez documented cultural bias in intelligence tests for children and adolescents.

We have described some important sociohistorical circumstances experienced by adolescents, and we have evaluated how society viewed adolescents at different points in history. Next we will explore why caution needs to be exercised in generalizing about the adolescents of any era.

Stereotyping Adolescents

It is easy to stereotype a person, groups of people, or classes of people. A **stereotype** *is a broad category that reflects our impressions and beliefs about people. All stereotypes refer to an image of what the typical member of a particular group is like.* We live in a complex world and strive to simplify this complexity. Stereotyping people is one way we do this. We simply assign a label to a group of people—for example, we say that youth are *promiscuous*. Then we have much less to consider when we think about this set of people. Once we assign stereotypes, it is difficult to abandon them, even in the face of contradictory evidence.

Stereotypes about adolescents are plentiful: "They say they want a job, but when they get one, they don't want to work"; "They are all lazy"; "They are all sex fiends"; "They are all into drugs, every last one of them"; "Kids today don't have the moral fiber of my generation"; "The problem with adolescents today is that they all have it too easy"; "They are a bunch of egotistical smart alecks"; and so it goes.

Indeed, during most of the twentieth century, adolescents have been described as abnormal and deviant, rather than normal and nondeviant. Consider Hall's image of storm and stress. Consider also media portrayals of adolescents as rebellious, conflicted, faddish, delinquent, and self-centered—*Rebel Without a Cause* in the late 1950s, and *Easy Rider* in the 1960s, for example. Consider also the image of adolescents as

stereotype

A broad category that reflects our impressions and beliefs about people. All stereotypes refer to an image of what the typical member of a particular group is like.

In case you're worried about what's going to become of the younger generation, it's going to grow up and start worrying about the younger generation.

—Roger Allen
Contemporary American Writer

THROUGH THE EYES OF ADOLESCENTS

Wanting to Be Treated as an Asset

"Many times teenagers are thought of as a problem that no one really wants to deal with. People are sometimes intimidated and become hostile when teenagers are willing to challenge their authority. It is looked at as being disrespectful. Teenagers are, many times, not treated like an asset and as innovative thinkers who will be the leaders of tomorrow. Adults have the power to teach the younger generation about the world and allow them to feel they have a voice in it."

—Zula, Age 16
Brooklyn, New York

adolescent generalization gap
Adelson's concept of widespread generalizations about adolescents based on information about a limited, highly visible group of adolescents.

Teens Only!
Three Teenagers
Profile of America's Youth
Trends in the Well-Being of America's Youth
Youth Information Directory
http://www.mhhe.com/santrocka9

stressed and disturbed, from *Sixteen Candles* and *The Breakfast Club* in the 1980s to *Boyz N the Hood* in the 1990s.

Such stereotyping of adolescents is so widespread that adolescence researcher Joseph Adelson (1979) called it the **adolescent generalization gap,** *meaning that widespread generalizations about adolescents have developed that are based on information about a limited, often highly visible group of adolescents.*

A Positive View of Adolescence

The negative stereotyping of adolescents is overdrawn (Howe & Strauss, 2000; Stepp, 2000). In a cross-cultural study by Daniel Offer and his colleagues (1988) no support for such as negative view of adolescence was found. The self-images of adolescents around the world—in the United States, Australia, Bangladesh, Hungary, Israel, Italy, Japan, Taiwan, Turkey, and West Germany—were sampled. A healthy self-image characterized at least 73 percent of the adolescents studied. They were moving toward adulthood with a healthy integration of previous experiences, self-confidence, and optimism about the future. Although there were some differences in the adolescents, they were happy most of the time, they enjoyed life, they perceived themselves as able to exercise self-control, they valued work and school, they expressed confidence about their sexual selves, they showed positive feelings toward their families, and they felt they had the capability to cope with life's stresses—not exactly a storm-and-stress portrayal of adolescence.

Old Centuries and New Centuries   Beginning with G. Stanley Hall's portrayal of adolescence as a period of storm and stress, for much of this century in the United States and other Western cultures, adolescence has unfortunately been perceived as a problematic period of the human life span that youth, their families, and society had to endure. But as the research study just described indicated, a large majority of adolescents are not nearly as disturbed and troubled as the popular stereotype of adolescence suggests.

The end of old centuries and the beginning of new centuries have a way of stimulating reflections on what was and visions of what could be and should be. In the field of psychology in general, like its subfield of adolescent development, this has meant a look back at a century in which the field of psychology became too negative (Larson, 2000; Santrock, 2003; Seligman & Csikszentmihalyi, 2000). Psychology had become an overly grim science with people too often characterized as passive and victimized. The calling now is for a new focus on the positive side of psychology and greater emphasis on such topics as hope, optimism, positive individual traits, creativity, and positive group and civic values, such as responsibility, nurturance, civility, and tolerance.

As you read earlier in the chapter, in psychology's subfield of adolescent development, at the beginning of the twentieth century, G. Stanley Hall (1974) proposed a negative, storm-and-stress view of adolescents that strongly influenced perceptions of adolescence for much of that century. Now at the beginning of the twenty-first century, as we look back on the twentieth century, adolescents were stereotyped too negatively.

Generational Perceptions and Memories   Adults' perceptions of adolescents emerge from a combination of personal experience and media portrayals, neither of which produce an objective picture of how normal adolescents develop (Feldman & Elliott, 1990). Some of the readiness to assume the worst about adolescents likely involves the short memories of adults. Many adults measure their current perceptions of adolescents by memories of their own adolescence. Adults often portray today's adolescents as more troubled, less respectful, more self-centered, more assertive, and more adventurous than they were.

However, in matters of taste and manners, the youth of every generation have seemed radical, unnerving, and different from adults—different in how they look, how they behave, the music they enjoy, their hairstyles, and the clothing they choose. It is an enormous error to confuse adolescents' enthusiasm for trying on new identities and enjoying moderate amounts of outrageous behavior with hostility toward parental and societal standards. Acting out and boundary testing are time-honored ways in which adolescents move toward accepting, rather than rejecting, parental values.

Practical Resources and Research
Youth Information Directory
Adolescent Issues
Profile of America's Youth
American Youth Policy Forum
http://www.mhhe.com/santrocka9

At this point we have examined many ideas about the historical perspective on adolescence. This review should help you to reach your learning goals related to this topic.

☐ FOR YOUR REVIEW

Learning Goal 1
Explain the historical perspective on adolescence

- Plato said that reasoning first develops in adolescence and Aristotle argued that self-determination is the hallmark of adolescence. In the Middle Ages, knowledge about adolescence moved a step backward: children were viewed as miniature adults and developmental transformations in adolescence were ignored. Rousseau provided a more enlightened view of adolescence, including an emphasis on different phases of development.
- Between 1890 and 1920, a cadre of psychologists, urban reformers, and others began to mold the concept of adolescence.
- G. Stanley Hall is the father of the scientific study of adolescence. In 1904, he proposed the storm-and-stress view of adolescence, which has strong biological foundations.
- In contrast to Hall's biological view, Margaret Mead argued for a sociocultural interpretation of adolescence. In the inventionist view, adolescence is a sociohistorical invention. Legislation was enacted early in the twentieth century that ensured the dependency of adolescents and delayed their entry into the workforce. From 1900 to 1930, there was a 600 percent increase in the number of high school graduates in the United States.
- Adolescents gained a more prominent place in society from 1920 to 1950. By 1950, every state had developed special laws for adolescents. Barriers prevented many ethnic minority individuals and females from entering the field of studying adolescent development in the early and middle part of the twentieth century. Leta Hollingworth was a pioneering female, and Kenneth and Mamie Clark and George Sanchez were pioneering ethnic minority individuals in studying adolescents.

Learning Goal 2
Discuss stereotyping adolescents and a positive view of adolescence

- Negative stereotyping of adolescents in any historical era has been common.
- Joseph Adelson described the concept of the "adolescent generalization gap," which states that widespread generalizations are often based on a limited set of highly visible adolescents.
- For too long, adolescents have been viewed in negative ways. Research shows that a considerable majority of adolescents around the world have positive self-esteem. The majority of adolescents are not highly conflicted but rather are searching for an identity.

Now that we have explored the history of interest in adolescents, let's turn our attention to today's adolescents. Our discussion of today's adolescents will especially focus on how adolescents are characterized by heterogeneity and diversity.

TODAY'S ADOLESCENTS

Now that we have discussed historical perspectives on adolescents and stereotyping adolescents, let's explore the current status of adolescents.

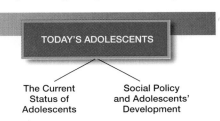

The Current Status of Adolescents

In many ways, it is both the best of times and the worst of times for today's adolescents. Their world possesses powers and perspectives inconceivable less than a century ago: computers; longer life expectancies; the entire planet accessible through television,

Growing up has never been easy. However, adolescence is not best viewed as a time of rebellion, crisis, pathology, and deviance. A far more accurate vision of adolescence describes it as a time of evaluation, of decision making, of commitment, and of carving out a place in the world. Most of the problems of today's youth are not with the youth themselves. What adolescents need is access to a range of legitimate opportunities and to long-term support from adults who deeply care about them. *What might some of these opportunities be?*

satellites, and air travel. However, today the temptations and hazards of the adult world descend upon children and adolescents so early that too often they are not cognitively and emotionally ready to handle them effectively.

Crack, for example, is far more addictive than marijuana, the drug of an earlier generation. Strange fragments of violence and sex flash out of the television set and lodge in the minds of youth. The messages are powerful and contradictory. Rock videos suggest orgiastic sex. Public health officials counsel safe sex. Various talk-show hosts present sensationalized accounts of exotic drugs and serial murders. Television pours a bizarre version of reality into the imaginations of adolescents.

Every stable society transmits values from one generation to the next. That is civilization's work. In today's world, a special concern is the nature of the values being communicated to adolescents. Only half a century ago, two of three families consisted of a father who was the breadwinner, a mother, and the children and adolescents they were raising. Today, less than one in five families fits that description. Phrases such as *quality time* have found their way into the American vocabulary. Absence is a motif in the lives of many adolescents—absence of authority, limits, emotional commitment (Morrow, 1988).

In many ways, today's adolescents are presented with an environment that is less stable than that of adolescents several decades ago (Weissberg & Greenberg, 1998). High divorce rates, high adolescent pregnancy rates, and increased geographic mobility of families contribute to this lack of stability. The rate of adolescent drug use in the United States is the highest in the industrialized world.

Copyright © 1986, Washington Post Writers Group. Reprinted with permission.

However, growing up has never been easy. In many ways, the developmental tasks of today's adolescents are no different from those of adolescents in the 1950s. Adolescence is not a time of rebellion, crisis, pathology, and deviance for a large majority of youth. It is far more accurate to see adolescence as a time of evaluation, of decision making, of commitment, and of carving out a place in the world.

Our discussion underscores an important point about adolescents. They are not a homogeneous group. Most adolescents successfully negotiate the lengthy path to adult maturity, but a large minority do not. Socioeconomic, ethnic, cultural, gender, age, and lifestyle differences influence the developmental trajectory of every adolescent.

Of special interest today in the study of adolescents is how contexts influence their development (Bronfenbrenner, 2000; Eccles, 2002; Lerner, 2000). **Contexts** *are the settings in which development occurs; settings influenced by historical, economic, social, and cultural factors.* To sense how important contexts are in understanding adolescent development, consider a researcher who wants to discover whether today's adolescents are more racially tolerant than those of a decade or two ago. Without reference to the historical, economic, social, and cultural aspects of race relations, adolescents' racial tolerance cannot be fully understood. Each adolescent's development occurs against a cultural backdrop of contexts (McLoyd, 1998, 2000). These contexts or settings include families, peers, schools, churches, neighborhoods, communities, university laboratories, the United States, China, Mexico, Egypt, and many others, each with meaningful historical, economic, social, and cultural legacies.

Contexts will be given special attention in this book. All of section 3 is devoted to contexts, with separate chapters on families, peers, schools, and culture. As we will see next, some experts argue that the social policy of the United States should place a stronger emphasis on improving the contexts in which adolescents live.

Social Policy and Adolescents' Development

Social policy *is a national government's course of action designed to influence the welfare of its citizens.* A current trend is to conduct adolescent development research that will lead to wise and effective decision making in the area of social policy (Bogenschneider, 2002; Carlson & McLanahan, 2002; Edelman, 1997; Ferber, 2002; Lerner, Fisher, & Weinberg, 2000; Shonkoff, 2000). Because more than 20 percent of adolescents are giving birth, because the use and

We need every human gift and cannot afford to neglect any gift because of artificial barriers of sex or race or class or national origin.

—Margaret Mead
American Anthropologist, 20th Century

contexts
The settings in which development occurs. These settings are influenced by historical, economic, social, and cultural factors.

social policy
A national government's course of action designed to influence the welfare of its citizens.

 THROUGH THE EYES OF ADOLESCENTS

Land of Diminished Dreams

The year is two-thousand fifty-four,
The world is full of curses.
People walk the streets no more,
No women carry purses.

The name of the game is survival now—
Safety is far in the past.
Families are huge, with tons of kids
In hopes that one will last.

Drugs are no longer looked down on,
They are a way of life.
They help us escape the wrenching stress
Of our fast world's endless strife . . .

I wake up now—it was only a dream,
But the message was terribly clear.
We'd better think hard about the future
Before our goals and our dreams disappear.

—Jessica Inglis, Age 16

CAREERS IN ADOLESCENT DEVELOPMENT

Peter Benson
Director, Search Institute

Peter Benson has been the Director of the Search Institute in Minneapolis since 1985. The Search Institute is an independent, nonprofit organization whose mission is to advance the well-being of adolescents. The Institute conducts applied scientific research, provides information about many aspects of improving adolescents' lives, gives support to communities, and trains people to work with youth.

Peter obtained his undergraduate degree in psychology from Augustana College, master's degree in the psychology of religion from Yale University, and Ph.D. in social psychology from the University of Denver. Peter directs a staff of 80 individuals at the Search Institute, lectures widely about youth, and consults with a number of communities and organizations on adolescent issues.

Under Peter's direction, the Search Institute has determined through research that a number of assets (such as family support and good schools) serve as a buffer to prevent adolescents from developing problems and increase the likelihood that adolescents will competently make the transition from adolescence to adulthood. We will further discuss these assets in chapter 14, "Adolescent Problems."

Peter Benson, talking with adolescents.

As we face a new century and a new millennium, the overarching challenge for America is to rebuild a sense of community and hope and civility and caring for all of our children and youth.

—Marian Wright Edelman
Contemporary American Lawyer and Child Advocate

Children's Defense Fund
http://www.mhhe.com/santrocka9

generational inequity
The unfair treatment of younger members of an aging society in which older adults pile up advantages by receiving inequitably large allocations of resources, such as Social Security and Medicare.

abuse of drugs is widespread among adolescents, and because the specter of AIDS is spreading, the United States needs revised social policy related to adolescents.

Marian Wright Edelman, president of the Children's Defense Fund, has been a tireless advocate of children's rights. Especially troublesome to Edelman (1997) are the indicators of social neglect that place the United States at or near the bottom of industrialized nations in the treatment of children and adolescents. Edelman says that parenting and nurturing the next generation of children and youth is our society's most important function and that we need to take it more seriously than we have in the past. She points out that we hear a lot from politicians these days about "family values," but that when we examine our nation's policies for families, they don't reflect the politicians' words. Edelman says that we need a better health-care system for families, safer schools and neighborhoods, better parent education, and improved family support programs.

Who should get the bulk of government dollars for improved well-being? Children? Adolescents? Their parents? The elderly? **Generational inequity** *is the unfair treatment of younger members of an aging society in which older adults pile up advantages by receiving inequitably large allocations of resources, such as Social Security and Medicare.* Generational inequity raises questions about whether the young should have to pay for the old and whether an "advantaged" older population is using up resources that should go to disadvantaged children and adolescents. The argument is that older adults are advantaged because they have publicly provided pensions, health care, food stamps, housing subsidies, tax breaks, and other benefits that younger groups do not have. While the trend of greater services for the elderly has been occurring, the percentage of children and adolescents living in poverty has been rising. Adolescents have especially been underserved by the government.

Bernice Neugarten (1988) says the problem should not be viewed as one of generational inequity, but rather as a major shortcoming of our broader economic and social policies. She believes we should develop a spirit of support for improving the range of options of all people in society. Also, it is important to keep in mind that children will one day become older adults and in turn be supported by the efforts of their children.

If there was no Social Security system, in many instances adult children would have to bear the burden of supporting their older parents, which would reduce their ability to spend resources on educating their own children (Schaie, 2000).

In the twenty-first century, the well-being of adolescents should be one of America's foremost concerns. The future of our youth is the future of our society. Adolescents who do not reach their full potential, who are destined to make fewer contributions to society than it needs, and who do not take their place as productive adults diminish our society's future.

In one recent effort to capture what is needed for more positive youth development, Reed Larson (2000) argued that adolescents need more opportunities to develop the capacity for initiative. This involves becoming self-motivated and expending effort to reach challenging goals. Too often adolescents find themselves bored with life. To counter this boredom and help adolescents develop more initiative, Larson especially believes that structured voluntary activities such as sports, arts, and participation in organizations are important contexts.

At this point we have examined many ideas about today's adolescents. This review should help you reach your learning goals related to this topic.

FOR YOUR REVIEW

Learning Goal 3
Evaluate today's adolescents

- Adolescents are heterogeneous. Although a majority of adolescents successfully make the transition from childhood to adulthood, too large a percentage do not and are not provided with adequate opportunities and support. Different portraits of adolescents emerge depending on the particular set of adolescents being described.
- Contexts, the settings in which development occurs, play important roles in adolescent development. These contexts include families, peers, schools, and culture.
- Social policy is a national government's course of action designed to influence the welfare of its citizens. The U.S. social policy on adolescents needs revision to provide more services for youth.
- Some experts argue that adolescents as an age group have been underserved by the government and that a generational inequity has evolved with a much greater percentage of government support going to older adults.

So far in this chapter we have examined the history of interest in adolescence and today's adolescents. Next, we will explore the nature of development.

THE NATURE OF DEVELOPMENT

Each of us develops in certain ways like all other individuals, like some other individuals, and like no other individuals. Most of the time, our attention focuses on our individual uniqueness, but researchers who study development are drawn to our shared as well as our unique characteristics. As humans, each of us travels some common paths. Each of us—Leonardo da Vinci, Joan of Arc, George Washington, Martin Luther King, Jr., you, and I—walked at about the age of 1, talked at about the age of 2, engaged in fantasy play as a young child, and became more independent as a youth.

What do we mean when we speak of an individual's development? **Development** *is the pattern of change that begins at conception and continues through the life span. Most development involves growth, although it also includes decay (as in death and dying).* The pattern of movement is complex because it is the product of several processes.

THE NATURE OF DEVELOPMENT

Processes and Periods   Developmental Issues

Developmental Transitions

development
The pattern of change that begins at conception and continues through the life span. Most development involves growth, although it also includes decay (as in death and dying).

Processes and Periods

Adolescent development is determined by biological, cognitive, and socioemotional processes. Development also is often described in terms of periods.

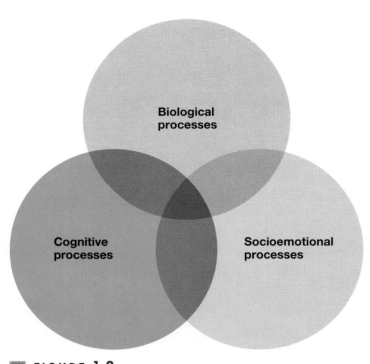

FIGURE 1.2
Biological, Cognitive, and Socioemotional Processes

Changes in development are the result of biological, cognitive, and socioemotional processes. These processes are interwoven as the adolescent develops.

biological processes
Physical changes in an individual's body.

cognitive processes
Changes in an individual's thinking and intelligence.

socioemotional processes
Changes in an individual's relationships with other people, emotions, personality, and social contexts.

prenatal period
The time from conception to birth.

infancy
The developmental period that extends from birth to 18 or 24 months.

early childhood
The developmental period extending from the end of infancy to about 5 or 6 years of age; sometimes called the preschool years.

middle and late childhood
The developmental period extending from about 6 to about 10 or 11 years of age; sometimes called the elementary school years.

Biological, Cognitive, and Socioemotional Processes   **Biological processes** *involve physical changes in an individual's body.* Genes inherited from parents, the development of the brain, height and weight gains, motor skills, and the hormonal changes of puberty all reflect the role of biological processes in the adolescent's development. Biological processes and physical development in adolescence are discussed extensively in chapter 3.

Cognitive processes *involve changes in an individual's thinking and intelligence.* Memorizing a poem, solving a math problem, and imagining what it would be like to be a movie star all reflect the role of cognitive processes in the adolescent's development. Chapters 4 and 5 discuss cognitive processes in detail.

Socioemotional processes *involve changes in an individual's relationships with other people, in emotions, in personality, and in the role of social contexts in development.* Talking back to parents, an aggressive attack on a peer, the development of assertiveness, an adolescent's joy at the senior prom, and a society's gender-role orientation all reflect the role of socioemotional processes in the adolescent's development. Sections 3 and 4 focus on socioemotional processes and adolescent development.

Biological, cognitive, and socioemotional processes are intricately interwoven. Socioemotional processes shape cognitive processes, cognitive processes advance or restrict socioemotional processes, and biological processes influence cognitive processes. Although the various processes involved in adolescent development are discussed in separate sections of the book, keep in mind that you are studying about the development of an integrated human being who has only one interdependent mind and body (see figure 1.2).

Periods of Development   Development is commonly described in terms of periods. We will consider developmental periods that occur in childhood, adolescence, and adulthood. Approximate age ranges are given for the periods to provide a general idea of when they begin and end.

Childhood   Childhood periods of development include the prenatal period, infancy, early childhood, and middle and late childhood.

The **prenatal period** *is the time from conception to birth.* It is a time of tremendous growth—from a single cell to an organism complete with a brain and behavioral capabilities—in approximately 9 months.

Infancy *is the developmental period that extends from birth to 18 or 24 months of age.* Infancy is a time of extreme dependency on adults. Many psychological activities—for example, language, symbolic thought, sensorimotor coordination, social learning, and parent-child relationships—are just beginning.

Early childhood *is the developmental period that extends from the end of infancy to about 5 or 6 years of age; sometimes the period is called the preschool years.* During this time, young children learn to become more self-sufficient and to care for themselves, develop school readiness (following instructions, identifying letters), and spend many hours in play and with peers. First grade typically marks the end of this period.

Middle and late childhood *is the developmental period that extends from about 6 to 10 or 11 years of age. Sometimes the period is called the elementary school years.* Children master the fundamental skills of reading, writing, and arithmetic, and they are formally exposed to the larger world and its culture. Achievement becomes a more central theme of the child's world, and self-control increases.

Adolescence   Our major interest in this book is in the development of adolescents. However, as our developmental timetable suggests, considerable development and experience have occurred before the individual reaches adolescence. No girl or boy enters adolescence as a blank slate with only a genetic blueprint determining thoughts, feelings, and behaviors. Rather, the combination of a genetic blueprint, childhood experiences, and adolescent experiences determines the course of adolescent development. Keep in mind this point about the continuity of development between childhood and adolescence. More about the issue of continuity and discontinuity in development appears shortly.

A definition of adolescence requires consideration of age and also sociohistorical influences. Remember our earlier discussion of the increased interest in the inventionist view of adolescence. With such limitations in mind, **adolescence** *is defined as the developmental period of transition between childhood and adulthood; it involves biological, cognitive, and socioemotional changes.* Although cultural and historical circumstances limit our ability to attribute an exact age range to adolescence, in America and most other cultures today, adolescence begins at approximately 10 to 13 years of age and ends between the ages of 18 and 22 for most individuals. The biological, cognitive, and socioemotional changes of adolescence range from the development of sexual functions to abstract thinking processes to independence.

Developmentalists increasingly describe adolescence in terms of early and late periods. **Early adolescence** *corresponds roughly to the middle school or junior high school years and includes most pubertal change.* **Late adolescence** *refers to approximately the latter half of the second decade of life. Career interests, dating, and identity exploration are often more pronounced in late adolescence than in early adolescence.* Researchers who study adolescents increasingly specify whether their results likely generalize to all adolescents or are more specific to early or late adolescence.

The old view of adolescence was that adolescence is a singular, uniform period of transition resulting in entry to the adult world. In contrast, current approaches in the study of adolescence often examine the precursors and outcomes of a variety of transitions, the constellation of events that define the transitional period, or the timing and sequence of events that take place within a transitional period (Graber, Brooks-Gunn, & Peterson, 1996; Lerner & others, 1996; Sarigiani & Petersen, 2000). For instance, puberty and school events are often investigated as key transitions signaling entry into adolescence; completing school or taking one's first full-time job are evaluated as transitional events that determine the exit from adolescence or the entry into adulthood.

Today, developmentalists do not believe that change ends with adolescence (Baltes, 2000; Baltes, Lindenberger, & Staudinger, 1998; Lerner, 1998; Santrock, 2002). Remember that development is defined as a lifelong process. Adolescence is part of the life course and, as such, is not an isolated period of development. Though adolescence has some unique characteristics, what takes place in adolescence is interconnected with development and experiences in childhood and adulthood. Figure 1.3 on page 20 portrays the developmental periods in the human life span and their approximate age ranges.

Adult Development   Like childhood, and like adolescence, adulthood is not a homogeneous period of development. Developmentalists often describe three periods of adult development: early adulthood, middle adulthood, and late adulthood. **Early adulthood** *usually begins in the late teens or early twenties and lasts through the thirties.* It is a time of establishing personal and economic independence. Career development becomes a more intensified theme than in adolescence.

Our discussion of developmental periods in the human life span continues with **middle adulthood,** *the developmental period entered at approximately 35 to 45 years of age and exited at some point between approximately 55 and 65 years of age.* This period

THINKING CRITICALLY

Imagining What Your Development as an Adolescent Might Have Been Like in Other Cultural Contexts

Imagine what your development as an adolescent would have been like in a culture that offered few choices compared to the Western world—Communist China during the Cultural Revolution. Young people could not choose their jobs or their mates in rural China. They also were not given the choice of migrating to the city. Imagine also another cultural context, this one in the United States. Some areas of inner cities can be effective contexts for raising youth, others not as effective. What would your life as an adolescent have been like if you had grown up in an area of an inner city where most services had moved out, schools were inferior, poverty was extreme, and crime was common? Unfortunately, some of you did grow up in these circumstances.

adolescence
The developmental period of transition from childhood to early adulthood; it involves biological, cognitive, and socioemotional changes.

early adolescence
The developmental period that corresponds roughly to the middle school or junior high school years and includes most pubertal change.

late adolescence
Approximately the latter half of the second decade of life. Career interests, dating, and identity exploration are often more pronounced in late adolescence than in early adolescence.

early adulthood
The developmental period beginning in the late teens or early twenties and lasting into the thirties.

middle adulthood
The developmental period that is entered at about 35 to 45 years and exited at about 55 to 65 years of age.

late adulthood
The developmental period that lasts from about 60 to 70 years of age until death.

Whatever is formed for long duration arrives slowly to its maturity.
—Samuel Johnson
English Writer, 18th Century

is especially important in the lives of adolescents because their parents either are about to enter this adult period or are already in it. Middle adulthood is a time of increasing interest in transmitting values to the next generation, enhanced concern about one's body, and increased reflection about the meaning of life. In chapter 5, we will study how the maturation of both adolescents and parents contributes to an understanding of parent-adolescent relationships.

Eventually, the rhythm and meaning of the human life span wend their way to **late adulthood,** *the developmental period that lasts from approximately 60 to 70 years of age until death.* It is a time of adjustment to decreasing strength and health, and to retirement and reduced income. Reviewing one's life and adapting to changing social roles also characterize late adulthood, as do lessened responsibility, increased freedom, and grandparenthood.

Developmental Transitions

Transitions in development are often important junctures in people's lives. Such transitions include going from being a fetus to a newborn and young infant, going from being an infant to a young child, and going from being a young child to a school-aged child. For our focus in this book, two important transitions are from childhood to adolescence and from adolescence to adulthood. Let's explore these transitions.

Childhood to Adolescence   The transition from being a child to being an adolescent involves a number of biological, cognitive, and socioemotional changes. Among the biological changes are puberty with its growth spurt, hormonal changes, and sexual maturation. In early adolescence, changes in the brain take place that allow for more advanced thinking. Also at this time, changes in sleep occur with adolescents staying up later and wanting to sleep later.

Along the cognitive changes in the transition from being a child to being an adolescent are increases in abstract, idealistic, and logical thinking. As they make the transition to adolescence, individuals begin to think in more egocentric ways in that they often sense they are onstage, unique, and invulnerable. More responsibility for decision making is placed on the young adolescents' shoulders than when they were children.

Among the socioemotional changes in the transition from being a child to being an adolescent are increases in seeking independence, conflict with parents, and a motivation to spend more time with peers. Conversations with friends become more intimate and include more self-disclosure. As individuals enter adolescence, they experience schools that are larger and more impersonal. Achievement becomes more serious business and academic challenges increase in early adolescence. Changes in sexual maturation produce a much greater interest in romantic relationships. Young adolescents also show greater mood swings than when they were children.

As can be seen, the transition from being a child to being an adolescent is complex and multidimensional, involving changes in many different aspects of an individual's

60/70 Years to Death	Late Adulthood
35/45 to 55/65 Years	Middle Adulthood
Late Teens/ Early 20s to 30s	Early Adulthood
10/13 to 18/22 Years	Adolescence
6 to 10/11 Years	Middle and Late Childhood
3 to 5 Years	Early Childhood
Birth to 18/24 Months	Infancy
Conception to Birth	Prenatal Period

■ FIGURE 1.3
Periods of Development

Developmental transitions from childhood to adolescence involve biological, cognitive, and socioemotional changes. *What are some of these changes?*

life. Developing competently through this transition requires considerable adaptation and thoughtful, sensitive support from caring adults.

Adolescence to Adulthood   Another important transition takes place when individuals change from being an adolescent to being an adult (Gutman, 2002; Jozefowicz, 2002; Raymore, Barber, & Eccles, 2001). It has been said that adolescence begins in biology and ends in culture. This means that the marker for the transition from childhood to adolescence involves the onset of pubertal maturation, while the marker for the transition from adolescence to adulthood is determined by cultural standards and experiences. Nonetheless, as seen earlier, the transition from being a child to being an adolescent not only involves biological changes but cognitive and socioemotional changes as well.

Do individuals abruptly enter adulthood? That is unlikely. Sociologist Kenneth Kenniston (1970) proposed that a transition occurs between being an adolescent and being an adult which can last two to eight years or even longer. **Youth** *is Kenniston's term for the transitional period between adolescence and adulthood, which is a time of economic and personal temporariness.* Faced with a complex world of work and highly specialized career preparation, many individuals spend an extended period of time in a technical institute, college, or graduate/professional school. During this transition, their income is often low and sporadic. Established residences may change frequently. Marriage and a family may be delayed.

youth
Kenniston's term for the transitional period between adolescence and adulthood, which is a time of economic and personal temporariness.

More recently, the transition from being an adolescent to being an adult has been referred to as *emerging adulthood* (Arnett, 2000). The approximate age range given for emerging adulthood is approximately 18 to 25 years of age. Experimentation and exploration characterize emerging adulthood. Many individuals at this point in development are still exploring which career path they want to follow, what they want their identity to be, and which lifestyle they want to adopt (such as single, cohabiting, or married).

Determining just when an individual becomes an adult is difficult. The most widely recognized marker of entry into adulthood is when an individual takes a more or less permanent, full-time job. This usually happens when individuals finish school—high school for some, college for others, graduate or professional school for others (Graber & Brooks-Gunn, in press). However, the criteria for determining when individuals leave adolescence behind them and enter the adult world are far from clear. Economic independence is considered a marker for adult status but developing this independence is often a long, drawn-out process. College graduates are increasingly returning to live with their parents as they seek to get their feet on the ground economically. About 40 percent of individuals in their late teens to early twenties move back to live with their parents at least once (Goldscheider & Goldscheider, 1999).

Self-responsibility and independent decision making are other possible markers of adulthood. Indeed, in one study, adolescents cited taking responsibility for oneself and independent decision making as what marks entry into adulthood (Scheer & Unger, 1994). In another study, more than 70 percent of college students said that being an adult means accepting responsibility for the consequences of one's actions, deciding on one's own beliefs and values, and establishing a relationship with parents as an equal adult (Arnett, 1995).

Is there a specific age at which individuals become an adult? In one study, 21-year-olds said that they reached adult status when they were 18 to 19 years old (Scheer, 1996). In this study, both social status factors (financial status and graduation/education) and cognitive factors (being responsible and making independent decisions) were cited as markers for reaching adulthood. Clearly,

What determines when adolescence ends and adulthood begins?

THINKING CRITICALLY

The Importance of Asking Questions—Exploring Your Own Development as an Adolescent

Asking questions reflects our active curiosity. Children—especially young children—are remarkable for their ability to ask questions. When my granddaughter Jordan was 4 years old, one of her favorite words was "Why?" As strong as question-asking is early in our lives, many of us ask far fewer questions as adults.

Asking questions can help us engage in critical thinking about adolescent development, including our own development as adolescents. As you go through this course, you might want to ask yourself questions about how you experienced a particular aspect of development. For example, consider your experiences in your family as you were growing up. Questions you could pose to yourself might include these: "How did my parents bring me up? How did the way they reared me influence what I'm like today? How did my relationship with my brothers or sisters affect my development?" Consider also questions like these about your experiences with peers and at school: "Did I have many close friends while I was growing up? How much time did I spend with my peers and friends at various points in childhood and adolescence compared with the time I spent with my parents? What were my schools like? How good were my teachers? How did the schools and teachers affect my achievement orientation today?"

Be curious. Ask questions. Ask your friends or classmates about their experiences as they were growing up and compare them with yours.

nature-nurture issue
Involves the debate about whether development is primarily influenced by nature or nurture. Nature refers to an organism's biological inheritance, nurture to its environmental experiences.

reaching adulthood involves more than just being a specific chronological age.

In sum, at some point in the late teens through the early twenties, individuals reach adulthood. In becoming an adult, they accept responsibility for themselves, become capable of making independent decisions, and gain financial independence (Arnett, 2000).

What we have said so far about the determinants of adult status mainly addresses individuals in industrialized societies, especially Americans. Are the criteria for adulthood the same in developing countries as they are in the United States? In developing countries, marriage is often a more significant marker for entry into adulthood and this usually occurs much earlier (Arnett, 2000; Davis & Davis, 1989).

So far in our coverage of the nature of development, we have focused on processes and periods in development, as well as developmental transitions. Next, we will explore some important issues in development.

Developmental Issues

A number of issues are raised in the study of adolescent development. The major issues include these: Is development due more to nature (heredity) or more to nurture (environment)? Is development more continuous and smooth or more discontinuous and stagelike? Is development due more to early experience or more to later experience?

Nature and Nurture   The **nature-nurture issue** *involves the debate about whether development is primarily influenced by nature or nurture. Nature refers to an organism's biological inheritance, nurture to its environmental experiences.* "Nature" proponents claim that the most important influence on development is biological inheritance. "Nurture" proponents claim that environmental experiences are the most important influence.

According to the nature advocates, just as a sunflower grows in an orderly way—unless flattened by an unfriendly environment—so does the human grow in an orderly way. The range of environments can be vast, but the nature approach argues that the genetic blueprint produces commonalities in growth and development. We walk before we talk, speak one word before two words, grow rapidly in infancy and less so in early childhood, experience a rush of sexual hormones in puberty, reach the peak of our physical strength in late adolescence and early adulthood, and then physically decline. The nature proponents acknowledge that extreme environments—those that are psychologically barren or hostile—can depress development. However, they believe that basic growth tendencies are genetically wired into humans.

By contrast, other psychologists emphasize the importance of nurture, or environmental experiences, in development. Experiences run the gamut from the individual's biological environment—nutrition, medical care, drugs, and physical accidents—to the social environment—family, peers, schools, community, media, and culture.

Some adolescent development researchers believe that, historically, too much emphasis has been placed on the biological changes of puberty as determinants of adolescent psychological development (Montemayor & Flannery, 1991). They recognize that biological change is an important dimension of the transition from childhood to adolescence, one that is found in all primate species and in all cultures throughout the world. However, they believe that social contexts (nurture) play important roles in adolescent psychological development as well, roles that until recently have not been given adequate attention.

Continuity and Discontinuity   Think about your development for a moment. Was your growth into the person you are today a gradual growth, like the slow, cumulative growth of a seedling into a giant oak, or did you experience sudden, distinct changes in your growth, like the way a caterpillar changes into a butterfly (see figure 1.4)? For the most part, developmentalists who emphasize experience have described development as a gradual, continuous process; those who emphasize nature have described development as a series of distinct stages.

The **continuity-discontinuity issue** *focuses on the extent to which development involves gradual, cumulative change (continuity) or distinct stages (discontinuity).* In terms of continuity, a child's first word, while seemingly an abrupt, discontinuous event, is actually the result of weeks and months of growth and practice. Puberty, while also seemingly an abrupt, discontinuous occurrence, is actually a gradual process occurring over several years.

In terms of discontinuity, each person is described as passing through a sequence of stages in which change is qualitatively, rather than quantitatively, different. As the oak moves from seedling to giant tree, it becomes *more* oak—its development is continuous. As a caterpillar changes into a butterfly, it does not become more caterpillar; it becomes a *different kind* of organism—its development is discontinuous. For example, at some point a child moves from not being able to think abstractly about the world to being able to. This is a qualitative, discontinuous change in development, not a quantitative, continuous change.

Early and Later Experience   Another important developmental topic is the **early-later experience issue,** *which focuses on the degree to which early experiences (especially early in childhood) or later experiences are the key determinants of development.* That is, if infants or young children experience negative, stressful circumstances in their lives, can those experiences be overcome by later, more positive experiences in adolescence? Or are the early experiences so critical, possibly because they are the infant's first, prototypical experiences, that they cannot be overridden by a later, more enriched environment in childhood or adolescence?

The early-later experience issue has a long history and continues to be hotly debated among developmentalists. Some believe that unless infants experience warm, nurturant caregiving in the first year or so of life, their development will never be optimal (Bowlby, 1989; Main, 2000; Sroufe, 1996). Plato was sure that infants who were rocked frequently became better athletes. Nineteenth-century New England ministers told parents in Sunday sermons that the way they handled their infants would determine their children's future character. The emphasis on the importance of early experience rests on the belief that each life is an unbroken trail on which a psychological quality can be traced back to its origin.

The early-experience doctrine contrasts with the later-experience view that, rather than achieving statuelike permanence after change in infancy, our development continues to be like the ebb and flow of a river. The later-experience advocates argue that children and adolescents are malleable throughout development and that later sensitive caregiving is just as important as earlier sensitive caregiving. A number of life-span developmentalists, who focus on the entire life span rather than only on child development, stress that too little attention has been given to later experiences in development (Baltes, 1987, 2000). They accept that early experiences are important contributors to development, but no more important than later experiences. Jerome Kagan (1992) points out that even children who show the qualities of an inhibited temperament, which is linked to heredity, have the capacity to change their behavior. In his research, almost one-third of a group of children who had an inhibited temperament at 2 years of age were not unusually shy or fearful when they were 4 years of age (Kagan, Snidmar, & Arcus, 1995).

People in Western cultures, especially those steeped in the Freudian belief that the key experiences in development are children's relationships with their parents in the first five years of life, have tended to support the idea that early experiences are more important than later experiences (Chan, 1963). In contrast, the majority of people in

continuity-discontinuity issue
The issue regarding whether development involves gradual, cumulative change (continuity) or distinct stages (discontinuity).

early-later experience issue
This issue focuses on the degree to which early experiences (especially early in childhood) or later experiences are the key determinants of development.

■ **FIGURE 1.4**
Continuity and Discontinuity in Development

Is human development like a seedling gradually growing into a giant oak? Or is it more like a caterpillar suddenly becoming a butterfly?

the world do not share this belief. For example, people in many Asian countries believe that experiences occurring after about 6 to 7 years of age are more important aspects of development than earlier experiences are. This stance stems from the long-standing belief in Eastern cultures that children's reasoning skills begin to develop in important ways in the middle childhood years.

Continuity and Discontinuity
http://www.mhhe.com/santrocka9

Evaluating the Developmental Issues   As we consider further these three salient developmental issues—nature and nurture, continuity and discontinuity, and early and later experience—it is important to realize that most developmentalists recognize that it is unwise to take an extreme position on these issues. Development is not all nature or all nurture, not all continuity or discontinuity, and not all early experience or all later experience. Nature and nurture, continuity and discontinuity, and early and later experience all affect our development through the human life span. For example, in considering the nature-nurture issue, the key to development is the interaction of nature and nurture rather than either factor alone (Loehlin, 1995, 2000). An individual's cognitive development, for instance, is the result of heredity-environment interaction, not heredity or environment alone. Much more about the role of heredity-environment interaction appears in chapter 3.

Consider also the behavior of adolescent males and females (Feldman & Elliott, 1990). Nature factors continue to influence differences between adolescent boys and girls in such areas as height, weight, and age at pubertal onset. On the average, girls are shorter and lighter than boys and enter puberty earlier. However, some previously well-established differences between adolescent females and males are diminishing, suggesting an important role for nurture. For example, adolescent females are pursuing careers in math and science in far greater numbers than in the past, and are seeking autonomy in a much stronger fashion. Unfortunately, adolescent females also are increasing their use of drugs and cigarette smoking compared to adolescent females in earlier eras. The shifting patterns of gender similarities and differences underscore the belief that simplistic explanations based only on biological or only on environmental causes are unwise.

Although most developmentalists do not take extreme positions on the developmental issues we have discussed, this consensus has not meant the absence of spirited debate about how strongly development is determined by these factors. Continuing with our example of the behavior of female and male adolescents, are girls less likely to do well in math because of their "feminine" nature or because of society's masculine bias? Consider also adolescents who, as children, experienced poverty, parental neglect, and poor schooling. Could enriched experiences in adolescence overcome the "deficits" they encountered earlier in development? The answers developmentalists give to such questions reflect their stance on the issues of nature and nurture, continuity and discontinuity, and early and later experiences. The answers also influence public policy about adolescents and how each of us lives through the human life span.

At this point we have examined many ideas about the nature of development. This review should help you to reach your learning goals related to this topic.

☐ FOR YOUR REVIEW

Learning Goal 4
Define development and describe processes and periods in development

- Development is the pattern of movement or change that occurs throughout the life span.
- Biological processes involve physical changes in the individual's body. Cognitive processes consist of changes in thinking and intelligence. Socioemotional changes focus on changes in relationships with people, in emotion, in personality, and in social contexts.
- Development is commonly divided into these periods: prenatal, infancy, early childhood, middle and late childhood, adolescence, early adulthood, middle adulthood, and late adulthood. Adolescence is the developmental period of transition between childhood and adulthood that involves biological, cognitive, and

socioemotional changes. In most cultures, adolescence begins at approximately 10 to 13 years of age and ends at about 18 to 22 years of age. Developmentalists increasingly distinguish between early adolescence and late adolescence.

Learning Goal 5
Discuss transitions and issues in development

- Two important transitions in development are from childhood to adolescence and adolescence to adulthood. In the transition from childhood to adolescence, pubertal change is prominent, although cognitive and socioemotional changes occur as well. It sometimes has been said that adolescence begins in biology and ends in culture. The concepts of youth and emerging adulthood have been proposed to describe the transition from adolescence to adulthood. Among the criteria for determining adulthood are self-responsibility, independent decision making, and economic independence.
- Three important issues in development are (1) the nature-nurture issue (Is development mainly due to heredity [nature] or environment [nurture]?), (2) the continuity-discontinuity issue (Is development more gradual, cumulative [continuity] or more abrupt and sequential [discontinuity]?), (3) the early-later experience issue (Is development due more to early experiences, especially in infancy and early childhood, or to later [more recent and current] experiences)? Most developmentalists do not take extreme positions on these issues although they are extensively debated.

So far in this chapter we have focused on the history of interest in adolescence, today's adolescents, and the nature of development. Next, we will explore what matters in adolescence, which will provide you with a menu of the main topics in the remainder of the book.

UNDERSTANDING ADOLESCENCE: WHAT MATTERS?

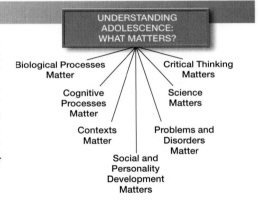

In adolescence, what matters? What is involved in understanding adolescence? What is at work when adolescents make a healthy journey from childhood to adulthood? What goes wrong when they fall off course and are not on track to reach their full potential? In thinking about what really matters in adolescence, let's examine some of the main themes of this book and explore contemporary thinking about these themes. For an understanding of adolescence, these things matter: biological processes, cognitive processes, contexts, social and personality development, problems and disorders, science, and critical thinking. Studying these aspects of adolescence scientifically and thinking critically about them also can substantially improve our understanding of adolescent development.

Biological Processes Matter

Earlier in the chapter, we examined the nature-nurture issue. Recall that this issue raises the question of how strongly adolescents' biological (nature) makeup influences their behavior and development.

Controversy swirls about this topic. In the early views of Hall and Freud, biology was dominant. Today we continue to believe that biology plays a key role in the adolescent's development, although current theorizing often seeks to determine how heredity and environment work together in producing adolescent development.

A current trend is to examine how evolution might have played a role in determining the nature of adolescent development (Buss, 1998, 2000; Buss & others, 2001; Csikszentmihalyi & Schmidt, 1998). The field of evolutionary psychology, the most recent major theoretical view in psychology, seeks to examine how adaptation, reproduction, and "survival of the fittest" can help to explain behavior and development. We especially evaluate evolution's role in chapter 3, "Puberty, Health, and Biological Foundations," and chapter 10, "Gender."

There also is considerable interest today in studying how heredity is involved in behavior and development (Lewis, 2002; Wahlsten, 2000). Scientists are making considerable progress in charting the role of genes in various diseases and disorders. We will explore heredity more extensively in chapter 3.

The health of today's adolescents is a special concern. Far too many adolescents engage in health-compromising behaviors, such as smoking, excessive drinking, and risk-taking adventures. We will examine adolescents' health throughout the book, but especially focus on it in chapter 3.

Cognitive Processes Matter

How important is the adolescent's mind in what she or he does? Adolescents not only are biological beings, they are mental beings. Considerable changes take place in cognition during adolescence (Byrnes, 2001; Kuhn, 2000). Adolescents have more sophisticated thinking skills than children, although there are considerable individual variations from one adolescent to another. Advances in adolescent thinking not only help them solve difficult academic problems in areas such as mathematics but change the way they examine their social lives as well. Increasingly, developmentalists are interested in learning more about adolescents' decision making and how it can be improved to help them adapt more competently. They also are motivated to find out ways to help adolescents think more critically and deeply about problems and issues. Another contemporary interest is determining what the components of intelligence are and creating educational programs that address these components (Torff, 1999). We will study cognitive processes in much greater detail in chapter 4, "Cognitive Development."

Contexts Matter

Earlier we described the increasing trend of examining contexts or settings to better understand adolescent development. Especially important contexts in adolescents' lives

Why do contexts matter in understanding adolescent development?

are their family, peer, school, and cultural contexts (Eccles, 2002; Harkness & Super, 2002). Families have a powerful influence on adolescent development, and today large numbers of researchers are charting many aspects of family life, such as conflict, attachment, and divorce, to determine how they affect adolescent outcomes (Buchanan, 2000; Dunn & others, 2001; Hetherington & Stanley-Hagan, 2002; Rutter, 2002). We will explore these and many other aspects of families in chapter 5.

Like families, peers play powerful roles in adolescents' lives. Researchers are studying how peer status (such as being isolated, rejected, or popular), friends, cliques, and dating and romantic relationships are involved in the adolescent's development (Brown, 2002). We will examine these and other aspects of peer relations in chapter 6.

Schools are another important context in adolescents' lives (Eccles & Wigfield, 2000; Pierce & Kurtz-Costes, 2001; Sadker & Sadker, 2003). Currently there is a great deal of concern about the quality of secondary education for adolescents. There also is controversy about the best way to teach adolescents (Ferrari, 2002). A current trend is for teachers to act as guides in providing adolescents with learning opportunities in which they can actively construct their understanding of a topic or issue (Cobb, 2000; Santrock, 2001). We will examine such concerns and trends in chapter 7, "Schools."

The Search Institute
http://www.mhhe.com/santrocka9

The culture in which adolescents live is another important context in their development (Greenfield, 2000, 2002; Triandis, 2000). Many researchers are comparing how adolescents in the United States are similar to or different from adolescents in other countries. And there is a special concern that far too many American adolescents are growing up in poverty (Fuligni & Yoshikawa, 2003; Magnuson & Duncan, 2002; McLoyd, 2000). In recent years, there also has been a considerable increase in studying the role of ethnicity in adolescent development (Cushner, McClelland, & Safford, 2003; Wong & Rowley, 2001). Another important aspect of culture today is technology (Calvert, 1999; Murray, 2000). We will examine these and many other aspects of culture in chapter 8, "Culture."

Social and Personality Development Matters

Other important aspects of adolescents' lives involve their social and personality development, such as their self and identity, gender, sexuality, moral development, and achievement. A key aspect of adolescents' development, especially for older adolescents, is their search for identity (Adams, Abraham, & Markstrom, 2000; Comas-Díaz, 2001). Researchers are interested in determining the contextual and developmental factors that promote healthy or unhealthy identity development (Rodriquez & Quinlan, 2002). We will examine these and many other aspects of the self and identity in chapter 9.

Gender is a pervasive aspect of adolescent development. Researchers are motivated to find out how contexts influence gender development, the role that sexuality plays in gender development during adolescence, how adolescence might be a critical juncture in gender development (especially for girls), gender similarities and differences, and adolescent male and female issues (Bumpas, Crouder, & McHale, 2001; Eagly, 2000). We will examine these and many other aspects of gender in chapter 10.

Sexuality has long been described as a key dimension of adolescent development. In adolescence, boys and girls

CAREERS IN ADOLESCENT DEVELOPMENT

Luis Vargas
Child Clinical Psychologist

Luis Vargas is Director of the Clinical Child Psychology Internship Program and a professor in the Department of Psychiatry at the University of New Mexico Health Sciences Center. He also is Director of Psychology at the University of New Mexico Children's Psychiatric Hospital.

Luis got an undergraduate degree is psychology from St. Edwards University in Texas, a master's degree in psychology from Trinity University in Texas, and his Ph.D. in clinical psychology from the University of Nebraska–Lincoln.

His main interests are cultural issues and the assessment and treatment of children, adolescents, and families. He is motivated to find better ways to provide culturally responsive mental health services. One of his special interests is the treatment of Latino youth for delinquency and substance abuse. He recently co-authored (with Joan Koss-Chioino) *Working with Latino Youth* (Koss-Chioino & Vargas, 1999), which spells out effective strategies for improving the lives of at-risk Latino youth.

Luis Vargas, counseling an adolescent girl.

take the journey to becoming men and women. It is a complex journey filled with mysteries and curiosities. An important point is that sexuality is a normal aspect of adolescent development. Developmentalists are motivated to discover adolescents' heterosexual and homosexual attitudes and behaviors, why the United States has the highest adolescent pregnancy rate in the industrialized world and what can be done about it, and strategies for reducing sexually transmitted diseases (Basen-Enquist & others, 2001; Ford, Sohn, & Lepkowski, 2001; Kelly, 2000; Leadbetter & Way, 2000). We will discuss these sexuality topics and many others in chapter 11.

Moral development is another important aspect of adolescents' lives. Researchers seek to find out the roles that thoughts, feelings, and contexts play in adolescents' moral development (Bandura & others, 2001; Damon, 2000). They want to know how important parents and peers are in adolescents' moral development. There also is considerable interest in the best way to morally educate adolescents, what adolescents' values are, and developmental changes in the way they think about religion. We will explore these and many other aspects of moral development in chapter 12.

In adolescence, achievement becomes a more serious matter. Researchers are interested in determining how such factors as being internally motivated, planning, setting goals, self-monitoring, and having a mastery motivation are involved in the adolescent's motivation to achieve (Elliott & McGregor, 2001; Weiner, 2000; Stipek, 2002). They also want to better understand the role of work in adolescent development and how adolescents think about careers (Spokane, 2000). We will examine these and other aspects of achievement in chapter 13.

Problems and Disorders Matter

Far too many adolescents have problems and disorders that restrict their ability to optimally reach adulthood (Miller & others, 2000). Researchers study such problems and disorders as drug use and abuse, delinquency, depression and suicide, and eating disorders (Mont, Colby, & O'Leary, 2001). They want to know what causes adolescents to develop these problems and disorders and what the best ways are to prevent them in the first place and intervene in them when they do develop (Alquzzine & Kay, 2002). A current trend is the understanding that many at-risk adolescents have more than one problem and that intervention programs need to take this into account. We will examine these and other aspects of problems and disorders in chapter 14.

Science Matters

Does science matter in understanding adolescent development? You probably have heard it said that experience is the most important teacher. However, much of the knowledge we get from personal experience is based on our individual observations and interpretations. How do we know if these are accurate? Sometimes we make errors in sight, hearing, and interpretation. Scientific studies help to correct our personal interpretations (Best & Kahn, 2003; McMillan & Wergin, 2002). In recent decades an increasing number of researchers have studied adolescents, and the result is a dramatic increase in our understanding of how they develop. Although we have much left to discover and there are many controversies about adolescent development, scientists are making considerable progress in improving our knowledge. An emphasis on research will appear throughout this book, and in chapter 2 you will explore in greater detail the scientific aspects of studying adolescent development.

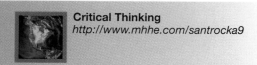

Critical Thinking
http://www.mhhe.com/santrocka9

Critical Thinking Matters

Are you a critical thinker? What does it mean to be a critical thinker? Critical thinkers think reflectively and productively and evaluate evidence. Thinking critically means asking yourself how you know something. Too often we have a tendency to recite, define, describe, state, and list rather than analyze, infer, connect, synthesize, criticize, create, evaluate, think, and rethink (Brooks & Brooks, 1993). Critical thinkers are open-minded and intellectually curious, look for multiple determinants of behavior, and often think like a scientist (Halpern, 1996). Thinking scientifically involves keeping in mind that personal experiences and interpretations are error-prone and that it is important to examine the evidence about a topic or issue in adolescent development. Take a critical thinking stance as you study adolescent development in this course. To encourage your critical thinking, many questions appear throughout the text, "Thinking Critically" boxes challenge you to think critically, and at the end of each chapter "Taking It to the Net" exercises encourage you to think critically about problems and issues that you can explore on the Internet. In addition, quotations are included periodically throughout the chapters to stimulate your critical thinking.

At this point we have examined many ideas about what matters in adolescence. This review should help you to reach your learning goals related to this topic.

☐ FOR YOUR REVIEW

Learning Goal 6
Know what matters in understanding adolescent development

- In terms of biological processes, there is considerable interest in the roles of heredity and environment, evolution, and health in adolescent development.
- In terms of cognitive processes, we need to understand changes in thinking skills and decision making. Also important is charting the nature of intelligence in adolescence.
- In terms of contexts, key contexts or settings for adolescent development are families, peers, schools, and culture.
- In terms of social and personality development, there is considerable interest in the self and identity, gender, sexuality, moral development, and achievement.
- In terms of science, scientific studies help us to correct our individual observations and personal interpretations of adolescence.
- In terms of critical thinking, to better understand adolescence it is important to think deeply and productively about this topic.

In this chapter, we have introduced the field of adolescent development. In exploring what matters in adolescent development, we indicated that science matters. In the next chapter, we will examine this topic in much greater depth.

CHAPTER MAP

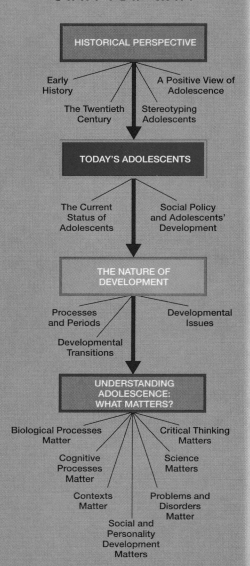

REACH YOUR LEARNING GOALS

At the beginning of the chapter, we stated six learning goals and encouraged you to review material related to these goals at four points in the chapter. This is a good time to return to these reviews and use them to guide your study and help you to reach your learning goals.

Page 13

Learning Goal 1   Explain the historical perspective on adolescence

Learning Goal 2   Discuss stereotyping adolescents and a positive view of adolescence

Page 17

Learning Goal 3   Evaluate today's adolescents

Page 24

Learning Goal 4   Define development and describe processes and periods in development

Learning Goal 5   Discuss transitions and issues in development

Page 29

Learning Goal 6   Know what matters in understanding adolescent development

KEY TERMS

storm-and-stress view 7
inventionist view 8
stereotype 11
adolescent generalization gap 12
contexts 15
social policy 15
generational inequity 16
development 17
biological processes 18
cognitive processes 18
socioemotional processes 18
prenatal period 18
infancy 18

early childhood 18
middle and late childhood 18
adolescence 19
early adolescence 19
late adolescence 19
early adulthood 19
middle adulthood 19
late adulthood 20
youth 21
nature-nurture issue 22
continuity-discontinuity issue 23
early-later experience issue 23

KEY PEOPLE

G. Stanley Hall 7
Margaret Mead 7
Leta Hollingworth 10
Kenneth and Mamie Clark 11
George Sanchez 11

Daniel Offer 12
Marian Wright Edelman 16
Bernice Neugarten 16
Reed Larson 17
Kenneth Kenniston 21

RESOURCES FOR IMPROVING THE LIVES OF ADOLESCENTS

Children's Defense Fund

> 25 E Street, NW
> Washington, DC 20001
> 202–628–8787

The Children's Defense Fund, headed by Marian Wright Edelman, exists to provide a strong and effective voice for children and adolescents who cannot vote, lobby, or speak for themselves.

Great Transitions

> (1995) by the Carnegie Council on Adolescent Development
> New York: Carnegie Corporation

This report by the Carnegie Council on Adolescent Development covers a wide range of topics, including reengaging families with their adolescents, educating adolescents, promoting adolescent health, strengthening communities, and redirecting the pervasive power of the media.

Search Institute

> Thresher Square West
> 700 South Third Street, Suite 210
> Minneapolis, MN 55415
> 612–376–8955

The Search Institute has available a large number of resources for improving the lives of adolescents. The brochures and books available address school improvement, adolescent literacy, parent education, program planning, and adolescent health, and include resource lists. A free quarterly newsletter is available.

Securing the Future

> (2000) by Sheldon Danziger and Jane Waldfogel (Eds.)
> New York: Russell Sage Foundation

This book includes articles from scholars in a number of different disciplines (such as economics, psychology, and sociology) to explore effective ways to improve social policy for children and youth.

TAKING IT TO THE NET

http://www.mhhe.com/santrocka9

1. About a century ago, G. S. Hall wrote that adolescence was an especially stressful period of time, a stereotype that continues today as evidenced in media representations of adolescence as well as in literary works. Adolescents often are portrayed as interested only in drugs, engaging in promiscuous and risky sex, and as alcohol abusers. *What is the evidence about the percentages of adolescents in these categories that you can cite to refute the stereotype?*

2. You are a student teacher for Ms. Masterson, who teaches tenth-grade English. She is trying to capitalize on the vast store of information on the Web by helping students integrate Web resources into their papers. Knowing that it is important to think critically when gleaning information from the Web, Ms. Masterson asks you to help her formulate guidelines students can use to evaluate websites. *What clues will you suggest Ms. Masterson provide her classes to help the students evaluate website information?*

3. Our version of adolescence evolved because of a variety of social reforms, including child labor laws that limit adolescent involvement in the workforce. When you took your first job, you likely were limited in the kind of work you could do because of these laws. *Do you think they are fair? How would you argue for a more individual case-by-case application of these laws?*

Connect to *http://www.mhhe.com/santrocka9* to research the answers and complete these exercises. In some cases, you'll also find further instructions on this site.

APPENDIX

CAREERS IN ADOLESCENT DEVELOPMENT

Some of you may be quite sure about what you plan to make your life's work. Others of you may not have decided on a major yet and are uncertain about which career path you want to follow. Each of us wants to find a rewarding career and enjoy the work we do. The field of adolescent development offers an amazing breadth of career options that can provide extremely satisfying work.

If you decide to pursue a career in adolescent development, what career options are available to you? There are many. College and university professors teach courses in many different areas of adolescent development, education, family development, and medicine. Teachers impart knowledge, understanding, and skills to adolescents. Counselors, clinical psychologists, and physicians help adolescents to cope more effectively with their lives and well-being. Various professionals work with families with adolescents to improve the quality of family functioning.

Although an advanced degree is not absolutely necessary in some areas of adolescent development, you usually can expand your opportunities (and income) considerably by obtaining a graduate degree. Many careers in adolescent development pay reasonably well. For example, psychologists earn well above the median salary in the United States. Also, by working in the field of adolescent development you can guide youth in improving their lives, understand yourself and others better, possibly advance the state of knowledge in the field, and have an enjoyable time while you are doing these things.

If you are considering a career in adolescent development, as you go through this term, try to spend some time with adolescents of different ages. Observe their behavior. Talk with them about their lives. Think about whether you would like to work with youth in your life's work.

Another important aspect of exploring careers is to talk with people who work in various jobs. For example, if you have some interest in becoming a school counselor, call a school, ask to speak with a counselor, and set up an appointment to discuss the counselor's career and work.

Something else that should benefit you is to work in one or more jobs related to your career interests while you are in college. Many colleges and universities have internships or work experiences for students who major in such fields as development. In some instances, these opportunities are for course credit or pay; in others, they are strictly on a volunteer basis. Take advantage of these opportunities. They can provide you with valuable experiences to help you decide if this is the right career area for you and they can help you get into graduate school, if you decide you want to go.

In the following sections, we will profile a number of careers in three areas: education/research; clinical/counseling/medical; and families/relationships. These are not the only career options in the field of adolescent development, but they should provide you with an idea of the range of opportunities available and information about some of the main career avenues you might pursue. In profiling these careers, we will address the amount of education required, the nature of the training, and a description of the work.

EDUCATION/RESEARCH

There are numerous career opportunities in adolescent development that involve education and/or research. These range from being a college professor to being a school psychologist.

College/University Professor

Courses in adolescent development are taught in different programs and schools in college and universities, including psychology, education, child and family studies, social work, and medicine. A Ph.D. or master's degree almost always is required to teach in some area of adolescent development in a college or university. Obtaining a doctoral degree usually takes four to six years of graduate work. A master's degree requires approximately two years of graduate work. The professorial job might be at a research university with one or more master's or Ph.D. programs in development, at a four-year college with no graduate programs, or at a community college.

The training involves taking graduate courses, learning to conduct research, and attending and presenting papers at professional meetings. Many graduate students work as teaching or research assistants for professors in an apprenticeship relationship that helps them to become competent teachers and researchers. The work that college professors do includes teaching courses either at the undergraduate or graduate level (or both), conducting research in a specific area, advising students and/or directing their research, and serving on college or university committees. Some college instructors do not conduct research as part of their job but instead focus mainly on teaching. In many instances, research is most likely to be part of the job description at universities with master's and Ph.D. programs.

If you are interested in becoming a college or university professor, you might want to make an appointment with your instructor in this class on adolescent development to learn more about the profession and what his or her career/work is like.

Researcher

Some individuals in the field of adolescent development work in research positions. In most instances, they will have either a master's or Ph.D. in some area of adolescent development. The researchers might work at a university, in some cases in a university professor's research program, in government at such agencies as the National Institute of Mental Health, or in private industry. Individuals who have full-time research positions in development generate innovative research ideas, plan studies, carry out the research by collecting data, analyze the data, and then interpret it. Then, they will usually attempt to publish the research in a scientific journal. A researcher often works in a collaborative manner with other researchers on a project and may present the research at scientific meetings, where she or he also learns about other research. One researcher might spend much of his or her time in a laboratory while another researcher might work out in the field, such as in schools, hospitals, and so on.

Secondary School Teacher

Becoming a secondary school teacher requires a minimum of an undergraduate degree. The training involves taking a wide range of courses with a major or concentration in education as well as completing a supervised practice-teaching internship. The work of a secondary school teacher involves teaching in one or more subject areas, preparing the curriculum, giving tests, assigning grades, monitoring students' progress, conducting parent-teacher conferences, and attending in-service workshops.

Exceptional Children (Special Education) Teacher

Becoming a teacher of exceptional children requires a minimum of an undergraduate degree. The training consists of taking a wide range of courses in education and a concentration of courses in educating children with disabilities or children who are gifted. The work of a teacher of exceptional children involves spending concentrated time with individual children who have a disability or are gifted. Among the children a teacher of exceptional children might work with are children with learning disabilities, ADHD (attention deficit hyperactivity disorder), mental retardation, or a physical disability such as cerebral palsy. Some of this work will usually be done outside of the student's regular classroom, some of it will be carried out when the student is in the regular classroom. The exceptional children teacher works closely with the student's regular classroom teacher and parents to create the best educational program for the student. Teachers of exceptional children often continue their education after obtaining their undergraduate degree and attain a master's degree.

Family and Consumer Science Educator

Family and consumer science educators may specialize in early childhood education or instruct middle and high school students about such matters as nutrition, interpersonal relationships, human sexuality, parenting, and human development. Hundreds of colleges and universities throughout the United States offer two- and four-year degree programs in family and consumer science. These programs usually include an internship requirement. Additional education courses may be needed to obtain a teaching certificate. Some family and consumer science educators go on to graduate school for further training, which provides a background for possible jobs in college teaching or research.

Educational Psychologist

An educational psychologist most often teaches in a college or university and conducts research in such areas of educational psychology as learning, motivation, classroom management, and assessment. Most educational psychologists have a doctorate in education, which takes four to six years of graduate work. They help to train students who will take various positions in education, including educational psychology, school psychology, and teaching.

School Psychologist

School psychologists focus on improving the psychological and intellectual well-being of elementary and secondary school students. They usually have a master's or doctoral degree in school psychology. In graduate school, they take courses in counseling, assessment, learning, and other areas of education and psychology. School psychologists may work in a centralized office in a school district or in one or more schools. They give psychological tests, interview students and their parents, consult with teachers, and may provide counseling to students and their families.

CLINICAL/COUNSELING/MEDICAL

There are a wide variety of clinical, counseling, and medical careers that involve working with adolescents. These range from clinical psychologist to adolescent drug counselor to adolescent medicine specialist.

Clinical Psychologist

Clinical psychologists seek to help people with psychological problems. They work in a variety of settings, including colleges and universities, clinics, medical schools, and private practice. Clinical psychologists have either a Ph.D. (which involves clinical and research training) or a Psy.D. degree (which involves only clinical training). This graduate training usually takes five to seven years and includes courses in clinical psychology and a one-year supervised internship in an accredited setting toward the end of the training. In most cases, they must pass a test to become licensed in a state and to call themselves a clinical psychologist. Some clinical psychologists only conduct psychotherapy, others do psychological assessment and psychotherapy, and some also do research. In regard to adolescent development, clinical psychologists may specialize in a particular age group, such as children and/or adolescents (child clinical psychologist).

Psychiatrist

Psychiatrists obtain a medical degree and then do a residency in psychiatry. Medical school takes approximately four years and the psychiatry residency another three to four years. Unlike psychologists, who do not go to medical school, psychiatrists can administer drugs to clients.

Like clinical psychologists, psychiatrists might specialize in working with children and/or adolescents (child psychiatry). Psychiatrists might work in medical schools in teaching and research roles, in a medical clinic, or in private practice. In addition to administering drugs to help improve the lives of people with psychological problems, psychiatrists also may conduct psychotherapy.

Psychiatric Nurse

Two to five years of education in a certified nursing program are required to work as a psychiatric nurse. Psychiatric nursing students take courses in the biological sciences, nursing care, psychology, and go through supervised clinical training in psychiatric settings. Psychiatric nurses specialize in helping adolescents with mental health problems and work closely with psychiatrists to improve adolescents' adjustment. A clinical specialist in adolescent nursing designation requires a master's degree or higher in nursing.

Counseling Psychologist

Counseling psychologists go through much of the same training as clinical psychologists, although in a graduate program in counseling rather than clinical psychology. Counseling psychologists have either a master's degree or a doctoral degree. They also must go through a licensing procedure. One type of master's degree in counseling leads to the designation of licensed professional counselor. They work in the same settings as clinical psychologists, and may do psychotherapy, teach, or conduct research. In many instances, counseling psychologists do not do therapy with individuals who have more severe mental disorders, such as schizophrenia.

School Counselor

School counselors help to identify students' abilities and interests, guide students in developing academic plans, and explore career options with students. They may help students cope with adjustment problems. They may work with students individually, in small groups, or even in a classroom. They often consult with parents, teachers, and school administrators when trying to help students with their problems. School counselors usually have a master's degree in counseling.

High school counselors advise students on choosing a major, admissions requirements for college, taking entrance exams, applying for financial aid, and on appropriate vocational and technical training.

Career Counselor

Career counselors help individuals to identify what the best career options are for them and guide them in applying for jobs. They may work in private industry or at a college/university. They usually interview individuals and give them vocational and/or psychological tests to help them provide students with information about appropriate careers that fit their interests and abilities. Sometimes they help individuals to create professional resumes or conduct mock interviews to help them feel comfortable in a job interview. They may create and promote job fairs or other recruiting events to help individuals obtain jobs.

Social Worker

Social workers often are involved in helping people with social or economic problems. They may investigate, evaluate, and attempt to rectify reported cases of abuse, neglect, endangerment, or domestic disputes. They can intervene in families if necessary and provide counseling and referral services to individuals and families. They have a minimum of an undergraduate degree from a school of social work that includes course work in various areas of sociology and psychology. Some social workers also have a master's or doctoral degree. They often work for publicly funded agencies at the city, state, or national level, although increasingly they work in the private sector in areas such as drug rehabilitation and family counseling.

In some cases, social workers specialize in a certain area. For example, family-care social workers often work with families with children or an older adult who needs support services.

Drug Counselor

Drug counselors provide counseling to individuals with drug-abuse problems. They may work on an individual basis with a substance abuser or conduct group therapy sessions. At a minimum, drug counselors go through an associate or certificate program. Many have an undergraduate degree in substance-abuse counseling, and some have master's and doctoral degrees. They may work in private practice, with a state or federal government agency, with a company, or in a hospital setting. Some drug counselors specialize in working with adolescents. Most states provide a certification procedure for obtaining a license to practice drug counseling.

Health Psychologist

Health psychologists might work with many different health-care professionals, including physicians, nurses, clinical psychologists, psychiatrists, and social workers, in an effort to improve the health of adolescents. Health psychologists may conduct research, provide clinical assessment, or give treatment.

Many health psychologists focus on prevention through research and clinical interventions that are designed to foster health and reduce the risk of disease. More than half of health psychologists include clinical services as part of their duties. Among the settings in which health psychologists work are primary care programs, inpatient medical units, and specialized care programs, such as women's health, drug treatment, smoking cessation, and others.

Health psychologists typically have a doctoral degree (Ph.D. or Psy.D.) in psychology. Some health psychologists receive training in clinical psychology as part of their graduate work and some have obtained a doctoral degree in some area other than health psychology, then pursued a postdoctoral degree in health psychology. A postdoctoral degree usually takes about two years beyond a Ph.D. Many doctoral programs in clinical, counseling, social, and experimental psychology have specialized tracks in health psychology.

Adolescent Medicine Specialist

To become an adolescent medicine specialist it is necessary to complete medical school and then further specialization, which usually involves at least three years beyond medical school. Adolescent medicine specialists must become board certified in either pediatrics or internal medicine.

Adolescent medicine specialists evaluate medical and behavioral problems of youth. Among the problems they examine and seek to treat are growth disorders (such as delayed puberty), acne, eating disorders, substance abuse, depression, anxiety, sexually transmitted diseases, contraception and pregnancy, and sexual identity concerns.

Adolescent medicine specialists may work in private practice, in a medical clinic, in a hospital, or in a medical school. As a medical doctor, they can administer drugs and may counsel parents and adolescents on ways to improve the adolescent's health. Many adolescent medicine specialists on the faculty of medical schools also teach and conduct research on adolescents' health and diseases.

FAMILIES/RELATIONSHIPS

One career that involves working with adolescents and their families focuses on marriage and family therapy.

Marriage and Family Therapist

Marriage and family therapists work on the principle that many individuals who have psychological problems benefit when psychotherapy is provided in the context of a marital or family relationship. Marriage and family therapists may provide marital therapy, couple therapy to individuals in a relationship who are not married, and family therapy to two or more members of a family.

Marriage and family therapists have a master's and/or doctoral degree. They go through a training program in graduate school similar to a clinical psychologist but with the focus on marital and family relationships. To practice marital and family therapy in most states it is necessary to go through a licensing procedure.

WEBSITE CONNECTIONS FOR CAREERS IN ADOLESCENT DEVELOPMENT

By going to the website for this book, you can obtain more detailed career information about the various careers in adolescent development described in this appendix. Go to the Web connections in the Career Appendix section, where you will read about a description of the websites. Then click on the title and you will be able to go directly to the website described. Following are the website connections.

Education/Research

Careers in Psychology
Elementary and Secondary School Teaching
Exceptional Children Teachers
Education Psychology
School Psychology

Clinical/Counseling/Medical

Clinical Psychology
Psychiatry
Counseling Psychology
School Counseling
Drug Counseling
Social Work
Health Psychology
Pediatrics
Adolescent Medicine

Families/Relationships

Marriage and Family Therapist

CHAPTER MAP

THEORIES OF ADOLESCENT
DEVELOPMENT

Psychoanalytic
Theories

Cognitive
Theories

Behavioral and
Social Cognitive
Theories

An Eclectic
Theoretical
Orientation

Ecological,
Contextual
Theory

EXPLORING RESEARCH

Why Research
on Adolescent
Development
Is Important

The Field of Adolescent
Development Research

The Scientific
Research Approach

RESEARCH METHODS

Participants

Measures

Correlational
and Experimental
Strategies

Time Span
of Research

Multiple Measures,
Sources, and Contexts

RESEARCH
CHALLENGES

Ethics

Gender

Ethnicity
and Culture

Being a Wise
Consumer of
Information
About
Adolescent
Development

■ THE YOUTHS OF ERIKSON AND PIAGET

Two important developmental theorists, whose views are described later in this chapter, are Erik Erikson and Jean Piaget. Let's examine a portion of their lives as they were growing up, to discover how their experiences might have contributed to the theories they developed.

Erik Homberger Erikson (1902–1994) was born near Frankfurt, Germany, to Danish parents. Before Erik was born, his parents separated, and his mother left Denmark to live in Germany. At age 3, Erik became ill, and his mother took him to see a pediatrician named Homberger. Young Erik's mother fell in love with the pediatrician, married him, and named Erik after his new stepfather.

Erik attended primary school from age 6 to 10 and then the *gymnasium* (high school) from ages 11 to 18. He studied art and a number of languages rather than science courses such as biology and chemistry. Erik did not like formal schooling, and this was reflected in his grades. Rather than go to college, at age 18 the adolescent Erikson wandered around Europe, keeping a diary of his experiences. After a year of travel through Europe, he returned to Germany and enrolled in an art school, became dissatisfied, and enrolled in another.

Jean Piaget (1896–1980) was born in Neuchâtel, Switzerland. Jean's father was an intellectual who taught young Jean to think systematically. Jean's mother was also very bright. His father had an air of detachment from his mother, whom Piaget described as prone to frequent neurotic outbursts.

At the age of 22, Piaget went to work in the psychology laboratory at the University of Zurich. There he was exposed to the insights of Alfred Binet, who developed the first intelligence test. By the time Piaget was 25, his experience in varied disciplines had helped him to see important links between philosophy, psychology, and biology.

These excerpts from Erikson's and Piaget's lives illustrate how personal experiences might influence a theorist's direction. Erikson's wanderings and search for self contributed to his theory of identity development, and Piaget's intellectual experiences with his parents and schooling contributed to his emphasis on cognitive development.

Truth is arrived at by the painstaking process of eliminating the untrue.

—Arthur Conan Doyle
British Physician and Detective-Story Writer, 20th Century

CHAPTER LEARNING GOALS

SOME INDIVIDUALS HAVE DIFFICULTY THINKING OF adolescent development as being a science in the same way that physics, chemistry, and biology are sciences. Can a discipline that studies pubertal change, parent-adolescent relationships, and adolescent thinking be equated with disciplines that investigate how gravity works and the molecular structure of compounds? Science is not defined by *what* it investigates but by *how* it investigates. Whether you are studying photosynthesis, butterflies, Saturn's moons, or adolescent development, it is the way you study that makes the approach scientific or not. By the time you have completed this chapter you should be able to reach these learning goals:

1 Discuss psychoanalytic theories

2 Know about cognitive theories

3 Explain behavioral and social cognitive theories

4 Understand ecological, contextual theory and an eclectic theoretical orientation

5 Explore research

6 Describe how participants are selected and measures

7 Understand the distinction between correlational and experimental strategies and know about the time span of research

8 Elaborate on research challenges

THEORIES OF ADOLESCENT DEVELOPMENT

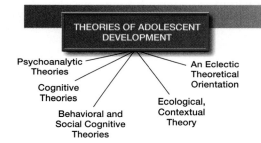

THEORIES OF ADOLESCENT DEVELOPMENT

Psychoanalytic Theories

Cognitive Theories

Behavioral and Social Cognitive Theories

Ecological, Contextual Theory

An Eclectic Theoretical Orientation

theory
An interrelated, coherent set of ideas that helps to explain and make predictions.

As researchers formulate a problem to study, they often draw on *theories*. A **theory** *is an interrelated, coherent set of ideas that helps to explain and make predictions.* We will briefly explore four major kinds of theories of adolescent development: psychoanalytic, cognitive, behavioral and social learning, and ecological. The diversity of theories makes understanding adolescent development a challenging undertaking. Just when one theory appears to correctly explain adolescent development, another theory crops up and makes you rethink your earlier conclusion. Remember that adolescent development is complex and multifaceted. Although no single theory has been able to account for all aspects of adolescent development, each theory has contributed an important piece to the puzzle. Although the theories sometimes disagree about certain aspects of adolescent development, much of their information is *complementary* rather than contradictory. Together, the various theories let us see the total landscape of adolescent development in all its richness.

Psychoanalytic Theories

psychoanalytic theory
Describes development as primarily unconscious and heavily colored by emotion. Behavior is merely a surface characteristic. It is important to analyze the symbolic meanings of behavior. Early experiences are important in development.

Psychoanalytic theory *describes development as primarily unconscious—that is, beyond awareness—and is heavily colored by emotion. Psychoanalytic theorists believe that behavior is merely a surface characteristic and that, to truly understand development, we have to analyze the symbolic meanings of behavior and the deep inner workings of the mind. Psychoanalytic theorists also stress that early experiences with parents extensively shape our development.* These characteristics are highlighted in the main psychoanalytic theory, that of Sigmund Freud.

Freud's Theory   Freud (1856–1939) developed his ideas about psychoanalytic theory from work with mental patients. A medical doctor who specialized in neurology, he spent most of his years in Vienna, though he moved to London near the end of his career because of the Nazis' anti-Semitism.

Personality Structure   Freud (1917) believed that personality has three structures: the id, the ego, and the superego. The *id* is the Freudian structure of personality that consists of instincts, which are an individual's reservoir of psychic energy. In Freud's view, the id is totally unconscious; it has no contact with reality. As children experience the demands and constraints of reality, a new structure of personality emerges—the *ego*, the Freudian structure of personality that deals with the demands of reality. The ego is called the "executive branch" of personality because it makes rational decisions. The id and the ego have no morality—they do not take into account whether something is right or wrong. The *superego* is the Freudian structure of personality that is the moral branch of personality. The superego takes into account whether something is right or wrong. Think of the superego as what we often refer to as our "conscience." You probably are beginning to sense that both the id and the superego make life rough for the ego. Your ego might say, "I will have sex only occasionally and be sure to take the proper precautions because I don't want a child to interfere with the development of my career." However, your id is saying, "I want to be satisfied; sex is pleasurable." Your super-ego is at work too: "I feel guilty about having sex."

Remember that Freud considered personality to be like an iceberg. Most of personality exists below our level of awareness, just as the massive part of an iceberg is beneath the surface of the water. Figure 2.1 illustrates this analogy.

Freud believed that adolescents' lives are filled with tension and conflict. To reduce this tension, adolescents keep information locked in their unconscious mind, said Freud. He believed that even trivial behaviors have special significance when the unconscious forces behind them are revealed. A twitch, a doodle, a joke, a smile—each might have an unconscious reason for appearing, according to Freud. For example, 17-year-old Barbara is kissing and hugging Tom. She says, "Oh, *Jeff*, I love you so much." Tom pushes her away and says, "Why did you call me Jeff? I thought you didn't think about him anymore. We need to have a talk!" You probably can remember times when these *Freudian slips* came out in your own behavior.

Defense Mechanisms   The ego resolves conflict between its demands for reality, the wishes of the id, and the constraints of the superego by using *defense mechanisms*. They are unconscious methods the ego uses to distort reality and protect itself from anxiety. In Freud's view, the conflicting demands of the personality structures produce anxiety. For example, when the ego blocks the id's pleasurable pursuits, we feel anxiety. This diffuse, distressed state develops when the ego senses that the id is going to cause harm to the individual. The anxiety alerts the ego to resolve the conflict by means of defense mechanisms.

Repression is the most powerful and pervasive defense mechanism, according to Freud. It pushes unacceptable id impulses out of awareness and back into the unconscious mind. Repression is the foundation from which all other defense mechanisms work; the goal of every defense mechanism is to repress, or push, threatening impulses out of awareness. Freud said that our early childhood experiences, many of which he believed are sexually laden, are too threatening and stressful for us to deal with consciously, and that we reduce the anxiety of this conflict through repression.

Both Peter Blos (1989), a British psychoanalyst, and Anna Freud (1966), Sigmund Freud's daughter, believe that defense mechanisms provide considerable insight into adolescent development. Blos states that regression during adolescence is actually not defensive at all, but rather an integral, normal, inevitable, and universal aspect of puberty. The nature of regression may vary from one adolescent to the next. It may involve childhood autonomy,

Sigmund Freud, the pioneering architect of psychoanalytic theory. *How did Freud believe each individual's personality is organized?*

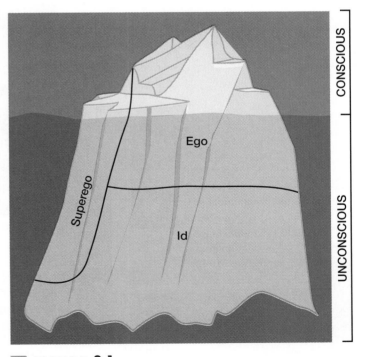

■ FIGURE 2.1

The Conscious and Unconscious Mind: The Iceberg Analogy

The analogy of the conscious and unconscious mind to an iceberg is often used to illustrate how much of the mind is unconscious in Freud's theory. The conscious mind is the part of the iceberg above water, the unconscious mind the part below water. Notice that the id is totally unconscious, while the ego and superego can operate at either the conscious or unconscious level.

Anna Freud, Sigmund Freud's daughter. *How did her view differ from her father's?*

compliance, and cleanliness, or it may involve a sudden return to the passiveness that characterized the adolescent's behavior during childhood.

Anna Freud (1966) developed the idea that defense mechanisms are the key to understanding adolescent adjustment. She believes that the problems of adolescence are not to be unlocked by understanding the id, or instinctual forces, but instead are to be discovered in the existence of "love objects" in the adolescent's past. She argues that the attachment to these love objects, usually parents, is carried forward from the infant years and merely toned down or inhibited during the latency years. During adolescence, these pregenital urges might be reawakened, or, worse, newly acquired genital (adolescent) urges might combine with the urges that developed in early childhood.

Two final points about defense mechanisms are important. First, they are unconscious; adolescents are not aware that they are calling on defense mechanisms to protect their ego and reduce anxiety. Second, when used in moderation or on a temporary basis, defense mechanisms are not necessarily unhealthy. For the most part, though, individuals should not let defense mechanisms dominate their behavior and prevent them from facing the demands of reality.

Psychosexual Stages As Freud listened to, probed, and analyzed his patients, he became convinced that their problems were the result of experiences early in life. Freud believed that we go through five stages of psychosexual development, and that at each stage of development we experience pleasure in one part of the body more than in others (see figure 2.2).

The *oral stage* is the first Freudian stage of development, occurring during the first 18 months of life, in which the infant's pleasure centers around the mouth. Chewing, sucking, and biting are the chief sources of pleasure. These actions reduce tension in the infant.

The *anal stage* is the second Freudian stage of development, occurring between 1½ and 3 years of age, in which the child's greatest pleasure involves the anus or the eliminative functions associated with it. In Freud's view, the exercise of anal muscles reduces tension.

The *phallic stage* is the third Freudian stage of development, which occurs between the ages of 3 and 6; its name comes from the Latin word, *phallus,* which means "penis." During the phallic stage, pleasure focuses on the genitals as the child discovers that self-manipulation is enjoyable.

In Freud's view, the phallic stage has a special importance in personality development because it is during this period that the Oedipus complex appears.

GENITAL STAGE

Adolescence and Adulthood

LATENCY STAGE

6 Years to Puberty

PHALLIC STAGE

3 to 6 Years

ANAL STAGE

$1\frac{1}{2}$ to 3 Years

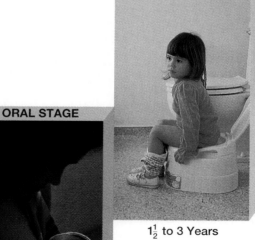

ORAL STAGE

0 to $1\frac{1}{2}$ Years

■ FIGURE 2.2
Freudian Stages

This name comes from Greek mythology, in which Oedipus, the son of the King of Thebes, unwittingly kills his father and marries his mother. The *Oedipus complex,* in Freudian theory, is the young child's intense desire to replace the parent of the same sex and enjoy the affections of the opposite-sex parent. Freud's concept of the Oedipus complex has been criticized by some psychoanalysts and writers.

How is the Oedipus complex resolved? At about 5 to 6 years of age, children recognize that their same-sex parent might punish them for their incestuous wishes. To reduce this conflict, the child identifies with the same-sex parent, striving to be like him or her. If the conflict is not resolved, though, the individual can become fixated at the phallic stage.

The *latency stage* is the fourth Freudian stage of development, which occurs between approximately 6 years of age and puberty; the child represses all interest in sexuality and develops social and intellectual skills. This activity channels much of the child's energy into emotionally safe areas and helps the child forget the highly stressful conflicts of the phallic stage.

The *genital stage* is the fifth and final Freudian stage of development, occurring from puberty on. The genital stage is a time of sexual reawakening; the source of sexual pleasure now becomes someone outside of the family. Freud believed that unresolved conflicts with parents reemerge during adolescence. When these are resolved, the individual is capable of developing a mature love relationship and functioning independently as an adult.

Revisions of Freud's Theory   Freud's theory has undergone significant revisions by a number of psychoanalytic theorists (Luborsky, 2000; Westen, 2000). Many contemporary psychoanalytic theorists place less emphasis on sexual instincts and more emphasis on

Freud's Theory
Horney's Theory
Erikson's Theory
http://www.mhhe.com/santrocka9

Karen Horney

Nancy Chodorow

 FIGURE 2.3
Feminist-Based Criticisms of Freud's Theory

The first feminist-based criticism of Freud's theory was proposed by psychoanalytic theorist Karen Horney (1967). She developed a model of women with positive feminine qualities and self-evaluation. Her critique of Freud's theory included reference to a male-dominant society and culture. Rectification of the male bias in psychoanalytic theory continues today. For example, Nancy Chodorow (1978, 1989) emphasizes that many more women than men define themselves in terms of their relationships and connections to others. Her feminist revision of psychoanalytic theory also stresses the meaningfulness of emotions for women, as well as the belief that many men use the defense mechanism of denial in self-other connections.

cultural experiences as determinants of an individual's development. Unconscious thought remains a central theme, but most contemporary psychoanalysts believe that conscious thought makes up more of the iceberg than Freud envisioned. Feminist criticisms of Freud's theory have also been made (see figure 2.3 on p. 43). Next, we explore the ideas of an important revisionist of Freud's ideas—Erik Erikson.

Erikson's Theory Erik Erikson (1902–1994) recognized Freud's contributions but believed that Freud misjudged some important dimensions of human development. For one, Erikson (1950, 1968) said we develop in *psychosocial stages,* in contrast to Freud's *psychosexual stages.* For Freud, the primary motivation for human behavior was sexual in nature, for Erickson it was social and reflected a desire to affiliate with other people. Erickson emphasized developmental change throughout the human life span, whereas Freud argued that our basic personality is shaped in the first five years of life. In **Erikson's theory** *eight stages of development unfold as we go through the life span* (see figure 2.4). *Each stage consists of a unique developmental task that confronts individuals with a crisis that must be faced.* According to Erikson, this crisis is not a catastrophe but a turning point of increased vulnerability and enhanced potential. The more an individual resolves the crises successfully, the healthier that individual's development will be (Hopkins, 2000).

Trust versus mistrust is Erikson's first psychosocial stage, which is experienced in the first year of life. A sense of trust requires a feeling of physical comfort and a minimal amount of fear and apprehension about the future. Trust in infancy sets the stage for a lifelong expectation that the world will be a good and pleasant place to live.

Autonomy versus shame and doubt is Erikson's second stage of development, occurring in late infancy and toddlerhood (ages 1 to 3). After gaining trust in their caregivers, infants begin to discover that their behavior is their own. They start to assert their sense of independence or autonomy. They realize their will. If infants are restrained too much or punished too harshly, they are likely to develop a sense of shame and doubt.

Initiative versus guilt is Erikson's third stage of development, occurring during the preschool years. As preschool children encounter a widening social world, they are challenged more than when they were infants. Active, purposeful behavior is needed to cope with these challenges. Children are asked to assume responsibility for their

Erikson's Stages	Developmental Period
Integrity versus despair	Late adulthood (60s–)
Generativity versus stagnation	Middle adulthood (40s, 50s)
Intimacy versus isolation	Early adulthood (20s, 30s)
Identity versus identity confusion	Adolescence (10 to 20 years)
Industry versus inferiority	Middle and late childhood (elementary school years, 6 years to puberty)
Initiative versus guilt	Early childhood (preschool years, ages 3 to 5)
Autonomy versus shame and doubt	Infancy (1 to 3 years)
Trust versus mistrust	Infancy (first year)

FIGURE 2.4
Erikson's Eight Life-Span Stages

Erikson's theory
He proposed that people go through eight stages of development with each stage consisting of a unique developmental task that confronts individuals with a crisis that must be faced.

bodies, their behavior, their toys, and their pets. Developing a sense of responsibility increases initiative. Uncomfortable guilt feelings may arise, though, in children who are irresponsible and are made to feel too anxious. Erikson has a positive outlook on this stage. He believes that most guilt is quickly compensated for by a sense of accomplishment.

Industry versus inferiority is Erikson's fourth developmental stage, occurring approximately in the elementary school years. Children's initiative brings them in contact with a wealth of new experiences. As they move into middle and late childhood, they direct their energy toward mastering knowledge and intellectual skills. At no other time is the child more enthusiastic about learning than at the end of early childhood's period of expansive imagination. The danger in the elementary school years is the development of a sense of inferiority—of feeling incompetent and unproductive. Erikson believes that teachers have a special responsibility for children's development of industry. Teachers should "mildly but firmly coerce children into the adventure of finding out that one can learn to accomplish things which one would never have thought of by oneself" (Erikson, 1968, p. 127).

Erik Erikson with his wife, Joan, who is an artist. Erikson generated one of the most important developmental theories of the twentieth century. *What is the nature of his theory?*

Identity versus identity confusion is Erikson's fifth developmental stage, which individuals experience during the adolescent years. At this time individuals are faced with finding out who they are, what they are all about, and where they are going in life. Adolescents are confronted with many new roles and adult statuses—vocational and romantic, for example. Parents need to allow adolescents to explore many different roles and different paths within a particular role. If the adolescent explores such roles in a healthy manner and arrives at a positive path to follow in life, then a positive identity will be achieved. If an identity is pushed on the adolescent by parents, if the adolescent does not adequately explore many roles, and if a positive future path is not defined, then identity confusion reigns.

Intimacy versus isolation is Erikson's sixth developmental stage, which individuals experience during the early adulthood years. At this time, individuals face the developmental task of forming intimate relationships with others. Erikson describes intimacy as finding oneself yet losing oneself in another. If the young adult forms healthy friendships and an intimate close relationship with another individual, intimacy will be achieved; if not, isolation will result.

Generativity versus stagnation is Erikson's seventh developmental stage, which individuals experience during middle adulthood. A chief concern is to assist the younger generation in developing and leading useful lives—this is what Erikson meant by generativity. The feeling of having done nothing to help the next generation is *stagnation.*

Integrity versus despair is Erikson's eighth and final developmental stage, which individuals experience during late adulthood. In our later years, we look back and evaluate what we have done with our lives. Through many different routes, the older person may have developed a positive outlook in most or all of the previous developmental stages. If so, the retrospective glances reveal a life well spent, and the person feels a sense of satisfaction—integrity is achieved. If the older adult resolved many of the earlier developmental stages negatively, the retrospective glances likely will yield doubt or gloom—the despair Erikson talks about.

Erikson does not believe that the proper solution to a stage crisis is always completely positive in nature. Some exposure or commitment to the negative end of a person's bipolar conflict is sometimes inevitable—you cannot trust all people under all circumstances and survive, for example. Nonetheless, positive resolutions to stage crises should dominate for optimal development (Hopkins, 2000).

Evaluating the Psychoanalytic Theories
The contributions of psychoanalytic theories include their emphases on these factors:

- Early experiences play an important part in development.
- Family relationships are a central aspect of development.
- Personality can be better understood if it is examined developmentally.

Jean Piaget, the famous Swiss developmental psychologist, changed the way we think about the development of children's minds. *What are some key ideas in Piaget's theory?*

Piaget's theory

He proposed that individuals actively construct their understanding of the world and go through four stages of cognitive development.

- The mind is not all conscious; unconscious aspects of the mind need to be considered.
- Changes take place in the adulthood as well as the childhood years (Erikson).

These are some of the criticisms of psychoanalytic theories:

- The main concepts of psychoanalytic theories have been difficult to test scientifically.
- Much of the data used to support psychoanalytic theories come from individuals' reconstruction of the past, often the distant past, and are of unknown accuracy.
- The sexual underpinnings of development are given too much importance (especially in Freud's theory).
- The unconscious mind is given too much credit for influencing development.
- Psychoanalytic theories present an image of humans that is too negative (especially Freud).

Cognitive Theories

Whereas psychoanalytic theories stress the importance of adolescents' unconscious thoughts, cognitive theories emphasize their conscious thoughts. Three important cognitive theories are Piaget's theory, Vygotsky's theory, and information-processing theory.

Piaget's Theory

The famous Swiss psychologist Jean Piaget (1896–1980) proposed an important theory of cognitive development. **Piaget's theory** *states that individuals actively construct their understanding of the world and go through four stages of cognitive development.* Two processes underlie this cognitive construction of the world: organization and adaptation. To make sense of our world, we organize our experiences. For example, we separate important ideas from less important ideas. We connect one idea to another. But not only do we organize our observations and experiences, we also *adapt* our thinking to include new ideas because additional information furthers understanding.

Piaget (1954) also believed that we go through four stages in understanding the world (see figure 2.5). Each of the stages is age-related and consists of distinct ways of thinking. Remember, it is the *different* way of understanding the world that makes one stage more advanced than another; knowing *more* information does not make the child's thinking more advanced in the Piagetian view. This is what Piaget meant when he said the child's cognition is *qualitatively* different in one stage compared to another. What are Piaget's four stages of cognitive development like?

The *sensorimotor stage,* which lasts from birth to about 2 years of age, is the first Piagetian stage. In this stage, infants construct an

FORMAL OPERATIONAL STAGE

The adolescent reasons in more abstract, idealistic, and logical ways.

11 Years of Age Through Adulthood

CONCRETE OPERATIONAL STAGE

The child can now reason logically about concrete events and classify objects into different sets.

7 to 11 Years of Age

PREOPERATIONAL STAGE

The child begins to represent the world with words and images. These words and images reflect increased symbolic thinking and go beyond the connection of sensory information and physical action.

2 to 7 Years of Age

SENSORIMOTOR STAGE

The infant constructs an understanding of the world by coordinating sensory experiences with physical actions. An infant progresses from reflexive, instinctual action at birth to the beginning of symbolic thought toward the end of the stage.

Birth to 2 Years of Age

■ FIGURE 2.5 Piaget's Four Stages of Cognitive Development

understanding of the world by coordinating sensory experiences (such as seeing and hearing) with physical, motoric actions—hence the term sensorimotor. At the beginning of this stage, newborns have little more than reflexive patterns with which to work. At the end of the stage, 2-year-olds have complex sensorimotor patterns and are beginning to operate with primitive symbols.

The *preoperational stage,* which lasts approximately from 2 to 7 years of age, is the second Piagetian stage. In this stage, children begin to represent the world with words, images, and drawings. Symbolic thought goes beyond simple connections of sensory information and physical action. However, although preschool children can symbolically represent the world, according to Piaget, they still lack the ability to perform *operations,* the Piagetian terms for internalized mental actions that allow children to do mentally what they previously did physically.

The *concrete operational stage,* which lasts from approximately 7 to 11 years of age, is the third Piagetian stage. In this stage, children can perform operations, and logical reasoning replaces intuitive thought as long as reasoning can be applied to specific or concrete examples. For instance, concrete operational thinkers cannot imagine the steps necessary to complete an algebraic equation, which is too abstract for thinking at this stage of development.

The *formal operational stage,* which appears between the ages of 11 and 15, is the fourth and final Piagetian stage. In this stage, individuals move beyond concrete experiences and think in abstract and more logical terms. As part of thinking more abstractly, adolescents develop images of ideal circumstances. They might think about what an ideal parent is like and compare their parents with this ideal standard. They begin to entertain possibilities for the future and are fascinated with what they can be. In solving problems, formal operational thinkers are more systematic, developing hypotheses about why something is happening the way it is, then testing these hypotheses in a deductive fashion. We will have much more to say about Piaget's theory in chapter 4, "Cognitive Development."

Vygotsky's Theory

Like Piaget, Russian Lev Vygotsky (1896–1934) also believed that children actively construct their knowledge. **Vygotsky's theory** *is a sociocultural cognitive theory that emphasizes developmental analysis, the role of language, and social relations.* Vygotsky was born in Russia in the same year as Piaget, but he died much earlier, at the age of 37. Both Piaget's and Vygotsky's ideas remained virtually unknown to American scholars for many years, not being introduced to American audiences through English translations until the 1960s. In the last several decades, American psychologists and educators have shown increased interest in Vygotsky's (1962) views.

Three claims capture the heart of Vygotsky's view (Tappan, 1998): (1) children's and adolescents' cognitive skills can be understood only when they are developmentally analyzed and interpreted; (2) cognitive skills are mediated by words, language, and forms of discourse, which serve as psychological tools for facilitating and transforming mental activity; and (3) cognitive skills have their origins in social relations and are embedded in a sociocultural backdrop.

For Vygotsky, taking a developmental approach means that in order to understand any aspect of the child's and adolescent's cognitive functioning, one must examine its origins and transformations from earlier to later forms. Thus, a particular mental act cannot be viewed accurately in isolation but should be evaluated as a step in a gradual developmental process.

Vygotsky's second claim, that to understand cognitive functioning it is necessary to examine the tools that mediate and shape it, led him to believe that language is the most important of these tools. Vygotsky argued that language is a tool that helps the child and adolescent plan activities and solve problems.

Vygotsky's third claim was that cognitive skills originate in social relations and culture. Vygotsky portrayed the child's and adolescent's development as inseparable from social and cultural activities. He believed that the development of memory, attention, and reasoning involves learning to use the inventions of society, such as language, mathematical systems, and memory strategies. In one culture, this might consist of

There is considerable interest today in Lev Vygotsky's sociocultural cognitive theory of child development. *What were Vygotsky's three basic claims about children's development?*

Vygotsky's theory
He proposed a sociocultural cognitive theory that emphasizes developmental analysis, the role of language, and social relations.

learning to count with the help of a computer. In another, it might consist of counting on one's fingers or using beads.

Vygotsky's theory has stimulated considerable interest in the view that knowledge is *situated* and *collaborative* (Greeno, Collins, & Resnick, 1996; Kozulin, 2000; Rogoff, 1998). That is, knowledge is distributed among people and environments, which include objects, artifacts, tools, books, and the communities in which people live. This suggests that knowing can best be advanced through interaction with others in cooperative activities.

Within these basic claims, Vygotsky articulated unique and influential ideas about the relation between learning and development. These ideas especially reflect his view that cognitive functioning has social origins. We will have much more to say about Vygotsky's theory in chapter 4, "Cognitive Development." Now that we have learned some basic ideas about Piaget's theory and Vygotsky's theory, we will examine a third cognitive theory—information processing.

Piaget's Theory
Vygotsky's Theory
http://www.mhhe.com/santrocka9

information-processing approach
Emphasizes that individuals manipulate information, monitor it, and strategize about it. Central to information process are the processes of memory and thinking.

The Information-Processing Approach

The **information-processing approach** *emphasizes that individuals manipulate information, monitor it, and strategize about it. Central to this approach are the processes of memory and thinking.* According to the information-processing approach, individuals develop a gradually increasing capacity for processing information, which allows them to acquire increasingly complex knowledge and skills (Bjorklund & Rosenbaum, 2000; Chen & Siegler, 2000). Unlike Piaget's cognitive developmental theory, the information-processing approach does not describe development as stagelike.

Although a number of factors stimulated the growth of the information-processing approach, none was more important than the computer, which demonstrated that a machine could perform logical operations. Psychologists began to wonder if the logical operations carried out by computers might tell us something about how the human mind works. They drew analogies to computers to explain the relation between cognition or thinking and the brain. The physical brain is described as the computer's hardware, cognition as its software. Although computers and software are not perfect analogies for brains and cognitive activities, the comparison contributed to our thinking about the mind as an active information-processing system.

Robert Siegler (1998), a leading expert on children's information processing, believes that thinking is information processing. He says that when individuals perceive, encode, represent, store, and retrieve information, they are thinking. Siegler especially thinks that an important aspect of development is to learn good strategies for processing information. For example, in becoming a better reader this might involve learning to monitor the key themes of the material being read.

Evaluating the Cognitive Theories

Among the contributions of the cognitive theories are these:

- The cognitive theories present a positive view of development, emphasizing individuals' conscious thinking.
- The cognitive theories (especially Piaget's and Vygotsky's) emphasize the individual's active construction of understanding.
- Piaget's and Vygotsky's theories underscore the importance of examining developmental changes in children's thinking.
- The information-processing approach offers detailed descriptions of cognitive processes.

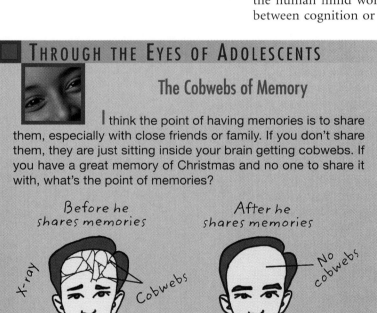

THROUGH THE EYES OF ADOLESCENTS

The Cobwebs of Memory

I think the point of having memories is to share them, especially with close friends or family. If you don't share them, they are just sitting inside your brain getting cobwebs. If you have a great memory of Christmas and no one to share it with, what's the point of memories?

Before he shares memories

After he shares memories

X-ray   Cobwebs   No cobwebs

Seventh-Grade Student
West Middle School
Ypsilanti, Michigan

Among the criticisms of the cognitive theories are these:

• There is skepticism about the pureness of Piaget's stages.
• The cognitive theories do not give adequate attention to individual variations in cognitive development.
• The information processing approach does not provide an adequate description of developmental changes in cognition.
• Psychoanalytic theorists argue that the cognitive theories do not give enough credit to unconscious thought.

At this point we have examined psychoanalytic and cognitive theories. The following review should help you to reach your learning goals related to these topics.

Learning Goal 1 **Discuss psychoanalytic theories**	• In Freud's theory, personality is made up of three structures: id, ego, and superego. The conflicting demands of these structures produce anxiety. Most of children's thoughts are unconscious, according to Freud. Freud was convinced that problems develop because of early experiences. Individuals go through five psychosexual stages: oral, anal, phallic, latency, and genital. • In Erikson's theory, eight psychosocial stages are emphasized: trust versus mistrust, autonomy versus shame and doubt, initiative versus guilt, industry versus inferiority, identity versus identity confusion, intimacy versus isolation, generativity versus stagnation, and integrity versus despair. • Among the contributions of psychoanalytic theory is an emphasis on a developmental framework; among the criticisms is a lack of scientific support.
Learning Goal 2 **Know about cognitive theories**	• Piaget proposed a cognitive developmental theory. Children go through four stages: sensorimotor, preoperational, concrete operational, and formal operational. • Vygotsky's theory consists of three basic claims about development: (1) cognitive skills need to be interpreted developmentally, (2) cognitive skills are mediated by language, and (3) cognitive skills have their origin in social relations and culture. • The information-processing approach emphasizes that individuals manipulate information, monitor it, and strategize about it. The development of computers stimulated interest in this approach. • Among the contributions of the cognitive approach is the active construction of understanding; among the criticisms is that too little attention is given to individual variations.

Now that we have discussed psychoanalytic and cognitive theories, we will turn our attention to another set of important theories about adolescent development: behavioral and social cognitive.

Behavioral and Social Cognitive Theories

Seventeen-year-old Tom is going steady with 16-year-old Ann. Both have warm, friendly personalities, and they enjoy being together. Psychoanalytic theorists would say that their warm, friendly personalities are derived from long-standing relationships with their parents, especially their early childhood experiences. They also would argue that the reason for their attraction to each other is unconscious; they are unaware of how their biological heritage and early life experiences have been carried forward to influence their personalities in adolescence.

Behaviorists and social learning theorists would observe Tom and Ann and see something quite different. They would examine their experiences, especially their most recent ones, to understand the reason for Tom and Ann's attraction to each other. Tom would be described as rewarding Ann's behavior, and vice versa, for example. No reference would be made to unconscious thoughts, the Oedipus complex, stages of development, and defense mechanisms. The **behavioral and social cognitive theories**

Skinner's View
Albert Bandura
http://www.mhhe.com/santrocka9

behavioral and social cognitive theories
Theories that emphasize the importance of studying environmental experiences and observable behavior. Social cognitive theorists emphasize person/cognitive factors in development.

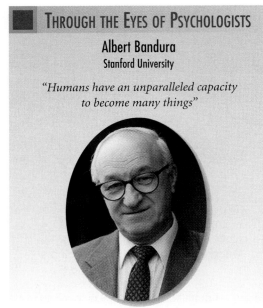

emphasize the importance of studying environmental experiences and observable behavior to understand adolescent development. Social cognitive theorists emphasize person/cognitive factors in development.

Skinner's Behaviorism

Behaviorism emphasizes the scientific study of observable behavioral responses and their environmental determinants. In the behaviorism of B. F. Skinner (1904–1990), the mind, conscious or unconscious, is not needed to explain behavior and development. For him, development is behavior. For example, observations of Sam reveal that his behavior is shy, achievement oriented, and caring. Why is Sam's behavior this way? For Skinner (1938) rewards and punishments in Sam's environment have shaped him into a shy, achievement-oriented, and caring person. Because of interactions with family members, friends, teachers, and others, Sam has *learned* to behave in this fashion.

Since behaviorists believe that development is learned and often changes according to environmental experiences, it follows that rearranging experiences can change development (Adams, 2000; Hayes, 2000). For behaviorists, shy behavior can be transformed into outgoing behavior; aggressive behavior can be shaped into docile behavior; lethargic, boring behavior can be turned into enthusiastic, interesting behavior.

Social Cognitive Theory

Some psychologists believe that the behaviorists are basically right when they say that personality is learned and influenced strongly by environmental factors. But they think Skinner went too far in declaring that characteristics of the person or cognitive factors are unimportant in understanding development. *Social cognitive theory* states that behavior, environment, and person/cognitive factors are important in understanding development.

Albert Bandura (1986, 1997, 2000) and Walter Mischel (1973, 1995) are the architects of the contemporary version of social cognitive theory, which initially was labeled *cognitive social learning theory* by Mischel (1973). As shown in figure 2.6, Bandura says that behavior, environment, and person/cognitive factors interact in a reciprocal manner. Thus, in Bandura's view, the environment can determine a person's behavior (which matches up with Skinner's view), but there is much more to consider. The person can act to change the environment. Person/cognitive factors can influence a person's behavior and vice versa. Person/cognitive factors include self-efficacy (a belief that one can master a situation and produce positive outcomes), plans, and thinking skills. We will have much more to say about self-efficacy in chapter 13, "Achievement, Careers, and Work."

Bandura believes observational learning is a key aspect of how we learn. Through observational learning, we form ideas about the behavior of others and then possibly adopt this behavior ourselves (Zimmerman & Schunk, 2002). For example, a boy might observe his father's aggressive outbursts and hostile exchanges with people; when the boy is with his peers, he interacts in a highly aggressive way, showing the same characteristics as his father's behavior.

Like Skinner's behavioral approach, the social cognitive approach emphasizes the importance of empirical research in studying development. This research focuses on the processes that explain development—the socioemotional and cognitive factors that influence what we are like as people.

Evaluating the Behavioral and Social Cognitive Theories

These are some of the contributions of the behavioral and social cognitive theories:

- An emphasis on the importance of scientific research
- A focus on the environmental determinants of behavior
- An underscoring of the importance of observational learning (Bandura)
- An emphasis on person and cognitive factors (social cognitive theory)

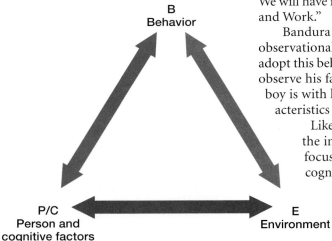

FIGURE 2.6
Bandura's Social Cognitive Theory

Bandura's social cognitive theory emphasizes reciprocal influences of behavior, environment, and person/cognitive factors.

These are some of the criticisms of the behavioral and social cognitive theories:

- Too little emphasis on cognition (Pavlov, Skinner)
- Too much emphasis on environmental determinants
- Inadequate attention to developmental changes
- Too mechanical and inadequate consideration of the spontaneity and creativity of humans

The behavioral and social cognitive theories emphasize the importance of environmental experiences in human development. Next we will turn our attention to another approach that underscores the importance of environmental influences on development—ecological, contextual theory.

Ecological, Contextual Theory

Urie Bronfenbrenner (1917–   ) has proposed a strong environmental view of children's development that is receiving increased attention. **Ecological, contextual theory** is Bronfenbrenner's view of development. It consists of five environmental systems, ranging from the fine-grained inputs of direct interactions with social agents to the broad-based inputs of culture. The five systems in Bronfenbrenner's ecological theory are the microsystem, mesosystem, exosystem, macrosystem, and chronosystem. Bronfenbrenner's (1986, 1995, 2000; Bronfenbrenner & Morris, 1998) ecological, contextual model is shown in figure 2.7 on page 52.

The *microsystem* in Bronfenbrenner's ecological, contextual theory is the setting in which an individual lives. This context includes the person's family, peers, school, and neighborhood. It is in the microsystem that most of the direct interactions with social agents take place—with parents, peers, and teachers, for example. The individual is viewed not as a passive recipient of experiences in these settings, but as someone who helps construct the settings. Bronfenbrenner points out that most of the research on sociocultural influences has focused on microsystems.

The *mesosystem* in Bronfenbrenner's ecological, contextual theory involves relations between microsystems, or connections between contexts. Examples are the relation of family experiences to school experiences, school experiences to work experiences, and family experiences to peer experiences. For instance, adolescents whose parents have rejected them may have difficulty developing positive relations with teachers. Developmentalists increasingly believe that it is important to observe behavior in multiple settings—such as family, peer, and school contexts—to obtain a more complete picture of adolescent development.

The *exosystem* in Bronfenbrenner's ecological, contextual theory is involved when experiences in another social setting—in which the individual does not have an active role—influence what the individual experiences in an immediate context. For example, work experiences might affect a woman's relationship with her husband and their adolescent. The woman might receive a promotion that requires more travel, which might increase marital conflict and change patterns of parent-adolescent interaction. Another example of an exosystem is city government, which is responsible for the quality of parks, recreation centers, and library facilities for children and adolescents.

The *macrosystem* in Bronfenbrenner's ecological, contextual theory involves the culture in which individuals live. Culture refers to the behavior patterns, beliefs, and all other products of a group of people that are passed on from generation to generation. *Cross-cultural studies*—the comparison of one culture with one or more other cultures—provide information about the generality of adolescent development.

The *chronosystem* in Bronfenbrenner's ecological, contextual theory involves the patterning of environmental events and transitions over the life course and sociohistorical circumstances. For example, in studying the effects of divorce on children, researchers have found that the negative effects often peak in the first year after the divorce and the effects are more negative for sons than for daughters

ecological, contextual theory
Bronfenbrenner's view of development, involving five environmental systems—microsystem, mesosystem, ecosystem, macrosystem, and chronosystem. These emphasize the role of social contexts in development.

Bronfenbrenner's Theory
Bronfenbrenner and a
Multicultural Framework
http://www.mhhe.com/santrocka9

THROUGH THE EYES OF PSYCHOLOGISTS
Urie Bronfenbrenner
Cornell University

"Perhaps even more in developmental science than in other fields, the pathways to discovery are not easy to find."

■ FIGURE 2.7
Bronfenbrenner's Ecological, Contextual Theory of Development

Bronfenbrenner's ecological, contextual theory consists of five environmental systems: microsystem, mesosystem, exosystem, macrosystem, and chronosystem.

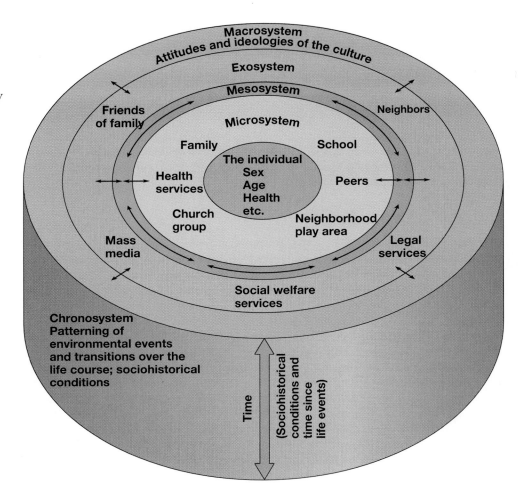

(Hetherington, 1995; Hetherington, Cox, & Cox, 1982). By two years after the divorce, family interaction is less chaotic and more stable. With regard to sociocultural circumstances, girls today are much more likely to be encouraged to pursue a career than they were 20 to 30 years ago. In ways such as these, the chronosystem has a powerful impact on adolescents' lives.

It should be pointed out that Bronfenbrenner (1995, 2000) recently added biological influences to his theory and now describes it as a bioecological theory. Nonetheless, the ecological, environmental contexts still predominate in Bronfenbrenner's theory.

Evaluating Ecological, Contextual Theory   These are some of the contributions of ecological, contextual theory:

- A systematic examination of macro and micro dimensions of environmental systems
- Attention to connections between environmental settings (mesosystem)
- Consideration of sociohistorical influences on development (chronosystem)

These are some of the criticisms of ecological theory:

- Even with the added discussion of biological influences in recent years, there is still too little attention to biological foundations of development.
- The theory gives inadequate attention to cognitive processes.

An Eclectic Theoretical Orientation

eclectic theoretical orientation

Not following any one theoretical approach, but rather selecting from each theory whatever is considered the best in it.

An **eclectic theoretical orientation** *does not follow any one theoretical approach, but rather selects and uses whatever is considered the best in each theory.* No single theory described in this chapter is infallible or capable of explaining entirely the rich complexity of adolescent development. Each of the theories has made important contributions to our understanding of adolescent development, but none provides a complete description and explanation.

For these reasons, the four major approaches to adolescent development are presented in this text in an unbiased fashion. As a result, you can view the field of adolescent development as it actually exists—with different theorists drawing different conclusions. Many other theories of adolescent development, not discussed in this chapter, are woven through the discussion of adolescent development in the remainder of the book. For example, chapter 9 examines the humanistic approach, which emphasizes adolescents' development of self, and chapter 13 discusses attribution theory, which emphasizes adolescents' motivation for understanding the causes of their own and others' behavior.

Many "local" theories or mini-models also guide research in specific areas of development (Kuhn, 1998). For example, in chapter 5, "Families," you will read about the new look in theorizing about parent-adolescent relationships. In chapter 7, "Schools," you will read about some models for improving adolescents' education. Throughout this book you will read about these local theories that focus on specific aspects of adolescent development. Together, the grand theories and micro approaches give us a more complete portrait of how the journey of adolescent development unfolds.

Since the last review we have examined behavioral and social cognitive theories; ecological, contextual theory; and an eclectic theoretical orientation. This review should help you to reach your learning goals related to these topics.

☐ FOR YOUR REVIEW

Learning Goal 3
Explain behavioral and social cognitive theories

- The behavioral and social cognitive theories emphasize the observation of behavior, learned through experience
- In Skinner's behaviorism, development is observed behavior, which is determined by rewards and punishments. In Bandura's social cognitive theory, the environment is an important determinant of behavior but so are person and cognitive factors. Bandura believes that self-efficacy is a key person factor.
- Contributions of the behavioral and social cognitive theories include an emphasis on scientific research; criticisms include inadequate attention to developmental changes.

Learning Goal 4
Understand ecological, contextual theory and an eclectic theoretical orientation

- Ecological, contextual theory states that development is influenced by five environmental systems: microsystem, mesosystem, exosystem, macrosystem, and chronosystem. It was proposed by Urie Bronfenbrenner.
- A contribution of ecological, contextual theory is its systematic analysis of environmental systems at different levels; a criticism is its lack of attention to biological factors.
- An eclectic theoretical orientation does not follow any particular theory but instead selects and uses the best from each theory.
- Research is not only guided by grand theories, such as Piaget's, but also by local or micro theories that focus on a specific aspect or time frame of development.

Now that we have discussed theories of adolescent development, let's further explore the science of adolescent development by examining how research is conducted.

EXPLORING RESEARCH

Recall from the beginning of the chapter that science is not investigated by *what* it investigates but rather by *how* it investigates. Let's further examine what it means to take a scientific approach in studying adolescent development.

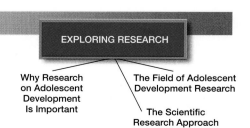

EXPLORING RESEARCH

Why Research on Adolescent Development Is Important

The Field of Adolescent Development Research

The Scientific Research Approach

Why Research on Adolescent Development Is Important

It sometimes is said that experience is the most important teacher. We do get a great deal of knowledge from personal experience. We generalize from what we observe and frequently turn memorable encounters into lifetime "truths." But how valid are these conclusions? Sometimes we err in making these personal observations or misinterpret what we see and hear. Chances are, you can think of many situations in which you thought other people read you the wrong way, just as they may have felt that you mis-read them. And when we base information only on personal experiences, we also aren't always completely objective because sometimes we make judgments that protect our ego and self-esteem (McMillan, 2000; McMillan & Wergin, 2002).

We get information not only from personal experiences, but also from authorities or experts. You might hear experts spell out a "best way" to educate adolescents or to deal with adolescent problems. But the authorities and experts don't always agree, do they? You might hear one expert proclaim that one strategy for teaching adolescents is the best and the next week see that another expert touts another strategy as the best. How can you tell which one to believe? One way to clarify the situation is to carefully examine research that has been conducted on the topic.

The Scientific Research Approach

Researchers take a skeptical, scientific attitude toward knowledge. When they hear someone claim that a particular method is effective in helping adolescents cope with stress, they want to know if the claim is based on *good* research (Beutler & Martin, 1999). The science part of adolescent development seeks to sort fact from fancy by using particular strategies for obtaining information.

Scientific research is objective, systematic, and testable. It reduces the likelihood that information will be based on personal beliefs, opinions, and feelings. Scientific research is based on the **scientific method,** *an approach that can be used to discover accurate information. It includes these steps: Conceptualize the problem, collect data, draw conclusions, and revise research conclusions and theory.*

Conceptualizing a problem involves identifying the problem, perhaps doing some theorizing, and developing one or more hypotheses. For example, suppose that a team of researchers decides that it wants to study ways to improve the achievement of adolescents from impoverished backgrounds. The researchers have *identified a problem,* which at a general level might not seem like a difficult task. However, as part of the first step, they also must go beyond a general description of the problem by isolating, analyzing, narrowing, and focusing more specifically on what aspect of it they hope to study. Perhaps the researchers decide to discover whether mentoring that involves sustained support, guidance, and concrete assistance to adolescents from impoverished backgrounds can improve their academic performance. At this point, even more narrowing and focusing needs to take place. What specific strategies do they want the mentors to use? How often will the mentors see the adolescents? How long will the mentoring program last? What aspects of the adolescents' achievement do the researchers want to assess?

As researchers formulate a problem to study, they often draw on theories and develop hypotheses. Remember from earlier in the chapter that a *theory* is an interrelated, coherent set of ideas that helps to explain and make predictions. *Hypotheses,* which are specific assumptions and predictions that can be tested to determine their accuracy, are derived from theories. For example, a theory on mentoring might attempt to explain and predict why sustained support, guidance, and concrete experience should make a difference in the lives of adolescents from impoverished backgrounds. The theory might focus on adolescents' opportunities to model the behavior and strategies of mentors, or it might focus on the effects of individual attention, which might be missing in the adolescents' lives.

The next step is to *collect information (data).* In the study of mentoring, the researchers might decide to conduct the mentoring program for six months. Their data

Science refines everyday thinking.
—Albert Einstein
*German-Born American Physicist,
20th Century*

scientific method
An approach that can be used to discover accurate information. It includes these steps: Conceptualize the problem, collect data, draw conclusions, and revise research conclusions and theory.

Generating Research Ideas
http://www.mhhe.com/santrocka9

Step 1: CONCEPTUALIZE THE PROBLEM

A researcher identifies this problem: Many adolescents from impoverished backgrounds have lower achievement than adolescents from higher socioeconomic backgrounds. The researcher develops the hypothesis that mentoring will improve the achievement of the adolescents from impoverished backgrounds.

Step 2: COLLECT INFORMATION (DATA)

The researcher conducts the mentoring program for 6 months and collects data before the program begins and after its conclusion using classroom observations, teachers' ratings, and achievement test scores.

Step 3: DRAW CONCLUSIONS

The researcher statistically analyzes the data and finds that adolescents' achievement improved over the 6 months of the study. The researcher concludes that mentoring is likely an important reason for the increase in the adolescent's achievement.

Step 4: REVISE RESEARCH CONCLUSIONS AND THEORY

This research on mentoring, along with other research that obtains similar results, increases the likelihood that mentoring will be considered as an important component of theorizing about how to improve the achievement of adolescents from low-income backgrounds.

FIGURE 2.8
The Scientific Method Applied to a Study of Mentoring

might consist of classroom observations, teachers' ratings, and achievement tests given to the mentored adolescents before the mentoring began and at the end of six months of mentoring.

Once data have been collected, adolescent development researchers use *statistical procedures* to understand the meaning of quantitative data. Then they try to draw *conclusions*. In the study of mentoring, statistics would help determine whether their own observations are due to chance. After data have been analyzed, researchers compare their findings with the findings of other researchers on the same topic.

The final step in the scientific method is *revising research conclusions and theory.* A number of theories have been generated to describe and explain adolescent development. Over time, some theories have been discarded, others revised. Throughout the text you will read about a number of theories of adolescent development. Figure 2.8 illustrates the steps in the scientific method applied to the study of mentoring we have been discussing.

The Field of Adolescent Development Research

Knowledge in the field of adolescence rests heavily on the development of a broad, competent research base. When I wrote the first edition of *Adolescence* in the late 1970s, only a small number of scholars were studying adolescent development. Researchers were studying adults and children, but not adolescents. Over the last two decades, and especially the last decade, the research base of adolescence has grown enormously as an increasing number of investigators have become intrigued by issues and questions that involve the developmental period between childhood and adulthood. The growth of research on adolescent development is reflected in the increasing number of research journals and scholars from different disciplines devoted to advancing scientific knowledge about adolescence.

Why were researchers so neglectful of adolescence until recently? For most of the twentieth century, experiences in childhood, especially the early childhood years, were thought to be so critical that later experiences, such as those occurring in adolescence, were believed to have little impact on development (Bruer, 1999). But beginning in the 1980s, developmentalists seriously challenged the early-experience doctrine, concluding that later experiences were more important in development than had been commonly believed (Brim & Kagan, 1980). The increased research interest in adolescence also has resulted from observations that extensive changes take place between childhood and adulthood (Dornbusch, Petersen, & Hetherington, 1991).

Adolescence Research Journals
http://www.mhhe.com/santrocka9

The main outlets for the vast amount of research being conducted on adolescence are journals and papers presented at scientific meetings. Whether or not you pursue a career in adolescent development, psychology, or a related scientific field, you can benefit by learning about the journal process. Possibly as a student you will be required to look up original research in journals as part of writing a term paper. As a parent, teacher, or nurse you might want to consult journals to obtain information that will help you understand and work more effectively with adolescents. As an inquiring person, you might look up information in journals after you have heard or read something that piqued your curiosity.

A *journal* publishes scholarly and academic information, usually in a specific domain—like physics, math, sociology, or, in the case of our interest, adolescence. Scholars in these fields publish most of their research in journals, which are the core sources of information in virtually every academic discipline.

Journal articles are usually written for other professionals in the field of the journal's focus—such as geology, anthropology, or, again in our case, adolescence. They often contain technical language and specialized terms related to a specific discipline that are difficult for nonprofessionals to understand. Most of you have already had one or more courses in psychology, and you will be learning a great deal more about the specialized field of adolescent development in this course. This should improve your ability to understand journal articles in this field.

An increasing number of journals publish information about adolescence. Some are devoted exclusively to adolescence; others include information about other periods of the human life span as well. Journals devoted exclusively to adolescence include *Journal of Research on Adolescence, Journal of Early Adolescence, Journal of Youth and Adolescence, Adolescence,* and *Journal of Adolescent Health Care.* Journals that include research on adolescence but also research on other age ranges include *Child Development, Developmental Psychology,* and *Human Development.* Also, a number of journals that do not focus on development include articles on adolescence, such as *Journal of Educational Psychology, Sex Roles, Journal of Marriage and the Family,* and *Journal of Consulting and Clinical Psychology.*

In psychology and the field of adolescence, most journal articles are reports of original research. Many journals also include review articles that present an overview of different studies on a particular topic—such as adolescent depression, attachment in adolescence, or adolescent decision making.

Many journals are selective about what they publish. Every journal has an editorial board of experts that evaluate

THINKING CRITICALLY
Isn't Everyone a Psychologist?

Each of us has theories about human behavior, and it is hard to imagine how we could get through life without them. In this sense, we are all psychologists. However, the theories of psychology that we carry around and the way we obtain support for our theories are often quite different from the way psychologists go about theorizing and collecting data about an issue or topic (Stanovich, 1998).

Think for a few moments about your views of human behavior. How did you arrive at them? Might at least some of them be biased? Now think about what you have read about theories and methods in this chapter. How is our personal psychology of adolescence different from the scientific psychology of adolescence? Which one is more likely to be accurate? Why? Although our personal psychology of adolescence and the scientific psychology of adolescence are often different, in what ways might they be similar?

the articles submitted for publication. Each submitted paper is carefully examined by one or more of the experts, who accept or reject it based on such factors as its contribution to the field, theoretical soundness, methodological excellence, and clarity of writing. Some of the most prestigious journals reject as many as 80 to 90 percent of the articles that are submitted because they fail to meet the journal's standards.

Where do you find journals? Your college or university library likely has one or more of the journals listed earlier. Some public libraries also carry journals. I encourage you to look up one or more of the journals that include material on adolescence.

To help you understand the journals, let's examine the format followed by many of them. Their organization often takes this course: abstract, introduction, method, results, discussion, and references.

The *abstract* is a brief summary that appears at the beginning of the article. The abstract lets readers quickly determine whether the article is relevant to their interests and whether they want to read the entire article. The *introduction,* as its title suggests, introduces the problem or issue that is being studied. It includes a concise review of research relevant to the topic, theoretical ties, and one or more hypotheses to be tested. The *method* section consists of a clear description of the participants evaluated in the study, the measures used, and the procedures that were followed. The method section should be sufficiently clear and detailed so that by reading it another researcher could repeat, or replicate, the study. The *results* section reports the analysis of the data collected. In most cases, the results section includes statistical analyses that are difficult for nonprofessionals to understand. The *discussion* section presents the author's conclusions, inferences, and interpretation of what was found. Statements are usually made about whether the hypotheses presented in the introduction were supported, limitations of the study, and suggestions for future research. The *references* section is the last part of the journal article, and gives a bibliographic listing for every source cited in the article. The references section is often a good source for finding other articles relevant to the topic you are interested in.

Research journals are the core of information in virtually every academic discipline. Those shown here are among the increasing number of research journals that publish information about adolescent development. *What are the main parts of a research article that present findings from original research?*

Since the last review we have explored a number of ideas about research. This review should help you to reach your learning goals related to this topic.

FOR YOUR REVIEW

Learning Goal 5
Explore research

- Research on adolescent development is important because when we base information on personal experience, we are not always objective. Research provides a vehicle for evaluating the accuracy of what experts and authorities say.
- Scientific research is objective, systematic, and testable. Scientific research is based on the scientific method, which includes these steps: conceptualize the problem, collect data, draw conclusions, and revise research conclusions and theory.
- The field of adolescent development research is growing. The main outlets for this research are journals and papers presented at professional meetings. Research journals follow this format: abstract, introduction, method, results, and discussion.

So far in this chapter we have described theories of adolescent development and explored some basic ideas about research. Next, we will continue to explore how research is conducted by examining the methods researchers use.

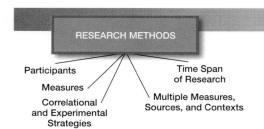

RESEARCH METHODS

When researchers conduct a study on adolescent development, they need to determine who the participants will be, which measure(s) they will use, whether to adopt a correlational or experimental strategy, and decide on the time span of the inquiry. Let's now explore these aspects of research.

Participants

Who the participants will be is an important question that every adolescent development researcher must tackle. Will they be females, males, or both? How old will they be? Will individuals in early and late adolescence be studied? Will they be of a single ethnicity, such as non-Latino White, or will they come from a diversity of ethnic groups.

When researchers conduct a study, they usually want to be able to draw conclusions that will apply to a larger group of people than the participants they actually study. Thus, a researcher might decide to study 100 adolescents from divorced families in Los Angeles, California, but the researcher would like for the results of the study to apply to all adolescents from divorced families in the United States.

A *population* is the entire group about which the investigator wants to draw conclusions. In this particular study of adolescents from divorced families, the population is all adolescents from divorced families in the United States. A *sample* is a subset of the population chosen by the investigator for study. In this adolescence study, the sample is 100 adolescents from divorced families in Los Angeles, California. Why does a sample need to be used rather than a population? Because it is impractical to collect data on the entire population.

Generalization from the sample to the population only can be made if the sample is representative (which means "typical") of the population. For example, in the study of 100 adolescents from divorced families, assume that a disproportionate number of them were in families undergoing psychotherapy. Thus, caution is warranted in generalizing to all adolescents from divorced families, especially those living in families not undergoing psychotherapy.

In a *random sample,* every member of the population has an equal chance of being selected. In the study of adolescents from divorced families, a representative sample would mirror the population in terms of such factors as age, socioeconomic status, ethnicity, geographic location, mental health status, religion, and so on.

It is easy to get the impression that research on adolescent development is worthless if it is not based on a random sample. However, random sampling is important in some types of research but less important in others. If a researcher wants to know how often divorce occurs in families with one or more adolescents in the United States, obtaining a random sample is important. But in many research studies, investigators are interested in studying specific aspects of development under specific conditions, in which case they deliberately do not obtain a random sample. In these studies, they might want to study adolescents with certain characteristics well represented. Thus, in a study of adolescents in divorced families, a researcher might investigate 50 families in which the divorce occurred prior to adolescence and 50 families in which it took place during adolescence. This researcher wants to know how the age at onset of the divorce is related to development.

It also should be pointed out that in adolescent development research, generalization often develops when similar findings occur across a number of studies rather than from random sampling in a single study. If five or six studies conducted with varied samples (maybe one from Los Angeles, another in Athens, Georgia, and others with somewhat similar or different characteristics) all arrive at similar conclusions, then we gain confidence in the generalization of the findings.

Now that we have explored who the participants will be in a study, let's examine another important aspect of research—which measure(s) will be used to collect data.

Measures

Among the measures that can be used in research are observation, interviews and questionnaires, standardized tests, physiological measures, and case studies.

Observation   Sherlock Holmes chided his assistant, Watson, "You see but you do not observe." We look at things all the time. However, casually watching two adolescents interacting is not the same as the type of observation used in scientific studies. Scientific observation is highly systematic. It requires knowing what you are looking for, conducting observations in an unbiased manner, accurately recording and categorizing what you see, and effectively communicating your observations.

When deciding on who the participants will be in a study on adolescent development, what are some decisions that have to be made?

A common way to record observations is write them down, often using shorthand or symbols. In addition, tape recorders, video cameras, special coding sheets, one-way mirrors, and computers increasingly are being used to make observations more efficient.

Observations can be made in laboratories or naturalistic settings. A **laboratory** *is a controlled setting from which many of the complex factors of the real world have been removed.* Some researchers conduct studies in laboratories at the colleges or universities where they teach. Although laboratories often help researchers to gain more control over the behavior of the participants, laboratory studies have been criticized as being artificial. In **naturalistic observation,** *behavior is observed outside of a laboratory in the "real world."* Researchers conduct naturalistic observations of adolescents in classrooms, at home, at youth centers, at museums, in neighborhoods, and in other settings (Leinhardt, Crowley, & Knutson, 2002).

One innovative strategy involving observation is the *video-recall technique* (Gottman & Levenson, 1985; Powers, Welsh, & Wright, 1994). In this method, participants serve as raters of their own videotaped behavior (Holmbeck & Shapera, 1999). After engaging in a task together, parents and adolescents, friends, or dating partners are asked to view the tape and make ratings of their own behavior and then the other person's behavior (Welsh & others, 1998). The focus of the ratings depends on the particular topic being investigated. This method provides information about individuals' subjective perceptions of what they believe their behavior and the other person's behavior was like.

Interviews and Questionnaires

Sometimes the quickest and best way to get information from adolescents is to ask them for it. Researchers use interviews and questionnaires (surveys) to find out about adolescents' experiences, beliefs, and feelings. Most interviews take place face-to-face, although they can be done in other ways, such as over the phone or via the Internet. Questionnaires are usually given to individuals in printed form and participants are asked to fill them out.

Good interviews and surveys involve concrete, specific, and unambiguous questions and some means of checking the authenticity of the respondents' replies. However, interviews and surveys are not without problems (Gall, Borg, & Gall, 2002). One crucial limitation is that many individuals give socially desirable answers, responding in a way they think is most socially acceptable and desirable rather than according to how they truly think or feel. For example, when asked whether they cheat on tests in school, some adolescents might say that they don't even though they do, because it is socially undesirable to cheat. Skilled interviewing techniques and questions that increase forthright responses are critical to obtaining accurate information.

Standardized Tests

Standardized tests *are commercially prepared tests that assess performance in different domains. A standardized test allows an adolescent's performance to be compared with that of other adolescents of the same age, in many cases on a national level.* Standardized tests can be given to adolescents to assess their intelligence, achievement, personality, career interests, and other skills. These tests might be for a variety of purposes, including outcome measures in research studies, information that helps psychologists make decisions about individual adolescents, or comparisons of students' performance across schools, states, and countries. In chapter 4, "Cognitive Development," we will further explore standardized tests of intelligence.

The most widely used standardized test of personality is the Minnesota Multiphasic Personality Inventory (MMPI) (Butcher, 2000). The MMPI-A (with the A standing for Adolescent) is a downward extension of the MMPI that was specifically constructed to assess the personality of adolescents in clinical and research settings (Butcher & others, 1992). The MMPI-A includes several scales not found in the MMPI-2, the current version of the MMPI for adults. These adolescent scales include Alienation, Conduct Problems, Low Aspirations, School Problems, Immaturity, Alcohol/Drug Problems Proneness, and Alcohol/Drug Problems Acknowledgment (Holmbeck & Shapera, 1999). The MMPI-A also includes a number of validity scales that can be used to detect whether the adolescent is providing truthful responses,

laboratory
A controlled setting from which many of the complex factors of the real world have been removed.

naturalistic observation
Observations that take place out in the real world instead of in a laboratory.

standardized tests
Commercially prepared tests that assess performance in different domains.

responding in a socially desirable way, or providing other nonvalid responses (Baer & others, 1997). In chapter 9, "The Self and Identity," we will explore assessment of self-worth and self-esteem, which are central dimensions of personality.

Physiological Measures   Physiological measures are increasingly being used in assessing adolescent development. Three major types of physiological measures involve assessment of (1) hormones in the bloodstream, (2) body composition, and (3) brain activity.

As puberty unfolds, hormone secretions in the blood increase. Researchers take blood samples of adolescents to determine the nature of these hormonal changes (Susman, 1997; Susman, Dorn, & Schiefelbein, in press).

The body composition of adolescents also is a focus of physiological assessment. There is a special interest in the increase in fat content in the body during pubertal development.

Until recently, little research had focused on the brain activity of adolescents. However, the development of neuroimaging techniques has led to a flurry of research studies on adolescents' brain activity (Blumenthal & others, 1999; Thompson & others, 2000). One technique that is being used in a number of studies is *magnetic resonance imaging (MRI),* which involves creating a magnetic field around a person's body and using radio waves to construct images of the person's brain tissues and biochemical activities. We will have much more to say about these physiological measures in chapter 3, "Puberty, Health, and Biological Foundations."

Brandi Binder is evidence of the brain's hemispheric flexibility and resilience. Despite having the right side of her cortex removed because of a severe case of epilepsy, Brandi engages in many activities often portrayed as only "right-brain" activities. She loves music, math, and art, and is shown here working on one of her paintings.

case study
An in-depth look at an individual.

Case Studies   A **case study** *is an in-depth look at an individual.* This method often is used when unique circumstances in a person's life cannot be duplicated, for either practical or ethical reasons. For example, consider the case study of Brandi Binder (Nash, 1997). She developed such a severe case of epilepsy that surgeons had to remove the right side of her cortex when she was 6 years old. Brandi lost virtually all of the control she had established over muscles on the left side of her body, the side controlled by the right side of her brain. Yet at age 14, after years of therapy ranging from leg lifts to mathematics and music training, Brandi is an A student. She loves music, mathematics, and art, which usually are associated with the right side of the brain. Her recuperation is not 100 percent. For example, she has not regained the use of her left arm. However, her case study shows that if there is a way to compensate, the human brain will find it. Brandi's remarkable recovery also provides evidence against the stereotype that the left side (left hemisphere) is the sole source of logical thinking and the right hemisphere exclusively the source of creativity. Brains are not that neatly split in terms of their functioning, as Brandi's case illustrated.

Although case studies provide dramatic, in-depth portrayals of people's lives, we need to exercise caution when interpreting the information in case studies (Davison, 2000). The subject of a case study is unique, with a genetic makeup and set of experiences that no one else shares. For these reasons, the findings might not generalize to other people.

Correlational and Experimental Strategies

An important research decision is whether to conduct a study using a correlational or experimental strategy.

Correlational Research   In **correlational research,** *the goal is to describe the strength of the relation between two or more events or characteristics.* Correlational research is useful because the more strongly two events are correlated (related or associated), the more effectively we can predict one from the other. For example, if researchers find that low-involved, permissive parenting is correlated with an adolescent's lack of self-control, this suggests that low-involved, permissive parenting might be one source of the lack of self-control.

correlational research
Research whose goal is to describe the strength of the relation between two or more events or characteristics.

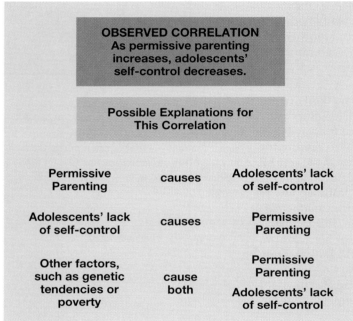

FIGURE 2.9
Possible Explanations of Correlational Data

From an observed correlation between two events, one cannot conclude that the first event causes the second event. Other possibilities are that the second event causes the first event or that a third, unknown event causes the correlation between the first two events.

experimental research

Research involving experiments that permit the determination of cause. A carefully regulated procedure in which one or more of the factors believed to influence the behavior being studied is manipulated and all other factors are held constant.

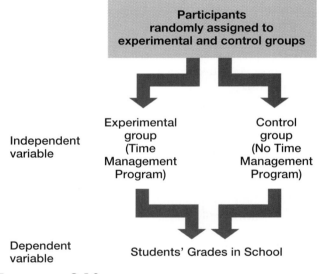

FIGURE 2.10
The Experimental Strategy Applied to a Study of the Effects of Time Management on Students' Grades

However, a caution is in order: *Correlation does not equal causation.* The correlational finding just mentioned does not mean that permissive parenting necessarily causes low self-control in adolescents. It could mean that, but it also could mean that the adolescent's lack of self-control caused the parents to simply throw up their arms in despair and give up trying to control the adolescent. It also could mean that other factors, such as heredity or poverty, caused the correlation between permissive parenting and low self-control in adolescents. Figure 2.9 illustrates these possible interpretations of correlational data.

Experimental Research **Experimental research** *allows researchers to determine the causes of behavior. They accomplish this task by performing an experiment, a carefully regulated procedure in which one or more of the factors believed to influence the behavior being studied is manipulated and all other factors are held constant. If the behavior under study changes when a factor is manipulated, we say the manipulated factor causes the* *behavior to change.* "Cause" is the event being manipulated. "Effect" is the behavior that changes because of the manipulation. Experimental research is the only reliable method of establishing cause and effect. Because correlational research does not involve manipulation of factors, it is not a dependable way to isolate cause.

Experiments involve at least one independent variable and one dependent variable. The **independent variable** *is the manipulated, influential, experimental factor.* The label *independent* indicates that this variable can be changed independently of any other factors. For example, suppose we want to design an experiment to study the effects of peer tutoring on adolescents' achievement. In this example, the amount and type of peer tutoring could be an independent variable. The **dependent variable** *is the factor that is measured in an experiment. It can change as the independent variable is manipulated.* The label *dependent* is used because this variable depends on what happens to the participants in an experiment as the independent variable is manipulated. In the peer tutoring study, achievement is the dependent variable. This might be assessed in a number of ways. Let's say that in this study it is measured by scores on a nationally standardized achievement test.

In experiments, the independent variable consists of differing experiences that are given to one or more experimental groups and one or more control groups. An **experimental group** *is a group whose experience is manipulated.* A **control group** *is a group that is treated in every way like the experimental group except for the manipulated factor.* The control group serves as the baseline against which the effects of the manipulated condition can be compared. In the peer tutoring study, we need to have one group of adolescents that gets peer tutoring (experimental group) and one that doesn't (control group).

Another important principle of experimental research is **random assignment**— *assigning participants to experimental and control groups by chance.* This practice reduces the likelihood that the experiment's results will be due to any preexisting differences between the groups. In our study of peer tutoring, random assignment greatly reduces the probability that the two groups will differ on such factors as age, family background, initial achievement, intelligence, personality, health, and so on.

To summarize the study of peer tutoring and adolescent achievement, participants are randomly assigned to two groups: One (the experimental group) is given peer tutoring, the other (the control group) is not. The independent variable consists of the differing experiences that the experimental and control groups receive. After the peer tutoring is completed, the adolescents are given a nationally standardized achievement test (dependent variable). Figure 2.10 on page 62 illustrates the experimental research method applied to a different problem: whether a time management program can improve adolescents' grades.

independent variable

The manipulated, influential, experimental factor in an experiment.

dependent variable

The factor that is measured as the result of an experiment.

experimental group

A group whose experience is manipulated in an experiment.

control group

A comparison group in an experiment that is treated in every way like the experimental group except for the manipulated factor.

random assignment

In experimental research, the assignment of participants to experimental and control groups by chance.

Multiple Measures, Sources, and Contexts

Methods have their strengths and weaknesses (Elmes, Kantowitz, & Roedinger, 2003). Direct observation is a valuable tool for obtaining information about adolescents, but some things cannot be directly observed in adolescents—their moral thoughts, their inner feelings, their arguments with parents, how they acquire information about sex, and so on. In such instances, other measures, such as interviews, questionnaires, and case studies, may be valuable. Because every method has limitations, researchers have increasingly turned to multiple measures in assessing adolescent development. For example, a researcher might ask adolescents about their aggressive or delinquent behavior, check with their friends, observe them at home and in the neighborhood, interview their parents, and talk with their teachers. Researchers hope that the convergence of multimeasure, multisource, and multicontext information will provide a more comprehensive and valid assessment of adolescent development.

These methods, along with the research issues discussed in chapter 1 and the theories presented earlier in this chapter, provide a sense of development's scientific nature. Figure 2.11 on page 64 compares the main theoretical perspectives in terms of

Correlational Research
Experimental Research
http://www.mhhe.com/santrocka9

Theory	Issues and Methods			
	Continuity/discontinuity, early versus later experience	Biological and environmental factors	Importance of cognition	Research methods
Psychoanalytic	Discontinuity between stages—continuity between early experiences and later development; early experiences very important; later changes in development emphasized in Erikson's theory	Freud's biological determination interacting with early family experiences; Erikson's more balanced biological-cultural interaction perspective	Emphasized, but in the form of unconscious thought	Clinical interviews, unstructured personality tests, psychohistorical analyses of lives
Cognitive	Discontinuity between stages—continuity between early experiences and later development in Piaget's theory; has not been important to information-processing psychologists	Piaget's emphasis on interaction and adaptation; environment provides the setting for cognitive structures to develop; information-processing view has not addressed this issue extensively, but mainly emphasizes biological-environmental interaction	The primary determinant of behavior	Interviews and observations
Behavioral and Social Cognitive	Continuity (no stages); experience at all points of development important	Environment viewed as the primary cause of behavior in both views	Strongly deemphasized in the behavioral approach but an important mediator in social cognitive	Observation, especially laboratory observation
Ecological, Contextual	Little attention to continuity/discontinuity in Bronfenbrenner's theory	Very strong environmental emphasis	Not emphasized in Bronfenbrenner's theory	Varied methods; collect data in a number of social contexts

FIGURE 2.11
A Comparison of Theories and the Issues and Methods in Adolescent Development

how they address important developmental issues and the methods often used in studying adolescents.

Time Span of Research

Another research decision involves the time span of the research. Two options are to study individuals all at one time or study the same individuals over time.

cross-sectional research
Research that studies people all at one time.

Cross-sectional research *involves studying people all at one time.* For example, a researcher might be interested in studying the self-esteem of 8-, 12-, and 16-year olds. In a cross-sectional study, all participants' self-esteem would be assessed at one time. The cross-sectional study's main advantage is that the researcher does not have to wait for the children to grow older. However, this approach provides no information about the stability of the children's and adolescents' self-esteem, or how it might change over time.

longitudinal research
Research that studies the same people over a period of time, usually several years or more.

Longitudinal research *involves studying the same individuals over a period of time, usually several years or more.* In a longitudinal study of self-esteem, the researcher might examine the self-esteem of a group of 8-year-old children, then assess their self-esteem again when they are 12 and then again when they are 16. One of the great values of longitudinal research is that we can evaluate how individual children and adolescents change or stay the same as they get older (Rosnow, 2000). However, because longitudinal research is time consuming and costly, most research is cross-sectional.

Since the last review, we have discussed a number of research methods. This review should help you to reach your learning goals related to this topic.

☐ FOR YOUR REVIEW

Learning Goal 6
Describe how participants are selected and measures

- A sample of participants is selected and in many cases the goal is for the data collected from this sample to generalize to a population. One strategy to accomplish this is to obtain a random sample. In some instances, researchers do not obtain a random sample because they may be interested in a specific research question about a specific sample of adolescents.
- Observations need to be conducted systematically. Observations can be made in laboratories or in natural settings.
- Most interviews take place face-to-face. Most questionnaires (surveys) are given to individuals in printed form and filled out.
- Standardized tests are commercially prepared tests that assess performance in different domains.
- Physiological measures include those that assess hormones, body composition, and brain activity.
- Case studies provide an in-depth look at an individual.
- Researchers increasingly are adopting a multimeasure, multisource, multicontext approach in an effort to obtain a more complete set of information about adolescents in a study.

Learning Goal 7
Understand the distinction between correlational and experimental strategies and know about the time span of research

- In correlational research, the goal is to describe the relation between two or more events or characteristics. Correlation does not equal causation. In experimental research, the influence of at least one independent variable on one or more dependent variables is examined; also, participants are randomly assigned to one or more experimental and one or more control groups.
- Cross-sectional research involves studying people all at one time. Longitudinal research consists of studying the same people over time.

So far in this chapter, we have examined theories of adolescent development, explored research, and described research methods. Next, we will discuss some research challenges.

RESEARCH CHALLENGES

Research on adolescent development poses a number of challenges. Some of the challenges involve the pursuit of knowledge itself. Others involve the effects of research on participants. Still others relate to achieving a better understanding of the information derived from research studies.

Ethics

Researchers must exercise considerable caution to ensure the well-being of adolescents participating in a study. Most colleges have review boards that evaluate whether the research is ethical.

The code of ethics adopted by the American Psychological Association (APA) instructs researchers to protect participants from mental and physical harm. The best interests of the participants always must be kept foremost in the researcher's mind (Kimmel, 1996; Sieber, 2000). Adolescents must give their informed consent to participate.

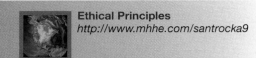

Ethical Principles
http://www.mhhe.com/santrocka9

Three important research ethics topics are informed consent, confidentiality, and debriefing. *Informed consent* means that all participants if they are old enough (typically 7 years or older) in a research study must know what their participation will involve and any risks that might develop. If they are not old enough, their parents' or guardians' consent must be obtained. Informed consent means that the participants (and/or their parents/legal guardians) have been told what their participation will entail and any risks that might be involved. For example, if researchers want to study the effects of conflict in divorced families on adolescents' self-esteem, the participants should be informed that in some instances discussion of a family's experiences might improve family relationships, but in other cases might raise unwanted family stress. After informed consent is given, participants retain the right to withdraw at any time (Jones, 2000).

Another important aspect of research ethics is *confidentiality,* which means that researchers are responsible for keeping all of the data they gather on individuals completely confidential, and, when possible, completely anonymous. Yet another responsibility of researchers is *debriefing,* which consists of informing participants of the purpose and methods used in a study after the study has been completed.

Gender

Traditionally, science has been presented as nonbiased and value-free. However, many experts on gender believe that psychological research often has involved gender bias (Anselmi, 1998; Doyle & Paludi, 1998; Crawford & Unger, 2000). They argue that for too long female experience was subsumed under male experience. For example, conclusions have been drawn routinely about females based on research conducted only with males. Similarly, with regard to socioeconomic bias, conclusions have been drawn about all males and females from studies that do not include participants from low-income backgrounds.

Here are three broad questions that female scholars have raised regarding gender bias in psychological research (Tetreault, 1997):

- How might gender be a bias that influences the choice of theory, questions, hypotheses, participants, and research design?
- How might research on topics of primary interest to females, such as relationships, feelings, and empathy, challenge existing theory and research?
- How has research that heretofore has exaggerated gender differences between females and males influenced the way parents, teachers, and others think about and interact with female and male adolescents? For example, gender differences in mathematics often have been exaggerated and fueled by societal bias.

In chapter 10, "Gender," we will explore many aspects of gender, including what researchers have found out about actual differences between females and males.

Ethnicity and Culture

We need to include more adolescents from ethnic minority backgrounds in research (Graham, 1992; Phinney & Landin, 1998; Wilson, 2000). Historically, ethnic minority adolescents essentially were ignored in research or simply viewed as variations from the norm or the average. Their developmental and educational problems have been viewed as "confounds" or "noise" in data. Researchers have deliberately excluded these adolescents from the samples they have selected to study (Ryan-Finn, Cauce, & Grove, 1995). Because ethnic minority adolescents have been excluded from research for so long, there likely is more variation in adolescents' real lives than research studies have indicated in the past.

Researchers also have tended to practice what is called "ethnic gloss" when they select and describe ethnic minority samples (Trimble, 1989). *Ethnic gloss* means using an ethnic label, such as African American or Latino, in a superficial way that makes an ethnic group look more homogeneous than it really is. For example, a researcher might describe a sample as "20 Latinos and 20 Anglo-Americans" when a more precise description of the Latino group would need to state: "The 20 Latino participants were Mexican Americans from low-income neighborhoods in the southwestern area of Los Angeles. Twelve were from homes in which Spanish is the dominant language spoken, 8 from homes in which English is the main spoken language. Ten were born in the United States, 10 in Mexico. Ten described themselves as Mexican Americans, 5 as Mexican, 3 as American, 2 as Chicano, and 1 as Latino." Ethnic gloss can cause researchers to obtain samples of ethnic groups that either are not representative or conceal the group's diversity, which can lead to overgeneralization and stereotyping.

Also historically, when researchers have studied ethnic minority adolescents, they have focused on their problems. It is important to study the problems, such as poverty, that many ethnic minority adolescents face, but it also is important to examine their strengths as well, such as their pride, self-esteem, improvised problem-solving skills, and extended-family support systems. Fortunately, now in the context of a more pluralistic view of our society, researchers are increasingly studying the positive dimensions of ethnic minority adolescents (Swanson, 1997).

Being a Wise Consumer of Information About Adolescent Development

We live in a society that generates a vast amount of information about adolescents in various media that range from research journals to newspaper and television accounts. The information varies greatly in quality. How can you evaluate this information?

Be Cautious of What Is Reported in the Popular Media

Television, radio, newspapers, and magazines frequently report research on adolescent development. Many researchers regularly supply the media with information about adolescents. In some cases, this research has been published in professional journals or presented at national meetings and then is picked up by the popular media. And most colleges have a media relations department that contacts the press about current faculty research.

However, not all research on adolescents that appears in the media comes from professionals with excellent credentials and reputations. Journalists, television reporters, and other media personnel are not scientifically trained. It is not an easy task for them to sort through the avalanche of material they receive and make sound decisions about which information to report.

Unfortunately, the media tend to focus on sensational, dramatic findings. They want you to stay tuned or buy their publication. When the information they gather from research journals is not sensational, they might embellish it and sensationalize it, going beyond what the researcher intended.

CAREERS IN ADOLESCENT DEVELOPMENT

Pam Reid
Educational and Developmental Psychologist

As a child, Pam Reid played with chemistry sets, and at the university she was majoring in chemistry, planning on becoming a medical doctor. Because some of her friends signed up for a psychology course as an elective, she decided to join them. She was so intrigued by learning more about how people think, behave, and develop that she changed her major to psychology. She says, "I fell in love with psychology." Pam went on to obtain her Ph.D. in educational psychology.

Today, Pam is a professor of education and psychology at the University of Michigan. She is also a research scientist for the University of Michigan Institute for Research on Women and Gender. Her main interest is how children and adolescents develop social skills, and especially how gender, socioeconomic status, and ethnicity are involved in development. Because many psychological findings have been based on research with middle-socioeconomic-status non-Latino White populations, Pam believes it is important to study people from different ethnic groups. She stresses that by understanding the expectations, attitudes, and behavior of diverse groups, we enrich the theory and practice of psychology. Currently Pam is working with her graduate students on a project involving middle school girls. She is interested in why girls, more often than boys, stop taking classes in mathematics.

Pam Reid (*back row, center*) with graduate students she is mentoring at the University of Michigan.

Another problem with research reported in the media is a lack of time or space to go into important details about a study. The media often only get a few lines or a few moments to summarize as best they can what might be complex findings. Too often this means that what is reported is overgeneralized and stereotyped.

Know How to Avoid Assuming Individual Needs on the Basis of Group Research

Nomothetic research is research conducted at the level of the group. Most research on adolescents is nomothetic research. Individual variations in how adolescents behave are not a common focus. For example, if researchers are interested in the effects of divorce on adolescents' school achievement, they might conduct a study with 50 adolescents from divorced families and 50 adolescents from intact, never-divorced families. They might find that adolescents from divorced families, as a group, have lower achievement in school than adolescents from intact families. That is a nomothetic finding that applies to adolescents from divorced families as a group. And that is what is commonly reported in the media and also in research journals. In this particular study, it likely was the case that some of the adolescents from divorced families had higher school achievement than the adolescents from intact families—not as many, but some. Indeed, it is entirely possible that, of the 100 adolescents in the study, the 2 or 3 adolescents who had the highest school achievement were from divorced families and this fact was not reported in the media.

Nomothetic research provides valuable information about the characteristics of a group of adolescents, revealing strengths and weaknesses of the group. However, in many instances, parents, teachers, and others want to know about how to help one particular adolescent cope and learn more effectively. *Idiographic needs* are needs of the individual, not of the group. Unfortunately, although nomothetic research can point up problems for certain groups of adolescents, its findings do not always hold for an individual adolescent.

Recognize How Easy It Is to Overgeneralize About a Small or Clinical Sample

There often isn't space or time in media presentations to go into details about the nature of the sample of adolescents on which the study is based. In many cases, samples are too small to let us generalize to a larger population. For example, if a study of adolescents from divorced families is based on only 10 or 20 adolescents, what is found in the study cannot be generalized to all adolescents from divorced families. Perhaps the sample was drawn from families who have substantial economic resources, are Anglo-American, live in a small southern town, and are undergoing therapy. From this study, we clearly would be making unwarranted generalizations if we thought the findings also characterize adolescents who are from low- to moderate-income families, are from other ethnic backgrounds, live in a different geographic region, and are not undergoing therapy.

Be Aware That a Single Study Usually Is Not the Defining Word

The media might identify an interesting research study and claim that it is something phenomenal with far-reaching implications. As a competent consumer of information, be aware that it is extremely rare for a single study to have earth-shattering, conclusive answers that apply to all adolescents. In fact, where there are large numbers of studies that focus on a particular issue, it is not unusual to find conflicting results from one study to the next. Reliable answers about adolescent development usually emerge only after many researchers have conducted similar studies and drawn similar conclusions. In our example of divorce, if one study reports that a counseling program for adolescents from divorced families improved their achievement, we cannot conclude that the counseling program will work as effectively with all adolescents from divorced families until many more studies have been conducted.

Remember That Causal Conclusions Cannot Be Drawn from Correlational Studies

Drawing causal conclusions from correlational studies is one of the most common mistakes made by the media. In nonexperimental studies (remember that in an experiment, participants are randomly assigned to treatments or experiences), two variables of factors might be related to each other. However, causal interpretations cannot be made when two or more factors simply are correlated. We cannot say that one factor causes the other. In the case of divorce, the headline might read: "Divorce causes adolescents to have low achievement." We read the story and find out that the information is based on the results of a research study. Because we obviously cannot, for ethical and practical reasons, randomly assign adolescents to families that will become divorced or remain intact, this headline is based on a correlational study and the causal statements are unproven. It could well be, for example, that both adolescents' poor school performance and parents' divorce are typically due to some other factor, such as family conflict or economic problems.

Always Consider the Source of the Information and Evaluate Its Credibility   Studies are not automatically accepted by the research community. As we discussed earlier in this chapter, researchers usually have to submit their findings to a research journal where they are reviewed by their colleagues, who make a decision about whether or not to publish the paper. The quality of research in journals is far from uniform, but in most cases the research has undergone far more scrutiny and careful consideration of the work's quality than in the case for research or any other information that has not gone through the journal process. And within the media, we can distinguish between what is presented in respected newspapers, such as the *New York Times* and *Washington Post*, as well as creditable magazines such as *Time* and *Newsweek*, and much less respected tabloids, such as the *National Inquirer* and *Star*.

THINKING CRITICALLY

Reading and Analyzing Reports About Adolescent Development

Information about adolescent development appears in research journals and in magazines and newspapers. Choose one of the topics covered in this book and course—such as identity, adolescent problems, or parenting. Find an article in a research journal (such as *Developmental Psychology, Child Development, Journal of Research on Adolescence, Journal of Early Adolescence,* or *Journal of Youth and Adolescence*) and an article in a newspaper or magazine on the same topic. How did the research article on the topic differ from the newspaper or magazine article? What did you learn from this comparison?

Since the last review, we have studied a number of research challenges. This review should help you to reach your learning goals related to this topic.

☐ FOR YOUR REVIEW

Learning Goal 8
Elaborate on research challenges

- Researchers recognize that a number of ethical concerns have to be met when conducting studies, including informed consent, confidentiality, and debriefing.
- Every effort should be made to make research equitable for both females and males.
- More adolescents from ethnic minority backgrounds need to be included in adolescent development research.
- Being a wise consumer of information about adolescent development includes being cautious about what is reported in the media, not overgeneralizing about a small or clinical sample, not taking a single study as the defining word, not accepting causal interpretations from correlational studies, and always considering the source of the information and evaluating its credibility.

In this chapter, we have examined how adolescent development is studied from a scientific research perspective. In the next chapter, we will focus on biological foundations, puberty, and health.

CHAPTER MAP

REACH YOUR LEARNING GOALS

At the beginning of the chapter, we stated eight learning goals and encouraged you to review material related to these goals at five points in the chapter. This is a good time to return to these reviews and use them to guide your study and help you to reach your learning goals.

Page 49

Learning Goal 1   Discuss psychoanalytic theories
Learning Goal 2   Know about cognitive theories

Page 53

Learning Goal 3   Explain behavioral and social cognitive theories
Learning Goal 4   Understand ecological, contextual theory and an eclectic theoretical orientation

Page 58

Learning Goal 5   Explore research

Page 65

Learning Goal 6   Describe how participants are selected and measures
Learning Goal 7   Understand the distinction between correlational and experimental strategies and know about the time span of research

Page 69

Learning Goal 8   Elaborate on research challenges

KEY TERMS

theory 40
psychoanalytic theory 40
Erikson's theory 44
Piaget's theory 46
Vygotsky's theory 47
information-processing approach 48
behavioral and social cognitive theories 49
ecological, contextual theory 51
eclectic theoretical orientation 52
scientific method 54
laboratory 60
naturalistic observation 60

standardized tests 60
case study 61
correlational research 61
experimental research 62
independent variable 63
dependent variable 63
experimental group 63
control group 63
random assignment 63
cross-sectional research 64
longitudinal research 64

KEY PEOPLE

Sigmund Freud 40
Peter Blos 41
Anna Freud 42
Karen Horney 43
Nancy Chodorow 43
Erik Erikson 44

Jean Piaget 46
Lev Vygotsky 47
Robert Siegler 48
B. F. Skinner 50
Albert Bandura 50
Urie Bronfenbrenner 51

RESOURCES FOR IMPROVING THE LIVES OF ADOLESCENTS

Identity: Youth and Crisis

(1968) by Erik H. Erikson
New York: W. W. Norton

Erik Erikson is one of the leading theorists in the field of life-span development. In *Identity: Youth and Crisis,* he outlines his eight stages of life-span development and provides numerous examples from his clinical practice to illustrate the stages. Special attention is given to the fifth stage in Erikson's theory, identity versus identity confusion.

Observational Strategies of Child Study

(1980) by D. M. Irwin and M. M. Bushnell
Fort Worth, TX: Harcourt Brace

Being a good observer can help you help children and adolescents reach their full potential. Observational skills can be learned. This practical book gives you a rich set of observational strategies that will make you a more sensitive observer of adolescent behavior.

Youth Policy
Youth Policy Institute

Cardinal Station
Washington, DC 20064
202–755–8078

A monthly publication issued by a cooperative venture of national organizations, foundations, and academic institutions interested in the future of adolescents. It provides information about federal and nonfederal programs for youth, and it includes a six-month calendar of events and conferences involving or concerned with youth.

TAKING IT TO THE NET   http://www.mhhe.com/santrocka9

1. Child neglect is a serious problem. It affects children and adolescents and has implications for how they will rear their own future children. *How might you use Bronfenbrenner's theory to organize information about the factors underlying child neglect in a paper or class presentation?*

2. Drinking and other drug use by college students is a serious concern on most college campuses. Suppose a representative of the Dean of Students office came into your classroom and distributed a survey of drinking and drug use, asking you to complete it anonymously. *Are any of your rights as a human subject being violated?*

3. A requirement for your methods course is to design and carry out an original research project. Among the many decisions you must make is what type of data you will collect. You decide to research adapting to college life. Your instructor asks if you will use an interview or a survey. *Which will you use, what is the distinction between an interview and a survey, and what are the benefits and difficulties of each?*

Connect to *http://www.mhhe.com/santrocka9* to research the answers and complete these exercises. In some cases, you'll also find further instructions on this site.

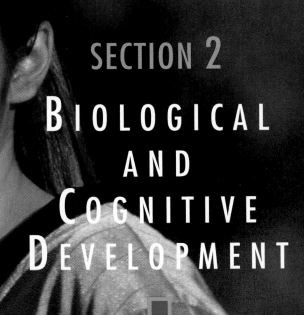

SECTION 2

BIOLOGICAL AND COGNITIVE DEVELOPMENT

◼

I think that what is happening to me is so wonderful and not only what can be seen on my body, but all that is taking place inside. I never discuss myself with anybody; that is why I have to talk to myself about them.

—Anne Frank
German Jewish Diarist, 20th Century

Adolescence, the transition from childhood to adulthood, involves biological, cognitive, and socioemotional development. These strands of development are interwoven in the adolescent's life. This section focuses on adolescents' biological and cognitive development and consists of two chapters: chapter 3, "Puberty, Health, and Biological Foundations," and chapter 4, "Cognitive Development."

PUBERTY, HEALTH, AND BIOLOGICAL FOUNDATIONS

In youth, we clothe ourselves with rainbows and go brave as the zodiac.
—Ralph Waldo Emerson
American Poet and Essayist, 19th Century

■ PUBERTY'S MYSTERIES AND CURIOSITIES

I am pretty confused. I wonder whether I am weird or normal. My body is starting to change, but I sure don't look like a lot of my friends. I still look like a kid for the most part. My best friend is only 13, but he looks like he is 16 or 17. I get nervous in the locker room during PE class because when I go to take a shower, I'm afraid somebody is going to make fun of me since I'm not as physically developed as some of the others.

—Robert, age 12

I don't like my breasts. They are too small, and they look funny. I'm afraid guys won't like me if they don't get bigger.

—Angie, age 13

I can't stand the way I look. I have zits all over my face. My hair is dull and stringy. It never stays in place. My nose is too big. My lips are too small. My legs are too short. I have four warts on my left hand, and people get grossed out by them. So do I. My body is a disaster!

—Ann, age 14

I'm short and I can't stand it. My father is 6 feet tall, and here I am only five foot four. I'm 14 already. I look like a kid, and I get teased a lot, especially by other guys. I'm always the last one picked for sides in basketball because I'm so short. Girls don't seem to be interested in me either because most of them are taller than I am.

—Jim, age 14

The comments of these four adolescents in the midst of pubertal change underscore the dramatic upheaval in our bodies following the calm, consistent growth of middle and late childhood. Young adolescents develop an acute concern about their bodies.

PUBERTY'S CHANGES ARE PERPLEXING to adolescents. Although these changes bring forth doubts, fears, and anxieties, most adolescents survive them quite well. By the time you have completed this chapter you should be able to reach these learning goals:

1 Understand pubertal change

2 Know about developmental changes in the brain

3 Evaluate adolescent health

4 Explain heredity and environment

PUBERTY

- Determinants of Puberty
- Growth Spurt
- Sexual Maturation
- Pubertal Timing and Health Care
- Psychological Dimensions
- Secular Trends In Puberty

puberty
A period of rapid physical maturation involving hormonal and bodily changes that take place primarily in early adolescence.

PUBERTY

Puberty involves a number of complex factors. We will begin our exploration of puberty by focusing on its determinants.

Determinants of Puberty

Puberty can be distinguished from adolescence. For virtually everyone, puberty has ended long before adolescence is exited. Puberty is often thought of as the most important marker for the beginning of adolescence. **Puberty** *is a period of rapid physical maturation involving hormonal and bodily changes that take place primarily in early adolescence.*

Among the most important factors involved in puberty are *heredity;* hormones; and weight, body fat, and leptin.

Heredity   Puberty is not an environmental accident. Programmed into the genes of every human being is a timing for the emergency of puberty (Adair, 2001). Puberty does not take place at 2 or 3 years of age and it does not occur in the twenties. In the future, we are likely to see molecular genetic studies that identify specific genes which are linked to the onset and progression of puberty. Nonetheless, as you will see in our further discussion of puberty, within the boundaries of about 9 to 16 years of age, environmental factors can influence the onset and duration of puberty.

Hormones   Behind the first whisker in boys and the widening of hips in girls is a flood of hormones. Let's explore the nature of these hormonal changes.

Hormones *are powerful chemical substances secreted by the endocrine glands and carried through the body by the bloodstream.* Two classes of hormones have significantly different concentrations in males and females. **Androgens** *are the main class of male sex hormones.* **Estrogens** *are the main class of female hormones.* It is important to note that although these hormones function more strongly in one sex or the other that they are produced by both males and females.

Testosterone is an androgen that plays an important role in male pubertal development. Throughout puberty, increasing testosterone levels are associated with a number of physical changes in boys—development of external genitals, increase in height, and voice changes. *Estradiol* is an estrogen that plays an important role in female pubertal development. As estradiol level rises, breast development, uterine development, and skeletal changes occur. In one study, testosterone levels increased 18-fold in boys but only 2-fold in girls across puberty; estradiol levels increased 8-fold in girls but only 2-fold in boys across puberty (Nottelman & others, 1987).

The level of sex hormones is low in the early part of childhood. As we have just seen, during puberty, the level of sex hormones rises. Next, we will explore how the endocrine system functions to maintain a certain concentration of sex hormones.

The Endocrine System   The endocrine system's role in puberty involves the interaction of the hypothalamus, the pituitary gland, and the gonads (sex glands) (see figure 3.1). The *hypothalamus* is a structure in the higher portion of the brain that monitors eating, drinking, and sex. The *pituitary gland* is an important endocrine gland that controls growth and regulates other glands. The *gonads* are the sex glands—the testes in males, the ovaries in females.

hormones
Powerful chemicals secreted by the endocrine glands and carried through the body by the bloodstream.

androgens
The main class of male sex hormones.

estrogens
The main class of female sex hormones.

Biological Changes
http://www.mhhe.com/santrocka9

Pituitary gland: This master gland produces hormones that stimulate other glands. Also, it influences growth by producing growth hormones; it sends gonadotropins to the testes and ovaries and a thyroid-stimulating hormone to the thyroid gland. It sends a hormone to the adrenal gland as well.

Hypothalamus: It is a structure in the brain that interacts with the pituitary gland to monitor the bodily regulation of hormones.

Thyroid gland: It interacts with the pituitary gland to influence growth.

Adrenal gland: It interacts with the pituitary gland and likely plays a role in pubertal development, but less is known about its function than about sex glands. Recent research, however, suggests it may be involved in adolescent behavior, particularly for boys.

The gonads, or sex glands: These consist of the testes in males, ovaries in females. The sex glands are strongly involved in the appearance of secondary sex characteristics, such as facial hair in males and breast development in females. The general class of hormones called estrogens is dominant in females, while androgens are dominant in males. More specifically, testosterone in males and estradiol in females are key hormones in pubertal development.

FIGURE 3.1
The Major Endocrine Glands Involved in Pubertal Change

How does the endocrine system work? The pituitary gland sends a signal via go-nadotropins (hormones that stimulate the testes and ovaries) to the appropriate gland to manufacture the hormone. Then the pituitary gland, through interaction with the hypothalamus, detects when the optimal level of hormones is reached and responds by maintaining gonadotropin secretion.

Levels of sex hormones are regulated by two hormones secreted by the pituitary gland: *FSH* (follicle-stimulating hormone) and *LH* (luteinizing hormone). FSH stimulates follicle development in females and sperm production in males. LH regulates estrogen secretion and ovum development in females and testosterone production in males (Hyde & DeLamater, 2000). Also, a substance called *GnRh* (gonadotropin-releasing hormone) is secreted by the hypothalamus.

These hormones are regulated by a *negative feedback system*. What this means is that if the level of sex hormones rises too high, the hypothalamus and pituitary gland reduce stimulation to the gonads and thus decrease production of sex hormones. If the level of sex hormones goes too low, then production of the hormones increases.

Figure 3.2 shows how the feedback system works. In males, the pituitary gland's production of LH stimulates the testes to produce testosterone. When testosterone levels get too high, the hypothalamus decreases its production of GnRH and the pituitary's production of LH is then also decreased. When the level of testosterone falls, the hypothalamus produces GnRH and the cycle starts again. The negative feedback system works similarly in females, involving LH, GnRH, the ovaries, and estrogen.

The negative feedback system in the endocrine system works much like a thermostat-furnace system. If a room is cold, the thermostat signals the furnace to turn on. The action of the furnace warms the air in the room, which eventually becomes warm enough to signal the furnace to turn off. Subsequently, the room temperature gradually falls off and the thermostat once again signals the furnace to produce more warm air, repeating the cycle. This is called a *negative* feedback loop because a *rise* in temperature turns *off* the furnace, while a *decrease* in temperature turns *on* the furnace.

We indicated earlier that the level of sex hormones is low in the early part of childhood but increases as puberty proceeds. In the analogy of the sex hormone system to a thermostat, it is as if the thermostat had been set at 50°F earlier in childhood and now becomes set at 80°F in puberty. At this higher level, the gonads have to produce more sex hormones, and that is what happens during puberty.

Growth Hormone   Not only does the pituitary gland release gonadotropins that stimulate the testes and ovaries, but through interaction with the hypothalamus the pituitary gland also secretes hormones that either directly lead to growth and skeletal maturation or produce growth effects through interaction with the *thyroid gland,* located in the neck region (see figure 3.1).

Growth hormone initially is secreted at night during puberty and subsequently also is secreted during the day, although daytime levels are usually very low (Susman, Dorn, & Schiefelbein, in press). Other endocrine factors can influence growth, such as cortisol, which is secreted by the adrenal cortex. Testosterone and estrogen also facilitate growth during puberty.

Adrenarche and Gonadarche   Puberty has two phases that are linked with hormonal changes: adrenarche and gonadarche (Susman, Dorn, & Schiefelbein, in press). *Adrenarche* involves hormonal changes in the adrenal glands, which are located just above the kidneys. These changes occur surprisingly early, from about 6 to 9 years of age and before what we generally consider to be the beginning of puberty. Adrenal androgens are secreted by the adrenal glands during adrenarche and continuing on through puberty.

Gonadarche is what most people think of as puberty and it follows adrenarche by approximately two years (Archibald, Graber, & Brooks-Gunn, in press). Gonadarche involves sexual maturation and the development of reproductive maturity. Gonadarche begins at approximately 9 to 10 years of age in non-Latino White girls, and 8 to 9 years in African American girls in the United States (Grumach & Styne, 1992). Gonadarche

FIGURE 3.2
The Feedback System of Sex Hormones

begins at about 10 to 11 years of age in boys. The culmination of gonadarche in girls is **menarche,** *a girl's first menstrual period,* and in boys **spermarche,** *a boy's first ejaculation of semen.*

Weight, Body Fat, and Leptin

One view is that critical body mass must be attained before puberty, especially *menarche* is attained. Some scientists even have proposed that a body weight of 106 ±3 pounds can trigger menarche and the end of the pubertal growth spurt (Friesch, 1984). However, this specific weight target is not well documented (Susman, 2001).

Other scientists have hypothesized that the onset of menarche is influenced by the percentage of body fat in total body weight with a minimum of 17 percent of body weight comprised of body fat required for menarche to occur. As with body weight, this specific percentage has not been consistently verified.

However, both anorexic adolescents whose weight drops dramatically and females who participate in certain sports (such as gymnastics and swimming) may become amenorrheic (having an absence or suppression of menstrual discharge). Undernutrition also may delay puberty in boys (Susman, Dorn, and Schiefelbein, in press).

The hormone *leptin* has been proposed as a possible signal of the beginning and progression of puberty (Mantzoros, 2000; Mantzoros, Flier, & Rogol, 1997). Leptin may be one of the messengers which signals the adequacy of fat stores for reproduction and

menarche
A girl's first menstrual period.

spermarche
A boy's first ejaculation of semen.

What are some of the differences in the ways girls and boys experience pubertal growth?

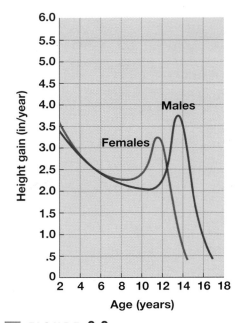

FIGURE 3.3
Pubertal Growth Spurt

On the average, the peak of the growth spurt that characterizes pubertal change occurs 2 years earlier for girls (11½) than for boys (13½).

maintenance of pregnancy at puberty (Kiess & others, 1999). Leptin concentrations are higher in girls than in boys. They also are related to the amount of fat in girls and androgen concentrations in boys (Roemmrich & others, 1999). Changes in leptin have not yet been studied in relation to adolescent behavior.

In sum, the determinants of puberty include heredity and hormones. Next, we will turn our attention to the growth spurt that characterizes puberty.

Growth Spurt

Growth slows throughout childhood, and puberty ushers in the most rapid increases in growth since infancy. As indicated in figure 3.3, the growth spurt associated with puberty occurs approximately two years earlier for girls than for boys. The mean beginning of the growth spurt is 9 years of age for girls and 11 years of age for boys. The peak of pubertal change occurs at 11.5 years for girls and 13.5 years for boys. During their growth spurt, girls increase in height about 3½ inches per year, boys about 4 inches.

Boys and girls who are shorter or taller than their peers before adolescence are likely to remain so during adolescence. In our society, there is a stigma attached to being a short boy. At the beginning of adolescence, girls tend to be as tall as or taller than boys of their age, but by the end of the middle school years most boys have caught up with, or in many cases even surpassed, girls in height. And even though height in elementary school is a good predictor of height later in adolescence, as much as 30 percent of the height of individuals in late adolescence is unexplained by height in the elementary school years.

The rate at which adolescents gain weight follows approximately the same developmental timetable as the rate at which they gain height. Marked weight gains coincide with the onset of puberty. Fifty percent of adult body weight is gained during adolescence (Rogol, Raemmich, & Clark, 1998). At the peak of weight gain during puberty, girls gain an average of 18 pounds in one year at about 12 years of age (approximately six months after their peak height increase). Boys' peak weight gain per year (20 pounds in one year) occurs at about the same time as their peak increase in height (about 13 to 14 years of age). During early adolescence, girls tend to outweigh boys, but, just as with height, by about 14 years of age, boys begin to surpass girls in weight.

In addition to increases in height and weight, changes in hip and shoulder width occur. Adolescent girls experience a spurt in hip width while boys undergo an increase in shoulder width. Increased hip width is linked with an increase in estrogen in girls. Increased shoulder width in boys is associated with an increase in testosterone.

The later growth spurt of boys also produces greater leg length in boys than is experienced by girls. Also, in many cases, the facial structure of boys becomes more angular during puberty while that of girls becomes more round and soft.

Sexual Maturation

Think back to the onset of your puberty. Of the striking changes that were taking place in your body, what was the first change that occurred? Researchers have found that male pubertal characteristics develop in this order: increase in penis and testicle size, appearance of straight pubic hair, minor voice change, first ejaculation (spermarche—this usually occurs through masturbation or a wet dream), appearance of kinky pubic hair, onset of maximum growth, growth of hair in armpits, more detectable voice changes, and growth of facial hair. Three of the most noticeable areas of sexual maturation in boys are penis elongation, testes development, and growth of facial hair. The normal range and average age of development for these sexual characteristics, along with height spurt, are shown in figure 3.4 on page 81. Figure 3.5 on page 82 shows the typical course of male sexual development during puberty.

What is the order of appearance of physical changes in females? First, either the breasts enlarge or pubic hair appears. Later, hair appears in the armpits. As these changes occur, the female grows in height, and her hips become wider than her shoulders. Her first menstruation (menarche) occurs rather late in the pubertal cycle.

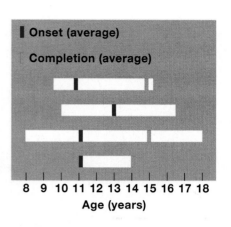

MALES

Height spurt
Penile growth
Testicular development
Growth of pubic hair

Age (years)

FEMALES

Height spurt
Menarche
Breast growth
Growth of pubic hair

Age (years)

■ **FIGURE 3.4**
Normal Range and Average Development of Sexual Characteristics in Males and Females

Initially, her menstrual cycles may be highly irregular. For the first several years, she might not ovulate every menstrual cycle. In some instances, she does not become fertile until two years after her period begins. No voice changes comparable to those in pubertal males occur for pubertal females. By the end of puberty, the female's breasts have become more fully rounded. Two of the most noticeable aspects of female pubertal change are pubic hair and breast development. Figure 3.4 shows the normal range and average development of these sexual characteristics and also provides information about menarche and height gain. Figure 3.5 on page 82 shows the typical course of female sexual development during puberty.

It is important to understand that there may be wide individual variations in the onset and progression of puberty. The pubertal sequence may begin as early as 10 years of age or as late as 13½ for boys. It may end as early as 13 years or as late as 17. The normal range is wide enough that, given two boys of the same chronological age, one might complete the pubertal sequence before the other one has begun it. For girls, the age range of menarche is even wider. It is considered within a normal range when it occurs between 9 and 15 years of age.

Secular Trends in Puberty

Imagine a toddler displaying all the features of puberty—a 3-year-old girl with fully developed breasts or a boy just slightly older with a deep male voice. That is what we would see by the year 2250 if the age at which puberty arrives would have been getting younger at the rate at which it was occurring for much of the twentieth century.

The term *secular trends* refers to patterns over time, especially across generations. For example, in Norway, menarche now occurs at just over 13 years of age compared to 17 years of age in the 1840s (de Muinich Keizer, 2001; Petersen, 1979). In the United States—where children physically mature up to a year earlier than in European countries—the average age of menarche declined an average of two to four months per decade for much of the twentieth century (see figure 3.6 on p. 83). In the United States, menarche occurred at an average of 15 years of age compared to about 12½ years today.

The earlier onset of puberty in the twentieth century was likely due to improved health and nutrition. One speculation about the earlier onset of puberty involves the increase of girlhood obesity. For example, in one recent study, the more sexually developed that girls were, the greater was their body mass (Kaplowitz & others, 2001). We will have more to say about obesity in adolescence.

■ **THROUGH THE EYES OF PSYCHOLOGISTS**

Christy Miller Buchanan
Wake Forest University

"A challenging aspect of measuring puberty is that it is not an event but a process involving many dimensions."

MALE SEXUAL DEVELOPMENT

    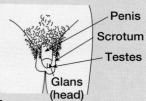

Penis
Scrotum
Testes
Glans
(head)

1.
No pubic hair. The testes, scrotum, and penis are about the same size and shape as those of a child.

2.
A little soft, long, lightly colored hair, mostly at the base of the penis. This hair may be straight or a little curly. The testes and scrotum have enlarged, and the skin of the scrotum has changed. The scrotum, the sack holding the testes, has lowered a bit. The penis has grown only a little.

3.
The hair is darker coarser, and more curled. It has spread to thinly cover a somewhat larger area. The penis has grown mainly in length. The testes and scrotum have grown and dropped lower than in stage 2.

4.
The hair is now as dark, curly, and coarse as that of an adult male. However, the area that the hair covers is not as large as that of an adult male; it has not spread to the thighs. The penis has grown even larger and wider. The glans (the head of the penis) is bigger. The scrotum is darker and bigger because the testes have gotten bigger.

5.
The hair has spread to the thighs and is now like that of an adult male. The penis, scrotum, and testes are the size and shape of those of an adult male.

FEMALE SEXUAL DEVELOPMENT

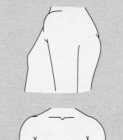  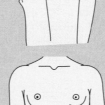 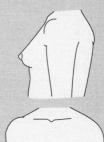 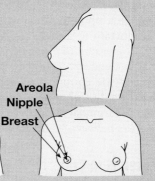

Areola
Nipple
Breast

1.
The nipple is raised just a little. The rest of the breast is still flat.

2.
The breast bud stage. The nipple is raised more than in stage 1. The breast is a small mound, and the areola is larger than in stage 1.

3.
The areola and the breast are both larger than in stage 2. The areola does not stick out from the breast.

4.
The areola and the nipple make up a mound that sticks up above the shape of the breast. (Note: This may not happen at all for some girls; some develop from stage 3 to stage 5, with no stage 4.)

5.
The mature adult stage. The breasts are fully developed. Only the nipple sticks out. The areola has moved back to the general shape of the breast.

◼ FIGURE 3.5
The Five Pubertal Stages of Male and Female Sexual Development

Keep in mind that we are unlikely to see pubescent toddlers in the future because there are some genetic limits on just how early puberty can come. So far we have been concerned mainly with the physical dimensions of puberty. However, as we see next, the psychological dimensions of puberty also involve some important changes.

Psychological Dimensions

A host of psychological changes accompany an adolescent's pubertal development (Sarigiani & Petersen, 2000). Try to remember when you were beginning puberty. Not only did you probably think of yourself differently, but your parents and peers also probably began acting differently toward you. Maybe you were proud of your changing body, even though you were perplexed about what was happening. Perhaps your parents no longer perceived you as someone they could sit in bed with to watch television or as someone who should be kissed goodnight.

There has been far less research on the psychosocial aspects of male pubertal transitions than on those of females, possibly because of the difficulty in defining when the male transitions occur. Wet dreams are one such marker, yet there has been little research on this topic (Susman & others, 1995).

Body Image   One psychological aspect of physical change in puberty is certain: Adolescents are preoccupied with their bodies and develop individual images of what their bodies are like. Perhaps you looked in the mirror on a daily and sometimes even hourly basis to see if you could detect anything different about your changing body. Preoccupation with one's body image is strong throughout adolescence, but it is especially acute during puberty, a time when adolescents are more dissatisfied with their bodies than in late adolescence (Wright, 1989).

There are gender differences in adolescents' perceptions of their bodies. In general, girls are less happy with their bodies and have more negative body images, compared to boys, throughout puberty (Brooks-Gunn & Paikoff, 1993; Henderson & Zivian, 1995). Also, as pubertal change proceeds, girls often become more dissatisfied with their bodies, probably because their body fat increases, while boys become more satisfied as they move through puberty, probably because their muscle mass increases (Seiffge-Krenke, 1998).

A current major concern about adolescent girls is their motivation to be very thin and that many adolescent girls believe they can't be too thin. This motivation has especially been fueled by the media's portrait of extremely thin as beautiful. We will have much more to say about this topic in chapter 14, "Adolescent Problems," where we will discuss eating disorders.

Hormones and Behavior   Are there links between concentrations of hormones and adolescent behavior? Hormonal factors are thought to account for at least part of the increase in negative and variable emotions that characterize adolescents (Archibald, Graber, & Brooks-Gunn, in press; Dorn, Williamson, & Ryan, 2002). Researchers have found that higher levels of androgens are associated with violence and acting-out problems in boys (van Goozen & others, 1998; Susman & others, 1987). Few studies have focused on estrogens; however, there is some indication that increased levels of estrogens are linked with depression in adolescent girls (Angold & others, 1999).

It is important to understand that hormonal factors alone are not responsible for adolescent behavior (Ge & Brody, 2002; Susman, Schiefelbein, & Heaton, 2002). For example, in one study, social factors accounted for two to four times as much variance as hormonal factors in young adolescent girls' depression and anger (Brooks-Gunn &

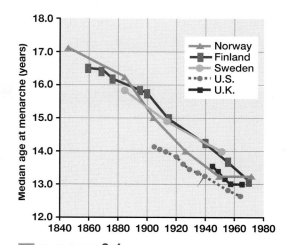

■ FIGURE 3.6

Median Ages at Menarche in Selected Northern European Countries and the United States from 1845 to 1969

Notice the steep decline in the age at which girls experienced menarche in five different countries. Recently the age at which girls experience menarche has been leveling off.

Adolescents show a strong preoccupation with their changing bodies and develop images of what their bodies are like. *Why might adolescent males have more positive body images than adolescent females?*

Warren, 1989). Stress, eating patterns, sexual activity, and depression can activate or suppress various aspects of the hormone system.

Menarche and the Menstrual Cycle   The onset of puberty and menarche has often been described as a "main event" in most historical accounts of adolescence (Erikson, 1968; Freud, 1917/1958; Hall, 1904). Basically, these views suggest that pubertal changes and events such as menarche produce a different body that requires considerable change in self-conception, possibly resulting in an identity crisis. Only recently has there been empirical research directed at understanding the female adolescent's adaptation to menarche and the menstrual cycle (Brooks-Gunn, Graber, & Paikoff, 1994).

In one study of 639 girls, a wide range of reactions to menarche appeared (Brooks-Gunn & Ruble, 1982). However, most of the reactions were quite mild, as girls described their first period as a little upsetting, a little surprising, or a little exciting and positive. In this study, 120 of the fifth- and sixth-grade girls were telephoned to obtain more personal, detailed information about their experience with menarche. The most frequent theme of the girls' responses was positive—namely, that menarche was an index of their maturity. Other positive reports indicated that the girls could now have children, were experiencing something that made them more like adult women, and now were more like their friends. The most frequent negative aspects of menarche reported by the girls were its hassle (having to carry supplies around) and its messiness. A minority of the girls also indicated that menarche involved physical discomfort, produced behavioral limitations, and created emotional changes.

Questions also were asked about the extent to which the girls communicated with others about the appearance of menarche, the extent to which the girls were prepared for menarche, and how the experience was related to early/late maturation. Virtually all of the girls told their mothers immediately, but most of the girls did not tell anyone else about menarche, with only one in five informing a friend. However, after two or three periods had occurred, most girls had talked with girlfriends about menstruation. Girls not prepared for menarche indicated more negative feelings about menstruation than those who were more prepared for its onset. Girls who matured early had more negative reactions than average- or late-maturing girls. In summary, menarche initially may be disruptive, especially for unprepared and early-maturing girls, but it typically does not reach the tumultuous, conflicting proportions described by some early theoreticians.

For many girls, menarche occurs on time, but for others it occurs early or late. Next, we examine the effects of early and late maturation on both boys and girls.

Early and Late Maturation   Some of you entered puberty early, others late, and yet others on time. When adolescents mature earlier or later than their peers, might they perceive themselves differently? In the Berkeley Longitudinal Study some years ago, early-maturing boys perceived themselves more positively and had more successful peer relations than did their late-maturing counterparts (Jones, 1965). The findings for early-maturing girls were similar but not as strong as for boys. When the late-maturing boys were studied in their thirties, however, they had developed a stronger sense of identity than had the early-maturing boys (Peskin, 1967). Late-maturing boys may have had more time to explore a wide variety of options. They may have focused on career development and achievement that would serve them better in life than their early-maturing counterparts' emphasis on physical status.

More-recent research, though, confirms that, at least during adolescence, it is advantageous to be an early-maturing rather than a late-maturing boy (Petersen, 1987). Roberta Simmons and Dale Blyth (1987) studied more than 450 individuals for five years, beginning in the sixth grade

THROUGH THE EYES OF ADOLESCENTS

Attractive Blond Females and Tall Muscular Males

When columnist Bob Greene (1988) called Connections in Chicago, a chatline for teenagers, to find out what young adolescents were saying to each other, the first things the boys and girls asked for—after first names—were physical descriptions. The idealism of the callers was apparent. Most of the girls described themselves as having long blond hair, being 5 feet 5 inches tall, and weighing 110 pounds. Most of the boys said that they had brown hair, lifted weights, were 6 feet tall, and weighed 170 pounds.

and continuing through the tenth grade, in Milwaukee, Wisconsin. Students were individually interviewed, and achievement test scores and grade point averages were obtained. The presence or absence of menstruation and the relative onset of menses were used to classify girls as early, middle, or late maturers. The peak of growth in height was used to classify boys according to these categories.

In the Milwaukee study, more mixed and complex findings emerged for girls (Simmons & Blyth, 1987). Early-maturing girls had more problems in school, were more independent, and were more popular with boys than late-maturing girls were. The time at which maturation was assessed also was a factor. In the sixth grade, early-maturing girls were more satisfied with their body image than late-maturing girls were, but by the tenth grade, late-maturing girls were more satisfied (see figure 3.7). Why? Because by late adolescence, early-maturing girls are shorter and stockier, while late-maturing girls are taller and thinner. The late-maturing girls in late adolescence have body images that more closely approximate the current American ideal of feminine beauty—tall and thin.

In the last decade an increasing number of researchers have found that early maturation increases girls' vulnerability to a number of problems (Brooks-Gunn & Paikoff, 1993; Sarigiani & Petersen, 2000; Stattin & Magnusson, 1990). Early-maturing girls are more likely to smoke, drink, be depressed, have an eating disorder, request earlier independence from their parents, and have older friends; and their bodies likely elicit responses from males that lead to earlier dating and earlier sexual experiences. In one study, early-maturing girls had lower educational and occupational attainment in adulthood (Stattin & Magnusson, 1990). Apparently as a result of their social and cognitive immaturity, combined with early physical development, early-maturing girls are easily lured into problem behaviors, not recognizing the possible long-term effects on their development (Petersen, 1993).

Complexity of On-Time and Off-Time Pubertal Events in Development   Being on-time or off-time in terms of pubertal events is a complex affair (Scholte & Dubas, 2002). For example, the dimensions can involve not just biological status and pubertal age, but also chronological age, grade in school, cognitive functioning, and social maturity (Petersen, 1987). Adolescents can be at risk when the demands of a particular social context do not match the adolescents' physical and behavioral characteristics (Lerner, 1993). Dancers whose pubertal status develops on time are one example. In general peer comparisons, on-time dancers should not show adjustment problems. However, they do not have the ideal characteristics for being a dancer, which generally are those associated with late maturity—a thin, lithe body build. The dancers, then, are on time in terms of pubertal development for their peer group in general, but there is an asynchrony to their development in terms of their more focused peer group—dancers.

Are Puberty's Effects Exaggerated?   Some researchers have begun to question whether puberty's effects are as strong as once believed (Montemayor, Adams, & Gulotta, 1990). Have the effects of puberty been exaggerated? Puberty affects some adolescents more strongly than others, and some behaviors more strongly than others. Body image, dating interest, and sexual behavior are quite clearly affected by pubertal change. In one study, early-maturing boys and girls reported more sexual activity and delinquency than did late maturers (Flannery, Rowe, & Gulley, 1993). The recent questioning of puberty's effects, however, suggests that, if we look at overall development and adjustment in the human life span, puberty and its variations have less-dramatic effects for most individuals than is commonly thought. For some young adolescents, the transition through puberty is stormy, but for most it is not. Each period of the human life span has its stresses. Puberty is no different. It imposes new challenges resulting from emerging developmental changes, but the vast majority of adolescents weather these stresses effectively. In addition, there are not only biological

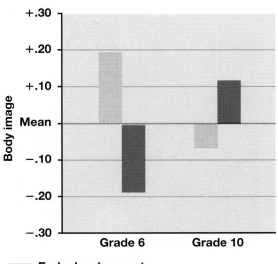

FIGURE 3.7
Early- and Late-Maturing Adolescent Girls' Perceptions of Body Image in Early and Late Adolescence

CAREERS IN ADOLESCENT DEVELOPMENT

Anne Petersen
Researcher and Administrator

Anne Petersen has had a distinguished career as a researcher and administrator with a main focus on adolescent development. Anne obtained three degrees (B.A., M.A., and Ph.D.) from the University of Chicago in math and statistics. Her first job after she obtained her Ph.D. was as a research associate/professor involving statistical consultation, and it was on this job that she was introduced to the field of adolescent development, which became the focus of her subsequent work.

Anne moved from the University of Chicago to Pennsylvania State University, where she became a leading researcher in adolescent development. Her research included a focus on puberty and gender. Anne also has held numerous administrative positions. In the mid-1990s, Anne became Deputy Director of the National Science Foundation and since 1996 has been Senior Vice-President for programs at the W. K. Kellogg Foundation.

Anne says that what inspired her to enter the field of adolescent development and take her current position at the Kellogg Foundation was her desire to make a difference for people, especially youth. In her position at Kellogg, Anne is responsible for all programming and services provided by the foundation for adolescents. Her goal is to make a difference for youth in this country and around the world. She believes that too often adolescents have been neglected.

Anne Petersen, interacting with adolescents.

influences on adolescent development, but also cognitive and social or environmental influences (Sarigiani & Petersen, 2000). As with all periods of human development, these processes work in concert to produce who we are in adolescence. Singling out biological changes as the dominating change in adolescence may not be a wise strategy.

Although extremely early and late maturation may be risk factors in development, we have seen that the overall effects of early or late maturation are often not great. Not all early maturers will date, smoke, and drink, and not all late maturers will have difficulty in peer relations. In some instances, the effects of school grade are stronger than maturational timing effects are (Petersen & Crockett, 1985). Because the adolescent's social world is organized by grade rather than by pubertal development, this finding is not surprising. However, this does not mean that maturation has no influence on development. Rather, we need to evaluate puberty's effects within the larger framework of interacting biological, cognitive, and socioemotional contexts (Brooks-Gunn, 1992; Sarigiani & Petersen, 2000).

Pubertal Timing and Health Care

What can be done to identify off-time maturers who are at risk for health problems? Many adolescents whose development is extremely early or extremely late are likely to come to the attention of a physician—such as a boy who has not had a spurt in height by the age of 16 or a girl who has not menstruated by the age of 15. Girls and boys who are early or late maturers but are well within the normal range are less likely to be taken to a physician because of their maturational status. Nonetheless, these boys and girls may have fears and doubts about being normal that they do not raise unless a physician, counselor, or other health-care provider takes the initiative. A brief discussion outlining the sequence and timing of events and the large individual variations in them may be all that is required to reassure many adolescents who are maturing very early or very late.

Health-care providers may want to discuss the adolescent's off-time development with the adolescent's parents as well. Information about the peer pressures of off-time development can be beneficial. Especially helpful to early-maturing girls is a discussion of peer pressures to date and to engage in adultlike behavior at an early age. The transition to middle school, junior high school, or high school may be more stressful for girls and boys who are in the midst of puberty than for those who are not (Brooks-Gunn, 1988).

If pubertal development is extremely late, a physician may recommend hormonal treatment. In one study of extended pubertal delay in boys, hormonal treatment worked to increase the height, dating interest, and peer relations in several boys but resulted in little or no improvement in other boys (Lewis, Money, & Bobrow, 1977).

In sum, most early- and late-maturing individuals weather puberty's challenges and stresses competently. For those who do not, discussions with sensitive and knowledgeable health-care providers and parents can improve the off-time maturing adolescent's coping abilities.

Since the last review, we have discussed many aspects of puberty. This review should help you to reach your learning goals related to this topic.

☐ FOR YOUR REVIEW

Learning Goal 1
Understand pubertal change

• Puberty is a period of rapid physical maturation involving hormonal and bodily changes that take place primarily in early adolescence. Puberty's determinants include heredity, hormones, and possibly weight, percent of body fat, and leptin. Two classes of hormones that are involved in pubertal change and have significantly different concentrations in males and females are androgens and estrogens. The endocrine system's role in puberty involves the interaction of the hypothalamus, pituitary gland, and gonads. FSH and LH, which are secreted by the pituitary gland, are important aspects of this system. So is GnRH produced by the hypothalamus. A negative feedback system characterizes the way the sex hormone system works. Growth hormone also contributes to pubertal change. Puberty has two phases: adrenarche and gonadarche. The culmination of gonadarche in boys is spermarche and in girls is menarche.

• The initial onset of pubertal growth occurs on the average at 9 years for girls and 11 years for boys. The peak of pubertal changes for girls is at 11.5 years while for boys it is at 13.5 years. Girls grow an average of 3½ inches per year during puberty, boys 4 inches. Sexual maturation is a key feature of pubertal change. Individual variation in puberty is extensive and within a wide range is considered to be normal. Secular trends in puberty took place in the twentieth century with puberty coming earlier.

• Adolescents show heightened interest in their bodies and body images. Younger adolescents are more preoccupied with these images than older adolescents are. Adolescent girls often have more negative body images than adolescent boys do. Researchers have found connections between pubertal change and behavior but environmental influences need to be taken into account. Menarche and the menstrual cycle produce a wide range of reactions in girls. Early maturation often favors boys, at least during early adolescence, but as adults, late-maturing boys have a more positive identity than early-maturing boys. Early-maturing girls are at risk for a number of developmental problems. Being on-time or off-time in pubertal development is complex. Some scholars have expressed doubt that puberty's effects on development are as strong as once envisioned. Most early- and late-maturing adolescents weather the challenges of puberty competently. For those who do not, discussions with knowledgeable health-care providers and parents can improve the coping abilities of off-time adolescents.

In our discussion of hormonal changes in puberty, we indicated that the hypothalamus and pituitary gland play important roles in regulating the level of sex hormones. Next, we will focus on further changes in the brain during adolescence.

THE BRAIN

Until recently, little research had been conducted on developmental changes in the brain during adolescence. While research in this area is still in its infancy, an increasing number of research studies are being carried out. Scientists now believe that the adolescent's brain is different than the child's brain and that during adolescence the brain is still growing (Crews, 2001).

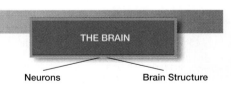

Neurons

Neurons, *or nerve cells, are the nervous system's basic units.* The three basic parts of the neuron are the cell body, the dendrites, and the axon (see figure 3.8 on p. 88). The

neurons
Nerve cells, which are the nervous system's basic units.

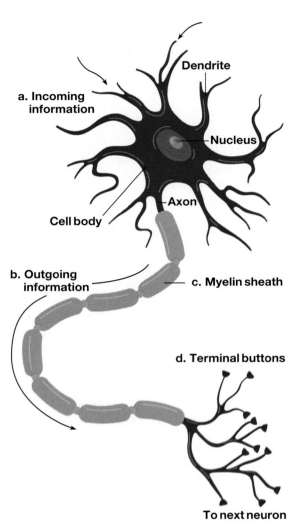

■ FIGURE 3.8
The Neuron

(*a*) The dendrites of the cell body receive information from other neurons, muscles, or glands through the axon. (*b*) Axons transmit information away from the cell body. (*c*) A myelin sheath covers most axons and speeds information transmission. (*d*) As the axon ends, it branches out into terminal buttons.

Neural Processes
Neuroimaging
Internet Neuroscience Resources
http://www.mhhe.com/santrocka9

dendrite is the receiving part of the neuron while the *axon* carries information away from the cell body to other cells. A *myelin sheath,* which is a layer of fat cells, encases most axons. The myelin sheath helps to insulate the axon and speeds up the transmission of the nerve impulse.

How do neurons change in adolescence? Researchers have found that cell bodies and dendrites do not change much during adolescence but that axons continue to develop through adolescence (Pfefferbaum & others, 1994; Rajapakse & others, 1996). The growth of axons is likely due to increased myelination (Giedd, 1998). Researchers have found that dendritic growth can continue even in older adults (Coleman, 1986), so further research may find more growth in dendrites during adolescence than these early studies are discovering.

In addition to dendritic spreading and the encasement of axons through myelination, another important aspect of the brain's development at the cellular level is the dramatic increase in connections between neurons (a process that is called synaptogenesis) (Ramey & Ramey, 2000). *Synapses* are gaps between neurons and are where connections between axons and dendrites take place.

Researchers have discovered an interesting aspect of synaptic connections. Nearly twice as many of these connections are made than will ever be used (Huttenlocher & others, 1991; Huttenlocher & Dabholkar, 1997). The connections that are used become strengthened and will survive, while the unused ones will be replaced by other pathways or disappear. That is, these connections will be "pruned" in the language of neuroscience. Figure 3.9 on page 89 vividly illustrates the dramatic growth and later pruning of synapses in the visual, auditory, and prefrontal cortex areas of the brain (Huttenlacher & Dabholkar, 1997). These are areas that are critical for higher-order cognitive functioning such as learning, memory, and reasoning.

As shown in figure 3.9, the time course for synaptic "blooming and pruning" varies considerably by brain region in humans. For example, the peak of synaptic overproduction in the visual cortex takes place at about the fourth postnatal month, following by a gradual retraction until the middle to end of the preschool years (Huttenlocher & Dabholkar, 1997). In areas of the brain involved in hearing and language, a similar although somewhat later course is detected. However, in the prefrontal cortex (the area of the brain where higher-level thinking and self-regulation occur), the peak of overproduction takes place at about 1 year of age and it is not until middle to late adolescence that the adult density of synapses is achieved.

What determines the timing and course of synaptic overproduction and subsequent retraction? Both heredity and experience are thought to be influential (Greenough, 2000; Greenough & Black, 1992).

Brain Structure

Neurons do not simply float in the brain. Connected in precise ways, they compose the various structures in the brain. Among structures of the brain that have recently been the focus of research in adolescent development are the brain's four lobes in the highest part of the brain—the cerebral cortex (see figure 3.10 on p. 89). The *occipital lobe* is involved in visual functioning. The *temporal lobe* is involved in hearing. The *parietal lobe* is involved in bodily sensations. The *frontal lobe* is involved in the control of voluntary muscles, personality, and intelligence. Another structure of the brain that has been studied during adolescent development is the *amygdala,* which is involved in emotion.

One of the main reasons that scientists only recently have begun to study brain development in adolescence is the lack of technology to do so. However, the creation of

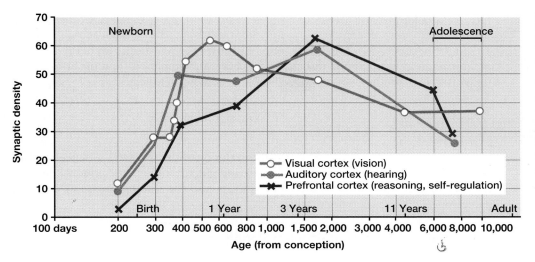

Synaptic Density in the Human Brain from Infancy to Adulthood

The graph shows the dramatic increase and then pruning in synaptic density for three regions of the brain: visual cortex, auditory cortex, and prefrontal cortex. Synaptic density is believed to be an important indication of the extent of connectivity between neurons.

sophisticated brain scanning devices, such as magnetic resonance imaging (MRI), is allowing better detection of brain changes during adolescence (Blumenthal & others, 1999). Magnetic resonance imaging consists of creating a magnetic field around a person's body and using radio waves to construct images of the brain's tissues and biochemical activities.

Using MRIs, scientists recently have discovered that children's and adolescents' brains undergo significant anatomical changes between 3 and 15 years of age (Thompson & others, 2000). By repeatedly obtaining brain scans of the same individuals for up to four years, it was discovered that rapid, distinct spurts of growth in the brain occur. The amount of brain material in some areas can nearly double within as little as one year of time, followed by a drastic loss of tissue as unneeded cells are purged and the brain continues to reorganize itself. In this research, the overall size of the brain did not change from 3 to 15 years of age. However, what did change dramatically were local patterns within the brain.

In this research, the most rapid growth from 3 to 6 years of age occurred in the frontal lobe areas that involve planning and organizing new actions, and in maintaining attention to tasks. From age 6 through puberty, the most growth took place in the temporal and parietal lobes, especially in the area of those lobes that function in language and spatial relations.

In one study, researchers used MRIs to discover if the brain activity of adolescents (10 to 18 years of age) differed from that of adults (20 to 40 years of age) during the processing of emotional information (Baird & others, 1999). In this study, the participants were asked to view pictures of faces displaying fearful expressions while undergoing an MRI. When adolescents (especially younger ones) processed emotional information, brain activity in the amygdala was more pronounced than in the frontal lobe but the reverse occurred in adults. As we indicated earlier, the amygdala is involved in emotion, while the frontal lobes are involved in higher level reasoning and thinking. The researchers interpreted these findings in this way: adolescents may respond with "gut" reactions to emotional stimuli while adults are more likely to respond in rational, reasoned ways. They also concluded that these changes are linked with growth in the frontal lobe of the brain from adolescence to adulthood. However, more research is needed to clarify these findings on

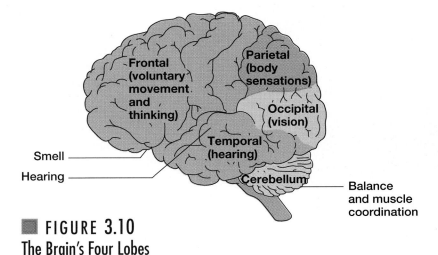

The Brain's Four Lobes

Shown here are the locations of the brain's four lobes: frontal, occipital, temporal, and parietal.

possible developmental changes in brain activity (Dahl, 2001; DeBellis & others, 2001; Spear, 2000).

In the next decade, we are likely to see far more research studies on brain development in adolescence. So far in this chapter we have studied puberty and the brain. Next, we will explore another very important topic in adolescence: health.

ADOLESCENT HEALTH

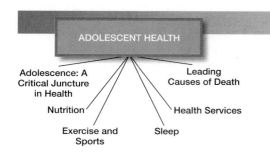

ADOLESCENT HEALTH

Adolescence: A Critical Juncture in Health

Nutrition

Exercise and Sports

Leading Causes of Death

Health Services

Sleep

We will begin our discussion of adolescent health by evaluating why adolescence may be a critical juncture in the health of many individuals. Other topics we will examine include nutrition, exercise and sports, sleep, and the leading causes of death in adolescence.

Adolescence: A Critical Juncture in Health

Adolescence is a critical juncture in the adoption of behaviors relevant to health (Maggs, Schulenberg, & Hurrelmann, 1997; Roth & Brooks-Gunn, 2000). Many of the factors linked to poor health habits and early death in the adult years begin during adolescence.

The early formation of healthy behavioral patterns, such as eating foods low in fat and cholesterol and engaging in regular exercise, not only has immediate health benefits but contributes to the delay or prevention of major causes of premature disability and mortality in adulthood—heart disease, stroke, diabetes, and cancer (Jessor, Turbin, & Costa, 1998, in press).

Even though America has become a health-conscious nation, many adults and adolescents still smoke, have poor nutritional habits, and spend too much of their lives as couch potatoes.

Many adolescents often reach a level of health, strength, and energy that they will never match during the remainder of their lives. They also have a sense of uniqueness and invulnerability that leads them to think that poor health will never enter their lives, or that if it does, they will quickly recoup from it. Given this combination of physical and cognitive factors, it is not surprising that many adolescents have poor health habits.

Many health experts believe that improving adolescent health involves far more than trips to a doctor's office when sick. The health experts increasingly recognize that whether adolescents will develop a health problem or be healthy is primarily based on their behavior. The goals are to (1) reduce adolescents' *health-compromising behaviors,* such as drug abuse, violence, unprotected sexual intercourse, and dangerous driving, and (2) increase *health-enhancing behaviors,* such as eating nutritiously, exercising, wearing seat belts, and getting adequate sleep.

Nutrition

The recommended range of energy intake for adolescents takes into account the different needs of adolescents, their growth rate, and their level of exercise. Males have higher energy needs than females. Older adolescent girls also have slightly lower energy needs than younger adolescent girls. Some adolescents' bodies burn energy faster than others. **Basal metabolism rate (BMR)** *is the minimum amount of energy an individual uses in a resting state.* As shown in figure 3.11 on page 91, BMR gradually declines from the beginning of adolescence through the end of adolescence.

Concern is often expressed over adolescents' tendency to eat between meals. However, the choice of foods is much more important than the time or place of eating. Fresh vegetables and fruits as well as whole-grain products are needed to complement the foods high in energy value and protein that adolescents commonly choose.

THROUGH THE EYES OF PSYCHOLOGISTS

Susan Millstein
University of California, San Francisco

"Identifying adolescents' unmet needs and setting goals for health promotion are important steps to take in maximizing adolescent development."

Adolescent Health
National Longitudinal Study of Adolescent Health
http://www.mhhe.com/santrocka9

---

basal metabolism rate (BMR)
The minimum amount of energy an individual uses in a resting state is the BMR.

A special concern in American culture is the amount of fat in our diet. Many of today's adolescents virtually live on fast-food meals, which contributes to the increased fat levels in their diet. Most fast-food meals are high in protein, especially meat and dairy products. But the average American adolescent does not have to worry about getting enough protein. What should be of concern is the vast number of adolescents who consume large quantities of fast foods that are not only high in protein but high in fat.

Medical personnel and psychologists have become increasingly concerned with the health hazards associated with obesity. Eating patterns established in childhood and adolescence are highly associated with obesity in adulthood—80 percent of obese adolescents become obese adults. Obesity is estimated to characterize 25 percent of today's American adolescents. We will further explore adolescent obesity in chapter 14, "Adolescent Problems."

In this section, we have focused on adolescent nutrition and obesity. In chapter 14, "Adolescent Problems," we will discuss two disorders that have increasingly characterized adolescent females—anorexia nervosa and bulimia. Next, we will continue to explore adolescent health by examining exercise and sports.

Exercise and Sports

Do American adolescents get enough exercise? How extensive is the role of sports in adolescents' lives?

Exercise   Are adolescents getting enough exercise? In three recent national studies, adolescents clearly were not getting enough exercise. The first study compared adolescents' exercise patterns in 1987 and 2001 (American Sports Data, 2001). In 1987, 31 percent of 12- to 17-year-olds said that they exercised frequently, compared to only 18 percent in 2001. In the second study, physical activity declined from early to late adolescence (National Center for Health Statistics, 2000). Adolescents in grade 9 were more likely to participate in moderate or vigorous physical activity than their counterparts in grades 10 through 12. Male adolescents were far more likely to exercise than female adolescents were. In the third study, few adolescents participated in school physical education (PE) classes (Gordon-Larsen, McMurray, & Popkin, 2000). Only about 20 percent took a PE class one or more days per week. Participation in PE classes was especially low for African American and Latino adolescents.

Do U.S. adolescents exercise less than their counterparts in other countries. In a recent comparison of adolescents in 28 countries. U.S. adolescents exercised less and ate more junk food than adolescents in most countries (World Health Organization, 2000). Just two-thirds of U.S. adolescents exercised at least twice a week compared to 80 percent or more adolescents in Ireland, Austria, Germany, and the Slovak Republic. U.S. adolescents were more likely to eat fried food and less likely to eat fruits and vegetables than adolescents in most other countries studied. U.S. adolescents' eating choices were similar to those of adolescents in England.

Some health experts blame television for the poor physical condition of American adolescents. In one investigation, adolescents who watched little television were much more physically fit than those who watched heavy doses of television (Tucker, 1987). The more adolescents watch television, the more likely they are to be overweight. No one is quite sure whether this is because they spend their leisure time in front of a television set, because they eat a lot of junk food they see advertised on television, or because less physically fit youth find physical activity less reinforcing than watching television.

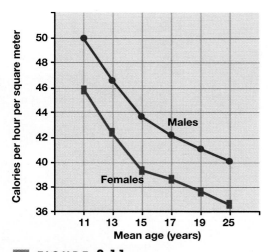

FIGURE 3.11
Basal Metabolic Rates (BMRs) for Adolescent Females and Males

THROUGH THE EYES OF ADOLESCENTS

Body Preoccupation and Concerns

After locking the bathroom door, 12-year-old Anya carefully examines her still shower-damp body. She pokes disgustedly at her stomach. A year ago she wasn't as concerned about her body and it felt more familiar. Now the body she looks at in the mirror has new curves and hair she is not sure she likes. She feels as though she is too heavy and thinks, "Maybe I should try that diet that Becky told me about." Sighing, she pulls on her oversize sweatshirt and wonders what to do (Lerner & Olson, 1995).

What is the nature of adolescents' physical activity? What might schools possibly do to improve adolescents' physical fitness?

Some of the blame for the poor physical condition of U.S. children and adolescents falls on U.S. schools, many of which fail to provide physical education class on a daily basis. One extensive investigation of behavior in physical education classes at four different schools revealed how little vigorous exercise takes place in these classes (Parcel & others, 1987). Boys and girls moved through space only 50 percent of the time they were in the classes, and they moved continuously an average of only 2.2 minutes. In sum, not only does the adolescent's school week include inadequate physical education classes, but the majority of adolescents do not exercise vigorously even when they are in physical education classes. Further, while we hear a lot about the exercise revolution among adults, most children and adolescents report that their parents are poor role models when it comes to vigorous physical exercise (Feist & Brannon, 1989).

Does it make a difference if children and adolescents are pushed to exercise more vigorously in school? One investigation provided an affirmative answer to this question (Tuckman & Hinkle, 1988). One hundred fifty-four boys and girls were randomly assigned to either three 30-minute running programs per week or to regular attendance in physical education classes. Although the results sometimes varied by sex, for the most part those in the running program had increased cardiovascular health and showed increased creativity. For example, the running-program boys had less body fat, and the running-program girls had more creative involvement in their classrooms.

An exciting possibility is that physical exercise might provide a buffer to adolescents' stress. In one investigation of 364 females in grades 7 through 11 in Los Angeles, the negative impact of stressful events on health declined as exercise levels increased, suggesting that exercise can be a valuable resource for combating adolescents' life stresses (Brown & Siegel, 1988). In another investigation, adolescents who exercised regularly coped more effectively with stress and had more positive identities than did adolescents who engaged in little exercise (Grimes & Mattimore, 1989). And in one recent study, high school seniors who exercised frequently had higher grade point averages, used drugs less frequently, were less depressed, and got along better with their parents than their counterparts who rarely exercised (Field, Diego, & Sanders, 2001).

In the fourth century B.C., Aristotle commented that the quality of life is determined by its activities. In today's world, we know that exercise is one of the principal activities that improves the quality of life, both adolescents' and adults' (Malina, 2001).

Sports   Sports play an important role in the lives of many adolescents (Kuchenbecker, 2000). Some estimates indicate that as many as 40 to 70 percent of American youths participate in various organized sports (Ferguson, 1999).

Sports can have positive and negative influences on adolescent development. Many sports activities can improve adolescents' physical well-being and health, self-confidence, motivation to excel, and ability to work with others (Cornock, Bowker, & Gadbois, 2001). In some cases, adolescents who spend considerable time in sports are less likely to engage in drugs and delinquency.

In one recent study of sports participation and health-related behaviors in more than 14,000 U.S. high school students, approximately 70 percent of the males and 53 percent of the females said that they had participated in one or more sports teams in school or nonschool settings (Pate & others, 2000). Male sports participants were more likely than nonparticipants to say they ate fruit and vegetables on the previous day and less likely to report cigarette smoking, cocaine and other illegal drug use, and trying to lose weight. Compared with female nonparticipants, female sports participants were more likely to say they ate vegetables on the previous day and less likely to report having sexual intercourse in the past three months.

The downside of the extensive participation in sports by American adolescents includes the increased high expectations by parents and coaches to win at all costs (Kuchenbecker, 2000). Researchers have found that adolescents' participation in competitive sports is linked with competition anxiety and self-centeredness (Bredemeier & Shields, 1996; Smith & Smoll, 1997). Another problem is that some adolescents spend so much time in sports that their academic skills suffer. And overuse injuries are increasing in adolescents who stretch their bodies beyond their capabilities. As they seek to become stars in their field, some adolescents increase the duration, intensity, and frequency of their training to a point that harms their bodies (Hellmich, 2000).

How might changing sleep patterns in adolescents affect their school performance?

Some of the problems that adolescents experience in sports involves coaches. Many youth coaches create a performance-oriented motivational climate focused on winning, public recognition, and performance relative to others. However, some coaches place more emphasis on mastery motivation that focuses adolescents' attention on the development of their skills and efforts to reach self-determined standards of success. Researchers have found that athletes with a mastery focus are more likely to see the benefits of practice, persist in the face of difficulty, and show more skill development over the course of a season (Roberts, Treasure, & Kavussanu, 1997).

Sleep

There has been a recent surge of interest in adolescent sleep patterns. This interest focuses on the belief that many adolescents are not getting enough sleep, that there are physiological underpinnings to adolescents' (especially older ones) desire to stay up later at night and sleep longer in the morning, and that these findings have implications for the hours that adolescents learn most effectively in school (Fukuda & Ishihara, 2001).

In one recent study, the sleep patterns of children in the second, fourth, and sixth grades were examined (Sadeh, Raviv, & Gruber, 2000). The children were evaluated with activity monitors, and the children and their parents completed sleep questionnaires and daily reports. Sixth-grade children went to sleep at night about one hour later (just after 10:30 P.M. versus just after 9:30 P.M.) and reported more daytime sleepiness than the second-grade children. Girls spent more time in sleep than boys. Also, family stress was linked with poor sleep, such as nightly wakings, in children.

Mary Carskadon and her colleagues (Acebo & others, 1999; Carskadon, Acebo, & Seifer, 2001; Carskadon & others, 1998; Carskadon & others, 1999; Wolfson & Carskadon, 1998) have conducted a number of research studies on adolescent sleep patterns. They found that adolescents would sleep an average of nine hours and 25 minutes when given the opportunity to sleep as long as they like. Most adolescents get considerably less than this nine hours of sleep, especially during the week. This creates a sleep debt, which adolescents often try to make up on the weekend. They also revealed that older adolescents are often more sleepy during the day than younger adolescents. Carskadon and her team of researchers theorized that this was not because of factors such as academic work and social pressures. Rather, their research suggests that adolescents' biological clocks undergo a hormonal phase shift as they get older. This pushes the time of wakefulness to an hour later than when they were young adolescents. The researchers found that this shift was caused by a delay in the nightly presence of the hormone melatonin, which is produced by the brain's pineal gland in preparation for the body to sleep. Melatonin is secreted at about 9:30 P.M. in younger adolescents but is produced approximately an hour later in older adolescents, which delays the onset of sleep.

Carskadon determined that early school starting times may result in grogginess and lack of attention in class and poor performance on tests. Based on this research, schools in Edina, Minnesota, made the decision to start classes at 8:30 A.M. rather than the earlier time they had been starting: 7:25 A.M. Under this later start time, there have been fewer referrals for discipline problems and the number of students who report an illness or depression has decreased. The Edina School System reports that test scores have improved for high school students, but not middle school students, which supports Carskadon's ideas about older adolescents being affected by earlier school start times than younger adolescents.

As we have just seen, changing sleep patterns in adolescence may have ramifications for how alert adolescents are in school. Next, we further explore the role of schools in adolescent health.

Health Services

Though adolescents have a greater number of acute health conditions than adults do, they use private physician services at a lower rate than any other age group does (Edelman, 1996). And adolescents often underutilize other health-care systems as well (Drotar, 2000; Klein & others, 2001; Millstein, 1993; Seiffge-Krenke, 1998). Health services are especially unlikely to meet the health needs of younger adolescents, ethnic minority adolescents, and adolescents living in poverty.

In the National Longitudinal Study of Adolescent Health, more than 12,000 adolescents were interviewed about the extent to which they needed health care but did not obtain it (Ford, Bearman, & Moody, 1999). Approximately 19 percent of the adolescents reported forgoing health care in the preceding year. Among the adolescents who especially needed health care but did not seek it were those who smoked cigarettes on a daily basis, frequently drank alcohol, and engaged in sexual intercourse.

Health Risks for Adolescents
http://www.mhhe.com/santrocka9

Among the chief barriers to better health services for adolescents are cost, poor organization, and availability of health services, as well as confidentiality of care. Also, few health-care providers receive any special training for working with adolescents. Many say that they feel unprepared to provide services such as contraceptive counseling and accurate evaluation of what constitutes abnormal behavior in adolescence (Irwin, 1993). Health-care providers might transmit to their patients their discomfort in discussing such topics as sexuality and drugs, which can lead to adolescents' unwillingness to discuss sensitive issues with them (Marcell & Millstein, 2001).

Leading Causes of Death

Medical improvements have increased the life expectancy of today's adolescents compared to their counterparts who lived early in the twentieth century. Still, life-threatening factors continue to exist in adolescents' lives.

The three leading causes of death in adolescence are accidents, homicide, and suicide (National Center for Health Statistics, 2000). More than half of all deaths in adolescents ages 10 to 19 are due to accidents, and most of those involve motor vehicles, especially for older adolescents. Risky driving habits, such as speeding, tailgating, and driving under the influence of alcohol or other drugs, might be more important causes of these accidents than lack of driving experience. In about 50 percent of the motor vehicle fatalities involving an adolescent, the driver has a blood alcohol level of 0.10 percent, twice the level needed to be "under the influence" in some states. A high rate of intoxication is also often present in adolescents who die as pedestrians or while using recreational vehicles.

Homicide also is a leading cause of death in adolescence. Homicide is especially high among African American male adolescents. They are three times more likely to be killed by guns than by natural causes (Simons, Finlay, & Yang, 1991).

Suicide accounts for 6 percent of the deaths in the 10 to 14 age group, a rate of 1.3 per 100,000 population. In the 15 to 19 age group, suicide accounts for 12 percent of deaths or 9 per 100,000 population. Since the 1950s, the adolescent suicide rate has tripled. We will discuss suicide further in chapter 14, "Adolescent Problems."

In this chapter we have discussed some important aspects of health. In later chapters, we will further explore many aspects of adolescent health. For example, we will examine many aspects of adolescent sexuality, such as unprotected sexual intercourse and sexually transmitted diseases in chapter 11, "Sexuality." We will evaluate drug abuse, violence, smoking, and eating disorders in chapter 14, "Adolescent Problems."

Since the last review, we have discussed developmental change in the brain and adolescent health. The following review should help you to reach your learning goals related to these topics.

☐ FOR YOUR REVIEW

Learning Goal 2
Know about developmental changes in the brain

- Neurons are the basic units of the nervous system and are made up of a cell body, dendrites, and an axon. So far, researchers have found that greater increases in the axon (probably because of increased myelination) take place in adolescence than in the cell body or dendrites. Synaptogenesis in the prefrontal cortex, where reasoning and self-regulation occur, continues through adolescence.
- Using magnetic resonance imaging (MRI), in one study, scientists found that between 3 to 15 years of age, rapid, distinct spurts of growth in the brain occur. In this study, from age 6 through puberty, the most growth took place in the temporal and parietal lobes, especially in areas that involve language and spatial relations. Other researchers have found that during adolescence, brain activity is more pronounced in the amygdala, which is involved in emotion, while in young adults, greater brain activity occurs in the frontal lobes, where higher reasoning takes place. Research on the development of the brain is in its infancy and the next decade is likely to see an increasing number of studies as technology in investigating the brain advances.

Learning Goal 3
Evaluate adolescent health

- Adolescence is a critical juncture in the adoption of positive health behaviors.
- A lower basal metabolism in adolescence means adolescents have to burn up more calories to maintain a healthy weight. There is concern about the eating habits of adolescents and obesity.
- Many adolescents do not get adequate exercise. Television, parents, and schools are possible contributors to the low exercise levels of adolescents. There are both positive and negative aspects of adolescents' participation in organized sports.
- Adolescents like to go to bed later and sleep later than children do. This may be linked with developmental changes in the brain. A special concern is the extent to which these changes in sleep patterns in adolescence affect academic behavior.
- Adolescents use health services far less than any other age group. There are a number of barriers to providing better health services for adolescents.
- The leading causes of death in adolescence are (1) accidents, (2) homicide, and (3) suicide.

Earlier in the chapter, we indicated that both heredity and environment are important influences on the onset of puberty. Let's now further explore the influence of heredity and environment on adolescent development.

By permission of Johnny Hart and Creators Syndicate, Inc.

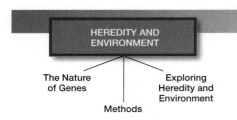

HEREDITY AND ENVIRONMENT

As with all other species, we must have some mechanism for transmitting characteristics from one generation to the next. Each adolescent carries a genetic code inherited from her or his parents. The genetic codes of all adolescents are alike in one important way—they all contain the human genetic code. Because of the human genetic code, a fertilized human egg cannot grow into an eel, an egret, or an elephant.

The Nature of Genes

We each begin life as a single cell weighing one twenty-millionth of an ounce! This tiny piece of matter housed our entire genetic code—the information about who we would become. These instructions orchestrated growth from that single cell to an adolescent made of trillions of cells, each containing a perfect replica of the original genetic code. Physically, the hereditary code is carried by biochemical agents called genes and chromosomes. Aside from the obvious physical similarity this code produces among adolescents (such as in anatomy, brain structure, and organs), it also may account for much of our psychological sameness (or universality).

No one possesses all the characteristics that our genetic structure makes possible. A **genotype** *is a person's genetic heritage, the actual genetic material*. However, not all of this genetic material is apparent in our observed and measurable characteristics. A **phenotype** *is the way an individual's genotype is expressed in observed and measurable characteristics*. Phenotypes include physical traits, such as height, weight, eye color, and skin pigmentation, as well as psychological characteristics, such as intelligence, creativity, personality, and social tendencies. For each genotype, a range of phenotypes can be expressed. Imagine that we could identify all of the genes that would make an adolescent introverted or extraverted. Would measured introversion-extraversion be predictable from knowledge of the specific genes? The answer is no, because even if our genetic model was adequate, introversion-extraversion is a characteristic shaped by experience throughout life. For example, a parent might push an introverted child into social situations and encourage the child to become more gregarious.

Methods

Among the ways that the effects of heredity on development are studied are behavior genetics and molecular genetics.

genotype
A person's genetic heritage; the actual genetic material.

phenotype
The way an individual's genotype is expressed in observed and measurable characteristics.

Behavior Genetics

Behavior genetics *is the study of the degree and nature of behavior's hereditary basis.* Behavior geneticists assume that behaviors are jointly determined by the interaction of heredity and environment (Plomin & others, 1997; Wahlsten, 2000). To study heredity's influence on behavior, behavior geneticists often use either twin studies or adoption studies.

In a **twin study,** *the behavioral similarity of identical twins is compared with the behavioral similarity of fraternal twins. Identical twins* (called monozygotic twins) develop from a single fertilized egg that splits into two genetically identical replicas, each of which becomes a person. *Fraternal twins* (called dizygotic twins) develop from separate eggs and separate sperm, making them genetically no more similar than nontwin siblings. Although fraternal twins share the same womb, they are no more alike genetically than are nontwin brothers and sisters, and they may be of different sexes. By comparing groups of identical and fraternal twins, behavior geneticists capitalize on the basic knowledge that identical twins are more similar genetically than are fraternal twins (Silberg & Rutter, 1997). In one twin study, 7,000 pairs of Finnish identical and fraternal twins were compared on the personality traits of extraversion (outgoingness) and neuroticism (psychological instability) (Rose & others, 1988). On both of these personality traits, identical twins were much more similar than fraternal twins were, suggesting the role of heredity in both traits. However, several issues crop up as a result of twin studies. Adults may stress the similarities of identical twins more than those of fraternal twins, and identical twins may perceive themselves as a "set" and play together more than fraternal twins. If so, observed similarities in identical twins could be environmentally influenced.

In an **adoption study,** *investigators seek to discover whether the behavior and psychological characteristics of adopted children are more like those of their adoptive parents, who provided a home environment, or those of their biological parents, who contributed their heredity. Another form of adoption study is to compare adoptive and biological siblings.* In one investigation, the educational levels attained by biological parents were better predictors of adopted children's IQ scores than were the IQs of the children's adopted parents (Scarr & Weinberg, 1983). Because of the genetic relation between the adopted children and their biological parents, the implication is that heredity influences children's IQ scores (Moldin, 1999).

Molecular Genetics

Studies of behavior genetics do not focus on the molecular makeup of genes. Rather behavior geneticists study the effects of heredity at a more global level by such methods as comparing the behavior of identical and fraternal twins.

Today, there is a great deal of enthusiasm about the use of molecular genetics to discover the specific locations on genes that determine an individual's susceptibility to many diseases and other aspects of health and well-being (Magee, Gordon, & Whelan, 2001; Peters & others, 2001; Sheffield, 1999).

The term *genome* is used to describe the complete set of instructions for making an organism. It contains the master blueprint for all cellular structures and activities for the life span of the organism. The human genome consists of tightly coiled threads of DNA.

The Human Genome Project, begun in the 1970s, has made stunning progress in mapping the human genome. A current goal for 2003 is to determine the sequences of the 3 billion chemical base pairs that make up human DNA (U.S. Department of Energy, 2001). In regard to adolescent development, we are likely to see efforts to identify

What is the nature of the twin study method?

behavior genetics
The study of the degree and nature of behavior's hereditary basis.

twin study
A study in which the behavioral similarity of identical twins is compared with the behavioral similarity of fraternal twins.

adoption study
A study in which investigators seek to discover whether, in behavior and psychological characteristics, adopted children and adolescents are more like their adoptive parents, who provided a home environment, or their biological parents, who contributed their heredity. Another form of adoption study is to compare adoptive and biological siblings.

Behavior Genetics
Twin Research
Human Genome Project
Heredity Resources
http://www.mhhe.com/santrocka9

specific genes that are linked with specific aspects of pubertal change and the development of sexual maturation. A special interest of the Human Genome Project is the identification of genetic markers for diseases. Once these genetic markers are found, what next? One strategy is to find a healthy copy of a missing gene and transplant it into the affected cells. Another is to develop drugs that will alter the genetic makeup of the affected cells.

Exploring Heredity and Environment

To begin our examination of heredity and environment, we will focus on heredity and environment correlations.

passive genotype-environment correlations

Correlations that occur when the biological parents, who are genetically related to the child, provide a rearing environment for the child.

evocative genotype-environment correlations

Correlations that occur when the adolescent's genotype elicits certain types of physical and social environments.

active (niche-picking) genotype-environment correlations

Correlations that occur when adolescents seek out environments they find compatible and stimulating.

Heredity-Environment Correlations   *Heredity-environment correlations* refers to the concept that an individual's genes influence the types of environments to which they are exposed. That is, individuals experience environments that are related or linked to their genetic propensities (Plomin & others, 1994). Behavior geneticist Sandra Scarr (1993) described three ways heredity and environment are correlated: passively, evocatively, and actively.

Passive genotype-environment correlations *occur when biological parents, who are genetically related to the child, provide a rearing environment for the child.* For example, suppose the parents have a genetic predisposition to be intelligent and read skillfully. Because they read well and enjoy reading, they provide their children with books to read. The likely outcome is that their children, given their own inherited predispositions, will become skilled readers.

Evocative genotype-environment correlations *occur because a child's genotype elicits certain types of physical and social environments.* For example, active, smiling children receive more social stimulation than passive, quiet children do. Cooperative, attentive adolescents evoke more pleasant and instructional responses from the adults around them than uncooperative, distractible adolescents do. Athletically inclined youth tend to elicit encouragement to engage in school sports and as a consequence tend to be the ones who try out for sports teams and go on to participate in athletically oriented environments.

Active (niche-picking) genotype-environment correlations *occur when children and adolescents seek out environments they find compatible and stimulating.* "Niche-picking" refers to finding a niche or setting that is suited to one's abilities. Adolescents select from their surrounding environment some aspect that they respond to, learn about, or ignore. Their active selections of environments are related to their particular genotype. For example, attractive adolescents tend to seek out attractive peers. Adolescents who are musically inclined are likely to select musical environments in which they can successfully perform their skills.

Scarr believes that the relative importance of the three genotype-environment correlations changes as children develop from infancy through adolescence. In infancy, much of the environment that children experience is provided by adults. Thus, passive genotype-environment correlations are more common in the lives of infants and young children than they are for older children and adolescents who can extend their experiences beyond the family's influences and create their environments to a greater degree.

THROUGH THE EYES OF PSYCHOLOGISTS

Sandra Scarr
University of Virginia

"It is hard to imagine anything that isn't in some way heritable."

Shared and Nonshared Environments   Behavior geneticists also believe that another way the environment's role in heredity-environment interactions can be carved up is to consider the experiences that adolescents have in families that are common with other adolescents living in the same home and those that are not common or shared (George, 1996; Hetherington, Reiss, & Plomin, 1994; Manke & Pike, 1997). Behavior geneticist Robert Plomin (1993) believes that common rearing, or shared environment, accounts for little of the variation in adolescents' personalities or interests. In other words, even though two adolescents live under the same roof with the same parents, their personalities are often very different.

Shared environmental influences *are adolescents' common experiences, such as their parents' personalities and intellectual orientation, the family's social class, and the neighborhood in which they live.* By contrast, **nonshared environmental influences** *are an adolescent's own unique experiences, both within the family and outside the family, that are not shared with another sibling.*

Parents often do not interact the same with all siblings, and siblings do not all interact the same with their parents (Feinberg & Hetherington, 2001; Mekos, Hetherington, & Reiss, 1996; O'Connor, 1994). Siblings often have different peer groups, different friends, and different teachers at school. In one study of nonshared environmental influences, the mother, the father, and two adolescent siblings were observed interacting in a problem-solving task (O'Connor & others, 1995). The results confirmed the importance of nonshared environmental influences—on the average, 67 percent of the adolescents' behavior and 65 percent of the parents' behavior could be explained by unique environmental experiences.

Eleanor Maccoby (1992) argues that there are a number of important aspects of family contexts that are shared by all family members. After all, adolescents observe how parents are treating their siblings, and they learn from what they observe as well as what they experience directly. And atmospheres and moods tend to be spread to whoever is present.

Conclusions About Heredity and Environment   In sum, both genes and environment are necessary for an adolescent to even exist ◀▐▐▐▐ P. 22. Without genes, there is no person; without environment, there is no person (Scarr & Weinberg, 1980). Heredity and environment operate together—or coorperate—to produce a person's intelligence, temperament, height, weight, ability to pitch a baseball, ability to read, and so on (Gottlieb, 2000; Gottlieb, Wahlsten, & Lickliter, 1998). If an attractive, popular, intelligent girl is elected president of her senior class in high school, is her success due to heredity or to environment? Of course, the answer is both. Because the environment's influence depends on genetically endowed characteristics, we say the two factors *interact* (Mader, 1999).

The relative contributions of heredity and environment are not additive, as in such-and-such a percentage of nature, such-and-such a percentage of experience. That's the old view. Nor is it accurate to say that full genetic expression happens once, around conception or birth, after which we take our genetic legacy into the world to see how far it gets us. Genes produce proteins throughout the life span, in many different environments. Or they don't produce these proteins, depending on how harsh or nourishing those environments are. The interaction is so extensive that

shared environmental influences
Adolescents' common environmental experiences that are shared with their siblings, such as their parents' personalities and intellectual orientation, the family's social class, and the neighborhood in which they live.

nonshared environmental influences
The adolescent's own unique experiences, both within a family and outside the family, that are not shared by another sibling.

The frightening part about heredity and environment is that we parents provide both.
—Notebook of a Printer

■ THINKING CRITICALLY
Heredity, Environment, and You

We have concluded that every individual's development is influenced by both heredity *and* environment. Think about your own development for a moment—some of your most important characteristics, like your temperament, personality, and intelligence. Now think about your mother's and your father's temperament, personality, and intelligence. For example, is your mother very bright, and are you also? Is your father introverted but you are more sociable? How closely do you match up with your mother's and your father's characteristics? Evaluate the extent to which you believe you inherited these characteristics or developed them through your experiences with your environment. Remember, chances are that both heredity and environment contributed to who you are today and who you were as an adolescent. And remember that determining heredity's and the environment's contributions in a scientific manner is an extremely complex undertaking. Your ability to come up with characteristics you share with one or both of your parents helps you to understand your similarities to your parents, but this does not tell you whether the characteristics are due to heredity or to environment.

William Greenough
University of Illinois

"The interaction of heredity and environment is so extensive that to ask which is more important, nature or nurture, is like asking which is more important to a rectangle, height or width."

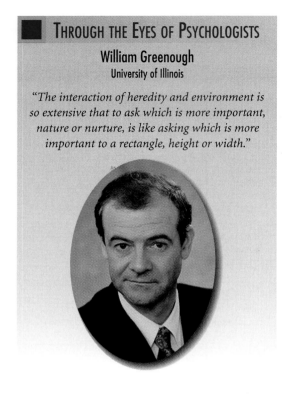

Genes and Parenting
http://www.mhhe.com/santrocka9

William Greenough (1997; Greenough & others, 1997) says that to ask which is more important, nature or nurture, is like asking which is more important to a rectangle, its length or width.

The emerging view is that many complex behaviors likely have some genetic loading that gives people a propensity for a particular developmental trajectory. But the actual development requires more: an environment. And that environment is complex, just like the mixture of genes we inherit. Environmental influences range from the things we lump together under "nurture" (such as parenting, family dynamics, schooling, and neighborhood quality) to biological encounters (such as viruses, birth complications, and even biological events in cells).

Imagine for a moment that there is a cluster of genes somehow associated with youth violence (this is hypothetical because we don't know of any such combination). The adolescent who carries this genetic mixture might experience a world of loving parents, regular nutritious meals, lots of books, and a series of masterful teachers. Or the adolescent's world might consist of parental neglect, a neighborhood where gunshots and crime are everyday occurrences, and inadequate schooling. In which of these environments are the adolescent's genes likely to manufacture the biological underpinnings of criminality? Also note that growing up with all of the "advantages" does not necessarily guarantee success. Adolescents from wealthy families might have access to books, excellent schools, travel, and tutoring but take such opportunities for granted and fail to develop the motivation to learn and achieve. In the same way, "poor" or "disadvantaged" does not equal "doomed"; many impoverished adolescents make the best of the opportunities available to them and learn to seek out advantages that can help them improve their lives.

The most recent nature–nurture controversy erupted when Judith Harris (1998) published *The Nurture Assumption*. In this provocative book, she argued that what parents do does not make a difference in their children's and adolescents' behavior. Yell at them. Hug them. Read to them. Ignore them. Harris says it won't influence how they turn out. She argues that genes and peers are far more important than parents in children's and adolescents' development.

Harris is right that genes matter, and she is right that peers matter. She is wrong that parents don't matter (Collins & others, 2000). There is a huge parenting literature with many research studies documenting the importance of parents in children's and adolescents' development. We will discuss parents' important roles in adolescent development throughout this book, giving them special attention in chapter 5, "Families." But for now, consider the research on just one area of development: child abuse. Many studies reveal that when parents abuse their children, the children have problems in regulating their emotions, becoming securely attached to others, developing competent peer relations, and adapting to school, and tend to develop anxiety and depression disorders, and in many instances these difficulties continue into adolescence (Cicchetti & Toth, 1998; Field, 2000; Rogatch & others, 1995). Child development expert T. Berry Brazelton (1998) commented, "*The Nurture Assumption* is so disturbing it devalues what parents are trying to do. . . . Parents might say, 'If I don't matter, why should I bother?' That's terrifying and it's coming when children and youth need a stronger home base." Even Jerome Kagan (1998), a champion of biological influences on development, when commenting about Harris' book, concluded that whether children are cooperative or competitive, achievement-oriented or not, they are strongly influenced by their parents for better or for worse.

At this point we have studied a number of ideas about the roles of evolution and heredity in adolescent development. This review should help you to reach your learning goals related to these topics.

☐ FOR YOUR REVIEW

Learning Goal 4
Explain heredity and environment

- Each adolescent inherits a genetic code from his or her parents. Physically, the heredity code is carried by biochemical agents called genes and chromosomes. Genotype refers to the unique configuration of genes, while phenotype involves observed and measurable characteristics. Behavior genetics is the field concerned with the degree and nature of behavior's hereditary basis. Twin and adoption studies are two methods behavior geneticists use to determine heredity and environment influences. Increasingly, molecular genetics is being used to pinpoint the effects of specific genes.

- Scarr argues that there are three types of genotype-environment correlations: passive, evocative, and active (niche-picking). Plomin believes that nonshared environmental experiences make up the main part of the environment's contribution to why one sibling's personality is different from another's. Heredity and environment are closely interwoven in their influence on development.

In this chapter, we have focused on puberty, health, and biological foundations in adolescence. In chapter 4, we will turn our attention to the cognitive changes that take place in adolescence.

CHAPTER MAP

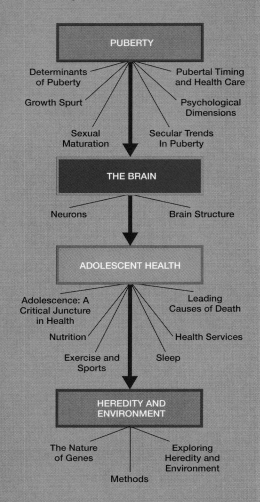

REACH YOUR LEARNING GOALS

At the beginning of the chapter, we stated four learning goals and encouraged you to review material related to these goals at three points in the chapter. This is a good time to return to these reviews and use them to guide your study and help you to reach your learning goals.

Page 87

Learning Goal 1   Understand pubertal change

Page 95

Learning Goal 2   Know about developmental changes in the brain
Learning Goal 3   Evaluate adolescent health

Page 101

Learning Goal 4   Explain heredity and environment

KEY TERMS

puberty 76
hormones 77
androgens 77
estrogens 77
menarche 79
spermarche 79
neurons 87
basal metabolism rate (BMR) 90
genotype 96
phenotype 96
behavior genetics 97

twin study 97
adoption study 97
passive genotype-environment
    correlations 98
evocative genotype-environment
    correlations 98
active (niche-picking) genotype-
    environment correlations 98
shared environmental influences 99
nonshared environmental influences 99

KEY PEOPLE

Roberta Simmons and Dale Blyth 84
Mary Carskadon 93
Sandra Scarr 98

RESOURCES FOR IMPROVING THE LIVES OF ADOLESCENTS

Journal of Adolescent Health Care

This journal includes articles about a wide range of health-related and medical issues, including reducing smoking, improving nutrition, health promotion, and physicians' and nurses' roles in reducing health-compromising behaviors of adolescents.

The Society for Adolescent Medicine

10727 White Oak Avenue
Granada Hills, CA 91344

This organization is a valuable source of information about competent physicians who specialize in treating adolescents. It maintains a list of recommended adolescent specialists across the United States.

TAKING IT TO THE NET

1. The growth spurt is accompanied by weight increases. Those whose weight increases too much are at an increased risk for negative health outcomes, including obesity, hypertension, and other health risks. One's body mass index (BMI) is a measure of the "fit" of one's weight to one's height. *Is your BMI in the "healthy" range or are you at risk for future health problems? How does your BMI relate to diet, exercise, and other measures of healthiness?*

2. Your instructor assigns a brief paper in which you are, first, to define the term "body image," including positive and negative aspects of it and, second, to devise procedures to improve an adolescent's negative body image, focusing on male body image as opposed to the

http://www.mhhe.com/santrocka9

more commonly researched and discussed female body image. *What procedures would you suggest to enhance a negative male body image?*

3. A major health concern during the adolescent years centers on the adolescent's diet. Keep track of everything you eat and drink for the next three days. *What is your daily caloric intake? Is it in the appropriate quantities recommended in the food pyramid? Are you eating healthy?*

Connect to *http://www.mhhe.com/santrocka9* to research the answers and complete these exercises. In some cases, you'll also find further instructions on this site.

CHAPTER MAP

THE COGNITIVE
DEVELOPMENTAL VIEW

Piaget's
Theory

Vygotsky's
Theory

THE INFORMATION-
PROCESSING VIEW

Characteristics

Metacognition
and Self-
Regulatory
Learning

Attention and
Memory

Creative
Thinking

Decision
Making

Critical
Thinking

THE PSYCHOMETRIC/
INTELLIGENCE VIEW

Intelligence
Tests

Controversies
and Issues in
Intelligence

Theories of
Multiple
Intelligences

Emotional
Intelligence

SOCIAL COGNITION

Adolescent
Egocentrism

Social Cognition
in the Rest of
This Text

Perspective
Taking

Implicit
Personality
Theory

COGNITIVE DEVELOPMENT

■

The thoughts of youth are long, long thoughts.
—Henry Wadsworth Longfellow
American Poet, 19th Century

■ THE DEVELOPING THOUGHTS OF ADOLESCENTS

When you were a young adolescent, what was your thinking like? Were your thinking skills as good as they are now? Could you solve difficult, abstract problems and reason logically about complex topics? Or did such skills improve in your high school years? Can you come up with any ways your thinking now is better than it was in high school?

Many young adolescents begin to think in more idealistic ways. How idealistic was your thinking when you were in middle school and high school? Did you think more about what is ideal versus what is real as an adolescent or as a child? Has your thinking gotten less idealistic now that you are in college, or do you still think a lot about an ideal world and how you might achieve it?

When we think about thinking, we usually consider it in terms of school subjects like math and English, or solving intellectual problems. But people's thoughts about social circumstances are also important. Psychologists are increasingly studying how adolescents think about social matters.

One of my most vivid memories of the adolescence of my oldest daughter, Tracy, is from when she was 12 years of age. I had accompanied her and her younger sister, Jennifer (10 at the time), to a tennis tournament. As we walked into a restaurant to have lunch, Tracy bolted for the restroom. Jennifer and I looked at each other, wondering what was wrong. Five minutes later Tracy emerged looking calmer. I asked her what had happened. Her response: "This one hair was out of place and every person in here was looking at me!"

Consider two other adolescents—Margaret and Adam. During a conversation with her girlfriend, 16-year-old Margaret says, "Did you hear about Catherine? She's pregnant. Do you think I would ever let that happen to me? Never." Thirteen-year-old Adam describes himself: "No one understands me, especially my parents. They have no idea of what I am feeling. They have never experienced the pain I'm going through." These experiences of Tracy, Margaret, and Adam represent the emergence of egocentric thought in adolescence. Later in the chapter we will explore adolescent egocentrism in greater detail.

CHAPTER LEARNING GOALS

WHEN PEOPLE THINK ABOUT CHANGES in adolescents, they often focus on the biological changes of puberty and socioemotional changes, such as independence, identity, relations with parents and peers, and so on. However, as you will see in this chapter, adolescents also undergo some impressive cognitive changes. When you have completed this chapter, you should be able to reach these learning goals:

1 Discuss Piaget's theory

2 Understand Vygotsky's theory

3 Evaluate the information-processing view

4 Explain the psychometric/intelligence view

5 Describe changes in social cognition

THE COGNITIVE DEVELOPMENTAL VIEW

Piaget's
Theory

Vygotsky's
Theory

Piaget's Theory
http://www.mhhe.com/santrocka9

schema

A concept or framework that exists in the individual's mind to organize and interpret information, in Piaget's theory.

assimilation

The incorporation of new information into existing knowledge.

accommodation

An adjustment to new information.

THE COGNITIVE DEVELOPMENTAL VIEW

In chapter 2, "The Science of Adolescent Development," we briefly examined Piaget's theory ◄‖‖ P. 46. Here we will explore his theory in more detail and describe another cognitive developmental theory that is receiving increased attention, that of Lev Vygotsky.

Piaget's Theory

Piaget had a number of things to say about adolescents' thinking being different from children's. We begin our coverage of Piaget's theory by describing its basic nature and the cognitive processes involved. Then we turn to his cognitive stages, giving special attention to concrete operational and formal operational thought.

The Nature of Piaget's Theory and Cognitive Processes Piaget's theory is the most well known, most widely discussed theory of adolescent cognitive development. Piaget stressed that adolescents are motivated to understand their world because doing so is biologically adaptive. In Piaget's view, adolescents actively construct their own cognitive worlds; information is not just poured into their minds from the environment. To make sense out of their world, adolescents organize their experiences. They separate important ideas from less important ones. They connect one idea to another. They not only organize their observations and experiences, they also adapt their thinking to include new ideas because additional information furthers understanding.

In actively constructing their world, adolescents use schemas. A **schema** *is a concept or framework that exists in an individual's mind to organize and interpret information.* Piaget's interest in schemas focused on how children and adolescents organize and make sense out of their current experiences.

Piaget (1952) said that two processes are responsible for how children and adolescents use and adapt their schemas: assimilation and accommodation.

Assimilation *occurs when individuals incorporate new information into existing knowledge.* In assimilation, the schema does not change. **Accommodation** *occurs when individuals adjust to new information.* In accommodation, the schema changes. Suppose that a 16-year-old girl wants to learn how to use a computer. Her parents buy her a computer for her birthday. She has never had the opportunity to use one. From her experience and observation, though, she realizes that software discs are inserted in a slot and a switch must be pressed to turn the computer on. Thus far she has incorporated her behavior into a conceptual framework she already had (assimilation). As she strikes several keys, she makes some errors. Soon she realizes that she needs to get someone to help her learn to use the computer efficiently or take a class on using a computer at her high school. These adjustments show her awareness of the need to alter her concept of computer use (accommodation).

Equilibration *is a mechanism in Piaget's theory that explains how children or adolescents shift from one state of thought to the next. The shift occurs as they experience cognitive conflict or a disequilibrium in trying to understand the world. Eventually, the child or adolescent resolves the conflict and reaches a balance, or equilibrium, of thought.* Piaget believed there is considerable movement between states of cognitive equilibrium and disequilibrium as assimilation and accommodation work in concert to produce cognitive change. For example, if a child believes that the amount of a liquid changes simply because the liquid is poured into a container with a different shape, she might be puzzled by such issues as where the "extra" liquid came from and whether there is actually more liquid to drink. The child will eventually resolve these puzzles as her thought becomes more advanced. In the everyday world, the child is constantly faced with such counterexamples and inconsistencies.

equilibration
A mechanism in Piaget's theory that explains how children or adolescents shift from one state of thought to the next. The shift occurs as they experience cognitive conflict or a disequilibrium in trying to understand the world. Eventually, the child or adolescent resolves the conflict and reaches a balance, or equilibrium.

Stages of Cognitive Development

Piaget said that individuals develop through four main cognitive stages: sensorimotor, preoperational, concrete operational, and formal operational. Each of the stages is age related and consists of distinct ways of thinking. It is the *different* way of understanding the world that makes one stage more advanced than the other; knowing *more* information does not make the adolescent's thinking more advanced, in the Piagetian view. This is what Piaget meant when he said that the person's cognition is *qualitatively* different in one stage compared to another. We will briefly again define the first two stages in Piaget's theory, which were first introduced in chapter 2, and then explain concrete and formal operational thought.

We are born capable of learning.
—Jean-Jacques Rousseau
*Swiss-Born French Philosopher,
18th Century*

Sensorimotor and Preoperational Thought

The **sensorimotor stage,** *which lasts from birth to about 2 years of age, is the first Piagetian stage. In this stage, infants construct an understanding of the world by coordinating sensory experiences (such as seeing and hearing) with physical, motoric actions—hence the term* sensorimotor. At the beginning of this stage, newborns have little more than reflexive patterns with which to work. By the end of the stage, 2-year-olds have complex sensorimotor patterns and are beginning to operate with primitive symbols.

The **preoperational stage,** *which lasts approximately from 2 to 7 years of age, is the second Piagetian stage. In this stage, children begin to represent the world with words, images, and drawings.* Symbolic thought goes beyond simple connections of information and action.

sensorimotor stage
Piaget's first stage of development, lasting from birth to about 2 years of age. In this stage, infants construct an understanding of the world by coordinating sensory experiences with physical, motoric actions.

preoperational stage
Piaget's second stage, which lasts approximately from 2 to 7 years of age. In this stage, children begin to represent their world with words, images, and drawings.

Concrete Operational Thought

The **concrete operational stage,** *which lasts approximately from 7 to 11 years of age, is the third Piagetian stage. In this stage, children can perform operations. Logical reasoning replaces intuitive thought as long as the reasoning can be applied to specific or concrete examples.*

Piaget said that concrete operational thought involves *operations*—mental actions that allow the individual to do mentally what was done before physically. And he said that the concrete operational thinker can engage in mental actions that are reversible. For example, the concrete operational thinker can mentally reverse liquid from one beaker to another and understand that the volume is the same even though the beakers differ in height and width. In Piaget's most famous task, a child is presented with two identical beakers, each filled with the same amount of liquid (see figure 4.1 on p. 108). Children are asked if these beakers have the same amount of liquid, and they usually say yes. Then, the liquid from one beaker is poured into a third beaker, which is taller and thinner than the first two (see figure 4.1 on p. 108). Children are then asked if the amount of liquid in the tall, thin beaker is equal to that which remains in one of the original beakers. Concrete operational thinkers answer yes and justify their answers appropriately. Preoperational thinkers (usually children under the age of 7) often answer no and justify their answer in terms of the differing height and width of the beakers. This example reveals the ability of the concrete operational thinker to decenter and

concrete operational stage
Piaget's third stage, which lasts approximately from 7 to 11 years of age. In this stage, children can perform operations. Logical reasoning replaces intuitive thought as long as the reasoning can be applied to specific or concrete examples.

■ FIGURE 4.1
Piaget's Conservation Task

The beaker test is a well-known Piagetian test to determine whether the child can think operationally—that is, can mentally reverse actions and show conservation of the substance. (*I*) Two identical beakers are presented to the child. Then the experimenter pours the liquid from B into C, which is taller and thinner than A or B. (*II*) The child is now asked if these beakers (A and C) have the same amount of liquid. The preoperational child says no. When asked to point to the beaker that has more liquid, the preoperational child points to the tall, thin beaker.

formal operational stage
Piaget's fourth and final stage of cognitive development, which he believed emerges at 11 to 15 years of age. It is characterized by abstract, idealistic, and logical thought.

coordinate several characteristics (such as height and width), rather than focusing on a single property of an object (such as height).

Conservation is Piaget's term for an individual's ability to recognize that the length, number, mass, quantity, area, weight, and volume of objects and substances do not change through transformations that alter their appearance.

Classification, or class inclusion reasoning, is Piaget's concept of concrete operational thought, in which children systematically organize objects into hierarchies of classes and subclasses.

Although concrete operational thought is more advanced than preoperational thought, it has limitations. Logical reasoning replaces intuitive thought as long as the principles can be applied to specific, *concrete* examples. For example, the concrete operational child cannot imagine the steps necessary to complete an algebraic equation, which is too abstract for thinking at this stage of cognitive development. A summary of the characteristics of concrete operational thought is shown in figure 4.2 on page 109.

Formal Operational Thought
The **formal operational stage** *is Piaget's fourth and final stage of cognitive development. Piaget believed that this stage emerges at 11 to 15 years of age.* Adolescents' developing power of thought opens up new cognitive and social horizons. What are the characteristics of formal operational thought, which Piaget believed develops in adolescence? Most significantly, formal operational thought is more *abstract* than concrete operational thought. Adolescents are no longer limited to actual, concrete experiences as anchors for thought. They can conjure up make-believe situations—events that are purely hypothetical possibilities or strictly abstract propositions—and try to reason logically about them.

The abstract quality of the adolescent's thought at the formal operational level is evident in the adolescent's verbal problem-solving ability. While the concrete operational thinker would need to see the concrete elements A, B, and C to be able to make the logical inference that if A = B and B = C, then A = C, the formal operational thinker can solve this problem merely through verbal presentation.

Another indication of the abstract quality of adolescents' thought is their increased tendency to think about thought itself. One adolescent commented, "I began thinking

Can use operations, mentally reversing action; shows conservation skills

Logical reasoning replaces intuitive reasoning, but only in concrete circumstances

Not abstract (can't imagine steps in algebraic equation, for example)

Classification skills—can divide things into sets and subsets and reason about their interrelations

FIGURE 4.2
Characteristics of Concrete Operational Thought

about why I was thinking what I was. Then I began thinking about why I was thinking about why I was thinking about what I was." If this sounds abstract, it is, and it characterizes the adolescent's enhanced focus on thought and its abstract qualities. Later in the chapter we will further discuss thinking about thinking, which is called *metacognition.*

Accompanying the abstract nature of formal operational thought in adolescence is thought full of idealism and possibilities. While children frequently think in concrete ways, or in terms of what is real and limited, adolescents begin to engage in extended speculation about ideal characteristics—qualities they desire in themselves and in others. Such thoughts often lead adolescents to compare themselves and others in regard to such ideal standards. And during adolescence, the thoughts of individuals are often fantasy flights into future possibilities. It is not unusual for the adolescent to become impatient with these newfound ideal standards and become perplexed over which of many ideal standards to adopt.

At the same time adolescents think more abstractly and idealistically, they also think more logically. Adolescents begin to think more as a scientist thinks, devising plans to solve problems and systematically testing solutions. This type of problem solving has an imposing name. **Hypothetical-deductive reasoning** *is Piaget's term for adolescents' ability, in the stage of formal operational thought, to develop hypotheses, or best guesses, about ways to solve problems, such as an algebraic equation. They then systematically deduce, or conclude, the best path to follow in solving the problem.* By contrast, children are more likely to solve problems in a trial-and-error fashion.

One example of hypothetical-deductive reasoning involves a version of the familiar game "Twenty Questions." Individuals are shown a set of 42 color pictures displayed in a rectangular array (six rows of seven pictures each) and asked to determine which picture the experimenter has in mind (that is, which is "correct"). The subjects are only allowed to ask questions to which the experimenter can answer yes or no. The object of the game is to select the correct picture by asking as few questions as possible.

Adolescents who are deductive hypothesis testers formulate a plan and test a series of hypotheses, which considerably narrows the field of choices. The most effective plan

hypothetical-deductive reasoning
Piaget's term for adolescents' ability, in the formal operational stage, to develop hypotheses, or best guesses, about ways to solve problems; they then systematically deduce, or conclude, the best path to follow in solving the problem.

THINKING CRITICALLY

Formal Operational Thought, Politics, and Ideology

The development of formal operational thought expands adolescents' worlds by allowing them to consider possibilities, to conduct experiments and test hypotheses, and to think about thoughts. Part of the cognitive expansion of their worlds involves constructing theories involving politics and ideology. During adolescence, for the first time individuals become adept at generating ideas about the world as it *could* be. In the realm of moral development, adolescents often quickly make a leap from how the world could be to how it *should* be. And many adolescents believe the world *should* be transformed in the direction of some utopian ideal.

Suppose an 8-year-old and a 16-year-old are watching a political convention on television. In view of where each is likely to be in terms of Piaget's stages of cognitive development, how would their perceptions of the political proceedings likely differ? What would the 8-year-old "see" and comprehend? What Piagetian changes would these differences reflect?

"and give me good abstract-reasoning ability, interpersonal skills, cultural perspective, linguistic comprehension, and a high sociodynamic potential."

is a "halving" strategy (Q: Is the picture in the right half of the array? A: No. Q: OK. Is it in the top half? And so on.). A correct halving strategy guarantees the answer to this problem in seven questions or less. In contrast, the concrete operational thinker might persist with questions that continue to test some of the same possibilities that previous questions could have eliminated. For example, they might ask whether the correct picture is in row 1 and be told that it is not, then later ask whether the picture is *x*, which is in row 1.

Thus, formal operational thinkers test their hypotheses with judiciously chosen questions and tests. Concrete operational thinkers, on the other hand, often fail to understand the relation between a hypothesis and a well-chosen test of it, stubbornly clinging to ideas that already have been discounted.

Piaget believed that formal operational thought is the best description of how adolescents think. A summary of formal operational thought's characteristics is shown in figure 4.3 on page 111. As we see next, though, formal operational thought is not a homogeneous stage of development.

Not all adolescents are full-fledged formal operational thinkers. Some developmentalists believe that formal operational thought consists of two subperiods: early and late (Broughton, 1983). In *early formal operational thought,* adolescents' increased ability to think in hypothetical ways produces unconstrained thoughts with unlimited possibilities. In this early period, formal operational thought submerges reality, and there is an excess of assimilation as the world is perceived too subjectively and idealistically. *Late formal operational thought* involves a restoration of intellectual balance. Adolescents now test out the products of their reasoning against experience, and a consolidation of formal operational thought takes place. An intellectual balance is restored, as the adolescent accommodates to the cognitive upheaval that has occurred. Late formal operational thought may appear during the middle adolescent years. In this view, assimilation of formal operational thought marks the transition to adolescence; accommodation to formal operational thought marks a later consolidation (Lapsley, 1990).

Piaget's (1952) early writings indicated that the onset and consolidation of formal operational thought are completed during early adolescence, from about 11 to 15 years of age. Later, Piaget (1972) revised his view and concluded that formal operational thought is not completely achieved until later in adolescence, between approximately 15 and 20 years of age. As we see next, many developmentalists believe that there is considerable individual variation in adolescent cognition.

Piaget's theory emphasizes universal and consistent patterns of formal operational thought. His theory does not adequately account for the unique, individual differences that characterize the cognitive development of adolescents (Overton & Byrnes, 1991). These individual variations in adolescents' cognitive development have been documented in a number of investigations (Neimark, 1982).

Some individuals in early adolescence are formal operational thinkers; others are not. A review of formal operational thought investigations revealed that only about one of every three eighth-grade students is a formal operational thinker (Strahan, 1983). Some investigators find that formal operational thought increases with age in adolescence; others do not. Many college students and adults do not think in formal operational ways either. For example, investigators have found that from 17 to 67 percent of college students think in formal operational ways (Elkind, 1961; Tomlinson-Keasey, 1972).

Many young adolescents are at the point of consolidating their concrete operational thought, using it more consistently than in childhood. At the same time, many

Abstract	Idealistic	Logical
Adolescents think more abstractly than children. Formal operational thinkers can solve abstract algebraic equations, for example.	Adolescents often think about what is possible. They think about ideal characteristics of themselves, others, and the world.	Adolescents begin to think more like scientists, devising plans to solve problems and systematically testing solutions. Piaget called this type of logical thinking hypothetical-deductive reasoning.

■ FIGURE 4.3
Characteristics of Formal Operational Thought

Adolescents begin to think more as scientists think, devising plans to solve problems and systematically testing solutions. Piaget gave this type of thinking the imposing name of hypothetical-deductive reasoning.

young adolescents are just beginning to think in a formal operational manner. By late adolescence, many adolescents are beginning to consolidate their formal operational thought, using it more consistently. And there often is variation across the content areas of formal operational thought, just as there is in concrete operational thought in childhood. A 14-year-old adolescent might reason at the formal operational level when analyzing algebraic equations but not do so with verbal problem solving or when reasoning about interpersonal relations.

Formal operational thought is more likely to be used in areas in which adolescents have the most experience and knowledge. Children and adolescents gradually build up elaborate knowledge through extensive experience and practice in various sports, games, hobbies, and school subjects, such as math, English, and science. The development of expertise in different domains of life may make possible high-level, developmentally mature-looking thought. In some instances, the sophisticated reasoning of formal operational thought might be responsible. In other instances, however, the thought might be largely due to the accumulation of knowledge that allows more automatic,

■ THROUGH THE EYES OF ADOLESCENTS
We Think More Than Adults Think We Do

"I don't think adults understand how much kids think today. We just don't take something at face value. We want to understand why things are the way they are and the reasons behind things. We want it to be a better world and we are thinking all of the time how to make it that way. When we get to be adults, we will make the world better."

—Jason, Age 15
Dallas, Texas

memory-based processes to function. Some developmentalists wonder if the acquisition of knowledge could account for all cognitive growth. Most, however, argue that *both* cognitive changes in such areas as concrete and formal operational thought *and* the development of expertise through experience are at work in understanding the adolescent's cognitive world.

Piaget's Theory and Adolescent Education

Piaget's theory has been widely applied to education, although more extensively with children than with adolescents. Piaget was not an educator and never pretended to be. But he did provide a sound conceptual framework from which to view educational problems. What principles of Piaget's theory of cognitive development can be applied to education? David Elkind (1976) described two.

First, the foremost issue in education is *communication.* In Piaget's theory, the adolescent's mind is not a blank slate. To the contrary, the adolescent has a host of ideas about the physical and natural world. Adolescents come to school with their own ideas about space, time, causality, quantity, and number. Educators need to learn to comprehend what adolescents are saying and to respond to their ideas. Second, adolescents are, by nature, knowing creatures. The best way to nurture this motivation for knowledge is to allow adolescents to spontaneously interact with the environment. Educators need to ensure that they do not dull adolescents' eagerness to know by providing an overly rigid curriculum that disrupts adolescents' rhythm and pace of learning.

Why have applications to adolescent education lagged behind applications to children's education? Adolescents who are formal operational thinkers are at a level similar to that of their teachers and of the authors of textbooks. In Piaget's model, it is no longer necessary to pay attention to qualitative changes in cognition. Also, the structure of education itself changes considerably between elementary and secondary levels. For children, the basic focus of education is the classroom. Children might be involved with, at most, several teachers during the day. In secondary schools, the focus shifts to subject-matter divisions of curriculum. Each teacher sees a student for 45 to 60 minutes a day in connection with one content area (English, history, math, for example). Thus, both teachers and texts can become more focused on the development of curriculum than on the developmental characteristics of students. And when teachers *are* concerned about students' developmental characteristics in adolescence, they pay more attention to social-personality dimensions than to cognitive dimensions.

One main argument that has emerged from the application of Piaget's theory to education is that instruction may too often be at the formal operational level, even though the majority of adolescents are not actually formal operational thinkers. That is, the instruction might be too formal and too abstract. Possibly, it should be less formal and more concrete. Researchers have found that adolescents construct a view of the world on the basis of observations and experiences and that educators should take this into account when developing a curriculum for adolescents (Linn, 1991).

Evaluating Piaget's Theory

What were Piaget's main contributions? Has his theory withstood the test of time?

Contributions Piaget is a giant in the field of developmental psychology. We owe to him the present field of cognitive development and a long list of masterful concepts of enduring power and fascination: assimilation, accommodation, conservation, hypothetical-deductive reasoning, and others. We also owe to him the current vision of children as active, constructive thinkers (Vidal, 2000).

Piaget also was a genius when it came to observing children. His careful observations showed us inventive ways to discover how children act on and adapt to their world. Piaget showed us some important things to look for in cognitive development, such as the shift from preoperational to concrete operational thinking. He also showed us how children need to make their experiences fit their schemas (cognitive frameworks) yet simultaneously adapt their schemas to experience. Piaget also revealed how cognitive change is likely to occur if the context is structured to allow gradual movement to the next-higher level. And we owe him the current belief that a concept does not emerge all of a sudden, full-blown, but instead develops through a series of partial accomplishments that lead to increasingly comprehensive understanding (Haith & Benson, 1998).

Criticisms   Piaget's theory has not gone unchallenged. Questions are raised about these areas:

- *Estimates of children's competence.* Some cognitive abilities emerge earlier than Piaget thought. For example, some aspects of object permanence emerge earlier in infancy than he believed. Even 2-year-olds are nonegocentric in some contexts. When they realize that another person will not see an object, they investigate whether the person is blindfolded or looking in a different direction. Conservation of number has been demonstrated as early as age 3, although Piaget thought it did not emerge until 7. Young children are not as uniformly "pre-" this and "pre-" that (precausal, preoperational) as Piaget thought.

  Other cognitive abilities can emerge later than Piaget thought. Many adolescents still think in concrete operational ways or are just beginning to master formal operations. Even many adults are not formal operational thinkers. In sum, recent theoretical revisions highlight more cognitive competencies of infants and young children and more cognitive shortcomings of adolescents and adults (Flavell, Miller, & Miller, 2001; Wertsch, 2000).
- *Stages.* Piaget conceived of stages as unitary structures of thought. Thus, his theory assumes developmental synchrony: various aspects of a stage should emerge at the same time. However, some concrete operational concepts do not appear in synchrony. For example, children do not learn to conserve at the same time as they learn to cross-classify. Thus, most contemporary developmentalists agree that children's cognitive development is not as stagelike as Piaget thought (Brainerd, 2002; Kuhn, 2000a).
- *Training children to reason at a higher level.* Some children who are at one cognitive stage (such as preoperational) can be trained to reason at a higher cognitive stage (such as concrete operational). This poses a problem for Piaget's theory. Piaget argued that such training is only superficial and ineffective, unless the child is at a maturational transition point between the stages (Gelman & Williams, 1998).
- *Culture and education.* Culture and education exert stronger influences on development than Piaget envisioned. The age at which individuals acquire conservation skills is associated to some extent with the degree to which their culture provides relevant practice (Cole, 1997). And in many developing countries, formal operational thought is rare. Shortly, you will read about Lev Vygotsky's theory of cognitive development in which culture and education are given more prominent roles than in Piaget's theory.

Piaget, shown sitting on a bench, was a genius at observing children. By carefully observing and interviewing children, Piaget constructed his comprehensive theory of children's cognitive development. *What are some other contributions, as well as criticisms, of Piaget's theory?*

One group of cognitive developmentalists believe that Piaget's theory needs to be modified. These **neo-Piagetians** *argue that Piaget got some things right, but that his theory needs considerable revision. In their revision of Piaget, they give more emphasis to how children process information through attention, memory, and strategies and to more precise explanations of cognitive changes.* They especially believe that a more accurate vision of children's and adolescents' thinking requires more knowledge of strategies, how fast and automatically information is processed, the particular cognitive task involved, and dividing cognitive problems into smaller, more precise steps.

The leading proponent of the neo-Piagetian view is Canadian developmental psychologist Robbie Case (1992, 1998, 2000). He accepts Piaget's four main stages of cognitive development but believes that a more precise description of changes within each

neo-Piagetians

Theorists who argue that Piaget got some things right but that his theory needs considerable revision. In their revision, they give more emphasis to information processing that involves attention, memory, and strategies; they also seek to provide more precise explanations of cognitive changes.

stage needs to be carried out. Case also argues that children's and adolescents' ability to process information more efficiently is linked to their brain growth and memory development. He especially cites the increasing ability to hold information in working memory (a workbench for memory similar to short-term memory) and manipulate it more effectively as critical to understanding cognitive development.

Is There a Fifth, Postformal Stage?   As we saw earlier in the chapter, Piaget did not believe there is a fifth, postformal stage. He argued that formal operational thought is the highest *qualitative* stage of thought and that it is entered in early adolescence. However, some theorists argue that Piaget was wrong about formal operations being the most advanced stage of thought. They believe that young adults can enter a fifth, postformal stage.

postformal thought

A form of thought, proposed as a fifth stage, that is qualitatively different from Piaget's formal operational thought. It involves understanding that the correct answer to a problem can require reflective thinking, that the correct answer can vary from one situation to another, and that the search for truth is often an ongoing, never-ending process.

Postformal thought *is qualitatively different from Piaget's formal operational thought. Postformal thought involves understanding that the correct answer to a problem requires reflective thinking and can vary from one situation to another, and that the search for truth is often an ongoing, never-ending process.* Also part of the fifth stage is the belief that solutions to problems need to be realistic and that emotion and subjective factors can influence thinking (Kitchener & King, 1981). Researchers have found that young adults are more likely to engage in this postformal thinking than adolescents are (Commons & others, 1989).

As young adults engage in more reflective judgment when solving problems, they might think deeply about many aspects of politics, their career and work, relationships, and other areas of life (Labouvie-Vief & Diehl, 1999). They might understand that what might be the best solution to a problem at work (with a co-worker or boss) might not be the best solution at home (with a romantic partner). Many young adults also become more skeptical about there being a single truth and often are not willing to accept an answer as final. They also often recognize that thinking can't just be abstract but rather has to be realistic and pragmatic. And many young adults understand that emotions can play a role in thinking—for example, that one likely thinks more clearly in a calm, collected state than in an angry, highly aroused state.

How strong is the research evidence for a fifth, postformal stage of cognitive development? The fifth stage is controversial, and some critics argue that the research evidence has yet to be provided to document it as clearly a qualitatively more advanced stage than formal operational thought.

William Perry (1970, 1999) especially believes that changes in reflective and relativistic thinking take place as individuals make the transition from adolescence to adulthood, a time referred to as emerging adulthood. He said that younger adolescents tend to view the world in terms of polarities—right/wrong, we/they, good/bad. As adolescents make the transition to adulthood, they gradually move away from this type of absolute thinking. This change occurs as they become aware of the diverse opinions and multiple perspectives of others.

Perry said that college is a pivotal time for the change from absolute to more relativistic thinking. Indeed, researchers have found that individuals who go to college think in more relativistic ways than those who do not attend college (King & Kitchener, 1994). This likely occurs because of the exposure to instructors and peers with views that are quite different from one's own.

Vygotsky's Theory

We introduced Vygotsky's theory in chapter 2, "The Science of Adolescent Development." Here we expand on those ideas ◀IIII P. 47.

Vygotsky's (1962) theory has stimulated considerable interest in the view that knowledge is *situated* and *collaborative* (Greeno, Collins, & Resnick, 1996; Rogoff, 1998)—that knowledge is distributed among people and environments, which include objects, artifacts, tools, books, and the communities in which people live. This suggests that knowing can best be advanced through interaction with others in cooperative activities (Glassman, 2001; Gojdamaschko, 1999; Kozulin, 2000; Tudge & Scrimsher, 2002).

One of Vygotsky's most important concepts is the **zone of proximal development** (**ZPD**), *which refers to the range of tasks that are too difficult for an individual to master alone, but that can be mastered with the guidance and assistance of adults or more-skilled peers.* Thus, the lower level of the ZPD is the level of problem solving reached by the adolescent working independently. The upper limit is the level of additional responsibility the adolescent can accept with the assistance of an able instructor (see figure 4.4). Vygotsky's emphasis on the ZPD underscored his belief in the importance of social influences on cognitive development.

In Vygotsky's approach, formal schooling is but one cultural agent that determines adolescents' growth (Keating, 1990). Parents, peers, the community, and the technological orientation of the culture are other forces that influence adolescents' thinking. For example, the attitudes toward intellectual competence that adolescents encounter through relationships with their parents and peers affect their motivation for acquiring knowledge. So do the attitudes of teachers and other adults in the community. Media influences, especially through the development of television and the computer, play increasingly important roles in the cognitive socialization of adolescents. For example, does television train adolescents to become passive learners and detract significantly from their intellectual pursuit? We will consider television's role in adolescent development in chapter 8.

The cognitive socialization of adolescents can be improved through the development of more cognitively stimulating environments and additional focus on the role of social factors in cognitive growth (Brown, Metz, & Campione, 1996). Approaches that take into account adolescents' self-confidence, achievement expectations, and sense of purpose are likely to be just as effective as, or even more effective than, more narrow cognitive approaches in shaping adolescents' cognitive growth. For example, a knowledge of physics could be of limited use to inner-city youth with severely limited prospects of employment (Keating, 1990).

Exploring Some Contemporary Concepts A number of contemporary concepts are compatible with Vygotsky's theory. These include the concepts of scaffolding, cognitive apprenticeship, tutoring, cooperative learning, and reciprocal teaching.

Scaffolding *Scaffolding* refers to changing the level of support over the course of a teaching session: a more-skilled person (teacher or more-advanced peer of the adolescent) adjusts the amount of guidance to fit the adolescent's current level of performance. When the task the adolescent is learning is new, direct instruction might be used. As the adolescent's competence increases, less guidance is provided. Think of scaffolding in learning as like the scaffolding used to build a bridge—it is used for support when needed, but is adjusted or removed as the project unfolds.

Cognitive Apprenticeship Barbara Rogoff (1990, 1998) believes that an important aspect of learning is *cognitive apprenticeship,* in which an expert stretches and supports the novice's understanding of and use of the culture's skills. The term *apprenticeship* underscores the importance of activity in learning and highlights the situated nature of learning. In a cognitive apprenticeship, adults often model strategies for adolescents then support their efforts at doing the task. Finally, they encourage adolescents to work independently.

zone of proximal development (ZPD)
Vygotsky's concept that refers to the range of tasks that are too difficult for an individual to master alone, but that can be mastered with the guidance or assistance of adults or more-skilled peers.

Lev Vygotsky: Revolutionary Scientist
Vygotsky Links
http://www.mhhe.com/santrocka9

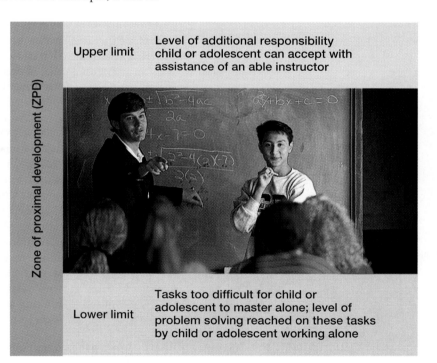

Upper limit Level of additional responsibility child or adolescent can accept with assistance of an able instructor

Zone of proximal development (ZPD)

Lower limit Tasks too difficult for child or adolescent to master alone; level of problem solving reached on these tasks by child or adolescent working alone

◻ FIGURE 4.4
Vygotsky's Zone of Proximal Development (ZPD)

Vygotsky's zone of proximal development has a lower limit and an upper limit. Tasks in the ZPD are too difficult for the child or adolescent to perform alone. They require assistance from an adult or a more-skilled youth. As children and adolescents experience the verbal instruction or demonstration, they organize the information in their existing mental structures so they can eventually perform the skill or task alone.

Scaffolding
Cognitive Apprenticeship
Peer Tutoring
http://www.mhhe.com/santrocka9

A key aspect of a cognitive apprenticeship is the expert's evaluation of when the learner is ready to take the next step with support from the expert. In one study of secondary school science and math students, experts used the timing of the students' participation in discourse to infer student understanding of the points of the lesson; the experts provided pauses to allow students to take responsibility for an idea by anticipating or completing the experts' ideas (Fox, 1993). Experts also used information regarding the length of each response opportunity students passed up and what the students were doing during the passed-up opportunity (such as calculating or expressing a blank stare). When students passed up two or three opportunities, experts continued with an explanation. If no evidence of understanding occurred during the explanation, the expert repeated or reformulated it. The experts also used "hint" questions to get students unstuck and observed the looks on their faces and how they responded to questions for discerning their understanding.

Tutoring   Tutoring involves a cognitive apprenticeship between an expert and a novice. Tutoring can take place between an adult and an adolescent or between a more-skilled adolescent and a less-skilled adolescent. Fellow students can be effective tutors. Cross-age tutoring usually works better than same-age tutoring. Researchers have found that peer tutoring often benefits students' achievement (Mathes & others, 1998). And tutoring can benefit the tutor as well as the tutee, especially when the older tutor is a low-achieving student. Teaching something to someone else is one of the best ways to learn.

Cooperative Learning   *Cooperative learning* involves students working in small groups to help each other learn. Cooperative learning groups vary in size, although a typical group will have about four students. Researchers have found that cooperative learning can be an effective strategy for improving achievement, especially when these two conditions are met (Slavin, 1995): (1) group rewards are generated (these help group members see that it is in their best interest to help each other learn), and (2) individuals are held accountable (that is, some method of evaluating an individual's contribution, such as an individual quiz, is used). Cooperative learning helps promote interdependence and connection with other students. In chapter 7, "Schools," we will further examine the concept of cooperative learning.

Cooperative Learning
Schools for Thought
http://www.mhhe.com/santrocka9

Reciprocal Teaching   *Reciprocal teaching* involves students taking turns leading a small-group discussion. Reciprocal teaching also can involve an adult and an adolescent. As in scaffolding, the teacher gradually assumes a less active role, letting the student assume more initiative. This technique has been widely used to help students learn to read more effectively. For example, Ann Brown and Annemarie Palincsar (1984) used reciprocal teaching to improve students' abilities to enact certain strategies to improve their reading comprehension. In this teacher-scaffolded instruction, teachers worked with students to help them *generate questions* about the text they had read, *clarify* what they did not understand, *summarize* the text, and *make predictions*.

Ann Brown's most recent efforts focused on transforming schools into communities of thinking and learning. Her ideas have much in common with Vygotsky's emphasis on learning as a collaborative process.

Comparing Piaget and Vygotsky   Awareness of Vygotsky's theory came later than awareness of Piaget's, so it has not yet been thoroughly evaluated. However, Vygotsky's theory has been embraced by many teachers and successfully applied to education. His view of the importance of sociocultural influences on development fits with the current belief in the importance of contextual factors in learning (Greenfield, 2000). However, criticisms of his theory have emerged; for example, it has been argued that he overemphasized the role of language in thinking.

Vygotsky's and Piaget's theories are constructivist. *Constructivism* emphasizes that individuals actively construct knowledge and understanding. In the constructivist view, information is not directly given to children and adolescents and

THROUGH THE EYES OF PSYCHOLOGISTS

Barbara Rogoff
University of California—Santa Cruz

"Cognitive development occurs as new generations collaborate with older generations in varying forms of interpersonal engagement and institutional practices."

Topic	Vygotsky	Piaget
Constructivism	Social constructivist	Cognitive constructivist
Stages	No general stages of development proposed	Strong emphasis on stages (sensorimotor, preoperational, concrete operational, and formal operational)
Key processes	Zone of proximal development, language, dialogue, tools of the culture	Schema, assimilation, accommodation, operations, conservation, classification, hypothetical-deductive reasoning
Role of language	A major role; language plays a powerful role in shaping thought	Language has a minimal role; cognition primarily directs language
View on education	Education plays a central role, helping children learn the tools of the culture.	Education merely refines the child's cognitive skills that already have emerged.
Teaching implications	Teacher is a facilitator and guide, not a director; establish many opportunities for children to learn with the teacher and more skilled peers	Also views teacher as a facilitator and guide, not a director; provide support for children to explore their world and discover knowledge

■ FIGURE 4.5
Comparison of Vygotsky's and Piaget's Theories

poured into their minds. Rather, they are encouraged to explore their world, discover knowledge, and think critically (Perkins, 1999).

Distinctions can be drawn between cognitive and social constructivist approaches. In a *cognitive constructivist approach,* emphasis is on the individual's cognitive construction of knowledge and understanding. Piaget's theory is cognitive constructivist. In a *social constructivist approach,* emphasis is on collaboration with others to produce knowledge and understanding. Vygotsky's theory is social constructivist.

In Piaget's and Vygotsky's theories, teachers serve as facilitators and guides rather than directors and molders of learning. Figure 4.5 on page 117 provides a comparison of Piaget's and Vygotsky's theories.

At this point we have studied a number of ideas about Piaget's and Vygotsky's theories. This review should help you to reach your learning goals related to these topics.

☐ FOR YOUR REVIEW

Learning Goal 1
Discuss Piaget's theory

- Piaget's widely acclaimed theory stresses adaptation, schemas, assimilation, accommodation, and equilibration.
- Piaget said that individuals develop through four cognitive stages: sensorimotor, preoperational, concrete operational, and formal operational. Formal operational thought, which Piaget believed appears from 11 to 15 years of age, is characterized by abstract, idealistic, and hypothetical-deductive thinking. Some experts argue that formal operational thought has two phases: early and late. Individual variation in adolescent cognition is extensive. Many young adolescents are still consolidating their concrete operational thought or are early formal operational thinkers rather than full-fledged ones.
- Although Piaget was not an educator, his constructivist ideas have been applied to education.
- In terms of Piaget's contributions, we owe to him the entire field of cognitive development and a masterful list of concepts. He also was a genius at observing children. Criticisms of Piaget's theory focus on estimates of competence, stages, training to reason at higher stages, and the role of culture and education. Neo-Piagetians have proposed some substantial changes in Piaget's theory.
- Piaget did not believe there is a fifth, postformal stage of thought. However, some theorists argue that this stage is entered by many young adults. Perry believed that emerging adulthood is a time when individuals think more reflectively and relativistically, especially if they go to college.

Learning Goal 2
Understand Vygotsky's theory

- Vygotsky's view stimulated considerable interest in the idea that knowledge is situated and collaborative. One of his important concepts is the zone of proximal development, which involves guidance by more-skilled peers and adults. Vygotsky argued that learning the skills of the culture is a key aspect of development.
- Some contemporary concepts linked with Vygotsky's theory include scaffolding, cognitive apprenticeship, tutoring, cooperative learning, and reciprocal teaching.
- Piaget's and Vygotsky's views are both constructivist—Piaget's being cognitive constructivist, Vygotsky's social constructivist. In both views, teachers should be facilitators, not directors, of learning.

Now that we have discussed the cognitive developmental views of Piaget and Vygotsky, we will turn our attention to another major framework for understanding adolescent cognition: information processing.

THE INFORMATION-PROCESSING VIEW

In chapter 2, "The Science of Adolescent Development," we briefly described the information-processing view ◀▥ P. 48. We indicated that information processing includes how information gets into adolescents' minds, how it is stored, and how it is retrieved to think about and solve problems.

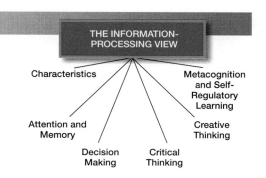

Information processing is both a framework for thinking about adolescent development and a facet of that development. As a framework, the information-processing view includes certain ideas about how adolescents' minds work and the best methods for studying this (Logan, 2000). As a facet of development, different aspects of information processing change as children make the transition through adolescence to adulthood. For example, changes in attention and memory are essentially changes in the way individuals process information. In our exploration of information processing, we will discuss developmental changes in attention and memory, as well as other cognitive processes, but first let's examine some basic characteristics of the information-processing approach.

Characteristics

Robert Siegler (1998) described three main characteristics of the information-processing approach:

• *Thinking*. In Siegler's view, thinking is information processing. In this regard, Siegler provides a broad perspective on thinking. He says that when adolescents perceive, encode, represent, and store information from the world, they are engaging in thinking. Siegler believes that thinking is highly flexible, which allows individuals to adapt and adjust to many changes in circumstances, task requirements, and goals. However, the human's remarkable thinking abilities have some constraints. Individuals can attend to only a limited amount of information at one point in time, and they are constrained by how fast they can process information.

• *Change mechanisms*. Siegler (2000) argues that the information-processing approach should focus on the role of mechanisms of change in development. He believes that four main mechanisms—encoding, automatization, strategy construction, and generalization—work together to create changes in children's and adolescents' cognitive skills. *Encoding* is the process by which information gets into memory. Siegler states that a key aspect of solving problems is encoding the relevant information and ignoring the irrelevant parts. Because it often takes time and effort to construct new strategies, children and adolescents must practice them in order to eventually execute them automatically and maximize their effectiveness. The term *automaticity* refers to the ability to process information with little or no effort. With age and experience, information processing becomes increasingly automatic on many tasks, allowing children and adolescents to detect connections among ideas and events that they otherwise would miss. An able 12-year-old zips through a practice list of multiplication problems with little conscious effort, and a 16-year-old picks up the newspaper and quickly scans the entertainment section for the location and time of a movie. In both cases, the information processing of these adolescents is more automatic and less effortful than that of children.

Recall that earlier in the chapter we described Robbie Case's neo-Piagetian view. Case's view includes an emphasis on changes in the way that adolescents process information differently than children. His view includes an aspect of information processing emphasized by Siegler: automaticity. In Case's (1992, 1998, 2000) view adolescents have more cognitive resources available to them because of automaticity, increased information-processing capacity, and more familiarity with a range of content knowledge. These advances in information processing reduce the load on cognitive systems, allowing adolescents to hold in mind several dimensions of a topic or a problem simultaneously. In contrast, children are more prone to focus on only one dimension.

The third and fourth change mechanisms proposed by Siegler are strategy construction and generalization. *Strategy construction* involves the discovery of a new procedure for processing information. Siegler says that adolescents need to encode key information about a problem and coordinate the information with relevant prior knowledge to solve the problem. To fully benefit from a newly constructed strategy, adolescents need to *generalize* it, or apply it to other problems.

• *Self-modification.* The contemporary information-processing approach argues, as does Piaget's theory of cognitive development, that adolescents play an active role in their development. They use knowledge and strategies that they have learned in previous circumstances to adapt their responses to a new learning situation. In this manner, adolescents build newer and more sophisticated responses from prior knowledge and strategies.

Attention and Memory

Although the bulk of research on information processing has been conducted with children and adults, the information-processing perspective is important in understanding adolescent cognition. As we saw in the example of the adolescent solving an algebraic equation, attention and memory are two important cognitive processes.

Attention   *Pay attention* is a phrase children and adolescents hear all of the time. Just what is *attention? Attention* is the concentration and focusing of mental effort. Attention also is both selective and shifting. For example, when adolescents take a test, they must attend to it. This implies that they have the ability to focus their mental effort on certain stimuli (the test questions) while excluding other stimuli, an important aspect of attention called *selectivity.* When selective attention fails adolescents, they have difficulty ignoring information that is irrelevant to their interest or goals. For example, if a television set is blaring while the adolescent is studying, the adolescent could have difficulty concentrating.

Not only is attention selective, but it is also *shiftable.* If a teacher asks students to pay attention to a certain question and they do so, their behavior indicates that they can shift the focus of their mental effort from one stimulus to another. If the telephone rings while the adolescent is studying, the adolescent may shift attention from studying to the telephone. An external stimulus is not necessary to shift attention. At any moment, adolescents can shift their attention from one topic to another, virtually at will. They might think about the last time they went to a play, then think about an upcoming musical recital, and so on.

In one investigation, 12-year-olds were markedly better than 8-year-olds and slightly worse than 20-year-olds at allocating their attention in a situation involving two tasks (Manis, Keating, & Morrison, 1980). Adolescents might have more resources available (through increased processing speed, capacity, and automaticity), or they might be more skilled at directing these resources.

Memory   There are few moments when adolescents' lives are not steeped in memory. Memory is at work with each step adolescents take, each thought they think, and each word they utter. *Memory* is the retention of information over time. It is central to mental life and to information processing. To successfully learn and reason, adolescents need to hold on to information and to retrieve the information they have tucked away. Three important memory systems are short-term memory, working memory, and long-term memory.

Short-Term Memory   *Short-term memory* is a limited-capacity memory system in which information is retained for as long as 30 seconds, unless the information is rehearsed, in which case it can be retained longer. A common way to assess short-term memory is to present a list of items to remember, which is often referred to as a memory span task. If you have taken an IQ test, you probably were asked to remember a string of numbers or words. You simply

What changes in attention characterize adolescence?

hear a short list of stimuli—usually digits—presented at a rapid pace (one per second, for example). Then you are asked to repeat the digits back. Using the memory span task, researchers have found that short-term memory increases extensively in early childhood and continues to increase in older children and adolescents, but at a slower pace. For example, in one investigation, memory span increased by 1½ digits between the ages of 7 and 13 (Dempster, 1981). Keep in mind, though, memory span's individual differences, which is why IQ and various aptitude tests are used.

How might short-term memory be used in problem solving? In a series of experiments, Robert Sternberg and his colleagues (Sternberg, 1977; Sternberg & Nigro, 1980; Sternberg & Rifkin, 1979) attempted to answer this question by giving third-grade, sixth-grade, ninth-grade, and college students analogies to solve. The main differences occurred between the younger (third- and sixth-grade) and older (ninth-grade and college) students. The older students were more likely to complete the information processing required to solve the analogy task. The children, by contrast, often stopped their processing of information before they had considered all of the necessary steps required to solve the problems. Sternberg believes that information processing was incomplete because the children's short-term memory was overloaded. Solving problems such as analogies requires individuals to make continued comparisons between newly encoded information and previously coded information. Sternberg argues that adolescents probably have more storage space in short-term memory, which results in fewer errors on problems like analogies.

In addition to more storage space, are there other reasons adolescents might perform better on memory span tasks and in solving analogies? Though many other factors could be involved, information-processing psychologists believe that changes in the speed and efficiency of information processing are important, especially the speed with which information can be identified.

Working Memory   An increasing number of psychologists believe that the way short-term memory has been historically described is too passive and does not do justice to the amount of cognitive work that is done over the short term in memory (Kail & Hall, 2001; Murdock, 1999). They prefer the concept of working memory to describe how memory works on a short-term basis (Sussman, 2001; Waters & Caplan, 2001). British psychologist Alan Baddeley (1992, 2000) proposed the concept of *working memory,* which is a kind of "mental workbench" where information is manipulated and assembled to help make decisions, solve problems, and comprehend written and spoken language.

In one recent study across the life span, the performances of individuals from 6 to 57 years of age were examined on both verbal and visuospatial working memory tasks (Swanson, 1999). The two verbal tasks were auditory digit sequence (the ability to remember numerical information embedded in a short sentence, such as "Now suppose somebody wanted to go to the supermarket at 8651 Elm Street") and semantic association (the ability to organize words into abstract categories). In the semantic association task, the participant was presented with a series of words and then asked to remember how they go together (such as shirt, saw, pants, hammer, shoes, and nails).

The two visuospatial tasks used in this study involved mapping/directions and a visual matrix. In the mapping/directions task, the participant was shown a street map in which the lines connected to a number of dots illustrating the direction the bicycle (child/young adolescent) or car (adult) would go to get through the city. The dots represented stoplights and the lines the direction of the vehicle. After briefly looking at the map, participants were asked to draw the directions and dots on a blank map. In the visual matrix task, participants were asked to remember visual sequences within a matrix that involved a series of dots. After looking at the visual matrix for five seconds, it was removed and the participants were asked questions about the location of the dots.

As shown in figure 4.6 on page 122, there was a substantial increase in the working memory of individuals from 8 through 24 years of age on all four tasks. Thus, it is likely that the adolescent years are an important developmental time frame for improvement

I come into the fields and spacious palaces of my memory, where are treasures of countless images of things of every manner.
—St. Augustine
Christian Church Father, 5th Century

Memory Links
http://www.mhhe.com/santrocka9

▣ FIGURE 4.6
Developmental Changes in Working Memory

Note: The scores shown here are the means for each age group and the age also represents a mean age. Higher scores reflect superior working memory performance.

		Task			
		Verbal		Visuospatial	
		Semantic Association	Digit/ Sentence	Mapping/ Directions	Visual Matrix
Age	8	1.33	1.75	3.13	1.67
	10	1.70	2.34	3.60	2.06
	13	1.86	2.94	4.09	2.51
	16	2.24	2.98	3.92	2.68
	24	2.60	3.71	4.64	3.47
	Highest Working Memory Performance				
		3.02 (age 45)	3.97 (age 35)	4.90 (age 35)	3.47 (age 24)

in working memory and that working memory continues to improve through the transition to adulthood and beyond.

Long-Term Memory   *Long-term memory* is a relatively permanent memory system that holds huge amounts of information for a long period of time. Long-term memory increases substantially in the middle and late childhood years and likely continues to improve during adolescence, although this has not been well documented by researchers. If anything at all is known about long-term memory, it is that it depends on the learning activities engaged in when learning and remembering information (Pressley & Schneider, 1997; Siegler, 1996). Most learning activities fit under the category of *strategies,* activities under the learner's conscious control. They sometimes are also called control processes. There are many of these activities, but one of the most important is organization, the tendency to group or arrange items into categories. We will have more to say about strategies shortly.

Attention and memory are important dimensions of information processing, but other dimensions also are important. Once adolescents attend to information and retain it, they can use the information to engage in a number of cognitive activities, such as making decisions, thinking critically, and thinking creatively. Let's begin our exploration of these cognitive activities by examining what is involved in decision making.

Decision Making

Adolescence is a time of increased decision making—about the future, which friends to choose, whether to go to college, which person to date, whether to have sex, whether to buy a car, and so on (Byrnes, 1997; Galotti & Kozberg, 1996; Parker & Fischhoff, 2002). How competent are adolescents at making decisions? In some reviews, older adolescents are described as more competent than younger adolescents, who, in turn, are more competent than children (Keating, 1990). Compared to children, young adolescents are more likely to generate options, to examine a situation from a variety of perspectives, to anticipate the consequences of decisions, and to consider the credibility of sources.

One study documents that older adolescents are better at decision making than younger adolescents are (Lewis, 1981). Eighth-, tenth-, and twelfth-grade students were presented with dilemmas involving the choice of a medical procedure. The oldest students were most likely to spontaneously mention a variety of risks, to recommend consultation with an outside specialist, and to anticipate future consequences. For example, when asked a question about whether to have cosmetic surgery, a twelfth-grader said that different aspects of the situation need to be examined along with its effects on the individual's future, especially relationships with other people. In contrast, an eighth-grader presented a more limited view, commenting on the surgery's effects on getting turned down for a date, the money involved, and being teased by peers.

In sum, older adolescents often make better decisions than do younger adolescents, who, in turn, make better decisions than children do. But the decision-making skills of older adolescents are far from perfect, as are those of adults (Klaczynski, 1997). Indeed, some researchers have recently found that adolescents and adults do not differ in their decision-making skills (Quadrel, Fischoff, & Davis, 1993).

Being able to make competent decisions does not guarantee that one will make them in everyday life, where breadth of experience often comes into play (Jacobs & Potenza, 1990; Keating, 1990). For example, driver-training courses improve adolescents' cognitive and motor skills to levels equal to, or sometimes superior to, those of adults. However, driver training has not been effective in reducing adolescents' high rate of traffic accidents (Potvin, Champagne, & Laberge-Nadeau, 1988). An important research agenda is to study the ways adolescents make decisions in practical situations.

Adolescents need more opportunities to practice and discuss realistic decision making (Jones, Rasmussen, & Moffitt, 1997). Many real-world decisions occur in an atmosphere of stress that includes such factors as time constraints and emotional involvement. One strategy for improving adolescent decision making about real-world choices involving such matters as sex, drugs, and daredevil driving is for schools to provide more opportunities for adolescents to engage in role-playing and group problem solving related to such circumstances.

Another strategy is for parents to involve their adolescents in appropriate decision-making activities. In one study of more than 900 young adolescents and a subsample of their parents, adolescents were more likely to participate in family decision making when they perceived themselves as in control of what happens to them and if they thought that their input would have some bearing on the outcome of the decision-making process (Liprie, 1993).

Critical Thinking

Closely related to making competent decisions is engaging in critical thinking, a current buzzword in education and psychology (Brooks & Brooks, 1999; Halonen, 1995) ◀◀◀ IIII P. 28. **Critical thinking** *involves thinking reflectively and productively and evaluating the evidence.* In a recent study of fifth-, eighth-, and eleventh-graders, critical thinking increased with age but still only occurred in 43 percent of even the eleventh-graders, and many adolescents showed self-serving biases in their reasoning (Klaczynski & Narasimham, 1998).

Adolescence is an important transitional period in the development of critical thinking (Keating, 1990). Among the cognitive changes that allow improved critical thinking in adolescence are:

- Increased speed, automaticity, and capacity of information processing, which free cognitive resources for other purposes
- More breadth of content knowledge in a variety of domains
- Increased ability to construct new combinations of knowledge
- A greater range and more spontaneous use of strategies or procedures for applying or obtaining knowledge, such as planning, considering alternatives, and cognitive monitoring

Although adolescence is an important period in the development of critical-thinking skills, if a solid basis of fundamental skills (such as literacy and math skills) is

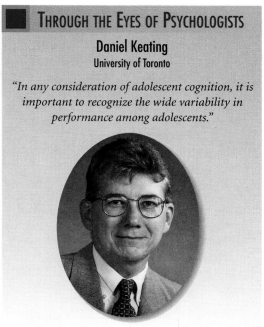

critical thinking
Thinking reflectively and productively and evaluating the evidence.

Exploring Critical Thinking
Critical Thinking Resources
Odyssey of the Mind
http://www.mhhe.com/santrocka9

Laura Bickford
Secondary School Teacher

Laura Bickford teaches English and journalism in grades 9 to 12 and she is Chair of the English Department at Nordhoff High School in Ojai, California.

Laura especially believes it is important to encourage students to think. Indeed, she says that "the call to teach is the call to teach students how to think." She believes teachers need to show students the value in asking their own questions, in having discussions, and in engaging in stimulating intellectual conversations. Laura says that she also encourages students to engage in metacognitive strategies (knowing about knowing). For example, she asks students to comment on their learning after particular pieces of projects have been completed. She requires students to keep reading logs so they can observe their own thinking as it happens.

Laura Bickford, working with students writing papers.

The Jasper Project
Teresa Amabile's Research
http://www.mhhe.com/santrocka9

creativity
The ability to think in novel and unusual ways and come up with unique solutions to problems.

convergent thinking
A pattern of thinking in which individuals produce one correct answer; characteristic of the items on conventional intelligence tests; coined by Guilford.

divergent thinking
A pattern of thinking in which individuals produce many answers to the same question; more characteristic of creativity than convergent thinking; coined by Guilford.

not developed during childhood, such critical-thinking skills are unlikely to mature in adolescence. For the subset of adolescents who lack such fundamental skills, potential gains in adolescent thinking are not likely.

Considerable interest has recently developed in teaching critical thinking in schools. Cognitive psychologist Robert J. Sternberg (1985) believes that most school programs that teach critical thinking are flawed. He thinks that schools focus too much on formal reasoning tasks and not enough on the critical-thinking skills needed in everyday life. Among the critical-thinking skills that Sternberg believes adolescents need in everyday life are these: recognizing that problems exist, defining problems more clearly, handling problems with no single right answer or any clear criteria for the point at which the problem is solved (such as selecting a rewarding career), making decisions on issues of personal relevance (such as deciding to have a risky operation), obtaining information, thinking in groups, and developing long-term approaches to long-term problems.

One educational program that embodies Sternberg's recommendations for increased critical thinking in schools is the *Jasper Project*, twelve videodisc-based adventures that focus on solving real-world math problems. The Jasper Project is the brainchild of the Cognition and Technology Group at Vanderbilt (1997). Figure 4.7 on page 125 shows one of the Jasper adventures. For students in grades 5 and up, Jasper helps them make connections with other disciplines including science, history, and social studies. Jasper's creators think that students need to be exposed to authentic, real-world problems that occur in everyday life. As students work together over several class periods, they have numerous opportunities to communicate about math, share their problem-solving strategies, and get feedback from others that refines their thinking. Jasper videodiscs for science also have been created.

For many years, the major debate in teaching critical thinking has been whether critical-thinking skills should be taught as general entities or in the context of specific subject matter instruction (math, English, or science, for example). A number of experts on thinking believe the evidence has come down on the side of teaching critical thinking embedded in a rich subject matter (Kuhn, 1999, 2000a).

Today, another debate regarding critical thinking has emerged. On the one side are traditionalists who see critical thinking as a set of mental competencies that reside in adolescents' heads. On the other side are advocates of a situated-cognition approach to critical thinking who regard intellectual skills as social entities that are exercised and shared within a community (Resnick & Nelson-Gall, 1997; Rogoff, 1998). This ongoing debate has not yet been resolved.

Creative Thinking

Creativity *is the ability to think in novel ways and come up with unique solutions to problems.* Thus, intelligence, which we will discuss shortly, and creativity are not the same thing. This was recognized by J. P. Guilford (1967), who distinguished between **convergent thinking,** *which produces one correct answer and is characteristic of the kind of thinking required on a conventional intelligence test,* and **divergent thinking,** *which produces many answers to the same question and is more characteristic of creativity.* For example, a typical item on a conventional intelligence test is "How many quarters will you get in return for 60 dimes?" In contrast, the following questions have many possible answers: "What image comes to mind when you hear the phrase *sitting alone in a dark room?*" or "Can you think of some unique uses for a paper clip?"

Are intelligence and creativity related? Although most creative adolescents are quite intelligent, the reverse is not necessarily true. Many highly intelligent adolescents are not very creative.

An important goal is to help adolescents become more creative (Csikszentmihalyi, 2000). Here are some good strategies for accomplishing this goal:

- *Have adolescents engage in brainstorming and come up with as many meaningful ideas as possible. Brainstorming* is a technique in which individuals are encouraged to come up with creative ideas in a group, play off each other's ideas, and say practically whatever comes to mind about a particular topic. Whether in a group or on an individual basis, a good creativity strategy is to generate as many new ideas possible. The famous twentieth-century Spanish artist Pablo Picasso produced more than 20,000 works of art. Not all of them were masterpieces. The more ideas adolescents produce, the better are their chance of creating something unique (Rickards, 1999).

- *Provide adolescents with environments that stimulate creativity.* Some settings nourish creativity, others depress it. People who encourage adolescents' creativity rely on adolescents' natural curiosity. Science and discovery museums offer rich opportunities for the stimulation of adolescents' creative thinking.

- *Don't overcontrol.* Telling adolescents exactly how to do things leaves them feeling that any originality is a mistake and any exploration is a waste of time (Amabile, 1993). Letting adolescents select their interests and supporting their inclinations is less likely to destroy their natural curiosity than dictating which activities they should pursue (Conti & Amabile, 1999; Runco, 2000).

- *Encourage internal motivation.* Excessive use of prizes, such as money, can stifle creativity by undermining the intrinsic pleasure adolescents derive from creative activities. Creative adolescents' motivation is the satisfaction generated by the work itself.

- *Foster flexible and playful thinking.* Creative thinkers are flexible and play with ideas and problems—which gives rise to a paradox: Although creativity takes effort, the effort goes more smoothly if adolescents take it lightly. In a way, humor can grease the wheels of creativity (Goleman, Kaufmann, & Ray, 1993). When adolescents are joking around, they are more likely to consider unusual solutions to problems (O'Quin & Dirks, 1999).

- *Introduce adolescents to creative people.* Poet Richard Lewis (1997) visits classrooms in New York City. He brings with him only the glassy spectrum that is encased in a circular glass case. He lifts it above his head so that every student can see its colored charm, asking "Who can see something playing inside?" Then he asks students to write about what they see. One middle school student named Snigdha wrote that she sees the rainbow rising and the sun sleeping with the stars. She also wrote that she sees the rain dropping on the ground, stems breaking, apples falling from trees, and the wind blowing the leaves.

- *Talk with adolescents about creative people or have them read about them.* Mihaly Csikszentmihalyi (pronounced ME-high CHICK-sent-me-high-ee) (1995) interviewed 90 leading figures in the sciences, government, business, and education about their creativity. One such individual was Mark Strand, a U.S. poet laureate, who said that his most creative moments come when he loses a sense of time and becomes totally absorbed in what he is doing. He commented that the absorbed state comes and goes; he can't stay in it for an

"Blueprint for Success"

Christina and Marcus, two students from Trenton, visit an architectural firm on Career Day. While learning about the work of architects, Christina and Marcus hear about a vacant lot being donated in their neighborhood for a playground. This is exciting news because there is no place in their downtown neighborhood for children to play. Recently, several students have been hurt playing in the street. The challenge is for students to help Christina and Marcus design a playground and ballfield for the lot.

■ FIGURE 4.7
A Problem-Solving Adventure in the Jasper Project

Harvard Project Zero
Csikszentmihalyi's Ideas
http://www.mhhe.com/santrocka9

"What do you mean 'What is it?' It's the spontaneous, unfettered expression of a young mind not yet bound by the restraints of narrative or pictorial representation."

entire day. When Strand gets an intriguing idea, he focuses intensely on it and transforms it into a visual image.

We have discussed some important aspects of the way adolescents process information, but we still need to explore adolescents' monitoring of their information processing and self-regulatory learning strategies.

Metacognition and Self-Regulatory Learning

What is metacognition? How can adolescents develop better information-processing and self-regulatory learning strategies?

What Is Metacognition?   Earlier in the chapter when we discussed Piaget's theory, we indicated that adolescents increase their thinking about thinking. Today, cognitive psychologists define **metacognition** *as cognition about cognition, or "knowing about knowing"* (Flavell, 1999; Flavell, Miller, & Miller, 2002).

Metacognitive skills have been taught to students to help them solve math problems (Cardelle-Elawar, 1992). In each of thirty daily lessons involving math story problems, a teacher guided low-achieving students in learning to recognize when they did not know the meaning of a word, did not have all of the necessary information to solve a problem, did not know how to subdivide the problem into specific steps, or did not know how to carry out a computation. After the thirty daily lessons, the students who were given the metacognitive training had better math achievement and attitudes toward math.

One expert on thinking, Deanna Kuhn (2000b), believes that metacognition should be a stronger focus of efforts to help individuals become better critical thinkers, especially at the middle school and high school levels. She distinguishes between first-order cognitive skills that enable adolescents to know about the world (such skills have been the main focus of critical thinking programs) and second-order cognitive skills—*meta-knowing skills*—that entail knowing about one's own (and others') knowing.

Exploring Strategies and the Self-Regulation of Strategies   In the view of Michael Pressley (1983; McCormick & Pressley, 1997; Pressley & Roehrig, 2002), the key to education is helping students learn a rich repertoire of strategies that result in solutions to problems. Good thinkers routinely use strategies and effective planning to solve problems. Good thinkers also know when and where to use strategies (they have metacognitive knowledge about strategies). Understanding when and where to use strategies often results from the learner's monitoring of the learning situation.

Pressley argues that when students are given instruction about effective strategies that are new to them, they often can apply these strategies on their own. However, some strategies are not effective for young children. For example, young children cannot competently use mental imagery. Pressley emphasizes that students benefit when the teacher models the appropriate strategy and overtly verbalizes the steps in the strategy. Then, students subsequently practice the strategy. Their practice of the strategy is guided and supported by the teacher's feedback until the students can effectively execute the strategy autonomously. When instructing students about employing the strategy, it also is a good idea to explain to them how using the strategy will benefit them.

Having practice in the new strategy usually is not enough for students to continue to use the strategy and transfer it to new situations. For effective maintenance and transfer, encourage students to monitor the effectiveness of the new strategy relative to their use of old strategies by comparing their performance on tests and other assessments. Pressley says that it is not enough to say "Try it, you will like it"; you need to say "Try it and compare."

Learning how to use strategies effectively usually takes time and requires guidance and support from the teacher. With practice, strategies are executed faster and more competently. "Practice" means using the effective strategy over and over again until it is automatically performed. For learners to execute the strategies effectively, they need to have the strategies in long-term memory, and extensive practice makes this possible. Learners also need to be motivated to use the strategies.

Do children and adolescents use one strategy or multiple strategies in memory and problem solving? They often use more than one strategy (Schneider & Bjorklund, 1998; Siegler, 1998). Most children and adolescents benefit from generating a variety of alternative strategies and experimenting with different approaches to a problem, discovering what works well, when, and where (Schneider & Bjorklund, 1998).

Self-Regulatory Learning

Self-regulatory learning *consists of the self-generation and self-monitoring of thoughts, feelings, and behaviors to reach a goal.* These goals might be academic (improving comprehension while reading, becoming a more organized writer, learning how to do multiplication, asking relevant questions) or they might be socioemotional (controlling one's anger, getting along better with peers). What are some of the characteristics of self-regulated learners? Self-regulatory learners (Winne, 1995, 1997; Winne & Perry, 2000):

• Set goals for extending their knowledge and sustaining their motivation
• Are aware of their emotional makeup and have strategies for managing their emotions
• Periodically monitor their progress toward a goal
• Fine-tune or revise their strategies based on the progress they are making
• Evaluate obstacles that arise and make the necessary adaptations

Researchers have found that most high-achieving students are self-regulatory learners (Paris & Paris, 2001; Pressley, 1995; Rudolph & others, 2001; Schunk & Zimmerman, 1994; Zimmerman, 2000, 2002). For example, compared with low-achieving students, high-achieving students set more specific learning goals, use more strategies to learn, self-monitor their learning more, and more systematically evaluate their progress toward a goal (Schnuk & Ertmer, 2000).

Teachers, tutors, mentors, counselors, and parents can help students become self-regulatory learners. Barry Zimmerman, Sebastian Bonner, and Robert Kovach (1996) developed a model of turning low-self-regulatory students into students who engaged in these multistep strategies: (1) self-evaluation and monitoring, (2) goal setting and strategic planning, (3) putting a plan into action and monitoring it, and (4) monitoring outcomes and refining strategies (see figure 4.8).

They describe a seventh-grade student who is doing poorly in history and apply their self-regulatory model to her situation. In step 1, she self-evaluates her studying and test preparation by keeping a detailed record of them. The teacher gives her some guidelines for keeping these records. After several weeks, the student turns in the records and traces her poor test performance to low comprehension of difficult reading material.

In step 2, the student sets a goal, in this case of improving reading comprehension, and plans how to achieve the goal. The teacher assists her in breaking down the goal into component parts, such as locating main ideas and setting specific goals for understanding a series of paragraphs in her textbook. The teacher also provides the student with strategies, such as focusing initially on the first sentence of each paragraph and then scanning the others as a means of identifying main ideas. Another support the teacher might offer the student is adult or peer tutoring in reading comprehension if it is available.

In step 3, the student puts the plan into action and begins to monitor her progress. Initially she

self-regulatory learning
The self-generation and self-monitoring of thoughts, feelings, and behaviors to reach a goal.

Self-Regulatory Learning
http://www.mhhe.com/santrocka9

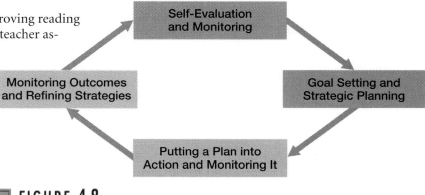

FIGURE 4.8
A Model of Self-Regulatory Learning

might need help from the teacher or tutor in identifying main ideas in the reading. This feedback can help her monitor her reading comprehension more effectively on her own.

In step 4, the student monitors her improvement in reading comprehension by evaluating whether it has had any impact on her learning outcomes. Most importantly: Has her improvement in reading comprehension led to better performance on history tests?

Since the last review, we have examined a number of ideas about the information-processing view. These questions should help you to reach your learning goals related to this topic.

☐ FOR YOUR REVIEW

Learning Goal 3
Evaluate the information-processing view

- Siegler states that the information-processing view emphasizes thinking, change mechanisms (encoding, automaticity, strategy construction, and generalization), and self-modification.
- Adolescents typically have better attentional skills than children do. They also have better short-term memory, working memory, and long-term memory than children.
- Adolescence is a time of increased decision making. Older adolescents make better decisions than younger adolescents, who in turn are better at this than children are. Being able to make competent decisions, however, does not mean they actually will be made in everyday life, where breadth of experience comes into play.
- Critical thinking involves thinking reflectively, productively, and evaluating the evidence. Adolescence is an important transitional period in critical thinking because of such cognitive changes as increased speed, automaticity, and capacity of information processing; more breadth of content knowledge; increased ability to construct new combinations of knowledge; and a greater range and spontaneous use of strategies. Debates about critical thinking involve whether it should be taught in a general way or tied to specific subject matter and whether it resides in adolescents' heads or involves situated cognition.
- Thinking creatively is the ability to think in novel and unusual ways and come up with unique solutions to problems. Guilford distinguished between convergent and divergent thinking. A number of strategies, including brainstorming, can be used to stimulate creative thinking.
- Metacognition is cognition about cognition, or knowing about knowing. In Pressley's view, the key to education is helping students learn a rich repertoire of strategies that results in solutions to problems. Kuhn argues that metacognition is the key to developing critical-thinking skills. Self-regulatory learning consists of the self-generation and self-monitoring of thoughts, feelings, and behaviors to reach a goal. Most high-achieving students are self-regulatory learners.

So far in this chapter we have explored two major approaches to adolescent cognition: cognitive developmental and information processing. Next, we will explore a third major approach: psychometric/intelligence.

THE PSYCHOMETRIC/INTELLIGENCE VIEW

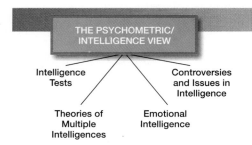

THE PSYCHOMETRIC/
INTELLIGENCE VIEW

Intelligence Tests

Controversies and Issues in Intelligence

Theories of Multiple Intelligences

Emotional Intelligence

psychometric/intelligence view
A view that emphasizes the importance of individual differences in intelligence; many advocates of this view also argue that intelligence should be assessed with intelligence tests.

The two views of adolescent cognition that we have discussed so far—cognitive developmental and information processing—do not emphasize IQ tests or individual variations in intelligence. The **psychometric/intelligence view** *does emphasize the importance of individual differences in intelligence, and many advocates of this view argue that intelligence should be assessed with intelligence tests.* An increasing issue in the field of intelligence involves pinning down what the components of intelligence really are (Embretson & McCollom, 2000).

Twentieth-century English novelist Aldous Huxley said that children are remarkable for their curiosity and intelligence. What did Huxley mean when he used the word *intelligence?* Intelligence is one of our most prized possessions, yet even the most intelligent people have not been able to agree on what intelligence is. Unlike height, weight, and age, intelligence cannot be directly measured. You can't peer into a student's head and observe the intelligence going on inside. We only can evaluate a student's intelligence *indirectly* by studying the intelligent acts that it generates. For the most part, we have relied on written intelligence tests to provide an estimate of a student's intelligence (Aiken, 2003; Kaufman, 2000a).

Some experts describe intelligence as including verbal ability and problem-solving skills. Others describe it as the ability to adapt to and learn from life's everyday experiences. Combining these ideas we can arrive at a fairly traditional definition of **intelligence** *as problem-solving skills and the ability to adapt to and learn from life's everyday experiences.* But even this broad definition doesn't satisfy everyone. As you will see shortly, some theorists propose that musical skills should be considered part of intelligence. And a definition of intelligence based on a theory like Vygotsky's would have to include the ability to use the tools of the culture with help from more-skilled individuals. Because intelligence is such an abstract, broad concept, it is not surprising that there are so many different possible definitions of it.

intelligence
Mental ability related to problem-solving skills, and the ability to adapt to and learn from life's everyday experiences; not everyone agrees on what constitutes intelligence.

Intelligence Tests

Robert J. Sternberg recalls being terrified of taking IQ tests as a child. He says that he literally froze when the time came to take such tests. Even as an adult, Sternberg feels stung by humiliation when he recalls being in the sixth grade and taking an IQ test with fifth-graders. Sternberg eventually overcame his anxieties about IQ tests. Not only did he begin to perform better on them, but at age 13 he devised his own IQ test and began using it to assess classmates—that is, until the school principal found out and scolded him. Sternberg became so fascinated by intelligence that he made its study one of his lifelong pursuits. Later in this chapter we will discuss his theory of intelligence. To begin, though, let's go back in time to examine the first valid intelligence test.

The Binet Tests   In 1904 the French Ministry of Education asked psychologist Alfred Binet to devise a method of identifying children who were unable to learn in school. School officials wanted to reduce crowding by placing in special schools students who did not benefit from regular classroom teaching. Binet and his student Theophile Simon developed an intelligence test to meet this request. The test is called the 1905 Scale. It consisted of 30 questions, ranging from the ability to touch one's ear to the ability to draw designs from memory and define abstract concepts.

Mental Measurements Yearbook
Alfred Binet
http://www.mhhe.com/santrocka9

Binet developed the concept of **mental age (MA),** *an individual's level of mental development relative to others.* Not much later, in 1912, William Stern created the concept of **intelligent quotient (IQ),** *which refers to a person's mental age divided by chronological age (CA), multiplied by 100. That is, IQ = MA/CA × 100.*

If mental age is the same as chronological age, then the person's IQ is 100. If mental age is above chronological age, then IQ is more than 100. If mental age is below chronological age, then IQ is less than 100. Scores noticeably above 100 are considered above-average. Scores noticeably below 100 are labeled below-average. For example, a 16-year-old with a mental age of 20 would have an IQ of 125, while a 16-year-old child with a mental age of 12 would have an IQ of 75.

mental age (MA)
An individual's level of mental development relative to others; a concept developed by Binet.

intelligent quotient (IQ)
A person's tested mental age divided by chronological age, multiplied by 100.

The Binet test has been revised many times to incorporate advances in the understanding of intelligence and intelligence testing (Naglieri, 2000). These revisions are called the Stanford-Binet tests (because the revisions were made at Stanford University). By administering the test to large numbers of people of different ages from different backgrounds, researchers have found that scores on a Stanford-Binet test approximate a normal distribution (see figure 4.9 on p. 130). A **normal distribution** *is symmetrical, with a majority of the scores falling in the middle of the possible range of scores and few scores appearing toward the extremes of the range.*

The current Stanford-Binet is administered individually to people from the age of 2 through the adult years. It includes a variety of items, some of which require verbal responses and others of which require nonverbal responses. For example, items that reflect a typical 6-year-old's level of performance on the test include the verbal ability to define at least six words, such as *orange* and *envelope,* as well as the nonverbal ability

normal distribution
A symmetrical distribution of values or scores, with a majority of scores falling in the middle of the possible range of scores and few scores appearing toward the extremes of the range; a distribution that yields what is called a "bell-shaped curve."

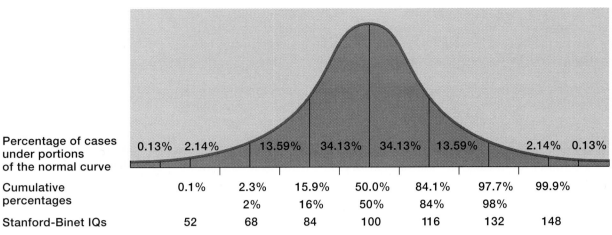

Percentage of cases under portions of the normal curve	0.13%	2.14%	13.59%	34.13%	34.13%	13.59%	2.14%	0.13%
Cumulative percentages		0.1%	2.3%	15.9%	50.0%	84.1%	97.7%	99.9%	
			2%	16%	50%	84%	98%		
Stanford-Binet IQs		52	68	84	100	116	132	148	

FIGURE 4.9
The Normal Curve and Stanford-Binet IQ Scores

The distribution of IQ scores approximates a normal curve. Most of the population falls in the middle range of scores. Notice that extremely high and extremely low scores are very rare. Slightly more than two-thirds of the scores fall between 84 and 116. Only about 1 in 50 individuals has an IQ of more than 132 and only about 1 in 50 individuals has an IQ of less than 68.

to trace a path through a maze. Items that reflect an average adult's level of performance include defining such words as *disproportionate* and *regard,* explaining a proverb, and comparing idleness and laziness.

The fourth edition of the Stanford-Binet was published in 1985. One important addition in this version was the analysis of the individual's responses in terms of four functions: verbal reasoning, quantitative reasoning, abstract/visual reasoning, and short-term memory. A general composite score is still obtained to reflect overall intelligence. The Stanford-Binet continues to be one of the tests most widely used to assess a student's intelligence.

The Wechsler Scales   Another set of tests widely used to assess students' intelligence is the Wechsler scales, developed by David Wechsler (Kaufman, 2000b). They include the Wechsler Preschool and Primary Scale of Intelligence–Revised (WPPSI-R) to test children 4 to 6½ years of age; the Wechsler Intelligence Scale for Children–Revised (WISC-R) for children and adolescents 6 to 16 years of age; and the Wechsler Adult Intelligence Scale–Revised (WAIS-R).

In addition to an overall IQ, the Wechsler scales also yield verbal and performance IQs. Verbal IQ is based on six verbal subscales, performance IQ on five performance subscales (Naglieri, 2000). This allows the examiner to quickly see patterns of strengths and weaknesses in different areas of the student's intelligence. Samples of WAIS-R subscales are shown in figure 4.10 on page 131.

Theories of Multiple Intelligences

Is it more appropriate to think of an adolescent's intelligence as a general ability or as a number of specific abilities?

Early Views   Binet and Stern both focused on a concept of general intelligence, which Stern called IQ. Wechsler believed it was possible and important to describe both a person's general intelligence and more specific verbal and performance intelligences. He was building on the ideas of Charles Spearman (1927), who said that people have both a general intelligence, which he called *g,* and specific types of intelligence, which he called *s.* As early as the 1930s, L. L. Thurstone (1938) said people have seven of these specific abilities, which he called primary mental abilities: verbal comprehension, number ability, word fluency, spatial visualization, associative memory, reasoning,

VERBAL SUBSCALES

SIMILARITIES
An individual must think logically and abstractly to answer a number of questions about how things might be similar.

For example, "In what ways are boats and trains the same?"

PERFORMANCE SUBSCALES

BLOCK DESIGN
An individual must assemble a set of multicolored blocks to match designs that the examiner shows. Visual-motor coordination, perceptual organization, and the ability to visualize spatially are assessed.

For example, "Use the four blocks on the left to make the pattern at the right."

Remember that the Wechsler includes 11 subscales, 6 verbal and 5 nonverbal. Two of the subscales are shown here.

■ FIGURE 4.10
Sample Subscales of the Wechsler Adult Intelligence Scale—Revised
Remember that the Wechsler includes 11 subscales, 6 verbal and 5 nonverbal. Two of the subscales are shown here.

Simulated items from the Wechsler Adult Intelligence Scale–Revised. Copyright © 1981, 1955 by The Psychological Corporation. All rights reserved.

and perceptual speed. More recently, the search for specific types of intelligence has heated up.

Sternberg's Triarchic Theory   Robert J. Sternberg (1986) developed the **triarchic theory of intelligence,** *which states that intelligence comes in three forms: analytical, creative, and practical.*

Analytical intelligence involves the ability to analyze, judge, evaluate, compare, and contrast. Creative intelligence consists of the ability to create, design, invent, originate, and imagine. Practical intelligence focuses on the ability to use, apply, implement, and put into practice (Wagner, 2000). Consider these three students:

- Ann scores high on traditional intelligence tests, such as the Stanford-Binet, and is a star analytical thinker.
- Todd does not have the best tests scores but has an insightful and creative mind.
- Art is street-smart and has learned to deal in practical ways with his world although his scores on traditional intelligence tests are low.

Some students are equally high in all three areas; others do well in one or two.

Sternberg (1997, 1999, 2000; Sternberg, Torff, & Grigorenko, 1998) says that students with different triarchic patterns "look different" in school. Students with high analytic ability tend to be favored in conventional schooling. They often do well in direct-instruction classes in which the teacher lectures and students are given objective tests. They often are considered to be "smart" students who get good grades, show up in high-level tracks, do well on traditional tests of intelligence and the SAT, and later get admitted to competitive colleges.

Students who are high in creative intelligence often are not on the top rung of their class. Sternberg says that many teachers have expectations about how assignments should be done, and that creatively intelligent students might not conform to these. Instead of giving conformist answers, they give unique answers, for which they sometimes are reprimanded or marked down. Most teachers do not want to discourage

triarchic theory of intelligence
Sternberg's view that intelligence comes in three main forms: analytical, creative, and practical.

Sternberg's Theory
http://www.mhhe.com/santrocka9

"You're wise, but you lack tree smarts."

creativity, but Sternberg believes that too often a teacher's desire to improve students' knowledge inhibits creative thinking.

Like students high in creative intelligence, students who are high in practical intelligence often do not relate well to the demands of school. However, these students often do well outside the classroom. They might have excellent social skills and good common sense. As adults, they sometimes become successful managers, entrepreneurs, or politicians, despite undistinguished school records.

Sternberg believes that few tasks are purely analytic, creative, or practical. Most require some combination of these skills. For example, when students write a book report, they might (1) analyze the book's main themes, (2) generate new ideas about how the book might have been written better, and (3) think about how the book's themes can be applied to people's lives.

He believes that in teaching it is important to balance instruction related to the three types of intelligence. That is, students should be given opportunities to learn through analytical, creative, and practical thinking, in addition to conventional strategies that focus on simply "learning" and remembering a body of information. You might be wondering whether there is a Sternberg triarchic intelligence test available. As yet, there isn't.

Gardner's Eight Frames of Mind   Howard Gardner (1983, 1993, 2002) believes there are eight types of intelligence. They are described here, along with examples of the types of individuals in which they are reflected as strengths (Campbell, Campbell, & Dickinson, 1999):

- *Verbal skills:* the ability to think in words and to use language to express meaning (authors, journalists, speakers)
- *Mathematical skills:* the ability to carry out mathematical operations (scientists, engineers, accountants)
- *Spatial skills:* the ability to think in three-dimensional ways (architects, artists, sailors)
- *Bodily-kinesthetic skills:* the ability to manipulate objects and be physically skilled (surgeons, craftspeople, dancers, athletes)
- *Musical skills:* possessing a sensitivity to pitch, melody, rhythm, and tone (composers, musicians, and sensitive listeners)
- *Interpersonal skills:* ability to understand and effectively interact with others (successful teachers, mental health professionals)
- *Intrapersonal skills:* ability to understand oneself and effectively direct one's life (theologians, psychologists)
- *Naturalist skills:* ability to observe patterns in nature and understand natural and human-made systems (farmers, botanists, ecologists, landscapers)

Gardner says that the different forms of intelligence can be destroyed by brain damage, that each involves unique cognitive skills, and that each shows up in unique ways in both the gifted and idiot savants (individuals with mental retardation who have an exceptional talent in a particular domain, such as drawing, music, or computing).

Evaluating the Multiple-Intelligences Approaches   Sternberg's and Gardner's approaches have much to offer. They have stimulated broader thinking about what makes up adolescents' competencies. And they have motivated educators to develop programs that instruct students in multiple domains (Torff, 2000). These approaches also have contributed to the interest in assessing intelligence in innovative ways that go beyond conventional standardized and paper-and-pencil memory tasks.

Some critics say that classifying musical skills as a main type of intelligence is off base. Why not also classify other skill domains as types of intelligence? For

An Interview with Howard Gardner
Multiple-Intelligences Links
http://www.mhhe.com/santrocka9

example, there are outstanding chess players, prizefighters, writers, politicians, physicians, lawyers, ministers, and poets, yet we do not refer to chess intelligence, prizefighter intelligence, and so on. Other critics say that the research has not yet been conducted to support the thesis that Sternberg's three intelligences and Gardner's eight intelligences are the best ways to categorize intelligence.

Emotional Intelligence

Both Sternberg's and Gardner's views include categories of social intelligence. In Sternberg's theory the category is called "practical intelligence" and in Gardner's theory the categories are "insights about self" and "insights about others." However, the greatest interest in recent years in the social aspects of intelligence has focused on the concept of emotional intelligence. **Emotional intelligence** *was proposed in 1990 as a form of social intelligence that involves the ability to monitor one's own and others' feelings and emotions, to discriminate among them, and to use this information to guide one's thinking and action* (Salovy & Mayer, 1990). However, the main interest in emotional intelligence was ushered in with the publication of Daniel Goleman's (1995) book, *Emotional Intelligence*. Goleman believes that when it comes to predicting an adolescent's competence, IQ as measured by standardized intelligence tests matters less than emotional intelligence. In Goleman's view, emotional intelligence involves these four main areas:

> **emotional intelligence**
> A form of social intelligence that involves the ability to monitor one's own and others' feelings and emotions, to discriminate among them, and to use this information to guide one's thinking and action.

- *Developing emotional self-awareness* (such as the ability to separate feelings from actions)
- *Managing emotions* (such as being able to control anger)
- *Reading emotions* (such as taking the perspectives of others)
- *Handling relationships* (such as the ability to solve relationship problems)

One private school in San Francisco, the Nueva School, has a class in self science that is closely related to the concept of emotional intelligence. The subject in self science is feelings—the adolescent's own and those involved in relationships. Teachers speak to such emotional issues as hurt over being left out, envy, and disagreements that can disrupt relationships. These are some of the topics in a fifth-grade self-science class at the Nueva School:

- Having self-awareness (in the sense of recognizing feelings and building a vocabulary for them; seeing links between thoughts, feelings, and reactions)
- Knowing if thoughts or feelings are governing a decision
- Seeing the consequences of alternative choices
- Applying these insights to decisions about such issues as drugs, smoking, and sex
- Managing emotions; learning to handle anxieties, anger, and sadness
- Taking responsibility for decisions and actions, such as following through on commitments
- Understanding that empathy, understanding others' feelings, and respecting differences in how people feel about things are key aspects of getting along in the social world
- Recognizing the importance of relationships and learning how to be a good listener and question asker; learning how to cooperate, resolve conflicts, and negotiate

Names for these classes range from "Social Development" to "Life Skills" to "Social and Emotional Learning." Their common goal is raise every child's and adolescent's emotional competence as part of regular education rather than focus on emotional skills as only something to be taught remedially to those who are faltering and identified as "troubled."

Measures of emotional intelligence have been and are being developed, but as yet none has reached the point of wide acceptance (Goleman, 1995; Rockhill & Greener, 1999; Salovy & Woolery, 2000). Especially lacking is research on the predictive validity of these measures (Mayer, Caruso, & Salovy, 2000).

Controversies and Issues in Intelligence

The topic of intelligence is surrounded by controversy. Among those controversies are whether nature or nurture is more important in determining intelligence, how much intelligence tests are culturally biased, and appropriate and inappropriate uses of intelligence tests (Brody, 2000).

Nature and Nurture   In chapters 1 and 3, we introduced the question of how extensively nature (heredity) and nurture (environment) influence adolescents' development ◀▦ Pp. 22, 97. Some scientists proclaim that intelligence is primarily inherited and that environmental experiences play only a minimal role in its manifestation (Herrnstein & Murray, 1994; Jensen, 1969). Heredity is an important part of the intelligence equation (Grigorenko, 2000; Loehlin, 2000; Scarr, 1996). However, the emerging view on the nature-nurture controversy is that many complicated qualities, such as intelligence, probably have a genetic basis for a *propensity* for a particular developmental trajectory, such as low, average, or high intelligence. If such genes exist, they certainly are found both in adolescents whose families and environments appear to promote the development of adolescents' abilities and in adolescents whose families and environments do not appear as supportive. Regardless of one's genetic background, growing up with "all the advantages" does not guarantee eventual high intelligence and success, especially if those advantages are taken for granted. Nor does the absence of such advantages guarantee eventual low intelligence or failure, especially if the family and adolescent can make the most of whatever opportunities are available to them.

One argument for the importance of environment in intelligence involves the increasing scores of IQ tests around the world. Scores on these tests have been increasing so fast that a high percentage of people who would have been regarded as having average intelligence at the turn of the twentieth century would be considered below average in intelligence today (Hall, 1998) (see figure 4.11). If a representative sample of people today took the Stanford-Binet test used in 1932, about one-fourth would be defined as having very superior intelligence, a label usually accorded to fewer than 3 percent of the population. Because the increase in scores has taken place in a relatively short period of time, it can't be due to heredity, but rather might be due to such environmental factors as the explosion in information people are exposed to as well as a much greater percentage of the population experiencing more education.

Ethnicity and Culture   Are there ethnic differences in intelligence? Are conventional tests of intelligence biased, and if so, can we develop culture-fair tests?

On average in the United States, adolescents from African American and Latino families score below adolescents from non-Latino White families on standardized intelligence tests. Most comparisons have focused on African Americans and Whites. African American adolescents score 10 to 15 points lower than White American adolescents (Neisser & others, 1996). Keep in mind that this represents an average difference. Many African American adolescents score higher than most White adolescents. Estimates are that 15 to 25 percent of African American adolescents score higher than half of all White adolescents.

Are these differences based on heredity or environment? The consensus answer is environment (Brooks-Gunn, Klebanov, & Duncan, 1996). One reason to think so is that in recent decades, as African Americans have experienced improved social, economic, and educational

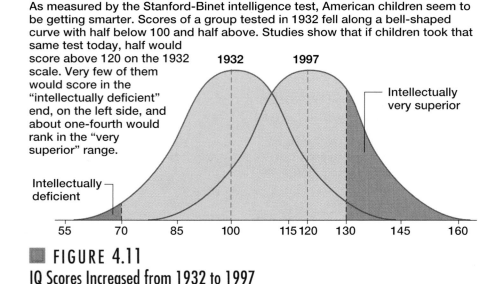

As measured by the Stanford-Binet intelligence test, American children seem to be getting smarter. Scores of a group tested in 1932 fell along a bell-shaped curve with half below 100 and half above. Studies show that if children took that same test today, half would score above 120 on the 1932 scale. Very few of them would score in the "intellectually deficient" end, on the left side, and about one-fourth would rank in the "very superior" range.

■ FIGURE 4.11
IQ Scores Increased from 1932 to 1997

opportunities, the gap between African American and White adolescents on conventional intelligence tests had declined (Jones, 1984). Between 1977 and 1996, as educational opportunities for African Americans increased, the gap between their SAT scores and those of their White counterparts also shrunk 23 percent (College Board, 1996). And when adolescents from low-income African American families are adopted by more-advantaged middle-socioeconomic-status families, their scores on intelligence tests are closer to the national average for middle-socioeconomic-status adolescents than to the national average for adolescents from low-income families (Scarr & Weinberg, 1983).

Many of the early tests of intelligence were culturally biased, favoring urban adolescents over rural adolescents, adolescents from middle-socioeconomic-status families over those from low-income families, and White adolescents over ethnic minority adolescents (Kaufman & Lindenberger, 2002; Miller-Jones, 1989). The standards for the early tests were almost exclusively based on White middle-socioeconomic-status adolescents.

Another problem can arise: even if the content of test items is unbiased, the language in which the items appear might not be. Some adolescents from ethnic minority groups might have trouble understanding the test's written language. Consider Gregory Ochoa. When he was in high school, he and his classmates were given an IQ test. Gregory looked at the test questions and didn't understand many of the words. Spanish was spoken at his home, and his English was not very good. Several weeks later Gregory was placed in a "special" class in which many of the other students had names like Ramirez and Gonzales. The class was for students who were mentally retarded. Gregory lost interest in school and eventually dropped out. He joined the Navy, where he took high school courses and earned enough credits to attend college. He graduated from San Jose City College as an honor student, continued his education, and eventually became a professor of social work at the University of Washington in Seattle.

Culture-fair tests *are tests of intelligence that are intended to be free of cultural bias.* Two types of culture-fair tests have been devised. The first includes items that are believed to be familiar to children from all socioeconomic and ethnic backgrounds, or items that at least are familiar to the children taking the test. For example, a child might be asked how a bird and a dog are different, on the assumption that all children have been exposed to birds and dogs. The second type of culture-fair test has all of the verbal items removed. Figure 4.12 shows a sample item from the Raven Progressive Matrices Test, which exemplifies this approach. Even though such tests are designed to be culture-fair, students with more education score higher on them than their less-educated counterparts do.

These attempts to produce culture-fair tests remind us that conventional intelligence tests probably are culturally biased, yet the effort to create a truly culture-fair test has not yielded a successful alternative. It is important to consider also that what is viewed as intelligent in one culture might not be thought of as intelligent in another culture (Lonner, 1990; Poortinga, 2000). In most Western cultures, adolescents are considered intelligent if they are both smart (have considerable knowledge and can solve verbal problems) and fast (can process information quickly). By contrast, in the Buganda culture in Uganda, adolescents who are wise, slow in thought, and say the socially correct thing are considered intelligent. And in the widely dispersed Caroline Islands, one of the most important dimensions of intelligence is the ability to navigate by the stars.

The Use and Misuse of Intelligence Tests   Psychological tests are tools. Like all tools, their effectiveness depends on the knowledge, skill, and integrity of the user. A hammer can be used to build a beautiful kitchen cabinet or it can be used as a weapon of assault. Like a hammer, psychological tests can be used for positive purposes or they can be badly abused. Here are some cautions about

culture-fair tests
Tests of intelligence that are intended to be free of cultural bias.

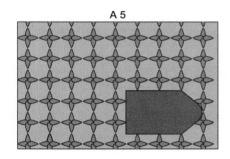
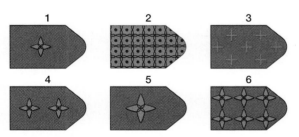

FIGURE 4.12
Sample Item from the Raven Progressive Matrices Test

Individuals are presented with a matrix arrangement of symbols, such as the one at the top of this figure, and must then complete the matrix by selecting the appropriate missing symbol from a group of symbols.

IQ tests that can help us to avoid the pitfalls of using information about an adolescent's intelligence in negative ways.

- *IQ test scores can easily lead to stereotypes and inappropriate expectations about adolescents.* Sweeping generalizations are too often made on the basis of an IQ score (Rosenthal, 2000). Imagine that you are in the teacher's lounge the day after school has started in the fall. You mention a student—Johnny Jones—and another teacher remarks that she had Johnny in class last year. She comments that he was a real dunce and scored 83 on an IQ test. How hard is it to ignore this information as you go about teaching your class? Probably difficult. But it is important that you not develop the expectation that, because Johnny scored low on an IQ test, it is useless to spend much time teaching him. An IQ test should always be considered a measure of current performance. It is not a measure of fixed potential. Maturational changes and enriched environmental experiences can advance a student's intelligence.
- *IQ test scores should not be used as the main or sole characteristic of competence.* As we have seen in this chapter, it is important to consider not only students' intellectual competence in areas such as verbal skills, but also their creative and practical skills.
- *Especially be cautious in interpreting the meaningfulness of an overall IQ score.* In evaluating an adolescent's intelligence, it is wiser to think of intelligence as being made up of a number of domains. Keep in mind the different types of intelligence described by Sternberg and Gardner. Remember that by considering different domains of intelligence, you can find that every adolescent has one or more strengths. Another important caution in interpreting intelligence tests is to recognize that they are an indicator of current performance, not fixed potential.

Since the last review, we have discussed many ideas about the psychometric/intelligence view. These questions should help you to reach your learning goals related to this topic.

FOR YOUR REVIEW

Learning Goal 4
Explain the psychometric/intelligence view

- This view emphasizes the importance of individual differences and assessment. Intelligence can be defined as problem-solving skills and the ability to adapt to and learn from everyday experiences.
- Binet and Simon developed the first intelligence test. Binet created the concept of mental age and Stern crafted the concept of IQ as MA/CA × 100. The range of scores on the Stanford-Binet approximates a normal distribution. The Wechsler scales also are widely used to assess intelligence. They provide an overall IQ, as well as verbal and performance IQs.
- Spearman proposed many years ago that people have a general intelligence (*g*) and specific intelligences (*s*). Thurstone believed that people have seven specific abilities, which he called primary mental abilities. More recently, Sternberg has stated that intelligence comes in three main forms: analytical, creative, and practical. Gardner recently has described eight types of intelligence: verbal, math, spatial, bodily-kinesthetic, interpersonal, intrapersonal, musical, and naturalist.
- Emotional intelligence is a form of social intelligence that involves the ability to monitor one's own and others' feelings and emotions, to discriminate among them, and to use this information to guide one's own thinking and action. Goleman believes that emotional intelligence consists of four main areas: emotional self-awareness, managing emotions, reading emotions, and handling relationships.
- Among the controversies and issues in intelligence are those involving nature and nurture, ethnicity and culture, and the use and misuse of intelligence tests.

So far in this chapter we have explored three major perspectives on adolescent cognition: cognitive developmental, information processing, and psychometric/intelligence. Next, we will examine another topic that involves adolescent cognition: how adolescents think about social matters.

SOCIAL COGNITION

Social cognition refers to how individuals conceptualize and reason about their social world—the people they watch and interact with, relationships with those people, the groups in which they participate, and how they reason about themselves and others. Developmentalists have recently shown a flourish of interest in how children and adolescents reason about social matters. For many years, the study of cognitive development focused primarily on cognition about nonsocial phenomena, such as logic, numbers, words, time, and the like. Now there is a lively interest in how children and adolescents reason about their social world as well (Flavell, Miller, & Miller, 2002). Our discussion of social cognition focuses on egocentrism, perspective taking, and implicit personality theory.

SOCIAL COGNITION

Adolescent Egocentrism — Perspective Taking — Implicit Personality Theory — Social Cognition in the Rest of This Text

Adolescent Egocentrism

Adolescent egocentrism *refers to the heightened self-consciousness of adolescents, which is reflected in their belief that others are as interested in them as they themselves are, and in their sense of personal uniqueness.*

David Elkind (1976) believes that adolescent egocentrism can be dissected into two types of social thinking—imaginary audience and personal fable. The *imaginary audience* involves attention-getting behavior—the desire to be noticed, visible, and "on stage." Tracy's comments and behavior, discussed in the Images introduction to the chapter, reflect the imaginary audience. Another adolescent might think that others are as aware of a small spot on his trousers as he is, possibly knowing that he has masturbated. Another adolescent, an eighth-grade girl, walks into her classroom and thinks that all eyes are riveted on her complexion. Adolescents especially sense that they are "on stage" in early adolescence, believing that they are the main actors and all others are the audience.

According to Elkind, the *personal fable* is the part of adolescent egocentrism involving an adolescent's sense of uniqueness. Adolescents' sense of personal uniqueness makes them feel that no one can understand how they really feel. For example, an adolescent girl thinks that her mother cannot possibly sense the hurt that she feels because her boyfriend broke up with her. As part of their effort to retain a sense of personal uniqueness, adolescents might craft a story about the self that is filled with fantasy, immersing themselves in a world that is far removed from reality. Personal fables frequently show up in adolescent diaries.

Developmentalists have increasingly studied adolescent egocentrism in recent years. The research interest focuses on what the components of egocentrism really are, the nature of self-other relationships, why egocentric thought emerges in adolescence, and the role of egocentrism in adolescent problems. For example, David Elkind (1985) believes that adolescent egocentrism is brought about by formal operational thought. Others, however, argue that adolescent egocentrism is not entirely a cognitive phenomenon. Rather, they think that the imaginary audience is due both to the ability to think hypothetically (formal operational thought) and the ability to step outside one's self and anticipate the reactions of others in imaginative circumstances (perspective taking) (Lapsley & Murphy, 1985).

adolescent egocentrism
The heightened self-consciousness of adolescents, which is reflected in their belief that others are as interested in them as they themselves are, and in their sense of personal uniqueness.

Many adolescent girls spend long hours in front of the mirror, depleting cans of hair spray, tubes of lipstick, and jars of cosmetics. *How might this behavior be related to changes in adolescent cognitive and physical development?*

Perspective Taking

Perspective taking is the ability to assume another person's perspective and understand his or her thoughts and feelings. Robert Selman (1980) proposed a developmental theory of perspective taking that has

I check my look in the mirror. I wanna change my clothes, my hair, my face.

—Bruce Springsteen
Contemporary American Rock Star

Social Cognition
http://www.mhhe.com/santrocka9

received considerable attention. He believes perspective taking involves a series of five stages, ranging from 3 years of age through adolescence (see figure 4.13 on p. 139). These stages begin with the egocentric viewpoint in early childhood and end with in-depth perspective taking in adolescence.

To study adolescents' perspective taking, Selman individually interviews the adolescents, asking them to comment on such dilemmas as the following:

> Holly is an eight-year-old girl who likes to climb trees. She is the best tree climber in the neighborhood. One day while climbing down from a tall tree, she falls . . . but does not hurt herself. Her father sees her fall. He is upset and asks her to promise not to climb trees any more. Holly promises.
>
> Later that day, Holly and her friends meet Shawn. Shawn's kitten is caught in a tree and can't get down. Something has to be done right away or the kitten may fall. Holly is the only one who climbs trees well enough to reach the kitten and get it down, but she remembers her promise to her father. (Selman, 1976, p. 302)

Subsequently, the interviewer asks the adolescents a series of questions about the dilemma, such as these:

> Does Holly know how Shawn feels about the kitten?
> How will Holly's father feel if he finds out she climbed the tree?
> What does Holly think her father will do if he finds out she climbed the tree?
> What would you do in this situation?

By analyzing children's and adolescents' responses to these dilemmas, Selman (1980) concluded that their perspective taking follows the developmental sequence described in figure 4.13. In this view, individuals move from the egocentric perspective of young children to the interdependent perspective of adolescents. Correspondingly, their interpersonal negotiation strategies change from the impulsiveness of young children to the more collaborative orientation of adolescents (Selman & Adalbjarnardottir, 2000; Selman & Schultz, 1999).

Selman's research has shown strong support for the sequential nature of perspective taking, although the ages at which children and adolescents reach the perspective-taking stages overlap considerably. Some researchers believe that the attainment of stage 3 perspective taking accounts for the imaginary audience and personal fable dimensions of adolescent egocentrism (Lapsley, 1993).

Although adolescents' perspective taking can increase their self-understanding, it also can improve their peer group status and the quality of their friendships. For example, in one investigation, the most popular children in the third and eighth grades had competent perspective-taking skills (Kurdek & Krile, 1982). Adolescents who are competent at perspective taking are better at understanding the needs of their companions so that they likely can communicate more effectively with them. And in one study, competence in social perspective coordination was an important influence on adolescent friendship formation following residential relocation (Vernberg & others, 1994).

The relation between the self and another individual is complex. Most major developmental theorists believe that development changes in self-other relationships are characterized by movement from egocentrism to perspectivism, but the considerable overlap in the age range at which various levels of perspective taking emerge make generalizations about clear-cut stages difficult. Next, we turn our attention to another aspect of social cognition that changes during adolescence—implicit personality theory.

■ THINKING CRITICALLY

Adolescent Egocentrism—Does It Ever Go Away?

In my course on adolescence, college students have occasionally commented that they know some people in their twenties who still show the characteristics we have associated with adolescent egocentrism. They want to know if it is maladaptive, when you are in your late teens and twenties, to act as if all eyes are riveted on you, to have a strong desire to be noticed, visible, and "on stage," and to feel as though all others are as interested in you as you are.

What do you think? How maladaptive is it for individuals in their late teens and their twenties to show adolescent egocentrism? Isn't it adaptive to show at least some interest in one-self? How can you draw the line between self-interest that is adaptive, protective, and appropriate and self-interest that is maladaptive, selfish, and inappropriate? One good strategy for coming to grips with this issue is to consider the extent to which the egocentrism overwhelms and dominates the individual's life.

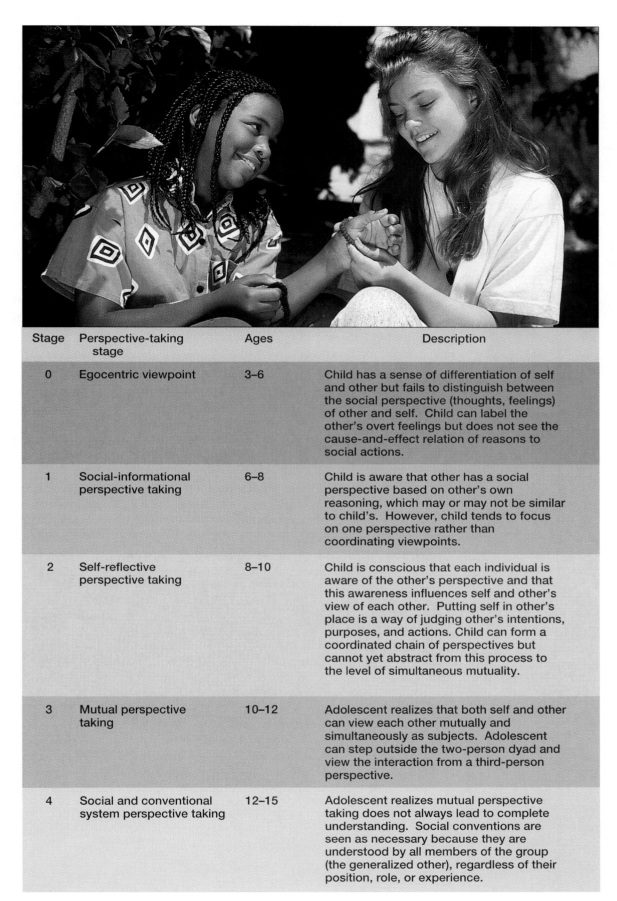

Stage	Perspective-taking stage	Ages	Description
0	Egocentric viewpoint	3–6	Child has a sense of differentiation of self and other but fails to distinguish between the social perspective (thoughts, feelings) of other and self. Child can label the other's overt feelings but does not see the cause-and-effect relation of reasons to social actions.
1	Social-informational perspective taking	6–8	Child is aware that other has a social perspective based on other's own reasoning, which may or may not be similar to child's. However, child tends to focus on one perspective rather than coordinating viewpoints.
2	Self-reflective perspective taking	8–10	Child is conscious that each individual is aware of the other's perspective and that this awareness influences self and other's view of each other. Putting self in other's place is a way of judging other's intentions, purposes, and actions. Child can form a coordinated chain of perspectives but cannot yet abstract from this process to the level of simultaneous mutuality.
3	Mutual perspective taking	10–12	Adolescent realizes that both self and other can view each other mutually and simultaneously as subjects. Adolescent can step outside the two-person dyad and view the interaction from a third-person perspective.
4	Social and conventional system perspective taking	12–15	Adolescent realizes mutual perspective taking does not always lead to complete understanding. Social conventions are seen as necessary because they are understood by all members of the group (the generalized other), regardless of their position, role, or experience.

■ FIGURE 4.13
Selman's Stages of Perspective Taking

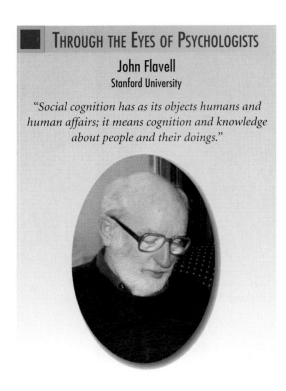

implicit personality theory
The layperson's conception of personality.

Implicit Personality Theory

Implicit personality theory *is the layperson's conception of personality.* Do adolescents conceptualize an individual's personality differently than children do? Adolescents are more likely to interpret an individual's personality in the way that many personality theorists in psychology do than children are (Barenboim, 1981). Adolescents interpret personality differently than children in three ways. First, when adolescents are given information about another person, they are more likely to consider both previously acquired information and current information, rather than relying only on the concrete information at hand, as children do. Second, adolescents are more likely to detect the situational or contextual variability in personality, rather than thinking that personality is always stable. Third, rather than merely accepting surface traits as a valid description of someone's personality, adolescents are more likely than children to look for deeper, more complex, even hidden causes of personality.

In these comments obtained in one developmental investigation of how individuals perceive others, we can see how the development of an implicit personality theory proceeds (Livesley & Bromley, 1973):

> Max sits next to me, his eyes are hazel and he is tall. He hasn't got a very big head, he's got a big pointed nose. (p. 213; age 7 years, 6 months)

> He smells very much and is very nasty. He has no sense of humor and is very dull. He is always fighting and he is cruel. He does silly things and is very stupid. He has brown hair and cruel eyes. He is sulky and eleven years old and has lots of sisters. I think he is the most horrible boy in the class. He has a croaky voice and always chews his pencil and picks his teeth and I think he is disgusting. (p. 217; age 9 years, 11 months)

> Andy is very modest. He is even shyer than I am when near strangers and yet is very talkative with people he knows and likes. He always seems good tempered and I have never seen him in a bad temper. He tends to degrade other people's achievements, and yet never praises his own. He does not seem to voice his opinions to anyone. He easily gets nervous. (p. 221; age 15 years, 8 months)

> . . . she is curious about people but naive, and this leads her to ask too many questions so that people become irritated with her and withhold information, although she is not sensitive enough to notice it. (p. 225; young adult)

Social Cognition in the Rest of This Text

Interest in social cognition has blossomed, and the approach has infiltrated many aspects of the study of adolescent development. In the discussion of families in chapter 5, the emerging cognitive abilities of the adolescent are evaluated in concert with parent-adolescent conflict and parenting strategies. In the description of peer relations in chapter 6, the importance of social knowledge and social information processing in peer relations is highlighted. In the overview of the self and identity in chapter 9, social cognition's role in understanding the self and identity is explored. And in the evaluation of moral development in chapter 12, considerable time is devoted to discussing Kohlberg's theory, which is a prominent aspect of the study of social cognition in adolescence.

Since the last review we have explored many ideas about social cognition. These questions should help you to reach your learning goals related to this topic.

☐ FOR YOUR REVIEW

Learning Goal 5
Describe changes in social cognition

- Social cognition refers to how people conceptualize and reason about their social world, including the relation of the self to others.
- Elkind proposed that adolescents, especially young adolescents, develop an egocentrism that consists of an imaginary audience and a personal fable. Critics argue that perspective taking rather than formal operational thought is the main factor in the development of adolescent egocentrism.
- Perspective taking is the ability to take another person's perspective and understand his or her thoughts and feelings. Adolescents are better at perspective taking than children are, but there is considerable overlap in the ages at which the higher states of perspective taking occur. Selman proposed a model that has served as the basis for thinking about developmental changes in perspective taking.
- Implicit personality theory is the public's or layperson's conception of personality. Adolescents' implicit personality theory is closer to that of scientists who study personality than is the implicit personality of children. Compared to children, adolescents describe personality as having more past-present connections, as more contextual, and as more unconscious.
- We will study social cognition throughout this text, especially in chapters on families, peers, the self and identity, and moral development.

In this chapter, we have examined cognitive development in adolescence. In the next chapter, we will explore families and adolescents, the first chapter in the main section of the book titled, "The Contexts of Adolescent Development."

CHAPTER MAP

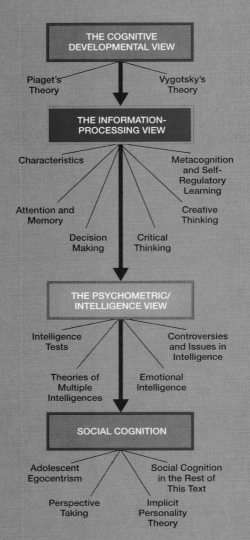

THE COGNITIVE DEVELOPMENTAL VIEW

Piaget's Theory

Vygotsky's Theory

THE INFORMATION-PROCESSING VIEW

Characteristics

Metacognition and Self-Regulatory Learning

Attention and Memory

Creative Thinking

Decision Making

Critical Thinking

THE PSYCHOMETRIC/ INTELLIGENCE VIEW

Intelligence Tests

Controversies and Issues in Intelligence

Theories of Multiple Intelligences

Emotional Intelligence

SOCIAL COGNITION

Adolescent Egocentrism

Social Cognition in the Rest of This Text

Perspective Taking

Implicit Personality Theory

REACH YOUR LEARNING GOALS

At the beginning of the chapter, we stated five learning goals and encouraged you to review material related to these goals at four points in the chapter. This is a good time to return to these reviews and use them to guide your study and help you to reach your learning goals.

Page 118

Learning Goal 1   Discuss Piaget's theory
Learning Goal 2   Understand Vygotsky's theory

Page 128

Learning Goal 3   Evaluate the information-processing view

Page 136

Learning Goal 4   Explain the psychometric/intelligence view

Page 141

Learning Goal 5   Describe changes in social cognition

KEY TERMS

schema 106
assimilation 106
accommodation 106
equilibration 107
sensorimotor stage 107
preoperational stage 107
concrete operational stage 107
formal operational stage 108
hypothetical-deductive reasoning 109
neo-Piagetians 113
postformal thought 114
zone of proximal development (ZPD) 115
critical thinking 123
creativity 124

convergent thinking 124
divergent thinking 124
metacognition 126
self-regulatory learning 127
psychometric/intelligence view 128
intelligence 129
mental age (MA) 129
intelligent quotient (IQ) 129
normal distribution 129
triarchic theory of intelligence 131
emotional intelligence 133
culture-fair tests 135
adolescent egocentrism 137
implicit personality theory 140

KEY PEOPLE

Jean Piaget 106
Lev Vygotsky 106
Annemarie Palincsar and Ann Brown 116
Robbie Case 113
Barbara Rogoff 115
Robert Siegler 119
Daniel Keating 123
J. P. Guilford 124
Mihaly Csikszentmihalyi 125
Deanna Kuhn 126
Michael Pressley 126

Alfred Binet 129
William Stern 129
David Wechsler 130
Charles Spearman 130
L. L. Thurstone 130
Robert Sternberg 131
Howard Gardner 132
Daniel Goleman 133
David Elkind 137
Robert Selman 137

RESOURCES FOR IMPROVING THE LIVES OF ADOLESCENTS

Apprenticeship in Thinking

(1990) by Barbara Rogoff
New York: Oxford University Press

Rogoff believes that children's and adolescents' cognitive development is best served by participation in social activity, guided by companions who stretch and support their understanding and use of the culture's tools.

Children's Thinking

(1998, 3rd ed.) by Robert Siegler
Upper Saddle River, NJ: Prentice Hall

In-depth coverage of information processing by one of the field's leading experts.

Encyclopedia of Creativity

(1999, Vols. 1 & 2) by Mark Runco & Steven Pritzker (Eds.)
San Diego: Academic Press

A wealth of information about virtually every imaginable aspect of creativity, written by leading experts.

How People Learn

(1999) by the Committee on Developments
in the Science of Learning
Washington, DC: National Academy Press

A prestigious panel headed by John Bransford and Ann Brown describes the current state of knowledge about how children and youth think and learn.

The Jasper Project

(1997) by the Cognition and Technology Group at Vanderbilt
Mahwah, NJ: Erlbaum

An innovative, problem-based learning approach is discussed; includes a CD of one of the Jasper adventures.

Teaching and Learning Through Multiple Intelligences

(1999, 2nd ed.) by Linda Campbell, Bruce Campbell,
and Dee Dickinson
Boston: Allyn & Bacon

Provides applications of Gardner's eight intelligences to classrooms.

TAKING IT TO THE NET

http://www.mhhe.com/santrocka9

1. Your psychology instructor notes that in surfing the Web one can find a large number of sites with IQ tests, including tests for emotional IQ, sports IQ, trivia IQ, social IQ, musical IQ, as well as tests for IQs in a variety of other areas. As an extra credit assignment the instructor challenges the class to write a two-page paper indicating whose theoretical stance about intelligence could encompass such IQ concepts and how it would do so. *What would you write?*

2. Suppose your roommate complains that there is just too much material to learn in his or her classes and that he or she has a lot of trouble getting all the information into memory. You recognize this as a metamemory problem. *What means would you suggest your roommate use to improve getting information into memory?*

3. As a dual major in biology and psychology, you realize that fundamental psychological processes such as memory, problem solving, and information processing must ultimately be tied to components of biological development. You decide to write your term paper on the links between neuroscience and cognitive development. *What themes will you write about?*

Connect to *http://www.mhhe.com/santrocka9* to research the answers and complete these exercises. In some cases, you'll also find further instructions on this site.

THE CONTEXTS OF ADOLESCENT DEVELOPMENT

Man is a knot, a web, a mesh into which relationships are tied.
—Antoine de Saint-Exupery
French Novelist and Aviator, 20th Century

Adolescent development takes place in social contexts, which provide the setting and sociohistorical, cultural backdrop for physical, cognitive, and socioemotional growth. This third section consists of four chapters: chapter 5, "Families"; chapter 6, "Peers"; chapter 7, "Schools"; and chapter 8, "Culture."

■ Variations in Adolescents' Perceptions of Parents

My mother and I depend on each other. However, if something separated us, I think I could still get along O.K. I know that my mother continues to have an important influence on me. Sometimes she gets on my nerves, but I still basically like her, and respect her, a lot. We have our arguments, and I don't always get my way, but she is willing to listen to me.

—Amy, age 16

You go from a point at which your parents are responsible for you to a point at which you want a lot more independence. Finally, you are more independent, and you feel like you have to be more responsible for yourself; otherwise you are not going to do very well in this world. It's important for parents to still be there to support you, but at some point, you've got to look in the mirror and say, "I can do it myself."

—John, age 18

I don't get along very well with my parents. They try to dictate how I dress, who I date, how much I study, what I do on weekends, and how much time I spend talking on the phone. They are big intruders in my life. Why won't they let me make my own decisions? I'm mature enough to handle these things. When they jump down my throat at every little thing I do, it makes me mad and I say things to them I probably shouldn't. They just don't understand me very well.

—Ed, age 17

My father never seems to have any time to spend with me. He is gone a lot on business, and when he comes home, he is either too tired to do anything or plops down and watches TV and doesn't want to be bothered. He thinks I don't work hard enough and don't have values that were as solid as his generation. It is a very distant relationship. I actually spend more time talking to my mom than to him. I guess I should work a little harder in school than I do, but I still don't think he has the right to say such negative things to me. I like my mom a lot better because I think she is a much nicer person.

—Tom, age 15

We have our arguments and our differences, and there are moments when I get very angry with my parents, but most of the time they are like heated discussions. I have to say what I think because I don't think they are always right. Most of the time when there is an argument, we can discuss the problem and eventually find a course that we all can live with. Not every time, though, because there are some occasions when things just remain unresolved. Even when we have an unresolved conflict, I still would have to say that I get along pretty good with my parents.

—Ann, age 16

FAMILIES

■

It is not enough for parents to understand children. They must accord children the privilege of understanding them.

—Milton Saperstein
American Author, 20th Century

THE COMMENTS OF THESE FIVE ADOLESCENTS offer a brief glimpse of the diversity that characterizes adolescents' relationships with their parents. Although parent-adolescent relationships vary considerably, researchers are finding that, for the most part, the relationships are both (1) very important aspects of development and (2) more positive than once was believed. When you have completed this chapter, you should be able to reach these learning goals:

1 Explain the nature of family processes

2 Discuss parent-adolescent relationships

3 Know about sibling relationships

4 Describe the effects of divorce, stepfamilies, and working parents

5 Understand culture, ethnicity, gender, and parenting

6 Evaluate social policy and families

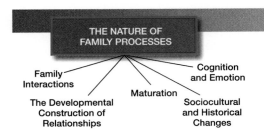

THE NATURE OF FAMILY PROCESSES

Family Interactions

Cognition and Emotion

Maturation

The Developmental Construction of Relationships

Sociocultural and Historical Changes

reciprocal socialization
The process by which children and adolescents socialize parents, just as parents socialize them.

THE NATURE OF FAMILY PROCESSES

We will begin our exploration of family processes by focusing on how family members interact with each other.

Family Interactions

For many years, the socialization of adolescents was viewed as a straightforward, one-way matter of indoctrination. The basic philosophy was that children and adolescents had to be trained to fit into the social world, so their behavior had to be shaped accordingly. However, socialization is much more than molding the child and adolescent into a mature adult. The child and adolescent are not like inanimate blobs of clay that the sculptor forms into a polished statue. **Reciprocal socialization** *is the process by which children and adolescents socialize parents just as parents socialize them.* To get a better feel for how reciprocal socialization works, consider two situations: the first emphasizing the impact of growing up in a single-parent home (parental influences), the second a talented teenage ice skater (adolescent influences). In the first situation, the speaker is 14-year-old Robert:

> I never have seen my father. He never married my mother, and she had to quit school to help support us. Maybe my mother and I are better off that he didn't marry her because he apparently didn't love her . . . but sometimes I get very depressed about not having a father, especially when I see a lot of my friends with their fathers at ball games and such. My father still lives around here, but he has married, and I guess he wants to forget about me and my mother. . . . A lot of times I wish my mother would get married and I could at least have a stepfather to talk with about things and do things with me.

In the second situation, the first speaker is 13-year-old Kathy:

> "Mother, my skating coach says that I have a lot of talent, but it is going to take a lot of lessons and travel to fully develop it." Her mother responds, "Kathy, I just don't know. We will have to talk with your father about it tonight when he gets home from work." That evening, Kathy's father tells his wife, "Look, to do that for Kathy, I will have to get a second job, or you will have to get a job. There is no way we can afford what she wants with what I make."

As developmentalists probe the nature of reciprocal socialization, they are impressed with the importance of synchrony in parent-child and parent-adolescent relationships. **Synchrony** *refers to the carefully coordinated interaction between the parent and the child or adolescent, in which, often unknowingly, they are attuned to each other's behavior.* The turn taking that occurs in parent-adolescent negotiation reflects the reciprocal, synchronous nature of parent-adolescent relationships. The interactions of parents and adolescents in synchronous relationships can be conceptualized as a dance or a dialogue in which successive actions of the partners are closely coordinated. This coordinated dance or dialogue can assume the form of mutual synchrony (each individual's behavior depends on the partner's previous behavior), or it can be reciprocal in a more precise sense: The actions of the partners can be matched, as when one partner imitates the other or there is mutual smiling.

Reciprocal socialization takes place within the social system of a family, which consists of a constellation of subsystems defined by generation, gender, and role (Kreppner, 2001; Minuchin, 2002). Divisions of labor among family members define particular subsystems, and attachments define others. Each family member is a participant in several subsystems—some dyadic (involving two people), some polyadic (involving more than two people) (Kramer & Lin, 1997). The father and adolescent represent one dyadic subsystem, the mother and father another. The mother-father-adolescent represent one polyadic subsystem.

Figure 5.1 shows an organizational scheme that highlights the reciprocal influences of family members and family subsystems (Belsky, 1981). As can be seen by following the arrows in the figure, marital relations, parenting, and adolescent behavior can have both direct and indirect effects on each other. An example of a direct effect is the influence of the parent's behavior on the adolescent. An example of an indirect effect is how the relationship between the spouses mediates the way a parent acts toward the adolescent (Emery & Tuer, 1993). For example, marital conflict might reduce the efficiency of parenting, in which case marital conflict would have an indirect effect on the adolescent's behavior (Wilson & Gottman, 1995).

Interaction between individuals in a family can change, depending on who is present. In one investigation, 44 adolescents were observed either separately with their mother and father (dyadic settings) or in the presence of both parents (triadic setting) (Gjerde, 1986). The presence of the father improved mother-son relationships, but the presence of the mother decreased the quality of father-son relations. This may have occurred because the father takes the strain off the mother by controlling the adolescent or because the mother's presence reduces father-son interaction, which may not be high in many instances. Indeed, in one recent investigation, sons directed more negative behavior toward their mothers than toward their fathers in dyadic situations (Buhrmester & others, in press). However, in a triadic context of adolescent-mother-father, fathers helped "rescue" mothers by attempting to control the sons'

synchrony
The carefully coordinated interaction between the parent and the child or adolescent in which, often unknowingly, they are attuned to each other's behavior.

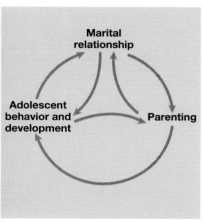

■ FIGURE 5.1
Interaction Between Adolescents and Their Parents: Direct and Indirect Effects

negative behavior. In one recent study that focused on adolescents in middle-socioeconomic-status African American families, both mothers' and fathers' communication was more positive in dyadic than triadic interactions (Smetana, Abernethy, & Harris, 2000).

The Developmental Construction of Relationships

developmental construction views
Views sharing the belief that as individuals grow up, they acquire modes of relating to others. There are two main variations of this view. One emphasizes continuity and stability in relationships throughout the life span; the other emphasizes discontinuity and changes in relationships throughout the life span.

continuity view
A developmental view that emphasizes the role of early parent-child relationships in constructing a basic way of relating to people throughout the life span.

Developmentalists have shown an increased interest in understanding how we construct relationships as we grow up (Collins & Madsen, 2002). Psychoanalytic theorists have always been interested in how this process works in families. However, the current explanations of how relationships are constructed is virtually stripped of Freud's psychosexual stage terminology and also is not always confined to the first five years of life, as has been the case in classical psychoanalytic theory. Today's **developmental construction views** *share the belief that as individuals grow up, they acquire modes of relating to others. There are two main variations within this view, one of which emphasizes continuity and stability in relationships throughout the life span and one of which emphasizes discontinuity and change in relationships throughout the life span.*

The Continuity View The **continuity view** *emphasizes the role that early parent-child relationships play in constructing a basic way of relating to people throughout the life span.* These early parent-child relationships are carried forward to later points in development to influence all subsequent relationships (with peers, with friends, with teachers, and with romantic partners, for example) (Ainsworth, 1979; Bowlby, 1989; Sroufe, 1996). In its extreme form, this view states that the basic components of social relationships are laid down and shaped by the security or insecurity of parent-infant attachment relationships in the first year or two of the infant's life. More about the importance of secure attachment in the adolescent's development appears later in the chapter when we discuss autonomy and attachment.

Close relationships with parents also are important in the adolescent's development because these relationships function as models or templates that are carried forward over time to influence the construction of new relationships. Clearly, close relationships do not repeat themselves in an endless fashion over the course of the child's and adolescent's development. And the quality of any relationship depends to some degree on the specific individual with whom the relationship is formed. However, the nature of earlier relationships that are developed over many years often can be detected in later relationships, both with those same individuals and in the formation of relationships with others at a later point in time (Gjerde, Block, & Block, 1991). Thus, the nature of parent-adolescent relationships does not depend only on what happens in the relationship during adolescence. Relationships with parents over the long course of childhood are carried forward to influence, at least to some degree, the nature of parent-adolescent relationships. And the long course of parent-child relationships also could be expected to influence, again at least to some degree, the fabric of the adolescent's peer relationships, friendships, and dating relationships.

In the research of Alan Sroufe and his colleagues, evidence for continuity is being found (Sroufe, 2001; Sroufe, Egeland, & Carson, 1999). Attachment history and early care were related to peer competence in adolescence, up to 15 years after the infant assessments. In interviews with adolescents, those who formed couple relationships during camp retreats had been securely attached in infancy. Also, ratings of videotaped behavior revealed that those with secure attachment histories were more socially competent, which included having confidence in social situations and showing leadership skills. For most children, there was a cascading effect in which early family relationships provided the necessary support for effectively engaging in the peer world, which in turn provided the foundation for more extensive, complex peer relationships.

How childhood experiences with parents are carried forward and influence the nature of the adolescent's development is important, but the nature of intergenerational relationships is significant as well. As the life-span perspective has taken on greater

To what extent is an adolescent's development likely to be influenced by early experiences with parents?

acceptance among developmental psychologists, researchers have become interested in the transmission of close relationships across generations (Elder, 2000; Kandel & Wu, 1995).

The middle generation in three generations is especially important in the socialization process. For example, the parents of adolescents can be studied in terms of their relationships with their own parents, when they were children and presently, and in terms of their relationships with their own adolescents, both when the adolescents were children and presently. Life-span theorists point out that the middle-aged parents of adolescents may have to give more help than they receive. Their adolescents probably are reaching the point where they need considerable financial support for education, and their parents, whose generation is living longer than past generations, may also require financial support, as well as more comfort and affection than earlier in the life span.

The Discontinuity View   The **discontinuity view** *emphasizes change and growth in relationships over time.* As people grow up, they develop many different types of relationships (with parents, with peers, with teachers, and with romantic partners, for example). Each of these relationships is structurally different. With each new type of relationship, individuals encounter new modes of relating (Buhrmester & Furman, 1987; Furman & Wehner, 1997; Piaget, 1932; Sullivan, 1953; Youniss, 1980). For example, Piaget (1932) argued that parent-child relationships are strikingly different from children's peer relationships. Parent-child relationships, he said, are more likely to consist of parents having unilateral authority over children. By contrast, peer relationships are more likely to consist of participants who relate to each other on a much more equal basis. In parent-child relationships, since parents have greater knowledge and authority, their children often must learn how to conform to rules and regulations laid down by parents. In this view, we use the parental-child mode when relating to authority figures (such as with teachers and experts) and when we act as authority figures (when we become parents, teachers, and experts).

In contrast, relationships with peers have a different structure and require a different mode of relating to others. This more egalitarian mode is later called upon in relationships with romantic partners, friends, and coworkers. Because two peers possess

discontinuity view
A developmental view that emphasizes change and growth in relationships over time.

relatively equal knowledge and authority (their relationship is reciprocal and symmetrical), children learn a democratic mode of relating that is based on mutual influence. With peers, children learn to formulate and assert their own opinions, appreciate the perspective of peers, cooperatively negotiate solutions to disagreements, and evolve standards for conduct that are mutually acceptable. Because peer relationships are voluntary (rather than obligatory, as in the family), children and adolescents who fail to become skillful in the symmetrical, mutual, egalitarian, reciprocal mode of relating have difficulty being accepted by peers.

Although the discontinuity view does not deny that prior close relationships (such as with parents) are carried forward to influence later relationships, it does stress that each new type of relationship that children and adolescents encounter (such as with peers, with friends, and with romantic partners) requires the construction of different and even more sophisticated modes of relating to others. Further, in the change/growth version, each period of development uniquely contributes to the construction of relationship knowledge; development across the life span is not solely determined by a sensitive or critical period during infancy.

Evidence for the discontinuity view of relationships was found in the longitudinal study conducted by Andrew Collins and his colleagues (Collins, Hennighausen, & Sroufe, 1998). Quality of friendship interaction (based on observations of coordinated behavior, such as turn-taking, sharing, eye contact, and touching, and their duration) in middle childhood was related to security with dating, and disclosure and intimacy with a dating partner, at age 16.

Maturation

Mark Twain once remarked that when he was 14 his father was so ignorant he could hardly stand to have the man around him, but when Mark got to be 21, he was astonished at how much his father had learned in those seven years! Mark Twain's comments suggest that maturation is an important theme of parent-adolescent relationships. Adolescents change as they make the transition from childhood to adulthood, but their parents also change during their adult years (Grotevant, 1998).

THROUGH THE EYES OF PSYCHOLOGISTS

W. Andrew Collins
University of Minnesota

"Expectancy violations on the part of parents and adolescents are especially likely during the transition to adolescence."

Adolescent Changes Among the changes in the adolescent that can influence parent-adolescent relationships are puberty, expanded logical reasoning, increased idealistic thought, violated expectations, changes in schooling, peers, friendships, dating, and movement toward independence. Several investigations have shown that conflict between parents and adolescents, especially between mothers and sons, is the most stressful during the apex of pubertal growth (Hill & others, 1985; Steinberg, 1988).

In terms of cognitive changes, the adolescent can now reason in more logical ways with parents than in childhood. During childhood, parents may be able to get by with saying, "O.K. That is it. We do it my way or else," and the child conforms. But with increased cognitive skills, adolescents no longer are likely to accept such a statement as a reason for conforming to parental dictates. Adolescents want to know, often in fine detail, why they are being disciplined. Even when parents give what seem to be logical reasons for discipline, adolescents' cognitive sophistication may call attention to deficiencies in the reasoning. Such prolonged bouts of discourse with parents are usually uncharacteristic of parent-child relationships but are frequent occurrences in parent-adolescent relationships.

In addition, the adolescent's increasing idealistic thought comes into play in parent-adolescent relationships. Parents are now evaluated vis-à-vis what an ideal parent is like. The very real interactions with parents, which inevitably involve some negative interchanges and flaws, are placed next to the adolescent's schema of an ideal parent. And, as part of their egocentrism, adolescents' concerns with how others view them are likely to produce overreactions to parents' comments. A mother may comment to her adolescent daughter that she needs a new blouse. The daughter might respond, "What's the matter? You don't think I have good taste? You think I look gross, don't you? Well, you are the one who is gross!" The same comment made to the daughter several years earlier in late childhood probably would have elicited a less intense response.

Another dimension of the adolescent's changing cognitive world related to parent-adolescent relations is the expectations parents and adolescents have for each other (Collins & Luebker, 1994; Collins & Repinski, in press). Preadolescent children are often compliant and easy to manage. As they enter puberty, children begin to question or seek rationales for parental demands (Maccoby, 1984). Parents might perceive this behavior as resistant and oppositional because it departs from the child's previously compliant behavior. Parents often respond to the lack of compliance with increased pressure for compliance. In this situation, expectations that were stabilized during a period of relatively slow developmental change are lagging behind the behavior of the adolescent in the period of rapid pubertal change.

What dimensions of the adolescent's social world contribute to parent-adolescent relationships? Adolescence brings with it new definitions of socially appropriate behavior. In our society, these definitions are associated with changes in schooling arrangements—transitions to middle or junior high school. Adolescents are required to function in a more anonymous, larger environment with multiple and varying teachers. More work is required, and more initiative and responsibility must be shown to adapt successfully. The school is not the only social arena that contributes to parent-adolescent relationships. Adolescents spend more time with peers than when they were children, and they develop more sophisticated friendships than in childhood. Adolescents also begin to push more strongly for independence. In sum, parents are called on to adapt to the changing world of the adolescent's schooling, peer relations, and push for autonomy (Grotevant, 1998).

Parental Changes

Parental changes that contribute to parent-adolescent relationships involve marital satisfaction, economic burdens, career reevaluation and time perspective, and health and body concerns (MacDermid & Crouter, 1995; Silverberg & Steinberg, 1990). Marital dissatisfaction is greater when the offspring is an adolescent than when the offspring is a child or an adult. This recently was documented in a longitudinal study of almost 7,000 spouses (Benin, 1997). In addition, parents feel a greater economic burden during the rearing of adolescents. Also during this time, parents may reevaluate their occupational achievement, deciding whether they have met their youthful aspirations of success. They may look to the future and think about how much time they have remaining to accomplish what they want. Adolescents, however, look to the future with unbounded optimism, sensing that they have an unlimited amount of time to accomplish what they desire. Health concerns and an interest in body integrity and sexual attractiveness become prominent themes of adolescents' parents. Even when their body and sexual attractiveness are not deteriorating, many parents of adolescents perceive that they are. By contrast, adolescents have reached or are beginning to reach the peak of their physical attractiveness, strength, and health. Although both adolescents and their parents show a heightened preoccupation with their bodies, adolescents' outcome probably is more positive.

In one study of middle-aged parents and their adolescents, the relation between parents' midlife concerns and their adolescents' pubertal development could not be characterized simply as positive, negative, or nil (MacDermid & Crouter, 1995). Parents reported less intense midlife concerns when their adolescents were further along in puberty. Spousal support in midlife emerged as an important factor in helping parents meet the challenges of pubertal changes in their adolescents.

The changes in adolescents' parents just described characterize development in middle adulthood. Most adolescents' parents either are in middle adulthood or are rapidly approaching middle adulthood. However, in the last two decades, the timing of

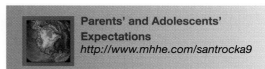
Parents' and Adolescents' Expectations
http://www.mhhe.com/santrocka9

The generations of living things pass in a short time, and like runners hand on the torch of life.
—Lucretius
Roman Poet, 1st Century B.C.

parenthood has undergone some dramatic shifts (Parke, 2001, in press; Parke & Buriel, 1998). Parenthood is taking place earlier for some, later for others, than in previous decades. First, the number of adolescent pregnancies substantially increased during the 1980s. Second, the number of women who postpone childbearing until their thirties and early forties simultaneously increased. The topic of adolescents as parents is discussed in chapter 11. Here we focus on sociohistorical changes related to postponement of childbearing until the thirties or forties.

There are many contrasts between becoming a parent in adolescence and becoming a parent 15 to 30 years later. Delayed childbearing allows for considerable progress in occupational and educational domains. For both males and females, education usually has been completed, and career development is well established.

The marital relationship varies with the timing of parenthood onset. In one investigation, couples who began childbearing in their early twenties were compared with those who began in their early thirties (Walter, 1986). The late-starting couples had more egalitarian relationships, with men participating in child care and household tasks more often.

Is parent-child interaction different for families in which parents delay having children until their thirties or forties? Investigators have found that older fathers are warmer, communicate better, encourage more achievement, and show less rejection with their children than younger fathers. However, older fathers also are less likely to place demands on children, to enforce rules, and to engage in physical play or sports with their children (MacDonald, 1987). These findings suggest that sociohistorical changes are resulting in different developmental trajectories for many families, trajectories that involve changes in the way marital partners and parents and adolescents interact.

Sociocultural and Historical Changes

Family development does not occur in a social vacuum. Important sociocultural and historical influences affect family processes (Day, 2002; Goldscheider, 1997; McHale & Grolnick, 2001). Family changes might be due to great upheavals in a nation, such as war, famine, or mass immigration. Or they could be due more to subtle transitions in ways of life. The Great Depression in the early 1930s had some negative effects on families. During its height, the depression produced economic deprivation, adult discontent, depression about living conditions, marital conflict, inconsistent child rearing, and unhealthy lifestyles—heavy drinking, demoralized attitudes, and health disabilities—especially in the father (Elder, 1998). Subtle changes in a culture that have significant influences on the family were described by the famous anthropologist Margaret Mead (1978). The changes focus on the longevity of the elderly and the role of the elderly in the family, the urban and suburban orientation of families and their mobility, television, and a general dissatisfaction and restlessness.

Fifty years ago, the older people who survived were usually hearty and still closely linked to the family, often helping to maintain the family's existence. Today, older people live longer, which means that their middle-aged children are often pressed into a caretaking role for their parents or the elderly parents might be placed in a nursing home. Elderly parents may have lost some of their socializing role in the family during the twentieth century as many of their children moved great distances away.

THROUGH THE EYES OF ADOLESCENTS

Why Don't You Understand Me? Why Do You Blame Me for Everything?

Andrea is 12 years old. Yesterday she wrote her parents a note. She began the note by thanking her parents for all of the wonderful things they had done for her. Then, very quickly, she nailed them right between the eyes with her criticism. She wanted to know why they never listen to her. Why they don't understand her. Why they blame her for everything. Why they yell at her so much. Andrea went on to say that she feels left out of the family and that she's not sure they (her parents) really love her. Andrea's increasingly idealistic thinking led her to compare her real parents with what ideal parents are like. Like all real parents, Andrea's came up far short.

Many of these family moves are away from farms and small towns to urban and suburban settings. In the small towns and farms, individuals were surrounded by life-long neighbors, relatives, and friends. Today, neighborhood and extended-family support systems are not nearly as prevalent. Families now move all over the country, often uprooting adolescents from school and peer groups they have known for a considerable length of time. And for many families, this type of move occurs every year or two, as one or both parents are transferred from job to job.

Television also plays a major role in the changing family. Many children who watch television find that parents are too busy working to share this experience with them. Children increasingly experience a world their parents are not a part of. Instead of participating in neighborhood peer groups, children come home after school and plop down in front of the television set. And television allows children and their families to see new ways of life. Lower-SES families can look into the family lives of higher-SES families by simply pushing a button.

Another dramatic change in families is the increasing number of adolescents who grow up in a hodgepodge of family structures, with far greater numbers of single-parent and stepparent families than ever before in history (Hetherington & Kelly, 2002). Later in the chapter, we discuss such aspects of the changing social world of the adolescent and the family in greater detail.

Cognition and Emotion

Cognitive processes are increasingly believed to be central to understanding socialization in the family (Bugental & Goodnow, 1998; Parke, 2001; Parke & Buriel, 1998). Cognition in family socialization comes in many forms, including parents' cognitions, beliefs, and values about their parental role, as well as how parents perceive, organize, and understand their adolescents' behaviors and beliefs.

One study found a link between mothers' beliefs and their children's social problem-solving skills (Rubin, Mills, & Rose-Krasnor, 1989). Mothers who placed higher values on such skills as making friends, sharing with others, and leading or influencing other children had children who were more assertive, prosocial, and competent problem solvers.

Emotion also is increasingly viewed as central to understanding family processes (Parke & Buriel, 1998). Some of the areas that studies of emotion in family processes have focused on include the development of emotional regulation, the development of emotional production and understanding, and the role of emotion in carrying out the parental role.

Especially important in effective parenting is helping children and youth learn to manage their emotions. Children's social competence is often linked to the emotional lives of their parents. For example, one study found that parents who displayed positive emotional expressiveness had children who were high in social competence (Boyum & Parke, 1995). Through interactions with parents, children learn to express their emotions in socially appropriate ways.

Researchers also are finding that parental support and acceptance of children's emotions are related to children's ability to manage their emotions in positive ways (Parke & Buriel, 1998). Parental comforting of children when they experience negative emotion is linked with constructive handling of anger (Eisenberg & Fabes, 1994). Also, parental motivation to discuss emotions with their children is related to children's awareness and understanding of others' emotions (Denham, Cook, & Zoller, 1992; Dunn & Brown, 1994).

Underlying much of the current research on socialization processes in families is the belief that cognition and emotion generally operate together in determining parenting practices (Dix, 1991).

THROUGH THE EYES OF PSYCHOLOGISTS

Ross Parke
University of California–Riverside

"Cognition and emotion are increasingly viewed as important socialization processes in families."

At this point we have studied a number of ideas about the nature of family processes. This review should help you to reach your learning goals related to this topic.

☐ FOR YOUR REVIEW

Learning Goal 1
Explain the nature of family processes

- Adolescents socialize parents just as parents socialize adolescents. Synchrony involves the carefully coordinated interaction between parent and adolescent, in which, often unknowingly, they are attuned to each other's behavior. The family is a system of interacting individuals with different subsystems—some dyadic, some polyadic.
- The developmental construction views share the belief that as individuals develop they acquire modes of relating to others. There are two main variations within this view, one that emphasizes continuity and one that stresses discontinuity and change in relationships.
- Relationships are influenced by the maturation of the adolescent and the maturation of parents. Adolescent changes include puberty, expanded logical reasoning, increased idealistic and egocentric thought, violated expectations, changes in schooling, peers, friendships, dating, and movement toward independence. Changes in parents might include marital dissatisfaction, economic burdens, career reevaluation, time perspective, and healthy/body concerns.
- Sociocultural and historical changes can be due to great upheavals such as war or to more subtle changes such as television and the mobility of families.
- Among the roles of cognition in parent-adolescent relationships are beliefs about the parental role and understanding adolescent behavior. Among the roles of emotion are regulation of emotion in adolescents and emotional aspects of the parental role.

Now that we have examined some basic aspects of family processes, let's focus in greater depth on parent-adolescent relationships.

PARENT-ADOLESCENT RELATIONSHIPS

Parents as Managers — Autonomy and Attachment — Parenting Techniques — Parent-Adolescent Conflict

Parenting Adolescents
Exploring Parent-Adolescent Relationships
http://www.mhhe.com/santrocka9

Parent-Adolescent Relationships

We have seen how the expectations of adolescents and their parents often seem violated as adolescents change dramatically during the course of puberty. Many parents see their child changing from a compliant being into someone who is noncompliant, oppositional, and resistant to parental standards. Parents often clamp down and put more pressure on the adolescent to conform to parental standards. Many parents often deal with the young adolescent as if they expect the adolescent to become a mature being within the next 10 to 15 minutes. But the transition from childhood to adulthood is a long journey with many hills and valleys. Adolescents are not going to conform to adult standards immediately. Parents who recognize that adolescents take a long time "to get it right" usually deal more competently and calmly with adolescent transgressions than do parents who demand immediate conformity to parental standards. Yet other parents, rather than placing heavy demands on their adolescents for compliance, do virtually the opposite, letting them do as they please in a very permissive manner.

As we discuss parent-adolescent relationships, we will discover that neither high-intensity demands for compliance nor an unwillingness to monitor and be involved in the adolescent's development is likely to be a wise parenting strategy. Further, we will explore another misperception that parents of adolescents sometimes entertain. Parents may perceive that virtually all conflict with their adolescent is bad. We will discover that a moderate degree of conflict with parents in adolescence is not only inevitable but may also serve a positive developmental function.

Parents as Managers

In our discussion of the increased interest in studying the roles of cognition and emotion in family processes, we indicated that an important aspect of parenting is helping children and youth manage their emotions. Likewise, an increasing trend in

CHEEVERWOOD   by Michael Fry

© 1986, Washington Post Writers Group, reprinted with permission.

conceptualizing and researching parent-child relationships is to think of parents as managers of children's lives.

Parents can play important roles as managers of children's opportunities, as monitors of children's social relationships, and as social initiators and arrangers (Parke & Buriel, 1998). Parents serve as regulators of opportunities for their children's social contact with peers, friends, and adults. From infancy through adolescence, mothers are more likely than fathers to have a managerial role in parenting. In infancy, this might involve taking a child to a doctor, and arranging for day care; in early childhood, it might involve a decision about which preschool the child should attend; in middle and late childhood, it might include directing the child to take a bath, to match their clothes and wear clean clothes, and to put away toys; in adolescence, it could involve participating in a parent-teacher conference and subsequently managing the adolescent's homework activity.

An important aspect of the managerial role of parenting is effective monitoring of the adolescent. This is especially important as children move into the adolescent years. Monitoring includes supervising an adolescent's choice of social settings, activities, and friends. As we will see in chapter 14, "Adolescent Problems," a lack of adequate parental monitoring is the parental factor that is related to juvenile delinquency more than any other (Patterson & Stouthamer-Loeber, 1984).

Parenting Techniques

Parents want their adolescents to grow into socially mature individuals, and they often feel a great deal of frustration in their role as parents. Psychologists have long searched for parenting ingredients that promote competent social development in adolescents. For example, in the 1930s, behaviorist John Watson argued that parents were too affectionate with their charges. Early research focused on a distinction between physical and psychological discipline, or between controlling and permissive parenting. More recently, there has been greater precision in unraveling the dimensions of competent parenting.

Especially widespread is the view of Diana Baumrind (1971, 1991), who believes that parents should be neither punitive nor aloof from their adolescents, but rather should develop rules and be affectionate with them. She emphasizes four types of parenting that are associated with different aspects of the adolescent's social behavior: authoritarian, authoritative, neglectful, and indulgent.

Authoritarian parenting *is a restrictive, punitive style in which the parent exhorts the adolescent to follow the parent's directions and to respect work and effort. The authoritarian parent places firm limits and controls on the adolescent and allows little verbal exchange. Authoritarian parenting is associated with adolescents' socially incompetent*

authoritarian parenting
This is a restrictive, punitive style in which the parent exhorts the adolescent to follow the parent's directions and to respect work and effort. Firm limits and controls are placed on the adolescent, and little verbal exchange is allowed. This style is associated with adolescents' socially incompetent behavior.

behavior. For example, an authoritarian parent might say, "You do it my way or else. There will be no discussion!" Adolescents of authoritarian parents often are anxious about social comparison, fail to initiate activity, and have poor communication skills.

Authoritative parenting *encourages adolescents to be independent but still places limits and controls on their actions. Extensive verbal give-and-take is allowed, and parents are warm and nurturant toward the adolescent. Authoritative parenting is associated with adolescents' socially competent behavior.* An authoritative father, for example, might put his arm around the adolescent in a comforting way and say, "You know you should not have done that. Let's talk about how you can handle the situation better next time." The adolescents of authoritative parents are self-reliant and socially responsible.

Authoritative parents also monitor their adolescents' lives. In one recent study, increased parental monitoring was effective in reducing adolescent problem behaviors and improving school performance.

Permissive parenting comes in two forms: neglectful and indulgent. **Neglectful parenting** *is a style in which the parent is very uninvolved in the adolescent's life. It is associated with adolescents' socially incompetent behavior, especially a lack of self-control.* The neglectful parent cannot answer the question, "It is 10:00 P.M. Do you know where your adolescent is?" Adolescents have a strong need for their parents to care about them; adolescents whose parents are neglectful develop the sense that other aspects of the parents' lives are more important than they are. Adolescents whose parents are neglectful are socially incompetent: They show poor self-control and do not handle independence well.

Closely related to the concept of neglectful parenting is a lack of *parental monitoring.* In one recent study, parental monitoring of adolescents was linked with higher grades, lower sexual activity, and less depression in adolescents (Jacobson & Crockett, 2000). In chapter 14, "Adolescent Problems," we will further discuss how a lack of parental monitoring is related to juvenile delinquency.

Indulgent parenting *is a style in which parents are highly involved with their adolescents but place few demands or controls on them. Indulgent parenting is associated with adolescents' social incompetence, especially a lack of self-control.* Indulgent parents allow their adolescents to do what they want, and the result is that the adolescents never learn to control their own behavior and always expect to get their way. Some parents deliberately rear their adolescents in this way because they believe that the combination of warm involvement with few restraints will produce a creative, confident adolescent. In one family with indulgent parents, the 14-year-old son moved his parents out of their master bedroom suite and claimed it—along with their expensive stereo system and color television—as his. The boy is an excellent tennis player but behaves in the manner of John McEnroe, raving and ranting around the tennis court. He has few friends, is self-indulgent, and has never learned to abide by rules and regulations. Why should he? His parents never made him follow any.

In our discussion of parenting styles, we have talked about parents who vary along the dimensions of acceptance, responsiveness, demand, and control. As shown in figure 5.2 on page 159, the four parenting styles—authoritarian, authoritative, neglectful, and indulgent—can be described in terms of these dimensions.

In one investigation, Diana Baumrind (1991) analyzed parenting styles and social competence in adolescence. The comprehensive assessment involved observations and interviews with 139 boys and girls 14 years of age and their parents. More than any other factor, the responsiveness (considerateness and supportiveness, for example) of the parents was related to the adolescents' social competence. And when parents had problem behaviors themselves (alcohol problems and marital conflict, for example), adolescents were more likely to have problems and show decreased social competence. Other researchers continue to find support for the belief that authoritarian and permissive parenting are less effective strategies than authoritative parenting (Durbin & others, 1993).

Several caveats about parenting styles are in order. First, the parenting styles do not capture the important themes of reciprocal socialization and synchrony.

authoritative parenting
This style encourages adolescents to be independent but still places limits and controls on their actions. Extensive verbal give-and-take is allowed, and parents are warm and nurturant toward the adolescent. This style is associated with adolescents' socially competent behavior.

neglectful parenting
A style in which the parent is very uninvolved in the adolescent's life. It is associated with adolescents' social incompetence, especially a lack of self-control.

indulgent parenting
A style in which parents are highly involved with their adolescents but place few demands or controls on them. This is associated with adolescents' social incompetence, especially a lack of self-control.

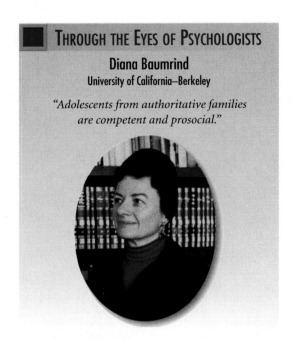

THROUGH THE EYES OF PSYCHOLOGISTS

Diana Baumrind
University of California–Berkeley

"Adolescents from authoritative families are competent and prosocial."

Keep in mind that adolescents socialize parents, just as parents socialize adolescents. Second, many parents use a combination of techniques rather than a single technique, although one technique may be dominant. Although consistent parenting is usually recommended, the wise parent may sense the importance of being more permissive in certain situations, more authoritarian in others, and yet more authoritative in others.

Parent-Adolescent Conflict

A common belief is that there is a huge gulf that separates parent and adolescents in the form of a so-called *generation gap*—that is, that during adolescence the values and attitudes of adolescents become increasingly distanced from those of their parents. For the most part, the generation gap is a stereotype. For example, most adolescents and their parents have similar beliefs about the value of hard work, achievement, and career aspirations (Gecas & Seff, 1990). They also often have similar religious and political beliefs. As we will see in our discussion of research on parent-adolescent conflict, a minority of adolescents (perhaps 20 to 25 percent) have a high degree of conflict with their parents, but for a substantial majority the conflict is moderate or low.

Early adolescence is a time when parent-adolescent conflict escalates beyond parent-child conflict (Montemayor, 1982; Weng & Montemayor, 1997). This increase may be due to a number of factors already discussed involving the maturation of the adolescent and the maturation of parents: the biological changes of puberty, cognitive changes involving increased idealism and logical reasoning, social changes focused on independence and identity, violated expectations, and physical, cognitive, and social changes in parents associated with middle adulthood. In an analysis of a number of studies, it was concluded that parent-adolescent conflict decreases from early adolescence through late adolescence (Laursen, Coy, & Collins, 1998).

Although conflict with parents does increase in early adolescence, it does not reach the tumultuous proportions envisioned by G. Stanley Hall at the beginning of the twentieth century (Holmbeck, 1996; Steinberg & Silk, 2002). Rather, much of the conflict involves the everyday events of family life, such as keeping a bedroom clean, dressing neatly, getting home by a certain time, not talking on the phone forever, and so on. The conflicts rarely involve major dilemmas like drugs and delinquency. In one recent study of middle-socioeconomic-status African American families, parent-adolescent conflict was common but low in intensity and focused on everyday living issues such as the adolescent's room, chores, choice of activities, and homework (Smetana & Gaines, 1999). Nearly

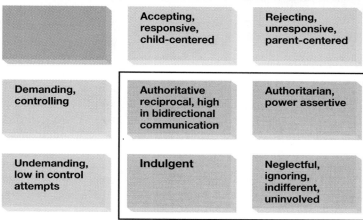

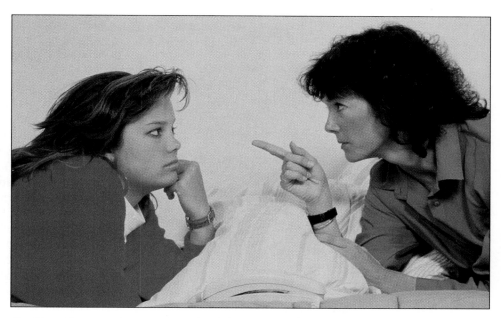
FIGURE 5.2
A Fourfold Scheme of Parenting Styles

Conflict with parents increases in early adolescence. *What is the nature of this conflict in a majority of American families?*

all conflicts were resolved by adolescents giving in to parents but adolescent concession declined with age.

In one study of conflict in a number of social relationships, adolescents reported having more disagreements with their mother than with anyone else—followed in order by friends, romantic partners, siblings, fathers, other adults, and peers (Laursen, 1995). In another study of 64 high school sophomores, interviews were conducted in their homes on three randomly selected evenings during a three-week period (Montemayor, 1982). The adolescents were asked to tell about the events of the previous day, including any conflicts they had with their parents. Conflict was defined as "either you teased your parent or your parent teased you; you and your parent had a difference of opinion; one of you got mad at the other; you and your parent had a quarrel or an argument; or one of you hit the other." During a period of 192 days of tracking the 64 adolescents, an average of 68 arguments with parents was reported. This represents a rate of 0.35 arguments with parents per day or about one argument every 3 days. The average length of the arguments was 11 minutes. Most conflicts were with mothers, and the majority were between mothers and daughters.

Still, a high degree of conflict characterizes some parent-adolescent relationships. It has been estimated that in about 20 percent of families, parents and adolescents engage in prolonged, intense, repeated, unhealthy conflict (Montemayor, 1982). While this figure represents a minority of adolescents, it indicates that 4 to 5 million American families encounter serious, highly stressful parent-adolescent conflict. And this prolonged, intense conflict is associated with a number of adolescent problems—moving away from home, juvenile delinquency, school dropout rates, pregnancy and early marriage, membership in religious cults, and drug abuse (Brook & others, 1990).

Although in some cases these problems may be caused by intense, prolonged parent-adolescent conflict, in others the problems might have originated before the onset of adolescence. Simply because children are physically much smaller than parents, parents might be able to suppress oppositional behavior. But by adolescence, increased size and strength can result in an indifference to or confrontation with parental dictates.

Judith Smetana (1988, 1993, 1997) believes that parent-adolescent conflict can be better understood by considering the adolescent's changing social cognitive abilities. In her research, she has found that parent-adolescent conflict is related to the different approaches parents and adolescents take when addressing various points of contention. For example, consider an adolescent whose parents are displeased with the way the adolescent dresses. The adolescent often defines the issue as a personal one ("It's my body and I can do what I want to with it"), whereas parents usually define such issues in broader terms ("Look, we are a family and you are part of it. You have a responsibility to us to present yourself in a better fashion"). Many such issues punctuate the lives of parents and adolescents (keeping a room clean, curfew, choice of friends, and so on). As adolescents grow older, they are more likely to see their parents' perspective and look at issues in broader terms.

It should be pointed out that there is less conflict in some cultures than in others. American psychologist Reed Larson (1999) recently spent six months in India studying middle-SES adolescents and their families. He observed that in India there seems to be little parent-adolescent conflict and that many families likely would be described as "authoritarian" in Baumrind's categorization. Larson also observed that in India adolescents do not go through a process of breaking away from their parents and that parents choose their youths' marital partners. Conflict between parents and adolescents also has been observed as lower in Japan than in the United States (Rothbaum & others, 2000; White, 1993).

> *We never know the love of our parents until we have become parents.*
> —Henry Ward Beecher
> *American Clergyman, 19th Century*

Parent-Adolescent Conflict
http://www.mhhe.com/santrocka9

CAREERS IN ADOLESCENT DEVELOPMENT

Martha Chan
Marriage and Family Therapist

Martha Chan is a marriage and family therapist who works for Adolescent Counseling Services in Palo Alto, California. She has been the program director of adolescent counseling services for more than a decade.

Among her activities, Martha counsels parents and adolescents about family issues, conducts workshops for parents at middle schools, and writes a monthly column that addresses such topics as "I'm a single mom: How do I talk with my son about sex?", "My daughter wants to dye her hair purple," and "My son is being bullied."

Next, we will explore autonomy and attachment. As with most topics in this chapter, this discussion will focus on mainstream U.S. families. Keep in mind that there can be cultural variations in autonomy and attachment in adolescence, just as there are in parent-adolescent conflict.

Autonomy and Attachment

It has been said that there are only two lasting bequests that we can leave our offspring—one is roots, the other wings. These words reflect the importance of attachment and autonomy in the adolescent's successful adaptation to the world. Historically, developmentalists have shown far more interest in autonomy than in attachment during the adolescent period. Recently, however, interest has heightened in attachment's role in healthy adolescent development. Adolescents and their parents live in a coordinated social world, one involving autonomy *and* attachment. In keeping with the historical interest in these processes, we discuss autonomy first.

Autonomy   The increased independence that typifies adolescence is labeled as rebelliousness by some parents, but in many instances the adolescent's push for autonomy has little to do with the adolescent's feelings toward the parents. Psychologically healthy families adjust to adolescents' push for independence by treating the adolescents in more adult ways and including them more in family decision making. Psychologically unhealthy families often remain locked into power-oriented parent control, and parents move even more heavily toward an authoritarian posture in their relationships with their adolescents.

However, it is important to recognize that parental control comes in different forms. In one study, adolescent adjustment depended on the type of parental control exerted (Keener & Boykin, 1996). Control characterized by psychological manipulation and the imposition of guilt was linked with lower levels of adolescent adjustment; control characterized by parental awareness of the adolescent's activities, efforts to control the adolescent's deviance, and low harshness was associated with better adjustment.

The adolescent's quest for autonomy and sense of responsibility creates puzzlement and conflict for many parents. Parents begin to see their teenagers slipping away from their grasp. Often, the urge is to take stronger control as the adolescent seeks autonomy and personal responsibility. Heated, emotional exchanges might ensue, with either side calling names, making threats, and doing whatever seems necessary to gain control. Parents can become frustrated because they expected their teenager to heed their advice, to want to spend time with the family, and

Families as Asset Builders
http://www.mhhe.com/santrocka9

Adolescents make a strong push for independence. *As the adolescent pursues autonomy, what are some good strategies parents can adopt?*

to grow up to do what is right. To be sure, they anticipated that their teenager would have some difficulty adjusting to the changes adolescence brings, but few parents are able to accurately imagine and predict the strength of adolescents' desires to be with their peers and how much they want to show that it is they, not the parents, who are responsible for their success or failure.

The Complexity of Adolescent Autonomy   Defining adolescent autonomy is more complex and elusive than it might seem at first (Collins, Gleason, & Sesma, 1997; Collins, Hyson, & Meyer, 2000). For most individuals, the term autonomy connotes self-direction and independence. But what does it really mean? Is it an internal personality trait that consistently characterizes the adolescent's immunity from parental influence? Is it the ability to make responsible decisions for oneself? Does autonomy imply consistent behavior in all areas of adolescent life, including school, finances, dating, and peer relations? What are the relative contributions of peers and other adults to the development of the adolescent's autonomy?

Adolescent autonomy is *not* a unitary personality dimension that consistently comes out in all behaviors (Hill & Holmbeck, 1986). For example, in one investigation, high school students were asked 25 questions about their independence from their families (Psathas, 1957). Four distinct patterns of adolescent autonomy emerged from analyses of the high school students' responses. One dimension was labeled "permissiveness in outside activities" and was represented by such questions as "Do you have to account to parents for the way you spend your money?" A second dimension was called "permissiveness in age-related activities" and was reflected in such questions as "Do your parents help you buy your clothes?" A third independent aspect of adolescent autonomy was referred to as "parental regard for judgment," indicated by responses to items like "In family discussions, do your parents encourage you to give your opinion." And a fourth dimension was characterized as "activities with status implications" and was indexed by parental influence on choice of occupation.

emotional autonomy
The capacity to relinquish childlike dependencies on parents.

One aspect of autonomy that is especially important is **emotional autonomy,** *the capacity to relinquish childlike dependencies on parents.* In developing emotional autonomy, adolescents increasingly de-idealize their parents, perceive them as people rather simply as parenting figures, and become less dependent on them for immediate emotional support.

Gender   Gender differences characterize autonomy granting in adolescence with boys usually being given more independence than girls. In one recent study, this gender difference was especially present in families with a traditional gender-role orientation (Bumpus, Crouter, & McHale, 2001).

Parental Attitudes   A number of investigators have studied the relation between parental attitudes and adolescent autonomy. In general, authoritarian parenting is associated with low adolescent autonomy (Hill & Steinberg, 1976). Democratic parenting (much like authoritative parenting) is usually associated with increased adolescent autonomy (Kandel & Lesser, 1969), although findings in this regard are less consistent.

Culture, Demographic Factors, and Adolescent Autonomy   Expectations about the appropriate timing of adolescent autonomy often vary across cultures, parents, and adolescents. For example, expectations for early autonomy on the part of adolescents are more prevalent in Whites, single parents, and adolescents themselves than they are in Asian Americans or Latinos, married parents, and parents themselves (Feldman & Rosenthal, 1990).

In one recent cross-cultural analysis, it was concluded that adolescents in the United States strive for autonomy from parents earlier than adolescents in Japan (Rothbaum & others, 2000). Even Asian adolescents raised in the United States do not usually seek autonomy as early as their Anglo-American peers (Greenberger & Chu, 1996). In the transition to adulthood, many Japanese are surprised by the U.S. habit of taking out loans to pay for their education, a practice they believe implies a distance between family members that is uncomfortable (Lebra, 1994). Also in the transition to adulthood, Japanese are less likely to live outside the home than Americans (Hendry, 1999).

Developmental Transition in Autonomy Involved in Going Away to College

Many youth experience a transition in the development of autonomy when they leave home and go away to college (Bleeker & others, 2002; Silver, Levitt, & Santos, 2002). The transition from high school to college involves increased autonomy for most individuals. For some, homesickness sets in; for others, sampling the privileges of life without parents hovering around is marvelous. For the growing number of students whose families have been torn by separation and divorce, though, moving away can be especially painful. Adolescents in such families may find themselves in the roles of comforter, confidant, and even caretaker of their parents as well as their siblings. In the words of one college freshman, "I feel responsible for my parents. I guess I shouldn't, but I can't help it. It makes my separation from them, my desire to be free of others' problems, my motivation to pursue my own identity more difficult." For yet other students, the independence of being a college freshman is not always as stressful. According to 18-year-old Brian, "Becoming an adult is kind of hard. I'm having to learn to balance my own checkbook, make my own plane reservations, do my own laundry, and the hardest thing of all is waking up in the morning. I don't have my mother there banging on the door."

In one investigation, the psychological separation and adjustment of 130 college freshmen and 123 college upperclassmen were studied (Lapsley, Rice, & Shadid, 1989). As expected, freshmen showed more psychological dependency on their parents and poorer social and personal adjustment than upperclassmen. Female students also showed more psychological dependency on their parents than male students did. In another recent study, parent-child relationships were less satisfactory prior to the high school-to-college transition (Silver, 1995). And in another recent study, students who went away to college reported feeling closer to their mother, less conflict with parents, and more decision-making control and autonomy than did college students who lived at home (Holmbeck, Durbin, & Kung, 1995).

Adolescent Runaways

Why do adolescents run away from their homes? Generally, runaways are very unhappy at home. The reasons many of them leave seem legitimate by almost anyone's standards. When they run away, they usually do not leave a clue to their whereabouts—they just disappear.

Many runaways are from families in which a parent or another adult beats them or sexually exploits them. Their lives may be in danger daily. Their parents may be drug addicts or alcoholics. In some cases, the family may be so poor that the parents are unable to feed and clothe their teenagers adequately. The parents may be so overburdened by their material inadequacies that they fail to give their adolescents the attention and understanding they need. So teenagers hit the streets in search of the emotional and material rewards they are not getting at home.

But runaways are not all from our society's lower-SES tier. Teenage lovers, confronted by parental hostility toward their relationship, might decide to run off together and make it on their own. Or the middle-SES teenager might decide that he has seen enough of his hypocritical parents—people who try to make him live by one set of moral standards, while they live by a loose, false set of ideals. Another teen might live with parents

This adolescent has run away from home. *What is it about family relationships that causes adolescents to run away from home? Are there ways society could better serve runaways?*

THROUGH THE EYES OF ADOLESCENTS

Needing Parents as Guides

Stacey Christensen, age 16: "I am lucky enough to have open communication with my parents. Whenever I am in need or just need to talk, my parents are there for me. My advice to parents is to let your teens grow at their own pace, be open with them so that you can be there for them. We need guidance; our parents need to help but not be too overwhelming."

Stacey Christensen

Prevention of Parent-Adolescent Problems
http://www.mhhe.com/santrocka9

who constantly bicker. Any of these adolescents might decide that they would be happier away from home. In one recent study, homeless adolescents experienced more parental maltreatment, were scolded more often, and reported that their parents loved them less, than housed adolescents (Wolfe, Toro, & McCaskill, 1999).

Running away often is a gradual process, as adolescents begin to spend less time at home and more time on the streets or with a peer group. The parents might be telling them that they really want to see them, to understand them; but runaways often feel that they are not understood at home and that the parents care much more about themselves.

Adolescent runaways are especially susceptible to drug abuse (MacLean & Paradise, 1997). In one investigation, as part of the National Longitudinal Study of Youth Survey, runaway status at ages 14 to 15 was associated with drug abuse and alcohol problems four years later at ages 18 to 19 (Windle, 1989). Repeat runaways were more likely to be drug abusers than one-time runaways were. Both one-time and repeat runaways were more likely to be school dropouts when this was assessed four years later.

Some provision must be made for runaways' physical and psychological well-being. In recent years, nationwide hotlines and temporary shelters for runaways have been established. However, there are still too few of these shelters, and there is often a noted lack of professional psychological help for the runaways at such shelters.

One exception is the temporary shelter in Dallas, Texas, called Casa de los Amigos (house of friends). At the Casa, there is room for 20 runaways, who are provided with the necessities of life as well as medical and legal assistance. In addition, a professional staff of 13 includes counselors and case managers, assisted by VISTA volunteers and high school and college interns. Each runaway is assigned a counselor, and daily group discussion sessions expose the youth to one another's feelings. Whenever possible, the counselors explore the possibility of working with the runaways' families to see if all of the family members can learn to help each other in more competent ways than in the past. It is hoped that more centers like Casa de los Amigos will appear in cities in the United States.

Conclusions   In sum, the ability to attain autonomy and gain control over one's behavior in adolescence is acquired through appropriate adult reactions to the adolescent's desire for control. At the onset of adolescence, the average individual does not have the knowledge to make appropriate or mature decisions in all areas of life. As the adolescent pushes for autonomy, the wise adult relinquishes control in those areas in which the adolescent can make reasonable decisions and continues to guide the adolescent in areas in which the adolescent's knowledge is more limited. Gradually, adolescents acquire the ability to make mature decisions on their own. The discussion that follows reveals in greater detail how it is erroneous to view the development of autonomy apart from connectedness to parents.

Attachment and Connectedness

Adolescents do not simply move away from parental influence into a decision-making world all their own. As they become more autonomous, it is psychologically healthy for them to be attached to their parents.

Secure and Insecure Attachment   Attachment theorists such as British psychiatrist John Bowlby (1989) and American developmental psychologist Mary Ainsworth (1979) argue that secure attachment in infancy is central to the development of social competence. In **secure attachment,** *infants use the caregiver, usually the mother, as a secure base from which to explore the environment. Secure attachment is theorized to be an important foundation for psychological development later in childhood, adolescence, and adulthood.* In **insecure attachment,** *infants either avoid the caregiver or show considerable resistance or ambivalence toward the caregiver. Insecure attachment is theorized to be related to difficulties in relationships and problems in later development.*

In the last decade, developmentalists have begun to explore the role of secure attachment and related concepts, such as connectedness to parents, in adolescence (Allen, Hauser, & Borman-Spurrell, 1996; Becker & others, 2000; Easterbrooks & Biesecker, 2002; Kobak, 1999). They believe that secure attachment to parents in adolescence can facilitate the adolescent's social competence and well-being, as reflected in such characteristics as self-esteem, emotional adjustment, and physical health (Cooper, Shaver, & Collins, 1998; Juang & Nyugen, 1997). In the research of Joseph Allen and his colleagues (Allen & others, 1994, 1996; Allen & Kuperminc, 1995), securely attached adolescents have somewhat lower probabilities of engaging in problem behaviors. In one recent study, secure attachment to both the mother and the father was related positively to adolescents' peer and friendship relations (Lieberman, Doyle, & Markiewicz, 1999).

Many studies that assess secure and insecure attachment in adolescence use the Adult Attachment Interview (AAI) (George, Main, & Kaplan, 1984). This measure examines an individual's memories of significant attachment relationships. Based on the responses to questions on the AAI, individuals are classified as *secure-autonomous* (which corresponds to secure attachment in infancy) or as being in one of three insecure categories:

Dismissing/avoidant attachment *is an insecure category in which individuals deemphasize the importance of attachment. This category is associated with consistent experiences of rejection of attachment needs by caregivers.* One possible outcome of dismissing/avoidant attachment is that parents and adolescents mutually distance themselves from each other, which lessens parents' influence. In one study, dismissing/avoidant attachment was related to violent and aggressive behavior on the part of the adolescent.

Preoccupied/ambivalent attachment *is an insecure category in which adolescents are hypertuned to attachment experiences. This is thought to mainly occur because parents are inconsistently available to the adolescent.* This can result in a high degree of attachment-seeking behavior, mixed with angry feelings. Conflict between parents and adolescents in this type of attachment classification can be too high for healthy development.

Unresolved/disorganized attachment *is an insecure category in which the adolescent has an unusually high level of fear and might be disoriented. This can result from such traumatic experiences as a parent's death or abuse by parents.*

Developmental Transformations

Transformations characterize adolescents' autonomy and connectedness with their families. In one study by Reed Larson and his colleagues (1996), 220 White middle-SES adolescents from 10 to 18 years of age carried beepers and, when beeped at random times, reported whom they were with, what they were doing, and how they were feeling. The amount of time adolescents spent with their families decreased from 35 percent for 10-year-olds to 14 percent for 18-year-olds, suggesting increased autonomy with age. However, increased family connectedness was evident with increased age, with more family conversation about interpersonal issues, especially for girls. As adolescents got older, they were more likely to perceive themselves as leading the interactions. Also, after a decrease in early adolescence, older teenagers reported more favorable affect with others during family interactions.

Conclusions

In sum, the old model of parent-adolescent relationships suggested that, as adolescents mature, they detach themselves from parents and move into a world of autonomy apart from parents. The old model also suggested that parent-adolescent

secure attachment
In this attachment pattern, infants use their primary caregiver, usually the mother, as a secure base from which to explore the environment. Secure attachment is theorized to be an important foundation for psychological development later in childhood, adolescence, and adulthood.

insecure attachment
In this attachment pattern, infants either avoid the caregiver or show considerable resistance or ambivalence toward the caregiver. This pattern is theorized to be related to difficulties in relationships and problems in later development.

dismissing/avoidant attachment
An insecure attachment category in which individuals deemphasize the importance of attachment. This category is associated with consistent experiences of rejection of attachment needs by caregivers.

preoccupied/ambivalent attachment
An insecure attachment category in which adolescents are hypertuned to attachment experiences. This is thought to mainly occur because parents are inconsistently available to the adolescents.

unresolved/disorganized attachment
An insecure category in which the adolescent has an unusually high level of fear and is disoriented. This can result from such traumatic experiences as a parent's death or abuse by parents.

FIGURE 5.3
The Old and New Models of Parent-Adolescent Relationships

Old model		New model	
Autonomy, detachment from parents; parent and peer worlds are isolated	Intense, stressful conflict throughout adolescence; parent-adolescent relationships are filled with storm and stress on virtually a daily basis	Attachment and autonomy; parents are important support systems and attachment figures; adolescent-parent and adolescent-peer worlds have some important connections	Moderate parent-adolescent conflict common and can serve a positive developmental function; conflict greater in early adolescence, especially during the apex of puberty

Reengaging Families with Adolescents
http://www.mhhe.com/santrocka9

conflict is intense and stressful throughout adolescence. The new model emphasizes that parents serve as important attachment figures, resources, and support systems as adolescents explore a wider, more complex social world. The new model also emphasizes that, in the majority of families, parent-adolescent conflict is moderate rather than severe and that everyday negotiations and minor disputes are normal, serving the positive developmental function of promoting independence and identity (see figure 5.3).

So far in this chapter we have examined the nature of family processes and parent-adolescent relationships. In addition to parent-adolescent relationships, there is another aspect to the family worlds of most adolescents—sibling relationships—which we discuss next.

SIBLING RELATIONSHIPS

Sibling Roles   Birth Order

Developmental
Changes

SIBLING RELATIONSHIPS

Sandra describes to her mother what happened in a conflict with her sister:

> We had just come home from the ball game. I sat down on the sofa next to the light so I could read. Sally (the sister) said, "Get up. I was sitting there first. I just got up for a second to get a drink." I told her I was not going to get up and that I didn't see her name on the chair. I got mad and started pushing her—her drink spilled all over her. Then she got really mad; she shoved me against the wall, hitting and clawing at me. I managed to grab a handful of hair.

At this point, Sally comes into the room and begins to tell her side of the story. Sandra interrupts, "Mother, you always take her side." Sound familiar? How much does conflict characterize sibling relations? As we examine the roles siblings play in social development, you will discover that conflict is a common dimension of sibling relationships but that siblings also play many other roles in social development.

Sibling Roles

More than 80 percent of American adolescents have one or more siblings—that is, sisters and brothers. As anyone who has had a sibling knows, the conflict experienced by Sally and Sandra in their relationship with each other is a common interaction style of siblings. However, conflict is only one of the many dimensions of sibling relations. Adolescent sibling relations include helping, sharing, teaching, fighting, and playing, and adolescent siblings can act as emotional supports, rivals, and communication partners (Zukow-Goldring, 2002). In a recent study, positive sibling relationships in adolescence contributed to a sense of emotional and school-related support (Seginer, 1998).

In some instances, siblings can be stronger socializing influences on the adolescent than parents are (Teti, 2002). Someone close in age to the adolescent—such as a sibling—might be able to understand the adolescent's problems and communicate more effectively than parents can. In dealing with peers, coping with difficult teachers, and discussing taboo subjects (such as sex), siblings might be more influential in socializing adolescents than parents are. In one recent study, both younger and older adolescent siblings viewed older siblings as sources of social support for social and scholastic activities (Tucker, McHale, & Crouter, 2001). Furthermore, in one study, children showed more consistent behavior when interacting with siblings and more varied behavior when interacting with parents (Baskett & Johnson, 1982). In this study, children interacted in much more aggressive ways with their siblings than with their parents. In another study, adolescents reported a higher degree of conflict with their siblings than with anyone else (Buhrmester & Furman, 1990).

Developmental Changes

Although adolescent sibling relations reveal a high level of conflict in comparison to adolescents' relationships with other social agents (parents, peers, teachers, and romantic partners, for example), there is evidence that sibling conflict is actually lower in adolescence than in childhood. In a recent study, the lessened sibling conflict during adolescence was due partly to a dropoff in the amount of time siblings spent playing and talking with each other during adolescence (Buhrmester & Furman, 1990). The decline also reflected a basic transformation in the power structure of sibling relationships that seems to occur in adolescence. In childhood, there is an asymmetry of power, with older siblings frequently playing the role of "boss" or caregiver. This asymmetry of power often produces conflicts when one sibling tries to force the other to comply with his or her demands. As younger siblings grow older and their maturity level "catches up" to older siblings', the power asymmetry decreases. As siblings move through adolescence, most learn how to relate to each other on a more equal footing and, in doing so, come to resolve more of their differences than in childhood. Nonetheless, as we said earlier, sibling conflict in adolescence is still reasonably high.

More than 80 percent of us have one or more siblings. *What are some developmental changes in siblings?*

Birth Order

Birth order has been of special interest to sibling researchers, who want to identify the characteristics associated with being born into a particular slot in a family. Firstborns have been described as more adult oriented, helpful, conforming, anxious, and self-controlled, and less aggressive than their siblings. Parental demands and high standards established for firstborns may result in firstborns realizing higher academic and professional achievements than their siblings (Furman & Lanthier, 2002). For example, firstborns are overrepresented in *Who's Who* and among Rhodes Scholars. However, some of the same pressures placed on firstborns for high achievement can be the reason firstborns also have more guilt, anxiety, difficulty in coping with stressful situations, and higher admission to guidance clinics.

Birth order also plays a role in siblings' relationships with each other (Vandell, Minnett, & Santrock, 1987). Older siblings invariably take on the dominant role in sibling interaction, and older siblings report feeling more resentful that parents give preferential treatment to younger siblings.

What are later-borns like? Characterizing later-borns is difficult because they can occupy so many different sibling positions. For example, a later-born might be the second-born male in a family of two siblings or a third-born female in a family of four siblings. In two-child families, the profile of the later-born child is related to the sex of his or her sibling. For example, a boy with an older sister is more likely to develop "feminine" interests than a boy with an older brother. Overall, later-borns usually enjoy better relations with peers than firstborns. Last-borns, who are often described as the "baby" in the family even after they have outgrown infancy, run the risk of becoming overly dependent. Middle-borns tend to be more diplomatic, often performing the role of negotiator in times of dispute (Sutton-Smith, 1982).

The popular conception of the only child is of a "spoiled brat" with such undesirable characteristics as dependency, lack of self-control, and self-centered behavior. But research presents a more positive portrayal of the only child, who often is achievement oriented and displays a desirable personality, especially in comparison to later-borns and children from large families (Thomas, Coffman, & Kipp, 1993).

So far our consideration of birth-order effects suggest that birth order might be a strong predictor of adolescent behavior. However, an increasing number of family researchers believe that birth order has been overdramatized and overemphasized. The critics argue that, when all of the factors that influence adolescent behavior are considered, birth order itself shows limited ability to predict adolescent behavior. Consider just sibling relationships alone. They vary not only in birth order, but also in number of siblings, age of siblings, age spacing of siblings, and sex of siblings. For example, in one recent study male sibling pairs had a less-positive relationship (less caring, less intimate, and lower conflict resolution) than male/female or female/female sibling pairs (Cole & Kerns, 2001).

Consider also the temperament of siblings. Researchers have found that siblings' temperamental traits (such as "easy" and "difficult"), as well as differential treatment of siblings by parents, influence how siblings get along (Brody, Stoneman, & Burke, 1987). Siblings with "easy" temperaments who are treated in relatively equal ways by parents tend to get along with each other the best, whereas siblings with "difficult" temperaments, or siblings whose parents gave one sibling preferential treatment, get along the worst.

Beyond temperament and differential treatment of siblings by parents, think about some of the other important factors in adolescents' lives that influence their behavior beyond birth order. They include heredity, models of competency or incompetency that parents present to adolescents on a daily basis, peer influences, school influences, socioeconomic factors, sociohistorical factors, cultural variations, and so on. When someone says firstborns are always like this, but last-borns are always like that, you now know that they are making overly simplistic statements that do not adequately take into account the complexity of influences on an adolescent's behavior. Keep in mind,

Big sisters are the crab grass in the lawn of life.
—Charles Schultz
American Cartoonist, 20th Century

though, that, although birth order itself may not be a good predictor of adolescent behavior, sibling relationships and interaction are important dimensions of family processes in adolescence.

Since the last review, you have studied many aspects of parent-adolescent relationships and sibling relationships. This review should help you to reach your learning goals related to this topic.

☐ FOR YOUR REVIEW

Learning Goal 2
Discuss parent-adolescent relationships

- An increasing trend is to conceptualize parents as managers of adolescents' lives.
- Authoritarian, authoritative, neglectful, and indulgent are four main parenting styles. Authoritative parenting is associated with socially competent adolescent behavior more than the other styles.
- Conflict with parents does increase in early adolescence, but such conflict is usually moderate and can serve a positive developmental function of increasing independence and identity exploration. The generation gap is exaggerated, although in as many as 20 percent of families parent-adolescent conflict is too high and is linked with adolescent problems.
- Many parents have a difficult time handling the adolescent's push for autonomy. Autonomy is a complex concept with many referents. Developmental transitions in autonomy include the onset of early adolescence and the time when individuals leave home and go to college. A special concern about autonomy involves runaways. The wise parent relinquishes control in areas where the adolescent makes mature decisions and retains more control in areas where the adolescent makes immature decisions. Adolescents do not simply move away into a world isolated from parents. Attachment to parents in adolescence increases the probability that an adolescent will be socially competent and explore a widening social world in a healthy way. Increasingly, researchers classify attachment in adolescence into one secure category (secure-autonomous) and three insecure categories (dismissing/avoidant, preoccupied/ambivalent, and unresolved/disorganized).

Learning Goal 3
Know about sibling relationships

- Sibling relationships often involve more conflict than relationships with other individuals. However, adolescents also share many positive moments with siblings through emotional support and social communication.
- Although sibling conflict in adolescence is reasonably high, it is usually less than in childhood.
- Birth order has been of special interest and differences between firstborns and later-borns have been reported. The only child often is more socially competent than the stereotype "spoiled child" suggests. An increasing number of family researchers believe that birth-order effects have been overdramatized and that other factors are more important in predicting the adolescent's behavior.

So far in this chapter we have examined the nature of family processes, parent-adolescent relationships, and sibling relationships. Next, we will explore the changing family in a changing society.

THE CHANGING FAMILY IN A CHANGING SOCIETY

More adolescents are growing up in a greater variety of family structures than ever before in history (Hernandez, 1997). Many mothers spend the greater part of their day away from their children. More than one of every two mothers with a child under the age of 5, and more than two of every three with a child from 6 to 17 years of age, is in the labor force. The number of adolescents growing up in single-parent families is staggering. The United States has the highest percentage of single-parent families, compared to virtually all other countries (see figure 5.4 on p. 170). Also, by age 18, approximately one-fourth of all American children will have lived a portion of their lives in a stepfamily.

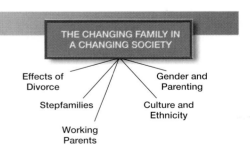

THE CHANGING FAMILY IN A CHANGING SOCIETY

Effects of Divorce

Stepfamilies

Working Parents

Gender and Parenting

Culture and Ethnicity

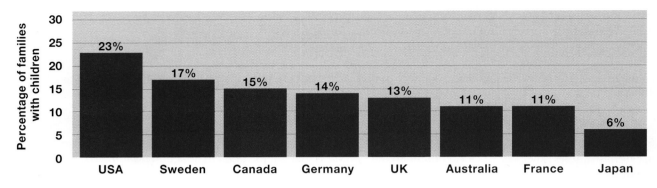

Note: Children are under 18 years of age.

FIGURE 5.4
Single-Parent Families in Different Countries

This graph shows the percentage of families with children under 18 that are single-parent families.

Adolescents and Divorce for Adolescents: Dealing with Parents' Divorce
Divorce Resources
http://www.mhhe.com/santrocka9

Effects of Divorce

These are the questions that we will explore that focus on the effects of divorce: Are adolescents better adjusted in intact, never-divorced families than in divorced families? Should parents stay together for the sake of their children and adolescents? How much do parenting skills matter in divorced families? What factors affect the adolescent's individual risk and vulnerability in a divorced family? What role does socioeconomic status play in the lives of adolescents in divorced families? (Hetherington, 1999, 2000; Hetherington & Kelly, 2002; Hetherington & Stanley-Hagan, 2002).

Adolescents' Adjustment in Divorced Families   Most researchers agree that children and adolescents from divorced families show poorer adjustment than their counterparts in nondivorced families (Amato & Keith, 1991). Those that have experienced multiple divorces are at greater risk. Adolescents in divorced families are more likely than adolescents from nondivorced families to have academic problems, to show externalized problems (such as acting out and delinquency) and internalized problems (such as anxiety and depression), to be less socially responsible, to have less-competent intimate relationships, to drop out of school, to become sexually active at an earlier age, to take drugs, to associate with antisocial peers, and to have lower self-esteem (Conger & Chao, 1996).

Although there is a consensus that adolescents from divorced families show these adjustment problems to a greater extent than adolescents from nondivorced families, there is less agreement about the size of the effects (Buchanan, in press; Hetherington, Bridges, & Insabella, 1998). Some researchers report that the divorce effects are modest and have become smaller as divorce has become more commonplace in society (Amato & Keith, 1991). However, others argue that significantly more adolescents in divorced families (20 to 25 percent) have these types of adjustment problems than adolescents in nondivorced families (10 percent) (Hetherington & Jodl, 1994; Hetherington & Stanley-Hagan, 2002). Nonetheless, the majority of adolescents in divorced families do not have these problems (Emery, 1999). The weight of the research evidence underscores that most adolescents competently cope with their parents' divorce.

Should Parents Stay Together for the Sake of Their Children and Adolescents?
Whether parents should stay in an unhappy or conflicted marriage for the sake of their children and adolescents is one of the most commonly asked questions about divorce (Hetherington, 1999, 2000; Hetherington & Kelly, 2002). The stresses and disruptions in family relationships associated with an unhappy, conflictual marriage might erode the well-being of the children and adolescents; if these negative effects can be reduced

by the move to a divorced single-parent family, divorce might be advantageous. However, if the diminished resources and increased risks associated with divorce also are accompanied by inept parenting and sustained or increased conflict, not only between the divorced couple but also between parents and the children/adolescents and siblings, the best choice for the children/adolescents might be for an unhappy marriage to be retained. These are "ifs," and it is difficult to determine how these will play out when parents either remain together in an acrimonious marriage or become divorced.

How Much Do Family Processes Matter in Divorced Families?   In divorced families, family processes matter a lot. When the divorced parents have a harmonious relationship and use authoritative parenting, the adjustment of adolescents is improved (Hetherington, 2000; Hetherington, Bridges, & Insabella, 1998; Hetherington & Stanley-Hagan, 2002). A number of researchers have shown that a disequilibrium, including diminished parenting skills, occurs in the year following the divorce but that by two years after the divorce restabilization has occurred and parenting skills have improved (Hetherington, 1989). About one-fourth to one-third of adolescents in divorced families, compared to 10 percent in nondivorced families, become disengaged from their families, spending as little time as possible at home and in interaction with family members (Hetherington & Jodl, 1994). This disengagement is higher for boys than for girls in divorced families. However, if there is a caring adult outside the home, such as a mentor, the disengagement can be a positive solution to a disrupted, conflicted family circumstance.

What roles do noncustodial parents play in the lives of children and adolescents in divorced families? Most nonresidential fathers have a friendly, companionable relationship with their children and adolescents rather than a traditional parental relationship (Munsch, Woodward, & Darling, 1995). They want their visits to be pleasant and entertaining, so they are reluctant to assume the role of a disciplinarian or teacher. They are less likely than nondivorced fathers to criticize, control, and monitor the child's or adolescent's behavior or to help them with such tasks as homework (Bray & Berger, 1993). Frequency of contact with noncustodial fathers and adjustment of children and adolescents are usually found to be unrelated (Amato & Keith, 1991). The quality of the contact matters more. Under conditions of low conflict, when noncustodial fathers participate in a variety of activities with their offspring and engage in authoritative parenting, children and adolescents, especially boys, benefit (Lindner-Gunnoe, 1993). We know less about noncustodial mothers than fathers, but these mothers are less adept than custodial mothers at controlling and monitoring their child's or adolescent's behavior (Furstenberg & Nord, 1987). Noncustodial mothers' warmth, support, and monitoring can improve children's and adolescents' adjustment (Lindner-Gunnoe, 1993).

What Factors Are Involved in the Adolescent's Individual Risk and Vulnerability in a Divorced Family?   Among these factors are the adolescent's adjustment prior to the divorce, personality and temperament, developmental status, gender, and custody. Children and adolescents whose parents later divorce show poorer adjustment before the breakup (Amato & Booth, 1996). When antecedent levels of problem behaviors are controlled, differences in the adjustment of children and adolescents in divorced and nondivorced families are reduced (Cherlin & others, 1991).

Personality and temperament also play a role in adolescent adjustment in divorced families. Adolescents who are socially mature and responsible, who show few behavioral problems, and who have an easy temperament are better able to cope with their parents' divorce. Children and adolescents with a difficult temperament often have problems coping with their parents' divorce (Hetherington, 1995).

Focusing on the developmental status of the child or adolescent involves taking into account the age of onset of the divorce and the time when the child's or adolescent's adjustment is assessed. In most studies, these factors are confounded

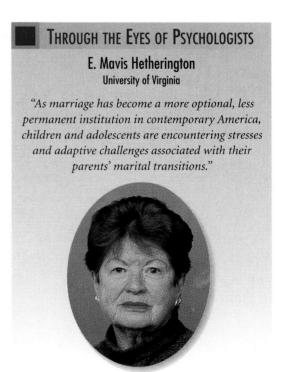

THROUGH THE EYES OF PSYCHOLOGISTS

E. Mavis Hetherington
University of Virginia

"As marriage has become a more optional, less permanent institution in contemporary America, children and adolescents are encountering stresses and adaptive challenges associated with their parents' marital transitions."

THINKING CRITICALLY

Communicating About Divorce

If parents decide to obtain a divorce, how should they communicate with their adolescent about the divorce? For one thing, they should explain the separation as soon as daily activities in the home make it obvious that one parent is leaving. If possible, both parents should be present when the adolescent is told about the separation. Adolescents also should be told that anytime they want to talk with someone about the separation, they should come to the parents. It is healthy for adolescents to get their pent-up emotions out in the open in discussions with their parents and to learn that their parents are willing to listen to their feelings and fears. Can you think of other strategies divorcing parents can use to effectively communicate with their adolescents?

Single Fathers
http://www.mhhe.com/santrocka9

with length of time since the divorce occurred. Some researchers have found that preschool children whose parents divorce are at greater risk for long-term problems than are older children (Zill, Morrison, & Coiro, 1993). The explanation for this focuses on their inability to realistically appraise the causes and consequences of divorce, their anxiety about the possibility of abandonment, their self-blame for the divorce, and their inability to use extrafamilial protective resources. However, problems in adjustment can emerge or increase during adolescence, even if the divorce occurred much earlier.

Earlier studies reported gender differences in response to divorce, with divorce being more negative for boys than for girls in mother-custody families. However, more-recent studies have shown that gender differences are less pronounced and consistent than was previously believed. Some of the inconsistency could be due to the increase in father-custody and joint-custody families and increased involvement of noncustodial fathers, especially in their sons' lives. Female adolescents in divorced families are more likely to drop out of high school and college than are their male counterparts. Male and female adolescents from divorced families are similarly affected in the likelihood of becoming teenage parents, but single parenthood affects girls more adversely (McLanahan & Sandefur, 1994).

In recent decades, an increasing number of children and adolescents have lived in father-custody and joint-custody families. What is their adjustment like, compared to the adjustment of children and adolescents in mother-custody families? Although there have been few thorough studies of the topic, there appear to be few advantages of joint custody over custody by one parent (Hetherington, Bridges, & Insabella, 1998). Some studies have shown that boys adjust better in father-custody families and that girls adjust better in mother-custody families, but other studies have not. In one study, adolescents in father-custody families had higher rates of delinquency, believed to be due to less-competent monitoring by the fathers (Maccoby & Mnookin, 1992).

What Role Does Socioeconomic Status Play in the Lives of Adolescents in Divorced Families?

On the average, custodial mothers lose about 25 to 50 percent of their predivorce income, in comparison to a loss of only 10 percent of custodial fathers (Emery, 1999). This income loss for divorced mothers typically is accompanied by increased workloads, high rates of job instability, and residential moves to less desirable neighborhoods with inferior schools (Carlson & McLanahan, 2002).

Stepfamilies

Parents are divorcing in greater numbers than ever before, but many of them remarry (Dunn & others, 2001; White & Gilbreth, 2001). It takes time for parents to marry, have children, get divorced, and then remarry. Consequently, there are far more elementary and secondary school children than infant or preschool children in stepfamilies.

The number of remarriages involving children has grown steadily in recent years as the divorce rate has increased. Also, divorces occur at a 10 percent higher rate in remarriages than in first marriages (Cherlin & Furstenberg, 1994). As a result of their parents' successive marital transitions, about half of all children whose parents divorce will have a stepfather within four years of parental separation.

Types of Stepfamilies

There are different types of stepfamilies. Some types are based on family structure, others on relationships.

Family Structure Types   In some, the stepfamily may have been preceded by a circumstance in which a spouse died. However, a large majority of stepfamilies are preceded by a divorce rather than a death.

Three common types of stepfamily structure are (1) stepfather, (2) stepmother, and (3) blended or complex. In stepfather families, the mother typically had custody of the children and became remarried, introducing a stepfather into her children's lives. In stepmother families, the father usually had custody and became remarried, introducing a stepmother into his children's lives. And in a blended or complex stepfamily, both parents bring children from previous marriages to live in the newly formed stepfamily.

Researchers have found that children's relationships with custodial parents (mother in stepfather families, father in stepmother families) are often better than with stepparents (Santrock, Warshak, & Sitterle, 1998). However, when adolescents have a positive relationship with their stepfather, it is related to fewer adolescent problems (White & Gilbreth, 2001). Also, children in simple stepfamilies (stepfather, stepmother) often show better adjustment than their counterparts in complex (blended) families (Anderson & others, 1999).

Relationship Types   In addition to their structure (stepfather, stepmother, or blended), stepfamilies also develop certain patterns of relationships. In a study of 200 stepfamilies, James Bray and his colleagues (Bray & Berger, 1993; Bray, Berger, & Boethel, 1999; Bray & Kelly, 1998) found that over time stepfamilies often fall into three types based on their relationships: neo-traditional, matriarchal, and romantic.

- *Neo-traditional.* Both adults want a family and are able to successfully cope with the challenges of new stepfamily. After three to five years, these families often look like intact, never-divorced families with positive relationships often characterizing the stepfamily members.
- *Matriarchal.* In this type of stepfamily, the mother has custody and is used to managing the family herself. The stepfather married her not because he especially wanted to be a father. She runs the family and the stepfather is sort of just there, often ignoring the children or occasionally engaging in some enjoyable activities with them. This type of stepfamily may function adequately except when the mother wants help and the stepfather doesn't want to give it. This type of stepfamily also may not function well if he decides to become very involved (which typically occurs after they have a baby of their own) and she feels that her turf has been invaded.
- *Romantic.* These adults married with very high, unrealistic expectations for their stepfamily. They try to create an instant, very happy family and can't understand why it doesn't happen immediately. This type of stepfamily is the one that is most likely to end in a divorce.

Adjustment   As in divorced families, children in stepfamilies have more adjustment problems than their counterparts in nondivorced families (Hetherington, Bridges, & Insabella, 1998; Hetherington & Kelly, 2002). The adjustment problems of children are much like those of children in divorced families—academic problems, externalizing and internalizing problems, lower self-esteem, early sexual activity, delinquency, and so on (Anderson & others, 1999). Adjustment for parents and children may take longer in stepfamilies, up to five years or more, than in divorced families, in which a restabilization is more likely to occur within two years (Anderson & others, 1999). One aspect of a stepfamily that makes adjustment difficult is **boundary ambiguity,** *the uncertainty in stepfamilies about who is in or out of the family and who is performing or responsible for certain tasks in the family system.*

There is an increase in adjustment problems of children in newly remarried families (Hetherington & Clingempeel, 1992). This occurred in the study conducted by Bray and his colleagues (Bray & Berger, 1993; Bray & Kelly, 1998). In this study, the formation of a stepfamily often meant that children had to move, which involved

boundary ambiguity
The uncertainty in stepfamilies about who is in or out of the family and who is performing or responsible for certain tasks in the family system.

changing schools and friends. It took time for the stepparent to get to know the stepchildren. The new spouses had to learn how to cope with the challenges of their relationship and parenting together. In Bray's view, the formation of a stepfamily was like merging two cultures.

Bray and his colleagues also found that it was not unusual for the following problems to develop early in the stepfamily's existence. When the stepparent tried to discipline the stepchild, this often did not work well. Most experts recommend that in the early part of a stepfamily the biological parent should be the parent doing any disciplining of the child that is needed. The stepparent-stepchild relationship develops best when the stepparent spends time with the stepchild in activities that the child enjoys.

The newly formed stepfamily sometimes had difficulty coping with changes that they could not control. For example, the husband and wife may be looking forward to going away without the children the next weekend. Then the other biological parent calls at the last minute and cancels taking the children. The new spouse may get angry and unfortunately, both parents may take their frustration out on the children. Successful stepfamilies adjust to such unexpected circumstances and have backup plans.

In terms of the age of the child, researchers have found that early adolescence is an especially difficult time for the formation of a stepfamily (Bray & Kelly, 1998; Hetherington, 1993; Hetherington & others, 1999). This may occur because the stepfamily circumstances exacerbate normal adolescent concerns about identity, sexuality, and autonomy.

Now that we have considered the changing social worlds of adolescents when their parents divorce and remarry, we turn our attention to another aspect of the changing family worlds of adolescents—the situation when both parents work.

Stepfamily Resources
Stepfamily Support
Stepfathers
Working Mothers
http://www.mhhe.com/santrocka9

Working Parents

Interest in the effects of parental work on the development of children and adolescents has increased in recent years (Gottfried, Gottfried, & Bathurst, 2002; Hoffman, 2000). Our examination of parental work focuses on the following issues: the role of working mothers in adolescents' development, the adjustment of latchkey adolescents, the effects of relocation on adolescent development, and the influence of unemployment on adolescents' lives.

Working Mothers   Most of the research on parental work has focused on young children. Little attention has been given to early adolescence, even though it is during this period that many mothers return to full-time work, in part due to presumed independence of their young adolescents. In one study, 10- to 13-year olds carried electronic pagers for one week and completed self-report forms in response to random signals sent to them every other hour (Richards & Duckett, 1994). The most striking aspect of the study was the absence of significant differences associated with maternal employment. There were few differences in the quantity and quality of time associated with maternal employment. Other researchers have arrived at similar conclusions (Lerner, Jacobson, & del Gaudio, 1992). As a leading authority on maternal employment, Lois Hoffman (1989), stated, maternal employment is a fact of modern life. It is not an aberrant aspect of it, but a response to other social changes that meets the needs not met by the previous family ideal of a full-time mother and homemaker. Not only does it meet the parents' needs, but in many ways, it may be a pattern better suited to socializing children for the adult roles they will occupy. This is especially true for daughters, but it is true for sons, too. The broader range of emotions and skills that each parent presents is more consistent with this adult role. Just as the father shares the breadwinning role and the child-rearing role with the mother, so the son, too, will be more likely to share these roles. The rigid gender-role stereotyping perpetuated by the divisions of labor in the traditional family is not appropriate for the demands children of both sexes will have made on them as adults. The needs of the growing child require the mother to loosen her hold on the child, and this task may be easier for the working woman whose job is an additional source of identity and self-esteem.

Gender differences have sometimes been associated with parental work patterns. In some studies, no gender differences are found, but in others, maternal employment has greater benefits for adolescent daughters than for sons (Law, 1992), and in yet others, adolescent sons benefit academically and emotionally when they identify with the work patterns of their fathers more than with those of their mothers (Orthner, Giddings, & Quinn, 1987).

In one study, Nancy Galambos and her colleagues (1995) studied the effects of parents' work overload on their relationships with their adolescent and on the adolescent's development. They found some evidence for the impact of work overload, but the effects differed for mothers and fathers. The mother's warmth and acceptance shown toward the adolescent helped to reduce the negative impact of her work overload on the adolescent's development. The key factor for fathers was parent-adolescent conflict—when it was lower, the negative impact of the father's work overload on the adolescent's development was reduced. Also, when both parents were stressed, parent-adolescent conflict was highest.

Latchkey Adolescents   Although the mother's working is not necessarily associated with negative outcomes for adolescents, a certain set of adolescents from working-mother families bears further scrutiny—those called latchkey adolescents. Latchkey adolescents typically do not see their parents from the time they leave for school in the morning until about 6:00 or 7:00 P.M. They are called "latchkey" children or adolescents because they often are given the key to their home, take the key to school, and let themselves into the home while their parents are still at work. Many latchkey adolescents are largely unsupervised for two to four hours a day during each school week, or for entire days, five days a week, during the summer months.

Thomas and Lynette Long (1983) interviewed more than 1,500 latchkey children. They concluded that a slight majority of these children had negative latchkey experiences. Some latchkey children grow up too fast, hurried by the responsibility placed on them. How do latchkey children handle the lack of limits and structure during the latchkey hours? Without limits and parental supervision, it becomes easier for latchkey children and adolescents to find their way into trouble—possibly abusing a sibling, stealing, or vandalizing. The Longs found that 90 percent of the adjudicated juvenile delinquents in Montgomery County, Maryland, were from latchkey families. In another investigation of more than 4,900 eighth-graders in Los Angeles and San Diego, those who cared for themselves 11 hours a week or more were twice as likely to have abused alcohol and other drugs than were their counterparts who did not care for themselves at all before or after school (Richardson & others, 1989). Adolescence expert Joan Lipsitz (1983), testifying before the Select Committee on Children, Youth, and Families, called the lack of adult supervision of children and adolescents in the after-school hours one of the nation's major problems. Lipsitz called it the "3:00 to 6:00 P.M. problem" because it was during this time frame that the Center for Early Adolescence in North Carolina, where she was director, experienced a peak of adolescent referrals for clinical help.

Although latchkey adolescents can be vulnerable to problems, keep in mind that the experiences of latchkey adolescents vary enormously, just as do the experiences of all children with working mothers. Parents need to give special attention to the ways their latchkey adolescents' lives can be monitored effectively. Variations in latchkey experiences suggest that parental monitoring and authoritative parenting help the adolescent to cope more effectively with latchkey experiences, especially in resisting peer pressure (Galambos & Maggs, 1991; Steinberg, 1986). The degree to which latchkey adolescents are at developmental risk remains unsettled. A positive sign is that researchers are beginning to conduct more precise analyses of adolescents' latchkey experiences in an effort to determine which aspects of latchkey circumstances are the most detrimental and which aspects foster better adaptation. In one recent study that focused on the after-school hours, unsupervised peer contact, lack of neighborhood safety, and low monitoring were linked with externalizing problems (such as acting-out and delinquency) in young adolescents (Pettit & others, 1999).

Relocation   Geographical moves or relocations are a fact of life for many American families. Each year, about 17 percent of the population changes residences. This figure does not include multiple moves within the same year, so it may even underestimate the mobility of the U.S. population. The majority of these moves are made because of job demands. Moving can be especially stressful for children and adolescents, disrupting friendship ties and adolescent activities. The sources of support to which adolescents and their parents turn, such as extended-family members and friends, are often unavailable to recently moved families.

Although relocations are often stressful for all individuals involved, they may be especially stressful for adolescents because of their developing sense of identity and the importance of peer relations in their lives. In one study, geographical relocation was detrimental to the well-being of 12- to 14-year-old females but not of their male counterparts (Brown & Orthner, 1990). The adolescent girls' life satisfaction was negatively related both to recent moves and to a high number of moves in their history, and a history of frequent moves was also associated with the girls' depression. However, the immediate negative effects on the girls disappeared over time. The researchers concluded that female adolescents might require more time to adapt to family relocations. Male adolescents might use sports and other activities in their new locale to ease the effects of relocation.

Unemployment   What effects does unemployment have on families and on adolescents' development? During the Great Depression, unemployment dramatically increased parental stress and undermined the school achievement and health of children and adolescents (Elder, 2000). In one investigation, the effects of changes in parental work status on young adolescents' school adjustment were explored (Flanagan & Eccles, 1993). Four groups were compared. *Deprived* families reported a layoff or demotion at time 1 but no recovery two years later. *Declining* families experienced a layoff or demotion between times 1 and 2. *Recovery* families reported similar losses at time 1 but reemployment two years later. *Stable* families reported no layoffs or demotion between times 1 and 2. Adolescents in deprived and declining families showed less competent peer interaction, and adolescents in deprived families were the most disruptive in school. The transition to adolescence was especially difficult for children whose parents were coping with changes in their work status. Other researchers have also recently found that economic downturn and joblessness can have negative effects on the adolescent's development (Gomel, Tinsley, & Clark, 1995; Lord, 1995).

Culture and Ethnicity

Cultures vary on a number of issues involving families, such as what the father's role in the family should be, the extent to which support systems are available to families, and how children should be disciplined (Harkness & Super, 1995, 2002) ◀||||| P. 27. Although there are cross-cultural variations in parenting (Whiting & Edwards, 1988), in one study of parenting behavior in 186 cultures around the world, the most common pattern was a warm and controlling style, one that was neither permissive nor restrictive (Rohner & Rohner, 1981). The investigators commented that the majority of cultures have discovered, over many centuries, a "truth" that only recently emerged in the Western world—namely, that children's and adolescents' healthy social development is most effectively promoted by love and at least some moderate parental control.

The family reunion of the Limon family in Austin, Texas (above). Mexican American children often grow up in families with a network of relatives that runs into scores of individuals.

A 14-year-old adolescent, his 6-year-old sister, and their grandmother (right). The African American cultural tradition of an extended family household has helped many African American parents cope with adverse social conditions.

Ethnic minority families differ from White American families in their size, structure and composition, reliance on kinship networks, and level of income and education (Chen & Yu, 1997; Coll & Pachter, 2002; Hughes, 1997). Large and extended families are more common among ethnic minority groups than among White Americans. For example, more than 30 percent of Latino families consist of five or more individuals. African American and Latino children interact more with grandparents, aunts, uncles, cousins, and more distant relatives than do White American children (Lyendecker & others, 2002; McAdoo, 2002).

As we saw earlier in our discussion of divorce, single-parent families are more common among African Americans and Latinos than among White Americans. In comparison with two-parent households, single-parent households often have more-limited resources of time, money, and energy. This shortage of resources can prompt them to encourage early autonomy among their adolescents. Also, ethnic minority parents are less well educated and engage in less joint decision making than White American parents. And ethnic minority adolescents are more likely to come from low-income families than White American adolescents are (Magnuson & Duncan, 2002; McLoyd, 2000). Although impoverished families often raise competent youth, poor parents can have a diminished capacity for supportive and involved parenting (McLoyd, 1990).

Family Diversity
http://www.mhhe.com/santrocka9

Some aspects of home life can help to protect ethnic minority youth from social patterns of injustice. The community and family can filter out destructive racist messages, parents can provide alternate frames of reference than those presented by the majority, and parents can also provide competent role models and encouragement. And the extended-family system in many ethnic minority families provides an important buffer to stress.

Gender and Parenting

What is the mother's role in the family? The father's role? How can mothers and fathers become cooperative, effective partners in parenting?

The Mother's Role   What do you think of when you hear the word *motherhood?* If you are like most people, you associate motherhood with a number of positive qualities, such as being warm, selfless, dutiful, and tolerant (Matlin, 1993). And while most women expect that motherhood will be happy and fulfilling, the reality is that motherhood has been accorded relatively low prestige in our society. When stacked up against money, power, and achievement, motherhood unfortunately doesn't fare too well and mothers rarely receive the appreciation they warrant. When children and adolescents don't succeed or they develop problems, our society has had a tendency to attribute the lack of success or the development of problems to a single source—mothers. One of psychology's most important lessons is that behavior is multiply determined. So it is with adolescent development—when development goes awry, mothers are not the single cause of the problems even though our society stereotypes them in this way.

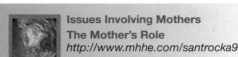

Issues Involving Mothers
The Mother's Role
http://www.mhhe.com/santrocka9

The reality of motherhood today is that while fathers have increased their child-rearing responsibilities somewhat, the main responsibility for children and adolescents still falls on the mother's shoulders (Barnard & Solchany, 2002; Brooks & Bronstein, 1996). In one recent study, adolescents said that their mothers were more involved in parenting than fathers in both the ninth and twelfth grades (Sputa & Paulson, 1995). Mothers do far more family work than fathers do—two to three times more (Thompson & Walker, 1989). A few "exceptional" men do as much family work as their wives; in one study the figure was 10 percent of the men (Berk, 1985). Not only do women do more family work than men, the family work most women do is unrelenting, repetitive, and routine, often involving cleaning, cooking, child care, shopping, laundry, and straightening up. The family work most men do is infrequent, irregular, and nonroutine, often involving household repairs, taking out the garbage, and yard work. Women report that they often have to do several tasks at once, which helps to explain why they find domestic work less relaxing and more stressful than men do.

Because family work is intertwined with love and embedded in family relations, it has complex and contradictory meanings. Most women feel that family tasks are mindless but essential. They usually enjoy tending to the needs of their loved ones and keeping the family going, even if they do not find the activities themselves enjoyable and fulfilling. Family work is both positive and negative for women. They are unsupervised and rarely criticized, they plan and control their own work, and they have only their own standards to meet. However, women's family work is often worrisome, tiresome, menial, repetitive, isolating, unfinished, inescapable, and often unappreciated. It is not surprising that men report that they are more satisfied with their marriage than women do.

What do you think the father's role in adolescent development should be? What role did your father play in your development?

In sum, the role of the mother brings with it benefits as well as limitations. Although motherhood is not enough to fill most women's entire lives, for most mothers, it is one of the most meaningful experiences in their lives (Hoffnung, 1984).

The Father's Role   The father's role has undergone major changes (Lamb, 1997; Parke, 1995, 2001, 2002; Parke & others, 2002). During the colonial period in America, fathers were primarily responsible for moral teaching. Fathers provided guidance and values, especially through religion. With the Industrial Revolution, the father's role changed; he gained the responsibility as the breadwinner, a role that continued through the Great Depression. By the end of World War II, another role for fathers emerged, that of a gender-role model. Although being a breadwinner and moral guardian continued to be important father roles, attention shifted to his role as a male, especially for sons. Then, in the 1970s, the current interest in the father as an active, nurturant, caregiving parent emerged. Rather than being responsible only for the discipline and control of older children and for providing the family's economic base, the father now is being evaluated in terms of his active, nurturant involvement with his children (Perry-Jenkins, Payne, & Hendricks, 1999).

How actively are today's fathers involved with their children and adolescents? One longitudinal study of adolescents in fifth to twelfth grade found that fathers spend only a small portion of their time with adolescents (Larson & others, 1996). Studies reveal that fathers spend from one-third to three-fourths as much time with children and adolescents as mothers do (Biller, 1993; Pleck, 1997; Yeung & others, 1999). In one recent study, fathers of more than 1,700 children up to 12 years old were spending an increasing amount of time with their children, compared to their counterparts in the early 1990s, but still less time than mothers were (Yeung & others, 1999). Though some fathers are exceptionally committed parents, others are virtual strangers to their adolescents even though they reside in the same household (Burton & Synder, 1997).

Adolescents' social development can significantly benefit from interaction with a caring, accessible, and dependable father who fosters a sense of trust and confidence (Carlson & McLanahan, 2002; Parke, 2002; Way, 1997). In one investigation, Frank Furstenberg and Kathleen Harris (1992) documented how nurturant fathering can overcome children's difficult life circumstances. In low-income African American families, children who reported close attachments and feelings of identification with their fathers during adolescence were twice as likely as young adults to have found a stable job or to have entered college, and were 75 percent less likely to have become unwed parents, 80 percent less likely to have been in jail, and 50 percent less likely to have developed depression. Unfortunately, however, only 10 percent of the economically disadvantaged children they studied experienced a stable, close relationship with their father during childhood and adolescence. In two other studies, college females and males reported better personal and social adjustment when they had grown up in a home with a nurturant, involved father rather than a negligent or rejecting father (Fish & Biller, 1973; Reuter & Biller, 1973). And in another study, fathers characterized by positive affect had adolescents who were less likely to be depressed (Duckett & Richards, 1996).

Partners in Parenting   Parents' cooperation, mutual respect, balanced communication, and attunement to each other's needs help the adolescent to develop positive attitudes toward both males and females (Biller, 1993; Parke, 2002; Tamis-LeMonda & Cabrera, 2002). It is much easier for working parents to cope with changing family circumstances when the father and the mother equitably share child-rearing responsibilities. Mothers feel less stress and have more positive attitudes toward their husbands when their husbands are supportive partners. Researchers have found that egalitarian marital relationships have positive effects on adolescent development, fostering their trust and encouraging communication (Yang & others, 1996).

It is clear that most American children suffer too . . . little father.

—Gloria Steinem
*American Feminist and Author,
20th Century*

Fathering
The Fatherhood Project
http://www.mhhe.com/santrocka9

SOCIAL POLICY AND FAMILIES

We have seen in this chapter that parents play very important roles in adolescent development. Although adolescents are moving toward independence, they are still connected with their families, which are far more important to them than is commonly believed. We know that competent adolescent development is most likely to happen when adolescents have parents who (Small, 1990):

- Show them warmth and respect
- Demonstrate sustained interest in their lives
- Recognize and adapt to their changing cognitive and socioemotional development
- Communicate expectations for high standards of conduct and achievement
- Display authoritative, constructive ways of dealing with problems and conflict

However, compared to families with young children, families with adolescents have been neglected in community programs and public policies ◀▌▌▌ P. 15. The Carnegie Council on Adolescent Development (1995) identified some key opportunities for improving social policy regarding families with adolescents. These are some of the council's recommendations:

- School, cultural arts, religious and youth organizations, and health-care agencies, should examine the extent to which they involve parents in activities with adolescents and should develop ways to engage parents and adolescents in activities they both enjoy.
- Professionals such as teachers, psychologists, nurses, physicians, youth specialists, and others who have contact with adolescents need to not only work with the individual adolescent but increase the time they spend interacting with the adolescent's family.
- Employers should extend to the parents of young adolescents the workplace policies now reserved only for the parents of young children. These policies include flexible work schedules, job sharing, telecommuting, and part-time work with benefits. This change in work/family policy would free parents to spend more time with their teenagers.
- Community institutions such as businesses, schools, and youth organizations should become more involved in providing after-school programs. After-school programs for elementary school children are increasing, but such programs for adolescents are rare. More high-quality, community-based programs for adolescents are needed in the after-school, weekend, and vacation time periods.

Since the last review, you have studied many aspects of the changing family in a changing social world and social policy related to families. This review should help you to reach your learning goals related to this topic.

☐ FOR YOUR REVIEW

Learning Goal 4
Describe the effects of divorce, stepfamilies, and working parents

- Adolescents in divorced families have more adjustment problems than their counterparts in nondivorced families, although the size of the effects is debated. Whether parents should stay together for the sake of the adolescent is difficult to determine, although conflict has a negative effect on the adolescent. Adolescents are better adjusted in divorced families when their parents have a harmonious relationship with each other and use authoritative parenting. Among other factors to be considered in adolescent adjustment are adjustment prior to the divorce, personality and temperament, developmental status, gender, and custody. Income loss for divorced mothers is linked to a number of other stresses that can affect adolescent adjustment.
- An increasing number of children are growing up in stepfamilies. Stepfamilies involve different types of structure (stepfather, stepmother, blended) and relationships (neo-traditional, matriarchal, and romantic). Children in stepfamilies have more adjustment

problems than children in nondivorced homes. Adjustment is especially difficult in the first several years of a stepfamily's existence and is difficult for young adolescents.
- Overall, the mother's working outside the home does not have an adverse effect on the adolescent. Latchkey experiences do not have a uniformly negative effect on adolescents. Parental monitoring and structured activities in the after-school hours benefit latchkey adolescents. Relocation can have a more adverse effect on adolescents than children, although research on this issue is sparse. Unemployment of parents has detrimental effects on adolescents.

Learning Goal 5
Understand culture, ethnicity, gender, and parenting

- Authoritative parenting is the most common form of parenting around the world.
- Ethnic minority families differ from non-Latino White families in their size, structure, and composition, their reliance on kinship networks, and their levels of income and education.
- Most people associate motherhood with a number of positive images, but the reality is that motherhood is accorded a relatively low status in American society. Over time, the father's role in the child's development has changed. Fathers are less involved in child-rearing than mothers are, but fathers are increasing the time they spend with children. Father-mother cooperation and mutual respect help the adolescent to develop positive attitudes toward males and females.

Learning Goal 6
Evaluate social policy and families

- Families with adolescents have been neglected in social policy. A number of recommendations for improving social policy for families with adolescents were made.

In this chapter, we have examined many aspects of families. In chapter 6, we will turn our attention to peer relations. We will revisit the concept discussed earlier in this chapter that parent and peer worlds are often connected, not isolated.

CHAPTER MAP

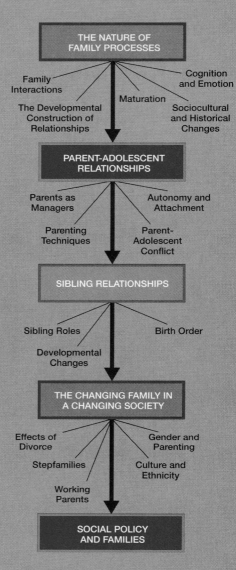

THE NATURE OF
FAMILY PROCESSES

Family
Interactions

Cognition
and Emotion

Maturation

The Developmental
Construction of
Relationships

Sociocultural
and Historical
Changes

PARENT-ADOLESCENT
RELATIONSHIPS

Parents as
Managers

Autonomy and
Attachment

Parenting
Techniques

Parent-
Adolescent
Conflict

SIBLING RELATIONSHIPS

Sibling Roles

Birth Order

Developmental
Changes

THE CHANGING FAMILY IN
A CHANGING SOCIETY

Effects of
Divorce

Gender and
Parenting

Stepfamilies

Culture and
Ethnicity

Working
Parents

SOCIAL POLICY
AND FAMILIES

REACH YOUR LEARNING GOALS

At the beginning of the chapter, we stated six learning goals and encouraged you to review material related to these goals at three points in the chapter. This is a good time to return to these reviews and use them to guide your study and help you to reach your learning goals.

Page 156

Learning Goal 1   Explain the nature of family processes

Page 169

Learning Goal 2   Discuss parent-adolescent relationships

Learning Goal 3   Know about sibling relationships

Page 180

Learning Goal 4   Describe the effects of divorce, stepfamilies, and working parents

Learning Goal 5   Understand culture, ethnicity, gender, and parenting

Learning Goal 6   Evaluate social policy and families

KEY TERMS

reciprocal socialization 148
synchrony 149
developmental construction views 150
continuity view 150
discontinuity view 151
authoritarian parenting 157
authoritative parenting 158
neglectful parenting 158

indulgent parenting 158
emotional autonomy 162
secure attachment 165
insecure attachment 165
dismissing/avoidant attachment 165
preoccupied/ambivalent attachment 165
unresolved/disorganized attachment 165
boundary ambiguity 173

KEY PEOPLE

Andrew Collins 152
Diana Baumrind 157
John Bowlby and Mary Ainsworth 164
Joseph Allen 165
E. Mavis Hetherington 171
Lois Hoffman 174

RESOURCES FOR IMPROVING THE LIVES OF ADOLESCENTS

Between Parent & Teenager

> (1969) by Haim Ginott
> New York: Avon

Despite the fact that *Between Parent & Teenager* is well past its own adolescence (it was published in 1969), it continues to be one of the most widely read and recommended books for parents who want to communicate more effectively with their teenagers.

Big Brothers/Big Sisters of America

> 17 South 17th Street, Suite 1200
> Philadelphia, PA 19103
> 215–567–2748

Single mothers and single fathers who are having problems with a son or daughter might want to get a responsible adult to spend at least one afternoon every other week with the son or daughter.

Stepfamily Association of America

> 602 East Joppa Road
> Baltimore, MD 21204
> 410–823–7570

This organization provides a support network for stepparents, remarried parents, and their children.

Raising Black Children

> (1992) by James P. Comer and Alvin E. Poussaint
> New York: Plume

This excellent book includes many wise suggestions for raising African American children.

You and Your Adolescent

> (1997, 2nd ed.) by Laurence Steinberg and Ann Levine
> New York: Harper Perennial

You and Your Adolescent provides a broad, developmental overview of adolescence, with parental advice mixed in along the way.

TAKING IT TO THE NET

http://www.mhhe.com/santrocka9

1. Parents are a valuable resource for adolescents who need to cope with the extreme stress, such as that which often is felt when parents divorce, when the adolescent must deal with the death of a friend or family member, or when a disaster occurs. *What tips would you include in a list that parents could use to help their adolescents cope with extreme stress?*

2. All parents must determine how to discipline their children. Discipline techniques used during childhood may have important implications for adolescent development and behavior. *What would you advise parents about spanking their children? Does it have important consequences for later adolescent behavior?*

3. Some evidence suggests that the way we parent is influenced by how our parents parented us. *How did your parents rear you? What was their style? Will yours be the same?*

Connect to *http://www.mhhe.com/santrocka9* to research the answers and complete these exercises. In some cases, you'll also find further instructions on this site.

CHAPTER 6

CHAPTER MAP

THE NATURE OF PEER RELATIONS

- Peer Group Functions
- Bullying
- Family-Peer Linkages
- Conglomerate Strategies for Improving Social Skills
- Peer Conformity
- Emotional Regulation in Peer Relations
- Peer Statuses
- Social Cognition

FRIENDSHIP

- Its Importance
- Mixed-Age Friendships
- Sullivan's Ideas
- Intimacy and Similarity

ADOLESCENT GROUPS

- Group Function and Formation
- Youth Organizations
- Children Groups and Adolescent Groups
- Cliques and Crowds
- Ethnic and Cultural Variations

DATING AND ROMANTIC RELATIONSHIPS

- Functions of Dating
- Romantic Love and Its Construction
- Types of Dating and Developmental Changes
- Emotion and Romantic Relationships
- Culture and Dating
- Male and Female Dating Scripts

■ YOUNG ADOLESCENT GIRLS' FRIENDS AND RELATIONAL WORLDS

Lynn Brown and Carol Gilligan (1992) conducted in-depth interviews of 100 girls 10 to 13 years of age who were making the transition to the relational worlds of adolescence. They listened to what these girls were saying about how important friends were to them. The girls were very curious about the human world they lived in and kept track of what was happening to the peers and friends in their world. The girls spoke about the pleasure they derived from the intimacy and fun of human connection, and about the potential for hurt in relationships. They especially highlighted the importance of clique formation in their lives.

One girl, Noura, says that she learned about what it feels like to be the person that everyone doesn't like and that it was very painful. Another girl, Gail, reflected on her life over the last year and says that she is now getting along better with people, probably because she is better at understanding how they think and at accepting them. A number of the girls talked about "whitewashing" in the adolescent relational world. That is, many girls say nice and kind things to be polite but often don't really mean them. They know the benefits of being perceived as the perfect, happy girl, at least on the surface. Suspecting that people prefer the "perfect girl," they experiment with her image and the happiness she might bring. The perfectly nice girl seems to gain popularity with other girls, and as many girls strive to become her, jealousies and rivalries break out. Cliques can provide emotional support for girls who are striving to be perfect but know they are not. One girl, Victoria, commented that some girls like her, who weren't very popular, nonetheless were accepted into a "club" with three other girls. She now feels that when she is sad or depressed she can count on the "club" for support. Though they were "leftovers" and did not get into the most popular cliques, these four girls say they know they are liked and it feels great.

Another girl, Judy, at age 13, spoke about her interest in romantic relationships. She says that although she and her girlfriends are only 13, they want to have romantic relationships. She covers her bodily desires and sexual feelings with romantic ideals. She describes a girl who goes out with guys and goes farther than most girls would and says the girl's behavior is "disgusting." Rather than sex, Judy says she is looking for a really good relationship with a guy.

PEERS

■

A man's growth is seen in the successive choirs of his friends.
—Ralph Waldo Emerson, 1841
American Poet and Essayist, 19th Century

WHEN YOU THINK BACK TO YOUR ADOLESCENT years, many of your most enjoyable moments were spent with peers—on the telephone, in school activities, in the neighborhood, on dates, at dances, or just hanging out. Peer relations undergo important changes during adolescence. In childhood, the focus of peer relations is on being liked by classmates and being included in games or lunchroom conversations. Being overlooked or, worse yet, being disliked and rejected by peers can have damaging effects on children's development that sometimes carry forward to adolescence. Adolescents have a larger number of acquaintances in their peer networks than children do. Beginning in early adolescence, teenagers typically prefer to have a smaller number of friendships that are more intense and intimate than those of younger children. Cliques and crowds usually take on more importance, as adolescents begin to "hang out" together. Dating and romantic relationships become important for most adolescents. By the time you have completed this chapter, you should be able to reach these learning goals:

1 Discuss peer group functions and family-peer linkages

2 Describe peer conformity, peer statuses, and other dimensions of peer relations

3 Know about friendship in adolescence

4 Evaluate adolescent groups

5 Discuss cliques, crowds, and youth organizations

6 Describe dating in adolescence

7 Explain romantic love and its construction

THE NATURE OF
PEER RELATIONS

Peer Group
Functions

Bullying

Family-Peer
Linkages

Conglomerate
Strategies for
Improving
Social Skills

Peer Conformity

Emotional
Regulation
in Peer
Relations

Peer Statuses

Social
Cognition

Adolescent Peer Relations
http://www.mhhe.com/santrocka9

peers
Children or adolescents who are of about the same age or maturity level.

THE NATURE OF PEER RELATIONS

Peers play very important roles in the lives of adolescents. Let's explore what these roles are.

Peer Group Functions

To many adolescents, how they are seen by peers is the most important aspect of their lives. Some adolescents will go along with anything, just to be included as a member of the group. To them, being excluded means stress, frustration, and sadness. Contrast Bob, who has no close friends, with Steve, who has three close buddies he pals around with all of the time. Sally was turned down by the club at school that she was working for six months to get into, in contrast to Sandra, who is a member of the club and who frequently is told by her peers how "super" her personality is.

Some friends of mine have a 13-year-old daughter. Last year, she had a number of girlfriends—she spent a lot of time on the phone talking with them, and they frequently visited each other's homes. Then her family moved, and this 13-year-old girl had to attend a school with a lower socioeconomic mix of students than at her previous school. Many of the girls at the new school feel that my friend's daughter is "too good" for them, and because of this she is having difficulty making friends this year. One of her most frequent complaints is, "I don't have any friends. . . . None of the kids at school ever call me. And none of them ever ask me over to their houses. What can I do?"

Peers *are children or adolescents who are of about the same age or maturity level.* Same-age peer interaction serves a unique role in U.S. culture (Hartup, 1983). Age grading would occur even if schools were not age graded and adolescents were left alone to determine the composition of their own societies. After all, one can learn to be a good fighter only among age-mates: The bigger guys will kill you, and the little ones are no challenge. One of the most important functions of the peer group is to provide a source of information about the world outside the family. From the peer group, adolescents receive feedback about their abilities. Adolescents learn whether what they do is better than, as good as, or worse than what other adolescents do. Learning this at home is difficult because siblings are usually older or younger.

Developmental Changes in Peer Time   Children spend an increasing amount of time in peer interaction during middle and late childhood and adolescence. In one investigation, children interacted with peers 10 percent of their day at age 2, 20 percent at age 4, and more than 40 percent between the ages of 7 and 11 (Barker & Wright, 1951). In a typical school day, there were 299 episodes with peers per day. By adolescence, peer relations occupy large chunks of an individual's life. In one investigation, over the course of one weekend, young adolescent boys and girls spent more than twice as much time with peers as with parents (Condry, Simon, & Bronfenbrenner, 1968).

What do adolescents do when they are with their peers? In one study, sixth-graders were asked what they do when they are with their friends (Medrich & others, 1982). Team sports accounted for 45 percent of boys' activities but only 26 percent of girls'. General play, going places, and socializing were common listings for both sexes. Most peer interactions occur outside the home (although close to home), occur more often in private than public places, and occur more between children of the same sex than of the opposite sex.

Are Peers Necessary for Development?   When peer monkeys who have been reared together are separated from one another, they become depressed and less advanced socially (Suomi, Harlow, & Domek, 1970). The human development literature contains a classic example of the importance of peers in social development. Anna Freud (Freud & Dann, 1951) studied six children from different families who banded together after their parents were killed in World War II. Intensive peer attachment was observed; the children were a tightly knit group, dependent on one another and aloof with outsiders. Even though deprived of parental care, they became neither delinquent nor psychotic.

Good peer relations might be necessary for normal social development in adolescence. Social isolation, or the inability to "plug in" to a social network, is linked with many different forms of problems and disorders, ranging from delinquency and problem drinking to depression (Hops & others, 1997; Kupersmidt & Coie, 1990). In one study of adolescents, positive peer relationships were associated with positive social adjustment (Ryan & Patrick, 1996). Peer relations in childhood and adolescence are also related to later development. In one study, poor peer relations in childhood were associated with dropping out of school and delinquency in late adolescence (Roff, Sells, & Golden, 1972). In another study, harmonious peer relations during adolescence were linked with positive mental health at midlife (Hightower, 1990).

And in a more recent study, children who had a stable best friend in fifth grade and their fifth-grade counterparts who were friendless were assessed 12 years later as adults (Bagwell, Newcomb, & Bukowski, 1998). Children who had a stable best friend in fifth grade had a more positive sense of self-worth as adults than their counterparts who had been friendless in fifth grade.

Positive and Negative Peer Relations   As you might have detected from our discussion of peer relations thus far, peer influences can be both positive and negative (Rubin, Bukowski & Parker, 1998; Shaffer, 2000; Urberg, 1999). Both Jean Piaget (1932) and Harry Stack Sullivan (1953) were influential theorists who stressed that it is through peer interaction that children and adolescents learn the symmetrical reciprocity mode of relationships discussed in chapter 5. Children explore the principles of fairness and justice by working through disagreements with peers. They also learn to be keen observers of peers' interests and perspectives in order to smoothly integrate themselves into ongoing peer activities. In addition, Sullivan argued that adolescents learn to be

What are some links between parent-adolescent and adolescent-peer relations?

skilled and sensitive partners in intimate relationships by forging close friendships with selected peers. These intimacy skills are carried forward to help form the foundation of later dating and marital relationships, according to Sullivan.

In contrast, some theorists have emphasized the negative influences of peers on children's and adolescents' development. Being rejected or overlooked by peers leads some adolescents to feel lonely or hostile. Further, such rejection and neglect by peers are related to an individual's subsequent mental health and criminal problems. Some theorists have also described the adolescent peer culture as a corrupt influence that undermines parental values and control. Further, peers can introduce adolescents to alcohol, drugs, delinquency, and other forms of behavior that adults view as maladaptive.

As you read about peers, also keep in mind that although peer experiences have important influences on children's development, those influences vary according to the way peer experience is measured, the outcomes specified, and the developmental trajectories traversed (Hartup, 1999). "Peers" and "peer group" are global concepts. These can be beneficial concepts in understanding peer influences as long as they are considered as "setting conditions" and the specific type of setting in which the child participates, such as "acquaintance," "clique," "neighborhood associates," "friendship network," and "activity group," is taken into account. For example, one analysis of the peer groups describes these aspects of the youth culture: membership crowd, neighborhood crowd, reference crowd, church crowd, sports team, friendship group, and friend (Brown, 1999).

Family-Peer Linkages

For many years, parents and peers were thought of as disparate, if not oppositional, forces in the adolescent's development. Adolescents do show a strong motivation to be with their peers and become independent. However, it is incorrect to assume that movement toward peer involvement and autonomy are unrelated to parent-adolescent relationships. Recent studies have provided persuasive evidence that adolescents live in a connected world with parents and peers, not a disconnected one (Ladd & Le Sieur, 1995; Ladd & Pettit, 2002; Scharf & Schulman, 2000; Tilton-Weaver & Leighter, 2002).

What are some of the ways the worlds of parents and peers are connected? Parents' choices of neighborhoods, churches, schools, and their own friends influence the pool from which their adolescents select possible friends (Cooper & Ayers-Lopez, 1985). For example, parents can choose to live in a neighborhood with playgrounds, parks, and youth organizations or in a neighborhood where houses are far apart, few adolescents live, and youth organizations are not well developed.

■ THINKING CRITICALLY

Parent-Peer Linkages in Your Adolescence

Think back to your middle school/junior high and high school years. What was your relationship with your parents like? Were you securely attached or insecurely attached to them? How do you think your relationship with your parents affected your friendship and peer relations in adolescence? Later in the chapter we will discuss dating and romantic relationships. As a preview to that material, consider this question: Do you think that observing your parents' marital lives and interacting with your parents while you were growing up have influenced your dating and romantic relationships? If so, how?

Parents can model or coach their adolescents in ways of relating to peers. In one study, parents acknowledged that they recommended specific strategies to their adolescents to help them develop more positive peer relations (Rubin & Sloman, 1984). For example, parents discussed with their adolescents ways that disputes could be mediated and how to become less shy. They also encouraged them to be tolerant and to resist peer pressure. And in one study, young adolescents talked more frequently about peer-related problems with their mothers than with their fathers (Gauze, 1994).

In addition, as we discussed in chapter 5, an increasing number of researchers have found that secure attachment to parents is related to the adolescent's positive peer relations (Allen & others, 2001) ◀▦ P. 164. In one study, adolescents who were securely attached to parents were also securely attached to their peers; adolescents who were insecurely attached to their parents were likewise insecurely attached to their peers (Armsden & Greenberg, 1984). And in another study, older adolescents who had an ambivalent attachment history with their parents reported less satisfaction in their relationship with their best friend than did their securely attached counterparts (Fisher, 1990).

In chapter 5, we indicated that Japanese adolescents seek autonomy later from their parents and have less conflict with them than American adolescents do. In a recent cross-cultural analysis, it also was concluded that the peer group is more important to U.S. adolescents than to Japanese adolescents (Rothbaum & others, 2000). Japanese adolescents spend less time outside the home, have less recreational leisure time, and engage in fewer extracurricular activities with peers than U.S. adolescents (White, 1993). Also, U.S. adolescents are more likely to put pressure on their peers to resist parental influence than Japanese adolescents are (Rothblum & others, 2000).

As can be seen, there is much more connectedness between the family and peer worlds of adolescents than once was believed. Throughout adolescence, the worlds of parents and peers work in coordinated, although sometimes different, ways to influence the adolescent's development.

Peer Conformity

Peer Pressure
http://www.mhhe.com/santrocka9

Conformity comes in many forms and affects many aspects of adolescents' lives. Do adolescents take up jogging because everyone else is doing it? Do adolescents let their hair grow long one year and cut it short the next because of fashion? Do adolescents take cocaine if pressured by others, or do they resist the pressure? **Conformity** *occurs when individuals adopt the attitudes or behavior of others because of real or imagined pressure from them.* The pressure to conform to peers becomes very strong during the adolescent years. Consider the comments of Kevin, an eighth-grader:

conformity
This occurs when individuals adopt the attitudes or behaviors of others because of real or imagined pressure from them.

> I feel a lot of pressure from my friends to smoke and steal and things like that. My parents do not allow me to smoke, but my best friends are really pushing me to do it. They call me a pansy and a momma's boy if I don't. I really don't like the idea of smoking, but my good friend Steve told me in front of some of our friends, "Kevin, you are an idiot and a chicken wrapped up in one little body." I couldn't stand it any more, so I smoked with them. I was coughing and humped over, but I still said, "This is really fun—yeah, I like it." I felt like I was part of the group.

Also, think about the statement by 14-year-old Andrea:

> Peer pressure is extremely influential in my life. I have never had very many friends, and I spend quite a bit of time alone. The friends I have are older. . . . The closest friend I have had is a lot like me in that we are both sad and depressed a lot. I began to act even more depressed than before when I was with her. I would call her up and try to act even more depressed than I was because that is what I thought she liked. In that relationship, I felt pressure to be like her.

Each of you, individually, walkest with the tread of a fox, but collectively ye are geese.
—Solon
Greek Statesman and Poet,
6th Century B.C.

Conformity to peer pressure in adolescence can be positive or negative. Teenagers engage in all sorts of negative conformity behavior—use seedy language, steal, vandalize, and make fun of parents and teachers. However, a great deal of peer conformity is not negative and consists of the desire to be involved in the peer world, such as dressing like friends and wanting to spend huge chunks of time with members of a clique. Such circumstances may involve prosocial activities as well, as when clubs raise money for worthy causes.

In a study focused on negative, neutral, and positive aspects of peer conformity, Thomas Berndt (1979) studied 273 third-grade through twelfth-grade students. Hypothetical dilemmas that were presented to the students required the students to make choices about conformity with friends on prosocial and antisocial behavior and about conformity with parents on neutral and prosocial behaviors. For example, one prosocial item questioned whether students relied on their parents' advice in such situations as deciding about helping at the library or instructing another child to swim. An antisocial question asked a boy what he would do if one of his peers wanted him to help steal some candy. A neutral question asked a girl if she would follow peer suggestions to engage in an activity she wasn't interested in—such as going to a movie she did not want to see.

Some interesting developmental patterns were found in this investigation. In the third grade, parent and peer influences often directly contradicted each other. Since parent conformity is much greater for third-grade children, children of this age are probably still closely tied to and dependent on their parents. However, by the sixth grade, parent and peer influences were found to be no longer in direct opposition. Peer conformity had increased, but parent and peer influences were operating in different situations—parents had more impact in some situations, while peers had more clout in others.

By the ninth grade, parent and peer influences were once again in strong opposition to each other, probably because the conformity of adolescents to the social behavior of peers is much stronger at this grade level than at any other. At this time, adolescent adoption of antisocial standards endorsed by the peer group inevitably leads to conflict between adolescents and parents. Researchers have also found that the adolescent's attempt to gain independence meets with more parental opposition around the ninth grade than at any other time (Douvan & Adelson, 1966).

A stereotypical view of parent-child relationships suggests that parent-peer opposition continues into the late high school and college-age years. But Berndt (1979) found that adolescent conformity to antisocial, peer-endorsed behavior decreases in the late high school years, and agreement between parents and peers begins to increase in some areas. In addition, by the eleventh and twelfth grades, students show signs of developing a decision-making style more independent of peer and parental influence.

Though most adolescents conform to peer pressure and societal standards, some adolescents are nonconformist or anticonformist. **Nonconformity** *occurs when individuals know what people around them expect but do not use those expectations to guide their behavior.* Nonconformists are independent, as when a high school student chooses to not be a member of a clique. **Anticonformity** *occurs when individuals react counter to a group's expectations and deliberately move away from the actions or beliefs the group advocates.* Two contemporary versions of anticonformist teenagers are "skinheads" and "punks."

In sum, peer pressure is a pervasive theme of adolescents' lives. Its power can be observed in almost every dimen-

nonconformity
This occurs when individuals know what people around them expect but do not use those expectations to guide their behavior.

anticonformity
This occurs when individuals react counter to a group's expectations and deliberately move away from the actions or beliefs the group advocates.

What distinguishes anticonformity from nonconformity?

sion of adolescents' behavior—their choice of dress, music, language, values, leisure activities, and so on. Parents, teachers, and other adults can help adolescents to deal with peer pressure (Clasen & Brown, 1987). Adolescents need many opportunities to talk with both peers and adults about their social worlds and the pressures involved. The developmental changes of adolescence often bring forth a sense of insecurity. Young adolescents may be especially vulnerable because of this insecurity and the many developmental changes taking place in their lives. To counter this stress, young adolescents need to experience opportunities for success, both in and out of school, that increase their sense of being in control. Adolescents can learn that their social world is reciprocally controlled. Others might try to control them, but they can exert personal control over their actions and influence others in turn. Next, in our discussion of peer popularity, neglect, and rejection, we discuss further the powerful role that peer relations play in adolescent development.

Peer Statuses

Peer Conflicts
http://www.mhhe.com/santrocka9

Every adolescent wants to be popular—you probably thought about popularity a lot when you were in junior and senior high school. Teenagers commonly think, "What can I do to have all of the kids at school like me?" "How can I be popular with both girls and guys?" "What's wrong with me? There must be something wrong, or I would be more popular." Sometimes, adolescents go to great lengths to be popular; and in some cases, parents go to even greater lengths to try to insulate their adolescents from rejection and to increase the likelihood that they will be popular. Students show off and cut up because it gets attention and makes their peers laugh. Parents set up elaborate parties, buy cars and clothes for their teens, and drive adolescents and their friends all over in the hope that their sons or daughters will be popular.

Popular children *are frequently nominated as a best friend and rarely are disliked by their peers.* Researchers have discovered that popular children and adolescents give out reinforcements, listen carefully, maintain open lines of communication with peers, are happy, act like themselves, show enthusiasm and concern for others, and are self-confident without being conceited (Hartup, 1983). In one study, popular youth were more likely than unpopular youth to communicate clearly with their peers, elicit their peers' attention, and maintain conversation with peers (Kennedy, 1990).

popular children
Children who are frequently nominated as a best friend and are rarely disliked by their peers.

Certain physical and cultural factors also affect adolescents' popularity. Adolescents who are physically attractive are more popular than those who are not (Kennedy, 1990) and, contrary to what some believe, brighter adolescents are more popular than less intelligent ones. Adolescents growing up in middle-SES surroundings tend to be more popular than those growing up in lower-SES surroundings, presumably in part because they are more in control of establishing standards for popularity (Hollingshead, 1975). But remember that findings such as these reflect group averages—there are many physically attractive teenagers who are unpopular, and some physically unattractive ones who are very well liked. Sociologist James Coleman (1980) points out that, for adolescents in the average range, there is little or no relation between physical attractiveness and popularity. It is only in the extremes (very attractive and very unattractive) that a link between popularity and attractiveness holds.

Teenagers are people who express a burning desire to be different by dressing exactly alike.
—Anonymous

Developmentalists distinguish three types of children who have a different status than popular children: Those who are (1) neglected, (2) rejected, or (3) controversial (Wentzel & Asher, 1995). **Neglected children** *are infrequently nominated as a best friend but are not disliked by their peers.* **Rejected children** *are infrequently nominated as someone's best friend and are actively disliked by their peers.* **Controversial children** *are frequently nominated both as someone's best friend and as being disliked.*

neglected children
Children who are infrequently nominated as a best friend but are not disliked by their peers.

rejected children
Children who are infrequently nominated as a best friend and are actively disliked by their peers.

Rejected children and adolescents often have more serious adjustment problems later in life than those who are neglected (Dishion & Spracklen, 1996). For example, in one study, 112 fifth-grade boys were evaluated over a period of 7 years until the end of high school (Kupersmidt & Coie, 1990). The key factor in predicting whether rejected children would engage in delinquent behavior or drop out of school later during adolescence was their aggression toward peers in elementary school.

controversial children
Children who are frequently nominated both as a best friend and as being disliked.

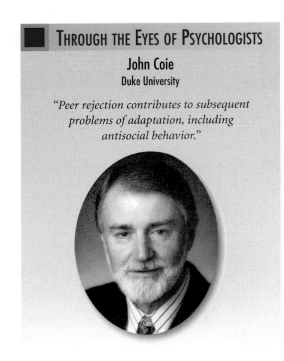
Not all rejected children and adolescents are aggressive (Coie, 1999). Although aggression and its related characteristics of impulsiveness and disruptiveness underlie rejection about half the time, approximately 10 to 20 percent of rejected children and adolescents are shy (Cillessen & others, 1992).

How can neglected children and adolescents be trained to interact more effectively with their peers? The goal of training programs with neglected children and adolescents is often to help them attract attention from their peers in positive ways and to hold their attention by asking questions, by listening in a warm and friendly way, and by saying things about themselves that relate to the peers' interests. They also are taught to enter groups more effectively.

The goal of training programs with rejected children and adolescents is often to help them listen to peers and "hear what they say" instead of trying to dominate peer interactions. Rejected children and adolescents are trained to join peers without trying to change what is taking place in the peer group.

One issue that has been raised about improving the peer relations of rejected children and adolescents is whether the focus should be on improving their prosocial skills (better empathy, careful listening, improved communication skills, and so on) or on reducing their aggressive, disruptive behavior and improving their self-control (Coie & Koeppl, 1990). In one study, socially rejected young adolescents were coached on the importance of showing behaviors that would improve their chance of being liked by others (Murphy & Schneider, 1994). The intervention was successful in improving the friendships of the socially rejected youth.

Improving the prosocial skills of rejected adolescents, though, does not automatically eliminate their aggressive or disruptive behavior. Aggression often leads to reinforcement because peers give in to aggressive youths' demands. Thus, in addition to teaching better prosocial skills to rejected adolescents, direct steps must also be taken to eliminate their aggressive actions. Further, acquiring positive status with peers may take time to achieve because it is hard for peers to change their opinions if adolescents frequently engage in aggressive conduct (Coie & Dodge, 1998).

The controversial peer status had not been studied until recently. In one study, girls who had controversial peer status in the fourth grade were more likely to become adolescent mothers than were girls of other peer statuses (Underwood, Kupersmidt, & Coie, 1996). Also, aggressive girls had more children than nonaggressive girls did.

Next, we will turn our attention to the role of social cognition in understanding peer relations. Part of this discussion further considers ideas about reducing the aggression of children and adolescents in their peer encounters.

Social Cognition

A distinction can be made between knowledge and process in cognition. In studying cognitive aspects of peer relations, this distinction can be made. Learning about the social knowledge adolescents bring with them to peer relations is important, as is studying how adolescents process information during peer interaction.

As children move into adolescence, they acquire more social knowledge, and there is considerable individual variation in how much one adolescent knows about what it takes to make friends, to get peers to like him or her, and so forth. For example, does the adolescent know that giving out reinforcements will increase the likelihood that he or she will be popular? That is, does Mary consciously know that, by telling Barbara such things as "I really like that sweater you have on today" and "Gosh, you sure are popular with the guys," she will enhance the likelihood Barbara will want her to be her friend? Does the adolescent know that, when others perceive that he or she is similar to them, he or she will be liked better by the others? Does the adolescent know that friendship involves sharing intimate conversations and that a friendship likely is improved when the adolescent shares private, confidential information with another adolescent? To what extent does the adolescent know that comforting and listening skills will improve friendship relations? To what extent does the adolescent know what it takes to become a leader? Think back to your adolescent years. How sophisticated were you in knowing about such social matters? Were you aware of the role of nice statements and perceived similarity in determining popularity and friendship? While you may not have been aware of these factors, those of you who were popular and maintained close friendships likely were competent at using these strategies.

From a social cognitive perspective, children and adolescents may have difficulty in peer relations because they lack appropriate social cognitive skills (Coie & Dodge, 1998; Crick & Dodge, 1994; Dodge, 1993; Lochman & Dodge, 1998). One investigation explored the possibility that social cognitive skill deficits characterize children who have peer-related difficulties (Asarnow & Callan, 1985). Boys with and without peer adjustment difficulties were identified, and then a number of social cognitive processes or skills were assessed. These included the boys' ability to generate alternative solutions to hypothetical problems, to evaluate these solutions in terms of their effectiveness, to describe self-statements, and to rate the likelihood of self-statements. It was found that boys without peer adjustment problems generated more alternative solutions, proposed more assertive and mature solutions, gave less intense aggressive solutions, showed more adaptive planning, and evaluated physically aggressive responses less positively than the boys with peer adjustment problems. For example, as shown in figure 6.1, negative-peer-status sixth-grade boys were not as likely to generate alternative solutions and were much less likely to ada tively plan ahead than their positive-peer-status counterparts.

In one study of sixth- and seventh-graders, knowledge of both appropriate and inappropriate strategies for making friends was related positively to prosocial behavior and peer acceptance and negatively to antisocial behavior (Wentzel & Erdley, 1993). The appropriate and inappropriate strategies generated by students are listed in figure 6.2 on page 194.

Now let's examine how social information processing might be involved in peer relations. For example, consider the situation when a peer accidentally trips and knocks a boy's soft drink out of his hand. The boy misinterprets the encounter as hostile, which leads him to retaliate aggressively against the peer. Through repeated encounters of this kind, peers come to perceive the boy as having a habit of acting inappropriately. Kenneth Dodge (1983) argues that children go through five steps in processing information about their social world: decoding of social cues, interpretation, response search, selecting an optimal response, and enactment. Dodge has found that aggressive boys are more likely to perceive another child's actions as hostile when the peer's intention is ambiguous. And when aggressive boys search for cues to determine a peer's intention, they respond more rapidly, less efficiently, and less reflectively than nonaggressive children. These are among the social cognitive factors believed to be involved in children's and adolescents' conflicts with each other.

Emotional Regulation in Peer Relations

The ability to regulate emotion plays an important role in successful peer relations (Rubin, 2000; Underwood & Hurley, 2000; Workman & others, 2000). Moody and emotionally negative individuals experience greater rejection by peers, whereas emotionally positive individuals are more popular (Saarni, 1999). Adolescents who have effective self-regulatory skills can modulate their emotional expressiveness in contexts that evoke intense emotions, as when a peer says something negative. In one study, rejected children were more likely than popular children to use negative gestures in a provoking situation (Underwood & Hurley, 1997).

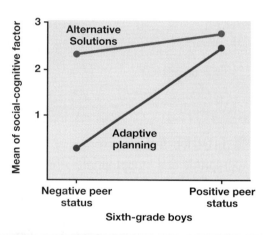

FIGURE 6.1

Generation of Alternative Solutions and Adaptive Planning by Negative- and Positive-Peer-Status Boys

Notice that negative-peer-status boys were less likely to generate alternative solutions and plan ahead than were their positive-peer-status counterparts.

Category	Examples
Strategies Appropriate for Making Friends	
Initiate interaction	Learn about friends: ask for their name, age, favorite activities. Prosocial overtures: introduce self, start a conversation, invite them to do things.
Be nice	Be nice, kind, considerate.
Prosocial behavior	Honesty and trustworthiness: tell the truth, keep promises. Be generous, sharing, cooperative.
Respect for self and others	Respect others, have good manners: be polite, courteous, listen to what others say. Have a positive attitude and personality: be open to others, be friendly, be funny. Be yourself. Enhance your own reputation: be clean, dress neatly, be on best behavior.
Provide social support	Be supportive: help, give advice, show you care. Engage in activities together: study or play, sit next to one another, be in same group. Enhance others: compliment them.
Strategies Inappropriate for Making Friends	
Psychological aggression	Show disrespect, bad manners: be prejudiced, inconsiderate, use others, curse, be rude. Be exclusive, uncooperative: don't invite them to do things, ignore them, isolate them, don't share or help them. Hurt their reputation or feelings: gossip, spread rumors, embarrass them, criticize them.
Negative self-presentation	Be self-centered: be snobby, conceited, jealous, show off, care only about yourself. Be mean, have bad attitude or affect: be mean, cruel, hostile, a grouch, angry all the time. Hurt own reputation: be a slob, act stupid, throw temper tantrums, start trouble, be a sissy.
Antisocial behavior	Physical aggression: fight, trip, spit, cause physical harm. Verbal aggression or control: yell at others, pick on them, make fun of them, call them names, be bossy. Dishonesty, disloyalty: tell lies, steal, cheat, tell secrets, break promises. Break school rules: skip school, drink alcohol, use drugs.

■ FIGURE 6.2

Appropriate and Inappropriate Strategies for Making Friends at School

Conglomerate Strategies for Improving Social Skills

Cooperative Groups and Conflict Resolution
http://www.mhhe.com/santrocka9

conglomerate strategies
The use of a combination of techniques, rather than a single approach, to improve adolescents' social skills; also called coaching.

Conglomerate strategies, *also referred to as coaching, involve the use of a combination of techniques, rather than a single approach, to improve adolescents' social skills.* A conglomerate strategy might consist of demonstration or modeling of appropriate social skills, discussion, and reasoning about the social skills, as well as the use of reinforcement for their enactment in actual social situations. In one coaching study, students with few friends were selected and trained in ways to have fun with peers (Oden & Asher, 1975). The "unpopular" students were encouraged to participate fully, to show interest in others, to cooperate, and to maintain communication. A control group of students (who also had few friends) was directed in peer experiences but was not coached specifically in terms of improved peer strategies. Subsequent assessment revealed that the coaching was effective, with the coached group members showing more sociability when observed in peer relationships than their noncoached counterparts.

Other efforts to teach social skills also have used conglomerate strategies (Merrell & Gimpel, 1997; Repinski & Leffert, 1994). In one study, middle school adolescents were instructed in ways to improve their self-control, stress management, and social problem solving (Weissberg & Caplan, 1989). For example, as problem situations arose, teachers modeled and students practiced six sequential steps: (1) stop, calm down, and think before you act; (2) go over the problem and state how you feel; (3) set a positive goal; (4) think of lots of solutions; (5) plan ahead for the consequences; (6) go ahead and try the best plan. The 240 adolescents who participated in the program improved their ability to devise cooperative solutions to problem situations, and their teachers reported that the students showed improved social relations in the classroom following the program. In another study, boys and girls in a low-income area of New Jersey were given instruction in social decision making, self-control, and group awareness (Clabby & Elias, 1988). When compared with boys and girls who did not receive the training, the program participants were more sensitive to the feelings of others, more mindful of the consequences of their actions, and better able to analyze problem situations and act appropriately.

Social skills training programs have generally been more successful with children 10 years of age or younger than with adolescents (Malik & Furman, 1993). Peer reputations become more fixed as cliques and peer groups become more salient in adolescence. Even if adolescents develop new skills and engage in appropriate interactions, their peers might not change their evaluation of them. In such instances, intervention that changes such perceptions is needed.

One such intervention strategy involves cooperative group training. In this approach, children or adolescents work toward a common goal that holds promise for changing reputations. Most cooperative group programs have been conducted in academic settings, but other contexts might be used. For example, participation in cooperative games and sports increases sharing and feelings of happiness. And some Nintendo and video games require cooperative efforts by the players.

Bullying

Reducing Bullying
http://www.mhhe.com/santrocka9

Significant numbers of children and adolescents are victimized by bullies (Slee & Taki, 1999; Parker, 2002). In one recent national survey of more than 15,000 sixth- through tenth-graders, 30 percent said they had been involved in moderate or frequent bullying (Nansel & others, 2001). Middle school students and boys were more likely to be involved in bullying than high school boys or girls. In another recent study of more than 4,000 middle school students in Maryland, 31 percent reported being victimized three or more times in the past year (Haynie & others, 2001).

Victims of bullying have been found to have certain characteristics (Card, Isaacs & Hodges, 2000; Nansel & Overpeck, 2002; Pellegrini, 2000). One recent study found that victims of bullies had parents who were intrusive, demanding, and unresponsive with their children (Ladd & Kochenderfer, in press). Also in this study, parent-child relationships characterized by intense closeness were linked with higher levels of peer victimization in boys. Overly close and emotionally intense relationships between parents and sons might not foster assertiveness and independence. Rather, they might foster self-doubts and worries that are perceived as weaknesses when expressed in male peer groups. Another study (Olweus, 1980) found that for both bullies and victims, the parenting they experienced was linked with their peer interaction. Bullies' parents were more likely to be rejecting, authoritarian, or permissive about their son's aggression, whereas victims' parents were more likely to be anxious and overprotective.

In another recent study, third- and sixth-grade boys and girls who internalized problems (for instance, were anxious and withdrawn), were physically weak, and were rejected by peers increasingly were victimized over time (Hodges & Perry, 1999). Yet another study found that the relation between internalizing problems and increased victimization was reduced for children with a protective friendship (Hodges & others, 1999).

Victims of bullies can suffer both short-term and long-term effects (Limber, 1997). Short-term, they can become depressed, lose interest in schoolwork, or even avoid going to school. The effects of bullying can persist into adulthood. One longitudinal study of male victims who were bullied during childhood found

What is the nature of bullying in adolescence?

that in their twenties they were more depressed and had lower self-esteem than their counterparts who had not been bullied in childhood (Olweus, 1993). Bullying also can indicate a serious problem for the bully as well as the victim. In the study just mentioned, about 60 percent of the boys who were identified as bullies in middle school had at least one criminal conviction (and about one-third had three or more convictions) in their twenties, rates that are far higher than the rates for nonbullies. Some strategies that teachers can use to reduce bullying are (Limber, 1997; Olweus, 1994; Stevens, De Bourdeaudhuij, & Van Oost, 2001):

- Get older peers to serve as monitors for bullying and intervene when they see it taking place.
- Develop schoolwide rules and sanctions against bullying and post them throughout the school.
- Form friendship groups for adolescents who are regularly bullied by peers.
- Incorporate the message of the antibullying program into church, school, and other community activities where adolescents are involved.

At this point we have studied a number of ideas about peer relations. These questions should help you to reach your learning goals related to this topic.

☐ FOR YOUR REVIEW

Learning Goal 1
Discuss peer group functions and family-peer linkages

- Peers are individuals who are about the same age or maturity level. Peers provide a means of social comparison and a source of information beyond the family. Good peer relations may be necessary for normal social development. The inability to "plug in" to a social network is associated with a number of problems. Peer relations can be negative or positive.
- Piaget and Sullivan stressed that peer relations provide the context for learning the symmetrical reciprocity mode of relationships.
- Hartup states that peer relations are complex and may vary according to the way they are measured, the outcomes specified, and the developmental trajectories traversed.
- Healthy family relations usually promote healthy peer relations. Parents can model or coach their child in ways of relating to peers. Parents' choice of neighborhoods, churches, schools, and their own friends influence the pool from which their children select possible friends.

Learning Goal 2
Describe peer conformity, peer statuses, and other dimensions of peer relations

- Conformity occurs when individuals adopt the attitudes or behavior of others because of real or imagined pressure to do so. Conformity to antisocial peer standards peaks around the eighth or ninth grade, then diminishes by the twelfth grade. Nonconformists know what people expect of them but don't use those expectations to guide their behavior. Anticonformists react counter to a group's expectations.
- Popular children are frequently nominated as a best friend and are rarely disliked by their friends. Neglected children are infrequently nominated as a best friend but are not disliked by their peers. Rejected children are rarely nominated as a best friend and are disliked by their peers. Controversial children are frequently nominated both as a best friend and as being disliked by peers.
- Social knowledge and social information-processing skills are associated with improved peer relations.
- Self-regulation of emotion is associated with positive peer relations.
- Conglomerate strategies, also referred to as coaching, involve the use of a combination of techniques, rather than a single strategy, to improve adolescents' social skills.
- Significant numbers of students are bullied, and bullying can result in short-term and long-term negative effects for the victim.

Now that we have examined many aspects of the nature of peer relations, let's turn our attention to friendships in adolescence.

FRIENDSHIP

The important role of friendships in adolescent development is exemplified in this description by a 13-year-old girl:

> My best friend is nice. She's honest, and I can trust her. I can tell her my innermost secrets and know that nobody else will find out about them. I have other friends, too, but she is my best friend. We consider each other's feelings and don't want to hurt each other. We help each other out when we have problems. We make up funny names for people and laugh ourselves silly. We make lists of which boys are the sexiest and which are the ugliest, which are the biggest jerks, and so on. Some of these things we share with other friends; some we don't.

Its Importance

Adolescents' friendships serve six functions (Gottman & Parker, 1987) (see figure 6.3):

1. *Companionship.* Friendship provides adolescents with a familiar partner, someone who is willing to spend time with them and join in collaborative activities.
2. *Stimulation.* Friendship provides adolescents with interesting information, excitement, and amusement.
3. *Physical support.* Friendship provides time, resources, and assistance.
4. *Ego support.* Friendship provides the expectation of support, encouragement, and feedback that helps adolescents to maintain an impression of themselves as competent, attractive, and worthwhile individuals.
5. *Social comparison.* Friendship provides information about where adolescents stand vis-à-vis others and whether adolescents are doing okay.
6. *Intimacy/affection.* Friendship provides adolescents with a warm, close, trusting relationship with another individual, a relationship that involves self-disclosure.

Sometimes, though, conflicts arise in friendships. One recent study focused on conflict with parents and friends (Adams & Laursen, 2001). Parent-adolescent conflicts were more likely to be characterized by a combination of daily hassle topics, neutral or angry affect afterward, power-assertive outcomes, and win-lose outcomes. Friend conflicts were more likely to involve a combination of relationship topics, friendly affect afterward, disengaged resolutions, and equal or no outcomes.

Sullivan's Ideas

Harry Stack Sullivan (1953) was the most influential theorist to discuss the importance of adolescent friendships. He argued that there is a dramatic increase in the psychological importance and intimacy of close friends during early adolescence. In contrast to other psychoanalytic theorists' narrow emphasis on the importance of parent-child relationships, Sullivan contended that friends also play important roles in shaping children's and adolescents' well-being and development. In terms of well-being, he argued that all people have a number of basic social needs, including the need for tenderness (secure attachment), playful companionship, social acceptance, intimacy, and sexual relations. Whether or not these needs are fulfilled largely determines our emotional well-being. For example, if the need for playful companionship goes unmet, then we become bored and depressed; if the need for social acceptance is not met, we suffer a lowered sense of self-worth. Developmentally, friends become increasingly depended upon to

Friendship
http://www.mhhe.com/santrocka9

■ FIGURE 6.3
The Functions of Friendships

satisfy these needs during adolescence, and thus the ups-and-downs of experiences with friends increasingly shape adolescents' state of well-being. In particular, Sullivan believed that the need for intimacy intensifies during early adolescence, motivating teenagers to seek out close friends. He felt that, if adolescents failed to forge such close friendships, they would experience painful feelings of loneliness coupled with a reduced sense of self-worth.

Research findings support many of Sullivan's ideas. For example, adolescents report more often disclosing intimate and personal information to their friends than do younger children (Buhrmester & Furman, 1987). Adolescents also say they depend more on friends than parents to satisfy needs for companionship, reassurance of worth, and intimacy (Furman & Buhrmester, 1992). In one study, daily interviews with 13- to 16-year-old adolescents over a five-day period were conducted to find out how much time they spent engaged in meaningful interactions with friends and parents (Buhrmester & Carbery, 1992). Adolescents spent an average of 103 minutes per day in meaningful interactions with friends compared to just 28 minutes per day with parents. In addition, the quality of friendship is more strongly linked to feelings of well-being during adolescence than during childhood. Teenagers with superficial friendships, or no close friendships at all, report feeling lonelier and more depressed, and they have a lower sense of self-esteem than teenagers with intimate friendships (Buhrmester, 1990; Yin, Buhrmester, & Hibbard, 1996). And in another study, friendship in early adolescence was a significant predictor of self-worth in early adulthood (Bagwell, Newcomb, & Bukowski, 1994).

The increased closeness and importance of friendship challenges adolescents to master evermore sophisticated social competencies (Porter, 2000). Viewed from the developmental constructionist perspective described in chapter 5, adolescent friendship represents a new mode of relating to others that is best described as a *symmetrical intimate mode* ◀‖‖‖ P. 151. During childhood, being a good friend involves being a good playmate: Children must know how to play cooperatively and must be skilled at smoothly entering ongoing games on the playground. By contrast, the greater intimacy of adolescent friendships demands that teenagers learn a number of close relationship competencies, including knowing how to self-disclose appropriately, being able to provide emotional support to friends, and managing disagreements in ways that do not undermine the intimacy of the friendship. These competencies require more sophisticated skills in perspective taking, empathy, and social problem solving than were involved in childhood playmate competencies.

In addition to the role they play in the socialization of social competence, friendship relationships are often important sources of support (Berndt, 1996; Hartup & Collins, 2000). Sullivan described how adolescent friends support one another's sense of personal worth. When close friends disclose their mutual insecurities and fears about themselves, they discover that they are not "abnormal" and that they have nothing to be ashamed of. Friends also act as important confidants that help adolescents work through upsetting problems (such as difficulties with parents or the breakup of romance) by providing both emotional support and informational advice. Friends can also protect "at risk" adolescents from victimization by peers (Bukowski, Sippola, & Boivin, 1995). In addition, friends can become active partners in building a sense of identity. During countless hours of conversation, friends act as sounding boards as teenagers explore issues ranging from future plans to stances on religious and moral issues.

Willard Hartup (1996), who has studied peer relations across four decades, recently concluded that children and adolescents often use friends as cognitive and social resources on a regular basis. Hartup also commented that normative transitions, such as moving from elementary to middle school, are negotiated more competently by children who have friends than by those who don't. The quality of friendship is also important to consider. Supportive friendships between socially skilled individuals are developmentally advantageous, whereas coercive and conflict-ridden friendships are not. Friendship and its developmental significance can vary from one adolescent to another. Adolescents' characteristics, such as temperament ("easy" versus "difficult," for example) likely influence the nature of friendships.

Each friend represents a world in us, a world possibly not born until they arrive, and it is only by this meeting that a new world is born.

—Anaïs Nin
*French-Born American Writer,
20th Century*

Intimacy and Similarity

Two important characteristics of friendship are intimacy and similarity.

Intimacy   In the context of friendship, *intimacy* has been defined in different ways. For example, it has been defined broadly to include everything in a relationship that makes the relationship seem close or intense. In most research studies, though, **intimacy in friendship** *is defined narrowly as self-disclosure or sharing of private thoughts.* Private or personal knowledge about a friend also has been used as an index of intimacy (Selman, 1980; Sullivan, 1953).

intimacy in friendship
In most research, this is defined narrowly as self-disclosure or sharing of private thoughts.

The most consistent finding in the last two decades of research on adolescent friendships is that intimacy is an important feature of friendship (Berndt & Perry, 1990; Bukowski, Newcomb, & Hoza, 1987; Sesma, 2000). When young adolescents are asked what they want from a friend or how they can tell someone is their best friend, they frequently say that a best friend will share problems with them, understand them, and listen when they talk about their own thoughts or feelings. When young children talk about their friendships, comments about intimate self-disclosure or mutual understanding are rare. In one investigation, friendship intimacy was more prominent in 13- to 16-year-olds than in 10- to 13-year-olds (Buhrmester, 1989).

Are the friendships of adolescent girls more intimate than the friendships of adolescent boys? When asked to describe their best friends, girls refer to intimate conversations and faithfulness more than boys do. For example, girls are more likely to describe their best friend as "sensitive just like me" or "trustworthy just like me" (Duck, 1975). The assumption behind this gender difference is that girls are more oriented toward interpersonal relationships. Boys may discourage one another from openly disclosing their problems, as part of their masculine, competitive nature (Maccoby, 1995). Boys make themselves vulnerable to being called "wimps" if they can't handle their own problems and insecurities. However, in one recent study, sex differences in initial self-disclosure were not found for African American adolescents (Jones, Costin, & Ricard, 1994).

In one study of adolescent peer networks, the most robust finding was that female students were more integrated into school social networks than males were (Urberg & others, 1995). Girls were also more likely than boys to have a best friend and to be a clique member.

Adolescents also regard loyalty or faithfulness as more critical in friendships than children do (Rotenberg, 1993). When talking about their best friend, adolescents frequently refer to the friend's willingness to stand up for them when around other people. Typical comments are: "Bob will stick up for me in a fight," "Sally won't talk about me behind my back," or "Jennifer wouldn't leave me for somebody else." In these descriptions, adolescents underscore the obligations of a friend in the larger peer group.

In one study of adolescent peer networks in the sixth grade through the twelfth grade, adolescents were more selective in naming friends (Urberg & others, 1995). In the twelfth grade, they made and received fewer friendship choices and had fewer mutual friends. This increased selectivity might be due to increased social cognitive skills that allow older adolescents to make more accurate inferences about who likes them.

Similarity   Another predominant characteristic of friendship is that, throughout the childhood and adolescent years, friends are generally similar—in terms of age, sex,

THROUGH THE EYES OF ADOLESCENTS
We Defined Each Other with Adjectives

"I was funky. Dana was sophisticated. Liz was crazy. We walked to school together, went for bike rides, cut school, got stoned, talked on the phone, smoked cigarettes, slept over, discussed boys and sex, went to church together, and got angry at each other. We defined each other with adjectives and each other's presence. As high school friends, we simultaneously resisted and anticipated adulthood and womanhood.

"What was possible when I was 15 and 16? We still had to tell our parents where we were going! We wanted to do excitedly forbidden activities like going out to dance clubs and drinking whiskey sours. Liz, Dana, and I wanted to do these forbidden things in order to feel: to have intense emotional and sensual experiences that removed us from the suburban sameness we shared with each other and everyone else we knew. We were tired of the repetitive experiences that our town, our siblings, our parents, and our school offered to us. . . .

"The friendship between Dana, Liz, and myself was born out of another emotional need: the need for trust. The three of us had reached a point in our lives when we realized how unstable relationships can be, and we all craved safety and acceptance. Friendships all around us were often uncertain. We wanted and needed to be able to like and trust each other."

One of the most important aspects of friendship is being able to share private thoughts. *What are some other characteristics of adolescent friendships?*

ethnicity, and many other factors (Luo, Fang, & Aro, 1995). Friends often have similar attitudes toward school, similar educational aspirations, and closely aligned achievement orientations. Friends like the same music, wear the same kind of clothes, and prefer the same leisure activities (Berndt, 1982). If friends have different attitudes about school, one of them may want to play basketball or go shopping rather than do homework. If one friend insists on completing homework while the other insists on playing basketball, the conflict may weaken the friendship, and the two may drift apart.

In one recent study of young adolescents, students usually selected friends who had achievement levels similar to their own (Ryan, 2001). Of course, not all adolescents associate with friends whose characteristics are all similar to their own, and this can make a difference in attitudes toward school. For example, in the study just mentioned, students who "hung out" with a group of friends who disliked school showed a greater decrease in their own enjoyment of school over the course of the school year compared to students who spent time with friends who liked school (Ryan, 2001).

Mixed-Age Friendships

Although most adolescents develop friendships with individuals who are close to their own age, some adolescents become best friends with younger or older individuals. A common fear, especially among parents, is that adolescents who have older friends will be encouraged to engage in delinquent behavior or early sexual behavior. Researchers have found that adolescents who interact with older youths do engage in these behaviors more frequently, but it is not known whether the older youths guide younger adolescents toward deviant behavior or whether the younger adolescents were already prone to deviant behavior before they developed the friendship with the older youths (Billy, Rodgers, & Udry, 1984).

In a longitudinal study of eighth-grade girls, early-maturing girls developed friendships with girls who were chronologically older but biologically similar to them (Magnusson, 1988). Because of their associations with older friends, the early-maturing girls were more likely than their peers to engage in a number of deviant behaviors, such as being truant from school, getting drunk, and stealing. Also, as adults (26 years of age), the early-maturing girls were more likely to have had a child and were less likely to be vocationally and educationally oriented than their later-maturing counterparts. Thus, parents do seem to have reason to be concerned when their adolescents become close friends with individuals who are considerably older than they are.

At this point, we have discussed many ideas about friendship. A review of these ideas is presented in summary table 6.2. Next, we will explore another aspect of the adolescent's social world—groups.

Since the last review we have studied many aspects of friendship in adolescence. This review should help you to reach your learning goals related to this topic.

☐ For Your Review

Learning Goal 3 **Know about friendship in adolescence**	• The functions of friendship include companionship, stimulation, physical support, ego support, social comparison, and intimacy/affection. • Sullivan argued that there is a dramatic increase in the psychological importance and intimacy of close friends in adolescence. Research supports this view. • Intimacy and similarity are two of the most important characteristics of friendships. • Children and adolescents who become close friends with older individuals engage in more deviant behaviors than their counterparts with same-age friends. Early-maturing girls are more likely than late-maturing girls to have older friends, which can contribute to problem behaviors.

So far in this chapter we have explored the nature of peer relations and friendship. Next, we will focus on adolescent groups.

Adolescent Groups

During your adolescent years, you probably were a member of both formal and informal groups. Examples of formal groups include the basketball team or drill team, the Girl Scouts or Boy Scouts, the student council, and so on. A more informal group could be a group of peers, such as a clique. Our study of adolescent groups focuses on the functions of groups and how groups are formed, differences between children groups and adolescent groups, cultural variations, cliques, and youth organizations.

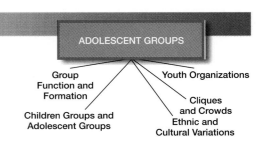

Group Function and Formation

Why does an adolescent join a study group? A church? An athletic team? A clique? Groups satisfy adolescents' personal needs, reward them, provide information, raise their self-esteem, and give them an identity. Adolescents might join a group because they think that group membership will be enjoyable and exciting and satisfy their need for affiliation and companionship. They might join a group because they will have the opportunity to receive rewards, either material or psychological. For example, an adolescent may reap prestige and recognition from membership on the school's student council. Groups also are an important source of information. As adolescents sit in a study group, they learn effective study strategies and valuable information about how

norms
Rules that apply to all members of a group.

roles
Certain positions in a group that are governed by rules and expectations. Roles define how adolescents should behave in those positions.

to take tests. The groups in which adolescents are members—their family, their school, a club, a team—often make them feel good, raise their self-esteem, and provide them with an identity.

Any group to which adolescents belong has two things in common with all other groups: norms and roles. **Norms** *are rules that apply to all members of a group.* An honor society, for example, might require all members to have a 3.5 grade point average. A school might require its male students to have hair that does not go below the collar of their shirt. A football team might require its members to work on weight lifting in the off-season. **Roles** *are certain positions in a group that are governed by rules and expectations. Roles define how adolescents should behave in those positions.* In a family, parents have certain roles, siblings have other roles, and grandparents have still other roles. On a basketball team, many different roles must be filled: center, forward, guard, rebounder, defensive specialist, and so on.

Children Groups and Adolescent Groups

Children groups differ from adolescent groups in several important ways. The members of children groups often are friends or neighborhood acquaintances, and the groups usually are not as formalized as many adolescent groups. During the adolescent years, groups tend to include a broader array of members; in other words, adolescents other than friends or neighborhood acquaintances often are members of adolescent groups. Try to recall the student council, honor society, or football team at your junior high school. If you were a member of any of these organizations, you probably remember that they were made up of many individuals you had not met before and that they were a more heterogeneous group than your childhood peer groups. Rules and regulations were probably well defined, and captains or leaders were formally elected or appointed in the adolescent groups.

A well-known observational study by Dexter Dunphy (1963) indicates that opposite-sex participation in groups increases during adolescence. In late childhood, boys and girls participate in small, same-sex groups. As they move into the early adolescent years, the same-sex groups begin to interact with each other. Gradually, the leaders and high-status members form further groups based on mixed-sex relationships. Eventually, the newly created mixed-sex groups replace the same-sex groups. The mixed-sex groups interact with each other in large crowd activities, too—at dances and athletic events, for example. In late adolescence, the crowd begins to dissolve as couples develop more serious relationships and make long-range plans that may include engagement and marriage. A summary of Dunphy's ideas is presented in figure 6.4 on page 203.

Ethnic and Cultural Variations

Whether adolescents grow up as part of the peer culture in a ghetto or in a middle-socioeconomic-status (SES) suburban area influences the nature of the groups to which they belong. For example, in a comparison of middle- and lower-SES adolescent groups, lower-SES adolescents displayed more aggression toward the low-status members of the group but showed less aggression toward the president of the class or group than their middle-SES counterparts (Maas, 1954).

In many schools, peer groups are strongly segregated according to socioeconomic status and ethnicity. In schools with large numbers of middle- and lower-SES students, middle-SES students often assume the leadership roles in formal organizations, such as student council, the honor society, fraternity-sorority groups, and so on. Athletic teams are one type of adolescent group in which African American adolescents and adolescents from low-income families have been able to gain parity or even surpass adolescents from middle- and upper-SES families in achieving status.

Ethnic minority adolescents, especially immigrants, may rely on peer groups more than White adolescents (Spencer & Dornbusch, 1990). This is especially true when ethnic minority adolescents' parents have not been very successful in their careers. The desire to be accepted by the peer group is especially strong among refugee adolescents,

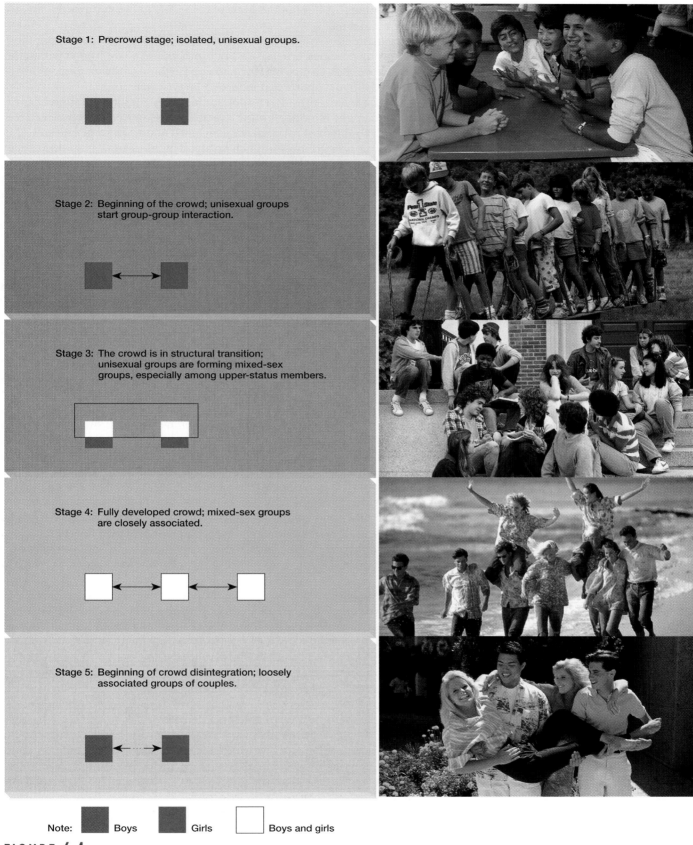

Note: ■ Boys   ■ Girls   □ Boys and girls

FIGURE 6.4
Dunphy's Progression of Peer Group Relations in Adolescence

whose greatest threat is not the stress of belonging to two cultures but the stress of belonging to none.

For many ethnic minority youth, especially immigrants, peers from their own ethnic group provide a crucial sense of brotherhood or sisterhood within the majority culture. Peer groups may form to oppose those of the majority group and to provide adaptive supports that reduce feelings of isolation.

So far, we have considered adolescents' peer relations in different socioeconomic and ethnic minority groups. Are there also some cultures in which the peer group plays a different role than in the United States? In some cultures, children are placed in peer groups for much greater lengths of time at an earlier age than they are in the United States. For example, in the Murian culture of eastern India, both male and female children live in a dormitory from the age of 6 until they get married (Barnouw, 1975). The dormitory is a religious haven where members are devoted to work and spiritual harmony. Children work for their parents, and the parents arrange the children's marriages. When the children wed, they must leave the dormitory.

Adolescent cliques have been mentioned on several occasions in this chapter. For example, in the discussion of Dunphy's work, the importance of heterosexual relationships in the evolution of adolescent cliques was noted. Let's now examine adolescent cliques in more detail.

Cliques and Crowds

Cliques and crowds assume more important roles in the lives of adolescents than children.

cliques
Small groups that range from two to about twelve individuals and average about five to six individuals.

Cliques   **Cliques** *are small groups that range from two to about twelve individuals and average about five to six individuals.* These clique members usually are of the same sex and are similar in age.

Cliques can form because adolescents engage in similar activities, such as being in a club together or on a sports team (Ennet & Bauman, 1996). Some cliques also form because of friendship. Several adolescents may form a clique because they have spent time with each other and enjoy each other's company. Not necessarily friends before forming the clique, they often develop a friendship if they stay in the clique.

What do adolescents do in cliques? They share ideas, hang out together, and often develop an in-group identity in which they believe their clique is better than other cliques.

crowds
A larger group structure than cliques. Adolescents are usually members of a crowd based on reputation and may or may not spend much time together.

Crowds   **Crowds** *are a larger group structure than cliques. Adolescents are usually members of a crowd based on reputation and may or may not spend much time together.* Crowds are less personal than cliques. Many crowds are defined by the activities adolescents engage in (such as "jocks" who are good at sports or "druggies" who take drugs), although some crowds are defined more by the nature of their interaction. For example, in Dexter Dunphy's developmental sequence that was described earlier in the chapter, the crowds were interactional-based crowds, not reputation-based crowds.

In one study, Bradford Brown and Jane Lohr (1987) examined the self-esteem of 221 seventh- through twelfth-graders. The adolescents were either associated with one of the five major school crowds or were relatively unknown by classmates and not associated with any school crowd. Crowds included the following: jocks (athletically oriented), populars (well-known students who lead social activities), normals (middle-of-the-road students who make up the masses), druggies/toughs (known for illicit drug use or other delinquent activities), and nobodies (low in social skills or intellectual abilities). The self-esteem of the jocks and the populars was highest, that of the nobodies was lowest. But one group of adolescents not in a crowd had self-esteem equivalent to the jocks and the populars. This group was the independents, who indicated that crowd membership was not important to them. Keep in mind that these data are correlational—self-esteem could increase an adolescent's probability of becoming a crowd member just as clique membership could increase the adolescent's self-esteem.

One of the main factors that distinguish crowds is group norms regarding school orientation (Brown & Theobald, 1998). In one study of adolescents in nine Midwestern and West Coast high schools, grade-point differences of almost two full letter grades were found between the highest achievers ("brains") and lowest achievers ("druggies") (Brown & others, 1993). The norms of particular crowds can place adolescents on a trajectory for school failure. Members of deviantly oriented crowds are more likely to drop out of school early (Cairns & Cairns, 1994).

Crowd membership is also associated with drug use and sexual behavior. In one study, five adolescent crowds were identified: jocks (athletes), brains (students who enjoy academics), burnouts (adolescents who get into trouble), populars (social, student leaders), nonconformists (adolescents who go against the norm), as well as a none/average group (Prinstein, Fetter, & La Greca, 1996). Burnouts and nonconformists were the most likely to smoke cigarettes, drink alcohol, and use marijuana; brains were the least likely. Jocks were the most sexually active clique.

Bradford Brown made these conclusions about adolescent crowds (Brown, Dolcini, & Leventhal, 1995; Brown, Mory, & Kinney, 1994):

1. *The influence of crowds is not entirely negative.* Crowds emerge in adolescence to provide youth with provisional identities they can adopt, at least temporarily, on their way to a more integrated identity later in development. In Brown's research with 1,000 Midwestern middle school and high school students, peer pressure was strongest regarding getting good grades, finishing high school, and spending time with friends. The students reported little pressure to engage in drinking, drug use, sexual intercourse, and other potentially health-compromising behaviors.

2. *The influence of crowds is not uniform for all adolescents.* Crowds vary not only in terms of dress, grooming styles, musical tastes, and hangouts at school, but also in terms of more-consequential activities such as effort in school or deviant behavior (Youniss, McLellan, & Strouse, 1994). Thus, whether crowds are "friend" or "foe" depends largely on the particular crowd with which the adolescent is associated. Furthermore, in Brown's research, one-third of the student body floated among several crowds; some students—isolates—were totally detached from crowds.

3. *Developmental changes occur in crowds.* In Brown's research, barriers against moving from one crowd to another were much stronger in the ninth grade than in the twelfth grade. It was easier for high school seniors than for freshmen to shift affiliations among crowds or forge friendships across crowd lines.

Youth Programs
Youth-Serving Organizations
Boys and Girls Clubs
http://www.mhhe.com/santrocka9

Youth Organizations

Youth organizations can have an important influence on the adolescent's development (Holditch & others, 2002; Roth & others, 1998; Snider & Miller, 1993). More than 400 national youth organizations currently operate in the United States (Erickson, 1996). The organizations include career groups, such as Junior Achievement; groups aimed at building character, such as Girl Scouts and Boy Scouts; political groups, such as Young Republicans and Young Democrats; and ethnic groups, such as Indian Youth of America (Price & others, 1990). They serve approximately 30 million young people each year. The largest youth organization is 4-H, with nearly 5 million participants. The smallest are ASPIRA, a Latino youth organization that provides intensive educational enrichment programs for about

THROUGH THE EYES OF ADOLESCENTS

King of the Geeks

"The place to meet girls in the eighth grade was school. At the beginning of the eighth grade, having come from a smaller public school, a feeder school, into a sea of strange faces, I would characterize my social situation as 'King of the Geeks.' I was the coolest of the geeks (smart, weird, nonathletic types who had not entered the ranks of the popular). I sat at the far end of the geek table in the cafeteria, closest to the 'cool' tables, in a very hierarchical set-up. . . .

"Appearances were very important in creating an image. After a month or so of dressing cool, I found myself being eyed by a girl from the cool group. She was very nice, an intelligent talkative girl who also gave me a chance to enter the popular crowd."

These adolescents are participating in Girls Club and Boys Club activities. *What effects do youth organizations have on adolescents?*

I didn't belong as a kid, and that always bothered me. If only I'd known that one day my differentness would be an asset, then my early life would have been much easier.

—Bette Midler
Contemporary American Actress

13,000 adolescents each year, and WAVE, a dropout-prevention program that serves about 8,000 adolescents each year.

Adolescents who join such groups are more likely to participate in community activities in adulthood and have higher self-esteem, are better educated, and come from families with higher incomes than their counterparts who do not participate in youth groups (Erickson, 1982). Participation in youth groups can help adolescents practice the interpersonal and organizational skills that are important for success in adult roles.

The Search Institute (1995) conducted a study that sheds light on both the potential for and barriers to participation in youth programs. The study focused on Minneapolis, which faces many of the same challenges regarding youth as other cities. The after-school hours represent an important time frame in which adolescents could form positive relationships with adults and peers. Yet this study found that more than 50 percent of the youth said they don't participate in any type of youth program in a typical week. More than 40 percent reported no participation in youth programs during the summer months.

About 350 youth programs were identified in Minneapolis, about one program for every 87 adolescents. However, about one-half of the youth and their parents agree that there are not enough youth programs. Parents with the lowest incomes were the least satisfied with program availability.

Some of the reasons given by middle school adolescents for not participating in youth programs were a lack of interest in available activities, a lack of transportation, and lack of awareness about what is available. Here are several adolescents' comments about why they don't participate in youth programs:

"Some things I don't like, like sports stuff because I'm not good at it."
"Nobody is going to take a bus across town just to get to a program."
"I have enough time but my parents don't. I need them to take me there."

Parents see similar barriers, especially transportation and costs.

Adolescents express an interest in activities that would foster their peer relations. They want more informal programs or places where their time is not highly structured—places where they can drop by, hang out, and spontaneously choose what they want to do. However, many adolescents also reported having an interest in participating more in structured activities such as taking lessons, playing sports, dances, youth-led programs, and youth service.

To increase the participation of low-income and ethnic minority adolescents in youth groups, Girls Clubs and Boys Clubs are being established in locations where young adolescents are at high risk for dropping out of school, becoming delinquents, and developing substance-abuse problems. The locations include 15 housing projects in different American cities. The club programs are designed to provide individual, small-group, and drop-in supportive services that enhance educational and personal development. Preliminary results suggest that the Boys and Girls Clubs help to reduce vandalism, drug abuse, and delinquency (Boys and Girls Clubs of America, 1989).

One example of how participation in a youth organization can influence adolescent development focuses on observations of Girl Scouts engaged in their campaign to sell cookies (Rogoff & others, 1995). Both alone and in groups, the Girl Scouts developed plans for their sales and as they gained experience modified the plans. Sales pitches became more refined and they improved their ability to track orders. Initially, tracking sales was controlled by their mothers and eventually the girls learned how to do this themselves.

According to Reed Larson (2000), such structured voluntary youth activities as selling Girl Scout cookies are especially well-suited for the development of initiative. Another study of structured youth activities that led to increased initiative involves adolescents in low-income areas who began participating in art and drama groups, sports teams, Boys and Girls Clubs, YMCA gang intervention programs, and other community organizations (Heath, 1997, 1999; Heath & McLaughlin, 1993). When the adolescents first joined these organizations, they seemed bored. Within three to four weeks, though, they reported greater confidence in their ability to affect their world and adjusted their behavior in pursuit of a goal.

In sum, youth activities and organizations provide excellent developmental contexts in which to provide adolescents opportunities to develop many positive qualities. Participation in these contexts can help to increase achievement and decrease delinquency (Dworkin & others, 2001; Hughes, Alfano, & Harkness, 2002; Larson, 2000).

Since the last review we have studied many aspects of adolescent groups. This review should help you to reach your learning goals related to this topic.

☐ FOR YOUR REVIEW

Learning Goal 4
Evaluate adolescent groups

- Groups satisfy adolescents' personal needs, reward them, provide information, can raise their self-esteem, and contribute to their identity. Norms are the rules that apply to all members of a group. Roles are rules and expectations that govern certain positions in the group.
- Children groups are less formal, less heterogeneous, and less mixed-sex than adolescent groups. Dunphy's study found that adolescent group development proceeds through five stages.
- More aggression is directed at low-status members in lower-SES groups. In many schools, peer groups are segregated according to ethnic group and socioeconomic status. Ethnic minority adolescents often have two sets of peers—one at school, one in the community. A special concern is peer support for ethnic minority achievement. Ethnic minority adolescents, especially immigrants, might turn to the peer group more than non-Latino White adolescents do.
- In some cultures, children are placed in peer groups for greater lengths of time than in the United States.

(continued on p. 208)

- Cliques are small groups that range from two to about twelve individuals and average about five to six individuals. Crowds are a larger group structure than cliques. Adolescents are members of crowds usually based on reputation and may or may not spend much time together.
- Youth organizations can have important influences on adolescent development. More than 400 national youth organizations currently exist in the United States. Boys' and Girls' Clubs are examples of youth organizations designed to increase membership in youth organizations in low-income neighborhoods. Participation in youth organizations may increase achievement and decrease delinquency. Youth activities and organizations also may provide opportunities for adolescents to develop initiative.

So far in this chapter we have examined the nature of adolescent peer relations, friendships, and groups. Next, we will explore the dating and romantic relationships.

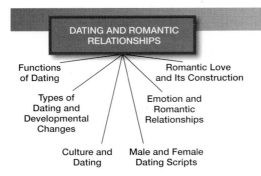

DATING AND ROMANTIC RELATIONSHIPS

Functions of Dating

Romantic Love and Its Construction

Types of Dating and Developmental Changes

Emotion and Romantic Relationships

Culture and Dating

Male and Female Dating Scripts

DATING AND ROMANTIC RELATIONSHIPS

Though many adolescent boys and girls have social interchanges through formal and informal peer groups, it is through dating that more serious contacts between the sexes occur (Furman, Brown, & Feiring, 1999; ; Furman & Shaffer, 2002; Shulman & Collins, 1998). Young male adolescents spend many agonizing moments worrying about whether they should call a certain girl and ask her out: "Will she turn me down?" "What if she says yes, what do I say next?" "How am I going to get her to the dance? I don't want my mother to take us!" "I want to kiss her, but what if she pushes me away?" "How can I get to be alone with her?" And, on the other side of the coin, young adolescent girls wonder: "What if no one asks me to the dance?" "What do I do if he tries to kiss me?" Or, "I really don't want to go with him. Maybe I should wait two more days and see if Bill will call me."

In this discussion, we will focus on heterosexual dating and romantic relationships. But many adolescents are gay, lesbian, or bisexual. Although these youth experience additional and somewhat different pressures, they also experience the same sorts of fears and expectations about dating as heterosexual adolescents feel.

Exploring Dating
http://www.mhhe.com/santrocka9

Functions of Dating

Dating is a relatively recent phenomenon. It wasn't until the 1920s that dating as we know it became a reality, and even then, its primary role was for the purpose of selecting and winning a mate. Prior to this period, mate selection was the sole purpose of dating, and "dates" were carefully monitored by parents, who completely controlled the nature of any heterosexual companionship. Often, parents bargained with each other about the merits of their adolescents as potential marriage partners and even chose mates for their children. In recent times, of course, adolescents have gained much more control over the dating process and who they go out with. Furthermore, dating has evolved into something more than just courtship for marriage.

Dating today can serve at least eight functions (Paul & White, 1990):

1. Dating can be a form of recreation. Adolescents who date seem to have fun and see dating as a source of enjoyment and recreation.
2. Dating is a source of status and achievement. Part of the social comparison process in adolescence involves evaluating the status of the people one dates: are they the best looking, the most popular, and so forth.
3. Dating is part of the socialization process in adolescence: It helps the adolescent to learn how to get along with others and assists in learning manners and sociable behavior.
4. Dating involves learning about intimacy and serves as an opportunity to establish a unique, meaningful relationship with a person of the opposite sex.

In the first half of the twentieth century, dating served mainly as a courtship for marriage.

Today the functions of dating include courtship but also many others. *What are some of these other functions of dating?*

5. Dating can be a context for sexual experimentation and exploration.
6. Dating can provide companionship through interaction and shared activities in an opposite-sex relationship.
7. Dating experiences contribute to identity formation and development; dating helps adolescents to clarify their identity and to separate from their families of origin.
8. Dating can be a means of mate sorting and selection, thereby retaining its original courtship function.

Types of Dating and Developmental Changes

In their early romantic relationships, many adolescents are not motivated to fulfill attachment or even sexual needs. Rather, early romantic relationships serve as a context for adolescents to explore how attractive they are, how they should romantically interact with someone, and how all of this looks to the peer group (Brown, in press). Only after adolescents acquire some basic competencies in interacting with romantic partners does the fulfillment of attachment and sexual needs become a central function of these relationships (Furman & Wehner, 1998).

In their early exploration of romantic relationships, today's adolescents often find comfort in numbers and begin hanging out together in mixed-sex groups. Sometimes they just hang out at someone's house or get organized enough to get someone to drive them to a mall or a movie (Peterson, 1997).

Yet another form of dating recently has been added. *Cyberdating* is dating over the Internet (Thomas, 1998). One 10-year-old girl posted this ad on the net:

> Hi! I'm looking for a Cyber Boyfriend! I'm 10. I have brown hair and brown eyes. I love swimming, playing basketball, and think kittens are adorable!!!

THROUGH THE EYES OF ADOLESCENTS

They Were Thinking About Having Sex with Girls from Budweiser Ads

"During ninth and tenth grade, I constantly fell in love with older boys I knew only slightly and shy boys my own age I knew well. I never went out on any dates with these boys; I just thought about them a lot. I knew some older guys from school government and committees. They were nice to me. Some flirted quite a bit with me. But I never went on dates with the older guys because they never asked me out. They usually had girlfriends who were seniors. The shy boys my own age were not quite ready for dating. While I was thinking about true love and romantic walks through the park, they were thinking about videogames, rock music, and having sex with girls from Budweiser ads. I never quite felt much like 'dating material.' I was tall and liked school and talked a lot in class. I wore weird clothes and wrote articles for the school newspaper and about local political candidates. Sometimes bizarre boys who wanted to be comic strip heroes or felt as stifled as I did by our relatively small town would confess their true love for me. These incidents never led to sexual relationships with these boys. I would tell them I knew how they felt, seeing that I had a few unfruitful crushes of my own. I never liked any of the boys who liked me."

Teen Chat
http://www.mhhe.com/santrocka9

Cyberdating is especially becoming popular among middle school students. By the time they reach high school and are able to drive, dating usually has evolved into a more traditional real-life venture. Cyberdating can especially be a dangerous experience for adolescents unaware of the predators that may be present.

Most girls in the United States begin dating at the age of 14, while most boys begin sometime between the ages of 14 and 15 (Sorenson, 1973). Most adolescents have their first date sometime between the ages of 12 and 16. Fewer than 10 percent have a first date before the age of 10, and by the age of 16, more than 90 percent have had at least one date. More than 50 percent of the tenth-, eleventh-, and twelfth-graders in one study averaged one or more dates per week (Dickinson, 1975). About 15 percent of these high school students dated less than once per month, and about three out of every four students had "gone with" someone at least once. A special concern is early dating and "going with" someone, which is associated with adolescent pregnancy and problems at home and school (Degirmencioglu, Saltz, & Ager, 1995; Downey & Bonica, 1997; Neeman, Hubbard, & Masten, 1995).

As shown in figure 6.5, announcing that "I like someone" occurred earliest—by the sixth grade almost 40 percent had done this. However, it was not until the tenth grade that 50 percent of adolescents had a sustained romantic relationship that lasted two months or more. By their senior year, 25 percent still had not engaged in this type of sustained romantic relationship. Also in this study, girls' early romantic involvement was linked to their lower grades, less active participation in class discussions, and school problems.

In one study of 15-year-olds' romantic relationships, although most said that they had had a girlfriend or boyfriend in the past three years, most were not currently dating (Feiring, 1996). Most of the 15-year-olds had had short-term dating relationships, averaging four months. Less than 10 percent had had a dating relationship that lasted for a year or longer. Although the length of their dating relationships was relatively brief, contact was very frequent. The adolescents reported seeing each other in person and talking on the phone almost daily. Dating occurred more in a group than in a couples-alone context. What did adolescents say they did when they were on a date? The most frequent dating activities were going to a movie, dinner, hanging out at a mall or school, parties, and visiting each others' homes. In another study, the average length of a dating relationship for tenth-graders was five to six months, increasing to more than eight months for twelfth-graders (Dowdy & Kliewer, 1996). In this study, dating-related conflict between adolescents and parents was less frequent for twelfth-graders than for tenth-graders.

One recent study had fifth- to eighth-grade adolescents carry electronic pagers for one week and complete self-report forms in response to signals sent to them at random times (Richards & others, 1998). Four years later the participants underwent the same procedure. Time with, and thoughts about, the opposite sex occupied more of the adolescents' week in high school than in fifth and sixth grades. Fifth- and sixth-grade girls spent approximately one hour a week in the presence of a boy, and their male counterparts spent even less time in the presence of a girl. Although more time was spent thinking about an individual of the opposite sex, it still added up to less than two hours a week for girls, and less than one hour per week for boys, in fifth and sixth grades. By eleventh and twelfth grade, girls were spending about 10 hours a week with a boy, boys about half that time with a girl. Frequency of thoughts had increased as well. The high school girls spent about eight hours a week thinking about a boy, the high school boys about five or six hours thinking about a girl.

In sum, during early adolescence, individuals spent more time thinking about the opposite sex than they actually spent with them. In seventh and eighth grade, they spent four to six hours thinking about them but only about one hour actually with them. By eleventh and

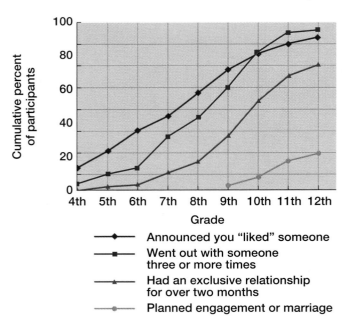

FIGURE 6.5

Age Onset of Romantic Activity

twelfth grade, this had shifted to more time spent in their actual presence than thinking about them.

Culture and Dating

The sociocultural context exerts a powerful influence on adolescent dating patterns and on mate selection (Coates, 1999; Xiaohe & Whyte, 1990). Values and religious beliefs of people in various cultures often dictate the age at which dating begins, how much freedom in dating is allowed, whether dates must be chaperoned by adults or parents, and the roles of males and females in dating. For example, Latino and Asian American cultures have more conservative standards regarding adolescent dating than the Anglo-American culture. Dating can be a source of cultural conflict for many immigrants and their families who have come from cultures in which dating begins at a late age, little freedom in dating is allowed, dates are chaperoned, and adolescent girls' dating is especially restricted.

In one recent study, Latino young adults living in the Midwestern region of the United States reflected on their socialization for dating and sexuality (Raffaelli & Ontai, in press). Because U.S. style dating was viewed as a violation of traditional courtship styles by most of their parents, the parents placed strict boundaries on their romantic involvement. As a result many of the Latinos described their adolescent dating experiences as filled with tension and conflict. The average age at which the girls began dating was 15.7 years with early dating experiences usually occurring without parental knowledge or permission. Over half of the girls engaged in "sneak dating."

Male and Female Dating Scripts

Do male and female adolescents bring different motivations to the dating experience? Candice Feiring (1996) found that they did. Fifteen-year-old girls were more likely to describe romance in terms of interpersonal qualities, boys in terms of physical attraction. For young adolescents, the affiliative qualities of companionship, intimacy, and support were frequently mentioned as positive dimensions of romantic relationships, but love and security were not. Also, the young adolescents described physical attraction more in terms of being cute, pretty, or handsome than in terms of sexuality (such as being a good kisser). Possibly the failure to discuss sexual interests was due to the adolescents' discomfort in talking about such personal feelings with an unfamiliar adult.

Dating scripts *are the cognitive models that adolescents and adults use to guide and evaluate dating interactions.* In one recent study, first dates were highly scripted along gender lines (Rose & Frieze, 1993). Males followed a proactive dating script, females a reactive one. The male's script involved initiating the date (asking for and planning it), controlling the public domain (driving and opening doors), and initiating sexual interaction (making physical contact, making out, and kissing). The female's script focused on the private domain (concern about appearance, enjoying the date), participating in the structure of the date provided by the male (being picked up, having doors opened), and responding to his sexual gestures. These gender differences give males more power in the initial stage of a relationship.

dating scripts
The cognitive models that adolescents and adults use to guide and evaluate dating interactions.

Emotion and Romantic Relationships

Romantic emotions can envelop adolescents' lives (Harper, Welsh, & Woody, 2002; Larson, Clore, & Wood, 1999; Larson & Richards, 1999). A 14-year-old reports feeling in love and can't think about anything else. A 15-year-old is distressed that "everyone else has a boyfriend but me." As we just saw, adolescents spend a lot of time thinking about romantic involvement. Some of this thought can involve positive emotions of compassion and joy, but it also can include negative emotions such as worry, disappointment, and jealousy.

Romantic relationships often are involved in an adolescent's emotional experiences. In one study of ninth- to twelfth-graders, girls gave real and fantasized heterosexual

Types of Love
http://www.mhhe.com/santrocka9

*L*ove is a canvas furnished by nature and embroidered by imagination.
—Voltaire
French Philosopher, 18th Century

Love
Exploring Close Relationships
http://www.mhhe.com/santrocka9

romantic love
Also called passionate love or eros, this love has strong sexual and infatuation components, and it often predominates in the early part of a love relationship.

relationships as the explanation for more than one-third of their strong emotions, and boys gave this reason for 25 percent of their strong emotions (Wilson-Shockley, 1995). Strong emotions were attached far less to school (13 percent), family (9 percent), and same-sex peer relations (8 percent). The majority of the emotions were reported as positive, but a substantial minority (42 percent), were reported as negative, including feelings of anxiety, anger, jealousy, and depression.

Adolescents who have a boyfriend or girlfriend reported wider daily emotional swings than their counterparts who did not (Richards & Larson, 1990). In a period of three days, one eleventh-grade girl went from feeling "happy because I'm with Dan," to upset because they had a "huge fight" and "he won't listen to me and keeps hanging up on me," to feeling "suicidal because of the fight," to feeling "happy because everything between me and Dan is fine."

In one recent study of more than 8,000 adolescents, those in love had a higher risk for depression than their counterparts who did not get romantically involved (Joyner & Udry, 2000). Young adolescent girls who were in love were especially at risk for depression.

Romantic Love and Its Construction

Romantic love *is also called passionate love or eros; it has strong sexual and infatuation components, and it often predominates in the early part of a love relationship.* The fires of passion burn hot in romantic love. It is the type of love Juliet had in mind when she cried, "O Romeo, Romeo, wherefore art thou Romeo?" It is the type of love portrayed in new songs that hit the charts virtually every week.

Romantic love characterizes most adolescent love, and romantic love is also extremely important among college students. In one investigation, unattached college males and females were asked to identify their closest relationship (Berscheid, Snyder, & Omoto, 1989). More than half named a romantic partner, rather than a parent, sibling, or friend.

How is emotion involved in adolescent romantic relationships?

Another type of love is **affectionate love,** *also called companionate love, which occurs when individuals desire to have another person near and have a deep, caring affection for that person.* There is a strong belief that affectionate love is more characteristic of adult love than adolescent love and that the early stages of love have more romantic ingredients than the later stages.

Similarity, physical attractiveness, and sexuality are important ingredients of dating relationships. So is intimacy, which is discussed in greater detail in chapter 9. But to fully understand dating relationships in adolescence, we need to know how experiences with family members and peers contribute to the way adolescents construct their dating relationships, as first discussed in chapter 5 with regard to the developmental construction view of relationships (Day & others, 2001) ◄IIII P. 150.

In the continuity version of the developmental construction view, relationships with parents are carried forward to influence the construction of other relationships, such as dating (Fangs & Bryant, 2000) ◄IIII P. 150. Thus, adolescents' relationships with opposite-sex parents, as well as same-sex parents, contribute to adolescents' dating. For example, the adolescent male whose mother has been nurturant but not smothering probably feels that relationships with females will be rewarding. By contrast, the adolescent male whose mother has been cold and unloving toward him likely feels that relationships with females will be unrewarding.

In chapter 5, "Families," we saw that attachment history and early child care were precursors to forming positive couple relationships in adolescence (Sroufe, Egeland, & Carson, 1999) ◄IIII P. 150. For example, infants who had an anxious attachment with their caregiver in infancy were less likely to develop positive couple relationships in adolescence than were their securely attached counterparts. It might be that adolescents with a history of secure attachment are better able to control their emotions and more comfortable self-disclosing romantic relationships.

Wyndol Furman and Elizabeth Wehner (1998) discussed how specific insecure attachment styles might be related to adolescents' romantic relationships. Adolescents with a secure attachment to parents are likely to approach romantic relationships expecting closeness, warmth, and intimacy. Thus, they are likely to feel comfortable developing close, intimate romantic relationships. Adolescents with a dismissing/avoidant attachment to parents are likely to expect romantic partners to be unresponsive and unavailable. Thus, they might tend to behave in ways that distance themselves from romantic relationships. Adolescents with a preoccupied/ambivalent attachment to parents are likely to be disappointed and frustrated with intimacy and closeness in romantic relationships.

According to Peter Blos (1962, 1989), at the beginning of adolescence, boys and girls try to separate themselves from the opposite-sex parent as a love object. As adolescents separate themselves, they often are self-centered. Blos believes that this narcissism gives adolescents a sense of strength. Especially in early adolescence, this narcissistic self-orientation is likely to produce self-serving, highly idealized, and superficial dating relationships.

Adolescents' observations of their parents' marital relationship also contribute to their own construction of dating relationships. Consider an adolescent girl from a divorced family who grew up watching her parents fight on many occasions. Her dating relationships may take one of two turns: She may immerse herself in dating

THROUGH THE EYES OF ADOLESCENTS

Where Is He?

Where is he?
I thought I was his bumble
bee
I cried and cried
Like someone just died
My love from him is so strong
Cause I had him for so long
I love him with all my heart
And when I see him he
makes
me tremble in that spot
But where is he?
Please, please tell me
I cannot see
I looked and looked all the
way around
But I saw nothing
And my heart hit the ground
I love him with all my heart
and soul
But the way he left me
Was so, so cold
Please, please tell me
I cannot see
WHERE IS HE?

—Kelly Excellus, Age 13
East Boston, Massachusetts

affectionate love
Also called companionate love, this love occurs when an individual desires to have another person near and has a deep, caring affection for that person.

relationships to insulate herself from the stress she has experienced, or she may become aloof and untrusting with males and not wish to become involved heavily in dating relationships. Even when she does date considerably, she may find it difficult to develop a trusting relationship with males because she has seen promises broken by her parents.

Mavis Hetherington (1972, 1977) found that divorce was associated with a stronger heterosexual orientation of adolescent daughters than was the death of a parent or living in an intact family. Further, the daughters of divorced parents had a more negative opinion of males than did the girls from other family structures. And girls from divorced and widowed families were more likely to marry images of their fathers than were girls from intact families. Hetherington believes that females from intact families likely have had a greater opportunity to work through relationships with their fathers and therefore are more psychologically free to date and marry someone different than their fathers. Parents also are more likely to be involved or interested in their daughters' dating patterns and relationships than their sons'. For example, in one investigation, college females were much more likely than their male counterparts to say that their parents tried to influence whom they dated during adolescence (Knox & Wilson, 1981). They also indicated that it was not unusual for their parents to try to interfere with their dating choices and relationships.

So far we have been discussing the continuity version of the developmental construction view. In contrast, in the discontinuity version peer relations and friendships provide the opportunity to learn modes of relating that are carried over into romantic relationships (Furman & Wehner, 1993, 1999; Sullivan, 1953). Remember that in chapter 5, "Families," we described longitudinal research in which friendship in middle childhood was linked with security in dating, as well as intimacy in dating at age 16 (Collins, Henninghausen, & Sroufe, 1998) ◄▐▐▐ P. 152.

Harry Stack Sullivan (1953) believed that it is through intimate friendships that adolescents learn a mature form of love he referred to as "collaboration." Sullivan felt that it was this collaborative orientation, coupled with sensitivity to the needs of the friend, that forms the basis of satisfying dating and marital relationships. He also pointed out that dating and romantic relationships give rise to new interpersonal issues that youths had not encountered in prior relationships with parents and friends. Not only must teenagers learn tactics for asking partners for dates (and gracefully turning down requests), but they must also learn to integrate sexual desires with psychological intimacy desires. These tactics and integration are not easy tasks and it is not unusual for them to give rise to powerful feelings of frustration, guilt, and insecurity.

In addition to past relationships with parents and friends influencing an adolescent's dating relationships, family members and peers can directly influence dating experiences (Day & others, 2001; Niederjohn, Welsch & Scheussler, 2000; Shulman & Seiffge-Krenke, 2001). For example, sibling relationships influence adolescent dating. In one investigation, siblings were important resources for dating (O'Brien, 1990). In this study, adolescents said that they got more support for dating from siblings than from their mothers. In late adolescence, siblings were viewed as more important advisors and confidants than mothers when concerns about dating were involved. Sometimes, adolescents use siblings to their advantage when dealing with parents. In one study, younger siblings pointed to how their older siblings were given dating privileges that they had been denied (Place, 1975). In this investigation, an adolescent would sometimes side with a sibling when the sibling was having an argument with parents in the hope that the sibling would reciprocate when the adolescent needed dating privileges the parents were denying.

Peer relations are also involved in adolescent dating (Morales & Roberts, 2002). In Dunphy's research, discussed earlier in the chapter, all large peer crowds in adolescence were mixed-sex, and males in these crowds were consistently older than females (Dunphy, 1963). In this research, group leaders also played an important role. Both the leaders of large crowds and smaller cliques were highly involved with the opposite sex. Leaders dated more frequently, were more likely to go steady, and achieved these dating patterns earlier than nonleaders in the cliques. Leaders also were ascribed the task of maintaining a certain level of mixed-sex involvement in the group. Peer leaders functioned as dating confidants and advisors, even putting partners together in the case of "slow learners."

Recent studies by Jennifer Connolly and her colleagues (Connolly, Furman, & Konarksi, 1995, 2000; Connolly & Goldberg, 1999; Connolly & Stevens, 1999) document the role of peers in the emergence of romantic involvement in adolescence. In one study, adolescents who were part of mixed-sex peer groups moved more readily into romantic relationships than their counterparts whose mixed-sex peer groups were more limited (Connolly, Furman, & Konarksi, 2000). In another study, there was a similar degree of romantic involvement described by adolescents and their friends (Connolly & Stevens, 1999).

Since the last review we have studied many aspects of dating and romantic relationships. This review should help you to reach your learning goals related to this topic.

☐ FOR YOUR REVIEW

Learning Goal 6
Describe dating in adolescence

- Dating can be a form of recreation, a source of social status and achievement, an aspect of socialization, a context for learning about intimacy and sexual experimentation, a source of companionship, and a means of mate sorting.
- Younger adolescents often begin to hang out together in mixed-sex groups. Hooking up, seeing each other, and going out represent different forms of commitment. Recently, cyberdating has occurred. A special concern is early dating, which is associated with a number of problems. In early adolescence, individuals spend more time thinking about the opposite sex than actually being with them, but this often reverses in the high school years.
- Culture can exert a powerful influence on dating. Many adolescents from immigrant families face conflicts with their parents about dating.
- Romantic relationships can envelop adolescents' lives. The emotions of romantic relationships are sometimes positive, sometimes negative, and can change very quickly.

Learning Goal 7
Explain romantic love and its construction

- Romantic love, also called passionate love, involves sexuality more than affectionate love. Romantic love is especially prominent among adolescents and traditional-aged college students. Affectionate love is more common in middle and late adulthood, characterizing love that endures over time.
- The developmental construction view emphasizes how relationships with parents, siblings, and peers influence how adolescents construct their romantic relationships.
- Dunphy's study found that group leaders play a role in dating and Connolly's research revealed the importance of peers and friends in adolescent romantic relationships.

In this chapter, we have focused on peers. One context in which adolescents spend considerable time with peers is at school. Next, we will explore the roles of school in adolescent development in greater depth.

CHAPTER MAP

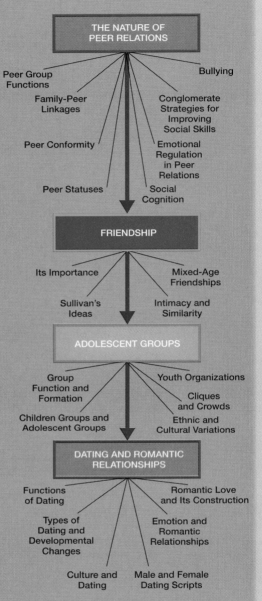

THE NATURE OF PEER RELATIONS

- Peer Group Functions
- Family-Peer Linkages
- Peer Conformity
- Peer Statuses
- Bullying
- Conglomerate Strategies for Improving Social Skills
- Emotional Regulation in Peer Relations
- Social Cognition

FRIENDSHIP

- Its Importance
- Sullivan's Ideas
- Mixed-Age Friendships
- Intimacy and Similarity

ADOLESCENT GROUPS

- Group Function and Formation
- Children Groups and Adolescent Groups
- Youth Organizations
- Cliques and Crowds
- Ethnic and Cultural Variations

DATING AND ROMANTIC RELATIONSHIPS

- Functions of Dating
- Types of Dating and Developmental Changes
- Culture and Dating
- Romantic Love and Its Construction
- Emotion and Romantic Relationships
- Male and Female Dating Scripts

REACH YOUR LEARNING GOALS

At the beginning of the chapter, we stated seven learning goals and encouraged you to review material related to these goals at four points in the chapter. This is a good time to return to these reviews and use them to guide your study and help you to reach your learning goals.

Page 196

Learning Goal 1   Discuss peer group functions and family-peer linkages

Learning Goal 2   Describe peer conformity, peer statuses, and other dimensions of peer relations

Page 201

Learning Goal 3   Know about friendship in adolescence

Page 207

Learning Goal 4   Evaluate adolescent groups

Learning Goal 5   Discuss cliques, crowds, and youth organizations

Page 215

Learning Goal 6   Describe dating in adolescence

Learning Goal 7   Explain romantic love and its construction

KEY TERMS

peers 186
conformity 189
nonconformity 190
anticonformity 190
popular children 191
neglected children 191
rejected children 191
controversial children 191
conglomerate strategies 194

intimacy in friendship 199
norms 202
roles 202
cliques 204
crowds 204
dating scripts 211
romantic love 212
affectionate love 213

KEY PEOPLE

Thomas Berndt 190
John Coie 192
Kenneth Dodge 193
Harry Stack Sullivan 197
Willard Hartup 198
Dexter Dunphy 202

Bradford Brown 204
Reed Larson 207
Candice Feiring 211
Wyndol Furman 213
Jennifer Connolly 215

RESOURCES FOR IMPROVING THE LIVES OF ADOLESCENTS

Boys and Girls Clubs of America

771 First Avenue
New York, NY 10017
213–351–5900

The Boys and Girls Clubs of America is a national, nonprofit youth organization that provides support services to almost 1,500 Boys and Girls Club facilities.

Boys and Girls Clubs of Canada/Clubs des Garçons et Filles du Canada

7030 Woodbine Avenue, Suite 703
Markham, Ontario L3R 6G2
416–477–7272

Boys and Girls Clubs, with families and other adults, offer children and youth opportunities to develop skills, knowledge, and values to become fulfilled individuals.

The Development of Romantic Relationships in Adolescence

(1999) by Wyndol Furman, Brad Brown, and
Candice Feiring (Eds.)
New York: Cambridge University Press

A number of experts address the much-neglected topic of romantic relationships in adolescence.

Just Friends

(1985) by Lillian Rubin
New York: HarperCollins

Just Friends explores the nature of friendship and intimacy.

National Peer Helpers Association

818–240–2926

This association has publications and information on peer programs across the United States.

Peer Interactions, Relationships, and Groups

(1998) by Kenneth Rubin, William Bukowski, and Jeffrey Parker
In W. Damon (Ed.), *Handbook of Child Psychology* (5th ed., Vol. 3)
New York: Wiley

An in-depth examination of many areas of peer relations research by leading experts.

Peer Relationships and Social Competence in Early and Middle Childhood

(1999) by Gary Ladd
Annual Review of Psychology, Vol. 50
Palo Alto, CA: Annual Reviews

An up-to-date, authoritative review of peer relations research from the 1970s to the present.

Youth-Reaching-Youth Project

202–783–7949

The Youth-Reaching-Youth Project offers a model peer program that involves young people and students in preventing and reducing alcohol use among high-risk youth.

TAKING IT TO THE NET   http://www.mhhe.com/santrocka9

1. Media portrayals of adolescents' peer interactions often involve negative instances of peer pressure, including drinking and smoking, delinquency, and drug use. *What would you and your friends say to a reporter from the campus newspaper to illustrate the positive side of peer pressure and influence?*

2. Having stressed the importance of adolescence as a period of transition from childhood to adult forms of behavior, your psychology of adolescent instructor assigns as a paper topic the emergence of romantic relationships. *How would you describe adolescence as a transition from immature to adult forms of romantic relationships?*

3. Cyberdating is increasing in popularity, particularly among older children and younger adolescents. *What would you advise your younger sibling who is dabbling in cyberdating about important cautions?*

Connect to *http://www.mhhe.com/santrocka9* to research the answers and complete these exercises. In some cases, you'll also find further instructions on this site.

CHAPTER MAP

■ FROM NO MORE "WHAT IF" QUESTIONS TO AUTHORS' WEEK

SCHOOLS

■

The whole art of teaching is only the art of awakening the natural curiosity of young minds.

—Anatole France,
French Novelist, 20th Century

Some schools for adolescents are ineffective, others effective, as revealed in these excerpts (Lipsitz, 1984):

A teacher in a social studies class squelches several imaginative questions, exclaiming, "You're always asking 'what if' questions. Stop asking 'what if.'" When a visitor asks who will become president if the president-elect dies before the electoral college meets, the teacher explodes, "You're as bad as they are! That's another 'what if' question!"

A teacher drills students for a seemingly endless amount of time on prime numbers. After the lesson, not one student can say why it is important to learn prime numbers.

A visitor asks a teacher if hers is an eighth-grade class. "It's called eighth grade," the teacher answers harshly, "but we know it's really kindergarten, right class?"

In a predominantly Latino school, only the one adult hired as a bilingual teacher speaks Spanish.

In a biracial school, the principal and the guidance counselor cite test scores with pride. They are asked if the difference between the test scores of African American and white students is narrowing: "Oh, that's an interesting question!" says the guidance counselor with surprise. The principal agrees. It has never been asked by or of them before.

The preceding vignettes are from middle schools where life seems to be difficult and unhappy for students. By contrast, consider these circumstances in effective middle schools (Lipsitz, 1984):

Everything is peaceful. There are open cubbies instead of locked lockers. There is no theft. Students walk quietly in the corridors. "Why?" they are asked. "So as not to disturb the media center," they answer, which is self-evident to them, but not the visitor. . . . When asked, "Do you like this school?" [They] answer, "No, we don't like it. We love it!"

When asked how the school feels, one student answered, "It feels smart. We're smart. Look at our test scores." Comments from one of the parents of a student at the school are revealing: "My child would have been a dropout. In elementary school, his teacher said to me, 'That child isn't going to give you anything but heartaches.' He had perfect attendance here. He didn't want to miss a day. Summer vacation was too long and boring. He got here and someone cared for him."

The humane environment that encourages teachers' growth is translated by the teachers into a humane environment that encourages students' growth. The school feels cold when one first enters. It has the institutional feeling of any large school building with metal lockers and impersonal halls. Then one opens the door to a team area, and it is filled with energy, movement, productivity, doing. There is a lot of informal relating among students and between students and teachers. Visible from one vantage point are students working on written projects, putting the last touches on posters, watching a film, and working independently from reading kits. . . . Most know what they are doing, can say why it is important, and go back to work immediately after being interrupted.

Authors' Week is a special activity built into the school's curriculum that entices students to consider themselves in relation to the rich variety of making and doing in peoples' lives. Based on student interest, availability, and diversity, authors are invited to discuss their craft. Students sign up to meet with individual authors. They must have read one individual book by the author. Students prepare questions for their sessions with the authors. Sometimes, an author stays several days to work with a group of students on his or her manuscript.

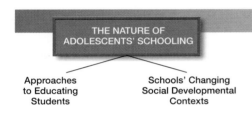

THE NATURE OF
ADOLESCENTS' SCHOOLING

Approaches
to Educating
Students

Schools' Changing
Social Developmental
Contexts

AskERIC
Phi Delta Kappan
http://www.mhhe.com/santrocka9

THE NATURE OF ADOLESCENTS' SCHOOLING

Today, virtually all American adolescents under the age of 16 and most 16- to 17-year-olds are in school. More than half of all youth continue their education after graduating from high school by attending technical schools, colleges, or universities. Schools for adolescents are vast and varied settings with many functions, diverse make-ups, and varying approaches to educating students.

Approaches to Educating Students

Let's explore the historical background of schools in adolescents' lives, some contemporary approaches to how student learning should take place, cross-cultural comparisons, and social policy.

Historical Aspects of Educating Students   During the twentieth century, American schools assumed a more prominent role in the lives of adolescents. From 1890 to 1920, virtually every state developed laws that excluded youth from work and required them to attend school ◀▥ P. 8. In this time frame, the number of high school graduates increased by 600 percent. By making secondary education compulsory, the adult power structure placed adolescents in a submissive position and made their move into the adult world of work more manageable. In the nineteenth century, high schools were mainly for the elite, with the educational emphasis on classical, liberal arts courses. By the 1920s, educators perceived that the secondary school curriculum needed to be changed. Schools for the masses, it was thought, should not just involve intellectual training but training for work and citizenship. The curriculum of secondary schools became more comprehensive and grew to include general education, college preparatory, and vocational education courses. As the twentieth century unfolded, secondary schools continued to expand their orientation, adding courses in music, art, health, physical education, and other topics. By the middle of the twentieth century, schools had moved further toward preparing students for comprehensive roles in life (Conant, 1959). Today, secondary schools have retained their comprehensive orientation, designed to train adolescents intellectually but vocationally and socially as well.

Although school attendance has consistently increased for more than 150 years, the distress over alienated and rebellious youth brought up the issue of whether secondary schools actually benefit adolescents. In the 1970s, three independent panels agreed that high schools contributed to adolescent alienation and actually impeded the transition to adulthood (Brown, 1973; Coleman & others, 1974; Martin, 1976). The argument is that high schools segregate adolescents into "teenage warehouses," isolating them in their own self-contained world with their own values away from adult society. The prestigious panels stressed that adolescents should be given educational alternatives to the comprehensive high school, such as on-the-job community work, to increase their exposure to adult roles and to decrease their isolation from adults. Partially in response to these reports, a number of states lowered the age at which adolescents could leave school from 16 to 14.

In the 1980s, the back-to-basics movement gained momentum. The **back-to-basics movement** *stresses that the function of schools should be the rigorous training of intellectual skills through such subjects as English, mathematics, and science.* Back-to-basics advocates point to the excessive fluff in secondary school curricula, with too many alternative subjects that do not give students a basic education in intellectual subjects. They also believe that schools should be in the business of imparting knowledge to adolescents and should not be concerned about adolescents' social and emotional lives. Critics of the fluff in schools also sometimes argue that the school day should be longer and that the school year should be extended into the summer months. Back-to-basics advocates want students to have more homework, more tests, and more discipline. They usually believe that adolescents should be behind their desks and not roaming around the room, while teachers should be at the head of the classroom, drilling knowledge into adolescents' minds.

Much of the current back-to-basics emphasis is a reaction against the trend toward open education in the 1970s. The open-education approach, which was based on the British educational system, allowed adolescents to learn and develop at their own pace within a highly structured classroom. However, too many school systems that implemented open education in the United States thought it meant tearing down classroom walls and letting adolescents do whatever they wanted. Incorrect application of open education in American schools resulted in a strong backlash against it.

Adolescent educators Arthur Powell, Eleanor Farrar, and David Cohen (1985) conducted an in-depth examination of fifteen diverse high schools across the United States by interviewing students, teachers, and school personnel, as well as by observing and interpreting what was happening in the schools. The metaphor of the "shopping mall" high school emerged as the authors tried to make sense of the data they had collected.

Variety, choice, and neutrality are important dimensions of the "shopping mall" high school. Variety appears in the wide range of courses offered (in one school, 480 courses in the curriculum!), with something for apparently every student. Variety usually stimulates choice. Choice is often cited as a positive aspect of curricula, but the choice often rests in the hands of students, who, in too many instances, make choices based on ignorance rather than information. The investigators found that the diversity of individuals, multiple values, and wide range of course offerings combined to produce neutrality. Because they try to accommodate the needs of different student populations, high schools may become neutral institutions that take few stands on the products and services they offer. The shopping mall is an intriguing metaphor for America's high schools and provides insight into some general characteristics that have emerged.

Should the main and perhaps only major goal of schooling for adolescents be the development of an intellectually mature individual? Or should schools also focus on the adolescent's maturity in social and emotional development? Should schools be comprehensive and provide a multifaceted curriculum that includes many electives and alternative subjects to a basic core? These provocative questions continue to be heatedly debated in educational and community circles (Alexander, 2000; Sadker & Sadker, 2003).

In one recent study, participation on school teams was linked with a lower sense of social isolation (Stone, Barber, & others, 2001). Participation in academic clubs (debate, foreign language, math club, chess club, science fair, or tutoring) and in school band, drama, and/or dance was related to higher self-esteem in adolescents.

back-to-basics movement
This philosophy stresses that the function of schools should be the rigorous training of intellectual skills through such subjects as English, mathematics, and science.

No one can be given an education. All you can give is the opportunity to learn.
—Carolyn Warner
American Author, 20th Century

In the first place God made idiots. That was for practice. Then he made school boards.
—Mark Twain
American Author, 20th Century

The debate about the function of schools produces shifts of emphases, much like a swinging pendulum, moving toward basic skills at one point in time, toward options, frills, or comprehensive training for life at another, and so on back and forth. What we should strive for, though, is not a swinging pendulum but something like a spiral staircase; that is, we should continually be developing more sophisticated ways of fulfilling the varied and changing functions of schools (Reynolds, 2000).

So far in our discussion of the function of schools, we have been examining the nature of U.S. secondary schools. Secondary schools around the world are the focus of the next section.

Cross-Cultural Comparisons Secondary schools in different countries share a number of similar features, but differ on others (Cameron & others, 1983). Let's explore the similarities and differences in secondary schools in six countries: Australia, Brazil, Germany, Japan, Russia, and the United States.

Most countries mandate that children begin school at 6 to 7 years of age and stay in school until they are 14 to 17 years of age. Brazil requires students to go to school only until they are 14 years of age, while Russia mandates that students stay in school until they are 17. Germany, Japan, Australia, and the United States require school attendance until 15 to 16 years of age.

Most secondary schools around the world are divided into two or more levels, such as middle school (or junior high school) and high school. However, Germany's schools are divided according to three educational ability tracks: (1) the main school provides a basic level of education, (2) the middle school gives students a more advanced education, and (3) the academic school prepares students for entrance to a university. German schools, like most European schools, offer a classical education, which includes courses in Latin and Greek.

Japanese secondary schools have an entrance exam, but secondary schools in the other five countries do not. Only Australia and Germany have comprehensive exit exams.

The United States is the only country in the world in which sports are an integral part of the public school system. Only a few private schools in other countries have their own sports teams, sports facilities, and highly organized sports events.

Curriculum is often similar in secondary schools in different countries, although there are some differences in content and philosophy. For example, at least until recently, the secondary schools in Russia have emphasized the preparation of students for work. The "labor education program," which is part of the secondary school curriculum, includes vocational training and on-the-job experience. The idea is to instill in

The juku or "cramming school," is available to Japanese adolescents in the summertime and after school. It provides coaching to help them improve their grades and their entrance exam scores for high schools and universities. The Japanese practice of requiring an entrance exam for high school is a rarity among the nations of the world.

youth a love for manual work and a positive attitude about industrial and work organizations. Russian students who are especially gifted—academically, artistically, or athletically—attend special schools where the students are encouraged to develop their talents and are trained to be the very best in their vocation. With the breakup of the Soviet Union, it will be interesting to follow what changes in education take place in Russia.

In Brazil, students are required to take Portuguese (the native language) and four foreign languages (Latin, French, English, and Spanish). Brazil requires these languages because of the country's international character and emphasis on trade and commerce. Seventh-grade students in Australia take courses in sheep husbandry and weaving, two areas of economic and cultural interest in the country. In Japan, students take a number of Western courses in addition to their basic Japanese courses; these courses include Western literature and languages (in addition to Japanese literature and language), Western physical education (in addition to Japanese martial arts classes), and Western sculpture and handicrafts (in addition to Japanese calligraphy). The Japanese school year is also much longer than that of other countries (225 days, versus 180 days in the United States, for example).

Contemporary Approaches to Student Learning   What is the best way for educators to promote student learning? This is a controversial topic. The back-to-basics movement still has strong advocates who believe that children should mainly be taught in a **direct instruction approach,** *a teacher-centered approach that is characterized by teacher direction and control, mastery of academic skills, high expectations for students' progress, and maximum time spent on learning tasks.* This approach has much in common with the behavioral approach we discussed in chapter 2, "The Science of Adolescent Development."

In the 1990s there appeared a wave of interest in constructivist approaches to school reform (Santrock, 2001). **Cognitive constructivist approaches** *emphasize the adolescent's active, cognitive construction of knowledge and understanding. Piaget's theory* (discussed in chapters 2 and 4) *is an example of a cognitive constructivist approach.* The implications of Piaget's theory are that teachers should provide support for students to explore their world and develop understanding. **Social constructivist approaches** *focus on collaboration with others to produce knowledge and understanding. Vygotsky's theory* (also discussed in chapters 2 and 4) *is an example of a social constructivist approach.* The implications of Vygtosky's theory are that teachers should create many opportunities for students to learn with the teacher and the peers in co-constructing understanding (Bearison & Dorval, 2002).

Advocates of the cognitive and social constructivist approaches argue that the direct instruction approach turns adolescents into passive learners and does not adequately challenge them to think in critical and creative ways (Perkins, 1999). The direct instruction enthusiasts say that the constructivist approaches often do not give enough attention to the content of a discipline, such as history or science. They also point out that many constructivist approaches are too relativistic and vague.

The APA's Learner-Centered Principles   Learner-centered principles move instruction away from the teacher and toward the student. The increased interest in learner-centered principles has resulted in the publication by the APA of *Learner-Centered Psychological Principles: A Framework for School Reform and Redesign* (Learner-Centered Principles Work Group, 1997; Presidential Task Force on Psychology in Education, 1992; Work Group of the American Psychological Association's Board of Educational Affairs, 1995). These principles were constructed, and are periodically revised, by a prestigious group of scientists and educators from a wide range of disciplines and interests. The principles have important implications for the way teachers instruct students.

The 14 learner-centered principles involve cognitive and metacognitive factors, motivational and affective factors, developmental and social factors, and individual difference factors. To read more about these learner-centered principles, see figure 7.1 on page 224.

direct instruction approach

A teacher-centered approach characterized by teacher direction and control, mastery of academic skills, high expectations for students' progress, and maximum time spent on learning tasks.

cognitive constructivist approaches

Approaches that emphasize the adolescent's active, cognitive construction of knowledge and understanding; an example is Piaget's theory.

social constructivist approaches

Approaches that focus on collaboration with others to produce knowledge and understanding; an example is Vygotsky's theory.

Constructivist Teaching and Learning
APA's Learner-Centered Psychological Principles
http://www.mhhe.com/santrocka9

COGNITIVE AND METACOGNITIVE FACTORS

1. Nature of the Learning Process
   The learning of complex subject matter is most effective when it is an intentional process of constructing meaning and experience.
2. Goals of the Learning Process
   Successful learners, over time and with support and instructional guidance, can create meaningful, coherent representations of knowledge.
3. Construction of Knowledge
   Successful learners can link new information with existing knowledge in meaningful ways.
4. Strategic Thinking
   Successful learners can create a repertoire of thinking and reasoning strategies to achieve complex goals.
5. Thinking About Thinking
   Higher order strategies for selecting and monitoring mental operations facilitate creative and critical thinking.
6. Context of Learning
   Learning is influenced by environmental factors, including culture, technology, and instructional practices.

MOTIVATIONAL AND INSTRUCTIONAL FACTORS

7. Motivational and Emotional Influences on Learning
   What and how much is learned is influenced by the learner's motivation. Motivation to learn, in turn, is influenced by the learner's emotional states, beliefs, interests, goals, and habits of thinking.
8. Intrinsic Motivation to Learn
   The learner's creativity, higher-order thinking, and natural curiosity all contribute to motivation to learn. Instrinsic (internal, self-generated) motivation is stimulated by tasks of optimal novelty and difficulty, tasks that are relevant to personal interests, and when learners are provided personal choice and control.
9. Effects of Motivation on Effort
   Acquiring complex knowledge and skills requires extended learner effort and guided practice. Without the learner's motivation to learn, the willingness to exert this effort is unlikely without coercion.

DEVELOPMENTAL AND SOCIAL FACTORS

10. Developmental Influences on Learning
    As individuals develop, there are different opportunities and constraints for learning. Learning is most effective when differential development within and across physical, cognitive, and socioemotional domains is taken into account.
11. Social Influences on Learning
    Learning is influenced by social interactions, interpersonal relations, and communication with others.

INDIVIDUAL DIFFERENCE FACTORS

12. Individual Differences in Learning
    Learners have different strategies, approaches, and capabilities for learning that are a function of prior experience and heredity.
13. Learning and Diversity
    Learning is most effective when differences in learners' linguistic, cultural, and social backgrounds are considered.
14. Standards and Assessment
    Setting appropriately high and challenging standards and assessing the learner as well as learning progress are integral aspects of the learning experience.

FIGURE 7.1
Learner-Centered Psychological Principles

Social Policy   In *Turning Points,* the Carnegie Council on Adolescent Development (1989) issued a set of eight principles for transforming adolescents' education. These principles can form the core of social policy initiatives for improving the education of adolescents, especially young adolescents. The eight principles are these:

- *Create communities for learning.* Many American middle and high schools are large, impersonal institutions. Teachers have few opportunities to develop the stable relationships with students that are essential to teaching them effectively. Unacceptably large schools should be brought to a human scale by creating "schools-within-schools," or "houses" within the school, and then dividing these subunits into smaller "teams" of teachers and students. Such smaller groupings can enable each student to receive increased individual attention in a supportive context.
- *Teach a core of common knowledge.* An important task for educators is to identify the most important principles and concepts within each academic discipline and concentrate their efforts on integrating these ideas into a connected, interdisciplinary curriculum. Depth and quality of information should be emphasized rather than coverage of a large quantity of information (Bereiter, 2002). *Turning Points* also considers community service to be an integral part of the curriculum. Community service can stimulate adolescents to think critically about real-world problems.
- *Provide an opportunity for all students to succeed.* A troubling dimension of schools is the inequitable distribution of opportunities to learn among youth. Educators can do a great deal more to teach students of diverse abilities. One strategy is to expand cooperative learning. Researchers have found that cooperative learning in mixed-ability learning groups helps high achievers deepen their understanding of material by explaining it to lower achievers, who in turn benefit by receiving help as needed from their peers. Cooperative learning can also help students to become acquainted with classmates from different ethnic and cultural backgrounds.
- *Strengthen teachers and principals.* States and school districts need to give teachers and principals more authority in transforming their schools. The teachers and principals know more about what will effectively work in their schools than do administrators and government officials, who are often far removed from the classrooms. The creation of governance committees composed of teachers, principals, support staff, parents, and community representatives can make schools more effective.
- *Prepare teachers for the middle grades.* Most teachers in middle schools are not specifically educated to teach young adolescents. Teacher education programs need to develop curricula that train middle school teachers to work with the special needs of young adolescents.
- *Improve academic performance through better health and fitness.* Schools for adolescents do not often have the support of health and social service agencies to address adolescents' physical and mental health needs. Developmentally appropriate health facilities, based in or near schools, need to be established.
- *Engage families in the education of adolescents.* Despite the clearly documented positive effects of parental involvement in education, parental involvement of all types declines considerably in adolescence, often to the point where it is nonexistent. An important social policy recommendation is to involve parents in decision making in significant ways, especially in low-income and ethnic minority neighborhoods (Epstein & Sanders, 2002). Parents who are involved in planning the school's work feel useful, develop confidence in their relations with the school staff, and are more likely to attend school functions, which signals to their adolescents that education is important.
- *Connect schools with communities.* "Full-service schools" should be considered in many locations. They represent a variety of school-based efforts to assist students and their families. These efforts include comprehensive youth-service programs, community schools, and family resource centers. Strengthening the academic environment in conjunction with supporting students and the basic needs of their families is the common core of all such efforts.

Schools' Changing Social Developmental Contexts

The social context differs at the preschool, elementary, and secondary level. The preschool setting is a protected environment, whose boundary is the classroom. In this limited social setting, preschool children interact with one or two teachers, almost always female, who are powerful figures in the young child's life. The preschool child also interacts with peers in a dyadic relationship or in small groups. Preschool children have little concept of the classroom as an organized social system, although they are learning how to make and maintain social contacts and communicate their needs. The preschool serves to modify some patterns of behavior developed through family experiences. Greater self-control may be required in the preschool years than earlier in development.

The classroom is still the major context for the elementary school child, although it is more likely to be experienced as a social unit than in the preschool. The network of social expression also is more complex now. Teachers and peers have a prominent influence on children during the elementary school years. The teacher symbolizes authority, which establishes the climate of the classroom, conditions of social interaction, and the nature of group functioning. The peer group becomes more salient, with increased interest in friendship, belonging, and status. And the peer group also becomes a learning community in which social roles and standards related to work and achievement are formed.

As children move into middle or junior high schools, the school environment increases in scope and complexity. The social field is the school as a whole rather than the classroom. Adolescents socially interact with many different teachers and peers from a range of social and ethnic backgrounds. Students are often exposed to a greater mix of male and female teachers. And social behavior is heavily weighted toward peers, extracurricular activities, clubs, and the community. The student in secondary schools is usually aware of the school as a social system and may be motivated to conform and adapt to the system or challenge it (Minuchin & Shapiro, 1983).

At this point we have examined a number of ideas about the nature of adolescents' schooling. This review should help you to reach your learning goals related to this topic.

☐ FOR YOUR REVIEW

Learning Goal 1
Describe approaches to educating students

- In the nineteenth century, secondary schools were for the elite. By the 1920s, they had become more comprehensive and trained adolescents not only for intellect, but also for work and citizenship. The comprehensive high school remains today, but the functions of schools continue to be debated.
- Contemporary approaches to student learning include the direct instruction and constructivist approaches. The American Psychological Association has proposed 14 learner-centered psychological principles to guide education.
- Schools vary across cultures. For example, U.S. schools have by far the strongest emphasis on athletics.
- Social policy recommendations include creating communities for learning, teaching a core of common knowledge, providing an opportunity for students to succeed, and strengthening teachers and principals.

Learning Goal 2
Know about schools' changing social developmental contexts

- The social context differs at the preschool, elementary school, and secondary school levels, increasing in complexity and scope for adolescents.

Now that we have discussed the nature of adolescents' schooling, let's turn our attention to transitions in schooling.

TRANSITIONS IN SCHOOLING

As children become adolescents and as adolescents develop and then become adults, they experience transitions in schooling (Seidman, 2000). We have just seen how the social setting changes from preschools through secondary schools. Additional important considerations involve transitions from elementary school to middle school or junior high school, from high school to college, and from school to work for noncollege youth, either after completing high school or after dropping out of school.

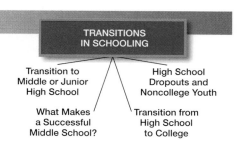

TRANSITIONS IN SCHOOLING

Transition to Middle or Junior High School

What Makes a Successful Middle School?

High School Dropouts and Noncollege Youth

Transition from High School to College

Transition to Middle or Junior High School

The emergence of junior high schools in the 1920s and 1930s was justified on the basis of physical, cognitive, and social changes that characterize early adolescence, as well as on the need for more schools in response to the growing student population. Old high schools became junior high schools, and new, regional high schools were built. In most systems, the ninth grade remained a part of the high school in content, although physically separated from it in a 6-3-3 system (a system whereby students are grouped as follows: first through sixth grade, seventh through ninth grade, and tenth through twelfth grade). Gradually, the ninth grade has been restored to the high school, as many school systems have developed middle schools that include the seventh and eighth grades, or sixth, seventh, and eighth grades. The creation of middle schools has been influenced by the earlier onset of puberty in recent decades. Figure 7.2 on page 228 reveals the dramatic increase in sixth- through eighth-grade middle schools and the corresponding decrease in seventh- through ninth-grade junior high schools.

One worry of educators and psychologists is that junior highs and middle schools have become simply watered-down versions of high schools, mimicking high schools' curricular and extracurricular schedules. The critics argue that unique curricular and extracurricular activities reflecting a wide range of individual differences in biological and psychological development in early adolescence should be incorporated into junior high and middle schools. The critics also stress that too many high schools foster passivity rather than autonomy and that schools should create a variety of pathways for students to achieve an identity.

The transition to middle school or junior high school from elementary school is a normative experience for virtually all children. However, the transition can be stressful because it occurs simultaneously with many other changes—in the individual, in the family, and in school (Eccles & Wigfield, 2000; Hawkins & Berndt, 1985; Seidman, 2000). These changes include puberty and related concerns about body image; the emergence of at least some aspects of formal operational thought, including accompanying changes in social cognition; increased responsibility and independence in association with decreased dependency on parents; change from a small, contained classroom structure to a larger, more impersonal school structure; change from one teacher to many teachers and a small, homogeneous set of peers to a larger, more heterogeneous set of peers; and increased focus on achievement and performance, and their assessment. This list includes a number of negative, stressful features, but aspects of the transition can also be positive. Students are more likely to feel grown up, have more subjects from which to select, have more opportunities to spend time with peers and to locate compatible friends, enjoy increased independence from direct parental monitoring, and may be more challenged intellectually by academic work.

When students make the transition from elementary school to middle or junior high school, they experience the **top-dog phenomenon,** *the circumstance of moving from the*

Educating Young Adolescents for a Changing World
http://www.mhhe.com/santrocka9

top-dog phenomenon
The circumstance of moving from the top position (in elementary school, the oldest, biggest, and most powerful students) to the lowest position (in middle or junior high school, the youngest, smallest, and least powerful).

THROUGH THE EYES OF ADOLESCENTS

Hoping a Pill Will Be Invented to Get You Through School

"I do good in school, but I don't want to do it. I want to get a good job and a good education and stuff, but I wish there was a pill or something that you could take to get you through school.

I try to stay away from fights at school. I try to settle things just by talking, but if somebody pushes me too far I'll take them on.

I wish everybody would pay more attention to kids. Sometimes grown-ups pay attention, but not a lot. They are kind of wrapped up in their jobs and don't pay attention to us kids. I don't think kids would get into as much trouble if people spent more time with kids."

—Howard, Age 11

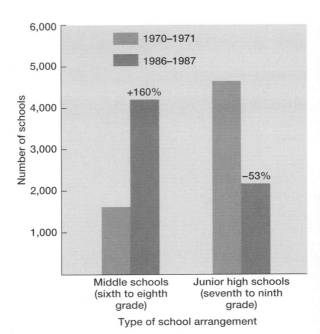

■ FIGURE 7.2
The Middle School Movement

top position (in elementary school, the oldest, biggest, and most powerful students in the school) to the lowest position (in middle or junior high school, the youngest, smallest, and least powerful students in the school). Researchers who have charted the transition from elementary to middle or junior high school find that the first year of middle or junior high school can be difficult for many students. For example, in one investigation of the transition from sixth grade in an elementary school to the seventh grade in a junior high school, adolescents' perceptions of the quality of their school life plunged in the seventh grade (Hirsch & Rapkin, 1987). In the seventh grade, the students were less satisfied with school, were less committed to school, and liked their teachers less. The drop in school satisfaction occurred regardless of how academically successful the students were.

Is the transition to sixth- through eighth-grade middle schools easier for students than the transition to seventh- through ninth-grade junior high schools? It is hard to say. The middle school transition does guarantee that more girls will experience pubertal change when they are in the large, impersonal context of the middle school, but middle schools do not reduce the number of times adolescents are "bottom dogs." And with another arrangement, in which the middle school consists of the fifth, sixth, and seventh grades, boys may be subjected to more stress than in the past because their pubertal change coincides with school change. The old two-tier system (the 8-4 arrangement: kindergarten through eighth grade, and ninth grade through twelfth grade) probably is the best for minimizing school transition stress because it reduces the number of transitions and because the main transition occurs after many adolescents are already well into puberty.

Roberta Simmons and Dale Blyth (1987) studied students in school systems with a 6-3-3 arrangement and with an 8-4 arrangement. The adolescents in the 8-4 arrangement (who only had to make one change of schools) had higher self-esteem and participated more in extracurricular activities than the adolescents in the 6-3-3 arrangement, who had to change schools twice. The adolescents' grades and sense of anonymity did not differ in the two types of school arrangements. The researchers concluded that all school transitions have a temporary negative influence on student's competence but that, the earlier the school change occurs in adolescence, the more difficult it likely is for students.

The transition from elementary to middle or junior high school occurs at the same time a number of other changes take place in development. Biological, cognitive, and socioemotional changes converge with this schooling transition to make it a time of considerable adaptation.

Schools that provide more support, less anonymity, more stability, and less complexity improve student adjustment during the transition from elementary to middle or junior high school (Fenzel, Blyth, & Simmons, 1991). In one investigation, 101 students were studied at three points in time: spring of the sixth grade (pretransition), fall of the seventh grade (early transition), and spring of the seventh grade (late transition) (Hawkins & Berndt, 1985). Two different schools were sampled—one a traditional junior high school, the other a junior high in which the students were grouped into small teams (100 students, four teachers). Students' adjustment was assessed through self-reports, peer ratings, and teacher ratings. Adjustment dropped during the posttransition—for example, seventh-grade students' self-esteem was lower than that of sixth-grade students. Students in the team-oriented junior high reported that they received more support from teachers. Friendship patterns also influenced the students' adjustment. Students who reported more contact with their friends and higher-quality friendships had more positive perceptions of themselves and of their junior high school than their low-friendship counterparts.

Two studies further highlight the factors that mediate school transition during early adolescence. In the first study, when parents were attuned to their young adolescents' developmental needs and supported their autonomy in decision-making situations, the young adolescents showed better adjustment and higher self-esteem across the transition from elementary school to junior high school (Eccles, Lord, & Buchanan, 1996). In the second study, support from parents and friends was associated with better adjustment of young adolescents following the school transition of both sixth- and ninth-graders (Costin & Jones, 1994).

First Days of Middle School
Resources for Middle School
Teachers
Middle School Issues
Middle School Programs
http://www.mhhe.com/santrocka9

What Makes a Successful Middle School?

Joan Lipsitz (1984) searched the nation for the best middle schools. Extensive contacts and observations were made. Based on the recommendations of education experts and observations in schools in different parts of the United States, four middle schools were chosen for their outstanding ability to educate young adolescents. The most striking feature of these middle schools was their willingness and ability to adapt all school practices to the individual differences in physical, cognitive, and social development of their students. The schools took seriously the knowledge investigators have developed about young adolescents. This seriousness was reflected in decisions about different aspects of school life. For example, one middle school fought to keep its schedule of mini-courses on Friday so that every student could be with friends and pursue personal interests. Two other middle schools expended considerable energy on a complex school organization so that small groups of students worked with small groups of teachers who could vary the tone and pace of the school day, depending on students' needs. Another middle school developed an advisory scheme so that each student had daily contact with an adult who was willing to listen, explain, comfort, and prod the adolescent. Such school policies reflect thoughtfulness and personal concern about individuals whose developmental needs are compelling. Another aspect observed was that, early in their existence—the first year in three of the schools and the second year in the fourth school—these effective middle schools emphasized the importance of creating an environment that was positive for the adolescent's social and emotional development. This goal was established not only because such environments contribute to academic excellence but also because social and emotional development are intrinsically valued as important in themselves in adolescents' schooling.

What does education often do? It makes a straight-cut ditch of a free, meandering brook.

—Henry David Thoreau
American Philosopher, Author, Naturalist, 19th Century

Recognizing that the vast majority of middle schools do not approach the excellent schools described by Joan Lipsitz (1984), in 1989 the Carnegie Council on Adolescent Development issued an extremely negative evaluation of U.S. middle schools. In the report—*Turning Points: Preparing American Youth for the Twenty-First Century*—the conclusion was reached that most young adolescents attend massive, impersonal schools; learn from seemingly irrelevant curricula; trust few adults in school; and lack access to health care and counseling. The Carnegie report recommends:

• Developing smaller "communities" or "houses" to lessen the impersonal nature of large middle schools
• Lowering student-to-counselor ratios from several hundred-to-1 to 10-to-1
• Involving parents and community leaders in schools
• Developing curricula that produce students who are literate, understand the sciences, and have a sense of health, ethics, and citizenship
• Having teachers team-teach in more flexibly designed curriculum blocks that integrate several disciplines, instead of presenting students with disconnected, rigidly separated 50-minute segments
• Boosting students' health and fitness with more in-school programs and helping students who need public health care to get it

Joan Lipsitz (shown here talking with young adolescents) has been an important spokesperson for the needs of adolescents. Former director of the Center for Early Adolescence at the University of North Carolina, she wrote the widely acclaimed book *Successful Schools for Young Adolescents*.

Through its Middle Grade School State Policy Initiative, the Carnegie Foundation of New York is implementing the *Turning Points* recommendations in nearly 100 schools and 15 states nationwide. A national evaluation of this initiative is currently under way. Data from the state of Illinois already show that in 42 schools participating in at least one year of the study since 1991, enactment of the *Turning Points* recommendations is associated with significant improvements in students' reading, math, and language arts achievement. In 31 schools with several years of data, the same pattern of positive results has been found *within* schools over time. That is, as schools continue to implement the *Turning Points* recommendations, students' achievement continues to improve (Carnegie Council on Adolescent Development, 1995).

Transition from High School to College

Just as the transition from elementary school to middle or junior high school involves change and possible stress, so does the transition from high school to college (Johnson, 2002; Rog, Hunsberger & Alisat, 2002). In many ways, the two transitions involve parallel changes. Going from a senior in high school to a freshman in college replays the "top-dog" phenomenon of going from the oldest and most powerful group of students to the youngest and least powerful group of students. For many of you, the transition from high school to college was not too long ago. You may vividly remember the feeling of your first days, weeks, and months on campus. You were called a freshman. Dictionary definitions of *freshmen* describe them not only as being in the first year of high school or college but as being novices or beginners. *Senior* not only designates the fourth year of high school or college, but also implies being above others in decision-making power. The transition from high school to college involves a move to a larger, more impersonal school structure, interaction with peers from more diverse geographical and sometimes more diverse ethnic backgrounds, and increased focus on achievement and performance, and their assessment.

But as with the transition from elementary school to middle or junior high school, the transition from high school to college can have positive aspects. Students are more likely to feel grown up, have more subjects from which to select, have more time to spend with peers, have more opportunities to explore different lifestyles and values,

THINKING CRITICALLY

Evaluating Your Own Middle or Junior High School

What was your own middle or junior high school like? How did it measure up to Lipsitz's criteria for effective schools for young adolescents? Did the school characteristically take individual differences into account? Did the administrators and teachers adequately address the unique needs of young adolescents as separate from those of children and older adolescents? Was socioemotional development emphasized as much as cognitive development? Suppose you could redesign the middle school you attended in one or two significant ways to improve students' socioemotional development. What changes would you make?

High Schools
Friendship and the Transition
to College
http://www.mhhe.com/santrocka9

(a)

(b)

(*a*) The transition from high school to college has a number of parallels with the transition from elementary school to middle or junior high school, including the "top-dog" phenomenon. (*b*) An especially important aspect of the transition to college is reduced interaction with parents.

enjoy greater independence from parental monitoring, and may be more challenged intellectually by academic work.

In one study, the transition from high school to college or full-time work was characterized as a time of growth rather than hardship (Aseltine & Gore, 1993). During this transition, the individuals showed lower levels of depression and delinquency than when they were in the last two years of high school. The improvement was related to better relationships with their parents.

For many individuals, a major change from high school to college is reduced contact with parents. One investigation revealed that going away to college might not only benefit the individual's independence but also improve relationships with parents (Sullivan & Sullivan, 1980). Two groups of parents and their sons were studied. One group of sons left home to board at college; the other group remained home and commuted daily to college. The students were evaluated both before they had completed high school and after they were in college. Those who boarded at college were more affectionate toward their parents, communicated better with them, and were more independent from them than their counterparts who remained at home and attended college. In another study, preestablished affective relationships were related to college adjustment (Takahashi & Majima, 1994). Peer-oriented students adjusted better to the high school/college transition than family-dominant students did. However, in one recent study, secure attachment with parents was linked with positive socioemotional adjustment in the transition to the first year of college (Larose & Boivin, 1998).

The large number of individuals who go directly to college after completing high school delay formal entry into the adult world of work. You might remember from chapter 1 the description of *youth,* a post–high-school age period involving a sense of economic and personal "temporariness" (Kenniston, 1970). For many individuals, going to college postpones career or marriage/family decisions. The major shift to college attendance occurred in the post–World War II years, as the GI Bill opened up a college education for many individuals. Since the 1960s, college attendance has steadily increased.

Students often go to college expecting something special. As one high school student said, "My main concern is that, without a college education, I won't have much chance in today's world. I want a better life, which to me, means going to college." Though high school students usually approach college with high expectations, their transition from high school to college may be less than ideal. In a study of undergraduate education in the United States, the Carnegie Foundation for the Advancement of Teaching pointed out the disturbing discontinuity between public high schools and institutions of higher learning (Boyer, 1986). Almost half of the prospective college students surveyed said that trying to select a college is confusing because there is no sound basis for making a decision. Many high school seniors choose a college almost blindfolded. Once enrolled, they might not be satisfied with their choice and might transfer or drop out, sometimes for the wrong reasons. The transition from high school to college needs to become smoother (Stevenson, Kochanek, & Schneider, 1998). As a first step, public schools should take far more responsibility for assisting students in the transition from high schools to college. Public high schools could learn considerably from the best private schools, which have always taken this transition seriously, according to the Carnegie Foundation report. Colleges also need to provide more helpful guidance to prospective students, going beyond glossy brochures and becoming more personalized in their interaction with high school students. Figure 7.3 on page 233 suggests that college representatives, high school counselors, comparative guides, and college publications have a long way to go.

Today's college freshmen appear to be experiencing more stress and depression than in the past, according to a UCLA survey of more than 300,000 freshmen at more than 500 colleges and universities (Sax & others, 2001). In 1987, 16 percent of college freshmen said they frequently felt overwhelmed; in 2001 that figure had risen slightly to 17 percent. Fear of failing in a success-oriented world is frequently given as a reason for stress and depression among college students. The pressure to succeed in college, get an outstanding job, and make lots of money is pervasive, according to many of the students.

		Students %	Parents %
College representatives at "College Nights"	Relevant	62	65
	Accurate	73	68
High school counselors	Relevant	57	49
	Accurate	70	62
Comparative guides	Relevant	53	50
	Accurate	65	59
College publications	Relevant	32	34
	Accurate	59	49

■ FIGURE 7.3
Evaluation of Major Sources of College Information by College-Bound High School Seniors and Their Parents (percentage agreeing)

High School Dropouts and Noncollege Youth

Dropping out of high school has been viewed as a serious educational and societal problem for many decades. By leaving high school before graduating, many dropouts have educational deficiencies that severely curtail their economic and social well-being throughout their adult lives. In this section, we study the scope of the problem, the causes of dropping out, and ways to reduce dropout rates.

Issues in Dropping Out of School
High School Dropouts and Ethnicity
Raising Achievement and Reducing Dropout Rates
http://www.mhhe.com/santrocka9

High School Dropout Rates Over the past 40 years, the proportion of adolescents who have not finished high school to those who have has decreased considerably. In 1940, more than 60 percent of 25- to 29-year-olds had not completed high school. Today, this figure is approximately 15 percent.

Despite the overall decline in high school dropout rates, the higher dropout rate of ethnic minority students and low-income students, especially in large cities, remains a major concern. Although the dropout rates of most ethnic minority students have been declining (the exception being Asian American adolescents), the rates remain above those of White students. Thirty-five percent of 20- to 21-year-old Latinos have dropped out of school. Dropout rates are extremely high for Native Americans: fewer than 10 percent graduate from high school. In some inner-city areas, the dropout rate for ethnic minority students is especially high, reaching more than 50 percent in Chicago, for example (Hahn, 1987). Latino dropout rates have declined little, if at all, in the past decade (National Center for Education Statistics, 2000). The dropout rate of African Americans has declined considerably and is now approaching the level for Whites (recent figures are about 13 percent for non-Latino Whites, 14 percent for African Americans) (U.S. Bureau of the Census, 2000).

The Causes of Dropping Out Students drop out of school for school-related, economic, family-related, peer-related, and personal reasons. School-related problems are consistently associated with dropping out of school (Ianni & Orr,

THROUGH THE EYES OF ADOLESCENTS

Adolescents Who Hate School

For some adolescents, school is a miserable place. Here are four of them:

- I'm 16 years old and I hate school. How do I get out of school? I'm in the eleventh grade. I don't like my teachers. They are jerks. How do I get through all of this?
- I'm 15 and I have one teacher who really hacks me off. He makes me want to hit him sometimes. One of these days I'm going to hit him. I don't care about school, anyway. My dad hits me. I steal from stores.
- I'm thinking about dropping out of school. I just don't want to put my time in on it. It's not what I want. What's going to happen to me if I do drop out? What are my parents going to do to me? I know they could kick me out of the house.
- I'm 14 and I hate school!!! It's too much pressure and I can't deal with it. What am I supposed to do? I don't even have time for myself. I need time to exercise, to sing, and to organize my life. I wish I liked school but I doubt if I ever will.

CAREERS IN ADOLESCENT DEVELOPMENT

Donna Smith
School Psychologist

Donna Smith is a school psychologist with the Cape Slattery School District in the state of Washington. After studying psychology at Brigham Young University and teaching in an elementary school (including teaching English as a second language), she furthered her education at Seattle University to become a school psychologist.

Donna has been working the past seven years at the elementary and high schools on the Neah Bay Makah Indian Reservation. One of her responsibilities is assessing children's needs for special education and other services. Although she engages in a limited amount of direct counseling, Donna often works with counselors and others who provide a range of services to children and adolescents.

The Makah tribe has been relatively isolated from the mainstream culture until recently. One positive aspect of this isolation is that the Makah community still provides some types of support that usually do not exist in mainstream communities. For example, when a traumatic incident occurs (as when a young boy disappears in the wood and can't be found), tribal elders come to the school to talk with the children and share their own experiences to help them through the stressful circumstance.

The Makah tribe continues to believe that "it takes a village to raise a child." Although there are many family problems in the community, there also are the added resources of caring aunts/uncles, grandparents, and neighbors who may become involved to help a child or adolescent with a problem.

Donna values her role as the facilitator of a team approach with teachers and other professionals in designing individual educational and coping programs for students. Donna says that "working with teams is a positive and powerful aspect of my job."

Donna Smith, counseling an adolescent girl.

1996; McDougall, Schonert-Reichl, & Hymel, 1996; Sewell, 2000). In one investigation, almost 50 percent of the dropouts cited school-related reasons for leaving school, such as not liking school, being suspended, or being expelled (Rumberger, 1983). Twenty percent of the dropouts (but 40 percent of the Latino students) cited economic reasons for dropping out. Many of these students quit school and go to work to help support their families. Socioeconomic status is the main factor in family background that is strongly related to dropping out of school: Students from low-income families are more likely to drop out than those from middle-income families. Many school dropouts have friends who also are school dropouts. Approximately one-third of the girls who drop out of school do so for personal reasons, such as pregnancy or marriage. However, overall, males are more likely than females to drop out.

Most research on dropouts has focused on high school students. One study focused on middle school dropouts (Rumberger, 1983). The observed differences in dropout rates among ethnic groups were related to differences in family background—especially socioeconomic status. Lack of parental academic support, low parental supervision, and low parental educational expectations for their adolescents were also related to dropping out of middle school.

Many of the factors just mentioned were related to dropping out of school in one large-scale investigation called *The High School and Beyond Study,* in which 30,000 high school sophomores were followed through graduation (Goertz, Ekstrom, & Rock, 1991). High school dropouts were more likely to come from low-income families, be in vocational programs, be males, be an ethnic minority (but not Asian American), and be in an urban school district (compared to rural or suburban). In addition, high school dropouts had lower grades in school (especially in reading), more disciplinary problems, lower rates of homework completion, lower self-esteem, lower educational expectations, and a more externalized sense of control. In one longitudinal study, high school dropouts had less language stimulation early in their development, compared to students who graduated from high school in a normal time frame (Cohen, 1994). And in another longitudinal study, very high, cumulative, early family stress had an impact on about one-half of the adolescents who subsequently dropped out of school (Jacobs, Garnier, & Weisner, 1996). In this same study, children at risk for dropping out of school who subsequently showed resilience and did not drop out of school had a more positive relational system within the family.

Reducing the Dropout Rate and Improving the Lives of Noncollege Youth

The dropout rate can be reduced and the lives of noncollege youth improved by strengthening the schools and by bridging the gap between school and work (William T. Grant Foundation Commission on Work, Family, and Citizenship, 1988).

Part of the solution lies within schools. Students may work hard through twelve grades of school, attain adequate records, learn basic academic skills, graduate in good standing, and still experience problems in getting started in a productive career. Others may drop out of school because they see little benefit from the type of education they are getting. Although no complete cure-all, strengthening schools is an important dimension of reducing dropout rates. While the education reform movements of the 1980s have encouraged schools to set higher standards for students and teachers, most of the focus has been on college-bound students. But reform movements should not penalize students who will not go to college. One way non-college-bound youth are being helped is through Chapter 1 of the Education Consolidation and Improvement Act, which provides extra services for low-achieving students. States and communities need to establish clear goals for school completion, youth employment, parental involvement, and youth community service. For example, it should be the goal of every state to reduce the dropout rate to 10 percent or less.

One innovative program is the "I Have a Dream" (IHAD) Program, a comprehensive, long-term dropout prevention program administered by the National "I Have a Dream" Foundation in New York. Local IHAD projects around the country "adopt" entire grades (usually the third or fourth) from public elementary schools, or corresponding age-cohorts from public housing developments. These children—"Dreamers"—are then provided with a program of academic, social, cultural, and recreational activities throughout their elementary, middle school, and high school years. An important part of this program is that it is personal rather than institutional: IHAD sponsors and staff develop close long-term relationships with the children. When participants complete high school, IHAD provides the tuition assistance necessary for them to attend a state or local college or vocational school.

These adolescents participate in the "I Have a Dream" Program, a comprehensive, long-term dropout prevention program that has been very successful.

The IHAD Program was created in 1981, when philanthropist Eugene Lang made an impromptu offer of college tuition to a class of graduating sixth-graders at P.S. 121 in East Harlem. Statistically, 75 percent of the students should have dropped out of school; instead, 90 percent graduated and 60 percent went on to college. Since the National IHAD Foundation was created in 1986, it has grown to number over 150 Projects in 57 cities and 28 states, serving some 12,000 children.

Community institutions, especially schools, need to break down the barriers between work and school. Many youth step off the education ladder long before reaching the level of a professional career, often with nowhere to step next, left to their own devices to search for work. These youth need more assistance than they are now receiving. Among the approaches worth considering are these:

• Monitored work experiences, such as through cooperative education, apprenticeships, internships, preemployment training, and youth-operated enterprises
• Community and neighborhood services, including voluntary service and youth-guided services
• Redirected vocational education, the principal thrust of which should not be preparation for specific jobs but acquisition of basic skills needed in a wide range of work
• Guarantees of continuing education, employment, or training, especially in conjunction with mentoring programs
• Career information and counseling to expose youth to job opportunities and career options as well as to successful role models
• School volunteer programs, not only for tutoring but to provide access to adult friends and mentors

At this point, we have examined a number of ideas about transitions in schooling. This review should help you to reach your learning goals related to this topic.

☐ FOR YOUR REVIEW

Learning Goal 3
Evaluate the transition to middle/junior high school and successful middle schools

- The emergence of junior high schools in the 1920s and 1930s was justified on the basis of the developmental changes of early adolescence and meeting the needs of a growing student population. Middle schools have become more popular and their appearance coincided with earlier pubertal development. The transition to middle/junior high school is often stressful because it occurs at the same time as a number of physical, cognitive, and socioemotional changes. This transition involves going from the "top-dog" to the "bottom-dog" position.
- Lipsitz concluded that successful middle schools take individual differences seriously, show a deep concern for what is known about early adolescence, and emphasize socioemotional development at least as much as cognitive development. In 1989, the Carnegie Foundation recommended a major redesign of American middle schools.

Learning Goal 4
Explain the transition from high school to college and school dropouts/noncollege youth

- In many ways, the transition to college parallels the transition from elementary to middle/junior high school. Reduced interaction with parents is usually involved in this transition. A special problem today is the discontinuity between high schools and colleges.
- Many school dropouts have educational deficiencies that limit their economic and social well-being for much of their adult lives. Progress has been made in lowering the dropout rate for African American youth, but the dropout rate for Native American and Latino youth remains very high. Dropping out of school is associated with demographic, family-related, peer-related, school-related, economic, and personal factors. The dropout rate could be reduced by strengthening schools and bridging the gap between school and work.

So far in this chapter we have discussed the nature of adolescents' schooling and transitions in schooling. Next, we will turn our attention to classrooms, teachers, and parents.

SCHOOLS, CLASSROOMS, TEACHERS, AND PARENTS

SCHOOLS, CLASSROOMS, TEACHERS, AND PARENTS

Size and Climate of Schools

Person-Environment Fit and Aptitude-Treatment Interaction

Teachers and Parents

Schools and classrooms vary along many dimensions, including size of school or class and school or class atmosphere. Adolescents' school life also involves thousands of hours of interactions with teachers. A special concern is parent involvement in the adolescent's schooling.

Size and Climate of Schools

What size were the schools you went to as an adolescent? Do you think they were too big? too small? Let's explore the effects of school size, as well as classroom size, on adolescent development.

School Size and Classroom Size   A number of factors led to the increased size of secondary schools in the United States: increasing urban enrollments, decreasing budgets, and an educational rationale of increased academic stimulation in consolidated institutions. But is bigger really better? No systematic relation between school size and academic achievement has been found, but more prosocial and possibly less antisocial behavior occur in small schools (Rutter & others, 1979). Large schools, especially those with more than 500 to 600 students, might not provide a personalized climate that allows for an effective system of social control. Students may feel alienated and not take responsibility for their conduct. This might be especially true for unsuccessful students who do not identify with their school and who become members of oppositional peer groups. The responsiveness of the school can mediate the impact of school size on adolescent behavior. For example, in one investigation, low-responsive schools (which offered few rewards for desirable behavior) had higher crime rates than high-responsive schools (McPartland & McDill, 1976). Although school responsiveness may mediate adolescent conduct, small schools may be more flexible and responsive than larger schools.

Besides the belief that smaller schools provide adolescents with a better education, there also is a belief that smaller classes are better than larger classes. Traditional schools in the Untied States have 30 to 35 students per classroom. The balance of the evidence suggests that substantial reductions in class size do improve student achievement (Blatchford & Mortimore, 1994; Glass & Smith, 1978; Kirst, 1998; Mosteller, 1995). The effects are strongest for students in the early primary grades, for low-achieving students, and for students from low-SES backgrounds. The greatest gains in achievement occur when the class size is 20 or fewer students.

Classroom Climate   It is important for classrooms to present a positive environment for learning. Two effective general strategies for creating positive classroom environments are using an authoritative strategy and effectively managing the group's activities.

The idea of an authoritative classroom management strategy is derived from Diana Baumrind's (1971, 1996) typology of parenting styles, which was discussed in chapter 5, "Families." Like authoritative parents, authoritative teachers have students who tend to be self-reliant, delay gratification, get along well with their peers, and show high self-esteem. An **authoritative strategy of classroom management** *encourages students to be independent thinkers and doers but still involves effective monitoring. Authoritative teachers engage students in considerable verbal give-and-take and show a caring attitude toward them. However, they still declare limits when necessary.* Teachers clarify rules and regulations, establishing these standards with input from students.

The authoritative strategy contrasts with two ineffective strategies: authoritarian and permissive. The **authoritarian strategy of classroom management** *is restrictive and punitive. The focus is mainly on keeping order in the classroom rather than on instruction and learning.* Authoritarian teachers place firm limits and controls on students and have little verbal exchange with them. Students in authoritarian classrooms tend to be passive learners, fail to initiate activities, express anxiety about social comparison, and have poor communication skills.

The **permissive strategy of classroom management** *offers students considerable autonomy but provides them with little support for developing learning skills or managing their behavior.* Not surprisingly, students in permissive classrooms tend to have inadequate academic skills and low self-control.

Overall, an authoritative strategy will benefit students more than authoritarian or permissive strategies. An authoritative strategy will help students become active, self-regulated learners (Evertson, Emmer, & Worsham, 2003; Marcella, Nelson, & Marchand-Martella, 2003).

In Jacob Kounin's (1970) classic research on classroom management, effective teachers did not differ from ineffective ones in the way they responded to students' misbehaviors; where they differed was in how competently they managed the group's activities. The effective teachers closely monitored students on a regular basis, which allowed them to detect problem behavior before it got out of hand. Effective teachers also kept the flow of a lesson moving smoothly, maintaining students' interest and not giving them opportunities to be easily distracted. And effective teachers engaged students in a variety of challenging, but not impossible, classroom activities.

To function smoothly, classrooms need clearly defined rules and routines (Emmer, Evertson, & Worsham, 2000, 2003). Students need to know how they are expected to behave. Without clearly defined classroom rules and routines, the misunderstandings that can breed chaos are inevitable. Rules should be reasonable and necessary, clear and comprehensible, and consistent with instructional and learning goals (Weinstein, 1997, 2003). Teachers can improve the likelihood that students will cooperate with them if they develop a positive relationship with students, get students to share and assume responsibility, and reward appropriate behavior.

The Metamorphosis of Classroom Management
Managing Today's Classroom
http://www.mhhe.com/santrocka9

authoritative strategy of classroom management

This teaching strategy encourages students to be independent thinkers and doers, but still involves effective monitoring. Authoritative teachers engage students in considerable verbal give-and-take and show a caring attitude toward them. However, they still declare limits when necessary.

authoritarian strategy of classroom management

This teaching strategy is restrictive and punitive. The focus is mainly on keeping order in the classroom rather than on instruction and learning.

permissive strategy of classroom management

This strategy offers students considerable autonomy but provides them with little support for developing learning skills or managing their behavior.

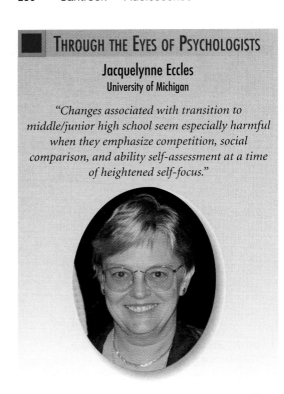
aptitude-treatment interaction (ATI)
This interaction stresses the importance of both the attitudes and the characteristics of the adolescent, such as academic potential or personality traits, and the treatments or experiences, such as the educational techniques, that the adolescent receives. *Aptitude* refers to such characteristics as the academic potential and personality characteristics on which students differ; *treatment* refers to educational techniques, such as structured versus flexible classrooms.

The role of the teacher remains the highest calling of a free people. To the teacher, America trusts its most important resource: children.
—Shirley Hufstedler
    American Government Official,
    20th Century

The effectiveness of classroom climate is often linked to a teacher's beliefs and practices (Eccles, Wigfield, & Schiefele, 1998). For example, student satisfaction, personal growth, and achievement are maximized only when teacher warmth and support are accompanied by efficient organization, an emphasis on academics, and provision of goal-oriented activities (Trickett & Moos, 1974).

Researchers have examined the climate not only of the classroom but also of the entire school. Schools with a climate of self-efficacy and positive expectations for students' success benefit student learning and achievement (Bandura, 1997; Bryk, Lee, & Holland, 1993). Other investigators argue that an emphasis on ability tracking, comparative performance evaluations, and ego, rather than a mastery focus, undermines the motivation of both students and teachers (Maehr & Midgely, 1996). Later, in chapter 13, "Achievement, Careers, and Work," we will further explore aspects of achievement that are important in understanding classroom and school climate.

Person-Environment Fit and Aptitude-Treatment Interaction

Some of the negative psychological changes associated with adolescent development might result from a mismatch between the needs of developing adolescents and the opportunities afforded them by the schools they attend. Adolescent expert Jacquelynne Eccles and her colleagues (Eccles & Wigfield, 2000; Eccles & others, 1993) described ways in which developmentally appropriate school environments can be created that match up better with adolescents' needs. Their recommendations are based on a large-scale study of 1,500 young adolescents in middle-income communities in Michigan. These adolescents were studied as they made the change from the sixth grade in an elementary school to the seventh grade in a junior high school.

Both the early adolescents and their teachers reported less opportunity for adolescent participation in classroom decision making in the seventh grade than in the sixth grade. By contrast, the students wanted to participate more in classroom decision making in the seventh grade than in the sixth grade. According to Eccles and her colleagues, such findings represent a person-environment mismatch that harms adolescent development.

As we have just seen, the characteristics and motivation of the adolescent need to be considered in determining what form of education is developmentally appropriate for them. In education, this match is usually referred to as **aptitude-treatment interaction (ATI)**, *which stresses the importance of both adolescents' characteristics and motivation and the treatments or experiences they receive in schools. Aptitude refers to such characteristics as the academic potential and personality characteristics on which students differ;* treatment *refers to educational techniques, such as structured versus flexible classrooms.*

Researchers have found that adolescents' achievement level (aptitude) interacts with classroom structure (treatment) to produce the best learning (Cronbach & Snow, 1977). For example, students who are highly achievement oriented usually do well in a flexible classroom and enjoy it; low-achievement-oriented students usually fare worse and dislike such flexibility. The reverse often appears in structured classrooms.

Teachers and Parents

Adolescents' development is influenced by teachers. In addition, an increasingly important issue is parent involvement in schooling.

Interactions with Teachers   Virtually everyone's life is affected in one way or another by teachers (Oakes & Lipton, 2002; Newman, 2002). You probably were influenced by teachers as you grew up. One day you may have, or perhaps you already have, children and adolescents whose lives will be guided by many different teachers. You likely can remember several of your teachers vividly. Perhaps one never smiled, another required you to memorize everything in sight, and yet another always appeared vibrant and encouraged question asking. Psychologists and educators have tried to compile a profile of a good teacher's personality traits, but the complexity of personality, education, learning, and individuals makes this a difficult task. Nonetheless, some teacher traits are associated with positive student outcomes more than others—enthusiasm, ability to plan, poise, adaptability, warmth, flexibility, and awareness of individual differences, for example. And in one study, positive teacher expectations were linked with higher student achievement (Jussim & Eccles, 1993).

Erik Erikson (1968) believes that good teachers produce a sense of industry, rather than inferiority, in their students. Good teachers are trusted and respected by the community and know how to alternate work and play, study and games, says Erikson. They know how to recognize special efforts and to encourage special abilities. They also know how to create a setting in which adolescents feel good about themselves and know how to handle those adolescents to whom school is not important. In Erikson's (1968) own words, adolescents should be "mildly but firmly coerced into the adventure of finding out that one can learn to accomplish things which one would never have thought of by oneself."

Other recommendations for successful teaching with young adolescents have been offered by adolescent educator Stephanie Feeney (1980). She believes that meaningful learning takes place when the developmental characteristics of the age group are understood, when trust has been established, and when adolescents feel free to explore, to experiment, and to make mistakes. The variability and change that characterizes young adolescents make them a difficult age group to instruct. The student who leans on the teacher one day for help may be strutting around independently the next day. Teachers who work successfully with young adolescents probably have vivid memories of their own adolescence and likely have mastered the developmental tasks of those years. Able to recall their youthful vulnerability, they understand and respect their students' sensitivity to criticism, desire for group acceptance, and feelings of being acutely conspicuous. Successful teachers of adolescents are secure in their own identity and comfortable with their sexuality. Possessing clear values, they use power and authority wisely and are sensitive to their students' feelings. Young adolescents respond best to teachers who exercise natural authority—based on greater age, experience, and wisdom—rather than arbitrary authority or abdication of authority by being pals with the adolescent. Young adolescents need teachers who are fair and consistent, who set reasonable limits, and who realize that adolescents need someone to push against while testing those limits.

In the study of adolescents and schooling by Jacquelynne Eccles and her colleagues (1993), some characteristics of the teachers in the seventh grade have implications for the quality of adolescent education. Seventh-grade teachers had less confidence in their teaching efficacy than their sixth-grade counterparts did. Also, students who moved from high-efficacy teachers in the sixth grade to low-efficacy teachers in the seventh grade had lower expectations for themselves and said school was more difficult at the end of the seventh grade than did adolescents who experienced no change in teacher efficacy or who moved from low-efficacy to high-efficacy teachers.

Student-teacher relationships began to deteriorate after the transition to junior high school. Also, students who moved from elementary school teachers they perceived to be supportive to junior high school teachers they perceived to be unsupportive showed a decline in the value they attached to an important school subject—math. Low-achieving students were especially at risk when they moved to less facilitative classroom environments after the junior high transition.

Parents and Schools   It is commonly believed that parent involvement is important in the child's schooling but that parents play a much smaller role in the adolescent's schooling. Increasingly, though, researchers are finding that parents can be key factors in schooling at all grade levels (Connors & Epstein, 1995). However, parents are not as involved in their adolescents' schooling as they or the schools would like (Comer, 1988; Epstein & Sanders, 2002). Even though parental involvement is minimal in elementary school, it is even less in secondary school (Eccles & Harold, 1993). In one study, teachers listed parental involvement as the number one

I touch the future. I teach.
—Christa McAuliffe
*American Educator and Astronaut,
20th Century*

Teaching Resources
http://www.mhhe.com/santrocka9

"My mom told me to tell you that I am the educational challenge you were told about in college."

Jimmy Furlow
Secondary School Teacher

Ninth-grade history teacher Jimmy Furlow believes that students learn best when they have to teach others. He has groups of students summarize textbook sections and put them on transparencies to help the entire class prepare for a test. Furlow lost both legs in Vietnam but he rarely stays in one place, moving his wheelchair around the room, communicating with students at eye level. When the class completes their discussion of all the points on the overhead, Furlow edits their work to demonstrate concise, clear writing and help students zero in on an important point (Marklein, 1998).

Ninth-grade history teacher Jimmy Furlow converses with a student in his class.

Parent Involvement in Schools
http://www.mhhe.com/santrocka9

priority in improving education (Chira, 1993). In an analysis of 16,000 students, the students were more likely to get A's and less likely to repeat a grade or be expelled if both parents were highly involved in their schooling (National Center for Education Statistics, 1997).

One example of a successful school-family partnership involves the New York City School System and the Children's Aid Society, which provide school-based programs for 1,200 adolescents and their families (Carnegie Council on Adolescent Development, 1995). The participating school's family resource center is open from 8:30 A.M. to 8:30 P.M. Staffed by social workers, parents, and other volunteers, the center houses adult education, drug-abuse prevention, and other activities. Because many of the families who send adolescents to the school are of Dominican origin, the school offers English-as-a-second-language classes for parents, 400 of whom recently were enrolled.

Joyce Epstein (1990, 1996; Epstein & Sanders, 2002) has provided a framework for understanding how parental involvement in adolescents' schooling can be improved. First, *families have a basic obligation to provide for the safety and health of their adolescents.* Many parents are not knowledgeable about the normal age-appropriate changes that characterize adolescents. School-family programs can help to educate parents about the normal course of adolescent development. Schools also can offer programs about health issues in adolescence, including sexually transmitted diseases, depression, drugs, delinquency, and eating disorders. Schools also can help parents find safe places for their adolescents to spend time away from home. Schools are community buildings that could be used as program sites by youth organizations and social service agencies.

Second, *schools have a basic obligation to communicate with families about school programs and the individual progress of their adolescents.* Teachers and parents rarely get to know each other in the secondary school years. Programs are needed to facilitate more direct and personalized parent-teacher communication. Parents also need to receive better information about curricular choices that may be related to eventual career choices. This is especially important with regard to females and ethnic minority students enrolling in science and math courses.

Third, *parents' involvement at school needs to be increased.* Parents and other family members may be able to assist teachers in the classroom in a variety of ways, such as tutoring, teaching special skills, and providing clerical or supervisory assistance. Such involvement is especially important in inner-city schools.

Fourth, *parent involvement in the adolescent's learning activities at home needs to be encouraged.* Secondary schools often raise a concern about parents' expertise and ability in helping their adolescents with homework. Given this concern, schools could provide parents with supplementary educational training so that parents can be more helpful and confident in their ability. "Family Math" and "Family Computers" are examples of programs that have been developed by some secondary schools to increase parent involvement in adolescent learning.

Fifth, *parents need to be increasingly involved in decision making at school.* Parent-teacher associations are the most common way for parents to be involved in school decision making. In some school districts, school improvement teams consisting of school staff and parents have been formed to address specific concerns.

Sixth, *collaboration and exchange with community organizations need to be encouraged.* Agencies and businesses can join with schools to improve adolescents' educational experiences. Business personnel can especially provide insights into careers and the world of work. Some schools have formed partnerships with businesses, which provide some financial backing for special projects.

In summary, the collaborative relationship between parents and schools has usually decreased as children move into the adolescent years. Yet parent involvement might be just as important in the adolescent's schooling as in the child's schooling. For example, Epstein (1996) created a program designed to increase parents' involvement in the education of their middle school students and it had positive effects on the students' school performance. It is to be hoped that the future will bring much greater family/school/community collaboration in the adolescent years (Eccles & Harold, 1993).

We have discussed a number of ideas about schools, classrooms, teachers, and parents. Next, we will explore the roles of socioeconomic status and ethnicity in schools.

SOCIOECONOMIC STATUS AND ETHNICITY IN SCHOOLS

Adolescents from low-income, ethnic minority backgrounds often have more difficulties in school than their middle-socioeconomic status, White counterparts. Why? Critics argue that schools have not done a good job of educating low-income, ethnic minority students to overcome the barriers to their achievement (Scott-Jones, 1995). Let's examine the roles of socioeconomic status (SES) and ethnicity in schools.

SOCIOECONOMIC STATUS
AND ETHNICITY IN SCHOOLS

Socioeconomic   Ethnicity
Status

Socioeconomic Status

Adolescents in poverty often face problems at home and at school that present barriers to their learning (McLoyd, 2000; Spring, 2002). At home, they might have parents who don't set high educational standards for them, who are incapable of helping them read or with their homework, and who don't have enough money to pay for educational materials and experiences such as books and trips to zoos and museums. They might experience malnutrition and live in areas where crime and violence are a way of life.

The schools that adolescents from impoverished backgrounds attend often have fewer resources than schools in higher-SES neighborhoods (Shade, Kelly, & Oberg, 1997). Schools in low-SES areas are more likely to have a higher percentage of students with lower achievement test scores, lower graduation rates, and fewer students going to college. They also are more likely to have young teachers with less experience than schools in higher-SES neighborhoods. In some instances, though, federal aid has provided a context for improved learning in schools located in low-income areas. Schools in low-SES areas are more likely to encourage rote learning, whereas schools in higher-SES areas are more likely to work with adolescents to improve their thinking skills (Spring, 1998). In sum, far too many schools in low-SES neighborhoods provide students with environments that are not conducive to effective learning and the schools' buildings and classrooms often are old, crumbling, and poorly maintained.

Jonathan Kozol (1991) vividly described some of these problems adolescents in poverty face in their neighborhood and at school in *Savage Inequalities*. Following are some of his observations in East St. Louis, Illinois, an inner-city area that is 98 percent African American and has no obstetric services, no regular trash collection, and few jobs. Nearly one-third of the families live on less than $7,500 a year, and

Poverty and Learning
Interview with Jonathan Kozol
http://www.mhhe.com/santrocka9

THINKING CRITICALLY

Looking Back at Your Own School

Think back on your own secondary school experiences. How diverse were your classmates in terms of

- ethnic or religious background?
- socioeconomic background?
- place of birth?

How diverse were your teachers in these respects? How sensitive were they to ethnic and cultural diversity?

In your experience, how fairly did the curriculum and the general educational programs of the school address the histories, traditions, and other needs of different groups in your schools? Were some groups favored over others?

What problems arose that reflected ethnic, religious, or socioeconomic differences?

If you had been a teacher back then instead of a student, are there things you would have wanted to change about your school to produce more social harmony and meet unmet needs related to diversity? What would you have tried to change?

Dr. Henry Gaskins began an after-school tutorial program for ethnic minority students in 1983 in Washington, D.C. For four hours every weeknight and all day Saturday, 80 students receive one-on-one assistance from Gaskins and his wife, two adult volunteers, and academically talented peers. Those who can afford it contribute five dollars to cover the cost of school supplies. In addition to tutoring in specific subjects, Gaskins' home-based academy helps students to set personal goals and to commit to a desire to succeed. Many of his students come from families in which the parents are high school dropouts and either cannot or are not motivated to help their adolescents achieve in school. In addition, the academy prepares students to qualify for scholarships and college entrance exams. Gaskins was recently awarded the President's Volunteer Action Award at the White House.

75 percent of the population lives on some form of welfare. Blocks upon blocks of housing consist of dilapidated, skeletal buildings. Residents breathe in chemical pollution from the nearby Monsanto Chemical Company. Raw sewage repeatedly backs up into homes. Lead from nearby smelters poisons the soil. Malnutrition is common. Fear of violence is real.

The problems of the streets spill over into the East St. Louis schools, where sewage also backs up from time to time. Classrooms and hallways are old and unattractive, athletic facilities inadequate. Teachers run out of chalk and paper, the science labs are 30 to 50 years out of date, and the school's heating system never has worked right. A history teacher has 110 students but only 26 books.

Kozol says that anyone who visits places like East St. Louis, even for a brief time, comes away profoundly shaken. Kozol's interest was in describing what life is like in the nation's inner-city neighborhoods and schools, which are predominantly African American and Latino. However, there are many non-Latino White adolescents who also live in poverty, mainly in suburban and rural areas. Kozol argues that many inner-city schools still are segregated, are grossly underfunded, and do not provide anywhere near adequate opportunities for students to learn effectively.

Ethnicity

School segregation is still a factor in the education of children and adolescents of color in the United States (Simons, Finlay, & Yang, 1991). Almost one-third of African American and Latino students attend schools in which 90 percent or more of the students are from ethnic minority groups.

The school experiences of students from different ethnic groups vary considerably (Meece & Kurtz-Costes, 2001; Wong & Rowley, 2001; Yeakey & Henderson, 2002). African American and Latino students are much less likely than non-Latino White or Asian American students to be enrolled in academic, college preparatory programs, and much more likely to be enrolled in remedial and special education programs. Asian American students are far more likely than other ethnic minority groups to take advanced math and science courses in high school. African American students are twice as likely as Latinos, Native Americans, or Whites to be suspended from school. Ethnic minorities of color constitute the majority in 23 of the 25 largest school districts in the United States, a trend that is increasing (Banks, 1997). However, 90 percent of the teachers in America's schools are non-Latino White and the percentage of minority teachers is projected to decrease even further in coming years.

In one recent study, African American adolescents were more likely to have U.S.-born, college-educated parents while Latino adolescents were more likely to have immigrant parents with a high school education or less (Cooper & others, 2001). In this study, resources and challenges across social worlds (parents' and teachers' help and siblings' challenges) were positively linked with adolescents' higher grade point average, eligibility, and admission to more prestigious colleges.

In another recent study, it was concluded that U.S. schools are especially doing a poor job of meeting the needs of America's fastest-growing minority population—Latinas (the term used for Latino females) (Ginorio & Huston, 2001). The study focuses on how Latinas' futures—or "possible selves"—are influenced by their families, culture, peers, teachers, and media. The report indicates that many high school counselors view success as "going away to college," yet some Latinas, because of family responsibilities, believe it is important to stay close to home. The high school graduation rate for Latinas lags behind that for girls of any other ethnic minority group. Latinas also are less likely to take the SAT exam than other non-Latino White and other ethnic group females. Thus, a better effort needs to be made at encouraging Latinas' academic success and involve the Latina's family more in the process of college preparation.

American anthropologist John Ogbu (1989; Ogbu & Stern, 2001) proposed the view that ethnic minority students are subordinated and exploited in the American educational system. He believes that students of color, especially African American and Latino students, have inferior educational opportunities, have teachers and school administrators who have low academic expectations for them, and encounter negative stereotypes of ethnic minority groups. In one study of middle schools in predominantly Latino areas of Miami, Latino and non-Latino White teachers rated African American students as having more behavior problems than African American teachers rated the same students as having (Zimmerman & others, 1995).

Like Ogbu, Margaret Beale Spencer (Spencer & Dornbusch, 1990) says that a form of institutional racism permeates many American schools. That is, well-meaning teachers, acting out of misguided liberalism, fail to challenge students of color to achieve. Such teachers prematurely accept a low level of performance from these students, substituting warmth and affection for high standards of academic success.

Here are some strategies for improving relations between ethnically diverse students (Santrock, 2001):

Exploring Multicultural Education
Multicultural Education Resources
Multicultural Pavilion
http://www.mhhe.com/santrocka9

- *Turn the class into a jigsaw.* When Elliot Aronson was a professor at the University of Texas at Austin, the Austin School system asked him for ideas on how to reduce the increasing racial tension in the classrooms. Aronson (1986) developed the concept of the **jigsaw classroom,** *where students from different cultural backgrounds are placed in a cooperative group in which they have to construct different parts of a project to reach a common goal.* Aronson used the term *jigsaw* because he envisioned the technique as being like a group of students cooperating to put together different pieces of a jigsaw puzzle.

  How might this work? Consider a class of students, some White, some African American, some Latino, and some Asian American. The lesson to be learned by the groups focuses on the life of Joseph Pulitzer. The class might be broken up into groups of six students each, with the groups being as equal as possible in terms of ethnic composition and achievement level. The lesson about Pulitzer's life is divided into six parts, with each part given to a member of each six-person group. The parts might be paragraphs from Pulitzer's biography, such as how the Pulitzer family came to the United States, Pulitzer's childhood, his early work, and so on. All students in each group are given an allotted time to study their parts. Then group members teach their parts to the group. Learning depends on the students' interdependence and cooperation in reaching the same goal.

jigsaw classroom
A strategy in which students from different cultural backgrounds are placed in a cooperative group in which, together, they have to construct different parts of a project to reach a common goal.

- *Encourage students to have positive personal contact with diverse other students.* Contact alone does not do the job of improving relationships with diverse others. For example, busing ethnic minority students to predominantly White schools, or vice versa, has not reduced prejudice or improved interethnic relations (Minuchin & Shapiro, 1983). What matters is what happens after children and adolescents get to school. Especially beneficial in improving interethnic relations is for people of different ethnicities to share with one another their worries, successes, failures, coping strategies, interests, and other personal information. This helps them see other people more as individuals than as members of a stereotyped cultural group.

Cooperative Learning
http://www.mhhe.com/santrocka9

- *Encourage students to engage in perspective taking.* Exercises and activities that help students see other's perspective can improve interethnic relations. This helps students "step into the shoes" of students who are culturally different and feel what it is like to be treated in fair or unfair ways (Cushner, McClelland, & Safford, 2003).
- *Help students to think critically and be emotionally intelligent when cultural issues are involved.* Students who learn to think critically and deeply about interethnic relations are likely to decrease their prejudice (Bennett, 2003; Diaz, 2003). Students who think in narrow ways are more likely to be prejudiced. Becoming emotionally intelligent includes understanding the causes of one's feelings, managing anger, listening to what others are saying, and being motivated to share and cooperate.

CAREERS IN ADOLESCENT DEVELOPMENT

James Comer
Psychiatrist

James Comer grew up in a low-income neighborhood in East Chicago, Indiana, and credits his parents with leaving no doubt about the importance of education. He obtained a BA degree from Indiana University. He went on to obtain a medical degree from Howard University College of Medicine, a Master of Public Health degree from the University of Michigan School of Public Health, and psychiatry training at the Yale University School of Medicine's Child Study Center. He currently is the Maurice Falk Professor of Child Psychiatry at the Yale University Child Study Center and an associate dean at the Yale University Medical School. During his years at Yale, Comer has concentrated his career on promoting a focus on child development as a way of improving schools. His efforts in support of healthy development of young people are known internationally.

Dr. Comer, perhaps, is best known for the founding of the School Development Program in 1968, which promotes the collaboration of parents, educators, and community to improve social, emotional, and academic outcomes for children. His concept of teamwork is currently improving the educational environment in more than 600 schools throughout America.

James Comer (*left*) is shown with some of the inner-city African American children who attend a school that became a better learning environment because of Comer's intervention. Comer is convinced that a strong, familylike atmosphere is a key to improving the quality of inner-city schools.

- *View the school and community as a team to help support teaching efforts.* James Comer (1988; Comer & others, 1996) believes that a community, team approach is the best way to educate students. Three important aspects of the Comer Project for Change are (1) a governance and management team that develops a comprehensive school plan, assessment strategy, and staff development plan; (2) a mental health or school support team; and (3) a parents program. Comer believes the entire school community should have a cooperative rather than an adversarial attitude. The Comer program is currently operating in more than 600 schools in 26 states.

  Evaluation of the effectiveness of the Comer program has been mixed. However, in one recent evaluation of the Comer School Development Program with fifth- through eighth-grade students in 10 inner-city Chicago schools over four years, students in the Comer schools did slightly better on reading and math, engaged in less acting-out behavior, and showed greater ability to control their anger than comparable students in non-Comer schools (Cook, Hunt, & Murphy, 2001).

- *Be a competent cultural mediator.* Teachers can play a powerful role as a cultural mediator (Banks, 1997, 2002). This includes being sensitive to racist content in materials and classroom interactions, learning more about different ethnic groups, being sensitive to students' ethnic attitudes, viewing students of color positively, and thinking of positive ways to get parents of color more involved as partners with teachers in educating students.

Since the last review we have studied classrooms, teachers, and parents, as well as socioeconomic status, and ethnicity, in schools. This review should help you to reach your learning goals related to these topics.

☐ FOR YOUR REVIEW

Learning Goal 5
Understand schools, classrooms, teachers, and parents

- In terms of school size and class size, smaller is usually better. Large schools might not provide a personalized climate that allows for effective social control. Most class sizes are 25 to 35 but a class size of 15 or fewer benefits learning. A positive classroom climate, which is promoted by an authoritative management strategy and effective management of group activities, improves student learning and achievement. The effectiveness of classroom climate is often linked to the teacher's beliefs and practices. Researchers also have studied the effects of the entire school's climate on achievement.
- Person-environment fit involves the concept that some of the negative psychological changes associated with adolescent development might result from a mismatch between adolescents' developing needs and the lack of opportunities afforded by schools. Aptitude-treatment interaction is closely linked with person-environment fit.
- Teacher characteristics involve many different dimensions and compiling a profile of the competent teacher's characteristics has been difficult. Parent involvement usually decreases as the child moves into adolescence. Epstein argues that greater collaboration between schools, families, and communities is needed.

Learning Goal 6
Clarify the roles of socioeconomic status and ethnicity in schools

- At home, in their neighborhoods, and at school, adolescents in poverty face problems that present barriers to effective learning.
- Schools in low-SES neighborhoods have fewer resources, have less experienced teachers, and encourage rote learning more than thinking skills than schools in higher-SES neighborhoods.
- The school experiences of students from different ethnic groups vary considerably. It is important for teachers to have positive expectations and challenge students of color to achieve.
- Strategies that teachers can use to improve relations among ethnically diverse students include turning the classroom into a "jigsaw," encouraging positive personal contact, stimulating perspective taking, viewing the school and community as a team, and being a competent cultural mediator.

So far in this chapter we have focused on the nature of schools for adolescents; transitions in schooling; schools, classrooms, teachers, and parents; and socioeconomic status and ethnicity. Another important aspect of schools for adolescents involves students who are exceptional, a topic to which we now turn.

ADOLESCENTS WHO ARE EXCEPTIONAL

For many years, public schools did little to educate adolescents with disabilities. However, in the last several decades, federal legislation has mandated that all children and adolescents with disabilities receive a free, appropriate education. And increasingly, these students are being educated in the regular classroom (Hardman, Drew, & Egan, 2002; Walther-Thomas & others, 2000). We will examine these aspects of adolescents who are exceptional: who they are, learning disabilities, attention deficit hyperactivity disorder, educational issues, and gifted adolescents.

Who Are Adolescents with Disabilities?

Approximately 10 percent of all students receive special education or related services (Reschly, 1996). Figure 7.4 on page 246 shows the approximate percentages, of all who receive special education services, of children and adolescents who have various disabilities (U.S. Department of Education, 1996). Slightly more than half have a learning disability. Substantial percentages also have speech or language impairments (21 percent of those with disabilities), mental retardation (12 percent), and serious

FIGURE 7.4
The Diversity of Children and Adolescents with Disabilities

[a]The total number of children and adolescents with this disability who received special education services in the 1994–1995 school year.

[b]Of all children and adolescents who received special education services in the 1994–1995 school year, the percentage who had this disability.

DISABILITY	TOTAL[a]	PERCENTAGE[b]
Specific learning disabilities	2,513,977	51.1
Speech or language impairments	1,023,665	20.8
Mental retardation	570,855	11.6
Serious emotional disturbance	428,168	8.7
Multiple disabilities	89,646	1.8
Hearing impairments	65,568	1.3
Orthopedic impairments	60,604	1.2
Other health impairments	106,509	2.2
Visual impairments	24,877	0.5
Autism	22,780	0.5
Deaf-blindness	1,331	0.0
Traumatic brain injury	7,188	0.1
All disabilities	4,915,168	100.0

Only the educated are free.
—Epicurius
Greek Philosopher, 3rd Century B.C.

learning disability
Individuals with a learning disability are of normal intelligence or above, have difficulties in at least one academic area and usually several, and their difficulties cannot be attributed to any other diagnosed problem or disorder, such as mental retardation.

Learning Disabilities Association
Learning Disabilities Resources
ADHD Resources
http://www.mhhe.com/santrocka9

emotional disturbance (9 percent). Educators prefer to speak of "adolescents with disabilities" rather than "disabled adolescents," to emphasize the person rather than the disability. Also, the term *disability* is now preferred over *handicap*—the current view being that a handicap is a limitation imposed by society or institutions in response to an individual's disability.

Learning Disabilities

Children and adolescents with a **learning disability** *are of normal intelligence or above and have difficulties in at least one academic area and usually several, and their difficulty cannot be attributed to any other diagnosed problem or disorder, such as mental retardation.* The global concept of learning disabilities includes problems in listening, concentrating, speaking, and thinking.

About three times as many boys as girls are classified as having a learning disability (U.S. Department of Education, 1996). Explanations for this gender difference include a greater biological vulnerability of boys as well as referral bias (boys are more likely to be referred by teachers because of their disruptive, hyperactive behavior).

By definition, adolescents do not have a learning disability unless they have an academic problem. The academic areas in which adolescents with a learning disability most commonly have problems are reading, written language, and math (Hallahan & Kaufmann, 2003). About 5 percent of all school-age children receive special education or related services because of a learning disability. In the federal classification of children receiving special education and services, attention deficit hyperactivity disorder (ADHD) is included in the learning disability category. Because of the significant increase in ADHD today, we will discuss it by itself in the next section.

Adolescents with a learning disability most commonly have problems with reading (Kamphaus, 2000). They especially show problems with phonological skills, which involve understanding how sounds and letters match up to make words. They often have difficulties with handwriting, spelling, or composition.

Many interventions have focused on improving the child's reading ability (Lyon & Moats, 1997). Most children whose reading disability is not diagnosed until third grade or later and receive standard instruction fail to show noticeable improvement (Lyon, 1996). However, intensive instruction over a period of time by a competent teacher can remediate the deficient reading skills of many children and adolescents. The success of even the best-designed reading intervention depends on the training and skills of the teacher.

Improving outcomes for adolescents with a learning disability is a challenging task and generally has required intensive intervention for even modest improvement in outcomes. No model program has proven to be effective for all adolescents with learning disabilities (Terman & others, 1996).

THINKING CRITICALLY

Reflecting on Learning Disabilities

Think back on your own schooling and how students with learning disabilities either were or were not diagnosed. Were you aware of such individuals in your classes? Were they helped by teachers and/or specialists? You might now know one or more people with a learning disability. Interview them about their school experiences. Ask them what they believe could have been done better to help with their disability.

Attention Deficit Hyperactivity Disorder

Attention deficit hyperactivity disorder (ADHD) *is a disability in which children and adolescents show one or more of the following characteristics over a period of time: inattention, hyperactivity, and impulsivity.* Adolescents who are inattentive have difficulty focusing on any one thing and might become bored with a task after only a few minutes. Adolescents who are hyperactive show high levels of physical activity, seeming to almost always be in motion. Adolescents who are impulsive have difficulty curbing their reactions and don't do a good job of thinking before they act.

The U.S. Department of Education statistics shown in figure 7.4 include children and adolescents with ADHD in the category of children with specific learning disabilities, an overall category that comprises slightly more than one-half of all children and adolescents who receive special education or related services. The number of children and adolescents with ADHD has increased substantially, by some estimates doubling in the 1990s. The disorder occurs as much as 4 to 9 times more in boys than in girls. There is controversy about the increased diagnosis of ADHD (Guyer, 2000; Terman & others, 1996). Some experts attribute the increase mainly to heightened awareness of the

attention deficit hyperactivity disorder (ADHD)
Children and adolescents with ADHD show one or more of the following characteristics over a period of time: inattention, hyperactivity, and impulsivity.

Many children and adolescents show impulsive behavior, such as this boy who is jumping out of his seat and throwing a paper airplane at classmates. *What is the best way for teachers to handle such situations?*

THROUGH THE EYES OF PSYCHOLOGISTS

Daniel Hallahan
University of Virginia

"The goal of special education is to prepare individuals with disabilities for success and a high quality of life in a mainstream society."

disorder. Others are concerned that many children and adolescents are being misdiagnosed without undergoing extensive professional evaluation based on input from multiple sources (Whalen, 2000).

It used to be thought that ADHD decreased in adolescence, but it now is believed that it often does not. Estimates suggest that ADHD decreases in only about one-third of adolescents with this disorder. Increasingly it is recognized that these problems can continue into adulthood.

Definitive causes of ADHD have not been found. For example, scientists have not been able to identify causal sites in the brain. However, a number of causes have been proposed, such as low levels of certain neurotransmitters (chemical messengers in the brain), prenatal and postnatal abnormalities, and environmental toxins such as lead. Heredity might play a role; 30 to 50 percent of children and adolescents with ADHD have a sibling or parent who has the disorder (Woodrich, 1994).

It is estimated that about 85 to 90 percent of students with ADHD are taking prescription medication such as Ritalin to control their behavior (Dennla, 2001; Whalen, 2001). A child or adolescent should be given medication only after a complete assessment that includes a physical examination (Whalen, 2000). The problem behaviors of many students with ADHD can be controlled by these prescriptive stimulants. However, not all students with ADHD respond positively to prescription stimulants, and some critics argue that physicians are too quick to prescribe stimulants for students with milder forms of ADHD (Clay, 1997). Many experts recommend a combination of academic, behavioral, and medical interventions to help students with ADHD learn and adapt more effectively. For example, in one recent study, a combination of Ritalin and behavioral intervention (such as note-taking instruction and social skills training) increased the likelihood by 17 percent that adolescents with ADHD did their homework and increased their test scores (Evans & others, 2001).

Educational Issues Involving Adolescents with Disabilities

The legal requirement that schools serve all children and adolescents with a disability is a fairly recent one. Beginning in the mid-1960s to mid-1970s, legislatures, the federal courts, and the U.S. Congress established special educational rights for children and adolescents with disabilities. Prior to that time, most children and adolescents with a disability were either refused enrollment or inadequately served by schools. In 1975, Congress enacted **Public Law 94-142,** *the Education for All Handicapped Children Act, which requires that all students with disabilities to be given a free, appropriate public education. It also provides funding to help implement this education.*

In 1990, Public Law 94-142 was renamed the **Individuals with Disabilities Education Act (IDEA).** *The IDEA spells out broad mandates for services to all children and adolescents with disabilities. These include evaluation and eligibility determination, appropriate education, the individualized education program (IEP), and a least restrictive environment.*

The IDEA has many specific provisions, such as requiring schools to send notices to parents of proposed actions, attendance of parents at meetings regarding the adolescent's placement, and the right to appeal school decisions to an impartial evaluator. The IDEA, including its 1997 amendments, requires that technology devices and services be provided to students when these are necessary to ensure a free, appropriate education (Bryant & Seay, 1998; Male, 2003).

Under the IDEA, the child or adolescent with a disability must be educated in the **least restrictive environment,** *a setting that is as similar as possible to the one in which the children or adolescents without a disability are educated.* This has given a legal basis to make an effort to educate children and adolescents with a disability in the regular classroom. The term for educating children and adolescents with a disability in the regular classroom used to be *mainstreaming.* However, that term has been replaced by the term **inclusion,** *which means educating a child or adolescent with special education needs full-time in a general school program* (Friend & Bursuck, 2002; Idol, 1997).

Public Law 94-142
The Education for All Handicapped Children Act, which requires all students with disabilities to be given a free, appropriate education and provides the funding to help implement this education.

Individuals with Disabilities Education Act (IDEA)
This spells out broad mandates for services to all children and adolescents with disabilities. These include evaluation and eligibility determination, appropriate education and the individualized education program (IEP), and a least restrictive environment.

least restrictive environment
A setting that is as similar as possible to the one in which the children or adolescents without a disability are educated; under the Individuals with Disabilities Education Act, the child or adolescent must be educated in this setting.

inclusion
Educating a child or adolescent with special education needs full-time in a general school program.

The principle of "least restrictive environment" compels schools to examine possible modifications of the regular classroom before moving the child or adolescent with a disability to a more restrictive placement (Hallahan & Kaufmann, 2003; Heward, 2000). Also, regular classroom teachers often need specialized training to help some children and adolescents with a disability, and state educational agencies are required to provide that training (Sitlington, Clark, & Kolstoe, 2000). For many children and adolescents, inclusion in the regular classroom, with modifications or supplemental services, is appropriate (Choate, 2000; Coleman & Webber, 2002). However, some experts believe that separate programs can be more effective and appropriate for other children and adolescents with disabilities (Martin, Martin, & Terman, 1996).

Adolescents Who Are Gifted

The final type of exceptionality we will discuss is quite different from the disabilities we have described so far. **Adolescents who are gifted** *have above-average intelligence (usually defined as an IQ of 130 or higher) and/or superior talent in some domain, such as art, music, or mathematics.* Programs for gifted adolescents in schools typically base admission to the programs on intelligence and academic aptitude, although experts increasingly advocate widening the criteria to include such factors as creativity and commitment (Davidson, 2000).

Some critics argue that too many adolescents in gifted programs really aren't gifted in a particular area but are just somewhat bright (there can be a substantial difference in giftedness between adolescents with IQs in the 130s and their counterparts with IQs of 150+), usually cooperative, and usually White. They believe the mantle of brilliance is cast on many adolescents who are not that far from simply being "smart normal." General intelligence as defined by an overall IQ score still remains a key component of many states' criteria for placing an adolescent in a gifted program. But changing conceptions of intelligence increasingly include ideas such as Gardner's theory of multiple intelligences, so there is likely to be movement away from a specific IQ score as a criterion for giftedness (Castellano & Diaz, 2002).

Ellen Winner (1996), an expert on giftedness, describes three characteristics of adolescents who are gifted:

1. *Precocity.* Adolescents who are gifted are precocious when given the opportunity to use their gift or talent (Howe, 2000). They begin to master an area earlier than their peers do. Learning in their domain is more effortless for them than for adolescents who are not gifted. Most adolescents who are gifted are precocious because they have an inborn high ability in a particular domain or domains, although this inborn precocity has to be identified and nourished.
2. *Marching to their own drummer.* Adolescents who are gifted learn in a qualitatively different way than their nongifted counterparts do. One way they march to a different drummer is that they require less support, or scaffolding, from adults to learn than their nongifted peers do. Often they resist explicit instruction. They also make discoveries on their own and find unique solutions to problems within their area of giftedness.
3. *A passion to master.* Adolescents who are gifted are driven to understand the domain in which they have high ability. They display an intense, obsessive interest and an ability to focus. They do not need to be pushed by their parents. They frequently have a high degree of internal motivation.

At 10 years of age, Alexandra Nechita burst onto the child prodigy scene. She paints quickly and impulsively on large canvases, some as large as 5 feet by 9 feet. It is not unusual for her to complete several of these large paintings in a week. Her modernist paintings sell for up to $80,000 apiece. When she was only 2 years old, Alexandra colored

Eighteen-year-old Chandra "Peaches" Allen was born without arms. Despite this disability, she has learned to write, eat, type, paint, and draw with her feet. She can even put on earrings. She is well-known for her artistic skills. She has won three grand-prize awards for her art in various shows. She is getting ready to enter college and plans to pursue a career in art and physical therapy. Chandra Allen's accomplishments reflect remarkable adaptation and coping. She is an excellent example of how adolescents can conquer a disability and pursue meaningful goals.

adolescents who are gifted
Adolescents who have above-average intelligence (usually defined as an IQ of 130 or higher) and/or superior talent in some domain, such as art, music, or mathematics.

Special Education Resources
The Council for Exceptional Children
Legal Issues and Disabilities
Inclusion
http://www.mhhe.com/santrocka9

In giving rights to others that belong to them, we give rights to ourselves.
—John F. Kennedy
U.S. President, 20th Century

in coloring books for hours. She never has had an interest in dolls or friends. Once she started going to school, she couldn't wait to get home to paint. And she continues to paint, relentlessly and passionately. It is, she says, what she loves to do.

In addition to the three characteristics of giftedness that we just mentioned (precocity, marching to the tune of a different drummer, and a passion to master), a fourth area in which gifted adolescents excel is *information-processing skills.* Researchers have found that adolescents who are gifted learn at a faster pace, process information more rapidly, are better at reasoning, use better strategies, and monitor their understanding better than their nongifted peers (Jackson & Butterfield, 1996; Sternberg & Clickenbeard, 1995).

When adolescents who are gifted are underchallenged, they can become disruptive, skip classes, and lose interest in achieving. Sometimes these adolescents just disappear into the woodwork, becoming passive and apathetic toward school (Rosselli, 1996). Here are four program options for adolescents who are gifted (Hertzog, 1998):

- Special classes. Historically, this has been the common way to educate adolescents who are gifted. The special classes during the regular school day are called "pullout" programs (Schiever & Maker, 1997). Some special classes also are arranged after school, on Saturdays, or in the summer.
- Acceleration and enrichment in the regular classroom setting.
- Mentor and apprenticeship programs. Some experts believe these are important, underutilized ways to motivate, challenge, and effectively educate adolescents who are gifted (Pleiss & Feldhusen, 1995).
- Work/study and community service programs.

Gifted and Talented Resources
Gifted Education
http://www.mhhe.com/santrocka9

The wave of educational reform has brought into the regular classroom many strategies that once were the domain of separate gifted programs. These include an emphasis on problem-based learning, projects, learning portfolios, and critical thinking. Combined with the increasing emphasis on educating all adolescents in the regular classroom, many schools now try to challenge and motivate adolescents who are gifted in the regular classroom (Hertzog, 1998). Some schools include after-school or Saturday programs or develop mentor/apprenticeship, work/study, or community service programs. In this way, an array of in-school and out-of-school opportunities can be provided.

Ellen Winner (1996) says that too often adolescents who are gifted are socially isolated and underchallenged in the classroom. It is not unusual for them to be ostracized and labeled "nerds" or "geeks" (Silverman, 1993). An adolescent who is the only gifted student in the room does not have the opportunity to learn with students of like ability. Many eminent adults report that for them school was a negative experience, that they were bored and sometimes knew more than their teachers (Bloom, 1985). Winner believes that American education will benefit when standards are raised for all adolescents. For adolescents who are still underchallenged, she recommends that they be allowed to attend advanced classes in their domain of exceptional ability. For example, some especially precocious middle school students are allowed to take college classes in their area of expertise.

According to Winner (2000), many children who are gifted do not turn out to be gifted adults. One reason for this is that some of them are pushed so hard by overzealous parents and teachers that they lose their intrinsic (internal) motivation. As adolescents, they may ask themselves, "Who am I doing this for?" If the answer is not for one's self, they may not want to do it anymore.

CAREERS IN ADOLESCENT DEVELOPMENT

Sterling Jones
Supervisor of Gifted and Talented Education

Sterling Jones is program supervisor for gifted and talented children in the Detroit Public School system. Sterling has

Sterling Jones with students in the gifted program in the Detroit Public Schools.

been working for more than three decades with children who are gifted. He believes that students' mastery of skills mainly depends on the amount of time devoted to instruction and the length of time allowed for learning. Thus, he believes that many basic strategies for challenging children who are gifted to develop their skills can be applied to a wider range of students than once believed. He has written several pamphlets for use by teachers and parents, including *How to Help Your Child Succeed* and *Gifted and Talented Education for Everyone.*

Sterling has undergraduate and graduate degrees from Wayne State University and taught English for a number of years before becoming involved in the program for gifted children. He also has written materials on African Americans, such as *Voices from the Black Experience,* that are used in the Detroit schools.

Since the last review we have studied many aspects of students who are exceptional. This review should help you to reach your learning goals related to this topic.

FOR YOUR REVIEW

Learning Goal 7
Describe adolescents with disabilities

- An estimated 10 percent of U.S. students receive special education services. Slightly more than 50 percent of these students are classified as having a learning disability.
- Students with a learning disability are of normal intelligence or above and have difficulties in at least one academic area and usually several, and their difficulty cannot be traced to another diagnosed problem. Reading difficulties represent the most common problem of students with a learning disability.
- Attention deficit hyperactivity disorder (ADHD) involves problems in one or more of these areas: inattention, hyperactivity, and impulsivity. Most experts recommend a combination of interventions for ADHD—medical (stimulants such as Ritalin), behavioral, and academic.
- Public Law 94-142 requires that all children and youth be given a free, appropriate education. IDEA spells out broad mandates for services to all children and youth with disabilities. The concept of least restrictive environment (LRE) also has been set forth. Inclusion means educating students with disabilities in the regular classroom.

Learning Goal 8
Discuss adolescents who are gifted

- Adolescents who are gifted have above-average intelligence (usually defined by an IQ of 120 or higher) and/or superior talent in some domain, such as art, music, or math.
- Characteristics of adolescents who are gifted include precocity, marching to their own drummer, a passion to master, and superior information-processing skills.

In this chapter, we have examined schools for adolescents. As part of our discussion, we explored schools in different countries as well as the roles of socioeconomic status and ethnicity in schools. In chapter 8, we will more extensively study the influence of culture, socioeconomic status, and ethnicity on adolescent development.

CHAPTER MAP

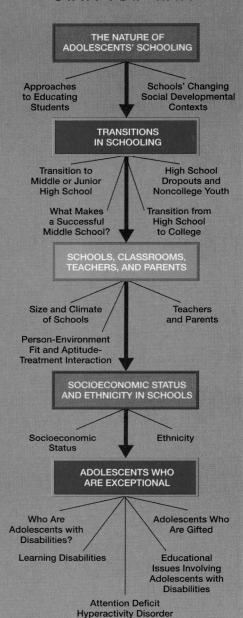

THE NATURE OF ADOLESCENTS' SCHOOLING

Approaches to Educating Students

Schools' Changing Social Developmental Contexts

TRANSITIONS IN SCHOOLING

Transition to Middle or Junior High School

High School Dropouts and Noncollege Youth

What Makes a Successful Middle School?

Transition from High School to College

SCHOOLS, CLASSROOMS, TEACHERS, AND PARENTS

Size and Climate of Schools

Teachers and Parents

Person-Environment Fit and Aptitude-Treatment Interaction

SOCIOECONOMIC STATUS AND ETHNICITY IN SCHOOLS

Socioeconomic Status

Ethnicity

ADOLESCENTS WHO ARE EXCEPTIONAL

Who Are Adolescents with Disabilities?

Adolescents Who Are Gifted

Learning Disabilities

Educational Issues Involving Adolescents with Disabilities

Attention Deficit Hyperactivity Disorder

REACH YOUR LEARNING GOALS

At the beginning of the chapter, we stated eight learning goals and encouraged you to review material related to these goals at four points in the chapter. This is a good time to return to these reviews and use them to guide your study and help you to reach your learning goals.

Page 226

Learning Goal 1   Describe approaches to educating students

Learning Goal 2   Know about schools' changing social developmental contexts

Page 236

Learning Goal 3   Evaluate the transition to middle/junior high school and successful middle schools

Learning Goal 4   Explain the transition from high school to college and school dropouts/noncollege youth

Page 245

Learning Goal 5   Understand schools, classrooms, teachers, and parents

Learning Goal 6   Clarify the roles of socioeconomic status and ethnicity in schools

Page 251

Learning Goal 7   Describe adolescents with disabilities

Learning Goal 8   Discuss adolescents who are gifted

KEY TERMS

back-to-basics movement 221
direct instruction approach 223
cognitive constructivist approaches 223
social constructivist approaches 223
top-dog phenomenon 227
authoritative strategy of classroom management 237
authoritarian strategy of classroom management 237
permissive strategy of classroom management 237

aptitude-treatment interaction (ATI) 238
jigsaw classroom 243
learning disability 246
attention deficit hyperactivity disorder (ADHD) 247
Public Law 94-142 248
Individuals with Disabilities Education Act (IDEA) 248
least restrictive environment 248
inclusion 248
adolescents who are gifted 249

KEY PEOPLE

Joan Lipsitz 230
Jacquelynne Eccles 238
Erik Erikson 239
Joyce Epstein 240
Jonathan Kozol 241

John Ogbu 243
Elliot Aronson 243
James Comer 244
Ellen Winner 249

RESOURCES FOR IMPROVING THE LIVES OF ADOLESCENTS

Adolescence in the 1990s

(1993) edited by Ruby Takanishi
New York: Teachers College Press

A number of experts on adolescence discuss the risk and opportunity for adolescents in today's world. Many chapters focus on improving the quality of schooling for adolescents.

Council for Exceptional Children (CEC)

1920 Association Drive
Reston, VA 22091
703–620–3660

The CEC maintains an information center on the education of children and adolescents who are exceptional and publishes materials on a wide variety of topics.

National Dropout Prevention Center

205 Martin Street
Clemson University
Clemson, SC 29634
803–656–2599

The center operates as a clearinghouse for information about dropout prevention and at-risk youth and publishes the *National Dropout Prevention Newsletter*.

School-Based Youth Services Program

New Jersey Department of Human Services
222 South Warren Street
Trenton, NJ 08625-0700
609–292–1617

This program operates in 37 sites in or near schools. The sites are open during and after school, on weekends, and all summer. They offer a core set of services, all of which require parental consent. Services include primary and preventive health care, individual and family counseling, drug- and alcohol-abuse counseling, recreation, and summer and part-time job development.

Successful Schools for Young Adolescents

(1984) by Joan Lipsitz
New Brunswick, NJ: Transaction Books

This book is a classic response for people involved in middle school education.

Turning Points

(1989) Carnegie Council on Adolescent Development
2400 N Street, NW
Washington, DC 20037-1153
202–429–7979

This comprehensive report concludes that the education most of the nation's young adolescents are receiving is seriously inadequate. The report includes a number of recommendations for meeting the educational needs of young adolescents.

TAKING IT TO THE NET   http://www.mhhe.com/santrocka9

1. The dramatic increase in the number of prescriptions for Ritalin due to the large increase in the diagnosis of ADD and ADHD has sparked considerable controversy, particularly among parents. *What are the pros and cons surrounding the use of Ritalin?*

2. Much has been made of means of altering curricula, lowering student/teacher ratios, and providing special programs for varying groups of students as means of enhancing the high school experience. *As a future parent, what types of educational experiences and career-planning opportunities would you want to see if you had a gifted child?*

3. Some have argued that larger schools are better because they offer greater curricular and extracurricular opportunities to students. Others have noted that smaller schools provide a more personalized instructional atmosphere that benefits students. *What are the major issues that a school board should address when considering concerns over school size?*

Connect to *http://www.mhhe.com/santrocka9* to research the answers and complete these exercises. In some cases, you'll also find further instructions on this site.

CHAPTER MAP

```
              CULTURE AND
              ADOLESCENCE

What Is                      Rites of
Culture?                     Passage

The Relevance               Models of
of Culture to               Cultural Change
the Study of
Adolescence        Cross-Cultural
                   Comparisons


            SOCIOECONOMIC STATUS
              AND POVERTY

The Nature of                Poverty
Socioeconomic
Status             Socioeconomic
                   Variations in Families,
                   Neighborhoods, and
                   Schools


                ETHNICITY

Ethnicity                    The United States
Issues                       and Canada:
                             Nations with
Ethnic Minority              Many Cultures
Adolescents


            TELEVISION AND
            OTHER MEDIA

Functions                    Social Policy
and Use of                   and the Media
Media

    Television          Technology,
                        Computers,
                        and the Internet

         The Media
         and Music
```

DATING PROBLEMS OF A 16-YEAR-OLD JAPANESE AMERICAN GIRL AND SCHOOL PROBLEMS OF A 17-YEAR-OLD CHINESE AMERICAN BOY

Sonya, a 16-year-old Japanese girl, was upset over her family's re-action to her White American boyfriend. Her parents refused to meet him and more than once threatened to disown her. Her older brothers also reacted angrily to Sonya's dating a White American, warning that they were going to beat him up. Her parents were also disturbed that Sonya's grades, above average in middle school, were beginning to drop.

Generational issues contributed to the conflict between Sonya and her family (Nagata, 1989). Her parents had experienced strong sanctions against dating Whites when they were growing up and were legally prevented from marrying anyone but a Japanese. As Sonya's older brothers were growing up, they valued ethnic pride and solidarity. The brothers saw her dating a White as "selling out" her own ethnic group. Sonya's and her family members' cultural values obviously differ.

Michael, a 17-year-old Chinese American high school student, was referred to an outpatient adolescent crisis center by the school counselor for depression and suicidal tendencies (Huang & Ying, 1989). Michael was failing several subjects and was repeatedly absent or late for school. Michael's parents were successful professionals who told the therapist that there was nothing wrong with them or with Michael's younger brother and sister, so what, they wondered, was wrong with Michael! What was wrong was that the parents expected all of their children to become doctors. They were frustrated and angered by Michael's school failures, especially since he was the firstborn son, who in Chinese families is expected to achieve the highest standards of all siblings.

The therapist underscored the importance of the parents' putting less pressure for achievement on Michael and gradually introduced more realistic expectations for Michael (who was not interested in becoming a doctor and did not have the necessary academic record anyway). The therapist supported Michael's desire not to become a doctor and empathized with the pressure he had experienced from his parents. As Michael's school attendance improved, his parents noted his improved attitude toward school and supported a continuation of therapy. Michael's case illustrates how expectations that Asian American youth will be "whiz kids" can become destructive.

Sonya's and Michael's circumstances underscore the importance of culture in understanding adolescent development.

CULTURE

■

Consider the flowers of a garden: Though differing in kind, color, form, and shape, yet, inasmuch as they are refreshed by the waters of one spring, revived by the breath of one wind, invigorated by the rays of one sun, this diversity increases their charm and adds to their beauty. . . . How unpleasing to the eye if all the flowers and plants, the leaves and blossoms, the fruits, the branches, and the trees of that garden were all of the same shape and color! Diversity of hues, form, and shape enriches and adorns the garden and heightens its effect.

—'Abdu'l Baha
Persian Baha'i Religious Leader, 19th/20th Century

ALTHOUGH WE ON PLANET EARTH have much in common with others, we also may vary according to our cultural and ethnic backgrounds. The sociocultural worlds of adolescents are described throughout this book. However, because culture and ethnicity are such pervasive dimensions of adolescence, we devote most of this chapter to these topics. Our culture also involves media and technology, topics we also will explore. By the time you have concluded this chapter, you should be able to reach these learning goals:

1 Understand culture and adolescent development

2 Discuss socioeconomic status and adolescence

3 Describe the role of poverty in adolescent development

4 Evaluate issues related to ethnicity

5 Know about ethnic minority adolescents

6 Discuss television and other media influences

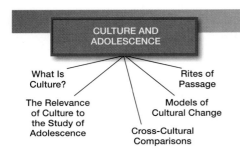

CULTURE AND ADOLESCENCE

What Is Culture?

The Relevance of Culture to the Study of Adolescence

Rites of Passage

Models of Cultural Change

Cross-Cultural Comparisons

culture
The behavior, patterns, beliefs, and all other products of a particular group of people that are passed on from generation to generation.

CULTURE AND ADOLESCENCE

What is culture, and why is it relevant to the study of adolescence? What is the importance of cross-cultural comparisons? How does change take place within and across cultures? What are rites of passage?

What Is Culture?

Culture *is the behavior, patterns, beliefs, and all other products of a particular group of people that are passed on from generation to generation.* The products result from the interaction between groups of people and their environment over many years (Kottak, 2002; Triandis, 2000). For example, in the section at the beginning of this chapter, we read about how the cultural values of Sonya's parents and brothers conflicted with her dating interests. We also read how the Chinese American cultural tradition of Michael's parents led to Michael's school-related problems.

Culture is a broad concept—it includes many components and can be analyzed in many ways. We already have analyzed the effects of three important cultural settings on adolescent development—the family, peers, and school. Later in this chapter, we will examine how much time adolescents spend in these and other settings.

Cross-cultural expert Richard Brislin (1993) described a number of features of culture, including these:

- Culture is made up of ideals, values, and assumptions about life that guide people's behaviors.
- Culture is made by people.
- Culture is transmitted from generation to generation, with the responsibility for transmission resting on the shoulders of parents, teachers, and community leaders.
- Culture's influence often becomes noticed the most in well-meaning clashes between people from very different cultural backgrounds.
- Despite compromises, cultural values still remain.
- When their cultural values are violated or when their cultural expectations are ignored, people react emotionally.
- It is not unusual for people to accept a cultural value at one point in their life and reject it at another point. For example, rebellious adolescents and young adults might accept a culture's values and expectations after having children of their own.

Two additional important dimensions of culture in adolescents' lives are socioeconomic status and ethnicity. **Socioeconomic status (SES)** *refers to a grouping of people with similar occupational, educational, and economic characteristics.* In this chapter, for example, we evaluate what it is like for an adolescent to grow up in poverty. **Ethnicity** *is based on cultural heritage, nationality characteristics, race, religion, and language.* Nowhere are sociocultural changes more profound than in the increasing ethnic diversity of America's adolescents. In this chapter, we study African American adolescents, Latino adolescents, Asian American adolescents, and Native American adolescents, and the sociocultural issues involved in their development. This chapter concludes with an overview of how an important dimension of culture—television and other media—affects adolescent development.

The Relevance of Culture to the Study of Adolescence

If the study of adolescence is to be a relevant discipline in the twenty-first century, increased attention will have to be focused on culture and ethnicity (Cooper & Denner, 1998; Eccles, 2002; Matsumoto 2000). The future will bring extensive contact between people from varied cultural and ethnic backgrounds. Schools and neighborhoods can no longer be the fortresses of one privileged group whose agenda is the exclusion of those with a different skin color or different customs. Immigrants, refugees, and ethnic minority individuals increasingly refuse to become part of a homogeneous melting pot, instead requesting that schools, employers, and governments honor many of their cultural customs. Adult refugees and immigrants might find more opportunities and better-paying jobs here, but their children and adolescents might learn attitudes in school that challenge traditional authority patterns at home (Brislin, 1993).

For the most part, the study of adolescents has, so far, been ethnocentric, emphasizing American values, especially middle-socioeconomic-status, White, male values (Spencer, 2000). Cross-cultural psychologists point out that many of the assumptions about contemporary ideas in fields like adolescence were developed in Western cultures (Triandis, 1994). One example of **ethnocentrism**—*the tendency to favor one's own group over other groups*—is the American emphasis on the individual or self. Many Eastern countries, such as Japan, China, and India, are group oriented. So is the Mexican culture. The pendulum may have swung too far in the individualistic direction in many Western cultures.

People in all cultures have a tendency to (Brewer & Campbell, 1976):

- Believe that what happens in their culture is "natural" and "correct" and that what happens in other cultures is "unnatural" and "incorrect"
- Perceive their cultural customs as universally valid; that is, what is good for us is good for everyone
- Behave in ways that favor their cultural group
- Feel proud of their cultural group
- Feel hostile toward other cultural groups

In fact, many cultures define being human by reference to their own cultural group. The ancient Greeks distinguished between those who spoke Greek and those whose language was incomprehensible and sounded like "barber" (a repetitive chatter), so they called them *barbarians.* The ancient Chinese labeled themselves "the central kingdom." In many languages, the word for *human* is the same as the name of the tribe. The implication is that people from other cultures are not perceived as fully human (Triandis, 1994).

Global interdependence is no longer a matter of belief or choice. It is an inescapable reality. Adolescents are not just citizens of the United States or Canada. They are citizens of the world, a world that through advances in technology and transportation has become increasingly interactive. By understanding the behavior and values of cultures around the world, we may be able to interact more effectively with each other and make this planet a more hospitable, peaceful place to live (Brislin, 2000; Matsumoto, 2000; Valisner, 2000).

socioeconomic status (SES)
A grouping of people with similar occupational, educational, and economic characteristics.

ethnicity
A dimension of culture based on cultural heritage, nationality, race, religion, and language.

The Web of Culture
Global Internet Communication
The Global Lab Project
Worldwide Classroom
http://www.mhhe.com/santrocka9

ethnocentrism
A tendency to favor one's own group over other groups.

Culture has a powerful impact on people's lives. In Xinjian, China, a woman prepares for horseback courtship. Her suitor must chase her, kiss her, and evade her riding crop—all on the gallop. A new marriage law took effect in China in 1981. The law sets a minimum age for marriage—22 years for males, 20 years for females. Late marriage and late childbirth are critical aspects of China's effort to control population growth.

Cross-Cultural Comparisons
http://www.mhhe.com/santrocka9

cross-cultural studies

Studies that compare a culture with one or more other cultures. Such studies provide information about the degree to which adolescent development is similar, or universal, across cultures or about the degree to which it is culture-specific.

Cross-Cultural Comparisons

Early in the twentieth century, overgeneralizations about the universal aspects of adolescents were made based on data and experience in a single culture—the middle-socioeconomic-status culture of the United States (Havighurst, 1976). For example, it was believed that adolescents everywhere went through a period of "storm and stress" characterized by self-doubt and conflict. However, as we saw in chapter 1, when Margaret Mead visited the island of Samoa, she found that the adolescents of the Samoan culture were not experiencing much stress ◀▐▐▐ P. 7.

Cross-cultural studies *involve the comparison of a culture with one or more other cultures, which provides information about the degree to which adolescent development is similar, or universal, across cultures, or the degree to which it is culture-specific.* The study of adolescence has emerged in the context of Western industrialized society, with the practical needs and social norms of this culture dominating thinking about adolescents. Consequently, the development of adolescents in Western cultures has evolved as the norm for all adolescents of the human species, regardless of economic and cultural circumstances. This narrow viewpoint can produce erroneous conclusions about the nature of adolescents (Berry, 2000; Goldstein, 2000; Miller, 2001). To develop a more global, cosmopolitan perspective on adolescents, we will consider adolescents' achievement behavior and sexuality in different cultures, as well as rites of passage.

Achievement The United States is an achievement-oriented culture, and U.S. adolescents are more achievement oriented than the adolescents in many other countries. Many American parents socialize their adolescents to be achievement oriented and

Cross-cultural studies involve the comparison of a culture with one or more other cultures. Shown here is a 14-year-old !Kung girl who has added flowers to her beadwork during the brief rainy season in the Kalahari desert in Botswana, Africa. Delinquency and violence occur much less frequently in the peaceful !Kung culture than in most other cultures around the world.

independent. In one investigation of 104 societies, parents in industrialized countries like the United States placed a higher value on socializing adolescents for achievement and independence than did parents in nonindustrialized countries like Kenya, who placed a higher value on obedience and responsibility (Bacon, Child, & Barry, 1963).

Anglo-American adolescents are more achievement oriented than Mexican and Mexican American adolescents are. For example, in one study, Anglo-American adolescents were more competitive and less cooperative than their Mexican and Mexican American counterparts (Kagan & Madsen, 1972). In this study, Anglo-Americans were more likely to discount the gains of other students when they could not reach the goals themselves. In other investigations, Anglo-American youth were more individual centered, while Mexican youth were more family centered (Holtzmann, 1982). Some developmentalists believe that the American culture is too achievement oriented for rearing mentally healthy adolescents (Elkind, 1981).

Although Anglo-American adolescents are more achievement oriented than adolescents in many other cultures, they are not as achievement oriented as many Japanese, Chinese, and Asian American adolescents. For example, as a group, Asian American adolescents demonstrate exceptional achievement patterns (Stevenson, 1995). Asian American adolescents exceed the national average for high school and college graduates. Eighty-six percent of Asian Americans, compared to 64 percent of White Americans, are in some higher-education program two years after high school graduation. Clearly, education and achievement are highly valued by many Asian American youth. More about Asian American youth appears later in this chapter and in chapter 13, where we discuss achievement.

Sexuality   Culture also plays a prominent role in adolescent sexuality. Some cultures consider adolescent sexual activity normal; others forbid it. Consider the Ines Beag and Mangaian cultures: Ines Beag is a small island off the coast of Ireland. Its inhabitants are among the most sexually repressed in the world. They know nothing about French kissing or hand stimulation of the penis. Sex education does not exist. They believe that, after marriage, nature will take its course. The men think that intercourse is bad for their health. Individuals in this culture detest nudity. Only babies are allowed to bathe nude, and adults wash only the parts of their body that extend beyond their clothing. Premarital sex is out of the question. After marriage, sexual partners keep their underwear on during intercourse! It is not difficult to understand why females in the Ines Beag culture rarely, if ever, achieve orgasm (Messinger, 1971).

By contrast, consider the Mangaian culture in the South Pacific. Boys learn about masturbation as early as age 6 or 7. At age 13, boys undergo a ritual that introduces them to manhood in which a long incision is made in the penis. The individual who conducts the ritual instructs the boy in sexual strategies, such as how to help his partner achieve orgasm before he does. Two weeks after the incision ceremony, the 13-year-old boy has intercourse with an experienced woman. She helps him to hold back his ejaculation so she can achieve orgasm with him. Soon after, the boy searches for girls to further his sexual experience, or they seek him, knowing that he now is a "man." By the end of adolescence, Mangaians have sex virtually every night.

American adolescents experience a culture more liberal than that of the Ines Beag but one that does not come close to matching the liberal sexual behavior of the Mangaians. The cultural diversity in the sexual behavior of adolescents is testimony to the power of environmental experiences in determining sexuality. As we move up in the animal kingdom, experience seems to take on more power as a determinant of sexuality. Although human beings cannot mate in midair like bees or display their plumage as magnificently as peacocks, adolescents can talk about sex with one another, read about it in magazines, and watch it on television and at the movies.

assimilation

The absorption of ethnic minority groups into the dominant group, which often means the loss of some or virtually all of the behavior and values of the ethnic minority group.

acculturation

Cultural change that results from continuous, firsthand contact between two distinctive cultural groups.

Models of Cultural Change

HUNTER-GATHERERS, NORTH AMERICA, LATE 20TH CENTURY

The models that have been used to understand the process of change that occurs in transitions within and between cultures are (1) assimilation, (2) acculturation, (3) alternation, and (4) multiculturalism.

Assimilation *occurs when individuals relinquish their cultural identity and move into the larger society.* The nondominant group might be absorbed into an established "mainstream," or many groups might merge to form a new society (often called a "melting pot"). Individuals often suffer from a sense of alienation and isolation until they have been accepted into, and perceive their acceptance in, the new culture.

Acculturation *is cultural change that results from continuous, firsthand contact between two distinctive cultural groups.* In contrast to assimilation (which emphasizes that people will eventually become full members of the majority group's culture and lose their identification with their culture of origin), the acculturation model stresses that people can become competent participants in the majority culture while still being identified as members of a minority culture (Hurtado, 1997).

The **alternation model** *assumes that it is possible for an individual to know and understand two different cultures. It also assumes that individuals can alter their behavior to fit a particular social context.* The alternation model differs from the assimilation and acculturation models in the following way: In the alternation model, it is possible to maintain a positive relationship with both cultures (LaFromboise, Coleman, & Gerton, 1993).

The **multicultural model** *promotes a pluralistic approach to understanding two or more cultures. This model argues that people can maintain their distinct identities while working with others from different cultures to meet common national or economic needs.* Cross-cultural psychologist John Berry (1990) believes that a multicultural society encourages all groups to (a) maintain and/or develop their group identity, (b) develop other-group acceptance and tolerance, (c) engage in intergroup contact and sharing, and (d) learn each other's language. In the multicultural model, people can maintain a positive identity as members of their culture of origin while simultaneously developing a positive identity with another culture.

Depending on the situation and person, any of these models might explain people's experiences as they acquire competency in a new culture. For example, consider an African American family that has moved from the rural South to live in a city. One member of the family might assimilate into the dominant Anglo culture, another might follow the path of acculturation, a third member might choose to actively alternate between the two cultures, and yet a fourth member might choose to live in a context in which the two cultures exist side by side as described in the multicultural model. Teresa LaFromboise and her colleagues (1993) argue that the more people are able to maintain active and effective relationships through alternation between the cultures, the less difficulty they will have in acquiring and maintaining competency in both cultures.

Now that we have discussed the nature of culture, cross-cultural comparisons, and models of cultural change, we will turn our attention to an aspect of adolescent life that is more pronounced in some cultures than others.

Rites of Passage

Rites of passage *are ceremonies or rituals that mark an individual's transition from one status to another, especially into adulthood.* Some societies have elaborate rites of passage that signal the adolescent's transition to adulthood; others do not. In many primitive cultures, rites of passage are the avenue through which adolescents gain access to sacred adult practices, knowledge, and sexuality (Sommer, 1978). These rites often involve dramatic practices intended to facilitate the adolescent's separation from the immediate family, especially the mother. The transformation usually is characterized by some form of ritual death and rebirth, or by means of contact with the spiritual world. Bonds are forged between the adolescent and the adult instructors through shared rituals, hazards, and secrets to allow the adolescent to enter the adult world. This kind of ritual provides a forceful and discontinuous entry into the adult world at a time when the adolescent is perceived to be ready for the change.

Africa, especially sub-Saharan Africa, has been the location of many rites of passage for adolescents. Under the influence of Western culture, many of the rites are disappearing today, although some vestiges remain. In locations where formal education is not readily available, rites of passage are still prevalent.

Americans do not have formal rites of passage that mark the transition from adolescence to adulthood. Some religious and social groups, however, have initiation ceremonies that indicate an advance in maturity—the Jewish bar mitzvah, the Catholic confirmation, and social debuts, for example.

alternation model
This model assumes that it is possible for an individual to know and understand two different cultures. It also assumes that individuals can alter their behavior to fit a particular social context.

multicultural model
This model promotes a pluralistic approach to understanding two or more cultures. It argues that people can maintain their distinctive identities while working with others from different cultures to meet common national or economic needs.

rites of passage
Ceremonies or rituals that mark an individual's transition from one status to another, especially into adulthood.

The Apache Indians of the American Southwest celebrate a girl's entrance into puberty with a four-day ritual that includes special dress, day-long activities, and solemn spiritual ceremonies.

These Congolese Kota boys painted their faces as part of a rite of passage to adulthood. *What kinds of rites of passage do American adolescents have?*

School graduation ceremonies come the closest to being culturewide rites of passage in the United States. The high school graduation ceremony has become nearly universal for middle-SES adolescents and increasing numbers of adolescents from low-income backgrounds (Fasick, 1994). Nonetheless, high school graduation does not result in universal changes—many high school graduates continue to live with their parents, to be economically dependent on them, and to be undecided about career and lifestyle matters. Another rite of passage for increasing numbers of American adolescents is sexual intercourse (Halonen & Santrock, 1999). By the end of adolescence, more than 70 percent of American adolescents have had sexual intercourse.

The absence in America of clear-cut rites of passage makes the attainment of adult status ambiguous. Many individuals are unsure whether they have reached adult status or not. In Texas, the age for beginning employment is 15, but many younger adolescents and even children are employed, especially Mexican immigrants. The age for driving is 16, but when emergency need is demonstrated, a driver's license can be obtained at age 15. Some parents might not allow their son or daughter to obtain a driver's license even at age 16, believing that 16-year-olds are too young for this responsibility. The age for voting is 18, and the age for drinking recently has been raised to 21. Exactly when adolescents become adults in America has not been clearly delineated as it has in some primitive cultures, where rites of passage are universal.

At this point we have examined a number of ideas about culture and adolescence. This review should help you to reach your learning goals related to this topic.

☐ FOR YOUR REVIEW

Learning Goal 1
Understand culture and adolescent development

- Culture is the behavior, patterns, beliefs, and all other products of a particular group of people that are passed on from generation to generation. If the study of adolescence is to be a relevant discipline in the twenty-first century, increased attention will need to be focused on culture and ethnicity.
- Cross-cultural studies involve the comparison of a culture with one or more other cultures, which provides information about the degree to which information about adolescent development is culture-specific. The study of adolescence emerged in the context of Western industrialized society.
- The models that have been used to understand cultural changes within and across cultures include assimilation, acculturation, alternation, and multiculturalism. The multicultural model promotes a pluralistic approach to understanding two or more cultures.
- Rites of passage are ceremonies that mark an individual's transition from one status to another, especially into adulthood. In primitive cultures, rites of passage are well defined but in contemporary America they are not.

Now that we have studied the nature of culture and adolescent development, let's turn our attention to these important aspects of culture: socioeconomic status and poverty.

SOCIOECONOMIC STATUS AND POVERTY

Many subcultures exist within countries. For example, the values and attitudes of adolescents growing up in an urban ghetto or rural Appalachia may differ from those of adolescents growing up in a wealthy suburb.

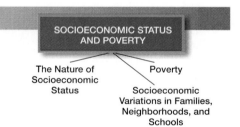

The Nature of Socioeconomic Status

Earlier in this chapter, we defined *socioeconomic status (SES)* as the grouping of people with similar occupational, educational, and economic characteristics. Socioeconomic status carries with it certain inequalities. Generally, members of a society have (1) occupations that vary in prestige, and some individuals have more access than others to higher-status occupations; (2) different levels of educational attainment, and some individuals have more access than others to better education; (3) different economic resources; and (4) different levels of power to influence a community's institutions. These differences in the ability to control resources and to participate in society's rewards produce unequal opportunities for adolescents (Bornstein & Bradley, 2003).

The number of visibly different socioeconomic statuses depends on the community's size and complexity. In most investigators' descriptions of socioeconomic status, two categories, low and middle, are used, although as many as five categories have been delineated. Sometimes low socioeconomic status is described as low-income, working class, or blue collar; sometimes the middle category is described as middle-income, managerial, or white collar. Examples of low-SES occupations are factory worker, manual laborer, welfare recipient, and maintenance worker. Examples of middle-SES occupations include salesperson, manager, and professional (doctor, lawyer, teacher, accountant, and so on).

Socioeconomic Variations in Families, Neighborhoods, and Schools

The families, schools, and neighborhoods of adolescents have socioeconomic characteristics (Bornstein & Bradley, 2003; Leventhal & Brooks-Gunn, 2000, 2003). Some adolescents have parents who have a great deal of money, and who work in prestigious occupations. These adolescents live in attractive houses and neighborhoods, and attend schools where the mix of students is primarily from middle- and upper-SES backgrounds. Other adolescents have parents who do not have very much money and who work in less prestigious occupations. These adolescents do not live in very attractive houses and neighborhoods, and they attend schools where the mix of students is mainly from lower-SES backgrounds. Such variations in neighborhood settings can influence adolescents' adjustment (Blyth, 2000; Booth & Crouter, 2000; Duncan, 2000; Leffert & Blyth, 1996). In one study, neighborhood crime and isolation were linked with low self-esteem and psychological distress in adolescents (Roberts, Jacobson, & Taylor, 1996).

In America and most other Western cultures, socioeconomic differences in child rearing exist (Hoff, Laursen, & Tardif, 2002; Hoff-Ginsberg & Tardif, 1995). Low-SES parents often place a high value on external characteristics, such as obedience and neatness, whereas higher (middle and upper) SES parents often place a high value on internal characteristics, such as self-control and delay of gratification. SES differences in parenting behaviors also exist. Higher-SES parents are more likely to explain something, use verbal praise, accompany their discipline with reasoning, and ask their children and adolescents questions. By contrast, low-SES parents are more likely to discipline their children and adolescents with physical punishment and criticize them (Heath, 1983).

SES differences also are involved in an important aspect of adolescents' intellectual orientation. Most school tasks require adolescents to use and process language. As a part of developing language skills, students must learn to read efficiently, write effectively, and give competent oral reports. Although variations exist within SES students, in one study students from low-SES families read less and watched television more than their middle-SES counterparts (see figure 8.1) (Erlick & Starry, 1973). Although television involves some verbal activity, it is primarily a visual medium, which suggests that adolescents from low-SES families prefer a visual medium over a verbal medium.

In one study, socioeconomic status, parenting, and skill-building activities were examined in divorced families (DeGarmo, Forgatch, & Martinez, 1998). Each of three indicators of socioeconomic status—education, occupation, and income—were studied independently to determine their effects on achievement in elementary school boys. Each indicator was associated with better parenting in the divorced families in the direction expected. Especially noteworthy was the finding that the effects of maternal education on boys' achievement was mediated by skill-building activities in the home that included time spent reading and engaging in other skill-building activities and time not spent watching television.

Like their parents, children and adolescents from low-SES backgrounds are at high risk for experiencing mental health problems (Magnuson & Duncan, 2002; McLoyd, 1993, 1998, 2000). Social maladaptation and psychological problems, such as depression, low self-confidence, peer conflict, and juvenile delinquency, are more prevalent among poor adolescents than among economically advantaged adolescents (Gibbs & Huang, 1989). Although psychological problems are more prevalent among adolescents from low-SES backgrounds, these adolescents vary considerably in intellectual and psychological functioning. For

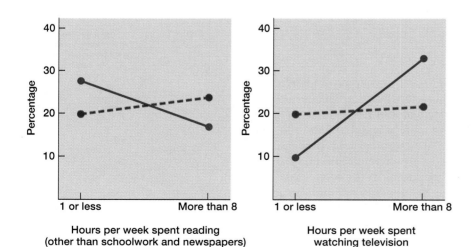

FIGURE 8.1
The Reading and Television Habits of High School Students from Low- and Middle-SES Families

example, a sizable portion of adolescents from low-SES backgrounds perform well in school; some perform better than many middle-SES students. When adolescents from low-SES backgrounds are achieving well in school, it is not unusual to find a parent or parents making special sacrifices to provide the necessary living conditions and support that contribute to school success.

In one study, although positive times occurred in the lives of ethnically diverse young adolescents growing up in poverty, many of their negative experiences were worse than those of their middle-SES counterparts (Richards & others, 1994). These adversities involved (1) physical punishment and lack of structure at home, (2) violence in the neighborhood, and (3) domestic violence in their buildings.

In chapter 7, "Schools," we read about schools in low-SES neighborhoods having fewer resources than schools in higher-SES neighborhoods ◀‖‖ P. 264. The schools in the low-SES areas also are more likely to have more students with lower achievement test scores, lower rates of graduation, and smaller percentages of students going to college (Garbarino & Asp, 1981). In some instances, however, federal aid to schools has provided a context for enhanced learning in low-income areas.

Poverty

**Children, Youth, and Poverty
Poverty in Canada
Research on Poverty**
http://www.mhhe.com/santrocka9

In a report on the state of America's children and adolescents, the Children's Defense Fund (1992) described what life is like for all too many youth. When sixth-graders in a poverty-stricken area of St. Louis were asked to describe a perfect day, one boy said he would erase the world, then he would sit and think. Asked if he wouldn't rather go outside and play, the boy responded, "Are you kidding, out there?"

The world is a dangerous and unwelcoming place for too many of America's youth, especially those whose families, neighborhoods, and schools are low-income (Edelman, 1997). Some adolescents are resilient and cope with the challenges of poverty without any major setbacks, but too many struggle unsuccessfully. Each child of poverty who reaches adulthood unhealthy, unskilled, or alienated keeps our nation from being as competent and productive as it can be (Children's Defense Fund, 1992).

The Nature of Poverty   Poverty is defined by economic hardship, and its most common marker is the federal poverty threshold (Huston, McLoyd, & Coll, 1994). The poverty threshold was originally based on the estimated cost of food (a basic diet) multiplied by 3. This federal poverty marker is adjusted annually for family size and inflation.

Based on the U.S. government's criteria for poverty, the proportion of children under the age of 18 living in families below the poverty threshold has increased from approximately 15 percent in the 1970s to 17 percent in the late 1990s (National Center for Health Statistics, 2001).

The U.S. figure of 17 percent of adolescents living in poverty is much higher than other industrialized nations. For example, Canada has a child/youth poverty rate of 9 percent, and Sweden has a rate of 2 percent. Poverty in the United States has demarcated along ethnic lines. Almost 40 percent of African American and Latino adolescents live in poverty (National Center for Health Statistics, 2001). Compared to White adolescents, ethnic minority adolescents are more likely to experience persistent poverty over many years and live in isolated poor neighborhoods where social supports are minimal and threats to positive development are abundant (Jarrett, 1995) (see figure 8.2).

Why is poverty among American youth so high? Three reasons are apparent (Huston, McLoyd, & Coll, 1994): (1) Economic changes have eliminated many blue-collar jobs that paid reasonably well, (2) the percentage of youth living in single-parent families headed by the mother has increased, and (3) government benefits were reduced during the 1970s and 1980s.

Poor children and their families are often exposed to poor health conditions, inadequate housing and homelessness, environmental toxins, and

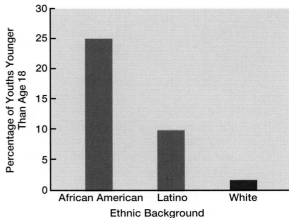

Note: A distressed neighborhood is defined by high levels (at least one standard deviation above the mean) of (1) poverty, (2) female-headed families, (3) high school dropouts, (4) unemployment, and (5) reliance on welfare.

FIGURE 8.2
Living in Distressed Neighborhoods

violent or unsupportive neighborhoods. Unlike income loss or unemployment due to job loss, poverty is not a homogeneous variable or distinct event. Also unemployment, unstable work history, and income loss do not always push families into poverty.

Let's further consider some of the psychological ramifications of living in poverty. First, the poor are often powerless. In occupations, they rarely are the decision makers. Rules are handed down to them in an authoritarian manner. Second, the poor are often vulnerable to disaster. They are not likely to be given notice when they are laid off from work and usually do not have financial resources to fall back on when problems arise. Third, their range of alternatives is often restricted. Only a limited number of jobs are open to them. Even when alternatives are available, the poor might not know about them or be prepared to make a wise decision, because of inadequate education and inability to read well. Fourth, being poor means having less prestige. This lack of prestige is transmitted to children early in their lives. The child in poverty observes that many other children wear nicer clothes and live in more attractive houses.

When poverty is persistent and long-standing, it can have especially damaging effects on children. In one study, the longer children lived in families with income below the poverty line, the lower was the quality of their home environments (Garrett, Ng'andu, & Ferron, 1994). Also in this study, improvements in family income had their strongest effects on the home environments of chronically poor children. In another study, children in families experiencing both persistent and occasional poverty had lower IQs and more internalized behavior problems than never-poor children, but persistent poverty had a much stronger negative effect on these outcomes than occasional poverty did (Duncan, Brooks-Gunn, & Klebanov, 1994).

A special concern is the high percentage of single mothers in poverty, more than one-third of whom are in poverty, compared to only 10 percent of single fathers. Vonnie McLoyd (1998, 2000) concludes that because poor, single mothers are more distressed than their middle-class counterparts are, they often show low support, nurturance, and involvement with their children. Among the reasons for the high poverty rate of single mothers are women's low pay, infrequent awarding of alimony payments, and poorly enforced child support by fathers (Graham & Beller, 2002). The term **feminization of poverty** *refers to the fact that far more women than men live in poverty. Women's low income, divorce, and the resolution of divorce cases by the judicial system, which leaves women with less money than they and their children need to adequately function, are the likely causes of the feminization of poverty.*

One recent trend in antipoverty programs is to conduct two-generation interventions (McLoyd, 1998). This involves providing both services for children (such as educational day care or preschool education) and services for parents (such as adult education, literacy training, and job skill training). Recent evaluations of the two-generation programs suggest that they have more positive effects on parents than they do on children (St. Pierre, Layzer, & Barnes, 1996). Also discouraging, regarding children, is the finding that when the two-generational programs show benefits, they are more likely to be in health benefits than in cognitive gains.

A downward trajectory is not inevitable for youth living in poverty (Carnegie Council on Adolescent Development, 1995). One potential positive path for such youth is to become involved with a caring mentor. The Quantum Opportunities Program, funded by the Ford Foundation, was a four-year, year-round mentoring effort. The students were entering the ninth grade at a high school with high rates of poverty, were minorities, and came from families that received public assistance. Each day for four years, mentors provided sustained support, guidance, and concrete assistance to their students.

What happens to a dream deferred?
Does it dry up
like a raisin in the sun?
    —Langston Hughes
      American Poet and Author, 20th Century

feminization of poverty
The fact that far more women than men live in poverty. Women's low income, divorce, and the resolution of divorce cases by the judicial system, which leaves women with less money than they and their children need to adequately function, are the likely causes.

THROUGH THE EYES OF ADOLESCENTS

Being Poor Was Awful

"Kids were mean there, not physically, but with their words. 'Who does your shopping for you? You've *never* been to the Calhoun Club? *Where* do you get your clothes from? You mean you *haven't* been out of the U.S.? You *rent* your home? You mean you don't get an *allowance?*' I couldn't have what they had or really understand the importance of it all, and I felt it acutely. There were the times when I would be talking with someone, and instead of listening to whatever it was I was saying, they'd be staring at my clothes.

". . . Being poor was awful, the bills were too many and too much. It didn't help me in dealing with the daily questionings or scornful looks from my peers. When they did that, I just looked away or down, shoulders slumped, because I felt self-conscious."

—Native American Adolescent Girl

These adolescents participate in the programs of El Puente, located in a predominantly low-SES Latino neighborhood in Brooklyn, New York. The El Puente program stresses five areas of youth development: health, education, achievement, personal growth, and social growth.

The Quantum program required students to participate in (1) academic-related activities outside school hours, including reading, writing, math, science, and social studies, peer tutoring, and computer skills training; (2) community service projects, including tutoring elementary school students, cleaning up the neighborhood, and volunteering in hospitals, nursing homes, and libraries; and (3) cultural enrichment and personal development activities, including life skills training, and college and job planning. In exchange for their commitment to the program, students were offered financial incentives that encouraged participation, completion, and long-range planning. A stipend of $1.33 was given to students for each hour they participated in these activities. For every 100 hours of education, service, or development activities, students received a bonus of $100. The average cost per participant was $10,600 for the four years, which is one-half the cost of one year in prison.

An evaluation of the Quantum project compared the mentored students with a nonmentored control group. Sixty-three percent of the mentored students graduated from high school but only 42 percent of the control group did; 42 percent of the mentored students are currently enrolled in college but only 16 percent of the control group are. Furthermore, control-group students were twice as likely as the mentored students to receive food stamps or welfare, and they had more arrests. Such programs clearly have the potential to overcome the intergenerational transmission of poverty and its negative outcomes.

Another effort to improve the lives of adolescents living in poverty is the El Puente program, which is primarily aimed at Latino adolescents living in low-SES areas.

El Puente ("the bridge") was opened in New York City in 1983 because of community dissatisfaction with the health, education, and social services youth were receiving (Simons, Finlay, & Yang, 1991). El Puente emphasizes five areas of youth development: health, education, achievement, personal growth, and social growth.

El Puente is located in a former Roman Catholic church on the south side of Williamsburg in Brooklyn, a neighborhood made up primarily of low-income Latino families, many of which are far below the poverty line. Sixty-five percent of the residents receive some form of public assistance. The neighborhood has the highest school dropout rate for Latinos in New York City and the highest felony rate for adolescents in Brooklyn.

When the youths, aged 12 through 21, first enroll in El Puente, they meet with counselors and develop a four-month plan that includes the programs they are interested in joining. At the end of four months, youth and staff develop a plan for continued participation. Twenty-six bilingual classes are offered in such subjects as the fine arts, theater, photography, and dance. In addition, a medical and fitness center, GED night school, and mental health and social services centers are also a part of El Puente.

El Puente is funded through state, city, and private organizations and serves about three hundred youth. The program has been replicated in Chelsea and Holyoke, Massachusetts, and two other sites in New York are being developed.

Since the last review, we have studied a number of ideas about socioeconomic status and poverty. This review should help you to reach your learning goals for these topics.

☐ FOR YOUR REVIEW

Learning Goal 2
Discuss socioeconomic status and adolescence

- Socioeconomic status (SES) is the grouping of people with similar occupational, educational, and economic characteristics. Socioeconomic status often involves certain inequalities.
- The families, neighborhoods, and schools of adolescents have socioeconomic characteristics that are related to the adolescent's development.
- Parents in low-SES families are more likely to value external characteristics and use physical punishment than their middle-SES counterparts.

Learning Goal 3
Describe the role of poverty in adolescent development

- Poverty is defined by economic hardship, and its most common marker is the federal poverty threshold (based on the estimated cost of food multiplied by 3). Based on this threshold, the percentage of children in poverty increased from 15 percent in the 1970s to 17 percent in the late 1990s.
- The subculture of the poor often is characterized not only by economic hardship, but also by social and psychological difficulties. When poverty is persistent and longstanding, it especially can have devastating effects on child and adolescent development.

So far in this chapter, we have discussed the nature of culture, socioeconomic status, and poverty. Next, we will focus on this important aspect of culture: ethnicity.

ETHNICITY

ETHNICITY

Ethnicity Issues

Ethnic Minority Adolescents

The United States and Canada: Nations with Many Cultures

Adolescents live in a world that has been made smaller and more interactive by dramatic improvements in travel and communication. Adolescents also live in a world that is far more diverse in its ethnic makeup than it was in past decades. Ninety-three languages are spoken in Los Angeles alone!

As mentioned earlier in the chapter, *ethnicity* refers to the cultural heritage, national characteristics, race, religion, and language of individuals. As evidenced by the waves of ethnic animosity around the world today, we need to better understand ethnicity.

Relatively high rates of immigration among minorities are contributing to the growth in the proportion of ethnic minorities in the U.S. population (McLoyd, 1998, 2000; Phinney, 2000). Because immigrants often experience stressors uncommon to or less prominent among longtime residents (such as language barriers, dislocations, and separations from support networks, dual struggle to preserve identity and to acculturate, and changes in SES status), adaptations in intervention programs might be required to achieve optimal cultural sensitivity when working with adolescents and their immigrant families (Suárez-Orozco, 1999).

Though the United States has an increasing immigrant population, psychologists have been slow to study these families. One recent study looked at the cultural values and intergenerational value discrepancies in immigrant (Vietnamese, Armenian, and Mexican) and nonimmigrant (African American and European American) families (Phinney, Madden, & Ong, 2000). Family obligations were endorsed more by parents than adolescents in all groups, and the intergenerational value discrepancy generally increased with time in the United States.

Exploring Diversity
Diversity Resources
Ethnic Groups
http://www.mhhe.com/santrocka9

Ethnicity Issues

What are ethnicity, socioeconomic status, differences, and diversity? Is adolescence a special juncture in the development of ethnic minority adolescents? How do prejudice, discrimination, and bias affect adolescents? What is the nature of value conflicts, assimilation, and pluralism?

Ethnicity, Socioeconomic Status, Differences, and Diversity   Much of the research on ethnic minority adolescents has failed to tease apart the influences of ethnicity and socioeconomic status (SES). Ethnicity and SES can interact in ways that exaggerate the influence of ethnicity because ethnic minority individuals are overrepresented in the lower socioeconomic levels of American society (Spencer & Dornbusch, 1990). Consequently, too often researchers have given ethnic explanations of adolescent development that were largely based on socioeconomic status rather than ethnicity. For example, decades of research on group differences in self-esteem failed to consider the socioeconomic status of African American and White American children and adolescents (Hare & Castenell, 1985). When the self-esteem of African American adolescents from low-income backgrounds is compared with that of White American adolescents from middle-SES backgrounds, the differences are often large but not informative because of the confounding of ethnicity and social class (Scott-Jones, 1995).

Some ethnic minority youth are from middle-SES backgrounds, but economic advantage does not entirely enable them to escape their ethnic minority status. Middle-SES ethnic minority youth still encounter much of the prejudice, discrimination, and bias associated with being a member of an ethnic minority group. Often characterized as a "model minority" because of their strong achievement orientation and family cohesiveness, Japanese Americans still experience stress associated with ethnic minority status (Sue, 1990). Although middle-SES ethnic minority adolescents have more resources available to counter the destructive influences of prejudice and discrimination, they still cannot completely avoid the pervasive influences of negative stereotypes about ethnic minority groups.

Not all ethnic minority families are poor, but poverty contributes to the stressful life experiences of many ethnic minority adolescents (Fuligni & Yoshikawa, 2003). Vonnie McLoyd (1990) concluded that ethnic minority youth experience a disproportionate share of the adverse effects of poverty and unemployment in America today. Thus, many ethnic minority adolescents experience a double disadvantage: (1) prejudice, discrimination, and bias because of their ethnic minority status, and (2) the stressful effects of poverty.

Historical, economic, and social experiences produce legitimate differences between various ethnic minority groups, and between ethnic minority groups and the majority White group (Halonen & Santrock, 1999). Individuals living in a particular ethnic or cultural group adapt to the values, attitudes, and stresses of that culture. Their

Migration and Ethnic Relations
Immigration: Journals and
Newsletter
Immigration and Ethnicity:
Research Centers
Immigrant Families
http://www.mhhe.com/santrocka9

behavior, while possibly different from our own, is, nonetheless, often functional for them. Recognizing and respecting these differences is an important aspect of getting along with others in a diverse, multicultural world (Leong, 2000). Adolescents, as well as each of us, need to take the perspective of individuals from ethnic and cultural groups that are different from ours and think, "If I were in their shoes, what kind of experiences might I have had?" "How would I feel if I were a member of their ethnic or cultural group?" "How would I think and behave if I had grown up in their world?" Such perspective taking often increases our empathy and understanding of individuals from ethnic and cultural groups different from ours.

Unfortunately, the emphasis often placed by society and science on the differences between ethnic minority groups and the White majority has been damaging to ethnic minority individuals. Ethnicity has defined who will enjoy the privileges of citizenship and to what degree and in what ways (Jones, 1994). An individual's ethnic background has determined whether the individual will be alienated, oppressed, or disadvantaged.

The current emphasis on differences between ethnic groups underscores the strengths of various ethnic minority groups and is long overdue (Cushner, McClelland, & Safford, 2000, 2003). For example, the extended-family support system that characterizes many ethnic minority groups is now recognized as an important factor in coping. And researchers are finding that African American males are better than Anglo males at nonverbal cues, multilingual/multicultural expression, improvised problem solving, and using body language in communication (Evans & Whitfield, 1988).

For too long, the ways ethnic minority groups differed from Whites were conceptualized as *deficits* or inferior characteristics on the part of the ethnic minority group. Indeed, research on ethnic minority groups often focused only on a group's negative, stressful aspects. For example, research on African American adolescent females invariably examined such topics as poverty, unwed motherhood, and dropping out of school. These topics continue to be important research areas of adolescent development, but research on the positive aspects of African American adolescent females in a pluralistic society is also much needed and sorely neglected. The self-esteem, achievement, motivation, and self-control of adolescents from different ethnic minority groups deserve considerable study.

Another important dimension of ethnic minority adolescents is their diversity (Spring, 2000; Wilson, 2000). Ethnic minority groups are not homogeneous; they have different social, historical, and economic backgrounds (Stevenson, 1998). For example, Mexican, Cuban, and Puerto Rican immigrants are Latinos but they had different reasons for migrating, came from varying socioeconomic backgrounds in their native countries, and experience different rates and types of employment in the United States (Ramirez, 1989). The U.S. federal government now recognizes the existence of 511 *different* Native American tribes, each having a unique ancestral background with differing values and characteristics. Asian Americans include the Chinese, Japanese, Filipinos, Koreans, and Southeast Asians, each group having distinct ancestries and languages. The diversity of Asian Americans is reflected in their educational attainment: Some achieve a high level of education, while many others have no education whatsoever. For

CAREERS IN ADOLESCENT DEVELOPMENT

Carola Suárez-Orozco
Lecturer, Researcher, and Co-Director of Immigration Projects

Carola Suárez-Orozco is a researcher and lecturer in the Human Development and Psychology area at Harvard University. She also is co-director of the Harvard Immigration Projects. She obtained her undergraduate degree (development studies) and graduate (clinical psychology) degree from the University of California at Berkeley.

Carola has worked both in clinical and public school settings in California and Massachusetts. She currently is co-directing a five-year longitudinal study of immigrant adolescents' (coming from Central America, China, and the Dominican Republic) adaptation to schools and society. One of the courses she teaches at Harvard is on the psychology of immigrant youth. She especially believes that more research needs to be conducted on the intersection of cultural and psychological factors in the adaptation of immigrant and ethnic minority youth (Suárez-Orozco, 2002; Suárez-Orozco & Suárez-Orozco, 2002).

Carola Suárez-Orozco, with her husband Marcelo, who also studies the adaptation of immigrants.

example, 90 percent of Korean American males graduate from high school, but only 71 percent of Vietnamese American males do.

Sometimes, well-meaning individuals fail to recognize the diversity within an ethnic group (Sue, 1990). For example, a sixth-grade teacher went to a human relations workshop and was exposed to the necessity of incorporating more ethnicity into her instructional planning. She had two Mexican American adolescents in her class, and she asked them to be prepared to demonstrate to the class on the following Monday how they danced at home. The teacher expected both of them to perform Mexican folk dances, reflecting their ethnic heritage. The first boy got up in front of the class and began dancing in a typical American fashion. The teacher said, "No, I want you to dance like you and your family do at home, like you do when you have Mexican American celebrations." The boy informed the teacher that his family did not dance that way. The second boy demonstrated a Mexican folk dance to the class. The first boy was highly assimilated into the American culture and did not know how to dance Mexican folk dances. The second boy was less assimilated and came from a Mexican American family that had retained more of its Mexican heritage.

This example illustrates the diversity and individual differences that exist within any ethnic minority group. Failure to recognize diversity and individual variations results in the stereotyping of an ethnic minority group.

Prejudice, Discrimination, and Bias

Prejudice *is an unjustified negative attitude toward an individual because of the individual's membership in a group.* The group toward which the prejudice is directed can be made up of people of a particular ethnic group, sex, age, religion, or other detectable difference. Our concern here is prejudice against ethnic minority groups. In one recent study, African American adolescents' connection to their ethnic group served as a buffer against threats of discrimination (Wong, Eccles, & Sameroff, 2001).

In a Gallup poll, Americans stated that they believe that the United States is ethnically tolerant and that overt racism is basically unacceptable ("Poll Finds Racial Tension Decreasing," 1990). However, many ethnic minority individuals continue to experience persistent forms of prejudice, discrimination, and bias (Monteith, 2000; Sue, 1990). Ethnic minority adolescents are taught in schools that often have a middle-SES, White bias and in classroom contexts that are not adapted to ethnic minority adolescents' learning styles. They are assessed by tests that are often culturally biased and are evaluated by teachers whose appreciation of their abilities may be hindered by negative stereotypes about ethnic minorities (Spencer & Dornbusch, 1990). Discrimination and prejudice continue to be present in the media, interpersonal interactions, and daily conversations. Crimes, strangeness, poverty, mistakes, and deterioration are often mistakenly attributed to ethnic minority individuals or foreigners (van Dijk, 1987).

As Asian American researcher Stanley Sue (1990) points out, people frequently have opposing views about discrimination and prejudice. On one side are individuals who value and praise the significant strides made in civil rights in recent years, pointing to affirmative action programs as proof of these civil rights advances. On the other side are individuals who criticize American institutions, such as education, because they believe that many forms of discrimination and prejudice still characterize these institutions.

For several reasons, the "browning" of America portends heightened racial/ethnic prejudice and conflict, or at least sharper racial and ethnic cleavages (McLoyd, 1998,

prejudice
An unjustified negative attitude toward an individual because of her or his membership in a group.

THINKING CRITICALLY

Reconstructing Prejudice

No matter how well intentioned adolescents are, their life circumstances have probably given them some prejudices. If they don't maintain particular prejudices toward people with different cultural and ethnic backgrounds, there might be other kinds of people who bring out prejudices in them. For example, prejudices can be developed about people who have certain religious beliefs or political convictions, people who are unattractive or too attractive, people with unpopular occupations (police officers, lawyers), people with a disability, and people from bordering towns.

Psychologist William James once observed that one function of education is to rearrange prejudices. How could adolescents' education rearrange prejudices like the ones we have listed? Consider prejudice toward ethnic minority groups, the main focus of our discussion of prejudice in this chapter. One strategy might be to adopt the jigsaw classroom concept involving cooperative learning, which was discussed in chapter 7. What other strategies might work?

Margaret Beale Spencer, shown here talking with adolescents, believes that adolescence is a critical juncture in the identity development of ethnic minority individuals. Most ethnic minority individuals consciously confront their ethnicity for the first time in adolescence.

Ethnic Minority Families
Prejudice
http://www.mhhe.com/santrocka9

2000). First, it is occurring against a backdrop of long-standing White privilege and an ingrained sense of entitlement and superiority among non-Latino Whites. Second, the youth of today's immigrants are less likely than their counterparts in the early twentieth century to believe that rejection of the values and ways of their parents' homeland is needed to succeed in American society. Many espouse economic, but not cultural, assimilation into mainstream society. Third, today's immigrants often settle in inner-city neighborhoods where assimilation often means joining a world that is antagonistic to the American mainstream because of its experience of racism and economic barriers.

Progress has been made in ethnic minority relations, but discrimination and prejudice still exist, and equality has not been achieved. Much remains to be accomplished (Murrell, 2000).

Adolescence: A Special Juncture for Ethnic Minority Individuals For ethnic minority individuals, adolescence is often a special juncture in their development (Rodriquez & Quinlan, 2002; Spencer & Dornbusch, 1990). Although children are aware of some ethnic and cultural differences, most ethnic minority individuals first consciously confront their ethnicity in adolescence. In contrast to children, adolescents have the ability to interpret ethnic and cultural information, to reflect on the past, and to speculate about the future. As they cognitively mature, ethnic minority adolescents become acutely aware of how the majority White culture evaluates their ethnic group (Comer, 1993). As one researcher commented, the young African American child may learn that Black is beautiful but conclude as an adolescent that White is powerful (Semaj, 1985).

Ethnic minority youths' awareness of negative appraisals, conflicting values, and restricted occupational opportunities can influence their life choices and plans for the future (Spencer & Dornbusch, 1990). As one ethnic minority youth stated, "The future seems shut off, closed. Why dream? You can't reach your dreams. Why set goals? At least if you don't set any goals, you don't fail."

For many ethnic minority youth, a special concern is the lack of successful ethnic minority role models (Blash & Unger, 1992). The problem is especially acute for inner-city ethnic minority youth. Because of the lack of adult ethnic minority role models, some ethnic minority youth may conform to middle-SES White values and identify with successful White role models. However, for many ethnic minority adolescents, their ethnicity and skin color limit their acceptance by the White culture. Thus, they face a difficult task: negotiating two values systems—that of their own ethnic group and that of the White society. Some adolescents reject the mainstream, forgoing the rewards controlled by White Americans; others adopt the values and standards of the majority White culture; and still others take the difficult path of biculturality.

The nature of identity development in ethnic minority adolescents is discussed further in chapter 9, "The Self and Identity."

Ethnic Minority Adolescents

Now that we have considered a number of ideas about ethnic minority adolescents in general, we turn our attention to specific ethnic minority groups in America, beginning with African American adolescents.

African American Adolescents African American adolescents make up the largest easily visible ethnic minority group in the United States. African American adolescents are distributed throughout the socioeconomic structure, although they constitute a larger proportion of poor and lower-SES individuals than does the majority White group (McLoyd, 1993, 1998). No cultural characteristic is common to all or nearly all African Americans and absent in Whites, unless it is the experience of being African American and the ideology that develops from that experience (Havighurst, 1987).

The majority of African American youth stay in school, do not take drugs, do not prematurely get married and become parents, are employed and eager to work, are not involved in crime, and grow up to lead productive lives in spite of social and economic disadvantage. While much of the writing and research about African American adolescents has focused on low-SES youth from families mainly residing in inner cities, the majority of African American youth do not reside in the ghettos of inner cities. At the heart of the new model of studying African American youth is recognition of the growing diversity in African American communities in the United States (McHale, 1995; Stevenson, 1998).

Prejudice against African Americans in some occupations still persists, but the proportion of African American males and females in middle-SES occupations has been increasing since 1940. A substantial and increasing proportion of African American adolescents are growing up in middle-SES families and share middle-class values and attitudes with White middle-SES adolescents. Nonetheless, large numbers of African American adolescents still live in poverty-enshrouded ghettos.

In one investigation of African Americans, a mixture of factors was related to the problems of adolescents in the inner city (Wilson, 1987). Increased social isolation in concentrated areas of poverty and little interaction with the mainstream society were related to the difficulties experienced by inner-city African American youth. Unattractive jobs and a lack of community standards to reinforce work increased the likelihood that inner-city African American youth would turn to either underground illegal activity, idleness, or both.

In the inner city, African American youth often have difficulty in finding legitimate employment, to some extent because of the lack of even low-paying jobs (Spencer & Dornbusch, 1990). The exodus of middle-SES African Americans from the cities to the suburbs has removed leadership, reduced the tax base, decreased the educated political constituency, and diminished the support of churches and other organizations.

In many ethnic minority communities, religious institutions play an important role. Many African Americans report that their religious beliefs help them to get along with others and to accept the realities of the American occupational system (Spencer & Dornbusch, 1990). In one research study of successful African American students, a strong religious faith was common (Lee, 1985). In this study, regular church attendance characterized the lives of the successful African American students, many of whom mentioned Jesus Christ, Martin Luther King, and deacons as important influences in their lives. For many African American families, the church has served as an important resource and support system, not only in spiritual matters, but in the development of a social network as well. In other research, Howard Stevenson (1997) found that African American adolescents were more angry, the more they were aware of the need for cultural pride and society's racism struggles. Their anger was controlled or inhibited if they received communication about spirituality or religion connected to cultural pride.

As mentioned earlier, there is a high percentage of single-parent African American families, many of whom are in low-SES categories. These family circumstances tax the coping ability of single parents and can have negative effects on children and adolescents (Wilson, Cook & Arrington, 1997). However, a characteristic of many African American families that helps to offset the high percentage of single-parent households is the extended-family household—in which one or several grandparents, uncles, aunts, siblings, or cousins either live together or provide support. The extended-family system has helped many African American parents to cope with adverse social conditions and economic impoverishment. The African American extended family can be traced to the African heritage of many African Americans; in many African cultures, a newly married couple does not move away from relatives. Instead, the extended family assists

THROUGH THE EYES OF PSYCHOLOGISTS

Vonnie McLoyd
University of Michigan

"Poverty and stress are common in the lives of many ethnic minority women who are single parents, and too often this translates into stressful lives for their children."

African Americans
http://www.mhhe.com/santrocka9

THROUGH THE EYES OF ADOLESCENTS

Seeking a Positive Image for African American Youth

"I want America to know that most of us black teens are not troubled people from broken homes and headed to jail. . . . In my relationships with my parents, we show respect for each other and we have values in our house. We have traditions we celebrate together, including Christmas and Kwanza."

—Jason Leonard, Age 15

Jason Leonard

Chicano

The name politically conscious Mexican American adolescents give themselves, reflecting the combination of their Spanish-Mexican-Indian heritage and Anglo influence.

its members with basic family functions. Researchers have found that the extended family helps to reduce the stress of poverty and single-parenting through emotional support, sharing of income and economic responsibility, and surrogate parenting (McAdoo, 1996). The presence of grandmothers in the households of many African American adolescents and their infants has also been an important support system for the teenage mother and the infant (Stevens, 1984).

Latino Adolescents   In the year 2000, the number of Latino Americans in the United States swelled to 30 million people, 15 percent of the total U.S. population. Most trace their roots to Mexico (almost two-thirds), Puerto Rico (12 percent), and Cuba (5 percent), the rest to Central and South American countries and the Caribbean. About one-third of all Latino Americans marry non-Latinos, promising a day when the Latino culture will be even more intertwined with other cultures in the United States.

By far the largest group of Latino adolescents consists of those who identify themselves as having a Mexican origin, although many of them were born in the United States (Domino, 1992). Their largest concentration is in the U.S. Southwest. They represent more than 50 percent of the student population in the schools of San Antonio and close to that percentage in the schools of Los Angeles. Mexican Americans have a variety of lifestyles and come from a range of socioeconomic statuses—from affluent professional and managerial status to migrant farm worker and welfare recipient in big-city barrios. Even though they come from families with diverse backgrounds, Latino adolescents have one of the lowest educational levels of any ethnic minority group in the United States. Social support from parents and school personnel may be especially helpful in developing stronger academic achievement in Latino youth (Romo, 2000; Salas, 2000).

Many Latino adolescents have developed a new political consciousness and pride in their cultural heritage (Comas-Díaz, 2001). Some have fused strong cultural links to Mexican and Indian cultures with the economic limitations and restricted opportunities in the barrio. **Chicano** *is the name politically conscious Mexican American adolescents give themselves to reflect the combination of their Spanish-Mexican-Indian heritage and Anglo influences.*

As for African American adolescents, the church and family play important roles in Latino adolescents' lives. Many, but not all, Latino families are Catholic. And a basic value in Mexico is represented by saying, "As long as our family stays together, we are strong." Mexican children are brought up to stay close to their family, a tradition continued by Mexican Americans. Unlike the father in many Anglo-American families, the Mexican father is the undisputed authority on all family matters and is usually obeyed without question. The mother is revered as the primary source of affection and care. This emphasis on family attachment leads the Mexican to say, "I will achieve mainly because of my family, and for my family, rather than myself." By contrast, the self-reliant American would say, "I will achieve mainly because of my ability and initiative, and for myself, rather than for my family." Unlike most American families, Mexican families tend to stretch out in a network of relatives that often runs to scores of individuals. Mexican American families also tend to be large and have a strong extended-family orientation.

Asian American Adolescents   Asian American adolescents are the fastest-growing segment of the American adolescent population, and they, too, show considerable

The tapestry of American society is rapidly changing with an increasing number of ethnic minority youth. *What issues are involved in the development of African American, Latino, Asian American, and Native American youth in America?*

diversity. In the 1970 census, only three Asian American groups were prominent—Japanese, Chinese, and Filipino. But in the last two decades, there has been rapid growth in three other groups—Koreans, Pacific Islanders (Guam and Samoa), and Vietnamese.

Adolescents of Japanese or Chinese origin can be found in virtually every large city. While their grasp of the English language is usually good, they have been raised in a subculture in which family loyalty and family influence are powerful. This has tended to maintain their separate subcultures. The Japanese American adolescents are somewhat more integrated into the Anglo lifestyle than are the Chinese American adolescents. However, both groups have been very successful in school. They tend to take considerable advantage of educational opportunities.

Asian families and practices, such as high expectations for success, induction of guilt about parental sacrifices and the need to fulfill obligations, parental control of after-school time, and respect for education, are among the reasons identified to explain the high achievement of Asian adolescents (Sue & Okazaki, 1990).

One recent study compared the achievement experiences of Asian American and White American adolescents (Asakawa & Csikszentmihalyi, 1998). When studying, Asian American students reported that it was a more positive experience and saw the studying as more connected to their future goals than their white American counterparts did. We will have more to say about the achievement of Asian American adolescents in chapter 13, "Achievement, Careers, and Work."

Latinos and Native Americans
Asian Americans
http://www.mhhe.com/santrocka9

Native American Adolescents   Approximately 100,000 Native American (American Indian) adolescents are scattered across many tribal groups in about 20 states. About 90 percent are enrolled in school. About 15,000 are in boarding schools, many of which are maintained by the federal government's Bureau of Indian Affairs. Another 45,000 are in public schools on or near Indian reservations. In these schools, Native American adolescents make up more than 50 percent of the students. The remaining 30,000 are in public schools where they are an ethnic minority. A growing proportion of Native American adolescents have moved to large cities.

Native American adolescents have experienced an inordinate amount of discrimination. While virtually any minority group experiences some discrimination in being a member of a larger, majority-group culture, in the early years of the United States, Native Americans were the victims of terrible physical abuse and punishment. Injustices that these 800,000 individuals experienced are reflected in their having the lowest standard of living, the highest teenage-pregnancy rate, the highest suicide rate, and the highest school dropout rate of any ethnic group in the United States (Chandler, 2002; LaFromboise & Low, 1989).

The United States and Canada: Nations with Many Cultures

The United States has been and continues to be a great receiver of ethnic groups (Glazer, 1997). It has embraced new ingredients from many cultures. The cultures often collide and cross-pollinate, mixing their ideologies and identities. Some of the culture of origin is retained, some of it lost, some of it mixed with the American culture. One after another, immigrants have come to the United States and been exposed to new channels of awareness and, in turn, exposed Americans to new channels of awareness. African American, Latino, Asian American, Native American, and other cultural heritages mix with the mainstream, receiving a new content and giving a new content.

Not only is there considerable diversity in the United States, but the United States' northern American neighbor, Canada, also is a country with diverse ethnic groups. Although Canada shares many similarities with the United States, there are some important differences (Majhanovich, 1998; Siegel & Wiener, 1993). Canada comprises a mixture of cultures that are loosely organized along the lines of economic power. The Canadian cultures include these:

- Native peoples, or First Nations, who were Canada's original inhabitants
- Descendants of French settlers who came to Canada during the seventeenth and eighteenth centuries
- Descendants of British settlers who came to Canada during and after the seventeenth century, or from the United States after the American Revolution in the latter part of the eighteenth century

The late nineteenth century brought three more waves of immigrants:

- From Asia, mainly China, immigrants came to the west coast of Canada in the latter part of the nineteenth and early twentieth centuries.
- From various European countries, immigrants came to central Canada and the prairie provinces during the early twentieth century and following World War II.
- From countries in economic and political turmoil (in Latin America, the Caribbean, Asia, Africa, the Indian subcontinent, the former Soviet Union, and the Middle East), immigrants have come to many different parts of Canada.

Canada has two official languages—English and French. Primarily French-speaking individuals reside mainly in Quebec; primarily English-speaking individuals reside mainly in other Canadian provinces. In addition to its English- and French-speaking populations, Canada has a large multicultural community. In three large Canadian cities—Toronto, Montreal, and Vancouver—more than 50 percent of the children and adolescents come from homes in which neither English nor French is the native language (Siegel & Wiener, 1993).

Since the last review, we have studied many aspects of ethnicity. This review should help you to reach your learning goals related to this topic.

☐ FOR YOUR REVIEW

Learning Goal 4
Evaluate issues related to ethnicity

- Too often researchers do not adequately tease apart SES and ethnicity when they study ethnic minority groups.
- Historical, economic, and social experiences produce many legitimate differences among ethnic minority groups, and between ethnic minority groups and the White majority. Too often differences have been interpreted as deficits in ethnic minority groups.
- Failure to recognize the diversity within an ethnic minority group can lead to stereotyping.
- Many ethnic minority adolescents continue to experience prejudice, discrimination, and bias.
- Adolescence often is a critical juncture in the development of ethnic minority individuals.

Learning Goal 5
Know about ethnic minority adolescents

- African American adolescents make up the largest visible ethnic minority group. The church and extended family have helped many African American adolescents cope with stressful circumstances.
- Latino adolescents trace their roots to many countries, including Mexico, Cuba, Puerto Rico, and Central America.
- Asian American adolescents are a diverse group and the fastest-growing ethnic minority group in the United States.
- Native American adolescents have faced painful discrimination and have the highest school dropout rate of any ethnic group.
- The United States has been and continues to be a great receiver of ethnic groups. The cultures mix their ideologies and identities.
- Adolescents in Canada are exposed to some cultural dimensions that are similar and different to their counterparts in the United States. Canada's main cultural ties are British and French.

So far in this chapter we have examined the nature of culture, socioeconomic status, poverty, and ethnicity. Next, we will explore some aspects of culture that have become increasingly important in the lives of adolescents: television and other media.

TELEVISION AND OTHER MEDIA

Few developments in society over the last 40 years have had a greater impact on adolescents than television (Calvert, 1999; Huston & Wright, 1998). The persuasion capabilities of television are staggering. As they have grown up, many of today's adolescents have spent more time in front of the television set than with their parents or in the classroom. Radio, records, rock music, and music video are other media that are especially important influences in the lives of many adolescents.

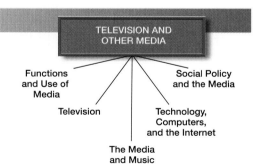

Functions and Use of Media

The functions of media for adolescents include these (Arnett, 1991):

1. *Entertainment.* Adolescents, like adults, often use media simply for entertainment and an enjoyable diversion from everyday concerns.
2. *Information.* Adolescents use media to obtain information, especially about topics that their parents may have been reluctant to discuss in the home, such as sexuality.
3. *Sensation.* Adolescents tend to be higher in sensation seeking than adults are; certain media provide intense and novel stimulation that appeals to adolescents.

4. *Coping.* Adolescents use media to relieve anxiety and unhappiness. Two of the most frequently endorsed coping responses of adolescents are "listen to music" and "watch TV."

5. *Gender-role modeling.* Media present models of female and male gender roles; these media images of females and males can influence adolescents' gender attitudes and behavior.

6. *Youth culture identification.* Media use gives many adolescents a sense of being connected to a larger peer network and culture, which is united by the kinds of values and interests conveyed through adolescent-oriented media.

If the amount of time spent in an activity is any indication of its importance, then there is no doubt that the mass media play important roles in adolescents' lives (Fine, Mortimer, & Roberts, 1990). Adolescents spend a third or more of their waking hours with some form of mass media, either as a primary focus or as a background for other activities. Estimates of adolescent television viewing range from two to four hours per day, with considerable variation around the averages: Some adolescents watch little or no television; others view as much as eight hours a day. Television viewing often peaks in late childhood and then begins to decline at some point in early adolescence in response to competing media and the demands of school and social activities (Huston & Alvarez, 1990). Figure 8.3 shows the extensive amount of time young adolescents spend watching television compared to doing homework and reading.

As television viewing declines, the use of music media—radio, CDs, tapes, and music video—increases four to six hours per day by the middle of adolescence (Fine, Mortimer, & Roberts, 1990; Larson, Kubey, & Colletti, 1989). As adolescents get older, movie attendance increases—more than 50 percent of 12- to 17-year-olds report at least monthly attendance. In recent years, viewing of videocassettes has become a common adolescent activity, with adolescent involvement at 5 to 10 hours per week (Wartella & others, 1990).

Adolescents also use the print media more than children do (Anderson & others, 2001). Newspaper reading often begins at about 11 to 12 years of age and gradually increases until 60 to 80 percent of late adolescents report at least some newspaper reading. In similar fashion, magazine and book reading gradually increase during adolescence. Approximately one-third of high school juniors and seniors say that they read magazines daily, while 20 percent say that they read nonschool books daily, reports that are substantiated by the sales of teen-oriented books and magazines. However, comic book reading declines steeply between the ages of 10 and 18.

Large, individual differences characterize all forms of adolescent media use. In addition to the age differences just described, gender, ethnicity, socioeconomic status, and intelligence are all related to which media are used, to what extent, and for what purposes. For example, female adolescents watch more television and listen to more music than male adolescents do; African American adolescents view television and listen to more music than White American adolescents do, with African American females showing the most frequent viewing and listening (Greenberg, 1988). Brighter adolescents and adolescents from middle-SES families are more likely to read the newspaper and news magazines, and also are more likely to watch television news, than are less intelligent adolescents and adolescents from low-income backgrounds (Chafee & Yang, 1990).

Television

The messages of television are powerful (Murray, 2000). What are television's functions? How extensively does television affect adolescents? What is MTV's role in adolescents' lives?

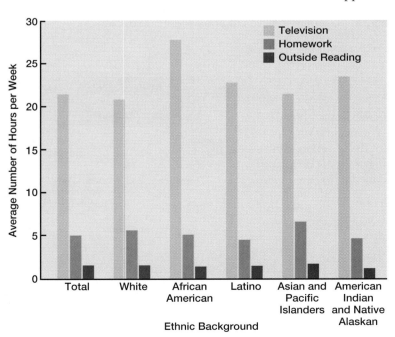

FIGURE 8.3
Weekly After-School Activities of Eighth-Graders

Television's Functions   Television has been called a lot of things, not all of them good. Depending on one's point of view, it is a "window to the world," the "one-eyed monster," or the "boob tube." Scores on national achievement tests in reading and mathematics, while showing a small improvement recently, have generally been lower than in the past decades—and television has been attacked as one of the reasons. Television may take adolescents away from the printed media and books. One study found that children who read books and the printed media watched television less than those who did not (Huston, Siegle, & Bremer, 1983). It is argued that television trains individuals to become passive learners. Rarely, if ever, does television require active responses from the observer. Heavy television use may produce not only a passive learner, but a passive lifestyle. In one investigation of 406 adolescent males, those who watched little television were more physically fit and physically active than those who watched a lot (Tucker, 1987). In a recent study, heavy TV viewing was correlated with obesity in adolescent girls (Anderson & others, 2001).

Exploring Television Violence
Children, Youth, Media, and
Violence
Cultural and TV Violence
http://www.mhhe.com/santrocka9

Television also can deceive. It can teach adolescents that problems are easily resolved and that everything turns out all right in the end. For example, it takes only about 30 to 60 minutes for detectives to sort through a complex array of clues and discover the killer—and they always find the killer. Violence is pictured as a way of life in many shows, and police are shown to use violence and break moral codes in their fight against evildoers. And the lasting results of violence are rarely brought home to the viewer. An individual who is injured in a TV show suffers for only a few seconds. In real life, the individual might take months or even years to recover, or perhaps does not recover at all.

A special concern is how ethnic minority groups are portrayed on television. Ethnic minorities have historically been underrepresented and misrepresented on television (Schiff & Truglio, 1995; Williams & Cox, 1995). Ethnic minority characters—whether African American, Asian, Latino, or Native American—have often been presented as less dignified and less positive than White characters.

But there are some positive aspects to television's influence on adolescents (Clifford, Gunter, & McAleer, 1995). For one thing, television presents adolescents with a world that is different from the one in which they live. This means that, through television, adolescents are exposed to a wider variety of views and knowledge than when they are informed only by their parents, teachers, and peers. Before television's advent, adolescents' identification models came in the form of parents, relatives, older siblings, neighborhood peers, famous individuals heard about in conversation or on the radio and read about in newspapers or magazines, and the film stars seen in movies. In the past, many of the identification figures came from family or peers whose attitudes, clothing styles, and occupational objectives were relatively homogeneous. The imagery and pervasiveness of television have exposed children and adolescents to hundreds of different neighborhoods, cultures, clothing fashions, career possibilities, and patterns of intimate relationships.

"The Cosby Show" was an excellent example of how television can present positive models for ethnic minority children and adolescents.

Television and Violence   How strongly does televised violence influence a person's behavior? In one longitudinal investigation, the amount of violence viewed on television at age 8 was significantly related to the seriousness of criminal acts performed as an adult (Huesmann, 1986). In another investigation, long-term exposure to television violence was significantly related to the likelihood of aggression in 1,565 12- to 17-year-old boys (Belson, 1978). Boys who watched the most aggression on television were the most likely to commit a violent crime, swear, be aggressive in sports, threaten violence toward another boy, write graffiti, or break windows.

These investigations are *correlational,* so we cannot conclude from them that television violence causes individuals to be more aggressive, only that watching television violence is *associated with* aggressive behavior. In one experiment, children were randomly assigned to one of two groups: One group watched shows taken directly from violent Saturday morning cartoon offerings on 11 different days; the second group watched cartoon shows with all of the violence removed (Steur, Applefield, & Smith, 1971). The children then were observed during play. The children who saw the TV cartoon violence kicked, choked, and pushed their playmates more than the children who watched nonviolent TV cartoon shows did. Because the children were assigned randomly to the two conditions (TV cartoons with violence versus TV cartoons with no violence), we can conclude that exposure to TV violence *caused* the increased aggression in this study.

In an extensive study of television violence, a number of conclusions were reached (Federman, 1997). Television violence can have at least three types of harmful effects on viewers: A viewer can learn aggressive attitudes and behaviors from watching television violence, become sensitized to the seriousness of the violence, and feel frightened of becoming a victim of real-life violence. The effects are more likely to occur in certain types of violent portrayals. Contextual features of television violence like an attractive perpetrator, justification for violence, and violence that goes unpunished can increase the risk of harmful effects. Other features, such as showing the harmful consequences, may reduce the likelihood of violence.

An example of a high-risk portrayal of violence on television involves a hostile motorcycle gang that terrorizes a neighborhood. In their harassment, they kidnap a well-known rock singer. A former boyfriend of the singer then tries to rescue her. He sneaks up on the gang and shoots six of them, one at a time. Some of the gunfire causes the motorcycles to blow up. The scene ends with the former boyfriend rescuing the singer.

This violence contains all of the features that encourage aggression in adolescents. The ex-boyfriend, one of the perpetrators of violence, is young and good looking, and cast as a rugged hero. His attack on the gang is depicted as justified—the gang members are ruthless and uncontrollable and have kidnapped an innocent woman. This "hero" is never punished or disciplined even though it appears that he has taken the law into his own hands. As the ultimate reward, the young woman proclaims her love for him after he rescues her. Also, in spite of the extensive violence in this movie, no one is shown as being seriously hurt. The focus quickly shifts away from the gang members after they have been shot, and we don't see them suffer or die.

The television that young children watch may influence their behavior as adolescents. If so, then this supports the continuity view of adolescence discussed in chapter 1. In one recently completed longitudinal study, girls who were more frequent preschool viewers of violent TV programs had lower grades than those who were infrequent viewers of such violence in preschool (Anderson & others, 2001). Also, viewing educational TV programs as preschoolers was associated with higher grades, reading more books, and less aggression, especially for boys, in adolescence.

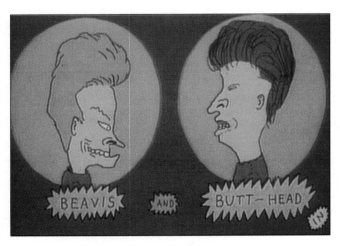

"Beavis and Butt-head" has been one of MTV's most popular TV programs. What kind of models do these characters provide for adolescents? They torture animals, harass girls, and sniff paint thinner. They like to burn things. And they emit an insidious laugh, "Huh-huh, huh-huh, huh-huh." They were initially created by a beginner animator for a festival of "sick and twisted" cartoons, but quickly gained fame—their own nightly MTV program, T-shirts, dolls, a book, a comic book, a movie, CDs (including one with Cher), and a Christmas special. *What age group are Beavis and Butt-head mostly likely to appeal to? Why? Are some adolescents more likely than others to be attracted to them?*

Television and Sex   Adolescents like to watch television programs with sexual content. In one study, the four TV programs preferred most by adolescents were the ones with the highest percentage of interactions containing sexual messages (Ward, 1994). Watching television sex can influence some adolescents' behavior. In one study, college students who frequently watched soap operas (with their heavy dose of sexual themes) gave higher estimates of the number of real-life love affairs, out-of-wedlock children, and divorces than did their infrequently viewing counterparts (Buerkel-Rothfuss & Mayes, 1981). High school and college students who attributed great sexual proficiency and satisfaction to television characters reported less satisfaction with their own first experience with intercourse than did students not making such attributions (Baran, 1976). And in another study, adolescents who were frequent viewers of television had more difficulty separating the world of television from real life (Truglio, 1990).

These studies, along with a number of others, lead to the conclusion that television teaches children and adolescents about sex (Bence, 1989, 1991; Caruthers & others, 2000; Ward, 2000). Over the past decade, sexual content on television has increased and become more explicit. The consistent sexual messages adolescents learn from television's content are that sexual behaviors usually occur between unmarried couples, that contraception is rarely discussed, and that the negative consequences of sexuality (such as an unwanted pregnancy and sexually transmitted diseases) are rarely shown (Greenberg & others, 1986).

A special concern about adolescents and television sex is that while parents and teachers often feel comfortable discussing occupational and educational choices, independence, and consumer behavior with adolescents, they usually don't feel comfortable discussing sex with them (Roberts, 1993). The resulting absence of competing information (peers do talk about sex but often perpetuate ignorance) intensifies television's role in imparting information about sex. Nonetheless, as with television aggression, whether television sex influences the behavior of adolescents depends on a number of factors, including the adolescent's needs, interests, concerns, and maturity (Strasburger & Donnerstein, 1999).

The Media and Music

Anyone who has been around adolescents very long knows that many of them spend huge amounts of time listening to music on the radio, playing CDs or tapes of their favorite music, or watching music videos on television. Approximately two-thirds of all records and tapes are purchased by the 10- to 24-year-old age group. And one-third of the nation's 8,200 radio stations aim their broadcast rock music at adolescent listeners.

Music tastes become more specific and differentiated from the beginning to the end of adolescence (Christenson & Roberts, 1991). In early adolescence, individuals often prefer middle-of-the road, top 40 rock music. By high school, however, adolescents frequently identify with much narrower music types, such as heavy metal, new wave, rap, and so on. Boys prefer "harder" forms of rock, girls softer, more romantic forms of "pop."

Music meets a number of personal and social needs for adolescents (Nicholas & Daniel, 2000). The most important personal needs are mood control and silence filling. Somewhat surprisingly, relatively few adolescents say that popular music lyrics are very important to them. Few use music "to learn about the world," although African American adolescents are more likely than their White counterparts to say popular music fulfills this function for them.

Popular music's social functions range from providing a party atmosphere to expressing rebellion against authority. However, the latter function is not as common as popular stereotypes suggest.

The music adolescents enjoy on records, tapes, radio, and television is an important dimension of their culture. Rock music does not seem to be a passing fad, having been around now for more than 45 years. Recently, it has had its share of controversy. Starting in 1983, MTV (the first music video television channel) and music videos in general were targets of debate in the media. About a year later, rock music lyrics were attacked by the Parents Music Resource Center (PMRC). This group charged in a congressional hearing that rock music lyrics were dangerously shaping the minds

THINKING CRITICALLY

How Sexist Is MTV?

MTV is very popular with adolescents, yet, as we have indicated, its programming sometimes is sexist. Construct a rating scale that assesses sexism. Then with rating scale and pen in hand, watch one evening's fare of MTV (two hours is enough) and evaluate it according to your scale. One strategy for developing your rating scale would be to concretely describe some sexist behaviors (like degrading comments about females, provocative sexist lyrics, and so on) and use these behaviors as categories for your ratings. Try to come up with five to ten behavioral categories that reflect sexism. Then, each time you observe one of the behaviors, place a checkmark in its column. After two hours of observing, total the number of checkmarks in each of the columns and overall. Evaluate your findings— Does MTV contain sexist fare? How much?

of adolescents in the areas of sexual morality, violence, drugs, and satanism. The national Parent Teacher Association agreed. And Tipper Gore (1987), a PMRC founder, voiced her views about the dangers of rock music lyrics in a book.

Associations have been found between a preference for heavy metal music and reckless or antisocial behavior. For example, researchers have found that heavy metal music is more popular among antisocial youth than among the general population (Wass, Miller, & Redditt, 1991). In one study, male fans of heavy metal music were more likely to engage in reckless driving and casual sex and to use drugs than were males who were not fans of heavy metal music (Arnett, 1991). In this same study, female heavy metal fans were more likely to engage in unprotected sex, marijuana use, shoplifting, and vandalism than were females who were not fans of heavy metal. In yet another study, heavy metal music was more popular among adolescents who used drugs than among those who did not (King, 1988). However, these studies are correlational in nature, so we cannot conclude that the music causes problem behaviors in adolescents—it is only related to the problem behaviors. That is, young people with particular views are attracted to a particular kind of music, such as punk. At the same time, it may be these particular young people who pay attention to, comprehend, and are vulnerable to the lyrics' influence.

One of the most frightening claims made by detractors of heavy metal music is that the music causes adolescents to attempt or commit suicide. This was exemplified in highly publicized cases in which parents charged that songs by Judas Priest and Ozzy Osbourne were related to their adolescents' suicides. However, no research data link depression or suicide to heavy metal or rap music.

Motivation, experience, and knowledge are factors in the interpretation of lyrics. In one investigation, preadolescents and adolescents often missed sexual themes in lyrics (Prinsky & Rosenbaum, 1987). Adult organizations such as the PMRC interpret rock music lyrics in terms of sex, violence, drugs, and satanism more than adolescents themselves do. In this investigation, it was found that, in contrast to these adult groups, adolescents interpreted their favorite songs in terms of love, friendship, growing up, life's struggles, having fun, cars, religion, and other topics in teenage life.

Technology, Computers, and the Internet

Culture involves change, and nowhere is that change greater than in the technological revolution today's adolescents are experiencing with increased use of computers and the Internet. If adolescents are to be adequately prepared for tomorrow's jobs, technology needs to become an integral part of their lives (Bereiter, 2002; Sharp, 1999). In a poll of seventh- to twelfth-graders jointly conducted by CNN and the National Science Foundation (1997), 82 percent predicted that they would not be able to make a good living unless they have computer skills and understand other technology. The technology revolution is part of the information society in which we now live.

People are using computers to communicate today the way they used to use pens, postage stamps, and telephones. The new information society still relies on some basic nontechnological competencies: good communication skills, the ability to solve problems, thinking deeply, thinking creatively, and having positive attitudes. However, how people pursue these competencies is being challenged and extended in ways and at a speed that few people had to cope with in previous eras (Bissell, Manning, & Rowland, 1999).

The Internet   The **Internet** *is the core of computer-mediated communication. The Internet system is worldwide and connects thousands of computer networks, providing an incredible array of information adolescents can access.* In many cases, the Internet has more current, up-to-date information than books. In 1996, President Clinton proposed that every school in the United States should be connected to the Internet because of how it has revolutionized access to information. By 1998, 89 percent of public schools had

**Tips for Using the Internet
Webliography
Internet Pals
Critical Analysis of the Internet**
http://www.mhhe.com/santrocka9

Internet
The core of computer-mediated communication. The Internet system is worldwide and connects thousands of computer networks, providing an incredible array of information adolescents can access.

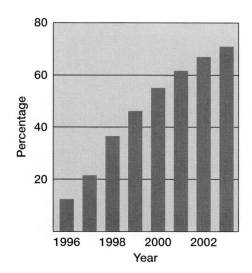

E-mail	83%
Search engine	78
Music sites	59
General research	58
Games	51
TV/movie sites	43
Chat room	42
Own Web page	38
Sport sites	35

■ **FIGURE 8.4**
Percentage of American Adolescents Who Go Online—Actual and Projected

■ **FIGURE 8.5**
Percentage of American Adolescents Who Go Online Engaging in a Particular Activity

been connected to the Internet. As indicated in figure 8.4, 47 percent of adolescents used computers to go online in 1999, a figure that is expected to rise to more than 70 percent by 2002.

What do adolescents do when they are online? As shown in figure 8.5, e-mail is the most frequent activity they engage in, and more than 40 percent of the adolescents who go online connect with a chat room.

E-mail *(electronic mail) is another valuable way that the Internet can be used. Messages can be sent to and received from individuals as well as large numbers of people.*

Special concerns have emerged about children's and adolescents' access to information on the Internet, which has been largely unregulated. Adolescents can access adult sexual material, instructions for making bombs, and other information that is inappropriate for them.

With as many as 11 million American adolescents now online, more and more of adolescent life is taking place in a landscape that is inaccessible to many parents. Many adolescents have a computer in their bedroom, and most parents don't have any idea what information their adolescents are obtaining online. Some psychologists recommend putting the computer in the family room, where adults and adolescents have more opportunities to discuss what information is being accessed online. Every Web browser records what sites users visit. With just elementary computer knowhow, parents can monitor their adolescents' computer activities.

Technology and Sociocultural Diversity Technology brings with it certain social issues. A special concern is whether increased use of technology (especially computers) in homes and schools will widen the learning gap between rich and poor and male and female students (Maddux, Johnson, & Willis, 1997; Roblyer & Edwards, 2000). For example, in 1996 less than one-third of schools with a majority of students from low-SES backgrounds had Internet access, whereas two-thirds of schools with students from primarily higher-SES backgrounds had Internet access. There are gaps in computer availability across ethnic groups as well. In 1998, 49.3 percent of Whites had Internet access, compared to 35.5 percent of African Americans (Hoffman & Novak, 1999). And families with a male adolescent are more likely to own a computer than those with a female adolescent (DeVillar & Faltis, 1991).

e-mail
Electronic mail, a valuable way the Internet can be used. Messages can be sent to and received by individuals as well as large numbers of people.

What do adolescents do when they go online?

Technology and Education
Educational Technology Journal
Critical Issues in Technology and
Education
Technology Standards in
Education
http://www.mhhe.com/santrocka9

Just a step away is the creation of a global, interactive, multimedia database to make the most current information available to all teachers anywhere in the world.

—Dee Dickinson
Contemporary American Teacher and Author

Mediascope
http://www.mhhe.com/santrocka9

Technology and Education   The number of computers in schools has increased dramatically. Yet despite the potential of computers to improve student learning, schools continue to lag behind other segments of society, such as businesses, in the use of technology. Computers are still used too often for drill-and-practice activities rather than constructive learning. In one survey, a majority of middle and high school students reported using computers only minimally over a 30-week time frame (Becker, 1994). In this survey, 1 of 11 students said they used school computers for English class, 1 of 15 for a math class, and only 1 of 40 for a social science class.

Many teachers do not have adequate training in using computers, and school districts have been slow to provide much-needed technology workshops. And with rapidly changing technology, the computers that many schools purchase quickly become outdated. Others computers break and sit in need of repair.

Such realities mean that in most schools, learning has not yet been technologically revolutionized. Only when schools have technologically trained teachers and current, workable technologies will classrooms have the opportunity to be truly transformed by the technology revolution (Newby & others, 2000).

It is important to keep in mind that technology itself does not improve an adolescent's ability to learn. Several essential conditions are necessary to create learning environments that adequately support students' learning. These include vision and support from educational leaders, educators who are skilled in the use of technology for learning, access to contemporary technologies, and an emphasis on the adolescent as an active, constructivist learner (International Society for Technology in Education, 1999).

Social Policy and the Media

Adolescents are exposed to an expanding array of media that carry messages that shape adolescents' judgments and behavior. The social policy initiatives listed here were recommended by the Carnegie Council on Adolescent Development (1995):

- *Encourage socially responsible programming.* There is good evidence of a link between media violence and adolescent aggression. The media also shape many other dimensions of adolescents' development—gender, ethnic, and occupational roles, as well as standards of beauty, family life, and sexuality. Writers, producers, and media executives need to recognize how powerful their messages are to adolescents

and work with experts on adolescent development to provide more positive images to youth.
- *Support public efforts to make the media more adolescent friendly.* Essentially, the American media regulate themselves in regard to their influence on adolescents. All other Western nations have stronger regulations than the United States to foster appropriate educational programming.
- *Encourage media literacy programs as part of school curricula, youth and community organizations, and family life.* Many adolescents do not have the knowledge and skills to critically analyze media messages. Media literacy programs should focus not only on television, but also on the Internet, newspapers, magazines, radio, videos, music, and electronic games.
- *Increase media presentations of health promotions.* Community-wide campaigns using public service announcements in the media have been successful in reducing smoking and increasing physical fitness in adolescents. Use of the media to promote adolescent health and well-being should be increased.
- *Expand opportunities for adolescents' views to appear in the media.* The media should increase the number of adolescent voices in their presentations by featuring editorial opinions, news stories, and videos authored by adolescents. Some schools have shown that this strategy of media inclusion of adolescents can be an effective dimension of education.

One organization that is trying to do something about the media's impact on adolescents is Mediascope, which is developing an ethics curriculum on violence to be used in courses that train the thousands of film students who hope to become moviemakers. Mediascope is also monitoring the entire television industry to assess such issues as the gratuitous use of violence.

THROUGH THE EYES OF PSYCHOLOGISTS
Sandra Calvert
Georgetown University

"It is timely and important for our society to make the journey through the information age accessible and interesting to all youth, and to ensure them a safe passage during the journey."

Since the last review, we have discussed many aspects of television and other media. This review should help you to reach your learning goals related to this topic.

FOR YOUR REVIEW

Learning Goal 6
Discuss television and other media influences

- The functions of the media include entertainment, information, sensation, coping, gender-role modeling, and youth culture identification. Adolescents spend more than a third of their waking hours with some form of mass media. Estimates of TV viewing range from two to four hours a day on average for adolescents. Television viewing often declines in adolescence while the use of music media increases. Adolescents also use the print media more than children do. There are large individual variations in adolescent media use.
- The functions of television include providing information and entertainment, as well as a portrait of the world beyond the immediate context in which they live. One negative aspect of television is that it involves passive learning. Special concerns are the ways ethnic minorities, sex, and aggression are portrayed on television.
- Adolescents are heavy consumers of CDs, tapes, and rock music. Music meets a number of personal and social needs of adolescents.
- Today's adolescents are experiencing a technology revolution through computers and the Internet.
- Social policy recommendations regarding the media include encouraging socially responsible programming, supporting public efforts to make the media more adolescent friendly, and encouraging media literacy campaigns.

In this chapter, we have focused on the role of culture in adolescent development. This chapter concludes the main section of the book on the social contexts of adolescence. In the next main section of the book, we will focus our attention to the social and personality aspects of adolescent development, beginning with chapter 9, "The Self and Identity."

CHAPTER MAP

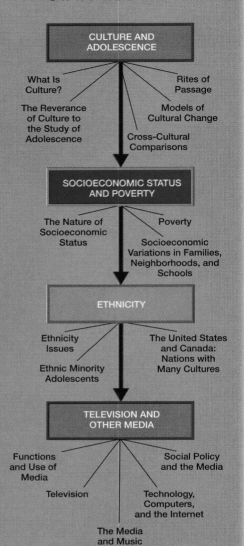

REACH YOUR LEARNING GOALS

At the beginning of this chapter we stated six learning goals and encouraged you to review material related to these goals at four points in the chapter. This is a good time to return to these reviews and use them to guide your study and help you to reach your learning goals:

Page 263

    Learning Goal 1   Understand culture and adolescent development

Page 268

    Learning Goal 2   Discuss socioeconomic status and adolescence

    Learning Goal 3   Describe the role of poverty in adolescent development

Page 277

    Learning Goal 4   Evaluate issues related to ethnicity

    Learning Goal 5   Know about ethnic minority adolescents

Page 285

    Learning Goal 6   Discuss television and other media influences

KEY TERMS

culture 256
socioeconomic status (SES) 257
ethnicity 257
ethnocentrism 257
cross-cultural studies 258
assimilation 260
acculturation 260
alternation model 261

multicultural model 261
rites of passage 261
feminization of poverty 266
prejudice 271
Chicano 274
Internet 282
e-mail 283

KEY PEOPLE

Richard Brislin 256
Carola Suárez-Orozco 270
Stanley Sue 271
James Jones 271
Vonnie McLoyd 273
Sandra Calvert 285

RESOURCES FOR IMPROVING THE LIVES OF ADOLESCENTS

The Adolescent & Young Adult Fact Book

(1991) by Janet Simons, Belva Finlay, and
Alice Yang
Washington, DC: Children's Defense Fund

This book is filled with valuable charts that describe the roles that poverty and ethnicity play in adolescent development.

Advocates for Youth Media Project

3733 Motor Avenue, Suite 204
Los Angeles, CA 90034
310–559–5700

This project promotes responsible portrayals of sexuality in the entertainment media. The project members work with media professionals by sponsoring informational events and offering free consultation services to writers, producers, and other media personnel.

Canadian Ethnocultural Council/Conseil Ethnoculturel du Canada

251 Laurier Avenue West, Suite 110
Ottawa, Ontario K1P 5J6
613–230–3867

CEC's objective is to secure equality of opportunity, of rights, and of dignity for ethnocultural minorities and all other Canadians.

Children's Journey Through the Information Age

(1999) by Sandra Calvert
New York: McGraw-Hill

This is an excellent, contemporary treatment of many dimensions of the information age, such as television and computers.

Cybereducator

(1999) by Joan Bissell, Anna Manring, and Veronica Roland

A guide to using the Internet for K–12 education.

Quantum Opportunity Program

1415 North Broad Street
Philadelphia, PA 19122
215–236–4500

This is a year-round youth development program funded by the Ford Foundation. It has demonstrated that intervening in the lives of 13-year-old African Americans from poverty backgrounds can significantly improve their prospects.

Studying Ethnic Minority Adolescents

(1998) by Vonnie McLoyd & Laurence Steinberg (Eds.)
Mahwah, NJ: Erlbaum

An excellent resource book for learning about the best methods for studying ethnic minority adolescents.

Understanding Culture's Influence on Behavior

(1993) by Richard Brislin
Fort Worth, TX: Harcourt Brace

This is an excellent book on culture's role in behavior and development.

TAKING IT TO THE NET

http://www.mhhe.com/santrocka9

1. Adolescents who come from severe poverty, who experience parental divorce, who are the subjects of discrimination, and who attend very poor schools are at risk for various psychological and behavioral disorders. Yet, it is not at all inevitable that those who are at risk will experience poor development. *How do they develop the resilience that insulates them from the negative environmental conditions?*

2. Rites of passage mark important developmental milestones. Some are more formal, for example, a religious ceremony, and others are less formal, for example, entrance into sexual behavior. *How might you use the concept of rites of passage to explain various aspects of ado-*

lescent behavior (for example, body piercing, tattooing) to high school teachers?

3. The multicultural model of cultural change promotes a pluralistic approach to meeting common needs. *As a student in higher education, how would you explain the role of education, and particularly multicultural education, in achieving this form of cultural change?*

Connect to *http://www.mhhe.com/santrocka9* to research the answers and complete these exercises. In some cases, you'll also find further instructions on this site.

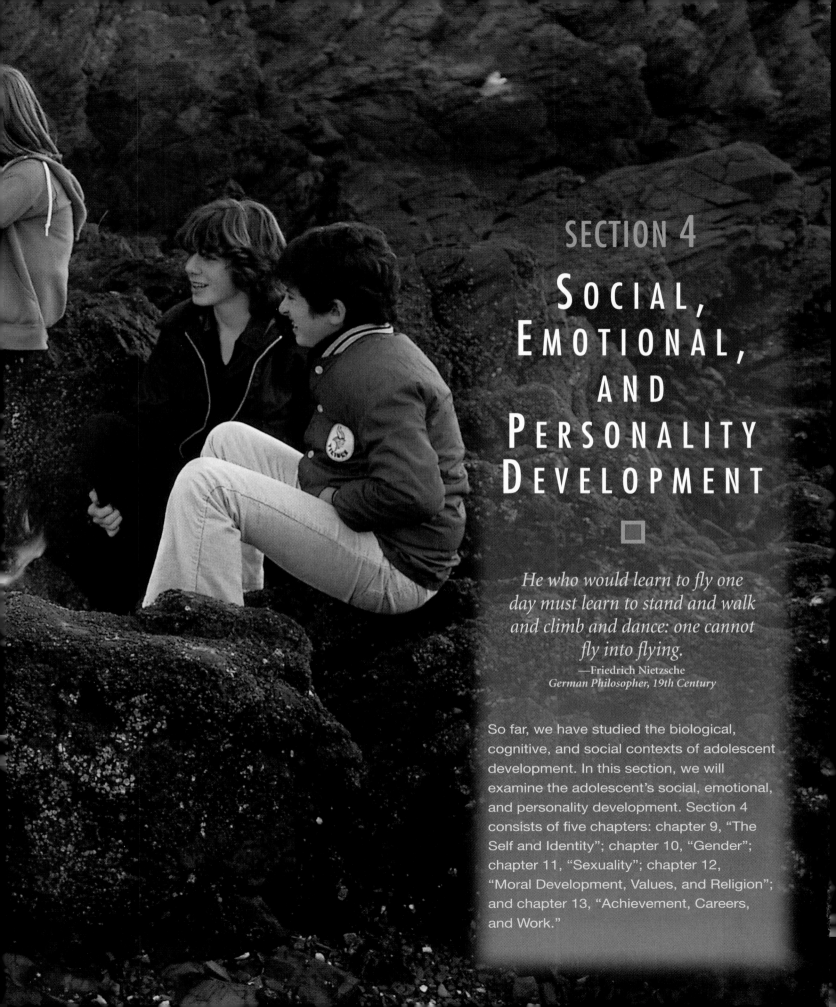

SECTION 4

SOCIAL, EMOTIONAL, AND PERSONALITY DEVELOPMENT

He who would learn to fly one day must learn to stand and walk and climb and dance: one cannot fly into flying.
—Friedrich Nietzsche
German Philosopher, 19th Century

So far, we have studied the biological, cognitive, and social contexts of adolescent development. In this section, we will examine the adolescent's social, emotional, and personality development. Section 4 consists of five chapters: chapter 9, "The Self and Identity"; chapter 10, "Gender"; chapter 11, "Sexuality"; chapter 12, "Moral Development, Values, and Religion"; and chapter 13, "Achievement, Careers, and Work."

CHAPTER MAP

```
┌─────────────────────────┐
│        THE SELF         │
└─────────────────────────┘
        /           \
   Self-          Self-Esteem
   Understanding   and Self-Concept


┌─────────────────────────┐
│        IDENTITY         │
└─────────────────────────┘
```

Erikson's   Gender and
Ideas on   Identity
Identity   Development

The Four   Cultural
Statuses of   and Ethnic
Identity   Aspects
                             of Identity

Developmental   Family
Changes   Influences
                             on Identity

```
┌─────────────────────────┐
│      IDENTITY AND       │
│        INTIMACY         │
└─────────────────────────┘
```
        /   \
   Intimacy   Loneliness

THE SELF AND IDENTITY

■ A 15-Year-Old Girl's Self-Description

How do adolescents describe themselves? How would you have described yourself when you were 15 years old? What features would you have emphasized? The following is a self-portrait of one 15-year-old girl:

> What am I like as a person? Complicated! I'm sensitive, friendly, outgoing, popular, and tolerant, though I can also be shy, self-conscious, and even obnoxious. Obnoxious! I'd *like* to be friendly and tolerant all of the time. That's the kind of person I *want* to be, and I'm disappointed when I'm not. I'm responsible, even studious now and then, but on the other hand, I'm a goof-off, too, because if you're too studious, you won't be popular. I don't usually do that well at school. I'm a pretty cheerful person, especially with my friends, where I can even get rowdy. At home I'm more likely to be anxious around my parents. They expect me to get all A's. It's not fair! I worry about how I probably *should* get better grades. But I'd be mortified in the eyes of my friends. So I'm usually pretty stressed-out at home, or sarcastic, since my parents are always on my case. But I really don't understand how I can switch so fast. I mean, how can I be cheerful one minute, anxious the next, and then be sarcastic? Which one is the *real* me? Sometimes, I feel phony, especially around boys. Say I think some guy might be interested in asking me out. I try to act different, like Madonna. I'll be flirtatious and fun-loving. And then everybody, I mean *everybody* else is looking at me like they think I'm totally weird. Then I get self-conscious and embarrassed and become radically introverted, and I don't know who I really am! Am I just trying to impress them or what? But I don't really care what they think anyway. I don't *want* to care, that is. I just want to know what my close friends think. I can be my true self with my close friends. I can't be my real self with my parents. They don't understand me. What do *they* know about what it's like to be a teenager? They still treat me like I'm still a kid. At least at school people treat you more like you're an adult. That gets confusing, though. I mean, which am I, a kid or an adult? It's scary, too, because I don't have any idea what I want to be when I grow up. I mean, I have lots of *ideas.* My friend Sheryl and I talk about whether we'll be flight attendants, or teachers, or nurses, veterinarians, maybe mothers, or actresses. I know I *don't* want to be a waitress or a secretary. But how do you decide all of this? I really don't know. I mean, I think about it a lot, but I can't resolve it. There are days when I wish I could just become immune to myself. (Harter, 1990b, pp. 352–353)

"Who are you?" said the Caterpillar. Alice replied, rather shyly, "I—I hardly know, Sir, just at present—at least I know who I was when I got up this morning, but I must have changed several times since then."

—Lewis Carroll
English Writer, 19th Century

HALLMARKS OF ADOLESCENT DEVELOPMENT are an increased effort at self-understanding and exploring one's identity. Far more than in childhood, adolescents, especially older adolescents, seek to know who they are, what they are all about, and where they are going in life. This produces considerable self-reflection as adolescents search for their identity. By the time you have completed this chapter, you should be able to reach these learning goals:

1 Evaluate the adolescent's self-understanding

2 Know about the adolescent's self-esteem and self-concept

3 Discuss Erikson's ideas on identity, identity statuses, and developmental changes

4 Describe links between identity and family influences, culture and ethnicity, and gender

5 Explain identity and intimacy

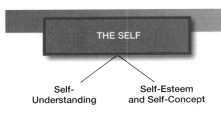

THE SELF

Adolescents carry with them a sense of who they are and what makes them different from everyone else. They cling to this identity and develop a sense that this identity is becoming more stable. Consider one adolescent male's self-description: "I am male, bright, an athlete, a political liberal, an extravert, and a compassionate individual." He takes comfort in his uniqueness: "No one else is quite like me. I am 5 feet 11 inches tall and weigh 160 pounds. I live in a suburb and plan to attend the state university. I want to be a sports journalist. I am an expert at building canoes. When I am not going to school and studying, I write short stories about sports figures, which I hope to publish someday." Real or imagined, an adolescent's developing sense of self and uniqueness is a motivating force in life. Our exploration of the self begins with information about adolescents' self-understanding and then turns to their self-esteem and self-concept.

Concepts of Person and Self
Recent and Forthcoming Books on the Self
International Society for Self and Identity
http://www.mhhe.com/santrocka9

Self-Understanding

Adolescents' self-understanding becomes more introspective, but it is not completely interiorized. Rather, self-understanding is a social-cognitive construction (Bosma & Kunnen, 2001; Tesser, Fleeson, & Suls, 2000). That is, adolescents' developing cognitive capacities interact with their sociocultural experiences to influence self-understanding. The questions about self-understanding that we will examine include these: What is self-understanding? What are some important dimensions of adolescents' self-understanding? How integrated is adolescents' self-understanding?

self-understanding
The adolescent's cognitive representation of the self, the substance and content of the adolescent's self-conceptions.

What Is Self-Understanding?   **Self-understanding** *is the adolescent's cognitive representation of the self, the substance and content of the adolescent's self-conceptions.* For example, a 12-year-old boy understands that he is a student, a boy, a football player, a family member, a video game lover, and a rock music fan. A 14-year-old girl understands that she is a cheerleader, a student council member, and a movie fan. An adolescent's self-understanding is based, in part, on the various roles and membership categories that define who adolescents are (Harter, 1990a). Though not the whole of personal identity, self-understanding provides identity's rational underpinnings.

Dimensions of Adolescents' Self-Understanding   The development of self-understanding in adolescence is complex and involves a number of aspects of the self (Harter, 1998, 1999). Let's examine how the adolescent's self-understanding differs from the child's.

Abstract and Idealistic   Remember from our discussion of Piaget's theory of cognitive development in chapters 2 and 4 that many adolescents begin to think in more *abstract* and *idealistic* ways ◀▥ Pp. 47, 108. When asked to describe themselves, adolescents are more likely than children to use abstract and idealistic labels. Consider 14-year-old Laurie's abstract description of herself: "I am a human being. I am indecisive. I don't know who I am." Also consider her idealistic description of herself: "I am a naturally sensitive person who really cares about people's feelings. I think I'm pretty good-looking." Not all adolescents describe themselves in idealistic ways, but most adolescents distinguish between the real self and the ideal self.

Differentiated   Adolescents' self-understanding becomes increasingly *differentiated*. Adolescents are more likely than children to describe themselves with contextual or situational variations (Harter, Waters, & Whitesell, 1996). For example, a 15-year-old girl might describe herself with one set of characteristics in relation to her family and another set of characteristics in relation to her peers and friends. Yet another set of characteristics appears in her self-description regarding her romantic relationship. In sum, adolescents are more likely than children to understand that one possesses different selves, depending on one's role or particular context.

The Fluctuating Self   Given the contradictory nature of the self in adolescence, it is not surprising that the self fluctuates across situations and across time (Harter, 1990a; Harter & Whitesell, 2002). The 15-year-old girl quoted at the beginning of the chapter remarked that she could not understand how she could switch so fast—from being cheerful one moment, to being anxious the next, and then sarcastic a short time later. One researcher described the fluctuating nature of the adolescent's self with the metaphor of "the barometric self" (Rosenberg, 1979). The adolescent's self continues to be characterized by instability until the adolescent constructs a more unified theory of self, usually not until late adolescence or even early adulthood.

Contradictions within the Self   After adolescence ushers in the need to differentiate the self into multiple roles in different relational contexts, this naturally leads to potential contradictions between these differentiated selves. In one study, Susan Harter (1986) asked seventh-, ninth-, and eleventh-graders to describe themselves. She found that the number of contradictory self-descriptions (moody *and* understanding, ugly *and* attractive, bored *and* inquisitive, caring *and* uncaring, introverted *and* fun-loving, and so on) dramatically increased between the seventh and ninth grades. The contradictory self-descriptions declined in the eleventh grade but still were higher than in the seventh grade. Adolescents develop the cognitive ability to detect these inconsistencies in the self as they strive to construct a general theory of the self or of their personality (Harter & Monsour, 1992).

Real and Ideal, True and False Selves   The adolescent's emerging ability to construct ideal selves in addition to actual ones can be perplexing to the adolescent. The capacity to recognize a discrepancy between *real* and *ideal* selves represents a cognitive advance, but humanistic theorist Carl Rogers (1950) believed that when the real and ideal selves are too discrepant, it is a sign of maladjustment. Depression can result from a substantial discrepancy between one's actual self and one's ideal self (the person one wants to be) because an awareness of this discrepancy can produce a sense of failure and self-criticism.

Although some theorists consider a strong discrepancy between the ideal and real selves maladaptive, others argue that this is not always true, especially in adolescence. For

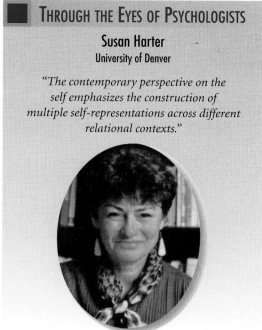

THROUGH THE EYES OF PSYCHOLOGISTS
Susan Harter
University of Denver

"The contemporary perspective on the self emphasizes the construction of multiple self-representations across different relational contexts."

THINKING CRITICALLY
Examining Possibilities

Think about what your future selves might be. What do you envision will make you the happiest about the future selves you aspire to become? What prospective selves hold negative possibilities?

possible self
What individuals might become, what they would like to become, and what they are afraid of becoming.

example, in one view, an important aspect of the ideal or imagined self is the **possible self,** *what individuals might become, what they would like to become, and what they are afraid of becoming* (Cota-Robles, Neiss, & Hunt, 2000; Markus & Nurius, 1986). Thus, adolescents' possible selves include both what adolescents hope to be as well as what they dread they will become (Martin, 1997). In this view, the presence of both hoped-for as well as dreaded selves is psychologically healthy, providing a balance between positive, expected selves and negative, feared selves. The attributes of future positive selves (getting into a good college, being admired, having a successful career) can direct future positive states, while attributes of future negative selves (being unemployed, being lonely, not getting into a good college) can identify what is to be avoided in the future.

In one recent study, the relation of possible selves to negative health behaviors was explored in more than 1,600 sixth- through ninth-grade students (Aloise-Young, Hennigan, & Leong, 2001). Cigarette smoking and alcohol consumption were negatively related to the number of positive future selves.

Can adolescents distinguish between their *true* and *false* selves? In one research study, they could (Harter & Lee, 1989). Adolescents are most likely to show their false self in romantic or dating situations, and with classmates; they are least likely to show their false self with close friends. Adolescents display a false self to impress others, to try out new behaviors or roles, because others force them to behave in false ways, and because others do not understand their true self. Some adolescents report that they do not like their false-self behavior, but others say that it does not bother them. Harter and her colleagues (1996) found that experienced authenticity of the self is highest among adolescents who say they receive support from their parents.

Social Comparison   Some developmentalists believe that adolescents are more likely than children to use *social comparison* to evaluate themselves (Ruble & others, 1980). However, adolescents' willingness to *admit* that they engage in social comparison to evaluate themselves declines in adolescence because they view social comparison as socially undesirable. They think that acknowledging their social comparison motives will endanger their popularity. Relying on social comparison information in adolescence can be confusing because of the large number of reference groups. For example, should adolescents compare themselves to classmates in general? to friends? to their own gender? to popular adolescents? to good-looking adolescents? to athletic adolescents? Simultaneously considering all of these social comparison groups can be perplexing for adolescents.

Self-Conscious   Adolescents are more likely than children to be *self-conscious* about and *preoccupied* with their self-understanding. As part of their self-conscious and preoccupied self-exploration, adolescents become more introspective. However, the introspection is not always done in social isolation. Sometimes, adolescents turn to their friends for support and self-clarification, obtaining their friends' opinions of an emerging self-definition. As one researcher on self-development commented, adolescents' friends are often the main source of reflected self-appraisals, becoming the social mirror into which adolescents anxiously stare (Rosenberg, 1979). This self-consciousness and self-preoccupation reflect the concept of adolescent egocentrism, which we discussed in chapter 4.

Self-Protective   In adolescence, self-understanding includes more mechanisms to *protect the self.* Although adolescents often display a sense of confusion and conflict stimulated by introspective efforts to understand themselves, they also call on mechanisms to protect and enhance the self. In protecting the self, adolescents are prone to denying their negative characteristics. For example, in Harter's investigation of self-understanding, positive self-descriptions, such as *attractive, fun-loving, sensitive, affectionate,* and *inquisitive,* were more likely to be described as central, important aspects of the self, whereas negative self-descriptions, such as *ugly, mediocre, depressed, selfish,* and *nervous,* were more likely to be described as peripheral, less important aspects of the self

(Harter, 1986). Adolescents' tendency to protect themselves fits with the earlier description of adolescents' tendency to describe themselves in idealistic ways.

Unconscious   In adolescence, self-understanding involves greater recognition that the self includes *unconscious,* as well as conscious, components, a recognition not likely to occur until late adolescence (Selman, 1980). That is, older adolescents are more likely than younger adolescents to believe that certain aspects of their mental experience are beyond their awareness or control.

Self-Integration   In adolescence, self-understanding becomes more *integrative,* with the disparate parts of the self more systematically pieced together, especially in late adolescence. Older adolescents are more likely to detect inconsistencies in their earlier self-descriptions as they attempt to construct a general theory of self, an integrated sense of identity.

Because the adolescent creates multiple self-concepts, the task of integrating these varying self-conceptions becomes problematic. At the same time that adolescents are faced with pressures to differentiate the self into multiple roles, the emergence of formal operational thought presses for *integration* and the development of a consistent, coherent theory of self. These budding formal operational skills initially present a liability because they first allow adolescents to *detect* inconsistencies in the self across varying roles, only later providing the cognitive capacity to *integrate* such apparent contradictions. In the narrative that opened the chapter, the 15-year-old girl could not understand how she could be cheerful yet depressed and sarcastic, wondering "which is the real me." Researchers have found that 14- to 15-year-olds not only detect inconsistencies across their various roles (with parents, friends, and romantic partners, for example) but are much more troubled by these contradictions than younger (11- to 12-year-old) and older (17- to 18-year-old) adolescents are (Damon & Hart, 1988).

Conclusions   As we have seen, the development of self-understanding in adolescence is complex and involves a number of aspects of the self. Rapid changes that occur in the transition from childhood to adolescence result in heightened self-awareness and consciousness. This heightened self-focus leads to consideration of the self and the many changes that are occurring in it, which can produce doubt about who the self is and which facets of the self are "real" (Hart, 1996).

James Marcia (1996) believes that changes in the self in adolescence can best be understood by dividing them into early ("deconstruction"), middle ("reconstruction"), and late ("consolidation") phases. That is, the adolescent initially is confronted by contradictory self-descriptions, followed by attempts to resolve contradictions, and subsequently develops a more integrated self-theory (identity).

At this point we have discussed a number of ideas about self-understanding. Remember, from the introduction of the self, that self-conception involves not only self-understanding but also self-esteem and self-concept. That is, not only do adolescents try to define and describe attributes of the self (self-understanding), but they also evaluate these attributes (self-esteem and self-concept).

Self-Understanding and Sociocultural Contexts   The increasing proliferation of selves in adolescence can vary across relationships with people, social roles, and sociocultural contexts. Researchers have found that adolescents' portraits of themselves can change depending on whether they describe themselves when they are with their mother, father, close friend, romantic partner, or peer. They also can change depending on whether they describe themselves in the role of the student, athlete, or employee. And adolescents might create different selves depending on their ethnic and cultural background and experiences.

The multiple selves of ethnically diverse youth reflect their experiences in navigating their multiple worlds of family, peers, school, and community (Cooper, in press; Cooper & others, 1995). Research with American youth of African, Chinese, Filipino, Latino, European, Japanese, and Vietnamese descent, as well as Japanese youth, shows that as youth move across cultural worlds, they can encounter barriers related to language, racism, gender, immigration, and poverty. In each of their different worlds, they might also find resources in other people, in institutions, and in themselves. Youth who find it too difficult to move between worlds can become alienated from their school, family, and peers. However, youth who effectively navigate their various worlds can develop bicultural or multicultural selves and become "culture brokers" for others.

Hazel Markus and her colleagues (Markus & Kitayama, 1994; Markus, Mullally, & Kitayama, 1999) believe that it is important to understand how multiple selves emerge through participation in cultural practices. They argue that all selves are culture-specific selves that emerge as individuals adapt to their cultural environments. In North American contexts (especially middle-SES contexts), individuality is promoted and maintained. North Americans, when given the opportunity to describe themselves, often provide not only portraits of their current selves but also notions of their future selves. They also frequently show a need to have multiple selves that are stable and consistent. In Japan, multiple selves are often described in terms of relatedness to others (Dedikdes & Brewer, 2001). Self-improvement also is an important aspect of the multiple selves of many Japanese. Markus and her colleagues recognize that cultural groups are characterized by diversity but nonetheless conclude that it is helpful to understand the dominant aspects of multiple selves within a culture.

Hazel Markus Talks About Selfways
Culture and the Self
http://www.mhhe.com/santrocka9

At this point, we have studied many aspects of self-understanding in adolescence. This review should help you to reach your learning goals related to this topic.

☐ FOR YOUR REVIEW

Learning Goal 1
Evaluate the adolescent's self-understanding

- Self-understanding is the adolescent's cognitive representation of the self, the substance and content of the adolescent's self-conceptions.
- Dimensions of the adolescent's self-understanding include abstract and idealistic; differentiated; contradictions within the self; real and ideal, true and false selves, social comparison; self-conscious; unconscious; and self-integrative.
- The increasing number of selves in adolescence can vary across relationships with people, social roles, and sociocultural contexts.

Next, we will continue to examine the self in adolescence by focusing on the adolescent's self-esteem and self concept.

Self-Esteem and Self-Concept

What are self-esteem and self-concept? How are they measured? Are some domains more salient to the adolescent's self-esteem than others are? How do relationships with parents and peers influence adolescents' self-esteem? What are the consequences of adolescents' low self-esteem? How can adolescents' self-esteem be increased?

What Are Self-Esteem and Self-Concept? **Self-esteem** *is the global evaluative dimension of the self. Self-esteem is also referred to as self-worth or self-image.* For example, an adolescent might perceive that she is not merely a person, but a good person. Of course, not all adolescents have an overall positive image of themselves. **Self-concept** *involves domain-specific evaluations of the self.* Adolescents can make self-evaluations in many domains of their lives—academic, athletic, appearance, and so on. In sum, self-esteem refers to global self-evaluations, self-concept to more domain-specific evaluations.

Investigators have not always made clear distinctions between self-esteem and self-concept, sometimes using the terms interchangeably or not precisely defining them. As you read the remaining discussion of self-esteem and self-concept, the distinction between self-esteem as global self-evaluation and self-concept as domain-specific self-evaluation should help you to keep the terms straight.

self-esteem
The global evaluative dimension of the self. Self-esteem is also referred to as self-worth or self-image.

self-concept
Domain-specific evaluations of the self.

Measuring Self-Esteem and Self-Concept   Measuring self-esteem and self-concept hasn't always been easy, especially in assessments of adolescents (Owens, Stryker, & Goodman, 2001; Wylie, 1979). For many years measures were designed primarily for children or for adults, with little attention given to adolescents. Susan Harter (1989b) developed a separate measure for adolescents: the Self-Perception Profile for Adolescents. It taps eight domains—scholastic competence, athletic competence, social acceptance, physical appearance, behavioral conduct, close friendship, romantic appeal, and job competence—plus global self-worth. The adolescent measure has three skill domains not present in her child measure—job competence, romantic appeal, and close friendship.

Some assessment experts argue that a combination of several methods should be used in measuring self-esteem. In addition to self-reporting, rating of an adolescent's self-esteem by others and observations of the adolescent's behavior in various settings could provide a more complete and more accurate self-esteem picture. Peers, teachers, parents, and even others who do not know the adolescent can be asked to rate the adolescent's self-esteem. Adolescents' facial expressions and the extent to which they congratulate or condemn themselves are also good indicators of how they view themselves. For example, adolescents who rarely smile or rarely act happy are revealing something about their self-esteem. One investigation that used behavioral observations in the assessment of self-esteem shows some of the positive as well as negative behaviors that can provide clues to the adolescent's self-esteem (see figure 9.1) (Savin-Williams & Demo, 1983). By using a variety of methods (such as self-report and behavioral observations) and obtaining information from various sources (such as the adolescent, parents, friends, and teachers), investigators probably can construct a more accurate picture of the adolescent's self-esteem.

Are Some Domains More Salient Than Others to Adolescents' Self-Esteem?   Physical appearance is an especially powerful contributor to self-esteem in adolescence. For example, in Harter's (1989a) research, physical appearance consistently correlates the most strongly with global self-esteem, followed by peer social acceptance. Harter also has found that the strong association between perceived appearance and general self-worth is not confined to adolescence but holds across the life span, from early childhood through middle age. And in one recent study, adolescents' self-concepts regarding their physical attractiveness were the strongest predictor of their overall self-esteem (Lord & Eccles, 1994).

An Adolescent Talks About Self-Esteem
Exploring Self-Esteem
Research
Self-Esteem Websites
http://www.mhhe.com/santrocka9

Positive Indicators	Negative Indicators
1. Gives others directives or commands	1. Puts down others by teasing, name-calling, or gossiping
2. Uses voice quality appropriate for situation	2. Uses gestures that are dramatic or out of context
3. Expresses opinions	3. Engages in inappropriate touching or avoids physical contact
4. Sits with others during social activities	4. Gives excuses for failures
5. Works cooperatively in a group	5. Glances around to monitor others
6. Faces others when speaking or being spoken to	6. Brags excessively about achievements, skills, appearance
7. Maintains eye contact during conversation	7. Verbally puts self down; self-deprecation
8. Initiates friendly contact with others	8. Speaks too loudly, abruptly, or in a dogmatic tone
9. Maintains comfortable space between self and others	9. Does not express views or opinions, especially when asked
10. Has little hesitation in speech, speaks fluently	10. Assumes a submissive stance

FIGURE 9.1
Behavioral Indicators of Self-Esteem

College of Positive Self-Image 7.
University of Low Self-Esteem 0.

Parental and Peer Influences on Self-Esteem

Two important sources of social support that contribute to adolescents' self-esteem are relationships with parents and peers. In the most extensive investigation of parent-child relationships and self-esteem, a measure of self-esteem was given to boys, and the boys and their mothers were interviewed about their family relationships (Coopersmith, 1967). Based on these assessments, these parenting attributes were associated with boys' high self-esteem:

• Expression of affection
• Concern about the boys' problems
• Harmony in the home
• Participation in joint family activities
• Availability to give competent, organized help to the boys when they needed it
• Setting clear and fair rules
• Abiding by these rules
• Allowing the boys freedom within well-prescribed limits

Remember that because these findings are correlational, researchers cannot say that these parenting attributes *cause* children's high self-esteem. Such factors as expression of affection and allowing children freedom within well-prescribed limits probably are important determinants of children's self-esteem, but researchers still must say that *they are related* to rather than *they cause* children's self-esteem, based on the available research data that are correlational.

Peer judgments gain increasing importance among older children and adolescents. In one investigation, peer support contributed more strongly to the self-esteem of young adolescents than to that of children, although parenting support was an important factor in self-esteem for both children and young adolescents (Usher & others, 2000; Harter, 1987). In this study, peer support was a more important factor than parenting support for late adolescents. Two types of peer support were studied: classmate support and close-friend support. Classmate support contributed more strongly to adolescents' self-esteem at all ages than close-friend support. Given that, in most instances, close friends provide considerable support, it may be that their regard is not perceived as enhancing; rather, the adolescent may need to turn to somewhat more objective sources of support to validate his or her self-esteem.

Consequences of Low Self-Esteem

For most adolescents, low self-esteem results in only temporary emotional discomfort. But in some adolescents, low self-esteem can translate into other problems (Usher & others, 2000; Zimmerman, Copeland, & Shope, 1997). Low self-esteem has been implicated in depression, suicide, anorexia nervosa, delinquency, and other adjustment problems (Fenzel, 1994). The seriousness of the problem depends not only on the nature of the adolescent's low self-esteem but on other conditions as well. When low self-esteem is compounded by difficult school transitions or family life, or by other stressful events, the adolescent's problems can intensify.

Increasing Adolescents' Self-Esteem

Four ways adolescents' self-esteem can be improved are through (1) identifying the causes of low self-esteem and the domains of competence important to the self, (2) emotional support and social approval, (3) achievement, and (4) coping (see figure 9.2 on p. 299).

Identifying adolescents' sources of self-esteem—that is, competence in domains important to the self—is critical to improving self-esteem. Self-esteem theorist and researcher Susan Harter (1990b) points out that the self-esteem enhancement programs of the 1960s, in which self-esteem itself was the target and individuals were encouraged to simply feel good about themselves, were ineffective. Rather, Harter (1998) believes that intervention must occur at the level of the *causes* of self-esteem if the individual's self-esteem is to improve significantly.

It is difficult to make people miserable when they feel worthy of themselves.
—Abraham Lincoln
American President, 19th Century

Building Self-Esteem
Improving Young Adolescents'
Self-Esteem
http://www.mhhe.com/santrocka9

Identifying the causes of low self-esteem and which domains of competence are important to the self

Emotional support and social approval

Achievement

Coping

FIGURE 9.2
Four Main Ways to Improve Self-Esteem

Adolescents have the highest self-esteem when they perform competently in domains important to the self. Therefore, adolescents should be encouraged to identify and value their areas of competence.

Emotional support and social approval in the form of confirmation from others also powerfully influence adolescents' self-esteem (Harter, 1990b). Some youth with low self-esteem come from conflicted families or conditions in which they experienced abuse or neglect—situations in which support is unavailable. In some cases, alternative sources of support can be implemented, either informally through the encouragement of a teacher, a coach, or another significant adult, or more formally, through programs such as Big Brothers and Big Sisters. While peer approval becomes increasingly important during adolescence, both adult and peer support are important influences on the adolescent's self-esteem. In one recent study, both parental and peer support were related to the adolescent's general self-worth (Robinson, 1995).

Achievement also can improve adolescents' self-esteem (Bednar, Wells, & Peterson, 1995). For example, the straightforward teaching of real skills to adolescents often results in increased achievement and, thus, in enhanced self-esteem. Adolescents develop higher self-esteem because they know what tasks are important for achieving goals, and they have experienced performing them or similar behaviors. The emphasis on the importance of achievement in improving self-esteem has much in common with Bandura's social cognitive concept of *self-efficacy*, which refers to individuals' beliefs that they can master a situation and produce positive outcomes.

Self-esteem also is often increased when adolescents face a problem and try to cope with it rather than avoid it (Lazarus, 1991). If coping rather than avoidance prevails, adolescents often face problems realistically, honestly, and nondefensively. This produces favorable self-evaluative thoughts, which lead to the self-generated approval that raises self-esteem. The converse is true of low self-esteem. Unfavorable self-evaluations trigger denial, deception, and avoidance in an attempt to disavow that which has already been glimpsed as true. This process leads to self-generated disapproval as a form of feedback to the self about personal adequacy.

At this point, we have studied many aspects of self-esteem and self-concept in adolescence. This review should help you to reach your learning goals related to these topics.

☐ FOR YOUR REVIEW

Learning Goal 2
Know about the adolescent's self-concept and self-esteem

- Self-esteem is the global, evaluative dimension of the self, and also is referred to as self-worth or self-image. According to Harter, self-concept involves domain-specific self-evaluations.
- For too long, little attention was given to developing measures of self-esteem and self-concept specifically tailored to adolescents. Harter's Self-Perception Profile is one adolescent measure.
- Perceived physical appearance is an especially strong contributor to global self-esteem. Peer acceptance also is linked to global self-esteem in adolescence.
- In Coopersmith's study, children's self-esteem was associated with such parenting practices as affection and allowing children freedom within well-prescribed limits. Peer and friendship relations also are linked with self-esteem.
- For most adolescents, low self-esteem results in only temporary emotional discomfort. However, for others, especially when low self-esteem persists, it is linked with depression, suicide, anorexia nervosa, and delinquency.
- Four ways to increase adolescents' self-esteem are (1) identify the causes of low self-esteem and which domains of competence are important to the adolescent, (2) provide emotional support and social approval, (3) help the adolescent to achieve, and (4) improve the adolescent's coping skills.

So far in this chapter, we have examined the adolescent's self-understanding, self-esteem, and self-concept. Next, we will turn our attention to the adolescent's identity development, which is closely linked to self-understanding.

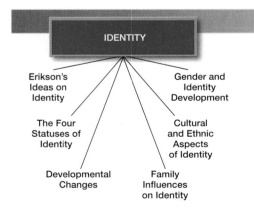

identity versus identity confusion
Erikson's fifth developmental stage, which individuals experience during the adolescent years. At this time, individuals are faced with finding out who they are, what they are all about, and where they are going in life.

IDENTITY

By far the most comprehensive and provocative theory of identity development has been told by Erik Erikson. Some experts on adolescence consider Erikson's ideas to be the single most influential theory of adolescent development. Erikson's theory was introduced in chapter 2 ◀▌▎▎ P. 44. Here that introduction is expanded, beginning with a reanalysis of his ideas on identity.

Erikson's Ideas on Identity

Who am I? What am I all about? What am I going to do with my life? What is different about me? How can I make it on my own? Not usually considered during childhood, these questions surface as common, virtually universal, concerns during adolescence. Adolescents clamor for solutions to these questions that revolve around the concept of identity, and it was Erik Erikson (1950, 1968) who first understood how central such questions are to understanding adolescent development. That today identity is believed to be a key concept in adolescent development is a result of Erikson's masterful thinking and analysis.

Revisiting Erikson's Views on Identity and the Human Life Span **Identity versus identity confusion** is *Erikson's fifth developmental stage, which individuals experience during the adolescent years. At this time, adolescents examine who they are, what they are*

all about, and where they are going in life. Adolescents are confronted with many new roles, such as vocational and romantic roles. **Psychosocial moratorium** *is Erikson's term for the gap between childhood security and adult autonomy that adolescents experience as part of their identity exploration.* As adolescents explore and search their culture's identity files, they often experiment with different roles. Youths who successfully cope with these conflicting identities emerge with a new sense of self that is both refreshing and acceptable. Adolescents who do not successfully resolve this identity crisis suffer what Erikson calls identity confusion. The confusion takes one of two courses: Individuals withdraw, isolating themselves from peers and family, or they immerse themselves in the world of peers and lose their identity in the crowd.

Erikson's ideas about adolescent identity development reveal rich insights into adolescents' thoughts and feelings. Reading one or more of his original writings is worthwhile. A good starting point is *Identity: Youth and Crisis* (1968). Other works that portray identity development are *Young Man Luther* (1962) and *Gandhi's Truth* (1969)—the latter won a Pulitzer Prize.

Personality and Role Experimentation   Two core ingredients in Erikson's theory of identity development are personality and role experimentation. As indicated earlier, Erikson believes that adolescents face an overwhelming number of choices and at some point during youth enter a period of psychological moratorium (Hopkins, 2000). During this moratorium, they try out different roles and personalities before they reach a stable sense of self. They might be argumentative one moment, cooperative the next moment. They might dress neatly one day, sloppily the next day. They might like a particular friend one week, despise the friend the next week. This personality experimentation is a deliberate effort on the part of adolescents to find out where they fit in the world.

As they gradually come to realize that they will be responsible for themselves and their own lives, adolescents search for what those lives are going to be. Many parents and other adults, accustomed to having children go along with what they say, may be bewildered or incensed by the wisecracks, the rebelliousness, and the rapid mood changes that accompany adolescence. It is important for these adults to give adolescents the time and the opportunities to explore different roles and personalities. In turn, most adolescents eventually discard undesirable roles.

There are literally hundreds of roles for adolescents to try out, and probably just as many ways to pursue each role. Erikson believes that, by late adolescence, vocational roles are central to identity development, especially in a highly technological society like the United States. Youth who have been well trained to enter a workforce that offers the potential of reasonably high self-esteem will experience the least stress during the development of identity. Some youth have rejected jobs offering good pay and traditionally high social status, choosing instead to work in situations that allow them to be more genuinely helpful to their fellow humans, such as in the Peace Corps, in mental health clinics, or in schools for children from low-income backgrounds. Some youth prefer unemployment to the prospect of working at a job they feel they would be unable to perform well or at which they would feel useless. To Erikson, this attitude reflects the desire to achieve a meaningful identity through being true to oneself, rather than burying one's identity in that of the larger society.

According to Erikson, identity is a self-portrait composed of many pieces, including these:

- The career and work path the person wants to follow (vocational/career identity)
- Whether the person is conservative, liberal, or a middle-of-the roader (political identity)
- The person's spiritual beliefs (religious identity)

psychosocial moratorium
Erikson's term for the gap between childhood security and adult autonomy that adolescents experience as part of their identity exploration.

Exploring Identity
The Society for Research on Identity Development
Identity Development in Literature
http://www.mhhe.com/santrocka9

One of Erik Erikson's strategies for explaining the nature of identity development was to analyze the lives of famous individuals. One such individual was Mahatma Gandhi (*center*), the spiritual leader of India in the mid-twentieth century, about whom Erikson (1969) wrote about in *Gandhi's Truth.*

- Whether the person is single, married, divorced, and so on (relationship identity)
- The extent to which the person is motivated to achieve and is intellectual (achievement, intellectual identity)
- Whether the person is heterosexual, homosexual, or bisexual (sexual identity)
- Which part of the world or country the person is from and how intensely the person identifies with his or her cultural heritage (cultural/ethnic identity)
- The kind of things a person likes to do, which can include sports, music, hobbies, and so on (interest)
- The individual's personality characteristics (such as being introverted or extraverted, anxious or calm, friendly or hostile, and so on) (personality)
- The individual's body image (physical identity)

Some Contemporary Thoughts on Identity   Contemporary views of identity development suggest several important considerations. First, identity development is a lengthy process, in many instances a more gradual, less cataclysmic transition than Erikson's term *crisis* implies (Baumeister, 1991). Second, as just indicated, identity development is extraordinarily complex (Marcia, 1989). Identity formation neither begins nor ends with adolescence. It begins with the appearance of attachment, the development of a sense of self, and the emergence of independence in infancy, and reaches its final phase with a life review and integration in old age. What is important about identity development in adolescence, especially late adolescence, is that, for the first time, physical development, cognitive development, and social development advance to the point at which the individual can sort through and synthesize childhood identities and identifications to construct a viable path toward adult maturity. Resolution of the identity issue at adolescence does not mean that identity will be stable through the remainder of life. An individual who develops a healthy identity is flexible and adaptive, open to changes in society, in relationships, and in careers (Adams, Gulotta, & Montemayor, 1992). This openness assures numerous reorganizations of identity's contents throughout the identity-achieved individual's life.

Just as there is an increasing tendency to describe the adolescent's self system in terms of multiple selves, so have experts on adolescence begun to characterize the adolescent's identity system in terms of multiple identities (Brooks-Gunn & Graber, 1999). While identities during the adolescent years are preceded by childhood identities, central questions such as "Who am I?" and "What aspects of my identities come out in different contexts?" are asked more frequently in the adolescent years. During adolescence, identities are more strongly characterized by the search for balance between the needs for autonomy and for connectedness.

Identity formation does not happen neatly, and it usually does not happen cataclysmically. At the bare minimum, it involves commitment to a vocational direction, an ideological stance, and a sexual orientation. Synthesizing the identity components can be a long and drawn-out process, with many negations and affirmations of various roles and faces. Identity development gets done in bits and pieces. Decisions are not made once and for all, but have to be made again and again. And the decisions might seem trivial at the time: whom to date, whether or not to break up, whether or not to have intercourse, whether or not to take drugs, whether or not to go to college or finish high school and get a job, which major, whether to study or to play, whether or not to be politically active, and so on. Over the years of adolescence, the decisions begin to form a core of what the individual is all about as a human being—what is called her or his identity.

When I say, "I," I mean something absolutely unique not to be confused with any other.
—Ugo Betti
Italian Playwright, 20th Century

Identity Status Research
http://www.mhhe.com/santrocka9

The Four Statuses of Identity

Eriksonian researcher James Marcia (1980, 1994) believes that Erikson's theory of identity development contains four statuses of identity, or ways of resolving the identity crisis: identity diffusion, identity foreclosure, identity moratorium, and identity achievement. The extent of an adolescent's crisis and commitment are used to classify the individual according to one of the four identity statuses. **Crisis** *is defined as a period of identity development during which the adolescent is choosing among meaningful alternatives.* Most researchers use the term *exploration* rather than *crisis,* although, in the spirit of Marcia's formulation, the term *crisis* is used here. **Commitment** *is a part of identity development in which adolescents show a personal investment in what they are going to do.*

Identity diffusion *is Marcia's term for the state adolescents are in when they have not yet experienced a crisis (that is, they have not yet explored meaningful alternatives) or made any commitments.* Not only are they undecided about occupational and ideological choices, they are also likely to show little interest in such matters. **Identity foreclosure** *is Marcia's term for the state adolescents are in when they have made a commitment but have not experienced a crisis.* This occurs most often when parents hand down commitments to their adolescents, usually in an authoritarian way. In these circumstances, adolescents have not had adequate opportunities to explore different approaches, ideologies, and vocations on their own. **Identity moratorium** *is Marcia's term for the state of adolescents who are in the midst of a crisis, but whose commitments either are absent or are only vaguely defined.* **Identity achievement** *is Marcia's term for an adolescent's having undergone a crisis and having made a commitment.* Marcia's four statuses of identity development are summarized in figure 9.3.

The identity status approach has been sharply criticized by some researchers and theoreticians (Blasi, 1988; Bosma & Kunnen, 2001; Cote & Levine, 1988; Goosens, 1995;

crisis
A period of identity development during which the adolescent is choosing among meaningful alternatives.

commitment
The part of identity development in which adolescents show a personal investment in what they are going to do.

identity diffusion
Marcia's term for the state adolescents are in when they have not yet experienced a crisis or made any commitments.

identity foreclosure
Marcia's term for the state adolescents are in when they have made a commitment but have not experienced a crisis.

identity moratorium
Marcia's term for the state of adolescents who are in the midst of a crisis, but whose commitments either are absent or are only vaguely defined.

identity achievement
Marcia's term for an adolescent's having undergone a crisis and made a commitment.

Identity status				
Position on occupation and ideology	Identity moratorium	Identity foreclosure	Identity diffusion	Identity achievement
Crisis	Present	Absent	Absent	Present
Commitment	Absent	Present	Absent	Present

■ FIGURE 9.3
Marcia's Four Statuses of Identity

THINKING CRITICALLY

Exploring Your Identity

Think deeply about your exploration and commitment in the areas listed here. For each area, check whether your identity status is diffused, foreclosed, moratorium, or achieved.

Identity Component	Identity Status			
	Diffused	Foreclosed	Moratorium	Achieved
Vocational (career)				
Political				
Religious				
Relationship				
Achievement				
Sexual				
Gender				
Ethnic/ cultural				
Interests				
Personality				
Physical				

If you checked "diffused" or "foreclosed" for any areas, take some time to think about what you need to do to move into a moratorium identity status in those areas. How much has your identity in each of these areas listed changed in recent years?

Kruger, 2000; Lapsley & Power, 1988; Van Hoof, 1999). They believe that the identity status approach distorts and trivializes Erikson's notions of crisis and commitment. For example, concerning crisis, Erikson emphasized youths' questioning the perceptions and expectations of one's culture and developing an autonomous position with regard to one's society. In the identity status approach, these complex questions are dealt with by simply evaluating whether a youth has thought about certain issues and has considered alternatives. Erikson's idea of commitment loses the meaning of investing oneself in certain lifelong projects and is interpreted simply as having made a firm decision or not. Others still believe that the identity status approach is a valuable contribution to understanding identity (Archer, 1989; Berzonsky & Adams, 1999; Marcia, 1994; Waterman, 1989, 1999).

Michael Berzonsky (2000; Berzonsky & Kuk, 2002) has proposed an alternative way of conceptualizing identity to Marcia's identity statuses. His social cognitive view emphasizes differences in how individuals process self-relevant information, negotiate identity conflicts, and make personal decisions. Berzonsky describes three identity processing styles: (1) informational, (2) normative, and (3) diffuse/avoidant. In the informational identity style, individuals actively seek out, process, and use self-relevant information when dealing with identity issues and forming personal commitments. In the normative identity style, individuals conform to the expectations and prescriptions of significant others. In the diffuse/avoidant identity style, individuals deliberately avoid having to deal with personal conflicts and decisions.

Developmental Changes

In Marcia's terms, young adolescents are primarily in the identity statuses of diffusion, foreclosure, or moratorium. At least three aspects of the young adolescent's development are important in identity formation (Marcia, 1987, 1996): Young adolescents must be confident that they have parental support, must have an established sense of industry, and must be able to adopt a self-reflective stance toward the future.

Some researchers believe the most important identity changes take place in youth rather than earlier in adolescence. For example, Alan Waterman (1985, 1989, 1992, 1999) has found that from the years preceding high school through the last few years of college, there is an increase in the number of individuals who are identity achieved, along with a decrease in those who are identity diffused. College upperclassmen are more likely to be identity achieved than college freshmen or high school students are. Many young adolescents are identity diffused. These developmental changes are especially true for vocational choice. For religious beliefs and political ideology, fewer college students have reached the identity-achieved status, with a substantial number characterized by foreclosure and diffusion. Thus, the timing of identity may depend on the particular life area involved, and many college students are still wrestling with ideological commitments (Arehart & Smith, 1990; Harter, 1990b).

Many identity status researchers believe that a common pattern of individuals who develop positive identities is to follow what are called "MAMA" cycles of moratorium–achievement–moratorium–achievement (Archer, 1989). These cycles may be repeated throughout life (Francis, Fraser, & Marcia, 1989). Personal, family, and societal changes are inevitable, and as they occur, the flexibility and skill required to

"Do you have any idea who I am?"

explore new alternatives and develop new commitments are likely to enhance an individual's coping skills. Regarding commitment, Marcia (1996) believes that the first identity is just that—it is not, and should not be expected to be, the final product.

Family Influences on Identity

Parents are important figures in the adolescent's development of identity. In studies that relate identity development to parenting styles, democratic parents, who encourage adolescents to participate in family decision making, foster identity achievement. Autocratic parents, who control the adolescent's behavior without giving the adolescent an opportunity to express opinions, encourage identity foreclosure. Permissive parents, who provide little guidance to adolescents and allow them to make their own decisions, promote identity diffusion (Enright & others, 1987).

In addition to studies on parenting styles, researchers have also examined the role of individuality and connectedness in the development of identity. Developmentalist Catherine Cooper and her colleagues (Carlson, Cooper, & Hsu, 1990; Cooper & Grotevant, 1989; Grotevant & Cooper, 1985, 1998) believe that the presence of a family atmosphere that promotes both individuality and connectedness is important in the adolescent's identity development. **Individuality** *consists of two dimensions: self-assertion, the ability to have and communicate a point of view; and separateness, the use of communication patterns to express how one is different from others.* **Connectedness** *also consists of two dimensions: mutuality, sensitivity to and respect for others' views; and permeability, openness to others' views.* In general, Cooper's research findings reveal that identity formation is enhanced by family relationships that are both individuated, which encourages adolescents to develop their own point of view, and connected, which provides a secure base from which to explore the widening social worlds of adolescence. However, when connectedness is strong and individuation weak, adolescents often have an identity foreclosure status; in contrast, when connectedness is weak, adolescents often reveal an identity confusion status (Archer & Waterman, 1994).

individuality

An important element in adolescent identity development. It consists of two dimensions: self-assertion, the ability to have and communicate a point of view; and separateness, the use of communication patterns to express how one is different from others.

connectedness

An important element in adolescent identity development. It consists of two dimensions: mutuality, sensitivity to and respect for others' views; and permeability, openness to others' views.

Stuart Hauser and his colleagues (Hauser & Bowlds, 1990; Hauser & others, 1984) also have illuminated family processes that promote the adolescent's identity development. They have found that parents who use *enabling* behaviors (such as explaining, accepting, and giving empathy) facilitate the adolescent's identity development more than do parents who use *constraining* behaviors (such as judging and devaluing). In sum, family interaction styles that give the adolescent the right to question and to be different, within a context of support and mutuality, foster healthy patterns of identity development (Harter, 1990b).

Cultural and Ethnic Aspects of Identity

Let's examine Erik Erikson's view on culture and identity and then turn to the development of ethnic identity.

Erikson's View   Erikson was especially sensitive to the role of culture in identity development. He pointed out that, throughout the world, ethnic minority groups have struggled to maintain their cultural identities while blending into the dominant culture (Erikson, 1968). Erikson said that this struggle for an inclusive identity, or identity within the larger culture, has been the driving force in the founding of churches, empires, and revolutions throughout history.

Adolescence: A Special Juncture   For ethnic minority individuals, adolescence is often a special juncture in their development (Bat-Chava & others, 1997; Kurtz, Cantu, & Phinney, 1996; Spencer & Dornbusch, 1990). Although children are aware of some ethnic and cultural differences, most ethnic minority individuals consciously confront their ethnicity for the first time in adolescence. In contrast to children, adolescents have the ability to interpret ethnic and cultural information, to reflect on the past, and to speculate about the future (Wong, 1997).

ethnic identity
An enduring, basic aspect of the self that includes a sense of membership in an ethnic group and the attitudes and feelings related to that membership.

Exploring Ethnic Identities
An Adolescent Talks About
Ethnic Identity
Ethnic Identity Research
http://www.mhhe.com/santrocka9

Defining and Exploring Ethnic Identity   Jean Phinney (1996) defined **ethnic identity** *as an enduring, basic aspect of the self that includes a sense of membership in an ethnic group and the attitudes and feelings related to that membership.* Thus, for adolescents from ethnic minority groups, the process of identity formation has an added dimension due to exposure to alternative sources of identification, their own ethnic group and the mainstream or dominant culture (Phinney, 2000). Researchers have found that ethnic identity increases with age and that higher levels of ethnic identity are linked with more positive attitudes not only toward one's own ethnic group but toward members of other ethnic groups as well (Phinney, Ferguson, & Tate, 1997). Many ethnic minority adolescents have bicultural identities—identifying in some ways with their ethnic minority group, in other ways with the majority culture (Kuperminc & others, 2002; Moje & others, 2002; Phinney & Devich-Navarro, 1997; Sidhu, 2000; Tupuola, 2000) ◀▥ P. 268.

The ease or difficulty with which ethnic minority adolescents achieve healthy identities depends on a number of factors (Phinney & Rosenthal, 1992). Many ethnic minority adolescents have to confront issues of prejudice and discrimination, and barriers that limit their goals and aspirations.

In one investigation, ethnic identity exploration was higher among ethnic minority than among White American college students (Phinney & Alipuria, 1990). In this same investigation, ethnic minority college students who had thought about and resolved issues involving their ethnicity had higher self-esteem than did their ethnic minority counterparts who had not. In another investigation, the ethnic identity development of Asian American, African American, Latino, and White American tenth-grade students in Los Angeles was studied (Phinney, 1989). Adolescents from each of the three ethnic minority groups faced a similar need to deal with their ethnic-group identification in a predominantly White American culture. In some instances, the adolescents from the three ethnic minority groups perceived different issues to be important in their resolution of ethnic identity. For Asian American adolescents, pressures to achieve academically and concerns about quotas that make it difficult to get into good colleges were salient issues. Many African American adolescent females discussed their realization that White American standards of beauty (especially hair and skin color) did not apply to them; African American adolescent males were concerned with possible job discrimination and the need to distinguish themselves from a negative societal image of African American male adolescents. For Latino adolescents, prejudice was a recurrent theme, as was the conflict in values between their Latino culture heritage and the majority culture.

Helms' Model of Ethnic Identity Development

Janet Helms (1990, 1996) has proposed a model of ethnic identity development that consists of four stages.

- *Stage 1: Preencounter.* In this first stage, ethnic minority individuals prefer dominant cultural values to those of their own culture. Their role models, lifestyles, and value systems are adopted from the dominant group, while the physical and/or cultural characteristics that single them out as ethnic minority individuals are a source of pain and stress. For example, African Americans may perceive their own physical features as undesirable and their African American cultural values and ways a handicap to success in American society.

- *Stage 2: Encounter.* While moving to the encounter stage is usually a gradual process, reaching this stage may occur because of an event that makes individuals realize that they will never be members of mainstream White America. A monumental event, such as the assassination of Martin Luther King, Jr., or more personal "identity-shattering" events may serve as triggers. In the encounter stage, ethnic minority individuals begin to break through their denial. For example, Latinos who feel ashamed of their cultural upbringing may have conversations with Latinos who are proud of their cultural heritage. Ethnic minority individuals become aware during the encounter stage that not all cultural values of the dominant group are beneficial to them. Conflicting attitudes about the self, minority group culture, and the dominant culture are characteristic of the encounter stage. Ethnic minority individuals want to identify with the minority group but do not know how to develop this identity. The recognition that an identity must be developed and not found leads to the third stage: immersion/emersion.

- *Stage 3: Immersion/Emersion.* At the beginning of this stage—immersion—ethnic minority individuals completely endorse minority views and reject the dominant society. Movement into this stage likely occurs because (1) individuals begin to resolve some conflicts from the previous stage and develop a better understanding of such societal forces as racism and discrimination; and (2) individuals begin to ask themselves, "Why should I feel ashamed of who I am?" The answer at this point often elicits both guilt and anger—the guilt of "selling out" in the past and anger at having been "brainwashed" by the dominant group.

  In the second phase of this stage—emersion—individuals experience feelings of discontent and discomfort with their rigid views of the immersion phase and develop notions of greater individual autonomy. Emersion allows them to vent the anger that characterized the beginning of this stage, through rap groups, explorations of their own culture, discussions of racial/ethnic issues, and so on. Education and opportunities to expel hostile feelings allow individuals' emotions to level off, so that they can think more clearly and adaptively. They no longer find it necessary to reject everything from the dominant culture and accept everything from their own culture. They now have the autonomy to determine the strengths and weaknesses of their culture, and to decide which parts of the culture will become a part of their identity.

- *Stage 4: Internalization/Commitment.* The main theme of this stage of ethnic minority identity development is that individuals experience a sense of fulfillment regarding the integration of their personal and cultural identities. They have resolved the conflicts and discomforts of the immersion/emersion stage and attained greater

THROUGH THE EYES OF PSYCHOLOGISTS

Catherine Cooper
University of California, Santa Cruz

"Many ethnic minority youth must bridge 'multiple worlds' in constructing their identities."

THROUGH THE EYES OF ADOLESCENTS

Identity Exploring

Michelle Chin, age 16: "Parents do not understand that teenagers need to find out who they are, which means a lot of experimenting, a lot of mood swings, a lot of emotions and awkwardness. Like any teenager, I am facing an identity crisis. I am still trying to figure out whether I am a Chinese American or an American with Asian eyes."

Michelle Chin

Cultural Identity in Canada
Identity, Ethnicity, Religion, and
Political Violence
Research on Gender and Identity
Some Developmental Models of
Girls and Women
http://www.mhhe.com/santrocka9

self-control and flexibility. They also more objectively examine the cultural values of other ethnic minority individuals and groups, as well as those of the dominant group. At this stage, individuals want to eliminate all forms of discrimination. The commitment in this stage refers to the behavioral enactment of the newly realized identity. Individuals take actions—whether large, such as engaging in large-scale political or social activism, or small, such as performing everyday activities that are consistent with their ethnic identity—to eliminate discrimination.

Contexts The contexts in which ethnic minority youth live influence their identity development (Hecht, Jackson, & Ribeau, 2002; Spencer, 1999, 2000; Spencer & others, 2001). Many ethnic minority youth in the United States live in low-SES urban settings where support for developing a positive identity is absent. Many of these youth live in pockets of poverty, are exposed to drugs, gangs, and criminal activities, and interact with other youth and adults who have dropped out of school and/or are unemployed. In such settings, effective organizations and programs for youth can make important contributions to developing a positive identity.

Shirley Heath and Milbrey McLaughlin (1993) studied sixty youth organizations that involved 24,000 adolescents over a period of five years. They found that these organizations were especially good at building a sense of ethnic pride in inner-city ethnic youth. Heath and McLaughlin believe that many inner-city youth have too much time on their hands, too little to do, and too few places to go. Inner-city youth want to participate in organizations that nurture them and respond positively to their needs and interests. Organizations that perceive youth as fearful, vulnerable, and lonely but also frame them as capable, worthy, and eager to have a healthy and productive life contribute in positive ways to the identity development of ethnic minority youth.

Gender and Identity Development

In Erikson's (1968) classic presentation of identity development, the division of labor between the sexes was reflected in his assertion that males' aspirations were mainly oriented toward career and ideological commitments, while females' were centered around marriage and childbearing. In the 1960s and 1970s researchers found support for Erikson's assertion about gender differences in identity. For example, vocational concerns were more central to the identity of males, and affiliative concerns were more important in the identity of females (La Voie, 1976). However, in the last decade, as females have developed stronger vocational interests, these gender differences are disappearing (Madison & Foster-Clark, 1996; Waterman, 1985).

Some investigators believe that females and males go through Erikson's stages in different order. One view is that for males, identity formation precedes the stage of intimacy, while for females, intimacy precedes identity (Douvan & Adelson, 1966). These ideas are consistent with the belief that relationships and emotional bonds are more important concerns of females, while autonomy and achievement are more important concerns of males (Gilligan, 1992). In one study, the development of a clear sense of self by adolescent girls was related to their concerns about care and response in relationships (Rogers, 1987). In another investigation, a strong sense of self in college women was associated with their ability to solve problems of care in relationships while staying connected with both self and others (Skoe & Marcia, 1988). Indeed, conceptualization and measurement of identity development in females should include interpersonal content (Patterson, Sochting, & Marcia, 1992).

The task of identity exploration might be more complex for females than for males, in that females might try to establish identities in more domains than males do. In today's world, the options for females have increased and thus can at times be confusing and conflicting, especially for females who hope to successfully integrate family and career roles (Archer, 1994, 2000; Josselson, 1994; Streitmatter, 1993).

At this point we have studied many aspects of identity. This review should help you to reach your learning goals related to this topic.

☐ FOR YOUR REVIEW

Learning Goal 3
Discuss Erikson's ideas on identity, identity statuses, and developmental changes

- Identity versus identity confusion is Erikson's fifth developmental stage, which individuals experience during adolescence. As adolescents are confronted with new roles, they enter a psychosocial moratorium. Personality and role experimentation are two key ingredients of Erikson's view. In technological societies like the United States, the vocational role is especially important. Identity development is extraordinarily complex and is done in bits and pieces.
- Marcia proposed four identity statuses: diffused, foreclosed, moratorium, and achieved. A combination of crisis (exploration) and commitment yields one of the statuses. Some critics argue that Marcia's four identity statuses oversimplify identity development.
- Some experts believe that the main identity changes take place in late adolescence or youth, rather than in early adolescence. College upperclassmen are more likely to be identity achieved than are freshmen or high school students, although many college students are still wrestling with ideological commitments. Individuals often follow "moratorium-achievement-moratorium-achievement" cycles.

Learning Goal 4
Describe links between identity and family influences, culture and ethnicity, and gender

- Parents are important figures in adolescents' identity development. Researchers have found that democratic parenting, individuality, connectedness, and enabling behaviors are linked with positive aspects of identity.
- Erikson was especially sensitive to the role of culture in identity development, underscoring the fact that throughout the world ethnic minority groups have struggled to maintain their cultural identities while blending into majority culture. Adolescence is often a special juncture in the identity development of ethnic minority individuals because for the first time they consciously confront their ethnic identity. Many ethnic minority adolescents have a bicultural identity. Helms proposed a model of ethnic identity development. Contexts influence ethnic identity development.
- Erikson believed that adolescent males have a stronger vocational identity, female adolescents a stronger social identity. Some researchers find that these gender differences are disappearing; others argue that a social identity is a stronger aspect of female identity development.

So far in this chapter, we have studied many aspects of the self and identity. As we see next, Erikson believed that another important aspect of identity was to examine its connection with intimacy.

IDENTITY AND INTIMACY

Earlier in this book, in chapter 6, "Peers," we explored a number of ideas about intimacy. For example, we studied the important role of intimacy in friendship and in dating and romantic relationships ◀‖‖ Pp. 199, 211. Later we will further examine intimacy in chapter 11, "Sexuality." Here we will focus on the concept of intimacy in

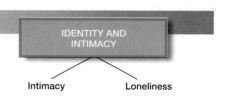

IDENTITY AND INTIMACY

Intimacy   Loneliness

Erikson's theory, different styles of intimate interaction, and the loneliness that often ensues for a person who has little intimacy with others.

Intimacy

Erikson (1968) believes that intimacy should come after individuals are well on their way to establishing a stable and successful individual identity. Intimacy is another life crisis in Erikson's scheme—if intimacy is not developed in early adulthood, the individual may be left with what Erikson calls isolation. **Intimacy versus isolation** *is Erikson's sixth developmental stage, which individuals experience during early adulthood. At this time, individuals face the task of forming intimate relationships with others.* Erikson describes intimacy as finding oneself, yet losing oneself in another. If young adults form healthy friendships and an intimate relationship with another individual, intimacy will be achieved; if not, isolation will result.

In one study of unmarried college students 18 to 23 years of age, a strong sense of self, expressed through identity achievement and an instrumental orientation, was an important factor in forming intimate connections, for both males and females (Madison & Foster-Clark, 1996). However, insecurity and a defensive posture in relationships were expressed differently in males' and females' relationships, with males displaying greater superficiality and females more dependency.

An inability to develop meaningful relationships with others can harm an individual's personality. It may lead individuals to repudiate, ignore, or attack those who frustrate them. Such circumstances account for the shallow, almost pathetic attempts of youth to merge themselves with a leader. Many youths want to be apprentices or disciples of leaders and adults who will shelter them from the harm of the "out-group" world. If this fails, and Erikson believes that it must, sooner or later the individuals retreat to search themselves to discover where they went wrong. This introspection sometimes leads to painful depression and isolation and can contribute to a mistrust of others and restrict the youths' willingness to act on their own initiative.

Adolescents and young adults show different styles of intimate interaction. Jacob Orlofsky (1976) developed one classification with five styles: intimate, preintimate, stereotyped, pseudointimate, and isolated (Orlofsky, Marcia, & Lesser, 1973). In the **intimate style,** *the individual forms and maintains one or more deep and long-lasting love relationships.* In the **preintimate style,** *the individual shows mixed emotions about commitment, an ambivalence reflected in the strategy of offering love without obligations or long-lasting bonds.* In the **stereotyped style,** *the individual has superficial relationships that tend to be dominated by friendship ties with same-sex rather than opposite-sex individuals.* In the **pseudointimate style,** *the individual maintains a long-lasting sexual attachment with little or no depth or closeness.* In the **isolated style,** *the individual withdraws from social encounters and has little or no attachment to same- or opposite-sex individuals.* Occasionally, the isolate shows signs of developing close interpersonal relationships, but usually the interactions are stressful. In one investigation, intimate and preintimate individuals were more sensitive to their partners' needs and were more open in their friendships than individuals in the other three intimacy statuses were (Orlofsky, Marcia, & Lesser, 1973).

A desirable goal is to develop a mature identity and have positive, close relationships with others. Kathleen White and her colleagues (1987) developed a model of relationship maturity that includes this goal at its highest level. Individuals are described as moving through three levels of relationship maturity: self-focused, role-focused, and individuated-connected.

The **self-focused level** *is the first level of relationship maturity, at which one's perspective of another or a relationship is concerned only with how it affects oneself.* The individual's own wishes and plans overshadow those of others, and the individual shows little concern for others. Intimate communication skills are in the early developing, experimental stages. In terms of sexuality, there is little understanding of mutuality or consideration of another's sexual needs.

---

intimacy versus isolation
Erikson's sixth developmental stage, which individuals experience during the early adulthood years. At this time, individuals face the developmental task of forming intimate relationships with others.

Intimacy
http://www.mhhe.com/santrocka9

intimate style
The individual forms and maintains one or more deep and long-lasting love relationships.

preintimate style
The individual shows mixed emotions about commitment, an ambivalence reflected in the strategy of offering love without obligations.

stereotyped style
The individual has superficial relationships that tend to be dominated by friendship ties with same-sex rather than opposite-sex individuals.

pseudointimate style
The individual maintains a long-lasting sexual attachment with little or no depth or closeness.

isolated style
The individual withdraws from social encounters and has little or no attachment to same- or opposite-sex individuals.

self-focused level
The first level of relationship maturity, at which one's perspective of another or of a relationship is concerned only with how it affects oneself.

The **role-focused level** *is the second or intermediate level of relationship maturity, at which perceiving others as individuals in their own right begins to develop. However, at this level, the perspective is stereotypical and emphasizes social acceptability.* Individuals at this level know that acknowledging and respecting another is part of being a good friend or a romantic partner. Yet commitment to an individual, rather than the romantic partner role itself, is not articulated. Generalizations about the importance of communication in relationships abound, but underlying this talk is a shallow understanding of commitment.

The **individuated-connected level** *is the highest level of relationship maturity, at which there is evidence of self-understanding, as well as consideration of others' motivations and anticipation of their needs. Concern and caring involve emotional support and individualized expression of interest.* Commitment is made to specific individuals with whom a relationship is shared. At this level, individuals understand the personal time and investment needed to make a relationship work. In White's view, the individuated-connected level is not likely to be reached until adulthood. She believes that most individuals making the transition from adolescence to adulthood are either self-focused or role-focused in their relationship maturity.

role-focused level

The second or intermediate level of relationship maturity, at which perceiving others as individuals in their own right begins to develop. However, at this level the perspective is stereotypical and emphasizes social acceptability.

individuated-connected level

The highest level of relationship maturity, at which there is evidence of an understanding of oneself, as well as consideration of others' motivations and anticipation of their needs. Concern and caring involve emotional support and individualized expression of interest.

Loneliness

We often think of older adults as the loneliest individuals, but surveys have found that the highest levels of loneliness often appear during late adolescence and youth (Cutrona, 1982). Some adolescents feel lonely because they have strong needs for intimacy but have not yet developed the social skills or relationship maturity to satisfy these needs. They might feel isolated and sense that they do not have anyone they can turn to for intimacy. In one study, teenage loneliness appeared to be part of a depressive complex for girls while signaling poor scholastic functioning for boys (Koenig & Faigeles, 1995). Society's contemporary emphasis on self-fulfillment and achievement, the importance attached to commitment in relationships, and the decline in stable, close relationships are among the reasons feelings of loneliness are common today.

Loneliness
Shyness
http://www.mhhe.com/santrocka9

Loneliness is associated with an individual's sex, attachment history, self-esteem, and social skills. A lack of time spent with females, on the part of both males and females, is associated with loneliness. Lonely adolescents are not adequately integrated into the peer system and might not have close friends (Hicks & Connolly, 1995). Also, individuals who are lonely often have a poor relationship with their parents. Early experiences of rejection and loss (as when a parent dies) can cause a lasting effect of feeling alone. Lonely individuals often have low self-esteem and tend to blame themselves more than they deserve for their inadequacies. Lonely individuals also are often deficient in social skills. For example, they show inappropriate self-disclosure, self-attention at the expense of attention to a partner, or an inability to develop comfortable intimacy.

The social transition to college is a time when loneliness might develop, as individuals leave behind the familiar world of hometown and family. Many college freshmen feel anxious about meeting new people and developing a new social life. As one student commented:

> My first year here at the university has been pretty lonely. I wasn't lonely at all in high school. I lived in a fairly small town—I knew everyone and everyone knew me. I was a member of several clubs and played on the basketball team. It's not that way at the university. It is a big place, and I've felt like a stranger on so many occasions. I'm starting to get used to my life here, and the last few months I've been making myself meet people and get to know them, but it has not been easy.

As reflected in the comments of this freshman, individuals usually cannot bring their popularity and social standing from high school into the college environment. There might be a dozen high school basketball stars, National Merit scholars, and former student council presidents on a single dormitory floor. Especially if students attend college away from home, they face the task of forming completely new social relationships.

In one investigation conducted two weeks after the school year began, 75 percent of the 354 college freshmen said that they had felt lonely at least part of the time since arriving on campus (Cutrona, 1982). More than 40 percent said that their loneliness was moderate to severe in intensity. Students who were the most optimistic and had the highest self-esteem were more likely to overcome their loneliness by the end of the freshman year. Loneliness is not reserved only for college freshmen, though. It is not uncommon to find a number of upperclassmen who are also lonely.

Researchers have developed measures of loneliness. Individuals are asked to respond to statements such as these:

"I don't feel in tune with the people around me."
"I can't find companionship when I want it."

Individuals who consistently respond that they never or rarely feel in tune with people around them and rarely or never can find companionship when they want it are likely to fall into the category of moderately or intensely lonely.

According to Robert Weiss (1973), loneliness is virtually always a response to the absence of some particular type of relationship. Weiss distinguished two forms of loneliness—*emotional isolation* and *social isolation*—which correspond to the absence of different types of social provisions. **Emotional isolation** *is a type of loneliness that arises when a person lacks an intimate attachment relationship; single, divorced, and widowed adults often experience this type of loneliness.* In contrast, **social isolation** *is a type of loneliness that occurs when a person lacks a sense of integrated involvement. Being deprived of participation in a group or community involving companionship, shared interests, organized activities, and meaningful roles causes a person to feel alienated, bored, and uneasy.* Recently relocated married couples often experience social isolation and long for involvement with friends and community.

It is common for adolescents to experience both types of loneliness. Being left out of clique and crowd activities can give rise to painful feelings of social isolation. Not having an intimate dating or romantic partner can give rise to the loneliness of emotional isolation.

Individuals can reduce their loneliness by either changing their social relations or changing their social needs and desires (Peplau & Perlman, 1982). Probably the most direct and satisfying choice is to improve their social relations by forming new relationships, by using their existing social network more competently, or by creating "surrogate" relationships with pets, television personalities, and the like. The second way to reduce loneliness is to reduce one's desire for social contact. Over the short run,

emotional isolation
A type of loneliness that arises when a person lacks an intimate attachment relationship; single, divorced, and widowed adults often experience this type of loneliness.

social isolation
A type of loneliness that occurs when a person lacks a sense of integrated involvement. Being deprived of participation in a group or community involving companionship, shared interests, organized activities, and meaningful roles causes a person to feel alienated, bored, and uneasy.

individuals can accomplish this by selecting activities they can enjoy alone rather than those that require another's company. Over the long run, though, effort should be made to form new relationships. A third coping strategy that some individuals unfortunately adopt involves distracting themselves from their painful feelings of loneliness by consuming alcohol or other drugs to "drown their sorrows" or by becoming a workaholic. Some of the negative health consequences of loneliness may be the product of such maladaptive coping strategies. If you perceive yourself to be a lonely individual, you might consider contacting the counseling center at your college for advice on ways to reduce your loneliness and to improve your social skills in relationships.

Since the last review, we have studied many aspects of identity and intimacy. This review should help you to reach your learning goals related to this topic.

☐ FOR YOUR REVIEW

Learning Goal 5
Explain identity and intimacy

- Intimacy versus isolation is Erikson's sixth stage of human development, which individuals experience during early adulthood.
- Orlofsky described five styles of intimate interaction: intimate, preintimate, stereotyped, pseudointimate, and isolated. White proposed a model of relationship maturity with these three stages: self-focused, role-focused, and individuated-connected.
- Surveys often find that the highest levels of loneliness occur during late adolescence and youth. The social transition to college is a time when loneliness is often present. Weiss distinguished between emotional isolation and social isolation.

In this chapter, we examined many aspects of the self and identity. In our discussion of identity, we evaluated the role of gender in identity. In chapter 10, we will further explore gender and adolescent development.

CHAPTER MAP

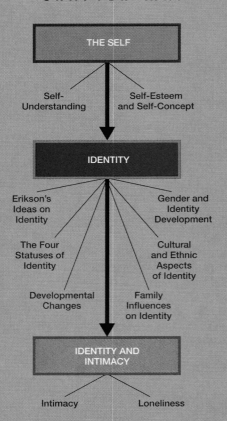

REACH YOUR LEARNING GOALS

At the beginning of this chapter, we stated five learning goals and encouraged you to review material related to these goals at four points in this chapter. This is a good time to return to these reviews. Use them to guide your study and help you to reach your learning goals.

Page 296

Learning Goal 1   Evaluate the adolescent's self-understanding

Page 300

Learning Goal 2   Know about the adolescent's self-esteem and self-concept

Page 309

Learning Goal 3   Discuss Erikson's ideas on identity, identity statuses, and developmental changes

Learning Goal 4   Describe the links between identity and family influences, culture and ethnicity, and gender

Page 313

Learning Goal 5   Explain identity and intimacy

KEY TERMS

self-understanding 292
possible self 294
self-esteem 296
self-concept 296
identity versus identity confusion 300
psychosocial moratorium 301
crisis 303
commitment 303
identity diffusion 303
identity foreclosure 303
identity moratorium 303
identity achievement 303
individuality 305

connectedness 305
ethnic identity 306
intimacy versus isolation 310
intimate style 310
preintimate style 310
stereotyped style 310
pseudointimate style 310
isolated style 310
self-focused level 310
role-focused level 311
individuated-connected level 311
emotional isolation 312
social isolation 312

KEY PEOPLE

Susan Harter 293
Erik Erikson 300
James Marcia 302
Alan Waterman 304
Catherine Cooper 305

Stuart Hauser 306
Jean Phinney 306
Jacob Orlofsky 310
Kathleen White 310
Robert Weiss 312

RESOURCES FOR IMPROVING THE LIVES OF ADOLESCENTS

Adolescent Identity Formation

(1992) by Gerald Adams, Thomas Gulotta,
and Raymond Montemayor (Eds.)
Newbury Park, CA: Sage

This book provides an up-to-date portrayal of a number of aspects of identity development in adolescence. It includes chapters on a feminist's approach to identity, ethnic identity, and the role of identity in adolescent problems.

Adolescent Psychological Development: Rationality, Morality, and Identity

(1999) by David Moshman
Mahwah, NJ: Erlbaum

A contemporary analysis of several important dimensions of adolescent development, including identity.

The Construction of the Self

(1999) by Susan Harter
New York: Guilford

A leading self theorist and researcher, Susan Harter provides an in-depth analysis of how children and adolescents see themselves.

Gandhi's Truth

(1969) by Erik Erikson
New York: W. W. Norton

This Pulitzer Prize–winning book by Erik Erikson, who developed the concept of identity as a central aspect of adolescent development, analyzes the life of Mahatma Gandhi, the spiritual leader of India in the middle of the twentieth century.

Intimate Connections

(1985) by David D. Burns
New York: William Morrow

Intimate Connections presents a program for overcoming loneliness.

Self-Esteem: The Puzzle of Low Self-Regard

(1991) by Roy Baumeister (Ed.)
New York: Plenum

An excellent book on low self-esteem and how it can be raised. Includes a chapter by Susan Harter on causes and consequences of low self-esteem in children and adolescents.

TAKING IT TO THE NET

http://www.mhhe.com/santrocka9

1. Your roommate returns from the computer lab and announces he took a self-esteem test on the web and scored really high. Knowing something about test reliability and validity, you are really skeptical about such tests. *What will you advise your roommate about the reliability and validity of online self-esteem tests?*

2. Your sister returns home from her first few weeks at college and seems to be not as confident and self-assured as she was when she left. She complains about her friends at school tugging her in different directions, about feeling awkward in various social situations, and of having lost control of her attention and concentration. *Is it possible that she is undergoing a change in identity?*

3. In Erikson's theory, the quality of resolution of earlier crises impacts on the quality of resolution of later crises. *What might be some of the outcomes of a less desirable resolution of the identity crisis on the resolution of the intimacy crisis that follows it?*

Connect to *http://www.mhhe.com/santrocka9* to research the answers and complete these exercises. In some cases, you'll also find further instructions on this site.

CHAPTER
10

CHAPTER MAP

WHAT IS GENDER?

BIOLOGICAL, SOCIAL,
AND COGNITIVE INFLUENCES
ON GENDER

Biological
Influences

Cognitive
Influences

Social
Influences

GENDER STEREOTYPES,
SIMILARITIES, AND
DIFFERENCES

Gender
Stereotyping

Gender in
Context

Gender
Similarities and
Differences

Gender
Controversy

GENDER-ROLE
CLASSIFICATION

Traditional
Gender Roles

Gender-Role
Transcendence

Androgyny

Traditional
Masculinity and
Problem Behaviors
in Adolescent Males

DEVELOPMENTAL CHANGES
AND JUNCTURES

Early
Adolescence
and Gender
Intensification

Is Early
Adolescence a
Critical Juncture
for Females?

■ Tomorrow's Gender Worlds of Today's Adolescents

GENDER

■

It is fatal to be man or woman pure and simple; one must be woman-manly or man-womanly.

—Virginia Woolf
English Novelist, 20th Century

Controversy characterizes today's females and males. Females increasingly struggle to gain influence and change the worlds of business, politics, and relationships with males. The changes are far from complete, but social reformers hope that a generation from now the struggles of the last decades of the twentieth century will have generated more freedom, influence, and flexibility for females (Denmark, Rabinowitz, & Sechzer, 2000; Lopez, 2001). Possibly in the next generation, when today's adolescents become tomorrow's adults, such issues as equal pay, child care, abortion, rape, and domestic violence will no longer be discussed as "women's issues" but, rather, as economic issues, family issues, and ethical issues—reflecting the equal concern of females *and* males. Possibly one of today's adolescent females will become the head of a large corporation several decades from now and the appointment will not make headlines by virtue of her gender. Half the presidential candidates may be women and nobody will notice.

What would it take for today's adolescent females to get from here to there? The choices are not simple ones. When Barbara Bush celebrated motherhood and wifely virtues in a commencement address at Wellesley College, she stimulated a national debate among the young on what it means to be a successful woman. The debate was further fueled by TV anchorwoman Connie Chung's announcement that she would abandon the fast track at CBS in a final drive to become a mother at age 44. At the same time, male role models are also in flux. Wall Street star Peter Lynch, the head of Fidelity Investment's leading mutual fund, resigned to have more time with his family and to pursue humanitarian projects (Gibbs, 1990). In 1993, both Chung and Lynch returned to work.

When asked to sketch their futures, many of today's youth say they want good careers, good marriages, and two or three children, but they don't want their children to be raised by strangers (Spade & Reese, 1991). Idealistic? Maybe. Some will reach these goals; some will make other choices as they move from adolescence into adulthood, and then through the adult years. Some of today's adolescents will choose to remain single as they move into adulthood and pursue their career goals; others will become married but not have children; and yet others will balance the demands of family and work. In a word, not all of today's females have the same goals; neither do all of today's males. What is important is to develop a society free of barriers and discrimination, one that allows females and males to freely choose, to meet their expectations, and to realize their potential.

GENDER PLAYS AN IMPORTANT ROLE in the lives of adolescents. A new dimension is added to gender development with the onset of puberty and the sexual maturation it brings. When you have completed this chapter you should be able to reach these learning goals:

1 Know what is meant by gender

2 Explain biological, social, and cognitive influences on gender

3 Describe gender stereotypes, similarities, and differences

4 Discuss gender controversy and gender in context

5 Evaluate traditional gender roles and androgyny

6 Understand possible problems with masculinity and explain gender-role transcendence

7 Describe developmental changes and junctures

WHAT IS GENDER?

WHAT IS GENDER?

gender
The sociocultural and psychological dimensions of being male or female.

gender role
A set of expectations that prescribes how females and males should think, act, and feel.

Nowhere in adolescents' social development have more sweeping changes occurred in recent years than in the area of gender. What exactly is meant by *gender?* Whereas the term *sex* refers to the biological dimension of being male or female, **gender** *refers to the psychological and sociocultural dimensions of being male or female.* Few aspects of adolescents' development are more central to their identity and to their social relationships than gender. One aspect of gender bears special mention: A **gender role** *is a set of expectations that prescribes how females or males should think, act, and feel.* For example, should males be more assertive than females, and should females be more sensitive than males to others' feelings?

BIOLOGICAL, SOCIAL, AND COGNITIVE INFLUENCES ON GENDER

BIOLOGICAL, SOCIAL, AND COGNITIVE INFLUENCES ON GENDER

Biological Influences

Cognitive Influences

Social Influences

How strong is biology's influence on gender? How extensively do children's and adolescents' experiences shape their gender development? How do cognitive factors influence gender development? We will explore the answers to each of these questions.

Biological Influences

In our examination of biological influences on gender behavior in adolescence, we will first discuss pubertal change, especially its role in increasing sexual interest, and second we will examine Freud's and Erikson's ideas about anatomy and destiny.

Pubertal Change and Sexuality Biology's influence on gender behavior involves pubertal change ◀IIII P. 76. Pubertal change contributes to an increased incorporation of sexuality into the gender attitudes and behavior of adolescents. As their bodies are flooded with hormones, many girls desire to be the very best female possible, and many boys strive to be the very best male possible. The increased incorporation of sexuality into gender behavior means that adolescent girls often display increased stereotypical female behavior and adolescent boys often display increased stereotypical male behavior. In many cases, adolescent girls and boys show these behaviors even more intensely when they interact with opposite-sex peers, especially with individuals they would like to date. Thus, female adolescents might behave in an affectionate, sensitive, charming, and soft-spoken manner, and male adolescents might behave in an assertive, cocky, cynical, and forceful way, because they perceive that such behaviors enhance their sexuality and attractiveness.

There have been few attempts to relate puberty's sexual changes to gender behavior. Researchers have found that sexual behavior is related to hormonal changes in puberty, at least for boys. For example, in one study, adolescent sex researcher Robert Udry (1990) found that rising androgen levels were related to boys' increased sexual activity. For adolescent girls, androgen levels and sexual activity were associated, but girls' sexual activity was more strongly influenced by the type of friends they had than by their hormone levels. In the same study, Udry investigated whether hormone increases in puberty were related to gender behaviors, such as being affectionate, charming, assertive, and cynical, but found no significant associations.

While puberty's biological changes set the stage for increased incorporation of sexuality into gender behavior, how sexuality becomes a part of gender is determined by such social influences as cultural standards for sex and peer group norms for dating. One explanation for increased differences in gender behavior was the increased socialization to conform to traditional masculine and feminine roles. However, puberty plays a role in gender intensification because it is a signaling to socializing others—such as parents, peers, and teachers—that the adolescent is beginning to approach adulthood and, therefore, should begin to act in ways that resemble the stereotypical female or male adult.

In sum, gender intensification in adolescence likely includes not only increased social pressures to conform to traditional masculine and feminine roles but also pubertal changes that introduce sexuality into gender behavior. Masculinity and femininity are renegotiated during adolescence, and much of this renegotiation involves sexuality. Further discussion of gender intensification appears later in the chapter.

Freud and Erikson—Anatomy Is Destiny   Both Sigmund Freud and Erik Erikson argued that an individual's genitals influence his or her gender behavior and, therefore, that anatomy is destiny ◀▥ Pp. 40, 44. One of Freud's basic assumptions was that human behavior and history are directly related to reproductive processes. From this assumption arose his belief that gender and sexual behavior are essentially unlearned and instinctual. Erikson (1968) extended Freud's argument, claiming that the psychological differences between males and females stem from their anatomical differences. Erikson argued that, because of genital structure, males are more intrusive and aggressive, females more inclusive and passive. Critics of the anatomy-is-destiny view believe that experience is not given enough credit. The critics say that females and males are more free to choose their gender roles than Freud and Erikson allow. In response to the critics, Erikson modified his view, saying that females in today's world are transcending their biological heritage and correcting society's overemphasis on male intrusiveness.

Evolutionary Psychology and Gender   The evolutionary psychology view emphasizes that evolutionary adaptations produced psychological sex differences (Buss, 1995, 2000; Buss & Kenrick, 1998). Evolutionary psychologists argue that women and men faced different evolutionary pressures in primeval environments when the human species was evolving and that the sexes' different status regarding reproduction was the key feature that framed different adaptive problems of females and males.

The area of behavior that has been discussed the most by evolutionary psychologists to support their view involves sexual selection. In this view, sex-typed features evolved through male competition and led to a reproductive advantage for dominant males. Men sought short-term mating strategies because this allowed them to increase their reproductive advantage by fathering more children. In contrast, women devoted more effort to parenting, and they chose mates who could provide their offspring with resources or protection.

As the man beholds the woman
As the woman sees
the man,
Curiously they note
each other,
As each other they only can.
—Bryan Procter
English Poet, 19th Century

Gender Resources
http://www.mhhe.com/santrocka9

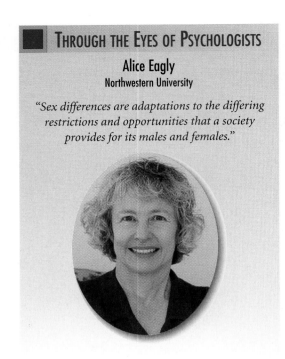

Alice Eagly's Research
http://www.mhhe.com/santrocka9

social cognitive theory of gender
This theory emphasizes that children's and adolescents' gender development occurs through observation and imitation of gender behavior, and through rewards and punishments they experience for gender-appropriate and -inappropriate behavior.

In the contemporary view of evolutionary psychology, because men competed with other men for access to women, men's evolved dispositions favor violence, competition, and risk taking. Women in turn developed a preference for long-term mates who could support a family. As a consequence, men strived to acquire more resources than other men in order to attract women, and women developed preferences for successful, ambitious men who could provide these resources.

Critics of the evolutionary psychology view argue that humans have the decision-making ability to change their gender behavior and therefore are not locked into the evolutionary past. They also stress that the extensive cross-cultural variation in sex differences and mate preferences provides stronger evidence for a social influence view of gender differences than for an evolutionary view. Next, we will explore what some of these social influences are.

Social Influences

Many social scientists, such as Alice Eagly (1997, 2000, 2001), locate the cause of psychological sex differences not in biologically evolved dispositions but in the contrasting positions and social roles of women and men. In contemporary American society and in most cultures around the world, women have less power and status than men and control fewer resources. Women perform more domestic work than men and spend fewer hours in paid employment. Although most women are in the workforce, they receive lower pay than men and are thinly represented in the highest levels of organizations. Thus, from the perspective of social influences, gender hierarchy and sexual division of labor are important causes of sex-differentiated behavior. As women adapted to roles with less power and less status in society, they showed more cooperative, less dominant profiles than men.

Parental Influences   Parents, by action and example, influence their children's and adolescents' gender development. During the transition from childhood to adolescence, parents allow boys more independence than girls, and concern about girls' sexual vulnerability may cause parents to monitor their behavior more closely and ensure that they are chaperoned. Families with young adolescent daughters indicate that they experience more intense conflict about sex, choice of friends, and curfews than do families with young adolescent sons (Papini & Sebby, 1988). When parents place severe restrictions on their adolescent sons, it is disruptive to their sons' development (Baumrind, 1991).

Parents often have different expectations for their adolescent sons and daughters, especially in such academic areas as math and science. For example, many parents believe that math is more important for their sons' futures than for their daughters', and their beliefs influence the value adolescents place on math achievement (Eccles, 1987). More about gender and achievement appears later in this chapter.

Social cognitive theory has been especially important in understanding social influences on gender ◀⦚⦚⦚ P. 50. The **social cognitive theory of gender** *emphasizes that children's and adolescents' gender development occurs through observation and imitation of gender behavior, and through rewards and punishments they experience for gender-appropriate and -inappropriate behavior.* By observing parents and other adults, as well as peers, at home, at school, in the neighborhood, and in the media, adolescents are exposed to a myriad of models who display masculine and feminine behavior. And parents often use rewards and punishments to teach their daughters to be feminine ("Karen, that dress you are wearing makes you look so pretty.") and their sons to be masculine ("Bobby, you were so aggressive in that game. Way to go!").

One major change in the gender-role models adolescents have been exposed to in recent years is the increasing number of working mothers. Most adolescents today have a mother who is employed at least part-time. Although maternal employment is not specific to adolescence, it does influence gender-role development, and its influence likely depends on the age of the child or adolescent involved. Young adolescents may be especially attuned to understanding adult roles, so their mothers' role choices may be important influences on their concepts and attitudes about women's roles (Huston & Alvarez, 1990). Adolescents with working mothers have less-stereotyped concepts of female roles (and sometimes male roles as well) than do adolescents whose mothers are full-time homemakers. They also have more positive attitudes about nontraditional roles for women. Daughters of employed mothers have higher educational and occupational aspirations than do daughters of homemakers (Hoffman, 1989, 2000). Thus, working mothers often serve as models who combine traditional feminine home roles with less traditional activities away from home.

Peers   Parents provide the earliest discrimination of gender behavior, but before long, peers join in the societal process of responding to and modeling masculine and feminine behavior. In middle and late childhood, children show a clear preference for being with and liking same-sex peers (Maccoby, 1996, 1998). After extensive observations of elementary school playgrounds, two researchers characterized the play settings as "gender school," pointing out that boys teach one another the required masculine behavior and reinforce it, and that girls also teach one another the required feminine behavior and reinforce it (Luria & Herzog, 1985).

In earlier chapters, we learned that adolescents spend increasing amounts of time with peers  P. 186. In adolescence, peer approval or disapproval is a powerful influence on gender attitudes and behavior. Peers can socialize gender behavior partly by accepting or rejecting others on the basis of their gender-related attributes. Deviance from sex-typed norms often leads to low peer acceptance, but within a broad range of normal behavior it is not clear that conformity to sex-typed personality attributes is a good predictor of peer acceptance (Huston & Alvarez, 1990).

School and Teacher Influences   In certain ways, both girls and boys might receive an education that is not fair (Sadker & Sadker, 1994). For example:

- Girls' learning problems are not identified as often as boys' are.
- Boys are given the lion's share of attention in schools.
- Girls start school testing higher than boys in every academic subject, yet they graduate from high school scoring lower than boys do on the SAT exam.
- Pressure to achieve is more likely to be heaped on boys than on girls.

A special concern is that, because they are more impersonal and encourage independence more than elementary schools do, most middle and junior high schools are better suited to the learning styles of males.

Consider this research study (Sadker & Sadker, 1986). Observers were trained to collect data in more than 100 fourth-, sixth-, and eighth-grade classrooms. At all three grade levels, male students were involved in more interactions with teachers than female students were, and male students were given more attention than their female counterparts were. Male students were also given more remediation, more criticism, and more praise than female students. Further, girls with strong math abilities are given lower-quality instruction than their male counterparts are (Eccles, 1993).

Myra Sadker and David Sadker (1994, 2003), who have been studying gender discrimination in schools for more than two decades, believe that many educators are unaware of the subtle ways in which gender infiltrates the school's environment. Their hope is that sexism can be eradicated in the nation's schools.

A special concern is that most middle and junior high schools consist of independent, masculine learning environments, which appear better suited to the learning style of the average adolescent boy than to that of the average adolescent girl (Huston & Alvarez, 1990). Compared to elementary schools, middle and junior high schools provide a more impersonal environment, which meshes better with the autonomous

Shortchanging Girls,
Shortchanging America
Positive Expectations for Girls
War on Boys
Center for Gender Equity
Gender and Television
http://www.mhhe.com/santrocka9

orientation of male adolescents than with the relationship, connectedness orientation of female adolescents.

There is concern about gender equity not only in secondary schools, but in colleges and universities as well (Paludi, 1998). In some colleges, male students dominate class discussions. In one study, numerous hours of videotape supplied by 24 professors at Harvard University were analyzed (Krupnick, 1985). Males usually dominated the class discussion, especially in classes in which the instructor and the majority of the students were male. At one state university, female and male students participated virtually equally in class discussion (Crawford & MacLeod, 1990). Reports from all-female institutions (such as Smith and Wellesley) suggest that females there are often assertive in the classroom (Matlin, 1993).

Females interested in the sciences hear the message that they don't fit in this area not only from society but also sometimes from professors themselves. Another group of females who are vulnerable to the "don't fit in" message are women of color. In one study, female and male Latino students who were enrolled at two Ivy League colleges were interviewed (Ethier & Deaux, 1990). Some of the Latina students especially felt uncomfortable, tense, and aware of being different at the predominantly Anglo institutions. Other Latina students perceived little discomfort or prejudicial treatment, reflecting individual variations in these ethnic minority females.

Mass-Media Influences   As already described, adolescents encounter male and female roles in their everyday interactions with parents, peers, and teachers. The messages about gender roles carried by the mass media also are important influences on adolescents' gender development (Huston & Alvarez, 1990).

Television directed at adolescents might be the most extreme in its portrayal of the sexes, especially of teenage girls (Beal, 1994). In one study, teenage girls were shown as primarily concerned with dating, shopping, and their appearance (Campbell, 1988). They were rarely depicted as interested in school or career plans. Attractive girls were often portrayed as "airheads" and intelligent girls as unattractive.

Another highly stereotyped form of programming specifically targeted toward teenage viewers is rock music videos. What adolescents see on MTV and some other TV shows (for example, the "Beavis and Butt-head" and "South Park" shows) is highly stereotyped and slanted toward a male audience. Females are twice as likely to be dressed provocatively in music videos as in prime-time programming, and aggressive acts are often perpetrated by females in music videos—for example, in one scene a woman pushes a man to the ground, holds him down, and kisses him (Sherman & Dominick, 1986). MTV has been described as a teenage boy's "dreamworld," filled with

Females are often portrayed in sexually provocative ways on MTV and in rock videos.

beautiful, aroused women who outnumber men, who seek out and even assault men to have sex, and who always mean yes even when they say no (Jhally, 1990).

Early adolescence may be a period of heightened sensitivity to television messages about gender roles. Young adolescents increasingly view programs designed for adults that include messages about gender-appropriate behavior, especially in heterosexual relationships. Cognitively, adolescents engage in more idealistic thoughts than children do, and television certainly has its share of idealized characters with whom adolescents can identify and imitate—highly appealing models who are young, glamorous, and successful.

The world of television is highly gender-stereotyped and conveys clear messages about the relative power and importance of women and men (Calvert, 1999; Huston & Alvarez, 1990). Males are overrepresented, and females are underrepresented. On virtually every type of program, males outnumber females by approximately two or three to one (Williams & others, 1986). Men and women usually engage in sex-typed occupational and family roles. In the 1970s, female characters appeared more often than males in the contexts of the home, romance, and physical appearance, males more frequently than females in the contexts of work, cars, and sports. By the mid 1980s, when females were portrayed outside the home, their roles were almost as likely to be nontraditional (for example, police officer or attorney) as traditional (for example, secretary or nurse). Men continued to be shown almost entirely in traditional male occupations. In one analysis, women were shown as sexual objects (that is, in scanty clothing or engaged in sexually provocative behavior) in 35 percent of the commercial television programs in 1985 (Williams & others, 1986). Such portrayals are even more frequent on music videos. Male characters are portrayed more often than female characters as aggressive, dominant, competent, autonomous, and active, while female characters are more often portrayed as passive.

Researchers have studied how early adolescent television viewing influences gender attitudes and behavior (Morgan, 1984, 1987). The researchers adopt the assumption that television carries sexist messages and that the more the adolescent is exposed, the greater the number of stereotyped messages the adolescent likely receives. In one investigation of eighth-grade boys and girls, heavy television viewing predicted an increased tendency to endorse traditional gender-role divisions of labor with respect to household chores (Morgan, 1987).

If television can communicate sexist messages and influence adolescents' gender behavior, might nonstereotyped gender messages on television reduce sexist behavior? One major effort to reduce gender stereotyping was the television series "Freestyle" (Johnston, Etteman, & Davidson, 1980). The series was designed to counteract career stereotypes in 9- to 12-year-olds. After watching "Freestyle," both girls and boys were more open to nontraditional career possibilities. The benefits of "Freestyle" were greatest for students who viewed the TV series in the classroom and who participated in discussion groups about the show led by their teacher. Classroom discussion was especially helpful in altering boys' beliefs, which were initially more stereotyped than girls'.

However, in one study with young adolescents 12 to 13 years of age, the strategy of nonstereotyped television programming backfired (Durkin & Hutchins, 1984). The young adolescents watched sketches about people who held nontraditional jobs, such as a male secretary, a male nurse, and a female plumber. After viewing the series, the adolescents still held traditional views about careers, and in some cases they were even more disapproving of the alternative careers than they had been before watching the TV series. Thus, once stereotypes are strongly in place, it is difficult to modify them.

Cognitive Influences

So far, we have discussed a number of biological and social influences on adolescents' gender behavior. Cognitive theories stress that adolescents actively construct their gender world. In this section, we look at two cognitive theories: the cognitive developmental theory of gender and gender schema theory.

Cognitive Developmental Theory   According to the **cognitive developmental theory of gender,** *children's gender-typing occurs after they have developed a concept of gender. Once they begin to consistently conceive of themselves as male or female, children often organize their world on the basis of gender.* Based on Piaget's theory and initially proposed by developmentalist Lawrence Kohlberg (1966), the cognitive developmental theory of gender proceeds in the following fashion: A young girl decides, "I am a girl. I want to do girl things; therefore, the opportunity to do girl things is rewarding." Having acquired the ability to categorize, children strive toward consistency in using categories and in their behavior.

Kohlberg's cognitive developmental theory emphasizes that the main changes in gender development occur in childhood. By the concrete operational stage (the third stage in Piaget's theory, entered at 6 to 7 years of age), children understand gender constancy—that a male is still a male regardless of whether he wears pants or a skirt, or whether his hair is short or long, for example (Tavris & Wade, 1984).

Are there any cognitive developmental changes in adolescence that might influence gender behavior? The abstract, idealized, logical characteristics of formal operational

cognitive developmental theory of gender
In this view, children's gender-typing occurs after they have developed a concept of gender. Once they begin to consistently conceive themselves as male or female, children often organize their world on the basis of gender.

thought mean that adolescents now have the cognitive capacity to analyze their self and decide what they want their gender identity to be. Adolescence is the developmental period when individuals begin to focus increased attention on vocational and lifestyle choices. With their increased cognitive skills, adolescents become more aware of the gender-based nature of vocational and lifestyle behavior. As adolescents pursue an identity—"Who am I, what am I all about, and where am I going in life?"—gender roles are one area in which they have choices to make. Recall the discussion of gender and identity in the last chapter ◀▥ P. 308. As females have developed stronger vocational interests, sex differences (adolescent males explore and make commitments to a vocational role more than adolescent females) are now turning into similarities. However, as adolescent females pursue an identity, they often show a greater interest in relationships and emotional bonds than adolescent males do. In sum, both the changes ushered in by formal operational thought and the increased interest in identity concerns lead adolescents to examine and redefine their gender attitudes and behavior.

Gender Schema Theory   A **schema** *is a concept or framework that exists in the individual's mind to organize and interpret information.* A **gender schema** *organizes the world in terms of female and male.* **Gender schema theory** *states that an individual's attention and behavior are guided by an internal motivation to conform to gender-based sociocultural standards and stereotypes.* Gender schema theory suggests that "gender typing" occurs when individuals are ready to encode and organize information along the lines of what is considered appropriate or typical for males and females in society. Gender schema theory emphasizes the active construction of gender but also accepts that societies determine which schemas are important and the associations involved (Rodgers, 2000; Ruble & Martin, 1998). In most cultures, these definitions involve a sprawling network of gender-linked associations, which encompass not only features directly related to female and male persons—such as anatomy, reproductive function, division of labor, and personality attributes—but also features more remotely or metaphorically related to sex, such as an abstract shape's angularity or roundness and the periodicity of the moon. No other dichotomy of life's experiences seems to have as many features linked to it as does the distinction between being male and being female (Paludi, 1998).

As a real-life example of gender schema's influence on adolescents, consider a 17-year-old high school student deciding which hobby to try from among the many available possibilities. The student could ask about how expensive each possibility is, whether it can be done in cold weather, whether or not it can be done during the school week, whether it will interfere with studying, and so on. But the adolescent also is likely to look at the hobby through the lens of gender and ask: "What sex is the hobby? What sex am I? Do they match? If they do, I will consider the hobby further. If not, I will reject it." This student consciously may not be aware of his or her gender schema's influence on the decision of which hobby to pursue. Indeed, in many of our everyday encounters, we consciously are not aware of how gender schemas affect our behavior.

schema
A concept or framework that exists in the individual's mind to organize and interpret information.

gender schema
A cognitive structure that organizes the world in terms of male and female.

gender schema theory
According to this theory, an individual's attention and behavior are guided by an internal motivation to conform to gender-based sociocultural standards and stereotypes.

At this point we have studied a number of ideas about what gender is and biological, social, and cognitive influences. This review should help you to reach your learning goals related to these topics.

☐ FOR YOUR REVIEW

Learning Goal 1
Know what is meant by gender

- Gender involves the psychological and sociocultural dimension of being male or female.
- A gender role is a set of expectations that prescribes how females or males should think, act, and feel.

Learning Goal 2
Explain biological, social, and cognitive influences on gender

- Because of pubertal change, sexuality plays a more important role in gender development for adolescents than for children. Freud's and Erikson's ideas promote the idea that anatomy is destiny. Today's developmentalists are interactionists when biological and environmental influences on gender are at issue. In the evolutionary psychology view, evolutionary adaptations produced psychological sex differences especially in the area of mate selection. Criticisms of the evolutionary psychology view have been made.

- In the social roles view, women have less power and status than men do and control fewer resources. In this view, gender hierarchy and sexual division of labor are important causes of sex-differentiated behavior. Social cognitive theory emphasizes the adoption of parents' gender-appropriate behavior. Peers are especially adept at rewarding gender-appropriate behavior. There is still concern about gender inequity in education. Despite improvements, TV still portrays males as more competent than females.

- Kohlberg proposed a cognitive developmental theory of gender development. Gender schema theory states that individuals develop a schema for gender influenced by sociocultural standards and stereotypes of gender.

Now that we have examined what gender is and biological, social, and cognitive influences, let's turn our attention to how gender roles are classified.

GENDER STEREOTYPES, SIMILARITIES, AND DIFFERENCES

How pervasive is gender stereotyping? What are the real differences between boys and girls?

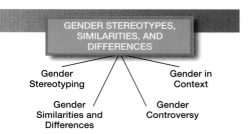

Gender Stereotyping

Gender stereotypes *are broad categories that reflect our impressions and beliefs about females and males.* All stereotypes, whether they are based on gender, ethnicity, or other groupings, refer to an image of what the typical member of a particular social category is like. The world is extremely complex. Every day we are confronted with thousands of different stimuli. The use of stereotypes is one way we simplify this complexity. If we simply assign a label (such as the quality of softness) to someone, we then have much less to consider when we think about the individual. However, once labels are assigned they are remarkably difficult to abandon, even in the face of contradictory evidence.

Many stereotypes are so general they are ambiguous. Consider the stereotypes for "masculine" and "feminine." Diverse behaviors can be called on to support each stereotype, such as scoring a touchdown or growing facial hair for "masculine" and playing with dolls or wearing lipstick for "feminine." The stereotype may be modified in the face of cultural change. At one point in history, muscular development may be thought of as masculine; at another point, masculinity might be associated with a more lithe, slender physique. The behaviors popularly agreed upon as reflecting a stereotype can also fluctuate according to socioeconomic circumstances. For example, lower socioeconomic groups might be more likely than higher socioeconomic groups to include "rough and tough" as part of a masculine stereotype.

Even though the behaviors that are supposed to fit the stereotype often do not, the label itself can have significant consequences for the individual. Labeling a male "feminine" and a female "masculine" can produce significant social reactions to the individuals in terms of status and acceptance in groups, for example.

How widespread is feminine and masculine stereotyping? According to a far-ranging study of college students in thirty

gender stereotypes
Broad categories that reflect our impressions and beliefs about females and males.

"So according to the stereotype, you can put two and two together, but I can read the handwriting on the wall."

countries, stereotyping of females and males is pervasive (Williams & Best, 1982). Males were widely believed to be dominant, independent, aggressive, achievement oriented, and enduring, while females were widely believed to be nurturant, affiliative, less esteemed, and more helpful in times of distress.

In another investigation, women and men who lived in more highly developed countries perceived themselves as more similar than did women and men who lived in less-developed countries (Williams & Best, 1989). In the more highly developed countries, women were more likely to attend college and be gainfully employed. Thus, as sexual equality increases, male and female stereotypes, as well as actual behavioral differences, may diminish. In this investigation, women were more likely to perceive similarity between the sexes than men were (Williams & Best, 1989). And the sexes were perceived more similarly in Christian than in Muslim societies.

Stereotypes often are negative and sometimes involve prejudice and discrimination. **Sexism** *is prejudice and discrimination against an individual because of her or his sex.* A person who says that women cannot be competent lawyers is expressing sexism; so is a person who says that men cannot be competent nursery school teachers. Prejudice and discrimination against women have a long history, and they continue. Consider a true story about Ann Hopkins, one of only a few female accountants employed by the very large firm Price Waterhouse (Fiske & others, 1991). Hopkins had performed admirably in her work at Price Waterhouse. She had more billable hours than any of her 87 male co-workers and had brought in $25 million in new business for the firm. However, when a partnership in the firm opened up, Hopkins was not chosen. The executives at Price Waterhouse said that she had weak interpersonal skills, needed a "charm school" course, and was too "macho." Hopkins' filed a lawsuit against Price Waterhouse. After a lengthy trial, the U.S. Supreme Court ruled in Hopkins' favor, stating that gender-based stereotyping played a significant role in her being denied a partnership in the firm.

Sexism can be obvious, as when a chemistry professor tells a female premed student that women belong in the home (Matlin, 1993). Sexism can also be more subtle, as when the word *girl* is used to refer to a mature woman. In one recent analysis, an attempt was made to distinguish between old-fashioned and modern sexism (Swim & others, 1995). *Old-fashioned sexism* is characterized by endorsement of traditional gender roles, differential treatment for men and women, and a stereotype that females are less competent than males. Like modern racism, *modern sexism* is characterized by the denial that there is still discrimination, antagonism toward women's demands, and lack of support for policies designed to help women (for example, in education and work). Figure 10.1 on page 327 shows the types of items that were developed to measure old-fashioned and modern sexism.

Gender Similarities and Differences

There is a growing consensus in gender research that differences between the sexes have often been exaggerated, especially in terms of cognitive abilities (Hyde & Mezulis, 2001; Hyde & Plant, 1995). Remember our discussion of gender bias in research in chapter 2 ◀▐▐▐ P. 66. It is not unusual to find statements such as the following: "While only 32 percent of females were found to . . . , fully 37 percent of the males were. . . ." This difference of 5 percent likely is a very small difference, and might or might not even be statistically significant or capable of being replicated in a separate study (Denmark & Paludi, 1993). And generalizations that claim that males outperform females, such as "males outperform females in math," do not mean that all males outperform all females. Rather, such a statement means, in the case of our example, that the average math achievement scores for males at certain ages are higher than the average math achievement scores for females at those ages. The math achievement scores of females and males overlap considerably, so that although an *average* difference might favor males, many females have higher math achievement than many males. Further, there is a tendency to think of differences between females and males as biologically based. Remember that when differences occur, they might be socioculturally based.

sexism
Prejudice and discrimination against an individual because of her or his sex.

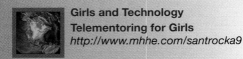
Girls and Technology
Telementoring for Girls
http://www.mhhe.com/santrocka9

There is more difference within the sexes than between them.
—Ivy Compton-Burnett
English Novelist, 20th Century

Old-Fashioned Sexism
Women are generally not as smart as men.
I would not be as comfortable having a woman for a boss as I would be having a man for a boss.
It is more important to encourage boys than to encourage girls to participate in athletics.
Women are not as capable as men of thinking logically.
When both parents are employed and their child gets sick at school, the school should call the mother rather than the father.

Modern Sexism
Discrimination against women is no longer a problem in the United States.
Women rarely miss out on good jobs because of sexist discrimination.
It is rare to see women treated in a sexist manner on television.
On the average, people in our society treat husbands and wives equally.
Society has reached the point where women and men have equal opportunities for achievement.
It is not easy to understand why women's groups are still concerned about societal limitations on women's opportunities.
It is not easy to understand the anger of women's groups in America.
Over the past few years, the government and news media have been showing more concern about the treatment of women than is warranted by women's actual experiences.
Note: Endorsement of the above items reflects old-fashioned sexism and modern sexism, respectively. The wording of the items has been changed from the original research for ease of understanding.

■ FIGURE 10.1
Types of Items Developed to Measure Old-Fashioned and Modern Sexism

Let's now examine some of the differences between the sexes, keeping in mind that (a) the differences are averages—not all females versus all males; (b) even when differences are reported, there is considerable overlap between the sexes; and (c) the differences may be due primarily to biological factors, sociocultural factors, or both (Caplan & Caplan, 1994, 1999). We'll discuss physical, cognitive, and socioemotional differences.

Physical/Biological Differences   From conception on, females are less likely than males to die, and females are less likely than males to develop physical or mental disorders. Estrogen strengthens the immune system, making females more resistant to infection, for example. Female hormones also signal the liver to produce more "good" cholesterol, which makes their blood vessels more elastic than males'. Testosterone triggers the production of low-density lipoprotein, which clogs blood vessels. Males have twice the risk of coronary disease as females. Higher levels of stress hormones cause faster clotting in males, but also higher blood pressure than in females. Adult females have about twice the body fat of their male counterparts, most of it concentrated around breasts and hips. In males, fat is more likely to go to the abdomen. On the average, males grow to be 10 percent taller than females. Male hormones promote the growth of long bones; female hormones stop such growth at puberty.

Similarity was the rule rather than the exception in a recent study of metabolic activity in the brains of females and males (Gur & others, 1995). The exceptions involved areas of the brain that involve emotional expression and physical expression (which are more active in females). Overall, though, there are many physical differences between females and males. Are there as many cognitive differences?

Cognitive Differences   According to a classic review of gender differences in 1974, Eleanor Maccoby and Carol Jacklin (1974) concluded that males have better math skills and better visuospatial ability (the kind of skills an architect needs to design a building's angles and dimensions), while females have better verbal abilities. More recently,

THROUGH THE EYES OF PSYCHOLOGISTS

Deborah Tannen
Georgetown University

"Understanding the other's ways of talking is a giant leap across the communication gap between women and men, and a giant step toward opening lines of communication."

rapport talk
The language of conversation, establishing connections, and negotiating relationships.

report talk
Talk that gives information; public speaking is an example.

THINKING CRITICALLY
Rethinking the Words We Use in Gender Worlds

Several decades ago the word *dependency* was used to describe the relational orientation of females. Dependency took on a negative connotation. For example, the implication was that females can't take care of themselves but males can. Today, the word *dependency* is being replaced with the term *relational abilities,* which has a much more positive connotation. Rather than being thought of as dependent, females now are more often described as having skills that enable them to form and maintain positive relationships (Caplan & Caplan, 1999).

Make up a list of words that you associate with masculinity and femininity. Do the words have any negative connotations for males or females? For the words that do, think about replacements that have more positive connotations.

Maccoby (1987) revised her conclusion about several gender dimensions. She said that the accumulation of research evidence now suggests that differences in verbal ability between females and males have virtually disappeared, but that the math and visuospatial differences still exist. However, in analyses involving the National Assessment of Educational Progress (1996, 1997), there were no differences in the average math scores of eighth- and twelfth-grade females and males, although in fourth grade boys did outperform girls in math.

Some experts in the gender area, such as Janet Shibley Hyde (1993; Hyde & Mezulis, 2001), believe that the cognitive differences between females and males have been exaggerated. For example, Hyde argues that there is considerable overlap in the distributions of females' and males' scores on math and math tasks. Figure 10.2 on page 329 shows that although males outperform females on math tasks, their scores overlap substantially with females' scores. Thus, though the *average* difference favors males, many females have higher scores on math tasks than most males do.

Socioemotional Differences   Four areas of socioemotional development in which gender has been studied are relationships, aggression, emotion, and achievement. Sociolinguist Deborah Tannen (1990) distinguishes between rapport talk and report talk. **Rapport talk** *is the language of conversation and a way of establishing connections and negotiating relationships.* **Report talk** *is talk that gives information. Public speaking is an example of report talk.* Males hold center stage through report talk with such verbal performances as story telling, joking, and lecturing with information. In contrast, females prefer private rapport talk and conversation that is relationship-oriented.

Tannen says that boys and girls grow up in different worlds of talk—parents, siblings, peers, teachers, and others talk to boys and girls differently. The play of boys and girls is also different. Boys tend to play in large groups that are hierarchically structured, and their groups usually have a leader who tells the others what to do and how to do it. Boys' games have winners and losers and often are the subject of arguments. And boys often boast of their skill and argue about who is best at what. Girls, on the other hand, are more likely to play in small groups or pairs, and at the center of a girl's world is often a best friend. In girls' friendships and peer groups, intimacy is pervasive. Turn taking is more characteristic of girls' games than of boys' games. And much of the time, girls simply like to sit and talk with each other, concerned more about being liked by others than about jockeying for status in some obvious way.

In sum, Tannen, like other gender experts such as Carol Gilligan, whose ideas you will read about later in the chapter, believes that girls are more relationship-oriented than boys—and that this relationship orientation should be highly valued in our culture.

One of the most consistent gender differences is that boys are more physically aggressive than girls. Boys also are more active than girls. The physical aggression difference is especially pronounced when adolescents are provoked. These differences occur across cultures and appear very early in children's development. However, researchers have found fewer gender differences in verbal aggression and in some cases no differences.

An important skill is to be able to regulate and control your emotions and behavior. Males usually show less self-regulation than females (Eisenberg, Martin, & Fabes, 1996), and this low self-control can translate into behavioral problems.

For some areas of achievement, gender differences are so large they can best be described as nonoverlapping. For example, no major league baseball players are female, and

96 percent of all registered nurses are female. In contrast, many measures of achievement-related behaviors do not reveal gender differences. For example, girls show just as much persistence at tasks. The question of whether males and females differ in their expectations for success at various achievement tasks is not yet settled.

Gender Controversy

Not all psychologists agree that differences between females and males are rare or small. Alice Eagly (1995) stated that such a belief arose from a feminist commitment to similarity between the sexes as a route to political equality, and from piecemeal and inadequate interpretations of relevant empirical research. Many feminists express a fear that differences between females and males will be interpreted as deficiencies in females and as biologically based, which could promote the old stereotypes that women are inferior to men (Crawford & Unger, 2000; Unger & Crawford, 1992). According to Eagly, contemporary psychology has produced a large body of research that reveals that behavior is sex differentiated to varying extents.

Evolutionary psychologist David Buss (1995, 2000) argues that men and women differ psychologically in those domains in which they have faced different adaptive problems across their evolutionary history. In all other domains, predicts Buss, the sexes will be found to be psychologically similar. He cites males' superiority in the cognitive domain of spatial rotation. This ability is essential for hunting, in which the trajectory of a projectile must anticipate the trajectory of a prey animal as each moves through space and time. Buss also cites a sex difference in casual sex, with men engaging in this behavior more than women do. In one study, men said that ideally they would like to have more than eighteen sex partners in their lifetime, whereas women stated that ideally they would like to have only four or five (Buss & Schmitt, 1993). In another study, 75 percent of the men but none of the women approached by an attractive stranger of the opposite sex consented to a request for sex (Clark & Hatfield, 1989). Such sex differences, says Buss, are exactly the type predicted by evolutionary psychology.

In sum, controversy characterizes the issue of whether sex differences are rare and small or common and large (Maracek, 1995), evidence that negotiating the science and politics of gender is not an easy task (Paul, 2000).

Gender in Context

When thinking about gender similarities and differences, keep in mind that the context in which females and males are thinking, feeling, and behaving should be taken into account ◀‖‖ P. 26. To see how context affects gender, let's further explore gender in relation to helping behavior and emotion.

Males are more likely to help in contexts in which a perceived danger is present and they feel competent to help (Eagly & Crowley, 1986). For example, males are more likely than females to help a person who is stranded by the roadside with a flat tire; automobile problems are an area about which many males feel a sense of competence. In contrast, when the context involves volunteering time to help a child with a personal problem, females are more likely to help than males are, because there is little danger present and females feel more competent at nurturing. In many cultures, girls show more caregiving behavior than boys do (Blakemore, 1993). However, in the few cultures where they both care for

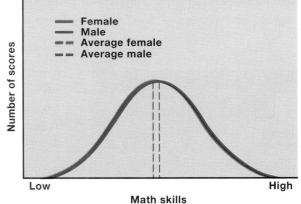

■ FIGURE 10.2
Math Skills of Males and Females

Notice that, although an average male's math skills are higher than an average female's, the overlap between the sexes is substantial. Not all males have better math skills than all females—the substantial overlap indicates that, although the average score of males is higher, many females outperform many males on such tasks.

younger siblings on a regular basis, girls and boys are similar in their tendencies to nurture (Whiting, 1989).

Context is also relevant to gender differences in the display of emotions (Anderson & Leaper, 1996; Shields, 1991). Consider anger. Males are more likely to show anger toward strangers, especially other males, when they feel that they have been challenged. Males also are more likely than females to turn their anger into aggressive action (Tavris & Wade, 1984). Differences between males and females in the display of emotion occur most often in the contexts that highlight social roles and relationships. For example, females are more likely than males to discuss emotion in terms of interpersonal relationships (Saarni, 1988) and to express fear and sadness, especially when communicating with their friends and family.

Since the last review we have examined a number of ideas about gender stereotypes, similarities, and differences. This review should help you to reach your learning goals related to these topics.

☐ FOR YOUR REVIEW

Learning Goal 3
Describe gender stereotypes, similarities, and differences

- Gender stereotypes are widespread around the world, especially emphasizing the male's power and the female's nurturance.
- There are a number of physical/biological differences between females and males.
- Some experts, such as Hyde, argue that cognitive differences between males and females have been exaggerated.
- Females enjoy engaging in rapport talk, males in report talk. Males are more physically aggressive, more active, and show less control of their emotions than females do. For some areas of achievement, gender differences exist, for others they do not.

Learning Goal 4
Discuss gender controversy and gender in context

- Currently, there is considerable controversy over how similar or different females and males are in a number of areas.
- Context is an important factor in understanding gender.

So far in this chapter, we have studied what gender is; biological, social, and cognitive influences; and gender stereotypes, similarities, and differences. Next, we will explore another important aspect of gender—how gender roles are classified.

GENDER-ROLE CLASSIFICATION

```
         GENDER-ROLE
         CLASSIFICATION

Traditional                    Gender-Role
Gender Roles                   Transcendence

      Androgyny          Traditional
                         Masculinity and
                         Problem Behaviors
                         in Adolescent Males
```

How were gender roles classified in the past? What is androgyny? Is a strong masculine orientation related to problem behaviors in adolescent males? What is gender-role transcendence?

Traditional Gender Roles

Not too long ago, it was accepted that boys should grow up to be masculine and that girls should grow up to be feminine, that boys are made of frogs and snails and puppy dogs' tails, and that girls are made of sugar and spice and all that's nice. Today, diversity characterizes gender roles and the feedback individuals receive from their culture. A girl's mother might promote femininity, the girl might be close friends with a tomboy, and the girl's teachers at school might encourage her assertiveness.

In the past, the well-adjusted male was expected to be independent, aggressive, and power oriented. The well-adjusted female was expected to be dependent, nurturant, and uninterested in power. Further, masculine characteristics were considered to be healthy and good by society; female characteristics were considered to be undesirable. A classic study in the early 1970s summarized the traits and behaviors that college students believed were characteristic of males and those they believed were characteristic of females (Broverman & others, 1972). The traits clustered into two groups that were

Gender Around the World
Gender Socialization in Six Countries
http://www.mhhe.com/santrocka9

labeled "instrumental" and "expressive." The instrumental traits paralleled the male's purposeful, competent entry into the outside world to gain goods for his family; the expressive traits paralleled the female's responsibility to be warm and emotional in the home. Such stereotypes harm females more than males because the characteristics assigned to males are more valued than those assigned to females.

Traditional gender roles continue to be practiced in many countries around the world. For example, in Egypt the division of labor between Egyptian males and females is dramatic: Egyptian males are socialized to work in the public sphere, females in the private world of home and child-rearing. The Islamic religion dictates that the man's duty is to provide for his family, the woman's duty to care for her family and household (Dickersheid & others, 1988). Any deviations from this traditional gender-role orientation are severely disapproved of.

Egypt is not the only country in which males and females are socialized to behave, think, and feel in strongly gender-specific ways. Kenya and Nepal are two other cultures in which children are brought up under very strict gender-specific guidelines (Munroe, Himmin, & Munroe, 1984). In the People's Republic of China, the female's status has historically been lower than the male's. The teachings of the fifth-century B.C. Chinese philosopher Confucius were used to reinforce the concept of the female as an inferior being. Beginning with the 1949 revolution in China, women began to achieve more economic freedom and more-equal status in marital relationships. However, even with the sanctions of a socialist government, the old patriarchal traditions of male supremacy in China have not been completely uprooted. Chinese women still make considerably less money than Chinese men in comparable positions, and in rural China a tradition of male supremacy still governs many women's lives.

In Egypt near the Aswan Dam, women are returning from the Nile River, where they have filled their water jugs. *How might gender-role socialization for girls in Egypt compare to that in the United States?*

Thus, although females in China have made considerable strides, complete equality remains a distant objective. And in many cultures, such as Egypt and other countries where the Muslim religion predominates, gender-specific behavior is pronounced, and females are not given access to high-status positions.

Access to education for girls has improved somewhat around the world, but girls' education still lags behind boys' education. For example, according to recent UNICEF (2000) analysis of education around the world, by age 18, girls have received, on average 4.4 years less education than boys have. This lack of education reduces their chances of developing to their future potential.

Androgyny

In the last 30 to 40 years in the United States, a decline in the adoption of traditional gender roles has occurred. For example, in recent years U.S. female college students have shown a propensity for turning in their aprons for careers. For example, in 1967, more than 40 percent of college females and more than 60 percent of college males agreed with the statement, "The activities of married women are best confined to home and family." In 1999, those percentages had dropped to 23 percent for college females and 35 percent for college males (Sax & others, 1999). As shown in figure 10.3 on page 332, the greatest change in these attitudes occurred in the 1960s and early 1970s. Interestingly, in the last several years, there has been a slight upturn in traditional gender-role adoption by U.S. college students. Similar patterns of marital role expectations were also found in another recent study (Botkin, Weeks, & Morris, 2000).

In the 1970s, as both males and females became dissatisfied with the burdens imposed by their strictly stereotyped roles, alternatives to "masculinity" and "femininity" were explored. Instead of thinking of masculinity and femininity as a continuum, with more of one meaning less of the other, it was proposed that individuals could show both expressive and instrumental traits. This thinking led to the development of the concept of **androgyny,** *the presence of a high degree of desirable masculine and feminine*

androgyny
The presence of a high degree of desirable feminine and masculine characteristics in the same individual.

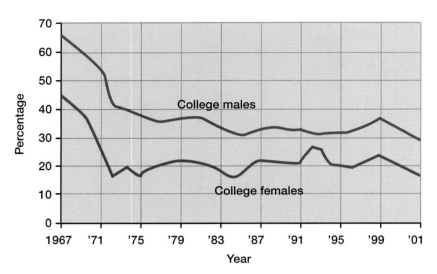

FIGURE 10.3
Changing Attitudes About Gender Roles

Note: Data show the percentage of first-year college students agreeing with the statement, "The activities of married women are best confined to home and family" from 1967 through 2001.

characteristics in the same individual (Bem, 1977; Spence & Helmreich, 1972). The androgynous individual might be a male who is assertive (masculine) and nurturant (feminine), or a female who is dominant (masculine) and sensitive to others' feelings (feminine).

Measures have been developed to assess androgyny. One of the most widely used gender measures, the Bem Sex-Role Inventory, was constructed by a leading early proponent of androgyny, Sandra Bem. To see what the items on Bem's measure are like, see figure 10.4 on page 333. Based on their responses to the items in the Bem Sex-Role Inventory, individuals are classified as having one of four gender-role orientations: masculine, feminine, androgynous, or undifferentiated. The androgynous individual is simply a female or a male who has a high degree of both feminine (expressive) and masculine (instrumental) traits. No new characteristics are used to describe the androgynous individual. A feminine individual is high on feminine (expressive) traits and low on masculine (instrumental) traits; a masculine individual shows the reverse of these traits. An undifferentiated person is not high on feminine or masculine traits.

Androgynous individuals are described as more flexible and more mentally healthy than either masculine or feminine individuals. In one recent study, androgyny was linked with well-being and lower levels of stress (Stake, 2000). Individuals who are undifferentiated are the least competent. To some degree, though, the context influences which gender role is most adaptive. In close relationships, a feminine or androgynous gender role may be more desirable because of the expressive nature of close relationships. However, a masculine or androgynous gender role might be more desirable in academic and work settings because of the instrumental nature of these settings. And the culture in which individuals live also plays an important role in determining what is adaptive. On the one hand, increasing numbers of children in the United States and other modernized countries such as Sweden are being raised to behave in androgynous ways. On the other hand, traditional gender roles continue to dominate the cultures of many countries around the world as we saw earlier in this chapter.

In one recent study, the masculine trait of most importance involved being self-sufficient, rather than being dominant or assertive, and the feminine trait of most importance was sensitivity or compassion, rather than dependency or subservience (Auster & Ohm, 2000). These traits were belived to be important for both males and females.

Can and should androgyny be taught to children and adolescents in school? In one investigation, tenth- through twelfth-grade students from three high schools in British Columbia were given a 20-unit course in gender roles (Kahn & Richardson, 1983). Students analyzed the history and modern development of male and female gender roles and evaluated the function of traditionally accepted stereotypes of females and males. The course centered on student discussion, supplemented by films, videotapes, and guest speakers. The materials included exercises to heighten students' awareness of their attitudes and beliefs, role reversal of typical gender-role behavior, role-playing of difficult work and family conflict circumstances, and assertiveness training for direct, honest communication.

A total of 59 students participated in the gender-role course. To determine whether the course changed the adolescents' gender-role orientation, these students were compared to 59 students from the same schools who did not take the gender-role

To help you think about the gender-role orientations of adolescents and what gender-role orientation you will present when you interact with them, rate yourself on the following items from 1 (never or almost never true) to 7 (always or almost always true). Then after you have completed all of the items, you will be able to determine whether you have a masculine, feminine, or androgynous gender-role orientation. These items are from the Bem Sex-Role Inventory.

1. self-reliant
2. yielding
3. helpful
4. defends own beliefs
5. cheerful
6. moody
7. independent
8. shy
9. conscientious
10. athletic
11. affectionate
12. theatrical
13. assertive
14. flatterable
15. happy
16. strong personality
17. loyal
18. unpredictable
19. forceful
20. feminine
21. reliable
22. analytical
23. sympathetic
24. jealous
25. has leadership abilities
26. sensitive to the needs of others
27. truthful
28. willing to take risks
29. understanding
30. secretive
31. makes decisions easily
32. compassionate
33. sincere
34. self-sufficient
35. eager to soothe hurt feelings
36. conceited
37. dominant
38. soft-spoken
39. likable
40. masculine
41. warm
42. solemn
43. willing to take a stand
44. tender
45. friendly
46. aggressive
47. gullible
48. inefficient
49. acts as a leader
50. childlike
51. adaptable
52. individualistic
53. does not use harsh language
54. unsystematic
55. competitive
56. loves children
57. tactful
58. ambitious
59. gentle
60. conventional

Scoring
(a) Add up your ratings for items 1, 4, 7, 10, 13, 16, 19, 22, 25, 28, 31, 34, 37, 40, 43, 46, 49, 55, and 58. Divide the total by 20. That is your masculinity score.
(b) Add up your ratings for items 2, 5, 8, 11, 14, 17, 20, 23, 26, 29, 32, 35, 38, 41, 44, 47, 50, 53, 56, and 59. Divide the total by 20. That is your femininity score.
(c) If your masculinity score is above 4.9 (the approximate median for the masculinity scale) and your femininity score is above 4.9 (the approximate femininity median) then you would be classified as androgynous on Bem's scale.

FIGURE 10.4
What Gender-Role Orientation Will You Present to Adolescents?

course. Prior to the start of the course, all students were given the Bem Sex-Role Inventory. No differences between the two groups were found at that time. After the students completed the course, they and the control group were given the Attitudes Toward Women Scale (Spence & Helmreich, 1972). In two of the schools, students who took the gender-role course had more-liberal attitudes about the female's role in society than students who did not take the course. In these schools, the students were primarily girls who chose to take the course as an elective. In the third school, students who took the gender-role course actually had more conservative attitudes toward the female's role in society than those who did not take the course. The gender-role class in the third school was required and was made up almost equally of males and females.

Another attempt to produce a more androgynous gender-role orientation in students also met with mixed results (Guttentag & Bray, 1976). The curriculum lasted for one year and was implemented in the kindergarten, fifth, and ninth grades. It involved books, discussion materials, and classroom exercises. The program was most successful with the fifth-graders and least successful with the ninth-graders, who displayed a boomerang effect of developing a more rigid gender-role orientation. The program's success varied from class to class, being most effective when the teacher produced sympathetic reaction in the peer group. However, some classes ridiculed and rejected the curriculum.

Ethical concerns are raised when the program involves teaching children and adolescents to depart from socially approved behavior patterns, especially when there is no evidence of extreme sex typing in the groups to whom the interventions are applied. The advocates of androgyny programs believe that traditional sex typing is psychologically harmful for all children and adolescents and that it has prevented many girls and women from experiencing equal opportunity. While some people believe that androgyny is more adaptive than either a traditional masculine or a traditional feminine pattern, ignoring the imbalance within our culture that values masculinity more than femininity is impossible.

Traditional Masculinity and Problem Behaviors in Adolescent Males

In our discussion of masculinity so far, we have discussed how the masculine role has been accorded a prominent status in the United States, as well as in most other cultures. However, might there be a negative side to traditional masculinity, especially in adolescence? An increasing number of gender theorists and researchers believe there is (Levant, 1999).

Joseph Pleck and his colleagues (Pleck, 1983; Pleck, Sonnenstein, & Ku, 1994) believe that what defines traditional masculinity in many Western societies includes engaging in certain behaviors that, although officially socially disapproved, validate masculinity. That is, in the male adolescent culture, male adolescents perceive that they are more masculine, and that others will perceive them as more masculine, if they engage in premarital sex, drink alcohol and take drugs, and participate in delinquent activities.

In one investigation, the gender-role orientation and problem behaviors of 1,680 15- to 19-year-old males were assessed (Pleck, Sonnenstein, & Ku, 1994). In this study—referred to as the National Survey of Adolescent Males—there was strong evidence that problem behaviors in adolescent males are associated with their attitudes toward masculinity. The adolescent males who reported traditional beliefs about masculinity (for example, endorsing such items as "A young man should be tough, even if he's not big"; "It is essential for a guy to get respect from others";

THINKING CRITICALLY

Gender Roles and the Future

In the last two decades, there has been considerable change in gender roles in the United States. How much change have you personally experienced? What changes do you think will occur in gender roles as we go through the twenty-first century? Or do you believe that gender roles will stay about the way they are now?

There is a practical side to considering these questions. How will you attempt to raise your children, in terms of gender roles? Will gender neutrality be your goal? Will you encourage more traditional distinctions?

and "Men are always ready for sex") also were likely to say that they had school difficulties, engaged in alcohol and drug use, participated in delinquent activities, and were sexually active.

In the investigation by Joseph Pleck and his colleagues (1994), the roles of risk and protective influences in adolescent males' problem behaviors were studied. Risk factors for problems included low parental education, being the son of a teenage mother, living in a mother-headed household or a nonmaternal family (father only, foster family, grandparents, alone), lenient family rules, and infrequent church attendance. Protective factors included strict family rules and frequent church attendance.

According to Pleck's (1981, 1995) *role-strain* view, male roles are contradictory and inconsistent. Men not only experience stress when they violate men's roles, they also are harmed when they *do* act in accord with expectations for men's roles (Levant, 1995). Here are some of the areas where men's roles can cause considerable strain (Levant, 1999; Levant & Brooks, 1997; Philpot & others, 1997):

The Men's Bibliography
Psychological Study of Men and Masculinity
Male Issues
Men's Movement Organizations
http://www.mhhe.com/santrocka9

- *Health.* Men live 8 to 10 years less than women do. They have higher rates of stress-related disorders, alcoholism, car accidents, and suicide. Men are more likely than women to be the victims of homicide. In sum, the male role is hazardous to men's health (Copenhaver, Lash, & Eisler, 2000).
- *Male-female relationships.* Too often, the male's role involves images that men should be dominant, powerful, and aggressive and should control women. Also, the male role has involved looking at women in terms of their bodies rather than their minds and feelings. Earlier, we described Deborah Tannen's (1990) concept that men show too little interest in rapport talk and relationships. And the male role has included the view that women should not be considered equal to men in work, earnings, and many other aspects of life. Too often these dimensions of the male role have produced men who have denigrated women, been violent toward women, and been unwilling to have equal relationships with women.
- *Male-male relationships.* Too many men have had too little interaction with their fathers, especially fathers who are positive role models. Nurturing and being sensitive to others have been considered aspects of the female role, and not the male role. And the male role emphasizes competition rather than cooperation. All of these aspects of the male role have left men with inadequate positive, emotional connections with other males (Kilmartin, 2000).

To reconstruct their masculinity in more positive ways, Ron Levant (1995) believes, every man should (1) reexamine his beliefs about manhood, (2) separate out the valuable aspects of the male role, and (3) get rid of those parts of the masculine role that are destructive. All of this involves becoming more "emotionally intelligent"—that is, becoming more emotionally self-aware, managing emotions more effectively, reading emotions better (one's own emotions and others'), and being motivated to improve those relationships. The hope is that if adult males can make these changes, they will serve as better role models for adolescent males.

Gender-Role Transcendence

Although the concept of androgyny was an improvement over exclusive notions of femininity and masculinity, it has turned out to be less of a panacea than many of its early proponents envisioned (Paludi, 1998). Some theorists, such as Pleck (1983), believe that the idea of androgyny should be replaced with **gender-role transcendence,** *the belief that, when an individual's competence is at issue, it should not be conceptualized on the basis of masculinity, femininity, or androgyny, but rather on a person basis.* Thus, rather than merging gender roles or stereotyping people as "masculine" or "feminine," Pleck believes we should begin to think about people as people. However, both the concepts of androgyny and gender-role transcendence draw attention away from women's unique needs and the power imbalance between women and men in most cultures (Hare-Muston & Maracek, 1988).

gender-role transcendence
The belief that, when an individual's competence is at issue, it should be conceptualized not on the basis of masculinity, femininity, or androgyny but, rather, on a person basis.

Since the last review, we have examined a number of ideas about gender-role classification. This review should help you to reach your learning goals related to this topic.

☐ FOR YOUR REVIEW

Learning Goal 5
Evaluate traditional gender roles and androgyny

- In the past, a well-adjusted male was supposed to be masculine (powerful, assertive, and so on), and the well-adjusted female was supposed to be feminine (nurturant, relationship-oriented, and so on). Historically, masculine traits have been valued more than feminine traits and sexism has been widespread.
- Alternatives to traditional masculinity and femininity began to surface in the 1970s. The concept of androgyny—that the most competent individuals have both positive masculine and feminine traits—was proposed. Gender-role classification began to focus on a fourfold scheme: masculine, feminine, androgynous, or undifferentiated. Many androgynous individuals are competent and flexible. Context and culture influence an individual's gender-role classification.

Learning Goal 6
Understand possible problems with masculinity and explain gender-role transcendence

- What defines traditional masculinity in many Western cultures includes behaviors that can be problematic for many male adolescents. Researchers have found that adolescents who are high in masculinity often show problem behaviors, such as school-related problems, drug use, and delinquency. Recommendations have been made for improving the male role.
- One alternative to androgyny is gender-role transcendence: evaluating individuals not on the basis of their gender but instead on the basis of what they are like as a person.

We have covered many aspects of gender in this chapter so far. Next, we explore some important developmental aspects of gender in adolescence.

DEVELOPMENTAL CHANGES
AND JUNCTURES

Early
Adolescence
and Gender
Intensification

Is Early
Adolescence a
Critical Juncture
for Females?

gender intensification hypothesis
This hypothesis states that psychological and behavioral differences between boys and girls become greater during early adolescence because of increased socialization pressures to conform to masculine and feminine gender roles.

DEVELOPMENTAL CHANGES AND JUNCTURES

What changes take place during early adolescence that might affect gender roles? Is early adolescence a critical juncture in female development?

Early Adolescence and Gender Intensification

As females and males experience many physical and social changes during early adolescence, they have to come to terms with new definitions of their gender roles (Belansky & Clements, 1992; Feiring, in press; Huston & Alvarez, 1990). During early adolescence, individuals develop the adult, physical aspects of their sex. Some theorists and researchers have proposed that, with the onset of puberty, girls and boys experience an intensification in gender-related expectations. The **gender intensification hypothesis** *states that psychological and behavioral differences between boys and girls become greater during early adolescence because of increased socialization pressures to conform to traditional masculine and feminine gender roles* (Hill & Lynch, 1983; Lynch, 1991). Puberty's role in gender intensification might involve a signaling to socializing others—parents, peers, and teachers, for example—that the adolescent is beginning to approach adulthood and, therefore, should begin to act more in ways that resemble the stereotypical female or male adult. In one study, sex differences in gender-role attitudes increased across the early adolescent years. Gender-role attitudes were measured by the Attitudes Toward Women Scale (Galambos & others, 1985), which assesses the extent to which adolescents approve of gender-based division of roles. For example, the adolescent is asked such questions as whether girls should have the same freedom as boys. Other researchers also have reported evidence of gender intensification in early adolescence (Hill & Lynch, 1983). However, not every female and male shows gender intensification during puberty, and the family context influences how strongly gender intensification occurs (Crouter, Manke, & McHale, 1995).

The gender intensification hypothesis states that psychological and behavioral differences between boys and girls become greater during early adolescence because of increased socialization pressures to conform to traditional masculine and feminine gender roles. Puberty's role in gender intensification may involve a signaling to socializing others—parents, peers, and teachers, for example—that the adolescent is beginning to approach adulthood and, therefore, should begin to act in ways that resemble the stereotypical female or male adult.

In one study of eighth- and eleventh-graders, the eleventh-grade boys and girls were more similar to each other on both masculine and feminine traits than were eighth-grade boys and girls (Karniol & others, 1998). Irrespective of gender, the eleventh-graders showed less masculinity than the eighth-graders. However, the eleventh-grade girls were lower in femininity than the eighth-grade girls, while the eleventh-grade boys were higher on femininity than the eighth-grade boys. Thus, it appears that as adolescent boys and girls grow older, they show less stereotypic adoption of gender roles. Indeed, it is noteworthy in this study that there were no eighth-grade boys in the low-masculinity/high-femininity category, which supports the concept of gender intensification in early adolescence.

Is Early Adolescence a Critical Juncture for Females?

Carol Gilligan has conducted extensive interviews with girls from 6 to 18 years of age (Gilligan, 1996; Gilligan, Brown, & Rogers, 1990). She and her colleagues have reported that girls consistently reveal detailed knowledge about human relationships that is based on listening and watching what happens between people. According to Gilligan, girls can sensitively pick up different rhythms in relationships and often are able to follow the pathways of feelings. Gilligan believes that girls experience life differently than boys do; in Gilligan's words, girls have a "different voice."

Gilligan also states that girls come to a critical juncture in their development when they reach adolescence. Gilligan says that, in early adolescence, (usually around 11 to 12 years of age), girls become aware that their intense interest in intimacy is not prized by

CAREERS IN ADOLESCENT DEVELOPMENT

Carol Gilligan
Professor and Chair of Gender Studies Program

Carol Gilligan obtained an undergraduate degree from Swarthmore College, a master's degree in clinical psychology from Radcliffe College, and a Ph.D. in social psychology from Harvard University. Her teaching career at Harvard began in 1967, when she co-taught a developmental psychology class with Erik Erikson. In 1997, Carol was appointed to the first position at Harvard in Gender Studies and is now the Chair of the gender studies program.

Carol Gilligan's work has expanded the understanding of gender development. Her research has shown that the inclusion of girls' voices can make an important difference in development, especially in the domains of gender and morality.

Carol's ideas especially became well known with the publication of *In a Different Voice* (1982). In another book, *Between Voice and Silence: Women and Girls, Race and Relationship* (with J. McLean Taylor and A. Sullivan) (1996), she studied girls from low-income families and their struggles to be heard and taken seriously. Her recent work includes the Harvard Project on Women's Psychology and Girls' Development, as well as a prevention project, Strengthening Healthy Resistance and Courage in Girls. Carol also is currently writing a new book, *The Birth of Pleasure.*

Carol Gilligan (right, in maroon dress) with some of the females she has interviewed about their relationships with others.

the male-dominated culture, even though society values women as caring and altruistic. The dilemma, says Gilligan, is that girls are presented with a choice that makes them appear either selfish (if they become independent and self-sufficient) or selfless (if they remain responsive to others). Gilligan states that, as young adolescent girls experience this dilemma, they increasingly "silence" their "different voice." They become less confident and more tentative in offering their opinions, which often persists into adulthood. Some researchers believe that this self-doubt and ambivalence too often translates into depression and eating disorders among adolescent girls.

Contextual variations influence whether adolescent girls silence their "voice." In one recent study, Susan Harter and her colleagues (Harter, Waters, & Whitesell, 1996) found evidence for a refinement of Gilligan's position, in that feminine girls reported lower levels of voice in public contexts (at school with teachers and classmates) but not in more private interpersonal relationships (with close friends and parents). However, androgynous girls reported a strong voice in all contexts. Harter and her colleagues also found that adolescent girls who buy into societal messages that females should be seen and not heard are at most risk in their development. The greatest liabilities occurred for females who not only lacked a "voice" but who emphasized the importance of appearance. In focusing on their outer selves, these girls face formidable challenges in meeting the punishing cultural standards of attractiveness.

Some critics argue that Gilligan and her colleagues overemphasize differences in gender. One of those critics is developmentalist Eleanor Maccoby, who says that Gilligan exaggerates the differences between males and females in intimacy and connectedness. Other critics fault Gilligan's research strategy, which rarely includes a comparison group of boys or statistical analysis. Instead, Gilligan conducts extensive interviews with girls and then provides excerpts from the girls' narratives to buttress her ideas. Other critics fear that Gilligan's findings reinforce stereotypes—females as nurturing and sacrificing, for example—that might undermine females' struggle for equality. These critics say that Gilligan's "different voice" perhaps should be called "the voice of the victim." What we should be stressing, say these critics, is more opportunities for females to reach higher levels of achievement and self-determination.

In reply, revisionists such as Gilligan say that their work provides a way to liberate females and transform a society that has far too long discriminated against females. They also say that if females' approach to life is acknowledged as authentic, women will no longer have to act like men. The revisionists argue that females' sensitivity in relationships is a special gift in our culture (Brown, Way, & Duff, 1999). Influenced by Gilligan's and other feminists' thinking, some schools are beginning to incorporate the feminine voice into their curriculum. For example, at the Emma Willard School in Troy, New York, the entire curriculum has been revamped to emphasize cooperation rather than competition, and to encourage girls to analyze and express ideas from their own perspective rather than responding in stereotyped or conformist ways.

Whether you believe the connectionist arguments of Gilligan or the achievement/self-determination arguments of her critics, there is increasing evidence that adolescence is a critical juncture in the psychological development of females. In a national survey conducted by the American Association of University Women, girls revealed a significantly greater drop in self-esteem during adolescence than boys did. And in another recent study, the self-esteem of girls declined during adolescence (Rosner & Rierdan, 1994). At ages 8 and 9, 60 percent of the girls were confident and assertive and felt positive about themselves, compared to 67 percent of the boys. However, over the next eight years, the girls' self-esteem fell 31 percentage points—only 29 percent of high school girls felt positive about themselves. Across the same age range, boys' self-worth dropped 21 points—leaving 46 percent of the high school boys with high self-esteem, which makes for a gender gap of 17 percentage points.

Since the last review we have examined a number of ideas about developmental changes and junctures. This review should help you to reach your learning goals related to this topic.

☐ FOR YOUR REVIEW

Learning Goal 7
Describe developmental changes and junctures

- The gender intensification hypothesis states that psychological and behavioral differences between boys and girls become greater during adolescence because of increased socialization pressures to conform to traditional gender roles.
- Gilligan believes that girls come to a critical juncture in their development during early adolescence. Girls become aware that their intense interest in intimacy is not prized by the male-dominant society. Some critics say that Gilligan exaggerates gender differences in intimacy

In this chapter we have examined many aspects of gender. We saw that in adolescence gender becomes influenced by sexuality more than in childhood. In chapter 11, we will more extensively explore adolescent sexuality.

CHAPTER MAP

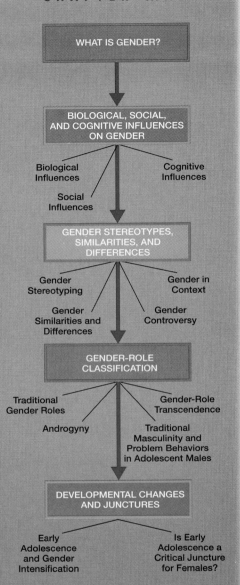

REACH YOUR LEARNING GOALS

At the beginning of the chapter we stated seven learning goals and encouraged you to review material related to these goals at four points in the chapter. This is a good time to return to these reviews. Use them to guide your study and help you to reach your learning goals.

Page 324

Learning Goal 1   Know what is meant by gender

Learning Goal 2   Explain biological, social, and cognitive influences on gender

Page 330

Learning Goal 3   Describe gender stereotypes, similarities, and differences

Learning Goal 4   Discuss gender controversy and gender in context

Page 336

Learning Goal 5   Evaluate traditional gender roles and androgyny

Learning Goal 6   Understand possible problems with masculinity and explain gender-role transcendence

Page 339

Learning Goal 7   Describe developmental changes and junctures

KEY TERMS

gender 318
gender role 318
social cognitive theory of gender 320
cognitive developmental theory
    of gender 323
schema 324
gender schema 324
gender schema theory 324

gender stereotypes 325
sexism 326
rapport talk 328
report talk 328
androgyny 331
gender-role transcendence 335
gender intensification hypothesis 336

KEY PEOPLE

Sigmund Freud 319
Erik Erikson 319
Alice Eagly 320
Myra Sadker and David Sadker 321
Lawrence Kohlberg 323
Eleanor Maccoby 327
Carol Jacklin 327

Janet Shibley Hyde 328
Deborah Tannen 328
David Buss 329
Sandra Bem 332
Joseph Pleck 334
Carol Gilligan 337

RESOURCES FOR IMPROVING THE LIVES OF ADOLESCENTS

Beyond Appearance

(1999) by Norine Johnson, Michael Roberts, and Judith Worrell (Eds.)
Washington, DC: American Psychological Association

In this book you can read about many aspects of girls' development in adolescence.

The Mismeasure of Woman

(1992) by Carol Tavris
New York: Simon & Schuster

This is an excellent book on gender stereotyping, similarities and differences between the sexes, and how females should be measured by their own standards, not males'.

A New Psychology of Men

(1995) by Ronald Levant and William Pollack
New York: Basic Books

This edited volume includes chapters by leading authorities in men's issues and gender roles related to the male's development. The contributors detail how some male problems are unfortunate by-products of the current way males are socialized.

The Two Sexes

(1998) by Eleanor Maccoby
Cambridge, MA: Harvard University Press

In this book you can explore how gender differences emerge in children's groups.

YMCA

101 North Wacker Drive
Chicago, IL 60606

The YMCA provides a number of programs for teenage boys. A number of personal health and sports programs are available.

You Just Don't Understand

(1990) by Deborah Tannen
New York: Ballantine

This is a book about how women and men communicate—or, all too often, miscommunicate—with each other.

YWCA

726 Broadway
New York, NY 10003

The YWCA promotes health, sports participation, and fitness for women and girls. Its programs include instruction in health, teen pregnancy prevention, family life education, self-esteem enhancement, parenting, and nutrition.

TAKING IT TO THE NET   http://www.mhhe.com/santrocka9

1. Gender roles influence how we perceive ourselves and others, our desires and goals, and our personalities. But they also impact on the everyday lives of adults in very basic and fundamental ways. *What might the issues of balancing home and career be and how are they similar and different for males and females?*

2. Great changes have occurred in gender roles since the 1970s, particularly in the lives of women. But have these changes impacted on the nature and quality of married life? *How do you view the relation between gender roles and marriage? How might your spouse view that relationship?*

3. Gender differences in humans in part reflect physical/biological differences. *How might other disciplines such as biology inform your understanding of how these physical differences came into play?*

Connect to *http://www.mhhe.com/santrocka9* to research the answers and complete these exercises. In some cases, you'll also find further instructions on this site.

CHAPTER 11

CHAPTER MAP

EXPLORING ADOLESCENT SEXUALITY

A Normal Aspect of Adolescent Development

Sexual Attitudes and Behavior

ADOLESCENT SEXUAL PROBLEMS

Adolescent Pregnancy

Forcible Sexual Behavior and Sexual Harassment

Sexually Transmitted Diseases

SEXUAL KNOWLEDGE AND SEX EDUCATION

Sexual Knowledge

Sex Education in the Schools

Sources of Sex Information

SEXUAL WELL-BEING, SOCIAL POLICY, AND ADOLESCENTS

Sexual Well-Being and Developmental Transitions

Social Policy and Adolescent Sexuality

■ THE MYSTERIES AND CUROSITIES OF ADOLESCENT SEXUALITY

I am 16 years old, and I really like this one girl. She wants to be a virgin until she marries. We went out last night, and she let me go pretty far, but not all the way. I know she really likes me, too, but she always stops me when things start getting hot and heavy. It is getting hard for me to handle. She doesn't know it, but I'm a virgin, too. I feel I am ready to have sex. I have to admit I think about having sex with other girls, too. Maybe I should be dating other girls.

—Frank C.

If we listen to boys and girls at the very moment they seem most pimply, awkward, and disagreeable, we can penetrate a mystery most of us once felt heavily within us, and have now forgotten. This mystery is the very process of creation of man and woman.

—Colin McInnes
Contemporary Scottish Author

I'm 14 years old. I have a lot of sexy thoughts. Sometimes, just before I drift off to sleep at night, I think about this hunk who is 16 years old and plays on the football team. He is so gorgeous, and I can feel him holding me in his arms and kissing and hugging me. When I'm walking down the hall between classes at school, I sometimes start daydreaming about guys I have met and wonder what it would be like to have sex with them. Last year I had this crush on the men's track coach. I'm on the girls' track team, so I saw him a lot during the year. He hardly knew I thought about him the way I did, although I tried to flirt with him several times.

—Amy S.

Is it weird to be a 17-year-old guy and still be a virgin? Sometimes, I feel like the only 17-year-old male on the planet who has not had sex. I feel like I am missing out on something great, or at least that's what I hear. I'm pretty religious, and I sometimes feel guilty when I think about sex. The thought runs through my mind that maybe it is best to wait until I'm married or at least until I have a long-term relationship that matters a lot to me.

—Tom B.

I'm 15 years old, and I had sex for the first time recently. I had all of these expectations about how great it was going to be. He didn't have much experience either. We were both pretty scared about the whole thing. It was all over in a hurry. My first thought was, "Is that all there is?" It was a very disappointing experience.

—Claire T.

I've felt differently than most boys for a long time and I had my first crush on another boy when I was 13. I'm 16 years old now and I'm finally starting to come to grips with the fact that I am gay. I haven't told my parents yet. I don't know if they will be able to handle it. I'm still a little confused by all of this. I know I will have to "come out" at some point.

—Jason R.

CHAPTER LEARNING GOALS

DURING ADOLESCENCE, THE LIVES of males and females become wrapped in sexuality. In chapter 3, we studied the biological basis of sexual maturation, including the timing of these changes and the hormones involved. Here we will focus on the sexual attitudes and experiences of adolescents. By the time that you have completed this chapter, you should be able to reach these learning goals:

1　Understand that sexuality is a normal aspect of adolescence

2　Know about adolescent heterosexual attitudes and behavior

3　Describe adolescent homosexual attitudes and behavior

4　Discuss self-stimulation and evaluate contraceptive use

5　Know about adolescent pregnancy

6　Describe sexually transmitted diseases

7　Explain forcible sexual behavior and sexual harassment

8　Evaluate sexual knowledge and sex education

9　Explore sexual well-being, social policy, and adolescents

EXPLORING ADOLESCENT SEXUALITY

EXPLORING ADOLESCENT SEXUALITY

- A Normal Aspect of Adolescent Development
- Sexual Attitudes and Behavior

Adolescence is a time of sexual exploration and experimentation, of sexual fantasies and realities, of incorporating sexuality into one's identity. Adolescents have an almost insatiable curiosity about the mysteries of sex. They think about whether they are sexually attractive, how to perform sexually, and what the future holds for their sexual lives. Most adolescents eventually manage to develop a mature sexual identity, even though there are always times of vulnerability and confusion along life's sexual journey.

A Normal Aspect of Adolescent Development

Much of what we hear about adolescent sexuality involves problems, such as adolescent pregnancy and sexually transmitted diseases. These are important concerns. However, it is important not to lose sight of the fact that sexuality is a normal part of adolescence.

A Bridge Between the Asexual Child and Sexual Adult　An important theme of adolescence that we have underscored in this book is that too often adolescents are negatively stereotyped. We presented this theme in chapter 1, "Introduction," and will return to it again in chapter 14, "Adolescent Problems," and in the Epilogue ◀ P. 11. The themes of negative stereotyping and adolescent problems also apply to the topic of adolescent sexuality (Crockett, Raffaelli, & Molilanen, in press).

We will discuss a number of problems that can occur in the area of adolescent sexuality, such as adolescent pregnancy and sexually transmitted diseases. However, it is important to keep in mind that sexual development and interest are normal aspects of adolescent development and that the majority of adolescents have healthy sexual attitudes and engage in sexual behaviors that will not compromise their journey to adulthood.

Adolescence is a bridge between the asexual child and the sexual adult (Feldman, 1999). Every society pays some attention to adolescent sexuality. In some societies, adults chaperone adolescent females to protect them from males. Other societies promote very early marriage. Yet other societies, such as the United States, allow some sexual experimentation, although there is controversy about just how far sexual experimentation should be allowed to go.

Previous chapters introduced topics that are a backdrop for understanding sexual attitudes and behavior in adolescence:

- Chapter 3, "Puberty, Health, and Biological Foundations": An important aspect of pubertal change involves sexual maturation and a dramatic increase in androgens in males and estrogens in females ◀▮▮▮ P. 80. Puberty is coming earlier today, and girls enter puberty approximately two years earlier than boys do. Early maturation in girls can lead to early dating and early sexual activity.
- Chapter 4, "Cognitive Development": Young adolescents tend to have adolescent egocentrism—they perceive themselves as unique and invulnerable ◀▮▮▮ P. 137. This can lead them to take sexual risks. In emotional moments like those involved in sexual experimentation, adolescents' sexual urges and desire to experience adult temptations can overwhelm their ability to make competent decisions. A few moments of irresponsible sexual activity can have negative consequences even into the adult years.
- Chapter 5, "Families": Intense, prolonged conflict with parents is associated with problems in areas like sexuality, as is a lack of parental monitoring ◀▮▮▮ P. 159. Adolescents' need for autonomy and attempts to engage in adult behaviors (like sexual intercourse) to prove their maturity can contribute to conflict with parents. Better relationships with parents are correlated with postponing sexual intercourse, less frequent intercourse, and fewer partners in adolescence (Miller, Benson, & Galbraith, in press). When adolescents are close to their parents and perceive that their parents disapprove of them having sexual intercourse, adolescents are more likely to abstain from having sex (Dittus & Jaccard, 2000; Sieving, McNeily, & Blum, 2000). Later in this chapter, we will see that adolescents receive very little sex education from parents and that parents and adolescents rarely discuss sex.
- Chapter 6, "Peers": Peers and friends provide settings for learning about and discussing sexuality (Caruthers & Ward, 2002) ◀▮▮▮ P. 186. Though parents and adolescents rarely talk with each other about sex, same-sex siblings, peers, and friends often do. In thinking about adolescent sexuality, remember that sex is not an individual behavior but rather a dyadic behavior. Sexuality takes place within the context of opposite-sex or same-sex relationships. In adolescence, sexual attractiveness and interest is linked with peer popularity and acceptance. Having older friends is associated with more problems than having same-age friends, early dating is associated with a number of adolescent problems, and romantic love is important (especially for girls) in adolescence. The main ingredient of romantic love is sexual interest, but it also involves both positive and negative emotions. There are different dating scripts for adolescent boys (proactive scripts) and girls (reactive scripts). In this chapter, we will examine how adolescent sexual scripts often play out differently along gender lines.
- Chapter 7, "Schools": We did not address sex education in schools in chapter 7, but schools increasingly are playing an important role in this area. As we will see later in this chapter, most parents now recognize that sex education in schools is an important aspect of education.
- Chapter 8, "Culture": There are vast cultural variations in sexuality; in some cultures sexuality is extremely repressed, other cultures have far more liberal standards for sexuality ◀▮▮▮ P. 260. The media often present sexuality to adolescents in an unrealistic way (Kim, 2002). An increasing concern is adolescents' access to sexual material on the Internet.
- Chapter 9, "The Self and Identity": Sexual identity is one of the dimensions of personal identity (Russell & Trong, 2002) ◀▮▮▮ P. 304. Intimacy with another is an important aspect of the dyadic nature of adolescent sexuality.

THROUGH THE EYES OF PSYCHOLOGISTS

Shirley Feldman
Stanford University

"Sexual arousal emerges as a new phenomenon in adolescence and it is important to view sexuality as a normal aspect of adolescent development."

We are born twice over; the first time for existence, the second for life; Once as human beings and later as men or as women.

—Jean-Jacques Rousseau
*Swiss-Born French Philosopher,
18th Century*

Sex is virtually everywhere in the American culture and is used to sell just about everything. *Is it surprising, then, that adolescents are so curious about sex and tempted to experiment with sex?*

• Chapter 10, "Gender": There are a number physical and biological differences between females and males ◄‖‖ P. 318. As children move into adolescence, a new dimension is added to their gender: sexuality. According to the gender intensification hypothesis, pubertal changes can lead boys and girls to conform to traditional masculine and feminine behavior, respectively.

As you can see, sexuality has ties to virtually all areas of adolescent development that we discuss in this book, because sexuality is an important theme of normal adolescent development. Let's now explore the sexual culture American adolescents are exposed to.

The Sexual Culture   It is important to put adolescent sexuality into the context of sexuality in the American culture (Crockett, Raffaeli, & Moilanen, in press). Shortly we will examine the increased permissiveness that emerged in the twentieth century in the culture as a whole. Whereas at one time sex was reserved for married couples, today adult sex occurs among divorcees, with extramarital partners, and so on. There has been an enormous increase in births to unmarried women who are adults. Sex among unmarried teenagers is an extension of this general trend toward greater sexual permissiveness in the adult culture.

Many Americans are ambivalent about sex. Sex is used to sell just about everything, from cars to detergents. Sex is explicitly portrayed in movies, TV shows, videos, lyrics of popular music, MTV, and Internet websites. Why, then, are we so surprised that adolescents are so curious and want to experiment with sex, when the sexual culture obviously encourages the adolescent's biological sexual urges?

Sexuality often involves more tension between parents and adolescents in the United States than in most cultures. In one analysis, it was concluded that parent-adolescent tension about sex is greater in the United States than in Japan because U.S. adolescents engage in more sexual activity and because sexual activity is embued with certain social meanings, such as high status for males (Rothbaum & others, 2000).

Developing a Sexual Identity   Mastering emerging sexual feelings and forming a sense of sexual identity is multifaceted (Brooks-Gunn & Graber, 1999; Brooks-Gunn

& Paikoff, 1997; Graber & Brooks-Gunn, in press; Graber, Brooks-Gunn, & Galen, 1999). This lengthy process involves learning to manage sexual feelings, such as sexual arousal and attraction, developing new forms of intimacy, and learning the skills to regulate sexual behavior to avoid undesirable consequences. Developing a sexual identity also involves more than just sexual behavior. It includes interfaces with other developing identities. Sexual identities emerge in the context of physical factors, social factors, and cultural factors, with most societies placing constraints on the sexual behavior of adolescents.

An adolescent's sexual identity involves an indication of sexual orientation (homosexual, heterosexual, bisexual) and it also involves activities, interests, and styles of behavior. A study of 470 tenth- to twelfth-grade Australian youth characterized an adolescent's sexual identity as following one of five different styles (Buzwell & Rosenthal, 1996):

- *Sexually naive.* This group had low sexual self-esteem, suggesting a lack of confidence and some discontent regarding their sexuality and physical characteristics. They also had high anxiety about sex and were lower than any other group on sexual arousal and exploration. This group consisted primarily of tenth-grade females, the vast majority of whom were virgins.
- *Sexually unassured.* This group reported especially low sexual self-esteem and high anxiety about sex. They felt sexually unattractive, were dissatisfied with their sexual behavior, and perceived their bodies as underdeveloped and unappealing. This group was predominantly male, and most were virgins.
- *Sexually competent.* This group had high sexual self-esteem, appearing confident of their sexual appeal and body and comfortable about their sexual behavior. They had a moderate level of sexual commitment and were only somewhat anxious about sex. This group was composed mainly of twelfth-graders, with slightly more girls than boys. A majority of them were sexually experienced.
- *Sexually adventurous.* This group had high sexual self-esteem, low sexual anxiety, low sexual commitment, and high interest in exploring sexual options. This group included substantially more girls than boys, and most were nonvirgins.
- *Sexually driven.* These adolescents had high sexual self-esteem, felt sexually attractive, and were confident in their ability to manage sexual situations. They had the lowest score of all groups on sexual commitment. This group was almost entirely male and had the largest number of sexually experienced adolescents.

Obtaining Information About Adolescent Sexuality

Gathering information about sexual attitudes and behavior is not always a straightforward affair. Consider how you would respond if someone asked you, "How often do you have intercourse?" or "How many different sexual partners have you had?" The people most likely to respond to sexual surveys are those with liberal sexual attitudes who engage in liberal sexual behaviors. Thus, research is limited by the reluctance of individuals to candidly answer questions about extremely personal matters and by researchers' inability to get any answer, candid or otherwise, from individuals who simply refuse to talk to strangers about sex (Halonen & Santrock, 1999). In addition, when asked about their sexual activity, do individuals respond truthfully or with socially desirable answers? For example, might a ninth-grade boy report that he has had sexual intercourse even if he has not because he is afraid someone will find out that he is sexually inexperienced.

Methods have been developed to increase the validity of sexual self-report information. In one study, interviewers who were the same sex as the adolescents individually asked questions of increasing sexual involvement until the respondent reported that he or she had not engaged in a behavior, at which point the interview was ended (Paikoff & others, 1997). This strategy might be preferable to a checklist, which can lead to over- or under-reporting and embarrassment. Some researchers also have presented adolescents with audiotaped questions to reduce adolescents' embarrassment about reporting sexual behaviors to an interviewer.

At this point, we have discussed a number of ideas about sexuality being a normal aspect of adolescent development. This review should help you to reach your learning goals related to this topic.

☐ FOR YOUR REVIEW

Learning Goal 1
Understand that sexuality is a normal aspect of adolescence

- Too often the problems adolescents encounter with sexuality are emphasized rather than the fact that sexuality is a normal aspect of adolescent development. Adolescence is a bridge between the asexual child and the sexual adult. Discussions in a number of other chapters serve as a backdrop for understanding adolescent sexuality.
- Increased permissiveness in adolescent sexuality is linked with increased sexual permissiveness in the larger culture.
- Developing a sexual identity is multifaceted. An adolescent's sexual identity involves an indication of sexual orientation and activities, interests, and styles of behavior. One study identified five sexual styles: naive, unassured, competent, adventurous, and driven.
- Obtaining valid information about adolescent sexuality is not easy. Much of the data are based on interviews and questionnaires, which can involve untruthful or socially desirable responses.

Now that we have examined sexuality as a normal aspect of adolescent development, let's turn our attention to the sexual attitudes and behaviors of adolescents.

How is it that, in the human body, reproduction is the only function to be performed by an organ of which an individual carries only one half so that he has to spend an enormous amount of time and energy to find another half?

—Francois Jacob
French Biologist, 20th Century

Sexual Attitudes and Behavior

Let's now explore adolescents' sexual attitudes and behavior—first heterosexual, then homosexual.

Heterosexual Attitudes and Behavior   What is the progression of adolescent sexual behaviors? How extensively have heterosexual attitudes and behaviors changed in the twentieth century? What sexual scripts do adolescents follow? Are some adolescents more vulnerable to irresponsible sexual behavior than others? We will examine each of these questions.

The Progression of Adolescent Sexual Behaviors   Adolescents engage in a rather consistent progression of sexual behaviors (DeLamater & MacCorquodale, 1979). Necking usually comes first, followed by petting. Next comes intercourse, or, in some cases, oral sex, which has increased substantially in adolescence in recent years. In an investigation of tenth- through twelfth-graders, 25 percent of the males and 15 percent of the females who reported not having had intercourse reported having had oral sex (Newcomer & Udry, 1985). In one recent study 452 individuals 18 to 25 years of age were asked about their own past sexual experiences (Feldman, Turner, & Araujo, 1999). The following progression of sexual behaviors occurred: kissing preceded petting, which preceded sexual intercourse and oral sex. Figure 11.1 on page 349 shows the approximate ages at which males and females typically first engaged in a variety of sexual behaviors. Notice that male adolescents reported engaging in these sexual behaviors approximately one year earlier than female adolescents.

Adolescent Heterosexual Behavior—Trends and Incidence   Had you been a college student in 1940, you probably would have had a different attitude about many aspects of sexuality than you do today. A review of college students' sexual practices in the twentieth century reveals two important trends (Darling, Kallen, & VanDusen, 1984). First, the percentage of youth who say they have had sexual intercourse has increased dramatically. Second, the proportion of female college students who report that they have had sexual intercourse has increased more rapidly than that of males, although the initial base for males was greater.

What is the current profile of sexual activity of adolescents? Based on a national survey of adolescents, sexual intercourse is uncommon in early adolescence but becomes more common in the high school and college years (see figure 11.2 on page 350) (Alan Guttmacher Institute, 1995, 1998; Centers for Disease Control and Prevention, 2000). These are some of the findings:

• Eight in 10 girls and seven in 10 boys are virgins at age 15.
• The probability that adolescents will have sexual intercourse increases steadily with age, but 1 in 5 individuals have not yet had sexual intercourse by age 19.
• Initial sexual intercourse occurs in the mid- to late-adolescent years for a majority of teenagers, about eight years before they marry; more than one-half of 17-year-olds have had sexual intercourse.
• The majority of adolescent females' first voluntary sexual partners are younger, the same age, or no more than two years older; 27 percent are three or four years older; and 12 percent are five or more years older.

Most studies report that adolescent males are more likely than adolescent females to say that they have had sexual intercourse and are sexually active (Feldman, Turner, & Araujo, 1999; Hayes, 1987). Adolescent males also are more likely than their female counterparts to report that sexual intercourse is an enjoyable experience. And African American are more likely to have a less restrictive timetable for sexual behaviors than other groups, whereas Asian Americans are more likely to have a more restrictive one (Feldman, Turner, & Araujo, 1999) (see figure 11.3 on page 350).

In some areas of the United States, the percentages of sexually active young adolescents might even be greater. In an inner-city area of Baltimore, 81 percent of the males at age 14 said that they already had engaged in sexual intercourse. Other surveys in inner-city, low-SES areas also reveal a high incidence of early sexual intercourse (Clark, Zabin, & Hardy, 1984).

Some reports of an increase in oral sex among adolescents have recently appeared (Remez, 2000; Schuster, 2000). Possible reasons for the increase in oral sex include freedom from pregnancy and a belief that oral sex is safe from disease, although as we will see later believing that oral sex is always disease-free is a misperception. Talking about oral sex has become commonplace in the media and has exposed adolescents to the sexual practice.

In sum, in the United States by the end of adolescence the majority of individuals have had sexual intercourse. Male, African American, and inner-city adolescents report being the most sexually active. Though sexual intercourse can be a meaningful experience for older, mature adolescents, many adolescents are not emotionally prepared to handle sexual experiences, especially in early adolescence. In one study, the earlier in adolescence boys and girls engaged in sexual intercourse, the more likely they were to show adjustment problems (Bingham & Crockett, 1996).

The timing of teenage sexual initiation varies widely by country and gender. In one recent study, among females, the proportion having first intercourse by age 17 ranged from 72 percent in Mali to 47 percent in the United States, and 45 percent in Tanzania (Singh & others, 2000). The proportion of males who had their first intercourse by age 17 ranged from 76 percent in Jamaica to 64 percent in the United States and 63 percent in Brazil.

Sexual activity patterns for 15- to 19-year-olds follow very different patterns for males and females in almost every geographic region of the world (Singh & others, 2000). The vast majority of sexually experienced males in this age group are unmarried, while two-thirds or more of the sexually experienced females at these ages are married

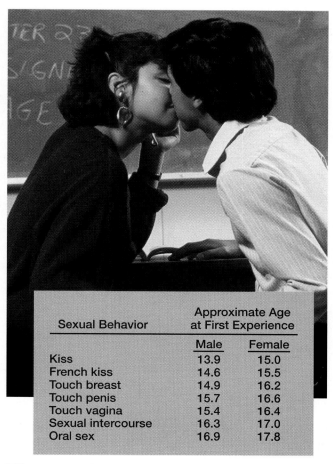

Sexual Behavior	Approximate Age at First Experience	
	Male	Female
Kiss	13.9	15.0
French kiss	14.6	15.5
Touch breast	14.9	16.2
Touch penis	15.7	16.6
Touch vagina	15.4	16.4
Sexual intercourse	16.3	17.0
Oral sex	16.9	17.8

FIGURE 11.1
Age at First Experience of Various Sexual Behaviors

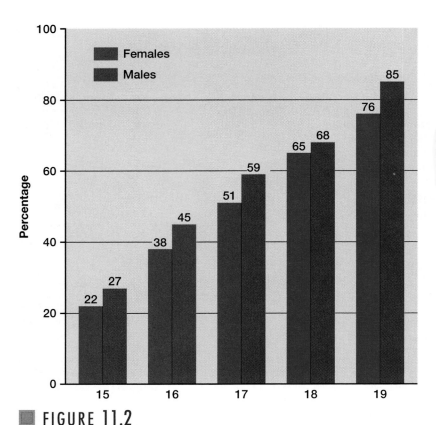

■ **FIGURE 11.2**

Percentage of Youth Who Say They Have Had Sexual Intercourse at Various Ages

sexual script
A stereotyped pattern of role prescriptions for how individuals should behave sexually. Females and males have been socialized to follow different sexual scripts.

in developing countries. However, in the United States, the overwhelming majority of 15- to 19-year-old females are unmarried.

Adolescent Female and Male Sexual Scripts

As adolescents explore their sexual identities, they are guided by sexual scripts. A **sexual script** *is a stereotyped pattern of role prescriptions for how individuals should sexually behave. Females and males have been socialized to follow different sexual scripts.* Differences in female and male sexual scripting can cause problems and confusions for adolescents as they work out their sexual identities. Female adolescents learn to link sexual intercourse with love (Michael & others, 1994). They often rationalize their sexual behavior by telling themselves that they were swept away by the passion of the moment. A number of studies have found that adolescent females are more likely than their male counterparts to report being in love as the main reason they are sexually active (Cassell, 1984). Other reasons that females give for being sexually active include giving in to male pressure, gambling that sex is a way to get a boyfriend, curiosity, and sexual desire unrelated to loving and caring.

The majority of adolescent sexual experiences involve the male making sexual advances, and it is up to the female to set the limits on the male's sexual overtures (Goodchilds & Zellman, 1984). Adolescent boys experience considerable peer pressure to have sexual intercourse. As one adolescent remarked, "I feel a lot of pressure from my buddies to go for the score." I vividly remember the raunchy conversation that filled our basketball locker room in junior high school. By the end of the ninth grade, I was sure that I was the only virgin left on the 15-member team, but I wasn't about to acknowledge that to my teammates.

One study found that adolescent boys expected to have sex, put pressure on girls to have sex with them, but said that they do not force girls to have sex with them (Crump & others, 1996). And in a national survey, 12- to 18-year-olds said these are "often a reason" teenagers have sex (Kaiser Family Foundation, 1996):

- A boy or girl is pressuring them (61 percent of girls, 23 percent of boys)
- They think they are ready (59 percent of boys, 51 percent of girls)
- They want to be loved (45 percent of girls, 28 percent of boys)
- They don't want people to tease them for being a virgin (43 percent of boys, 38 percent of girls)

Risk Factors for Sexual Problems

Most adolescents become sexually active at some point during adolescence. Many adolescents are at risk for sexual problems and other problems when they have sexual intercourse before 16 years of age. Adolescents who have sex before they are 16 are often ineffective users of contraceptives and are at risk for adolescent pregnancy and sexually transmitted diseases. Early sexual activity is also linked with other at-risk behaviors such as excessive drinking, drug use, delinquency, and school-related problems (Rosenbaum & Kandel, 1990).

In one recent longitudinal study, sexual involvement by girls in early adolescence was linked with their lower

SEXUAL TIMETABLE	WHITE	AFRICAN AMERICAN	LATINO	ASIAN AMERICAN
Kiss	14.3	13.9	14.5	15.7
French kiss	15.0	14.0	15.3	16.2
Touch breast	15.6	14.5	15.5	16.9
Touch penis	16.1	15.0	16.2	17.8
Touch vagina	16.1	14.6	15.9	17.1
Sexual intercourse	16.9	15.5	16.5	18.0
Oral sex	17.1	16.9	17.1	18.3

■ **FIGURE 11.3**

Sexual Timetables of White, African American, Latino, and Asian American Adolescents

What is the nature of adolescent sexual scripts?

self-esteem, greater depression, greater sexual activity, and lower grades in the high school years (Buhrmester, 2001). Early sexual involvement by boys was related to greater substance abuse and sexual activity in the high school years.

Risk factors for sexual problems in adolescence include contextual factors such as socioeconomic status (SES) and family/parenting circumstances. In one recent review, living in a dangerous and/or a low-income neighborhood were at-risk factors for adolescent pregnancy (Miller, Benson, & Galbraith, 2001). Also in this review, these aspects of parenting were linked with reduced risk of adolescent pregnancy: parent/adolescent closeness or connectedness, parental supervision or regulation of adolescents' activities, and parental values against intercourse or unprotected intercourse in adolescence (Miller, Benson, and Galbraith, 2001). Further, having older sexually active siblings or pregnant/parenting teenage sisters place adolescents at an elevated risk of adolescent pregnancy (Miller, Benson, & Galbraith, 2001).

Now that we have considered a number of ideas about heterosexual attitudes and behaviors in adolescence, we will turn our attention to homosexual attitudes and behaviors.

Homosexual Attitudes and Behavior Most individuals think that heterosexual behavior and homosexual behavior are distinct patterns that can be easily defined. In fact, however, preference for a sexual partner of the same or opposite sex is not always a fixed decision, made once in life and adhered to forever. For example, it is not unusual for an individual, especially a male, to engage in homosexual experimentation in adolescence, but not engage in homosexual behavior as an adult. And some individuals engage in heterosexual behavior during adolescence, then turn to homosexual behavior as adults.

A Continuum of Heterosexuality and Homosexuality Until the end of the nineteenth century, it was generally believed that people were either heterosexual or homosexual. Today, it is

The Kinsey Institute
Sexuality Research Information Service
http://www.mhhe.com/santrocka9

THROUGH THE EYES OF ADOLESCENTS

Struggling with a Sexual Decision

Elizabeth is an adolescent girl who is reflecting on her struggle with whether to have sex with a guy she is in love with. She says it is not a question of whether she loves him or not. She does love him, but she still doesn't know if it is right or wrong to have sex with him. He wants her to have sex, but she knows her parents don't. With her friends, some say yes others say no. So Elizabeth is confused. After a few days of contemplation, in a moment of honesty, she admits that she is not his special love. This finally tilts the answer to not having sex with him. She realizes that if the relationship falls through, she will look back and regret it if she does have sex. In the end, Elizabeth decided not to have sex with him.

Elizabeth's reflections reveal her struggle to understand what is right and what is wrong, whether to have sex or not. In her circumstance, the fact that in a moment of honesty she admitted that she was not his special love made a big difference in her decision.

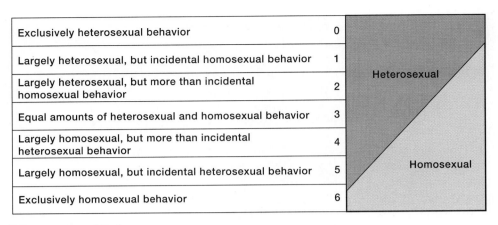

Exclusively heterosexual behavior	0
Largely heterosexual, but incidental homosexual behavior	1
Largely heterosexual, but more than incidental homosexual behavior	2
Equal amounts of heterosexual and homosexual behavior	3
Largely homosexual, but more than incidental heterosexual behavior	4
Largely homosexual, but incidental heterosexual behavior	5
Exclusively homosexual behavior	6

FIGURE 11.4
The Continuum of Sexual Orientation

The continuum ranges from exclusive heterosexuality, which Kinsey and associates (1948) rated as 0, to exclusive homosexuality (6). People who are about equally attracted to both sexes (ratings 2 to 4) are bisexual.

bisexual
A person who is attracted to people of both sexes.

The International Lesbian and Gay Association
National Gay and Lesbian Task Force
Supporting Gay and Lesbian Rights
Lesbian and Gay Issues
http://www.mhhe.com/santrocka9

more acceptable to view sexual orientation as a continuum from exclusive heterosexuality to exclusive homosexuality. Pioneering this view were Alfred Kinsey and his associates (1948), who described sexual orientation as a continuum on a six-point scale, with 0 signifying exclusive heterosexuality and 6 indicating exclusive homosexuality (see figure 11.4). Some individuals are **bisexual,** *being sexually attracted to people of both sexes.* In Kinsey's research, approximately 1 percent of individuals reported being bisexual (1.2 percent of males and 0.7 percent of females) and between 2 to 5 percent of individuals reported being homosexual (4.7 percent of males and 1.8 percent of females). In one national survey, only 2.3 percent of males said they have had same-sex experience and only 1.1 percent said they are exclusively gay (Alan Guttmacher Institute, 1995). And in another national study, the percentage of individuals who reported being active homosexuals was much lower (2.7 percent of males and 1.3 percent of females) than the ofttimes reported 10 percent (Michael & others, 1994).

Causes of Homosexuality   Why are some individuals homosexual and others heterosexual? Speculation about this question has been extensive, but no firm answers are available. Homosexual and heterosexual males and females have similar physiological responses during sexual arousal and seem to be aroused by the same types of tactile stimulation. Investigators find no differences between homosexuals and heterosexuals for a wide range of attitudes, behaviors, and adjustments (Bell, Weinberg, & Mammersmith, 1981; Savin-Williams, 1995). Both the American Psychiatric Association and the American Psychological Association recognized that homosexuality is not a form of mental illness and discontinued classification of homosexuality as a disorder in the 1970s.

Recently researchers have explored the possible biological basis of homosexuality (D'Augelli, 2000; Herek, 2000). In this regard, we will evaluate hormone, brain, and twin studies regarding homosexual orientation. The results of hormone studies have been inconsistent. Indeed, if male homosexuals are given male sexual hormones (androgens), their sexual orientation does not change; their sexual desire merely increases. A very early critical period might influence sexual orientation. In the second to fifth months after conception, exposure of the fetus to hormone levels characteristic of females might cause the individual (female or male) to become attracted to males (Ellis & Ames, 1987). If this critical-period hypothesis turns out to be correct, it would explain why clinicians have found that sexual orientation is difficult, if not impossible, to modify (Meyer-Bahlburg & others, 1995).

With regard to anatomical structures, neuroscientist Simon LeVay (1991) found that an area of the hypothalamus that governs sexual behavior is twice as large (about the size of a grain of sand) in heterosexual men as in homosexual men. The area is about the same size in homosexual men as in heterosexual women. Critics of LeVay's work point out that many of the homosexuals in the study had AIDS and their brains could have been altered by the disease.

One study investigated homosexual orientation in pairs of twins (Whitman, Diamond, & Martin, 1993). The researchers began with a group of homosexuals, each of whom had a twin sibling, and investigated the sexual orientation of the siblings. The siblings who were a monozygotic twin of a homosexual came from the same fertilized egg as the homosexual and thus were genetically identical to the homosexual. Of these, almost two-thirds had a homosexual orientation. The siblings who were a dizygotic twin of a homosexual came from a different fertilized egg than the homosexual and thus were genetically no more similar to the homosexual than a nontwin sibling would be. Of these, less than one-third had a homosexual orientation. The authors interpret their results as supporting a biological interpretation of homosexuality. However, not all of the monozygotic twins had a homosexual orientation, so clearly environmental factors were involved in at least those cases.

An individual's sexual orientation—heterosexual, homosexual, or bisexual—is most likely determined by a combination of genetic, hormonal, cognitive, and environmental factors (Strickland, 1995). Most experts on homosexuality believe that no one factor alone causes homosexuality and that the relative weight of each factor may vary from one individual to the next. In effect, no one knows exactly what causes an individual to be homosexual. Scientists have a clearer picture of what does not cause homosexuality. For example, children raised by gay or lesbian parents or couples are no more likely to be homosexual than are children raised by heterosexual parents (Patterson, 1995). There also is no evidence that male homosexuality is caused by a dominant mother or a weak father, or that female homosexuality is caused by girls' choosing male role models.

Gay or Lesbian Identity in Adolescence   Although the development of gay or lesbian identity has been widely studied in adults, few researchers have investigated the gay or lesbian identity (often referred to as the coming-out process) in adolescents (Flowers & Buston, 2001). In one study of gay male adolescents, coming out was conceptualized in three stages: sensitization; awareness with confusion, denial, guilt, and shame; and acceptance (Newman & Muzzonigro, 1993). The majority of the gay adolescents said they felt different from other boys as children. The average age at having their first crush on another boy was 12.7 years, and the average age at realizing they were gay was 12.5 years. Most of the boys said they felt confused when they first became aware that they were gay. About half of the boys said they initially tried to deny their identity as a gay.

Reactions to homosexual self-recognition range from relief and happiness ("Now I understand and I feel better") to anxiety, depression, and suicidal thoughts ("I can't let anybody know; I've got to kill myself"). Gay adolescents often develop a number of defenses against self-recognition and labeling. The defenses include these (Savin-Williams & Rodriguez, 1993):

"I guess I was drunk."
"It was just a phase I was going through."
"I've heard that all guys do it once."
"I just love her and not all girls."
"I was lonely."
"I was just curious."

THROUGH THE EYES OF ADOLESCENTS

Not Interested in the "Oogling" That My Friends Engaged In

"In middle school I was very involved with the drama club. My singing voice is a cross between Elvis and Roger Rabbit, but I was always on stage in the school musicals. I was an attention 'addict.' . . . I was very charismatic and self-confident until the subject of sex was brought up. I just couldn't participate in the 'oogling' that my friends engaged in. I didn't find Danissa and her chest as inviting as everyone else did. John's conquest of Cindy wasn't the least bit interesting to me, particularly because I didn't have the sex drive to engage in these behaviors myself. When I did develop this drive, I guess in the eighth grade, I found myself equally disinterested in Danissa and her chest. Instead, I found myself very interested in Tony and his sharp features and muscular build."

—Gay Adolescent Male

Why are some individuals homosexual and others heterosexual? How do adolescents disclose their gay, lesbian, or bisexual identity to family members?

Such defenses might be temporary, or they might be life-long. They might have some positive outcomes (such as redirecting sexual energies into successful academic pursuits) or destructive outcomes (such as marrying a person whom one does not find erotically or emotionally attractive).

Disclosure   Based on empirical research, these conclusions can be reached about adolescents who disclose their gay or lesbian identity (Savin-Williams, 1998, 2000):

- Parents are seldom the first person an adolescent tells about his or her same-sex attractions.
- Mothers are usually told before fathers, possibly because adolescents have more distant relationships with fathers.
- Mothers are more likely than fathers to know about their adolescent's (son's or daughter's) same-sex attractions.
- Approximately 50 to 60 percent of lesbian, gay, and bisexual adolescents have disclosed to at least one sibling, but siblings are still seldom the first person to whom a sexual-minority youth discloses.
- The first person to whom adolescents may disclose their homosexual or bisexual identity is likely to be a friend.

Discrimination and Bias   Having irrational negative feelings against homosexuals is called *homophobia*. In its more extreme forms, homophobia can lead individuals to ridicule, beat, or even murder people they believe to be homosexual. More typically it is associated with avoidance of homosexuals, faulty beliefs about the homosexual lifestyle (such as believing the falsehood that most child molesters are homosexuals), and subtle or overt discrimination in housing, employment, and other areas of life.

One of the harmful aspects of the stigmatization of homosexuality is the self-devaluation engaged in by gay individuals (Patterson, 1995; Rose & Rodgers, 2000; Savin-Williams & Rodriguez, 1993). One common form of self-devaluation is called passing, the process of hiding one's real social identity. Passing strategies include giving out information that hides one's homosexual identity or avoiding one's true sexual identity. Passing behaviors include lying to others and saying, "I'm straight and attracted to opposite-sex individuals." Such defenses against self-recognition are heavily entrenched in our society. Without adequate support, and with fear of stigmatization, many gay and lesbian youth return to the closet and then reemerge at a safer time later, often in college. A special concern is the lack of support gay adolescents receive from parents, teachers, and counselors (Davis & Stewart, 1997; Savin-Williams, 2001).

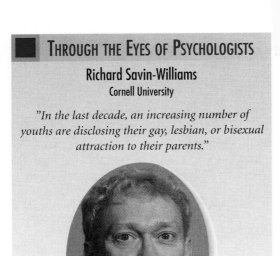

THROUGH THE EYES OF PSYCHOLOGISTS

Richard Savin-Williams
Cornell University

"In the last decade, an increasing number of youths are disclosing their gay, lesbian, or bisexual attraction to their parents."

Another concern is the link between suicide risk and sexual orientation (Morrison & L'Heureux, 2001; Rose & Rogers, 2000). In one study of junior high and high school students, suicide attempts were reported by 28 percent of the bisexual/homosexual males, 21 percent of the bisexual/homosexual females, 15 percent of the heterosexual females, and only 4 percent of the heterosexual males (Remafedi & others, 1998).

Now that we have explored adolescent heterosexual and homosexual attitudes and behavior, let's examine another dimension of adolescent sexuality: self-stimulation.

Self-Stimulation   Regardless of whether adolescents have a heterosexual or homosexual orientation, they must equally confront increasing feelings of sexual arousal. One way in which many youths who are not dating or who consciously choose not to engage in sexual intercourse or sexual explorations deal with these insistent feelings of sexual arousal is through masturbation or self-stimulation.

As indicated earlier, a heterosexual continuum of necking, petting, and intercourse or oral sex characterizes many adolescents' sexual experiences. Substantial numbers of adolescents, though, have sexual experience outside of this heterosexual continuum through masturbation or same-sex behavior. Most boys have an ejaculation for the first time at about 12 to 13 years of age. Masturbation, genital contact with a same-sex or other-sex partner, or a wet dream during sleep are common circumstances for ejaculation.

Masturbation is the most frequent sexual outlet for many adolescents (Gates & Sonnenstein, 2000). In one investigation, masturbation was commonplace among adolescents (Haas, 1979). More than two-thirds of the boys and one-half of the girls masturbated once a week or more. Adolescents today do not feel as guilty about masturbation as they once did, although they still may feel embarrassed or defensive about it. In past eras, masturbation was denounced as causing everything from warts to insanity. Today, as few as 15 percent of adolescents attach any stigma to masturbation (Hyde & DeLamater, 2000).

In one study, the masturbation practices of female and male college students were studied (Leitenberg, Detzer, & Srebnik, 1993). Almost twice as many males as females said they had masturbated (81 percent versus 45 percent), and the males who masturbated did so three times more frequently during early adolescence and early adulthood than did the females who masturbated during the same age periods. No association was found between engaging in masturbation during preadolescence and/or early adolescence and sexual adjustment in adulthood.

Contraceptive Use   Sexual activity, while normal activity necessary for procreation, carries with it considerable risks if appropriate safeguards are not taken (Zimmer-Gembeck, Doyle, & Daniels, 2001). There are two kinds of risks that youth encounter: unintended unwanted pregnancy and sexually transmitted diseases. Both of these risks can be reduced significantly if contraception is used. While gay and lesbian youth are spared the risk of pregnancy, like their heterosexual peers, they still face the risk of sexually transmitted diseases.

The good news is that adolescents are increasing their use of contraceptives (Child Trends, 2000). Adolescent girls' contraceptive use at first intercourse rose from 48 percent to 65 percent during the 1980s (Forrest & Singh, 1990). By 1995, use at first intercourse reached 78 percent, with two-thirds of that figure involving condom use. A sexually active adolescent who does not use contraception has a 90 percent chance of pregnancy within 1 year (Alan Guttmacher Institute, 1998). The method adolescent girls use most frequently is the pill (44 percent), followed by the condom (38 percent). About 10 percent rely on an injectable contraception, 4 percent on withdrawal, and 3 percent on

Adolescents are increasing their use of contraceptives, although large numbers of sexually active adolescents still do not use contraceptives, especially at first intercourse.

an implant (Alan Guttmacher Institute, 1998). Approximately one-third of adolescent girls who rely on condoms also take the pill or practice withdrawal.

Although adolescent contraceptive use is increasing, many sexually active adolescents still do not use contraceptives, or they use them inconsistently (Ford, John, & Lepkowski, 2001). Sexually active younger adolescents are less likely to take contraceptive precautions than older adolescents. Younger adolescents are more likely to use a condom or withdrawal, whereas older adolescents are more likely to use the pill or a diaphragm. In one study, adolescent females reported changing their behavior in the direction of safer-sex practices more than did adolescent males (Rimberg & Lewis, 1994).

In thinking about contraceptive use in adolescence, it is important to consider the interpersonal context of adolescents' lives. For example, one reason adolescent girls do not encourage their partners to use condoms is that they don't want to risk losing their partners. That is, in the eyes of the adolescent girl the potential risk of pregnancy or sexually transmitted diseases is not as threatening as the potential loss of a partner (Feldman, 1999).

The issue of contraception is more difficult for adolescents than adults because of differing patterns of sexual activity (Feldman, 1999). Whereas many adults, especially married adults, have sex on a regular and predictable schedule, and typically with one partner (or relatively few partners), adolescents' sexual activity often reflects a pattern of feast or famine. Their sexual encounters tend to occur unpredictably and intermittently rather than on a predictable and regular basis. Thus, some forms of contraception that are most effective and widely used by adults (such as the pill and IUD) are not as well suited for adolescents' patterns of sexual activity. Also, married couples often discuss the form of contraception that they plan to use; such discussions are far less likely to occur among adolescent partners and unmarried young adults. This means that adolescents frequently resort to the use of condoms, which are not completely reliable. The good news, though, is that condoms (unlike the pill or IUD) are effective against sexually transmitted diseases.

What factors are related to contraceptive use? Being from a low-SES family is one of the best predictors of adolescents' nonuse of contraceptives. Younger adolescents are less likely to use contraceptives than older adolescents (Hofferth, 1990). Not being involved in a steady, committed dating relationship is also associated with a lack of contraceptive use (Chilman, 1979). In addition, adolescents with poor coping skills, lack of a future orientation, high anxiety, poor social adjustment, and a negative attitude toward contraceptives are not as likely to use contraceptives. Further, degree of personal concern about AIDS and the perception that a partner would appreciate condom use are associated with more consistent use of condoms by male adolescents (Pleck, Sonenstein, & Ku, 1991). Condom use is inhibited by concerns about embarrassment and reduced sexual pleasure. Educational efforts that include information about AIDS and pregnancy prevention may promote more consistent use of condoms by adolescent males.

While American adolescents' use of contraceptives increased in the last two decades, adolescents in Canada, Great Britain, France, Sweden, and the Netherlands are still more likely to use contraceptives than are adolescents in the United States (Child Trends, 2000; Forrest, 1990). U.S. adolescents are especially less likely to use effective contraceptives like the pill than their counterparts in other countries.

The Alan Guttmacher Institute
http://www.mhhe.com/santrocka9

Since the last review, we have studied many ideas about heterosexual and homosexual attitudes and behavior, self-stimulation, and contraceptive use. This review should help you to reach your learning goals related to these topics.

☐ FOR YOUR REVIEW

Learning Goal 2	
Know about adolescent heterosexual attitudes and behavior	• The progression of sexual behaviors is typically necking, petting, sexual intercourse, or, in some cases, oral sex.
	• The number of adolescents reporting having had sexual intercourse increased significantly in the twentieth century. The proportion of females engaging in intercourse increased more rapidly than for males. National data indicate that slightly more than half of all adolescents today have had sexual intercourse by age 17,

although the percentage varies by sex, ethnicity, and context. Male, African American, and inner-city adolescents report the highest sexual activity.
- A common adolescent sexual script involves the male making sexual advances, and it is left up to the female to set limits on the male's sexual overtures. Adolescent females' sexual scripts link sex with love more than adolescent males' sexual scripts do.
- Risk factors for sexual problems include early sexual activity, having a number of sexual partners, not using contraception, engaging in other at-risk behaviors such as drinking and delinquency, living in a low-SES neighborhood, and ethnicity.

Learning Goal 3
Describe adolescent homosexual attitudes and behavior

- Today, it is widely accepted that sexual orientation should be viewed as a continuum from exclusive heterosexuality to exclusive homosexuality.
- An individual's sexual orientation—whether bisexual, heterosexual, or homosexual—is likely caused by a mix of genetic, hormonal, cognitive, and environmental factors.
- Recent research has focused on adolescents' disclosure of same-sex attractions and the struggle they often go through in doing this.
- Discrimination and bias against homosexuality produces considerable stress for adolescents with a homosexual interest.

Learning Goal 4
Discuss self-stimulation and evaluate contraceptive use

- Self-stimulation is part of the sexual activity of virtually all adolescents and one of their most frequent sexual outlets.
- Adolescents are increasing their use of contraceptives, but large numbers of sexually active adolescents still do not use them. Young adolescents and those from low-SES backgrounds are less likely to use contraceptives than their older, middle-SES counterparts.

So far in this chapter, we have examined the normal aspects of adolescent sexuality and sexual attitudes/behavior. In our coverage of sexual attitudes and behavior, we discussed some factors that are linked with sexual problems in adolescence. Next, we will more extensively explore adolescent sexual problems.

ADOLESCENT SEXUAL PROBLEMS

Sexual problems in adolescence include adolescent pregnancy, sexually transmitted diseases, and forcible sexual behavior and sexual harassment.

ADOLESCENT SEXUAL PROBLEMS

Adolescent Pregnancy

Sexually Transmitted Diseases

Forcible Sexual Behavior and Sexual Harassment

Adolescent Pregnancy

Angela is 15 years old and pregnant. She reflects, "I'm three months pregnant. This could ruin my whole life. I've made all of these plans for the future, and now they are down the drain. I don't have anybody to talk with about my problem. I can't talk to my parents. There is no way they can understand." Pregnant adolescents were once virtually invisible and unmentionable. But yesterday's secret has become today's national dilemma. Our exploration of adolescent pregnancy focuses on its incidence and nature, its consequences, cognitive factors that may be involved, adolescents as parents, and ways adolescent pregnancy rates can be reduced.

Incidence and Nature of Adolescent Pregnancy   Adolescent girls who become pregnant are from different ethnic groups and from different places, but their circumstances have the same stressfulness. They represent a flaw in America's social fabric. Like Angela, far too many become pregnant in their early or middle adolescent years. More than 200,000 females in the United States have a child before their eighteenth birthday. As one 17-year-old Los Angeles mother of a 1-year-old son said, "We are children having children."

In recent cross-cultural comparisons, the United States continued to have one of the highest rates of adolescent pregnancy and childbearing in the developed world,

What are some changes that have taken place in adolescent pregnancy since the 1950s and 1960s?

despite a considerable decline in the 1990s (Alan Guttmacher Institute, 2000; Centers for Disease Control and Prevention, 2001). U.S. adolescent pregnancy rates are similar to that in Russia and several Eastern European countries, such as Bulgaria, and at least four times the rates in France, Germany, and Japan. The U.S. adolescent pregnancy rate is approximately eight times as high as in the Netherlands. While U.S. adolescents are no more sexually active than their counterparts in the Netherlands, their adolescent pregnancy rate is much higher.

There are encouraging trends, though, in U.S. adolescent pregnancy rates (Ventura & others, 2001). In 2000, births to adolescent girls fell to a record low (Centers for Disease Control & Prevention, 2001a). For every 1,000 girls 15 to 19 years of age, there were 49 births—the lowest rate in the six decades this statistic has been kept. The rate of births to adolescent girls has dropped 22 percent since 1991. Reasons for the decline include increased contraceptive use, fear of sexually transmitted diseases such as AIDS, and the economic prosperity of the 1990s, which may have caused many adolescents to delay starting a family so that they could take jobs.

The greatest drop in the U.S. adolescent pregnancy rate in the 1990s was for 15- to 17-year-old African American girls. Fear of sexually transmitted diseases, especially AIDS, school/community health classes, and a greater hope for the future are the likely reasons for the decrease in U.S adolescent pregnancy rates in the 1990s. Latino adolescents are more likely than African American and non-Latino White adolescents to become pregnant (Child Trends, 2001). Births to Latino and African American adolescents are more likely to be repeat births than births to non-Latino White adolescents.

Consequences of Adolescent Pregnancy   The consequences of America's high adolescent pregnancy rate are cause for great concern (Kalil & Konz, 2000). Adolescent pregnancy creates health risks for both the offspring and the mother. Infants born to adolescent mothers are more likely to have low birth weights—a prominent factor in infant mortality—as well as neurological problems and childhood illness (Dryfoos, 1990). Adolescent mothers often drop out of school. Although many adolescent mothers resume their education later in life, they generally do not catch up with women who postpone childbearing. In the National Longitudinal Survey of Work Experience of Youth, it was found that only half of the 20- to 26-year-old women who first gave birth at age 17 had completed high school by their twenties (the percentage was even lower for those who gave birth at a younger age) (Mott & Marsiglio, 1985). By contrast, among young females who waited until age 20 to have a baby, more than 90 percent had obtained a high school education (Kenney, 1987). Among the younger adolescent mothers, almost half had obtained a general equivalency diploma (GED), which does not often open up good employment opportunities.

These educational deficits have negative consequences for the young females themselves and for their children (Kenney, 1987). Adolescent parents are more likely than those who delay childbearing to have low-paying, low-status jobs, or to be unemployed. The mean family income of White females who give birth before age 17 is approximately half that of families in which the mother delays birth until her middle or late twenties.

Though the consequences of America's high adolescent pregnancy rate are cause for great concern, it often is not pregnancy alone that leads to negative consequences for an adolescent mother and her offspring (Brooks-Gunn & Paikoff, 1997; Feldman, 1999; Pittman, 2000). Adolescent mothers are more likely to come from low-SES backgrounds (Hoffman, Foster, & Furstenberg, 1993). Many adolescents mothers also were not good students before they became pregnant. Also keep in mind that not every adolescent female who bears a child lives a life of poverty and low achievement. Thus, although adolescent pregnancy is a high-risk circumstance and in general adolescents who do not become pregnant fare better than those who do, some adolescent mothers do well in school and have positive outcomes (Ahn, 1994; Leadbetter & Way, 2000).

Cognitive Factors in Adolescent Pregnancy Cognitive changes have intriguing implications for adolescents' sex education (Lipsitz, 1980). With their developing idealism and ability to think in more abstract and hypothetical ways, young adolescents may get caught up in a mental world far removed from reality, one that may involve a belief that things cannot or will not happen to them and that they are omnipotent and indestructible. Having information about contraceptives is not enough—what seems to predict whether or not adolescents will use contraceptives is their acceptance of themselves and their sexuality. This acceptance requires not only emotional maturity but cognitive maturity.

Most discussions of adolescent pregnancy and its prevention assume that adolescents have the ability to anticipate consequences, to weigh the probable outcome of behavior, and to project into the future what will happen if they engage in certain acts, such as sexual intercourse. That is, prevention is based on the belief that adolescents have the cognitive ability to approach problem solving in a planned, organized, and analytical manner. However, many adolescents are just beginning to develop these capacities, and others have not developed them at all.

The personal fable described in chapter 4 may be associated with adolescent pregnancy. The young adolescent might say, "Hey, it won't happen to me." If adolescents are locked into this personal fable, they might not respond well to a course on sex education that preaches prevention. A developmental perspective on cognition suggests what can be taught in sex education courses for young adolescents.

Late adolescents (18 to 19 years of age) are to some degree realistic and future oriented about sexual experiences, just as they are about careers and marriage. Middle adolescents (15 to 17 years of age) often romanticize sexuality. But young adolescents (10 to 15 years of age) seem to experience sex in a depersonalized way that is filled with anxiety and denial. This depersonalized orientation toward sex is not likely to lead to preventive behavior.

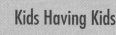

THROUGH THE EYES OF ADOLESCENTS

Kids Having Kids

Here are some comments by adolescents and adults about adolescent pregnancy:

Having children too young is not fair to the child or yourself. Love is not enough. I was 16 and unmarried when I had my first child, I dropped out of school and had the baby in a different state. My mother made arrangements to put the child up for adoption. How I suffered, cried, and worried all alone in a room far from home. I wanted to die, then wanted to live to see the child I was carrying. I saw him briefly after he was born, and then many years later I contacted him. He could not forgive me.

—Hope, an adult reflecting on her youth

Create a comfortable atmosphere where teenagers can ask questions. Then more teenagers will want to get condoms and birth control pills.

—Sarah, 17 years old

We should be asking "Why are so many parents so negligent?" instead of "Why do so many teens end up pregnant?"

—Susan, American teenager

High school programs should show teens what life is like with a baby. Experience, even simulated, is the best method of learning.

—Russell, who became a father when he was 17 years old

CAREERS IN ADOLESCENT DEVELOPMENT

Lynn Blankenship
Family and Consumer Science Educator

Lynn Blankenship is a family and consumer science educator. She has an undergraduate degree in this area from the University of Arizona. She has taught for more than 20 years, the last 14 at Tucson High Magnet School.

Lynn was awarded the Tucson Federation of Teachers Educator of the Year Award for 1999–2000 and the Arizona Association of Family and Consumer Science Teacher of the Year in 1999.

Lynn especially enjoys teaching life skills to adolescents. One of her favorite activities is having students care for an automated baby that imitates the needs of real babies. Lynn says that this program has a profound impact on students because the baby must be cared for around the clock for the duration of the assignment. Lynn also coordinates real-world work experiences and training for students in several child care facilities in the Tucson area.

Lynn Blankenship with students carrying their automated babies.

Adolescent Pregnancy
Teen Pregnancy Reduction
Initiative
http://www.mhhe.com/santrocka9

Adolescents as Parents Children of adolescent parents face problems even before they are born. Only one of every five pregnant adolescent girls receives any prenatal care at all during the important first three months of pregnancy. Pregnant adolescents are more likely to have anemia and complications related to prematurity than are mothers aged 20 to 24. The problems of adolescent pregnancy double the normal risk of delivering a low birth weight baby (one that weighs under 5.5 pounds), a category that places that infant at risk for physical and mental deficits (Dryfoos, 1990).

Infants who escape the medical hazards of having an adolescent mother might not escape the psychological and social perils (Brooks-Gunn & Chase-Lansdale, 1995; Luster & others, 1995). Children born to adolescent mothers do not do as well on intelligence tests and have more behavioral problems than do those born to mothers in their twenties (Silver, 1988). Adolescent mothers have less desirable child-rearing practices and less realistic expectations for their infants' development than do older mothers (Osofsky, 1990). Said one 18-year-old adolescent mother, "Not long after he was born, I began to resent him. I wouldn't play with him the first year. He didn't talk until he was two—he would just grunt. I'm sure some of his slow development is my fault. Now I want to make up for it and try to give him extra attention, but he still is behind his age." Other adolescent mothers might get excited about having "this little adorable thing" and anticipate that their world with their child will be marvelous. But as the infant demands more and more of their attention and they have to take care of the infant instead of going out on dates, their positive expectations turn sour.

So far, we have talked exclusively about adolescent mothers. Although some adolescent fathers are involved with their children, the majority are not. In one study, only one-fourth of adolescent mothers with a 3-year-old child said the father had a close relationship with her and the child (Leadbetter, Way, & Raden, 1994). Another study showed that in the last two decades there was a dramatic decline in father involvement with the children of adolescent mothers (Leadbetter, 1994).

Adolescent fathers have lower incomes, less education, and more children than do men who delay having children until their twenties. One reason for these difficulties is that the adolescent father compounds his problem of getting his girlfriend pregnant by dropping out of school (Resnick, Wattenberg, & Brewer, 1992). As soon as he leaves school, the adolescent father moves directly into a low-paying job. Adolescent fathers are saying to themselves, "You need to be a good father. The least you can do is get a job and provide some support."

Many young fathers have little idea of what a father is supposed to do. They may love their baby but not know how to behave. American society has given them few guidelines and few supports. Programs designed to help adolescent fathers are still relatively rare, but they are increasing. Terry, who is now 21, has a 17-month-old child and is himself the child of adolescent parents. After receiving support from the Teenage Pregnancy and Parenting Project in San Francisco, he is now a counselor there. He reports, "My father was a parent when he was an adolescent. So was my grandfather. I know it will stop with my son" (Stengel, 1985).

Reducing Adolescent Pregnancy   Serious, extensive efforts are needed to help pregnant adolescents and young mothers enhance their educational and occupational opportunities. Adolescent mothers also need extensive help in obtaining competent day care and in planning for the future (Klaw & Saunders, 1994). John Conger (1988) offered the following four recommendations for attacking the high rate of adolescent pregnancy: (1) sex education and family planning, (2) access to contraceptive methods, (3) the life options approach, and (4) broad community involvement and support, each of which we consider in turn.

Age-appropriate family-life education benefits adolescents. Much more about sex education appears later in this chapter.

In addition to age-appropriate family-life and sex education, sexually active adolescents need access to contraceptive methods. These needs often can be handled through adolescent clinics that provide comprehensive, high-quality health services. At four of the nation's oldest adolescent clinics, in St. Paul, Minnesota, the overall annual rate of first-time pregnancies has dropped from 80 per 1,000 to 29 per 1,000 (Schorr, 1989). These clinics offer everything from immunizations to sports physicals to treatment for sexually transmitted diseases. Significantly, they also advise adolescents on contraception and dispense prescriptions for birth control (provided parents have agreed beforehand to allow their adolescents to visit the clinic). An important aspect of the clinics is the presence of individuals trained to understand the special needs and confusions of the adolescent age group.

Better sex education, family planning, and access to contraceptive methods alone will not remedy the adolescent pregnancy crisis, especially for high-risk adolescents. Adolescents have to become *motivated* to reduce their pregnancy risk. This motivation will come only when adolescents look to the future and see that they have an opportunity to become self-sufficient and successful. Adolescents need opportunities to improve their academic and career-related skills, job opportunities, life-planning consultation, and extensive mental health services.

Finally, for adolescent pregnancy prevention to ultimately succeed, we need broad community involvement and support (Duckett, 1997). This support is a major reason for the success of pregnancy prevention efforts in other developed nations where rates of adolescent pregnancy, abortion, and childbearing are much lower than in America despite similar levels of sexual activity. In Holland, as well as other European countries such as Sweden, sex does not carry the mystery and conflict it does in American society. Holland does not have a mandated sex education program, but adolescents can obtain contraceptive counseling at government-sponsored clinics for a small fee. The Dutch media also have played an important role in educating the public about sex through

These are not adolescent mothers, but rather adolescents who are participating in the Teen Outreach Program (TOP) which engages adolescents in volunteer community service. These adolescent girls are serving as volunteers in a daycare center for crack babies. Researchers have found that such volunteer experiences can reduce the rate of adolescent pregnancy.

frequent broadcasts focused on birth control, abortion, and related matters. Dutch adolescents do not consider having sex without contraception.

One strategy for reducing adolescent pregnancy, called the Teen Outreach Program (TOP), focuses on engaging adolescents in volunteer community service and stimulates discussions that help adolescents appreciate the lessons they learn through volunteerism. In one study, 695 adolescents in grades 9 to 12 were randomly assigned to either a Teen Outreach group or a control group (Allen & others, 1997). They were assessed at both program entry and at program exit nine months later. The rate of pregnancy was substantially lower for the Teen Outreach adolescents. These adolescents also had a lower rate of school failure and academic suspension.

Girls, Inc., has four programs that are intended to increase adolescent girls' motivation to avoid pregnancy until they are mature enough to make responsible decisions about motherhood (Roth & others, 1998). Growing Together, a series of five two-hour workshops for mothers and adolescents, and Will Power/Won't Power, a series of six two-hour sessions that focus on assertiveness training, are for 12- to 14-year-old girls. For older adolescent girls, Taking Care of Business provides nine sessions that emphasize career planning as well as information about sexuality, reproduction, and contraception. Health Bridge coordinates health and education services—girls can participate in this program as one of their club activities. Research on girls' participation in these programs revealed a significant drop in their likelihood of getting pregnant, compared to girls who did not participate (Girls, Inc., 1991).

So far, we have discussed four ways to reduce adolescent pregnancy: sex education and family planning, access to contraceptive methods, life options, and broad community involvement and support. A fifth consideration, which is especially important for young adolescents, is abstinence. Abstinence is increasingly being included as a theme in sex education classes (Darroch, Landry, & Singh, 2000).

Since the last review, we have discussed a number of ideas about adolescent pregnancy. This review should help you to reach your learning goals related to this topic.

☐ FOR YOUR REVIEW

Learning Goal 5
Know about adolescent pregnancy

- Four of nine adolescent pregnancies are unintended. The U.S. adolescent pregnancy rate is the highest in the Western world. Fortunately, the U.S. adolescent pregnancy rate has recently started to decline.
- Adolescent pregnancy increases health risks for the mother and the offspring. Adolescent mothers are more likely to drop out of school and have lower-paying jobs than their adolescent counterparts who do not bear children. It is important to remember, though, that it often is not pregnancy alone that places adolescents at risk. Adolescent mothers often come from low-income families and were not doing well in school prior to their pregnancy.
- Cognitive factors, such as egocentric and immature thought, may be involved in adolescent pregnancy.
- The infants of adolescent parents are at risk both medically and psychologically. Adolescent parents are less effective in rearing their children than older parents are. Many adolescent fathers do not have a close relationship with their baby and the adolescent mother.
- Recommendations for reducing adolescent pregnancy include sex education and family planning, access to contraception, life options, community involvement and support, and abstinence. In one study, volunteer community service was linked with a lower incidence of adolescent pregnancy.

Now that we have studied adolescent pregnancy, let's turn our attention to other adolescent sexuality problems that may develop: sexually transmitted diseases.

Sexually Transmitted Diseases

Tammy, age 15, just finished listening to an expert lecture in her health class. We overhear her talking to one of her girlfriends as she walks down the school corridor: "That was a disgusting lecture. I can't believe all the diseases you can get by having sex. I think she was probably trying to scare us. She spent a lot of time talking about AIDS, which I have heard that normal people do not get. Right? I've heard that only homosexuals and drug addicts get AIDS. And I've also heard that gonorrhea and most other sexual diseases can be cured, so what is the big deal if you get something like that?" Tammy's view of sexually transmitted diseases—that they always happen to someone else, that they can be easily cured without any harm done, that they are too disgusting for a nice young person to hear about, let alone get—is common among adolescents. Tammy's view is wrong. Adolescents who are having sex run the risk of getting sexually transmitted diseases.

Sexually transmitted diseases (STDs) *are diseases that are contracted primarily through sexual contact. This contact is not limited to vaginal intercourse but includes oral-genital and anal-genital contact as well. STDs are an increasing health problem.* Approximately 25 percent of sexually active adolescents are estimated to become infected with an STD each year (Alan Guttmacher Institute, 1998).

Types   Among the main STDs adolescents can get are bacterial infections (such as gonorrhea and syphilis), chlamydia, and two STDs caused by viruses—genital herpes and AIDS (acquired immune deficiency syndrome).

Gonorrhea   **Gonorrhea** *is a sexually transmitted disease that is commonly called the "drip" or the "clap." It is reported to be one of the most common STDs in the United States and is caused by a bacterium called* Neisseria gonorrhoeae, *which thrives in the moist mucous membranes lining the mouth, throat, vagina, cervix, urethra, and anal tract.* The bacterium is spread by contact between the infected moist membranes of one individual and the membranes of another.

Early symptoms of gonorrhea are more likely to appear in males, who are likely to have a discharge from the penis and burning during urination. The early sign of gonorrhea in females, often undetectable, is a mild, sometimes irritating vaginal discharge. Complications of gonorrhea in males include prostate, bladder, and kidney problems, as well as sterility. In females, gonorrhea may lead to pelvic inflammatory disease, sterility, and abdominal adhesions (Crooks & Bauer, 2002).

Gonorrhea can be successfully treated in its early stages with penicillin or other antibiotics. Although the incidence of gonorrhea has declined, more than 500,000 cases are still reported annually, and the highest rates among women and second highest among men are in adolescence (Centers for Disease Control, 2000).

Syphilis   **Syphilis** *is a sexually transmitted disease caused by the bacterium* Treponema pallidum, *a member of the spirochete family.* The spirochete needs a warm, moist environment to survive, and it is transmitted by penile-vaginal, oral-genital, or anal contact. It can also be transmitted from a pregnant woman to her fetus after the fourth month of pregnancy. If the mother is treated before this time with penicillin, the syphilis will not be transmitted to the fetus.

If untreated, syphilis may progress through four phases: primary (chancre sores appear), secondary (general skin rash occurs), latent (can last for several years in which no overt symptoms are present), and tertiary (cardiovascular disease, blindness, paralysis, skin ulcers, liver damage, and mental problems may occur) (Crooks & Bauer, 2002). In its early phases, syphilis can be effectively treated with penicillin. Approximately 100,000 cases of syphilis are reported in the United States each year.

Chlamydia   **Chlamydia,** *the most common of all sexually transmitted diseases, is named for* Chlamydia trachomatis, *an organism that spreads by sexual contact and infects the genital organs of both sexes.* Although fewer individuals have heard of chlamydia than

sexually transmitted diseases (STDs)
Diseases that are contracted primarily through sexual contact. This contact is not limited to vaginal intercourse but includes oral-genital contact and anal-genital contact as well.

gonorrhea
Reported to be one of the most common STDs in the United States, this sexually transmitted disease is caused by a bacterium called *Neisseria gonorrhoeae,* which thrives in the moist mucous membranes lining the mouth, throat, vagina, cervix, urethra, and anal tract. This disease is commonly called the "drip" or the "clap."

syphilis
A sexually transmitted disease caused by the bacterium *Treponema pallidum,* a spirochete.

chlamydia
The most common of all sexually transmitted diseases, named for *Chlamydia trachomatis,* an organism that spreads by sexual contact and infects the genital organs of both sexes.

have heard of gonorrhea and syphilis, its incidence is much higher (Morris, Warren, & Aral, 1993). About 4 million Americans are infected with chlamydia each year. About 10 percent of all college students have chlamydia. This STD is highly infectious, and women run a 70 percent risk of contracting it in a single sexual encounter. The male risk is estimated at between 25 and 50 percent.

Many females with chlamydia have few or no symptoms. When symptoms do appear, they include disrupted menstrual periods, pelvic pain, elevated temperature, nausea, vomiting, and headache. Possible symptoms of chlamydia in males are a discharge from the penis and burning during urination.

Because many females with chlamydia are asymptomatic, the disease often goes untreated and the chlamydia spreads to the upper reproductive tract where it can cause pelvic inflammatory disease (PID). The resultant scarring of tissue in the fallopian tubes can result in infertility or in ectopic pregnancies (tubal pregnancies), or a pregnancy in which the fertilized egg is implanted outside the uterus. One-quarter of females who have PID become infertile; multiple cases of PID increase the rate of infertility to half. Some researchers suggest that chlamydia is the number one preventable cause of female infertility.

We now turn to two STDs that are caused by viruses—genital herpes and acquired immune deficiency syndrome (AIDS). Neither of these STDs is curable.

genital herpes
A sexually transmitted disease caused by a large family of viruses of different strains. These strains produce other, nonsexually transmitted diseases such as chicken pox and mononucleosis.

Genital Herpes   *Genital herpes is a sexually transmitted disease caused by a large family of viruses with many different strains. These strains produce other, nonsexually transmitted diseases such as chicken pox and mononucleosis.* Three to five days after contact, itching and tingling can occur, followed by an eruption of sores and blisters. The attacks can last up to three weeks and can recur in a few weeks or a few years.

Although drugs such as acyclovir can be used to alleviate symptoms, there is no known cure for herpes. Therefore, people infected with herpes often experience severe emotional distress in addition to the considerable physical discomfort. The virus can be transmitted through nonlatex condoms and foams, making infected individuals reluctant about sex, angry about the unpredictability of their lives, and fearful that they won't be able to cope with the pain of the next attack. For these reasons, support groups for victims of herpes have been established.

AIDS
Acquired immune deficiency syndrome, a primarily sexually transmitted disease caused by the HIV virus, which destroys the body's immune system.

AIDS   No single STD has had a greater impact on sexual behavior, or created more public fear in the last two decades, than AIDS. We will explore its nature and incidence, how it is transmitted, stages of the disease, and prevention.

AIDS is a sexually transmitted disease that is caused by a virus, the human immunodeficiency virus (HIV), that destroys the body's immune system. Following exposure to HIV, an individual is vulnerable to germs that a normal immune system could destroy.

As of June, 2000, there were almost 4,000 cases of AIDS in 13- to 19-year-olds in the United States (Centers for Disease Control and Prevention, 2001b). Among those 20 to 24 years of age, more than 26,000 AIDS cases had been reported. Because of its long incubation period between infection with the HIV virus and AIDS diagnosis, most of the 20- to 24-year-olds were infected during adolescence.

The greatest concern about AIDS is in sub-Saharan Africa, where it has reached epidemic proportions (Pisani, 2000; World Health Organization, 2000). Adolescent girls in many African countries are especially vulnerable to infection with the HIV virus by adult men. Approximately six times as many adolescent girls as boys have AIDS in these countries. In Kenya, 25 percent of the 15- to 19-year-old girls are HIV positive, compared to only 4 percent of this age group of boys. In Botswana, more than 30 percent of the adolescent girls who are pregnant are infected with the HIV virus.

In the United States, more adolescent boys than adolescent girls are infected with the HIV virus (Centers for Disease Control and Prevention, 2001b). The Africa and U.S. gender difference is likely due to the much higher transmission of the HIV virus to adolescent girls by adult men in sub-Saharan Africa and the higher transmission in homosexual males than heterosexual individuals in the United States.

There continues to be great concern about AIDS in many parts of the world, not just sub-Saharan Africa. In the United States, prevention is especially targeted at groups that show the highest incidence of AIDS. These include drug users, individuals with other sexually transmitted diseases, young homosexual males, individuals living in low-income circumstances, Latinos, and African Americans (Centers for Disease Control and Prevention, 2001b). Also, in recent years, there has been increased heterosexual transmission of the HIV virus in the United States.

There are some differences in AIDS cases in U.S. adolescents, compared to AIDS cases in U.S. adults:

• A higher percentage of adolescent AIDS cases are acquired by heterosexual transmission.
• A higher percentage of adolescents are asymptomatic individuals (who will become symptomatic in adulthood).
• A higher percentage of African American and Latino cases occur in adolescence.
• A special set of ethical and legal issues are involved in testing and informing partners and parents of adolescents.
• There is less use and availability of contraceptives in adolescence.

In one study, condom use among U.S. adolescents who are at the greatest risk of contracting AIDS—for example, intravenous drug users—was significantly below average (Sonenstein, Pleck, & Ku, 1989). Only 21 percent of the adolescents who had used intravenous drugs or whose partners had used intravenous drugs used condoms. Among adolescents who reported having sex with prostitutes, only 17 percent said that they used condoms. And among adolescents who reported having sex with five or more partners in the last year, only 37 percent reported using condoms. Adolescents who reported homosexual intercourse reported the highest condom use—66 percent.

Transmission of HIV Experts say that AIDS can be transmitted only by sexual contact, the sharing of needles, or blood transfusion (which in the last few years has been tightly monitored) (Kelly, 2000). Although 90 percent of AIDS cases in the United States, continue to occur among homosexual males and intravenous drug users, a disproportionate increase among females who are heterosexual partners of bisexual males or of intravenous drug users has been recently noted. This increase suggests that the risk of AIDS may be increasing among heterosexual individuals who have multiple sex partners. Figure 11.5 on page 366 describes what's risky and what's not, regarding AIDS.

Just asking a date about his or her sexual behavior does not guarantee protection from AIDS and other sexually transmitted diseases. For example, in one investigation, 655 college students were asked to answer questions about lying and sexual behavior (Cochran & Mays, 1990). Of the 422 respondents who said they were sexually active, 34 percent of the men and 10 percent of the women said they had lied so their partner would have sex with them. Much higher percentages—47 percent of the men and 60 percent of the women—said they had been lied to by a potential sexual partner. When asked what aspects of their past they would be most likely to lie about, more than 40 percent of the men and women said they would understate the number of their sexual partners. Twenty percent of the men, but only 4 percent of the women, said they would lie about their results from an AIDS blood test.

THINKING CRITICALLY

Sexual Behavior and Moral Choices: Privacy and Protection

Caroline contracted genital herpes from her boyfriend whom she had been dating for the past three years. After breaking off that relationship and spending some time on her own, Caroline began dating Charles. Before becoming sexually involved with him, Caroline told Charles about her herpes infection, thinking that it was the right thing to do. Charles seemed accepting of the news, but soon after the discussion he began treating Caroline differently. He became distant and cold toward her, and eventually broke off their relationship saying that it "just wasn't working." Caroline firmly believed it was because she had told him about the herpes.

Caroline later met Jeff, whom she really liked and wanted to start dating. As they became closer to developing a sexual relationship, Caroline felt that she should tell Jeff about the herpes, but she was afraid that he also would abandon her. She thought that if she arranged it so that they never had sexual contact when she had herpes blisters (the time when infecting someone else is most likely to occur), she could protect him. She also thought that if they used latex condoms for protection, he would be safe, even though condoms can break.

Is it acceptable for Caroline to withhold this information from Jeff? If Jeff should know, in what ways would it be best to tell him? If Caroline did tell Jeff, and he did end their relationship, would telling him have been a mistake? Does Jeff have a right to know? Does Caroline have a right to privacy?

The AIDS virus is not transmitted like colds or the flu, but by an exchange of infected blood, semen, or vaginal fluids. This usually occurs during sexual intercourse, in sharing drug needles, or to babies infected before or during birth.

You Won't Get AIDS From:

Everyday contact with individuals around you in school or the workplace, at parties, child-care centers, or stores

Swimming in a pool, even if someone in the pool has the AIDS virus

A mosquito bite, or from bedbugs, lice, flies, or other insects

Saliva, sweat, tears, urine, or feces

A kiss

Clothes, telephones, or toilet seats

Using a glass or eating utensils that someone else has used

Being on a bus, train, or crowded elevator with an individual who is infected with the virus or who has AIDS

Blood Donations and Transfusions:

You will not come into contact with the AIDS virus by donating blood at a blood bank.

The risk of getting AIDS from a blood transfusion has been greatly reduced. Donors are screened for risk factors, and donated blood is tested for HIV antibodies.

Risky Behavior:

Your chances of coming into contact with the virus increase if you:

Have more than one sex partner

Share drug needles and syringes

Engage in anal, vaginal, or oral sex without a condom

Perform vaginal or oral sex with someone who shoots drugs

Engage in sex with someone you don't know well or with someone who has several sex partners

Engage in unprotected sex (without a condom) with an infected individual

Safe Behavior:

Not having sex

Having sex that does not involve fluid exchange (rubbing, holding, massage)

Sex with one mutually faithful, uninfected partner

Sex with proper protection

Not shooting drugs

Source: *America Responds to AIDS*. U.S. Government educational pamphlet, 1988.

▇ FIGURE 11.5
Understanding AIDS: What's Risky, What's Not

HIV InfoWeb
Center for AIDS Prevention Studies
HIV/STD Education
Signs of HIV Infection in Females
http://www.mhhe.com/santrocka9

Prevention   Because it is possible, and even probable among high-risk groups, to have more than one STD at a time, efforts to prevent one disease help reduce the prevalence of other diseases. Efforts to prevent AIDS can also help prevent adolescent pregnancy and other sexually related problems. Because of the high rate of sexually transmitted diseases, it is crucial that both teenagers and adults understand these diseases (Klaus, 1997).

One study evaluated 37 AIDS prevention projects with children and adolescents (Janz & others, 1996). Small-group discussions, outreach to populations engaged in high-risk behaviors, and training of peers and volunteers were the activities rated the most effective. Small-group discussions, with an emphasis on open communication and repetition of messages, are excellent opportunities for adolescents to learn and share information about AIDS. The best outreach programs are culturally tailored and include incentives to participate. Outreach workers who are familiar and respected might be able to break through the barriers of fear and mistrust to ensure that appropriate messages are heard and heeded. For incentives to work, they also must be tailored for specific populations. School-age children might be attracted by academic credit or a stipend. For injection drug users, food, shelter, and a safe place to congregate might attract participants. For working women, child care and an opportunity to spend time with other adults might draw participants. The use of peer educators is often an effective strategy. As role models, peers can mirror healthy lifestyles for the target population as well as provide reinforcement and shape group norms in support of behavioral change. Peer educators often are effective at getting adolescents involved in AIDS prevention projects.

So far we have discussed these problems that involve adolescent sexuality: adolescent pregnancy and sexually transmitted diseases. Next, we will explore these adolescent sexuality problems: forcible sexual behavior and sexual harassment.

Forcible Sexual Behavior and Sexual Harassment

Most people choose to engage in sexual intercourse or other sexual activities, but, unfortunately, some people force others to engage in sex.

Forcible Sexual Behavior   **Rape** *is forcible sexual intercourse with a person who does not give consent.* Legal definitions of rape vary from state to state. In some states, husbands are allowed to force their wives to have sex, in others they are not, for example. Because of the difficulties involved in reporting rape, the actual incidence is not easily determined. It appears that rape occurs most often in large cities, where it has been reported that 8 of every 10,000 women 12 years old and older are raped each year. Nearly 200,000 rapes are reported each year in the United States. Ninety-five percent of rapes are committed by males.

Why is rape so pervasive in the American culture? Feminist writers believe that males are socialized to be sexually aggressive, to regard females as inferior beings, and to view their own pleasure as the most important objective. Researchers have found the following characteristics common among rapists: Aggression enhances the offender's sense of power or masculinity; rapists are angry at females generally; and they want to hurt their victims.

An increasing concern is **date, or acquaintance, rape,** *which is coercive sexual activity directed at someone with whom the perpetrator is at least casually acquainted.* Date rape is an increasing problem in high schools and on college campuses. About two-thirds of college men admit that they fondle women against their will, and one-half admit to forcing sexual activity. In one recent study, about two-thirds of the sexual victimization incidents were perpetrated by a romantic acquaintance (Flanagan, 1996). And in another recent study, 15 percent of adolescent girls reported that they had experienced what they considered to be date rape (Vicary, Klingaman, & Harkness, 1995).

Rape is a traumatic experience for the victim and those close to her or him. The rape victim initially feels shock and numbness, and often is acutely disorganized. Some women show their distress through words and tears, others show more internalized suffering. As victims strive to get their lives back to normal, they might experience depression, fear, and anxiety for months or years. Sexual dysfunctions, such as reduced sexual desire and the inability to reach orgasm, occur in 50 percent of rape victims. Many rape victims make lifestyle changes, moving to a new apartment or refusing to go out at night. About one-fifth of rape victims have made a suicide attempt—a rate eight times higher than that of women who have not been raped.

A female's recovery depends on both her coping abilities and psychological adjustment prior to the assault. Social support from parents, partner, and others close to her are important factors in recovery, as is the availability of professional counseling, which sometimes is obtained through a rape crisis center (Koss, 1993). Many rape victims become empowered by reporting their rape to the police and assisting the prosecution of the rapist if caught. However, women who take a legal approach are especially encouraged to use supportive counselors to aid them throughout the legal ordeal. Each female must be allowed to make her own, individual decision about whether to report the rape or not.

Although most victims of rape are female, rape of men does occur. Men in prisons are especially vulnerable to rape, usually by heterosexuals who are using rape to establish their domination and power within the prison. Though it might seem impossible for a man to be raped by a woman, a man's erection is not completely under his voluntary control, and some cases of male rape by women have been reported (Sarrel & Masters, 1982). Although male victims account for fewer than 5 percent of all rapes, the trauma that males suffer is just as great as that experienced by females.

Sexual Harassment   Females encounter sexual harassment in many different forms—ranging from sexist remarks and covert physical contact (patting, brushing against bodies) to blatant propositions and sexual assaults (Fitzgerald, 2000; Paludi, 1998). Literally millions of females experience such sexual harassment each year in educational and work settings. In one study, 85 percent of eighth- to eleventh-grade girls reported that

rape
Forcible sexual intercourse with a person who does not give consent.

date, or acquaintance, rape
Coercive sexual activity directed at someone with whom the perpetrator is at least casually acquainted.

Sexual Assault
Sexual Harassment
Sexual Harassment in Schools
http://www.mhhe.com/santrocka9

they were often sexually harassed (American Association of University Women, 1993). A surprisingly large percentage (75 percent) of boys also said they often were sexually harassed. Sexual comments, jokes, gestures, and looks were the most common forms of harassment. Students also reported other objectionable behavior, ranging from being the subject of sexual rumors to being forced to do something sexual.

The Office for Civil Rights in the U.S. Department of Education published a 40-page policy guide on sexual harassment. In this guide, a distinction is made between quid pro quo and hostile environment sexual harassment (Chmieleski, 1997). **Quid pro quo sexual harassment** *occurs when a school employee threatens to base an educational decision (such as a grade) on a student's submission to unwelcome sexual conduct.* For example, a teacher gives a student an A for allowing the teacher's sexual advances, or the teacher gives the student an F for resisting the teacher's approaches. **Hostile environment sexual harassment** *occurs when students are subjected to unwelcome sexual conduct that is so severe, persistent, or pervasive that it limits the students' ability to benefit from their education.* Such a hostile environment is usually created by a series of incidents, such as repeated sexual overtures.

Sexual harassment is a form of power and dominance of one person over another, which can result in harmful consequences for the victim. Sexual harassment can be damaging especially when the perpetrators are teachers and other adults who have considerable power and authority over students (Lee & others, 1995). As a society, we need to be less tolerant of sexual harassment (Firpo-Triplett, 1997).

Sexual abuse in adolescent dating relationships also is a major concern. In one recent study, approximately 2,000 ninth- through twelfth-grade females were asked about the extent to which they had experienced physical and sexual violence (Silverman & others, 2001). About 20 percent of the females said they had been physically or sexually abused by a dating partner. Further, the physical and sexual abuse was linked with substance use.

quid pro quo sexual harassment
Sexual harassment in which a school employee threatens to base an educational decision (such as a grade) on a student's submission to unwelcome conduct.

hostile environment sexual harassment
Sexual harassment in which students are subjected to unwelcome sexual conduct that is so severe, persistent, or pervasive that it limits the students' ability to benefit from their education.

Since the last review, we have discussed a number of ideas about sexually transmitted diseases, forcible sexual behavior, and sexual harassment. This review should help you to reach your learning goals related to these topics.

FOR YOUR REVIEW

Learning Goal 6
Describe sexually transmitted diseases

- Sexually transmitted diseases (STDs) are contracted primarily through sexual contact. The contact is not limited to vaginal intercourse but includes oral-genital and anal-genital contact as well.
- Commonly called the "drip" or "clap," gonorrhea is reported to be one of the most common STDs in the United States. Syphilis is caused by the bacterium *Treponema pallidum,* a spirochete. Chlamydia is the most common STD. Genital herpes is caused by a family of viruses with different strains.
- AIDS (acquired immune deficiency syndrome) is caused by the HIV virus, which destroys the body's immune system. Currently, the rate of AIDS in U.S. adolescents is relatively low, but it has reached epidemic proportions in sub-Sahara Africa, especially in adolescent girls. Because of the long incubation period, many 20- to 24-year-olds who are diagnosed with AIDS were infected during adolescence. AIDS can be transmitted through sexual contact, sharing needles, and blood transfusions. A number of projects are focusing on AIDS prevention.

Learning Goal 7
Explain forcible sexual behavior and sexual harassment

- Some individuals force others to have sex with them, Rape is forcible sexual intercourse with a person who does not give consent. About 95 percent of rapes are committed by males. An increasing concern is date, or acquaintance, rape.
- Sexual harassment is a form of power of one person over another. Sexual harassment of adolescents is widespread. Two forms are quid pro quo and hostile environment sexual harassment.

So far in this chapter we have studied sexuality as a normal aspect of adolescent development, sexual attitudes and behaviors, and adolescent sexual problems. Next, we will turn our attention to adolescents' sexual knowledge and sexual education.

SEXUAL KNOWLEDGE AND SEX EDUCATION

Given the high rate of sexually transmitted diseases, a special concern is the knowledge that both adolescents and adults have about these diseases and about other aspects of sexuality. How sexually literate are Americans? What are adolescents' sources of sex education? What is the role of schools in sex education?

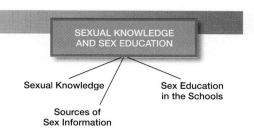

Sexual Knowledge

In one investigation of American females aged 15 to 17, one-third did not know at what stage of their monthly menstrual cycle they were most likely to get pregnant (Loewen & Leigh, 1986). In another study, a majority of adolescents believed that pregnancy risk is greatest during menstruation (Zelnick & Kantner, 1977). In yet another study, 12 percent of more than 8,000 students thought that birth control pills provide some protection against AIDS, and 23 percent believed they could tell by just looking at a potential sexual partner whether he or she was infected with HIV (Hechinger, 1992). In one recent national survey of more than 1,500 adolescents 12 to 18 years old, the respondents said that they have enough information to understand pregnancy but not enough about how to obtain and use birth control (Kaiser Family Foundation, 1996).

According to June Reinisch (1990), director of the Kinsey Institute for Sex, Gender, and Reproduction, U.S. citizens know more about how their automobiles function than about how their bodies function sexually. American adolescents and adults are not sheltered from sexual messages. According to Reinisch, adolescents too often are inundated with sexual messages, but not sexual facts. Sexual information is abundant, but much of it is misinformation. In some cases, even sex education teachers display sexual ignorance. One high school sex education teacher referred to erogenous zones as "erroneous zones," possibly causing students to wonder if their sexually sensitive zones were in error!

Sources of Sex Information

One 14-year-old adolescent recently was asked where he learned about sex. He responded, "In the streets." Asked if this was the only place, he said, "Well, I learned some more from *Playboy* and the other sex magazines." What about school, he was asked. He responded, "No, they talk about hygiene, but not much that could help you out." When asked about his parents' contributions, he replied, "They haven't told me one thing."

Parents are an important missing ingredient in the fight against adolescent pregnancy and sexually transmitted diseases (Brock & Jennings, 1993). A large majority of adolescents say that they cannot talk freely with their parents about sexual matters. Surveys indicate that about 17 percent of adolescents' sex education comes from mothers and only about 2 percent from fathers (Thornburg, 1981). While parents, especially fathers, have seldom been sources of sex education for adolescents, adolescents report that, when they can talk with their parents openly and freely about sex, they are less likely to be sexually active. Contraceptive use by female adolescents also increases when adolescents report that they can communicate about sex with their parents (Fisher, 1987).

As just noted, adolescents are far more likely to have conversations about sex with their mothers than with their fathers. This is true of both female and male adolescents, although female adolescents report having more frequent conversations about sex with their mothers than their male counterparts do (Feldman & Rosenthal, 1999; Lefkowitz & others, 1999). Also, in one recent study that involved videotaped conversations about sexual matters between mothers and adolescents, adolescent girls were more responsive and enthusiastic than adolescent boys were (Lefkowitz & others, 1999).

In a survey of all 1,152 students at a midwestern high school, students were asked where they learned about various aspects of sex (Thornburg, 1981). As in other investigations, the most common source of sex information was peers, followed by literature, mothers, schools, and experience. Though schools are usually thought of as a main source of sex education, only 15 percent of the adolescents' information about sex came from school instruction. In one study, college students said that they got more sex education from reading than from any other source (Andre, Frevert, & Schuchmann, 1989).

Sex Education in the Schools

A recent survey found that 93 percent of Americans support the teaching of sex education in high schools and 84 percent support its teaching in middle/junior high schools (SIECUS, 1999). The dramatic increase in HIV/AIDS and other sexually transmitted diseases is the main reason that Americans have increasingly supported sex education in schools in recent years. This survey also found that more than 8 of 10 Americans think that adolescents should be given information to protect themselves from unwanted pregnancies and STDs, as well as about abstinence. And more than 8 of 10 Americans rejected the idea that providing such sex education encourages sexual activity.

The nature of sex education in schools is changing. In one recent study, trends in sex education in American public schools from 1988 through 1999 were examined (Darroch, Landy, & Singh, 2000). Among the results of the survey:

- Some topics—how HIV is transmitted, STDs, abstinence, how to resist peer pressure to have intercourse, and the correct way to use a condom—were taught in earlier grades in 1999 than in 1988.
- In 1999, 23 percent of secondary school sex education teachers taught abstinence as the only way of preventing pregnancy and STDs, compared to only 2 percent in 1988. Teachers surveyed in 1999 also were more likely than those in 1988 to cite abstinence as the most important message they wished to convey (41 percent versus 25 percent).
- Steep declines occurred between 1988 and 1999 in the percentage of teachers who supported teaching about birth control, abortion, and sexual orientation.

In sum, sex education in U.S. schools today is increasingly focused on abstinence and is less likely to present students with comprehensive teaching that includes information about birth control, abortion, and sexual orientation.

In one recent study, 1,789 fifth- and sixth-grade U.S. teachers were asked about the nature of their sex education instruction in 1999 (Landry, Singh, & Darroch, 2000). The results included:

- Seventy-two percent said that sex education is taught in their schools at either the fifth grade, sixth grade, or both.
- More than 75 percent of teachers who include sex education in their instruction cover these topics: puberty, HIV and AIDS transmission, alcohol and drug use, and how to stick to a decision. However, many fifth- and sixth-grade teachers do not teach sex education at all. It was estimated that overall these topics are taught in about half of fifth- and sixth-grade classrooms.
- More than half of the teachers include the topic of abstinence in the sex education instruction.

Sex education programs in schools might not by themselves prevent adolescent pregnancy and sexually transmitted diseases. Researchers have found that sex education classes do improve adolescents' knowledge about human sexuality but do not always change their sexual behavior. When sex education programs are combined with contraceptive availability, the pregnancy rates of adolescents are more likely to drop (Wallis, 1985). This has led to the development of *school-linked* rather than school-based approaches to sex education and pregnancy prevention (Kirby & others, 1993). In one program pioneered by some Baltimore public schools in cooperation with Johns Hopkins University, family-planning clinics are located adjacent to the schools (Zabin, 1986).

"I don't like this A in sex education."

Copyright © Glenn Bernhardt.

The clinics send a nurse and social worker into the schools, where they make formal presentations about the services available from the clinics and about sexuality. They also are available to the students for counseling several hours each day. The same health personnel also conduct after-school sessions at the clinics. These sessions involve further counseling, films, and family-planning information. The results have been very positive. Students who participated in the programs delayed their first intercourse longer than did students in a control group. After 28 months, the pregnancy rate had declined by 30 percent in the program schools, while it rose 60 percent in the control-group schools. This program demonstrates that a key dimension of pregnancy prevention is the link between information and support services (Kenney, 1987).

However, some critics argue that school-linked health clinics promote premarital sex and encourage abortion for pregnant adolescents. These critics believe that more effort should be devoted to promoting adolescents' abstention from sex. Supporters of the school-linked clinics argue that sexual activity in adolescence has become a normative behavior and, therefore, that interventions should focus on teaching responsible sexual behavior and providing access to contraception (Dryfoos, 1995). Further, in one recent study, the effects of a school-wide program called "Safer Choices," which discussed pregnancy prevention and condom use, was effective in decreasing the number of adolescents who had sex without a condom and in decreasing the number of individuals with whom adolescents engaged in sex (Basen-Enquist & others, 2001).

THINKING CRITICALLY

Applying Psychology Concepts to Your Own Sexual History

Think about how you learned the "facts of life." Did most of your information come from well-informed sources? Were you able to talk freely and openly with your own parents about what to expect sexually? Did you acquire some false beliefs through your trial-and-error efforts? As you grew older, did you discover any aspects of your sexual knowledge that had to be revised because it was in error? Based on your experience in learning about sexuality, how do you think sex education should be addressed as a larger health issue in society? How would you develop your psychological argument based on the evidence?

The AIDS epidemic has led to an increased awareness of the importance of sex education in adolescence.

Sex is more demystified and less dramatized in Sweden than in the United States. Adolescent pregnancy rates are much lower in Sweden than in the United States.

In the United States, adolescents are enticed with stories of romantic love and portrayals of sex in the media. Boy-girl contact is encouraged but we are reluctant to discuss sex openly, unwilling to make contraceptives including condoms available to adolescents, and fail to offer alternatives other than abstinence (Crockett, Raffaelli, & Moilanen, in press). The contrast between the United States and other Western nations is remarkable. For example, the Swedish State Commission on Sex Education recommends that students should gain knowledge that will help them to experience sexual life as a source of happiness and fellowship with others. In contrast, U.S. sex education typically has focused on the hazards of sex and on the need to protect adolescent females from their male predators (Fine, 1988).

Swedish adolescents are sexually active at an earlier age than are American adolescents, and they are exposed to even more explicit sex on television. However, the Swedish National Board of Education has developed a curriculum that ensures that every child in the country, beginning at age 7, will experience a thorough grounding in reproductive biology and, by the age of 10 or 12, will have been introduced to information about various forms of contraception. Teachers are expected to handle the subject of sex whenever it becomes relevant, regardless of the subject they are teaching. The idea is to dedramatize and demystify sex so that familiarity will make students less vulnerable to unwanted pregnancy and sexually transmitted diseases. American society is not nearly so open about sex education.

Sweden has been quite successful in preventing adolescent pregnancy. Despite a relatively early onset of sexual activity, the adolescent pregnancy rate in Sweden is one of the lowest in the world.

SEXUAL WELL-BEING, SOCIAL POLICY, AND ADOLESCENTS

Sexual Well-Being and Developmental Transitions   Social Policy and Adolescent Sexuality

SEXUAL WELL-BEING, SOCIAL POLICY, AND ADOLESCENTS

Earlier in the chapter, we discussed some of the things that can go wrong in adolescent sexuality, such as unintended pregnancy, sexually transmitted diseases, forcible sexual behavior, and sexual harassment. It is important to remember that in general sexual interest and activity are a normal—not an abnormal—aspect of adolescent development. However, as we mentioned earlier in the chapter, American society dispenses mixed messages. We expect children to be asexual but normal adults to be sexually responsive (in the context of marriage). Yet we provide no clear agreements about how this transition from the asexual child to the sexual adult should take place. This is one of life's most important transitions, and it deserves more attention. Let's now explore some links between developmental transitions in adolescence and sexual well-being.

Sexual Well-Being and Developmental Transitions

All societies have mechanisms for regulating adolescent sexuality, and some are more successful than others (Brooks-Gunn & Paikoff, 1997; Graber & Brooks-Gunn, in press). Variations in parental control, peer group influence, societal norms, and neighborhood settings occur within and across societies. Historical changes also affect how much a culture's subgroups adhere to societal norms. In traditional societies, marriage is often linked with sexual maturity, and the first marriage occurs during the adolescent years (Paige & Paige, 1985). But in more industrialized societies, which require more formal educational skills, first marriages are delayed until early adulthood. The trends of an earlier occurrence of puberty and a later age of marriage have increased the time period between onset of reproductive maturity and marriage. In 1890, the interval was just over 7 years; today it is about 12 years, which might seem a long time to an adolescent or young adult experiencing sexual arousal.

No matter how much some adults might like to ignore the fact, sex has great meaning in adolescents' lives. Adolescents form their sexual identity, engage in sexual exploration (whether kissing, intercourse, or just dreaming about sex), and negotiate autonomy and intimacy in sexual contexts.

Most research on adolescent sexuality has focused on understanding sexual intercourse and the use of contraception rather than examining its multifaceted, contextual dimensions. The study of adolescent sexuality can be broadened by exploring adolescents' feelings about puberty and their bodies, sexual arousal and desire, sexual behavior as more than intercourse, and safe sex as being more than the use of condoms (Graber, Brooks-Gunn, & Galen, 1999). According to Jeanne Brooks-Gunn and Roberta Paikoff (1997), five developmental issues need to be examined more thoroughly in the study of adolescent sexuality:

- *Timing of behaviors associated with behavior.* Being an early-maturing girl is associated with having sexual intercourse. Indeed, maturing early sometimes results in a cascade of events, such as early dating, having older friends, being pursued by older males, demanding more autonomy from parents, and spending more time in activities that are not supervised by adults. Thus, special attention needs to be given to the sexual vulnerability of early-maturing girls (Graber, Britto, & Brooks-Gunn, 1999).
- *Co-occurrence of health-related behaviors.* Early maturation is linked not only with sexual intercourse but also with early drinking and smoking. Many high-risk youth don't have just a single problem; they have multiple problems. The confluence of such problems as unprotected sexual intercourse, drug abuse, delinquency, and school-related difficulties places adolescents on a precarious developmental trajectory, especially when these problems appear in early adolescence.
- *The contexts of sexual behavior.* Sexual behavior in adolescence is influenced by contextual factors, such as poverty and how long it persists, neighborhood quality, school characteristics, and peer group norms (Brooks-Gunn & others, 1993). At many different points in this chapter, we have seen that the incidences of sexual intercourse and adolescent pregnancy differ across and within cultures.
- *The timing of sexual experiences.* Young adolescents should not have sexual intercourse. They are less likely to engage in protected intercourse than older adolescents, increasing the probability of pregnancy. Cognitively and emotionally, young adolescents have difficulty handling sexuality's intense, varied feelings and understanding sexuality's complex meanings.
- *Gender and sexuality.* The sexual experiences of many young adolescent girls are involuntary or at the very least occur in settings in which male dominance plays a role. Further, as we saw earlier in the chapter, sexual scripts are often different for females and males.

The study of adolescent sexuality can be reframed to take into account behaviors and feelings, to promote a more multidimensional approach, and to explore sexual transitions beyond first intercourse and first contraceptive use. Healthy sexual pathways include (Brooks-Gunn & Paikoff, 1997):

- Practicing sexual abstinence but having positive feelings about one's body
- Not engaging in sexual intercourse with another individual but engaging in sexual exploration
- Engaging in sexual intercourse with another individual in the context of a committed relationship in late adolescence or early adulthood and using safe sex practices
- Participating in preintercourse behaviors with another individual in early adolescence, which might or might not result in sexual intercourse in late adolescence

Adolescents should be encouraged to do community service in childcare centers. This can help them to see first-hand what is required to raise children.

An important social policy agenda is to educate adolescents about parenthood.

Social Policy and Adolescent Sexuality

Adolescents should learn about human sexuality and reproduction early, *before* they become sexually active. Programs that promote sexual health should not begin any later than early adolescence. Information about preventing transmission of the AIDS virus should be included in education about sexuality. For example, many young adolescents do not know that the incubation period for AIDS can be 10 or more years and that a pregnant female can transmit HIV to her fetus. Interventions should identify the sexually oriented encounters that adolescents are likely to experience and provide life skills training on ways to avoid such situations or manage them more effectively. Schools, families, and the media can contribute to this effort.

Adolescent pregnancy is also an important target of social policy initiatives (Dannhausen-Brun, Shalowitz, & Berry, 1997). Most adolescent pregnancies are unintended. Any sound educational approach needs to make it very clear that becoming a parent at the right time—after adolescence—is critical to optimal development, for both the parent and the offspring.

The Carnegie Foundation's report *Starting Points: Meeting the Needs of Our Youngest Children* (1994) emphasized the importance of preparing adolescents for responsible parenthood. When individuals make an informed, thoughtful commitment to having children, they are more likely to become good parents. Individuals who are unprepared for the opportunities and responsibilities of parenthood create great risks for their children.

Our nation needs a substantial expansion of efforts to educate adolescents about parenthood. Families are an important source of such information, but so are schools, places of worship, and community organizations. Adolescents should be encouraged to do community service in childcare centers, because this will help them understand what is required to raise young children.

If adolescents do have children, what policy recommendations could help them? Four such recommendations are these (Chase-Lansdale & Brooks-Gunn, 1994): First, the life-course diversity of adolescent mothers suggests that no single service delivery program is universally applicable. Rather, different types of programs should be developed for different types of adolescent mothers. For example, those who have dropped out of school need different services than those who graduate from high school and are employed. Second, services should be expanded to include elementary-age children. Despite the fact that most studies show more negative consequences for older rather than younger children, most child-oriented services target infants and preschool children.

Two other policy implications involve the coordination of services and family systems. Better coordination of services for mothers and children is needed. Historically, programs have targeted either mothers (emphasizing work training) or children (emphasizing early enrichment) but have not linked the lives of adolescent mothers and their children. Also, a family systems perspective is missing from policy perspectives. Grandmothers are often significant members of teenage mothers' families, and service programs need to take this into account. Virtually no programs target grandmothers themselves. In addition, the family system might help or hinder the young mother's efforts to be an effective parent or to achieve economic security.

Since the last review, we have discussed a number of ideas about sexual knowledge and sex education, as well as about sexual well-being, social policy, and adolescents. This review should help you to reach your learning goals related to these topics.

☐ FOR YOUR REVIEW

Learning Goal 8
Evaluate sexual knowledge and sex education

- American adolescents and adults are not very knowledgeable about sex. Sex information is abundant but too often it is misinformation. Adolescents get the most information about sex from peers, followed by literature, mothers, schools, and experience.
- A majority of American parents support sex education in schools and this support has increased in concert with increases in STDs, especially AIDS. Some experts believe that school-linked sex education that ties in with community health centers is a promising strategy.

Learning Goal 9
Explore sexual well-being, social policy, and adolescents

- We need to examine five issues more thoroughly: the timing of behaviors associated with adolescent sexuality, the co-occurrence of sexual behaviors and other health-related behaviors, the contexts of sexual behavior, the age at which transitions take place, and gender.
- We also need improved and expanded initiatives to reduce adolescent pregnancy and educate adolescents about the responsibilities of parenting.

In this chapter, we have focused on adolescent sexuality. On several occasions, we raised moral issues about sexual conduct. In chapter 12, we will explore moral development in much greater depth.

CHAPTER MAP

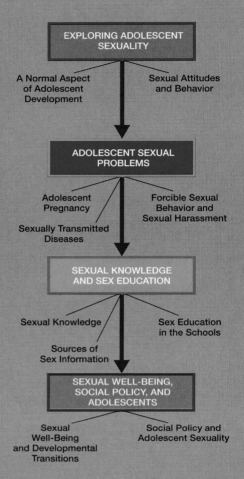

REACH YOUR LEARNING GOALS

At the beginning of the chapter we stated nine learning goals and encouraged you to review material related to these goals at five points in the chapter. This is a good time to return to these reviews. Use them to guide your study and help you to reach your learning goals.

Page 348

Learning Goal 1   Understand that sexuality is a normal aspect of adolescence

Page 356

Learning Goal 2   Know about adolescent heterosexual attitudes and behavior
Learning Goal 3   Describe adolescent homosexual attitudes and behavior
Learning Goal 4   Discuss self-stimulation and evaluate contraceptive use

Page 362

Learning Goal 5   Know about adolescent pregnancy

Page 368

Learning Goal 6   Describe sexually transmitted diseases
Learning Goal 7   Explain forcible sexual behavior and sexual harassment

Page 375

Learning Goal 8   Evaluate sexual knowledge and sex education
Learning Goal 9   Explore sexual well-being, social policy, and adolescents

KEY TERMS

sexual script 350
bisexual 352
sexually transmitted diseases (STDs) 363
gonorrhea 363
syphilis 363
chlamydia 363

genital herpes 364
AIDS 364
rape 367
date, or acquaintance, rape 367
quid pro quo sexual harassment 368
hostile environment sexual harassment 368

KEY PEOPLE

Shirley Feldman 345
Alfred Kinsey 352
Simon LeVay 353
Richard Savin-Williams 354
June Reinisch 369
Jeanne Brooks-Gunn 373

RESOURCES FOR IMPROVING THE LIVES OF ADOLESCENTS

AIDS Hotline

National AIDS Information Clearinghouse
P.O. Box 6003
Rockville, MD 20850
800–342–AIDS; 800–344–SIDA (Spanish);
800–AIDS–TTY (Deaf)

The people answering the hotline will respond to any questions children, youth, or adults have about HIV infection or AIDS. Pamphlets and other materials on AIDS are available.

Alan Guttmacher Institute

111 Fifth Avenue
New York, NY 10003
212–254–5656

The Alan Guttmacher Institute is an especially good resource for information about adolescent sexuality. The Institute publishes a well-respected journal, *Family Planning Perspectives,* which includes articles on many dimensions of sexuality, such as adolescent pregnancy, statistics on sexual behavior and attitudes, and sexually transmitted diseases.

Boys and Sex

(1991) by Wardell Pomeroy
New York: Delacorte Press

This book was written for adolescent boys and stresses the responsibility that comes with sexual maturity.

Girls and Sex

(1991) by Wardell Pomeroy
New York: Delacorte Press

The author poses a number of questions that young girls often ask about sex and then answers them. Many myths that young girls hear about sex are also demystified.

Mom, Dad, I'm Gay

(2001) by Ritch Savin-Williams
Washington, DC: American Psychological Association

Leading researcher on adolescent homosexual relationships, Ritch Savin-Williams examines how gay and lesbian adolescents develop their sexual identity.

National Sexually Transmitted Diseases Hotline

800–227–8922

This hotline provides information about a wide variety of sexually transmitted diseases.

Sex Information and Education Council of the United States (SIECUS)

130 West 42nd Street
New York, NY 10036
212–819–9770

This organization serves as an information clearinghouse about sex education. The group's objective is to promote the concept of human sexuality as an integration of physical, intellectual, emotional, and social dimensions.

TAKING IT TO THE NET

http://www.mhhe.com/santrocka9

1. Adolescence is a time when we not only are learning about sexuality but also are dealing with emerging sexuality and learning sexual scripts. Your instructor assigns a paper in which you are to evaluate the importance of sexual scripts in the change, or not, of gender roles. *What information will you include?*

2. While home for vacation you notice that your younger sister says that she wants to break up with her boyfriend but she fears he will hurt himself or someone else. She seems to feel guilty about wanting to break up because she seems to be the only person who loves and understands him. You begin to wonder if she might be in an abusive relationship. *What are the signs of an abusive dating relationship?*

3. Do you or any of your friends know a teenage father? *How does he cope with being a father? What special needs might he have in becoming a responsible father?*

Connect to *http://www.mhhe.com/santrocka9* to research the answers and complete these exercises. In some cases, you'll also find further instructions on this site.

CHAPTER MAP

WHAT IS MORAL DEVELOPMENT?

↓

MORAL THOUGHT

Piaget's Ideas and Cognitive Disequilibrium Theory

Reasoning in Different Social Cognitive Domains

Kohlberg's Ideas on Moral Development

Kohlberg's Critics

MORAL BEHAVIOR

Basic Processes

Altruism

Social Cognitive Theory of Moral Development

MORAL FEELINGS

Psychoanalytic Theory

The Contemporary Perspective

Child-Rearing Techniques

Empathy

MORAL EDUCATION

The Hidden Curriculum

Service Learning

Character Education

Cognitive Moral Education

Values Clarification

VALUES, RELIGION, AND CULTS

Values

Cults

Religion

MORAL DEVELOPMENT, VALUES, AND RELIGION

THE MORALS OF A HIGH SCHOOL NEWSPAPER

Fred, a senior in high school, wanted to publish a mimeographed newspaper for students so that he could express many of his opinions. He wanted to speak out against some of the school's rules, like the rule forbidding boys to have long hair.

Before Fred started his newspaper, he asked his principal for permission. The principal said that it would be all right if, before every publication, Fred would turn over all his articles for the principal's approval. Fred agreed and turned in several articles for approval. The principal approved all of them, and Fred published two issues of the paper in the next two weeks.

But the principal had not expected that Fred's newspaper would receive so much attention. Students were so excited about the paper that they began to organize protests against the hair regulation and the other school rules. Angry parents objected to Fred's opinions. They phoned the principal, telling him that the newspaper was unpatriotic and should not be published. As a result of the rising excitement, the principal ordered Fred to stop publishing. He gave as a reason that Fred's activities were disruptive to the operation of the school. (Rest, 1986, p.194)

The preceding story about Fred and his newspaper raises a number of questions related to adolescents' moral development:

Should the principal have stopped the newspaper?

When the welfare of the school is threatened, does the principal have the right to give orders to students?

Does the principal have the freedom of speech to say no in this case?

When the principal stopped the newspaper, was he preventing full discussion of an important problem?

Is Fred actually being loyal to his school and patriotic to his country?

What effect would stopping the newspaper have on the students' education in critical thinking and judgments?

Was Fred in any way violating the rights of others in publishing his own opinions?

It is one of the beautiful compensations of this life that no one can sincerely try to help another without helping himself.
—Charles Dudley Warner
American Essayist, 19th Century

What moral dilemmas might crop up for adolescents who are responsible for the school newspaper?

THIS CHAPTER IS ABOUT ADOLESCENTS' moral development, values, and religion. These topics have to do with right and wrong, what matters to people, and what people should do in their interactions and relationships with others. By the time you have completed this chapter, you should be able to reach these learning goals:

1 Know what moral development is

2 Explain moral thought

3 Discuss moral behavior

4 Understand moral feelings

5 Describe moral education

6 Evaluate values in adolescence

7 Discuss religion in adolescence

8 Know about cults

WHAT IS MORAL
DEVELOPMENT?

WHAT IS MORAL DEVELOPMENT?

moral development
Thoughts, feelings, and behaviors regarding standards of right and wrong.

Moral development is one of the oldest topics of interest to those who are curious about human nature. Today, most people have strong opinions about acceptable and unacceptable behavior, ethical and unethical behavior, and ways in which acceptable and ethical behaviors are to be fostered in adolescents.

Moral development *involves thoughts, feelings, and behaviors regarding standards of right and wrong.* Moral development has an *intrapersonal* dimension (a person's basic values and sense of self) and an *interpersonal* dimension (a focus on what people should do in their interactions with other people) (Walker, 1996; Walker & Pitts, 1998). The intrapersonal dimension regulates a person's activities when she or he is not engaged in social interaction. The interpersonal dimension regulates people's social interactions and arbitrates conflict. Let's now further explore some basic ideas about moral thoughts, feelings, and behaviors.

First, how do adolescents *reason* or *think* about rules for ethical conduct? For example, an adolescent can be presented with a story in which someone has a conflict about whether or not to cheat in a particular situation, such as taking an exam in school. The adolescent is asked to decide what is appropriate for the character to do and why. This was the strategy used in the section regarding Fred's newspaper. The focus is placed on the reasoning adolescents use to justify their moral decisions.

Second, how do adolescents actually *behave* in moral circumstances? For example, with regard to cheating, the emphasis is on observing adolescents' cheating and the environmental circumstances that produced and maintain the cheating. Adolescents might be observed through a one-way mirror as they are taking an exam. The observer might note whether they take out "cheat" notes, look at another student's answers, and so on.

Third, how do adolescents *feel* about moral matters? In the example of cheating, do the adolescents feel enough guilt to resist temptation? If adolescents do cheat, do feelings of guilt after the transgression keep them from cheating the next time they face temptation? The remainder of this discussion of moral development focuses on these three facets—thought, behavior, and feelings. Keep in mind that although we have separated moral development into three components—thought, behavior, and feelings—the components often are interrelated. For example, if the focus is on the individual's behavior, it is still important to evaluate the person's intentions (moral thought). And emotions accompany moral reasoning and can distort moral reasoning.

MORAL THOUGHT

How do adolescents think about standards of right and wrong? Piaget had some thoughts about this question. So did Lawrence Kohlberg.

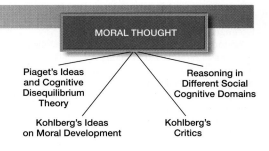

Piaget's Ideas and Cognitive Disequilibrium Theory

Interest in how children and adolescents think about moral issues was stimulated by Piaget (1932), who extensively observed and interviewed children from the ages of 4 to 12. Piaget watched children play marbles to learn how they used and thought about the game's rules. He also asked children questions about ethical issues—theft, lies, punishment, and justice, for example. Piaget concluded that children think in two distinct ways about morality, depending on their developmental maturity. **Heteronomous morality** *is the first stage of moral development in Piaget's theory, occurring at 4 to 7 years of age. Justice and rules are conceived of as unchangeable properties of the world, removed from the control of people.* **Autonomous morality,** *the second stage of moral development in Piaget's theory, is displayed by older children (about 10 years of age and older). The child becomes aware that rules and laws are created by people, and that, in judging an action, one should consider the actor's intentions as well as the consequences.* Children 7 to 10 years of age are in a transition between the two stages, evidencing some features of both.

A heteronomous thinker judges the rightness or goodness of behavior by considering the consequences of the behavior, not the intentions of the actor. For example, the heteronomous thinker says that breaking twelve cups accidentally is worse than breaking one cup intentionally while trying to steal a cookie. For the moral autonomist, the reverse is true. The actor's intentions assume paramount importance. The heteronomous thinker also believes that rules are unchangeable and are handed down by all-powerful authorities. When Piaget suggested to a group of young children that new rules be introduced into the game of marbles, they resisted. By contrast, older children—moral autonomists—accept change and recognize that rules are merely convenient, social agreed-upon conventions, subject to change by consensus.

According to Piaget, the heteronomous thinker also believes in **immanent justice,** *the idea that, if a rule is broken, punishment will be meted out immediately.* The young child somehow believes that the violation is connected automatically to the punishment. Thus, young children often look around worriedly after committing a transgression, expecting inevitable punishment. Immanent justice also implies that if something unfortunate happens to someone, it must be because the person had transgressed earlier. Older children, who are moral autonomists, recognize that punishment is socially mediated and occurs only if a relevant person witnesses the wrongdoing and that, even then, punishment is not inevitable.

Piaget argued that, as children develop, they become more sophisticated in thinking about social matters, especially about the possibilities and conditions of cooperation. Piaget believed that this social understanding comes about through the mutual give-and-take of peer relations. In the peer group, where others have power and status similar to the child's, plans are negotiated and coordinated, and disagreements are reasoned about and eventually settled. Parent-child relations, in which parents have the power and children do not, are less likely to advance moral reasoning, because rules are often handed down in an authoritarian way.

As discussed in earlier chapters, Piaget believed that adolescents usually become formal operational thinkers ◀▦ P. 108. Thus, they no longer are tied to immediate and concrete phenomena but are more logical, abstract, and deductive reasoners. Formal operational thinkers frequently compare the real to the ideal; create contrary-to-fact propositions; are cognitively capable of relating the distant past to the present;

heteronomous morality

The first stage of moral development in Piaget's theory, occurring at 4 to 7 years of age. Justice and rules are conceived of as unchangeable properties of the world, removed from the control of people.

autonomous morality

The second stage of moral development in Piaget's theory, displayed by older children (about 10 years of age and older). The child becomes aware that rules and laws are created by people and that, in judging an action, one should consider the actor's intentions as well as the consequences.

immanent justice

Piaget's concept that if a rule is broken, punishment will be meted out immediately.

understand their roles in society, in history, and in the universe; and can conceptualize their own thoughts and think about their mental constructs as objects. For example, around age 11 or 12, boys and girls spontaneously introduce concepts of belief, intelligence, and faith into their definitions of their religious identities.

Stimulated by Piaget's ideas, Martin Hoffman (1980) developed **cognitive disequilibrium theory,** *which states that adolescence is an important period in moral development, especially as individuals move from the relatively homogeneous grade school to the more heterogeneous high school and college environments, where they are faced with contradictions between the moral concepts they have accepted and experiences outside their family and neighborhood. Adolescents come to recognize that their set of beliefs is but one of many and that there is considerable debate about what is right and what is wrong.* Many adolescents and youth start to question their former beliefs and, in the process, develop their own moral system.

Kohlberg's Ideas on Moral Development

One of the most provocative views of moral development was crafted by Lawrence Kohlberg (1958, 1976, 1981, 1984, 1986). Kohlberg believed that moral development is based primarily on moral reasoning and unfolds in a series of stages. He arrived at his view after about 20 years of research involving unique interviews with individuals of different ages. In the interviews, children were presented with a series of stories in which characters face moral dilemmas. The following is the most popular of the Kohlberg dilemmas:

> In Europe, a woman was near death from a special kind of cancer. There was one drug that the doctors thought might save her. It was a form of radium that a druggist in the same town had recently discovered. The drug was expensive to make, but the druggist was charging ten times what the drug cost him to make. He paid $200 for the radium and charged $2,000 for a small dose of the drug. The sick woman's husband, Heinz, went to everyone he knew to borrow the money, but he could only get together $1,000, which is half of what it cost. He told the druggist that his wife was dying and asked him to sell it cheaper or let him pay later. But the druggist said, "No, I discovered the drug, and I am going to make money from it." So Heinz got desperate and broke into the man's store to steal the drug for his wife. (Kohlberg, 1969, p. 379)

This story is one of eleven that Kohlberg devised to investigate the nature of moral thought. After reading the story, interviewees are asked a series of questions about the moral dilemma: Should Heinz have stolen the drug? Was stealing it right or wrong? Why? Is it a husband's duty to steal the drug for his wife if he can get it no other way? Would a good husband steal it? Did the druggist have the right to charge that much when there was no law setting a limit on the price? Why?

From the answers interviewees gave for this and other moral dilemmas, Kohlberg hypothesized three levels of moral development, each of which is characterized by two stages. A key concept in understanding moral development is **internalization,** *the developmental change from behavior that is externally controlled to behavior that is controlled by internal standards and principles.* As children and adolescents develop, their moral thoughts become more internalized. Let's look further at Kohlberg's three levels of moral development.

Kohlberg's Level 1: Preconventional Reasoning **Preconventional reasoning** *is the lowest level in Kohlberg's theory of moral development. At this level, the individual shows no internalization of moral values—moral reasoning is controlled by external rewards and punishments.*

- Stage 1. *Heteronomous morality* is the first stage in Kohlberg's theory. At this stage, moral thinking is often tied to punishment. For example, children and adolescents obey adults because adults tell them to obey.
- Stage 2. *Individualism, instrumental purpose, and exchange* is the second Kohlberg stage of moral development. At this stage, individuals pursue

---

cognitive disequilibrium theory
Hoffman's theory that adolescence is an important period in moral development, in which, because of broader experiences associated with the move to high school or college, individuals recognize that their set of beliefs is but one of many and that there is considerable debate about what is right and wrong.

Exploring Moral Development
Kohlberg's Theory of Moral Development
Kohlberg's Moral Dilemmas
Kohlberg's Moral Stages
http://www.mhhe.com/santrocka9

internalization
The developmental change from behavior that is externally controlled to behavior that is controlled by internal standards and principles.

preconventional reasoning
The lowest level in Kohlberg's theory of moral development. The individual shows no internalization of moral values—moral reasoning is controlled by external rewards and punishment.

THROUGH THE EYES OF PSYCHOLOGISTS

Lawrence Kohlberg
(1927–1987)

"Moral development consists of a sequence of qualitative changes in a way an individual thinks."

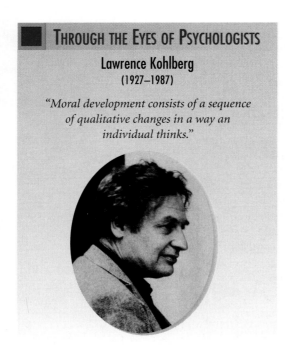

their own interests but also let others do the same. Thus, what is right involves an equal exchange. People are nice to others so that they will be nice to them in return.

Kohlberg's Level 2: Conventional Reasoning

Conventional reasoning *is the second, or intermediate, level in Kohlberg's theory of moral development. At this level, internalization is intermediate. Individuals abide by certain standards (internal), but they are the standards of others (external), such as parents or the laws of society.*

- Stage 3. *Mutual interpersonal expectations, relationships, and interpersonal conformity* is Kohlberg's third stage of moral development. At this stage, individuals value trust, caring, and loyalty to others as a basis of moral judgments. Children and adolescents often adopt their parents' moral standards at this stage, seeking to be thought of by their parents as a "good girl" or a "good boy."
- Stage 4. *Social systems morality* is the fourth stage in Kohlberg's theory of moral development. At this stage, moral judgments are based on understanding the social order, law, justice, and duty. For example, adolescents may say that, for a community to work effectively, it needs to be protected by laws that are adhered to by its members.

conventional reasoning
The second, or intermediate, level in Kohlberg's theory of moral development. Internalization is intermediate. Individuals abide by certain standards (internal), but they are the standards of others (external), such as parents or the laws of society.

Kohlberg's Level 3: Postconventional Reasoning

Postconventional reasoning *is the highest level in Kohlberg's theory of moral development. At this level, morality is completely internalized and is not based on others' standards. The individual recognizes alternative moral courses, explores the options, and then decides on a personal moral code.*

- Stage 5. *Social contract or utility and individual rights* is the fifth Kohlberg stage. At this stage, individuals reason that values, rights, and principles undergird or transcend the law. A person evaluates the validity of actual laws and social systems can be examined in terms of the degree to which they preserve and protect fundamental human rights and values.
- Stage 6. *Universal ethical principles* is the sixth and highest stage in Kohlberg's theory of moral development. At this stage, the person has developed a moral standard based on universal human rights. When faced with a conflict between law and conscience, the person will follow conscience, even though the decision might involve personal risk. A summary of the three levels and six stages is presented in figure 12.1 on page 384.

postconventional reasoning
The highest level in Kohlberg's theory of moral development. Morality is completely internalized.

Kohlberg believed that these levels and stages occur in a sequence and are age related: Before age 9, most children reason about moral dilemmas in a preconventional way; by early adolescence, they reason in more conventional ways. Most adolescents reason at stage 3, with some signs of stages 2 and 4. By early adulthood, a small number of individuals reason in postconventional ways. In a 20-year longitudinal investigation, the uses of stages 1 and 2 decreased (Colby & others, 1983). Stage 4, which did not appear at all in the moral reasoning of 10-year-olds, was reflected in 62 percent of the moral thinking of 36-year-olds. Stage 5 did not appear until age 20 to 22 and never characterized more than 10 percent of the individuals. Thus, the moral stages appeared somewhat later than Kohlberg initially envisioned, and the higher stages, especially stage 6, were extremely elusive. Recently, stage 6 was removed from the Kohlberg moral judgment scoring manual, but it still is considered to be theoretically important in the Kohlberg scheme of moral development. A review of data from

THINKING CRITICALLY

Exploring Your Moral Thinking

What do you think about the following circumstances?

- A man who had been sentenced to serve 10 years for selling a small amount of marijuana walked away from a prison camp after six months. Twenty-five years later he was caught. He is now in his fifties and has been a model citizen. Should he be sent back to prison? Why or why not? At which Kohlberg stage should your response be placed?
- A young woman who had been in a tragic accident is brain dead and has been kept on life support systems for four years without ever regaining consciousness. Should the life support systems be removed? Explain your response. At which Kohlberg stage should your response be placed?

45 studies in 27 diverse world cultures provided support for the universality of Kohlberg's first four stages, although there was more cultural diversity at stages 5 and 6 (Snarey, 1987).

Influences on the Kohlberg Stages   Kohlberg believed that the individual's moral orientation unfolds as a consequence of cognitive development. Children and adolescents construct their moral thoughts as they pass from one stage to the next, rather than passively accepting a cultural norm of morality (Brabeck, 2000). Investigators have sought to understand factors that influence movement through the moral stages, among them modeling, cognitive conflict, peer relations, and role-taking opportunities.

Several investigators have attempted to advance individuals' levels of moral development by having a model present arguments that reflect moral thinking one stage above the individuals' established levels. These studies are based on the cognitive developmental concepts of equilibrium and conflict (Walker & Taylor, 1991). By presenting moral information slightly beyond the individual's cognitive level, a disequilibrium is created that motivates a restructuring of moral thought. The resolution of the disequilibrium and conflict should be toward increased competence. In one study, subjects did prefer stages higher than their own more than stages lower than their own

LEVEL 3

**Postconventional Level
Full Internalization**

**Stage 5
Social Contract
or Utility and
Individual
Rights**

**Stage 6
Universal Ethical
Principles**

Individuals reason that values, rights, and principles undergird or transcend the law.

The person has developed moral judgments that are based on universal human rights. When faced with a dilemma between law and conscience, a personal, individualized conscience is followed.

LEVEL 2

**Conventional Level
Intermediate Internalization**

**Stage 3
Mutual
Interpersonal
Expectations,
Relationships,
and Interpersonal
Conformity**

**Stage 4
Social System
Morality**

Individuals value trust, caring, and loyalty to others as a basis for moral judgments.

Moral judgments are based on understanding and the social order, law, justice, and duty.

(Walker, de Vries, & Bichard, 1984). In sum, moral thought can be moved to a higher level through exposure to models or discussion that is more advanced than the adolescent's level.

Like Piaget, Kohlberg believed that peer interaction is a critical part of the social stimulation that challenges individuals to change their moral orientation. Whereas adults characteristically impose rules and regulations on children, the mutual give-and-take in peer interaction provides the child with an opportunity to take the role of another person and to generate rules democratically. Kohlberg stressed that role-taking opportunities can, in principle, be engendered by any peer group encounter. While Kohlberg believed that such role-taking opportunities are ideal for moral development, he also believed that certain types of parent-child experiences can induce the child and adolescent to think at more advanced levels of moral thinking. In particular, parents who allow or encourage conversation about value-laden issues promote more advanced moral thought in their children and adolescents. Unfortunately, many parents do not systematically

LEVEL 1

**Preconventional Level
No Internalization**

**Stage 1
Heteronomous
Morality**

**Stage 2
Individualism,
Purpose, and
Exchange**

Children obey because adults tell them to obey. People base their moral decisions on fear of punishment.

Individuals pursue their own interests but let others do the same. What is right involves equal exchange.

FIGURE 12.1
Kohlberg's Three Levels and Six Stages of Moral Development

provide their children and adolescents with such role-taking opportunities. Nonetheless, in one study, children's moral development was related to their parents' discussion style, which involved questioning and supportive interaction (Walker & Taylor, 1991). There is increasing emphasis on the role of parenting in moral development (Eisenberg & Murphy, 1995).

Why Is Kohlberg's Theory Important for Understanding Moral Development in Adolescence?   Kohlberg's theory is essentially a description of the progressive conceptions people use to understand social cooperation. In short, it tells the developmental story of people trying to understand things like society, rules and roles, and institutions and relationships. Such basic conceptions are fundamental to adolescents, for whom ideology becomes important in guiding their lives and making life decisions.

Kohlberg's Critics

Kohlberg's provocative theory of moral development has not gone unchallenged (Gilligan, 1982, 1992; Lapsley, 1996; Rest & others, 1999; Turiel, 1998). The criticisms involve the link between moral thought and moral behavior, the quality of the research, inadequate consideration of culture's role in moral development, and underestimation of the care perspective.

Moral Thought and Moral Behavior   Kohlberg's theory has been criticized for placing too much emphasis on moral thought and not enough emphasis on moral behavior. Moral reasons can sometimes be a shelter for immoral behavior. Bank embezzlers and presidents endorse the loftiest of moral virtues when commenting about moral dilemmas, but their own behavior may be immoral. No one wants a nation of cheaters and thieves who can reason at the postconventional level. The cheaters and thieves may know what is right, yet still do what is wrong.

In evaluating the relation between moral thought and moral behavior, consider the corrupting power of rationalizations and other defenses that disengage us from self-blame; these include reconstrual of the situation, euphemistic labeling, and attribution of blame to authorities, circumstances, or victims (Bandura, 1991). One area in which a link between moral judgment and behavior has been found is higher Kohlberg-stage reasoning acting as a buffer against criminality (Taylor & Walker, 1997).

Assessment of Moral Reasoning   Some developmentalists fault the quality of Kohlberg's research and believe that more attention should be paid to the way moral development is assessed (Boyes, Giordano, & Galperyn, 1993). For example, James Rest (1986) argued that alternative methods should be used to collect information about moral thinking instead of relying on a single method that requires individuals to reason about hypothetical moral dilemmas. Rest also said that Kohlberg's stories are extremely difficult to score. To help remedy this problem, Rest developed his own measure of moral development, called the Defining Issues Test (DIT).

The DIT attempts to determine which moral issues individuals feel are more critical in a given situation by presenting them with a series of dilemmas and a list of definitions of the major issues involved (Kohlberg's procedure does not make use of such a list). In the dilemma of Heinz and the druggist, individuals might be asked whether a community's laws should be upheld or whether Heinz should be willing to risk being injured or caught as a burglar. They might also be asked to list the most important values that govern human interaction. They are given six stories and asked to rate the importance of each issue involved in deciding what ought to be done. Then they are asked to list what they believe are the four most important issues. Rest argued that this method provides a more valid and reliable way to assess moral thinking than Kohlberg's method.

Researchers also have found that the hypothetical moral dilemmas posed in Kohlberg's stories do not match the moral dilemmas many children and adults

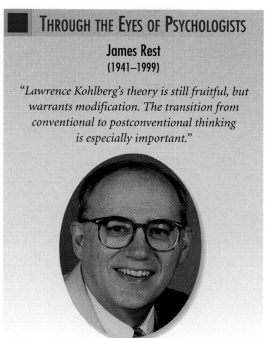

THROUGH THE EYES OF PSYCHOLOGISTS

James Rest
(1941–1999)

"Lawrence Kohlberg's theory is still fruitful, but warrants modification. The transition from conventional to postconventional thinking is especially important."

Story subject	Grade		
	7	9	12
	Percentage		
Alcohol	2	0	5
Civil rights	0	6	7
Drugs	7	10	5
Interpersonal relations	38	24	35
Physical safety	22	8	3
Sexual relations	2	20	10
Smoking	7	2	0
Stealing	9	2	0
Working	2	2	15
Other	1	26	20

■ FIGURE 12.2
Actual Moral Dilemmas Generated by Adolescents

This 14-year-old boy in Nepal is thought to be the sixth holiest Buddhist in the world. In one study of 20 adolescent male Buddhist monks in Nepal, the issue of justice, a basic theme in Kohlberg's theory, was not a central focus in the monks' moral views. Also, the monks' concerns about prevention of suffering and the importance of compassion are not captured in Kohlberg's theory.

face in their everyday lives (Walker, de Vries, & Trevethan, 1987; Yussen, 1977). Most of Kohlberg's stories focus on the family and authority. However, when one researcher invited adolescents to write stories about their own moral dilemmas, the adolescents generated dilemmas that were broader in scope, focusing on friends, acquaintances, and other issues, as well as family and authority (Yussen, 1977). The adolescents' moral dilemmas also were analyzed in terms of their content. As shown in figure 12.2, the moral issue that concerned adolescents more than any other was interpersonal relationships.

Some moral development researchers believe that a valuable method is to have research participants recall and discuss real-life dilemmas from their own experience (Walker, de Vries, & Trevethan, 1987). This strategy can provide a valid assessment not only of subjects' moral stage but also of how they interpret moral situations that are relevant to them.

Culture and Moral Development   Yet another criticism of Kohlberg's view is that it is culturally biased (Glassman, 1997; Haidt, 1997; Miller, 1995). A review of research on moral development in 27 countries concluded that moral reasoning is more culture-specific than Kohlberg envisioned and that Kohlberg's scoring system does not recognize higher-level moral reasoning in certain cultural groups (Snarey, 1987). Examples of higher-level moral reasoning that would not be scored as such by Kohlberg's system are values related to communal equity and collective happiness in Israel, the unity and sacredness of all life-forms in India, and the relation of the individual to the community in New Guinea. These examples of moral reasoning would not be scored at the highest level in Kohlberg's system because they do not emphasize the individual's rights and abstract principles of justice. One study assessed the moral development of 20 adolescent male Buddhist monks in Nepal (Huebner & Garrod, 1993). The issue of justice, a basic theme in Kohlberg's theory, was not of paramount importance in the monks' moral views, and their concerns about prevention of suffering and the role of compassion are not captured by Kohlberg's theory.

According to moral development theorist and researcher William Damon (1988), where culturally specific practices take on profound moral and religious significance, as in India, the moral development of children focuses extensively on their adherence to custom and convention. In contrast, Western moral doctrine tends to elevate abstract principles, such as justice and welfare, to a higher moral status than customs or conventions. As in India, socialization practices in many Third World countries actively instill in children a great respect for their culture's traditional codes and practices.

In Richard Shweder's (1991) view of culture and moral development, there are three ethical orientations or world views that appear: (1) an ethic of autonomy (dominant in Western cultures), (2) an ethic of community (prominent in cultures that emphasize communitarian values and tradition), and (3) an ethic of divinity (characteristic of cultures in which morality is mainly derived from religious prescriptions).

In sum, although Kohlberg's approach does capture much of the moral reasoning voiced in various cultures around the world, as we have just seen, there are some important moral concepts in particular cultures that his approach misses or misconstrues (Walker, 1996).

Gender and the Care Perspective   In chapter 11, we discussed Carol Gilligan's view that relationships and connections to others are critical aspects of female development ◀▥ P. 337. Gilligan (1982, 1992) also has criticized Kohlberg's theory of moral development. She believes that his theory does not adequately reflect relationships and concern for others. The **justice perspective** *is a moral perspective that focuses on the rights of the individual; individuals stand alone and independently make moral decisions. Kohlberg's theory is a justice perspective.* By contrast, the **care perspective** *is a moral perspective that views people in terms of their connectedness with others and emphasizes interpersonal communication, relationships with others, and concern for others. Gilligan's theory is a care perspective.* According to Gilligan, Kohlberg greatly underplayed the care perspective in moral development. She believes that this may have happened because he was a male, because most of his research was with males rather than females, and because he used male responses as a model for his theory.

In extensive interviews with girls from 6 to 18 years of age, Gilligan and her colleagues found that girls consistently interpret moral dilemmas in terms of human relationships and base these interpretations on listening and watching other people (Gilligan, 1990; Gilligan, Brown, & Rogers, 1990). According to Gilligan, girls have the ability to sensitively pick up different rhythms in relationships and often are able to follow the pathways of feelings. Gilligan believes that girls reach a critical juncture in their development when they reach adolescence. Usually around 11 to 12 years of age, girls become aware that their intense interest in intimacy is not prized by the male-dominated culture, even though society values women as caring and altruistic. The dilemma is that girls are presented with a choice that makes them look either selfish or selfless. Gilligan believes that, as adolescent girls experience this dilemma, they increasingly silence their "distinctive voice."

Researchers have found support for Gilligan's claim that females' and males' moral reasoning often centers around different concerns and issues (Galotti, Kozberg, & Farmer, 1990; Garmon, Basinger, & Gibbs, 1995; Skoe & Gooden, 1993). However, one of Gilligan's initial claims—that traditional Kohlbergian measures of moral development are biased against females—has been extensively disputed. For example, most research studies using the Kohlberg stories and scoring system do not find sex differences (Jafee & Hyde, 2000; Walker, 1984, 1991). Thus, the strongest support for Gilligan's claims comes from studies that focus on items and scoring systems pertaining to close relationships, pathways of feelings, sensitive listening, and the rhythm of interpersonal behavior (Galotti, Kozberg, & Farmer, 1990).

Though females often articulate a care perspective and males a justice perspective, the gender difference is not absolute, and the two orientations are not mutually exclusive (Lyons, 1990). For example, in one study, 53 of 80 females and males showed either a care or a justice perspective, but 27 participants used both orientations, with neither predominating (Gilligan & Attanucci, 1988).

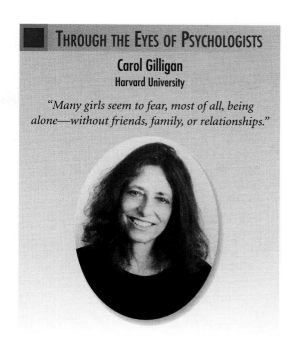

justice perspective
A moral perspective that focuses on the rights of the individual; individuals independently make moral decisions.

care perspective
The moral perspective of Carol Gilligan, which views people in terms of their connectedness with others and emphasizes interpersonal communication, relationships with others, and concern for others.

In a Different Voice
Exploring Girls' Voices
http://www.mhhe.com/santrocka9

Reasoning in Different Social Cognitive Domains

An increasing number of theorists and researchers believe it is important to make distinctions about different domains when considering adolescents' reasoning about various sociocognitive issues (Killen, 1991; Nucci, 1996, 2001; Smetana, 1995; Turiel, 1998). The three domains that have been given the most attention are moral, social, and personal.

In focusing on different domains, the *moral domain* is thought to involve issues about justice (such as fairness, the welfare of others, and rights). Moral concepts are believed to be generalized and unchangeable (Ardila-Rey & Killen, in press). For example, research studies of children in a number of countries consistently view acts of harm as wrong in any context (Killen, McGlotlin, & Lee-Kim, in press).

The *social-conventional domain* pertains to regularities designed to ensure the smooth functioning of social groups (customs and etiquette, for example). Thus, not eating with one's fingers and raising one's hand in class before asking a question are social-conventional concepts. Social-conventional concepts are believed to be context specific and changeable. Both moral and social-conventional concepts are viewed as issues that are regulated by adults.

The *personal domain* reflects decisions that are based on personal choice (such as choice of friends and choice of activities). The personal domain often involves issues of individual autonomy, personal prerogatives, and personal goals. For example, in chapter 5, "Families," we discussed how conflict between parents and adolescents sometimes occurs because parents and adolescents may interpret the events as belonging to different domains. Thus, an adolescent may regard smoking as an issue of personal choice while his parents view it as a moral issue. Concepts in the personal domain are thought to involve decision making that is not regulated by adults (Nucci, 1996).

At this point, we have studied a number of ideas about what moral development is and moral thought. This review should help you to reach your learning goals related to these topics.

☐ FOR YOUR REVIEW

Learning Goal 1
Know what moral development is

- Moral development involves thoughts, feelings, and behaviors regarding standards of right and wrong. Moral development consists of intrapersonal and interpersonal dimensions.

Learning Goal 2
Explain moral thought

- Piaget distinguished between the heteronomous morality of younger children and the autonomous morality of older children. Formal operational thought might undergird changes in adolescents' moral reasoning. Hoffman proposed cognitive disequilibrium theory, which describes individuals as moving from a relatively homogeneous grade school to the more heterogeneous secondary school and college environments, where individuals often experience contradictions regarding their moral stance.
- Kohlberg developed a provocative theory of moral reasoning. He argued that moral development consists of three levels—preconventional, conventional, and postconventional—and six stages (two at each level). Increased internalization characterized movement to levels 2 and 3. Influences on the stages include cognitive development, imitation and cognitive conflict, peer relations, and perspective taking.
- Kohlberg's critics say that he gave inadequate attention to moral behavior, did not adequately assess moral development, underestimated cultural influences, and underestimated the care perspective (Gilligan's theory).
- Distinctions are made between these social cognitive domains: (1) moral, (2) social conventional, and (3) personal.

So far we have studied what moral development is and moral thought. One of the criticisms of Kohlberg's theory is that it does not adequately address moral behavior. Let's now explore the nature of moral behavior.

MORAL BEHAVIOR

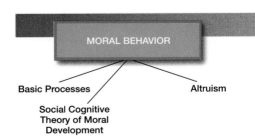

MORAL BEHAVIOR

Basic Processes — Altruism

Social Cognitive Theory of Moral Development

What are the basic processes that behaviorists believe are responsible for adolescents' moral behavior? How do social cognitive theorists view adolescents' moral development? What is the nature of altruistic behavior?

Basic Processes

Behavioral views emphasize the moral behavior of adolescents. The familiar processes of reinforcement, punishment, and imitation have been invoked to explain how and why adolescents learn certain moral behaviors and why their behaviors differ from one another. The general conclusions to be drawn are the same as for other domains of social behavior. When adolescents are reinforced for behavior that is consistent with laws and social conventions, they are likely to repeat that behavior. When models who behave "morally" are provided, adolescents are likely to adopt their behavior. And when adolescents are punished for immoral or unacceptable behavior, those behaviors can be eliminated, but at the expense of sanctioning punishment by its very use and of causing emotional side effects for the adolescent.

To these general conclusions can be added several qualifiers. The effectiveness of reinforcement and punishment depends on how consistently they are administered and the schedule that is adopted. The effectiveness of modeling depends on the characteristics of the model (such as power, warmth, uniqueness, and so on) and the presence of cognitive processes, such as symbolic codes and imagery, to enhance retention of the modeled behavior.

What kind of adult moral models are adolescents being exposed to in American society? Do such models usually do what they say? Adolescents are especially tuned in to adult hypocrisy, and evidence indicates that they are right to believe that many adults display a double standard, their moral actions not always corresponding to their moral thoughts. A poll of 24,000 adults sampled views on a wide variety of moral issues. Detailed scenarios of everyday moral problems were developed to test moral decision making. Consider the example of whether the adult would knowingly buy a stolen color television set. More than 20 percent said that they would, even though 87 percent said that this act is probably morally wrong. And approximately 31 percent of the adults said that they would be more likely to buy the stolen television if they knew they would not get caught. While moral thought is an important dimension of moral development, these data glaringly underscore that what people believe about right and wrong does not always correspond with how they will act in moral situations.

In addition to emphasizing the role of environmental determinants and the gap between moral thought and moral action, behaviorists also emphasize that moral behavior is situationally dependent. That is, they say that adolescents are not likely to display consistent moral behavior in diverse social settings. In a classic investigation of moral behavior—one of the most extensive ever conducted—Hugh Hartshorne and Mark May (1928–1930) observed the moral responses of 11,000 children and adolescents who were given the opportunity to lie, cheat, and steal in a variety of circumstances—at home, at school, at social events, and in athletics. A completely honest or a completely dishonest child or adolescent was difficult to find. Situation-specific moral behavior was the rule. Adolescents were more likely to cheat when their friends pressured them to do so and when the chance of being caught was slim. Other analyses suggest that some adolescents are more likely to lie, cheat, and steal than others, indicating more consistency of moral behavior in some adolescents than in others (Burton, 1984).

Social Cognitive Theory of Moral Development

The **social cognitive theory of moral development** *emphasizes a distinction between adolescents' moral competence—the ability to produce moral behaviors—and moral performance—those behaviors in specific situations* (Mischel & Mischel, 1975). Competence, or acquisition, depends primarily on cognitive-sensory processes; it is the outgrowth of these processes. Competencies include what adolescents are capable of doing, what they know, their skills, their awareness of moral rules and regulations, and their cognitive ability to construct behaviors. Adolescents' moral performance, or behavior, however, is determined by their motivation and the rewards and incentives to act in a specific moral way. Albert Bandura (1991; Bandura & others, 2001) also believes that moral development is best understood by considering a combination of social and cognitive factors, especially those involving self-control ◀▥ P. 50.

One reason that behaviorists and social cognitive theorists have been critical of Kohlberg's view is that, as mentioned earlier, they believe that he placed too little emphasis on moral behavior and the situational determinants of morality. However, while Kohlberg argued that moral judgment is an important determinant of moral behavior, he, like the Mischels, stressed that the individual's interpretation of both the moral and the factual aspects of a situation leads him or her to a moral decision (Kohlberg & Candee, 1979). For example, Kohlberg mentioned that "extramoral" factors, like the desire to avoid embarrassment, may cause individuals to avoid doing what they believe

social cognitive theory of moral development
The theory that distinguishes between *moral competence* (the ability to produce moral behaviors) and *moral performance* (performing those behaviors in specific situations).

to be morally right. In sum, both the Mischels and Kohlberg believe that moral action is influenced by a complex of factors. Overall, the findings are mixed with regard to the association of moral thought and behavior (Arnold, 1989), although one investigation with college students found that individuals with both highly principled moral reasoning and high ego strength were less likely to cheat in a resistance-to-temptation situation than were their low-principled and low-ego-strength counterparts (Hess, Lonky, & Roodin, 1985).

Moral behavior includes both negative aspects of behavior—cheating, lying, and stealing, for example—and positive aspects of behavior—being considerate to others and giving to a worthy cause, for example. Let's now explore the positive side of moral behavior—altruism.

Altruism

altruism
Unselfish interest in helping another person.

Altruism *is an unselfish interest in helping another person.* While adolescents have often been described as egocentric and selfish, adolescent acts of altruism are, nevertheless, plentiful—the hardworking adolescent who places a one-dollar bill in the church offering plate each week; the adolescent-sponsored car washes, bake sales, and concerts organized to make money to feed the hungry and help children who are mentally retarded; and the adolescent who takes in and cares for a wounded cat. How do psychologists account for such altruistic acts?

Reciprocity and exchange are involved in altruism (Brown, 1986). Reciprocity is found throughout the human world. Not only is it the highest moral principle in Christianity, but it is also present in every widely practiced religion in the world—Judaism, Hinduism, Buddhism, and Islam. Reciprocity encourages adolescents to do unto others as they would have others do unto them. In one recent study, adolescents showed more helping behavior around the house when mothers were involved with and spent time helping the adolescent (Eberly & Montemayor, 1996).

Not all adolescent altruism is motivated by reciprocity and exchange, but self-other interactions and relationships help us to understand altruism's nature (Eisenberg & others, 1995). The circumstances most likely to involve altruism by adolescents are empathetic or sympathetic emotion for an individual in need or a close relationship between the benefactor and the recipient (Clark & others, 1987). Altruism occurs more often in adolescence than in childhood, although examples of caring for others and comforting someone in distress occur even during the preschool years (Eisenberg & Fabes, 1998).

forgiveness
This is an aspect of altruism that occurs when an injured person releases the injurer from possible behavioral retaliation.

Forgiveness *is an aspect of altruism that occurs when the injured person releases the injurer from possible behavioral retaliation.* In one investigation, individuals from the fourth grade through college and adulthood were asked questions about forgiveness (Enright, Santos, & Al-Mabuk, 1989). The adolescents were especially swayed by peer pressure in their willingness to forgive others. Consider one 12-year-old girl's response to Kohlberg's dilemma of Heinz and the druggist:

Interviewer: "Suppose all of Heinz's friends come to see him and say, 'Please be more mature about this. We want you to be friends with the druggist.' Would it help him to forgive the druggist? Why/why not?"

Girl: "Probably, because Heinz would think they wanted him to. They would influence him."

In response to the same question, a 15-year-old girl said, "Yes, it would be his friends showing him the outside view. They would help him." The adolescent forgiveness theme that emerged was that the injured party often fails to see the best course of action. Outside aid, especially from friends, helps the harmed person to clarify the problem and then forgive.

Emerson once said, "The meaning of good and bad, better, and worse, is simply helping or hurting." By developing adolescents' capacity for empathy and altruism, America can become a nation of people who *help* rather than hurt. Later in the chapter in our coverage of moral education, we will explore adolescent helping in the context of service learning.

So far we have examined two of the three main domains of moral development: thought and behavior. Next, we will explore the third main domain: moral feelings.

MORAL FEELINGS

Among the ideas formulated about the development of moral feelings are the concepts developed by psychoanalytic theorists, the role of child-rearing techniques, the nature of empathy, and the role of emotions in moral development.

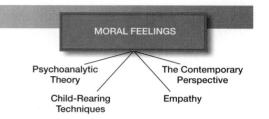

Psychoanalytic Theory

As discussed in chapter 2, Sigmund Freud's psychoanalytic theory describes the *super-ego* as one of the three main structures of personality (the id and the ego being the other two) ◀▥ P. 40. In Freud's classical psychoanalytic theory, an individual's superego—the moral branch of personality—develops in early childhood when the child resolves the Oedipus conflict and identifies with the same-sex parent. According to Freud, one reason why children resolve the Oedipus conflict is to alleviate the fear of losing their parents' love and of being punished for their unacceptable sexual wishes toward the opposite-sex parent. To reduce anxiety, avoid punishment, and maintain parental affection, children form a superego by identifying with the same-sex parent. In Freud's view, through this identification, children internalize the parents' standards of right and wrong that reflect societal prohibitions. Also, children turn inward the hostility that was previously aimed at the same-sex parent. This inwardly directed hostility is then experienced self-punitively (and unconsciously) as guilt. In the psychoanalytic account of moral development, self-punitiveness of guilt keeps children, and later on, adolescents from committing transgressions. That is, children and adolescents conform to societal standards to avoid guilt.

In Freud's view, the superego consists of two main components—the ego ideal and the conscience—which promote children's and adolescents' development of moral feelings. The **ego ideal** *is the component of the superego that involves ideal standards approved by parents,* whereas the **conscience** *is the component of the superego that involves behaviors not approved of by parents.* An individual's ego-ideal rewards the individual by conveying a sense of pride and personal value when the individual acts according to moral standards. The conscience punishes the individual for acting immorally by making the individual feel guilty and worthless. In this way, self-control replaces parental control.

Erik Erikson (1970) argued that there are three stages of moral development: specific moral learning in childhood, ideological concerns in adolescence, and ethical consolidation in adulthood. According to Erikson, during adolescence, individuals search for an identity. If adolescents become disillusioned with the moral and religious beliefs they acquired during childhood, they are likely to lose, at least temporarily, their sense of purpose and feel that their lives are empty. This may lead to adolescents' search for an ideology that will give some purpose to their life. For the ideology to be acceptable, it must both fit the evidence and mesh with adolescents' logical reasoning abilities. If others share this ideology, a sense of community is felt. For Erikson, ideology surfaces as the guardian of identity during adolescence because it provides a sense of purpose, assists in tying the present to the future, and contributes meaning to the behavior (Hoffman, 1980).

ego ideal
The component of the superego that involves ideal standards approved by parents.

conscience
The component of the superego that involves behaviors disapproved of by parents.

Child-Rearing Techniques

Both Piaget and Kohlberg held that parents do not provide any unique or essential inputs to children's moral development. However, they did believe that parents are responsible for providing general role-taking opportunities and cognitive conflict.

What role do parents play in their adolescent's moral development?

love withdrawal
A discipline technique in which a parent removes attention or love from a child.

power assertion
A discipline technique in which a parent attempts to gain control over a child or a child's resources.

induction
A discipline technique in which a parent uses reason and explanation of the consequences for others of a child's actions.

Through the Eyes of Psychologists

Nancy Eisenberg
Arizona State University

"Parents play an important role in children's moral development."

Nonetheless, Piaget and Kohlberg did not see parents as playing the primary role in moral development, reserving that role for peers (Walker, 1996).

In Freud's psychoanalytic theory, the aspects of child rearing that encourage moral development are practices that instill the fears of punishment and of losing parental love. Developmentalists who have studied child-rearing techniques and moral development have focused on parents' discipline. These discipline techniques include love withdrawal, power assertion, and induction (Hoffman, 1970). Love withdrawal comes closest to the psychoanalytic emphasis on fear of losing parental love. **Love withdrawal** *is a discipline technique in which a parent removes attention or love from the child,* as when the parent refuses to talk to the child or states a dislike for the child. For example, the parent might say, "I'm going to leave you if you do that again," or "I don't like you when you do that." **Power assertion** *is a discipline technique in which a parent attempts to gain control over the child or the child's resources.* Examples include spanking, threatening, or removing privileges. **Induction** *is the discipline technique in which a parent uses reason and explanation of the consequences for others of the child's actions.* Examples of induction include, "Don't hit him. He was only trying to help," and "Why are you yelling at her? She didn't mean to trip you."

Moral development theorist and researcher Martin Hoffman (1970) believes that any discipline produces arousal on the child's part. Love withdrawal and power assertion are likely to evoke a very high level of arousal, with love withdrawal generating considerable anxiety and power assertion considerable hostility. Induction is more likely to produce a moderate level of arousal in adolescents, a level that permits them to attend to the cognitive rationales parents offer. When a parent uses power assertion and love withdrawal, the adolescent may be so aroused that, even if the parent gives accompanying explanations about the consequences for others of the adolescent's actions, the adolescent might not attend to them. Power assertion presents parents as weak models of self-control—as individuals who cannot control their feelings. Accordingly, adolescents may imitate this model of poor self-control when they face stressful circumstances. The use of induction, however, focuses the adolescent's attention on the action's consequences for others, not on the adolescent's own shortcomings. For these reasons, Hoffman (1988) believes that parents should use induction to encourage adolescents' moral development. In research on parenting techniques, induction is more positively related to moral development than is love withdrawal or power assertion, although the findings vary according to developmental level and socioeconomic status. Induction works better with elementary-school-aged children than with preschool children (Brody & Shaffer, 1982) and better with middle-SES than with lower-SES children (Hoffman, 1970). Older children and adolescents are probably better able to understand the reasons given to them and are better at perspective taking. Some theorists believe that the internalization of society's moral standards is more likely among middle-SES than among lower-class individuals because internalization is more rewarding in the middle-SES culture (Kohn, 1977).

In sum, a number of developmentalists believe that family processes play a more important role in moral development than Kohlberg did (Eisenberg & Valiente, 2002). They argue that inductive discipline contributes to moral motivation and that parental values influence children's and adolescents' developing moral thoughts (Boyes & Allen, 1993; Walker, 1993).

In one recent longitudinal study over a four-year period, both parent/child and peer relationships were linked with children's developing moral maturity (Walker, Hennig, & Krettenauer, 2000). A general Socratic style of eliciting the other's opinion and checking for understanding (as when using appropriate probes) was effective in advancing in both parent/child and peer contexts.

However, excessive information giving was associated with lower rates of moral growth, possibly being interpreted as overly opinionated lecturing. Parents provided a more cognitively stimulating environment than did children's friends; friends engaged in more simple sharing of information.

Empathy

Positive feelings, such as empathy, contribute to adolescents' moral development. Feeling **empathy** *means reacting to another's feelings with an emotional response that is similar to that person's feelings.* Although empathy is experienced as an emotional state, it often has a cognitive component—the ability to discern another's inner psychological states, or what we have previously called *perspective taking.*

At about 10 to 12 years of age, individuals develop an empathy for people who live in unfortunate circumstances (Damon, 1988). Children's concerns are no longer limited to the feelings of particular persons in situations they directly observe. Instead, 10- to 12-year-olds expand their concerns to the general problems of people in unfortunate circumstances—the poor, the handicapped, and the socially outcast, for example. This newfound sensitivity may lead older children to behave altruistically, and later may give a humanitarian flavor to adolescents' development of ideological and political views.

Although every adolescent may be capable of responding with empathy, not all do. Adolescents' empathic behavior varies considerably. For example, in older children and adolescents, empathic dysfunctions can contribute to antisocial behavior. Some delinquents convicted of violent crimes show a lack of feeling for their victims' distress. A 13-year-old boy convicted of violently mugging a number of elderly people, when asked about the pain he had caused one blind woman, said, "What do I care? I'm not her" (Damon, 1988). In one recent study, parental empathy was associated with adolescent empathy (Marshall & others, 1994).

empathy
Reacting to another's feelings with an emotional response that is similar to the other's response.

Developing Empathy in Children and Youth
Moral Development, Empathy, and Violent Boys
Exploring Emotions and Emotional Intelligence
International Society for Research on Emotions
http://www.mhhe.com/santrocka9

The Contemporary Perspective

We have seen that classical psychoanalytic theory emphasizes the power of unconscious guilt in moral development but that other theories, such as that of Damon, emphasize the role of empathy. Today, many developmentalists believe that both positive feelings, such as empathy, sympathy, admiration, and self-esteem, and negative feelings, such as anger, outrage, shame, and guilt, contribute to adolescents' moral development (Damon, 1988, 2000; Eisenberg & Fabes, 1998). When strongly experienced, these emotions influence adolescents to act in accord with standards of right and wrong. Such emotions as empathy, shame, guilt, and anxiety over other people's violations of standards are present early in development and undergo developmental change throughout childhood and adolescence. These emotions provide a natural base for adolescents' acquisition of moral values, both orienting adolescents toward moral events and motivating them to pay close attention to such events. However, moral emotions do not operate in a vacuum to build adolescents' moral awareness, and they are not sufficient in themselves to generate moral responsivity. They do not give the "substance" of moral regulation—the rules, values, and standards of behavior that adolescents need to understand and act on. Moral emotions are inextricably interwoven with the cognitive and social aspects of adolescents' development.

In one study of fifth-, eighth-, and eleventh-graders, parents were the individuals most likely to evoke guilt (Williams & Bybee, 1994). With development, guilt evoked by members of the extended family and siblings was less prevalent, but guilt engendered by girlfriends or boyfriends was more frequent. At the higher grade levels, the percentage of students reporting guilt over aggressive, externalizing behavior declined, whereas those mentioning guilt over internal thoughts and inconsiderateness increased. Males were more likely to report guilt over externalizing behaviors, whereas females reported more guilt over violating norms of compassion and trust.

At this point, we have studied a number of ideas about moral behavior and moral feelings. This review should help you to reach your learning goals related to these topics.

☐ FOR YOUR REVIEW

Learning Goal 3
Discuss moral behavior

- Behaviorists argue that moral behavior is determined by the processes of reinforcement, punishment, and imitation. Situational variability in moral behavior is stressed by behaviorists. Hartshorne and May's classic study found considerable variation in moral behavior across situations.
- The social cognitive theory of moral development emphasizes a distinction between moral competence (the ability to produce moral behaviors) and moral performance (performing those behaviors in specific situations). Social cognitive theorists believe Kohlberg gave inadequate attention to moral behavior and situational variations.

Learning Goal 4
Understand moral feelings

- In Freud's theory, the superego—the moral branch of personality—is one of personality's three main structures. Freud also believed that through identification children internalize a parent's standards of right and wrong. Children may conform to moral standards in order to avoid guilt, in the Freudian view. The two main components of the superego are the ego ideal and conscience.
- The main child-rearing techniques that have been studied in relation to moral development are power assertion, induction, and love withdrawal. The most consistent links have been found between positive moral development and parental use of induction.
- Feeling empathy means reacting to another's feelings with an emotional response that is similar to that person's feelings. Empathy involves perspective taking as a cognitive component. Empathy changes developmentally.
- The contemporary perspective on emotions and moral development is that both positive feelings (such as empathy) and negative feelings (such as guilt) contribute to moral development. Emotions are interwoven with the cognitive and social dimensions of moral development.

Now that we have studied what moral development is and its three main components (thought, behavior, and feeling), let's turn our attention to moral education.

MORAL EDUCATION

MORAL EDUCATION

The Hidden Curriculum

Character Education

Values Clarification

Service Learning

Cognitive Moral Education

hidden curriculum
The pervasive moral atmosphere that characterizes schools.

Moral education is hotly debated in educational circles. We will study one of the earliest analyses of moral education, then turn to some contemporary views.

The Hidden Curriculum

More than 60 years ago, educator John Dewey (1933) recognized that even when schools do not have specific programs in moral education, they provide moral education through a "hidden curriculum." The **hidden curriculum** *is conveyed by the moral atmosphere that is a part of every school.* The moral atmosphere is created by school and classroom rules, the moral orientation of teachers and school administrators, and text materials. Teachers serve as models of ethical or unethical behavior. Classroom rules and peer relations at school transmit attitudes about cheating, lying, stealing, and showing consideration for others. And through its rules and regulations, the school administration infuses the school with a value system.

Character Education

character education
A direct moral education approach that involves teaching students a basic moral literacy to prevent them from engaging in immoral behavior or doing harm to themselves or others.

Character education *is a direct approach that involves teaching students a basic moral literacy to prevent them from engaging in immoral behavior and doing harm to themselves or others.* The argument is that such behaviors as lying, stealing, and cheating are wrong and students should be taught this throughout their education. Every school should have an explicit moral code that is clearly communicated to students. Any violations of the code should be met with sanctions (Bennett, 1993). Instruction in specified moral concepts, like cheating, can take the form of example and definition, class discussions and role-playing, or rewarding students for proper behavior.

Some character education movements are the Character Education Partnership, the Character Education Network, the Aspen Declaration on Character Education, and the publicity campaign "Character Counts." Books that promote character education include William Bennett's *Book of Virtues* (1993) and William Damon's *Greater Expectations* (1995).

Values Clarification

Values clarification *is an educational approach that is intended to help people clarify what their lives are for and what is worth working for.* In this approach, students are encouraged to define their own values and understand the values of others. Values clarification differs from character education in not telling students what their values should be.

In the following values clarification example, students are asked to select from among ten people the six who will be admitted to a safe shelter because a third world war has broken out (Johnson, 1990):

> You work for a government agency in Washington and your group has to decide which six of the following ten people will be admitted to a small fallout shelter. Your group has only 20 minutes to make the decision. These are your choices:
>
> • A 30-year-old male bookkeeper
> • The bookkeeper's wife, who is six months pregnant
> • A second-year African American male medical student who is a political activist
> • A 42-year-old male who is a famous historian and author
> • A Hollywood actress who is a singer and dancer
> • A female biochemist
> • A 54-year-old male rabbi
> • A male Olympic athlete who is good in all sports
> • A female college student
> • A policeman with a gun

In this type of values clarification exercise, there are no right or wrong answers. The clarification of values is left up to the individual student. Advocates of values clarification say it is value-free. However, critics argue that its controversial content offends community standards. They also say that because of its relativistic nature, values clarification undermines accepted values and fails to stress right behavior.

Cognitive Moral Education

Cognitive moral education *is an educational approach based on the belief that students should learn to value things like democracy and justice as their moral reasoning develops.* Kohlberg's theory, which we discussed earlier in this chapter has been the basis for a number of cognitive moral education programs. In a typical program, high school students meet in a semester-long course to discuss a number of moral issues. The instructor acts as a facilitator rather than as a director of the class. The hope is that students will develop more advanced notions of such concepts as cooperation, trust, responsibility, and community. Toward the end of his career, Kohlberg (1986) recognized that the moral atmosphere of the school is more important than he initially envisioned. For example, in one study, a semester-long moral education class based on Kohlberg's theory was successful in advancing moral thinking in three democratic schools but not in three authoritarian schools (Higgins, Power, & Kohlberg, 1983).

Recall from earlier in the chapter that Carol Gilligan (1982, 1996) believes that moral development should focus more on social relationships than Kohlberg does.

values clarification
An educational approach that focuses on helping people clarify what their lives are for and what is worth working for. Students are encouraged to define their own values and understand others' values.

cognitive moral education
An approach based on the belief that students should learn to value things like democracy and justice as their moral reasoning develops; Kohlberg's theory has been the basis for many of the cognitive moral education approaches.

Exploring Character Education
The Center for the Fourth and Fifth RS
Character Education Topics
Exploring Values Education
Variations in Moral Education
Association for Moral Education
Moral Education in Japan
http://www.mhhe.com/santrocka9

service learning
A form of education that promotes social responsibility and service to the community.

Thus, applying Gilligan's view to moral education, emphasis should be placed on such topics as caring, sensitivity to others' feelings, and relationships. In her view, schools should better recognize the importance of relationships in the development of adolescent girls.

THROUGH THE EYES OF ADOLESCENTS

Finding a Way to Get a Playground

Twelve-year-old Katie Bell more than just about anything else wanted a playground in her New Jersey town. She knew that other kids also wanted one so she put together a group, which generated fund-raising ideas for the playground. They presented their ideas to the town council. Her group got more youth involved. They helped raise money by selling candy and sandwiches door-to-door. Katie says, "We learned to work as a community. This will be an important place for people to go and have picnics and make new friends." Katie's advice, "You won't get anywhere if you don't try."

Katie Bell (*front*) and some of her volunteers.

Service Learning

Service learning *is a form of education that promotes social responsibility and service to the community.* In service learning, adolescents might engage in tutoring, help the elderly, work in a hospital, assist at a daycare center, or clean up a vacant lot to make a play area. An important goal of service learning is for adolescents to become less self-centered and more strongly motivated to help others (Santilli, Falbo, & Harris, 2002; Waterman, 1997).

Service learning takes education out into the community (Levesque & Prosser, 1996; Sherrod & Brabeck, 2002; Youniss, 2002). One eleventh-grade student worked as a reading tutor for students from low-SES backgrounds with reading skills well below their grade levels. She commented that until she did the tutoring she did not realize how many students had not experienced the same opportunities that she had when she was growing up. An especially rewarding moment was when one young girl told her, "I want to learn to read like you so I can go to college when I grow up." Thus, service learning can benefit not only adolescents but also the recipients of their help.

Researchers have found that service learning benefits adolescents in a number of ways:

- Their grades improve and they become more motivated and set more goals (Johnson & others, 1998; Serow, Ciechalski, & Daye, 1990).
- Their self-esteem improves (Hamburg, 1997; Johnson & others, 1998).
- They become less alienated (Calabrese & Schumer, 1986).
- They increasingly reflect on society's moral order and social concerns (Metz & McLellan, 2000; Yates, 1995).

In a study conducted with a sample of adolescents in Camden, New Jersey, one of the poorest cities in the United States, a number of African American and Latino American adolescents were nominated by community leaders for having demonstrated unusual commitments to caring for others or serving the community (Hart & Fegley, 1995). Even in the face of trying circumstances, these adolescents had a strong caring orientation.

More high schools are now requiring community service. In one survey, 15 percent of the nation's largest school districts had such a requirement (National and Community Service Coalition, 1995). Even though required community service has increased in high schools, in one survey of 40,000 adolescents, two-thirds said that they had never done any volunteer work to help other people (Benson, 1993). The benefits of service learning, for both the volunteer and the recipient, suggest that more adolescents should be required to participate in such programs.

Since the last review, we have studied a number of ideas about moral education. This review should help you reach your learning goals related to this topic.

☐ FOR YOUR REVIEW

Learning Goal 5
Describe moral education

- The hidden curriculum concept was proposed by John Dewey to refer to the moral atmosphere of a school.
- Character education is a direct education approach that advocates teaching adolescents a basic moral literacy.
- Values clarification focuses on helping people clarify what their lives are for and what is worth working for.
- Cognitive moral education, based on Kohlberg's theory, stresses that adolescents should learn to value things like democracy and justice as their moral reasoning develops.
- Service learning is a form of education that promotes social responsibility and service to the community. Participation in service learning is linked with a number of positive aspects of adolescent development.

In our discussion of moral education, we have seen that developing positive values is thought to be important. Next, we will further explore values in adolescents' lives.

VALUES, RELIGION, AND CULTS

What are adolescents' values like today? How powerful is religion in adolescents' lives? Why do some adolescents run away to join cults? We consider each of these questions in turn.

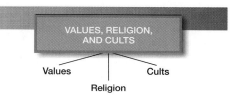

VALUES, RELIGION, AND CULTS

Values   Cults

Religion

Values

Adolescents carry with them a set of values that influences their thoughts, feelings, and actions (Flanagan, 1997). **Values** *are beliefs and attitudes about the way things should be.* They involve what is important to us. We attach values to all sorts of things: politics, religion, money, sex, education, helping others, family, friends, career, cheating, self-respect, and so on.

values
Beliefs and attitudes about the way things should be.

Over the past two decades, adolescents have shown an increased concern for personal well-being and a decreased concern for the well-being of others, especially for the disadvantaged (Sax & others, 2001). As shown in figure 12.3 on page 398, today's college freshmen are more strongly motivated to be well off financially and less motivated to develop a meaningful philosophy of life than were their counterparts of 20 or even 10 years ago. Student commitment to becoming very well off financially as a "very important" reason for attending college was at a high level in the 2000 survey (73 percent), compared to the 1970s (50 percent in 1971).

However, two aspects of values that increased during the 1960s continue to characterize many of today's youth: self-fulfillment and self-expression (Conger, 1981, 1988). As part of their motivation for self-fulfillment, many adolescents show great interest in their physical health and well-being. Greater self-fulfillment and self-expression can be laudable goals, but if they become the only goals, self-destruction, loneliness, or alienation can result. Young people also need to develop a corresponding sense of commitment to others' welfare. Encouraging adolescents to have a strong commitment to others, in concert with an interest in self-fulfillment, is an important task for America at the beginning of the twenty-first century.

However, there are some signs that today's college students are shifting toward a stronger interest in the welfare of our society. For example, between 1986 and 2001, there was an increase in the percentage of college freshmen who said they will

Values of American College Freshmen
National Service Learning Clearinghouse
Give Five
Kids Who Care
Volunteer Matching Online
http://www.mhhe.com/santrocka9

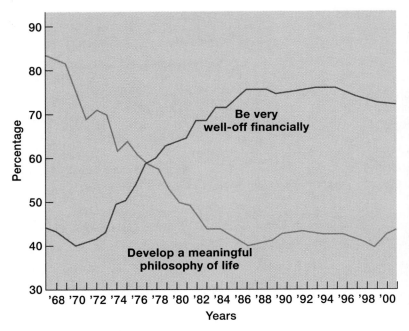

█ FIGURE 12.3
Changing Freshmen Life Goals, 1968–2001

In the last three decades, a significant change has occurred in freshmen students' life goals. A far greater percentage of today's college freshmen state that a "very important" life goal is to be well off financially, and far fewer state that developing a meaningful philosophy of life is a "very important" life goal.

participate in volunteer or community service work (23 percent in 2001 compared to 18 percent in 1986) (Sax & others, 2001). For successful adjustment in life, it is important to seek self-fulfillment *and* have a strong commitment to others.

Research on adolescents in seven different countries revealed that family values of compassion and social responsibility were the values that were most consistently linked with adolescent participation in community service, commitment to serving their country, and empathy for disenfranchised groups (Bowes & Flanagan, 2000; Flanagan & others, 1998). In one recent analysis, it was revealed that middle school civics textbooks are far more likely to discuss an individual's rights rather than social responsibility (Simmons & Avery, in press). Thus, adolescents may benefit from a stronger emphasis on social responsibility in both family and school contexts.

Religion

Many children and adolescents show an interest in religion, and religious institutions created by adults are designed to introduce certain beliefs to them and ensure that they will carry on a religious tradition. For example, societies have invented Sunday schools, parochial education, tribal transmission of religious traditions, and parental teaching of children at home.

Does this indoctrination work? In many cases it does (Paloutzian, 2000). In general, adults tend to adopt the religious teachings of their upbringing. For instance, individuals who are Catholics by the time they are 25 years of age, and who were raised as Catholics, likely will continue to be Catholics throughout their adult years. If a religious change or reawakening occurs, it is most likely to take place during adolescence.

CAREERS IN ADOLESCENT DEVELOPMENT

Constance Flanagan
Professor of Youth Civic Development

Connie Flanagan with adolescents.

Constance (Connie) Flanagan is a professor of youth civic development in the College of Agricultural Sciences at Pennsylvania State University. Her research focuses on youths' views about justice and the factors in families, schools, and communities that promote civic values, connections, and skills in youth (Flanagan, 2002).

Connie obtained her undergraduate degree in psychology from Duquesne University, her master's degree in education from the University of Iowa, and her Ph.D. from the University of Michigan. She has a special interest in improving the U.S. social policy for adolescents and serves as co-chair of the Committee on Child Development, Public Policy, and Public Information for the Society for Research in Child Development. In addition to teaching undergraduate and graduate classes, conducting research, and serving on various committees, Connie also evaluates research for potential publication as a member of the editorial board of *Journal of Adolescent Research* and *Journal of Research on Adolescence*. She also presents her ideas and research at numerous national and international meetings.

Religious issues are important to adolescents (Paloutzian & Santrock, 2000). In one survey, 95 percent of 13- to 18-year-olds said that they believe in God or a universal spirit (Gallup & Bezilla, 1992). Almost three-fourths of adolescents said that they pray, and about one-half indicated that they had attended religious services within the past week. Almost one-half of the youth said that it is very important for a young person to learn religious faith.

In one recent study of 9,700 adolescents, going to church was linked with better grades for students from low-income backgrounds (Regnerus, 2001). Churchgoing may benefit students because religious communities encourage socially acceptable behavior, which includes doing well in school. Churchgoing also may benefit students because churches often offer positive role models for students.

Developmental Changes   Adolescence can be an especially important juncture in religious development. Even if children have been indoctrinated into a religion by their parents, because of advances in their cognitive development they may begin to question what their own religious beliefs truly are.

During adolescence, especially in late adolescence and the college years, identity development becomes a central focus (Erikson, 1968). Adolescents want to know answers to questions like these: "Who am I?" "What am I all about as a person?" "What kind of life do I want to lead?" As part of their search for identity, adolescents begin to grapple in more sophisticated, logical ways with such questions as "Why am I on this planet?" "Is there really a God or higher spiritual being, or have I just been believing what my parents and the church imprinted in my mind?" "What really are my religious views?"

The cognitive developmental theory of famous Swiss psychologist Jean Piaget (1952) provides a theoretical backdrop for understanding religious development in

Religion enlightens, terrifies, subdues; it gives faith, inflicts remorse, inspires resolutions, and inflames devotion.

—Henry Newman
*English Churchman and Writer,
19th Century*

Many children and adolescents show an interest in religion, and many religious institutions created by adults (such as this Muslim school in Malaysia) are designed to introduce them to religious benefits and ensure that they will carry on a religious tradition.

Exploring the Psychology of Religion
Psychology of Religion Resources
Psychology of Religion Journals
http://www.mhhe.com/santrocka9

children and adolescents ◀‖‖ P. 46. For example, in one study children were asked about their understanding of certain religious pictures and Bible stories (Goldman, 1961). The children's responses fell into three stages closely related to Piaget's theory.

In the first stage (up until 7 or 8 years of age)—*preoperational intuitive religious thought*—children's religious thoughts were unsystematic and fragmented. The children often either did not fully understand the material in the stories or did not consider all of the evidence. For example, one child's response to the question "Why was Moses afraid to look at God?" (Exodus 3:6) was "Because God had a funny face!"

In the second stage (occurring from 7 or 8 to 13 or 14 years of age)—*concrete operational religious thought*—children focused on particular details of pictures and stories. For example, in response to the question about why Moses was afraid to look at God, one child said, "Because it was a ball of fire. He thought he might burn him." Another child voiced, "It was a bright light and to look at it might blind him."

In the third stage (age 14 through the remainder of adolescence)—*formal operational religious thought*—adolescents revealed a more abstract, hypothetical religious understanding. For example, one adolescent said that Moses was afraid to look at God because "God is holy and the world is sinful." Another youth responded, "The awesomeness and almightiness of God would make Moses feel like a worm in comparison."

Other researchers have found similar developmental changes in children and adolescents. For example, in one study, at about 17 or 18 years of age adolescents increasingly commented about freedom, meaning, and hope—abstract concepts—when making religious judgments (Oser & Gmünder, 1991).

Religiousness and Sexuality in Adolescence   One area of religion's influence on adolescent development involves sexual activity. Although variability and change in church teachings make it difficult to characterize religious doctrines simply, most churches

How do religious thought and behavior change as children and adolescents develop? How are children's and adolescents' religious conceptions influenced by their cognitive development?

discourage premarital sex. Thus, the degree of adolescent participation in religious organizations may be more important than religious affiliation as a determinant of premarital sexual attitudes and behavior. Adolescents who attend religious services frequently might hear messages about abstaining from sex. Involvement of adolescents in religious organizations also enhances the probability that they will become friends with adolescents who have restrictive attitudes toward premarital sex. In one study, adolescents who attend church frequently and valued religion in their lives were less experienced sexually and had less permissive attitudes toward premarital sex than did their counterparts who attended church infrequently and said that religion did not play a strong role in their lives (Thornton & Camburn, 1989). In one recent study, the link between religion and sexuality was confirmed (Fehring & others, 1998). In college students, guilt, prayer, organized religious activity, and religious well-being were associated with fewer sexual encounters. However, though religious involvement is associated with a lower incidence of sexual activity among adolescents, adolescents who are religiously involved and sexually active are less likely to use medical methods of contraception (especially the pill) than are their sexually active counterparts with low religious involvement (Studer & Thornton, 1987, 1989).

As we have seen, religion is a pervasive influence throughout the world. Next, we will focus on cults, which in some cases have been described as fringe religions.

Cults

Cults have been defined in various ways, ranging from "dangerous institutions that cause severe emotional harm" to "marginal and deviant groups" to "fringe, often new, religious movements." Cults have been described as being controlled by a charismatic

Cult 101
Cults and Mind Control
Social Psychological Aspects
of Cults
The Heaven's Gate Website
Dangerous Cults
http://www.mhhe.com/santrocka9

leader, as fostering the idea that there is only one correct set of beliefs and practices, as demanding unquestionable loyalty and obedience, as using mind-control techniques, as using deception and deceit in recruiting and interacting with the outside world, and as exploiting members' labor and finances (Galanter, 1999, 2000).

What is the difference between a cult and a church, a service club, or groups like Alcoholics Anonymous? There are many differences, but one major one involves the ultimate goal of the group (Cialdini & Rhoad, 1999). Established religions and altruistic movements focus outward, attempting to better the lives of members as well as non-members. Cults serve the purposes of the cult's leader. Their energies are directed inward rather than outward. Also, religions and altruistic movements usually do not involve overbearing authoritarian control by a leader, the use of deception in recruiting members, coercive influence techniques, and the replacement of one identity with a new identity that would not have been freely chosen by the individual before joining the group.

Who joins cults? For the most part, normal, average people. Approximately two-thirds of cult members are psychologically healthy individuals who come from normal families (Cialdini & Rhoad, 1999). The remaining one-third often have depressive symptoms, in many cases linked with personal loss such as a death in the family, a failed romantic relationship, or career problems. Only about 5 percent of cult members have major psychological problems before joining the cult. Cults prefer intelligent, productive individuals who can contribute money and talent to "the cause," whatever that might be.

Many individuals who become cult members are in a transitional phase of life. They have moved to a new city, lost a job, dropped out of school, or given up traditional religion as personally irrelevant. Potential cult members might find their work boring or stressful, their education meaningless, their social life not going well, their family remote or dysfunctional, their friends too busy to spend time with them, or their trust in government lost. Cults promise to fulfill most of a person's individual needs and to make their life safe, healthy, caring, and predictable. Cult leaders offer followers simple paths to happiness.

Some cult leaders have total authority over their disciples in both spiritual and material matters (Saliba, 1996). These leaders might portray themselves as inspired by, and receiving special revelations from, God. Some cults are based on a book by the cult leader that is believed to be revealed or inspired, as in the case of L. Ron Hubbard (deceased), founder of the Church of Scientology.

One all-powerful cult leader was Marshall Herff Applewhite, who recruited followers to the Heaven's Gate cult, a blend of New Age occultism and science-fiction fantasy. In 1997, 39 cult members died when they swallowed pudding laced with barbiturates and washed it down with vodka. After swallowing the lethal concoction, they reclined on their beds so their spirits could ascend to the "Level Above Human," as Applewhite called it. He had convinced the followers that a UFO was in the Hale-Bopp comet's slipstream and that the comet's appearance was a sign that it was time to go home.

What makes cults dangerous? Philip Zimbardo (1997) believes it depends to some degree on the kind of cult, since they come in so many sizes, purposes, and disguises (at last count there were more than 2,500 cults in the United States). Some cults are in the business of power and money, needing members to give money, work for free, or beg and to recruit new members. Some cults require members to turn over exorbitant amounts of money or property, some require exhausting labor, most demand that members sever ties with former friends and family (which creates total dependence on the cult for one's identity), and many cults destroy the individual's freedom of thought. The potential for abuse is highest in cults that are physically and socially isolated from the outside community.

Since the last review, we have studied a number of ideas about values, religion, and cults. The following review should help you reach your learning goals related to these topics.

☐ FOR YOUR REVIEW

Learning Goal 6
Evaluate values in adolescence

- Values are the beliefs and attitudes about the way things should be.
- Over the last two decades, adolescents have shown an increased concern for personal well-being and a decreased interest in the welfare of others. Recently, adolescents have shown an increased interest in community values and societal issues.

Learning Goal 7
Discuss religion in adolescence

- Many children and adolescents show an interest in religion, and religious institutions are designed to introduce them to religious beliefs.
- Adolescence may be a special juncture in religious development for many individuals. Piaget's theory provides a theoretical foundation for understanding developmental changes in religion. Links have been found between adolescent sexuality and religiousness.

Learning Goal 8
Know about cults

- Cults have been defined in various ways, ranging from dangerous institutions to fringe, often new, religious movements.
- Many people who join cults are in a transitional phase in their lives, and cults promise to fulfill their needs.
- The potential for the worst abuse is when a cult is physically and socially isolated from the outside community.

In this chapter, we have focused on moral development, values, and religions. In chapter 13, we will turn our attention to achievement, careers, and work.

CHAPTER MAP

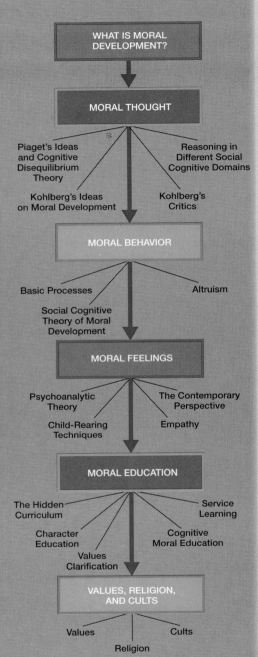

WHAT IS MORAL DEVELOPMENT?

MORAL THOUGHT

Piaget's Ideas and Cognitive Disequilibrium Theory

Reasoning in Different Social Cognitive Domains

Kohlberg's Ideas on Moral Development

Kohlberg's Critics

MORAL BEHAVIOR

Basic Processes

Altruism

Social Cognitive Theory of Moral Development

MORAL FEELINGS

Psychoanalytic Theory

The Contemporary Perspective

Child-Rearing Techniques

Empathy

MORAL EDUCATION

The Hidden Curriculum

Service Learning

Character Education

Cognitive Moral Education

Values Clarification

VALUES, RELIGION, AND CULTS

Values

Cults

Religion

REACH YOUR LEARNING GOALS

At the beginning of the chapter, we stated eight learning goals and encouraged you to review material related to these goals at four points in the chapter. This is a good time to return to these reviews. Use them to guide your study and help you to reach your learning goals.

Page 388

Learning Goal 1   Know what moral development is
Learning Goal 2   Explain moral thought

Page 394

Learning Goal 3   Discuss moral behavior
Learning Goal 4   Understand moral feelings

Page 397

Learning Goal 5   Describe moral education

Page 403

Learning Goal 6   Evaluate values in adolescence
Learning Goal 7   Discuss religion in adolescence
Learning Goal 8   Know about cults

KEY TERMS

moral development 380
heteronomous morality 381
autonomous morality 381
immanent justice 381
cognitive disequilibrium theory 382
internalization 382
preconventional reasoning 382
conventional reasoning 383
postconventional reasoning 383
justice perspective 387
care perspective 387
social cognitive theory of moral development 389
altruism 390

forgiveness 390
ego ideal 391
conscience 391
love withdrawal 392
power assertion 392
induction 392
empathy 393
hidden curriculum 394
character education 394
values clarification 395
cognitive moral education 395
service learning 396
values 397

KEY PEOPLE

Jean Piaget 381
Martin Hoffman 382
Lawrence Kohlberg 382
James Rest 385
Richard Shweder 386
Carol Gilligan 386

Hugh Hartshorne and Mark May 389
Albert Bandura 389
Sigmund Freud 391
Erik Erikson 391
Nancy Eisenberg 392
John Dewey 394

Resources for Improving the Lives of Adolescents

Cults

(1999) by Marc Galanter
New York: Oxford University Press

This recent book explores many aspects of cults, including their social psychological characteristics.

Four-One-One

7304 Beverly Street
Annandale, VA 22003
703–354–6270

This is a clearinghouse for information on community and national volunteer organizations.

Invitation to the Psychology of Religion

(2000, 3rd ed.) by Raymond Paloutzian
Needham Heights, MA: Allyn & Bacon

This book provides a broad overview of topics in the psychology of religion, including religious development, conversion, religious experience, attitudes and behavior, and mental health.

Meeting at the Crossroads

(1992) by Lyn Mikel Brown and Carol Gilligan
Cambridge, MA: Harvard University Press

This book provides a vivid portrayal of how adolescent girls are often ignored and misunderstood as they make their passage through adolescence.

National Helpers Network, Inc.

245 Fifth Avenue, Suite 1705
New York, NY 10016-8728
212–679–7461

This network developed the Early Adolescent Helper Program, an approach to service learning.

Postconventional Thinking

(1999) by James Rest, Darcia Narvaez, Muriel Bebeau, and
   Stephen Thoma
Hillsdale, NJ: Erlbaum

James Rest and his colleagues provide a neo-Kohlbergian analysis of moral development.

Service-Learning

(1997) by Alan Waterman (Ed.)
Mahwah, NJ: Erlbaum

A number of leading experts discuss many aspects of service learning.

Taking It to the Net   http://www.mhhe.com/santrocka9

1. Young children do what they think is right and do not do what they think is wrong in order to avoid punishment. The reasons for doing "right" change as we grow into and through the adolescent years. *As a future parent, what can you do to foster this aspect of moral development in your children?*

2. You are discussing issues of right and wrong, punishment, and moral reasoning in your philosophy class. Your instructor has broken the class into groups, and your group is assigned to evaluate arguments, pro and con, concerning the death penalty and to classify them according to Kohlberg's stages of moral reasoning. *What are some of the arguments pro and con and how did your group classify them?*

3. The nature and content of sex education instruction in public schools often is a lightning rod, attracting large numbers of parents to school board meetings. In trying to explain why, your adolescent psychology professor mentions issues of moral education, the hidden curriculum, and character education. *How do these concerns relate to the large parental turnout at school board meetings?*

Connect to *http://www.mhhe.com/santrocka9* to research the answers and complete these exercises. In some cases, you'll also find further instructions on this site.

ACHIEVEMENT, CAREERS, AND WORK

They can because they think they can.
—Virgil
Roman Poet, 1st Century B.C.

■ KIM-CHI AND THUY

Kim-Chi Trinh was only 9 years old in Vietnam when her father used his savings to buy passage for her on a fishing boat. It was a costly and risky sacrifice for the family, who placed Kim-Chi on the small boat, among strangers, in the hope that she eventually would reach the United States, where she would get a good education and enjoy a better life.

Kim made it to the United States and coped with a succession of three foster families. When she graduated from high school in San Diego in 1988, she had a straight-A average and a number of college scholarship offers. When asked why she excels in school, Kim-Chi says that she has to do well because she owes it to her parents, who are still in Vietnam.

Kim-Chi is one of a wave of bright, highly motivated Asians who are immigrating to America. Asian Americans are the fastest-growing ethnic minority group in the United States—two out of five immigrants are now Asian. Although Asian Americans make up only 2.4 percent of the U.S. population, they constitute 17 percent of the undergraduates at Harvard, 18 percent at MIT, 27 percent at the University of California at Berkeley, and a staggering 35 percent at the University of California at Irvine.

Not all Asian American youth do this well, however. Poorly educated Vietnamese, Cambodian, and Hmong refugee youth are especially at risk for school-related problems. Many refugee children's histories are replete with losses and trauma. Thuy, a 12-year-old Vietnamese girl, has been in the United States for two years and resides with her father in a small apartment with a cousin's family of five in the inner city of a West Coast metropolitan area (Huang, 1989). While trying to escape from Saigon, the family became separated, and the wife and two younger children remained in Vietnam. Thuy's father has had an especially difficult time adjusting to the United States, struggling with English classes and being unable to maintain several jobs as a waiter. When Thuy received a letter from her mother saying that her 5-year-old brother had died, Thuy's schoolwork began to deteriorate, and she showed marked signs of depression—lack of energy, loss of appetite, withdrawal from peer relations, and a general feeling of hopelessness. At the insistence of the school, she and her father went to the child and adolescent unit of a community mental health center. It took the therapist a long time to establish credibility with Thuy and her father, but eventually they began to trust the therapist as a good listener who had competent advice about how to handle different experiences in the new country. The therapist also contacted Thuy's teacher, who said that Thuy had been involved in several interethnic skirmishes at school. With the assistance of the mental health clinic, the school initiated interethnic student panels to address cultural differences and discuss reasons for ethnic hostility. Thuy was selected to participate in these panels. Her father became involved in the community mutual assistance association, and Thuy's academic performance began to improve.

THIS CHAPTER FOCUSES ON ACHIEVEMENT, careers, and work. As adolescence unfolds, achievement takes a more central role in development, a stronger interest in potential careers occurs, and work becomes a common theme. By the time you have completed this chapter, you should be able to reach these learning goals:

1   Explain why adolescence is a critical juncture in achievement

2   Discuss achievement processes

3   Describe the roles of ethnicity and culture in achievement

4   Understand how to motivate hard-to-reach, low-achieving adolescents

5   Know about career development

6   Discuss the role of work in adolescence

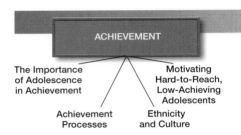

ACHIEVEMENT

Some developmentalists worry that the United States is rapidly becoming a nation of hurried, wired people who are raising their youth to become the same way—too uptight about success and failure, and far too worried about how personal accomplishments compare with those of others (Elkind, 1981). Others worry that our achievement expectations for youth have been too low (Honig, 1996; Stevenson, Hofer, & Randell, 2000).

The Importance of Adolescence in Achievement

Adolescence is a critical juncture in achievement (Eccles & Wigfield, 2000; Henderson & Dweck, 1990). New social and academic pressures force adolescents toward different roles, roles that often involve more responsibility. Achievement becomes a more serious business in adolescence, and adolescents begin to sense that the game of life is now being played for real (Yoon & others, 1996). They even may begin to perceive current successes and failures as predictors of future outcomes in the adult world. And as demands on adolescents intensify, different areas of their lives may come into conflict. Adolescents' social interests may cut into the time they need to pursue academic matters, or ambitions in one area may undermine the attainment of goals in another, as when academic achievement leads to social disapproval.

Whether or not adolescents effectively adapt to these new academic and social pressures is determined, in part, by psychological, motivational, and contextual factors (Eccles & Wigfield, 2000; Eccles, Wigfield, & Schiefele, 1998; Stipek, 2002; Wigfield & Eccles, 2001). Indeed, adolescents' achievement is due to much more than their intellectual ability. Students who are less bright than others often show an adaptive motivational pattern—persistent at tasks and confident about their ability to solve problems, for example—and turn out to be high achievers. In contrast, some of the brightest students show maladaptive achievement patterns—give up easily and do not have confidence in their academic skills, for example—and turn out to be low achievers.

Achievement Processes

A number processes are involved in achievement. We will explore these processes, beginning with the distinction between intrinsic and extrinsic motivation.

Calvin and Hobbes   by Bill Watterson

Intrinsic and Extrinsic Motivation   We begin our coverage of extrinsic and intrinsic motivation by examining what they are, then turn to a number of ideas about how they work best in learning and achievement.

The behavioral perspective emphasizes the importance of extrinsic motivation in achievement. **Extrinsic motivation** *involves external incentives such as rewards and punishments.* The humanistic and cognitive approaches stress the importance of intrinsic motivation in achievement. **Intrinsic motivation** *is based on internal factors such as self-determination, curiosity, challenge, and effort.* Some adolescents study hard because they want to make good grades or avoid parental disapproval (extrinsic motivation). Other adolescents study hard because they are internally motivated to achieve high standards in their work (intrinsic motivation) (Gottfried, Fleming, & Gottfried, 2001).

Self-Determination and Personal Choice
One view of intrinsic motivation emphasizes self-determination (deCharms, 1984; Deci & Ryan, 1994). In this view, adolescents want to believe that they are doing something because of their own will, not because of external success or rewards.

Researchers have found that giving adolescents some choice and providing opportunities for personal responsibility increases their internal motivation and intrinsic interest in school tasks (Covington & Mueller, 2001; Stipek, 1996). For example, one study found that high school science students who were encouraged to organize their own experiments demonstrated more care and interest in laboratory work than their counterparts who were given detailed instructions and directions (Rainey, 1965). In another study that included mainly African American students from low-SES backgrounds, teachers were encouraged to give them more responsibility for their school program (deCharms, 1984). This consisted of opportunities to set their own goals, plan how to reach the goals, and monitor their progress toward the goals. Students were given some choice in the activities they wanted to engage in and when they would do them. They also were encouraged to take personal responsibility for their behavior, including reaching the goals they had set. Compared to a control group, students in the intrinsic motivation/self-determination group had higher achievement gains and were more likely to graduate from high school.

Optimal Experiences and Flow
Mihaly Csikszentmihalyi (1990, 1993), whose work on creativity was discussed in chapter 4, also has developed ideas that are relevant to understanding motivation ◀‖‖ P. 125. He has studied the optimal experiences of people for more than two decades. These optimal experiences occur when people report feelings of deep enjoyment and happiness. Csikszentmihalyi uses the term **flow** *to*

extrinsic motivation
External motivational factors such as rewards and punishments.

intrinsic motivation
Internal motivational factors such as self-determination, curiosity, challenge, and effort.

Motivation and Achievement
Intrinsic Motivation
http://www.mhhe.com/santrocka9

flow
Csikszentmihalyi's concept of optimal life experiences, which he believes occur most often when people develop a sense of mastery and are absorbed in a state of concentration when they're engaged in an activity.

Students' Perceived Level of Their Own Skill

		Low	High
Students' Perceived Level of Challenge	Low	Apathy	Boredom
	High	Anxiety	Flow

FIGURE 13.1
Outcomes of Perceived Levels of Challenge and Skill

attribution theory
The concept that individuals are motivated to discover the underlying causes of their own behavior or performance in their effort to make sense of it.

Attribution
Effort, Expectations, and Motivation
http://www.mhhe.com/santrocka9

describe optimal experiences in life. Flow occurs most often when people develop a sense of mastery and are absorbed in a state of concentration while they engage in an activity. He argues that flow occurs when individuals are engaged in challenges they find neither too difficult nor too easy.

Perceived levels of challenge and skill can result in different outcomes (see figure 13.1) (Brophy, 1998). Flow is most likely to occur in areas in which adolescents are challenged and perceive themselves as having a high degree of skill. When adolescents' skills are high but the activity provides little challenge, the result is boredom. When both challenge and skill levels are low, apathy occurs. And when adolescents perceive themselves as not having adequate skills to master a challenging task they face, they experience anxiety.

At this point we have discussed a number of ideas about the importance of adolescence in achievement and extrinsic and intrinsic motivation. Next we will explore another important aspect of understanding achievement: attribution. As you read about attribution, you will see that intrinsic and extrinsic motivation are often one set of causes that adolescents look to as they attempt to explain their behavior.

Attribution   **Attribution theory** *states that in their effort to make sense out of their own behavior or performance, individuals are motivated to discover its underlying causes. Attributions are perceived causes of outcomes.* In a way, attribution theorists say, adolescents are like intuitive scientists, seeking to explain the cause behind what happens. For example, an adolescent asks "Why am I not doing well in this class?" "Did I get a good grade because I studied hard or the teacher made up an easy test, or both?" The search for a cause or an explanation is most likely to be initiated when unexpected and important events end in failure, such as when a good student gets a low grade (Graham & Weiner, 1996). Some of the most frequently inferred causes of success and failure are ability, effort, task ease or difficulty, luck, mood, and help or hindrance from others.

Bernard Weiner (1986, 1992, 2000) identified three dimensions of causal attributions: (1) *locus* refers to whether the cause is internal or external to the actor, (2) *stability* focuses on the extent to which the cause remains the same or changes, and (3) *controllability* is the extent to which the individual can control the cause. For example, an adolescent might perceive his aptitude as internally located, stable, and uncontrollable. The adolescent also might perceive chance or luck as external to himself, variable, and uncontrollable. Figure 13.2 on page 411 lists eight possible combinations of locus, stability, and controllability and how they match up with various common explanations of failure.

An adolescent's perception of success or failure as due to internal or external factors influences the adolescent's self-esteem (Alderman, 1999). Adolescents who perceive their success as due to internal reasons, such as effort, are more likely to increase their self-esteem following success than are adolescents who believe that their success was due to external reasons, such as luck.

An adolescent's perception of the stability of a cause influences her expectation of success. If she ascribes a positive outcome to a stable cause, such as aptitude, she expects future success. Similarly, if she ascribes a negative outcome to a stable cause, she expects future failure. When adolescents attribute failure to unstable causes such as bad luck or lack of effort, they can develop expectations that they will be able to succeed in the future, because they perceive the cause of their failure as changeable.

An adolescent's perception of the controllability of a cause is related to a number of emotional outcomes such as anger, guilt, pity, and shame (Graham & Weiner, 1996). When adolescents perceive themselves as prevented from succeeding because of external factors that other people could have controlled (such as noise or bias), they often become angry. When adolescents perceive themselves as not having done well because of internally controllable causes (such as not making enough effort or being negligent), they often feel guilty. When students perceive others as not achieving their goals because of uncontrollable causes (such as lack of ability or a physical handicap), they feel pity or sympathy. And when adolescents perceive themselves as failing because of internally uncontrollable factors (such as low ability), they feel shame, humiliation, and embarrassment.

To see how attributions affect subsequent achievement strivings, consider these two adolescents (Graham & Weiner, 1996):

1. Jane flunks her math test. She subsequently seeks tutoring and increases her study time.
2. Susan also fails her math test but decides to drop out of school.

Jane's negative outcome (failing the test) motivated her to search for the reasons behind her low grade. She attributes the failure to herself, not blaming her teacher or bad luck. She also attributes the failure to an unstable factor—lack of preparation and study time. Thus, she perceives that her failure is due to internal, unstable, and controllable factors. Because the factors are unstable, Jane has a reasonable expectation that she can still succeed in the future. And because the factors are controllable, she also feels guilty. Her expectations for success enable her to overcome her deflated sense of self-esteem. Her hope for the future results in renewed goal-setting and increased motivation to do well on the next test.

Susan's negative outcome (also failing the test) led her to drop out of school rather than resolve to study harder. Her failure also stimulates her to make causal attributions. Susan ascribes failure to herself and attributes her poor performance to lack of ability, which is internal, stable, and uncontrollable. Because the cause is internal, her self-esteem suffers. Because it is stable, she sees failure in her future and has a helpless feeling that she can't do anything about it. And because it is uncontrollable, she feels ashamed and humiliated. In addition, her parents and teacher tell her they feel sorry for her but don't provide any recommendations or strategies for success, furthering her belief that she is incompetent. With low expectations for success, low self-esteem, and a depressed mood, Susan decides to drop out of school.

What are the best strategies for teachers to use in helping students like Susan change their attributions? Educational psychologists often recommend providing students with a planned series of experiences in achievement contexts in which modeling, information about strategies, practice, and feedback are used to help them (1) concentrate on the task at hand rather than worry about failing, (2) cope with failures by retracing their steps to discover their mistake or analyzing the problem to discover another approach, and (3) attribute their failures to a lack of effort rather than a lack of ability (Brophy, 1998; Dweck & Elliott, 1983).

The current strategy is that rather than exposing adolescents to models who handle tasks with ease and demonstrate success, they should be presented with models who struggle to overcome mistakes before finally succeeding (Brophy, 1998). In this way, adolescents learn how to deal with frustration, persist in the face of difficulties, and constructively cope with failure.

When students fail or do poorly on a test or assignment, they often generate causal attributions in an attempt to explain the poor performance. The following explanations reflect eight combinations of Weiner's three main categories of attributions: locus (internal-external), stability (stable-unstable), and controllability (controllable-uncontrollable).	
Combination of Causal Attributions	**Reason Students Give for Failure**
Internal-stable-uncontrollable	Low aptitude
Internal-stable-controllable	Never study
Internal-unstable-uncontrollable	Sick the day of the test
Internal-unstable-controllable	Did not study for this particular test
External-stable-uncontrollable	School has tough requirements
External-stable-controllable	The instructor is biased
External-unstable-uncontrollable	Bad luck
External-unstable-controllable	Friends failed to help

■ FIGURE 13.2
Combinations of Causal Attributions and Explanations for Failure

When students fail or do poorly on a test or assignment, they often generate causal attributions in an attempt to explain the poor performance. The following explanations reflect eight combinations of Weiner's three main categories of attributions: locus (internal-external), stability (stable-unstable), and controllability (controllable-uncontrollable).

Mastery Motivation   Closely related to intrinsic motivation and attribution is mastery motivation. Researchers have identified mastery as one of three types of achievement orientation: mastery, helpless, and performance.

Carol Dweck and her colleagues (Henderson & Dweck, 1990; Dweck & Leggett, 1988) have found that adolescents show two distinct responses to challenging or difficult circumstances: a mastery orientation or a helpless orientation. Adolescents with a **mastery orientation** *focus on the task rather than on their ability, have positive affect (suggesting they enjoy the challenge), and generate solution-oriented strategies that*

mastery orientation

An outlook in which individuals focus on the task rather than on their ability, have positive affect, and generate solution-oriented strategies that improve their performance.

helpless orientation
An outlook in which individuals focus on their personal inadequacies, often attribute their difficulty to a lack of ability, and display negative affect (including boredom and anxiety). This orientation undermines performance.

improve performance. Mastery-oriented students often instruct themselves to pay attention, to think carefully, and to remember strategies that worked for them in the past (Anderman, Maehr, & Midgeley, 1996). In contrast, adolescents with a **helpless orientation** *focus on their personal inadequacies, often attribute their difficulty to a lack of ability, and display negative affect (including boredom and anxiety).* This orientation undermines their performance.

Mastery- and helpless-oriented adolescents do not differ in general ability. However, they have different theories about their abilities. Mastery-oriented adolescents believe their ability can be changed and improved. They endorse such statements as "Smartness is something you can increase as much as you want to." Helpless-oriented adolescents believe that ability is basically fixed and cannot be changed. They endorse such statements as "You can learn new things, but how smart you are pretty much stays the same." The mastery orientation is much like the attributional combination of internal locus, unstable, and controllable cause. The helpless orientation is much like the attributional combination of internal locus, stable, and uncontrollable cause.

A mastery orientation also can be contrasted with a **performance orientation,** *which involves being concerned with outcome rather than process.* For performance-oriented adolescents, winning is what matters and happiness is thought to be a result of winning. For mastery-oriented adolescents, what matters is the sense that they are effectively interacting with their environment. Mastery-oriented adolescents do like to win, but winning isn't as important to them as it is to performance-oriented adolescents. Developing their skills is more important.

performance orientation
An outlook in which individuals are concerned with performance outcome rather than performance process. For performance-oriented students, winning is what matters.

Mastery motivation has much in common with Csikszentmihalyi's concept of flow, which occurs when adolescents become absorbed in a state of concentration during an activity. Mastery-oriented adolescents immerse themselves in a task and focus their concentration on developing their skills rather than on worrying about whether they are going to outperform others. In a state of flow, adolescents become so attuned to what they are doing that they are oblivious to distractions.

Performance-oriented adolescents who are not confident of their success face a special problem (Stipek, 1996). If they try and fail, they often take their failure as evidence of low ability. By not trying at all, they can maintain an alternative, personally more acceptable explanation for their failure. This dilemma leads some students to engage in behavior that protects them from an image of incompetence in the short run but interferes with their learning and achievement in the long run (Covington, 1992). To avoid the attribution of low ability, some of these adolescents simply don't try, or they cheat, or they resort to more subtle image-protecting strategies such as procrastinating, making excuses, working halfheartedly, or setting unrealistic goals.

Mastery Motivation
http://www.mhhe.com/santrocka9

Self-Efficacy **Self-efficacy** *is the belief that one can master a situation and produce favorable outcomes.* Albert Bandura (1994, 1997, 2000), whose social cognitive theory we described in chapter 2, "The Science of Adolescent Development," believes that self-efficacy is a critical factor in whether or not adolescents achieve ◀‖‖ P. 50. Self-efficacy has much in common with mastery motivation and intrinsic motivation. Self-efficacy is the belief that "I can"; helplessness is the belief that "I cannot" (Stipek, 1996). Adolescents with high self-efficacy endorse such statements as "I know that I will be able to learn the material in this class" and "I expect to be able to do well at this activity."

self-efficacy
The belief that one can master a situation and produce positive outcomes.

Dale Schunk (1991, 2001) has applied the concept of self-efficacy to many aspects of students' achievement. In his view, self-efficacy influences a student's choice of activities. Students with low self-efficacy for learning might avoid many learning tasks, especially those that are challenging. In contrast, their high-self-efficacy counterparts eagerly work at learning tasks. High-self-efficacy students are more likely to expend effort and persist longer at a learning task than low-self-efficacy students.

A teacher's self-efficacy will have a major impact on the quality of learning that students experience (Pintrich & Schunk, 2002). Teachers with a low sense of self-efficacy often become mired in classroom problems. Low-self-efficacy teachers don't have confidence in their ability to manage their classrooms, become stressed and angered at students' misbehavior, are pessimistic about students' ability to improve, take a custodial view of their job, often resort to restrictive and punitive modes of discipline, and say that if they had it to do all over again they would not choose teaching as a profession (Melby, 1995).

In one study, teachers' instructional self-efficacy was linked with their students' mathematical and language achievement over the course of an academic year (Ashton & Webb, 1986). Students learned much more from teachers with a sense of efficacy than from those beset by self-doubts. Teachers with high self-efficacy tend to view difficult students as reachable and teachable. They regard learning problems as surmountable with extra effort and ingenious strategies to help struggling students. Low-self-efficacy teachers are inclined to say that low student ability is the reason that their students are not learning.

Bandura (1997) also addressed the characteristics of efficacious schools. School leaders seek ways to improve instruction. They figure out ways to work around stifling policies and regulations that impede academic innovations. Masterful academic leadership by the principal builds teachers' sense of instructional efficacy. In low-achieving schools, principals function more as administrators and disciplinarians.

High expectations and standards for achievement pervade efficacious schools. Teachers regard their students as capable of high academic achievement, set challenging academic standards for them, and provide support to help them reach these high standards. In contrast, in low-achieving schools not much is expected academically of students; teachers spend less time actively teaching and monitoring students' academic progress, and they tend to write off a high percentage of students as unteachable (Brookover & others, 1979). Not surprisingly, students in such schools have low self-efficacy and a sense of academic futility.

THROUGH THE EYES OF PSYCHOLOGISTS

Dale Schunk
Purdue University

"Self-efficacy is especially important in school learning and other achievement situations."

Exploring Self-Efficacy
Self-Efficacy Resources
http://www.mhhe.com/santrocka9

Goal-Setting, Planning, and Self-Monitoring Goal-setting, planning, and self-monitoring are important aspects of adolescent achievement (Maehr, 2001; Midgley, 2002). Researchers have found that self-efficacy and achievement improve when adolescents set goals that are specific, proximal, and challenging (Bandura, 1997; Schunk, 2001). A nonspecific, fuzzy goal is "I want to be successful." A more concrete, specific goal is "I want to make the honor roll by the end of the semester."

Adolescents can set both long-term (distal) and short-term (proximal) goals. It is okay to let adolescents set some long-term goals, such as "I want to graduate from high school" or "I want to go to college," but they also need to create short-term goals, which are steps along the way. "Getting an A on the next math test" is an example of a short-term, proximal goal. So is "Doing all of my homework by 4 P.M. Sunday." David McNally, author of *Even Eagles Need a Push* (1990), advises that when adolescents set goals and plan, they should be reminded to live their lives one day at a time. Have them make their commitments in bite-size chunks. A house is built one brick at a time, a cathedral one stone at a time. The artist paints one stroke at a time. The student should also work in small increments.

Another good strategy is for adolescents to set challenging goals (Elliot & Thrash, 2001; Kaplan & others, 2002). A challenging goal is a commitment to self-improvement. Strong interest and involvement in activities is sparked by challenges. Goals that are easy to reach generate little interest or effort. However, goals should be optimally matched to the adolescent's skill level. If goals are unrealistically high, the result will be repeated failures that lower the adolescent's self-efficacy.

Carol Dweck (1996; Dweck & Leggett, 1988) and John Nicholls (1979) define goals in terms of immediate achievement-related focus and definition of success. For example, Nicholls distinguishes between ego-involved goals, task-involved goals, and work-avoidant goals. Adolescents who have ego-involved goals strive to maximize favorable evaluations and minimize unfavorable ones. For example, ego-involved adolescents focus on how smart they will look and how effectively they can outperform other adolescents. In contrast, adolescents who have task-involved goals focus on mastering tasks. They concentrate on how they can do the task and what they will learn. Adolescents with work-avoidant goals try to exert as little effort as possible when faced with a task.

*L*ife is a gift . . . Accept it.
Life is an adventure . . . Dare it.
Life is a mystery . . . Unfold it.
Life is a struggle . . . Face it.
Life is a puzzle . . . Solve it.
Life is an opportunity . . . Take it.
Life is a mission . . . Fulfill it.
Life is a goal . . . Achieve it.

—Author Unknown

Goal-Setting
Anxiety
http://www.mhhe.com/santrocka9

anxiety
A vague, highly unpleasant feeling of fear and apprehension.

It is not enough just to get adolescents to set goals. It also is important to encourage them to plan how they will reach their goals. Being a good planner means managing time effectively, setting priorities, and being organized.

Adolescents not only should plan their next week's activities but also monitor how well they are sticking to their plan. Once adolescents engage in a task, they need to monitor their progress, judge how well they are doing on the task, and evaluate the outcomes to regulate what they do in the future (Eccles, Wigfield, & Schiefele, 1998). Researchers have found that high-achieving adolescents often are self-regulatory learners (Schunk & Zimmerman, 1994). For example, high-achieving adolescents self-monitor their learning more and systematically evaluate their progress toward a goal more than low-achieving students do. Encouraging adolescents to self-monitor their learning conveys to them the message that they are responsible for their own behavior and that learning requires their active, dedicated participation (Zimmerman, Bonner, & Kovach, 1996).

Anxiety   **Anxiety** *is a vague, highly unpleasant feeling of fear and apprehension.* It is normal for students to be concerned or worried when they face school challenges, such as doing well on a test. Indeed, researchers have found that many successful students have moderate levels of anxiety (Bandura, 1997). However, some students have high levels of anxiety and worry constantly, which can significantly impair their ability to achieve.

Some adolescents' high anxiety levels are the result of parents' unrealistic achievement expectations and pressure. For many individuals, anxiety increases across the school years as they face more frequent evaluation, social comparison, and, for some, experiences of failure (Eccles, Wigfield, & Schiefele, 1998). When schools create such circumstances, they likely increase students' anxiety.

A number of programs have been created to reduce high anxiety levels (Wigfield & Eccles, 1989). Some intervention programs emphasize relaxation techniques. These programs often are effective at reducing anxiety but do not always lead to improved achievement. Anxiety intervention programs linked to the worry aspect of anxiety emphasize changing the negative, self-damaging thoughts of anxious students and replacing them with positive, task-focused thoughts (Meichenbaum & Butler, 1980). These programs have been more effective than the relaxation programs in improving students' achievement.

At this point, we have examined a number of ideas about adolescence as a critical juncture in achievement and achievement processes. This review should help you to reach your learning goals related to these topics.

FOR YOUR REVIEW

Learning Goal 1
Explain why adolescence is a critical juncture in achievement

- Social and academic pressures force adolescents to cope with achievement in new ways. Achievement expectations increase in secondary schools.
- Whether adolescents effectively adapt to these new pressures is determined in part by psychological and motivational factors.

Learning Goal 2
Discuss achievement processes

- Extrinsic motivation involves external incentives such as rewards and punishment. Intrinsic motivation is based on internal factors such as self-determination, curiosity, challenge, and effort. One view is that giving students some choice and providing opportunities for personal responsibility increase intrinsic motivation. Flow is most likely to occur in areas in which adolescents are challenged and perceive themselves as having a high degree of skill.

- Attribution theory states that individuals are motivated to discover the underlying causes of behavior in an effort to make sense out of the behavior. Weiner identified three dimensions of causal attributions: locus, stability, and controllability.
- A mastery orientation is preferred over helpless or performance orientations in achievement situations.
- Self-efficacy is the belief that one can master a situation and attain positive outcomes. Self-efficacy has been shown to be an important process in achievement.
- Goal-setting, planning, and self-monitoring are important aspects of achievement.
- A special concern is when adolescents have too much anxiety in achievement situations, which sometimes is linked to unrealistic parental expectations.

Now that we have explored adolescence as a critical juncture in achievement and a number of achievement processes, let's turn our attention to the important contexts of ethnicity and culture to see how they are linked to adolescent achievement.

Ethnicity and Culture

What is the nature of achievement in ethnic minority children? How does culture influence children's achievement?

Ethnicity The diversity that exists among ethnic minority adolescents is evident in their achievement. For example, many Asian American students have a strong academic achievement orientation, but some do not.

In addition to recognizing the diversity that exists within every cultural group in terms of their achievement, it also is important to distinguish between difference and deficiency. Too often the achievement of ethnic minority students—especially African American, Latino, and Native American students—has been interpreted as *deficits* by middle-socioeconomic-status White standards, when they simply are *culturally different and distinct* (Jones, 1994) ◀IIII P. 269.

At the same time, many investigations overlook the socioeconomic status (SES) of ethnic minority students (Graham & Taylor, 2001) ◀IIII P. 270. In many instances, when ethnicity *and* socioeconomic status are investigated in the same study, socioeconomic status predicts achievement better than ethnicity. Students from middle- and upper-SES families fare better than their counterparts from low-SES backgrounds in a host of achievement situations—expectations for success, achievement aspirations, and recognition of the importance of effort, for example (Gibbs, 1989).

Sandra Graham (1986, 1990) has conducted a number of studies that reveal not only stronger differences in socioeconomic status than in ethnicity in achievement, but also the importance of studying ethnic minority student motivation in the context of general motivational theory. Her inquiries fall within the framework of attribution theory and focus on the causes African American students cite for their achievement orientation, such as why they succeed or fail. She has found that middle-SES African American students do not fit the stereotype of being unmotivated. Like their White middle-SES counterparts, they have high achievement expectations and understand that failure is usually due to a lack of effort rather than bad luck.

A special challenge for many ethnic minority students, especially those living in poverty, is dealing with racial prejudice, conflict between the values of their group and the majority group, and a lack of high-achieving adults in their cultural group who can serve as positive role models (McLoyd, 1998, 2000; Spencer & Dornbusch, 1990).

It also is important to consider the nature of the schools that primarily serve ethnic minority students (Eccles, Wigfield, & Schiefele, 1998) ◀IIII P. 242. More than one-third of African American and almost one-third of Latino students attend schools in the 47 largest city school districts in the United States, compared with only 5 percent of White and 22 percent of Asian American students. Many of these ethnic minority students come from low-SES families (more than one-half are eligible for free or reduced-cost lunches). These inner-city schools are less likely than other schools to serve more

Jaime Escalante
Secondary School Math Teacher

An immigrant from Bolivia, Jaime Escalante became a math teacher at Garfield High School in East Los Angeles in the 1970s. When he began teaching at Garfield, many of the students had little confidence in their math abilities and most of the teachers had low expectations for the students' success. Escalante took it as a special challenge to improve the students' math skills and even get them to the point where they could perform well on the Educational Testing Service Advanced Placement (AP) calculus exam.

The first year was difficult. Escalante's calculus class began at 8 A.M. He told the students the doors would be open at 7 A.M. and that instruction would begin at 7:30 A.M. He also worked with them after school and on weekends. He put together lots of handouts, told the students to take extensive notes, and required them to keep a folder. He gave them a five-minute quiz each morning and a test every Friday. He started with fourteen students but within two weeks only half remained. Only five students lasted through the spring. One of the boys who quit said, "I don't want to come at 7 o'clock. Why should I?"

Due to Escalante's persistent, challenging, and inspiring teaching, Garfield High—a school plagued by poor funding, violence, and inferior working conditions—became ranked seventh in the United States in calculus. Escalante's commitment and motivation were transferred to his students, many of whom no one believed in before Escalante came along. Escalante's contributions were portrayed in the film *Stand and Deliver*. Escalante, his students, and celebrity guests also introduce basic math concepts for sixth- to twelfth-grade students on the *Futures with Jaime Escalante* PBS series. Now retired from teaching, Escalante continues to work in a consulting role to help improve students' motivation to do well in math and improve their math skills. Escalante's story is testimony to how *one* teacher can make a major difference in students' motivation and achievement.

Jaime Escalante in a classroom teaching math.

advantaged populations or to offer high-quality academic support services, advanced courses, and courses that challenge students' active thinking skills. Even students who are motivated to learn and achieve can find it difficult to perform effectively in such contexts.

Culture   In the last decade, the poor performance of American children in math and science has become well publicized (Peak, 1996). For example, in one cross-national comparison of the math and science achievement of 9- to 13-year-old students, the United States finished 13th (out of 15) in science and 15th (out of 16) in math achievement (Educational Testing Service, 1992). In this study, Korean and Taiwanese students placed first and second, respectively.

Harold Stevenson's research (Stevenson, 1992, 1995; Stevenson, Hofer, & Randell, 2000) explores reasons for the poor performance of American students. Stevenson and his colleagues have completed five cross-cultural comparisons of students in the United States, China, Taiwan, and Japan. In these studies, the Asian students consistently outperform American students. And the longer they are in school, the wider the gap between Asian and American students becomes—the lowest difference is in first grade, the highest is in the eleventh grade (the highest grade studied).

Harold Stevenson and his colleagues have found that Asian schools embrace many of the ideals Americans have for their own schools, but are more successful in implementing them in interesting and productive ways that make learning more enjoyable for children and adolescents.

To learn more about the reasons for these large cross-cultural differences, Stevenson and his colleagues spent thousands of hours observing in classrooms, as well as interviewing and surveying teachers, students, and parents. They found that Asian teachers spent more of their time teaching math than American teachers did. For example, in Japan more than one-fourth of total classroom time in first grade was spent on math instruction, compared with only one-tenth of the time in U.S. first-grade classrooms. Also, Asian students were in school an average of 240 days a year compared to 178 days in the United States.

In addition to the substantially greater time spent on math instruction in Asian schools than in American schools, differences were found between Asian and American parents. American parents had much lower expectations for their children's education and achievement than the Asian parents did. Also, American parents were more likely to believe that their children's math achievement is due to innate ability, whereas Asian parents were more likely to say that their children's math achievement is the consequence of effort and training. Asian students were more likely than American students to do math homework, and Asian parents were far more likely to help their children with their math homework than American parents were (Chen & Stevenson, 1989).

Critics of the cross-national comparisons argue that in many comparisons virtually all U.S. students are being compared with a "select" group of students from other countries, especially in the secondary school comparisons. Therefore, they conclude, it is no wonder that American students don't fare so well. That criticism holds for some international comparisons. However, when the top 25 percent of students in different countries were recently compared, U.S. students did not rank much better (Mullis & others, 1998).

Harold Stevenson's Research
http://www.mhhe.com/santrocka9

Motivating Hard-to-Reach, Low-Achieving Adolescents

Jere Brophy (1998) recently described strategies for improving the motivation of hard-to-reach, low-achieving adolescents. These adolescents include (1) low achievers with low ability who have difficulty keeping up and have developed low achievement expectations, (2) adolescents with failure syndrome, and (3) adolescents obsessed with protecting their self-worth by avoiding failure.

Low Achievers with Low Ability   Adolescents with low ability need to be consistently reassured that they can meet goals and challenges and that they will be given the help and support that they need to succeed. However, they need to be reminded that they will make progress only as long as they make a real effort. They might require individualized instruction materials or activities to provide an optimal challenge for their skill level. They need to be guided in setting learning goals and provided with support for reaching these goals. These students need to be required to put forth considerable effort and make progress, even though they might not have the ability to perform at the level of many other adolescents.

Adolescents with Failure Syndrome   **Failure syndrome** *involves having low expectations for success and giving up at the first sign of difficulty.* Adolescents with failure syndrome are different from low-achieving adolescents who fail despite putting forth their best effort. Adolescents with failure syndrome don't put forth enough effort, often beginning tasks in a halfhearted manner and giving up quickly at the first hint of a challenge. They often have low self-efficacy or attribution problems, ascribing failure to internal, stable, and uncontrollable causes, such as low ability.

A number of strategies can be used to increase the motivation of adolescents who display failure syndrome. Especially beneficial are cognitive retraining methods, such as efficacy retraining, attribution retraining, and strategy retraining, which are described in figure 13.3 on page 418.

failure syndrome
Having low expectations for success and giving up at the first sign of difficulty.

FIGURE 13.3
Cognitive Retraining Methods for Increasing the Motivation of Students Who Display Failure Syndrome

TRAINING METHOD	PRIMARY EMPHASIS	MAIN GOALS
Efficacy Retraining	Improve Students' Self-efficacy Perceptions	Teach students to set, and strive to reach, specific, proximal, and challenging goals. Monitor students' progress and frequently support students by saying things like "I know you can do it." Use adult and peer modeling effectively. Individualize instruction and tailor it to the student's knowledge and skills. Keep social comparison to a minimum. Be an efficacious teacher who has confidence in your abilities. View students with failure syndrome as challenges rather than losers.
Attribution and Achievement Orientation Retraining	Change Students' Attributions and Achievement Orientation	Teach students to attribute failures to factors that can be changed, such as insufficient knowledge or effort and ineffective strategies. Work with students to develop a mastery orientation rather than a performance orientation by helping them focus on the achievement process (learning the task) rather than the achievement product (winning or losing).
Strategy Retraining	Improve Students' Domain- and Task-Specific Skills and Strategies	Help students acquire, and self-regulate their use of, effective learning and problem-solving strategies. Teach students what to do, how to do it, when to do it, and why to do it.

Adolescents Motivated to Protect Their Self-Worth by Avoiding Failure Some adolescents are so interested in protecting their self-worth and avoiding failure that they become distracted from pursuing learning goals and engage in ineffective learning strategies. These self-esteem and failure-avoiding strategies include (Covington, 2002; Covington & Teel, 1996):

- *Nonperformance.* The most obvious strategy for avoiding failure is to not try. Adolescents' nonperformance tactics include appearing eager to answer a teacher's question but hoping the teacher will call on another student, sliding down in the seat to avoid being seen by the teacher, and avoiding eye contact. These can seem like minor deceptions, but they might portend other, more chronic forms of noninvolvement such as dropping out and excessive absences.
- *Sham effort.* To avoid being criticized for not trying, some adolescents appear to participate but do so more to avoid punishment than to succeed. Adolescent behaviors that reflect a sham effort include asking a question even though they already know the answer, adopting a pensive, quizzical expression, and feigning focused attention during a class discussion.
- *Procrastination.* Adolescents who postpone studying for a test until the last minute can blame failure on poor time management, thus deflecting attention away from the possibility that they are incompetent. A variation on this theme involves students who take on so many activities and responsibilities that they have an excuse for not doing any one of them in a highly competent manner.
- *Setting unreachable goals.* By setting goals so high that success is virtually impossible, adolescents can avoid the implication that they are incompetent, because virtually all adolescents would fail to reach this goal.
- *The academic wooden leg.* This strategy involves admitting to a minor personal weakness in order to avoid acknowledging the greater, feared weakness of being incompetent. One example is to blame a failing test score on anxiety. Having test anxiety is not as devastating to a personal sense of self-worth as lack of ability.

The effort of adolescents to avoid failure have been grouped as **self-handicapping strategies** (Urdan & Midgely, 2001; Urdan, Midgely, & Anderman, 1998). *That is, some adolescents deliberately do not try in school, put off studying until the last minute, fool around the night before a test, and use other self-handicapping strategies so that if their subsequent performance is at a low level, these circumstances, rather than lack of ability, will be seen as the cause.*

In contrast to attributions, self-handicapping strategies precede success or failure. They are proactive efforts to protect oneself and to manipulate others' perceptions of causes of performance outcomes. For example, saying that you did not perform well on a test because you were tired is an attribution, whereas deliberately staying up late to use lack of sleep as an excuse in case you do poorly is a self-handicapping strategy.

What are some predictors of self-handicapping? Boys are more likely than girls to use self-handicapping strategies (Midgely & Urdan, 1995). Students with good grades and perceptions of academic competence are less likely to use self-handicapping than students with low grades and perceptions of academic incompetence (Urdan, Midgley, & Anderman, 1998).

Martin Covington and his colleagues (Covington, 1992, 1998; Covington & Teel, 1996; Covington, Teel, & Parecki, 1994) proposed a number of strategies teachers can use to help adolescents reduce their preoccupation with protecting their self-worth and avoiding failure:

- Give these adolescents assignments that are inherently interesting and stimulate their curiosity. The assignments should challenge, but not overwhelm, their skills. Allow them some choice of which learning activities they pursue. As their expertise increases, increase the level of challenge correspondingly.
- Establish a reward system so that all adolescents, not just the brightest, highest-achieving adolescents, can attain rewards if they put forth enough effort. Make sure that rewards reinforce students for setting meaningful goals. Also, try to make the act of learning itself a desirable goal.
- Help adolescents set challenging but realistic goals, and provide them with the academic and emotional support to reach those goals.
- Strengthen adolescents' association between effort and self-worth. Encourage adolescents to take pride in their effort and minimize social comparison.
- Encourage adolescents to have positive beliefs about their abilities.
- Improve teacher-adolescent relationships by emphasizing your role as a resource person who will guide and support learning efforts rather than an authority figure who controls student behavior.

self-handicapping strategies
Some adolescents deliberately do not try in school, put off studying until the last minute, and use other self-handicapping strategies so that if their subsequent performance is at a low level, these circumstances, rather than lack of ability, will be seen as the cause.

Since the last review, we have examined these aspects of achievement: ethnicity and culture, and motivating hard-to-reach, low-achieving adolescents. This review should help you to reach your learning goals related to these topics.

☐ FOR YOUR REVIEW

Learning Goal 3
Describe the roles of ethnicity and culture in achievement

- Too often research has failed to tease apart effects of ethnicity and socioeconomic status. It is always important to consider diversity of achievement within an ethnic group.
- American adolescents are more achievement-oriented than their counterparts in many countries, but in recent years Asian adolescents have outperformed American adolescents in math and science achievement.

Learning Goal 4
Understand how to motivate hard-to-reach, low-achieving adolescents

- One main type of hard-to-reach, low-achieving student is the discouraged student who lacks confidence and motivation to learn. This might be an adolescent with low ability and low expectations for success who needs reassurance and support, but who also needs to be reminded that progress only can be made when considerable effort is put forth.

(continued on p. 420)

So far in this chapter, we have examined many aspects of achievement in adolescence. Next, we will turn our attention to career development.

CAREER DEVELOPMENT

What theories have been developed to direct our understanding of adolescents' career choices? What roles do exploration, decision making, and planning play in career development? How do sociocultural factors affect career development?

Theories of Career Development

Three main theories describe the manner in which adolescents make choices about career development: Ginzberg's developmental theory, Super's self-concept theory, and Holland's personality type theory.

developmental career choice theory
Ginzberg's theory that children and adolescents go through three career choice stages: fantasy, tentative, and realistic.

Ginzberg's Developmental Theory **Developmental career choice theory** *is Eli Ginzberg's theory that children and adolescents go through three career choice stages: fantasy, tentative, and realistic* (Ginzberg, 1972; Ginzberg & others, 1951). When asked what they want to be when they grow up, young children may answer "a doctor," "a superhero," "a teacher," "a movie star," "a sports star," or any number of other occupations. In childhood, the future seems to hold almost unlimited opportunities. Ginzberg argues that, until about the age of 11, children are in the *fantasy stage* of career choice. From the ages of 11 to 17, adolescents are in the *tentative stage* of career development, a transition from the fantasy stage of childhood to the realistic decision making of young adulthood. Ginzberg believes that adolescents progress from evaluating their interests (11 to 12 years of age) to evaluating their capacities (13 to 14 years of age) to evaluating their values (15 to 16 years of age). Thinking shifts from less subjective to more realistic career choices at around 17 to 18 years of age. Ginzberg calls the period from 17 to 18 years of age through the early twenties the *realistic stage* of career choice. During this time, the individual extensively explores available careers, then focuses on a particular career, and finally selects a specific job within the career (such as family practitioner or orthopedic surgeon, within the career of doctor).

Critics have attacked Ginzberg's theory on a number of grounds. For one, the initial data were collected from middle-SES youth, who probably had more career options open to them. And, as with other developmental theories (such as Piaget's), the time frames are too rigid. Moreover, Ginzberg's theory does not take into account individual differences—some adolescents make mature decisions about careers (and stick with them) at much earlier ages than specified by Ginzberg. Not all children engage in career fantasies, either. In a revision of his theory, Ginzberg (1972) conceded that lower-SES individuals do not have as many options available as middle-SES individuals do. Ginzberg's general point—that at some point during late adolescence or early adulthood more realistic career choices are made—probably is correct.

career self-concept theory
Super's theory that individuals' self-concepts play a central role in their career choices and that in adolescence individuals first construct their career self-concept.

Super's Self-Concept Theory **Career self-concept theory** *is Donald Super's theory that individuals' self-concept plays a central role in their career choice. Super believes that it is during adolescence that individuals first construct a career self-concept* (Super, 1967, 1976). He emphasizes that career development consists of five different phases. First, at about 14 to 18 years of age, adolescents develop ideas about work that mesh with their already existing global self-concept—this phase is called *crystallization*. Between 18 and 22 years of age, they narrow their career choices and initiate behavior that enables them to enter some type of career—this phase is called *specification*. Between 21 and 24 years of age, young adults complete their education or training and enter the world of work—this phase is called *implementation*. The decision on a specific, appropriate career is made between 25 and 35 years of age—this phase is called *stabilization*. Finally, after the age of 35, individuals seek to advance their careers and to reach higher-status positions—this phase is called *consolidation*. The age ranges should be thought of as approximate rather than rigid. Super believes that career exploration in adolescence is a key ingredient of adolescents' career self-concept. He constructed the Career Development Inventory to assist counselors in promoting adolescents' career exploration.

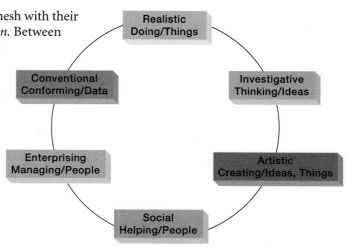

FIGURE 13.4
Holland's Model of Personality Types and Career Choices

Holland's Personality Type Theory **Personality type theory** *is John Holland's theory that an effort should be made to match an individual's career choice with his or her personality* (Holland, 1973, 1987). According to Holland, once individuals find a career that fits their personality, they are more likely to enjoy that particular career and to stay in a job for a longer period of time than individuals who work at jobs not suited to their personality. Holland believes that six basic personality types need to be considered when matching the individual's psychological makeup to a career (see figure 13.4):

personality type theory
Holland believes that an effort should be made to match an individual's career choice with his or her personality.

1. *Realistic*. These individuals are physically strong, deal in practical ways with problems, and have very little social know-how. They are best oriented toward practical careers, such as labor, farming, truck driving, and construction.
2. *Investigative*. These individuals are conceptually and theoretically oriented. They are thinkers rather than doers. They often avoid interpersonal relations and are best suited to careers in math and science.
3. *Social*. These individuals often have good verbal skills and interpersonal relations. They are likely to be best equipped to enter "people" professions, such as teaching, social work, counseling, and the like.
4. *Conventional*. These individuals show a distaste for unstructured activities. They are best suited for jobs as subordinates, such as bank tellers, secretaries, and file clerks.
5. *Enterprising*. These individuals energize their verbal abilities toward leading others, dominating individuals, and selling people on issues or products. They are best counseled to enter careers such as sales, politics, and management.
6. *Artistic*. These individuals prefer to interact with their world through artistic expression, avoiding conventional and interpersonal situations in many instances. These youth should be oriented toward such careers as art and writing.

Holland's Personality Types
Journal of Vocational Behavior
Career Development Quarterly
Journal of Counseling
Psychology
http://www.mhhe.com/santrocka9

If all individuals fell conveniently into Holland's personality types, career counselors would have an easy job. But individuals are more varied and complex than Holland's theory suggests. Even Holland (1987) now admits that most individuals are not pure types. Still, the basic idea of matching the abilities and attitudes of individuals to particular careers is an important contribution to the career field (Vondracek, 1991). Holland's personality types are incorporated into the Strong-Campbell Vocational Interest Inventory, a widely used measure in career guidance.

Criticism of Career Choice Theories Career development theories have been criticized on a number of fronts. Some critics argue that they are too simple. Others stress that there is little data to support them. Also, theories such as Holland's assume that interests and abilities are fixed during adolescence and early adulthood; critics emphasize that individuals can continue to change and develop as they grow older (Mortimer & Lorence, 1979). Further, career choice is influenced by many factors other than

Like on any other long journey, you need markers along your career path to tell you whether you are on track. These are your goals, the specific things that you will do and accomplish as you move through your career development. Every dream and vision you might have about your future career development can be broken down into specific goals and time frames.

Keeping your career dreams in focus, write down some of the specific work, job, and career goals you have for the next 20, 10, and 5 years. Be as concrete and specific as possible. In making up goals, start from the farthest point—20 years from now—and work backward. If you start from a near point, you run the risk of adopting goals that are not precisely and clearly related to your dream.

personality; such factors include individual preferences, the influences of parents, peers, and teachers, and sociocultural dimensions.

Cognitive Factors

Exploration, decision making, and planning play important roles in adolescents' career choices (Spokane, 2000). In countries where equal employment opportunities have emerged—such as the United States, Canada, Great Britain, and France—exploration of various career paths is critical in adolescents' career development. Adolescents often approach career exploration and decision making with considerable ambiguity, uncertainty, and stress. Many of the career decisions made by youth involve floundering and unplanned changes. Many adolescents do not adequately explore careers on their own and also receive little direction from guidance counselors at their schools. On the average, high school students spend less than three hours per year with guidance counselors, and in some schools the average is even less (National Assessment of Educational Progress, 1976). In many schools, students not only do not know what information to seek about careers, they do not know how to seek it.

One of the important aspects of planning in career development is awareness of the educational requirements for a particular career. In one investigation, a sample of 6,029 high school seniors from 57 different school districts in Texas was studied (Grotevant & Durrett, 1980). Students lacked accurate information about two aspects of careers: (1) the educational requirements of careers they desired and (2) the vocational interests predominantly associated with their career choices.

Career development is related to identity development in adolescence. Career decidedness and planning are positively related to identity achievement, whereas career planning and decidedness are negatively related to identity moratorium and identity diffusion statuses (Wallace-Broscious, Serafica, & Osipow, 1994). Adolescents farther along in the process of identity formation are better able to articulate their occupational choices and their next steps in obtaining short-term and long-term goals (Raskin, 1985). By contrast, adolescents in the moratorium and diffusion statuses of identity are more likely to struggle with making occupational plans and decisions.

In a large-scale longitudinal investigation, Mihaly Csikszentmihalyi and Barbara Schneider (2000) studied how U.S. adolescents develop attitudes and acquire skills to achieve their career goals and expectations. They assessed the progress of more than 1,000 students from 13 school districts across the United States. Students recorded at random moments their thoughts and feelings about what they did, and filled out questionnaires regarding school, family, peers, and career aspirations. The researchers also interviewed the adolescents, as well as their friends, parents, and teachers. Among the findings of the study:

- Girls anticipated the same lifestyles as boys in terms of education and income.
- Lower-income minority students were more positive about school than more affluent students were.
- Students who got the most out of school—and had the highest future expectations—were those who perceived school to be more playlike than worklike.
- Clear vocational goals and good work experiences did not guarantee a smooth transition to adult work. Engaging activities—with intensive involvement regardless of content—were essential to building the optimism and resilience that are important for achieving a satisfying work life. This finding fits with Csikszentmihalyi's concept of flow, which we explored earlier in the chapter.

In another study, adolescents were more ambitious in the 1990s than reports from adolescents in other studies conducted in the 1970s and 1980s (Schneider & Stevenson, 1999). The rising ambitions of adolescents were not confined to those from White middle-income families but also characterized adolescents from low-income and ethnic minority families.

Today, more than 90 percent of high school seniors expect to attend college and more than 70 percent anticipate working in professional jobs. Four decades ago the picture was different with only 55 percent expecting to go college and 42 percent anticipating working in professional jobs. In the study on adolescent ambitions in the 1990s, parents shared their adolescents' ambitious visions (Schneider & Stevenson, 1999). However, both adolescents and their parents often failed to make meaningful connections between educational credentials and future work opportunities. Parents can improve this by becoming more knowledgeable about which courses their adolescents are taking in school, developing a better understanding of the college admissions process, providing adolescents with better information about various careers, and realistically evaluating their adolescents' abilities and interests in relation to these careers.

Social Contexts

Not every individual born into the world can grow up to become a nuclear physicist or a doctor—there is a genetic limitation that keeps some adolescents from performing at the high intellectual levels necessary to enter such careers. Similarly, there are genetic limitations that restrict some adolescents from becoming professional football players or professional golfers. But there usually are many careers available to each of us, careers that provide a reasonable match with our abilities. Our sociocultural experiences exert strong influences on career choices from among the wide range available. Among the important social contexts that influence career development are socioeconomic status, parents and peers, schools, and gender.

Socioeconomic Status   The channels of upward mobility open to lower-SES youth are largely educational in nature ◀ⅢⅢ P. 241. The school hierarchy from grade school through high school, as well as through college and graduate school, is programmed to orient individuals toward some type of career. Less than 100 years ago, it was believed that only 8 years of education were necessary for vocational competence, and anything beyond that qualified the individual for advanced placement in higher-status occupations. By the middle of the twentieth century, the high school diploma had already lost ground as a ticket to career success. College rapidly became a prerequisite for entering a higher-status occupation. Employers reason that an individual with a college degree is a better risk than a high school graduate or a high school dropout.

Parents and Peers   Parents and peers also are strong influences on adolescents' career choices. Although some experts argue that American parents have achievement expectations that are too low, David Elkind (1981) believes that today's parents are pressuring their adolescents to achieve too much, too soon. In some cases, though, adolescents are not challenged enough by their parents. Consider the 25-year-old female who vividly describes the details of her adolescence that later prevented her from seeking a competent career. From early in adolescence, both of her parents encouraged her to

CAREERS IN ADOLESCENT DEVELOPMENT

Grace Leaf
College/Career Counselor

Grace Leaf is a counselor at Spokane Community College in Washington. She has a master's degree in educational leadership and is working toward a doctoral degree in educational leadership at Gonzaga University in Washington. Her job involves teaching, orientation for international students, conducting individual and group advising, and doing individual and group career planning. Grace tries to connect students with goals and values and helps them design an educational program that fits their needs and visions.

Grace Leaf (standing) advising college students about potential careers.

Career Planning
National Career Development
Association
http://www.mhhe.com/santrocka9

Parents play an important role in the adolescent's achievement. It is important for parents to neither pressure the adolescent too much nor challenge the adolescent too little.

Occupational Outlook Handbook
http://www.mhhe.com/santrocka9

finish high school, but at the same time they emphasized that she needed to get a job to help them pay the family's bills. She was never told that she could not go to college, but both parents encouraged her to find someone to marry who could support her financially. This very bright girl is now divorced and feels intellectually cheated by her parents, who socialized her in the direction of marriage and away from a college education.

From an early age, children see and hear about what jobs their parents have. In some cases, parents even take their children to work with them on jobs. Recently, when we were building our house, the bricklayer brought his two sons to help with the work. They were only 14 years old, yet they were already engaging in apprenticeship work with their father.

Unfortunately, some parents want to live vicariously through their son's or daughter's career achievements. The mother who did not get into medical school and the father who did not make it as a professional athlete may pressure their youth to achieve a career status beyond the youth's talents.

Many factors influence parents' role in adolescents' career development (Young, 1994). For one, mothers who work regularly outside the home and show effort and pride in their work probably have strong influences on their adolescents' career choices. A reasonable conclusion is that when both parents work and enjoy their work, adolescents learn work values from both parents.

Anna Roe (1956) argued that parent-child relationships play an important role in occupation selection. For example, she said that individuals who have warm and accepting parents are likely to choose careers that include work with people, such as sales positions and public relations jobs. By contrast, she stated, individuals who have rejecting or neglectful parents are more likely to choose careers that do not require a good "personality" or strong social skills, such as accounting and engineering. Critics argue that Roe's ideas are speculative, might not hold in today's world, and are too simple (Grotevant, 1996).

Parents can potentially influence adolescents' occupational choices through the way they present information about occupations and values, as well as through the experiences they provide adolescents (Eccles, 1993). For example, parents can communicate to their children and adolescents that they value the importance of going to college and attaining a professional degree as a means to attaining a career in medicine, law, or business. Other parents might communicate that college is not as important and place a higher value on being a sports or movie star.

In terms of the experiences they provide children, parents who read to their children, take them to the library on a regular basis, and make sure they go to the museums in the area send a message about the value of academic pursuits compared to parents who use their spare time to coach their children's Little League team. In this manner, parenting behaviors can influence adolescents' activity preferences and ultimately their educational and occupational choices. Of course, some parents try to develop both academic and sports orientations in their children, but many parents spend more time with their children in one area or the other.

In one recent research study, parents' roles in shaping early adolescents' occupational aspirations in two domains—academics (such as doctor, lawyer, architect) and sports (such as professional football or baseball player)—were examined (Jodl & others, 2001). In terms of the adolescent's interest in a career that requires a strong academic background, parents' values (which included their belief in positive outcomes for their youth, their educational aspirations for their youth, and their perception of their youths' academic ability) were closely related to their young adolescents' values (which included self-concept of academic ability, value of education in the future, and educational aspirations). However, in terms of the adolescent's interest in a sports career, the father's behavior (which included sports activity involvement, support of the adolescent's sports talent, and involvement as a coach) played a more important role.

Peers also can influence adolescents' career development. In one investigation, when adolescents had friends and parents with high career standards, they were more likely to seek higher-status careers, even if they came from low-income families (Simpson, 1962).

School Influences   Schools, teachers, and counselors can exert a powerful influence on adolescents' career development. School is the primary setting where individuals first encounter the world of work. School provides an atmosphere for continuing self-development in relation to achievement and work. And school is the only institution in society that is presently capable of providing the delivery systems necessary for career education—instruction, guidance, placement, and community connections.

"Your son has made a career choice, Mildred. He's going to win the lottery and travel a lot."

Copyright © 1986; Reprinted courtesy of Bunny Hoest and Parade Magazine.

A national survey revealed the nature of career information available to adolescents (Chapman & Katz, 1983). The most common single resource was the *Occupational Outlook Handbook (OOH),* with 92 percent of the schools having one or more copies. The second major source was the *Dictionary of Occupational Titles (DOT),* with 82 percent having this book available for students. Fewer than 30 percent had no established committee to review career information resources. When students talked to counselors, it was more often about high school courses than about career guidance.

School counseling has been criticized heavily, both inside and outside the educational establishment. Insiders complain about the large number of students per school counselor and the weight of noncounseling administrative duties. Outsiders complain that school counseling is ineffective, biased, and a waste of money. Short of a new profession, several options are possible (William T. Grant Foundation Commission, 1988). First, twice the number of counselors are needed to meet all students' needs. Second, there could be a redefinition of teachers' roles, accompanied by retraining and reduction in teaching loads, so that classroom teachers could assume a stronger role in handling the counseling needs of adolescents. The professional counselor's role in this plan would be to train and assist teachers in their counseling and to provide direct counseling in situations the teacher could not handle. Third, the whole idea of school counselors would be abandoned, and counselors would be located elsewhere—in neighborhood social service centers or labor offices, for example. (Germany forbids teachers to give career counseling, reserving this task for officials in well-developed networks of labor offices.)

The College Board Commission on Precollege Guidance and Counseling (1986) recommends other alternatives. It believes that local school districts should develop broad-based planning that actively involves the home, school, and community. Advocating better-trained counselors, the commission supports stronger partnerships between home and school to increase two-way communication about student progress and better collaboration among schools, community agencies, colleges, businesses, and other community resources.

Gender   Because many females have been socialized to adopt nurturing roles rather than career or achieving roles, they traditionally have not planned seriously for careers, have not explored career options extensively, and have restricted their career choices to careers that are gender-stereotyped (Gates, 2001; Jozefowicz, Barber, & Mollasis, 1994). The motivation for work is the same for both sexes. However, females and males make different choices because of their socialization experiences and the ways that social forces structure the opportunities available to them.

As growing numbers of females pursue careers, they are faced with questions involving career and family: Should they delay marriage and childbearing and establish

Yes, I am wise but it is wisdom for the pain.
Yes, I've paid the price but look how much
I've gained.
If I have to I can do anything.
I am strong, I am invincible, I am woman . . .
—Helen Reddy
American Singer, 20th Century

THROUGH THE EYES OF ADOLESCENTS

Thinking About Barriers

At 15, Monica Moffitt already has spent quite a bit of time thinking about the terrible "toos": too tall, according to some, to dance ballet, too black and female to aim for a career in neurosurgery, say others.

Monica's reply: "Too bad. I want to be a pioneer. If I'm the first one, that's even better."

Eighteen-year-old Trude Goodman says that the glass ceiling is still pretty powerful, but she thinks her generation of females has a lot more going for it than the generations that came before. Her classmate Kerri Geller agrees: "We have more confidence so we can achieve whatever we want to." However, another 18-year-old, Alison Fisher, says "I'm sometimes a little taken aback . . . shocked, really, at the prejudice I see in the workplace and academics. I hope we will be able to step above that but getting to college and work will definitely be a reality check."

Trude Goodman.

their career first? Or should they combine their career, marriage, and childbearing in their twenties? Some females in the last decade have embraced the domestic patterns of an earlier historical period. They have married, borne children, and committed themselves to full-time mothering. These "traditional" females have worked outside the home only intermittently, if at all, and have subordinated the work role to the family role.

Many other females, though, have veered from this time-honored path. They have postponed motherhood. They have developed committed, permanent ties to the workplace that resemble the pattern once reserved only for males. When they have had children, they have strived to combine a career and motherhood. While there have always been "career" females, today their numbers are growing at an unprecedented rate.

Special concerns are raised about the lack of modern technology equipment, such as computers and telecommunications equipment, in schools in low-SES areas. Such concerns are magnified further for many ethnic minority girls who attend schools in impoverished neighborhoods, because they often show less interest in technology than their male counterparts do.

In one recent effort to improve the interest of such girls in pursuing careers in the sciences and computer technology, the Young Women Scholars' Early Alert Initiative Program was created by Wayne State University, school districts in southeastern Michigan, and industry (Gipson, 1997). They surveyed elementary, middle school, and high school teachers from 18 school districts. Almost 40 percent of the teachers had no computer equipment in their classrooms, and even more lacked adequate computer training to fully utilize the computers they had.

Forty seventh-grade girls, primarily from low-SES ethnic minority families, were selected for the program. The girls were brought to Wayne State University on a number of occasions to participate in math, computer, and science workshops. The girls also were taken on field trips to the Medical School and the Information Technology Center, where they interacted with female scientists. These scientists described how they became interested in their specialty area, personal hardships, career paths, and current lives. Two field trips to industrial sites and three field trips to museums occurred during the five-month program. At each site, the girls met and spoke with scientists and museum staff. In addition, parents participated in some of the programs and assisted on at least one field trip.

Ethnic Minority Adolescents

African Americans, Asian Americans, Latinos, and Native Americans are four distinct subgroups of the American culture. Yet they share a history of exclusion from mainstream American society. This exclusion has occurred in history books, the educational system, the socioeconomic structure, and the labor force (Osipow & Littlejohn, 1995).

Math and science awareness interventions also are needed. One such intervention is a career-linking program that has been effectively used with inner-city middle school students (Fouad, 1995). The intervention combined printed career information,

CAREERS IN ADOLESCENT DEVELOPMENT

Armando Ronquillo
High School Counselor/College Advisor

Armando Ronquillo is a high school counselor and college advisor at Pueblo High School, which is in a low-socioeconomic-status area in Tucson, Arizona. More than 85 percent of the students have a Latino background. Armando was

Armando Ronquillo, counseling a Latina high school student about college.

named top high school counselor in the state of Arizona for the year 2000. He has especially helped to increase the number of Pueblo High School students who go to college.

Armando has an undergraduate degree in elementary and special education, and a master's degree in counseling. He counsels the students on the merits of staying in school and on the lifelong opportunities provided by a college education. Armando guides students in obtaining the academic preparation that will enable them to go to college, including how to apply for financial aid and scholarships. He also works with parents to help them understand that their child going to college is not only doable but also affordable.

Armando works with students on setting goals and planning. He has students plan for the future in terms of 1-year (short-term), 5-year (midrange), and 10-plus-year (long-term) time periods. Armando says he does this "to help students visualize how the educational plans and decisions they make today will affect them in the future." He also organizes a number of college campus visitations for students from Pueblo High School each year.

speakers and role models, field trips, and integration of career awareness into the curriculum. The intervention increased students' knowledge of careers, and the students performed better in math and science than a control group of students who did not get the career intervention experience. Two years after the intervention, the students also had chosen more difficult math courses than the control group students.

To intervene effectively in the career development of ethnic minority youth, counselors need to increase their knowledge of communication styles, values regarding the importance of the family, the impact of language fluency, and achievement expectations in various ethnic minority groups. Counselors need to be aware of and respect the cultural values of ethnic minority youth, but such values need to be discussed within the context of the realities of the educational and occupational world (Leong, 1995, 2000). For example, assertiveness training might be called for when Asian youth are following a cultural tradition of nonassertiveness. The counselor can emphasize to these youth that they can choose when and where to follow the more assertive style.

Since the last review, we have examined a number of ideas about career development. This review should help you to reach your learning goals related to this topic.

FOR YOUR REVIEW

Learning Goal 5 Know about career development	• Three theories of career development are Ginzberg's developmental theory, Super's self-concept theory, and Holland's personality type theory. Criticisms of each of these theories have been made. • Exploration, decision making, and planning are important cognitive dimensions of career development in adolescence.

(continued on p. 428)

So far in this chapter, we have examined achievement and careers. Next, we will turn our attention to the role of work in adolescents' lives.

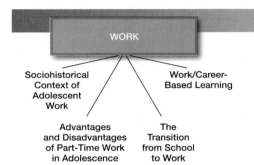

WORK

One of the greatest changes in adolescents' lives in recent years has been the increased number of adolescents who work in some part-time capacity and still attend school on a regular basis. Our discussion of adolescents and work includes information about the sociohistorical context of adolescent work, the advantages and disadvantages of part-time work, the transition from school to work, and work-based learning.

Sociohistorical Context of Adolescent Work

Over the past century, the percentage of youth who work full-time as opposed to those who are in school has decreased dramatically. In the late 1800s, fewer than one of every twenty high school age adolescents were in school. Today more than nine of every ten adolescents receive high school diplomas. In the nineteenth century, many adolescents learned a trade from their father or some other adult member of the community.

Even though prolonged education has kept many of today's youth from holding full-time jobs, it has not prevented them from working on a part-time basis while going to school. In 1940, only 1 of 25 tenth-grade males attended school and simultaneously worked part-time. In the 1970s, the number had increased to 1 in 4. Today, 3 of 4 combine school and part-time work. The typical part-time job for high school seniors involves 16 to 20 hours of work per week, although 10 percent work 30 hours or more. A similar increase has occurred for younger adolescents.

What kinds of jobs are adolescents working at today? About 17 percent who work do so in restaurants, such as McDonald's and Burger King, waiting on customers and cleaning up. Other adolescents work in retail stores as cashiers or salespeople (about 20 percent), in offices as clerical assistants (about 10 percent), or as unskilled laborers (about 10 percent). In one recent study, boys reported higher self-esteem and well-being when they perceived that their jobs were providing skills that would be useful to them in the future (Mortimer & others, 1992).

Do male and female adolescents take the same types of jobs, and are they paid equally? Some jobs (such as busboy, gardener, manual laborer, newspaper carrier) are held almost exclusively by male adolescents, while other jobs (such as baby-sitter, maid) are held almost exclusively by female adolescents. Male adolescents work longer hours and are paid more per hour than female adolescents (Helson, Elliot, & Leigh, 1989).

THROUGH THE EYES OF ADOLESCENTS

Being Raised to Be Responsible

"I am working in the Palace Theater. . . . It is my first job and I'm excited to be there. After all, I'm 14 years old, handling lots of money, candy, and late-night zaniness every weekend. I am the youngest worker there, but because I work hard my age isn't often remarked upon. Furthermore, I don't look 14, with my wide shoulders and 5'10" frame, my well-spoken manner and air of confidence. And I don't worry too much about being younger—I simply do what I have been raised to do: be responsible and work hard."

Advantages and Disadvantages of Part-Time Work in Adolescence

Does the increase in work have benefits for adolescents? In some cases, yes; in others, no. Ellen Greenberger and Laurence Steinberg (1981, 1986) examined the work experiences of students in four California high schools. Their findings disproved some common myths. For example, generally it is assumed that adolescents get extensive on-the-job training when they are hired for work. The reality is that they got little training at all. Also, it is assumed that youths—through work experiences—learn to get along better with adults. However, adolescents reported that they rarely felt close to the adults with whom they worked. The work experiences of the adolescents did help them to understand how the business world works, how to get and how to keep a job, and how to manage money. Working also helped adolescents to learn to budget their time, to take pride in their accomplishments, and to evaluate their goals. But working adolescents often have to give up sports, social affairs with peers, and sometimes sleep. And they have to balance the demands of work, school, family, and peers.

The Working Adolescent
http://www.mhhe.com/santrocka9

Greenberger and Steinberg asked students about their grade point averages, school attendance, satisfaction from school, and the number of hours spent studying and participating in extracurricular activities since they began working. They found that the working adolescents had lower grade point averages than nonworking adolescents. More than one of four students reported that their grades dropped when they began working; only one of nine said that their grades improved. But it was not just working that affected adolescents' grades—more important was *how long* they worked. Tenth-graders who worked more than 14 hours a week suffered a drop in grades. Eleventh-graders worked up to 20 hours a week before their grades dropped. When adolescents spend more than 20 hours per week working, there is little time to study for tests and to complete homework assignments.

In addition to work's affecting grades, working adolescents felt less involved in school, were absent more, and said that they did not enjoy school as much as their nonworking counterparts did. Adolescents who worked also spent less time with their families—but just as much time with their peers—as their nonworking counterparts. Adolescents who worked long hours also were more frequent users of alcohol and marijuana.

More-recent research confirms the link between part-time work during adolescence and problem behaviors. In one recent large-scale study, the role of part-time work in the adjustment of more than 70,000 high school seniors was investigated (Bachman & Schulenberg, 1993). Consistent with other research, part-time work in high school was associated with a number of problem behaviors: insufficient sleep, not eating breakfast, not exercising, not having enough leisure time, and using drugs. For the most part, the results occurred even when students worked 1 to 5 hours per week, but they became more pronounced after 20 hours of work per week. And in another study, taking on a job for more than 20 hours per week was associated with increasing

What are the effects of working and going to school on adolescents' grades and integration into school activities?

disengagement from school, increased delinquency and drug use, increased autonomy from parents, and self-reliance (Steinberg, Fegley, & Dornbusch, 1993). In sum, the overwhelming evidence is that working part-time while going to high school is associated with a number of problem behaviors when the work consumes 20 or more hours of the adolescent's week (Hansen, 1996).

Some states have responded to these findings by limiting the number of hours adolescents can work while they are attending secondary school. In 1986, in Pinellas County, Florida, a new law placed a cap on the previously unregulated hours that adolescents could work while school is in session. The allowable limit was set at 30 hours, which—based on research evidence—is still too high.

Although working too many hours may be detrimental to adolescent development, work may especially benefit adolescents in low-income, urban contexts by providing them with economic benefits and adult monitoring. This may increase school engagement and decrease delinquency. In one recent study, low-income, urban adolescents who never worked had more school-related difficulties than those who did work (Leventhal, Graber, & Brooks-Gunn, 2001). Stable work increased the likelihood that the adolescent males in low-income, urban contexts would go to college more so than for the adolescent females.

Several investigations have focused on the important question of how the costs and benefits of working in adolescence might vary as a function of the quality of the job (Larson & Verman, 1999). In one longitudinal study, adolescents in jobs with opportunities for advancement showed increases in mastery motivation, heightened work values, and reduced depression (Mortimer & others, 1996). Jobs that youth described as extrinsically rather than intrinsically rewarding appear to detract from schoolwork (Mortimer, Harley, & Johnson, 1998). In another study, positive effects of working were found (Marsh, 1991). Adolescents reported that their jobs encouraged good work habits and that they were using their earnings for high school or college costs. Negative effects occurred when adolescents perceived their job as more important than school and using their income for nonschool purposes.

The Transition from School to Work

In some cases, the media have exaggerated the degree of adolescent unemployment. For example, based on data collected by the U.S. Department of Labor, nine of ten adolescents are either in school, working at a job, or both. Only 5 percent are out of school, without a job, and looking for full-time employment. Most adolescents who are unemployed are not unemployed for long. Only 10 percent are without a job for six months or longer. Most unemployed adolescents are school dropouts.

Certain segments of the adolescent population, however, are more likely than others to be unemployed. For example, a disproportionate percentage of unemployed adolescents are African American. The unemployment situation is especially acute for African American and Latino youth between the ages of 16 and 19. The job situation, however, has improved somewhat for African American adolescents: In 1969, 44 percent of African American 16- to 19-year-olds were unemployed; today, that figure is approximately 32 percent.

How can adolescents be helped to bridge the gap between school and work? For adolescents bound for higher education and a professional degree, the educational system provides ladders from school to career. Most youth, though, step off the educational ladder before reaching the level of a professional career. Often, they are on their own in their search for work. Recommendations for bridging the gap from school to work were described briefly in chapter 7, on schools, but are expanded on here (William T. Grant Foundation Commission, 1988):

1. Monitored work experiences, including cooperative education, internships, apprenticeships, preemployment training, and youth-operated enterprises, should be implemented. These experiences provide opportunities for youth to gain work

**Improving School-Work Transitions
National Institute for Work and Learning
School-to-Work Transitions in Canada
Job Corps**
http://www.mhhe.com/santrocka9

experience, to be exposed to adult supervisors and models in the workplace, and to relate their academic training to the workplace.

2. Community and neighborhood services, including individual voluntary service and youth-guided services, should be expanded. Youth need experiences not only as workers but as citizens. Service programs not only expose youth to the adult world, but provide them with a sense of the obligations of citizenship in building a more caring and competent society.

3. Vocational education should be redirected. With few exceptions, today's vocational education does not prepare youth adequately for specific jobs. However, its hands-on methods can provide students with valuable and effective ways of acquiring skills they will need to be successful in a number of jobs. One promising approach is the career academy, which originated in Philadelphia and was replicated extensively in California (Glover & Marshall, 1993). At the end of the ninth grade, students at risk for failure are identified and invited to volunteer for a program based on a school-within-a-school format. The students and teachers remain together for three years. Students spend the tenth grade catching up on academic course work; computers and field trips are integrated into the curriculum. In the eleventh grade, every student has a mentor from industry who introduces the student to his or her workplace and joins the student for recreational activities at least once a month. By the end of the eleventh grade, the student obtains a summer job with one of the business partners. Students who stay in the program are promised a job when they graduate from high school.

4. Incentives need to be introduced. Low motivation and low expectations for success in the workplace often restrict adolescents' educational achievement. Recent efforts to guarantee postsecondary and continuing education and to provide guaranteed employment, and guaranteed work-related training for students who do well show promise of encouraging adolescents to work harder and be more successful in school.

5. Career information and counseling need to be improved. A variety of information and counseling approaches can be implemented to expose adolescents to job opportunities and career options. These services can be offered both in school and in community settings. They include setting up career information centers, developing the capacity of parents as career educators, and expanding the work of community-based organizations.

6. More school volunteers should be used. Tutoring is the most common form of school volunteer activity. However, adults are needed even more generally—as friends, as mentors for opening up career opportunities, and for assisting youth in mastering the dilemmas of living in a stressful time.

Improving education, elevating skill levels, and providing "hands-on" experience will help adolescents to bridge the gap between school and work. We need to address the needs of youth if we are to retain the confidence of youth who have been brought up to believe in the promise of the American Dream.

Work/Career-Based Learning

Work/career-based learning increasingly has become part of the effort to help youth make the transition from school to employment (Moore, 1998). Each year, approximately 500,000 high school students participate in cooperative education or other arrangements where learning objectives are met through part-time employment in office occupations, retailing, and other vocational fields. Vocational classes also involve large numbers of adolescents in school-based enterprises, through which they build houses, run restaurants, repair cars, operate retail stores, staff childcare centers, and provide other services.

As we begin the twenty-first century, some important changes are taking place in vocational education (Stern & Rahn, 1998). Today's high school diploma provides

National Center for Research in Vocational Education
Exploring Vocational Education
Roosevelt Renaissance 2000
Vocational Training in Europe
http://www.mhhe.com/santrocka9

access to fewer and fewer stable, high-paying jobs. Thus, more of the training for specific occupations is occurring in two-year colleges and postsecondary technical institutes.

In high schools, new forms of career-related education are creating options for many students, ranging from students with disabilities to students who are gifted. Among the new models are career academies, youth apprenticeships, and tech prep and career major programs. These models rely on work-related themes to focus the curriculum and prepare students for postsecondary education, including four-year colleges and universities. These new options are supported by the 1990 Perkins Act and the 1994 School-to-Work-Opportunities Act.

Three new types of high schools exemplify a college-and-career approach: single-theme schools; schools-within-schools; and majors, clusters, or pathways (Stern & Hallinan, 1997).

Most often found in large cities where the high population density allows more specialization, the *single-theme school* has a curriculum that is organized around a theme such as agriculture, aviation, fashion, or finance. Some of these schools have a strong college preparation orientation. Several examples of the single-theme school are the High School for Agricultural Sciences in Chicago and the High School of Economics and Finance in New York City.

The single-theme schools connect classroom learning with practical contexts through work-based learning, community service, and research projects. For example, at the High School for Agricultural Sciences, some class assignments are based on student internships at the Chicago Board of Trade or the Quaker Oats company. At the High School of Economics and Finance, students are required to spend time in paid internships at Wall Street firms and participate in unpaid community service.

A second variation of the college-and-career approach divides an entire high school into several *schools-within-schools*. These smaller groupings are referred to as "academies" or "houses." Their size can range from 80 to 300 students with 4 to 10 teachers each. The curriculum is organized around a career theme in an academy or house. A core academic curriculum is maintained but applied to broad occupational themes such as health careers, business and finance, natural resources, manufacturing sciences, communications media, law and government, graphic arts, and environmental studies. Some academies cover four years of schooling, others only the last two or three years.

A third version of the college-and-career approach divides high schools into *majors, clusters, or pathways*. In these schools, technical and vocational courses are organized according to broad themes, similar to academies, but academic classes usually are not composed of students who all major in the same field. Students in a career pathway, major, or cluster take academic classes in grades 9 through 12 with students from several other majors, but also take a sequence of electives specific to the pathway.

These different forms of high school organization also can be combined. For example, in a single-theme school, the range of student career interests can lead to the development of pathways or majors within the single theme. Gateway Institute of Technology in St. Louis uses this approach. The entire school is focused on preparing students for careers in high-tech science and engineering fields, but students can major in such areas as agriculture, biology, and health; engineering technology, applied physical sciences; or math and computer science.

Since the last review, we have examined a number of ideas about work in adolescence. This review should help you to reach your learning goals related to this topic.

☐ FOR YOUR REVIEW

Learning Goal 6	• Adolescents are not as likely to hold full-time jobs today as their counterparts from
Discuss the role of work in adolescence	the nineteenth century were. The number of adolescents who work part-time, though, has increased dramatically.

- Advantages of part-time work in adolescence include learning how the business world works, how to get and keep a job, how to manage money, how to budget time, how to take pride in accomplishments, and how to evaluate goals. Disadvantages include giving up extracurricular activities at school, social affairs with peers, and sometimes sleep; as well as balancing the demands of school, family, peers, and work.
- Rates of adolescent unemployment are sometimes exaggerated, but some adolescents—especially ethnic minority adolescents from low-SES backgrounds—face unemployment problems. To bridge the gap between school and work, better monitoring of adolescents' work experiences and better career counseling need to be accomplished.
- Interest in work-based learning in high school is increasing. Three new types of high schools exemplify a college-and-career approach: (1) single-theme schools; (2) schools-within-schools; and (3) majors, clusters, or pathways.

In this chapter, we have focused on achievement, careers, and work. In some cases, we have seen that adolescents have achievement-related problems. In chapter 14, we will focus more extensively on problems and disorders in adolescence.

CHAPTER MAP

ACHIEVEMENT

The Importance of Adolescence in Achievement

Motivating Hard-to-Reach, Low-Achieving Adolescents

Achievement Processes

Ethnicity and Culture

CAREER DEVELOPMENT

Theories of Career Development

Social Contexts

Cognitive Factors

WORK

Sociohistorical Context of Adolescent Work

Work/Career-Based Learning

Advantages and Disadvantages of Part-Time Work in Adolescence

The Transition from School to Work

REACH YOUR LEARNING GOALS

At the beginning of the chapter we stated six learning goals and reviewed material related to these goals at four points in the chapter. This is a good time to return to these reviews. Use them to guide your study and help you to reach your learning goals.

Page 414

Learning Goal 1   Explain why adolescence is a critical juncture in achievement

Learning Goal 2   Discuss achievement processes

Page 419

Learning Goal 3   Describe the roles of ethnicity and culture in achievement

Learning Goal 4   Understand how to motivate hard-to-reach, low-achieving adolescents

Page 427

Learning Goal 5   Know about career development

Page 432

Learning Goal 6   Discuss the role of work in adolescence

KEY TERMS

extrinsic motivation 409
intrinsic motivation 409
flow 409
attribution theory 410
mastery orientation 411
helpless orientation 412
performance orientation 412

self-efficacy 412
anxiety 414
failure syndrome 417
self-handicapping strategies 419
developmental career choice theory 420
career self-concept theory 420
personality type theory 421

KEY PEOPLE

Mihaly Csikszentmihalyi 409
Bernard Weiner 410
Carol Dweck 411
Albert Bandura 412
Dale Schunk 412
Sandra Graham 415
Harold Stevenson 416
Martin Covington 419

Eli Ginzberg 420
Donald Super 420
John Holland 421
David Elkind 423
Anna Roe 424
Ellen Greenberger
    and Laurence Steinberg 428

RESOURCES FOR IMPROVING THE LIVES OF ADOLESCENTS

All Grown Up & No Place to Go: Teenagers in Crisis

(1984) by David Elkind
Reading, MA: Addison-Wesley

Elkind believes that raising teenagers in today's world is more difficult than ever. He argues that teenagers are expected to confront adult challenges too early in their development.

Becoming Adult

(2000) by Mihaly Csikszentmihalyi and Barbara Schneider
New York: Basic Books

This report of a longitudinal study provides valuable information about the ways that work during adolescence influences developmental pathways into adulthood.

Motivating Students to Learn

(1998) by Jere Brophy
New York: McGraw-Hill

An excellent book on motivating students in the classroom.

Motivation for Achievement

(1999) by M. Kay Alderman
Mahwah, NJ: Erlbaum

This book explores contemporary ideas about motivating adolescents.

National Youth Employment Coalition

1501 Broadway, Room 111
New York, NY 10036
212–840–1801

This organization promotes youth employment.

Through Mentors

202–393–0512

Mentors are recruited from corporations, government agencies, universities, and professional firms. Their goal is to provide every youth in the District of Columbia with a mentor through high school. To learn how to become involved in a mentoring program or to start such a program, call the number listed here. Also, the National One-to-One Partnership Kit guides businesses in establishing mentoring programs (call 202–338–3844).

What Color Is Your Parachute?

(2000) by Richard Bolles
Berkeley, CA: Ten Speed Press

What Color Is Your Parachute? is an extremely popular book on job hunting.

What Kids Need to Succeed

by Peter Benson, Judy Galbraith, and Pamela Espeland
Minneapolis: Search Institute

This easy-to-read book presents commonsense ideas for parents, educators, and youth workers that can help youth succeed.

TAKING IT TO THE NET

http://www.mhhe.com/santrocka9

1. There are a number of career tests that are used as an aid in helping people select potential careers. *If you took several, would you get the same recommendations? How well did they do for you? What cautions would you advise friends taking such tests to keep in mind?*

2. One of your concerns as an undergraduate member of the College Curriculum Committee is making education relevant to the world of work that you and the other students will be entering. *How would you suggest the curriculum be structured in order to maximize its relevance to the world of work?*

3. The study of motivation is an important component of explaining human behavior. *How might the study of needs, attribution theory, and other aspects of motivation be important to the study of personality?*

Connect to *http://www.mhhe.com/santrocka9* to research the answers and complete these exercises. In some cases, you'll also find further instructions on this site.

SECTION 5

ADOLESCENT PROBLEMS

There is no easy path leading out of life, and few are the easy ones that lie within it.
—Walter Savage Landor
English Poet, 19th Century

Modern life is stressful and leaves its psychological scars on too many adolescents, who, unable to cope effectively, never reach their human potential. The need is not only to find better treatments for adolescents with problems, but to find ways to encourage adolescents to adopt healthier lifestyles, which can prevent problems from occurring in the first place. This section consists of one chapter (14), "Adolescent Problems."

CHAPTER
14

CHAPTER MAP

```
┌─────────────────────────────┐
│  EXPLORING ADOLESCENT       │
│         PROBLEMS            │
└─────────────────────────────┘
    Biological              Resilience
    Factors
    Psychological           Characteristics
    Factors                 of Adolescent
    Sociocultural           Problems
    Factors
    The Biopsychosocial     The Developmental
    Approach                Psychopathology
                            Approach
            │
            ▼
┌─────────────────────────────┐
│     PROBLEMS AND            │
│       DISORDERS             │
└─────────────────────────────┘
    Drugs and               Eating
    Alcohol                 Disorders

       Juvenile             Depression
       Delinquency          and Suicide
            │
            ▼
┌─────────────────────────────┐
│   INTERRELATION OF          │
│ PROBLEMS AND PREVENTION/    │
│       INTERVENTION          │
└─────────────────────────────┘
```

ADOLESCENT PROBLEMS

ANNIE AND ARNIE

Some mornings, Annie, a 15-year-old cheerleader, was too drunk to go to school. Other days, she would stop for a couple of beers or a screwdriver on the way to school. She was tall and blonde and good-looking, and no one who sold her liquor, even at 8:00 A.M., questioned her age. She got her money from baby-sitting and what her mother gave her to buy lunch. Finally, Annie was kicked off the cheerleading squad for missing practice so often. Soon she and several of her peers were drinking almost every morning. Sometimes, they skipped school and went to the woods to drink. Annie's whole life began to revolve around her drinking. It went on for two years, and, during the last summer, anytime she saw anybody she was drunk. After a while, her parents began to detect Annie's problem. But even when they punished her, she did not stop drinking. Finally, Annie started dating a boy she really liked and who would not put up with her drinking. She agreed to go to Alcoholics Anonymous and has just successfully completed treatment. She has stopped drinking for four consecutive months now, and continued abstinence is the goal.

Arnie is 13 years old. He has a history of committing thefts and physical assaults. The first theft occurred when Arnie was 8—he stole a cassette player from an electronics store. The first physical assault took place a year later, when he shoved his 7-year old brother up against the wall, bloodied his face, and then threatened to kill him with a butcher knife. Recently, the thefts and physical assaults have increased. In the last week, he stole a television set and struck his mother repeatedly and threatened to kill her. He also broke some neighborhood streetlights and threatened youths with a wrench and a hammer. Arnie's father left home when Arnie was 3 years old. Until the father left, his parents argued extensively, and his father often beat up his mother. Arnie's mother indicates that, when Arnie was younger, she was able to control him, but in the last several years she has not been able to enforce any sanctions on his antisocial behavior. Arnie's volatility and dangerous behavior have resulted in the recommendation that he be placed in a group home with other juvenile delinquents.

They cannot scare me with their empty spaces.
Between stars—on stars where no human race is.
I have it in me so much nearer home. To scare
myself with my own desert places.

—Robert Frost
American Poet, 20th Century

AT VARIOUS POINTS IN THIS BOOK, we have focused on adolescent problems. For example, we discussed school-related problems in chapter 7, "Schools," sexual problems in chapter 11, "Sexuality," and achievement problems in chapter 13, "Achievement, Careers, and Work." In this chapter, we exclusively examine adolescent problems. By the time you have completed this chapter, you should be able to reach these learning goals:

1 Know about the nature of adolescent problems

2 Discuss drugs and alcohol

3 Evaluate juvenile delinquency

4 Describe depression and suicide

5 Understand eating disorders

6 Discuss the interrelation of problems and prevention/intervention

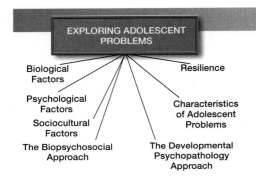

EXPLORING ADOLESCENT PROBLEMS

Let's explore what might cause adolescent problems, several approaches to understanding these causes, and the characteristics of adolescent problems.

Biological Factors

In the biological approach, adolescent problems are believed to be caused by a malfunctioning of the adolescent's body. Today, scientists who adopt a biological approach often focus on the brain and genetic factors as causes of adolescent problems. In the biological approach, drug therapy is frequently used to treat problems. For example, if an adolescent is depressed, in the biological approach, an antidepressant drug might be prescribed.

Psychological Factors

Among the psychological factors that have been proposed as causing adolescent problems are distorted thoughts, emotional turmoil, inappropriate learning, and troubled relationships. Two of the theoretical perspectives that we discussed in chapter 2, "The Science of Adolescent Development," address why adolescents might develop problems. Recall that psychoanalytic theorists attribute problems to stressful early experiences with parents. Also remember that behavioral and social cognitive theorists believe that adolescent problems are a consequence of social experiences with others.

Family and peer influences are especially believed to be important contributors to adolescent problems. For example, when we discuss substance abuse as well as juvenile delinquency, you will see that relationships with parents and peers are linked with these adolescent problems.

Sociocultural Factors

The psychological problems that adolescents develop appear in most cultures. However, the frequency and intensity of the problems vary across cultures with the variations being linked to social, economic, technological, and religious aspects of the cultures (Draguns, 1990; Tanaka-Matsumi, 2001).

Sociocultural factors that influence the development of adolescent problems include socioeconomic status and neighborhood quality (Brown & Adler, 1998). For example, poverty is a factor in the occurrence of delinquency.

The Biopsychosocial Approach

Some experts argue that all three factors—biological, psychological, and sociocultural—may be involved in determining whether an adolescent develops problems or not. Thus, if an adolescent engages in substance abuse it may be due to a combination of biological (heredity or brain processes), psychological (emotional turmoil or relationship difficulties), and sociocultural (poverty) factors. The combination of all three approaches is called the *biopsychosocial* approach.

American Psychiatric Association
Internet Mental Health
Mental Health Net
http://www.mhhe.com/santrocka9

The Developmental Psychopathology Approach

The field of **developmental psychopathology** *focuses on describing and exploring the developmental pathways of problems.* Many researchers in this field seek to establish links between early precursors of a problem (such as risk factors and early experiences) and outcomes (such as delinquency or depression) (Egeland, Pianta, & Ogawa, 1996; Egeland, Warren, & Aquilar, 2001; Harper, 2000; Popper, Ross, & Jennings, 2000). A developmental pathway describes continuities and transformations in factors that influence outcomes (Chang & Gjerde, 2000; Kremen & Block, 2000).

Adolescent problems can be categorized as internalizing or externalizing. **Internalizing problems** *occur when individuals turn their problems inward. Examples of internalizing disorders include anxiety and depression.* **Externalizing problems** *occur when problems are turned outward. An example of an externalizing problem is juvenile delinquency.* Links have been established between patterns of problems in childhood and outcomes in adulthood. In one study, males with internalizing patterns (such as anxiety and depression) in the elementary school years were likely to have similar forms of problems at age 21, but they did not have an increased risk of externalizing problems as young adults (Quinton, Rutter, & Gulliver, 1990). Similarly, the presence of an externalizing pattern (such as aggression or antisocial behavior) in childhood elevated risk for antisocial problems at age 21. For females in the same study, early internalizing and externalizing patterns both predicted internalizing problems at age 21.

Alan Sroufe and his colleagues (1999) have found that anxiety problems in adolescence are linked with anxious/resistant attachment in infancy, and that conduct problems in adolescence are related to avoidant attachment in infancy. Sroufe believes that a combination of early supportive care (attachment security) and early peer competence help to buffer adolescents from developing problems. In another recent developmental psychopathology study, Ann Masten and her colleagues (in press) followed 205 children for 10 years from childhood into adolescence. They found that good intellectual functioning and parenting served protective roles in keeping adolescents from engaging in antisocial behaviors. Later in this chapter, we will further explore such factors in our discussion of resilient adolescents.

developmental psychopathology
The area of psychology that focuses on describing and exploring the developmental pathways of problems.

internalizing problems
Occur when individuals turn problems inward. Examples include anxiety and depression.

externalizing problems
Occur when individuals turn problems outward. An example is juvenile delinquency.

Characteristics of Adolescent Problems

The spectrum of adolescent problems is wide. The problems vary in their severity and in how common they are for girls versus boys and for different socioeconomic groups. Some adolescent problems are short-lived; others can persist over many years. One 13-year-old adolescent might show a pattern of acting-out behavior that is disruptive to his classroom. As a 14-year-old, he might be assertive and aggressive, but no longer disruptive. Another 13-year-old might show a similar pattern of acting-out behavior. At age 16, she might have been arrested for numerous juvenile offenses and still be a disruptive influence in the classroom.

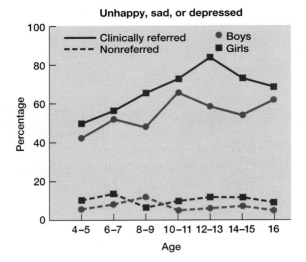

Unhappy, sad, or depressed

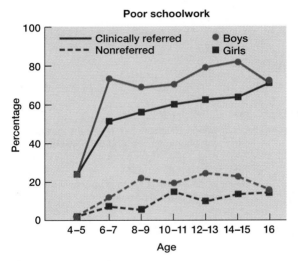

Poor schoolwork

FIGURE 14.1

The Two Items Most Likely to Differentiate Clinically Referred and Nonreferred Children and Adolescents

Developmental Assets
http://www.mhhe.com/santrocka9

Some problems are more likely to appear at one developmental level than at another. For example, fears are more common in early childhood, many school-related problems surface for the first time in middle and late childhood, and drug-related problems become more common in adolescence (Achenbach & Edelbrock, 1981). In one study, depression, truancy, and drug abuse were more common among older adolescents, while arguing, fighting, and being too loud were more common among younger adolescents (Edelbrock, 1989).

In the large-scale investigation by Thomas Achenbach and Craig Edelbrock (1981), adolescents from a lower-SES background were more likely to have problems than those from a middle-SES background. Most of the problems reported for adolescents from a lower-SES background were undercontrolled, externalizing behaviors—destroying others' things and fighting, for example. These behaviors also were more characteristic of boys than girls. The problems of middle-SES adolescents and girls were more likely to be overcontrolled and internalizing—anxiety or depression, for example.

The behavioral problems most likely to cause adolescents to be referred to a clinic for mental health treatment were feelings of unhappiness, sadness, or depression, and poor school performance (see figure 14.1). Difficulties in school achievement, whether secondary to other kinds of problems or primary problems in themselves, account for many referrals of adolescents.

In another investigation, Achenbach and his colleagues (1991) studied the problems and competencies of 2,600 children and adolescents 4 to 16 years old assessed at intake into mental health services and 2,600 demographically matched nonreferred children and adolescents. Lower-socioeconomic-status children and adolescents had more problems and fewer competencies than did their higher-socioeconomic-status counterparts. Children and adolescents had more problems when they had fewer related adults in their homes, had biological parents who were unmarried in their homes, had parents who were separated or divorced, lived in families who received public assistance, and lived in households in which family members had received mental health services. Children and adolescents who had more externalized problems came from families in which parents were unmarried, separated, or divorced, as well as from families receiving public assistance.

Many studies have shown that factors such as poverty, ineffective parenting, and mental disorders in parents *predict* adolescent problems. Predictors of problems are called *risk factors*. Risk factor means that there is an elevated probability of a problem outcome in groups of people who have that factor. Children with many risk factors are said to have a "high risk" for problems in childhood and adolescence, but not every one of these children will develop problems.

The Search Institute in Minneapolis has prescribed 40 developmental assets that they believe adolescents need to achieve positive outcomes in their lives (Benson, 1997). Half of these assets are external, half internal. The 20 *external* assets include support (such as family and neighborhood), empowerment (such as adults in the community valuing youth and youth being given useful community roles), boundaries and expectations (such as the family setting clear rules and consequences and monitoring the adolescent's whereabouts as well as positive peer influence), and constructive use of time (such as engaging in creative activities three or more times a week and participating three or more hours a week in organized youth programs). The 20 *internal* assets include commitment to learning (such as motivation to achieve in school and doing at least one hour of homework on school days), positive (values helping others and demonstrating integrity), social competencies (such as knowing how to plan and make decisions, and having interpersonal competencies like empathy and friendship skills), and positive identity (such as having a sense of control over life and high self-esteem). In research conducted by the Search Institute, adolescents with more assets reported engaging in fewer risk-taking behaviors, such as alcohol and tobacco use, sexual intercourse, and violence. For example, in one survey of more than 12,000 ninth- to twelfth-graders, 53 percent of the students with 0 to 10 assets reported using alcohol three or more times in the past month or getting drunk more than once in the past two weeks, compared to only 16 percent of the students with 21 to 30 assets or 4 percent of the students with 31 to 40 assets.

Resilience

Even when children and adolescents are faced with adverse conditions, such as poverty, are there characteristics that help buffer and make them resilient to developmental outcomes? Some children and adolescents do triumph over life's adversities (Garmezy, 1993; Luthar, Cicchetti, & Becker, 2000; Markstrom & Tryon, 1997; Taylor & Wong, 2000). Ann Masten (Masten & Coatsworth, 1998; Willis & others, 2001) analyzed the research literature on resilience and concluded that a number of individual factors (such as good intellectual functioning), family factors (close relationship to a caring parent figure), and extrafamilial factors (bonds to prosocial adults outside the family) characterize resilient children and adolescents (see figure 14.2).

Norman Garmezy (1993) described a setting in a Harlem neighborhood of New York City to illustrate resilience: In the foyer of the walkup apartment building is a large frame on a wall in the entranceway. It displays the photographs of children who live in the apartment building, with a written request that if anyone sees any of the children endangered on the street, they bring them back to the apartment house. Garmezy commented that this is an excellent example of adult competence and concern for the safety and well-being of children.

Source	Characteristic
Individual	Good intellectual functioning Appealing, sociable, easygoing disposition Self-efficacy, self-confidence, high self-esteem Talents Faith
Family	Close relationship to caring parent figure Authoritative parenting: warmth, structure, high expectations Socioeconomic advantages Connections to extended supportive family networks
Extrafamilial context	Bonds to prosocial adults outside the family Connections to prosocial organizations Attending effective schools

■ FIGURE 14.2
Characteristics of Resilient Children and Adolescents

Developing Resilience in Urban Youth
http://www.mhhe.com/santrocka9

At this point we have discussed a number of ideas about abnormality. This review should help you to reach your learning goals related to this topic.

☐ FOR YOUR REVIEW

Learning Goal 1
Know about the nature of adolescent problems

- Biological, psychological, and sociocultural factors have been proposed as causes of adolescent problems. In the biopsychosocial approach, all three factors—biological, psychological, and sociocultural—are emphasized.
- In the developmental psychopathology approach, the emphasis is on describing and exploring developmental pathways of problems.
- The spectrum of adolescent problems is wide, varying in severity, developmental level, sex, and socioeconomic status. One way of classifying problems is as internalizing or externalizing. Middle-SES adolescents and females have more internalizing problems, low-SES adolescents and males have more externalizing problems.
- Adolescents who have a number of external and internal assets have fewer problems than their counterparts with few external and internal assets.
- Three sets of characteristics are reflected in the lives of children and adolescents who show resilience in the face of adversity and disadvantage: (1) cognitive skills and positive responsiveness from others; (2) families marked by warmth, cohesion, and the presence of a caring adult; and (3) some source of external support.

Now that we have examined the basic nature of abnormality, let's turn our attention to specific problems in adolescence.

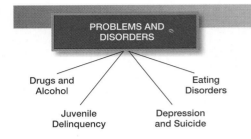

PROBLEMS AND
DISORDERS

Drugs and
Alcohol

Juvenile
Delinquency

Eating
Disorders

Depression
and Suicide

PROBLEMS AND DISORDERS

What are some of the major problems and disorders in adolescence? They include drugs and alcohol, juvenile delinquency, school-related problems, sexual problems, depression and suicide, and eating disorders. We discussed school-related and sexual problems in earlier chapters. Here we will examine the other problems, beginning with drugs and alcohol.

Drugs and Alcohol

Why do adolescents take drugs? How pervasive is adolescent drug use in the United States? What are the nature and effects of various drugs taken by adolescents? What factors contribute to adolescent drug use? These are among the questions we now evaluate.

Why Do Adolescents Take Drugs?   During one phase of his medical career, Sigmund Freud experimented with therapeutic uses of cocaine. He was searching for possible medical applications, such as a painkiller for eye surgery. He soon found that the drug induced ecstasy. He even wrote to his fiancée and told her how just a small dose of cocaine produced lofty, wonderful sensations. As it became apparent that some people become psychologically addicted to cocaine, and after several died from overdoses, Freud quit using the drug.

Since the beginning of history, humans have searched for substances that would sustain and protect them and also act on the nervous system to produce pleasurable sensations. Individuals are attracted to drugs because drugs help them to adapt to an ever-changing environment. Smoking, drinking, and taking drugs reduce tension and frustration, relieve boredom and fatigue, and in some cases help adolescents to escape the harsh realities of their world. Drugs provide pleasure by giving inner peace, joy, relaxation, kaleidoscopic perceptions, surges of exhilaration, or prolonged heightened sensation. They may help some adolescents to get along better in their world. For example, amphetamines might help the adolescent to stay awake to study for an exam.

Why do adolescents take drugs?

Drugs also satisfy adolescents' curiosity—some adolescents take drugs because they are intrigued by sensational accounts of drugs in the media, while others may listen to a popular song and wonder if the drugs described can provide them with unique, profound experiences. Drugs are taken for social reasons also, allowing adolescents to feel more comfortable and to enjoy the company of others.

But the use of drugs for personal gratification and temporary adaptation carries a very high price tag: drug dependence, personal and social disorganization, and a predisposition to serious and sometimes fatal diseases (Gullotta, Adams, & Montemayor, 1995; Ksir, 2000). Thus, what is intended as adaptive behavior is maladaptive in the long run. For example, prolonged cigarette smoking, in which the active drug is nicotine, is one of the most serious yet preventable health problems. Smoking has been described by some experts as "suicide in slow motion."

As adolescents continue to take a drug, their bodies develop **tolerance,** *which means that a greater amount of the drug is needed to produce the same effect.* The first time someone takes 5 milligrams of Valium, for example, the drug will make them feel very relaxed. But after taking the pill every day for six months, 10 milligrams might be needed to achieve the same calming effect.

Physical dependence *is the physical need for a drug that is accompanied by unpleasant withdrawal symptoms when the drug is discontinued.* **Psychological dependence** *is the strong desire and craving to repeat the use of a drug because of various emotional reasons, such as a feeling of well-being and reduction of stress.* Both physical and psychological dependence mean that the drug is playing a powerful role in the adolescent's life.

Trends in Overall Drug Use

The 1960s and 1970s were a time of marked increases in the use of illicit drugs. During the social and political unrest of those years, many youth turned to marijuana, stimulants, and hallucinogens. Increases in adolescent alcohol consumption during this period also were noted (Robinson & Greene, 1988). More precise data about drug use by adolescents have been collected in recent years.

Each year since 1975, Lloyd Johnston, Patrick O'Malley, and Gerald Bachman, working at the Institute of Social Research at the University of Michigan, have carefully monitored the drug use of America's high school seniors in a wide range of public and private high schools. Since 1991, they also have surveyed drug use by eighth- and tenth-graders. The University of Michigan study is called the Monitoring the Future Study.

The use of drugs among U.S. secondary school students declined in the 1980s but began to increase in the early 1990s (Johnston, O'Malley, & Bachman, 2001). In 2001, adolescents' use of any illicit was below the peaks attained in 1997 (Johnston, O'Malley, & Bachman, 2001). Figure 14.3 on page 446 shows the overall trends in drug use by high school seniors since 1975.

Nonetheless, even with the recent leveling off in use, the United States still has the highest rate of adolescent drug use of any industrialized nation. Also, the University of Michigan survey likely underestimates the percentage of adolescents who take drugs because it does not include high school dropouts, who have a higher rate of drug use than do students who are still in school. Johnston, O'Malley, and Bachman (1999) believe that "generational forgetting" contributed to the rise of adolescent drug use in the 1990s, with adolescents' beliefs about the dangers of drugs eroding considerably. Let's now consider separately a number of drugs that are used by adolescents.

Alcohol

To learn more about the role of alcohol in adolescents' lives, we examine how alcohol influences behavior and brain activity, the use and abuse of alcohol by adolescents, and risk factors in adolescents' alcohol abuse.

Effects of Alcohol on Adolescents' Behavior and Brain Activity

Alcohol is an extremely potent drug. It acts on the body as a depressant and slows down the brain's activities. If used in sufficient quantities, it will damage or even kill biological tissues, including muscle and brain cells. The mental and behavioral effects of alcohol include reduced inhibition and impaired judgment. Initially, adolescents feel more talkative and more confident

National Clearinghouse for Alcohol and Drug Information
National Institute of Drug Abuse
Drug Abuse and Adolescents
http://www.mhhe.com/santrocka9

tolerance
The condition in which a greater amount of a drug is needed to produce the same effect as a smaller amount used to produce.

physical dependence
Physical need for a drug that is accompanied by unpleasant withdrawal symptoms when the drug is discontinued.

psychological dependence
Strong desire and craving to repeat the use of a drug for various emotional reasons, such as a feeling of well-being and reduction of distress.

Monitoring the Future Study
http://www.mhhe.com/santrocka9

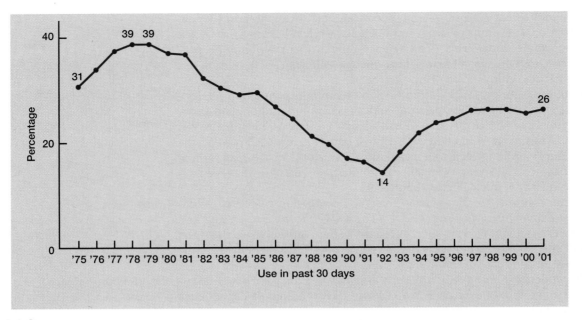

FIGURE 14.3
Trends in Drug Use by U.S. High School Seniors

This graph shows the percentage of high school seniors who say they have taken an illicit drug in the past 30 days. Notice the increased use in the last half of the 1970s, the decrease in the 1980s, and the increase in much of the 1990s.

Source: Johnston, O'Malley, & Bachman (2001).

Alcohol is a good preservative for everything but brains.

—Mary Pettibone Poole
American Author, 20th Century

when they use alcohol. However, skilled performances, such as driving, become impaired, and as more alcohol is ingested, intellectual functioning, behavioral control, and judgment become less efficient. Eventually, the drinker becomes drowsy and falls asleep. With extreme intoxication, the drinker may lapse into a coma. Each of these behavioral effects varies according to how the adolescent's body metabolizes alcohol, the individual's body weight, the amount of alcohol ingested, and whether previous drinking has led to tolerance.

Alcohol is the drug most widely used by U.S. adolescents. It has produced many enjoyable moments and many sad ones as well. Alcoholism is the third leading killer in the United States. Each year, approximately 25,000 individuals are killed, and 1.5 million injured, by drunk drivers. In 65 percent of the aggressive male acts against females, the offender has been under the influence of alcohol (Goodman & others, 1986). In numerous instances of drunk driving and assaults on females, the offenders have been adolescents. More than 13 million individuals are classified as alcoholics, many of whom established their drinking habits during adolescence.

In recent research, heavy, regular drinking in adolescence was linked with impairment to the brain:

• Brain scans of adolescents who abuse alcohol revealed damage to the hippocampus, a region of the brain especially involved in learning and memory. In one study, 24 adolescents and young adults with serious drinking problems were compared with similar-aged individuals without drinking problems (De Bellis & others, 2000). Brain scans revealed that the hippocampus of the heavy drinkers was 10 percent smaller than their peers, which is a substantial difference.

• Brain scans of females who drank heavily as adolescents but had quit as young adults were compared with young adult females who did not drink heavily as adolescents (Tapert & others, 2001). Images of their brains were taken while they completed a memory task in which they had to remember the location of an object on a screen. Compared with young women who were not heavy drinkers in adolescence, the adolescent drinkers had considerably more trouble remembering the

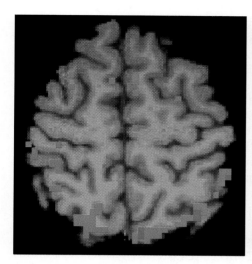
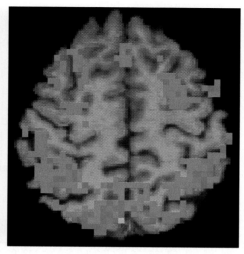

■ FIGURE 14.4
Brain Images of a Young Woman Who Abused Alcohol as an Adolescent and One Who Did Not

The brain image (MRI scan) on the left is the brain of the young woman who abused alcohol as an adolescent. The lack of color indicates sluggish brain activity. In contrast, the brain scan on the right of a young woman who did not abuse alcohol as an adolescent reveals more color, suggesting greater brain activity.

location of the object on the screen and the images of their brains revealed sluggish activity. Figure 14.4 shows the differences in the brains of two 20-year-old women, one who abused alcohol as an adolescent and one who did not.

More research needs to be carried out before definitive conclusions are reached about heavy alcohol use in adolescence and impairment to the brain. However, these recent studies suggest that there may be a harmful link.

Adolescent Alcohol Use and Abuse
Alcohol use remains very high among adolescents and has dropped only slightly in the last several years (Johnston, O'Malley, & Bachman, 2001). Monthly prevalence among high school seniors was 72 percent in 1980 but declined to 50 percent in 2001. Binge drinking (defined in the University of Michigan surveys as having five or more drinks in a row in the last two weeks) fell from 41 percent to 33 percent in 2001. A consistent sex difference occurs in binge drinking, with males engaging in this more than females. In 1997, 39 percent of male high school seniors said they had been drunk in the last two weeks, compared to 29 percent of their female counterparts.

Risk Factors in Adolescents' Alcohol Abuse
Among the risk factors in adolescents' abuse of alcohol are heredity, family influences, peer relations, personality characteristics, and the college transition. There is increasing evidence of a genetic predisposition to alcoholism, although it is important to remember that both genetic and environmental factors are involved (Moos, Finney, & Cronkite, 1990).

Adolescent alcohol use is related to parent and peer relations. Adolescents who drink heavily often come from unhappy homes in which there is a great deal of tension, have parents who give them little nurturance, are insecurely attached to their parents, have parents who use poor family management practices (low monitoring, unclear expectations, few rewards for positive behavior), and have parents who sanction alcohol use (Barnes, Farrell, & Banerjee, 1995: Peterson & others, 1994).

The peer group is especially important in adolescent alcohol abuse (Dielman & others, 1992). In one study, exposure to peer use and misuse of alcohol, along with susceptibility to peer pressure, were strong predictors of adolescent alcohol abuse

National Institute on Alcohol Abuse and Alcoholism Exploring Alcohol Abuse Research on Alcohol Abuse
http://www.mhhe.com/santrocka9

(Dielman, Shope, & Butchart, 1990). Whether adolescents have older, same-age, or younger peers as friends is also related to alcohol and drug abuse in adolescence. In one study, adolescents who took drugs were more likely to have older friends than were their counterparts who did not take drugs (Blyth, Durant, & Moosbrugger, 1985).

In another study, the Friendly PEERsuasion program reduced the incidence of drinking among girls who already drank and delayed the onset of drinking among girls who had not drunk previously (Girls, Inc., 1993). This program also improved the girls' resistance skills; the participants indicated that they were less likely than nonpartici-pants to stay in a drinking situation. The PEERsuasion program consists of fourteen one-hour sessions that include enjoyable, interactive activities related to using drugs. Adolescents are taught healthy ways to manage stress, detect media and peer pressure to use drugs, and practice skills for making responsible decisions about drug use. Then the girls serve as peer leaders to plan and implement substance-abuse prevention activities for 6- to 10-year-olds.

In one recent study of more than 3,000 eleventh-grade students, peer pressure was strongly related to alcohol use (Borden, Donnermeyer, & Scheer, 2001). Also in this study, participation in school-based and non-school-based activities was related to lower incidence of drug use and getting drunk less in the past year.

In another recent study, three types of tenth-grade adolescent drinkers were found: (1) those involved in problem behaviors at high rates; (2) highly anxious adolescents who report that they have performance anxiety; and (3) popular, well-functioning adolescents (these included crowds such as "jocks" and "brains" (Barber, Eccles, & Stone, 2001). Later, as they were making the transition to adulthood, the "jocks" and "criminals" showed the highest rates of being in substance abuse rehabilitation programs. Thus, associating with certain crowds in adolescence is linked with drinking behavior in adolescence and alcohol problems in the transition to adulthood.

Is there a personality profile that also might provide information about adolescents at risk for alcohol abuse? Alcohol researcher Robert Cloninger (1991) found that three traits present as early as 10 years of age are associated with alcoholism at the age of 28: (1) easily bored, needing constant activity and challenge; (2) driven to avoid negative consequences of actions; and (3) craving immediate external reward for effort. Cloninger advises parents who notice these traits in their children and young adolescents to ensure that their children have a structured, challenging environment and to provide them with considerable support.

A strong family support system is clearly an important preventive strategy in reducing alcohol abuse by adolescents (Waldron, Brody, & Slesnick, 2001). Are there others? Would raising the minimum drinking age have an effect? In one investigation, raising the minimum drinking age did lower the frequency of automobile crashes involving adolescents, but raising the drinking age alone did not reduce alcohol abuse (Wagennar, 1983). Another effort to reduce alcohol abuse involved a school-based program in which adolescents discussed alcohol-related issues with peers (Wodarski & Hoffman, 1984). At a one-year follow-up, students in the intervention schools reported less alcohol abuse and had discouraged each other's drinking more often than had students in other schools who had not been involved in the peer discussion of alcohol-related issues. Efforts to help the adolescent with a drinking problem vary enormously. Therapy may include working with other family members, peer-group discussion sessions, and specific behavioral techniques. Unfortunately, there has been little interest in identifying different types of adolescent alcohol abusers and then attempting to match treatment programs to the particular problems of the adolescent drinker. Most efforts simply assume that adolescents with drinking problems are a homogeneous group, and do not take into account the varying developmental patterns and social histories of different adolescents. Some adolescents with drinking problems may be helped more through family therapy, others through peer counseling, and yet others through intensive behavioral strategies, depending on the type of drinking problem and the social agents who have the most influence on the adolescent (Maguin, Zucker, & Fitzgerald, 1995).

In one recent study, binge-drinking trajectories from early adolescence to emerging adulthood were studied (Chassin, Pitts, & Prost, 2001). Individuals who were binge drinkers at 18 to 23 years of age often began drinking early and heavily, had parents who had alcohol problems, associated with peers who drank heavily, took other drugs, and engaged in antisocial behavior. These risk factors for binge drinking in emerging adulthood were assessed when the individuals were 13 years of age.

The transition from high school to college may be a critical transition in alcohol abuse (Schulenberg & Maggs, in press; Schulenberg & others, 2001). The large majority of older adolescents and youth who drink recognize that drinking is common among people their age and is largely acceptable, even expected by their peers. They also may perceive some social and coping benefits from alcohol use and even occasional heavy drinking. They also often diminish their drinking as they move further into the early adulthood years.

What kinds of problems are associated with binge drinking in college?

Heavy binge drinking can take a toll on college students. In a recent national survey of drinking patterns on college campuses, almost half of the binge drinkers reported problems that included missed classes, injuries, troubles with police, and unprotected sex (see figure 14.5) (Wechsler & others, 1994, 2000). Binge-drinking college students were 11 times more likely to fall behind in school, 10 times more likely to drive after drinking, and twice as likely to have unprotected sex than college students who did not binge drink.

While most youth drink long before they go to college, there often is an increase in heavy drinking during the first two years of college (Schulenberg, 1999; Schulenberg & Maggs, in press). For youth who do not go to college, there actually is a decline in drinking after high school (Schulenberg, 1999; Schulenberg & others, 2000). Chronic binge drinking for college students is more common for males than females and for students living away from home, especially males living at fraternity houses (Schulenberg, 1999). Clearly, it is important for colleges to recognize how critical the transition

THE TROUBLES THAT "FREQUENT BINGE DRINKERS" CREATE FOR...

Themselves[1] (% of those surveyed who admitted having had the problem)		and Others[2] (% of those surveyed who had been affected)	
Missed a class	61	Had study or sleep interrupted	68
Forgot where they were or what they did	54	Had to care for drunken student	54
Engaged in unplanned sex	41	Been insulted or humiliated	34
Got hurt	23	Experienced unwanted sexual advances	26
Had unprotected sex	22	Had serious argument	20
Damaged property	22	Had property damaged	15
Got into trouble with campus or local police	11	Been pushed or assaulted	13
Had five or more alcohol-related problems in school year	47	Had at least one of above problems	87

▪ FIGURE 14.5
The Hazardous Consequences of Binge Drinking in College

[1]Frequent binge drinkers were defined as those who had had at least four or five drinks at one time on at least three occasions in the previous two weeks.
[2]These figures are from colleges where at least 50% of students are binge drinkers.

from high school to college is and to develop programs that reduce binge drinking (Santrock & Halonen, 2002; Schulenberg & others, 2001).

Many young people decrease their use of alcohol as they move into adult roles, such as taking a permanent job, marriage or cohabitation, and parenthood (Schulenberg & Maggs, in press).

Hallucinogens

Hallucinogens *are drugs that modify an individual's perceptual experiences and produce hallucinations. Hallucinogens are called psychedelic (mind-altering) drugs.* First, we discuss LSD, which has powerful hallucinogenic properties, and then marijuana, a milder hallucinogen.

LSD

LSD, lysergic acid diethylamide, is a hallucinogen that, even in low doses, produces striking perceptual changes. Objects glow and change shape. Colors become kaleidoscopic. Fabulous images unfold as users close their eyes. Sometimes the images are pleasurable, sometimes unpleasant or frightening. In one drug trip, an LSD user might experience a cascade of beautiful colors and wonderful scenes; in another drug trip, the images might be frightening and grotesque. LSD's effects on the body may include dizziness, nausea, and tremors. Emotional and cognitive effects may include rapid mood swings or impaired attention and memory.

LSD's popularity in the 1960s and 1970s was followed by a reduction in use by the mid 1970s as its unpredictable effects become publicized. However, adolescents' use of LSD increased in the 1990s (Johnston, O'Malley, & Bachman, 2001). In 1985, 1.8 percent of U.S. high school seniors reported LSD use the last 30 days; in 1994, this increased to 4.0 percent but then declined to 2.3 percent in 2001.

Marijuana

Marijuana, a milder hallucinogen than LSD, comes from the hemp plant Cannabis sativa, which originated in Central Asia but is now grown in most parts of the world. Marijuana is made of the hemp plant's dry leaves; its dried resin is known as hashish. The active ingredient in marijuana is THC, which stands for the chemical delta-9-tetrahydrocannabinol. This ingredient does not resemble the chemicals of other psychedelic drugs. Because marijuana is metabolized slowly, its effects may be present over the course of several days.

The physical effects of marijuana include increases in pulse rate and blood pressure, reddening of the eyes, coughing, and dryness of the mouth. Psychological effects include a mixture of excitatory, depressive, and hallucinatory characteristics, making the drug difficult to classify. The drug can produce spontaneous and unrelated ideas; perceptions of time and place can be distorted; verbal behavior may increase or cease to occur at all; and sensitivity to sounds and colors might increase. Marijuana also can impair attention and memory, which suggests that smoking marijuana is not conducive to optimal school performance. When marijuana is used daily in heavy amounts, it also can impair the human reproductive system and may be involved in some birth defects.

Marijuana use by adolescents decreased in the 1980s. For example, in 1979, 37 percent of high school seniors said they had used marijuana in the last month, but in 1992 that figure had dropped to 12 percent. Figure 14.6 shows the increase in marijuana use by eighth-, tenth-, and twelfth-graders in the United States in the 1990s, although this use has started to level off. In one analysis, the increased use of marijuana in the 1990s was not related to such factors as religious commitment or grades but was linked with increased approval of using the drug and decreased perception that the drug is harmful (Johnston, O'Malley, & Bachman, 1999).

Stimulants

Stimulants *are drugs that increase the activity of the central nervous system.* The most widely used stimulants are caffeine, nicotine, amphetamines, and cocaine. Stimulants increase heart rate, breathing,

hallucinogens
Drugs that alter an individual's perceptual experiences and produce hallucinations; also called psychedelic or mind-altering drugs.

LSD
Marijuana
http://www.mhhe.com/santrocka9

stimulants
Drugs that increase the activity of the central nervous system.

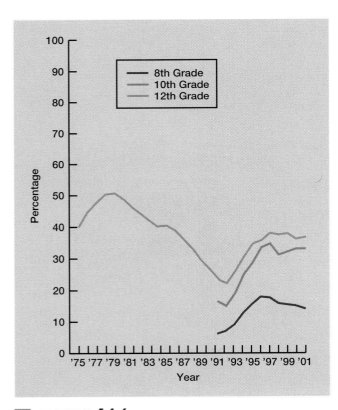

■ FIGURE 14.6
Trends in Marijuana Use by U.S. Eighth-, Tenth-, and Twelfth-Graders: Use in the Past Year

Note the increase in marijuana use in the last half of the 1970s, the decreased use in the 1980s, and the increased use in the 1990s.

and temperature but decrease appetite. Stimulants increase energy, decrease feelings of fatigue, and lift mood and self-confidence. After the effects wear off, though, the user often becomes tired, irritable, and depressed, and may experience headaches. Stimulants can be physically addictive.

Cigarette Smoking   Cigarette smoking (in which the active drug is nicotine) is one of the most serious yet preventable health problems. Smoking is likely to begin in grades 7 through 9, although sizable portions of youth are still establishing regular smoking habits during high school and college. Since the national surveys by Johnston, O'Malley, and Bachman began in 1975, cigarettes have been the substance most frequently used on a daily basis by high school seniors.

Smoking often begins in early adolescence. The peer group especially plays an important role in smoking (McRee & Gebelt, 2001). In one recent study, the risk of current smoking was linked with peer networks in which at least half of the members smoked, one or two best friends smoked, and smoking was common in the school (Alexander & others, 2001).

The good news is that cigarette smoking is decreasing among adolescents. In the national survey by the Institute of Social Research, the percentage of high school seniors who are current cigarette smokers continued to decline in 2001 (Johnston, O'Malley, & Bachman, 2001). Cigarette smoking peaked in 1997 among high school seniors and since then has been gradually declining. Among high school seniors, a decline from 36.5 percent in 1997 to 29.5 percent in 2001 occurred regarding smoking one or more cigarettes in the past 30 days. Among eighth- and tenth-graders, the decline was even greater. However, despite these recent improvements, approximately one-third of America's youth are active smokers at the end of their high school years.

The devastating effects of early smoking were brought home in a recent research study, which found that smoking in the adolescent years causes permanent genetic changes in the lungs and forever increases the risk of lung cancer, even if the smoker quits (Weincke & others, 1999). Such damage was much less likely among smokers in the study who started in their twenties. One of the remarkable findings in the study was that the early age of onset of smoking was more important in predicting genetic damage than how much the individuals smoked.

In two recent studies, cigarette smoking in adolescence was linked with emotional problems. In the first study, more than 15,000 adolescents were tracked for one year to assess the possible link between cigarette smoking and depression (Goodman & Capitman, 2000). Those who began smoking during the one-year duration of the study were four times more likely to become depressed at the end of that year. In the second study, more than 600 adolescents (average age 16) were followed into their early adulthood years (average age 22) to discover possible connections between cigarette smoking in adolescence and the prevalence of mental disorders in early adulthood (Johnson & others, 2000). Those who smoked heavily as adolescents were far more likely to have anxiety disorders as adults.

Cigarette Smoking and Cancer
National Cancer Institute
Cigarette Brands and
Adolescents
Addicted to Nicotine
Effective Prevention Programs
for Tobacco Use
http://www.mhhe.com/santrocka9

Cigarettes are readily available to these underage youth. Of the eighth-graders, most of whom are 13 to 14 years of age, three-fourths said that they can get cigarettes fairly easily if they want them. By the tenth grade, more than 90 percent say they can buy cigarettes easily.

In another study smoking initiation rates increased rapidly after 10 years of age and peaked at 13 to 14 years of age (Escobedo & others, 1993). Students who began smoking at 12 years of age or younger were more likely to be regular and heavy smokers than were students who began at older ages. Students who had participated in interscholastic sports were less likely to be regular and heavy smokers than were their counterparts who were not sports participants. In another study, adolescents whose parents smoked were more likely to be smokers themselves than were adolescents whose parents did not smoke (Kandel & Wu, 1995). Maternal smoking was more strongly related to smoking by young adolescents (especially girls) than paternal smoking was.

"I'll tell you one thing. As soon as I'm thirteen I'm gonna stop!"

Reprinted by permission of Tribune Media Services.

Traditional school health programs have often succeeded in educating adolescents about the long-term health consequences of smoking but have had little effect on adolescent smoking behavior. That is, adolescent smokers know as much about the health risks of smoking as do nonadolescent smokers, but this knowledge has had little impact on reducing their smoking behavior (Miller & Slap, 1989). The need for effective intervention has prompted investigators to focus on those factors that place young adolescents at high risk for future smoking, especially social pressures from peers, family members, and the media (Copeland, Heim, & Rome, 2001; Kulig & others, 2001).

A number of researchers have developed strategies for interrupting behavioral patterns that lead to smoking (Bruess & Richardson, 1992; Perry, Kelder, & Komro, 1993). In one investigation, high school students were recruited to help seventh-grade students resist peer pressure to smoke (McAlister & others, 1980). The high school students encouraged the younger adolescents to resist the influence of high-powered ads suggesting that liberated women smoke by saying, "She is not really liberated if she is hooked on tobacco." The students also engaged in role-playing exercises called "chicken." In these situations, the high school students called the younger adolescents "chicken" for not trying a cigarette. The seventh-graders practiced resistance to the peer pressure by saying, "I'd be a real chicken if I smoked just to impress you." Following several sessions, the students in the smoking prevention group were 50 percent less likely to begin smoking compared to a group of seventh-grade students in a neighboring junior high school, even though the parents of both groups of students had the same smoking rate.

One comprehensive health approach that includes an attempt to curb cigarette smoking by adolescents was developed by clinical psychologist Cheryl Perry and her colleagues (1988). Three programs were developed based on peer group norms, healthy role models, and social skills training. Elected peer leaders were trained as instructors. In seventh grade, adolescents were offered "Keep It Clean," a six-session course emphasizing the negative effects of smoking. In eighth grade, students were involved in "Health Olympics," an approach that included exchanging greeting cards on smoking and health with peers in other countries. In ninth grade, students participated in "Shifting Gears," which included six sessions focused on social skills. In the social skills program, students critiqued media messages and created their own positive health videotapes. At the same time as the school intervention, a community-wide smoking cessation program, as well as a diet and health awareness campaign, were initiated. After five years, students who were involved in the smoking and health program were much less likely to smoke cigarettes, use marijuana, or drink alcohol than their counterparts who were not involved in the program.

Cocaine   *Cocaine* is a stimulant that comes from the coca plant, native to Bolivia and Peru. For many years, Bolivians and Peruvians chewed on the plant to increase their stamina. Today, cocaine is either snorted or injected in the form of crystals or powder. The effect is a rush of euphoric feelings, which eventually wear off, followed by depressive feelings, lethargy, insomnia, and irritability. Cocaine can have a number of damaging effects on the body, resulting in heart attacks, strokes, and brain seizures.

How many adolescents use cocaine? Use of cocaine in the last 30 days by high school seniors dropped from a peak of 6.7 percent in 1985 to 2.1 percent in 2001 (Johnston, O'Malley, & Bachman, 2001). A growing percentage of high school students are reaching the conclusion that cocaine use entails considerable unpredictable risk. Still, the percentage of adolescents who have used cocaine is precariously high. About 1 of every 13 high school seniors has tried cocaine at least once.

A troublesome part of the cocaine story rests in the dangerous shift in how it is administered, due in large part to the advent of crack cocaine—an inexpensive, purified,

Cocaine
http://www.mhhe.com/santrocka9

smokable form of the drug. Crack use is especially heavy among non-college-bound youth in urban settings.

Amphetamines *Amphetamines* are widely prescribed stimulants, sometimes appearing in the form of diet pills. They are called "pep pills" and "uppers." Amphetamine use among high school seniors has decreased significantly. Use of amphetamines in the last 30 days by high school seniors declined from 10.7 percent in 1982 to 5.6 percent in 2001. However, use of over-the-counter stay-awake pills, which usually contain caffeine as their active ingredient, has sharply increased. Use of over-the-counter diet pills has decreased in recent years, although 40 percent of females have tried using diet pills by the time they graduate from high school.

Ecstasy Ecstasy, the street name for the synthetic drug MDMA, has stimulant and hallucinogenic effects. Its chemical structure is similar to methamphetamines. It usually comes in a pill form. Tolerance builds up rapidly so users may take three or four pills at a time. Ecstasy produces euphoric feelings and heightened sensations (especially touch and sight). The drug is popular at raves, where youth dance all night long with light sticks and other visual enhancements. Users often become hyperactive and sleepless. Ecstasy use can lead to dangerous increases in blood pressure, as well as stroke or a heart attack (Johnston, O'Malley, & Bachman, 2000). Repeated Ecstasy use may damage the areas of the brain that involve the regulation of mood, sexual response, sleep, and pain sensitivity.

There is a special concern about Ecstasy use by adolescents. In the national study conducted by the Institute of Social Research at the University of Michigan, the percentage of twelfth-graders who had used Ecstasy in the last year increased from 5.6 percent in 1998 to 9.2 percent in 2001 (Johnston, O'Malley, & Bachman, 2001). Similar increases in Ecstasy use, although at lower percentages, also occurred for eighth- and tenth-graders.

Depressants **Depressants** *are drugs that slow down the central nervous system, bodily functions, and behavior.* Medically, depressants have been used to reduce anxiety and to induce sleep. Among the most widely used depressants are alcohol, which we discussed earlier, barbiturates, and tranquilizers. Though used less frequently, the opiates are especially dangerous depressants.

Barbiturates, such as Nembutal and Seconal, are depressant drugs that induce sleep or reduce anxiety. *Tranquilizers,* such as Valium and Xanax, are depressant drugs that reduce anxiety and induce relaxation. They can produce symptoms of withdrawal when an individual stops taking them. Since the initial surveys, begun in 1975, of drug use by high school seniors, use of depressants has decreased. For example, use of barbiturates at least every 30 days in 1975 was 4.7 percent; in 2001, it was only 2.8 percent. Over the same time period, tranquilizer use also decreased, from 4.1 percent to 3.0 percent, for 30-day prevalence.

CAREERS IN ADOLESCENT DEVELOPMENT

Cheryl Perry
Epidemiologist, School of Public Health

Cheryl Perry is a professor of epidemiology in the School of Public Health at the University of Minnesota. She obtained her undergraduate degree in math from UCLA, a master's degree in education from the University of California at Davis, and a Ph.D. in education from Stanford.

Cheryl teaches courses in the prevention of high-risk behavior among adolescents and conducts a number of research studies. These currently include a cancer prevention program in the St. Paul, Minnesota, schools, a program to reduce alcohol use among U.S. adolescents, and a 30-school study of cardiovascular health in New Delhi, India.

Cheryl has received numerous awards for her outstanding contributions to understanding adolescent health and reducing at-risk adolescent behavior. She has served on the Board of Directors of the American School Health Association and as a scientific editor on the U.S. Surgeon General's Report on preventing tobacco use in young adolescents.

Cheryl Perry

depressants
Drugs that slow the central nervous system, bodily functions, and behavior.

Opiates, which consist of opium and its derivatives, depress the activity of the central nervous system. They are commonly known as narcotics. Many drugs have been produced from the opium poppy, among them morphine and heroin (which is converted to morphine when it enters the brain). For several hours after taking an opiate, an individual feels euphoria, pain relief, and an increased appetite for food and sex; however, the opiates are among the most physically addictive drugs. The body soon craves more heroin and experiences very painful withdrawal unless more is taken.

The rates of heroin use among adolescents are quite low, but they have risen significantly for grades 8, 10, and 12 in the 1990s (Johnston, O'Malley, & Bachman, 2001). In 2001, 0.4 percent of high school seniors said they had used heroin the last 30 days. A positive note occurred in the University of Michigan's recent surveys—more students perceived heroin as dangerous than in surveys conducted in the early to mid 1990s. Perceived dangerousness is usually a precursor to a drop in a drug's use.

At this point, we have discussed a number of depressants, stimulants, and hallucinogens. Their medical uses, duration of effects, overdose symptoms, health risks, physical addiction risk, and psychological dependence risk are summarized in figure 14.7 on page 455.

anabolic steroids

Drugs derived from the male sex hormone, testosterone. They promote muscle growth and lean body mass.

Anabolic Steroids
http://www.mhhe.com/santrocka9

Anabolic Steroids

Anabolic steroids *are drugs derived from the male sex hormone, testosterone. They promote muscle growth and increase lean body mass.* Anabolic steroids have medical uses, but they increasingly have been abused by some athletes and others who hope to improve their performance and physical attractiveness. Nonmedical uses of these drugs carry a number of physical and psychological health risks (National Clearinghouse for Alcohol and Drug Information, 1999).

Both males and females who take large doses of anabolic steroids usually experience changes in sexual characteristics. In males, this can involve a shrinking of the testicles, reduced sperm count, impotence, premature baldness, enlargement of the prostate gland, breast enlargement, and difficulty or pain in urinating. In females, their use can trigger severe acne on the face and body, a weakening of tendons (which can result in rupturing or tearing), reduction in HDL (the "good" cholesterol), and high blood pressure. Psychological effects in both males and females can involve irritability, uncontrollable bursts of anger, severe mood swings (which can lead to depression when individuals stop using the steroids), impaired judgment stemming from feelings of invincibility, and paranoid jealousy.

In the University of Michigan study (Johnston, O'Malley, & Bachman, 2001), 1.6 percent of eighth-graders, 2.1 percent of tenth-graders, and 2.4 percent of twelfth-graders said they had used anabolic steroids in the last year. In one recent study conducted in Sweden, use of anabolic steroids by high school students was linked with strength training, tobacco use, heavy alcohol consumption, and truancy (Kindlundh & others, 1999).

Factors in Adolescent Drug Abuse

Earlier, we discussed the factors that place adolescents at risk for alcohol abuse. Researchers also have examined the factors that are related to drug use in adolescence, especially the roles of development, parents, peers, and schools (Hops, 2002; Petraitis, Flay, & Miller, 1995).

Most adolescents become drug users at some point in their development, whether their use is limited to alcohol, caffeine, and cigarettes, or extended to marijuana, cocaine, and hard drugs. A special concern involves adolescents using drugs as a way of coping with stress, which can interfere with the development of competent coping skills and responsible decision making. Researchers have found that drug use in childhood or early adolescence has more detrimental long-term effects on the development of responsible, competent behavior than drug use that occurs in late adolescence (Newcomb & Bentler, 1989). When they use drugs to cope with stress, young adolescents often enter adult roles of marriage and work prematurely without adequate socioemotional growth and experience greater failure in adult roles.

How early are adolescents beginning drug use? National samples of eighth- and ninth-grade students were included in the Institute for Social Research survey of drug

DRUG CLASSIFICATION	MEDICAL USES	SHORT-TERM EFFECTS	OVERDOSE	HEALTH RISKS	RISK OF PHYSICAL/ PSYCHOLOGICAL DEPENDENCE
Depressants					
Alcohol	Pain relief	Relaxation, depressed brain activity, slowed behavior, reduced inhibitions	Disorientation, loss of consciousness, even death at high blood-alcohol levels	Accidents, brain damage, liver disease, heart disease, ulcers, birth defects	Physical: moderate; psychological: moderate
Barbiturates	Sleeping pill	Relaxation, sleep	Breathing difficulty, coma, possible death	Accidents, coma, possible death	Physical and psychological moderate to high
Tranquilizers	Anxiety reduction	Relaxation, slowed behavior	Breathing difficulty, coma, possible death	Accidents, coma, possible death	Physical: low to moderate; psychological: moderate to high
Opiates (narcotics)	Pain relief	Euphoric feelings, drowsiness, nausea	Convulsions, coma, possible death	Accidents, infectious diseases such as AIDS (when the drug is injected)	Physical: high; psychological: moderate to high
Stimulants					
Amphetamines	Weight control	Increased alertness, excitability; decreased fatigue, irritability	Extreme irritability, feelings of persecution, convulsions	Insomnia, hypertension, malnutrition, possible death	Physical: possible; psychological: moderate to high
Cocaine	Local anesthetic	Increased alertness, excitability, euphoric feelings; decreased fatigue, irritability	Extreme irritability, feelings of persecution, convulsions, cardiac arrest, possible death	Insomnia, hypertension, malnutrition, possible death	Physical: possible; psychological: moderate (oral) to very high (injected or smoked)
Hallucinogens					
LSD	None	Strong hallucinations, distorted time perception	Severe mental disturbance, loss of contact with reality	Accidents	Physical: none; psychological: low
Marijuana	Treatment of the eye disorder glaucoma	Euphoric feelings, relaxation, mild hallucinations, time distortion, attention and memory impairment	Fatigue, disoriented behavior	Accidents, respiratory disease	Physical: very low; psychological: moderate

■ FIGURE 14.7
Psychoactive Drugs: Depressants, Stimulants, and Hallucinogens

use for the first time in 1991 (Johnston, O'Malley, & Bachman, 1992). Early on in the increase in drug use in the United States (late 1960s, early 1970s), drug use was much higher among college students than among high school students, who in turn had much higher rates of drug use than did middle or junior high school students. However, today the rates for college and high school students are similar, and the rates for

"Just tell me where you kids get the idea to take so many drugs."

young adolescents are not as different from those for older adolescents as might be anticipated.

Drinking in the past year (2001) was reported by 42 percent of the eighth-graders, 64 percent of the tenth-graders, and 73 percent of the twelfth-graders (Johnston, O'Malley, & Bachman, 2001). Seventeen percent of the eighth-graders said they had engaged in binge drinking in the past year. Cigarette smoking had already been tried by 37 percent of the eighth-graders, with 12 percent of them (average age of 13) smoking in the past 30 days. Relatively few students had initiated cocaine use by the eighth grade (4.3 percent use ever) or the tenth grade (5.7 percent ever). An age differentiation also appeared for marijuana use, which tends to be one of the first illegal drugs tried by adolescents. Of the eighth-graders, 15 percent reported using marijuana in the prior year, compared with 33 percent of the tenth-graders and 37 percent of the high school seniors. Inhalant drugs, such as glues, aerosols, and butane, are rather commonly used by young adolescents—9 percent of eighth-graders reported use of inhalant drugs in the prior year, for example, while only 7 percent of the tenth- and 5 percent of the twelfth-graders reported such use.

Parents, peers, and social support play important roles in preventing adolescent drug abuse (Chapman & Saxman, 2000; Dishion, 2002; Mayes & Truman, 2002; Medler, 2000; Urberg, Goldstein, & Toro, 2002). A developmental model of adolescent drug abuse has been proposed by Judith Brook and her colleagues (1990). They believe that the initial step in adolescent drug abuse is laid down in the childhood years, when children fail to receive nurturance from their parents and grow up in conflict-ridden families. These children fail to internalize their parents' personality, attitudes, and behavior, and later carry this absence of parental ties into adolescence. Adolescent characteristics, such as lack of a conventional orientation and inability to control emotions, are then expressed in affiliations with peers who take drugs, which, in turn, leads to drug use. In recent studies, Brook and her colleagues have found support for their model.

In one recent national survey, parents who were more involved in setting limits (for everything from where the adolescents went after school to what they are exposed to on the Internet, TV, and music videos) were more likely to have adolescents who did not use drugs (National Center for Addiction and Substance Abuse, 2001). The researchers characterized these parents as "hands-on." By contrast, "hands-off" parents—those who were low in involvement and rarely set limits—had adolescents who were twice as likely to smoke cigarettes, drink alcohol, or take other drugs. Although adolescents often complain about such parental intrusion, it is likely that this close monitoring sends a message that their parents care about them.

In one recent study of more than 4,000 sixth- through eighth-grade students, parent involvement, parent expectations for not abusing drugs, and adolescents' positive regard for their parents were related to less smoking and drinking by the young adolescents (Simons-Morton & others, 2001). Also in this study, direct peer pressure and associating with problem-behaving friends were linked with drinking and smoking. In another study, heavy drug use by peers was linked with initial drug use by adolescents (Simons, Walker-Barnes, & Mason, 2001).

In a review of the role that schools can play in the prevention of drug abuse, Joy Dryfoos (1990) concluded that

1. Early intervention in schools is believed to be more effective than later intervention. This intervention works best when implemented before the onset of drug use. Middle school is often mentioned as an excellent time for the inclusion of drug-abuse programs in schools. In one evaluation of school-based drug prevention programs in the 1990s, early prevention was a key factor in the successful programs (Shin, 2001).

2. Nonetheless, school-based drug-abuse prevention requires a kindergarten-through-twelfth-grade approach, with age-appropriate components available. When school prevention programs are provided, the students need follow-up and

continuous attention. Counseling about drug abuse should be available throughout the school years.

3. Teacher training is an important element in school-based programs. The best-designed drug-abuse curriculum is ineffective in the hands of an inadequately prepared teacher. School systems need to provide time and resources for in-service training and supervision.

4. Social skills training, especially focused on coping skills and resistance to peer pressure, is the most promising of the new wave of school-based curricula. However, the effectiveness of these social skills training programs over the long term and whether or not they are as effective with high-risk youth as with others are not known.

5. Peer-led programs are often more effective than teacher-led or counselor-led programs, especially when older students (senior high) are the leaders and role models for younger students (junior high and middle school).

6. Most of the school-based programs have been general programs directed at all students, rather than specific programs targeted at high-risk adolescents. More programs aimed at the high-risk group are needed.

7. The most effective school-based programs are often part of community-wide prevention efforts that involve parents, peers, role models, media, police, courts, businesses, youth-serving agencies, as well as schools.

The basic philosophy of community-wide programs is that a number of different programs have to be in place. The Midwestern Prevention Program, developed by Mary Ann Pentz (1994), implemented a community-wide health-promotion campaign that used local media, community education, and parent programs in concert with a substance-abuse curriculum in the schools. Evaluations of the program after 18 months and after four years revealed significantly lower rates of alcohol and marijuana use by adolescents in the program than by their counterparts in other areas of the city where the program was not in operation.

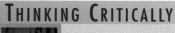

THINKING CRITICALLY

Developing a Drug-Abuse Prevention Program for Adolescents

Drug abuse is a major problem for adolescents in the United States. We have covered many different topics about drug abuse, including the nature of addiction, as well as the roles of development, parents, peers, and schools in drug abuse. Imagine that you have just been appointed the head of the President's Commission on Adolescent Drug Abuse. What would be the first program you would try to put in place? What would its components be? Would schools be a major locus of the intervention? Would the media play a key role in the program?

Since the last review, we have discussed a number of ideas about drugs and alcohol. This review should help you to reach your learning goals related to these topics.

☐ FOR YOUR REVIEW

Learning Goal 2
Discuss drugs and alcohol

- Drugs have been used since the beginning of human existence for pleasure, utility, curiosity, and social reasons. Understanding drugs requires an understanding of addiction and psychological dependence.

- The 1960s and 1970s were a time of marked increase in the use of illicit drugs. Drug use began to decline in the 1980s but increased again in the 1990s. The United States has the highest adolescent drug-use rate of any industrialized nation.

- Alcohol is a depressant and is the drug most widely used by adolescents. Alcohol abuse is a major adolescent problem. Risk factors for alcohol use include heredity, negative family and peer influences, certain personality factors, and the college transition.

- Other drugs that can be harmful to adolescents include hallucinogens (LSD and marijuana—their use increased in the 1990s), stimulants (such as nicotine, cocaine, and amphetamines), and depressants (such as barbiturates, tranquilizers, and alcohol). Anabolic steroid use by adolescents also has increased.

(continued on p. 458)

Learning Goal 2
Discuss drugs and alcohol
(concluded)

- Drug use in childhood and early adolescence has more negative long-term effects than when it first occurs in late adolescence. Parents and peers can provide important supportive roles in preventing adolescent drug use. Early intervention, a K-12 approach, teacher training, social skills training, and other strategies can be used in school-based efforts to reduce adolescent drug use.

Now that we have examined drug and alcohol use by adolescents, let's turn our attention to another major adolescent problem: juvenile delinquency.

Juvenile Delinquency

Thirteen-year-old Arnie, in the section that opened this chapter, has a history of thefts and physical assaults. Arnie is a juvenile delinquent. What is a juvenile delinquent? What are the antecedents of delinquency? What types of interventions have been used to prevent or reduce delinquency?

juvenile delinquency
A broad range of child and adolescent behaviors, including socially unacceptable behavior, status offenses, and criminal acts.

index offenses
Whether they are committed by juveniles or adults, these are criminal acts, such as robbery, rape, and homicide.

status offenses
Performed by youths under a specified age, these are juvenile offenses that are not as serious as index offenses. These offenses may include such acts as drinking under age, truancy, and sexual promiscuity.

Office of Juvenile Justice and Delinquency Prevention Justice Information Center Preventing Crime
http://www.mhhe.com/santrocka9

conduct disorder
The psychiatric diagnostic category for the occurrence of multiple delinquent activities over a six-month period. These behaviors include truancy, running away, fire setting, cruelty to animals, breaking and entering, and excessive fighting.

What Is Juvenile Delinquency?   The term **juvenile delinquency** *refers to a broad range of behaviors, from socially unacceptable behavior (such as acting out in school) to status offenses (such as running away) to criminal acts (such as burglary).* For legal purposes, a distinction is made between index offenses and status offenses. **Index offenses** *are criminal acts, whether they are committed by juveniles or adults. They include such acts as robbery, aggravated assault, rape, and homicide.* **Status offenses,** *such as running away, truancy, underage drinking, sexual promiscuity, and uncontrollability, are less serious acts. They are performed by youth under a specified age, which classifies them as juvenile offenses.* States often differ in the age used to classify an individual as a juvenile or an adult. Approximately three-fourths of the states have established age 18 as a maximum for defining juveniles. Two states use age 19 as the cutoff, seven states use age 17, and four states use age 16. Thus, running away from home at age 17 may be an offense in some states but not others.

One issue in juvenile justice is whether an adolescent who commits a crime should be tried as an adult (Cassel & Bernstein, 2001). One study found that trying adolescent offenders as adults increased rather than reduced their crime rate (Myers, 1999). The study evaluated more than 500 violent youths in Pennsylvania, which has adopted a "get tough" policy. Although these 500 offenders had been given harsher punishment than a comparison group retained in juvenile court, they were more likely to be rearrested—and rearrested more quickly—for new offenses once they were returned to the community. This suggests that the price of short-term public safety attained by prosecuting juveniles as adults might increase long-term criminal offenses.

In one analysis, it was proposed that individuals 12 and under should not be evaluated under adult criminal laws but that those 17 and older should be (Steinberg & Cauffman, 1999). It was recommended that individuals 13 to 16 years of age be given some type of individualized assessment in terms of whether to be tried in a juvenile court or an adult criminal court. This framework argues strongly against court placement based solely on the nature of an offense and takes into account the offender's developmental maturity.

In addition to the legal classifications of index offenses and status offenses, many of the behaviors considered delinquent are included in widely used classifications of abnormal behavior. **Conduct disorder** *is the psychiatric diagnostic category used when multiple behaviors occur over a six-month period. These behaviors include truancy, running away, fire setting, cruelty to animals, breaking and entering, excessive fighting, and others. When three or more of these behaviors co-occur before the age of 15 and the child or adolescent is considered unmanageable or out of control, the clinical diagnosis is conduct disorder.*

In sum, most children or adolescents at one time or another act out or do things that are destructive or troublesome for themselves or others. If these behaviors occur often in childhood or early adolescence, psychiatrists diagnose them as conduct disorders. If these behaviors result in illegal acts by juveniles, society labels them as *delinquents.*

In the Pittsburgh Youth Study, a longitudinal study that focused on more than 1,500 inner-city boys, three developmental pathways to delinquency were (Loeber & others, 1998).

- *Authority conflict.* Youth on this pathway showed stubborness prior to age 12, then moved on to defiance and avoidance of authority.
- *Covert.* This pathway included minor covert acts, such as lying, followed by property damage and moderately serious delinquency, then serious delinquency.
- *Overt.* This pathway included minor aggression followed by fighting and violence.

How many adolescents are arrested each year for committing juvenile delinquency offenses? In 1997, law enforcement agencies made an estimated 2.8 million arrests of individuals under the age of 18 in the United States (Office of Juvenile Justice and Prevention, 1998). This represents about 10 percent of adolescents 10 to 18 years of age in the United States. Note that this figure reflects only adolescents who have been arrested and does not include those who committed offenses but were not apprehended.

Recent U.S. government statistics reveal that 8 of 10 cases of juvenile delinquency involve males (Snyder & Sickmund, 1999). Although males are still far more likely to engage in juvenile delinquency, there has been a greater percentage increase in female than male juvenile delinquents in the last two decades (Hoyt & Scherer, 1998). For both male and female delinquents, rates for property offenses are higher than rates for other offenses (such as toward persons, drug offenses, and public order offenses).

Antecedents of Juvenile Delinquency   Predictors of delinquency include identity (negative identity), self-control (low degree), age (early initiation), sex (male), expectations for education (low expectations, little commitment), school grades (low achievement in early grades), peer influence (heavy influence, low resistance), socioeconomic status (low), family influence (lack of monitoring, low support, and ineffective discipline), and neighborhood quality (urban, high crime, high mobility). A summary of these antecedents of delinquency is presented in figure 14.8 on page 460.

Let's look in more detail at several of these factors that are related to delinquency. Erik Erikson (1968) believes that adolescents whose development has restricted them from acceptable social roles or made them feel that they cannot measure up to the demands placed on them might choose a negative identity. Adolescents with a negative identity may find support for their delinquent image among peers, reinforcing the negative identity. For Erikson, delinquency is an attempt to establish an identity, although it is a negative identity.

Although delinquency is less exclusively a lower-SES phenomenon than it was in the past, some characteristics of lower-SES culture might promote delinquency ◀▥ P. 263. The norms of many low-SES peer groups and gangs are antisocial, or counterproductive to the goals and norms of society at large. Getting into and staying out of trouble are prominent features of life for some adolescents in low-SES neighborhoods. Adolescents from low-SES backgrounds might sense that they can gain attention and status by performing antisocial actions. Being "tough" and "masculine" are high-status traits for low-SES boys, and these traits are often measured by the adolescent's success in performing and getting away with delinquent acts.

The nature of a community can contribute to delinquency (Farrington, 2000; Tolan, Guerra, & Kendall, 1995). A community with a high crime rate allows adolescents to observe many models who engage in criminal activities and might be rewarded for their criminal accomplishments. Such communities often are characterized by poverty, unemployment, and feelings of alienation. The quality of schools, funding for education, and organized neighborhood activities are other community factors that might be related to delinquency. Are there caring adults in the schools and neighborhood who can convince adolescents with

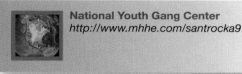

National Youth Gang Center
http://www.mhhe.com/santrocka9

■ THROUGH THE EYES OF PSYCHOLOGISTS

Gerald Patterson
University of Oregon

"Common parenting weaknesses in the families of antisocial boys include a lack of supervision, poor disciplining skills, limited problem-solving abilities, and a tendency to be uncommunicative with sons."

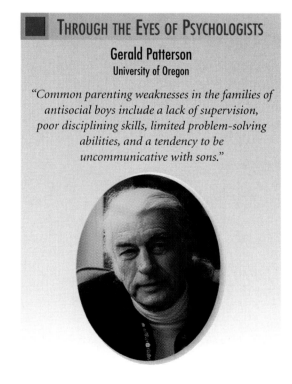

Antecedent	Association with delinquency	Description
Identity	Negative identity	Erikson believes delinquency occurs because the adolescent fails to resolve a role identity.
Self-control	Low degree	Some children and adolescents fail to acquire the essential controls that others have acquired during the process of growing up.
Age	Early initiation	Early appearance of antisocial behavior is associated with serious offenses later in adolescence. However, not every child who acts out becomes a delinquent.
Sex	Males	Boys engage in more antisocial behavior than girls do, although girls are more likely to run away. Boys engage in more violent acts.
Expectations for education and school grades	Low expectations and low grades	Adolescents who become delinquents often have low educational expectations and low grades. Their verbal abilities are often weak.
Family influences	Monitoring (low), support (low), discipline (ineffective)	Delinquents often come from families in which parents rarely monitor their adolescents, provide them with little support, and ineffectively discipline them.
Peer influences	Heavy influence, low resistance	Having delinquent peers greatly increases the risk of becoming delinquent.
Socioeconomic status	Low	Serious offenses are committed more frequently by lower-class males.
Neighborhood quality	Urban, high crime, high mobility	Communities often breed crime. Living in a high-crime area, which also is characterized by poverty and dense living conditions, increases the probability that a child will become a delinquent. These communities often have grossly inadequate schools.

FIGURE 14.8
The Antecedents of Juvenile Delinquency
After John W. Santrock. Copyright © The McGraw-Hill Companies.

delinquent tendencies that education is the best route to success? When family support becomes inadequate, then such community supports take on added importance in preventing delinquency.

Family support systems are also associated with delinquency (Henry, Tolan, & Gorman-Smith, 2001). Parents of delinquents are less skilled in discouraging antisocial behavior and in encouraging skilled behavior than are parents of nondelinquents. Parental monitoring of adolescents is especially important in determining whether an adolescent becomes a delinquent (Patterson, DeBarsyhe, & Ramsey, 1989; Pettit & others, 2001). "It's 10 P.M.; do you know where your children are?" seems to be an important question for parents to answer affirmatively. Family discord and inconsistent and inappropriate discipline are also associated with delinquency.

An increasing number of studies have found that siblings can have a strong influence on delinquency (Conger & Reuter, 1996; Lyons & others, 1995). In one recent study, high levels of hostile sibling relationships and older sibling delinquency were linked with younger sibling delinquency in both brother and sister pairs (Slomkowksi & others, 2001).

Peer relations also play an important role in delinquency. Having delinquent peers increases the risk of becoming delinquent (Henry, Tolan, & Gorman-Smith, 2001).

A current special concern in low-income areas is escalating gang violence.

Violence and Youth   An increasing concern is the high rate of adolescent violence (Price, 2001; Tolan, 2001; Weist & Cooley-Quille, 2001). In a recent school year, 57 percent of elementary and secondary school principals reported that one or more incidents of crime or violence occurred in their school and were reported to law enforcement officials (National Center for Education Statistics, 1998). Ten percent of all public schools experience one or more serious violent crimes (murder, rape, physical attack or fight with a weapon, robbery) each year (National Center for Education Statistics, 1998). Physical attacks or fights with a weapon lead the list of reported crimes. Each year more than 6,000 students are expelled for bringing firearms or explosives to school.

In a recent study, 17 percent of high school students reported carrying a gun or other weapon in the past 30 days (National Center for Health Statistics, 2000). In this same study, a smaller percentage (7 percent) reported bringing a gun or other weapon onto school property. Not all violence-related behaviors involve weapons. In this study 44 percent of male and 27 percent of female high school students said that they were involved in one or more physical fights.

In the late 1990s, a series of school shootings gained national attention. In April 1999, two Columbine High School (in Littleton, Colorado) students, Eric Harris (18) and Dylan Klebold (17) shot and killed 12 students and a teacher, wounded 23 others, and then killed themselves. In May 1998, slightly built Kip Kinkel strode into a cafeteria at Thurston High School in Springfield, Oregon, and opened fire on his fellow students, murdering two and injuring many others. Later that day, police went to Kip's home and found his parents lying dead on the floor, also victims of Kip's violence.

In 2001, 15-year-old Charles Andrew "Andy" Williams fired shots at Santana High School in Santee, California, that killed two classmates and injured 13 others. According to students at the school, Andy was a victim of bullying at the school and had joked

Oregon Social Learning Center
Center for the Prevention of School Violence
School-Based Violence Prevention in Canada
A Guide for Safe Schools
School Shootings
http://www.mhhe.com/santrocka9

Andrew "Andy" Williams, escorted by police after being arrested for killing two classmates and injuring 13 others at Santana High School. *What factors might contribute to youth murders?*

Violence and Gangs
Prevention of Youth Violence
Lost Boys
http://www.mhhe.com/santrocka9

the previous weekend of his violent plans, but no one took him seriously after he later said he was just kidding.

Is there any way that psychologists can predict whether a youth will turn violent? It's a complex task but they have pieced together some clues (Cowley, 1998). The violent youth are overwhelmingly male and many are driven by feelings of powerlessness. Violence seems to infuse these youth with a sense of power.

Small-town shooting sprees attract attention, but youth violence is far greater in poverty-infested areas of inner cities. Urban poverty fosters powerlessness and the rage that goes with it. Living in poverty is frustrating and many inner-city neighborhoods provide almost daily opportunities to observe violence. Many urban youth who live in poverty also lack adequate parent involvement and supervision.

James Garbarino (1999, 2001) says there is a lot of ignoring that goes on in these kinds of situations. Parents often don't want to acknowledge what might be a very upsetting reality. Harris and Klebold were members of the Trenchcoat Mafia clique of Columbine outcasts. The two even had made a video for a school video class the previous fall that depicted them walking down the halls at the school and shooting other students. Allegations were made that a year earlier the Sheriff's Department had been given information that Harris had bragged openly on the Internet that he and Klebold had built four bombs. Kip Kinkel had an obsession with guns and explosives, a history of abusing animals, and a nasty temper when crossed. When police examined his room, they found two pipe bombs, three larger bombs, and bomb-making recipes that Kip had downloaded from the Internet. Clearly, some signs were presented in these students' lives to suggest some serious problems, but it is still very difficult to predict whether youth like these will actually act on their anger and sense of powerlessness to commit murder.

Garbarino (1999, 2001) has interviewed a number of youth killers. He concludes that nobody really knows precisely why a tiny minority of youth kill but that it might be a lack of a spiritual center. In the youth killers he interviewed, Garbarino often found a spiritual or emotional emptiness in which the youth sought meaning in the dark side of life.

The following factors often are present in at-risk youths and seem to propel them toward violent acts (Walker, 1998):

• Early involvement with drugs and alcohol
• Easy access to weapons, especially handguns
• Association with antisocial, deviant peer groups
• Pervasive exposure to violence in the media

Many at-risk youths are also easily provoked to rage, reacting aggressively to real or imagined slights and acting on them, sometimes with tragic consequences. They might misjudge the motives and intentions of others toward them because of the hostility and agitation they carry (Coie & Dodge, 1998). Consequently, they frequently engage in hostile confrontations with peers and teachers. It is not unusual to find the anger-prone youth issuing threats of bodily harm to others.

In one recent study based on data collected in the National Longitudinal Study of Adolescent Health, secure attachment to parents, living in an intact family, and attending church services with parents were linked with lower incidences of engaging in violent behavior in seventh- through twelfth-graders (Franke, 2000).

These are some of the Oregon Social Learning Center's recommendations for reducing youth violence (Walker, 1998):

- *Recommit to raising children safely and effectively.* This includes engaging in parenting practices that have been shown to produce healthy, well-adjusted children. Such practices include consistent, fair discipline that is not harsh or severely punitive, careful monitoring and supervision, positive family management techniques, involvement in the child's daily life, daily debriefings about the child's experiences, and teaching problem-solving strategies.
- *Make prevention a reality.* Too often lip service is given to prevention strategies without investing in them at the necessary levels to make them effective.
- *Give more support to schools, which are struggling to educate a population that includes many at-risk children.*
- *Forge effective partnerships among families, schools, social service systems, churches, and other agencies to create the socializing experiences that will provide all youth with the opportunity to develop in positive ways.*

David and Roger Johnson (1995) believe it is important to go beyond violence prevention to include conflict resolution training in schools. Violence does need to be prevented in schools, but many violence prevention programs haven't worked because they are poorly targeted (too general and not focused on the relatively small group of students who need them the most), provide materials but don't focus on program implementation (too often they assume that a few hours will "fix" students who engage in violent behavior), and are unrealistic about the strength of social factors that produce violent behavior (schools alone can't solve all of our nation's social problems, such as decaying neighborhoods, lack of parental support, and so on).

Two approaches to conflict resolution programs are the cadre approach and the total student body approach. In the *cadre approach,* a small number of students are trained to serve as peer mediators for the entire school. Johnson and Johnson do not believe this approach is as effective as the *total student body approach,* in which every student learns how to manage conflicts constructively by negotiating agreements and mediating schoolmates' conflicts. A disadvantage of the total student body approach is the time and commitment required from school personnel to implement it. However, the more students there are who are trained in conflict resolution, the more likely it is that conflicts will be constructively managed.

One example of the total student body approach was developed by Johnson and Johnson (1991). Their Teaching Students to Be Peacemakers program involves both negotiation and mediation strategies. The steps students learn in negotiation are to (1) define what they want, (2) describe their feelings, (3) explain the reasons underlying the wants and feelings, (4) take the perspective of the other student to see the conflict from both sides, (5) generate at least three optional agreements that benefit both parties, and (6) come to an agreement about the best course of action.

CAREERS IN ADOLESCENT DEVELOPMENT

Rodney Hammond
Health Psychologist

When Rodney Hammond went to college at the University of Illinois in Champaign-Urbana, he had not decided on a major. To help finance his education, he took a part-time job in a child development research program sponsored by the psychology department. In this job, he observed inner-city children in contexts designed to improve their learning. He saw firsthand the contributions psychology can make and knew then that he wanted to be a psychologist.

Rodney Hammond went on to obtain a doctorate in school and community psychology with a focus on children's development. Today, he is Director of Violence Prevention at the National Center for Injury Prevention and Control in Atlanta. Rodney calls himself a "health psychologist," although when he went to graduate school, training for that profession did not exist as it does now. He and his associates teach at-risk youth how to use social skills to manage conflict effectively and to recognize situations that could become violent. They have shown in their research that with this intervention many youth are less likely to become juvenile delinquents. Hammond's message to undergraduates: "If you are interested in people and problem solving, psychology is a great way to combine the two."

Rodney Hammond, talking with an adolescent about strategies for coping with stress and avoiding risk-taking behaviors.

The steps students learn in mediation are to (1) stop the hostilities, (2) ensure that the disputants are committed to the mediation, (3) facilitate negotiations between the disputants, and (4) formalize the agreement.

When students have completed negotiation and mediation training, the school or teacher implements the Peacemakers program by choosing two student mediators for each day. Being a mediator helps students learn how to negotiate and resolve conflicts. Evaluations of the Peacemakers program have been positive, with participants showing more constructive conflict resolution than nonparticipants (Johnson & Johnson, 1995).

Since the last review, we have discussed a number of ideas about juvenile delinquency. This review should help you to reach your learning goals related to this topic.

☐ FOR YOUR REVIEW

Learning Goal 3
Evaluate juvenile delinquency

- Juvenile delinquency consists of a broad range of behaviors, from socially undesirable behavior to status offenses. For legal purposes, a distinction is made between index and status offenses. Conduct disorder is a psychiatric category often used to describe delinquent-type behaviors.
- Predictors of juvenile delinquency include a negative identity, low self-control, early initiation of delinquency, weak educational orientation, heavy peer influence, low parental monitoring, ineffective discipline, and living in a high-crime, urban area.
- The high rate of violence among youth is an increasing concern. Ten percent of public schools experience one or more serious violent incidents each year.
- A number of strategies have been proposed for reducing youth violence, including conflict resolution training.

So far in our coverage of adolescent problems, we have focused on drugs, alcohol, and juvenile delinquency. Next, we will explore depression and suicide.

Depression and Suicide

As mentioned earlier in the chapter, one of the most frequent characteristics of adolescents referred for psychological treatment is sadness or depression, especially among girls. In this section, we discuss the nature of adolescent depression and adolescent suicide.

major depressive disorder

The diagnosis when an individual experiences a major depressive episode and depressed characteristics, such as lethargy and depression, for two weeks or longer and daily functioning becomes impaired.

Depression   An adolescent who says "I'm depressed" or "I'm so down" may be describing a mood that lasts only a few hours or a much longer lasting mental disorder. In **major depressive disorder,** *an individual experiences a major depressive episode and depressed characteristics, such as lethargy and hopelessness, for at least two weeks or longer and daily functioning becomes impaired.* According to the *DSM-IV* classification of mental disorders (American Psychiatric Association, 1994), nine symptoms define a major depressive episode and to be classified as having major depressive disorder, at least five of these much be present during a two-week period:

1. Depressed mood most of the day
2. Reduced interest or pleasure in all or most activities
3. Significant weight loss or gain, or significant decrease or interest in appetite
4. Trouble sleeping or sleeping too much
5. Psychomotor agitation or retardation
6. Fatigue or loss of energy
7. Feeling worthless or guilty in an excessive or inappropriate manner
8. Problems in thinking, concentrating, or making decisions
9. Recurrent thoughts of death and suicide

In adolescence, pervasive depressive symptoms might be manifested in such ways as tending to dress in black clothes, writing poetry with morbid themes, or a preoccupation with music that has depressive themes. Sleep problems can appear as all-night television watching, difficulty in getting up for school, or sleeping during the day. Lack of interest in usually pleasurable activities may show up as withdrawal from friends or staying alone in the bedroom most of the time. A lack of motivation and energy level can show up in missed classes. Boredom might be a result of feeling depressed. Adolescent depression also can occur in conjunction with conduct disorder, substance abuse, or an eating disorder.

How serious a problem is depression in adolescence? Surveys have found that approximately one-third of adolescents who go to a mental health clinic suffer from depression (Fleming, Boyle, & Offord, 1993). Depression is more common in the adolescent years than the elementary school years (Compas & Grant, 1993). By about age 15, adolescent females have a rate of depression that is twice that of adolescent males. Some of the reasons for this sex difference that have been proposed are these:

Depression is more likely to occur in adolescence than in childhood and more likely to characterize female adolescents than male adolescents. *Why might female adolescents be more likely to develop depression than adolescent males?*

- Females tend to ruminate in their depressed mood and amplify it.
- Females' self-images, especially their body images, are more negative than males.
- Females face more discrimination than males do.
- Hormonal changes alter vulnerability to depression in adolescence, especially among girls.
- Puberty occurs earlier for girls than boys and as a result girls experience a piling up of changes and life experiences in the middle school years, which can increase depression.

Mental health professionals believe that depression often goes undiagnosed in adolescence. Why is depression often not detected in adolescence? Normal adolescents often show mood swings, ruminate in introspective ways, express boredom with life, and indicate a sense of hopelessness. These behaviors might simply be transitory and not reflect a mental disorder but rather normal adolescent behaviors and thoughts.

Follow-up studies of depressed adolescents indicate that the symptoms of depression experienced in adolescence predict similar problems in adulthood (Garber & others, 1988). This means that adolescent depression needs to be taken seriously. It does not just automatically go away. Rather, adolescents who are diagnosed as having depression are more likely to experience the problem on a continuing basis in adulthood than are adolescents not diagnosed as having depression. In one recent longitudinal study, transient problems in adolescence were related to situation specific factors (such as negative peer events), whereas chronic problems were defined by individual characteristics, such as internalizing behaviors (Brooks-Gunn & Graber, 1995).

Other family factors are involved in adolescent depression (Sheeber, Hops, & Davis, 2001). Having a depressed parent is a risk factor for depression in childhood and adolescence (Windle & Dumenci, 1998). Parents who are emotionally unavailable, immersed in marital conflict, and have economic problems may set the stage for the emergence of depression in their adolescent children (Marmorstein & Shiner, 1996; Sheeber & others, 1997).

Poor peer relationships also are associated with adolescent depression. Not having a close relationship with a best friend, having less contact with friends, and peer rejection increase depressive tendencies in adolescents (Vernberg, 1990).

The experience of difficult changes or challenges is associated with depressive symptoms in adolescence (Compas & Grant, 1993). Parental divorce increases depressive symptoms in adolescents. Also, when adolescents go through puberty at the same time as they move from elementary school to middle or junior high school, they report

Exploring Adolescent Depression
Pathways to Adolescent Depression
Information for Adolescents About Depression
Depression Research
http://www.mhhe.com/santrocka9

being depressed more than do adolescents who go through puberty after the school transition (Petersen, Sarigiani, & Kennedy, 1991).

Depression has been treated with drug therapy and psychotherapy techniques (Beckham, 2000). Antidepressant drugs reduce the symptoms of depression in about 60 to 70 percent of cases, often taking about two to four weeks to improve mood. Cognitive therapy also has been effective in treating depression (Beck, 1993; Hollon, 2000).

Suicide   Suicidal behavior is rare in childhood but escalates in early adolescence. Suicide is the third leading cause of death today among adolescents 13 through 19 years of age in the United States (National Center for Health Statistics, 2000). Although the incidence of suicide in adolescence has increased in recent decades, it is still a relatively rare event in adolescence. In 1998, 4,135 individuals from 15 through 24 years of age committed suicide in the United States, or approximately 11 of every 100,000 individuals in this age grouping (National Vital Statistics Reports, 2001).

Far more adolescents contemplate suicide or attempt suicide unsuccessfully. In a recent national study, one-fifth of high school students said they had seriously considered or attempted suicide in the last 12 months (National Center for Health Statistics, 2000). Less than 3 percent reported a suicide attempt that resulted in an injury, poisoning, or drug overdose that had been treated by a doctor. In this study, female adolescents were more likely to consider suicide than male adolescents. From the ninth through twelfth grades, females increasingly contemplated suicide, but this trend was not found in adolescent males. Adolescent males were more likely to actually commit suicide than adolescent females because they are more likely to use more lethal means, such as a gun, while adolescent females are more likely to cut their wrists or take an overdose of sleeping pills, which is less likely to result in death.

Why do adolescents attempt suicide? There is no simple answer to this important question. It is helpful to think of suicide in terms of proximal and distal factors. Proximal, or immediate, factors can trigger a suicide attempt. Highly stressful circumstances, such as the loss of a boyfriend or girlfriend, poor grades at school, or an unwanted pregnancy, can trigger a suicide attempt. Drugs may play a proximal risk for suicide and this risk may have increased in recent years (National Center for Health Statistics, 2000).

Distal, or earlier, experiences often are involved in suicide attempts as well. A long-standing history of family instability and unhappiness may be present (Reinherz & others, 1994). Just as a lack of affection and emotional support, high control, and pressure for achievement by parents during childhood are related to adolescent depression, such combinations of family experiences are also likely to show up as distal factors in suicide attempts. The adolescent might also lack supportive friendships. In a study of suicide among gifted women, previous suicide attempts, anxiety, conspicuous instability in work and in relationships, depression, or alcoholism also were present in the women's lives (Tomlinson-Keasey, Warren, & Elliot, 1986). These factors are similar to those found to predict suicide among gifted men.

In one recent study, family connectedness was linked with a lower incidence of suicide attempts by adolescents (Borowsky, Ireland, & Resnick, 2001). In this study, drug use and having a friend who committed suicide were related to a higher incidence of adolescent suicide attempts.

Just as genetic factors are associated with depression, they are also associated with suicide. The closer the genetic relationship a person has to someone who has committed suicide, the more likely that person is to commit suicide.

What is the psychological profile of the suicidal adolescent like? Most youth who commit suicide have a history of problems. Suicidal adolescents often have depressive symptoms (Gadpaille, 1996). Although not all depressed adolescents are suicidal, depression is the most frequently cited factor associated with adolescent suicide. A sense of hopelessness, low self-esteem, and high self-blame are also associated with adolescent suicide (Harter & Marold, 1992).

In some instances, suicides in adolescence occur in clusters. That is, when one adolescent commits suicide, other adolescents who find out about this also commit suicide.

Suicide Facts
What Do You Know About Suicide?
Suicide and Homicide
Research on Suicidal Behavior
Eating Disorders
http://www.mhhe.com/santrocka9

Such "copycat" suicides raise the issue of whether suicides should be reported in the media because if so they might plant the idea of committing suicide in other adolescents' minds.

Figure 14.9 provides valuable information about what to do and what not to do when you suspect someone is likely to commit suicide.

Eating Disorders

Eating disorders have become increasing problems in adolescence. Here are some research findings regarding adolescent eating disorders:

- Girls who felt negatively about their bodies in early adolescence were more likely to develop eating disorders two years later than their counterparts who did not feel negatively about their bodies (Attie & Brooks-Gunn, 1989).
- Girls who had positive relationships with both parents had healthier eating habits than girls who had negative relationships with one or both parents (Swarr & Richards, 1996). Negative parent-adolescent relationships were linked with increased dieting in adolescent girls over a one-year period (Archibald, Graber, & Brooks-Gunn, 1999).
- Girls who were both sexually active with their boyfriends and in pubertal transition were the most likely to be dieting or engaging in disordered eating patterns (Caufmann, 1994).
- Girls who were making a lot of effort to look like same-sex figures in the media were more likely than their peers to become very concerned with their weight (Field & others, 2001).
- Many adolescent girls have a strong desire to weigh less (Graber & Brooks-Gunn, 2001).

Let's now examine different types of eating disorders in adolescence, beginning with obesity.

Obesity   In a recent national survey, 14 percent of 12- to 19-year-olds in the United States were overweight (National Center for Health Statistics, 2000). Being overweight was determined by body mass index (BMI), which is computed by a formula that takes into account height and weight. Only adolescents at or above the 95th percentile of BMI were included in the overweight category. This represents a significant increase in obesity over past years (see figure 14.10 on p. 468).

Eating patterns established in childhood and adolescence are highly associated with obesity in adulthood. For example, 80 percent of obese adolescents become obese adults. Many obese adolescents feel that everything would be great in their lives if they only could lose weight. A typical example is Debby, who at 17 has been obese since she was 12. She came from a middle-SES family and her parents pressured her to lose weight, repeatedly sending her to weight reduction centers and physicians. One summer Debby was sent to a diet camp, where she went from 200 to 150 pounds. On returning home, she was terribly disappointed when her parents pressured her to lose more. With increased tension and parental preoccupation with her weight, she gave up her dieting efforts and her weight rose rapidly. Debby isolated herself and continued her preoccupation with food. Later, clinical help was sought and fortunately Debby was able to work through her hostility toward her parents and understand her self-destructive behavior. Eventually she gained a sense of self-control and became willing to reduce her weight for herself, not for her peers or her parents.

There have been few cross-cultural comparisons of obesity in childhood and adolescence. However, in one recent study, U.S. children and adolescents (6 to 18 years of age) were four times more likely to be classified as obese than their counterparts in

What to do

1. Ask direct, straightforward questions in a calm manner: "Are you thinking about hurting yourself?"

2. Assess the seriousness of the suicidal intent by asking questions about feelings, important relationships, who else the person has talked with, and the amount of thought given to the means to be used. If a gun, pills, a rope, or other means has been obtained and a precise plan developed, clearly the situation is dangerous. Stay with the person until help arrives.

3. Be a good listener and be very supportive without being falsely reassuring.

4. Try to persuade the person to obtain professional help and assist him or her in getting this help.

What not to do

1. Do not ignore the warning signs.

2. Do not refuse to talk about suicide if a person approaches you about it.

3. Do not react with humor, disapproval, or repulsion.

4. Do not give false reassurances by saying such things as "Everything is going to be OK." Also do not give out simple answers or platitudes, such as "You have everything to be thankful for."

5. Do not abandon the individual after the crisis has passed or after professional help has commenced.

FIGURE 14.9
What to Do and What Not to Do When You Suspect Someone Is Likely to Attempt Suicide

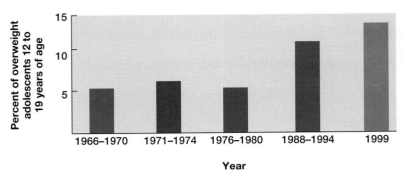

■ **FIGURE 14.10**

The Increase in Adolescent Obesity from 1966 to 1999 in the United States

China and almost three times as likely to be classified as obese than their counterparts in Russia (Wang, 2000).

In a recent U.S. study, adolescents who had an overweight mother or father were more likely to be overweight than their counterparts without an overweight parent (Dowda & others, 2001). Also in this study, adolescent girls who watched four or more hours of television a day were more likely to be overweight than those who watched less than four hours a day. Adolescent boys who participated in sports team and exercise programs were less likely to be overweight than those who did not participate in these programs.

Both heredity and environmental factors are involved in obesity (Stunkard, 2000). Some individuals inherit a tendency to be overweight. Only 10 percent of children who do not have obese parents become obese themselves, whereas 40 percent of children who become obese have one obese parent and 70 percent of children who become obese have two obese parents. Also, identical twins have similar weights, even when they are reared apart.

Strong evidence of the environment's role in obesity is the doubling of the rate of obesity in the United States since 1900, as well as the significant increase in adolescent obesity since the 1960s, which was described earlier. This dramatic increase in obesity likely is due to greater availability of food (especially food high in fat), energy-saving devices, and declining physical activity. American adolescents also are more obese than European adolescents and adolescents in many other parts of the world.

Anorexia Nervosa and Bulimia Nervosa   Two eating disorders that may appear in adolescence are anorexia nervosa and bulimia nervosa.

Anorexia Nervosa   **Anorexia nervosa** *is an eating disorder that involves the relentless pursuit of thinness through starvation.* Anorexia nervosa is a serious disorder that can lead to death. Three main characteristics of anorexia nervosa are (Davison & Neale, 2001):

- Weighing less than 85 percent of what is considered normal for their age and height.
- Having an intense fear of gaining weight. The fear does not decrease with weight loss.
- Having a distorted image of their body shape. Even when they are extremely thin, they see themselves as too fat. They never think they are thin enough, especially in the abdomen, buttocks, and thighs. They usually weigh themselves frequently, often take their body measurements, and gaze critically at themselves in mirrors.

Anorexia nervosa typically begins in the early to middle teenage years, often following an episode of dieting and the occurrence of some type of life stress. It is about 10 times more likely to characterize females than males. Although most U.S. adolescent girls have been on a diet at some point, slightly less than 1 percent ever develop anorexia nervosa (Walters & Kendler, 1994). When anorexia nervosa does occur in

anorexia nervosa
An eating disorder that involves the relentless pursuit of thinness through starvation.

Anorexia Nervosa and Other Eating Disorders
Anorexia Nervosa
http://www.mhhe.com/santrocka9

Anorexia nervosa has become an increasing problem for adolescent girls and young adult women. *What are some possible causes of anorexia nervosa?*

males, the symptoms and other characteristics (such as family conflict) are usually similar to those reported by females who have the disorder (Olivardia & others, 1995).

Most anorexics are White adolescent or young adult females from well-educated, middle- and upper-income families that are competitive and high-achieving. They set high standards, become stressed about not being able to reach the standards, and are intensely concerned about how others perceive them (Striegel-Moore, Silberstein, & Rodin, 1993). Unable to meet these high expectations, they turn to something they can control: their weight.

The fashion image in the American culture which emphasizes that "thin is beautiful" contributes to the incidence of anorexia nervosa. This image is reflected in the saying, "You never can be too rich or too thin." The media portrays thin as beautiful in their choice of fashion models, which many adolescent girls want to emulate.

About 70 percent of patients with anorexia nervosa eventually recover. Recovery often takes six to seven years and relapses are common before a stable pattern of eating and weight maintenance is achieved (Strober, Freeman & Morrel, 1997). In a longitudinal study of individuals diagnosed with anorexia nervosa in adolescence, 10 years later, approximately two-thirds were fully recovered, 3 percent still had anorexia nervosa, and none of them had died (Herpertz & others, 2001). However, in another longitudinal study, 21 years after being diagnosed with anorexia nervosa, 16 percent of the individuals had died because of factors related to anorexia nervosa (Lowe & others, 2001).

Bulimia Nervosa   While anorexics control their eating by restricting it, most bulimics cannot. **Bulimia nervosa** *is an eating disorder in which the individual consistently follows a binge-and-purge eating pattern.* The bulimic goes on an eating binge and then purges by self-inducing vomiting or using a laxative. As with anorexics, most bulimics are preoccupied with food, have a strong fear of becoming overweight, and are depressed or anxious (Davison & Neale, 2001). Unlike anorexia nervosa, the binge-and-purging of bulimia nervosa occurs within a normal weight range, which means that it often is difficult to detect (Mizes & Miller, 2000).

bulimia nervosa
In this eating disorder, the individual consistently follows a binge-and-purge eating pattern.

Bulimia nervosa typically begins in late adolescence or early adulthood. About 90 percent of the cases are women. Approximately 1 to 2 percent of women are estimated to develop bulimia nervosa (Gotesdam & Agras, 1995). Many women who develop bulimia nervosa were somewhat overweight before the onset of the disorder and the binge eating often began during an episode of dieting. As with anorexia nervosa, about 70 percent of individuals who develop bulimia nervosa eventually recover from the disorder (Keel & others, 1999).

Since the last review, we have discussed a number of ideas about depression, suicide, and eating disorders. This review should help you to reach your learning goals related to these topics.

☐ FOR YOUR REVIEW

Learning Goal 4
Describe depression and suicide

- Adolescents have a higher rate of depression than children do. Female adolescents are far more likely to develop depression than adolescent males are. Adolescents who develop depression are more likely than nondepressed adolescents to have depression as adults. Treatment of depression has involved both drug therapy and psychotherapy.
- The U.S. adolescent suicide rate has tripled since the 1950s. Both proximal and distal factors likely are involved in suicide.

Learning Goal 5
Understand eating disorders

- Studies suggest an increasing percentage of U.S. adolescents are obese. Both hereditary and environmental factors are involved in obesity.
- Anorexia nervosa is an eating disorder that involves the relentless pursuit of thinness through starvation. Anorexia nervosa primarily afflicts non-Latino White, middle- and upper-SES females.
- Bulimia nervosa is an eating disorder in which the individual consistently follows a binge-and-purge pattern.

So far in this chapter, we have examined the nature of abnormality and a number of adolescent problems and disorders. Next, we will explore the multiple problems that characterize many at-risk adolescents.

INTERRELATION OF
PROBLEMS AND PREVENTION/
INTERVENTION

INTERRELATION OF PROBLEMS AND PREVENTION/INTERVENTION

The adolescents most at risk have more than one problem. Researchers are increasingly finding that problem behaviors in adolescence are interrelated (Santelli & others, 2001; Tubman, Windle, and Windle, 1996). For example, heavy substance abuse is related to early sexual activity, lower grades, dropping out of school, and delinquency. Early initiation of sexual activity is associated with the use of cigarettes and alcohol, use of marijuana and other illicit drugs, lower grades, dropping out of school, and delinquency. Delinquency is related to early sexual activity, early pregnancy, substance abuse, and dropping out of school. As many as 10 percent of the adolescent population in the United States have serious multiple-problem behaviors (adolescents who have dropped out of school, or are behind in their grade level, are users of heavy drugs, regularly use cigarettes and marijuana, and are sexually active but do not use contraception). Many, but not all, of these very high-risk youth "do it all." Another 15 percent of adolescents participate in many of these same behaviors but with slightly lower frequency and less deleterious consequences. These high-risk youth often engage in two- or three-problem behaviors (Dryfoos, 1990).

In addition to understanding that many adolescents engage in multiple-problem behaviors, it also is important to develop programs that reduce adolescent problems. In a review of the programs that have been successful in preventing or reducing adolescent problems, adolescent researcher Joy Dryfoos (1990) described the common

Prevention Research
http://www.mhhe.com/santrocka9

components of these successful programs. The common components include these:

1. *Intensive individualized attention.* In successful programs, high-risk children are attached to a responsible adult who gives the child attention and deals with the child's specific needs. This theme occurred in a number of different programs. In a successful substance-abuse program, a student assistance counselor was available full-time for individual counseling and referral for treatment.

2. *Community-wide multiagency collaborative approaches.* The basic philosophy of community-wide programs is that a number of different programs and services have to be in place. In one successful substance-abuse program, a community-wide health promotion campaign was implemented that used local media and community education in concert with a substance-abuse curriculum in the schools.

3. *Early identification and intervention.* Reaching children and their families before children develop problems, or at the beginning of their problems, is a successful strategy (Botvin, 1999; Hill & others, 1999).

One preschool program serves as an excellent model for the prevention of delinquency, pregnancy, substance abuse, and dropping out of school. Operated by the High Scope Foundation in Ypsilanti, Michigan, the Perry Preschool has had a long-term positive impact on its students. This enrichment program, directed by David Weikart, services disadvantaged African American children. They attend a high-quality two-year preschool program and receive weekly home visits from program personnel. Based on official police records, by age 19 individuals who had attended the Perry Preschool program were less likely to have been arrested and reported fewer adult offenses than a control group. The Perry Preschool students also were less likely to drop out of school, and teachers rated their social behavior as more competent than that of a control group who did not receive the enriched preschool experience.

THINKING CRITICALLY

Why Might a Course of Risk Taking in Adolescence Likely Have More Serious Consequences Today Than in the Past?

The world is a dangerous place for too many of America's teenagers, especially those from low-SES families, neighborhoods, and schools. Many adolescents are resilient and cope with the challenges of adolescence without too many setbacks, but other adolescents struggle unsuccessfully to find jobs, are written off as losses by their schools, become pregnant before they are ready to become parents, or risk their health through drug abuse. Adolescents in virtually every era have been risk takers, testing limits and making shortsighted judgments. But why are the consequences of choosing a course of risk taking possibly more serious today than they have ever been?

Since the last review, we have discussed a number of ideas about the interrelation of problems and prevention/intervention. This review should help you to reach your learning goals related to these topics.

FOR YOUR REVIEW

Learning Goal 6
Discuss the interrelation of problems and prevention/intervention

- Researchers increasingly are finding that problem behaviors in adolescence are interrelated.
- In Dryfoos' analysis, these were the common components of successful prevention/intervention programs: (1) extensive individual attention, (2) community-wide intervention, and (3) early identification.

In this, the final chapter in the book, we have examined a number of ideas about problems and disorders. To conclude the book, following this chapter is an Epilogue that is designed to encourage you to think about some of the main themes we have discussed throughout the book and to consider what adolescents' lives will be like in the future.

CHAPTER MAP

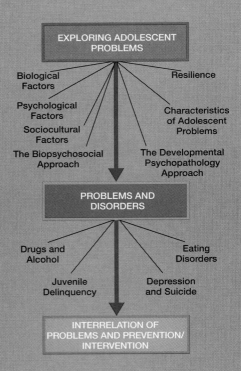

REACH YOUR LEARNING GOALS

At the beginning of the chapter we stated six learning goals and reviewed material related to these goals at five points in the chapter. This is a good time to return to these reviews. Use them as a guide for your study and to help you reach your learning goals.

Page 443

Learning Goal 1   Know about the nature of adolescent problems

Page 457

Learning Goal 2   Discuss drugs and alcohol

Page 464

Learning Goal 3   Evaluate juvenile delinquency

Page 470

Learning Goal 4   Describe depression and suicide
Learning Goal 5   Understand eating disorders

Page 471

Learning Goal 6   Discuss the interrelation of problems and prevention/intervention

KEY TERMS

developmental psychopathology 441
internalizing problems 441
externalizing problems 441
tolerance 445
physical dependence 445
psychological dependence 445
hallucinogens 450
stimulants 450
depressants 453

anabolic steroids 454
juvenile delinquency 458
index offenses 458
status offenses 458
conduct disorder 458
major depressive disorder 464
anorexia nervosa 468
bulimia nervosa 469

KEY PEOPLE

Thomas Achenbach and
   Craig Edelbrock 442
Norman Garmezy 443
Lloyd Johnston, Patrick O'Malley,
   and Gerald Bachman 445
Joy Dryfoos 456
James Garbarino 462
David and Roger Johnson 463

RESOURCES FOR IMPROVING THE LIVES OF ADOLESCENTS

Adolescents at Risk

(1990) by Joy Dryfoos
New York: Oxford University Press

This is an excellent book on adolescent problems.

American Anorexia/Bulimia Association

133 Cedar Lane
Teaneck, NJ 07666
201–836–1800

This organization provides information, referrals, and publications related to anorexia nervosa and bulimia.

Developmental Psychopathology

(1999) by Suniya Luthar, Jacob Burack, Dante Cicchetti, and John Weisz (Eds.)
New York: Cambridge University Press

This volume presents up-to-date explorations of many aspects of developmental psychopathology by leading experts.

Lost Boys

(1999) by James Garbarino
New York: Free Press

This book explores why some youth are violent and kill.

National Adolescent Suicide Hotline

800–621–4000

This hotline can be used 24 hours a day by teenagers contemplating suicide, as well as by their parents.

National Clearinghouse for Alcohol Information

P.O. Box 2345
1776 East Jefferson Street
Rockville, MD 20852
301–468–2600

This clearinghouse provides information about a wide variety of issues related to drinking problems, including adolescent drinking.

Violence Prevention for Young Adolescents

(1991) by Renee Wilson-Brewer, Stu Cohen, Lydia O'Donnell, and Irene Goodman
Carnegie Council on Adolescent Development
2400 N Street, NW
Washington, DC 20037
202–429–7979

This paper provides an overview of violence prevention programs. Eleven different programs are outlined, including several designed to curb gang violence.

TAKING IT TO THE NET

http://www.mhhe.com/santrocka9

1. Depression is one example of a mood disorder. *How common are mood disorders in adolescents? What are other examples of mood disorders, and how do the symptoms differ from "normal" behavior?*

2. Obesity is the major eating disorder. A common stereotype is that obese people simply eat too much and that they easily could achieve normal weight if they just watched how and what they ate. *If one of your friends expressed this view, how would you counter it?*

3. Think of an important stressful event or situation in which you found yourself sometime during the past three months. *What did you do; how did you deal with the stressor? Is that how you generally cope?* Take the coping test and find out.

Connect to *http://www.mhhe.com/santrocka9* to research the answers and complete these exercises. In some cases, you'll also find further instructions on this site.

EPILOGUE

ADOLESCENTS: THE FUTURE OF SOCIETY

In the end the power behind development is life.

—ERIK ERIKSON, *AMERICAN PSYCHOANALYST, 20TH CENTURY*

At the beginning of the twenty-first century, the well-being of adolescents is one of our most important concerns. We all cherish the future of adolescents, for they are the future of any society. Adolescents who do not reach their full potential, who are destined to make fewer contributions to society than society needs, and who do not take their place as productive adults diminish that society's future. In this epilogue, we will revisit a number of important themes and issues in adolescent development and then present a montage of thoughts that convey the beauty, power, and complexity of adolescents' development.

Our journey through adolescence has been long and complex, and you have read about many facets of adolescents' lives. This is a good time to stand back and ask yourself what you have learned. What theories, studies, and ideas struck you as more important than others? What did you learn about your own development as an adolescent? Did anything you learned stimulate you to rethink how adolescents develop? How did you develop into the person you are today?

Themes and Issues in Adolescent Development

As we look back across the chapters of *Adolescence,* some common themes and issues emerge. Let's explore what some of the most important themes and issues are.

The Storm-and-Stress View of Adolescence Has Been Overdramatized

Growing up has never been easy. However, adolescence is not best viewed as a time of rebellion, crisis, pathology, and deviance. A far more accurate vision of adolescence describes it as a time of evaluation, of decision making, of commitment, and of carving out a place in the world. Most problems of today's youth are not with the youth themselves. What adolescents need is access to a range of legitimate opportunities and long-term support from adults who deeply care about them.

In matters of taste and manners, the youth of every generation have seemed radical, unnerving, and different from adults—different in how they look, how they behave, the music they enjoy, their hairstyles, and the clothing they choose. But it is an enormous error to confuse the adolescent's enthusiasm for

trying on new identities and enjoying moderate amounts of outrageous behavior with hostility toward parental and societal standards. Acting out and boundary testing are time-honored ways in which adolescents move toward accepting, rather than rejecting, parental values.

Although adolescence has been portrayed too negatively for too long, many adolescents today are at risk for not reaching their full potential. They do experience far too much storm and stress. This discussion underscores an important point about adolescents: They are not a homogeneous group. Different portrayals of adolescence emerge, depending on the particular group of adolescents being described.

We Need to Dramatically Reduce the Number of Adolescents at Risk for Not Reaching Their Potential

Although we emphasized that the majority of adolescents navigate the long journey of adolescence successfully, far too many adolescents in America are not reaching their potential because they are not being adequately reared by caregivers, not being adequately instructed in school, and not being adequately supported by society. Adolescents who do not reach their full potential and do not grow up to make competent contributions to their world invariably have not been given adequate individual attention and support as they were growing up. Adolescents need parents who love them; monitor their development; are sensitive to their needs; have a sound understanding of their own, as well as their adolescents', development; and help to steer them away from health-compromising behaviors.

We also need schools that place a greater emphasis on a curriculum that is developmentally appropriate and pays closer attention to adolescent health and well-being. This needs to be accomplished at all levels of education, but especially in the middle school and junior high school years. And we need to give more attention to our nation's social policy, especially in terms of ways to break the poverty cycle that enshrouds more than 25 percent of adolescents in the United States. Our nation's political values need to reflect greater concern for the inadequate conditions in which far too many adolescents live. To reduce the number of adolescents at risk for not reaching their full potential, community-wide agency cooperation and integration, as well as early prevention or early intervention, need to be given special attention.

Adolescent Development Is Embedded in Sociocultural, Historical Contexts

Throughout this book we have emphasized the importance of considering the contexts in which the adolescent develops. *Context* refers to the setting in which development occurs, a setting that is influenced by historical, economic, social, and cultural factors. These contexts or settings include homes, schools, peer groups, churches, neighborhoods, communities, cities, the United States, Canada, Russia, France, Japan, Egypt, and many others—each with meaningful historical, economic, social, and cultural legacies.

In the twentieth century alone in the United States, successive waves of adolescents witnessed dramatic historical changes, including two world wars and their violence, the Great Depression and its economic woes, the advent of television and computers, increased levels of education, and altered gender roles. And as new generations appear, they increasingly have had an ethnic minority heritage.

Global interdependence is no longer a matter of belief or preference. It is an inescapable reality. By increasing our knowledge of the behavior, values, and nature of adolescent development in cultures around the world, we can learn about the universal aspects of adolescent development, cultural variations on their development, and how to interact with adolescents more effectively to make this planet a more hospitable, peaceful place to live.

Understanding our own culture better also can improve adolescents' lives. There is a special sense of urgency in addressing the nature of ethnicity and how it affects adolescent development because of the dramatic changes in the ethnic composition of America's population. The Asian, Latino, and African American populations are expected to increase at a much faster pace than the Anglo-American population in the foreseeable future. At a point early in the twenty-first century, one-third of the population in the United States will be members of ethnic minority groups.

To help adolescents of any ethnic heritage reach their full potential, we need to do the following:

• Recognize the diversity within every cultural and ethnic group. Not recognizing this diversity leads to unfortunate, harmful stereotyping.
• Understand that there are legitimate differences among cultural and ethnic groups. Recognizing and accepting these differences are important dimensions of getting along with others in a diverse, multicultural world. For too long, differences between ethnic minority individuals and Anglo-Americans were characterized as deficits on the part of ethnic minority individuals.
• Recognize and accept similarities among cultural and ethnic groups when differences have been incorrectly assumed. Through much of its history, America has had a White,

middle-SES bias. The search for legitimate similarities among White Americans and ethnic minority Americans is important because incorrectly assumed differences involve stereotyping and can lead to prejudice.
• Reduce discrimination and prejudice. Discrimination and prejudice continue to haunt too many adolescent lives—in interpersonal relations, in the media, and in daily conversations. Crimes, strangeness, poverty, mistakes, and deterioration too often are attributed to ethnic minority individuals without full consideration of the circumstances.
• Consider different sides of sensitive cultural and ethnic issues. We need to see things from different points of view and encourage adolescents to do likewise. If we don't seek alternative explanations and interpretations of problems and issues, our conclusions, and those of adolescents, may be based solely on expectations, prejudices, stereotypes, and personal experiences.

The Family Plays an Important Role in Adolescent Development

At a point not too long ago, we heard rumblings about the decreasing influence of the family in adolescents' lives and how the family as we had come to know it was breaking down. Although the structure of many families has changed as a result of increasing numbers of divorced, working-mother, and stepparent families, the family is still a powerful socializing influence on adolescent development. Regardless of the type of culture and family structure in which adolescents grow up, they benefit enormously when one or both parents are highly involved in their upbringing, provide them with warmth and nurturance, help them to develop self-control, and provide them with an environment that promotes their health and well-being.

Competent parents are knowledgeable about the nature of adolescent development, effectively monitor their adolescent's life, and adapt their behavior as the adolescent grows and matures.

A special concern is that too many of America's adolescents grow up in low-SES families and suffer the stressful and burdensome perils of poverty. In a number of places in *Adolescence* we called attention to programs that will benefit adolescents who live in low-SES settings. These programs currently are improving the lives of thousands of adolescents but need to be expanded to help far more adolescents than currently are being served by them.

For those of you who will become parents someday, or are already parents, I underscore how important it is for each of you to take seriously the rearing of your children and adolescents. Remember that good parenting takes an incredible amount of time—so if you become a parent, you should be willing to commit yourself, day after day, week after week, month after month, and year after year, to providing your children and adolescents with a warm, supportive, safe, and stimulating environment that will make them feel secure and allow them to reach their full potential as human beings. This is true for fathers as well as mothers. Although there has been an increase in the amount of time fathers spend with their adolescents, far too many fathers still do not develop adequate relationships with their adolescent daughters and sons.

Adolescents Deserve a Better Education

The importance of education in adolescent development was highlighted throughout *Adolescence.* There is a widespread agreement that something needs to be done about our nation's schools. We need schools that place a stronger emphasis on education that is developmentally appropriate. This needs to be accomplished at all levels of education, but especially in the middle school and junior high school grades.

The information and thinking society of the twenty-first century will not be content with products of education who have been trained to merely take in and recycle information handed out by teachers and other authority figures. Today's adolescents, who will become tomorrow's adults, need to experience an education that teaches them to think for themselves and to generate new information. This transformation is occurring in some, but not nearly enough, schools.

Schools and classrooms for adolescents also need to be smaller, place more emphasis on health and well-being, involve parents and community leaders, provide better counseling services, and be more sensitive to individual variations in adolescent development. In short, our nation's secondary schools need a major overhaul if we are to truly be sensitive to how adolescents develop.

Adolescents Deserve to Live and Develop in a More Equitable Gender World

Another important dimension of adolescents' lives that needs to be addressed in helping them reach their full potential is gender. Throughout *Adolescence* we emphasized how the world of adolescents and adults has not been a very fair gender world. Not only have ethnic minority adolescents grown up in a world that has confronted them with bias and discrimination, so have adolescent girls.

An important goal of this book has been to extensively evaluate the gender worlds of adolescents and to promote gender equity in adolescent development. I (your author) have two daughters who are now in their mid twenties. As Tracy and Jennifer were growing up, there were many instances when I felt they experienced bias and discrimination because they were females—in school, in athletics, and in many other contexts of their lives. My wife and I wanted them to have the opportunities to reach their full potential and not be limited by a gender-biased society and authority figures. Our hope was that they would not only develop strengths in traditional feminine domains, such as relationship skills, but also acquire a sense of self-assertiveness, a traditionally masculine domain, that would serve them well in their quest to become competent persons. I hope that all adolescents have this opportunity, and that Tracy's and Jennifer's adolescents will have fewer gender barriers to break through than they did.

Knowledge About Adolescent Development Has Benefitted from a Diversity of Theories and an Extensive Research Enterprise

A number of theories have made important contributions to our understanding of adolescent development. From the social theories of Erikson and Bronfenbrenner to the cognitive theory of Piaget, each has contributed an important piece of the developmental puzzle. However, no single theory is capable of predicting, explaining, and organizing the rich, complex, multifaceted landscape of the adolescent's developmental journey. The inability of a single theory to explain all of adolescent development should not be viewed as a shortcoming of the theory. Any theory that attempts to explain all of adolescent development is too general. The field of adolescent development has been moved forward by theories that are precise and zero in on key aspects of one or two dimensions of adolescents' lives rather than by theories that try to do everything.

Knowledge about adolescent development has also benefited from a research effort that has greatly expanded over the last two decades. The science of adolescent development is rapidly becoming a highly sophisticated field in which collecting evidence about adolescent development is based on well-defined rules, exemplary practices, mathematical procedures for handling the evidence, and drawing inferences from what has been found.

Adolescents Benefit from Both Basic and Applied Research

Across the fourteen chapters of *Adolescence,* we have discussed both basic research and applied research. Basic research, sometimes called pure research, is the study of issues to obtain knowledge for its own sake rather than for practical application. In contrast, applied research is the study of issues that have direct practical significance, often with the intent of changing human behavior. Social policy research is applied research, not basic research.

A developmentalist who conducts basic research might ask: How is the cognitive development of adolescents different from that of children? In contrast, a developmentalist who conducts applied research might ask: How can knowledge about adolescents' and children's cognitive development be used to educate them more effectively or help them cope more effectively with stress?

Most developmentalists believe that both basic and applied research contributes to improving adolescents' lives. Although basic research sometimes produces information that can be applied to improve the well-being of adolescents, it does not guarantee this application. But insisting that research always be relevant is like trying to grow flowers by focusing only on the blossoms and not tending to the roots.

Adolescent Development Is Influenced by an Interaction of Heredity and Environment

Both heredity and environment are necessary for adolescents to even exist. Heredity and environment operate together—or cooperate—to produce an adolescent's height and weight, ability to shoot a basketball, intelligence, reading skills, temperament, and all other dimensions of the adolescent's development.

In chapter 1, we discussed the nature-nurture controversy, the debate about whether development is primarily influenced by heredity and maturation (nature) or by environment and experience (nurture). The debate shows no signs of subsiding, but for now virtually all developmentalists are interactionists, accepting that adolescent development is determined by both heredity and environment. Behavior geneticists continue to specify more precisely the nature of heredity-environment interaction through concepts such as those of passive, evocative, and active genotype/environment interactions and shared and nonshared environmental influences.

Adolescent Development Involves Both Continuity and Discontinuity

Some developmentalists emphasize the continuity of development, the view that development involves gradual, cumulative change from conception to death. Others stress the discontinuity of development, the view that development consists of distinct stages in the life span.

Development involves both continuity and discontinuity. For example, although Piaget's stages reflect discontinuity, in the sense that adolescents change from being concrete to formal operational thinkers, researchers have found that children's and adolescents' intelligence shows more continuity than once was believed. Who is right? Probably both. As Piaget envisioned, most concrete operational children do not think hypothetically and don't solve problems in a scientific manner. In this aspect, development is stagelike, as Piaget proposed. However, as information-processing psychologists believe, adolescents' thinking is not as stagelike as Piaget believed.

Adolescent Development Is Determined by Both Early and Later Experiences

Adolescents' development is determined by both early and later experiences. However, developmentalists still debate how strong the contributions of each type of experience are. The early-experience advocates argue that early experiences, especially in infancy, are more important than later experiences are. They believe, for example, that warm, nurturant, sensitive parenting in the first year of life is necessary for optimal later development, even in adolescence or adulthood. Later experiences in childhood and adolescence are not as important in shaping the individual's developmental path, they say.

By contrast, other developmentalists stress that later experiences are just as important as early experiences in adolescent development. That is, warm, nurturant, sensitive parenting is just as important in the elementary school years and adolescence in shaping development as it is in infancy. People in Western cultures are stronger advocates of early experience, those in Eastern cultures of later experiences. The debate continues.

Adolescent Development Is Determined by an Interaction of Biological, Cognitive, and Socioemotional Processes

Biological processes involve changes in the adolescent's physical nature, such as genes inherited from parents and the hormonal changes of puberty. Cognitive processes involve changes in the adolescent's thought and intelligence, such as memorizing a poem or solving a math problem. Socioemotional processes involve changes in the adolescent's relationships with other people, emotions, and personality, such as the intimate conversation of two friends, an adolescent girl's sadness and depression, and a shy, introverted adolescent boy.

In many parts of the book, you read about how biological, cognitive, and socioemotional processes are intricately interwoven. For example, biology plays a role in adolescents' temperament, especially influencing how shy or gregarious they are. Inadequate parenting and schooling can harm the adolescent's intelligence. Cognitive changes substantially alter how adolescents think about their parents and peers. Both theory and research focused on adolescent development are becoming more integrated and less compartmentalized as links across different domains are sought.

Adolescent Development Involves Both Commonalities with Other Adolescents and Individual Variation

Most every adolescent develops like all other adolescents, in certain ways. Most every adolescent is reared by one or more adult caregivers who have more power than the adolescent does; most every adolescent engages in peer relations, goes to school, and becomes more independent and searches for an identity.

But adolescents are not always like collections of geese; they are unique, each adolescent writing an individual history. One adolescent may grow up in the well-manicured lawns of suburbia, another in the ghetto confines of an inner city. One adolescent may be tall, another short. One adolescent may be a genius, another might have mental retardation. One adolescent may have been abused as a child, another lavished with love. And one adolescent may be highly motivated to learn, another couldn't care less.

Adolescent Development Is Determined by Internal/External and Self/Other Influences

Controversy still surrounds whether adolescents are architects of their own development (internal, self-determined) or whether their development primarily is orchestrated by the external forces of others. However, most experts on adolescence recognize that development is not entirely external and other-determined and, likewise, not entirely internal and self-generated. Trying to tease apart internal/external and self/other influences is extraordinarily difficult because the adolescent is always embedded in a social context with others. To be certain, adolescents are not helplessly buffeted about by their environment. Adolescents bring certain developmental capacities to any situation and act on the situation. At the same time, however, they interact with others who offer their own versions of the world, which adolescents sometimes learn from and adopt for themselves. At times, adolescents are like solitary scientists, crafting their own books of dreams and reality as Piaget envisioned; at other times, they are socially intertwined with skilled teachers and peers, as Vygotsky conceived.

America, especially male America, has had a history of underscoring the importance of self-determination and individualism. Recently, however, females have challenged the status of self-determination as a more important human value than being connected to others and competent at relationships. And as psychologists have become more interested in cultures around the world, they have begun to recognize that many cultures, especially Eastern cultures, promote values that emphasize concern for others, interdependence, and harmonious relationships. It is important for us to raise a nation of adolescents who not only value a separate "I," uniqueness, and self-determination, but who also value connectedness with others, concern for others, and harmony in relationships.

Adolescents' Behavior Is Multiply Determined

An important aspect of thinking about the behavior of any adolescent is that the adolescent's behavior is multiply determined. When we think about what causes an adolescent's behavior, we often lean toward explaining it in terms of a single cause. Consider a 12-year-old adolescent boy named Bobby. His teachers say that he is having trouble in school because he is from a father-absent home. The implication is that not having a father present in the home causes Bobby's poor academic performance. Not having a father may be one factor in Bobby's poor performance in school, but many others also influence his behavior. These factors include his genetic heritage and a host of environmental and sociocultural experiences, both in the past and in the present. On closer inspection of Bobby's

circumstances, we learn that not only has his father been absent all of Bobby's life, but that his extended-family support system also has been weak. We also learn that he lives in a low-SES area with little community support for recreation, libraries, and families. The school system in which Bobby is enrolled has a poor record of helping low-achieving adolescents and has little interest in developing programs for adolescents from disadvantaged circumstances. We could find other reasons that help explain Bobby's poor school achievement, but these examples illustrate the importance of going beyond accepting a single cause as the reason for an adolescent's behavior. As with each of us, Bobby's behavior is multiply determined.

Adolescents Will Benefit from an Interdisciplinary Approach to Their Development

Some of you taking this class on adolescence are being taught by a developmental psychologist, others by someone who specializes in human development or family relationships, others by an educational psychologist or professor in an education department, others by a nurse or pediatrician, and yet others by professors from different disciplines. The field of adolescent development has become more interdisciplinary. Our knowledge about adolescents, and how to improve adolescents' lives, has benefited, and will continue to benefit, from the contributions of scholars and professionals in a number of disciplines, including developmental psychology, education and educational psychology, pediatrics and nursing, clinical psychology, counseling, psychiatry, sociology, anthropology, and law. The collaboration between developmental psychologists and pediatricians, nurses, and psychiatrists is one example of this interdisciplinary cooperation; the emerging area of how development influences adolescents' health reflects this cross-disciplinary trend.

THE JOURNEY OF ADOLESCENCE

We have come to the end of this book. I hope you can now look back and say that you learned a lot about adolescents, not only other adolescents but yourself as an adolescent and how your adolescent years contributed to who you are today. The insightful words of philosopher Søren Kierkegaard capture the importance of looking backward to understand ourselves: "Life is lived forward, but understood backwards." I also hope that those of you who become the parents of adolescents or work with adolescents in some capacity—whether as teacher, counselor, or community leader—feel that you now have a better grasp of what adolescence is all about. I leave you with the following montage of thoughts and images that convey the power, complexity, and beauty of adolescence in the human life span:

In no order of things is adolescence the time of simple life. Adolescents feel like they can last forever, think they know everything, and are quite sure about it. They clothe themselves with rainbows and go brave as the zodiac, flashing from one end of the world to the other both in mind and body. In many ways, today's adolescents are privileged, wielding unprecedented economic power. At the same time, they move through a seemingly endless preparation for life. They try on one face after another, seeking to find a face of their own. In their most pimply and awkward moments, they become acquainted with sex. They play furiously at "adult games" but are confined to a society of their own peers. They want their parents to understand them and hope that their parents will accord them the privilege of understanding them. Their generation of young people is the fragile cable by which the best and the worst of their parents' generation is transmitted to the present. In the end, there are only two lasting gifts parents can leave youth—one is roots, the other is wings.

John W. Santrock

GLOSSARY

A

accommodation an adjustment to new information. 106

acculturation cultural change that results from continuous, firsthand contact between two distinctive cultural groups. 260

active (niche-picking) genotype-environment correlations correlations that occur when adolescents seek out environments they find compatible and stimulating. 98

adolescence the developmental period of transition from childhood to early adulthood; it involves biological, cognitive, and socioemotional changes. 19

adolescent egocentrism the heightened self-consciousness of adolescents, which is reflected in their belief that others are as interested in them as they themselves are and in their sense of personal uniqueness. 137

adolescent generalization gap Adelson's concept of widespread generalizations about adolescents based on information about a limited, highly visible group of adolescents. 12

adolescents who are gifted adolescents who have above-average intelligence (usually defined as an IQ of 130 or higher) and/or superior talent in some domain, such as art, music, or mathematics. 249

adoption study a study in which investigators seek to discover whether, in behavior and psychological characteristics, adopted children and adolescents are more like their adoptive parents, who provided a home environment, or their biological parents, who contributed their heredity. Another form of adoption study is to compare adoptive and biological siblings. 97

affectionate love also called companionate love, this love occurs when an individual desires to have another person near and has a deep, caring affection for that person. 213

AIDS acquired immune deficiency syndrome, a primarily sexually transmitted disease caused by the HIV virus, which destroys the body's immune system. 364

alternation model this model assumes that it is possible for an individual to know and understand two different cultures. It also assumes that individuals can alter their behavior to fit a particular social context. 261

altruism unselfish interest in helping another person. 390

anabolic steroids drugs derived from the male sex hormone, testosterone. They promote muscle growth and lean body mass. 454

androgens the main class of male sex hormones. 77

androgyny the presence of a high degree of desirable feminine and masculine characteristics in the same individual. 331

anorexia nervosa an eating disorder that involves the relentless pursuit of thinness through starvation. 468

anticonformity this occurs when individuals react counter to a group's expectations and deliberately move away from the actions or beliefs the group advocates. 190

anxiety a vague, highly unpleasant feeling of fear and apprehension. 414

aptitude-treatment interaction (ATI) this interaction stresses the importance of both the attitudes and the characteristics of the adolescent, such as academic potential or personality traits, and the treatments or experiences, such as the educational techniques, that the adolescent receives. Aptitude refers to such characteristics as the academic potential and personality characteristics on which students differ; treatment refers to educational techniques, such as structured versus flexible classrooms. 238

assimilation (culture) the absorption of ethnic minority groups into the dominant group, which often means the loss of some or virtually all of the behavior and values of the ethnic minority group. 260

assimilation (Piaget) the incorporation of new information into existing knowledge. 106

attention deficit hyperactivity disorder (ADHD) children and adolescents with ADHD show one or more of the following characteristics over a period of time: inattention, hyperactivity, and impulsivity. 247

attribution theory states that in their effort to make sense out of their own behavior or performance, individuals are motivated to discover the underlying causes. 410

authoritarian parenting this is a restrictive, punitive style in which the parent exhorts the adolescent to follow the parent's directions and to respect work and effort. Firm limits and controls are placed on the adolescent, and little verbal exchange is allowed. This style is associated with adolescents' socially incompetent behavior. 157

authoritarian strategy of classroom management this teaching strategy is restrictive and punitive. The focus is mainly on keeping order in the classroom rather than on instruction and learning. 237

authoritative parenting this style encourages adolescents to be independent but still places limits and controls on their actions. Extensive verbal give-and-take is allowed, and parents are warm and nurturant toward the adolescent. This style is associated with adolescents' socially competent behavior. 158

authoritative strategy of classroom management this teaching strategy encourages students to be independent thinkers and doers, but still involves effective monitoring. Authoritative teachers engage students in considerable verbal give-and-take and show a caring attitude toward them. However, they still declare limits when necessary. 237

autonomous morality the second stage of moral development in Piaget's theory, displayed by older children (about 10 years of age and older). The child becomes aware that rules and laws are created by people and that, in judging an action, one should consider the actor's intentions as well as the consequences. 381

B

back-to-basics movement this philosophy stresses that the function of schools should be the rigorous training of intellectual skills through such subjects as English, mathematics, and science. 221

basal metabolism rate (BMR) the minimum amount of energy an individual uses in a resting state is the BMR. 90

behavior genetics the study of the degree and nature of behavior's hereditary basis. 97

behavioral and social cognitive theories theories that emphasize the importance of studying environmental experiences and observable behavior. Social cognitive theorists emphasize person/cognitive factors in development. 49

biological processes physical changes in an individual's body. 18

bisexual a person who is attracted to people of both sexes. 352

boundary ambiguity the uncertainty in stepfamilies about who is in or out of the family and who is performing or responsible for certain tasks in the family system. 173

bulimia nervosa in this eating disorder, the individual consistently follows a binge-and-purge eating pattern. 469

C

care perspective the moral perspective of Carol Gilligan, which views people in terms of their connectedness with others and emphasizes interpersonal communication, relationships with others, and concern for others. 387

career self-concept theory Super's theory that individuals' self-concept plays a central role in career choice and that in adolescence individuals first construct a career self-concept. 420

case study an in-depth look at an individual. 61

character education   a direct moral education approach that involves teaching students a basic moral literacy to prevent them from engaging in immoral behavior or doing harm to themselves or others.   394

Chicano   the name politically conscious Mexican American adolescents give themselves, reflecting the combination of their Spanish-Mexican-Indian heritage and Anglo influence.   274

chlamydia   the most common of all sexually transmitted diseases, named for *Chlamydia trachomatis,* an organism that spreads by sexual contact and infects the genital organs of both sexes.   363

cliques   are small groups that range from two to about twelve individuals and average about five to six individuals.   204

cognitive constructivist approaches   approaches that emphasize the adolescent's active, cognitive construction of knowledge and understanding; an example is Piaget's theory.   223

cognitive developmental theory of gender   in this view, children's gender-typing occurs after they have developed a concept of gender. Once they begin to consistently conceive themselves as male or female, children often organize their world on the basis of gender.   323

cognitive disequilibrium theory   Hoffman's theory that adolescence is an important period in moral development, in which, because of broader experiences associated with the move to high school or college, individuals recognize that their set of beliefs is but one of many and that there is considerable debate about what is right and wrong.   382

cognitive moral education   an approach based on the belief that students should learn to value things like democracy and justice as their moral reasoning develops; Kohlberg's theory has been the basis for many of the cognitive moral education approaches.   395

cognitive processes   changes in an individual's thinking and intelligence.   18

commitment   the part of identity development in which adolescents show a personal investment in what they are going to do.   303

concrete operational stage   Piaget's third stage, which lasts from approximately 7 to 11 years of age; children can perform operations, and logical reasoning replaces intuitive thought as long as the reasoning can be applied to specific concrete examples.   107

conduct disorder   the psychiatric diagnostic category for the occurrence of multiple delinquent activities over a six-month period. These behaviors include truancy, running away, fire setting, cruelty to animals, breaking and entering, and excessive fighting.   458

conformity   this occurs when individuals adopt the attitudes or behaviors of others because of real or imagined pressure from them.   189

conglomerate strategies   the use of a combination of techniques, rather than a single approach, to improve adolescents' social skills; also called coaching.   194

connectedness   an important element in adolescent identity development. It consists of two dimensions: mutuality, sensitivity to and respect for others' views; and permeability, openness to others' views.   305

conscience   the component of the superego that involves behaviors disapproved of by parents.   391

contexts   the settings in which development occurs. These settings are influenced by historical, economic, social, and cultural factors.   15

continuity view   a developmental view that emphasizes the role of early parent-child relationships in constructing a basic way of relating to people throughout the life span.   150

continuity-discontinuity issue   the issue regarding whether development involves gradual, cumulative change (continuity) or distinct stages (discontinuity).   23

control group   a comparison group in an experiment that is treated in every way like the experimental group except for the manipulated factor.   63

controversial children   children who are frequently nominated both as a best friend and as being disliked.   191

conventional reasoning   the second, or intermediate, level in Kohlberg's theory of moral development. Internalization is intermediate. Individuals abide by certain standards (internal), but they are the standards of others (external), such as parents or the laws of society.   383

convergent thinking   a pattern of thinking in which individuals produce one correct answer; characteristic of the items on conventional intelligence tests; coined by Guilford.   124

correlational research   research whose goal is to describe the strength of the relation between two or more events or characteristics.   61

creativity   the ability to think in novel and unusual ways and come up with unique solutions to problems.   124

crisis   a period of identity development during which the adolescent is choosing among meaningful alternatives.   303

critical thinking   thinking reflectively and productively and evaluating the evidence.   123

cross-cultural studies   studies that compare a culture with one or more other cultures. Such studies provide information about the degree to which adolescent development is similar, or universal, across cultures or about the degree to which it is culture-specific.   258

cross-sectional research   research that studies people all at one time.   64

crowds   are a larger group structure than cliques. Adolescents usually are members of a crowd based on reputation and may or may not spend much time together.   204

culture   the behavior, patterns, beliefs, and all other products of a particular group of people that are passed on from generation to generation.   256

culture-fair tests   tests of intelligence that are intended to be free of cultural bias.   135

date, or acquaintance, rape   coercive sexual activity directed at someone with whom the perpetrator is at least casually acquainted.   367

dating scripts   the cognitive models that adolescents and adults use to guide and evaluate dating interactions.   211

dependent variable   the factor that is measured as the result of an experiment.   63

depressants   drugs that slow the central nervous system, bodily functions, and behavior.   453

development   the pattern of change that begins at conception and continues through the life span. Most development involves growth, although it also includes decay (as in death and dying).   17

developmental career choice theory   Ginzberg's theory that children and adolescents go through three career-choice stages: fantasy, tentative, and realistic.   420

developmental construction views   views sharing the belief that as individuals grow up, they acquire modes of relating to others. There are two main variations of this view. One emphasizes continuity and stability in relationships throughout the life span; the other emphasizes discontinuity and changes in relationships throughout the life span.   150

developmental psychopathology   the area of psychology that focuses on describing and exploring the developmental pathways of problems and disorders.   441

direct instruction approach   a teacher-centered approach characterized by teacher direction and control, mastery of academic skills, high expectations for students' progress, and maximum time spent on learning tasks.   223

discontinuity view   a developmental view that emphasizes change and growth in relationships over time.   151

dismissing/avoidant attachment   an insecure attachment category in which individuals deemphasize the importance of attachment. This category is associated with consistent experiences of rejection of attachment needs by caregivers.   165

divergent thinking   a pattern of thinking in which individuals produce many answers to the same question; more characteristic of creativity than convergent thinking; coined by Guilford.   124

early adolescence   the developmental period that corresponds roughly to the middle school or junior high school years and includes most pubertal change.   19

early adulthood   the developmental period beginning in the late teens or early twenties and lasting into the thirties.   19

early childhood   the developmental period extending from the end of infancy to about 5 or 6 years of age; sometimes called the preschool years.   18

early-later experience issue   this issue focuses on the degree to which early experiences (especially early in childhood) or later experiences are the key determinants of development.   23

eclectic theoretical orientation   an approach that does not follow any one theoretical approach, but instead selects and uses whatever is considered the best in many different theories.   52

ecological contextual theory   Bronfenbrenner's view of development, involving five environmental systems—microsystem, mesosystem, exosystem, macrosystem, and chronosystem. These emphasize the role of social contexts in development.   51

ego ideal   the component of the superego that involves ideal standards approved by parents.   391

e-mail   electronic mail, a valuable way the Internet can be used. Messages can be sent to and received by individuals as well as large numbers of people.   283

emotional autonomy   the capacity to relinquish childlike dependencies on parents.   162

emotional intelligence   a form of social intelligence that involves the ability to monitor one's own and others' feelings and emotions, to discriminate among them, and to use this information to guide one's thinking and action.   133

emotional isolation   a type of loneliness that arises when a person lacks an intimate attachment relationship; single, divorced, and widowed adults often experience this type of loneliness.   312

empathy   reacting to another's feelings with an emotional response that is similar to the other's response.   393

equilibration   a mechanism in Piaget's theory that explains how children or adolescents shift from one state of thought to the next. The shift occurs as they experience cognitive conflict or a disequilibrium in trying to understand the world. Eventually, the child or adolescent resolves the conflict and reaches a balance, or equilibrium.   107

Erikson's theory   he proposed eight stages of psychosocial development that unfold throughout the human life span. Each stage consists of a unique developmental task that confronts individuals with a crisis that must be faced.   44

estrogens   the main class of female sex hormones.   77

ethnic identity   an enduring, basic aspect of the self that includes a sense of membership in an ethnic group and the attitudes and feelings related to that membership.   306

ethnicity   a dimension of culture based on cultural heritage, nationality, race, religion, and language.   257

ethnocentrism   a tendency to favor one's own group over other groups.   257

evocative genotype-environment correlations   correlations that occur when the adolescent's genotype elicits certain types of physical and social environments.   98

experimental group   a group whose experience is manipulated in an experiment.   63

experimental research   research involving experiments that permit the determination of cause. A carefully regulated procedure in which one or more of the factors believed to influence the behavior being studied is manipulated and all other factors are held constant.   63

externalizing problems   occur when individuals turn problems outward. An example is juvenile delinquency.   441

extrinsic motivation   involves external incentives such as rewards and punishments.   409

 F

failure syndrome   involves having low expectations for success and giving up at the first sign of difficulty.   417

feminization of poverty   the fact that far more women than men live in poverty. Women's low income, divorce, and the resolution of divorce cases by the judicial system, which leaves women with less money than they and their children need to adequately function, are the likely causes.   266

flow   involves optimal experiences in life; occurs most often when people are absorbed in a state of concentration while they engage in an activity.   409

forgiveness   this is an aspect of altruism that occurs when an injured person releases the injurer from possible behavioral retaliation.   390

formal operational stage   Piaget's fourth and final stage of cognitive development, which he believed emerges at 11 to 15 years of age. It is characterized by abstract, idealistic, and logical thought.   108

 G

gender   the sociocultural and psychological dimensions of being male or female.   318

gender intensification hypothesis   this hypothesis states that psychological and behavioral differences between boys and girls become greater during early adolescence because of increased socialization pressures to conform to masculine and feminine gender roles.   356

gender role   a set of expectations that prescribes how females and males should think, act, and feel.   318

gender-role transcendence   the belief that, when an individual's competence is at issue, it should be conceptualized not on the basis of masculinity, femininity, or androgyny but, rather, on a person basis.   335

gender schema   a cognitive structure that organizes the world in terms of male and female.   324

gender schema theory   according to this theory, an individual's attention and behavior are guided by an internal motivation to conform to gender-based sociocultural standards and stereotypes.   324

gender stereotypes   broad categories that reflect our impressions and beliefs about females and males.   325

generational inequity   the unfair treatment of younger members of an aging society in which older adults pile up advantages by receiving inequitably large allocations of resources, such as Social Security and Medicare.   16

genital herpes   a sexually transmitted disease caused by a large family of viruses of different strains. These strains produce other, nonsexually transmitted diseases such as chicken pox and mononucleosis.   364

genotype   a person's genetic heritage; the actual genetic material.   96

gonorrhea   reported to be one of the most common STDs in the United States, this sexually transmitted disease is caused by a bacterium called *Neisseria gonorrhoeae*, which thrives in the moist mucous membranes lining the mouth, throat, vagina, cervix, urethra, and anal tract. This disease is commonly called the "drip" or the "clap."   363

 H

hallucinogens   drugs that alter an individual's perceptual experiences and produce hallucinations; also called psychedelic or mind-altering drugs.   450

helpless orientation   involves focusing on personal inadequacies, attributing difficulty to lack of ability, and displaying negative affect.   412

heteronomous morality   the first stage of moral development in Piaget's theory, occurring at 4 to 7 years of age. Justice and rules are conceived of as unchangeable properties of the world, removed from the control of people.   381

hidden curriculum   the pervasive moral atmosphere that characterizes schools.   394

hormones   powerful chemical substances secreted by the endocrine glands and carried through the body by the bloodstream.   77

hostile environment sexual harassment   sexual harassment in which students are subjected to unwelcome sexual conduct that is so severe, persistent, or pervasive that it limits the students' ability to benefit from their education.   368

hypothetical-deductive reasoning   Piaget's term for adolescents' ability, in the formal operational stage, to develop hypotheses, or best guesses, about ways to solve problems; they then systematically deduce, or conclude, the best path to follow in solving the problem.   109

 I

identity achievement   Marcia's term for an adolescent's having undergone a crisis and made a commitment.   303

identity diffusion   Marcia's term for the state adolescents are in when they have not yet experienced a crisis or made any commitments.   303

identity foreclosure   Marcia's term for the state adolescents are in when they have made a commitment but have not experienced a crisis.   303

identity moratorium   Marcia's term for the state of adolescents who are in the midst of a crisis, but whose commitments either are absent or are only vaguely defined.   303

identity versus identity confusion   Erikson's fifth stage of development, which occurs during the adolescent years. Adolescents are faced with finding out who they are, what they are all about, and where they are going in life.   300

immanent justice   Piaget's concept that if a rule is broken, punishment will be meted out immediately.   381

implicit personality theory   the layperson's conception of personality.   140

inclusion   educating a child or adolescent with special education needs full-time in a general school program.   248

independent variable   the manipulated, influential, experimental factor in an experiment.   63

index offenses   whether they are committed by juveniles or adults, these are criminal acts, such as robbery, rape, and homicide.   458

individuality   an important element in adolescent identity development. It consists of two dimensions: self-assertion, the ability to have and communicate a point of view; and separateness, the use of communication patterns to express how one is different from others.   305

Individuals with Disabilities Education Act (IDEA)   this spells out broad mandates for services to all children and adolescents with disabilities. These include evaluation and eligibility determination, appropriate education and the individualized education program (IEP), and a least restrictive environment.   248

individuated-connected level   the highest level of relationship maturity, at which there is evidence of an understanding of oneself, as well as consideration of others' motivations and anticipation of their needs. Concern and caring involve emotional support and individualized expression of interest.   311

induction   a discipline technique in which a parent uses reason and explanation of the consequences for others of a child's actions.   392

indulgent parenting   a style in which parents are highly involved with their adolescents but place few demands or controls on them. This is associated with adolescents' social incompetence, especially a lack of self-control.   158

infancy   the developmental period that extends from birth to 18 or 24 months.   18

information-processing approach   emphasizes that individuals manipulate information, monitor it, and strategize about it. Central to this approach are the processes of memory and thinking.   48

insecure attachment   in this attachment pattern, infants either avoid the caregiver or show considerable resistance or ambivalence toward the caregiver. This pattern is theorized to be related to difficulties in relationships and problems in later development.   165

intelligence   mental ability related to verbal and problem-solving skills and the ability to adapt to and learn from life's everyday experiences; not everyone agrees on what constitutes intelligence.   129

intelligent quotient (IQ)   a person's tested mental age divided by chronological age, multiplied by 100.   129

internalization   the developmental change from behavior that is externally controlled to behavior that is controlled by internal standards and principles.   382

internalizing problems   occur when individuals turn problems inward. Examples include anxiety and depression.   441

Internet   the core of computer-mediated communication. The Internet system is worldwide and connects thousands of computer networks, providing an incredible array of information adolescents can access.   282

intimacy in friendship   in most research, this is defined narrowly as self-disclosure or sharing of private thoughts.   199

intimacy versus isolation   Erikson's sixth developmental stage, which individuals experience during the early adulthood years. At this time, individuals face the developmental task of forming intimate relationships with others.   310

intimate style   the individual forms and maintains one or more deep and long-lasting love relationships.   310

intrinsic motivation   based on internal factors such as self-determination, curiosity, challenge, and effort.   409

inventionist view   the view that adolescence is a sociohistorical creation. Especially important in this view are the sociohistorical circumstances at the beginning of the twentieth century, a time when legislation was enacted that ensured the dependency of youth and made their move into the economic sphere more manageable.   8

isolated style   the individual withdraws from social encounters and has little or no attachment to same- or opposite-sex individuals.   310

jigsaw classroom   a strategy in which students from different cultural backgrounds are placed in a cooperative group in which, together, they have to construct different parts of a project to reach a common goal.   243

justice perspective   a moral perspective that focuses on the rights of the individual; individuals independently make moral decisions.   387

juvenile delinquency   a broad range of child and adolescent behaviors, including socially unacceptable behavior, status offenses, and criminal acts.   458

laboratory   a controlled setting from which many of the complex factors of the real world have been removed.   60

late adolescence   approximately the latter half of the second decade of life. Career interests, dating, and identity exploration are often more pronounced in late adolescence than in early adolescence.   19

late adulthood   the developmental period that lasts from about 60 to 70 years of age until death.   20

learning disability   individuals with a learning disability (1) are of normal intelligence or above and (2) have difficulties in at least one academic area and usually several, and (3) their difficulties cannot be attributed to any other diagnosed problem or disorder, such as mental retardation.   246

least restrictive environment   a setting that is as similar as possible to the one in which the children or adolescents without a disability are educated; under the Individuals with Disabilities Education Act, the child or adolescent must be educated in this setting.   248

longitudinal research   research that studies the same people over a period of time, usually several years or more.   64

love withdrawal   a discipline technique in which a parent removes attention or love from a child.   392

major depressive disorder   the diagnosis when an individual experiences a major depressive episode and depressed characteristics, such as lethargy and depression, for two weeks or longer and daily functioning becomes impaired.   464

mastery orientation   involves focusing on the task rather than on their ability, having positive affect, generating solution-oriented strategies that improve performance.   411

menarche   a girl's first menstruation.   79

mental age (MA)   an individual's level of mental development relative to others; a concept developed by Binet.   129

metacognition   cognition about cognition, or "knowing about knowing."   126

middle adulthood   the developmental period that is entered at about 35 to 45 years and exited at about 55 to 65 years of age.   19

middle and late childhood   the developmental period extending from about 6 to about 10 or 11 years of age; sometimes called the elementary school years.   18

moral development   thoughts, feelings, and behaviors regarding standards of right and wrong.   380

multicultural model   this model promotes a pluralistic approach to understanding two or more cultures. It argues that people can maintain their distinctive identities while working with others from different cultures to meet common national or economic needs.   261

naturalistic observation observations that take place out in the real world instead of in a laboratory. 60

nature-nurture issue involves the debate about whether development is primarily influenced by nature or nurture. Nature refers to an organism's biological inheritance, nurture to its environmental experiences. 22

neglected children children who are infrequently nominated as a best friend but are not disliked by their peers. 191

neglectful parenting a style in which the parent is very uninvolved in the adolescent's life. It is associated with adolescents' social incompetence, especially a lack of self-control. 158

neo-Piagetians theorists who argue that Piaget got some things right but that his theory needs considerable revision. In their revision, they give more emphasis to information processing that involves attention, memory, and strategies; they also seek to provide more precise explanations of cognitive changes. 113

neurons nerve cells, which are the nervous system's basic units. 87

nonconformity this occurs when individuals know what people around them expect but do not use those expectations to guide their behavior. 190

nonshared environmental influences the adolescent's own unique experiences, both within a family and outside the family, that are not shared by another sibling. 99

normal distribution a symmetrical distribution of values or scores, with a majority of scores falling in the middle of the possible range of scores and few scores appearing toward the extremes of the range; a distribution that yields what is called a "bell-shaped curve." 129

norms rules that apply to all members of a group. 202

passive genotype-environment correlations correlations that occur when the biological parents, who are genetically related to the child, provide a rearing environment for the child. 98

peers children or adolescents who are of about the same age or maturity level. 187

performance orientation involves being concerned more with the outcome rather than the process of achievement. 412

permissive strategy of classroom management this strategy offers students considerable autonomy but provides them with little support for developing learning skills or managing their behavior. 237

personality type theory Holland's theory that an effort should be made to match career interests with an individual's personality type. 421

phenotype the way an individual's genotype is expressed in observed and measurable characteristics. 96

physical dependence physical need for a drug that is accompanied by unpleasant withdrawal symptoms when the drug is discontinued. 445

Piaget's theory he proposed that individuals actively construct their understanding of the world and go through four stages of cognitive development. 46

popular children children who are frequently nominated as a best friend and are rarely disliked by their peers. 191

possible self what individuals might become, what they would like to become, and what they are afraid of becoming. 294

postconventional reasoning the highest level in Kohlberg's theory of moral development. Morality is completely internalized. 383

postformal thought a form of thought, proposed as a fifth stage, that is qualitatively different from Piaget's formal operational thought. It involves understanding that the correct answer to a problem can require reflective thinking, that the correct answer can vary from one situation to another, and that the search for truth is often an ongoing, never-ending process. 114

power assertion a discipline technique in which a parent attempts to gain control over a child or a child's resources. 392

preconventional reasoning the lowest level in Kohlberg's theory of moral development. The individual shows no internalization of moral values—moral reasoning is controlled by external rewards and punishment. 382

preintimate style the individual shows mixed emotions about commitment, an ambivalence reflected in the strategy of offering love without obligations. 310

prejudice an unjustified negative attitude toward an individual because of her or his membership in a group. 271

prenatal period the time from conception to birth. 18

preoccupied/ambivalent attachment an insecure attachment category in which adolescents are hypertuned to attachment experiences. This is thought to mainly occur because parents are inconsistently available to the adolescents. 165

preoperational stage Piaget's second stage, which lasts approximately from 2 to 7 years of age. In this stage, children begin to represent their world with words, images, and drawings. 107

pseudointimate style the individual maintains a long-lasting sexual attachment with little or no depth or closeness. 310

psychoanalytic theory describes development as primarily unconscious and heavily colored by emotion. Behavior is merely a surface characteristic. It is important to analyze the symbolic meanings of behavior. Early experiences are important in development. 40

psychological dependence strong desire and craving to repeat the use of a drug for various emotional reasons, such as a feeling of well-being and reduction of distress. 445

psychometric/intelligence view a view that emphasizes the importance of individual differences in intelligence; many advocates of this view also argue that intelligence should be assessed with intelligence tests. 128

psychosocial moratorium Erikson's term for the gap between childhood security and adult autonomy that adolescents experience as part of their identity exploration. 301

puberty a period of rapid physical maturation involving hormonal and bodily changes that take place primarily in early adolescence. 76

Public Law 94-142 the Education for All Handicapped Children Act, which requires all students with disabilities to be given a free, appropriate education and provides the funding to help implement this education. 248

quid pro quo sexual harassment sexual harassment in which a school employee threatens to base an educational decision (such as a grade) on a student's submission to unwelcome conduct. 368

random assignment in experimental research, the assignment of participants to experimental and control groups by chance. 63

rape forcible sexual intercourse with a person who does not give consent. 367

rapport talk the language of conversation, establishing connections, and negotiating relationships. 328

reciprocal socialization the process by which children and adolescents socialize parents, just as parents socialize them. 148

rejected children children who are infrequently nominated as a best friend and are actively disliked by their peers. 191

report talk talk that gives information; public speaking is an example. 328

rites of passage ceremonies or rituals that mark an individual's transition from one status to another, especially into adulthood. 261

role-focused level the second or intermediate level of relationship maturity, at which perceiving others as individuals in their own right begins to develop. However, at this level the perspective is stereotypical and emphasizes social acceptability. 311

roles certain positions in a group that are governed by rules and expectations. Roles define how adolescents should behave in those positions. 202

romantic love also called passionate love or eros, this love has strong sexual and infatuation components, and it often predominates in the early part of a love relationship. 212

schema a concept or framework that exists in the individual's mind to organize and interpret information, as in Piaget's theory. 106

scientific method   an approach that can be used to discover accurate information. It includes these steps: conceptualize the problem, collect data, draw conclusions, and revise research conclusions and theory.   54

secure attachment   in this attachment pattern, infants use their primary caregiver, usually the mother, as a secure base from which to explore the environment. Secure attachment is theorized to be an important foundation for psychological development later in childhood, adolescence, and adulthood.   165

self-concept   domain-specific evaluations of the self.   269

self-efficacy   the belief that one can master a situation and produce favorable outcomes.   412

self-esteem   the global evaluative dimension of the self. Self-esteem is also referred to as self-worth or self-image.   296

self-focused level   the first level of relationship maturity, at which one's perspective of another or of a relationship is concerned only with how it affects oneself.   310

self-handicapping strategies   deliberately not trying in school, putting off studying until the last minute, fooling around the night before a test, and using other ineffective strategies that will be seen as the cause of poor performance rather than lack of ability.   419

self-regulatory learning   the self-generation and self-monitoring of thoughts, feelings, and behaviors to reach a goal.   127

self-understanding   the adolescent's cognitive representation of the self, the substance and content of the adolescent's self-conceptions.   292

sensorimotor stage   Piaget's first stage of development, lasting from birth to about 2 years of age. In this stage, infants construct an understanding of the world by coordinating sensory experiences with physical, motoric actions.   107

service learning   a form of education that promotes social responsibility and service to the community.   396

sexism   prejudice and discrimination against an individual because of her or his sex.   326

sexual script   a stereotyped pattern of role prescriptions for how individuals should behave sexually. Females and males have been socialized to follow different sexual scripts.   350

sexually transmitted diseases (STDs)   diseases that are contracted primarily through sexual contact. This contact is not limited to vaginal intercourse but includes oral-genital contact and anal-genital contact as well.   363

shared environmental influences   adolescents' common environmental experiences that are shared with their siblings, such as their parents' personalities and intellectual orientation, the family's social class, and the neighborhood in which they live.   99

social cognitive theory of gender   this theory emphasizes that children's and adolescents' gender development occurs through observation and imitation of gender behavior, and through rewards and punishments they experience for gender-appropriate and -inappropriate behavior.   320

social cognitive theory of moral development   the theory that distinguishes between *moral competence* (the ability to produce moral behaviors) and *moral performance* (performing those behaviors in specific situations).   389

social constructivist approaches   approaches that focus on collaboration with others to produce knowledge and understanding; an example is Vygotsky's theory.   223

social isolation   a type of loneliness that occurs when a person lacks a sense of integrated involvement. Being deprived of participation in a group or community involving companionship, shared interests, organized activities, and meaningful roles causes a person to feel alienated, bored, and uneasy.   312

social policy   a national government's course of action designed to influence the welfare of its citizens.   15

socioeconomic status (SES)   a grouping of people with similar occupational, educational, and economic characteristics.   257

socioemotional processes   changes in an individual's relationships with other people, emotions, personality, and social contexts.   18

spermarche   a boy's first ejaculation of semen.   79

standardized tests   commercially prepared tests that assess performance in different domains.   60

status offenses   performed by youths under a specified age, these are juvenile offenses that are not as serious as index offenses. These offenses may include such acts as drinking under age, truancy, and sexual promiscuity.   458

stereotype   a broad category that reflects our impressions and beliefs about people. All stereotypes refer to an image of what the typical member of a particular group is like.   11

stereotyped style   the individual has superficial relationships that tend to be dominated by friendship ties with same-sex rather than opposite-sex individuals.   310

stimulants   drugs that increase the activity of the central nervous system.   450

storm-and-stress view   G. Stanley Hall's concept that adolescence is a turbulent time charged with conflict and mood swings.   7

synchrony   the carefully coordinated interaction between the parent and the child or adolescent in which, often unknowingly, they are attuned to each other's behavior.   149

syphilis   a sexually transmitted disease caused by the bacterium *Treponema pallidum,* a spirochete.   363

theory   an interrelated, coherent set of ideas that helps to explain and make predictions.   40

tolerance   the condition in which a greater amount of a drug is needed to produce the same effect as a smaller amount used to produce.   445

top-dog phenomenon   the circumstance of moving from the top position (in elementary school, the oldest, biggest, and most powerful students) to the lowest position (in middle or junior high school, the youngest, smallest, and least powerful).   227

triarchic theory of intelligence   Sternberg's view that intelligence comes in three main forms: analytical, creative, and practical.   131

twin study   a study in which the behavioral similarity of identical twins is compared with the behavioral similarity of fraternal twins.   97

unresolved/disorganized attachment   an insecure category in which the adolescent has an unusually high level of fear and is disoriented. This can result from such traumatic experiences as a parent's death or abuse by parents.   165

values clarification   an educational approach that focuses on helping people clarify what their lives are for and what is worth working for. Students are encouraged to define their own values and understand others' values.   395

values   beliefs and attitudes about the way things should be.   397

Vygotsky's theory   a sociocultural cognitive theory that emphasizes developmental analysis, the role of language, and social relations.   47

youth   Kenniston's term for the transitional period between adolescence and adulthood, which is a time of economic and personal temporariness.   21

zone of proximal development (ZPD)   Vygotsky's concept that refers to the range of tasks that are too difficult for an individual to master alone, but that can be mastered with the guidance or assistance of adults or more-skilled peers.   115

REFERENCES

A

Acebo, C., Sadeh, A., Seifer, R., Tzischinsky, O., Wolfson, A.R., Hafer, A., & Carskadon, M.A. (1999). Estimating sleep patterns with activity monitoring in children and adolescents: How many nights are necessary for reliable measures? *Sleep, 22,* 95–103.

Achenbach, T.M., & Edelbrock, C.S. (1981). Behavioral problems and competencies reported by parents of normal and disturbed children aged four through sixteen. *Monographs of the Society for Research in Child Development, 46* (1, Serial No. 188).

Achenbach, T.M., Howell, C.T., Quay, H.C., & Conners, C.K. (1991). National survey of problems and competencies among four- to sixteen-year-olds. *Monographs of the Society for Research in Child Development,* Serial No. 225 (Vol. 56, No. 3).

Adair, L.S. (2001). Size at birth predicts age at menarche. *Pediatrics, 107,* E59.

Adams, G.R., Abraham, K.G., & Markstrom, C.A. (2000). The relations among identify development, self-consciousness, and self-focusing during middle and late adolescence. In G. Adams (Ed.), *Adolescent development: The essential readings.* Malden, MA: Blackwell.

Adams, G.R., Gullotta, T.P., & Montemayor, R. (Eds.). (1992). *Adolescent identity formation.* Newbury Park, CA: Sage.

Adams, H. (2000). Behavior therapy. In A. Kazdin (Ed.), *Encyclopedia of psychology.* Washington, DC, & New York: American Psychological Association and Oxford University Press.

Adams, R., & Laursen, B. (2001). The organization and dynamics of adolescent conflict with parents and friends. *Journal of Marriage and the Family, 63,* 97–110.

Adelson, J. (1979, January). Adolescence and the generalization gap. *Psychology Today,* pp. 33–37.

Ahn, N. (1994). Teenage childbearing and high school completion: Accounting for individual heterogeneity. *Family Planning Perspectives, 26,* 17–21.

Aiken, L.R., (2003). *Psychological testing and assessment* (11th ed.). Boston: Allyn & Bacon.

Ainsworth, M.D.S. (1979). Infant-mother attachment. *American Psychologist, 34,* 932–937.

Alan Guttmacher Institute. (1995). *National survey of the American male's sexual habits.* New York: Author.

Alan Guttmacher Institute. (1998). *Teen sex and pregnancy.* New York: Author.

Alan Guttmacher Institute. (2000, February 24). *United States and the Russian Federation lead the developed world in teenage pregnancy rates.* New York: Author.

Alderman, M.K. (1999). *Motivation for achievement.* Mahwah, NJ: Erlbaum.

Alexander, C., Piazza, M., Mekos, D., & Valente, T. (2001). Peers, schools, and cigarette smoking. *Journal of Adolescent Health, 29,* 22–30.

Alexander, P.A. (2000). Toward a model of academic development Schooling and the acquisition of knowledge. *Educational Researcher, 29,* 28–33.

Algozzine, B., & Kay, P. (2002). *Preventing problem behaviors.* Thousand Oaks, CA: Corwin Press.

Allen, J.P., Hauser, S., Eickholt, C., Bell, K., & O'Connor, T. (1994). Autonomy and relatedness in family interactions as predictors of expressions of negative adolescent affect. *Journal of Research on Adolescence, 4,* 535–552.

Allen, J.P., Hauser, S.T., & Borman-Spurrell, E. (1996). Attachment security and related sequelae of severe adolescent psychopathology: An eleven-year follow-up study. *Journal of Consulting and Clinical Psychology, 64,* 254–263.

Allen, J.P., McElhaney, C., Boykinik, & Land, D.J. (April, 2001). *Adolescent attachment and family relationships.* Paper presented at the meeting of the Society for Research in Child Development, Minneapolis.

Allen, J.P., Philliber, S., Herring, S., & Kuperminc, G.P. (1997). Preventing teen pregnancy and academic failure: Experimental evaluation of a developmentally-based approach. *Child Development, 68,* 729–742.

Aloise-Young, P.A., Hennigan, K.M., & Leong, C.W. (2001). Possible selves and negative health behaviors during early adolescence. *Journal of Early Adolescence, 21,* 158–181.

Amabile, T. (1993). Commentary. In D. Goleman, P. Kaufman, & M. Ray, *The creative spirit.* New York: Plume.

Amato, P.R., & Booth, A. (1996). A prospective study of divorce and parent-child relationships. *Journal of Marriage and the Family, 58,* 356–365.

Amato, P.R., & Keith, B. (1991). Parental divorce and the well-being of children: A meta-analysis. *Psychological Bulletin, 110,* 26–46.

American Association of University Women. (1993). *Hostile hallways.* Washington, DC: Author.

American Psychiatric Association. (1994). *Diagnostic and statistical manual of mental disorders* (4th ed.). Washington, DC: Author.

American Sports Data. (2001). *Superstudy of sports participation.* Hartsdale, NY: American Sports Data.

Anderman, E.M., Maehr, M.L., & Midgley, C. (1996). *Declining motivation after the transition to middle school: Schools can make a difference.* Unpublished manuscript, University of Kentucky, Lexington.

Anderson, D.R., Huston, A.C., Schmitt, K., Linebarger, D.L., & Wright, J.C. (2001). Early childhood television viewing and adolescent behavior: The Recontact Study. *Monographs of the Society for Research in Child Development, 66* (1, Serial No. 264).

Anderson, E., Greene, S.M., Hetherington, E.M., & Clingempeel, W.G. (1999). The dynamics of parental remarriage. In E.M. Hetherington (Ed.), *Coping with divorce, single parenting, and remarriage.* Mahwah, NJ: Erlbaum.

Anderson, K.J., & Leaper, C. (1996, March). *The social construction of emotion and gender between friends.* Paper presented at the meeting of the Society for Research on Adolescence, Boston.

Andre, T., Frevert, R.L., & Schuchmann, D. (1989). From whom have college students learned what about sex? *Youth and Society, 20,* 241–268.

Angold, A., Costello, E.J., & Worthman, C.M. (1999). Puberty and depression: The roles of age, pubertal status and pubertal timing. *Psychological Medicine, 28,* 51–61.

Anselmi, D.L. (1998). *Questions of gender.* Burr Ridge, IL: McGraw-Hill.

Archer, S.L. (1989). The status of identity: Reflections on the need for intervention. *Journal of Adolescence, 12,* 345–359.

Archer, S.L. (2000). Intimacy. In A. Kazdin (Ed.), *Encyclopedia of psychology.* Washington, DC, and New York: American Psychological Association and Oxford University Press.

Archer, S.L. (Ed.). (1994). *Intervention for adolescent identity development.* Newbury Park, CA: Sage.

Archer, S.L., & Waterman, A.S. (1994). Adolescent identity development: Contextual perspectives. In C.B. Fisher & R.M. Lerner (Eds.), *Applied developmental psychology.* New York: McGraw-Hill.

Archibald, A.B., Graber, J.A., & Brooks-Gunn, J. (1999). Associations among parent-adolescent relationships, pubertal growth, dieting, and body image in young adolescent girls: A short-term longitudinal study. *Journal of Research on Adolescence, 9,* 395–415.

Archibald, A.B., Graber, J.A., & Brooks-Gunn, J. (in press). Pubertal processes and physical growth in adolescence. In G.R. Adams & M. Berzonsky (Eds.), *Handbook on adolescence.* Malden, MA: Blackwell.

Ardila-Rey, A., & Killen, M. (in press). Middle-class Colombian children's evaluations of personal, moral, and social-conventional interactions in the classroom. *International Journal of Behavioral Development.*

Arehart, D.M., & Smith, P.H. (1990). Identity in adolescence: Influences on dysfunction and psychosocial task issues. *Journal of Youth and Adolescence, 19,* 63–72.

Armsden, G., & Greenberg, M.T. (1984). *The inventory of parent and peer attachment: Individual differences and their relationship to psychological well-being in adolescence.* Unpublished manuscript, University of Washington.

Arnett, J.J. (1991). Heavy metal music and reckless behavior among adolescents. *Journal of Youth and Adolescence, 20,* 573–592.

Arnett, J.J. (1995, March). *Are college students adults?* Paper presented at the meeting of the Society for Research in Child Development, Indianapolis.

Arnett, J.J. (2000). Emerging childhood. *American Psychologist, 55,* 469–480.

Arnold, M.L. (1989, April). *Moral cognition and conduct: A quantitative review of the literature.* Paper presented at the Society for Research in Child Development meeting, Kansas City.

Aronson, E. (1986, August). *Teaching students things they think they know all about: The case of prejudice and desegregation.* Paper presented at the meeting of the American Psychological Association, Washington, DC.

Asakawa, K., & Csikszentmihalyi, M. (1998). The quality of experience of Asian American adolescents in academic activities: An exploration of educational achievement. *Journal of Research on Adolescence, 8,* 241–262.

Asarnow, J.R., & Callan, J.W. (1985). Boys with peer adjustment problems: Social cognitive processes. *Journal of Consulting and Clinical Psychology, 53,* 80–87.

Aseltine, R.H., & Gore, S. (1993). Mental health and social adaptation following the transition from high school. *Journal of Research on Adolescence, 3,* 247–270.

Ashton, P.T., & Webb, R.B. (1986). *Making a difference: Teachers' sense of efficacy and student achievement.* White Plains, NY: Longman.

Attie, I., & Brooks-Gunn, J. (1989). Development of eating problems in adolescent girls: A longitudinal study. *Developmental Psychology, 25,* 70–79.

Auster, C.J., & Ohm, S.C. (2000). Masculinity and femininity in contemporary American society: A reevaluation using the Bem Sex-Role Inventory. *Sex Roles, 43,* 499–528.

Bachman, J.G., & Schulenberg, J. (1993). How part-time work intensity relates to drug use, problem behavior, time use, and satisfaction among high school seniors: Are these consequences or just correlates? *Developmental Psychology, 29,* 220–235.

Bacon, M.K., Child, I.L., & Barry, H. (1963). A cross-cultural study of correlates of crime. *Journal of Abnormal and Social Psychology, 66,* 291–300.

Baddeley, A. (1992). Working memory. *Science, 255,* 556–560.

Baddeley, A. (2000). Short-term and working memory. In E. Tulving & F.I.M. Craik (Eds.), *The Oxford handbook of memory.* New York: Oxford University Press.

Baer, R.A., Ballenger, J., Berry, D.T.R., & Wetter, M.W. (1997). Detection of random responding on the MMPI-A. *Journal of Personality Assessment, 68,* 139–151.

Bagwell, C.L., Newcomb, A.F., & Bukowski, W.M. (1994, February). *Early adolescent friendship as a predictor of adult adjustment: A twelve-year follow-up investigation.* Paper presented at the biennial meeting of the Society for Research on Adolescence, San Diego.

Bagwell, C.L., Newcomb, A.F., & Bukowski, W.M. (1998). Preadolescent friendship and peer rejection as predictors of adult adjustment. *Child Development, 69,* 140–153.

Baird, A.A., Gruber, S.A., Cohen, B.M., Renshaw, R.J., & Yureglun-Todd, D.A. (1999). FMRI of the amygdala in children and adolescents. *American Academy of Child and Adolescent Psychiatry, 38,* 195–199.

Baltes, P. B. (1987). Theoretical propositions of life-span developmental psychology: On the dynamics between growth and decline. *Developmental Psychology, 23,* 611–626.

Baltes, P.B. (2000). Life-span developmental theory. In A. Kazdin (Ed.), *Encyclopedia of psychology.* Washington, DC, & New York: American Psychological Association and Oxford University Press.

Baltes, P.B., Lindenberger, U., & Staudinger, U.M. (1998). Life-span theory in developmental psychology. In W. Damon (Ed.), *Handbook of child psychology* (5th ed., Vol. 1). New York: Wiley.

Bandura, A. (1982). Self-efficacy mechanism in human agency. *American Psychologist, 37,* 122–147.

Bandura, A. (1986). *Social foundations of thought and action: A social cognitive theory.* Englewood Cliffs, NJ: Prentice Hall.

Bandura, A. (1991). Social cognitive theory of moral thought and action. In W.M. Kurtines & J.L. Gewirtz (Eds.), *Handbook of moral behavior and development* (Vol. 1). Hillsdale, NJ: Erlbaum.

Bandura, A. (1994). *Self-efficacy: The exercise of self-control.* New York: W.H. Freeman.

Bandura, A. (1997). *Self-efficacy.* New York: W.H. Freeman.

Bandura, A. (2000). Self-efficacy. In A. Kazdin (Ed.), *Encyclopedia of psychology.* Washington, DC, and New York: American Psychological Association and Oxford University Press.

Bandura, A. (2000). Social cognitive theory. In A. Kazdin (Ed.), *Encyclopedia of psychology.* Washington, DC, and New York: American Psychological Association and Oxford University Press.

Bandura, A., Caprara, G.V., Barbaranelli, C., Pastorelli C., & Regalia, C. (2001). Sociocognitive self-regulatory mechanisms governing transgressive behavior. *Journal of Personality and Social Psychology, 80,* 125–135.

Banks, J.A. (1997). *Approaches to multicultural education reform.* In J.A. Banks and C.A.M. Banks (Eds.), *Multicultural education.* Boston: Allyn & Bacon.

Banks, J.A. (2002). *Introduction to multicultural education.* Boston: Allyn & Bacon.

Baran, S.J. (1976). How TV and film portrayals affect sexual satisfaction in college and adolescent sexual image. *Journal of Broadcasting, 20,* 61–88.

Barber, B.L., Eccles, J.S., & Stone, M.R. (2001, April). *Whatever happened to the jock, the brain, and the princess? Young adult pathways linked to adolescent activity involvement and identity.* Paper presented at the meeting of the Society for Research in Child Development, Minneapolis.

Barenboim, C. (1981). The development of person perception in childhood and adolescence: From behavioral comparisons to psychological constructs to psychological comparisons. *Child Development, 52,* 129–144.

Barker, R., & Wright, H.F. (1951). *One boy's day.* New York: Harper.

Barnard, K.E., & Solchany, J.E. (2002). Mothering. In M.H. Bornstein (Ed.), *Handbook of parenting* (2nd Ed.). Mahwah, NJ: Erlbaum.

Barnes, G.M., Farrell, M.P., & Banerjee, S. (1995). Family influences on alcohol abuse and other problem behaviors among Black and White Americans. In G.M. Boyd, J. Howard, & R.A. Zucker (Eds.), *Alcohol problems among adolescents.* Hillsdale, NJ: Erlbaum.

Barnouw, V. (1975). *An introduction to anthropology: Vol. 2. Ethnology.* Homewood, IL: Dorsey Press.

Basen-Enquist, K., Coyle, K.K., Parcel, G.S., Kirby, D., Bnanspach, S.W., Carvajal, S.C., & Baumler, E. (2001). Schoolwide effects of a multicomponent HIV, STD, and pregnancy prevention program for high school students. *Health Education and Behavior, 28,* 166–185.

Baskett, L.M., & Johnston, S.M. (1982). The young child's interaction with parents versus siblings. *Child Development, 53,* 643–650.

Bat-Chava, Y., Allen, L., Aber, J.L., & Seidman, E. (1997, April). *Racial and ethnic identity and the contexts of development.* Paper presented at the meeting of the Society for Research in Child Development, Washington, DC.

Baumeister, R.F. (1991). Identity crisis. In R.M. Lerner, A.C. Petersen, & J. Brooks-Gunn (Eds.), *Encyclopedia of adolescence* (Vol. 1). New York: Garland.

Baumrind, D. (1971). Current patterns of parental authority. *Developmental Psychology Monographs, 4* (1, Pt. 2).

Baumrind, D. (1991). Effective parenting during the early adolescent transition. In P.A. Cowan & E.M. Hetherington (Eds.), *Advances in family research* (Vol. 2). Hillsdale, NJ: Erlbaum.

Baumrind, D. (1996, April). Unpublished review of J.W. Santrock's *Children,* 5th ed. (New York: McGraw-Hill).

Beal, C.R. (1994). *Boys and girls: The development of gender roles.* New York: McGraw-Hill.

Bearison, D.J., & Dorval, B. (2002). *Collaborative cognition.* Westport, CT: Ablex.

Beck, A.T. (1993). Cognitive therapy: Past, present, and future. *Journal of Consulting and Clinical Psychology, 61,* 194–198.

Becker, B., Latendresse, S., Galen, B., & Luthar, S. (2000, April). *Parental attachment, peer relations, and academic competence.* Paper presented at the meeting of the Society for Research on Adolescence, Chicago.

Becker, H.J. (1994). *Analysis of trends of school use of new information technology.* Irvine: University of California.

Beckham, E.E. (2000). Depression. In A. Kazdin (Ed.), *Encyclopedia of psychology.* Washington, DC, and New York: American Psychological Association and Oxford University Press.

Bednar, R.L., Wells, M.G., & Peterson, S.R. (1995). *Self-esteem* (2nd ed.). Washington, DC: American Psychological Association.

Belansky, E.S., & Clements, P. (1992, March). *Adolescence: A crossroads for gender-role transcendence or gender-role intensification.* Paper presented at the meeting of the Society for Research on Adolescence, Washington, DC.

Bell, A.P., Weinberg, M.S., & Mammersmith, S.K. (1981). *Sexual preference: Its development in men and women.* New York: Simon & Schuster.

Belsky, J. (1981). Early human experience: A family perspective. *Developmental Psychology, 17,* 3–23.

Belson, W. (1978). *Television violence and the adolescent boy.* London: Saxon House.

Bem, S.L. (1977). On the utility of alternative procedures for assessing psychological androgyny. *Journal of Consulting and Clinical Psychology, 45,* 196–205.

Bence, P. (1989, April). *Adolescent dating behavior and TV soaps: Guided by "The Guiding Light"?* Paper presented at the biennial meeting of the Society for Research in Child Development, Kansas City.

Bence, P. (1991). Television, adolescents and development. In R.M. Lerner, A.C. Petersen, & J. Brooks-Gunn (Eds.), *Encyclopedia of adolescence* (Vol. 2). New York: Garland.

Benin, M. (1997, August). *A longitudinal study of marital satisfaction.* Paper presented at the meeting of the American Sociological Association, Toronto.

Bennett, C. (2003). *Comprehensive multicultural education* (5th Ed.). Boston: Allyn & Bacon.

Bennett, W. (1993). *The book of virtues.* New York: Simon & Schuster.

Benson, P.L. (1993). *The troubled journey.* Minneapolis: Search Institute.

Benson, P.L. (1997). *All kids are our kids: What communities must do to raise caring and responsible children and adolescents.* Minneapolis: Search Institute.

Bereiter, C. (2002). *Education and the mind in the knowledge age.* Mahwah, NJ: Erlbaum.

Berk, S.F. (1985). *The gender factory: The apportionment of work in American households.* New York: Plenum.

Berndt, T.J. (1979). Developmental changes in conformity to peers and parents. *Developmental Psychology, 15,* 608–616.

Berndt, T.J. (1982). The features and effects of friendship in early adolescence. *Child Development, 53,* 1447–1460.

Berndt, T.J. (1996). Transitions in friendship and friends' influence. In J.A. Graber, J. Brooks-Gunn, & A.C. Petersen (Eds.), *Transitions through adolescence.* Mahwah, NJ: Erlbaum.

Berndt, T.J., & Perry, T.B. (1990). Distinctive features and effects of early adolescent friendships. In R. Montemayor (Ed.), *Advances in adolescent research.* Greenwich, CT: JAI Press.

Berry, J.W. (1990). Psychology of acculturation: Understanding individuals moving between cultures. In R.W. Brislin (Ed.), *Applied cross-cultural psychology.* Newbury Park, CA: Sage.

Berry, J.W. (2000). Cultural foundations of human behavior. In A. Kazdin (Ed.), *Encyclopedia of psychology.* Washington, DC, and New York: American Psychological Association and Oxford University Press.

Berscheid, E., Snyder, M., & Omoto, A.M. (1989). Issues in studying close relationships. In C. Hendrick (Ed.), *Close relationships.* Newbury Park, CA: Sage.

Berzonsky, M. (2000, June). *A social cognitive approach to identity development: The role of identity style.* Paper presented at the meeting of the European Association for Research on Adolescence, Jena, Germany.

Berzonsky, M.D., & Adams, G.R. (1999). Reevaluating the identity status paradigm: Still useful after 35 years. *Developmental Review, 19,* 557–590.

Berzonsky, M.D., & Kuk, L.S. (2002, April). *Identity processing orientation, commitment, personal problems, and academic performance.* Paper presented at the meeting of the Society for Research on Adolescence, New Orleans.

BeShears, E., & McLeod, R. (2000, April). *The relationship of family and neighborhood effects on delinquency.* Paper presented at the meeting of the Society for Research on Adolescence, Chicago.

Best, J.W., & Kahn, J.V. (2003). *Research in education* (9th Ed.). Boston: Allyn & Bacon.

Beutler, L., & Martin, B. (1999). Scientific objectivity. In P. Kendall, J. Butcher, & G. Holmbeck (Eds.), *Handbook of research methods in clinical psychology.* New York: Wiley.

Biller, H.B. (1993). *Fathers and families: Paternal factors in child development.* Westport, CT: Auburn House.

Billy, J.O.G., Rodgers, J.L., & Udry, J.R. (1984). Adolescent sexual behavior and friendship choice. *Social Forces, 62,* 653–678.

Bingham, C.R., & Crockett, L.J. (1996). Longitudinal adjustment patterns of boys and girls experiencing early, middle, and late sexual intercourse. *Developmental Psychology, 32,* 647–658.

Bissell, J., Manring, A., & Rowland, V. (1999). *Cybereducator.* New York: McGraw-Hill.

Bjorklund, D.F., & Rosenbaum, K. (2000). Middle childhood: Cognitive development. In A. Kazdin (Ed.), *Encyclopedia of psychology.* Washington, DC, & New York: American Psychological Association and Oxford University Press.

Blakemore, J.E.O. (1993, March). *Preschool children's interest in babies: Observations in naturally occurring situations.* Paper presented at the biennial meeting of the Society for Research in Child Development, New Orleans.

Blasi, A. (1988). Identity and the development of the self. In D. Lapsley & F.C. Power (Eds.), *Self, ego, and identity: Integrative approaches.* New York: Springer-Verlag.

Blatchford, P., & Mortimore, P. (1994). The issue of class size for young children in school: What can we learn from research? *Oxford Review of Education, 20* (4), 411–428.

Bleeker, M.M., Kohler, K., Verson, M.K., & Messersmith, E. (2002, April). *Adolescence into young adulthood: The perspectives of parents and as their children grow up.* Paper presented at the meeting of the Society for Research on Adolescence, New Orleans.

Bloom, B. (Ed.). (1985). *Developing talent in young people.* New York: Ballantine Books.

Blos, P. (1962). *On adolescence.* New York: Free Press.

Blos, P. (1989). The inner world of the adolescent. In A.H. Esman (Ed.), *International annals of adolescent psychiatry* (Vol. 1). Chicago: University of Chicago Press.

Blumenthal, J., Jeffries, N.O., Castellanos, F.X., Liu, H., Zijdenbos, A., Paus, T., Evans, A.C., Rapoport, J.L., & Giedd, J.N. (1999). Brain development during childhood and adolescence: A longitudinal MRI study. *Nature Neuroscience 10,* 861–863.

Blyth, D.A. (2000). Community approaches to improving outcomes for urban children, youth, and families. In A. Booth & A.C. Crouter (Eds.), *Does it take a village?* Mahwah, NJ: Erlbaum.

Blyth, D.A., Durant, D., & Moosbrugger, L. (1985, April). *Perceived intimacy in the social relationships of drug- and nondrug-using adolescents.* Paper presented at the meeting of the Society for Research in Child Development, Toronto.

Blythe, M.J., & Rosenthal, S.L. (2000). Female adolescent sexuality. Promoting healthy sexual development. *Obstetrics & Gynecology in Clinics of North America, 27,* 125–141.

Bogenschneider, K. (2002). *Family policy matters.* Mahwah, NJ: Erlbaum.

Booth, A., & Crouter, A.C. (2000). *Does it take a village?* Mahwah, NJ: Erlbaum.

Borden, L.M., Donnermeyer, J.F., & Scheer, S.D. (2001). The influence of extra-curricular activities and peer influence on substance use. *Adolescent & Family Health, 2,* 12–19.

Bornstein, M.H., & Bradley, R.H. (Eds.) (2003). *Socioeconomic status, parenting, and child development.* Mahwah, NJ: Erlbaum.

Borowsky, I.W., Ireland, M., & Resnick, M.D. (2001). Adolescent suicide attempts: Risks and protectors. *Pediatrics, 107,* 485–493.

Bosma, H.A., & Kunnen, E.S. (Eds.). (2001). *Identity and emotion.* New York: Cambridge University Press.

Bosma, H.A., & Kunnen, E.S. (2001). Determinants and mechanisms in ego identity development: A review and synthesis. *Developmental Review, 21,* 39–66.

Botkin, D.R., Weeks, M.O., & Morris, J.E. (2000). Changing marital expectations: 1991–1996. *Sex Roles, 42,* 933–942.

Botvin, G.J. (1999, June). *Impact of preventive interventions on protection for drug use, onset, and progression.* Paper presented at the meeting of the Society for Prevention Research, New Orleans.

Bowes, J., & Flanagan, C.A. (2000, July). The relationship of empathy, sympathy, and altruism in adolescence: International comparisons. In L. Sherrod (Chair), *Youth civic engagement.* Symposium conducted at the biennial meeting of the International Society for the Study of Behavioral Development, Beijing, China.

Bowlby, J. (1989). *Secure attachment.* New York: Basic Books.

Boyer, E.L. (1986, December). Transition from school to college. *Phi Delta Kappan,* pp. 283–287.

Boyes, M.C., & Allen, S.G. (1993). Styles of parent-child interaction and moral reasoning in adolescence. *Merrill-Palmer Quarterly, 39,* 551–570.

Boyes, M.C., Giordano, R., & Galperyn, K. (1993, March). *Moral orientation and interpretive contexts of moral deliberation.* Paper presented at the biennial meeting of the Society for Research in Child Development, New Orleans.

Boys and Girls Clubs of America. (1989, May 12). *Boys and Girls Clubs in public housing projects: Interim report.* Minneapolis: Boys and Girls Clubs of America.

Boyum, L., & Parke, R.D. (1995). Family emotional expressiveness and children's social competence. *Journal of Marriage and the Family, 57,* 593–608.

Brabeck, M.M. (2000). Kohlberg, Lawrence. In A. Kazdin (Ed.), *Encyclopedia of psychology.* Washington, DC, and New York: American Psychological Association and Oxford University Press.

Brainard, C.J. (2002). Jean Piaget, learning research, and American education. In B.J. Zimmerman & D.H. Schunk (eds.), *Educational Psychology.* Mahwah, NJ: Erlbaum.

Bray, J., & Kelly, J. (1998). *Stepfamilies.* New York: Broadway.

Bray, J.H., & Berger, S.H. (1993). Developmental Issues in Stepfamilies Research Project: Family relationships and parent-child interactions. *Journal of Family Psychology, 7,* 76–90.

Bray, J.M., Berger, S.H., & Boethel, C.L. (1999). Marriage to remarriage and beyond. In E.M. Hetherington (Ed.), *Coping with divorce, single parenting, and remarriage.* Mahwah, NJ: Erlbaum.

Brazelton, T.B. (1998, Sept. 7). Commentary. *Dallas Morning News,* p. C2.

Bredemeier, B., & Shields, D. (1996). Moral development and children's sport. In F. Smoll & R. Smith (Eds.). *Children and youth in sport: A biopsychosocial perspective.* Chicago: Brown & Benchmark.

Brewer, M.B., & Campbell, D.T. (1976). *Ethnocentrism and intergroup attitudes.* New York: Wiley.

Brim, O.G., & Kagan, J. (1980). Constancy and change: A view of the issues. In O.G. Brim & J. Kagan (Eds.), *Constancy and change in human development.* Cambridge, MA: Harvard University Press.

Brislin, R. (1993). *Understanding culture's influence on behavior.* Fort Worth, TX: Harcourt Brace.

Brislin, R.W. (2000). Cross-cultural training. In A. Kazdin (Ed.), *Encyclopedia of psychology.* Washington, DC, and New York: American Psychological Association and Oxford University Press.

Brock, L.J., & Jennings, G.H. (1993). What daughters in their 30s wish their mothers had told them. *Family Relations, 42,* 61–65.

Brody, G.H., & Shaffer, D.R. (1982). Contributions of parents and peers to children's moral socialization. *Developmental Review, 2,* 31–75.

Brody, G.H., Stoneman, Z., & Burke, M. (1987). Child temperaments, maternal differential behavior and sibling relationships. *Developmental Psychology, 23,* 354–362.

Brody, N. (2000). Intelligence. In A. Kazdin (Ed.), *Encyclopedia of psychology.* Washington, DC, and New York: American Psychological Association and Oxford University Press.

Bronfenbrenner, U. (1986). Ecology of the family as a context for human development: Research perspectives. *Developmental Psychology, 22,* 723–742.

Bronfenbrenner, U. (1995). Developmental ecology through space and time: A future perspective. In P. Moen, G.H. Elder, & K. Lüscher (Eds.), *Examining lives in context.* Washington, DC: American Psychological Association.

Bronfenbrenner, U. (2000). Ecological theory. In A. Kazdin (Ed.), *Encyclopedia of psychology.* Washington, DC, and New York: American Psychological Association and Oxford University Press.

Bronfenbrenner, U., & Morris, P. (1998). The ecology of developmental processes. In W. Damon (Ed.), *Handbook of child psychology* (5th ed., Vol. 1). New York: Wiley.

Brook, J.S., Brook, D.W., Gordon, A.S., Whiteman, M., & Cohen, P. (1990). The psychological etiology of adolescent drug use: A family interactional approach. *Genetic Psychology Monographs, 116,* no. 2.

Brookover, W.B., Beady, C., Flood, P., Schweitzer, U., & Wisenbaker, J. (1979). *School social systems and student achievement: Schools make a difference.* New York: Praeger.

Brooks, J.G., & Brooks, M.G. (1993). *The case for constuctivist classrooms.* Alexandria, VA: Association for Supervision and Curriculum Development.

Brooks, M.G., & Brooks, J.G. (1999). The courage to be constructivist. *Educational Leadership, 57* (3), 18–24.

Brooks, T., & Bronstein, P. (1996, March). *Cross-cultural comparison of mothers' and fathers' behaviors toward girls and boys.* Paper presented at the meeting of the Society for Research on Adolescence, Boston.

Brooks-Gunn, J. (1988). Antecedents and consequences of variations in girls' maturational timing. In M.D. Levine & E.R. McAnarney (Eds.), *Early adolescent transitions.* Lexington, MA: Lexington Books.

Brooks-Gunn, J. (1992, March). *Revisiting theories of "storm and stress": The role of biology.* Paper presented at the meeting of the Society for Research on Adolescence, Washington, DC.

Brooks-Gunn, J., & Chase-Landsdale, P. L. (1995). Adolescent parenthood. In M.H. Bornstein (Ed.), *Children and parenting* (Vol. 3). Hillsdale, NJ: Erlbaum.

Brooks-Gunn, J., Duncan, G., Glebanov, P.K., & Sealand, N. (1993). Do neighborhoods influence child and adolescent development? *American Journal of Sociology, 99,* 353–395.

Brooks-Gunn, J., & Graber, J. A. (1995, March). *Depressive affect versus positive adjustment: Patterns of resilience in adolescent girls.* Paper presented at the meeting of the Society for Research in Child Development, Indianapolis.

Brooks-Gunn, J., & Graber, J.A. (1999). *What's sex got to do with it? The development of health and sexual identities during adolescence.* Unpublished manuscript, Department of Psychology, Columbia University, New York City.

Brooks-Gunn, J., Graber, J.A., & Paikoff, R.L. (1994). Studying links between hormones and negative affect: Models and measures. *Journal of Research on Adolescence, 4,* 469–486.

Brooks-Gunn, J., Klebanov, P.K., & Duncan, G.J. (1996). Ethnic differences in children's intelligence test scores: Role of economic deprivation, home environment, and maternal characteristics. *Child Development, 67,* 396–408.

Brooks-Gunn, J., & Paikoff, R.L. (1993). "Sex is a gamble, kissing is a game": Adolescent sexuality and health promotion. In S.G. Millstein, A.C. Petersen, & E.O. Nightingale (Eds.), *Promoting the health of adolescents.* New York: Oxford University Press.

Brooks-Gunn, J., & Paikoff, R.L. (1997). Sexuality and developmental transitions during adolescence. In J. Schulenberg, J. Maggs, & K. Hurrelmann (Eds.), *Health risks and developmental transitions during adolescence.* New York: Cambridge University Press.

Brooks-Gunn, J., & Ruble, D.N. (1982). The development of menstrual-related beliefs and behaviors during early adolescence. *Child Development, 53,* 1567–1577.

Brooks-Gunn, J., & Warren, M.P. (1989). The psychological significance of secondary sexual characteristics in 9- to 11-year-old girls. *Child Development, 59,* 161–169.

Brophy, J. (1998). *Motivating students to learn.* New York: McGraw-Hill.

Broughton, J. (1983). The cognitive developmental theory of adolescent self and identity. In B. Lee & G. Noam (Eds.), *Developmental approaches to self.* New York: Plenum.

Broverman, I., Vogel, S., Broverman, D., Clarkson, F., & Rosenkranz, P. (1972). Sex-role stereotypes: A current appraisal. *Journal of Social Issues, 28,* 59–78.

Brown, A.C., & Orthner, D.K. (1990). Relocation and personal well-being among early adolescents. *Journal of Early Adolescence, 10,* 366–381.

Brown, A.L., & Palincsar, A.M. (1984). Reciprocal teaching of comprehension-fostering and monitoring activities. *Cognition and Instruction, 1,* 175–177.

Brown, A.L., Metz, K.E., & Campione, J.C. (1996). Social interaction and individual understanding in a community of learners: The influence of Piaget and Vygotsky. In A. Tryphon & J. Voneche (Eds.), *Piaget-Vygotsky.* Mahwah, NJ: Erlbaum.

Brown, B.B. (1999). Measuring the peer environment of American adolescents. In S.L. Friedman & T.D. Wachs (Eds.), *Measuring environment across the life span.* Washington, DC: American Psychological Association.

Brown, B.B. (2002, April). *Changes and diversity in adolescents' social lives and interpersonal competence.* Paper presented at the meeting of the Society for Research on Adolescence, New Orleans.

Brown, B.B., Dolcini, M.M., & Leventhal, A. (1995, March). *The emergence of peer crowds: Friend or foe to adolescent health?* Paper presented at the meeting of the Society for Research on Child Development, Indianapolis.

Brown, B.B., Lambron, S.L., Mounts, N.S., & Steinberg, L. (1993). Parenting practices and peer group affiliation in adolescence. *Child Development, 64,* 467–482.

Brown, B.B., & Lohr, M.J. (1987). Peer-group affiliation and adolescent self-esteem: An integration of ego-identity and symbolic-interaction theories. *Journal of Personality and Social Psychology, 52,* 47–55.

Brown, B.B., Mory, M., & Kinney, D.A. (1994). Casting adolescent crowds in relational perspective: Caricature, channel, and context. In R. Montemayor, G.R. Adams, & T.P. Gullotta (Eds.), *Advances in adolescent development: Vol. 6. Personal relationships during adolescence.* Newbury Park, CA: Sage.

Brown, B.B., & Theobald, W. (1998). Learning contexts beyond the classroom: Extracurricular activities, community organizations, and peer groups. In K. Borman & B. Schneider (Eds.), *The adolescent years.* Chicago: University of Chicago Press.

Brown, F. (1973). *The reform of secondary education: Report of the national commission on the reform of secondary education.* New York: McGraw-Hill.

Brown, H.D., & Adler, N.E. (1998). Socioeconomic status. In H.S. Friedman (Ed.), *Encyclopedia of mental health* (Vol. 3). San Diego: Academic Press.

Brown, J.D., & Siegel, J.D. (1988). Exercise as a buffer of life stress: A prospective study of adolescent health. *Health Psychology, 7,* 341–353.

Brown, L.M., & Gilligan, C. (1992). *Meeting at the crossroads: Women's and girls' development.* Cambridge, MA: Harvard University Press.

Brown, L.M., Way, N., & Duff, J.L. (1999). The others in my I: Adolescent girls' friendships and peer relations. In N.G. Johnson, M.C. Roberts, & J. Worrell (Eds.), *Beyond appearance.* Washington, DC: American Psychological Association.

Brown, R. (1986). *Social psychology* (2nd ed.). New York: Macmillan.

Bruer, J.T. (1999). *The myth of the first three years.* New York: Free Press.

Bruess, C.E., & Richardson, G.E. (1992). *Decisions for health* (3rd ed.). Dubuque, IA: Brown & Benchmark.

Bryant, B.R., & Seay, P.C. (1998). The technology-related assistance to individuals with learning disabilities and their advocates. *Journal of Learning Disabilities, 31,* 4–15.

Bryk, A.S., Lee, V.E., & Holland, P.B. (1993). *Catholic schools and the common good.* Cambridge, MA: Harvard University Press.

Brynes, J.P. (2001). *Minds, brains, and learning.* New York: Guilford.

Buchanan, C.M. (2000). The impact of divorce on adjustment in adolescence. In R.D. Taylor & M.C. Wang (Eds.), *Resilience across contexts.* Mahwah, NJ: Erlbaum.

Buerkel-Rothfuss, D., & Mayes, S. (1981). Soap opera viewing: The cultivation effect. *Journal of Communication, 31,* 108–115.

Bugental, D.B., & Goodnow, J.J. (1998). Socialization processes. In W. Damon (Ed.), *Handbook of child psychology* (5th ed., Vol. 3). New York: Wiley.

Buhrmester, D. (1989). *Changes in friendship, interpersonal competence, and social adaptation during early adolescence.* Unpublished manuscript, Department of Psychology, UCLA, Los Angeles.

Buhrmester, D. (1990). Friendship, interpersonal competence, and adjustment in preadolescence and adolescence. *Child Development, 61,* 1101–1111.

Buhrmester, D. (2001, April). *Does age at which romantic involvement start matter?* Paper presented at the meeting of the Society for Research in Child Development, Minneapolis.

Buhrmester, D., & Carbery, J. (1992, March). *Daily patterns of self-disclosure and adolescent adjustment.* Paper presented at the biennial meeting of the Society for Research on Adolescence, Washington, DC.

Buhrmester, D., Camparo, L., Christensen, A., Gonzalez, L.S., & Hinshaw, S.P. (in press). Mothers and fathers interacting in dyads and triads with normal and hyperactive sons. *Developmental Psychology.*

Buhrmester, D., & Furman, W. (1987). The development of companionship and intimacy. *Child Development, 58,* 1101–1113.

Buhrmester, D., & Furman, W. (1990). Perceptions of sibling relationships during middle childhood and adolescence. *Child Development, 61,* 1387–1398.

Bukowski, W.M., Newcomb, A.F., & Hoza, B. (1987). Friendship conceptions among early adolescents: A longitudinal study of stability and change. *Journal of Early Adolescence, 7,* 143–152.

Bukowski, W.M., Sippola, L.K., & Boivin, M. (1995, March). *Friendship protects "at risk" children from victimization by peers.* Paper presented at the meeting of the Society for Research in Child Development, Indianapolis.

Bumpas, M.F., Crouter, A.C., & McHale, S.M. (2001). Parental autonomy granting during adolescence: Gender differences in context. *Developmental Psychology, 37,* 163–173.

Burton, L.M., & Synder, A.R. (1997). The invisible man revisited. In A. Booth & A.C. Crouter (Eds.), *Men in families.* Mahwah, NJ: Erlbaum.

Burton, R.V. (1984). A paradox in theories and research in moral development. In W.W. Kurtines & J.L. Gewirtz (Eds.), *Morality, moral behavior, and moral development.* New York: Wiley.

Buss, D., Shackelford, T.K., Kirkpatrick, L.A., & Larsen, R.J. (2001). A half century of mate preferences: The cultural evolution of values. *Journal of Marriage and the Family, 63,* 491–503.

Buss, D.M. (1995). Psychological sex differences: Origins through sexual selection. *American Psychologist, 50,* 164–168.

Buss, D.M. (1998). The psychology of human mate selection. In C.B. Crawford & D.L. Krebs (Eds.), *Handbook of evolutionary psychology.* Mahwah, NJ: Erlbaum.

Buss, D.M. (2000). Evolutionary psychology. In A. Kazdin (Ed.), *Encyclopedia of psychology.* Washington, DC, and New York: American Psychological Association and Oxford University Press.

Buss, D.M., & Kenrick, D.T. (1998). Evolutionary social psychology. In D.T. Gilbert, S.T. Fiske, & G. Lindzey (Eds.), *The handbook of social psychology* (4th ed., Vol. 2). New York: McGraw-Hill.

Buss, D.M., & Schmitt, D.P. (1993). Sexual strategies theory: An evolutionary perspective on human mating. *Psychological Review, 100,* 204–232.

Butcher, J. (2000). Computerized assessment. In A. Kazdin (Ed.), *Encyclopedia of psychology.* Washington, DC, and New York: American Psychological Association and Oxford University Press.

Butcher, J.N., Williams, C.L., Graham, J.R., Archer, R.P., Tellegen, A., Ben-Porath, Y.S., & Kaemmer, B. (1992). *MMPI-A (Minnesota Multiphasic Personality Inventory–Adolescent): Manual for administration, scoring, and interpretation.* Minneapolis: University of Minnesota Press.

Buzwell, S., & Rosenthal, D. (1996). Constructing a sexual self: Adolescents' sexual self-perceptions and sexual risk-taking. *Journal of Research on Adolescence, 6,* 489–513.

Byrnes, J.P. (1997). *The nature and development of decision making.* Mahwah, NJ: Erlbaum.

Cairnes, R.B., & Cairns, B.D. (1994). *Lifelines and risks: Pathways of youth in our time.* New York: Cambridge University Press.

Calabrese, R.L., & Schumer, H. (1986). The effects of service activities on adolescent alienation. *Adolescence, 21,* 675–687.

Calvert, S. (1999). *Children's journeys through the information age.* New York: McGraw-Hill.

Cameron, J., Cowan, L., Holmes, B., Hurst, P., & McLean, M. (Eds.). (1983). *International handbook of educational systems.* New York: Wiley.

Campbell, C.Y. (1988, August 24). Group raps depiction of teenagers. *Boston Globe,* p. 44.

Campbell, L., Campbell, B., & Dickinson, D. (1999). *Teaching and learning through multiple intelligences* (2nd ed.). Boston: Allyn & Bacon.

Caplan, P.J., & Caplan, J.B. (1994). *Thinking critically about research on sex and gender.* New York: McGraw-Hill.

Caplan, P.J., & Caplan, J.B. (1999). *Thinking critically about research on sex and gender* (2nd ed.). New York: Longman.

Card, N.A., Isaacs, J., & Hodges, E.V.E. (2000, April). *Dynamics of interpersonal aggression in the school context: Who aggresses against whom?* Paper presented at the meeting of the Society for Research on Adolescence, Chicago.

Cardelle-Elawar, M. (1992). Effects of teaching metacognitive skills to students with low mathematics ability. *Teaching & Teacher Education, 8,* 109–121.

Carlson, C., Cooper, C., & Hsu, J. (1990, March). *Predicting school achievement in early adolescence: The role of family process.* Paper presented at the meeting of the Society for Research in Adolescence, Atlanta.

Carlson, M.J., & McLanahan, S.S. (2002). Fragile families, father involvement, and public policy. In C.S. Tamis-LeMonda & N. Cabrera (Eds.), *The handbook of father involvement.* Mahwah, NJ: Erlbaum.

Carnegie Council on Adolescent Development. (1989). *Turning points: Preparing American youth for the twenty-first century.* New York: Carnegie Foundation.

Carnegie Council on Adolescent Development. (1995). *Great transitions.* New York: Carnegie Foundation.

Carnegie Foundation. (1994). *Starting points: Meeting the needs of our youngest children.* New York: Author.

Carskadon, M.A., Acebo, C., & Seifer, R. (2001). Extended nights, sleep loss, and recovery sleep in adolescence. *Archives of Italian Biology, 139,* 301–312.

Carskadon, M.A., Labyak, S.E., Acebo, C., & Seifer, R. (1999). Intrinsic circadian period of adolescent humans measured in conditions of forced desynchrony. *Neuroscience Letters, 260,* 129–132.

Carskadon, M.A., Wolfson, A.R., Acebo, C., Tzischinsky, O., & Seifer, R. (1998). Adolescent sleep patterns, circadian timing, and sleepiness at a transition to early school days. *Sleep, 21,* 873–884.

Caruthers, A., Jenkins, B., Reid, A., & Solomon, J. (2000, April). *From titillation to exploitation: The changing nature of television's sexual content.* Paper presented at the meeting of the Society for Research on Adolescence, Chicago.

Caruthers, A.S., & Ward, L.M. (2002, April). *Mixed messages: The divergent nature of sexual communication received from parents, peers, and the media.* Paper presented at the meeting of the Society for Research on Adolescence, New Orleans.

Case, R. (1998). The development of conceptual structures. In W. Damon (Ed.), *Handbook of child psychology* (5th Ed., Vol. 2). New York: Wiley.

Case, R. (2000). Conceptual development. In M. Bennett (Ed.), *Developmental psychology.* Philadelphia: Psychology Press.

Case, R. (Ed.). (1992). *The mind's staircase: Exploring the conceptual underpinnings of children's thought and knowledge.* Hillsdale, NJ: Erlbaum.

Castellano, J.A., & Diaz, E. (Eds.) (2002). *Reaching new horizons: Gifted and talented education for culturally and linguistically diverse students.* Boston: Allyn & Bacon.

Cassell, C. (1984). *Swept away: Why women fear their own sexuality.* New York: Simon & Schuster.

Cassell, E., & Bernstein, D.A. (2001). *Criminal behavior.* Boston: Allyn & Bacon.

Cauffman, B.E. (1994, February). *The effects of puberty, dating, and sexual involvement on dieting and disordered eating in young adolescent girls.* Paper presented at the meeting of the Society for Research on Adolescence, San Diego.

Centers for Disease Control and Prevention. (2000). Youth risk behavior surveillance— United States, 1999. *MMWR, 49* (No. SS-5).

Centers for Disease Control and Prevention. (2001a). *Data and statistics: Adolescent pregnancy.* Atlanta: Author.

Centers for Disease Control and Prevention. (2001b). *Sexually transmitted diseases.* Atlanta: Author.

Chafee, S.H., & Yang, S.M. (1990). Communication and political socialization. In O. Ichilov (Ed.), *Political socialization, citizen education, and democracy.* New York: Columbia University Press.

Chan, W.S. (1963). *A source book in Chinese philosophy.* Princeton, NJ: Princeton Books.

Chandler, M.J. (2002, April). *Suicide and the persistence of identity in the face of radical cultural and developmental change.* Paper presented at the meeting of the Society for Research on Adolescence, New Orleans.

Chang, R., & Gjerde, P.F. (2000, April). *Pathways toward and away from depression in young adult females: Person-centered analysis of longitudinal data.* Paper presented at the meeting of the Society for Research on Adolescence, Chicago.

Chapman, R.P., & Saxman, L.J. (2000, April). *Parental influence on early adolescent substance abuse.* Paper presented at the meeting of the Society for Research on Adolescence, Chicago.

Chapman, W., & Katz, M.R. (1983). Career information systems in secondary schools: A survey and assessment. *Vocational Guidance Quarterly, 31,* 165–177.

Chase-Lansdale, P.S., & Brooks-Gunn, J. (1994). Correlates of adolescent pregnancy. In C.B. Fisher & R.M. Lerner (Eds.), *Applied developmental psychology.* New York: McGraw-Hill.

Chassin, L., Pitts, S.C., & Prost, J. (2001, April). *Binge drinking trajectories from adolescence to emerging adulthood in a high risk sample: Predictors and substance abuse outcomes.* Paper presented at the meeting of the Society for Research in Child Development, Minneapolis.

Chen, C., & Stevenson, H.W. (1989). Homework: A cross-cultural examination. *Child Development, 60,* 551–561.

Chen, L.A., & Yu, P.P.H. (1997, April). *Parental ethnic socialization in Chinese American families.* Paper presented at the meeting of the Society for Research in Child Development, Washington, DC.

Chen, Z., & Siegler, R.S. (2000). Intellectual development in childhood. In R.J. Sternberg (Ed.), *Handbook of intelligence.* New York: Cambridge.

Cherlin, A.J., & Furstenberg, F.F. (1994). Stepfamilies in the United States: A reconsideration. In J. Blake & J. Hagen (Eds.), *Annual review of sociology.* Palo Alto, CA: Annual Reviews.

Cherlin, A.J., Furstenberg, F.F., Chase-Lansdale, P.L., Kiernan, K.E., Robins, P.K., Morrison, D.R., & Teitler, J.O. (1991). Longitudinal studies of effects of divorce in children in Great Britain and the United States. *Science, 252,* 1386–1389.

Child Trends. (2000). Trends in sexual activity and contraceptive use among teens. *Child trends research brief.* Washington, DC: Author.

Child Trends. (2001). *Trends among Hispanic children, youth, and families.* Washington, DC: Author.

Children's Defense Fund. (1992). *The state of America's children, 1992.* Washington, DC: Author.

Chilman, C. (1979). *Adolescent sexuality in a changing American society: Social and psychological perspectives.* Washington, DC: Public Health Service, National Institute of Mental Health.

Chira, S. (1993, June 23). What do teachers want most? Help from parents. *New York Times,* p. I7.

Chmielewski, C. (1997, September). Sexual harassment meet Title IX. *NEA Today, 16* (2), 24–25.

Choate, J.S. (2000). *Successful inclusive teaching* (3rd ed.). Boston: Allyn & Bacon.

Chodorow, N.J. (1978). *The reproduction of mothering.* Berkeley: University of California Press.

Chodorow, N.J. (1989). *Feminism and psychoanalytic theory.* New Haven, CT: Yale University Press.

Christenson, P.W., & Roberts, D.F. (1991, August). *Music media in adolescent health promotion: Problems and prospects.* Paper presented at the meeting of the American Psychological Association, San Francisco.

Cialdini, R., & Rhoad, K. (1999). *Cults: Questions and answers.* Retrieved from the World Wide Web: http://www.influenceatwork.com/cult.html.

Cicchetti, D., & Toth, S. (1998). Perspectives on research and practice in developmental psychopathology. In I.E. Siegel & K.A. Renninger (Eds.), *Handbook of child psychology* (5th ed., Vol. 4). New York: Wiley.

Cillessen, A.H.N., Van Ijzendoorn, H.W., Van Lieshout, C.F.M., & Hartup, W.W. (1992). Heterogeneity among peer-rejected boys: Subtypes and stabilities. *Child Development, 63,* 893–905.

Clabby, J.G., & Elias, M.J. (1988). Improving social problem-solving and awareness. *William T. Grant Foundation Annual Report,* p. 18.

Clark, K.B., & Clark, M.P. (1939). The development of the self and the emergence of racial identification in Negro preschool children. *Journal of Social Psychology, 10,* 591–599.

Clark, M.S., Powell, M.C., Ovellette, R., & Milberg, S. (1987). Recipient's mood, relationship type, and helping. *Journal of Personality and Social Psychology, 43,* 94–103.

Clark, R.D., & Hatfield, E. (1989). Gender differences in receptivity to sexual offers. *Journal of Psychology and Human Sexuality, 2,* 39–55.

Clark, S.D., Zabin, L.S., & Hardy, J.B. (1984). Sex, contraception, and parenthood: Experience and attitudes among urban black young men. *Family Planning Perspectives, 16,* 77–82.

Clasen, D.R., & Brown, B.B. (1987). Understanding peer pressure in the middle school. *Middle School Journal, 19,* 21–23.

Clay, R.A. (1997, December). Are children being overmedicated? *APA Monitor,* pp. 1, 27.

Clifford, B.R., Gunter, B., & McAleer, J.L. (1995). *Television and children.* Hillsdale, NJ: Erlbaum.

Cloninger, C.R. (1991, January). *Personality traits and alcoholic predisposition.* Paper presented at the conference of the National Institute on Drug Abuse, University of California at Los Angeles.

CNN and the National Science Foundation. (1997). *Poll on technology and education.* Washington, DC: National Science Foundation.

Coates, D.L. (1999) The cultured and culturing aspects of romantic experience in adolescence. In W. Furman, B.B. Brown, & C. Feiring (Eds.), *The development of romantic relationships in adolescence.* New York: Cambridge University Press.

Cobb, P. (2000). Constructivism. In A. Kazdin (Ed.), *Encyclopedia of psychology.* Washington, DC, and New York: American Psychological Association and Oxford University Press.

Cochran, S.D., & Mays, V.M. (1990). Sex, lies, and HIV. *New England Journal of Medicine, 322* (11) 774–775.

Cognition and Technology Group at Vanderbilt. (1997). *The Jasper Project.* Mahwah, NJ: Erlbaum.

Cohen, S.E. (1994, February). *High school dropouts.* Paper presented at the meeting of the Society for Research on Adolescence, San Diego.

Coie, J. (1999, April 9). *Some implications of children's peer relations for their future adjustment.* Invited presentation, Dept. of Psychology, University of Texas at Dallas, Richardson.

Coie, J.D., & Dodge, K.A. (1998). Aggression and antisocial behavior. In N. Eisenberg (Ed.), *Handbook of child psychology* (5th ed., Vol. 3). New York: Wiley.

Coie, J.D., & Koeppl, G.K. (1990). Adapting intervention to the problems of aggressive and disruptive rejected children. In S.R. Asher & J.D. Coie (Eds.), *Peer rejection in childhood.* New York: Cambridge University Press.

Colby, A., Kohlberg, L., Gibbs, J., & Lieberman, M. (1983). A longitudinal study of moral judgment. *Monographs of the Society for Research in Child Development, 48* (21, Serial No. 201).

Cole, A.K., & Kerns, K.A. (2001). Perceptions of sibling qualities and activities of early adolescents. *Journal of Early Adolescence, 21,* 204–226.

Cole, M. (1997). *Cultural psychology.* Cambridge, MA: Harvard University Press.

Coleman, J.S. (1980). The peer group. In J. Adelson (Ed.), *Handbook of adolescent psychology.* New York: Wiley.

Coleman, J.S., & others. (1974). *Youth: Transition to adulthood.* Report of the Panel on Youth of the President's Science Advisory Committee. Chicago: University of Chicago Press.

Coleman, M.C., & Webber, J. (2002). *Emotional and behavioral disorders* (4th Ed.). Boston: Allyn & Bacon.

Coleman, P.D. (1986, August). *Regulation of dendritic extent: Human aging brain and Alzheimer's disease.* Paper presented at the meeting of the American Psychological Association, Washington, DC.

Coll, C.T.G., & Pachter, L.M. (2002). Ethnic and minority parenting. In M. Bornstein (Ed.), *Handbook of parenting* (2nd ed., Vol. 4). Mahwah, NJ: Erlbaum.

College Board Commission on Precollege Guidance and Counseling. (1986). *Keeping the options open.* New York: College Entrance Examination Board.

College Board. (1996, August 22). *News from the College Board.* New York: College Entrance Examination Board.

Collins, W.A., Gleason, T., & Sesma, A. (1997). Internalization, autonomy, and relationships: Development during adolescence. In J.E. Grusec & L. Kuczynski (Eds.), *Parenting and children's internalization of values.* New York: Wiley.

Collins, W.A., Hennighausen, K.H., & Sroufe, L.A. (1998, June). *Developmental precursors of intimacy in romantic relationships: A longitudinal analysis.* Paper presented at the International Conference on Personal Relationships, Saratoga Springs, NY.

Collins, W.A., Hyson, D., & Meyer, S.E. (2000, April). *Are we all in this together? Relational and contextual correlates of autonomy during early and late adolescence.* Paper presented at the meeting of the Society for Research on Adolescence, Chicago.

Collins, W.A., & Luebker, C. (1994) Parent and adolescent expectancies: Individual and relational significance. In J.G. Smetana (Ed.), *New directions for child development: Beliefs about parenting.* San Francisco: Jossey-Bass.

Collins, W.A., Maccoby, E.E., Steinberg, L., Hetherington, E.M., & Bornstein, M.H. (2000). Contemporary research on parenting: the case for nature *and* nurture. *American Psychologist, 55,* 218–232.

Collins, W.A., & Madsen, S. (2002, April). *Relational roots of romance: Beyond "chumships."* Paper presented at the meeting of the Society for Research on Adolescence, New Orleans.

Collins, W.A., & Repinski, D.J. (in press). Parents and adolescents as transformers of relationships: Dyadic adaptations to developmental change. In J. Gerris (Ed.), *Dynamics of parenting: International perspectives.* Mahwah, NJ: Erlbaum.

Comas Díaz, L. (2001). Hispanics, Latinos, or Americanos: The evolution of identity. *Cultural Diversity and Ethnic Minority Psychology, 7,* 115–120.

Comer, J.P. (1988). Educating poor minority children. *Scientific American, 259,* 42–48.

Comer, J.P. (1993). *African-American parents and child development: An agenda for school success.* Paper presented at the biennial meeting of the Society for Research on Child Development, New Orleans.

Comer, J.P., Haynes, N.M., Joyner, E.T., & Ben-Avie, M. (1996). *Rallying the whole village: The Comer process for reforming urban education.* New York: Teachers College Press.

Commons, M.I., Sinnott, J.D., Richards, F.A., & Armon, C. (1989). *Adult development: Vol. I. Comparisons and applications of developmental models.* New York: Praeger.

Compas, B.E., & Grant, K.E. (1993, March). *Stress and adolescent depressive symptoms: Underlying mechanisms and processes.* Paper presented at the biennial meeting of the Society for Research in Child Development, New Orleans.

Conant, J.B. (1959). *The American high school today.* New York: McGraw-Hill.

Condry, J.C., Simon, M.L., & Bronfenbrenner, U. (1968). *Characteristics of peer- and adult-oriented children.* Unpublished manuscript, Cornell University, Ithaca, NY.

Conger, J.J. (1981). Freedom and commitment: Families, youth, and social change. *American Psychologist, 36,* 1475–1484.

Conger, J.J. (1988). Hostages to the future: Youth, values, and the public interest. *American Psychologist, 43,* 291–300.

Conger, R., & Reuter, M. (1996). Siblings, parents, and peers: A longitudinal study of social influences in adolescent risk for alcohol use and abuse. In G.H. Brody (Ed.), *Sibling relationships: Their causes and consequences.* Norwood, NJ: Ablex.

Conger, R.D., & Chao, W. (1996). Adolescent depressed mood. In R.L. Simons (Ed.), *Understanding differences between divorced and intact families: Stress, interaction, and child outcome.* Thousand Oaks, CA: Sage.

Connolly, J., Furman, W., & Konarski, R. (1995, April). *The role of social networks in the emergence of romantic relationships in adolescence.* Paper presented at the meeting of the Society for Research in Child Development, Indianapolis.

Connolly, J., Furman, W., & Konarski, R. (2000). The role of peers in the emergence of heterosexual romantic relationships in adolescence. *Child Development, 71,* 1395–1408.

Connolly, J., & Goldberg, A. (1999). Romantic relationships in adolescence: The role of friends and peers in their emergence and development. In W. Furman, B.B. Brown, and C. Feiring (Eds.), *The development of romantic relationships in adolescence.* New York: Cambridge University Press.

Connolly, J., & Stevens, V. (1999, April). *Best friends, cliques, and young adolescents' romantic involvement.* Paper presented at the meeting of the Society for Research in Child Development, Albuquerque.

Connors, L.J., & Epstein, J.L. (1995). Parent and school partnerships. In M.H. Bornstein (Ed.), *Children and parenting* (Vol. 4). Hillsdale, NJ: Erlbaum.

Conti, K., & Amabile, T. (1999). Motivation and creativity. In M.A. Runco & S. Pritzker (Eds.), *Encyclopedia of creativity.* San Diego: Academic Press.

Cook, T.D., Hunt, H.D., & Murphy, R.F. (2001, April). *Comer's school development program in Chicago: A theory-based evaluation.* Paper presented at the meeting of the Society for Research in Child Development, Minneapolis.

Cooper, C.R. (in press). *The weaving of maturity: Cultural perspectives on adolescent development.* New York: Oxford University Press.

Cooper, C.R., & Ayers-Lopez, S. (1985). Family and peer systems in early adolescence: New models of the role of relationships in development. *Journal of Early Adolescence, 5,* 9–22.

Cooper, C.R., Cooper, R.G., Azmitia, M., & Chavira, G. (2001). *Bridging multiple worlds: How African American and Latino youth in academic outreach programs navigate math pathways to college.* Unpublished manuscript, University of California at Santa Cruz.

Cooper, C.R., & Denner, J. (1998). Theories linking culture and psychology: Universal and community-specific processes. *Annual Review of Psychology, 49,* 559–584.

Cooper, C.R., & Grotevant, H.D. (1989, April). *Individuality and connectedness in the family and adolescents' self and relational competence.* Paper presented at the meeting of the Society for Research in Child Development, Kansas City.

Cooper, C.R., Jackson, J.F., Azmitia, M., Lopez, E., & Dunbar, N. (1995). Bridging students' multiple worlds: African American and Latino youth in academic outreach programs. In R.F. Macias & R.G. Garcia-Ramos (Eds.), *Changing schools for changing students.* Santa Barbara: University of California Linguistic Minority Research Institute.

Cooper, M.L., Shaver, P.R., & Collins, N.L. (1998). Attachment styles, emotional regulation, and adjustment in adolescence. *Journal of Personality and Social Psychology, 74,* 1380–1397.

Coopersmith, S. (1967). *The antecedents of self-esteem.* San Francisco: W. H. Freeman.

Copeland, H.L. Heim, A., & Rome E.S. (2001, March). *Developing a relevant and effective smoking program.* Paper presented at the meeting of the Society for Adolescent Medicine, San Diego.

Copenhaver, M.M., Lash, S.J., & Eisler, R.M. (2000). Masculine gender-role stress, anger, and male intimate abusiveness: Implications for men's relationships. *Sex Roles, 42,* 405–414.

Cornock, B., Bowker, A., & Gadbois, S. (2001, April). *Sports participation and self-esteem: Examining the goodness of fit.* Paper presented at the meeting of the Society for Research in Child Development, Minneapolis.

Costin, S.E., & Jones, F. (1994, February). *The stress-protective role of parent and friend support for 6th and 9th graders following a school transition.* Paper presented at the meeting of the Society for Research on Adolescence, San Diego.

Cota-Robles, S., Neiss, M., & Hunt, C. (2000, April). *Future parent, future scholars: A longitudinal study of adolescent "possible selves" and adult outcomes.* Paper presented at the meeting of the Society for Research on Adolescence, Chicago.

Cote, J.E., & Levine, C. (1988). On critiquing the identity status paradigm: A rejoinder to Waterman. *Developmental Review, 8,* 209–218.

Covington, M.V. (1992). *Making the grade: A self-worth perspective on motivation and school reform.* New York: Cambridge University Press.

Covington, M.V. (1998, April). *Caring about learning: The nature and nurturing of subject-matter appreciation.* Paper presented at the meeting of the American Educational Research Association, San Diego.

Covington, M.V. (2002). Patterns of adaptive learning study: Where do we go from here? In C. Midgley (Ed.), *Goals, goal structures, and patterns of adaptive learning.* Mahwah, NJ: Erlbaum.

Covington, M.V., & Mueller, K.J. (2001). Intrinsic and extrinsic motivation: An approach/avoidance reformulation. *Educational Psychology Review, 13,* 157–176.

Covington, M.V., & Teel, K.T. (1996). *Overcoming student failure.* Washington, DC: American Psychological Association.

Covington, M.V., Teel, K.T., & Parecki, A.D. (1994, April). *Motivation benefits of improved academic performance among middle-school African American students through an effort-based grading system.* Paper presented at the meeting of the American Educational Research Association, New Orleans.

Cowley, G. (1998, April 6). Why children turn violent. *Newsweek,* 24–25.

Crawford, M., & MacLeod, M. (1990). Gender in the college classroom: An assessment of the "chilly climate" for women. *Sex Roles, 23,* 101–122.

Crawford, M., & Unger, R. (2000). *Women and gender* (3rd ed.). New York: McGraw-Hill.

Crews, F. (2001, January 2). Commentary in "Brain growth gets blame for turbulent years." *USA Today,* p. 6D.

Crick, N.R., & Dodge, K.A. (1994). A review and reformulation of social information-processing mechanisms in children's social adjustment. *Psychological Bulletin, 115,* 74–101.

Crockett, I.J., Raffaeli, M., & Moilanen, K. (in press). Adolescent sexuality: Behavior and meaning. In G.R. Adams & M. Berzonsky (Eds.), *Blackwell handbook of adolescence.* Malden, MA: Blackwell Publishers.

Cronbach, L.J., & Snow, R.E. (1977). *Aptitudes and instructional methods.* New York: Irvington.

Crooks, R., & Bauer, K. (2002). *Our sexuality* (8th ed.). Belmont, CA: Wadsworth.

Crouter, A.C., Manke, B.A., & McHale, S.M. (1995). The family context of gender intensification in early adolescence. *Child Development, 66,* 317–329.

Crump, A.D., Haynie, D., Aarons, S., & Adair, E. (1996, March). *African American teenagers' norms, expectations, and motivations regarding sex, contraception, and pregnancy.* Paper presented at the meeting of the Society for Research on Adolescence, Boston.

Csikszentmihalyi, M. (1990). *Flow.* New York: HarperCollins.

Csikszentmihalyi, M. (1993). *The evolving self.* New York: Harper & Row.

Csikszentmihalyi, M. (1995). *Creativity.* New York: HarperCollins.

Csikszentmihalyi, M. (2000). Creativity: an overview. In A. Kazdin (Ed.), *Encyclopedia of psychology.* Washington, DC, and New York: American Psychological Association and Oxford University Press.

Csikszentmihalyi, M., & Schmidt, J.A. (1998). Stress and resilience in adolescence: An evolutionary perspective. In K. Borman & B. Schneider (Eds.) *The adolescent years: Social influences and educational challenges.* Chicago: University of Chicago Press.

Csikszentmihalyi, M., & Schneider, B. (2000). *Becoming adult.* New York: Basic Books.

Cushner, K.H., McClelland, A., & Safford, P. (2003). *Human diversity in education* (3rd ed.). Boston: Allyn & Bacon.

Cutrona, C.E. (1982). Transition to college: Loneliness and the process of social adjustment. In L.A. Peplau & D. Perlman (Eds.), *Loneliness: A sourcebook of current theory, research, and therapy.* New York: Wiley.

D'Augelli, A. (2000). Sexual orientation. In A. Kazdin (Ed.), *Encyclopedia of psychology.* Washington, DC, and New York: American Psychological Association and Oxford University Press.

Dahl, R.E. (2001). Affect regulation, brain development, and behavioral/emotional health in adolescence. *CNS Spectrums, 6,* 60–72.

Damon, W. (1988). *The moral child.* New York: Free Press.

Damon, W. (1995). *Greater expectations.* New York: Free Press.

Damon, W. (2000). Moral development. In A. Kazdin (Ed.), *Encyclopedia of psychology.* Washington, DC, and New York: American Psychological Association and Oxford University Press.

Damon, W., & Hart, D. (1988). *Self-understanding in childhood and adolescence.* New York: Cambridge University Press.

Dannhausen-Brun, C.A., Shalowitz, M.U., & Berry, C.A. (1997, April). *Challenging the assumptions: Teen moms and public policy.* Paper presented at the meeting of the Society for Research in Child Development, Washington, DC.

Darling, C.A., Kallen, D.J., & VanDusen, J.E. (1984). Sex in transition, 1900–1984. *Journal of Youth and Adolescence, 13,* 385–399.

Darroch, J.E., Landry, D.J., & Singh, S. (2000). Changing emphases in sexuality education in U.S. public secondary schools, 1988–1999. *Family Planning Perspectives, 32,* 204–211, 265.

Davidson, J. (2000). Giftedness In A. Kazdin (Ed.), *Encyclopedia of psychology.* Washington, DC, and New York: American Psychological Association and Oxford University Press.

Davis, L., & Stewart, R. (1997, July). *Building capacity for working with lesbian, gay, bisexual, and transgender youth.* Paper presented at the conference on Working with America's Youth, Pittsburgh.

Davis, S.S., & Davis, D.A. (1989). *Adolescence in a Moroccan town.* New Brunswick, NJ: Rutgers University Press.

Davison, G.C. (2000). Case study. In A. Kazdin (Ed.), *Encyclopedia of psychology.* Washington, DC, & New York: American Psychological Association and Oxford University Press.

Davison, G.C., & Neale, J.M. (2001). *Abnormal psychology* (8th ed.). New York: Wiley.

Day, R.D. (2002). *Introduction to family processes.* Mahwah, NJ: Erlbaum.

Day, S., Markiewitcz, D., Doyle, A.B., & Ducharme, J. (2001, April). *Attachment to mother, father, and best friend as predictors to the quality of adolescent romantic relationships.* Paper presented at the meeting of the Society for Research in Child Development, Minneapolis.

De Bellis, M.D., Clark, D.B., Beers, S.R., Soloff, P.H., Boring, A.M., Hall, J., Kersh, A., & Keshaan, M.S. (2000). Hippocampal volume in adolescent-onset alcohol use disorders. *American Journal of Psychiatry, 157,* 737–744.

De Bellis, M.D., Keshavan, M.S., Beers, S.R., Hall, J., Frustaci, K., Masalehdan, A., & Boring, N.J. (2001). Sex differences in brain maturation during childhood and adolescence. *Cerebral Cortex, 11,* 552–557.

de Munich Keizer, S.M., & Mul, D. (2001). Trends in pubertal development in Europe. *Human Reproduction Update, 7,* 287–291.

deCharms, R. (1984). Motivation enhancement in educational settings. In R. Ames & C. Ames (Eds.), *Research on motivation in education* (Vol. 1). Orlando: Academic Press.

Deci, E., & Ryan, R. (1994). Promoting self-determined education. *Scandinavian Journal of Educational Research, 38,* 3–14.

Dedikdes, C., & Brewer, M.B. (Eds.). (2001). *Individual self, relational self, and collective self.* Philadelphia: Psychology Press.

DeGarmo, D.S., Forgatch, M.S., & Martinez, C.R. (1998). *Parenting of divorced mothers as a link between social status and boys' academic outcomes: Unpacking the effects of SES.* Unpublished manuscript, Oregon Social Learning Center, University of Oregon, Eugene.

Degirmencioglu, S.M., Saltz, E., & Ager, J.W. (1995, March). *Early dating and "going steady": A retrospective and prospective look.* Paper presented at the meeting of the Society for Research in Child Development, Indianapolis.

DeLamater, J., & MacCorquodale, P. (1979). *Premarital sexuality.* Madison: University of Wisconsin Press.

Dempster, F.N. (1981). Memory span: Sources of individual and developmental differences. *Psychological Bulletin, 89,* 63–100.

Denham, S.A., Cook, M., & Zoller, D. (1992). Maternal emotional responsiveness to toddlers' social-emotional functioning. *Journal of Child Psychology and Psychiatry, 34,* 715–728.

Denmark, F.L., & Paludi, M.A. (Eds.). (1993). *Handbook on the psychology of women.* Westport, CT: Greenwood Press.

Denmark, F.L., Rabinowitz, V.C., & Sechzer, J.A. (2000). *Engendering psychology.* Boston: Allyn & Bacon.

Denny, C.B. (2001). Stimulant effects in attention deficit hyperactivity disorder. *Journal of Clinical Child Psychology, 30,* 98–109.

DeVillar, R.A., & Faltis, C.J. (1991). *Computers and cultural diversity: Restructuring for school success.* Albany: State University of New York Press.

Dewey, J. (1933). *How we think.* Lexington, MA: D.C. Heath.

Diaz, C. (2003). *Multicultural education in the 21st century.* Boston: Allyn & Bacon.

Dickerscheid, J.D., Schwarz, P.M., Noir, S., & El-Taliawy, T. (1988). Gender concept development of preschool-aged children in the United States and Egypt. *Sex Roles, 18,* 669–677.

Dickinson, G.E. (1975). Dating behavior of black and white adolescents before and after desegregation. *Journal of Marriage and the Family, 37,* 602–608.

Dielman, T.E., Schulenberg, J., Leech, S., & Shope, J.T. (1992, March). *Reduction of susceptibility to peer pressure and alcohol use/misuse through a school-based prevention program.* Paper presented at the meeting of the Society for Research on Adolescence, Washington, DC.

Dielman, T.E., Shope, J.T., & Butchart, A.T. (1990, March). *Peer, family, and intrapersonal predictors of adolescent alcohol use and misuse.* Paper presented at the meeting of the Society for Research in Adolescence, Atlanta.

Dishion, T., (2002, April). *Understanding and preventing adolescent drug abuse.* Paper presented at the meeting of the Society for Research on Adolescence, New Orleans.

Dishion, T.J., & Spracklen, K.M. (1996, March). *Childhood peer rejection in the development of adolescent substance abuse.* Paper presented at the meeting of the Society for Research on Adolescence, Boston.

Dittus, P.J., & Jaccard, J. (2000). *The relationship of adolescent perceptions of maternal disapproval of sex and of the mother-adolescent relationship to sexual outcomes.* Unpublished manuscript, Department of Psychology, State University of New York at Albany.

Dix, T. (1991). The affective organization of parenting: Adaptive and maladaptive processes. *Psychological Bulletin, 110,* 3–25.

Dodge, K.A. (1983). Behavioral antecedents of peer social status. *Child Development, 54,* 1386–1399.

Domino, G. (1992). Acculturation of Hispanics. In S.B. Knouse, P. Rosenfeld, & A. Culbertson (Eds.), *Hispanics in the workplace.* Newbury Park, CA: Sage.

Dorn, L.D., Williamson, D.E., & Ryan, N.D. (2002, April). *Maturational hormone differences in adolescents with depression and risk for depression.* Paper presented at the meeting of the Society for Research on Adolescence, New Orleans.

Dornbusch, S.M., Petersen, A.C., & Hetherington, E.M. (1991). Projecting the future of research on adolescence. *Journal of Research on Adolescence, 1,* 7–17.

Douvan, E., & Adelson, J. (1966). *The adolescent experience.* New York: Wiley.

Dowda, M., Ainsworth, B.E., Addy, C.L., Saunders, R., & Riner, W. (2001). Environmental influences, physical activity, and weight status in 8- to 16-year-olds. *Archives of Pediatric and Adolescent Medicine, 155,* 711–717.

Dowdy, B.B., & Kliewer, W. (1996, March). *Dating, parent-adolescent conflict, and autonomy.* Paper presented at the meeting of the Society for Research on Adolescence, Boston.

Downey, G., & Bonica, C.A. (1997, April). *Characteristics of early adolescent dating relationships.* Paper presented at the meeting of the Society for Research in Child Development, Washington, DC.

Doyle, J.A., & Paludi, M.A. (1998). *Sex and gender* (4th ed.). Burr Ridge, IL: McGraw-Hill.

Draguns, J.G. (1990). Applications of cross-cultural psychology in the field of mental health. In R.W. Brislin (Ed.), *Applied cross-cultural psychology.* Newbury Park, CA: Sage.

Drotar, D. (2000). *Promoting adherence to medical treatment in chronic childhood illness.* Mahwah, NJ: Erlbaum.

Dryfoos, J.G. (1990). *Adolescents at risk: Prevalence and prevention.* New York: Oxford University Press.

Dryfoos, J.G. (1995). Full service schools: Revolution or fad? *Journal of Research on Adolescence, 5,* 147–172.

Duck, S.W. (1975). Personality similarity and friendship choices by adolescents. *European Journal of Social Psychology, 5,* 351–365.

Duckett, E., & Richards, M.H. (1996, March). *Fathers' time in child care and the father-child relationship.* Paper presented at the meeting of the Society for Research on Adolescence, Boston.

Duckett, R.H. (1997, July). *Strengthening families/building communities.* Paper presented at the conference on Working with America's Youth, Pittsburgh.

Duncan, G.J. (2000). Neighborhoods and adolescent development: How can we determine the links? In A. Booth & A.C. Crouter (Eds.), *Does it take a village?* Mahwah, NJ: Erlbaum.

Duncan, G.J., Brooks-Gunn, J., & Klebanov, P.K. (1994). Economic deprivation and early childhood development. *Child Development, 65,* 296–318.

Dunn, J., & Brown, J. (1994). Affect expression in the family, children's understanding of emotions, and their interactions with others. *Merrill-Palmer Quarterly, 40,* 120–137.

Dunn, J., Davies, L.C., O'Connor, T.G., & Sturgess, W. (2001). Family lives and friendships: The perspectives of children in step-, single-parent, and nonstep families. *Journal of Family Psychology, 15,* 272–287.

Dunphy, D.C. (1963). The social structure of urban adolescent peer groups. *Society, 26,* 230–246.

Durbin, D.L., Darling, N., Steinberg, L., & Brown, B.B. (1993). Parenting style and peer group membership among European-American adolescents. *Journal of Research on Early Adolescence, 3,* 87–100.

Durkin, K., & Hutchins, G. (1984). Challenging traditional sex role stereotypes via career education broadcasts: The reactions of young secondary school pupils. *Journal of Educational Television, 10,* 25–33.

Dweck, C. (1996). Social motivation: Goals and social-cognitive processes. In J. Juvonen & K.R. Wentzel (Eds.), *Social motivation.* New York: Cambridge University Press.

Dweck, C., & Elliott, E. (1983). Achievement motivation. In P. Mussen (Ed.), *Handbook of child psychology* (4th ed., Vol. 4). New York: Wiley.

Dweck, C., & Leggett, E. (1988). A social cognitive approach to motivation and personality. *Psychological Review, 95,* 256–273.

Dworkin, J., Larson, R., Hansen, D., Jones, J., & Midle, T. (2001, April). *Adolescents' accounts of their growth experiences in youth activities.* Paper presented at the meeting of the Society for Research in Child Development, Minneapolis.

E

Eagly, A.H. (1995). The science and politics of comparing men and women. *American Psychologist, 50,* 145–158.

Eagly, A.H. (1997, August). *Social roles as an origin theory for sex-related differences.* Paper presented at the meeting of the American Psychological Association, Chicago.

Eagly, A.H. (2000). Gender roles. In A. Kazdin (Ed.), *Encyclopedia of psychology.* Washington, DC, and New York: American Psychological Association and Oxford University Press.

Eagly, A. H. (2001). Social role theory of sex differences and similarities. In J. Worrel (Ed.), *Encyclopedia of women and gender.* San Diego: Academic Press.

Eagly, A.H., & Crowley, M. (1986). Gender and helping behavior: A meta-analytic review of the social psychological literature. *Psychological Bulletin, 100,* 283–308.

Easterbrooks, M.A. & Giesecker, G. (2002, April). *Attachments to mothers, fathers , and peers: Connections with emotion regulation and working models of self and world.* Paper presented at the meeting of the Society for Research on Adolescence, New Orleans.

Eberly, M.B., & Montemayor, R. (1996, March). *Adolescent prosocial behavior toward mothers and fathers: A reflection of parent-adolescent relationships.* Paper presented at the meeting of the Society for Research on Adolescence, Boston.

Eccles, J.S. (1987). Gender roles and achievement patterns: An expectancy value perspective. In J.M. Reinisch, L.A. Rosenblum, & S.A. Sanders (Eds.), *Masculinity/femininity.* New York: Oxford University Press.

Eccles, J.S. (1993, March). *Psychological and social barriers to women's participation in mathematics and science.* Paper presented at the biennial meeting of the American Educational Research Association, Atlanta.

Eccles, J.S. (2002, April). *Ethnicity as a context for development.* Paper presented at the meeting of the Society for Research on Adolescence, New Orleans.

Eccles, J.S., & Harold, R.D. (1993). Parent-school involvement during the adolescent years. In R. Takanishi (Ed.), *Adolescence in the 1990s.* New York: Columbia University Press.

Eccles, J.S., Lord, S., & Buchanan, C.M. (1996). School transitions in early adolescence: What are we doing to our young people? In J.A. Graber, J. Brooks-Gunn, & A.C. Petersen (Eds.), *Transitions in adolescence.* Mahwah, NJ: Erlbaum.

Eccles, J.S., Midgley, C., Wigfield, A., Buchanan, C.M., Reuman, D., Flanagan, C., & Mac Iver, D. (1993). Development during adolescence: The impact of stage-environment fit on young adolescents' experiences in schools and families. *American Psychologist, 48,* 90–101.

Eccles, J.S., & Wigfield, A. (2000). Social patterns, achievements, and problems. In A. Kazdin (Ed.), *Encyclopedia of psychology.* Washington, DC, & New York: American Psychological Association and Oxford University Press.

Eccles, J.S., Wigfield, A., & Schiefele, U. (1998). Motivation to succeed. In W. Damon (Ed.), *Handbook of child psychology* (5th ed., Vol. 3). New York: Wiley.

Edelbrock, C.S. (1989, April). *Self-reported internalizing and externalizing problems in a community sample of adolescents.* Paper presented at the meeting of the Society for Research in Child Development, Kansas City.

Edelman, M.W. (1996). *The state of America's children.* Washington, DC: Children's Defense Fund.

Edelman, M.W. (1997, April). *Children, families, and social policy.* Paper presented at the meeting of the Society for Research in Child Development, Washington, DC.

Educational Testing Service. (1992, February). *Cross-national comparisons of 9–13 year olds' science and math achievement.* Princeton, NJ: Educational Testing Service.

Egeland, B., Pianta, R., & Ogawa, J. (1996). Early behavior problems: Pathways to mental disorders in adolescence. *Development and Psychopathology, 8,* 735–749.

Egeland, B., Warren, S., & Aguilar, B. (2001, April). *Perspectives on the development of psychopathology from the Minnesota Longitudinal Study.* Paper presented at the meeting of the Society for Research in Child Development, Minneapolis.

Eisenberg, N., Carolo, G., Murphy, B., & Van Court, P. (1995). Prosocial development in late adolescence: A longitudinal study. *Child Development, 66,* 1179–1197.

Eisenberg, N., & Fabes, R.A. (1994). Emotional regulation and the development of social competence. In M. Clark (Ed.), *Review of personality and social psychology.* Newbury Park, CA: Sage.

Eisenberg, N., & Fabes, R.A. (1998). Prosocial development. In N. Eisenberg (Ed.), *Handbook of child psychology* (5th ed., Vol. 3). New York: Wiley.

Eisenberg, N., Martin, C.L., & Fabes, R.A. (1996). Gender development and gender effects. In D.C. Berliner & R.C. Calfee (Eds.), *Handbook of educational psychology.* New York: Macmillan.

Eisenberg, N., & Murphy, B. (1995). Parenting and children's moral development. In M.H. Bornstein (Ed.), *Children and parenting* (Vol. 4). Hillsdale, NJ: Erlbaum.

Eisenberg, N., & Valiente, C. (2002). Parenting and children's prosocial and moral development. In M.H. Bornstein (Ed.), *Handbook of parenting.* Mahwah, NJ: Erlbaum.

Elder, G.H. (1975). Adolescence in the life cycle. In S.E. Dragastin & G.H. Elder (Eds.), *Adolescence in the life cycle: Psychological change and social context.* New York: Wiley.

Elder, G.H. (2000). Life course theory. In A. Kazdin (Ed.), *Encyclopedia of psychology.* Washington, DC, and New York: American Psychological Association and Oxford University Press.

Elder, G.H., Jr. (1998). The life course and human development. In W. Damon (Ed.), *Handbook of child psychology* (5th ed., Vol. 1). New York: Wiley.

Elkind, D. (1961). Quantity conceptions in junior and senior high school students. *Child Development, 32,* 551–560.

Elkind, D. (1976). *Child development and education: A Piagetian perspective.* New York: Oxford University Press.

Elkind, D. (1981). *The hurried child.* Reading, MA: Addison-Wesley.

Elkind, D. (1985). Reply to D. Lapsley and M. Murphy's *Developmental Review* paper. *Developmental Review, 5,* 218–226.

Elliot, A.J., & McGregor, H.A. (2001). A 2 × 2 achievement goal framework. *Journal of Personality and Social Psychology, 80,* 501–519.

Elliot, A.J., & Thrash, T.M. (2001). Achievement goals and the hierarchical model of achievement motivation. *Educational Psychology Review, 13,* 139–156.

Ellis, L., & Ames, M.A. (1987). Neurohormonal functioning and sexual orientation: A theory of homosexuality-heterosexuality. *Psychological Bulletin, 101,* 233–258.

Elmes, D.G., Kantowitz, B.H., & Roedinger, H.L. (2003). *Research methods in psychology* (7th Ed.). Belmont, CA: Wadsworth.

Embretson, S.E., & McCollam, K.M.S. (2000). Psychometric approaches to understanding and measuring intelligence. In R.J. Sternberg (Ed.), *Handbook of intelligence.* New York: Cambridge University Press.

Emery, R.E. (1999). *Renegotiating family relationships* (2nd ed.). New York: Guilford Press.

Emery, R.E., & Tuer, M. (1993). Parenting and the marital relationship. In T. Luster & L. Okagaki (Eds.), *Parenting: An ecological perspective.* Hillsdale, NJ: Erlbaum.

Emmer, E.T., Evertson, C.M., & Worsham, M.E. (2003). *Classroom management for secondary teachers* (6th ed.). Boston: Allyn & Bacon.

Ennett, S., & Bauman, K. (1996). Adolescent social networks: School, demographic, and longitudinal considerations. *Journal of Adolescent Research, 11,* 194–215.

Enright, R.D., Levy, V.M., Harris, D., & Lapsley, D.K. (1987). Do economic conditions influence how theorists view adolescents? *Journal of Youth and Adolescence, 16,* 541–559.

Enright, R.D., Santos, M.J.D., & Al-Mabuk, R. (1989). The adolescent as forgiver. *Journal of Adolescence, 12,* 95–110.

Epstein, J.L. (1990). School and family connections: Theory, research, and implications for integrating sociologies of education and family. In D.G. Unger & M.B. Sussman (Eds.), *Families in community settings: Interdisciplinary responses.* New York: Haworth Press.

Epstein, J.L. (1996). Perspectives and previews on research and policy for school, family, and community partnerships. In A. Booth & J.F. Dunn (Eds.), *Family-school links.* Mahwah, NJ: Erlbaum.

Epstein, J.L., & Sanders, M.G. (2002). Family, school, and community partnerships. In M. Bornstein (Ed.), *Handbook of parenting* (2nd ed., Vol. 5). Mahwah, NJ: Erlbaum.

Erickson, J.B. (1982). *A profile of community youth organization members, 1980.* Boys Town, NE: Boys Town Center for the Study of Youth Development.

Erickson, J.B. (1996). *Directory of American youth organizations* (2nd rev. ed.). Boys Town, NE: Boys Town, Communications and Public Services Division.

Erikson, E.H. (1950). *Childhood and society.* New York: W.W. Norton.

Erikson, E.H. (1962). *Young man Luther.* New York: W.W. Norton.

Erikson, E.H. (1968). *Identity: Youth and crisis.* New York: W.W. Norton.

Erikson, E.H. (1969). *Gandhi's truth.* New York: W.W. Norton.

Erikson, E.H. (1970). Reflections on the dissent of contemporary youth. *International Journal of Psychoanalysis, 51,* 11–22.

Erlick, A.C., & Starry, A.R. (1973, June). *Sources of information for career decisions.* Report of Poll No. 98, Purdue Opinion Panel.

Escobedo, L.G., Marcus, S.E., Holtzman, D., & Giovino, G.A. (1993). Sports participation, age at smoking initiation, and risk of smoking among U.S. high school students. *Journal of the American Medical Association, 269,* 1391–1395.

Ethier, K., & Deaux, K. (1990). Hispanics in ivy: Assessing identity and perceived threat. *Sex Roles, 20,* 59–70.

Evans, B.J., & Whitfield, J.R. (Eds.). (1988). *Black males in the United States: An annotated bibliography from 1967 to 1987.* Washington, DC: American Psychological Association.

Evans, S.W., Pelham, W.E., Smith, B.H., Bukstein, O., Gnagy, E.M., Greiner, A.R., Altenderfer, L., & Baron-Myak, C. (2001). Dose-response effects of methylphenidate on ecologically valid measures of academic performance and classroom behavior in adolescents with ADHD. *Experimental and Clinical Psychopharmacology, 9,* 163–175.

Evertson, C.M., Emmer, E.T., & Worsham, M.E. (2003). *Classroom management for elementary teachers* (6th ed.). Boston: Allyn & Bacon.

Fang, S., & Bryant, C.M. (2000, April). *Influence of parents on young adults' romantic relationships: A prospective analysis of parents' impact on attitudes and behavior.* Paper presented at the meeting of the Society for Research on Adolescence, Chicago.

Farrington, D.P. (2000). Delinquency. In A. Kazdin (Ed.), *Encyclopedia of psychology.* Washington, DC, and New York: American Psychological Association and Oxford University Press.

Fasick, F.A. (1994). On the "invention" of adolescence. *Journal of Early Adolescence, 14,* 6–23.

Feden, P.D., & Vogel, R.M. (2003). *Appyling cognitive science to promote student learning.* New York: McGraw-Hill.

Federman, J. (Ed.). (1997). *National television violence study* (Vol. 2). Santa Barbara: University of California.

Feeney, S. (1980). *Schools for young adolescents: Adapting the early childhood model.* Carrboro, NC: Center for Early Adolescence.

Fehring, R.J., Cheever, K.H., German, K., & Philpot, C. (1998). Religiosity and sexual activity among older adolescents. *Journal of Religion and Health, 37,* 229–239.

Feinberg, M., & Hetherington, E.M. (2001). Differential parenting as a within-family variable. *Journal of Family Psychology, 15,* 22–37.

Feiring, C. (1996). Concepts of romance in 15-year-old adolescents. *Journal of Research on Adolescence, 6,* 181–200.

Feiring, C. (in press). Gender identity and the development of romantic relationships in adolescence. In W. Furman, B.B. Brown, & C. Feiring (Eds.), *Heartaches and heartthrobs: Adolescent romantic relationships.* Cambridge, UK: Cambridge University Press.

Feist, J., & Brannon, L. (1989). *An introduction to behavior and health.* Belmont, CA: Wadsworth.

Feldman, S.S. (1999). Unpublished review of J.W. Santrock's *Adolescence,* 8th ed. (New York: McGraw-Hill).

Feldman, S.S., & Elliott, G.R. (1990). Progress and promise of research on normal adolescent development. In S.S. Feldman & G. Elliott (Eds.), *At the threshold: The developing adolescent.* Cambridge, MA: Harvard University Press.

Feldman, S.S., & Rosenthal, D.A. (1990). The acculturation of autonomy expectations in Chinese high schoolers residing in two Western nations. *International Journal of Psychology, 25,* 259–281.

Feldman, S.S., & Rosenthal, D.A. (1999). *Factors influencing parents' and adolescents' evaluations of parents as sex communicators.* Unpublished manuscript, Stanford Center on Adolescence, Stanford University.

Feldman, S.S., Turner, R., & Araujo, K. (1999). Interpersonal context as an influence on sexual timetables of youths: Gender and ethnic effects. *Journal of Research on Adolescence, 9,* 25–52.

Fenzel, L.M. (1994, February). *A prospective study of the effects of chronic strains on early adolescent self-worth and school adjustment.* Paper presented at the meeting of the Society for Research on Adolescence, San Diego.

Fenzel, L.M., Blyth, D.A., & Simmons, R.G. (1991). School transitions, secondary. In R.M. Lerner, A.C. Petersen, & J. Brooks-Gunn (Eds.), *Encyclopedia of adolescence* (Vol. 2). New York: Garland.

Ferber, T. (2002, April). *Social policy recommendations for adolescence in the 21st century.* Paper presented at the meeting of the Society for Research on Adolescence, New Orleans.

Ferguson, A. (1999, July 12). Inside the crazy culture of kids' sports. *Time,* pp. 52–60.

Ferrari, M. (Ed.) (2002). *The pursuit of excellence through education.* Mahwah, NJ: Erlbaum.

Field, A.E., Cambargo, C.A., Taylor, C.B., Berkey, C.S., Roberts, S.B., & Colditz, G.A. (2001). Peer, parent, and media influences on the development of weight concerns and frequent dieting among preadolescent and adolescent girls and boys. *Pediatrics, 107,* 54–60.

Field, T., Diego, M., & Sanders, C.E. (2001). Exercise is positively related to adolescents' relationships and academics. *Adolescence, 36,* 105–110.

Fine, G.A., Mortimer, J.T., & Roberts, D.F. (1990). Leisure, work, and the mass media. In S.S. Feldman & G.R. Elliott (Eds.), *At the threshold: The developing adolescent.* Cambridge, MA: Harvard University Press.

Fine, M. (1988). Sexuality, schooling, and adolescent females: The missing discourse of desire. *Harvard Educational Review, 58(1),* 29–53.

Firpo-Triplett, R. (1997, July). *Is it flirting or sexual harassment?* Paper presented at the conference on Working with America's Youth, Pittsburgh.

Fish, K.D., & Biller, H.B. (1973). Perceived childhood paternal relationships and college females' personal adjustment. *Adolescence, 8,* 415–420.

Fisher, D. (1990, March). *Effects of attachment on adolescents' friendships.* Paper presented at the meeting of the Society for Research in Adolescence, Atlanta.

Fisher, T.D. (1987). Family communication and the sexual behavior and attitudes of college students. *Journal of Youth and Adolescence, 16,* 481–495.

Fiske, S.T., Bersoff, D.N., Borgida, E., Deaux, K., & Heilman, M.E. (1991). Social science research on trial: Use of sex stereotyping research in *Price Waterhouse v. Hopkins. American Psychologist, 23,* 399–427.

Fitzgerald, L. (2000). Sexual harassment. In A. Kazdin (Ed.), *Encyclopedia of psychology.* Washington, DC, and New York: American Psychological Association and Oxford University Press.

Flanagan, A.S. (1996, March). *Romantic behavior of sexually victimized and nonvictimized women.* Paper presented at the meeting of the Society for Research on Adolescence, Boston.

Flanagan, C. (1997, April). *Youth, family values, and civil society.* Paper presented at the meeting of the Society for Research in Child Development, Washington, DC.

Flanagan, C. (2002, April). *Inclusion and reciprocity: Developmental sources of social trust and civic hope.* Paper presented at the meeting of the Society for Research on Adolescence, New Orleans.

Flanagan, C.A., & Eccles, J.S. (1993). Changes in parents' work status and adolescents' adjustment at school. *Child Development, 64,* 246–257.

Flanagan, C.A., Bowes, J., Jonsson, B., Csapo, B., & Sheblanova, E. (1998). Ties that bind: Correlates of male and female adolescents' civic commitments in seven countries. *Journal of Social Issues, 54,* 457–476.

Flannery, D.J., Rowe, D.C., & Gulley, B.L. (1993). Impact of pubertal status, timing, and age on adolescent sexual experience and delinquency. *Journal of Adolescent Research, 8,* 21–40.

Flavell, J.H. (1999). Cognitive development: Children's knowledge about the mind. *Annual Review of Psychology, Vol. 50.* Palo Alto, CA: Annual Reviews.

Flavell, J.H., & Miller, P.H. (1998). Social cognition. In D. Kuhn & R.S. Siegel (Eds.), *Handbook of child psychology* (5th ed., Vol. 3). New York: Wiley.

Flavell, J.H., Miller, P.H., & Miller, S.A. (2002). *Cognitive development* (4th ed.). Upper Saddle River, NJ: Prentice-Hall.

Fleming, J.E., Boyle, M., & Offord, D.R. (1993). The outcome of adolescent depression in the Ontario child health study follow-up. *Journal of the American Academy of Child and Adolescent Psychiatry, 32,* 28–29.

Flowers, P., & Buston, K. (2001). "I was terrified of being different," Exploring gay men's accounts of growing up in a heterosexist society. *Journal of Adolescence, 24,* 51–66.

Ford, C.A., Bearman, P.S., & Moody, J. (1999). Foregone health care among adolescents. *Journal of the American Medical Association, 282* (No. 23), 2227–2234.

Ford, K., Sohn, W., & Lepkowski, J. (2001). Characteristics of adolescents' sexual partners and their association with use of condoms and other contraceptive methods. *Family Planning Perspectives, 33,* 100–105, 132.

Forrest, J.D. (1990). Cultural influences on adolescents' reproductive behavior. In J. Bancroft & J.M. Reinisch (Eds.), *Adolescence and puberty.* New York: Oxford University Press.

Forrest, J.D., & Singh, S. (1990). The sexual and reproductive behavior of American women, 1982–1988. *Family Planning Perspectives, 22,* 206–214.

Fouad, N.A. (1995). Career behavior of Hispanics: Assessment and career intervention. In F.T.L. Leong (Ed.), *Career development and vocational behavior of racial and ethnic minorities.* Hillsdale, NJ: Erlbaum.

Fox, B.A. (1993). *The Human Tutorial Dialogue Project.* Mahwah, NJ: Erlbaum.

Francis, J., Fraser, G., & Marcia, J.E. (1989). *Cognitive and experimental factors in moratorium-achievement (MAMA) cycles.* Unpublished manuscript, Department of Psychology, Simon Fraser University, Burnaby, British Columbia.

Franke, T.M. (2000, winter). The role of attachment as a protective factor in adolescent violent behavior. *Adolescent & Family Health, 1,* 29–39.

Freeman, D. (1983). *Margaret Mead and Samoa.* Cambridge, MA: Harvard University Press.

Freud, A. (1966). Instinctual anxiety during puberty. In *The writings of Anna Freud: The ego and the mechanisms of defense.* New York: International Universities Press.

Freud, A., & Dann, S. (1951). Instinctual anxiety during puberty. In A. Freud, *The ego and its mechanisms of defense.* New York: International Universities Press.

Freud, S. (1917/1958). *A general introduction to psychoanalysis.* New York: Washington Square Press.

Friend, M., & Bursuck, W.D. (2002). *Including students with special needs* (3rd Ed.). Boston: Allyn & Bacon.

Friesch, R.E. (1984). Body fat, puberty and fertility, *Biological Review, 59,* 161–188.

Fukuda, K., & Ishihara, K. (2001). Age-related changes in sleeping patterns in adolescence. *Psychiatry and Clinical Neuroscience, 55,* 231–232.

Fuligni, A.J., & Yoshikawa, H. (2003). Socioeconomic resources, poverty, and child development among immigrant families. In M.H. Bornstein & R.H. Bradley (Eds.). *Socioeconomic status, parenting, and child development.* Mahwah, NJ: Erlbaum.

Furman, W., Brown, B.B., & Feiring, C. (Eds.) (1999). *Contemporary perspectives on romantic relationships.* New York: Cambridge University Press.

Furman, W., & Buhrmester, D. (1992). Age and sex differences in perceptions of networks of personal relationships. *Child Development, 63,* 103–115.

Furman, W., & Lanthier, R. (2002). Parenting siblings. In M. Bornstein (Ed.), Handbook *of parenting* (2nd ed., Vol. 1). Mahwah, NJ: Erlbaum.

Furman, W., & Wehner, E.A. (1997). Adolescent romantic relationships: A developmental perspective. In S. Shulman & W. A. Collins (Eds.), *New directions for child development: Adolescent romantic relationships.* San Francisco: Jossey-Bass.

Furman, W., & Wehner, E.A. (1998). Adolescent romantic relationships: A developmental perspective. In S. Shulman & W.A. Collins (Eds.), *New directions for child development: Adolescent romantic relationships.* San Francisco: Jossey-Bass.

Furstenberg, E.F. & Harris, K.Y. (1992). When fathers matter/where fathers matter. In R. Lerman and T. Oooms (Eds.), *Young unwed fathers.* Philadelphia: Temple University Press.

Furstenberg, F.F., Jr., & Nord, C.W. (1987). Parenting apart: Patterns of childrearing after marital disruption. *Journal of Marriage and the Family, 47,* 893–904.

Gadpaille, W.J. (1996). *Adolescent suicide.* Washington, DC: American Psychological Association.

Galambos, N.L., & Maggs, J.L. (1991). Out-of-school care of young adolescents and self-reported behavior. *Developmental Psychology, 27,* 644–655.

Galambos, N.L., Petersen, A.C., Richards, M., & Gitleson, I.B. (1985). The Attitudes toward Women Scale for Adolescents (AWSA): A Study of reliability and validity. *Sex Roles, 13,* 343–356.

Galambos, N.L., Sears, H.A., Almeida, D.M., & Kolaric, G.C. (1995). Parents' work overload and problem behavior in young adolescents. *Journal of Research on Adolescence, 5,* 201–224.

Galanter, M. (1999). *Cults.* New York: Oxford University Press.

Galanter, M. (2000). Cults. In A. Kazdin (Ed.), *Encyclopedia of psychology.* Washington, DC, and New York: American Psychological Association and Oxford University Press.

Gall, M.D., Borg, W.R., & Gall, J.P. (2003). *Educational research* (7th Ed.). Boston: Allyn & Bacon.

Gallup, G.W., & Bezilla, R. (1992). *The religious life of young Americans.* Princeton, NJ: Gallup Institute.

Galotti, K.M., & Kozberg, S.F. (1996). Adolescents' experience of a life-framing decision. *Journal of Youth and Adolescence, 25,* 3–16.

Galotti, K.M., Kozberg, S.F., & Farmer, M.C. (1990, March). *Gender and developmental differences in adolescents' conceptions of moral reasoning.* Paper presented at the meeting of the Society for Research in Adolescence, Atlanta.

Garbarino, J. (1999). *Lost boys: Why our sons turn violent and how we can save them.* New York: Free Press.

Garbarino, J. (2001). Violent children. *Archives of Pediatrics & Adolescent Medicine, 155,* 1–2.

Garbarino, J., & Asp, C.E. (1981). *Successful schools and competent students*. Lexington, MA: Lexington Books.

Garber, J., Kriss, M.R., Koch, M., & Lindholm, L. (1988). Recurrent depression in adolescents: A follow-up study. *Journal of the American Academy of Child and Adolescent Psychiatry, 27*, 49–54.

Gardner, H. (1983). *Frames of mind*. New York: Basic Books.

Gardner, H. (1993). *Multiple intelligences*. New York: Basic Books.

Gardner, H. (2002). Learning from extraordinary minds. In M. Ferrari (Ed.), *The pursuit of excellence through education*. Mahwah, NJ: Erlbaum.

Garmezy, N. (1993). Children in poverty: Resilience despite risk. *Psychiatry, 56*, 127–136.

Garmon, L., Basinger, K.S., & Gibbs, J.C. (1995, March). *Gender differences in the expression of moral judgment*. Paper presented at the meeting of the Society for Research in Child Development, Indianapolis.

Garrett, P., Ng'andu, N., & Ferron, J. (1994). Poverty experiences of young children and the quality of their home environments. *Child Development, 65*, 331–345.

Gates, G.J., & Sonnenstein, F.L. (2000). Heterosexual genital activity among adolescent males: 1988 and 1995. *Family Planning Perspectives, 32*, 295–297, 304.

Gates, J.L. (2001, April). *Women's career choices in math and science-related fields*. Paper presented at the meeting of the Society for Research in Child Development, Minneapolis.

Gauze, C.M. (1994, February). *Talking to Mom about friendship: What do mothers know?* Paper presented at the meeting of the Society for Research on Adolescence, San Diego.

Ge, X., & Brody, G.H. (2002, April). *The role of puberty, neighborhood, and life events in the development of internalizing problems*. Paper presented at the meeting of the Society for Research on Adolescence, New Orleans.

Gecas, V., & Seff, M. (1990). Families and adolescents: A review of the 1980s. *Journal of Marriage and the Family, 52*, 941–958.

Gelman, R., & Williams, E.M. (1998). Enabling constraints for cognitive development and learning. In W. Damon (Ed.), *Handbook of child psychology* (5th ed., Vol. 4). New York: Wiley.

George, C., Main, M., & Kaplan, N. (1984). *Attachment interview with adults*. Unpublished manuscript, University of California, Berkeley.

George, C.M. (1996, March). *Gene-environment interactions: Testing the bioecological model during adolescence*. Paper presented at the meeting of the Society for Research on Adolescence, Boston.

Gibbs, J.T. (1989). Black American adolescents. In J.T. Gibbs & L.N. Huang (Eds.), *Children of color*. San Francisco: Jossey-Bass.

Gibbs, J.T., & Huang, L.N. (1989). A conceptual framework for assessing and treating minority youth. In J.T. Gibbs & L.N. Huang (Eds.), *Children of color*. San Francisco: Jossey-Bass.

Gibbs, N. (1990, Fall). The dreams of youth. *Time* (Special Issue), pp. 10–14.

Giedd, J.N. (1998). Normal brain development ages 4–18. In K.R.R. Krishman & P.M. Doraiswamy (Eds.), *Brain imaging in clinical psychiatry*. New York: Marcel Dekker.

Gilligan, C. (1982). *In a different voice*. Cambridge, MA: Harvard University Press.

Gilligan, C. (1990). Teaching Shakespeare's sister. In C. Gilligan, N. Lyons, and T. Hanmer (Eds.), *Making connections: The relational worlds of adolescent girls at Emma Willard School*. Cambridge: Harvard University Press.

Gilligan, C. (1992, May). *Joining the resistance: Girls' development in adolescence*. Paper presented at the symposium on development and vulnerability in close relationships, Montreal, Quebec.

Gilligan, C. (1996). The centrality of relationships in psychological development: A puzzle, some evidence, and a theory. In G.G. Noam & K.W. Fischer (Eds.), *Development and vulnerability in close relationships*. Hillside, NJ: Erlbaum.

Gilligan, C., & Attanucci, J. (1988). Two moral orientations. In C. Gilligan, J.V. Ward, J.M. Taylor, & B. Bardige (Eds.), *Mapping the moral domain*. Cambridge, MA: Harvard University Press.

Gilligan, C., Brown, L.M., & Rogers, A.G. (1990). Psyche embedded: A place for body, relationships, and culture in personality theory. In A.I. Rabin, R.A. Zuker, R.A. Emmons, & S. Frank (Eds.), *Studying persons and lives*. New York: Springer.

Ginorio, A.B., & Huston, M. (2001). *Si! Se Puede! Yes, we can: Latinas in school*. Washington, DC: AAUW.

Ginzberg, E. (1972). Toward a theory of occupational choice: A restatement. *Vocational Guidance Quarterly, 20*, 169–176.

Ginzberg, E., Ginzberg, S.W., Axelrad, S., & Herman, J.L. (1951). *Occupational choice*. New York: Columbia University.

Gipson, J. (1997, March/April). Girls and computer technology: Barrier or key? *Educational Technology*, pp. 41–43.

Girls, Inc. (1991). *It's my party: Girls choose to be substance free*. Indianapolis: Author.

Girls, Inc. (1991). *Truth, trusting, and technology: New research on preventing adolescent pregnancy*. Indianapolis: Author.

Gjerde, P.F. (1986). The interpersonal structure of family interaction settings: Parent-adolescents relations in dyads and triads. *Developmental Psychology, 22*, 297–304.

Gjerde, P.F., Block, J., & Block, J.H. (1991). The preschool family context of 18-year-olds with depressive symptoms: A prospective study. *Journal of Research on Adolescence, 1*, 63–92.

Glass, G.V., & Smith, M.L. (1978, September). *Meta-analysis of research on the relationship of class size and achievement*. San Francisco: Far West Educational Laboratory.

Glassman, M. (2001). Dewey and Vygotsky: Society, experience, and inquiry in educational practice. *Educational Researcher, 30*, 3–14.

Glassman, M.J. (1997, April). *Moral action in the context of social activity*. Paper presented at the meeting of the Society for Research in Child Development, Washington, DC.

Glazer, N. (1997). *We are all multiculturalists now*. Cambridge, MA: Harvard University Press.

Glover, R.W., & Marshall, R. (1993). Improving the school-to-work transition of American adolescents. In R. Takanishi (Ed.), *Adolescence in the 1990s*. New York: Teachers College Record.

Goertz, M.E., Ekstrom, R.B., & Rock, D. (1991). Dropouts, high school: Issues of race and sex. In R.M. Lerner, A.C. Petersen, & J. Brooks-Gunn (Eds.), *Encyclopedia of adolescence* (Vol. 1). New York: Garland.

Gojdamaschko, N. (1999). Vygotsky. In M.A. Runco & S. Pritzker (Eds.), *Encyclopedia of creativity*. San Diego: Academic Press.

Goldman, R. (1964). *Religious thinking from childhood to adolescence*. London: Routledge & Kegan Paul.

Goldscheider, F.C. (1997). Family relationships and life course strategies for the 21st century. In S. Dreman (Ed.), *The family on the threshold of the 21st century*. Mahwah, NJ: Erlbaum.

Goldscheider, F., & Goldscheider, C. (1999). *The changing transition to adulthood: Leaving and returning home*. Thousand Oaks, CA: Sage.

Goldstein, S. (2000). *Cross-cultural explorations*. Boston: Allyn & Bacon.

Goleman, D. (1995). *Emotional intelligence*. New York: Basic Books.

Goleman, D., Kaufman, P., & Ray, M. (1993). *The creative spirit*. New York: Plume.

Gomel, J.N., Tinsley, B.J., & Clark, K. (1995, March). *Family stress and coping during times of economic hardship: A multi-ethnic perspective*. Paper presented at the meeting of the Society for Research in Child Development, Indianapolis.

Goodchilds, J.D., & Zellman, G.L. (1984). Sexual signaling and sexual aggression in adolescent relationships. In N.M. Malamuth & E.D. Donnerstein (Eds.), *Pornography and sexual aggression*. New York: Academic Press.

Goodman, E., & Capitman, J. (2000). Depressive symptoms and cigarette smoking among teens. *Pediatrics, 106*, 748–755.

Goodman, R.A., Mercy, J.A., Loya, F., Rosenberg, M.L., Smith, J.C., Allen, N.H., Vargas, L., & Kolts, R. (1986). Alcohol use and interpersonal violence: Alcohol detected in homicide victims. *American Journal of Public Health, 76*, 144–149.

Goosens, L. (1995). Identity status development and students' perception of the university environment: A cohort-sequential study. In A. Oosterwegel & R. Wicklund (Eds.), *The self in European and North American culture: Development and processes*. Dordrecht: Kluwer.

Gordon-Larson, P., McMurray, R.G., & Popkin, B.M. (2000). Determinants of adolescent physical activity patterns. *Pediatrics, 105*, E83–E84.

Gore, T. (1987). *Raising PG kids in an X-rated society*. Nashville, TN: Abingdon Press.

Gotesdam, K.G, & Agras, W.S. (1995). General population-based epidemiological survey of eating disorders in Norway. *International Journal of Eating Disorders, 18*, 119–126.

Gottfried, A.E., Fleming, J.S., & Gottfried, A.W. (2001). Continuity of academic intrinsic motivation from childhood through late adolescence: A longitudinal study. *Journal of Educational Psychology, 93.*

Gottfried, A.E., Gottfried, A.W., & Bathurst, K. (2002). Maternal and dual-earner employment status and parenting. In M. Bornstein (Ed.), *Handbook of parenting* (2nd ed., Vol. 2). Mahwah, NJ: Erlbaum.

Gottlieb, G. (2000). Nature and nurture theories. In A. Kazdin (Ed.), *Encyclopedia of psychology.* Washington, DC, & New York: American Psychological Association and Oxford University Press.

Gottlieb, G., Wahlsten, D., & Lickliter, R. (1998). The significance of biology for human development: A developmental psychobiological systems view. In W. Damon (Ed.), *Handbook of child psychology* (5th ed., Vol. 1). New York: Wiley.

Gottman, J.M., & Levenson, R.W. (1985). A valid procedure for obtaining self-report of affect in marital interaction. *Journal of Consulting and Clinical Psychology, 53,* 156–160.

Gottman, J.M., & Parker, J.G. (Eds.). (1987). *Conversations with friends.* New York: Cambridge University Press.

Graber, J.A., Britto, P.R., & Brooks-Gunn, J. (1999). What's love got to do with it? Adolescents' and young adults' beliefs about sexual and romantic relationships. In W. Furman, C. Feiring, & B.B. Brown (Eds.), *Contemporary perspectives on adolescent relationships.* New York: Cambridge University Press.

Graber, J.A., & Brooks-Gunn, J. (2001). *Co-occurring eating and depressive problems: An 8-year study of adolescent girls.* Unpublished manuscript, Center for Children and Families, Columbia University.

Graber, J.A., & Brooks-Gunn, J. (in press). Expectations for and precursors of leaving home in young women. In J.A. Graber & J.S. Dubas (Eds.), *Leaving home.* San Francisco: Jossey-Bass.

Graber, J.A., & Brooks-Gunn, J. (in press). In G.M. Wingood & R.J. Diclemente (Eds.), *Women's sexual and reproductive health: Social, psychological, and public health perspectives.* New York: Plenum.

Graber, J.A., Brooks-Gunn, J., & Galen, B.R. (1999). Betwixt and between: Sexuality in the context of adolescent transitions. In R. Jessor (Ed.), *New perspectives on adolescent risk behavior.* New York: Cambridge University Press.

Graber, J.A., Brooks-Gunn, J., & Petersen, A.C. (1996). Adolescent transitions in context. In J.A. Graber, J. Brooks-Gunn, & A.C. Petersen (Eds.), *Transitions through adolescence: Interpersonal domains and contexts.* Mahwah, NJ: Erlbaum.

Graham, J.H., & Beller, A.H. (2002). Non-resident fathers and their children: Child support and visitation from an economic perspective. In C.S. Tamis-LeMonda & N. Cabrera (Eds.), *The handbook of father involvement.* Mahwah, NJ: Erlbaum.

Graham, S. (1986, August). *Can attribution theory tell us something about motivation in blacks?* Paper presented at the meeting of the American Psychological Association, Washington, DC.

Graham, S. (1990). Motivation in Afro-Americans. In G.L. Berry & J.K. Asamen (Eds.), *Black students: Psychosocial issues and academic achievement.* Newbury Park, CA: Sage.

Graham, S. (1992). Most of the subjects were white and middle class. *American Psychologist, 47,* 629–637.

Graham, S. & Taylor, A.Z. (2001). Ethnicity, gender, and the development of achievement values. In A. Wigfield, & J.S. Eccles (Eds.), *Development of achievement motivation.* San Diego: Academic Press.

Graham, S., & Weiner, B. (1996). Theories and principles of motivation. In D.C. Berliner & R.C. Calfee (Eds.), *Handbook of educational psychology.* New York: Macmillan.

Greenberg, B.S. (1988). *Mass media and adolescents: A review of research reported from 1980–1987.* Manuscript prepared for the Carnegie Council on Adolescent Development.

Greenberg, B.S., Stanley, C., Siemicki, M., Heeter, C., Soderman, A., & Linsangan, R. (1986). *Sex content on soaps and prime-time television series most viewed by adolescents.* Project CAST Report /ns/2. East Lansing: Michigan State Department of Telecommunication.

Greenberger, E., & Chu, C. (1996). Perceived family relationships and depressed mood in early adolescence: A comparison of European and Asian Americans. *Developmental Psychology, 32,* 707–716.

Greenberger, E., & Steinberg, L. (1981). *Project for the study of adolescent work: Final report.* Report prepared for the National Institute of Education, U.S. Department of Education, Washington, DC.

Greenberger, E., & Steinberg, L. (1986). *When teenagers work: The psychological social costs of adolescent employment.* New York: Basic Books.

Greene, B. (1988, May). The children's hour. *Esquire Magazine,* pp. 47–49.

Greenfield, P.M. (2000). Culture and development. In A. Kazdin (Ed.), *Encyclopedia of psychology.* Washington, DC, & New York: American Psychological Association and Oxford University Press.

Greenfield, P.M. (2002, April). *The role of cultural values in adolescent peer conflict.* Paper presented at the meeting of the Society for Research on Adolescence, New Orleans.

Greeno, J.G., Collins, A.M., & Resnick, L.B. (1996). Cognition and learning. In D.C. Berliner & R.C. Chafee (Eds.), *Handbook of educational psychology.* New York: Macmillan.

Greenough, W.T. (1997, April 21). Commentary in article, "Politics of biology." *U.S. News & World Report,* p. 79.

Greenough, W.T. (2000). Brain development. In A. Kazdin (Ed.), *Encyclopedia of psychology.* Washington, DC, & New York: American Psychological Association and Oxford University Press.

Greenough, W.T., & Black, J.R. (1992). Induction of brain structure by experience: Substrates for cognitive development. In M.R. Gunnar & C.A. Nelson (Eds.), *Minnesota Symposia on Child Psychology: Vol. 24. Developmental behavioral neuroscience* (pp. 155–200). Hillsdale, NJ: Erlbaum.

Greenough, W.T., Wallace, C.S., Alcantara, A.A., Anderson, B.J., Hawrylak, R.B., Sirevaag, A.M., Weiler, I.J., & Withers, G.S. (1997, August). *The development of the brain.* Paper presented at the meeting of the American Psychological Association, Chicago.

Grigorenko, E.L. (2000). Heritability and intelligence. In R.J. Sternberg (Ed.), *Handbook of intelligence.* New York: Cambridge University Press.

Grimes, B., & Mattimore, K. (1989, April). *The effects of stress and exercise on identity formation in adolescence.* Paper presented at the biennial meeting of the Society for Research in Child Development, Kansas City.

Grizenko, N. (1998). Protective factors in development of psychopathology. In H.S. Friedman (Ed.), *Encyclopedia of mental health* (Vol. 3). San Diego: Academic Press.

Grotevant, H.D. (1996). Unpublished review of J.W. Santrock's *Adolescence,* 7th ed. (Dubuque, IA: Brown & Benchmark).

Grotevant, H.D. (1998). Adolescent development in family contexts. In W. Damon (Ed.), *Handbook of child psychology* (5th ed., Vol. 3). New York: Wiley.

Grotevant, H.D., & Cooper, C.R. (1985). Patterns of interaction in family relationships and the development of identity exploration in adolescence. *Child Development, 56,* 415–428.

Grotevant, H.D., & Cooper, C.R. (1998). Individuality and connectedness in adolescent development: Review and prospects for research on identity, relationships, and context. In E. Skoe & A. von der Lippe (Eds.), *Personality development in adolescence: A cross-national and life-span perspective.* London: Routledge.

Grotevant, H.D., & Durrett, M.E. (1980). Occupational knowledge and career development in adolescence. *Journal of Vocational Behavior, 17,* 171–182.

Grumbach, M.M., & Styne, D.M. (1992). Puberty: Ontogeny, neuroendocrinology, physiology, and disorders. In J.D. Wilson & P.W. Foster (Eds.), Williams textbook of endocrinology. (pp. 1139–1231). Philadelphia: W.B. Saunders.

Guilford, J.P. (1967). *The structure of intellect.* New York: McGraw-Hill.

Gullotta, T.P., Adams, G.R., & Montemayor, R. (Eds.). (1995). *Substance misuse in adolescence.* Newbury Park, CA: Sage.

Gur, R.C., Mozley, L.H., Mozley, P.D., Resnick, S.M., Karp, J.S., Alavi, A., Arnold, S.E., & Gur, R.E. (1995). Sex differences in regional cerebral glucose metabolism during a resting state. *Science, 267,* 528–531.

Gutman, L.M. (2002, April). *The role of stage-environment fit from early adolescence to young adulthood.* Paper presented at the meeting of the Society for Research on Adolescence, New Orleans.

Guttentag, M., & Bray, H. (1976). *Undoing sex stereotypes: Research and resources for educators.* New York: McGraw-Hill.

Guyer, B. (2000). *ADHD.* Boston: Allyn & Bacon.

Haas, A. (1979). *Teenage sexuality: A survey of teenage sexual behavior.* New York: Macmillan.

Hahn, A. (1987, December). Reaching out to America's dropouts: What to do? *Phi Delta Kappan,* pp. 256–263.

Haidt, J.D. (1997, April). *Cultural and class variations in the domain of morality and the morality of conventions.* Paper presented at the meeting of the Society for Research in Child Development, Washington, DC.

Haith, M.M., & Benson, J.B. (1998). Infant cognition. In W. Damon (Ed.), *Handbook of child psychology* (5th ed., Vol. 2). New York: Wiley.

Hall, G.S. (1904). *Adolescence* (Vols. 1 & 2). Englewood Cliffs, NJ: Prentice Hall.

Hall, W. (1998, February 24). I.Q. scores are up, and psychologists wonder why. *Wall Street Journal,* pp. B11–12.

Hallahan, D.P., & Kaufman, J.M. (2003). *Exceptional learners* (9th ed.). Boston: Allyn & Bacon.

Halonen, J. (1995). Demystifying critical thinking. *Teaching of Psychology, 22,* 75–81.

Halonen, J.A., & Santrock, J.W. (1999). *Psychology: Contexts and applications* (3rd ed.). New York: McGraw-Hill.

Halpern, D.F. (1996). *Thinking critically about critical thinking.* Mahwah, NJ: Erlbaum.

Hamburg, D.A. (1997). Meeting the essential requirements for healthy adolescent development in a transforming world. In R. Takanishi & D. Hamburg (Eds.), *Preparing adolescents for the 21st century.* New York: Cambridge University Press.

Hansen, D. (1996, March). *Adolescent employment and psychosocial outcomes: A comparison of two employment contexts.* Paper presented at the meeting of the Society for Research on Adolescence, Boston.

Hardman, M.L., Drew, C.J., & Egan, M.W. (2002). *Human exceptionality* (7th Ed.). Boston: Allyn & Bacon.

Hare, B.R., & Castenell, L.A. (1985). No place to run, no place to hide: Comparative status and future prospects of Black boys. In M.B. Spencer, G.K. Brookins, & W.R. Allen (Eds.), *Beginnings: The social and affective development of Black children.* Hillsdale, NJ: Erlbaum.

Hare-Muston, R., & Marecek, J. (1988). The meaning of difference: Gender theory, postmodernism, and psychology. *American Psychologist, 43,* 455–464.

Harkness, S., & Super, C.M. (1995). Culture and parenting. In M.H. Bornstein (Ed.), *Children and parenting* (Vol. 2). Hillsdale, NJ: Erlbaum.

Harkness, S., & Super, S.M. (2002). Culture and parenting. In M. Bornstein (Ed.), *Handbook of parenting* (2nd ed., Vol. 2). Mahwah, NJ: Erlbaum.

Harper, D.C. (2000). Developmental disorders. In A. Kazdin (Ed.), *Encyclopedia of psychology.* Washington, DC, and New York: American Psychological Association and Oxford University Press.

Harper, M.S., Welsch, D., & Woody, T. (2002, April). *Silencing the self: Depressive symptoms and loss of self in adolescent romantic relationships.* Paper presented at the meeting of the Society for Research on Adolescence, New Orleans.

Harris, J.R. (1998). *The nurture assumption.* New York: Free Press.

Hart, D. (1996). Unpublished review of J.W. Santrock's *Child development,* 8th ed. (Dubuque, IA: Brown & Benchmark).

Hart, D., & Fegley, S. (1995). Prosocial behavior and caring in adolescence: Relations to self-understanding and social judgment. *Child Development, 66,* 1346–1359.

Harter, S. (1986). Processes underlying the construction, maintenance, and enhancement of the self-concept of children. In J. Suls & A. Greenwald (Eds.), *Psychological perspective on the self* (Vol. 3). Hillsdale, NJ: Erlbaum.

Harter, S. (1987). The determinants and mediational role of global self-worth in children. In N. Eisenberg (Ed.), *Contemporary issues in developmental psychology.* New York: Wiley.

Harter, S. (1989a). Causes, correlates, and the functional role of global self-worth: A life-span perspective. In J. Kolligian & R. Sternberg (Eds.), *Perceptions of competence and incompetence across the life span.* New Haven, CT: Yale University Press.

Harter, S. (1989b). *Self-perception profile for adolescents.* Denver: University of Denver, Department of Psychology.

Harter, S. (1990a). Processes underlying adolescent self-concept formation. In R. Montemayor, G.R. Adams, & T.P. Gullotta (Eds.), *From childhood to adolescence: A transitional period?* Newbury Park, CA: Sage.

Harter, S. (1990b). Self and identity development. In S.S. Feldman & G.R. Elliott (Eds.), *At the threshold: The developing adolescent.* Cambridge, MA: Harvard University Press.

Harter, S. (1998). The development of self-representations. In W. Damon (Ed.), *Handbook of child psychology* (5th ed., Vol. 3). New York: Wiley.

Harter, S. (1999). *The construction of the self.* New York: Guilford.

Harter, S., & Lee, L. (1989). *Manifestations of true and false selves in adolescence.* Paper presented at the meeting of the Society for Research in Child Development, Kansas City.

Harter, S., & Marold, D.B. (1992). Psychosocial risk factors contributing to adolescent suicide ideation. In G. Noam & S. Borst (Eds.), *Child and adolescent suicide.* San Francisco: Jossey-Bass.

Harter, S., & Monsour, A. (1992). Developmental analysis of conflict caused by opposing attributes in the adolescent self-portrait. *Developmental Psychology, 28,* 251–260.

Harter, S., Waters, P., & Whitesell, N. (1996, March). *False self behavior and lack of voice among adolescent males and females.* Paper presented at the meeting of the Society for Research on Adolescence, Boston.

Harter, S., & Whitesell, N. (2002, April). *Global and relational features of the fluctuating and stable self among adolescents.* Paper presented at the meeting of the Society for Research on Adolescence, New Orleans.

Hartshorne, H., & May, M.S. (1928–1930). *Moral studies in the nature of character: Studies in deceit* (Vol. 1); *Studies in self-control* (Vol. 2); *Studies in the organization of character* (Vol. 3). New York: Macmillan.

Hartup, W.W. (1983). Peer relations. In P.H. Mussen (Ed.), *Handbook of child psychology* (4th ed., Vol. 4). New York: Wiley.

Hartup, W.W. (1996). The company they keep: Friendships and their developmental significance. *Child Development, 67,* 1–13.

Hartup, W.W. (1999, April). *Peer relations and the growth of the individual child.* Paper presented at the meeting of the Society for Research in Child Development, Albuquerque.

Hartup, W.W., & Collins, A. (2000) Middle childhood: Socialization and social contexts. In A. Kazdin (Ed.), *Encyclopedia of psychology.* Washington, DC, & New York: American Psychological Association and Oxford University Press.

Hauser, S.T., & Bowlds, M.K. (1990). Stress, coping, and adaptation. In S.S. Feldman & G.R. Elliott (Eds.), *At the threshold: The developing adolescent.* Cambridge, MA: Harvard University Press.

Hauser, S.T., Powers, S.I., Noam, G.G., Jacobson, A.M., Weisse, B., & Follansbee, D.J. (1984). Familial contexts of adolescent ego development. *Child Development, 55,* 195–213.

Havighurst, R.J. (1976). A cross-cultural view. In J.F. Adams (Ed.), *Understanding adolescence.* Boston: Allyn & Bacon.

Havighurst, R.J. (1987). Adolescent culture and subculture. In V.B. Van Hasselt & M. Hersen (Eds.), *Handbook of adolescent psychology.* New York: Pergamon.

Hawkins, J.A., & Berndt, T.J. (1985, April). *Adjustment following the transition to junior high school.* Paper presented at the biennial meeting of the Society for Research in Child Development, Toronto.

Hayes, C. (Ed.). (1987). *Risking the future: Adolescent sexuality, pregnancy, and childbearing* (Vol. 1). Washington, DC: National Academy Press.

Hayes, S.C. (2000). Applied behavior analysis. In A. Kazdin (Ed.), *Encyclopedia of psychology.* Washington, DC, & New York: American Psychological Association and Oxford University Press.

Haynie, D.L., Nansel, T., Eitel, P., Crump, A.D., Saylor, K., Yu, K., & Simons-Morton, B. (2001). Bullies, victims, and bully/victims: Distinct groups of at-risk youth. *Journal of Early Adolescence, 21,* 29–49.

Heath, S.B. (1983). *Ways with words.* Cambridge, England: Cambridge University Press.

Heath, S.B. (1997, April 21). *Language and work: Learning and identity development of older children in community settings* (George Miller Committee Lecture), University of Illinois.

Heath, S.B. (1999). Dimensions of language development: Lessons from older children. In A.S. Masten (Ed.), *Cultural processes in child development: The Minnesota symposium on child psychology* (Vol. 29). Mahwah, NJ: Erlbaum.

Heath, S.B., & McLaughlin, M.W. (Eds.). (1993). *Identity and inner-city youth: Beyond ethnicity and gender.* New York: Teachers College Press.

Hechinger, J. (1992). *Fateful choices.* New York: Hill & Wang.

Hecht, M.L., Jackson, R.L., & Ribeau, S.A. (2002). *African American communication* (2nd Ed.). Mahwah, NJ: Erlbaum.

Hellmich, N. (2000, November 7). Kids' bodies break down at play. *USA Today,* p. 1D.

Helms, J.E. (1996). *Where do we go from here? Affirmative action: Who benefits?* Washington, DC: American Psychological Association.

Helms, J.E. (Ed.). (1990). *Black and white racial identity: Theory, research, and practice.* Westport, CT: Greenwood Press.

Helson, R., Elliot, T., & Leigh, J. (1989). Adolescent antecedents of women's work patterns. In D. Stern & D. Eichorn (Eds.), *Adolescence and work.* Hillsdale, NJ: Erlbaum.

Henderson, K.A., & Zivian, M.T. (1995, March). *The development of gender differences in adolescent body image.* Paper presented at the meeting of the Society for Research in Child Development, Indianapolis.

Henderson, V.L., & Dweck, C.S. (1990). Motivation and achievement. In S.S. Feldman & G.R. Elliott (Eds.), *At the threshold: The developing adolescent.* Cambridge, MA: Harvard University Press.

Hendry, J. (1999). *Social anthropology.* New York: Macmillan.

Henry, D.B., Tolan, P.H., & Gorman-Smith, D. (2001). Longitudinal family and peer group effects on violence and nonviolent delinquency. *Journal of Clinical Child Psychology, 30,* 172–186.

Herek, G. (2000). Homosexuality. In A. Kazdin (Ed.), *Encyclopedia of psychology.* Washington, DC, and New York: American Psychological Association and Oxford University Press.

Hernandez, D.J. (1997). Child development and the social demography of childhood. *Child Development, 68,* 149–169.

Herpertz-Dahlmann, B., Muller, B., Herpertz, S., Heussen, N., Hebebrand, J., & Remschmidt, H. (2001). Prospective 10-year follow up in adolescent anorexia nervosa—course, outcome, psychiatric comorbidity, and psychosocial adaptation. *Journal of Child Psychology and Psychiatry, 42,* 603–612.

Herrnstein, R.J., & Murray, C. (1994). *The bell curve: Intelligence and class structure in modern life.* New York: Free Press.

Hertzog, N.B. (1998, Jan/Feb). Gifted education specialist. *Teaching Exceptional Children,* pp. 39–43.

Hess, L., Lonky, E., & Roodin, P.A. (1985, April). *The relationship of moral reasoning and ego strength to cheating behavior.* Paper presented at the meeting of the Society for Research in Child Development, Toronto.

Hetherington, E.M. (1972). Effects of father-absence on personality development in adolescent daughters. *Developmental Psychology, 7,* 313–326.

Hetherington, E.M. (1977). *My heart belongs to daddy: A study of the remarriages of daughters of divorcees and widows.* Unpublished manuscript, University of Virginia.

Hetherington, E.M. (1989). Coping with family transitions: Winners, losers, and survivors. *Child Development, 60,* 1–14.

Hetherington, E.M. (1995, March). *The changing American family and the well-being of children.* Paper presented at the meeting of the Society for Research in Child Development, Indianapolis.

Hetherington, E.M. (1999). *Should we stay together for the sake of the children?* Unpublished manuscript, Dept. of Psychology, University of Virginia, Charlottesville.

Hetherington, E.M. (2000). Divorce. In A. Kazdin (Ed.), *Encyclopedia of psychology.* Washington, DC, and New York: American Psychological Association and Oxford University Press.

Hetherington, E.M., Bridges, M., & Insabella, G.M. (1998). What matters? What does not? Five perspectives on the association between marital transitions and children's adjustment. *American Psychologist, 53,* 167–184.

Hetherington, E.M., & Clingempeel, W.G. (1992). Coping with marital transitions: A family systems perspective. *Monographs of the Society for Research in Child Development, 57,* (2–3, Serial No. 227).

Hetherington, E.M., Cox, M., & Cox, R. (1982). Effects of divorce on children and parents. In M.E. Lamb (Ed.), *Nontraditional families.* Hillsdale, NJ: Erlbaum.

Hetherington, E.M., Henderson, S.H., Reiss, D., & others. (1999). Adolescent siblings in stepfamilies: Family functioning and adolescent adjustment. *Monographs of the Society for Research in Child Development, 64* (No. 4).

Hetherington, E.M., & Jodl, K.M. (1994). Stepfamilies as settings for child development. In A. Booth & J. Dunn (Eds.), *Stepfamilies: Who benefits? Who does not?* Hillsdale, NJ: Erlbaum.

Hetherington, E.M., & Kelly, J. (2002). *For better or for worse: Divorce reconsidered.* New York: Norton.

Hetherington, E.M., Reiss, D., & Plomin, R. (1994). *Separate social worlds of siblings: Impact of nonshared environment on development.* Mahwah, NJ: Erlbaum.

Hetherington, E.M., & Stanley-Hagan, M. (2002). Parenting in divorced and remarried families. In M. Bornstein (Ed.), *Handbook of parenting* (2nd ed., Vol. 3). Mahwah, NJ: Erlbaum.

Heward, W.L. (2000). *Exceptional children* (6th ed.). Upper Saddle River, NJ: Merrill.

Hicks, R., & Connolly, J.A. (1995, March). *Peer relations and loneliness in adolescence: The interactive effects of social self-concept, close friends, and peer networks.* Paper presented at the meeting of the Society for Research in Child Development, Indianapolis.

Higgins, A., Power, C., & Kohlberg, L. (1983, April). *Moral atmosphere and moral judgment.* Paper presented at the biennial meeting of the Society for Research in Child Development, Detroit.

Hightower, E. (1990). Adolescent interpersonal and familial precursors of positive mental health at midlife. *Journal of Youth and Adolescence, 19,* 257–275.

Hill, J.P., & Holmbeck, G.N. (1986). Attachment and autonomy during adolescence. *Annals of Child Development, 3,* 145–189.

Hill, J.P., Holmbeck, G.N., Marlow, L., Green, T.M., & Lynch, M.E. (1985). Pubertal status and parent-child relations in families of seventh-grade boys. *Journal of Early Adolescence, 5,* 31–44.

Hill, J.P., & Lynch, M.E. (1983). The intensification of gender-related role expectations during early adolescence. In J. Brooks-Gunn & A.C. Petersen (Eds.), *Girls at puberty: Biological and psychosocial perspectives.* New York: Plenum.

Hill, J.P., & Steinberg, L.D. (1976, April 26–30). *The development of autonomy in adolescence.* Paper presented at the Symposium on Research on Youth Problems, Fundacion Orbegoza Eizaquirre, Madrid, Spain.

Hill, K., Battin-Pearson, S., Hawkins, J.D., & Jie, G. (1999, June). *The role of social developmental processes in facilitating or disrupting the link between early offending and adult crimes in males and females.* Paper presented at the meeting of the Society for Prevention Research, New Orleans.

Hirsch, B.J., & Rapkin, B.D. (1987). The transition to junior high school: A longitudinal study of self-esteem, psychological symptomatology, school life, and social support. *Child Development, 58,* 1235–1243.

Hodges, E.V.E., & Perry, D.G. (1999). Personal and interpersonal antecedents and consequences of victimization by peers. *Journal of Personality and Social Psychology, 76,* 677–685.

Hodges, E.V.E., Boivin, M., Vitaro, F., & Bukowski, W.M. (1999). The power of friendship: Protection against an escalating cycle of peer victimization. *Developmental Psychology, 35,* 94–101.

Hoff, E., Laursen, B., & Tardif, T. (2002). Socioeconomic status and parenting. In M.H. Bornstein (Ed.), *Handbook of parenting* (2nd Ed.). Mahwah, NJ: Erlbaum.

Hofferth, S.L. (1990). Trends in adolescent sexual activity, contraception, and pregnancy in the United States. In J. Bancroft & J.M. Reinisch (Eds.), *Adolescence and puberty.* New York: Oxford University Press.

Hoff-Ginsberg, E., & Tardif, T. (1995). Socioeconomic status and parenting. In M.H. Bornstein (Ed.), *Children and parenting* (Vol. 2). Hillsdale, NJ: Erlbaum.

Hoffman, D., & Novak, T. (1999). *Computer access, socioeconomic status, and ethnicity.* Unpublished manuscript, Vanderbilt University, Nashville.

Hoffman, L.W. (1989). Effects of maternal employment in the two-parent family. *American Psychologist, 44,* 283–292.

Hoffman, L.W. (2000). Maternal employment: Effects of social context. In R.D. Taylor & M.C. Wang (Eds.), *Resilience across contexts.* Mahwah, NJ: Erlbaum.

Hoffman, M.L. (1970). Moral development. In P.H. Mussen (Ed.), *Manual of child psychology* (3rd ed., Vol. 2). New York: Wiley.

Hoffman, M.L. (1980). Moral development in adolescence. In J. Adelson (Ed.), *Handbook of adolescent psychology.* New York: Wiley.

Hoffman, M.L. (1988). Moral development. In M.H. Bornstein & M.E. Lamb (Eds.), *Developmental psychology: An advanced textbook* (2nd ed.). Hillsdale, NJ: Erlbaum.

Hoffman, S., Foster, E., & Furstenberg, F. (1993). Reevaluating the costs of teenage childbearing. *Demography, 30,* 1–13.

Hoffnung, M. (1984). Motherhood: Contemporary conflict for women. In J. Freeman (Ed.), *Women: A feminist perspective* (3rd ed.). Palo Alto, CA: Mayfield.

Holditch, P., Broomfield, K., Foster, J., Emshoff, J., & Adamczak, J. (2002, April). *Cool Girls, Inc.: Evaluating a developmentally sensitive intervention for at-risk girls.* Paper presented at the meeting of the Society for Research on Adolescence, New Orleans.

Holland, J.L. (1973). *Making vocational choices: A theory of careers.* Englewood Cliffs, NJ: Prentice Hall.

Holland, J.L. (1987). Current status of Holland's theory of careers: Another perspective. *Career Development Quarterly, 36,* 24–30.

Hollingshead, A.B. (1975). *Elmtown's youth and Elmtown revisited.* New York: Wiley.

Hollingworth, L.S. (1914). *Functional periodicity: An experimental study of the mental and motor abilities of women during menstruation.* New York: Columbia University, Teachers College.

Hollingworth, L.S. (1916). Sex differences in mental tests. *Psychological Bulletin 13,* 377–383.

Hollon, S.D. (2000). Cognitive therapy. In A. Kazdin (Ed.), *Encyclopedia of psychology.* Washington, DC, and New York: American Psychological Association and Oxford University Press.

Holmbeck, G., & Shapera, W. (1999). Research methods with adolescents. In P. Kendall, J. Butcher, & G. Holmbeck (Eds.), *Handbook of research methods in clinical psychology.* New York: Wiley.

Holmbeck, G.N. (1996). A model of family relational transformations during the transition to adolescence: Parent-adolescent conflict and adaptation. In J.A. Graber, J. Brooks-Gunn, & A.C. Petersen (Eds.), *Transitions in adolescence.* Mahwah, NJ: Erlbaum.

Holmbeck, G.N., Durbin, D., & Kung, E. (1995, March). *Attachment, autonomy, and adjustment before and after leaving home: Sullivan and Sullivan revisited.* Paper presented at the meeting of the Society for Research in Child Development, Indianapolis.

Holmes, L.D. (1987). *Quest for the real Samoa: The Mead-Freeman controversy and beyond.* South Hadley, MA: Bergin & Garvey.

Holtzmann, W. (1982). Cross-cultural comparisons of personality development in Mexico and the United States. In D. Wagner & H.W. Stevenson (Eds.), *Cultural perspectives on child development.* San Francisco: W.H. Freeman.

Hopkins, J.R. (2000). Erikson, E.H. In A. Kazdin (Ed.), *Encyclopedia of psychology.* Washington, DC, & New York: American Psychological Association and Oxford University Press.

Hops, H. (2002, April). *Multiple pathways to adolescent drug use and abuse.* Paper presented at the meeting of the Society for Research on Adolescence, New Orleans.

Hops, H., Davis, B., Alpert, A., & Longoria, N. (1997, April). *Adolescent peer relations and depressive symptomatology.* Paper presented at the meeting of the Society for Research in Child Development, Washington, DC.

Horney, K. (1967). *Feminine psychology.* New York: W.W. Norton.

Howe, M.J.A. (2000). Prodigies. In A. Kazdin (Ed.), *Encyclopedia of psychology.* Washington, DC, and New York: American Psychological Association and Oxford University Press.

Howe, N., & Strauss, W. (2000). *Millenials rising: The next great generation.* New York: Vintage.

Hoyt, S., & Scherer, D.G. (1998). Female juvenile delinquency. *Law and Human Behavior, 22,* 81–107.

Huang, L.N. (1989). Southeast Asian refugee children and adolescents. In J.T. Gibbs & L.N. Huang (Eds.), *Children of color.* San Francisco: Jossey-Bass.

Huang, L.N., and Ying, Y. (1989). Chinese American children and adolescents. In J.T. Gibbs and L.N. Huang, (Eds.), *Children of color.* San Francisco: Jossey-Bass.

Huebner, A.M., & Garrod, A.C. (1993). Moral reasoning among Tibetan monks: A study of Buddhist adolescents and young adults in Nepal. *Journal of Cross-Cultural Psychology, 24,* 167–185.

Huesmann, L.R. (1986). Psychological processes promoting the relation between exposure to media violence and aggressive behavior by the viewer. *Journal of Social Issues, 42,* 125–139.

Huges, M., Alfano, M., & Harkness, S. (2002, April). *The GEAR UP Project: Strenghtening academic transitions and attainment through relationship building.* Paper presented at the meeting of the Society for Research on Adolescence, New Orleans.

Hughes, D.L. (1997, April). *Racial socialization in urban African-American and Hispanic families.* Paper presented at the meeting of the Society for Research in Child Development, Washington, DC.

Hurtado, M.T. (1997, April). *Acculturation and planning among adolescents.* Paper presented at the meeting of the Society for Research in Child Development, Washington, DC.

Huston, A.C., & Alvarez, M. (1990). The socialization context of gender-role development in early adolescence. In R. Montemayor, G.R. Adams, & T.P. Gulotta (Eds.), *From childhood to adolescence: A transitional period?* Newbury Park, CA: Sage.

Huston, A.C., McLoyd, V.C., & Coll, C.G. (1994). Children and poverty: Issues in contemporary research. *Child Development, 65,* 275–282.

Huston, A.C., Siegle, J., & Bremer, M. (1983, April). *Family environment television use by preschool children.* Paper presented at the biennial meeting of the Society for Research in Child Development, Detroit.

Huston, A.C., & Wright, J.C. (1998). Mass media and children's development. In I.E. Siegel & K.A. Renninger (Eds.), *Handbook of child psychology* (5th ed., Vol. 4). New York: Wiley.

Huttenlocher, J., Haight, W., Bruk, A., Seltzer, M., & Lyons, T. (1991). Early vocabulary growth: Relation to language input and gender. *Developmental Psychology, 27,* 236–248.

Huttenlocher, P.R., & Dabholkar, A.S. (1997). Regional differences in synaptogenesis in human cerebral cortex. *Journal of Comparative Neurology, 37* (2), 167–178.

Hyde, J.M., & Delamater, J.D. (2000). Understanding human sexuality (7th ed.). New York: McGraw-Hill.

Hyde, J.S. (1985). *Half the human experience* (3rd ed.). Lexington, MA: D. C. Heath.

Hyde, J.S. (1993). Meta-analysis and the psychology of women. In F.L. Denmark & M.A. Paludi (Eds.), *Handbook on the psychology of women.* Westport, CT: Greenwood.

Hyde, J.S., & Delamater, J.D. (2000). *Human sexuality* (7th ed.). New York: McGraw-Hill.

Hyde, J.S., & Mezulis, A.H. (2001). Gender difference research: Issues and critique. In J. Worell (Ed.), *Encyclopedia of women and gender.* San Diego: Academic Press.

Hyde, J.S., & Plant, E.A. (1995). Magnitude of psychological gender differences: Another side of the story. *American Psychologist, 50,* 159–161.

Ianni, F.A.J., & Orr, M.T. (1996). Dropping out. In J.A. Graber, J. Brooks-Gunn, & A.C. Petersen (Eds.), *Transitions in adolescence.* Mahwah, NJ: Erlbaum.

Idol, L. (1997). Key questions related to building collaborative and inclusive schools. *Journal of Learning Disabilities, 30,* 384–394.

International Society for Technology in Education. (1999). *National educational technology standards for students document.* Eugene, OR: International Society for Technology in Education.

Irwin, C.E. (1993). The adolescent, health, and society: From the perspective of the physician. In S.G. Millstein, A.C. Petersen, & E.O. Nightingale (Eds.), *Promoting the health of adolescents.* New York: Oxford University Press.

Jackson, N., & Butterfield, E. (1996). A conception of giftedness designed to promote research. In R.J. Sternberg & J.E. Davidson (Eds.), *Conceptions of giftedness.* New York: Cambridge University Press.

Jacobs, J.E., & Potenza, M. (1990, March). *The use of decision-making strategies in late adolescence.* Paper presented at the meeting of the Society for Research in Adolescence, Atlanta.

Jacobs, J.K., Garnier, H.E., & Weisner, T. (1996, March). *The impact of family life on the process of dropping out of high school.* Paper presented at the meeting of the Society for Research on Adolescence, Boston.

Jacobson, K.C., & Crockett, L.J. (2000). Parental monitoring and adolescent adjustment: An ecological perspective. *Journal of Research on Adolescence, 10,* 65–97.

Jaffe, S., & Hyde, J.S. (2000). Gender differences in moral orientation. *Psychological Bulletin, 126,* 703–726.

Janz, N.K., Zimmerman, M.A., Wren, P.A., Israel, B.A., Freudenberg, N., & Carter, R.J. (1996). Evaluation of 37 AIDS prevention projects: Successful approaches and barriers to program effectiveness. *Health Education Quarterly, 23,* 80–97.

Jarrett, R.L. (1995). Growing up poor: The family experiences of socially mobile youth in low-income African-American neighborhoods. *Journal of Adolescent Research, 10,* 111–135.

Jensen, A.R. (1969). How much can we boost IQ and scholastic achievement? *Harvard Educational Review, 39,* 1–123.

Jessor, R., Turbin, M.S., & Costa, F. (in press). Risk and protection in successful outcomes among disadvantaged adolescents. *Applied Developmental Science.*

Jhally, S. (1990). *Dreamworlds: Desire/sex/power in rock video* (Video). Amherst: University of Massachusetts at Amherst, Department of Communications.

Jodl, K.M., Michael, A., Malanchuk, O., Eccles, J.S., & Sameroff, A. (2001). Parents' roles in shaping early adolescents' occupational aspirations. *Child Development, 72,* 1247–1265.

Johnson, D.W. (1990). *Teaching out: Interpersonal effectiveness and self-actualization.* Upper Saddle River, NJ: Prentice-Hall.

Johnson, D.W., & Johnson, R. (1991). *Teaching students to be peacemakers.* Edina, MN: Interaction Book Company.

Johnson, D.W., & Johnson, R.T. (1995, February). Why violence prevention programs don't work—and what does. *Educational Leadership,* pp. 63–68.

Johnson, J.G., Cohen, P., Pine, D.S., Klein, D.F., Kasen, S., & Brook, J.S. (2000). Association between cigarette smoking and anxiety disorders during adolescence and adulthood. *Journal of the American Medical Association, 284,* 348–2351.

Johnson, M.K., Beebe, T., Mortimer, J.T., & Snyder, M. (1998). Volunteerism in adolescence: A process perspective. *Journal of Research on Adolescence, 8,* 309–332.

Johnson, V.K. (2002). *Managing the transition to college: The role of families and adolescents' coping strategies.* Paper presented at the meeting of the Society for Research on Adolescence, New Orleans.

Johnston, J., Etteman, J., & Davidson, T. (1980). *An evaluation of "Freestyle": A television series to reduce sex-role stereotypes.* Ann Arbor: University of Michigan, Institute for Social Research.

Johnston, L.D., O'Malley, P.M., & Bachman, J.G. (1992, January 25). *Most forms of drug use decline among American high school and college students.* News release, Institute of Social Research, University of Michigan, Ann Arbor.

Johnston, L.D., O'Malley, P.M., & Bachman, J.G. (1999, December 17). *Drug trends in the United States are mixed* (Press Release). Ann Arbor, MI: Institute of Social Research, University of Michigan.

Johnston, L.D., O'Malley, P.M., & Bachman, J.G. (2000). *The monitoring of the future: National results on adolescent drug use.* Washington, DC: National Institute on Drug Abuse.

Johnston, L.D., O'Malley, P.M., & Bachman, J.G. (2001, December 19). *Monitoring the Future: 2001.* Ann Arbor, MI: Institute for Social Research, University of Michigan.

Jones, B.F., Rasmussen, C.M., & Moffit, M.C. (1997). *Real-life problem solving.* Washington, DC: American Psychological Association.

Jones, D.C., Costin, S.E., & Ricard, R.J. (1994, February). *Ethnic and sex differences in best friendship characteristics among African-American, Mexican-American, and White adolescents.* Paper presented at the meeting of the Society for Research on Adolescence, San Diego.

Jones, J.M. (1994). The African American: A duality dilemma? In W.J. Lonner & R. Malpass (Eds.), *Psychology and culture.* Needham Heights, MA: Allyn & Bacon.

Jones, L.V. (1984). White-black achievement differences: The narrowing gap. *American Psychologist, 39,* 1207–1213.

Jones, M.C. (1965). Psychological correlates of somatic development. *Child Development, 36,* 899–911.

Jones, S.E. (2000). Ethics in research. In A. Kazdin (Ed.). *Encyclopedia of psychology.* Washington, DC, & New York: American Psychological Association and Oxford University Press.

Josselson, R. (1994). Identity and relatedness in the life cycle. In H.A. Bosma, T.L.G. Graafsma, H.D. Grotevant, & D.J. De Levita (Eds.), *Identity and development.* Newbury Park, CA: Sage.

Joyner, K., & Udry, J.R. (2000). "You don't bring me anything but down: Adolescent romance and depression. *Journal of Health and Social Behavior, 41,* 369–391.

Jozefowicz, D.M.H. (2002, April). *Quantitative and qualitative perspectives on the transition to adulthood.* Paper presented at the meeting of the Society for Research on Adolescence, New Orleans.

Jozefowicz, D.M., Barber, B.L., & Mollasis, C. (1994, February). *Relations between maternal and adolescent values and beliefs: Sex differences and implications for occupational choice.* Paper presented at the meeting of the Society for Research on Adolescence, San Diego.

Juang, L.P., & Nguyen, H.H. (1997, April). *Autonomy and connectedness: Predictors of adjustment in Vietnamese adolescents.* Paper presented at the meeting of the Society for Research in Child Development, Washington, DC.

Jussim, L., & Eccles, J.S. (1993). Teacher expectations II: Construction and reflection of student achievement. *Journal of Personality and Social Psychology, 63,* 947–961.

Kagan, J. (1992). Yesterday's premises, tomorrow's promises. *Developmental Psychology, 28,* 990–997.

Kagan, J. (1998). *The power of parents.* Available on the World Wide Web: *http://www.Psychplace.com.*

Kagan, J., Snidman, N., & Arcus, D. (1995, August). *Antecedents of shyness.* Paper presented at the meeting of the American Psychological Association, New York City.

Kagan, S., & Madsen, M.C. (1972). Experimental analysis of cooperation and competition of Anglo-American and Mexican children. *Developmental Psychology, 6,* 49–59.

Kahn, S.E., & Richardson, A. (1983). Evaluation of a course in sex roles for secondary school students. *Sex Roles, 9,* 431–440.

Kail, R., & Hall, L.K. (2001). Distinguishing short-term memory from working memory. *Memory and Cognition, 29,* 1–9.

Kail, R., & Pellegrino, J.W. (1985). *Human intelligence.* New York: W.H. Freeman.

Kaiser Family Foundation. (1996). *Kaiser Family Foundation survey of 1,500 teenagers ages 12–18.* San Francisco: Kaiser Foundation.

Kalil, A., & Kunz, J. (2000, April). *Psychological outcomes of adolescent mothers in young adulthood.* Paper presented at the meeting of the Society for Research on Adolescence, Chicago.

Kamphaus, R.W. (2000). Learning disabilities. In A. Kazdin (Ed.), *Encyclopedia of psychology.* Washington, DC, and New York: American Psychological Association and Oxford University Press.

Kandel, D.B., & Lesser, G.S. (1969). Parent-adolescent relationships and adolescence independence in the United States and Denmark. *Journal of Marriage and the Family, 31,* 348–358.

Kandel, D.B., & Wu, P. (1995). The contributions of mothers and fathers to the intergenerational transmission of cigarette smoking. *Journal of Research on Adolescence, 5,* 225–252.

Kaplan, M.J., Middleton, T., Urdan, C., & Midgley, C. (2002). Achievement goals and goal structures. In C. Midgley (Ed.), *Goals, goal structures, and patterns of adaptive learning.* Mahwah, NJ: Erlbaum.

Kaplowitz, P.B., Slora, E.J., Wasserman, R.C., Pedlow, S.E., & Herman-Giddens, M.E. (2001). Earlier onset of puberty in girls: Relation to increased body mass index and race. *Pediatrics, 108,* 347–353.

Karniol, R., Gabay, R., Ochioin, Y., & Harari, Y. (1998). *Sex Roles, 39,* 45–58.

Kaufman, A.S. (2000a). Tests of intelligence. In R.J. Sternberg (Ed.), *Handbook of intelligence.* New York: Cambridge University Press.

Kaufmann, A.S. (2000b). Wechsler, David. In A. Kazdin (Ed.), *Encyclopedia of psychology.* Washington, DC, and New York: American Psychological Association and Oxford University Press.

Kaufman, A.S., & Lindenberger, E.O. (2002). *Assessing adolescence and adult intelligence* (2nd Ed.). Boston: Allyn & Bacon.

Keating, D.P. (1990). Adolescent thinking. In S.S. Feldman & G.R. Elliott (Eds.), *At the threshold: The developing adolescent.* Cambridge, MA: Harvard University Press.

Keel, P.K., Mitchell, J.E., Miller, K.B., Davis, T.L., & Crowe, S.J. (1999). Long-term outcome of bulimia nervosa. *Archives of General Psychiatry, 56,* 63–69.

Keener, D.C., & Boykin, K.A. (1996, March). *Parental control, autonomy, and ego development.* Paper presented at the meeting of the Society for Research on Adolescence, Boston.

Kelly, J. (2000). Sexually transmitted diseases. In A. Kazdin (Ed.), *Encyclopedia of psychology.* Washington, DC, and New York: American Psychological Association and Oxford University Press.

Kennedy, J.H. (1990). Determinants of peer social status: Contributions of physical appearance, reputation, and behavior. *Journal of Youth and Adolescence, 19,* 233–244.

Kenney, A.M. (1987, June). Teen pregnancy: An issue for schools. *Phi Delta Kappan,* pp. 728–736.

Kenniston, K. (1970). Youth: A "new" stage of life. *American Scholar, 39,* 631–654.

Kiess, W., Reich, A., Meyer, K., Glasow, A., Deutscher, J., Klammt, J., Yang, Y., Muller, G., & Kratzsch, J. (1999). A role for leptin in sexual maturation and puberty? *Hormone Research, 51,* 55–3.

Killen, M. (1991). Social and moral development in early childhood. In W.M. Kurtines & J.L. Gewirtz (Eds.), *Handbook of moral behavior and development* (Vol. 2). Mahwah, NJ: Erlbaum.

Killen, M., McGlothlin, H., & Lee-Kim, J. (in press). Between individuals and culture: Individuals' evaluations of exclusion from groups. In H. Keller, Y. Poortinga, & A. Schoelmerich (Eds.), *Between biology and culture: Perspectives on ontogenetic development.* Cambridge, UK: Cambridge University Press.

Kilmartin, C. (2000). *The masculine self.* New York: McGraw-Hill.

Kim, J. (2002, April). *"Cosmo chicks": The impact of contemporary women's magazines on readers' sexual attitudes and self perceptions.* Paper presented at the meeting of the Society for Research on Adolescence, New Orleans.

Kimmel, A. (1996). *Ethical issues in behavioral research.* Cambridge, MA: Blackwell.

Kindlundh, A.M.S., Isacson, D.G.L., Berlund, L., & Nyberg, F. (1999). Factors associated with adolescence use of doping agents: Anabolic-androgenic steroids. *Addiction, 94,* 543–553.

King, P. (1988). Heavy metal music and drug use in adolescents. *Postgraduate Medicine, 83,* 295–304.

King, P.M., & Kitchener, K.S. (1994). *Developing reflective judgment: Understanding and promoting intellectual growth and critical thinking in adolescents and adults.* San Francisco: Jossey-Bass.

Kinsey, A.C., Pomeroy, W.B., & Martin, C.E. (1948). *Sexual behavior in the human male.* Philadelphia: Saunders.

Kirby, D., Resnick, M.D., Downes, B., Kocher, T., Gunderson, P., Pothoff, S., Zelterman, D., & Blum, R.W. (1993). The effects of school-based health clinics in St. Paul on school-wide birthrates. *Family Planning Perspectives, 25,* 12–16.

Kirst, M.W. (1998, April). *A plan for the evaluation of California's class-size reduction initiative.* Paper presented at the meeting of the American Educational Research Association, San Diego.

Kitchener, K.S., & King, P.M. (1981). Reflective judgment: Concepts of justification and their relationship to age and education. *Journal of Applied Developmental Psychology, 2,* 89–111.

Klaczynski, P.A. (1997). Bias in adolescents' everyday reasoning and its relationship with intellectual ability, personal theories, and self-serving motivation. *Developmental Psychology, 33,* 273–283.

Klaczynski, P.A., & Narasimham, G. (1998). Development of scientific reasoning biases: Cognitive versus ego-protective explanations. *Developmental Psychology, 34,* 175–187.

Klaus, T. (1997, July). *Seven scary sexuality subjects for males . . . and how to address them.* Paper presented at the conference on Working with America's Youth, Pittsburgh.

Klaw, E., & Saunders, N. (1994). *An ecological model of career planning in pregnant African American teens.* Paper presented at the biennial meeting of the Society for Research on Adolescence, San Diego.

Klein, J.D., Allan, M.J., Elster, A.B., Stevens, D., Cox, C., Hedberg, V.A., & Goodman, R.A. (2001). Improving adolescent preventative care in community health centers. *Pediatrics, 107,* 318–327.

Knox, D., & Wilson, K. (1981). Dating behaviors of university students. *Family Relations, 30,* 255–258.

Kobak, R. (1999). The emotional dynamics of disruptions in attachment relationships: Implications for theory, research, and clinical intervention. In J. Cassidy & P. Shaver (Eds.), *Handbook of attachment.* New York: Guilford.

Koenig, L.J., & Faigeles, R. (1995, March). *Gender differences in adolescent loneliness and maladjustment.* Paper presented at the meeting of the Society for Research in Child Development, Indianapolis.

Kohlberg, L. (1958). *The development of modes of moral thinking and choice in the years 10 to 16.* Unpublished doctoral dissertation, University of Chicago.

Kohlberg, L. (1966). A cognitive-developmental analysis of children's sex-role concepts and attitudes. In E. E. Maccoby (Ed.), *The development of sex differences.* Palo Alto, CA: Stanford University Press.

Kohlberg, L. (1969). Stage and sequence: The cognitive-developmental approach to socialization. In D.A. Goslin (Ed.), *Handbook of socialization theory and research.* Chicago: Rand McNally.

Kohlberg, L. (1976). Moral stages and moralization: The cognitive-developmental approach. In T. Lickona (Ed.), *Moral development and behavior.* New York: Holt, Rinehart & Winston.

Kohlberg, L. (1981). *Essays on moral development: Vol. 1. The philosophy of moral development.* San Francisco: Harper & Row.

Kohlberg, L. (1984). *Essays on moral development: Vol. 2. The philosophy of moral development.* San Francisco: Harper & Row.

Kohlberg, L. (1986). A current statement on some theoretical issues. In S. Modgil & C. Modgil (Eds.), *Lawrence Kohlberg.* Philadelphia: Falmer.

Kohlberg, L., & Candee, D. (1979). *Relationships between moral judgment and moral action.* Unpublished manuscript, Harvard University.

Kohn, M.L. (1977). *Class and conformity: A study in values* (2nd ed.). Chicago: University of Chicago Press.

Koss, M.P. (1993). Rape: Scope, impact, interventions, and public policy responses. *American Psychologist, 48,* 1062–1069.

Koss-Chiono, J.D., & Vargas, L.A. (Eds.). (1999). *Working with Latino youth.* San Francisco: Jossey-Bass.

Kottak, C.P. (2002). *Cultural anthropology* (9th ed.). New York: McGraw-Hill.

Kounin, J.S. (1970). *Discipline and management in classrooms.* New York: Holt, Rinehart & Winston.

Kozol, J. (1991). *Savage inequalities.* New York: Crown.

Kozulin, A. (2000). Vygotsky. In A. Kazdin (Ed.), *Encyclopedia of psychology.* Washington, DC, and New York: American Psychological Association and Oxford University Press.

Kramer, L., & Lin, L. (1997, April). *Mothers' and fathers' responses to sibling conflict.* Paper presented at the meeting of the Society for Research in Child Development, Washington, DC.

Kremen, A.M., & Block, J. (2000, April). *Maladaptive pathways in adolescence.* Paper presented at the meeting of the Society for Research in Adolescence, Chicago.

Kreppner, K. (2001). Retrospect and prospect in the psychological study of families as systems. In J.P. McHale & W.S. Grolnick (Eds.), *Retrospect and prospect in the psychological study of families.* Mahwah, NJ: Erlbaum.

Kroger, J. (2000). *Identity development.* Thousand Oaks, CA: Sage.

Krupnik, C.G. (1985). Women and men in the classroom: Inequality and its remedies. *On Teaching and Learning: The Journal of the Harvard University Derek Bok Center, 10,* 18–25.

Ksir, C. (2000). Drugs. In A. Kazdin (Ed.), *Encyclopedia of psychology.* Washington, DC and New York: American Psychological Association and Oxford University Press.

Kuchenbecker, S. (2000). *Raising winners.* New York: Times Books/Random House.

Kuhn, D. (1998). Afterword to Volume 2: Cognition, perception, and language. In W. Damon (Ed.), *Handbook of child psychology* (5th ed., Vol. 2). New York: Wiley.

Kuhn, D. (1999). A developmental model of critical thinking. *Educational Researcher, 28,* 26–37.

Kuhn, D. (2000). Adolescence: Adolescent thought processes. In A. Kazdin (Ed.), *Encyclopedia of psychology.* Washington, DC, & New York: American Psychological Association and Oxford University Press.

Kuhn, D. (2000a). Adolescence: Adolescent thought processes. In A. Kazdin (Ed.), *Encyclopedia of psychology.* Washington, DC, & New York: American Psychological Association and Oxford University Press.

Kuhn, D. (2000b). Metacognitive development. In L. Balter & S. Tamis-LeMonda (Eds.), *Child psychology.* Philadelphia: Psychology Press.

Kulig, J.W., Mandel, L., Ruthazer, R., & Stone, D. (2001, March). *School-based substance use prevention for female students.* Paper presented at the meeting of the Society for Adolescent Medicine, San Diego.

Kuperminc, G., Jurkovic, G., Perilla, J., Murphy, A., Casey, S., Ibanez, G., Parker, J., & Urruzmendi, A. (2002, April). *Latino self, American self: Mexican and immigrant Latino adolescents' bicultural identity constructions.* Paper presented at the meeting of the Society for Research on Adolescence, New Orleans.

Kupersmidt, J.B., & Coie, J.D. (1990). Preadolescent peer status, aggression, and school adjustment as predictors of externalizing problems in adolescence. *Child Development, 61,* 1350–1363.

Kurdek, L.A., & Krile, D. (1982). A developmental analysis of the relation between peer acceptance and both interpersonal understanding and perceived social self-competence. *Child Development, 53,* 1485–1491.

Kurtz, D.A., Cantu, C.L., & Phinney, J.S. (1996, March). *Group identities as predictors of self-esteem among African American, Latino, and White adolescents.* Paper presented at the meeting of the Society for Research on Adolescence, Boston.

Labouvie-Vief, G., & Diehl, M. (1999). Self and personality development. In J.C. Kavanaugh & S.K. Whitbourne (Eds.), *Gerentology: An interdisciplinary perspective.* New York: Oxford University Press.

Ladd, G.W., & Kochenderfer, B.J. (in press). Parenting behaviors and parent-child relationship: Correlates of peer victimization in kindergarten. *Developmental Psychology.*

Ladd, G.W., & Le Sieur, K.D. (1995). Parents and children's peer relationships. In M.H. Bornstein (Ed.), *Children and parenting* (Vol. 4). Hillsdale, NJ: Erlbaum.

Ladd, G.W., & Pettit, G. (2002). Parents and children's peer relationships. In M. Bornstein (Ed.), *Handbook of parenting* (2nd ed., Vol. 5). Mahwah, NJ: Erlbaum.

LaFromboise, T., & Low, K.G. (1989). American Indian children and adolescents. In J.T. Gibbs & L.N. Huang (Eds.), *Children of color.* San Francisco: Jossey-Bass.

LaFromboise, T., Coleman, H.L.K., & Gerton, J. (1993). Psychological impact of biculturalism: Evidence and theory. *Psychological Bulletin, 114,* 393–412.

Lamb, M.E. (1997). Fatherhood then and now. In A. Booth & A.C. Crouter (Eds.), *Men in families.* Mahwah, NJ: Erlbaum.

Landry, D.J., Singh, S., & Darroch, J.E. (2000). Sexuality education in fifth and sixth grades in U.S. public schools, 1999. *Family Planning Perspectives, 32,* 212–219.

Lapsley, D.K. (1990). Continuity and discontinuity in adolescent social cognitive development. In R. Montemayor, G. Adams, & T. Gulotta (Eds.), *From childhood to adolescence: A transitional period?* Newbury Park, CA: Sage.

Lapsley, D.K. (1993). *Moral psychology after Kohlberg.* Unpublished manuscript, Department of Psychology, Brandon University, Manitoba.

Lapsley, D.K. (1996). *Moral psychology.* Boulder, CO: Westview Press.

Lapsley, D.K., Enright, R.D., & Serlin, R.C. (1985). Toward a theoretical perspective on the legislation of adolescence. *Journal of Early Adolescence, 5,* 441–466.

Lapsley, D.K., & Murphy, M.N. (1985). Another look at the theoretical assumptions of adolescent egocentrism. *Developmental Review, 5,* 201–217.

Lapsley, D.K., & Power, F.C. (Eds.). (1988). *Self, ego, and identity.* New York: Springer-Verlag.

Lapsley, D.K., Rice, K.G., & Shadid, G.E. (1989). Psychological separation and adjustment to college. *Journal of Counseling Psychology, 36,* 286–294.

Larose, S., & Boivin, M. (1998). Attachment to parents, social support expectations, and socioemotional adjustment during the high school–college transition. *Journal of Research on Adolescence, 8,* 1–28.

Larson, R.W. (1999, September). Unpublished review of J.W. Santrock's *Adolescence,* 8th ed. (New York: McGraw-Hill).

Larson, R.W. (2000). Toward a psychology of positive youth development. *American Psychologist, 55,* 170–183.

Larson, R.W., Clore, G.L., & Wood, G.A. (1999). The emotions of romantic relationships. In W. Furman, B.B. Brown, & C. Feiring (Eds.), *Contemporary perspectives on romantic relationships.* New York: Cambridge University Press.

Larson, R.W., Kubey, R., & Colletti, J. (1989). Changing channels: Early adolescent media choices and shifting investments. *Journal of Youth and Adolescence, 18,* 583–599.

Larson, R.W., & Richards, M. (1999). Waiting for the weekend: The development of Friday and Saturday nights as the emotional climax of the week. In A.C. Crouter & R.W. Larson (Eds.), *Temporal rhythms in the lives of adolescents: Themes and variations.* San Francisco: Jossey-Bass.

Larson, R.W., Richards, M.H., Moneta, G., Holmbeck, G., & Duckett, E. (1996). Changes in adolescents' daily interactions with their families from 10 to 18: Disengagement and transformation. *Developmental Psychology, 32,* 744–754.

Larson, R.W., & Verman, S. (1999). How children and adolescents spend time across the world. *Psychological Bulletin, 125,* 701–736.

Lauren, B., Coy, K.C., & Collins, W.A. (1998). Reconsidering changes in parent-child conflict across adolescence: A meta-analysis. *Child Development, 69,* 817–832.

Laursen, B. (1995). Conflict and social interaction in adolescent relationships. *Journal of Research on Adolescence, 5,* 55–70.

LaVoie, J. (1976). Ego identity formation in middle adolescence. *Journal of Youth and Adolescence, 5,* 371–385.

Law, T.C. (1992, March). *The relationship between mothers' employment status and perception of child behavior.* Paper presented at the meeting of the Society for Research on Adolescence, Washington, DC.

Lazarus, R.S. (1991). *Emotion and adaptation.* New York: Oxford University Press.

Leadbeater, B.J. (1994, February). *Re-conceptualizing social supports for adolescent mothers: Grandmothers, babies, fathers, and beyond.* Paper presented at the meeting of the Society for Research on Adolescence, San Diego.

Leadbeater, B.J. & Way, N. (2000). *Growing up fast.* Mahwah, NJ: Erlbaum.

Leadbeater, B.J., Way, N., & Raden, A. (1994, February). *Barriers to involvement of fathers of the children of adolescent mothers.* Paper presented at the meeting of the Society for Research on Adolescence, San Diego.

Learner-Centered Principles Work Group. (1997). *Learner-centered psychological principles: A framework for school reform and redesign.* Washington, DC: American Psychological Association.

Lebra, T.S. (1994). Mother and child in Japanese socialization: A Japan-U.S. comparison. In P. Greenfield & R. Cocking (Eds.), *Cross-cultural roots of minority child development* (pp. 259–274). Hillsdale, NJ: Erlbaum.

Leinhardt, G., Crowley, K., Knutson, K. (Eds.) (2002). *Learning conversations in museums.* Mahwah, NJ: Erlbaum.

Lee, C.C. (1985). Successful rural black adolescents: A psychological profile. *Adolescence, 20,* 129–142.

Lee, V.E., Croninger, R.G., Linn, E., & Chen, X. (1995, March). *The culture of sexual harassment in secondary schools.* Paper presented at the meeting of the Society for Research in Child Development, Indianapolis.

Leffert, N., & Blyth, D.A. (1996, March). *The effects of community contexts on early adolescents.* Paper presented at the meeting of the Society for Research on Adolescence, Boston.

Lefkowitz, E.S., Afifi, T.L., Sigman, M., & Au, T.K. (1999, April). *He said, she said: Gender differences in mother-adolescent conversations about sexuality.* Paper presented at the meeting of the Society for Research in Child Development, Albuquerque.

Leinhardt, G., Crowley, K., & Knutson, K. (Eds.) (2002). *Learning conversations in museums.* Mahwah, NJ: Erlbaum.

Leitenberg, H., Detzer, M.J., & Srebnik, D. (1993). Gender differences in masturbation and the relation of masturbation experience in preadolescence and/or early adolescence to sexual behavior and adjustment in young adulthood. *Archives of Sexual Behavior, 22,* 87–98.

Leong, F.T.L. (1995). Introduction and overview. In F.T.L. Leong (Ed.), *Career development and vocational behavior in racial and ethnic minorities.* Hillsdale, NJ: Erlbaum.

Leong, F.T.L. (2000). Cultural pluralism. In A. Kazdin (Ed.), *Encyclopedia of psychology.* Washington, DC, and New York: American Psychological Association and Oxford University Press.

Lerner, J.V., Jacobson, L., & del Gaudio, A. (1992, March). *Maternal role satisfaction and family variables as predictors of adolescent adjustment.* Paper presented at the meeting of the Society for Research on Adolescence, Washington, DC.

Lerner, R.M. (1993). Early adolescence: Toward an agenda for the integration of research, policy, and intervention. In R.M. Lerner (Ed.), *Early adolescence.* Hillsdale, NJ: Erlbaum.

Lerner, R.M. (1998). Theories of human development: Contemporary perspectives. In W. Damon (Ed.), *Handbook of child psychology* (5th ed., Vol. 1). New York: Wiley.

Lerner, R.M. (2000). Developmental psychology: Theories. In A. Kazdin (Ed.), *Encyclopedia of psychology.* Washington, DC, & New York: American Psychological Association and Oxford University Press.

Lerner, R.M., Fisher, C.B., & Weinberg, R.A. (2000). Toward a science for and of the people: Promoting civil society through the application of developmental science. *Child Development, 71* 11–20.

Lerner, R.M., Lerner, J.V., von Eye, A., Ostrum, C.W., Nitz, K., Talwar-Soni, R., & Tubman, J. (1996). Continuity and discontinuity across the transition of early adolescence: A developmental contextual perspective. In J.A. Graber, J. Brooks-Gunn, & A.C. Petersen (Eds.), *Transitions through adolescence: Interpersonal domains and context.* Mahwah, NJ: Erlbaum.

Lerner, R.M., & Olson, C.K. (1995, February). "My body is so ugly." *Parents,* pp. 87–88.

Levant, R.F. (1995). *Masculinity reconstructed: Changing rules of manhood.* New York: Dutton.

Levant, R.F. (1999, August). *Boys in crisis.* Paper presented at the meeting of the American Psychological Association, Boston.

Levant, R.F., & Brooks, G.R. (1997). *Men and sex: New psychological perspectives.* New York: Wiley.

LeVay, S. (1991). A difference in hypothalamic structure between heterosexual and homosexual men. *Science, 253,* 1034–1037.

Leventhal, T., & Brooks-Gunn, J. (2000). The neighborhoods they live in: The effects of neighborhood residence on child and adolescent outcomes. *Psychological Bulletin, 126,* 309–337.

Leventhal, T., & Brooks-Gunn, J. (2003). Moving up: Neighborhood effects on children and families. In M.H. Bornstein & R.H. Bradley (Eds.), *Socioeconomics status, parenting, and child development.* Mahwah, NJ: Erlbaum.

Leventhal, T., Graber, J.A., & Brooks-Gunn, J. (2001). *Adolescent transitions into young adulthood.* Unpublished manuscript, Center for Children and Families, Columbia University, New York.

Levesque, J., & Prosser, T. (1996). Service learning connections. *Journal of Teacher Education, 47,* 325–334.

Lewis, C.G. (1981). How adolescents approach decisions: Changes over grades seven to twelve and policy implications. *Child Development, 52,* 538–554.

Lewis, R. (1997). With a marble and telescope: Searching for play. *Childhood Education, 36,* 346.

Lewis, R. (2002). *Human genetics* (4th ed.). New York: McGraw-Hill.

Lewis, V.G., Money, J., & Bobrow, N.A. (1977). Idiopathic pubertal delay beyond the age of 15: Psychological study of 12 boys. *Adolescence, 12,* 1–11.

Lieberman, M., Doyle, A., & Markiewicz, D. (1999). Developmental patterns in security of attachment to mother and father in late childhood and early adolescence: Associations with peer relations. *Child Development, 70,* 202–213.

Limber, S.P. (1997) Preventing violence among school children. *Family Futures, 1,* 27–28.

Lindner-Gunnoe, M. (1993). *Noncustodial mothers' and fathers' contributions to the adjustment of adolescent stepchildren.* Unpublished doctoral dissertation. University of Virginia.

Linn, M.C. (1991). Scientific reasoning, adolescent. In R.M. Lerner, A.C. Petersen, & J. Brooks-Gunn (Eds.), *Encyclopedia of adolescence* (Vol. 2). New York: Garland.

Liprie, M.L. (1993). Adolescents' contributions to family decision making. In B.H. Settles, R.S. Hanks, & M.B. Sussman (Eds.), *American families and the future: Analyses of possible destinies.* New York: Haworth Press.

Lipsitz, J. (1980, March). *Sexual development in young adolescents.* Invited speech given at the American Association of Sex Educators, Counselors, and Therapists, New York City.

Lipsitz, J. (1983, October). *Making it the hard way: Adolescents in the 1980s.* Testimony presented at the Crisis Intervention Task Force, House Select Committee on Children, Youth, and Families, Washington, DC.

Lipsitz, J. (1984). *Successful schools for young adolescents.* New Brunswick, NJ: Transaction Books.

Livesley, W.J., & Bromley, D.B. (1973). *Person perception in childhood and adolescence.* New York: Wiley.

Lochman, J.E., & Dodge, K.A. (1998). Distorted perceptions in dyadic interactions of aggressive and nonaggressive boys: Effects of prior expectations, context, and boys' age. *Development and Psychopathology, 10,* 495–512.

Loeber, R., Farrington, D.P., Stouthamer-Loeber, M., Moffitt, T., & Caspi, A. (1998). The development of male offending: Key findings from the first decade of the Pittsburgh Youth Study. *Studies in Crime and Crime Prevention, 7,* 141–172.

Loehlin, J. (1995, August). *Heritability of intelligence.* Paper presented at the meeting of the American Psychological Association, New York City.

Loehlin, J.C. (2000). Group differences in intelligence. In R. J. Sternberg (Ed.), *Handbook of intelligence.* New York: Cambridge University Press.

Loewen, I.R., & Leigh, G.K. (1986). *Timing of transition to sexual intercourse: A multivariate analysis of white adolescent females ages 15–17.* Paper presented at the meeting of the Society for the Scientific Study of Sex, St. Louis.

Logan, G. (2000). Information processing theories. In A. Kazdin (Ed.), *Encyclopedia of psychology.* Washington, DC, and New York: American Psychological Association and Oxford University Press.

Long, T., & Long, L. (1983). *Latchkey children.* New York: Penguin.

Lonner, W.J. (1990). An overview of cross-cultural testing and assessment. In R.W. Brislin (Ed.), *Applied cross-cultural psychology.* Newbury Park, CA: Sage.

Lopez, N. (2001, March). *Gender and culture.* Invited presentation at the Center on Women's Studies, University of Texas at Dallas.

Lord, S. (1995, March). *Parent psychological experiences as mediators of the influence of economic conditions on parenting in low income urban contexts.* Paper presented at the meeting of the Society for Research in Child Development, Indianapolis.

Lord, S.E., & Eccles, J.S. (1994, February). *James revisited: The relationship of domain self-concepts and values to Black and White adolescents' self-esteem.* Paper presented at the meeting of the Society for Research on Adolescence, San Diego.

Lowe, B., Zipfel, S., Buchholz, C., Dupont, Y., Reas, D.L., & Herzog, W. (2001). Long-term outcome of anorexia nervosa in a prospective 21-year follow-up study. *Psychology and Medicine, 31,* 881–890.

Luborsky, L.B. (2000) Psychoanalysis: Psychoanalytic psychotherapies. In A. Kazdin (Ed.), *Encyclopedia of psychology.* Washington, DC, & New York: American Psychological Association and Oxford University Press.

Luo, Q., Fang, X., & Aro, P. (1995, March). *Selection of best friends by Chinese adolescents.* Paper presented at the meeting of the Society for Research in Child Development, Indianapolis.

Luria, A., & Herzog, E. (1985, April). *Gender segregation across and within settings.* Paper presented at the biennial meeting of the Society for Research in Child Development, Toronto.

Luster, T.J., Perlstadt, J., McKinney, M.H., & Sims, K.E. (1995, March). *Factors related to the quality of the home environment adolescents provide for their infants.* Paper presented at the meeting of the Society for Research in Child Development, Indianapolis.

Luthar, S.S., Cicchetti, D., & Becker, B. (2000). The construct of resilience: A critical evaluation and guidelines for future work. *Child Development, 71,* 543–562.

Lyendecker, B., Carlson, V., Ascencio, M., & Miller, A. (2002). Parenting among Latino families in the United States. In M. Bornstein (Ed.), *Handbook of parenting* (2nd ed., Vol. 4). Mahwah, NJ: Erlbaum.

Lynch, M.E. (1991). Gender intensification. In R.M. Lerner, A.C. Petersen, & J. Brooks-Gunn (Eds.), *Encyclopedia of adolescence* (Vol. 1). New York: Garland.

Lyon, G.R. (1996). Learning disabilities. In *Special education for students with disabilities.* Los Altos, CA: Packard Foundation.

Lyon, G.R., & Moats, L.C. (1997). Critical conceptual and methodological considerations in reading intervention research. *Journal of Learning Disabilities, 30,* 578–588.

Lyons, M.J., True, W.R., Eisen, S.A., Goldberg, J., Meyer, J.M., Farone, S.V., Eaves, L.J., & Tsuang, M.T. (1995). Differential heritability of adult and juvenile antisocial traits. *Archives of General Psychiatry, 52,* 906–915.

Lyons, N.P. (1990). Listening to voices we have not heard. In C. Gilligan, N.P. Lyons, & T.J. Hanmer (Eds.), *Making connections.* Cambridge, MA: Harvard University Press.

M

Maas, H.S. (1954). The role of members in clubs of lower-class and middle-class adolescents. *Child Development, 25,* 241–251.

Maccoby, E.E. (1984). Middle childhood in the context of the family. In W.A. Collins (Ed.), *Development during middle childhood.* Washington, DC: National Academy Press.

Maccoby, E.E. (1987, November). Interview with Elizabeth Hall: All in the family. *Psychology Today,* pp. 54–60.

Maccoby, E.E. (1992). Trends in the study of socialization: Is there a Lewinian heritage? *Journal of Social Issues, 48,* 171–185.

Maccoby, E.E. (1995). The two sexes and their social systems. In P. Moen, G.H. Elder, & K. Luscher (Eds.), *Examining lives in context.* Washington, DC: American Psychological Association.

Maccoby, E.E. (1996). Peer conflict and intrafamily conflict: Are there conceptual bridges? *Merrill-Palmer Quarterly, 42,* 165–176.

Maccoby, E.E. (1998). *The two sexes.* Cambridge, MA: Harvard University Press.

Maccoby, E.E., & Jacklin, C.N. (1974). *The psychology of sex differences.* Palo Alto, CA: Stanford University Press.

Maccoby, E.E., & Mnookin, R.H. (1992). *Dividing the child: Social and legal dilemmas of custody.* Cambridge, MA: Harvard University Press.

MacDermid, S., & Crouter, A.C. (1995). Midlife, adolescence, and parental employment in family systems. *Journal of Youth and Adolescence, 24,* 29–54.

MacDonald, K. (1987). Parent-child physical play with rejected, neglected, and popular boys. *Developmental Psychology, 23,* 705–711.

MacLean, M.G., & Paradise, M.J. (1997, April). *Substance use and psychological health in homeless adolescents.* Paper presented at the meeting of the Society for Research in Child Development, Washington, DC.

Maddux, C.D., Johnson, D.L., & Willis, J.W. (1997). *Educational computing.* Boston: Allyn & Bacon.

Mader, S. (1999). *Biology* (6th ed.). New York: McGraw-Hill.

Madison, B.E., & Foster-Clark, F.S. (1996, March). *Pathways to identity and intimacy: Effects of gender and personality.* Paper presented at the meeting of the Society for Research on Adolescence, Boston.

Maehr, M.L. (2001). Goal theory is *not* dead—not yet, anyway: A reflection on the special issue. *Educational Psychology Review, 13,* 177–186.

Maehr, M.L., & Midgley, C. (1996). *Transforming school cultures.* Boulder, CO: Westview Press.

Magee, J., Gordon, J.I., & Whelan, A. (2001). Bringing the human genome and the revolution in bioinformatics to the medical school classroom. *Academic Medicine, 76,* 852–855.

Maggs, J.L., Schulenberg, J., & Hurrelmann, K. (1997). Developmental transitions in adolescence: Health promotion implications. In J. Schulenberg, J.L. Maggs, & K. Hurrelmann (Eds.), *Health risks and developmental transitions during adolescence.* New York: Cambridge University Press.

Magnuson, K.A., & Duncan, G.J. (2002). Parents in poverty. In M. Bornstein (Ed.), *Handbook of parenting* (2nd ed., Vol. 4). Mahwah, NJ: Erlbaum.

Magnuson, K.A., & Duncan, G.J. (2002). Poverty and parenting. In M.H. Bornstein (Ed.), *Handbook of parenting.* Mahwah, NJ: Erlbaum.

Magnusson, D. (1988). *Individual development from an interactional perspective: A longitudinal study.* Hillsdale, NJ: Erlbaum.

Maguin, E., Zucker, R.A., & Fitzgerald, H.E. (1995). The path to alcohol problems through conduct problems: A family-based approach to very early intervention with risk. In G.M. Boyd, J. Howard, & R.A. Zucker (Eds.), *Alcohol problems among adolescents.* Hillsdale, NJ: Erlbaum.

Main, M. (2000). Attachment theory. In A. Kazdin (Ed.), *Encyclopedia of psychology.* Washington, DC, & New York: American Psychological Association and Oxford University Press.

Majhanovich, S. (1998, April). *Unscrambling the semantics of Canadian multiculturalism.* Paper presented at the meeting of the American Educational Research Association, San Diego.

Male, M. (2003). *Technology for inclusion* (3rd Ed.). Boston: Allyn & Bacon.

Malik, N.M., & Furman, W. (1993). Practitioner review: Problems in children's peer relations: What can the clinician do? *Journal of Child Psychology and Psychiatry, 34,* 1303–1326.

Malina, R.M. (2001). Physical activity and fitness: Pathways from childhood to adulthood. *American Journal of Human Biology, 13,* 162–172

Manis, F.R., Keating, D.P., & Morrison, F.J. (1980). Developmental differences in the allocation of processing capacity. *Journal of Experimental Child Psychology, 29,* 156–169.

Manke, B., & Pike, A. (1997, April). *The search for new domains of nonshared environmental experience: Looking outside the family.* Paper presented at the meeting of the Society for Research in Child Development, Washington, DC.

Mantzoros, C.S. (2000). Role of leptin in reproduction. *Annals of the New York Academy of Sciences, 900,* 174–83.

Mantzoros, C.S., Flier, J.S., & Rogol, A.D. (1997). A longitudinal assessment of hormonal and physical alterations during normal puberty in boys. V. Rising leptin levels may signal the onset of puberty. *Journal of Clinical Endocrinology and Metabolism, 82,* 1066–1070.

Maracek, J. (1995). Gender, politics, and psychology's ways of knowing. *American Psychologist, 50,* 162–163.

Marcell, A.V., & Millstein, S.G. (2001, March). *Quality of adolescent preventive services: The role of physician attitudes and self-efficacy.* Paper presented at the meeting of the Society for Adolescent Medicine, San Diego.

Marcia, J. (1980). Ego identity development. In J. Adelson (Ed.), *Handbook of adolescent psychology.* New York: Wiley.

Marcia, J. (1987). The identity status approach to the study of ego identity development. In T. Honess & K. Yardley (Eds.), *Self and identity: Perspectives across the lifespan.* London: Routledge & Kegan Paul.

Marcia, J. (1989). Identity and intervention. *Journal of Adolescence, 12,* 401–410.

Marcia, J. (1994). The empirical study of ego identity. In H.A. Bosma, T.L.G. Graafsma, H.D. Grotevant, & D.J. De Levita (Eds.), *Identity and development.* Newbury Park, CA: Sage.

Marcia, J. (1996). Unpublished review of J.W. Santrock's *Adolescence,* 7th ed. (Dubuque, IA: Brown & Benchmark).

Marklein, M.B. (1998, November 24). An eye-level meeting of the minds. *USA Today,* p. 9D.

Markstrom, C.A., & Tryon, R.J. (1997, April). *Resiliency, social support, and coping among poor African-American and European-American Appalachian adolescents.* Paper presented at the meeting of the Society for Research in Child Development, Washington, DC.

Markus, H., & Nurius, P. (1986). Possible selves. *American Psychologist, 41,* 954–969.

Markus, H.R., & Kitayama, S. (1994). The cultural construction of self and emotion: Implications for social behavior. In S. Kitayama & H.R. Markus (Eds.), *Emotion and culture.* Washington, DC: American Psychological Association.

Markus, H.R., Mullally, P.R., & Kitayama, S. (1999). *Selfways: Diversity in modes of cultural participation.* Unpublished manuscript, Department of Psychology, University of Michigan.

Marmorstein, N.R., & Shiner, R.L. (1996, March). *The family environments of depressed adolescents.* Paper presented at the meeting of the Society for Research on Adolescence, Boston.

Marsh, H.W. (1991). Employment during high school: Character building or a subversion of academic goals? *Sociology of Education, 64,* 172–189.

Marshall, S., Adams, G.R., Ryan, B.A., & Keating, L.J. (1994, February). *Parental influences on adolescent empathy.* Paper presented at the meeting of the Society for Research on Adolescence, San Diego.

Martella, R.C., Nelson, J.R., & Marchand-Martella, N.E. (2003). *Managing disruptive behaviors in the classroom.* Boston: Allyn & Bacon.

Martin, E.W., Martin, R., & Terman, D.L. (1996). The legislative and litigation history of special education. *Future of Children, 6* (1), 25–53.

Martin, J. (1976). *The education of adolescents.* Washington, DC: U.S. Department of Education.

Martin, N.C. (1997, April). *Adolescents' possible selves and the transition to adulthood.* Paper presented at the meeting of the Society for Research in Child Development, Washington, DC.

Masten, A.S., & Coatsworth, J.D. (1998). The development of competence in favorable and unfavorable environments: Lessons from research on successful children. *American Psychologist, 53,* 205–220.

Masten, A.S., Hubbard, J.J., Gest, S.D., Tellegen, A., Garmezy, N., & Ramirez, M. (in press). Adaptation in the context of adversity: Pathways to resilience and maladaptation from childhood to late adolescence. *Development and Psychopathology.*

Mathes, P.G., Howard, J.K., Allen, S.H., & Fuchs, D. (1998). Peer-assisted learning strategies for first-grade readers: Responding to the needs of diverse learners. *Reading Research Quarterly, 33,* 62–94.

Matlin, M.W. (1993). *The psychology of women* (2nd ed.). San Diego: Harcourt Brace Jovanovich.

Matsumoto, D. (2000). Cross-cultural communication. In A. Kazdin (Ed.), *Encyclopedia of psychology.* Washington, DC, and New York: American Psychological Association and Oxford University Press.

Mayer, J.D., Caruso, D., & Salovy, P. (2000). Competing models of emotional intelligence. In R. Sternberg (Ed.), *Handbook of human intelligence.* New York: Cambridge University Press.

Mayes L.C., & Truman, S.D. (2002). Substance abuse and parenting. In M. Bornstein (Ed.), *Handbook of parenting* (2nd ed., Vol. 4). Mahwah, NJ: Erlbaum.

McAdoo, H.P. (1996). *Black families* (3rd ed.). Newbury Park, CA: Sage.

McAdoo, H.P. (2002). African-American parenting. In M. Bornstein (Ed.), *Handbook of parenting* (2nd ed., Vol. 4). Mahwah, NJ: Erlbaum.

McAlister, A., Perry, C., Killen, J., Slinkard, L.A., & Maccoby, N. (1980). Pilot study of smoking, alcohol, and drug abuse prevention. *American Journal of Public Health, 70,* 719–721.

McCormick, C.B., & Pressley, M. (1997). *Educational psychology.* New York: Longman.

McDougall, P., Schonert-Reichl, K., & Hymel, S. (1996, March). *Adolescents at risk for high school dropout: The role of social factors.* Paper presented at the meeting of the Society for Research on Adolescence, Boston.

McHale, J.P., & Grolnick, W.S. (Eds.). (2001). *Retrospect and prospect in the psychological study of families.* Mahwah, NJ: Erlbaum.

McHale, S.M. (1995). Lessons about adolescent development from the study of African-American youth. In L.J. Crockett & A.C. Crouter (Eds.), *Pathways through adolescence.* Hillsdale, NJ: Erlbaum.

McLanahan, S., & Sandefur, G. (1994). *Growing up with a single parent: What hurts, what helps?* Cambridge, MA: Harvard University Press.

McLoyd, V.C. (1990). The impact of economic hardship on Black families and children: Psychological distress, parenting, and socioemotional development. *Child Development, 61,* 311–346.

McLoyd, V.C. (1993, March). *Sizing up the future: Economic stress, expectations, and adolescents' achievement motivation.* Paper presented at the biennial meeting of the Society for Research in Child Development, New Orleans.

McLoyd, V.C. (1998). Children in poverty. In I.E. Siegel & K.A. Renninger (Eds.), *Handbook of child psychology* (5th ed., Vol. 4). New York: Wiley.

McLoyd, V.C. (2000). Poverty. In A. Kazdin (Ed.), *Encyclopedia of psychology.* Washington, DC, and New York: American Psychological Association and Oxford University Press.

McMillan, J.H. (2000). *Educational research* (3rd ed.). New York: HarperCollins.

McMillan, J.H., & Wergin, J.F. (2002). *Understanding and evaluating educational research* (2nd Ed.). Upper Saddle River, NJ: Prentice-Hall.

McNally, D. (1990). *Even eagles need a push.* New York: Dell.

McPartland, J.M., & McDill, E.L. (1976). *The unique role of schools in the causes of youthful crime.* Baltimore: Johns Hopkins University Press.

McRee, J.N., & Gebelt, J.L. (2001, April). *Pubertal development, choice of friends, and adolescent male tobacco use.* Paper presented the meeting of the Society for Research in Child Development, Minneapolis.

Mead, M. (1928). *Coming of age in Samoa.* New York: Morrow.

Mead, M. (1978, Dec. 30–Jan. 5). The American family: An endangered species. *TV Guide.*

Medler, S.M. (2000, April). *Adolescent and best friend smoking behavior: What role does attitude play?* Paper presented at the meeting of the Society for Research on Adolescence, Chicago.

Medrich, E.A., Rosen, J., Rubin, V., & Buckley, S. (1982). *The serious business of growing up.* Berkeley: University of California Press.

Meece, J.L., & Kurtz-Costes, B. (2001). Introduction: The schooling of ethnic minority children. *Educational Psychologist, 36,* 1–8.

Meichenbaum, D., & Butler, L. (1980). Toward a conceptual model of the treatment of test anxiety: Implications for research and treatment. In I.G. Sarason (Ed.), *Test anxiety.* Mahwah, NJ: Erlbaum.

Mekos, E., Hetherington, E.M., & Reiss, D. (1996). Sibling differences in problem behavior: The role of differential treatment in nondivorced and remarried families. *Child Development, 67,* 148–165.

Melby, J.N. (1995, March). *Early family and peer predictors of later adolescent tobacco use.* Paper presented at the meeting of the Society for Research in Child Development, Indianapolis.

Merrell, K.W., & Gimpel, G.A. (1997). *Social skills of children and adolescents.* Mahwah, NJ: Erlbaum.

Messinger, J.C. (1971). Sex and repression in an Irish folk community. In D.S. Marshal & R.C. Suggs (Eds.), *Human sexual behavior: Variations in the ethnographic spectrum* (pp. 3–37). New York: Basic Books.

Metz, E., & McLellan, J.A. (2000, April). *Challenging community service predicts civic engagement and social concerns.* Paper presented at the meeting of the Society for Research on Adolescence, Chicago.

Meyer-Bahlburg, H.F., Ehrhart, A.A., Rosen, L.R., Gruen, R.S., Veridiano, N.P., Vann, F.H., & Neuwalder, H.F. (1995). Prenatal estrogens and the development of homosexual orientation. *Developmental Psychology, 31,* 12–21.

Michael, R.T., Gagnon, J.H., Laumann, E.O., & Kolata, G. (1994). *Sex in America.* Boston: Little, Brown.

Midgley, C. (Ed.), *Goals, goal structures, and patterns of adaptive learning.* Mahwah, NJ: Erlbaum.

Midgley, C., & Urdan, T. (1995). Predictors of middle school students' use of self-handicapping strategies. *Journal of Early Adolescence, 15,* 389–411.

Miller, B.C., Benson, B., & Galbraith, K.A. (2001). Family relationships and adolescent pregnancy risk: A research synthesis. *Developmental Review, 21,* 1–38.

Miller, J.G. (1995, March). *Culture, context, and personal agency: The cultural grounding of self and morality.* Paper presented at the meeting of the Society for Research in Child Development, Indianapolis.

Miller, M.A., Alberts, J.K., Hecht, M.L., Trost, M.R., & Krizek, R.L. (2000). *Adolescent relationships and drug use.* Mahwah, NJ: Erlbaum.

Miller, P.J. (2001, April). *New insights from developmental cultural psychology: What the study of intra-cultural variation can contribute.* Paper presented at the meeting of the Society for Research on Child Development, Minneapolis.

Miller, S.K., & Slap, G.G. (1989). Adolescent smoking: A review of prevalence and prevention. *Journal of Adolescent Health Care, 10,* 129–135.

Miller-Jones, D. (1989). Culture and testing. *American Psychologist, 44,* 360–366.

Millstein, S.G. (1993). A view of health from the adolescent's perspective. In S.G. Millstein, A.C. Petersen, & E.O. Nightingale (Eds.), *Promoting the health of adolescents.* New York: Oxford University Press.

Minuchin, P. (2002). Looking toward the horizon: Present and future in the study of family systems. In J.P. McHale & W.S. Grolnick (Eds.), *Retrospect and prospect in the study of families.* Mahwah, NJ: Erlbaum.

Minuchin, P.P., & Shapiro, E.K. (1983). The school as a context for social development. In P.H. Mussen (Ed.), *Handbook of child psychology* (4th ed., Vol. 4). New York: Wiley.

Mischel, W. (1973). Toward a cognitive social learning reconceptualization of personality. *Psychological Review, 80,* 252–283.

Mischel, W. (1995, August). *Cognitive-affective theory of person-environment psychology.* Paper presented at the meeting of the American Psychological Association, New York City.

Mischel, W., & Mischel, H. (1975, April). *A cognitive social-learning analysis of moral development.* Paper presented at the meeting of the Society for Research in Child Development, Denver.

Mizes, J.S., & Miller, K.J. (2000). Eating disorders. In M. Herson & R.T. Ammerman (Eds.), *Advanced abnormal child psychology* (2nd ed.). Mahwah, NJ: Erlbaum.

Moje, E., Ciechanowski, K.M., Ellis, L., & Carrillo, R. (2002, April). *"I'm not White": Racial and ethnic identity representations among Latino/a youth.* Paper presented at the meeting of the Society for Research on Adolescence, New Orleans.

Moldin, S. (1999). Research methods in behavior genetics. In P. Kendall, J. Butcher, & G. Holmbeck (Eds.), *Handbook of research methods in clinical psychology.* New York: Wiley.

Monteith, M. (2000). Prejudice. In A. Kazdin (Ed.), *Encyclopedia of psychology.* Washington, DC, and New York: American Psychological Association and Oxford University Press.

Montemayor, R. (1982). The relationship between parent-adolescent conflict and the amount of time adolescents spend with parents, peers, and alone. *Child Development, 53,* 1512–1519.

Montemayor, R., & Flannery, D.J. (1991). Parent-adolescent relations in middle and late adolescence. In R.M. Lerner, A.C. Petersen, & J. Brooks-Gunn (Eds.), *Encyclopedia of adolescence* (Vol. 2). New York: Garland.

Montemayor, R., Adams, G.R., & Gulotta, T.P. (Eds.). (1990). *From childhood to adolescence: A transitional period?* Newbury Park, CA: Sage.

Monti, P.M., Colby, S.M., & O'Leary, T.A. (Eds.). (2001). *Adolescents, alcohol, and substance abuse.* New York: Guilford.

Moore, D. (1998, Fall). Gleanings: Focus on work-based learning. *CenterWork Newsletter* (NCRVE, University of California, Berkeley), pp. 1–4.

Moos, R.H., Finney, J.W., & Cronkite, R.C. (1990). *Alcoholism treatment: Context, process, and outcome.* New York: Oxford University Press.

Morales, J., & Roberts, J. (2002, April). *Developmental pathways from peer competence to romantic relationships.* Paper presented at the meeting of the Society for Research on Adolescence, New Orleans.

Morgan, M. (1984). Reward-induced decrements and increments in intrinsic motivation. *Review of Educational Research, 54,* 5–30.

Morgan, M. (1987). Television, sex-role attitudes, and sex-role behavior. *Journal of Early Adolescence, 7,* 269–282.

Morris, L., Warren, C.W., & Aral, S.O. (1993, September). Measuring adolescent sexual behaviors and related health outcomes. *Public Health Reports, 108,* 31–36.

Morrison, L.L., & L'Heureux, J. (2001). Suicide and gay/lesbian/bisexual youth: Implications for clinicians. *Journal of Adolescence, 24,* 39–50.

Morrow, L. (1988, August 8). Through the eyes of children. *Time,* pp. 32–33.

Mortimer, J., & Lorence, J. (1979). Work experience and occupational value socialization: A longitudinal study. *American Journal of Sociology, 84,* 1361–1385.

Mortimer, J., Finch, M., Ryu, S., Shanahan, M., & Call, K. (1996). The effects of work intensity on adolescent mental health, achievement, and behavioral adjustment: New evidence from a prospective study. *Child Development, 67,* 1243–1261.

Mortimer, J.T., Finch, M., Shanahan, M., & Ryu, S. (1992). Work experience, mental health, and behavioral adjustment in adolescence. *Journal of Research on Adolescence, 2,* 24–57.

Mortimer, J.T., Harley, C., & Johnson, M.K. (1998, February). *Adolescent work quality and the transition to adulthood.* Paper presented at the meeting of the Society for Research on Adolescence, San Diego, CA.

Moss, R., & Reyes, O. (2000, April). *The effects of exposure to community violence on urban youth and relevant protective factors.* Paper presented at the meeting of the Society for Research on Adolescence, Chicago.

Mosteller, F. (1995, Summer/Fall). The Tennessee study of class size in the early school grades. *Future of Children, 5* (2), 113–127.

Mott, F.L., & Marsiglio, W. (1985, September/October). Early childbearing and completion of high school. *Family Planning Perspectives,* p. 234.

Mullis, I.V.S., Martin, M.O., Beaton, A.E., Gonzales, E.J., Kelly, D.L., & Smith, T.A. (1998). *Mathematics and science achievement in the final year of secondary school.* Chestnut Hill, MA: Boston College, TIMSS International Study Center.

Munsch, J., Woodward, J., & Darling, N. (1995). Children's perceptions of their relationships with coresiding and non-custodial fathers. *Journal of Divorce and Remarriage, 23,* 39–54.

Murdock, B.B. (1999). Working memory and conscious awareness. In A.F. Collins, S.E. Gatherhole, M.A. Conway, & P.E. Morris (Eds.), *Theories of memory.* Mahwah, NJ: Erlbaum.

Murphy, K., & Schneider, B. (1994). Coaching socially rejected early adolescents regarding behaviors used by peers to infer liking: A dyad-specific intervention. *Journal of Early Adolescence, 14,* 83–95.

Murray, J.P. (2000). Media effects. In A. Kazdin (Ed.), *Encyclopedia of psychology.* Washington, DC, and New York: American Psychological Association and Oxford University Press.

Murrell, A.J. (2000). Discrimination. In A. Kazdin (Ed.), *Encyclopedia of psychology.* Washington, DC, and New York: American Psychological Association and Oxford University Press.

Myers, D.L. (1999). *Excluding violent youths from juvenile court: The effectiveness of legislative waiver.* Doctoral dissertation, University of Maryland, College Park.

Nagata, D.K. (1989). Japanese American children and adolescents. In J.T. Gibbs & L.N. Huang (Eds.), *Children of color.* San Francisco: Jossey-Bass.

Naglieri, J. (2000). The Stanford-Binet tests. In A. Kazdin (Ed.), *Encyclopedia of psychology.* Washington, DC, and New York: American Psychological Association and Oxford University Press.

Nansel, T., & Overpeck, M. (2002, April). *The relationship of bullying and being bullied to aggression/violence in a nationally representative sample of U.S. youth.* Paper presented at the meeting of the Society for Research on Adolescence, New Orleans.

Nansel, T.R., Overpeck, M., Pilla, R., Ruan, W., Simons-Morton, B., & Scheidt, P. (2001). Bullying behaviors among U.S. youth. *Journal of the American Medical Association, 285,* 2094–2100.

Nash, J.M. (1997, February 3). Fertile minds. *Time,* pp. 50–54.

National and Community Service Coalition. (1995). *Youth volunteerism.* Washington, DC: Author.

National Assessment of Educational Progress. (1976). *Adult work skills and knowledge* (Report No. 35-COD-01). Denver: National Assessment of Educational Progress.

National Assessment of Educational Progress. (1996). Gender Differences in motivation and strategy use in science. *Journal of Research in Science Teaching, 33,* 393–406.

National Assessment of Educational Progress. (1997). *NAEP 1996 mathematics report card for the nation and the states.* Washington, DC: National Center for Education Statistics.

National Center for Addiction and Substance Abuse. (2001). *2000 teen survey.* New York: Author.

National Center for Education Statistics. (1997). *School-family linkages* [Unpublished manuscript]. Washington, DC: U.S. Department of Education.

National Center for Education Statistics. (1998). *Violence and discipline problems in U.S. public schools.* Washington, DC: Author.

National Center for Education Statistics. (2000). *The condition of education.* Washington, DC: U.S. Department of Education, Office of Educational Research and Improvement.

National Center for Health Statistics. (2000). *Adolescent Health Chartbook in Health, United States, 2000.* Hyattsville, MD: U.S. Department of Health and Human Services.

National Center for Health Statistics. (2000). *Health United States, 2000, with adolescent health chartbook.* Bethesda, MD: U.S. Department of Health and Human Services.

National Center for Health Statistics. (2001). *Health, United States, socioeconomic status.* Atlanta, GA: Centers for Disease Control and Prevention.

National Clearinghouse for Alcohol and Drug Information. (1999). *Physical and psychological effects of anabolic steroids.* Washington, DC: Substance Abuse and Mental Health Services Administration.

National Vital Statistics Reports. (2001). Deaths and death rates for the 10 leading causes of death in specified age groups. *National Vital Statistics Reports, 48* (No. 11), Table 8.

Neemann, J., Hubbard, J., & Masten, A.S. (1995). The changing importance of romantic relationship involvement to competence from childhood to late adolescence. *Development and Psychopathology, 7,* 727–750.

Neimark, E.D. (1982). Adolescent thought: Transition to formal operations. In B.B. Wolman (Ed.), *Handbook of developmental psychology.* Englewood Cliffs, NJ: Prentice Hall.

Neisser, U., Boodoo, G., Bouchard, T.J., Boykin, A.W., Brody, N., Ceci, S.J., Halpern, D.F., Loehlin, J.C., Perloff, R., Sternberg, R.J., & Urbina, S. (1996). Intelligence: Knowns and unknowns. *American Psychologist, 51,* 77–101.

Neugarten, B.L. (1988, August). *Policy issues for an aging society.* Paper presented at the meeting of the American Psychological Association, Atlanta.

Newby, T.J., Stepich, D.A., Lehman, J.D., & Russell, J.D. (2000). *Instructional technology for teaching and learning* (2nd ed.). Upper Saddle River, NJ: Prentice Hall.

Newcomb, M.D., & Bentler, P.M. (1989). Substance use and abuse among children and teenagers. *American Psychologist, 44,* 242–248.

Newcomer, S.F., & Udry, J.R. (1985). Oral sex in an adolescent population. *Archives of Sexual Behavior, 14,* 41–46.

Newman, B.S., & Muzzonigro, P.G. (1993). The effects of traditional family values on the coming out process of gay male adolescents. *Adolescence, 28,* 213–226.

Newman, J.W. (2002). *America's teachers.* Boston: Allyn & Bacon.

Nicholas, G., & Daniel, J.H. (2000, April). *Music videos: Influential or entertaining?* Paper presented at the meeting of the Society for Research on Adolescence, Chicago.

Nicholls, J.G. (1979). Development of perception of own attainment and causal attribution for success and failure in reading. *Journal of Educational Psychology, 71,* 94–99.

Niederjohn, D.M., Welsh, D.P., & Scheussler, M. (2000, April). *Adolescent romantic relationships: Developmental influences of parents and peers.* Paper presented at the meeting of the Society for Research on Adolescence, Chicago.

Nottelmann, E.D., Susman, E.J., Blue, J.H., Inoff-Germain, G., Dorn, L.D., Loriaux, D.L., Cutler, G.B., & Chrousos, G.P. (1987). Gonadal and adrenal hormone correlates of adjustment in early adolescence. In R.M. Lerner & T.T. Foch (Eds.), *Biological-psychological interactions in early adolescence.* Hillsdale, NJ: Erlbaum.

Nucci, L. (1996). Morality and the personal sphere of actions. In E. Reed, E. Turiel, & T. Brown (Eds.), *Values and knowledge.* Mahwah, NJ: Erlbaum.

Nucci, L. (2001). *Education in the moral domain.* Cambridge, UK: Cambridge University Press.

O'Brien, R.W. (1990, March). *The use of family members and peers as resources during adolescence.* Paper presented at the meeting of the Society for Research in Adolescence, Atlanta.

O'Connor, T.G. (1994, February). *Patterns of differential parental treatment.* Paper presented at the meeting of the Society for Research on Adolescence, San Diego.

O'Connor, T.G., Hetherington, E.M., Reiss, D., & Plomin, R. (1995). A twin-sibling study of observed parent-adolescent interactions. *Child Development, 66,* 812–829.

O'Quin, K., & Dirks, P. (1999). Humor. In M.A. Runco & S. Pritzker (Eds.), *Encyclopedia of creativity.* San Diego: Academic Press.

Oakes, J., & Lipton, M. (2003). *Teaching to change the world* (2nd Ed.). New York: McGraw-Hill.

Oden, S.L., & Asher, S.R. (1975, April). *Coaching children in social skills for friendship making.* Paper presented at the meeting of the Society for Research in Child Development, Denver.

Offer, D., Ostrov, E., Howard, K.I., & Atkinson, R. (1988). *The teenage world: Adolescents' self-image in ten countries.* New York: Plenum.

Office of Juvenile Justice and Prevention. (1998). *Arrests in the United States under age 18: 1997.* Washington, DC: Author.

Ogbu, J.U. (1989, April). *Academic socialization of black children: An inoculation against future failure?* Paper presented at the meeting of the Society for Research in Child Development, Kansas City.

Ogbu, J., & Stern, P. (2001). Caste status and intellectual development. In R.J. Sternberg & E.L. Grigorenko (Eds.). *Environmental effects on cognitive abilities.* Mahwah, NJ: Erlbaum.

Olivardia, R., Pope, H.G., Mangweth, B., & Hudson, J.I. (1995). Eating disorders in college men. *American Journal of Psychiatry, 152,* 1279–1284.

Olweus, D. (1980). Bullying among schoolboys. In R. Barnen (Ed.), *Children and violence.* Stockholm: Acaemic Litteratur.

Olweus, D. (1993). *Bullying at school.* Cambridge, MA: Blackwell.

Olweus, D. (1994). Development of stable aggressive reaction patterns in males. *Advances in the study of aggression* (Vol. 1). Orlando: Academic Press.

Orlofsky, J. (1976). Intimacy status: Relationship to interpersonal perception. *Journal of Youth and Adolescence, 5,* 73–88.

Orlofsky, J., Marcia, J., & Lesser, I. (1973). Ego identity status and the intimacy vs. isolation crisis of young adulthood. *Journal of Personality and Social Psychology, 27,* 211–219.

Orthner, D.K., Giddings, M., & Quinn, W. (1987). *Youth in transition: A study of adolescents from Air Force and civilian families.* Washington, DC: U.S. Air Force.

Oser, F., & Gmünder, P. (1991). *Religious judgment: A developmental perspective.* Birmingham, AL: Religious Education Press.

Osipow, S.H., & Littlejohn, E.M. (1995). Toward a multicultural theory of career development: Prospects and dilemmas. In F.T.L. Leong (Ed.), *Career development and vocational behavior of racial and ethnic minorities.* Hillsdale, NJ: Erlbaum.

Osofsky, J.D. (1990, Winter). Risk and protective factors for teenage mothers and their infants. *SRCD Newsletter,* pp. 1–2.

Overton, W.F., & Byrnes, J.P. (1991). Cognitive development. In R.M. Lerner, A.C. Petersen, & J. Brooks-Gunn (Eds.), *Encyclopedia of adolescence* (Vol. 1). New York: Garland.

Owens, T., Stryker, S., & Goodman, N. (Eds.) (2001). *Extending self-esteem theory and research.* New York: Cambridge University Press.

Paige, K.E., & Paige, J.M. (1985). *Politics and reproductive rituals.* Berkeley: University of California Press.

Paikoff, R.L., Parfenoff, S.H., Williams, S.A., McCormick, A., Greenwood, G.L., & Holmbeck, G.N. (1997). Parenting, parent-child relationships, and sexual possibility situations among urban African American preadolescents: Preliminary findings and implications for HIV prevention. *Journal of Family Psychology, 11,* 11–22.

Paloutzian, R. (2000). *Invitation to the psychology of religion* (3rd ed.). Boston: Allyn & Bacon.

Paloutzian, R., & Santrock, J.W. (2000). The psychology of religion. In J.W. Santrock, *Psychology* (6th ed.). New York: McGraw-Hill.

Paludi, M.A. (1998). *The psychology of women.* Upper Saddle River, NJ: Prentice-Hall.

Papini, D., & Sebby, R. (1988). Variations in conflictual family issues by adolescent pubertal status, gender, and family member. *Journal of Early Adolescence, 8,* 1–15.

Parcel, G.S., Simons-Morton, G.G., O'Hara, N.M., Baranowski, T., Kolbe, L.J., & Bee, D.E. (1987). School promotion of healthful diet and exercise behavior: An integration of organizational change and social learning theory interventions. *Journal of School Health, 57,* 150–156.

Paris, S.G., & Paris, A.H. (2001). Classroom applications of research on self-regulated learning. *Educational Psychologist, 36,* 89–102.

Parke, R.D. (1995). Fathers and families. In M.H. Bornstein (Ed.), *Children and parenting* (Vol. 3). Hillsdale, NJ: Erlbaum.

Parke, R.D. (2001). Parenting in the new millennium: Prospects, promises, and pitfalls. In J.P. McHale & W.S. Grolnick (Eds.), *Retrospect and prospect in the psychological study of families.* Mahwah, NJ: Erlbaum.

Parke, R.D. (2002). Fathers and families. In M. Bornstein (Ed.), *Handbook of parenting* (2nd ed., Vol. 3). Mahwah, NJ: Erlbaum.

Parke, R.D., & Buriel, R. (1998). Socialization in the family. In N. Eisenberg (Ed.), *Handbook of child psychology* (5th ed., Vol. 3). New York: Wiley.

Parke, R.D., McDowell, D.J., Kim, M., Killian, C., Dennis, J., Flyr, M.L., & Wild, M.N. (2002). Fathers' contributions to chlidren's peer relationships. In C.S. Tamis-LeMonda & N. Cabrera (Eds.), *The handbook of father involvement.* Mahwah, NJ: Erlbaum.

Parker, A., & Fischhoff, B. (2002, April). *Individual differences in decision-making competence.* Paper presented at the meeting of the Society for Research on Adolescence, New Orleans.

Parker, L. (2002, April). *A correlational analysis of factors associated with bullying.* Paper presented at the meeting of the Society for Research on Adolescence, New Orleans.

Pate, R.R., Trost, S.G., Levin, S., & Dowda, M. (2000). Sports participation and health-related behaviors of U.S. youth. *Archives of Pediatric and Adolescent Medicine, 154,* 904–911.

Patterson, C.J. (1995). Sexual orientation and human development: An overview. *Developmental Psychology, 31,* 3–11.

Patterson, G.R., & Stouthamer-Loeber, M. (1984). The correlation of family management practices and delinquency. *Child Development, 55,* 1299–1307.

Patterson, G.R., DeBaryshe, B.D., & Ramsey, E. (1989). A developmental perspective on antisocial behavior. *American Psychologist, 44,* 329–335.

Patterson, S.J., Sochting, I., & Marcia, J.E. (1992). The inner space and beyond: Women and identity. In G.R. Adams, T.P. Gullotta, & R. Montemayor (Eds.), *Adolescent identity formation.* Newbury Park, CA: Sage.

Paul, E.L. (2000). *Taking Sides: Controversial issues in sex and gender.* New York: McGraw-Hill.

Paul, E.L., & White, K.M. (1990). The development of intimate relationships in late adolescence. *Adolescence, 25,* 375–400.

Peak, L. (1996). *Pursuing excellence: A study of U.S. eighth-grade mathematics and science teaching, learning, curriculum, and achievement in international context.* Washington, DC: U.S. Department of Education, National Center for Educational Statistics.

Pellegrini, A.D. (2000, April). *Longitudinal study of bullying, victimization, and peer affiliation during the transition to middle school.* Paper presented at the meeting of the Society for Research on Adolescence, Chicago.

Pentz, M.A. (1994). Primary prevention of adolescent drug abuse. In C. Fisher & R. Lerner (Eds.), *Applied developmental psychology.* New York: McGraw-Hill.

Peplau, L.A., & Perlman, D. (Eds.). (1982). *Loneliness: A sourcebook of current theory, research, and therapy.* New York: Wiley.

Perkins, D. (1999). The many faces of constructivism. *Educational Leadership, 57* (3), 6–11.

Perry, C., Hearn, M., Murray, D., & Klepp, K. (1988). *The etiology and prevention of adolescent alcohol and drug abuse.* Unpublished manuscript, University of Minnesota.

Perry, C.L., Kelder, S.H., & Komro, K.A. (1993). The social world of adolescents: Families, peers, schools, and the community. In S.G. Millstein, A.C. Petersen, & E.O. Nightingale (Eds.), *Promoting the health of adolescents.* New York: Oxford University Press.

Perry, W.G. (1970). *Forms of intellectual and ethical development in the college years.* New York: Holt, Rinehart & Winston.

Perry, W.G. (1999). *Forms of ethical and intellectual development in the college years: A scheme.* San Francisco: Jossey-Bass.

Perry-Jenkins, M., Payne, J., & Hendricks, E. (1999, April). *Father involvement by choice or necessity: Implications for parents' well-being.* Paper presented at the meeting of the Society for Research in Child Development, Albuquerque.

Peskin, H. (1967). Pubertal onset and ego functioning. *Journal of Abnormal Psychology, 72,* 1–15.

Peters, K.F., Menaker, T.J., Wilson, P.L., & Hadley, D.W. (2001). The Human Genome Project: An update. *Cancer and Nursing, 24,* 287–292.

Petersen, A. C. (1993). Creating adolescents: The role of context and process in developmental trajectories. *Journal of Research on Adolescence, 3,* 1–18.

Petersen, A.C. (1979, January). Can puberty come any faster? *Psychology Today,* pp. 45–56.

Petersen, A.C. (1987, September). Those gangly years. *Psychology Today,* pp. 28–34.

Petersen, A.C., & Crockett, L. (1985). Pubertal timing and grade effects on adjustment. *Journal of Youth and Adolescence, 14,* 191–206.

Petersen, A.C., Sarigiani, P.A., & Kennedy, R.E. (1991). Coping with adolescence. In M.E. Colte & S. Gore (Eds.), *Adolescent stress: Causes and consequences.* New York: Aldine de Gruyter.

Peterson, K.A. (1997, September 3). In high school, dating is a world unto itself. *USA Today,* pp. 1–2D.

Peterson, P.L., Hawkins, J.D., Abbott, R.D., & Catalano, R.F. (1994). Disentangling the effects of parent drinking, family management, and parental alcohol norms on current drinking by Black and White adolescents. *Journal of Research on Adolescence, 4,* 203–228.

Petraitis, J., Flay, B.R., & Miller, T.Q. (1995). Reviewing theories of adolescent substance use: Organizing pieces of the puzzle. *Psychological Bulletin, 17,* 67–86.

Pettit, G.S., Bates, J.E., Dodge, K.A., & Meece, D.W. (1999). The impact of after-school peer contact on early adolescent externalizing problems is moderated by parental monitoring, perceived neighborhood safety, and prior adjustment. *Child Development, 70,* 768–778.

Pettit, G.S., Laird, R.D., Dodge, K.A., Bates, J.A., & Criss, M.M. (2001). Antecedents and behavior-problem outcomes of parental monitoring and psychological control in early adolescence. *Child Development, 72,* 583–598.

Pfefferbaum, A., Mathalon, D.H., Sullivan, E.V., Rawles, J.M., Zipursky, R.B., & Lim, K.O. (1994). A quantitative magnetic resonance imaging study of changes in brain morphology from infancy to late adulthood. *Archives of Neurology, 51,* 874.

Philpot, C.L., Brooks, G.R., Lusterman, D., & Nutt, R.L. (1997). *Bridging separate gender worlds.* Washington, DC: American Psychological Association.

Phinney, J.S. (1989). Stages of ethnic identity development in minority group adolescents. *Journal of Early Adolescence, 9,* 34–49.

Phinney, J.S. (1996). When we talk about American ethnic groups, what do we mean? *American Psychologist, 51,* 918–927.

Phinney, J.S. (2000). Ethnic identity. In A. Kazdin (Ed.), *Encyclopedia of psychology.* Washington, DC, and New York: American Psychological Association and Oxford University Press.

Phinney, J.S. (2000, April). *Family obligations and life satisfaction among adolescents from immigrant families.* Paper presented at the meeting of the Society for Research on Adolescence, Chicago.

Phinney, J.S., & Alipuria, L.L. (1990). Ethnic identity in college students from four ethnic groups. *Journal of Adolescence, 13,* 171–183.

Phinney, J.S., & Devich-Navarro, M. (1997). Variations in bicultural identification among African American and Mexican American adolescents. *Journal of Research on Adolescence, 7,* 3–32.

Phinney, J.S., Ferguson, D.L., & Tate, J.D. (1997). Intergroup attitudes among ethnic minority adolescents: A causal model. *Child Development, 68,* 955–969.

Phinney, J.S., & Landin, J. (1998). Research paradigms for studying ethnic minority families within and across groups. In V.C. McLoyd & L. Steinberg (Eds.), *Studying minority adolescents.* Mahwah, NJ: Erlbaum.

Phinney, J.S., Madden, T., & Ong, A. (2000). Cultural values and intergenerational discrepancies in immigrant and non-immigrant families. *Child Development, 71,* 528–539.

Phinney, J.S., & Rosenthal, D.A. (1992). Ethnic identity in adolescence: Process, context, and outcome. In G.R. Adams, T.P. Gullotta, & R. Montemayor (Eds.), *Adolescent identity formation.* Newbury Park, CA: Sage.

Piaget, J. (1932). *The moral judgment of the child.* New York: Harcourt Brace Jovanovich.

Piaget, J. (1952). *The origins of intelligence in children.* New York: International Universities Press.

Piaget, J. (1954). *The construction of reality in the child.* New York: Basic Books.

Piaget, J. (1972). Intellectual evolution from adolescence to adulthood. *Human Development, 15,* 1–12.

Pintrich, P.R., & Schunk, D.H. (2002). *Motivation in education.* (2nd Ed.). Boston: Allyn & Bacon.

Pisani, E. (2001). AIDS in the 21st century: Some critical considerations. *Reproductive Health Matters, 8,* 63–76.

Pittman, L.D. (2000, April). *Links to parenting practices of African American mothers in impoverished neighborhoods.* Paper presented at the meeting of the Society for Research on Adolescence, Chicago.

Place, D.M. (1975). The dating experience for adolescent girls. *Adolescence, 38,* 157–173.

Pleck, J.H. (1981). *The myth of masculinity.* Beverly Hills, CA: Sage.

Pleck, J.H. (1983). The theory of male sex role identity: Its rise and fall, 1936–present. In M. Lewin (Ed.), *In the shadow of the past: Psychology portrays the sexes.* New York: Columbia University Press.

Pleck, J.H. (1995). The gender-role strain paradigm: An update: In R.F. Levant & W.S. Pollack (Eds.), *A new psychology of men.* New York: Basic.

Pleck, J.H. (1997). Paternal involvement: Levels, sources, and consequences. In M.E. Lamb (Ed.), *The role of the father in child development.* New York: Wiley.

Pleck, J.H., Sonnenstein, F., & Ku, L. (1991). Adolescent males' condom use: Relationships between perceived cost benefits and consistency. *Journal of Marriage and the Family, 53,* 733–745.

Pleck, J.H., Sonnenstein, F., & Ku, L. (1994). Problem behaviors and masculine ideology in adolescent males. In R. Ketterlinus & M.E. Lamb (Eds.), *Adolescent problem behaviors.* Hillsdale, NJ: Erlbaum.

Pleiss, M.K., & Feldhusen, J.F. (1995). Mentors, role models, and heroes in the lives of gifted children. *Educational Psychologist, 30,* 159–169.

Plomin, R. (1993, March). *Human behavioral genetics and development: An overview and update.* Paper presented at the biennial meeting of the Society for Research in Child Development, New Orleans.

Plomin, R., DeFries, J.C., McClearn, G.E., & Rutter, M. (1997). *Behavioral genetics* (3rd ed.). New York: W. H. Freeman.

Plomin, R., Reiss, D., Hetherington, E.N., & Howe, G.W. (1994). Nature and nurture: Contributions to measures of family environment. *Developmental Psychology, 30,* 32–43.

Poll finds racial tension decreasing. (1990, June 29). *Asian Week,* p. 4.

Pollack, W. (1999). *Real boys.* New York: Henry Holt.

Poortinga, Y.H. (2000). Cross-cultural test adaptation. In A. Kazdin (Ed.), *Encyclopedia of psychology.* Washington, DC, and New York: American Psychological Association and Oxford University Press.

Popper, S.D., Ross, S., & Jennings, K.D. (2000). Development and psychopathology. In M. Herson & R.T. Ammerman (Eds.), *Advanced abnormal child psychopathology.* Mahwah, NJ: Erlbaum.

Porter, M. (2000, April). *Social-cognitive development and friendship competence in adolescence.* Paper presented at the meeting of the Society for Research on Adolescence, Chicago.

Potvin, L., Champagne, F., & Laberge-Nadeau, C. (1988). Mandatory driver training and road safety: The Quebec experience. *American Journal of Public Health, 78,* 1206–1212.

Powell, A.G., Farrar, E., & Cohen, D.K. (1985). *The shopping mall high school: Winners and losers in the educational marketplace.* Boston: Houghton Mifflin.

Powers, S.I., Welsh, D.P., & Wright, V. (1994). Adolescents' affective experience of family behaviors: The role of subjective understanding. *Journal of Research in Adolescence, 4,* 585–600.

Presidential Task Force on Psychology and Education. (1992). *Learner-centered psychological principles: Guidelines for school redesign and reform (draft).* Washington, DC: American Psychological Association.

Pressley, M. (1983). Making meaningful materials easier to learn. In M. Pressley & J.R. Levin (Eds.), *Cognitive strategy research: Educational applications* (pp. 239–266). New York: Springer-Verlag.

Pressley, M. (1995). More about the development of self-regulation: Complex, long-term, and thoroughly social. *Educational Psychologist, 30,* 207–212.

Pressley, M., & Roehrig, A. (2002). Educational psychology in the modern period. In B.J. Zimmerman & D.H. Schunk (Eds.), *Educational psychology.* Mahwah, NJ: Erlbaum.

Pressley, M., & Schneider, W. (1997). *Introduction to memory development during childhood and adolescence.* Mahwah, NJ: Erlbaum.

Price, J.H. (2001). Violence, mental health, and youths. *American Journal of Health Education, 32,* 130–131.

Price, R.H., Cioci, M., Penner, W., & Trautlein, B. (1990). *School and community support programs that enhance adolescent health and education.* Washington, DC: Carnegie Council on Adolescent Development.

Prinsky, L.E., & Rosenbaum, J.L. (1987). Leerics or lyrics? *Youth and Society, 18,* 384–394.

Prinstein, M.J., Fetter, M.D., & La Greca, A.M. (1996, March). *Can you judge adolescents by the company they keep? Peer group membership, substance use, and risk-taking behaviors.* Paper presented at the meeting of the Society for Research on Adolescence, Boston.

Psathas, G. (1957). Ethnicity, social class, and adolescent independence. *Sociological Review, 22,* 415–523.

Quadrel, M.J., Fischoff, B., & Davis, W. (1993). Adolescent (in)vulnerability. *American Psychologist, 48,* 102–116.

Quinton, D., Rutter, M., & Gulliver, L. (1990). Continuities in psychiatric disorders from childhood to adulthood in the children of psychiatric patients. In L. Robins & M. Rutter (Eds.), *Straight and devious pathways from childhood to adulthood.* New York: Cambridge University Press.

Raffaelli, M., & Ontai, L. (in press). "She's sixteen years old and there's boys calling over to the house": An exploratory study of sexual socialization in Latino families. *Culture, Health, and Sexuality.*

Rainey, R. (1965). The effects of directed vs. non-directed laboratory work on high school chemistry achievement. *Journal of Research in Science Teaching, 3,* 286–292.

Rajapakse, J.C., DeCarli, C., McLaughlin, A., Giedd, J.N., Krain, A.L., Hamburger, S.D., & Rapoport, J.L. (1996). Cerebral magnetic resonance image segmentation using data fusion. *Journal of Computer Assisted Tomography, 20,* 206.

Ramey, S.L., & Ramey, C.T. (2000). Early childhood experiences and developmental competence. In S. Danzinger & J. Waldfogel (Eds.), *Securing the future: Investing in children from birth to college.* New York: Russell Sage Foundation.

Ramirez, O. (1989). Mexican American children and adolescents. In J.T. Gibbs & L.N. Huang (Eds.), *Children of color.* San Francisco: Jossey-Bass.

Raskin, P.M. (1985). Identity in vocational development. In A.S. Waterman (Ed.), *Identity in adolescence.* San Francisco: Jossey-Bass.

Raymore, L.A., Barber, B.L., & Eccles, J.S. (2001). Leaving home, attending college, partnership, and parenthood: The role of life transition events in leisure pattern stability from adolescence to early adulthood. *Journal of Youth and Adolescence, 30,* 197–223.

Regnerus, M.D. (2001). *Making the Grade: The Influence of Religion upon the Academic Performance of Youth in Disadvantaged Communities.* Report 01-04, Center for Research on Religion and Urban Civil Society, University of Pennsylvania.

Reinherz, H.Z., Giaconia, R.M., Silverman, A.B., & Friedman, A.C. (1994, February). *Early psychosocial risks for adolescent suicidal ideation and attempts.* Paper presented at the meeting of the Society for Research on Adolescence, San Diego.

Reinisch, J.M. (1990). *The Kinsey Institute new report on sex: What you must know to be sexually literate.* New York: St. Martin's Press.

Remafedi, G., French, S., Story, M., Resnick, M.D., & Blum, R. (1998). The relationship between suicide risk and sexual orientation: Results of a population-based study. *American Journal of Public Health, 88,* 57–60.

Remez, L. (2000). Oral sex among adolescents: Is it sex or is it abstinence? *Family Planning Perspectives, 32,* 212–226.

Repinski, D.J., & Leffert, N. (1994, February). *Adolescents' relationships with friends: The effects of a psychoeducational intervention.* Paper presented at the biennial meeting of the Society for Research on Adolescence, San Diego.

Reschly, D. (1996). Identification and assessment of students with disabilities. *Future of children, 6* (1), 40–53.

Resnick, L., & Nelson-Gall, S. (1997). Socializing intelligence. In L. Smith, J. Dockrell, & P. Tomlinson (Eds.), *Piaget, Vygotsky, and beyond.* London: Routledge Paul.

Resnick, M.D., Wattenberg, E., & Brewer, R. (1992, March). *Paternity avowal/disavowal among partners of low income mothers.* Paper presented at the meeting of the Society for Research on Adolescence, Washington, DC.

Rest, J.R. (1986). *Moral development: Advances in theory and research.* New York: Praeger.

Rest, J.R., Narvaez, D., Bebeau, M.J., & Thoma, S.J. (1999). *Postconventional moral thinking.* Mahwah, NJ: Erlbaum.

Reuter, M.W., & Biller, H.B. (1973). Perceived paternal nurturance-availability and personality adjustment among college males. *Journal of Consulting and Clinical Psychology, 40,* 339–342.

Reynolds, D. (2000). School effectiveness and improvement. In A. Kazdin (Ed.), *Encyclopedia of psychology.* Washington, DC, and New York: American Psychological Association and Oxford University Press.

Richards, M., Suleiman, L., Sims, B., & Sedeno, A. (1994, February). *Experiences of ethnically diverse young adolescents growing up in poverty.* Paper presented at the meeting of the Society for Research on Adolescence, San Diego.

Richards, M.H., Crowe, P.A., Larson, R., & Swarr, A. (1998). Developmental patterns and gender differences in the experience of peer companionship during adolescence. *Child Development, 69,* 154–163.

Richards, M.H., & Duckett, E. (1994). The relationship of maternal employment to early adolescent daily experiences with and without parents. *Child Development, 65,* 225–236.

Richards, M.H., & Larson, R. (1990, July). *Romantic relations in early adolescence.* Paper presented at the Fifth International Conference on Personal Relations, Oxford University, England.

Richardson, J.L., Dwyer, K., McGrugan, K., Hansen, W.B., Dent, C., Johnson, C.A., Sussman, S.Y., Brannon, B., & Glay, B. (1989). Substance use among eighth-grade students who take care of themselves after school. *Pediatrics, 84,* 556–566.

Rickards, T. (1999). Brainstorming. In M.A. Runco & S. Pritzker (Eds.), *Encyclopedia of creativity.* San Diego: Academic Press.

Rimberg, H.M., & Lewis, R.J. (1994). Older adolescents and AIDS: Correlates of self-reported safer sex practices. *Journal of Research on Adolescence, 4,* 453–464.

Roberts, D., Jacobson, L., & Taylor, R.D. (1996, March). *Neighborhood characteristics, stressful life events, and African-American adolescents' adjustment.* Paper presented at the meeting of the Society for Research on Adolescence, Boston.

Roberts, D.F. (1993). Adolescents and the mass media: From "Leave It to Beaver" to "Beverly Hills 90210." In R. Takanishi (Ed.), *Adolescence in the 1990s.* New York: Teachers College Press.

Roberts, G.C., Treasure, D.C., & Kavussanu, M. (1997). Motivation in physical activity contexts: An achievement goal perspective. *Advances in Motivation and Achievement, 10,* 413–447.

Robinson, D.P., & Greene, J.W. (1988). The adolescent alcohol and drug problem: A practical approach. *Pediatric Nursing, 14,* 305–310.

Robinson, N.S. (1995). Evaluating the nature of perceived support and its relation to perceived self-worth in adolescents. *Journal of Research on Adolescence, 5,* 253–280.

Roblyer, M.D., & Edwards, J. (2000). *Integrating educational psychology into teaching.* (2nd ed.). Upper Saddle River, NJ: Prentice Hall.

Rockhill, C.M., & Greener, S.M. (1999, April). *Development of the Meta-Mood Scale for elementary-school children.* Paper presented at the meeting of the Society for Research in Child Development, Albuquerque.

Rodgers, C. (2000). Gender schema. In A. Kazdin (Ed.), *Encyclopedia of psychology.* Washington, DC, and New York: American Psychological Association and Oxford University Press.

Rodriquez, M.L., & Quinlan, S.L. (2002, April). *Searching for a meaningful identity: Self/ethnic representations and family beliefs in Latino youth.* Paper presented at the meeting of the Society for Research on Adolescence, New Orleans.

Roe, A. (1956). *The psychology of occupations.* New York: Wiley.

Roemmich, J.N., Clark, P.A., Berr, S.S., Mai, V., Mantzoros, C.S., Flier, J.S., Weltman, A., & Rogol, A.D. (1999). Gender differences in leptin levels during puberty are related to the subcutaneous fat depot and sex steroids. *American Journal of Physiology, 275,* E543–551.

Roff, M., Sells, S.B., & Golden, M.W. (1972). *Social adjustment and personality development in children.* Minneapolis: University of Minnesota Press.

Rog, E., Hunsberger, B., & Alisat, S. (2002, April). *Bridging the gap between high-school and college through a social support intervention: A long-term evaluation.* Paper presented at the meeting of the Society for Research on Adolescence, New Orleans.

Rogatch, F.A., Cicchetti, D., Shields, A., & Toth, S.L. (1995). Parenting dysfunction in child maltreatment. In M.H. Bornstein (Ed.), *Handbook of parenting* (Vol. 4). Hillsdale, NJ: Erlbaum.

Rogers, A. (1987). *Questions of gender differences: Ego development and moral voice in adolescence.* Unpublished manuscript, Department of Education, Harvard University.

Rogers, C.R. (1950). The significance of the self regarding attitudes and perceptions. In M.L. Reymart (Ed.), *Feelings and emotions.* New York: McGraw-Hill.

Rogoff, B. (1990). *Apprenticeship in thinking.* New York: Oxford University Press.

Rogoff, B. (1998). Cognition as a collaborative process. In W. Damon (Ed.), *Handbook of child psychology* (5th ed., Vol. 2). New York: Wiley.

Rogoff, B., Baker-Sennett, J., Lacasa, P., & Goldsmith, D. (1995). Development through participation in sociocultural activity. *Cultural practices as contexts for development: New Directions for Child Development, 67* (Spring), 45–65.

Rogol, A.D., Roemmich, J.N., & Clark, P.A. (1998, September). *Growth at Puberty.* Paper presented at a workshop, Physical Development, Health Futures of Youth II: Pathways to Adolescent Health, Maternal and Child Health Bureau, Annapolis, MD.

Rohner, R.P., & Rohner, E.C. (1981). Parental acceptance-rejection and parental control: Cross-cultural codes. *Ethnology, 20,* 245–260.

Romo, H. (2000, April). *Keeping Latino youth in school.* Paper presented at the meeting of the Society for Research on Adolescence, Chicago.

Rose, H.A., & Rodgers, K.B. (2000, April). *Suicide ideation in adolescents who are confused about sexual orientation: A risk and resiliency approach.* Paper presented at the meeting of the Society for Research in Adolescence, Chicago.

Rose, S., & Frieze, I.R. (1993). Young singles' contemporary dating scripts. *Sex Roles, 28,* 499–509.

Rose, S.A., Feldman, J.F., McCarton, C.M., & Wolfson, J. (1988). Information processing in seven-month-old infants as a function of risk status. *Child Development, 59,* 489–603.

Rosenbaum, E., & Kandel, D.B. (1990). Early onset of adolescent sexual behavior and drug involvement. *Journal of Marriage and the Family, 52,* 783–798.

Rosenberg, M. (1979). *Conceiving the self.* New York: Basic Books.

Rosenthal, R. (2000). Expectancy effects. In A. Kazdin (Ed.), *Encyclopedia of psychology.* Washington, DC, & New York: American Psychological Association and Oxford University Press.

Rosner, B.A., & Rierdan, J. (1994, February). *Adolescent girls' self-esteem: Variations in developmental trajectories.* Paper presented at the meeting of the Society for Research on Adolescence, San Diego.

Rosnow, R.L. (2000). Longitudinal research. In A. Kazdin (Ed.), *Encyclopedia of psychology.* Washington, DC, & New York: American Psychological Association and Oxford University Press.

Rosselli, H.C. (1996, Feb/Mar). Gifted students. *National Association for Secondary School Principals,* pp. 12–17.

Rotenberg, K.J. (1993, March). *Development of restrictive disclosure to friends.* Paper presented at the biennial meeting of the Society for Research in Child Development, New Orleans.

Roth, J., & Brooks-Gunn, J. (2000). What do adolescents need for healthy development? Implications for youth policy. *Social Policy Report, Society for Research in Child Development, XIV* (No. 1), 1–19.

Roth, J., Brooks-Gunn, J., Murray, L., & Foster, W. (1998). Promoting healthy adolescents: Synthesis of youth development program evaluations. *Journal of Research on Adolescence, 8,* 423–459.

Rothbaum, F., Poll, M., Azuma, H., Miyake, K., & Weisz, J. (2000). The development of close relationships in Japan and the United States: Paths of symbiotic harmony and generative tension. *Child Development, 71,* 1121–1142.

Rubin, K.H. (2000). Middle childhood: Social and emotional development. In A. Kazdin (Ed.), *Encyclopedia of psychology.* Washington, DC, and New York: American Psychological Association and Oxford University Press.

Rubin, K.H., Bukowski, W., & Parker, J.G. (1998). Peer interactions, relationships, and groups. In N. Eisenberg (Ed.), *Handbook of child psychology* (5th ed., Vol. 3). New York: Wiley.

Rubin, K.H., Mills, R.S.L., & Rose-Krasnor, L. (1989). Maternal beliefs and children's competence. In B. Schneider, G. Attili, J. Nadel, & R. Weissberg (Eds.), *Social competence in developmental perspective.* Amsterdam: Kluwer Academic.

Rubin, Z., & Solman, J. (1984). How parents influence their children's friendships. In M. Lewis (Ed.), *Beyond the dyad.* New York: Plenum.

Ruble, D.N., & Martin, C.L. (1998). Gender development. In N. Eisenberg (Ed.), *Handbook of child psychology* (5th ed., Vol. 3). New York: Wiley.

Ruble, D.N., Boggiano, A.K., Feldman, N.S., & Loebl, J.H. (1980). Developmental analysis of the role of social comparison in self evaluation. *Developmental Psychology, 16,* 105–115.

Rudolph, K.D., Lambert, S.F., Clark, A.G., & Kurlakowsky, K.D. (2001). Negotiating the transition to middle school: The role of self-regulatory processes. *Child Development, 72,* 929–946.

Rumberger, R.W. (1983). Dropping out of high school: The influence of race, sex, and family background. *American Educational Research Journal, 20,* 199–220.

Rumberger, R.W. (1995). Dropping out of middle school: A multilevel analysis of students and schools. *American Educational Research Journal, 3,* 583–625.

Runco, M. (2000). Creativity: Research on the processes of creativity. In A. Kazdin (Ed.), *Encyclopedia of psychology.* Washington, DC, and New York: American Psychological Association and Oxford University Press.

Russell, S.T., & Truong, N.L. (2002, April). *Adolescent sexual orientation, family relationships, and emotional health.* Paper presented at the meeting of the Society for Research on Adolescence, New Orleans.

Rutter, M. (2002). Family influences on behavior and development. In J.P. McHale & W.S. Grolnick (Eds.), *Retrospect and prospect in the study of families.* Mahwah, NJ: Erlbaum.

Rutter, M., Maughan, B., Mortimore, P., & Ouston, J. (1979). *Fifteen thousand hours: Secondary schools and their effects on children.* Cambridge, MA: Harvard University Press.

Ryan, A.M. (2001). The peer group as a context for development of adolescent motivation and achievement. *Child Development, 72,* 1135–1150.

Ryan, A.M., & Patrick, H. (1996, March). *Positive peer relationships and psychosocial adjustment during adolescence.* Paper presented at the meeting of the Society for Research on Adolescence, Boston.

Ryan-Finn, K.D., Cause, A.M., & Grove, K. (1995, March). *Children and adolescents of color: Where are you? Selection, recruitment, and retention in developmental research.* Paper presented at the meeting of the Society for Research in Child Development, Indianapolis.

Saarni, C. (1988). Children's understanding of the interpersonal consequences of dissemblance of nonverbal emotional-expressive behavior. *Journal of Nonverbal Behavior, 12,* 275–294.

Saarni, C. (1999). *The development of emotional competence.* New York: Guilford.

Sadeh, A., Raviv, A., & Gruber, R. (2000). Sleep patterns and sleep disruptions in school-age children. *Developmental Psychology, 36,* 291–301.

Sadker, M., & Sadker, D. (1986, March). Sexism in the classroom: From grade school to graduate school. *Phi Delta Kappan,* pp. 512–515.

Sadker, M., & Sadker, D. (1994). *Failing at fairness.* New York: Touchstone.

Sadker, M., & Sadker, D. (2003). *Teachers, schools, and society* (6th Ed.). New York: McGraw-Hill.

Salas, J. (2000, April). *Special relationships with teachers facilitate school success: Perspectives of Mexican American students from poor and working-class families.* Paper presented at the meeting of the Society for Research on Adolescence, Chicago.

Saliba, J.A. (1996). *Understanding new religious movements.* Grand Rapids, MI: William B. Erdmans.

Salovy, P., & Mayer, J.D. (1990). Emotional intelligence. *Imagination, Cognition, and Personality, 9,* 185–211.

Salovy, P., & Woolery, A. (2000). Emotional intelligence: Categorization and measurement. In G. Fletcher & M.S. Clark (Eds.), *The Blackwell handbook of social psychology* (Vol. 2). Oxford, UK: Blackwell.

Santelli, J.S., Rogin, L., Brener, N.D., & Lowry, R. (2001, March). *Timing of alcohol and other drug use and sexual risk behaviors among unmarried adolescents.* Paper presented at the meeting of the Society for Research on Adolescence, San Diego.

Santilli, N.R., Falbo, M.C., & Harris, J.T. (2002, April). *The role of volunteer services, self perceptions, and relationships with others on prosocial development.* Paper presented at the meeting of the Society for Research on Adolescence, New Orleans.

Santrock, J. W. (2001). *Educational psychology.* New York: McGraw-Hill.

Santrock, J. W. (2002). *Life-span development* (8th ed.). New York: McGraw-Hill.

Santrock, J.W. (2003). *Psychology* (7th ed.). New York: McGraw-Hill.

Santrock, J.W., & Halonen, J.A. (2002). *Your guide to college success* (2nd ed.). Belmont, CA: Wadsworth.

Santrock, J.W., Sitterle, K.A., & Warshak, R.A. (1988). Parent-child relationships in stepfather families. In P. Bronstein & C.P. Cowan (Eds.), *Fatherhood today: Men's changing roles in the family.* New York: Wiley.

Sarigiani, P.A., & Petersen, A.C. (2000). Adolescence: Puberty and biological maturation. In A. Kazdin (Ed.), *Encyclopedia of psychology.* Washington, DC, & New York: American Psychological Association and Oxford University Press.

Sarrel, P., & Masters, W. (1982). Sexual molestation of men by women. *Archives of Human Sexuality, 11,* 117–131.

Savin-Williams, R.C. (1995). An exploratory study of pubertal maturation timing and self-esteem among gay and bisexual male youths. *Developmental Psychology, 31,* 56–64.

Savin-Williams, R.C. (1998). The disclosure to families of same-sex attractions by lesbian, gay, and bisexual youth. *Journal of Research on Adolescence, 8,* 49–68.

Savin-Williams, R.C. (2001). *Mom, dad, I'm gay.* Washington, DC: American Psychological Association.

Savin-Williams, R.C., & Demo, D.H. (1983). Conceiving or misconceiving the self: Issues in adolescent self-esteem. *Journal of Early Adolescence, 3,* 121–140.

Savin-Williams, R.C., & Rodriguez, R.G. (1993). A developmental, clinical perspective on lesbian, gay male, and bisexual youths. In T.P. Gullotta, G.R. Adams, & R. Montemayor (Eds.), *Adolescent sexuality.* Newbury Park, CA: Sage.

Sax, L.J., Astin, A.W., Korn, W.S., & Mahoney, K.M. (1999). *The American college freshman: Norms for fall 1999.* Los Angeles: Higher Education Research Institute, UCLA.

Sax, L.J., Astin, A.W., Korn, W.S., & Mahoney, K.M. (2000). *The American freshman; National norms for 2000.* Los Angeles: Higher Education Research Institute, UCLA.

Sax, L.J., Lindholm, J.A., Atin, A.W., Korn, W.S., & Mahoney, K.M. (2001). *The American Freshman: National norms for fall 2001.* Los Angeles: Higher Education Research Institute, UCLA.

Scarr, S. (1986). Best of human genetics. *Contemporary Psychology, 41,* 149–150.

Scarr, S. (1993). Biological and cultural diversity: The legacy of Darwin for development. *Child Development, 64,* 1333–1353.

Scarr, S., & Weinberg, R.A. (1980). Calling all camps! The war is over. *American Sociological Review, 45,* 859–865.

Scarr, S., & Weinberg, R.A. (1983). The Minnesota adoption studies: Genetic differences and malleability. *Child Development, 54,* 253–259.

Schaie, K.W. (2000). Review of Santrock *Life-span development,* 8th ed. (Boston: McGraw-Hill).

Scharf, M., & Shulman, S. (2000, April). *Adolescents' socio-emotional competence and parental representations of peer relationships in adolescence.* Paper presented at the meeting of the Society for Research on Adolescence, Chicago.

Scheer, S.D. (1996, March). *Adolescent to adult transitions: Social status and cognitive factors.* Paper presented at the meeting of the Society for Research on Adolescence, Boston.

Scheer, S.D., & Unger, D.G. (1994, February). *Adolescents becoming adults: Attributes for adulthood.* Paper presented at the meeting of the Society for Research on Adolescence, San Diego.

Schiever, S.W., & Maker, C.J. (1997). Enrichment and acceleration: An overview and new directions. In N. Colangelo & G.A. Davis (Eds.), *Handbook of gifted education.* Boston: Allyn & Bacon.

Schiff, J.L., & Truglio, R.T. (1995, March). *In search of the ideal family: The use of television family portrayals during early adolescence.* Paper presented at the meeting of the Society for Research in Child Development, Indianapolis.

Schneider, B., & Stevensen, D. (1999). *The ambitious generation.* New Haven, CT: Yale University.

Schneider, W., & Bjorklund, D. (1998). Memory. In W. Damon (Ed.), *Handbook of child psychology* (5th ed., Vol. 2). New York: Wiley.

Scholte, R., & Dubas, J.S. (2002, April). *The social context of early, on-time, and late maturing Dutch boys: Implications for adjustment.* Paper presented at the meeting of the Society for Research on Adolescence, New Orleans.

Schorr, L.B. (1989, April). *Within our reach: Breaking the cycle of disadvantage.* Paper presented at the biennial meeting of the Society for Research in Child Development, Kansas City.

Schulenberg, J. (June, 1999). *Binge drinking trajectories before, during, and after college: More reasons to worry from a developmental perspective.* Invited paper presented at the meeting of the American Psychological Society, Denver, Colorado.

Schulenberg, J., & Maggs, J.L. (in press). A developmental perspective on alcohol use and heavy drinking during adolescence and the transition to early adulthood. *NIAAA Monographs.*

Schulenberg, J., Maggs, J.L., Steinman, K.J., & Zucker, R.A. (2001). Development matters: Taking the long view on substance abuse etiology and intervention during adolescence. In P.M. Monti, S.M. Colbyk, & T.A. O'Leary (Eds.), *Adolescents, alcohol, and substance abuse.* New York: Guilford.

Schulenberg, J., O'Malley, P.M., Bachman, J.G., & Johnson, L.D. (2000). "Spread your wings and fly": The course of health and well-being during the transition to young adulthood. In L. Crockett & R. Silbereisen (Eds.), *Negotiating adolescence in times of social change.* New York: Cambridge University Press.

Schunk, D.H. (1989). Self-efficacy and academic motivation. *Educational Psychologist, 25,* 71–86.

Schunk, D.H. (1991). Self-efficacy and cognitive skill learning. In C. Ames & R. Ames (Eds.), *Research on motivation and education* (Vol. 3). Orlando: Academic Press.

Schunk, D.H. (2001). Social cognitive theory and self-regulated learning. In B.J. Zimmerman & D.H. Schunk (Eds.), *Self-regulated learning and academic achievement* (2nd ed.). Mahwah, NJ: Erlbaum.

Schunk, D.H., & Ertmer, P.A. (2000). Self-regulation and academic learning: Self-efficacy enhancing interventions. In M. Boekaerts, P.R. Pintrich, & M. Zeidner (Eds.), *Handbook of self-regulation.* San Diego: Academic Press.

Schunk, D.H., & Zimmerman, B.J. (Eds.). (1994). *Self-regulation of learning and performance.* Mahwah, NJ: Erlbaum.

Schuster, M. (2000, November 16). Commentary on the increase in oral sex in adolescence. *USA Today,* p. 2D.

Scott-Jones, D. (1995, March). *Incorporating ethnicity and socioeconomic status in research with children.* Paper presented at the meeting of the Society for Research in Child Development, Indianapolis.

Search Institute. (1995). *Barriers to participation in youth programs.* Unpublished manuscript, the Search Institute, Minneapolis.

Seginer, R. (1998). Adolescents' perception of relationships with older sibling in the context of other close relationships. *Journal of Research on Adolescence, 8,* 287–308.

Seidman, E. (2000). School transitions. In A. Kazdin (Ed.), *Encyclopedia of psychology.* Washington, DC, and New York: American Psychological Association and Oxford University Press.

Seiffge-Krenke, I. (1998). *Adolescents' health: A developmental perspective.* Mahwah, NJ: Erlbaum.

Seligman, M.E.P., & Csikszentmihalyi, M. (2000). Positive psychology. *American Psychologist, 55,* 5–14.

Selman, R. (1976). Social-cognitive understanding. In T. Lickona (Ed.), *Moral development and behavior.* New York: Holt, Rinehart & Winston.

Selman, R. (1980). *The growth of interpersonal understanding.* New York: Academic Press.

Selman, R.L., & Adalbjarnardottir, S. (2000). Developmental method to analyze the personal meaning adolescents make of risk and relationship: The case of "drinking." *Applied Developmental Science, 4,* 47–65.

Selman, R.L., & Schultz, L.H. (1999, August). *The GSID approach to developmental evaluation of conflict resolution and violence prevention programs.* Paper presented at the meeting of the American Psychological Association, Boston.

Semaj, L.T. (1985). Afrikanity, cognition, and extended self-identity. In M.B. Spencer, G.K. Brookins, & W.R. Allen (Eds.), *Beginnings: The social and affective development of Black children.* Hillsdale, NJ: Erlbaum.

Serow, R.C., Ciechalski, J., & Daye, C. (1990). Students as volunteers. *Urban Education, 25,* 157–168.

Sesma, A. (2000, April). *Friendship intimacy, adversity, and psychological well-being in adolescence.* Paper presented at the meeting of the Society for Research on Adolescence, Chicago.

Sewell, T.E. (2000). School dropout. In A. Kazdin (Ed.), *Encyclopedia of psychology.* Washington, DC, and New York: American Psychological Association and Oxford University Press.

Shade, S.C., Kelly, C., & Oberg, M. (1997). *Creating culturally responsive schools.* Washington, DC: American Psychological Association.

Shaffer, L. (2000, April). *From the mouths of babes and dudes: Pros and cons of different types of adolescent peer relationships.* Paper presented at the meeting of the Society for Research on Adolescence, Chicago.

Shaie, K.W. (2000). Review of Santrock *Life-span development,* 8th ed. (Boston: McGraw-Hill).

Sharp, V. (1999). *Computer education for teachers* (3rd ed.). New York: McGraw-Hill.

Sheeber, L., Hops, H., & Davis, B. (2001). Family processes in adolescent depression. *Clinical Child and Family Psychology Review, 4,* 19–32.

Sheeber, L., Hops, H., Andrews, J.A., & Davis, B. (1997, April). *Family support and conflict: Prospective relation to adolescent depression.* Paper presented at the meeting of the Society for Research in Child Development, Washington, DC.

Sheffield, V.C. (1999, May). *Application of genetic strategies and human genome project resources for the identification of human disease genes.* Paper presented at the meeting of the Society for Pediatric Research, San Francisco.

Sheidow, A.J., Groman-Smith, D., Henry, D.B., & Tolan, P.H. (2000, April). *Family and community characteristics: Risk factors for violence exposure in inner-city youth.* Paper presented at the meeting of the Society for Research on Adolescence, Chicago.

Sherman, B.L., & Dominick, J.R. (1986). Violence and sex in music videos: TV and rock 'n' roll. *Journal of Communication, 36,* 79–93.

Sherrod, L., & Brabek, K. (2002, April). *Community service and youths' political views.* Paper presented at the meeting of the Society for Research on Adolescence, New Orleans.

Shields, S.A. (1991). Gender in the psychology of emotion: A selective research review. In K.T. Strongman (Ed.), *International review of studies on emotion* (Vol. I). New York: Wiley.

Shin, H.S. (2001). A review of school-based drug prevention program evaluations in the 1990s. *American Journal of Health Education, 32,* 139–147.

Shonkoff, J.P. (2000). Science, policy, and practice: Three cultures in search of a shared mission. *Child Development, 71,* 181–187.

Short, R.J., & Talley, R.C. (1997). Rethinking psychology and the schools. *American Psychologist, 52,* 234–240.

Shulman, S., & Collins, W.A. (Eds.) (1998). *New directions for child development: Adolescent romantic relationships.* San Francisco: Jossey-Bass.

Shulman, S., & Seiffge-Krenke, I. (2001). Adolescent romance: Between experience and relationships. *Journal of Adolescence, 35,* 417–428.

Shweder, R.A. (1991). *Thinking through cultures: Expeditions in cultural psychology.* Cambridge, MA: Harvard University Press.

Sidhu, K.K. (2000, April). *Identity formation among second generation Canadian Sikh adolescent males.* Paper presented at the meeting of the Society for Research in Adolescence, Chicago.

Sieber, J.E. (2000). Ethics in research. In A. Kazdin (Ed.). *Encyclopedia of psychology.* Washington, DC, & New York: American Psychological Association and Oxford University Press.

SIECUS. (1999). *Public support for sexuality education.* Washington, DC: Author.

Siegel, L.S., & Wiener, J. (1993, Spring). Canadian special education policies: Children with learning disabilities in a bilingual and multicultural society. *Social Policy Report, Society for Research in Child Development, 7*, 1–16.

Siegler, R.S. (1996). Information processing. In J.W. Santrock, *Child development* (7th ed.). Dubuque, IA: Brown & Benchmark.

Siegler, R.S. (1998). *Children's thinking* (3rd ed.). Upper Saddle River, NJ: Prentice-Hall.

Siegler, R.S. (2000). Developmental research: Microgenetic method. In K. Lee (Ed.), *Childhood cognitive development*. Malden, MA: Blackwell.

Sieving, R.E., McNelly, C.S., & Blum, R.W. (2000). *Maternal expectations, mother-child connectedness, and adolescent sexual debut.* Unpublished manuscript, Department of Pediatrics, Medical School, University of Minnesota.

Silberg, J.L., & Rutter, M.L. (1997, April). *Pubertal status, life stress, and depression in juvenile twins: A genetic investigation.* Paper presented at the meeting of the Society for Research in Child Development, Washington, DC.

Silver, M.E. (1995, March). *Late adolescent-parent relations and the high school to college transition.* Paper presented at the meeting of the Society for Research in Child Development, Indianapolis.

Silver, M.E., Levitt, M.J., Santos, J., & Perdue, L. (2002, April). *Changes in family relationships as adolescents become young adults.* Paper presented at the meeting of the Society for Research on Adolescence, New Orleans.

Silver, S. (1988, August). *Behavior problems of children born into early-childbearing families.* Paper presented at the meeting of the American Psychological Association, Atlanta.

Silverberg, S.B., & Steinberg, L. (1990). Psychological well-being of parents with early adolescent children. *Developmental Psychology, 26*, 658–666.

Silverman, J.G., Raj, A., Mucci, L.A., & Hathaway, J.E. (2001). Dating violence against adolescent girls and associated substance use, unhealthy weight control, sexual risk behavior, pregnancy, and suicidality. *Journal of the American Medical Association, 386*, 572–579.

Silverman, L.K. (1993). A developmental model for counseling the gifted. In L.K. Silverman (Ed.), *Counseling the gifted and the talented.* Denver: Love.

Simmons, A.M., & Avery, P.G. (in press). Civic life as conveyed in U.S. civics and history textbooks. *Journal of Social Education.*

Simmons, R.G., & Blyth, D.A. (1987). *Moving into adolescence.* Hawthorne, NY: Aldine.

Simons, J.M., Finlay, B., & Yang, A. (1991). *The adolescent and young adult fact book.* Washington, DC: Children's Defense Fund.

Simons, J.S., Walker-Barnes, C., & Mason, C.A. (2001, April). *Predicting increases in adolescent drug use: A longitudinal investigation.* Paper presented at the meeting of the Society for Research in Child Development, Minneapolis.

Simons-Morton, B., Haynie, D.L., Crump, A.D., Eitel, P., & Saylor, K.E. (2001). Peer and parent influences on smoking and drinking among early adolescents. *Health Education & Behavior, 28*, 95–107.

Singh, S., Wulf, D., Samara, R., & Cuca, Y.P. (2000). Gender differences in the timing of first intercourse: Data from 14 countries. *International Family Planning Perspectives, 26*, 21–28, 43.

Sitlington, P.L., Clark, G.M., & Kolstoe, O.P. (2000). *Transition education and services for adolescents with disabilities* (3rd ed.). Boston: Allyn & Bacon.

Skinner, B.F. (1938). *The behavior of organisms: An experimental analysis.* New York: Appleton-Century-Crofts.

Skoe, E.E., & Gooden, A. (1993). Ethic of care and real-life moral dilemma content in male and female early adolescents. *Journal of Early Adolescence, 13*, 154–167.

Skoe, E.E., & Marcia, J.E. (1988). *Ego identity and care-based moral reasoning in college women.* Unpublished manuscript, Acadia University.

Slavin, R.E. (1995). *Cooperative learning: Theory, research, and practice* (2nd ed.). Boston: Allyn & Bacon.

Slee, P.T., & Taki, M. (1999, April). *School bullying.* Paper presented at the meeting of the Society for Research in Child Development, Albuquerque.

Slomkowski, C., Rende, R., Conger, K.J., Simons, R.L., & Conger, R.D. (2001). Sisters, brothers, and delinquency: Social influence during early and middle adolescence. *Child Development, 72*, 271–283.

Small, S.A. (1990). *Preventive programs that support families with adolescents.* Washington, DC: Carnegie Council on Adolescent Development.

Smetana, J. (1988). Concepts of self and social convention: Adolescents' and parents' reasoning about hypothetical and actual family conflicts. In M. Gunnar (Ed.), *21st Minnesota symposium on child psychology.* Hillsdale, NJ: Erlbaum.

Smetana, J. (1993, March). *Parenting styles during adolescence: Global or domain-specific?* Paper presented at the biennial meeting of the Society for Research in Child Development, New Orleans.

Smetana, J. (1997, April). *Parenting reconceptualized: A social domain analysis.* Paper presented at the meeting of the Society for Research in Child Development, Washington, DC.

Smetana, J., & Gaines, C. (1999). Adolescent-parent conflict in middle-class African-American families. *Child Development, 70*, 1447–1463.

Smetana, J.G. (1995). Parenting styles and conceptions of parental authority during adolescence. *Child Development, 66*, 299–316.

Smetana, J.G., Abernethy, A., & Harris, A. (2000). Adolescent-parent interactions in middle-class African-American families: Longitudinal change and contextual variations. *Journal of Family Psychology, 14*, 458–474.

Smith, R.C., & Crockett, L.J. (1997, April). *Positive adolescent peer relations: A potential buffer against family adversity.* Paper presented at the meeting of the Society for Research in Child Development, Washington, DC.

Smith, R.E., & Smoll, F.L. (1997). Coaching the coaches: Youth sports as a scientific and applied behavioral setting. *Current Directions in Psychological Science, 6*, 16–21.

Snarey, J. (1987, June). A question of morality. *Psychology Today*, pp. 6–8.

Snider, B.A., & Miller, J.P. (1993). The land-grant university system and 4-H: A mutually beneficial relationship of scholars and practitioners in youth development. In R.M. Lerner (Ed.), *Early adolescence.* Hillsdale, NJ: Erlbaum.

Snyder, H.N., & Sickmund, M. (1999, October). *Juvenile offenders and victims: 1999 national report.* Washington, DC: National Center for Juvenile Justice.

Sommer, B.B. (1978). *Puberty and adolescence.* New York: Oxford University Press.

Sonenstein, F.L., Pleck, J.H., & Ku, L.C. (1989). Sexual activity, condom use, and AIDS awareness among adolescent males. *Family Planning Perspectives, 21* (4), 152–158.

Sorensen, R.C. (1973). *Adolescent sexuality in contemporary America.* New York: World.

Spade, J.Z., & Reese, C.A. (1991). We've come a long way, maybe: College students' plans for work and family. *Sex Roles, 24*, 309–321.

Spear, L.P. (2000). Neurobehavioral changes. *Current Directions in Psychological Science, 9*, 111–114.

Spearman, C.E. (1927). *The abilities of man.* New York: Macmillan.

Spence, J.T., & Helmreich, R. (1972). The Attitudes Toward Women Scale: An objective instrument to measure the rights and roles of women in contemporary society. *JSAS Catalog of Selected Documents in Psychology, 2*, 66.

Spencer, M.B. (1999). Social and cultural influences on school adjustment: The application of an identity-focused cultural ecological perspective. *Educational Psychologist, 34*, 43–57.

Spencer, M.B. (2000). Ethnocentrism. In A. Kazdin (Ed.), *Encyclopedia of psychology.* Washington, DC, and New York: American Psychological Association and Oxford University Press.

Spencer, M.B., & Dornbusch, S.M. (1990). Challenges in studying minority youth. In S.S. Feldman & G.R. Elliott (Eds.), *At the threshold: The developing adolescent.* Cambridge, MA: Harvard University Press.

Spencer, M.B., Noll, E., Stoltzfuz, J., & Harpalani, V. (2001). Identity and school adjustment: Revisiting the "acting white" assumption. *Educational Psychologist, 36*, 21–30.

Spokane, A.R. (2000). Career choice. In A. Kazdin (Ed.), *Encyclopedia of psychology.* Washington, DC, and New York: American Psychological Association and Oxford University Press.

Spring, J. (2002). *American education* (10th ed.). New York: McGraw-Hill.

Spring, J. (2000). *The intersection of cultures.* New York: McGraw-Hill.

Sputa, C.L., & Paulson, S.E. (1995, March). *A longitudinal study of changes in parenting across adolescence.* Paper presented at the meeting of the Society for Research in Child Development, Indianapolis.

Sroufe, L.A. (1996). *Emotional development.* New York: Cambridge University Press.

Sroufe, L.A. (2001). From infant attachment to adolescent autonomy: Longitudinal data on the role of parents in development. In J. Borkowski, S. Ramey, & M. Bristol-Power (Eds.), *Parenting and your child's world*. Mahwah, NJ: Erlbaum.

Sroufe, L.A., Egeland, B., & Carlson, E.A. (1999). One social world: The integrated development of parent-child and peer relationships. In W.A. Collins & B. Laursen (Eds.), *Minnesota symposium on child psychology* (Vol. 31). Mahwah, NJ: Erlbaum.

St. Pierre, R., Layzer, J., & Barnes, H. (1996). *Regenerating two-generation programs*. Cambridge, MA: Abt Associates.

Stake, J.E. (2000). When situations call for instrumentality and expressiveness: Resource appraisal, coping strategy choice, and adjustment. *Sex Roles, 42*, 865–885.

Stanovich, K.E. (1998). *How to think straight about psychology* (4th ed.). New York: Longman.

Stattin, H., & Magnusson, D. (1990). *Pubertal maturation in female development: Paths through life* (Vol. 2). Hillsdale, NJ: Erlbaum.

Steinberg, L.D. (1986). Latchkey children and susceptibility to peer pressure: An ecological analysis. *Developmental Psychology, 22*, 433–439.

Steinberg, L.D. (1988). Reciprocal relation between parent-child distance and pubertal maturation. *Developmental Psychology, 24*, 122–128.

Steinberg, L.D., & Cauffman, E. (1999). A developmental perspective on jurisdictional boundary. In J. Fagan & F. Zimring (Eds.), *A developmental perspective on jurisdictional boundary*. Chicago: University of Chicago Press.

Steinberg, L.D., Fegley, S., & Dornbusch, S.M. (1993). Negative impact of part-time work on adolescent adjustment: Evidence from a longitudinal study. *Developmental Psychology, 29*, 171–180.

Steinberg, L.D., & Silk, J.S. (2002). Parenting adolescents. In M. Bornstein (Ed.), *Handbook of parenting* (2nd ed., Vol. 1). Mahwah, NJ: Erlbaum.

Stepp, L.S. (2000). *Our last best shot: Guiding our children through early adolescence*. New York: Riverhead Books.

Stern, D., & Hallinan, M.T. (1997, Summer). The high schools, they are a-changin'. *CenterWork Newsletter* (NCRVE, University of California, Berkeley), pp. 4–7.

Stern, D., & Rahn, M. (1998, Fall). How health career academies provide work-based learning. *CenterWork Newsletter* (NCRVE, University of California, Berkeley), pp. 5–8.

Sternberg, R.J. (1977). *Intelligence, information processing, and analogical reasoning: The componential analysis of human abilities*. Hillsdale, NJ: Erlbaum.

Sternberg, R.J. (1985, December). Teaching critical thinking, Part 2: Possible solutions. *Phi Delta Kappan*, pp. 277–280.

Sternberg, R.J. (1986). *Intelligence applied*. San Diego: Harcourt Brace Jovanovich.

Sternberg, R.J. (1997). Educating intelligence: Infusing the triarchic theory into instruction. In R.J. Sternberg & E. Grigorenko (Eds.), *Intelligence, heredity, and environment*. New York: Cambridge University Press.

Sternberg, R.J. (1999). Intelligence. In M.A. Runco & S. Pritzker (Eds.), *Encyclopedia of creativity*. San Diego: Academic Press.

Sternberg, R.J. (2000). Looking back and looking forward on intelligence: Toward a theory of successful intelligence. In M. Bennett (Ed.), *Developmental psychology*. Philadelphia: Psychology Press.

Sternberg, R.J., & Clinkenbeard, P.R. (1995, May/June). The triarchic model applied to identifying, teaching, and assessing gifted children. *Roeper Review*, 255–260.

Sternberg, R.J., & Nigro, C. (1980). Developmental patterns in the solution of verbal analogies. *Child Development, 51*, 27–38.

Sternberg, R.J., & Rifkin, B. (1979). The development of analogical reasoning processes. *Journal of Experimental Child Psychology, 27*, 195–232.

Sternberg, R.J., Torff, B., & Grigorenko, E. (1998, May). Teaching for successful intelligence raises school achievement. *Phi Delta Kappan*, pp. 667–669.

Steur, F.B., Applefield, J.M., & Smith, R. (1971). Televised aggression and the interpersonal aggression of preschool children. *Journal of Experimental Child Psychology, 11*, 442–447.

Stevens, J.H. (1984). Black grandmothers' and black adolescent mothers' knowledge about parenting. *Developmental Psychology, 20*, 1017–1025.

Stevens, V., De Bourdeaudhuij, & Van Oost, P. (2001). Anti-bullying interventions at school. *Health Promotion International, 16*, 155–167.

Stevenson, D.L., Kochanek, J., & Schneider, B. (1998). Making the transition from high school: Recent trends and policies. In K. Borman & B. Schneider (Eds.), *The adolescent years: Social influences and educational challenges*. Chicago: University of Chicago Press.

Stevenson, H.C. (1997). Managing anger: Protective, proactive, or adaptive racial socialization identity profiles and African-American manhood development. *Journal of Prevention & Intervention in the Community, 16*, 35–61.

Stevenson, H.C. (1998). Raising safe villages: Cultural-ecological factors that influence the emotional adjustment of adolescents. *Journal of Black Psychology, 24*, 44–59.

Stevenson, H.W. (1992, December). Learning from Asian schools. *Scientific American*, pp. 6, 70–76.

Stevenson, H.W. (1995). Mathematics achievement of American students: First in the world by the year 2000? In C.A. Nelson (Ed.), *Basic and applied perspectives on learning, cognition, and development*. Minneapolis: University of Minnesota Press.

Stevenson, H.W., Hofer, B.K., & Randell, B. (2000). Middle childhood: Education and schooling. In W. Damon (Ed.), *Encyclopedia of psychology*. Washington, DC, & New York: American Psychological Association and Oxford University Press.

Stevenson, H.W., Lee, S., Chen, C., Stigler, J.W., Hsu, C., & Kitamura, S. (1990). Contexts of achievement. *Monograph of the Society for Research in Child Development, 55* (Serial No. 221).

Stipek, D.J. (1996). Motivation and instruction. In D.C. Berliner & R.C. Calfee (Eds.), *Handbook of educational psychology*. New York: Macmillan.

Stipek, D.J. (2002). *Motivation to learn* (4th Ed.). Boston: Allyn & Bacon.

Stone, M.R., Barber, B.L., & Eccles, J.S. (2001, April). *How to succeed in high school by really trying: Does activity participation benefit students at all levels of social self-concept?* Paper presented at the meeting of the Society for Research in Child Development, Minneapolis.

Strahan, D.B. (1983). The emergence of formal operations in adolescence. *Transcendence, 11*, 7–14.

Strasburger, V.C., & Donnerstein, E. (1999). Children, adolescents, and the media: Issues and solutions. *Pediatrics, 103*, 129–137.

Streigel-Moore, R.H., Silberstein, L.R., & Rodin, J. (1993). The social self in bulimia nervosa: Public self-consciousness, social anxiety, and perceived fraudulence. *Journal of Abnormal Psychology, 102*, 297–303.

Streitmatter, J. (1993). Gender differences in identity development: An examination of longitudinal data. *Adolescence, 28*, 55–66.

Strickland, B.R. (1995). Research on sexual orientation and human development: A commentary. *Developmental Psychology, 31*, 137–140.

Strober, M., Freeman, R., & Morrell, W. (1997). The long-term course of severe anorexia nervosa in adolescents: Survival analysis of recovery, relapse, and outcome predictors over 10–15 years in a prospective study. *International Journal of Eating Disorders, 22*, 339–360.

Studer, M., & Thornton, A. (1987). Adolescent religiosity and contraceptive usage. *Journal of Marriage and the Family, 49*, 117–128.

Studer, M., & Thornton, A. (1989). The multifaceted impact of religiosity on adolescent sexual experience and contraceptive usage: A reply to Shornack and Ahmed. *Journal of Marriage and the Family, 51*, 1085–1089.

Stunkard, A.J. (2000). Obesity. In A. Kazdin (Ed.), *Encyclopedia of psychology*. Washington, DC, and New York: American Psychological Association and Oxford University Press.

Suárez-Orozco, C. (1999, August). *Conceptual considerations in our understanding of immigrant adolescent girls*. Paper presented at the meeting of the American Psychological Association, Boston.

Suárez-Orozco, C. (2002). Afterward: Understanding and serving the children of immigrants. *Harvard Educational Review, 71*, 579–589.

Suárez-Orozco, M., & Suárez-Orozco, C. (2002, April). *Global engagement: Immigrant youth and the social process of schooling.* Paper presented at the meeting of the Society for Research on Adolescence, New Orleans.

Sue, S. (1990, August). *Ethnicity and culture in psychological research and practice.* Paper presented at the meeting of the American Psychological Association, Boston.

Sue, S., & Okazaki, S. (1990). Asian-American educational achievements: A phenomenon in search of an explanation. *American Psychologist, 45,* 913–920.

Sullivan, H.S. (1953). *The interpersonal theory of psychiatry.* New York: W. W. Norton.

Sullivan, K., & Sullivan, A. (1980). Adolescent-parent separation. *Developmental Psychology, 16,* 93–99.

Suomi, S.J., Harlow, H.F., & Domek, C.J. (1970). Effect of repetitive infant-infant separations of young monkeys. *Journal of Abnormal Psychology, 76,* 161–172.

Super, D.E. (1967). *The psychology of careers.* New York: Harper & Row.

Super, D.E. (1976). *Career education and the meanings of work.* Washington, DC: U.S. Office of Education.

Susman, E.J. (1997). Modeling developmental complexity in adolescence: Hormones and behavior in context. *Journal of Research on Adolescence, 7,* 283–306.

Susman, E.J. (2001). Review of Santrock's *Adolescence,* 9th ed. (New York: McGraw-Hill).

Susman, E.J., Dorn, L.D., & Schiefelbein, V.L. (in press). Puberty, sexuality, and health. In R.M. Lerner, M.A. Easterbrooks, & J. Mistry (Eds.), *Comprehensive handbook of psychology: Developmental psychology* (Vol. 6). New York: Wiley.

Susman, E.J., Finkelstein J.W., Chinchilli, V.M., Schwab, J., Liben, L.S., D'Arcangelo, M.R., Meinke, J., Demers, L.M., Lookingbill, G., & Kulin, H.E. (1987). The effect of sex hormone replacement therapy on behavior problems and moods in adolescents with delayed puberty. *Journal of Pediatrics, 133* (4), 521–525.

Susman, E.J., Murowchick, E., Worrall, B.K., & Murray, D.A. (1995, March). *Emotionality, adrenal hormones, and context interactions during puberty and pregnancy.* Paper presented at the meeting of the Society for Research in Child Development, Indianapolis.

Susman, E.J., Schiefelbein, V., & Heaton, J.A. (2002, April). *Cortisol attenuations, puberty, and externalizing behavior: Family adjustment mediators.* Paper presented at the meeting of the Society for Research on Adolescence, New Orleans.

Sussman, A.L. (2001). Reality monitoring of performed and imagined interactive events: Developmental and contextual effects. *Journal of Experimental Child Psychology, 79,* 115–138.

Sutton-Smith, B. (1982). Birth order and sibling status effects. In M.E. Lamb & B. Sutton-Smith (Eds.), *Sibling relationships: Their nature and significance across the life span.* Hillsdale, NJ: Erlbaum.

Swanson, D.P. (1997, April). *Identity and coping styles among African-American females.* Paper presented at the meeting of the Society for Research in Child Development, Washington, DC.

Swanson, H.L. (1999). What develops in working memory? A life-span perspective. *Developmental Psychology, 35,* 986–1000.

Swarr, A.E., & Richards, M.H. (1996). Longitudinal effects of adolescent girls' pubertal development, perceptions of pubertal timing, and parental relations. *Developmental Psychology, 32,* 636–646.

Swim, J.K., Aikin, K.J., Hall, W.S., & Hunter, B.A. (1995). Sexism and racism: Old-fashioned and modern prejudices. *Journal of Personality and Social Psychology, 67,* 199–214.

Takahashi, K., & Majima, N. (1994). Transition from home to college dormitory: The role of preestablished affective relationships in adjustment to a new life. *Journal of Research on Adolescence, 4,* 367–384.

Takanishi, R., & DeLeon, P.H. (1994). A Head Start for the 21st century. *American Psychologist, 49,* 120–122.

Tamis-LeMonda, C.S., & Cabrera, N. (Eds.) (2002). *The handbook of father involvement.* Mahwah, NJ: Erlbaum.

Tanaka-Matsumi, J. (2001). Abnormal psychology and culture. In D. Matsumoto (Ed.), *The handbook of culture and psychology.* New York: Oxford University Press.

Tannen, D. (1990). *You just don't understand!* New York: Ballantine.

Tapert, S., Brown, G.S., Kindermann, S.S., Cheung, E.H., Frank, L.R., & Brown, S.A. (2001). fMRI measurement of brain dysfunction in alcohol-dependent young women. *Alcoholism: Clinical & Experimental Research, 25,* 236–245.

Tappan, M.B. (1998). Sociocultural psychology and caring psychology: Exploring Vygotsky's "hidden curriculum." *Educational Psychologist, 33,* 23–33.

Tavris, C., & Wade, C. (1984). *The longest war: Sex differences in perspective* (2nd ed.). San Diego: Harcourt Brace Jovanovich.

Taylor, J. McLean, Gilligan, C., & Sullivan, A.M. (1996). *Between voice and silence: Women and girls, race and relationship.* Cambridge, MA: Harvard University Press.

Taylor, J.H., & Walker, L.J. (1997). Moral climate and the development of moral reasoning: The effects of dyadic discussions between young offenders. *Journal of Moral Education, 26,* 21–43.

Taylor, R.D., & Wang, M.C. (2000). *Resilience across contexts.* Mahwah, NJ: Erlbaum.

Terman, D.L., Larner, M.B., Stevenson, C.S., & Behrman, R.E. (1996). Special education for students with disabilities: Analysis and recommendations. *Future of Children, 6* (1), 4–24.

Tesser, A., Fleeson, R.B., & Suls, J.M. (2000). *Psychological perspectives on self and identity.* Washington, DC: American Psychological Association.

Teti, D.M. (2002). Retrospect and prospect in the study of sibling relationships. In J.P. McHale & W.S. Grolnick (Eds.), *Retrospect and prospect in the study of families.* Mahwah, NJ: Erlbaum.

Tetreault, M.K.T. (1997). Classrooms for diversity: Rethinking curriculum and pedagogy. In J.A. Banks & C.A. Banks (Eds.), *Multicultural education* (3rd ed.). Boston: Allyn & Bacon.

Thomas, C.W., Coffman, J.K., & Kipp, K.L. (1993, March). *Are only children different from children with siblings? A longitudinal study of behavioral and social functioning.* Paper presented at the biennial meeting of the Society for Research in Child Development, New Orleans.

Thomas, K. (1998, November 4). Teen cyberdating is a new wrinkle for parents, too. *USA Today,* p. 9D.

Thompson, L., & Walker, A.J. (1989). Gender in families: Women and men in marriage, work, and parenthood. *Journal of Marriage and the Family, 51,* 845–871.

Thompson, P.M., Giedd, J.N., Woods, R.P., MacDonald, D., Evans, A.C., & Toga, A.W. (2000). Growth patterns in the developing brain detected by using continuum mechanical tensor maps. *Nature, 404,* 190–193.

Thompson, R.A., & Nelson, C.A. (2001). Developmental science and the media. *American Psychologist, 56,* 5–15.

Thornburg, H.D. (1981). Sources of sex education among early adolescents. *Journal of Early Adolescence, 1,* 171–184.

Thorton, A., & Camburn, D. (1989). Religious participation and sexual behavior and attitudes. *Journal of Marriage and the Family, 49,* 117–128.

Thurstone, L.L. (1938). *Primary mental abilities.* Chicago: University of Chicago Press.

Tilton-Weaver, L., & Leighter, S. (2002, April). *Peer management behavior: Linkages to parents' beliefs about adolescents and adolescents' friends.* Paper presented at the meeting of the Society for Research on Adolescence, New Orleans.

Tirozzi, G.N., & Uro, G. (1997). Education reform in the United States. *American Psychologist, 52,* 241–249.

Tolan, P.H. (2001). Emerging themes and challenges in understanding youth violence. *Journal of Clinical Child Psychology, 30,* 233–239.

Tolan, P.H., Guerra, N.G., & Kendall, P.C. (1995). A developmental-ecological perspective on antisocial behavior in children and adolescents: Toward a unified risk and intervention framework. *Journal of Consulting and Clinical Psychology, 63,* 579–584.

Tomlinson-Keasey, C. (1972). Formal operations in females from 11 to 54 years of age. *Developmental Psychology, 6,* 364.

Tomlinson-Keasey, C., Warren, L.W., & Elliott, J.E. (1986). Suicide among gifted women: A prospective study. *Journal of Abnormal Psychology, 95,* 123–130.

Torff, B. (2000). Multiple intelligences. In A. Kazdin (Ed.), *Encyclopedia of psychology.* Washington, DC, and New York: American Psychological Association and Oxford University Press.

Triandis, H.C. (1994). *Culture and social behavior.* New York: McGraw-Hill.

Triandis, H.C. (2000). Cross-cultural psychology. In A. Kazdin (Ed.), *Encyclopedia of psychology.* Washington, DC, & New York: American Psychological Association and Oxford University Press.

Trickett, E.J., & Moos, R.H. (1974). Personal correlates of contrasting environments: Student satisfaction in high school classrooms. *American Journal of Community Psychology, 2,* 1–12.

Trimble, J.E. (1989, August). *The enculturation of contemporary psychology.* Paper presented at the meeting of the American Psychological Association, New Orleans.

Tubman, J.G., Windle, M., & Windle, R.C. (1996). The onset and cross-temporal patterning of sexual intercourse in middle adolescence: Prospective relations with behavioral and emotional problems. *Child Development, 67,* 327–343.

Tucker, C.J., McHale, S.M., & Crouter, A.C. (2001). Conditions of sibling support in adolescence. *Journal of Family Psychology, 15,* 254–271.

Tucker, L.A. (1987). Television, teenagers, and health. *Journal of Youth and Adolescence, 16,* 415–425.

Tuckman, B.W., & Hinkle, J.S. (1988). An experimental study of the physical and psychological effects of aerobic exercise on schoolchildren. In B.G. Melamed & others (Eds.), *Child health psychology.* Hillsdale, NJ: Erlbaum.

Tudge, J.R.H., & Scrimsher, S. (2002). Lev S. Vygotsky on education. In B.J. Zimmerman & D.H. Schunk (Eds.), *Educational psychology.* Mahwah, NJ: Erlbaum.

Tupuola, A. (2000, April). *Shifting notions of personal identity for Samoan youth in New Zealand.* Paper presented at the meeting of the Society for Research on Adolescence, Chicago.

Turiel, E. (1998). The development of morality. In N. Eisenberg. (Ed.), *Handbook of child psychology* (5th ed., Vol. 3). New York: Wiley.

U.S. Bureau of the Census. (2000). *Statistical abstracts of the United States, 1999.* Washington, DC: U.S. Government Printing Office.

U.S. Department of Education. (1996). *Number and disabilities of children and youth served under IDEA.* Washington, DC: Office of Special Education Programs, Data Analysis System.

U.S. Department of Energy. (2001). *The Human Genome Project.* Washington, DC: Author.

Udry, J.R. (1990). Hormonal and social determinants of adolescent sexual initiation. In J. Bancroft & J.M. Reinisch (Eds.), *Adolescence and puberty.* New York: Oxford University Press.

Underwood, M.K., & Hurley, J.C. (1997, April). *Children's responses to angry provocation as a function of peer status and aggression.* Paper presented at the meeting of the Society for Research in Child Development, Washington, DC.

Underwood, M.K., & Hurley, J.C. (2000). Emotion regulation in peer relationships in middle childhood. In L. Balter & C.S. Tamis-LeMonda (Eds.), *Child psychology.* Philadelphia: Psychology Press.

Underwood, M.K., Kupersmidt, J.B., & Coie, J.D. (1996). Childhood peer sociometric status and aggression as predictors of adolescent childbearing. *Journal of Research on Adolescence, 6,* 201–223.

Unger, R., & Crawford, M. (1992). *Women and gender* (2nd ed.). New York: McGraw-Hill.

UNICEF. (2000). *Educating girls, transforming the future.* Geneva: UNICEF.

Updegraff, K.A. (1999, April). *Mothers' and fathers' involvement in adolescents' peer relationships: Links to friendship adjustment and peer competence.* Paper presented at the meeting of the Society for Research in Child Development, Albuquerque.

Urberg, K.A. (1999). Introduction: Some thoughts about studying the influence of peers on children and adolescents. *Merrill-Palmer Quarterly, 45,* 1–12.

Urberg, K.A., Degirmencioglu, S.M., Tolson, J.M., & Halliday-Scher, K. (1995). The structure of adolescent peer networks. *Developmental Psychology, 31,* 540–547.

Urberg, K.A., Goldstein, M.S., & Toro, P. (2002, April). *Social moderators of the effects of parent and peer drinking on adolescent drinking.* Paper presented at the meeting of the Society for Research on Adolescence, New Orleans.

Urdan, T., & Midgley, C. (2001). Academic self-handicapping: What we know, what more is there to learn. *Educational Psychology Review, 13,* 115–138.

Urdan, T., Midgely, C., & Anderman, E.M. (1998). The role of classroom goal structure in students' use of self-handicapping strategies. *American Educational Research Journal, 35,* 101–122.

Usher, B., Zahn-Waxler, C., Finch, C., & Gunlicks, M. (2000, April). *The relation between global self-esteem, perceived competence, and risk for psychopathology in adolescence.* Paper presented at the meeting of the Society for Research on Adolescence, Chicago.

Valisner, J. (2000). Cultural psychology. In A. Kazdin (Ed.), *Encyclopedia of psychology.* Washington, DC, and New York: American Psychological Association and Oxford University Press.

van Dijk, T.A. (1987). *Communicating racism.* Newbury Park, CA: Sage.

Van Goozen, S.H.M., Matthys, W., Cohen-Kettenis, P.T., Thisjssen, J.H.H., & van Engeland, H. (1998). Adrenal androgens and aggression in conduct disorder prepubertal boys and normal control. *Biological Psychiatry, 43,* 156–158.

Van Hoof, A. (1999). The identity status field re-reviewed: An update of unresolved and neglected issues with a view on some alternative approaches. *Developmental Review, 19,* 497–565.

Vandell, D.L., Minnett, A., & Santrock, J.W. (1987). Age differences in sibling relationships during middle childhood. *Applied Developmental Psychology, 8,* 247–257.

Ventura, S.J., Mosher, W.D., Curtin, S.C., Abma, J.C., & Henshaw, S. (2001). Trends in pregnancy rates for the United States, 1976–1997: An update. *National Vital Statistics Reports, 49,* 1–9.

Vernberg, E.M. (1990). Psychological adjustment and experience with peers during early adolescence: Reciprocal, incidental, or unidirectional relationships? *Journal of Abnormal Child Psychology, 18,* 187–198.

Vernberg, E.M., Ewell, K.K., Beery, S.H., & Abwender, D.A. (1994). Sophistication of adolescents' interpersonal negotiation strategies and friendship formation after relocation: A naturally occurring experiment. *Journal of Research on Adolescence, 4,* 5–19.

Vicary, J.R., Klingaman, L.R., & Harkness, W.L. (1995). Risk factors associated with date rape and sexual assault of adolescent girls. *Journal of Adolescence, 18,* 289–306.

Vidal, F. (2000). Piaget, Jean. In A. Kazdin (Ed.), *Encyclopedia of psychology.* Washington, DC, and New York: American Psychological Association and Oxford University Press.

Vondracek, F.W. (1991). Vocational development and choice in adolescence. In R.M. Lerner, A.C. Petersen, & J. Brooks-Gunn (Eds.), *Encyclopedia of adolescence* (Vol. 2). New York: Garland.

Vygotsky, L. (1962). *Thought and language.* Cambridge, MA: MIT Press.

Wagennar, A.C. (1983). *Alcohol, young drivers, and traffic accidents.* Lexington, MA: D.C. Heath.

Wagner, R.K. (2000). Practical intelligence. In A. Kazdin (Ed.), *Encyclopedia of psychology.* Washington, DC, & New York: American Psychological Association and Oxford University Press.

Wahlsten, D. (2000). Behavioral genetics. In A. Kazdin (Ed.), *Encyclopedia of psychology.* Washington, DC, & New York: American Psychological Association and Oxford University Press.

Waldron, H.B., Brody, J.L., & Slesnick, N. (2001). Integrative behavioral and family therapy for adolescent substance abuse. In P.M. Monti, S.M. Colbyk, & T.A. O'Leary (Eds.), *Adolescents, alcohol, and substance abuse.* New York: Guilford.

Walker, H. (1998, May 31). Youth violence: Society's problem. *Eugene Register Guard,* p. 1C.

Walker, L.J. (1984). Sex differences in the development of moral reasoning: A critical review. *Child Development, 51,* 131–139.

Walker, L.J. (1991). Sex differences in moral development. In W.M. Kurtines & J. Gewirtz (Eds.), *Moral behavior and development* (Vol. 2). Hillsdale, NJ: Erlbaum.

Walker, L.J. (1993, March). *Is the family a sphere of moral growth for children?* Paper presented at the biennial meeting of the Society for Research in Child Development, New Orleans.

Walker, L.J. (1996). Unpublished review of J.W. Santrock's *Child development,* 8th ed. (Dubuque, IA: Brown & Benchmark).

Walker, L.J., deVries, B., & Trevethan, S.D. (1987). Moral stages and moral orientation in real-life and hypothetical dilemmas. *Child Development, 58,* 842–858.

Walker, L.J., Hennig, K.H., & Krettenauer, R. (2000). Parent and peer contexts for children's moral reasoning development. *Child Development, 71,* 1033–1048.

Walker, L.J., & Pitts, R.C. (1998). Naturalistic conceptions of moral maturity. *Developmental Psychology, 34,* 403–419.

Walker, L.J., & Taylor, J.H. (1991). Family interaction and the development of moral reasoning. *Child Development, 62,* 264–283.

Wallace-Broscious, A., Serafica, F.C., & Osipow, S.H. (1994). Adolescent career development: Relationships to self-concept and identity status. *Journal of Research on Adolescence, 4,* 127–150.

Wallis, C. (1985, December 9). Children having children. *Time,* pp. 78–88.

Walter, C.A. (1986). *The timing of motherhood.* Lexington, MA: D.C. Heath.

Walters, E., & Kendler, K.S. (1994). Anorexia nervosa and anorexia-like symptoms in a population based twin sample. *American Journal of Psychiatry, 152,* 62–71.

Walther-Thomas, C., Korinek, L., McLaughlin, V.L., & Williams, B.T. (2000). *Collaboration for inclusive education.* Boston: Allyn & Bacon.

Wang, J.Q. (2000, November). *A comparison of two international standards to assess child and adolescent obesity in three populations.* Paper presented at the meeting of American Public Health Association, Boston.

Ward, L.M. (1994, February). *The nature and prevalence of sexual messages in the television programs adolescents view most.* Paper presented at the meeting of the Society for Research on Adolescence, San Diego.

Ward, L.M. (2000, April). *Does television exposure affect adolescents' sexual attitudes and expectations? Correlational and experimental confirmation.* Paper presented at the meeting of the Society for Research on Adolescence, Chicago.

Wartella, E., Heintz, K., Aidman, A., & Mazzarella, S. (1990). Television and beyond: Children's video media in one community. *Communications Research, 17,* 45–64.

Wass, H., Miller, M.D., & Redditt, C.A. (1991). Adolescents and destructive themes in rock music: A follow-up. *Omega, 23,* 199–206.

Waterman, A.S. (1985). Identity in the context of adolescent psychology. In A.S. Waterman (Ed.), *Identity in adolescence: Processes and contents.* San Francisco: Jossey-Bass.

Waterman, A.S. (1989). Curricula interventions for identity change: Substantive and ethical considerations. *Journal of Adolescence, 12,* 389–400.

Waterman, A.S. (1992). Identity as an aspect of optimal psychological functioning. In G.R. Adams, T.P. Gullotta, & R. Montemayor (Eds.), *Adolescent identity formation.* Newbury Park, CA: Sage.

Waterman, A.S. (1999). Identity, the identity statuses, and identity status development: A contemporary statement. *Developmental Review, 19,* 591–621.

Waters, G.S., & Caplan, D. (2001). Age, working memory, and on-line syntactic processing in sentence comprehension. *Psychology & Aging, 16,* 128–144.

Way, N. (1997, April). *Father-daughter relationships in urban families.* Paper presented at the meeting of the Society for Research in Child Development, Washington, DC.

Wechsler, H., Davenport, A., Sowdall, G., Moetykens, B., & Castillo, S. (1994). Health and behavioral consequences of binge drinking in college. *Journal of the American Medical Association, 272,* 1672–1677.

Weineke, J.K., Thurston, S.W., Kelsey, K.T., Varkonyi, A., Wain, J.C., Mark, E.J., & Christiani, D.C. (1999). Early age at smoking initiation and tobacco carcinogen DNA damage in the lung. *Journal of the National Cancer Institute, 91,* 614–619.

Weiner, B. (1986). *An attributional theory of motivation and emotion.* New York: Springer.

Weiner, B. (1992). *Human motivation: Metaphors, theories, and research.* Newbury Park, CA: Sage.

Weiner, B. (2000). Motivation: An overview. In A. Kazdin (Ed.), *Encyclopedia of psychology.* Washington, DC, and New York: American Psychological Association and Oxford University Press.

Weinstein, C.S. (2003). *Secondary classroom management* 2nd ed. New York: McGraw-Hill.

Weiss, R.S. (1973). *Loneliness: The experience of emotional and social isolation.* Cambridge, MA: MIT Press.

Weissberg, R., & Caplan, M. (1989, April). *A follow-up study of a school-based social competence program for young adolescents.* Paper presented at the meeting of the Society for Research in Child Development, Kansas City.

Weissberg, R.P., & Greenberg, M.T. (1998). School and community competence—Enhancement and prevention interventions. In I.E. Siegel & K.A. Renninger (Eds.), *Handbook of child psychology* (5th ed., Vol. 4). New York: Wiley.

Weist, M.D., & Cooley-Quille, M. (2001). Advancing efforts to address youth violence involvement. *Journal of Clinical Child Psychology, 30,* 147–151.

Welsh, D.P., Vickerman, R., Kawaguschi, M.C., & Rostosky, S.S. (1998). *Discrepancies adolescent romantic couples' and observers' perceptions of couple interaction and their relationship to mental health.* Unpublished manuscript, Dept. of Psychology, University of Massachusetts, Amherst.

Weng, A., & Montemayor, R. (1997, April). *Conflict between mothers and adolescents.* Paper presented at the meeting of the Society for Research in Child Development, Washington, DC.

Wentzel, K.R., & Asher, S.R. (1995). The academic lives of neglected, rejected, popular, and controversial children. *Child Development, 66,* 754–763.

Wentzel, K.R., & Erdley, C.A. (1993). Strategies for making friends: Relations to social behavior and peer acceptance in early adolescence. *Developmental Psychology, 29,* 819–826.

Wertsch, J. (2000). Cognitive development. In M. Bennett (Ed.), *Developmental psychology.* Philadelphia: Psychology Press.

Westen, D. (2000). Psychoanalytic theories. In A. Kazdin (Ed.), *Encyclopedia of psychology.* Washington, DC, & New York: American Psychological Association and Oxford University Press.

Whalen, C.K. (2001). ADHD treatment in the 21st century: Pushing the envelope. *Journal of Clinical Child Psychology, 30,* 136–140.

Whalen, C.O. (2000). Attention deficit hyperactivity disorder. In A. Kazdin (Ed.), *Encyclopedia of psychology.* Washington, DC, and New York: American Psychological Association and Oxford University Press.

White, K.M., Speisman, J.C., Costos, D., & Smith, A. (1987). Relationship maturity: A conceptual and empirical approach. In J. Meacham (Ed.), *Interpersonal relations: Family, peers, friends.* Basel, Switzerland: Karger.

White, L., & Gilbreth, J.G. (2001). When children have two fathers: Effects of relationships with stepfathers and noncustodial fathers on adolescent outcomes. *Journal of Marriage and the Family, 63,* 155–167.

White, M. (1993). *The material child: Coming of age in Japan and America.* New York: Free Press.

Whiting, B.B. (1989, April). *Culture and interpersonal behavior.* Paper presented at the biennial meeting of the Society for Research in Child Development, Kansas City.

Whiting, B.B., & Edwards, C.P. (1988). *Children of different worlds.* Cambridge, MA: Harvard University Press.

Whitman, F.L., Diamond, M., & Martin, J. (1993). Homosexual orientation in twins: A report on 61 pairs and three triplet sets. *Archives of Sexual Behavior, 22,* 187–206.

Wigfield, A., & Eccles, J.S. (1989). Test anxiety in elementary and secondary school students. *Journal of Educational Psychology, 24,* 159–183.

Wigfield, A., & Eccles, J.S. (Eds.) (2001). *Development of achievement motivation.* San Diego: Academic Press.

William T. Grant Foundation Commission on Work, Family, and Citizenship. (1988, February). *The forgotten half: Noncollege-bound youth in America.* New York: William T. Grant Foundation.

Williams, C., & Bybee, J. (1994). What do children feel guilty about? Developmental and gender differences? *Developmental Psychology, 30,* 617–623.

Williams, J.E., & Best, D.L. (1982). *Measuring sex stereotypes: A thirty-nation study.* Newbury Park, CA: Sage.

Williams, J.E., & Best, D.L. (1989). *Sex and psyche: Self-concept viewed cross-culturally.* Newbury Park, CA: Sage.

Williams, T.M., & Cox, R. (1995, March). *Informative versus other children's TV programs: Portrayals of ethnic diversity, gender, and aggression.* Paper presented at the meeting of the Society for Research in Child Development, Indianapolis.

Williams, T.M., Baron, D., Phillips, S., David, L., & Jackson, D. (1986, August). *The portrayal of sex roles on Canadian and U.S. television.* Paper presented at the conference of the International Association for Mass Media Research, New Delhi, India.

Wills, T.A., Sandy, J.M., Yaeger, A., & Shinar, O. (2001). Family risk factors and adolescent substance use: Moderation effects for temperament dimensions. *Developmental Psychology, 37,* 283–297.

Wilson, B.J., & Gottman, J.M. (1995). Marital interaction and parenting. In M.H. Bornstein (Ed.), *Children and parenting* (Vol. 4). Hillsdale, NJ: Erlbaum.

Wilson, J.W. (1987). *The truly disadvantaged: The inner city, the underclass, and public policy.* Chicago: University of Chicago Press.

Wilson, M.N. (2000). Cultural diversity. In A. Kazdin (Ed.), *Encyclopedia of psychology.* Washington, DC, and New York: American Psychological Association and Oxford University Press.

Wilson, M.N., Cook, D.Y., & Arrington, E.G. (1997). African-American adolescents and academic achievement: Family and peer influences. In R.D. Taylor & M.C. Wang (Eds.), *Social and emotional adjustment and relations in ethnic minority families.* Mahwah, NJ: Erlbaum.

Wilson-Shockley, S. (1995). *Gender differences in adolescent depression: The contribution of negative affect.* M.S. thesis, University of Illinois at Urbana-Champaign.

Windle, M. (1989). Substance use and abuse among adolescent runaways: A four-year follow-up study. *Journal of Youth and Adolescence, 18,* 331–341.

Windle, M., & Dumenci, L. (1998). An investigation of maternal and adolescent depressed mood using a latent trait-state model. *Journal of Research on Adolescence, 8,* 461–484.

Winne, P.H. (1995). Inherent details in self-regulated learning. *Educational Psychologist, 30,* 173–187.

Winne, P.H. (1997). Experimenting to bootstrap self-regulated learning. *Journal of Educational Psychology, 89,* 397–410.

Winne, P.H., & Perry, N.E. (2000). Measuring self-regulated learning. In M. Boekaerts, P.R. Pintrich, & M. Zeidner (Eds.), *Handbook of self-regulation.* San Diego: Academic Press.

Winner, E. (1996). *Gifted children: Myths and realities.* New York: Basic Books.

Winner, E. (2000). The origins and ends of giftedness. *American Psychologist, 55,* 159–169.

Wodarski, J.S., & Hoffman, S.D. (1984). Alcohol education for adolescents. *Social Work in Education, 6,* 69–92.

Wolery, M. (2000). Special education. In A. Kazdin (Ed.), *Encyclopedia of psychology.* Washington, DC, and New York: American Psychological Association and Oxford University Press.

Wolfe, S.M., Toro, P.A., & McCaskill, P.A. (1999). A comparison of homeless and matched housed adolescents on family environment variables. *Journal of Research on Adolescence, 9,* 53–66.

Wolfson, A.R., & Carskadon, M.A. (1998). Sleep schedules and daytime functioning in adolescents. *Child Development, 69,* 875–887.

Wong, C.A. (1997, April). *What does it mean to be an African-American or European-American growing up in a multi-ethnic community?* Paper presented at the meeting of the Society for Research in Child Development, Washington, DC.

Wong, C.A., & Rowley, S.J. (2001). The schooling of ethnic minority children: A commentary. *Educational Psychologist, 36,* 57–66.

Wong, C.A., Eccles, J.S., & Sameroff, A. (2001, April). *Ethnic discrimination and ethnic identification: The influence of African-Americans' and Whites' school and socioemotional development.* Paper presented at the meeting of the Society for Research in Child Development, Minneapolis.

Wood, M. (1998). Whose job is it anyway? Educational roles in inclusion. *Exceptional Children, 64,* 181–195.

Woodrich, D.L. (1994). *Attention-deficit hyperactivity disorder: What every parent should know.* Baltimore: Paul H. Brookes.

Work Group of the American Psychological Association's Board of Educational Affairs. (1995). *Learner-centered psychological principles: A framework for school redesign and reform (draft).* Washington, DC: American Psychological Association.

Workman, K.A., Jensen-Campbell, L.A., Nash, A., & Campbell, S.D. (2000, April). *Emotional regulation and responses to provocation: Does agreeableness make a difference?* Paper presented at the meeting of the Society for Research on Adolescence, Chicago.

World Health Organization. (2000). *The world health report.* Geneva: Author.

World Health Organization. (February 2, 2000). *Adolescent health behavior in 28 countries.* Geneva: Author.

Wright, M.R. (1989). Body image satisfaction in adolescent girls and boys. *Journal of Youth and Adolescence, 18,* 71–84.

Wylie, R. (1979). *The self concept. Vol. 2.: Theory and research on selected topics.* Lincoln: University of Nebraska Press.

Xiaohe, X., & Whyte, M.K. (1990). Love matches and arranged marriages. *Journal of Marriage and the Family, 52,* 709–722.

Yang, E., Satsky, M.A., Tietz, J.A., Garrison, S., Debus, J., Bell, K.L., & Allen, J.P. (1996, March). *Adolescent-father trust and communication: Reflections of marital relations between parents.* Paper presented at the meeting of the society for Research on Adolescence, Boston.

Yates, M. (1995, March). *Community service and political-moral discussions among Black urban adolescents.* Paper presented at the meeting of the Society for Research in Child Development, Indianapolis.

Yeakey, C.C., & Henderson, R.D. (Eds.) (2002). *Surmounting the odds: Equalizing educational opportunity in the new millenium.* Greenwich, CT: IAP.

Yeung, W.J., Sandberg, J.F., Davis-Kearn, P.E., & Hofferth, S.L. (1999, April). *Children's time with fathers in intact families.* Paper presented at the meeting of the Society for Research in Child Development, Albuquerque.

Yin, Y., Buhrmester, D., & Hibbard, D. (1996, March). *Are there developmental changes in the influence of relationships with parents and friends on adjustment during early adolescence?* Paper presented at the meeting of the Society for Research on Adolescence, Boston.

Yoon, K.S., Eccles, J.S., Wigfield, A., & Barber, B.L. (1996, March). *Developmental trajectories of early to middle adolescents' academic achievement and motivation.* Paper presented at the meeting of the Society for Research on Adolescence, Boston.

Young, R.A. (1994). Helping adolescents with career development: The active role of parents. *Career Development Quarterly, 42,* 195–203.

Youniss, J. (1980). *Parents and peers in the social environment: A Sullivan Piaget perspective.* Chicago: University of Chicago Press.

Youniss, J. (2002, April). *Youth civic engagement in the 21st century.* Paper presented at the meeting of the Society for Research on Adolescence, New Orleans.

Youniss, J., McLellan, J.A., & Strouse, D. (1994). "We're popular but we're not snobs": Adolescents describe their crowds. In R. Montemayor, G.R. Adams, & T.P. Gullotta (Eds.), *Advances in adolescent development: Vol. 6. Personal relationships during adolescence.* Newbury Park, CA: Sage.

Yussen, S.R. (1977). Characteristics of moral dilemmas written by adolescents. *Developmental Psychology, 13,* 162–163.

Zabin, L.S. (1986, May/June). Evaluation of a pregnancy prevention program for urban teenagers. *Family Planning Perspectives,* p. 119.

Zelnik, M., & Kantner, J.F. (1977). Sexual and contraceptive experiences of young unmarried women in the United States, 1976 and 1971. *Family Planning Perspectives, 9,* 55–71.

Zill, N., Morrison, D.R., & Coiro, M.J. (1993). Long-term effects of parental divorce on parent-child relationships, adjustment, and achievement in young adulthood. *Journal of Family Psychology, 7,* 91–103.

Zimbardo, P. (1997, May). What messages are behind today's cults? *APA Monitor,* p. 14.

Zimmer-Gembeck, M., Doyle, L., & Daniels, J.A. (2001). Contraceptive dispensing and selection in school-based health centers. *Journal of Adolescent Health, 29,* 177–185.

Zimmerman, B.J. (2000). Attaining self-regulation: A social cognitive perspective. In M. Boekaerts, P.R. Pintrich, & M. Zeidner (Eds.), *Handbook of self-regulation*. San Diego: Academic Press.

Zimmerman, B.J. (2002). Achieving academic excellence: A self-regulatory perspective. In M. Ferrari (Ed.), *The prusuit of excellence through education*. Mahwah, NJ: Erlabaum.

Zimmerman, B.J., Bonner, S., & Kovach, R. (1996). *Developing self-regulated learners*. Washington, DC: American Psychological Association.

Zimmerman, B.J., & Schunk, D.H. (2002). Albert Bandura: the scholar and his contributions to educational psychology. In B.J. Zimmerman & D.H. Schunk (Eds.), *Educational psychology.* Mahwah, NJ: Erlbaum.

Zimmerman, M.A., Copeland, L.A., & Shope, J.T. (1997, April). *A longitudinal study of self-esteem: Implications for adolescent development.* Paper presented at the meeting of the Society for Research in Child Development, Washington, DC.

Zimmerman, R.S., Khoury, E., Vega, W.A., Gil, A.G., & Warheit, G.J. (1995). Teacher and student perceptions of behavior problems among a sample of African American, Hispanic, and non-Hispanic White students. *American Journal of Community Psychology, 23,* 181–197.

Zukow-Goldring, P. (2002). Sibling caregiving. In M. Bornstein (Ed.), *Handbook of parenting* (2nd ed., Vol. 2). Mahwah, NJ: Erlbaum.

CREDITS

Photography; **11.1:** © Lawrence Migdale/Stock Boston; **p. 351:** © Peter Correz/Stone/Getty Images; **p. 354 (top):** © Marilyn Humphries; **p. 354 (bottom):** Courtesy of Ritch Savin-Williams; **p. 355:** © Bernard Gotfryd/Woodfin Camp & Associates; **p. 358:** © Dana Fineman/Corbis Sygma; **p. 360:** Courtesy of Lynn Blankinship; **p. 361:** © 1998 Frank Fournier; **p. 371:** © James D. Wilson/Woodfin Camp & Associates; **p. 372:** © SuperStock, Inc.; **p. 373:** Courtesy of Jeanne Brooks-Gunn; **p. 374 (left):** © Steve Skjold/Photo Edit; **p. 374 (right):** © Michael Newman/Photo Edit

CHAPTER 12

Opener: © Myrleen Ferguson Cate/Photo Edit; **p. 379:** © David R. Frazier Photolibrary; **p. 385:** Courtesy of Darcia Narvaez; **p. 386:** © Raghu-Rai/Magnum Photos; **p. 387:** Courtesy of Carol Gilligan and Royce Carlton Agency; **p. 392 (top):** © Paul Conklin/Photo Edit; **p. 392 (bottom):** Courtesy of Nancy Eisenberg; **p. 396:** © Ronald Cortes; **12.3:** © D.W. Productions/The Image Bank/Getty Images; **p. 399:** Courtesy of Connie Flanagan; **p. 400:** © Stone/Getty Images; **p. 401 (left):** © SuperStock, Inc.; **p. 401 (right):** © Bob Daemmrich/The Image Works

CHAPTER 13

Opener: © L.D. Gordon/The Image Bank/Getty Images; **p. 413:** Courtesy of Dale Schunk; **p. 416 (left):** © Michael Tweed/AP/Wide World Photos; **p. 416 (right):** © Robert A. Isaacs/Photo Researchers; **p. 423:** Courtesy of Grace Leaf; **p. 424:** © Bill Stanton; **p. 426:** The Dallas Morning News/Kim Ritzenthaler; **p. 427:** Courtesy of Armando Ronquillo; **p. 429:** © Richard Anderson

CHAPTER 14

Opener: © David Young-Wolff/Stone/Getty Images; **p. 444:** © Richard Hutchings/Photo Edit; **14.4 (left & right):** Courtesy of Susan Tapert; **p. 449:** © Joe Raedle/Newsmakers/Getty Images; **p. 453:** Courtesy of Cheryl Perry; **p. 459:** Courtesy of Gerald Patterson; **p. 461:** © Mark Richards/Photo Edit; **p. 462:** © Charlie Neuman/SDUT/Zuma; **p. 463:** Courtesy of Dr. Rodney Hammond; **p. 465:** © Jim Smith/Photo Researchers; **p. 469:** © Tony Freeman/Photo Edit

EPILOGUE

Opener: Girls in White Stockings by Leon Spilliaert. © Estate of Leon Spilliaert/Licensed by VAGA, New York, NY; and Lauros-Giraudon/Bridgeman Art Library; **p. E-6:** © Lisette Le Bon/SuperStock

FIGURES/TEXT CREDITS

CHAPTER 1

Eyes of Adolescents, pg. 15: From *Great Transitions,* October 1995. Copyright © Carnegie Corporation of New York. Reprinted with permission. **Figure 1.2:** From John W. Santrock, *Child Development.* Copyright © 1996 The McGraw-Hill Companies, Inc. Reprinted with permission. **Figure 1.4:** From John W. Santrock, *Child Development.* Copyright © 1996 The McGraw-Hill Companies, Inc. Reprinted with permission.

CHAPTER 2

Figure 2.5: From John W. Santrock, *Psychology.* Copyright © 1997 The McGraw-Hill Companies, Inc. Reprinted with permission. **Eyes of Adolescents, pg. 48:** From John W. Santrock, *Educational Psychology.* Copyright © The McGraw-Hill Companies, Inc. Reprinted with permission. **Figure 2.6:** From John W. Santrock, *Psychology.* Copyright © 1997 The McGraw-Hill Companies, Inc. Reprinted with permission. **Figure 2.7:** From Kopp and Krakow, *Child Development in Social Context.* Copyright © 1982 Pearson Education, Inc. Reprinted with permission. **Figure 2.9:** From John W. Santrock, *Psychology.* Copyright © 1997 The McGraw-Hill Companies, Inc. Reprinted with permission. **Figure 2.10:** From John W. Santrock, *Psychology.* Copyright © 1997 The McGraw-Hill Companies, Inc. Reprinted with permission.

CHAPTER 3

Cartoon, pg. 76: From *Penguin Dreams and Stranger Things* by Berke Breathed. Copyright © 1985 by Berke Breathed and The Washington Post Company. By permission of Little, Brown and Company, Inc. **Figure 3.1:** From John W. Santrock, *Children.* Copyright © 1997 The McGraw-Hill Companies, Inc. Reprinted with permission. **Figure 3.2:** From M. Grumbach, J. Roth, S. Kaplan, & R. Keich, "Hypothalamic-Pituitary Regulation of Puberty in Man," in M. Grumbach, G. Grave, and F. Mayer (eds.), *Control of the Onset of Puberty,* 1974. Reprinted with permission of Lippincott, Williams & Wilkins Publishers. **Figure 3.3:** From J.M. Tanner, R.H. Whitehouse, and M. Takaishi, "Standards from Birth to Maturity for Height, Weight, Height Velocity, and Weight Velocity: British Children, 1965," *Archives of Diseases in Childhood,* p. 41. Copyright © 1966. Used by permission of the British Medical Association. **Figure 3.5:** From John W. Santrock, *Children.* Copyright © 1997 The McGraw-Hill Companies, Inc. Reprinted with permission. **Figure 3.6:** From A.F. Roache, "Secular Trends in Stature, Weight and Maturation," *Monographs of the Society for Research in Child Development,* 44, Serial No. 179. Copyright © 1977 The Society for Research in Child Development, Inc. Reprinted by permission. **Figure 3.7:** From R.G. Simmons, D.A. Blyth, and K.L. McKinney, "The Social and Psychological Effects of Puberty on White Females," in J. Brooks-Gunn & A. Petersen (eds.), *Girls at Puberty: Biological and Psychosocial Perspectives, 1983.* Copyright © 1983 by Kluwer Academic/Plenum Publishers. Reprinted with permission. **Figure 3.8:** From John W. Santrock, *Child Development.* Copyright © 1996 The McGraw-Hill Companies, Inc. Reprinted with permission. **Figure 3.9:** From P.R. Huttenlacher and A.S. Dabholkar, "Regional Differences in Synaptogenesis in Human Cerebral Cortex," *Journal of Comparative Neurology,* 39 (2), 169–178, 1997. Copyright © 1997 by John Wiley & Sons, Inc. Reprinted with permission. **Figure 3.10:** From John W. Santrock, *Child Development.* Copyright © 1996 The McGraw-Hill Companies, Inc. Reprinted with permission.

CHAPTER 4

Cartoon, pg. 110: Copyright © The New Yorker Collection 1981 Ed Fisher from cartoonbank.com.

All rights reserved. **Figure 4.5:** From John W. Santrock, *Children.* Copyright © 1997 The McGraw-Hill Companies, Inc. Reprinted with permission. **Figure 4.6:** From L. Swanson, "What Develops in Working Memory? A Life-Span Perspective," *Developmental Psychology,* 35, 4, 986–1000. Copyright © by the American Psychological Association. Reprinted with permission. **Cartoon, pg. 125:** Copyright © 2000 Sidney Harris. Reprinted with permission. **Figure 4.8:** From Zimmerman, Bonner and Kovach, *Developing Self-Regulated Learners: Beyond Achievement to Self-Efficacy,* 1996. Copyright © 1996 by the American Psychological Association. Reprinted with permission. **Figure 4.9:** From John W. Santrock, *Psychology.* Copyright © 1997 The McGraw-Hill Companies, Inc. Reprinted with permission. **Figure 4.10:** From John W. Santrock, *Psychology.* Copyright © 1997 The McGraw-Hill Companies, Inc. Reprinted with permission. **Cartoon, pg. 132:** Copyright © The New Yorker Collection 1988 Donald Reilly from cartoonbank.com. All rights reserved. **Figure 4.11:** From John W. Santrock, *Psychology.* Copyright © 1997 The McGraw-Hill Companies, Inc. Reprinted with permission. **Figure 4.12:** Figure from the Raven Standard Progressive Matrices. Copyright © J.C. Raven Limited. Reprinted by permission. **Figure 4.13:** From R.L. Selman, "The Development of Social-Cognitive Understanding: A Guide to Educational and Clinical Practice," in *Moral Development and Behavior: Theory, Research, and Social Issues,* Thomas Lickona (ed.). Copyright © 1976 Holt, Rinehart and Winston, Inc. Reprinted by permission of Thomas Lickona.

CHAPTER 5

Figure 5.1: From J. Belsky, "Early Human Experiences: A Family Perspective," *Developmental Psychology,* 1981. Copyright © 1981 by the American Psychological Association. Reprinted with permission. **Figure 5.2:** From E.E. Maccoby and J.A. Martin, "Socialization in the Context of the Family: Parent-Child Interaction," in P.H. Mussen (ed.) *Handbook of Child Psychology,* 4th ed., Vol. 4. Copyright © 1983 John Wiley & Sons, Inc. Reprinted by permission of John Wiley & Sons, Inc. **Figure 5.4:** From John W. Santrock, *Children.* Copyright © 1997 The McGraw-Hill Companies, Inc. Reprinted with permission.

CHAPTER 6

Figure 6.1: From J.R. Asarnow and J.W. Callan, "Boys with Peer Adjustment Problems: Social Cognitive Processes," *Journal of Consulting and Clinical Psychology,* 53, 1985. Copyright © 1985 by the American Psychological Association. Reprinted with permission. **Figure 6.5:** Reprinted with permission of Duane Buhrmester, University of Texas at Dallas. **Eyes of Adolescents, pg. 213:** Written by a teen and posted on an Internet message board.

CHAPTER 7

Figure 7.2: From W.M. Alexander and C.K. McEwin, *Schools in the Middle: Status & Progress.* Copyright © 1989 National Middle School Association, Columbus, OH. Reprinted by permission. **Figure 7.3:** Copyright © The Carnegie Foundation for the

Advancement of Teaching. Reprinted by permission. **Cartoon, pg. 239:** Used by permission of Heiser Zedonek. **Figure 7.4:** U.S. Department of Educational Programs Data Analysis Systems, 1996. **Eyes of Adolescents, pg. 250:** Desilie (1984), pp. 55–73.

CHAPTER 8

Cartoon, pg. 260: Copyright © 1994 Sidney Harris. Reprinted with permission. **Eyes of Adolescents, pg. 274:** Jason Leonard (age 15), *USA Today,* Sept. 3, 1997.

CHAPTER 9

Images of Adolescence, pg. 291: From S. Harter, "Self and Identity Development," in S.S. Feldman and G.R. Elliott (eds.), *At the Threshold: The Developing Adolescent,* Harvard University Press, 1990. Reprinted with permission of the author. **Figure 9.1:** From R.C. Savin-Williams and D.H. Demo, "Conceiving or Misconceiving the Self: Issues in Adolescent Self-Esteem," *Journal of Early Adolescence,* 2, pp. 121–140, 1983. Copyright © 1983 by Sage Publications, Inc., Reprinted by permission of Sage Publications, Inc. **Cartoon, pg. 298:** IN THE BLEACHERS © Steve Moore. Reprinted with permission of Universal Press Syndicate. All rights reserved. **Cartoon, pg. 305:** Copyright © The New Yorker Collection 1988 Ed Koren from cartoonbank.com. All rights reserved.

CHAPTER 10

Figure 10.1: Adapted from Janet K. Swim, et al., "Sexism and Racism: Old-Fashioned and Modern Prejudices," *Journal of Personality and Social Psychology,* 68: 212, 1995 and J.B. McConahay, "Modern Racism Scale," in J.F. Dovidio & S.L. Gaertner (eds.), *Prejudice, Discrimination, and Racism,* 1986 Academic Press. **Figure 10.2:** From J.S. Hyde, "Gender Differences in Mathematics Performance," *Psychological Bulletin,* 107, 1990. Copyright © 1990 by the American Psychological Association. Reprinted with permission. **Figure 10.3:** L.J. Sax, A.W. Astin, W.S. Korn, K.M. Mahoney, 1999. *The American Freshman: National Norms for Fall 1999.* Higher Education Research Institute,

UCLA. Reprinted with permission. **Figure 10.4:** From John W. Santrock, *Psychology.* Copyright © 1997 The McGraw-Hill Companies, Inc. Reprinted with permission.

CHAPTER 11

Figure 11.1: Data from Feldman, Turner, & Aravjo (1999), Table 3, p. 35, *Journal of Research on Adolescence.* **Figure 11.2:** From Alan Guttmacher Institute, *1995 National Survey of Adolescent Growth & 1995 National Survey of Adolescent Males,* Allan Guttmacher Institute. **Figure 11.3:** Data from Feldman, Turner, & Aravjo (1999), Table 3, p. 35, *Journal of Research on Adolescence.* **Figure 11.4:** From John W. Santrock, *Psychology.* Copyright © 1997 The McGraw-Hill Companies, Inc. Reprinted with permission.

CHAPTER 12

Figure 12.1: From John W. Santrock, *Child Development.* Copyright © 1996 The McGraw-Hill Companies, Inc. Reprinted with permission. **Figure 12.2:** From S.R. Yussen, "Characteristics of Moral Dilemmas Written by Adolescents," *Developmental Psychology,* 13, 1977. Copyright © 1977 by the American Psychological Association. Reprinted with permission. **Figure 12.3:** Data from Deye, et al. *The American Freshman: National Norms for Fall 1992;* A.W. Austin, et al. *The American Freshman National Norms for Fall 1993.* A.W. Austin, et al. *The American Freshman Norms for Fall 1994.* All works © Higher Education Research Institute, UCLA.

CHAPTER 13

Cartoon, pg. 409: CALVIN AND HOBBES © Watterson. Reprinted with permission of Universal Press Syndicate. All rights reserved. **Figure 13.1:** From J. Brophy, *Motivating Students to Learn.* Copyright © 1988 The McGraw-Hill Companies, Inc. Reproduced with permission of The McGraw-Hill Companies Inc. **Figure 13.2:** From B. Weiner, *Human Motivation: Metaphors, Theories and Research,* 1992. Copyright © 1992 Sage Publications, Inc. Reprinted by permission of Sage Publications, Inc. **Figure 13.3:** From J. Brophy, *Motivating Students to Learn.* Copyright © 1988 The McGraw-

Hill Companies, Inc. Reproduced with permission of The McGraw-Hill Companies Inc. **Figure 13.4:** Reproduced by special permission of the Publisher, Psychological Assessment Resources, Inc., from *Making Vocational Choices.* Copyright © 1973, 1985 by Psychological Assessment Resources, Inc. All rights reserved.

CHAPTER 14

Figure 14.1: From T.M. Achenbach and C.S. Edelbrock, "Behavioral Problems and Competencies Reported by Parents of Normal and Disturbed Children Aged Four Through Sixteen," *Monographs of the Society for Research in Child Development,* #188. Reprinted with permission. **Figure 14.2:** From A.S. Masten and J.D. Coatsworth, "The Development of Competence in Favorable and Unfavorable Environments," *American Psychologist,* 53, 1998. Copyright © 1998 by the American Psychological Association. Reprinted with permission. **Figure 14.3:** Data from Johnston, O'Malley, & Bachman, 1988, Fig. 5.3, p. 103. University of Michigan Institute for Social Research. On Page Credit: After John W. Santrock. Copyright © The McGraw-Hill Companies. **Figure 14.5:** CREDIT TO COME AFTER THEY RECEIVE PAYMENT—INVOICE TO HANLEY 10/19/2001. **Figure 14.6:** Data from Johnston, O'Malley, & Bachman, 1988, Fig. 5.3, p. 103. University of Michigan Institute for Social Research. **Figure 14.7:** From John W. Santrock, *Psychology.* Copyright © 1997 The McGraw-Hill Companies, Inc. Reprinted with permission. **Cartoon, pg. 456:** Copyright © 2000 Sidney Harris. Reprinted with permission. **Figure 14.8:** From John W. Santrock, *Children.* Copyright © 1997 The McGraw-Hill Companies, Inc. Reprinted with permission. **Figure 14.9:** From John W. Santrock, *Children.* Copyright © 1997 The McGraw-Hill Companies, Inc. Reprinted with permission. **Figure 14.10:** Data from Center or Disease Control & Prevention, *Adolescent Chartbook 2000,* U.S. Department of Health and Human Statistics. **Eyes of Adolescents, pg. 469:** From M. Murphy, "I'm Okay," *St. Raphael's Better Health,* Nov./Dec. 1995, pp. 16–20. Reprinted by permission.

NAME INDEX

SUBJECT INDEX